6th European Edition

Philip Kotler

Gary Armstrong

Lloyd C. Harris

Nigel Piercy

Principles of

Marketing

PEARSON

Harlow, England • London • New York • Boston • San Francisco • Toronto • Sydney • Auckland • Singapore • Hong Kong
Tokyo • Seoul • Taipei • New Delhi • Cape Town • São Paulo • Mexico City • Madrid • Amsterdam • Munich • Paris • Milan

Pearson Education Limited
Edinburgh Gate
Harlow
Essex CM20 2JE
England

and Associated Companies throughout the world

Visit us on the World Wide Web at:
 www.pearson.com/uk

First European edition published 1996 by Prentice Hall Europe (print)
Second European edition published 1999 (print)
Third European edition published 2001 by Pearson Education (print)
Fourth European edition published 2005 (print)
Fifth European edition published 2008 (print)
Sixth European edition published 2013 (print and electronic)

© Prentice Hall Europe 1996, 1999 (print)
© Pearson Education Limited 2013 (print and electronic)

ISBN: 978-0-273-74297-5 (print)
         978-0-273-74315-6 (PDF)
         978-0-273-78111-0 (eText)

British Library Cataloguing-in-Publication Data
A catalogue record for this book is available from the British Library

Library of Congress Cataloging-in-Publication Data
A catalog record for this book is available from the Library of Congress

10 9 8 7 6 5 4 3 2
17 16 15 14

Typeset in Mundo Sans Std and Minion Pro 10/12 by 73
Printed and bound in Slovakia by Neografia

NOTE THAT ANY PAGE CROSS REFERENCES REFER TO THE PRINT EDITION

BRIEF CONTENTS

Lecturer Resources
For password-protected online resources tailored to support the use of this textbook in teaching, please visit www.pearsoned.co.uk/kotler

CONTENTS

Part 2: Understanding the marketplace and consumers

Chapter 3 Analysing the marketing environment

Chapter 4 Managing marketing information to gain customer insights

GUIDED TOUR

Objective outline

➤ **Objective 1** Define the consumer market and construct a simple model of consumer buyer behaviour.
Model of consumer behaviour (pp. 144–145)

➤ **Objective 2** Name four major factors that influence consumer buyer behaviour.
Characteristics affecting consumer behaviour (pp. 145–158)

➤ **Objective 3** List and define the major types of buying decision behaviour and the stages in the buyer decision process.

Types of buying decision behaviour (pp. 159–160)
The buyer decision process (pp. 161–163)

➤ **Objective 4** Describe the adoption and diffusion process for new products.
The buyer decision process for new products (pp. 164–165)

Learning objectives are clearly set out at the beginning of every chapter and then reviewed again at the end of every chapter

REVIEWING OBJECTIVES AND KEY TERMS

The European consumer market consists of more than 500 million people who consume more €8 billion worth of goods and services each year, making it one of the most attractive consumer markets in the world. The world consumer market consists of more than 6.8 billion people. Consumers around the world vary greatly in terms of cultural, social, personal and psychological makeup. Understanding how these differences affect *consumer buying behaviour* is one of the biggest challenges marketers face.

OBJECTIVE 1 Define the consumer market and construct a simple model of consumer buyer behaviour (pp. 144–145).

The *consumer market* consists of all the individuals and households who buy or acquire goods and services for personal consumption. The simplest model of consumer buyer behaviour is the stimulus-response model. According to this model, marketing stimuli (the four Ps) and other major forces (economic, technological, political, cultural) enter a consumer's 'black box' and produce certain responses. Once in the black box, these inputs produce observable buyer responses, such as product choice, brand choice, purchase timing and purchase amount.

OBJECTIVE 2 Name the four major factors that influence consumer buyer behaviour (pp. 145–158).

Consumer buyer behaviour is influenced by four key sets of buyer characteristics: cultural, social, personal, and psychological. Although many of these factors cannot be influenced by a marketer, they can be useful in identifying interested buyers and shaping products and appeals to serve consumer needs better. *Culture* is the most basic determinant of a person's wants and behaviour. *Subcultures* are 'cultures within cultures' that have distinct values and lifestyles and can be based on anything from age to ethnicity. Many companies focused their marketing programmes on the special needs of certain cultural and subcultural segments.

Social factors also influence a buyer's behaviour. A person's *reference groups* – family, friends, social networks, professional associations – strongly affect product and brand choices. A buyer's age, life-cycle stage, occupation, economic circumstances, personality and other *personal characteristics* influence his or her buying decisions. Consumer *lifestyles*–the whole pattern of acting and interacting in the world–are also an important influence on purchase decisions. Finally, consumer buying behaviour is influenced by four major *psychological factors*: motivation, perception, learning, and beliefs and attitudes.

Each of these factors provides a different perspective for understanding the workings of a buyer's black box.

OBJECTIVE 3 List and define the major types of buying decision behaviour and the stages in the buyer decision process (pp. 159–162).

Buying behaviour may vary greatly across different types of products and buying decisions. Consumers undertake *complex buying behaviour* when they are highly involved in a purchase and perceive significant differences among brands. *Dissonance-reducing behaviour* occurs when consumers are highly involved but see little difference among brands. *Habitual buying behaviour* occurs under conditions of low involvement and little significant brand difference. In situations characterised by low involvement but significant perceived brand differences, consumers engage in *variety-seeking buying behaviour*.

When making a purchase, a buyer goes through a decision process consisting of *need recognition, information search, evaluation of alternatives, purchase decision* and *postpurchase behaviour*. A marketer's job is to understand a buyer's behaviour at each stage and the influences that are operating. During *need recognition*, a consumer recognises a problem or a need that could be satisfied by a product or a service in the market. Once the need is recognised, a consumer is aroused to seek more information and moves into the *information search* stage. With information in hand, a consumer proceeds to *alternative evaluation*, during which the information is used to evaluate brands in the choice set. From there, a consumer makes a *purchase decision* and actually buys the product. In the final stage of the buyer decision process, *postpurchase behaviour*, a consumer takes action based on satisfaction or dissatisfaction.

OBJECTIVE 4 Describe the adoption and diffusion process for new products (pp. 164–165).

The product *adoption process* is made up of five stages: awareness, interest, evaluation, trial, and adoption. New-product marketers must think about how to help consumers move through these stages. With regard to the *diffusion process* for new products, consumers respond at different rates, depending on consumer and product characteristics. Consumers may be innovators, early adopters, early majority, late majority, or laggards. Each group may require different marketing approaches. Marketers often try to bring their new products to the attention of potential early adopters, especially those who are opinion leaders. Finally, several characteristics influence the rate of adoption: relative advantage, compatibility, complexity, divisibility, and communicability.

Case studies open every chapter to give insight into how the themes of the chapter are applied in practice.

Häagen-Dazs

Häagen-Dazs is one of today's top-selling super premium ice cream brands. But only a few years ago, the brand teetered on the verge of commodity status. A glut of top ice cream brands had turned to beating each other up on price in an increasingly frugal marketplace. Häagen-Dazs needed to find a way to strengthen its emotional connection to consumers – to stand out from the crowd of competing brands. 'We needed a socially relevant idea . . . linked to the brand's core essence,' says Katty Pien, brand director for Häagen-Dazs.

In response, the brand launched its 'Häagen-Dazs loves honey bees' campaign. The campaign centred on an issue that's important to both the brand and its customers – a mysterious colony-collapse disorder threatening the honey bee population. Honey bees pollinate one-third of all the natural products we eat and up to 40 per cent of the natural flavours used in Häagen-Dazs ice cream. Yet, honey bee populations are disappearing at an alarming rate. The 'Häagen-Dazs loves honey bees' ('HD loves HB') message is a natural one for the brand. 'We want to keep these little heroes buzzing,' says the company.

Perhaps even more important than the 'help the honey bees' message itself is the way that Häagen-Dazs communicates that message. More than just running a few ads and a website, Häagen-Dazs has created a fully fledged, beautiful IMC campaign, using a wide range of media and PR elements that work harmoniously for the cause. At the heart of the campaign is a website, www.helpthehoneybees.com, a kind of honey bee central where customers can learn about the problem and find out how they can help.

The campaign began with creative broadcast and print ads that were designed to drive traffic to the website. The first TV ad was a beautifully staged mini-opera that poignantly outlined the plight of the honey bee. 'Honey bees are dying, and we rely on them for many of our natural ingredients,' said the ad. 'Help us save them.' An early print ad introduced Häagen-Dazs' vanilla honey bee flavour ice cream and implored, 'Honey, please don't go. Nature needs honey bees. We all do.'

Once at the website, which is carefully integrated with other campaign elements, the emotional connections really blossom. With the sounds of birds chirping and bees buzzing, the site greets visitors with the headline 'Imagine a world without honey bees' and explains the colony-collapse disorder problem. 'Get involved,' the site suggests. 'Donate now! Buy a carton, save a bee. Plant a bee-friendly garden.' At the site, visitors can read more about the bee crisis and what Häagen-Dazs is doing, tap into a news feed called *The Buzz*, turn on Bee TV, purchase Bee-Ts with phrases like 'Long live the queen' and 'Bee a hero', create their own animated honeybee and 'Bee-mail' it to friends, or make a direct donation to support honeybee research.

At the grass roots level, to create even more bee buzz, Häagen-Dazs hands out samples of Vanilla Honey bee ice cream and wildflower seeds at local farmers markets across the country. It sponsors projects and fund-raisers by local community groups and schools. It also donates a portion of the sales of

The Häagen-Dazs loves honeybees IMC campaign uses a rich, well-coordinated blend of promotion elements to successfully deliver Häagen-Dazs' unique message.

Source: Häagen-Dazs

WHAT IS A PRICE?

In the narrowest sense, **price** is the amount of money charged for a product or a service. More broadly, price is the sum of all the values that customers give up to gain the benefits of having or using a product or a service. Historically, price has been the major factor affecting buyer choice. In recent decades, non-price factors have gained increasing importance. However, price still remains one of the most important elements that determines a firm's market share and profitability.

Price—The amount of money charged for a product or a service; the sum of the values that customers exchange for the benefits of having or using the product or service.

Price is the only element in the marketing mix that produces revenue; all other elements represent costs. Price is also one of the most flexible marketing mix elements. Unlike product features and channel commitments, prices can be changed quickly. At the same time, pricing is the number one problem facing many marketing executives, and many companies do not handle pricing well. Some managers view pricing as a big headache, preferring instead to focus on other marketing mix elements. However, smart managers treat pricing as a key strategic tool for creating and capturing customer value. Prices have a direct impact on a firm's bottom line. A small percentage improvement in price can generate a large percentage increase in profitability. More importantly, as part of a company's overall value proposition, price plays a key role in creating customer value and building customer relationships. 'Instead of running away from pricing,' says an expert, 'savvy marketers are embracing it.'[3]

AUTHOR COMMENT
Setting the right price is one of the marketer's most difficult tasks. A host of factors come into play. But finding and implementing the right price strategy is critical to success.

MAJOR PRICING STRATEGIES

The price the company charges will fall somewhere between one that is too high to produce any demand and one that is too low to produce a profit. Figure 10.1 summarises the major considerations in setting price. Customer perceptions of the product's value set the ceiling for prices. If customers perceive that the product's price is greater than its value, they will not buy the product. Product costs set the floor for prices. If the company prices the product below its costs, the company's profits will suffer. In setting its price between these two extremes, the company must consider several internal and external factors, including competitors' strategies and prices, the overall marketing strategy and mix, and the nature of the market and demand.

Figure 10.1 suggests three major pricing strategies: customer value-based pricing, cost-based pricing and competition-based pricing.

AUTHOR COMMENT
Like everything else in marketing, good pricing starts with *customers* and their perceptions of value.

Figure 10.1 Considerations in setting price

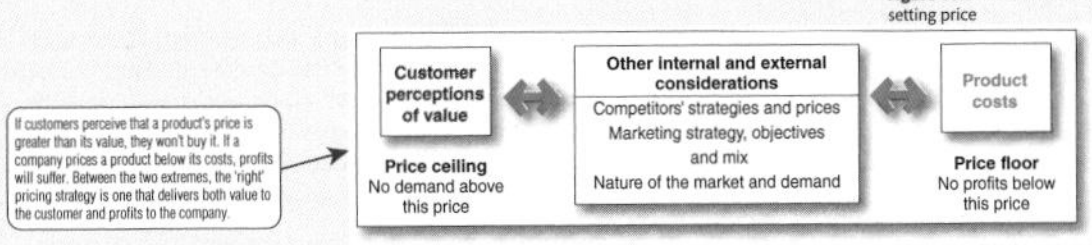

Author comment boxes provide guidance, tips and summaries of key points.

COMPANY CASE

Ocado – taking on the Internet giants direct

The online grocery market is one of the fastest-growing, most competitive retail markets in the UK. Worth £3.6 billion (€4.5 billion) in 2007, it is forecast to grow to at least £12 billion (€15 billion) in 2012. Institute of Grocery Distribution research suggests that the online grocery business was growing six times faster than in-store sales even in the tough conditions of the late 2000s.

Ocado is an upmarket British-based online grocery retailer, mainly selling Waitrose products (Waitrose is the supermarket division of the John Lewis Partnership in the UK – the country's 'posh' department store group). Sales are running at around £450 million (€562.5 million) and Ocado has around 1.6 million registered users.

The founders of Ocado were Tim Steiner, an investment banker, Jonathan Faiman, a friend of Steiner's since nursery school and also previously an investment banker, and Jason Gissing. In 2000, the John Lewis Partnership struck a deal to take a 40 per cent stake in Ocado and for its Waitrose business to act as Ocado's supplier (though Ocado has developed its own branded fresh food ranges as well). Intriguingly, in 2008 P&G took a stake in Ocado despite its loss-making status at that time, in its first-ever retailer investment.

Sir Terry Leahy, the respected Tesco boss, made no secret of his doubts about an upstart business set up by inexperienced youngsters in the early 2000s, when the dot-com boom was at its height, compared to his own Tesco Direct operation. The upstarts at Ocado retaliated with the claim that Teco's direct model was not profitable, with its results an artefact of misleading internal cost allocations – an accusation that Tesco vehemently rejects. Sir Terry's swipe at Ocado's business model, which he said was not viable, escalated the ferocity of competition in the online grocery business. Bitter rivalry emerged between Tesco and Ocado, as Ocado began to corner the online market within the M25, where it now controls an estimated 50 per cent of grocery delivery sales. Price wars ensued with Ocado targeting price parity with Tesco on its top 100 lines.

Ocado has pioneered its own approach to online grocery shopping and won awards for its customer service. Like the Boden 'posh' clothing catalogue, Pilates classes and honey-blonde highlights, the weekly Ocado delivery has become a 'must-have' for the affluent, urban tribe of yummy mummies. Ocado's fans are an emblem of middle-class aspirations. Its affluent customers, half of them inside the M25, love Ocado's emphasis on service. The company has cultivated an image of selling high-class food, while caring for the environment because customers don't need to drive to a store.

By 2010, the UK online grocery retailing market was divided as follows: Tesco (52 per cent), Asda (16 per cent), Sainsburys (16 per cent), Ocado (14 per cent) and Waitrose (2 per cent). Interestingly, most of Ocado's new customers were not acquired from Waitrose – 85 per cent were won from Tesco and Asda.

From the outset, Ocado's unique concept was to pick orders and despatch them direct to consumers from a huge, semi-automated, low-cost warehouse in Hertfordshire. The warehouse has the space of ten football pitches, with a 15 km network of conveyor belts handling as many as 7,200 grocery crates an hour, ready for despatch to customers. This is a much faster and more accurate way of picking orders. Direct distribution means Ocado can boast that every fresh item it delivers will have a shelf life of at least six days, and that its food waste is the lowest in the industry at 0.3 per cent of sales. By contrast, rivals such as Tesco began their Internet operations by picking goods from store shelves, meaning that some items would be out of stock and others towards the end of their shelf life (and stores were disrupted for regular shoppers by the order pickers with their giant shopping trolleys). Tesco is now getting its act together with Ocado-style warehouses. Indeed, 2010 saw Tesco and Asda opening 'ghost stores' in London, closed to customers, from which to pick online orders, to try and challenge Ocado's strong position in this important market.

Nonetheless, the floatation of the company in July 2010 saw Ocado's shares fall within weeks from the offer price of 180p to 135p. Ocado lost a quarter of its market value in its first month as a public company. Since then the shares have seen a slow and erratic recovery.

Ocado's critics doubted whether the business would ever gain enough scale to make a profit. One worry was Waitrose's plans to ramp up its own Internet operation (basically selling the same products as Ocado in much the same areas). Waitrose occupies the dual role of supplier and competitor to Ocado, and in 2011 Waitrose invested £6.5 million in its own online grocery business and rolling out its new website. Indeed, with John Lewis holding shares in Ocado, there is an ownership role as well. Nonetheless, in 2010, Ocado signed a further exclusive ten-year supply deal with Waitrose

There are also concerns that, as the online grocery market matures, latecomers like Marks & Spencer and Morrisons will enter at the same time that Waitrose expands, all threatening Ocado's current strong position.

In fact, some analysts, such as Morgan Stanley, believe that the online market is already mature and its relatively small share of the total grocery business is because over half of Britain's households have tried online and have gone back to shopping in-store, because they find it just as convenient as online. This

Detailed **Company Cases** close every chapter and provide Questions for discussion.

OBJECTIVE 4
Marketing strategy (p. 50)
Market segmentation (p. 51)
Market segment (p. 51)
Market targeting (p. 51)
Positioning (p. 52)
Differentiation (p. 52)
Marketing mix (p. 53)

OBJECTIVE 5
SWOT analysis (p. 54)
Marketing implementation (p. 57)
Marketing control (p. 58)
Return on marketing investment (p. 59)

Discussing and applying concepts sections at the end of each chapter provide a range of features and exercises that apply the theory to real-life scenarios.

DISCUSSING AND APPLYING THE CONCEPTS

Discussing the concepts

1. Explain what is meant by a *market-oriented* mission statement and discuss the characteristics of effective mission statements. (AACSB: Communication)

2. Define strategic planning and briefly describe the four steps that lead managers and a firm through the strategic planning process. Discuss the role marketing plays in this process. (AACSB: Communication)

3. Explain why it is important for all departments of an organisation – marketing, accounting, finance, operations management, human resources and so on to 'think consumer'. Why is it important that even people who are not in marketing understand it? (AACSB: Communication)

4. Define *positioning* and explain how it is accomplished. Describe the positioning for the following brands: BMW's X5, Amazon, Twitter and Marks and Spencer. (AACSB: Communication; Reflective Thinking)

5. Define each of the four Ps. What insights might a firm gain by considering the four Cs rather than the four Ps? (AACSB: Communication; Reflective Thinking)

6. What is marketing ROI? Why is it difficult to measure? (AACSB: Communication; Reflective Thinking)

Applying the concepts

1. In a small group, conduct a SWOT analysis, develop objectives, and create a marketing strategy for your school, a student organisation you might be involved in or a local business. (AACSB: Communication; Reflective Thinking)

2. Explain the role of a chief marketing officer. Summarise an article that describes the importance of this position, the characteristics of an effective officer, or any issues surrounding this position. (AACSB: Communication; Reflective Thinking)

3. Marketers are increasingly held accountable for demonstrating marketing success. Research the various marketing metrics, in addition to those described in the chapter and Appendix 2, used by marketers to measure marketing performance. Write a brief report of your findings. (AACSB: Communication; Reflective Thinking)

Focus on technology

Visit the websites of several car manufacturers and you will see the technological innovations and additions offered in today's vehicles. From navigation systems to audio enhancements and DVD systems, these technologies are enhancing today's cars. Microsoft, known mostly for its computer operating systems, has been working with Fiat to develop a new 'infotainment' system known as Blue&Me. Currently offered only in limited Fiat models, the system integrates mobile phones, MP3 players and an Internet connection through controls on the steering wheel. The new technology will also contain a navigation system, weather and traffic forecasts, and anti-theft devices.

1. According to the product/market expansion grid, which strategy best describes Microsoft's expansion into automobile applications?

2. Why is Fiat an important member of Microsoft's value-delivery network?

3. Describe why this advanced technology is important to Fiat in terms of positioning its products.

Focus on ethics

With around 15 per cent obesity in the EU and less than half participating in regular physical activity, athletic shoe marketers saw an opportunity: 'toning shoes'. Marketers tout these shoes as revolutionary; you can tone your muscles, lose weight, and improve your posture just by wearing them and going about your daily business. The claims are based on shoemaker-sponsored studies, and the Podiatric Medical Association agrees that toning shoes have some health value. They purportedly perform their magic by destabilising a person's gait, making leg muscles work harder. Consumers, particularly women, are buying it.

VIDEO CASE

TOMS Shoes MyMarketingLab

'Get involved: changing a life begins with a single step.' This sounds like a mandate from a non-profit volunteer organisation. But in fact, this is the motto of a for-profit shoe company located in Santa Monica, California. In 2006, Tom Mycoskie founded TOMS Shoes because he wanted to do something different. He wanted to run a company that would make a profit while at the same time helping the needy of the world.

Specifically, for every pair of shoes that TOMS sells, it gives a pair of shoes to a needy child somewhere in the world. So far, the company has given away tens of thousands of pairs of shoes and is on track to give away hundreds of thousands. Can TOMS succeed and thrive based on this idealistic concept? That all depends on how TOMS executes its strategy within the constantly changing marketing environment.

After viewing the video featuring TOMS Shoes, answer the following questions about the marketing environment:

1. What trends in the marketing environment have contributed to the success of TOMS Shoes?

2. Did TOMS Shoes first scan the marketing environment in creating its strategy, or did it create its strategy and fit the strategy to the environment. Does this matter?

3. Is TOMS' strategy more about serving needy children or about creating value for customers? Explain your answer.

Video cases at the end of each chapter provide questions to test your knowledge and understanding based on interviews with top management teams from a range of companies.

VIDEO CASE

Eaton MyMarketingLab

With nearly 60,000 employees doing business in 125 countries and sales last year of more than €8 billion, Eaton is one of the world's largest suppliers of diversified industrial goods. Eaton's products make cars more peppy, 18-wheelers safer to drive and airliners more fuel efficient. So why haven't you heard of the company? Because Eaton sells its products not to end consumers but to other businesses.

At Eaton, B-to-B marketing means working closely with customers to develop a better product. So the company partners with its sophisticated, knowledgeable clients to create total solutions that meet their needs. Along the way, Eaton maps the decision-making process to better understand the concerns and interests of decision makers. In the end, Eaton's success depends on its ability to provide high-quality, dependable customer service and product support.

This book is also available with MyMarketingLab.

Learn marketing your way with **self-assessment questions** with **feedback**, a recommended **study plan** to help you focus on where to improve and **podcasts** to provide alternative ways of looking at issues within the book.

Enhance your learning through specially developed **online resources**, designed to give you an extra edge in your coursework. My MarketingLab has been developed to help you make the most of your studies in marketing and get a better grade.

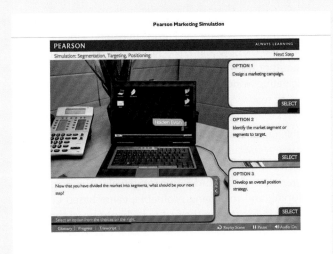

Put a spotlight on marketing in the real world with unique **mini-simulations**. Challenge yourself to make marketing decisions and see the impact of the decisions you've chosen.

Videos of real business professionals talking about issues relating to their day to day work and the strategic and marketing challenges which affect their business.

Keep up to date with what's happening in the marketing world with **bulletins** from *Marketing week* and the *Financial Times*.

Buy it now at www.mymktlab.com.

A MESSAGE FROM THE AUTHORS

Welcome to the sixth European edition of *Principles of Marketing*! Among many other changes and enhancements, this edition sees a change in the author team for the European edition: Lloyd C. Harris and Nigel Piercy of Warwick Business School in the UK now join Philip Kotler and Gary Armstrong to present this new edition. The goal of the new author team remains to bring you the freshest and most authoritative insights into the increasingly fascinating world of marketing. With the help and support of the millions of marketing students and marketing teachers who have used earlier editions of the book over the years, we hope that this book continues to be a market leader and international best seller.

The goal of every marketer is to create more value for customers. So it makes sense that our goal for the sixth edition is to create more value for you – *our customer*. How does this text bring you more value? First, it builds on a unique, integrative and intuitive marketing framework: simply put, marketing is the art and science of creating value *for* customers in order to capture value *from* customers in return. Marketers lead the way in developing and managing profitable, value-based customer relationships. We introduce this customer-value framework in the first two chapters and then build upon it throughout the book.

Beyond the strengthened customer-relationships framework, we emphasise four additional customer value themes. First, we expand our emphasis on *sustainable marketing*. Marketing is about caring for customers so there is nothing more important than not destroying the environment in which customers and their children will have to exist. Second, we focus on the importance of *measuring and managing return on marketing* – of capturing value in return for the customer value that the company creates. Third, we present all of the latest developments in the *marketing technologies* that are rapidly changing how marketers create and communicate customer value. Finally, we emphasise the importance of *marketing around the world*. As the world becomes an increasingly smaller place, marketers must be good at marketing their brands globally and in socially responsible ways that create long-term value to society as a whole.

Beyond providing all the latest marketing thinking, to add even more value, we have worked to make learning about and teaching marketing easier and more exciting for both students and teachers. The sixth edition presents marketing in a complete yet practical, exciting and easy-to-digest way. For example, to help bring marketing to life, we have filled the text with interesting examples and stories about real companies and their marketing practices. Moreover, the integrated, cutting-edge teaching and learning package lets you customise your learning and teaching experience. We highlight the sixth edition's many new features and enhancements in the pages that follow.

So, the sixth edition *creates more value for you* – more value in the content, more value in the supplements, more value in learning, and more value in YOUR classroom. We think that it's the best edition yet. We hope that you'll find *Principles of Marketing* the very best text from which to learn about and teach marketing.

Enjoy it and have a great time marketing to the world.

Yours sincerely,

Philip Kotler, Northwestern University, USA
Gary Armstrong, University of North Carolina – Chapel Hill, USA
Lloyd C. Harris, University of Warwick, UK
Nigel Piercy, University of Warwick, UK

PREFACE

The sixth European edition of *Principles of Marketing*! Still creating more value for you!

The goal of every marketer is to create more value for customers. So it makes sense that our goal for the sixth European edition is to continue creating more value for you – *our* customer. Our goal is to introduce new marketing students to the fascinating world of modern marketing in an innovative and comprehensive yet practical and enjoyable way. We've pored over every page, table, figure, fact and example in an effort to make this the best text from which to learn about and teach marketing. Enhanced by mymarketinglab, our online homework and personalised study tool, the sixth edition creates exceptional value for both students and teachers of marketing.

Marketing: creating customer value and relationships

Top marketers at outstanding companies share a common goal: putting the consumer at the heart of marketing. Today's marketing is all about creating customer value and building profit-able customer relationships. It starts with understanding consumer needs and wants, deter-mining which target markets the organisation can serve best, and developing a compelling value proposition by which the organisation can attract and grow valued consumers. If the organisation does these things well, it will reap the rewards in terms of market share, profits and customer equity.

Five major value themes

Form beginning to end, the sixth European edition of *Principles of Marketing* develops an innovative customer-value and customer-relationships framework that captures the essence of today's marketing. It builds on five major value themes:

1. **Creating value for customers in order to capture value from customers in return**. Today's marketers must be good at *creating customer value* and *managing customer relationships*. Outstanding marketing companies understand the marketplace and customer needs, design value-creating marketing strategies, develop integrated marketing programmes that deliver customer value and delight, and build strong customer relationships. In return, they capture value from customers in the form of sales, profits and customer loyalty.

    This innovative *customer-value framework* is introduced at the start of Chapter 1 in a five-step marketing process model, which details how marketing *creates* customer value and

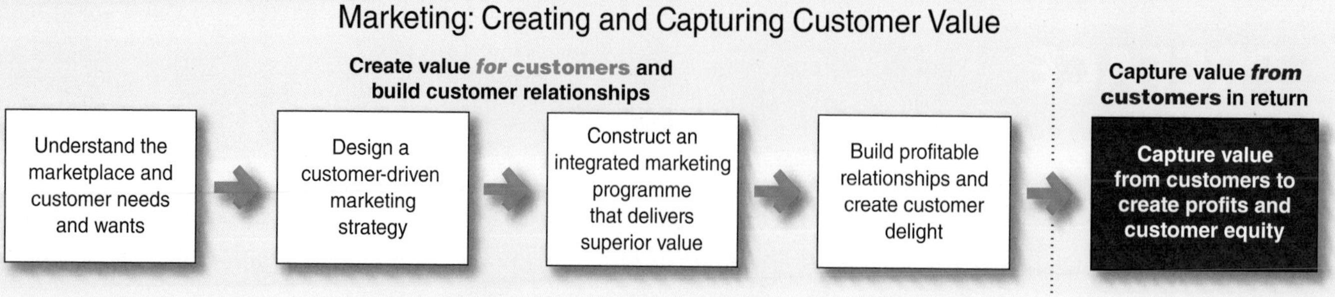

Marketing: Creating and Capturing Customer Value

Create value *for customers* and build customer relationships

Capture value *from* customers in return

| Understand the marketplace and customer needs and wants | → | Design a customer-driven marketing strategy | → | Construct an integrated marketing programme that delivers superior value | → | Build profitable relationships and create customer delight | → | **Capture value from customers to create profits and customer equity** |

Figure 1.1 A simple model of the marketing process

captures value in return. The framework is carefully developed in the first two chapters and then fully integrated throughout the remainder of the text.

2. **Building and managing strong, value-creating brands**. Well-positioned brands with strong brand equity provide the basis upon which to build customer value and profitable customer relationships. Today's marketers must position their brands powerfully and manage them well. They must build close brand relationships and experiences with customers.

3. **Measuring and managing return on marketing**. Marketing managers must ensure that their marketing money is being well spent. In the past, many marketers spent freely on big, expensive marketing programmes, often without thinking carefully about the financial returns on their spending. But all that has changed rapidly. 'Marketing accountability' – measuring and managing return on marketing investments – has now become an important part of strategic marketing decision making. This emphasis on marketing accountability is addressed throughout the new edition.

4. **Harnessing new marketing technologies**. New digital and other high-tech marketing developments are dramatically changing how consumers and marketers relate to one another. The sixth edition thoroughly explores the new technologies impacting marketing, from 'Web 3.0' in Chapter 1 to new digital marketing and online technologies in Chapters 15 and 17 to the exploding use of online social networks and customer-generated marketing in Chapters 1, 5, 14, 15, 17, and elsewhere.

5. **Sustainable marketing around the globe**. As technological developments make the world an increasingly smaller and more fragile place, marketers must be good at marketing their brands globally and in sustainable ways. New material throughout the sixth edition emphasises the concept of sustainable marketing – meeting the present needs of consumers and businesses while also preserving or enhancing the ability of future generations to meet their needs.

New in the sixth edition

We've thoroughly revised the sixth European edition of *Principles of Marketing* to reflect the major trends and forces impacting marketing in this era of customer value and relationships. Here are just some of the major and continuing changes you'll find in this edition:

• New coverage in every chapter of the sixth edition shows how companies and consumers are dealing with **marketing and the uncertain economy** in the aftermath of the recent economic downturn. Starting with a major new section in Chapter 1 and continuing with new sections, discussions and examples integrated throughout the text, the new edition shows how, now more than ever, marketers must focus on creating customer value and sharpening their value propositions to serve the needs of today's more frugal consumers. At the end of each chapter, a new feature – *Marketing and the Economy* – provides real examples for discussion and learning.

• Throughout the sixth edition, you will find revised coverage of the rapidly **changing nature of customer relationships** with companies and brands. Today's marketers aim to create deep consumer involvement and a sense of community surrounding a brand – to make the brand a meaningful part of consumers' conversations and their lives. Today's new relation-ship-building tools include everything from websites, blogs, in-person events and video sharing to online communities and social networks such as Facebook, YouTube, Twitter or a company's own social networking sites.

- The sixth edition contains new material on the continuing trend toward two-way interactions between customers and brands, including such topics as **customer-managed relationships, crowdsourcing** and **consumer-generated marketing**. Today's customers are giving as much as they get in the form of two-way relationships (Chapter 1), a more active role in providing customer insights (Chapter 4), crowdsourcing and shaping new products (Chapter 9), consumer-generated marketing content (Chapter 1, 14 and 15), developing or passing along brand messages (Chapters 1 and 15), interacting in customer communities (Chapters 5, 15 and 17), and other developments.
- *Marketing by the Numbers appendix.* An innovative Appendix 2 provides students with a comprehensive introduction to the marketing financial analysis that helps to guide, assess and support marketing decisions.
- Throughout every chapter of the sixth European edition we have included examples and illustrations that are relevant to today's marketer in Europe with an international perspective.

More than ever before, the sixth European edition of *Principles of Marketing* creates value for you – it gives you all you need to know about marketing in an effective and enjoyable total learning package!

A valuable total teaching and learning package

A successful marketing course requires more than a well-written book. A total package of resources extends this edition's emphasis on creating value for you. The following aids support *Principles of Marketing, sixth European edition*:

MyMarketingLab

mymarketinglab (www.mymktlab.com) gives you the opportunity to test yourself on key concepts and skills, track your own progress through the course, and use the personalised study plan activities – all to help you achieve success in the classroom.

The MyLab that accompanies *Principles of Marketing* includes:

- *Study Plan*: The Study Plan helps ensure that you have a basic understanding of course material before coming to class by guiding you directly to the pages you need to review.
- *Mini-Simulations*: Move beyond the basics with interactive simulations that place you in a realistic marketing situation and require you to make decisions based on marketing concepts.
- *Applied Theories*: Get involved with detailed videos, interactive cases and critical thinking exercises.
- *Videos*: The video library features a range of exciting videos for this edition including a video case at the end of each chapter.

Plus:

- *Interactive Elements*: A wealth of hands-on activities and exercises let you experience and learn firsthand. Whether it is with the online e-book where you can search for specific key-words or page numbers, highlight specific sections, enter notes right on the e-book page and print reading assignments with notes for later review or with other materials.

Find out more at www.mymktlab.com.

ABOUT THE AUTHORS

Philip Kotler is S.C. Johnson & Son Distinguished Professor of International Marketing at the J.L. Kellogg School of Management, Northwestern University. He received his master's degree at the University of Chicago and his PhD at MIT, both in Economics. Dr Kotler is author of *Marketing Management*, Thirteenth Edition (Prentice Hall). He has authored over 30 books and he has written over 100 articles for leading journals. He is the only three-time winner of the Alpha Kappa Psi Award for the best annual article in the *Journal of Marketing*. Dr Kotler's numerous honours include the Paul D. Converse Award given by the American Marketing Association to honour 'outstanding contributions to the science of marketing' and the Stuart Henderson Brit Award as Marketer of the Year. In 1985, he was named the first recipient of two major awards: the Distinguished Marketing Educator of the Year Award, given by the American Marketing Association, and the Philip Kotler Award for Excellence in Health Care Marketing. He has consulted on many US and foreign companies on marketing strategy. He has received over ten honorary doctorates from abroad.

Gary Armstrong is Crist W. Blackwell Distinguished Professor Emeritus of Undergraduate Education in the Kenan-Flagler Business School at the University of North Carolina at Chapel Hill. He received his PhD in marketing from Northwestern University. Professor Armstrong has contributed articles to leading research journals and consulted with many companies on marketing strategy. However, his first love is teaching. He has been very active in Kenan-Flagler's undergraduate business programme and he has received several campus-wide and business schools teaching awards. In 2004, Professor Armstrong received the UNC Board of Governors Award for Excellence in Teaching, the highest teaching honour bestowed at the University of North Carolina at Chapel Hill.

Lloyd C. Harris is the Head of the Marketing Group and Professor of Marketing at Warwick Business School, University of Warwick. After working in retail and service organisations he received his PhD in marketing from Cardiff University. His research results have been disseminated via a range of marketing, strategy, H.R.M. and general management journals. He has published widely in these fields and has published over one hundred pieces. He is particularly proud of papers that have been published in the *Journal of Retailing, Journal of the Academy of Marketing Science, Journal of Management Studies, Human Resource Management, Organization Studies* and the *Annals of Tourism Research*. He has consulted and run programmes for many leading private and public organisations, especially focusing on retailing and service organisations.

Nigel Piercy is Professor of Marketing and Strategy at Warwick Business School, University of Warwick. He was previously Professor of Strategic Marketing and Head of the Marketing Group at Cranfield School of Management. For several years he was the Sir Julian Hodge Professor of Marketing and Strategy at Cardiff University. He has also been visiting professor at Texas Christian University, the Fuqua School of Business at Duke University in North Carolina, the Columbia Graduate School of Business in New York, and at the University of California, Berkeley. He has managerial experience in retailing and was in business planning with Nycomed Amersham plc (now part of GE Healthcare). He has extensive experience as a consultant and management workshop speaker and facilitator with many organisations throughout the world, specializing in the issues of market strategy planning and implementation, and strategic sales management, and has been awarded many prizes for teaching excellence. Nigel has been awarded the distinction of a higher doctorate (Doctor of Letters) from Heriot-Watt University, Edinburgh, for his published research work. He is joint editor of the *Journal of Strategic Marketing* and serves on the editorial boards of several major scholarly journals.

ACKNOWLEDGEMENTS

We are grateful to the following for permission to reproduce copyright material:

Figures

Figure 1.5 adapted from Mismanagement of Customer Loyalty, *Harvard Business Review*, p. 93 (Werner Relnartz and V. Kumar 2002), Reprinted by permission of Harvard Business Review. Copyright © 2008 by the Harvard Business School Publishing Corporation; all rights reserved.; Figure 2.2 adapted from www.bcg.com/documents/file13904.pdf, Adapted from The BCG Portfolio Matrix from The Product Portfoilio Matrix, © 1970, The Boston Consulting Group; Figure 2.3 from Strategies for Diversification, *Harvard Business Review*, pp. 113–124 (H.IgorAnsoff 1957), Reprinted by permission of Harvard Business Review. Copyright © 1957 by the Harvard Business School Publishing Corporation; all rights reserved.; Figure 2.8 adapted from Return on Marketing: Using Consumer Equity to Focus on Marketing Strategy, *Journal of Marketing*, p. 112 (Roland T. Rust, Katherine Lemon and Valerie A. Zeithaml 2004), Reprinted with permission from Journal of Marketing, published by the American Marketing Association; Figure 5.5 adapted from *Consumer Behavior and Marketing Action*, Kent Publishing Company (Henry Assael 1987) p. 87, Reprinted with permission of Henry Assael; Figure 5.7 from *Diffusion of Innovations*, Free Press (Everett M.Rogers 2003), Reprinted with the permission of The Free Press, a Division of Simon & Schuster, Inc., from Diffusion of Innovations, 5th Ed. by Everett M. Rogers. Copyright © 1995, 2003 by Everett M. Rogers. Copyright © 1962, 1971, 1983 by The Free Press. All rights reserved.; Figure 11.2 adapted from Pricing and Public Policy: A Research Agenda and Overview of the Special Issue, *Journal of Public Policy and Marketing*, Spring 1999, pp. 3–10 (DhruvGrewal and Larry D. Compeau), Reprinted with permission from Journal of Public Policy and Marketing, published by the American Marketing; Association; Figure 18.2 adapted from Can You Say What the Strategy Is?, *Harvard Business Review*, p. 89 (David J. Collins and Michael Rukstad), April 2008, Reprinted by permission of Harvard Business Review. Copyright © 2008 by the Harvard Business School Publishing Corporation; all rights reserved.; Figure 20.2 from Innovation, creative Destruction and Sustainability, *Research Technology Management*, pp. 21–7 (Stuart L. Hart), September-October 2005, © The Industrial Research Institute. Reproduced with permission.

Screenshots

Screenshot on page 190 from http://www.peppol.eu/; Screenshot on page 206 from http://www.saga.co.uk/; Screenshot on page 211 from http://www.caci.co.uk/acorn-classification.aspx, CACI Limited; Screenshot on page 307 from http://www.ryanair.com/en; Screenshot on page 337 from http://www.cartrawler.com/about/company.php, Reprinted with permission; Screenshot on page 525 from http://www.fiskateers.com/, Project by StephenieHamen for Fiskateers.com. Reproduced by permission of Fiskars Group.

Tables

Table 9.2 from *Marketing Management*, 13th Ed., Prentice Hall (Philip Kotler and Kevin Lane Keller 2009) p. 288, Reproduced by permission of Pearson Education Inc., Upper Saddle River, New Jersey; Table on page 414 from *BusinessWeek*, 21/12/2008 (Carol Matlack); Table 20.2 from www.marketingpower.com/AboutAMA/Pages/Statement%20of%20Ethics.aspx#, Reprinted with permission of the American Marketing Association

Text

Quote on page 15 from www.klm.com, Reprinted with permission; Quote on page 18 from The CEO's Marketing Manifesto, *Marketing Management*, pp. 24–29 (Nirmalya Kumar 2008), Reprinted with permission from Marketing Management, published by the American Marketing Association.; Quote on page 26 from http://www.wateraid.org/uk/about_us/vision_and_mission/default.asp, Reprinted with permission.; Quote on page 26 from www.tiffany.com, Reprinted with permission.; Quote on pages 42-3 from State your Business; Too Many Mission Statements are Loaded with Fatheaded Jargon, *Business Week*, pp. 80 (Jack and Suzy Welch); Text on page 44 adapted from www.bcg.com/documents/file13904.pdf, Adapted from The BCG Portfolio Matrix from The Product Portfoilio Matrix, © 1970, The Boston Consulting Group; Quote on page 50 from www.loreal.com/_en/_ww/html/suppliers/index.aspx, © L'Oreal S.A. Reproduced with permission of L'Oreal; Quote on page 59 from ROI More Vital Than Ever, *Sales and Marketing Management*, pp. 51–52 (Mark McMaster 2002), Reprinted with permission of Mach 1 Business Media.; Case Study on pages 71-4 from Downwardly Mobile, *Financial Times*, 25/02/2011 (Andrew Parker and Andrew Ward); Nokia and Microsoft Talk Up Benefits of Co-Dependence, *Financial Times*, 12/01/2012, p. 23 (Richard Waters) © The Financial Times Limited. All Rights Reserved.; Case Study on pages 104-5 from Customers Feel the Quality Not the Width, *Financial Times*, 12/09/2006 (EoinCallan, Lucy Killgren and Elizabeth Rigby); Primark Slowdown Bodes III, *Financial Times*, 01/03/2011 (Claer Barrett and Andrea Felsted); Squeezed Buyers Halve Primark Sales Growth, *Financial Times*, 12/09/2011 (Claer Barrett); Strong Primark Sales Boost ABF, *Financial Times*, 19/01/2012 (Louise Lucas), © The Financial Times Limited. All Rights Reserved.; Case Study on pages 107-8 from Demand is Putting the Mobile into Automobile, *Financial Times*, 07/05/2010 (John Reed); Carmakers Tempt Cellphone Generation with Pay-as-you-go, *Financial Times*, 06/05/2010 (John Reed); Sharing: Flexible Hire is Talk of the Town, *Financial Times*, 12/09/2011 (John Reed), © The Financial Times Limited. All Rights Reserved.; Text on page 112 from Online Advertisers Issue Tracking Code, *Financial Times*, 15/04/2011 (Tim Bradshaw), © The Financial Times Limited. All Rights Reserved.; Text on pages 118-9 from Rank Sets Out to Discover Home Truths, *Financial Times*, 07/02/2011 (Rose Jacobs), © The Financial Times Limited. All Rights Reserved.; Text on pages 120-1 from Mecca Finds Gold Dust in Bingogoer Rituals, *Financial Times*, 07/02/2011 (Rose Jacobs), © The Financial Times Limited. All Rights Reserved.; Text on page 148 from Wii U kickstarts next generation of gaming, *Financial Times*, 10/06/2011 (Chris Nutall), © The Financial Times Limited. All Rights Reserved.; Case Study on pages 143-4 from Pretty, Posh and Profitable, *Financial Times*, 13/05/2011 (Lucie Greene); Text on pages 154-5 from Europe's cheap chic brands feel the pinch, *Financial Times*, 22/06/2011 (Andrea Felsted), © The Financial Times Limited. All Rights Reserved.; Case Study on pages 175-6 from Interview with Kim Väisänen; Lyytinen, J., and Yritäedes. 32 syytäryhtyäyrittäjäksi, GummerousKirjapainoOy, Jyväskylä 2004, http://www.blancco.com/en, Reprinted with permission of BlanccoOy Ltd.; Text on pages 187-8 from History proves the greatest teacher, *Financial Times*, 11/07/2007 (Andrew Baxter); Quote on page 190 from http://www.peppol.eu/; Case Study on pages 201-3 from Fast Fashion for Fast Consumers, *Financial Times*, 22/02/2011 (Claer Barrett), © The Financial Times Limited. All Rights Reserved.; Quote on page 223 from http://www.singaporeair.com/en_UK/about-us/, Reprinted with permission; Quote on page 242 from http://www.jordanscereals.co.uk/our-story/countryside-commitment/; Text on pages 245-6 from Coke vs Pepsi: The Taste They Don't Want You to Know About, *The 60-Second Marketer* (Andy Goldsmith), www.60secondmarketer.com/60SecondArticles/Branding/cokevs.pepsitast.html, © Andy Goldsmith, as published in 60SecondMarketer.com; Text on page 252 adapted from Clueing in Customers, *Harvard Business Review* (Leonard Berry and NeeliBendapudi

2003), Reprinted by permission of Harvard Business Review. Copyright © 2003 by the Harvard Business School Publishing Corporation; all rights reserved.; Text on pages 255-6 adapted from Customer Service Champs, *BusinessWeek*, 05/03/2007 (Jena McGregor); Quote on page 263 from TippingSprung Publishes Results from Fifth Annual Brand-Extensions Survey, http://www.brandchannel.com/papers_review.asp?sp_id=1222, Reprinted with permission of Martyn Tipping and Robert Sprung; Case Study on pages 270-1 from Consumer Trust sees John Lewis Set Retail Pace, *Financial Times*, 16/01/2010 (Andrea Felsted); Text on page 278 adapted from *A Group Effort* (Elisabeth Sullivan) p. 26; Text on page 282 adapted from http://www.insightsinretail.com/virtual-stores/the-use-of-virtual-store-simulations-in-marketing-research-and-beyond/, From "Shaping Retail: The Use of Virtual Store Simulations in Marketing Research & Beyond". Path to Purchase Institute, 2009; Quote on page 286 adapted from Innovation in Turbulent Times, *Harvard Business Review*, pp. 79–86 (Darrell K.Rigby, Karen Gruver and James Allen), June 2009, Reprinted by permission of Harvard Business Review. Copyright © 2009 by the Harvard Business School Publishing Corporation; all rights reserved.; Case Study on pages 299-300 from Succession Challenge for Incoming Reckitt Chief, *Financial Times*, 15/04/2011 (Alison Smith), © The Financial Times Limited. All Rights Reserved.; Text on page 332 from Scottish Scientists Develop Whisky Biofuel, *Financial Times*, 17/08/2010 (Andrew Bolger), © The Financial Times Limited. All Rights Reserved.; Text on page 338 from The World's Most Influential Companies: Unilever, *BusinessWeek*, 22/12/2008; Text on page 343 from Brussels targets online credit card fees, *Financial Times*, 23/06/2011 (Nikki Tait), © The Financial Times Limited. All Rights Reserved.; Case Study on pages 349-50 from "Kaisers predict riot of interest in new album", *Financial Times*, 02/06/2011 (Carl Wilkinson), © The Financial Times Limited. All Rights Reserved.; Text on pages 349-50 from CD price fall adds to music industry's blues, *Financial Times*, 12/05/2010 (Esther Bintliff); Radiohead MP3 release a tactic to lift CD sales, *Financial Times*, 07/10/2007 (Andrew Edgecliffe-Johnson); Text on page 359 adapted from Burger King franchises can have it their own way, *Wall Street Journal*, 21/01/2010 (Richard Gibson), Copyright © 2010, Dow Jones & Company, Inc. All Rights Reserved Worldwide. License numbers 2993091001021 & 2993091320061; Text on page 360 adapted from http://www.eff-franchise.com/; Quote on page 374 from https://raportal.riteaid.com/VN/VNBULLETIN/VNBU0003.ASPX?Type=S&Flg=F&EntryID=19; Text on page 398 adapted from Five Rules for Retailing in a Recession, *Harvard Business Review*, pp. 64–72 (Ken Favaro, Tim Romberger and David Meer), April 2009, Reprinted by permission of Harvard Business Review. Copyright © 2009 by the Harvard Business School Publishing Corporation; all rights reserved.; Text on page 401 adapted from Green Keeps Growing, *Private Label Magazine*, 01/10/2010 (Berlinski), www.privatelabelmag.com/feature.cfm; Text on page 402 adapted from Green Keeps Growing, *Private Label Magazine*, 01/10/2010 (Peter Berlinski); Case Study on pages 417-8 adapted from Marketing 50: Haagen-Dazs, KattyPien, Advertising Age, 17/11/2008 (Tiffany Meyers); Text on page 422 adapted from http://www.thinktank.org.uk/du_at_the_o2.php; Text on page 426 from Brands That Laugh all the Way to the Bank, *Financial Times*, 06/01/2011 (Rhymer Rigby); Text on page 450 adapted from Thinking Big Takes Audi from Obscure to Awesome, *Advertising Age*, 02/02/2009 (Jean Halliday); Text on page 455 adapted from How Etsy Made Us Rethink Consumer-Generated Ads, *Advertising Age*, 21/09/2009 (Bob Garfield); Text on page 483 adapted from Staying in the Game, *Pharmaceutical Executive*, pp. 158–9 (Sara Donnelly), May 2008, Reprinted with permission from Pharmaceutical Executive. Pharmaceutical Executive is a copyrighted publication of Advanstar Communications Inc. All Rights Reserved.; Text on page 484 adapted from Portal Powers GE Sales, *Computerworld*, 02/06/2003, pp. 31–2 (Gary H. Anthes); Text on page 485 adapted from Sales 2.0: How Soon Will It Improve Your Business?, *Selling Power*, pp. 58–61 (Pelin Wood Thorogood), November/December 2008; Text on page 493 from http://www.comscoredatamine.com/2011/02/groupon-contributes-to-significant-growth-for-coupon-sites-in-europe/, Reproduced with permission of comScore, Inc.; Text on page 512 adapted from PURL's of Wisdom, *Target Marketing*, pp. 27–9 (Heather Fletcher), January 2009, PURL's of Wisdom, Target Marketing, pp. 27–9 (Heather Fletcher), January 2009, Published by North American Publishing Company; Text on page 515 adapted from Going Mobile, *Supermarket News*, 12/01/2009 (Michael Garry); Text on page 554 adapted from Why Unilever Lost the Laundry War, *Advertising Age*, 06/08/2007 (Jack Neff); Text on pages 555-6 adapted from Strategies to Crack Well-Guarded Markets, *Harvard Business Review*, pp. 84–91 (David J. Bryce and Jeffrey H. Dyer), May 2007, Reprinted by permission of Harvard Business Review. Copyright © 2007 by the Harvard Business School Publishing Corporation; all rights reserved.; Text on pages 583-4 adapted from Cadbury Redefines Cheap Luxury - Marketing to India's Poor, Candy Makers Sells Small Bites for Pennies, *Wall Street Journal*, 08/06/2009 (Sonya Misquitta), © 2009 Dow Jones & Company, Inc. All Rights Reserved Worldwide. License numbers 2993100203743 & 2993100338903; Text on page 586 adapted from First Mover in Mobile: How It's Selling Cell Phones to the Developing World, *BusinessWeek*, 14/05/2007 (Jack Ewing); Case Study on pages 597-8 from Unilever Looks to Clean Up in Africa, *Financial Times*, 15/11/2007 (Barney Jopson); Case Study on pages 628-30 from GE Looks Out For a Cleaner Profit, *Financial Times*, 01/07/2005 (Fiona Harvey)

Photos

The publisher would like to thank the following for their kind permission to reproduce their photographs:

(Key: b-bottom; c-centre; l-left; r-right; t-top)

© 2010 Amazon.com, Inc. or its affiliates: 246; **3M Company:** 277; **Adidas:** 124; **Alamy Images:** 1Exposure 541, Alex Segre 313, Clynt Garnham Food & Drink 9, David Pearson 367, Finnbarr Webster 607, Friedhof Foster 237, Gallo Images 451, Helen Sessions 25, Ian Francis 247, 427, Ian Francis 247, 427, Image Broker 48, Image Source 121, Incamerastock 526l, Justin Kase 373, Lou Linwei 89, 329, Lynne Sutherland 602, M40S 201, Mark Mercer 255, Mark Richardson 181, MBI 152, Mike Finn-Kelcey 551, Oleg Shipov 175, Pictorial Press 363, Pixellover RM5 399, Shiny Pix 435, Stewart Goldstein 597; **American Association of Advertising Agencies:** 157; **Apple, Inc:** 71; **Bentley Houston:** 365; **Courtesy of Boots:** 514; **BuyMyFace.com:** 457; **Campbell Soup Company:** 161; **Climax Portable Machine Tools:** 480; **Consumer Electronics Association (CEA):** 496; **Copyright © Inditex:** 353; **Corbis:** 182, Sion Touhig 84; **Courtesy of © Red Bull Media House:** 115; **Courtesy of Steinway & Sons:** 306; **Courtesy of Waitrose Ltd:** 303; **European Union 2010:** 572; **Eyetracker:** 126; **Getty Images:** 341, 556, 612, AFP 91, 262, 403, 462, 575, Bloomberg 209, 390, 569, Boston Globe 220, Dan Kitwood 14, David Goddard 397, David Hecker 92, David McNew 429, Film Magic 619, Fred Duval 39, India Today Group 586, Justin Sullivan 109, Michael Loccisano 317, Michelle Pedone 156, Rebecca Sapp 360; **Glenkinchie Distillery:** 332; **H.J. Heinz Company Limited:** 290; **Haagen-Dazs:** 417; **Image courtesy of The Advertising Archives:** 41, 49, 151, 208, 286; **iStockphoto:** 526r; **Kurtis Meyers:** 257; **Eyevine Ltd:** 392t, 392b, Eros Hoagland 273; **Marketing NPV Corporation:** 59; **Microsoft Limited:** 445; **Morrisons:** 394; **NHS Blood and Transplant:** 241; **Ogilvy.com:** 584; **Pearson Education Ltd:** SteveShott 147; **Peugeot Citroen:** 107; **Photo by Jim Whitmer:** 333; **Press Association Images:** 355, 505, John Terhune 149, Paul Sakuma 339, Xu Ruiping 578; **Rex Features:** 1096104am 421, Geoff Wilkinson 225, MCP 216; **Saatchi & Saatchi:** 75; **Shutterstock.com:** 15, 22, 131, 327, 385, 476, Vlad61 52; **Specsavers:** 3; **Tata Motors Ltd:** 87; **The History of Advertising Trust:** 454; **Used by permission of Michelin, North America, Inc.:** 426; **Vivigo:** 46; **WaterAid:** 27

All other images © Pearson Education

In some instances we have been unable to trace the owners of copyright material, and we would appreciate any information that would enable us to do so.

PART ONE

Defining marketing and the marketing process

CHAPTER ONE

Marketing: creating and capturing customer value

Chapter preview

This chapter introduces you to the basic concepts of marketing. We start with a question: What is marketing? Simply put, marketing is managing profitable customer relationships. The aim of marketing is to create value for customers and capture value from customers in return. Next we discuss the five steps in the marketing process – from understanding customer needs, to designing customer-driven marketing strategies and integrated marketing programmes, to building customer relationships and capturing value for the firm. Finally, we discuss the major trends and forces affecting marketing in this age of customer relationships. Understanding these basic concepts and forming your own ideas about what they really mean to you will give you a solid foundation for all that follows.

We start with a good story about marketing in action at Specsavers, one of the world's fastest-growing optical and auditory retailers. What is the secret of its success? It's really no secret at all. Specsavers is completely customer obsessed. It has a passion for creating customer value and relationships. In return, customers reward Specsavers with their brand loyalty and buying euros. You'll see this theme of creating customer value to capture value in return repeated throughout this first chapter and the remainder of the text.

Objective outline

➤ **Objective 1** Define marketing and outline the steps in the marketing process.
What is marketing? (pp. 4–5)

➤ **Objective 2** Explain the importance of understanding customers and the marketplace and identify the five core marketplace concepts.
Understanding the marketplace and customer needs (pp. 6–8)

➤ **Objective 3** Identify the key elements of a customer-driven marketing strategy and discuss the marketing management orientations that guide marketing strategy.
Designing a customer-driven marketing strategy (pp. 8–12)

Preparing an integrated marketing plan and programme (p. 12)

➤ **Objective 4** Discuss customer relationship management (CRM) and identify strategies for creating value *for* customers and capturing value *from* customers in return.
Building customer relationships (pp. 13–19)
Capturing value from customers (pp. 19–21)

➤ **Objective 5** Describe the major trends and forces that are changing the marketing landscape in this age of relationships.
The changing marketing landscape (pp. 22–27)
So, what is marketing? pulling it all together (pp. 28–29)

Specsavers

The next time you are in a Specsavers store, trying on Karen Millen or Gok Wan designer frames, pay attention to the genial, well-dressed lady in her sixties wandering around, clutching shopping bags and chatting to customers. It is just possible that you've chanced upon the customer-obsessed Dame Mary Perkins, the co-founder of what is the world's biggest privately owned optical and auditory retailer, whose turnover is estimated to be around €1.75billion.

It is not fair to say that Dame Mary Perkins is merely interested with the customer experience of Specsavers; she is obsessed. Over 25 years ago, it was her frustration with the expensive, time-consuming and often intimidating process of buying glasses that led to Specsavers being established. Specsavers employs a firm called 'Retail Eyes' to evaluate their service using mystery shoppers. These undercover service sleuths write reports afterwards and sometimes shoot video using a hidden-button camera. Nevertheless, Dame Mary is so driven that she often covertly visits the group's shops across the country, often in disguise. 'We have professional mystery shoppers but I will go round on my own,' she smiles. 'I've got a couple of wigs and different glasses, and I'll go in with M&S carrier bags and people don't expect to see you. If it's a busy place you can sidle up to the customers and say: "what do you think of these?"'

Dame Mary has always been confident of knowing what customers want since she and her husband Doug, who she had met while they were training as opticians at Cardiff University in the UK, set up their first chain of opticians which they sold in the late 1970s. However, the experience of owning a chain of shops meant the couple knew it was not a model they wanted to revisit. 'We didn't want a big chain and worrying about a head office and whether staff were working properly. You lost touch with people,' she says.

Consequently, they devised a strategy that would allow opticians to become joint venture partners in each Specsavers store. 'We were very close to the opticians we employed in the last business and we knew that professional people were very much better working for themselves,' she says. 'But [if you] leave them on their own they are not going to make a very good business of it because there is so much back office stuff that needs doing. So we thought if they could own their own business but shelter under an umbrella with somebody else doing all the management services, that would leave them free to do what they are good at.'

Thriving with its joint venture partnership approach to eye care, Specsavers hit the milestone of 100 stores in July 1988, 200 in 1993, 300 in 1995, 400 in 2000, 500 in 2003, 600 in 2004 and 700 in 2005. The first Netherlands store opened in 1997, the first Swedish in 2004, and 2005 saw the first in Denmark and Norway. In 2006 the first store was opened in Spain, and in 2007 the company began supplying in Australia whilst opening the first store in Finland. In January 2008 Dame Mary Perkins opened the thousandth store in Roosendaal, Holland. Specsavers, which is still wholly owned by the couple, now has more than 1390 stores across the Channel Islands, UK, Ireland, the Netherlands, Scandinavia, Spain, Australia and New Zealand.

The explicit focus on customers is evident both in-store and online where posters and banners claim that 'customer satisfaction is our only priority'. Indeed, the prominently displayed Specsavers Customer Promise states that 'We want you to be completely happy with your purchase at Specsavers Opticians. If you have any concerns within three months of the date of your purchase we will put it right. No quibble, no fuss. Your statutory rights are not affected. Please ask in store for full details.' Customers are reminded that each outlet 'is owned and run by one or more store directors, who are responsible for the day-to-day running of the store and for the professional service provided.' Any suggestions, complaints or feedback are guaranteed to be personally handled by a Store Director who will respond directly to customers. The firm has even employed Simon Brown, a feng shui consultant and the author of *Practical Feng Shui for Business*, to ensure that stores have positive flows of energy.

The parent Specsavers group insists on rigorous customer service training and teams meet each partner every eight weeks. The in-store partners are explicitly deterred from becoming absentee owners of a number of Specsavers stores by a distinctive contract system that keeps them close to their customers on the shop floor. 'They are not only directors of the company, they are also employees of the company and under their contract they have to work 40 hours a week,' Dame Mary says. 'It is best to have the owner optician in that store. Otherwise we might as well have a chain.'

At Specsavers, taking good care of customers starts with a deep-down, customer-focused culture. The company is 'obsessed by service'.

Source: Specsavers

Specsavers has always been marketing-driven, and it employs a big marketing and creative team with almost all advertising generated in-house. They have produced a series of advertisements on the 'Should have gone to Specsavers' theme – one of which (admittedly the one with hundreds of bikini-clad models) has been viewed over 1.2 million times on YouTube. The firm sponsors 'Spectacle Wearer of the Year' and the 'Specsavers Crime Thriller Awards' with a major UK-based television channel, ITV. 'The two of us knew it was important to build that brand [from the start] – we got things in the paper and got the name bandied around, using different events and sponsorship,' Dame Mary says.

After the success of the Specsavers optician model, it is hardly surprising that the company is keen to drive into other areas, notably hearing aids. 'That was a golden opportunity with the database we have got and the customers we have,' says co-founder Dame Mary Perkins. She sees parallels with the optical industry of a couple of decades ago with high prices and lack of choice. After opening its first hearing centre five years ago, the company is now the biggest supplier of hearing aids in the UK, outside the NHS.[1]

Today's successful companies have one thing in common: they are strongly customer focused and heavily committed to marketing. These companies share a passion for understanding and satisfying customer needs in well-defined target markets. They motivate everyone in the organisation to help build lasting customer relationships based on creating value.

Customer relationships and value are especially important today. As Europe's economy slowly recovers following the worst downturn since the Great Depression, more frugal consumers are spending more carefully and reassessing their relationships with brands. In turn, it's more important than ever to build strong customer relationships based on real and enduring value.

WHAT IS MARKETING?

AUTHOR COMMENT

Stop here for a second and think about how you'd answer this question before studying marketing. Then see how your answer changes as you read the chapter.

Marketing, more than any other business function, deals with customers. Although we will soon explore more-detailed definitions of marketing, perhaps the simplest definition is this one: *Marketing is managing profitable customer relationships.* The two-fold goal of marketing is to attract new customers by promising superior value and keep and grow current customers by delivering satisfaction.

For example, Walmart has become the world's largest retailer – and the world's largest company – by delivering on its promise, 'Save money. Live better.' Nintendo surged ahead in the video-games market behind the pledge that 'Wii would like to play', backed by its wildly popular Wii console and a growing list of popular games and accessories for all ages. And McDonald's fulfils its 'I'm lovin it' motto by being 'our customers favourite place and way to eat' the world over, giving it a market share greater than that of its nearest three competitors combined.[2]

Sound marketing is critical to the success of every organisation. Large for-profit firms, such as Unilever, Nestlé, Shell and Santander use marketing. But so do not-for-profit organisations, such as schools, hospitals, museums, symphony orchestras and even churches.

You already know a lot about marketing; it's all around you. Marketing comes to you in the good old traditional forms: You see it in the abundance of products at your nearby shopping mall and the ads that fill your TV screen, spice up your magazines, or stuff your letter box. But in recent years, marketers have assembled a host of new marketing approaches, everything from imaginative websites and online social networks to your mobile phone. These new approaches do more than just blast out messages to the masses. They reach you directly and personally. Today's marketers want to become a part of your life and enrich your experiences with their brands – to help you *live* their brands.

At home, at school, where you work and where you play, you see marketing in almost everything you do. Yet, there is much more to marketing than meets the consumer's casual eye. Behind it all is a massive network of people and activities competing for your attention and purchases. This book will give you a complete introduction to the basic concepts and practices of today's marketing. In this chapter, we begin by defining marketing and the marketing process.

Marketing defined

What *is* marketing? Many people think of marketing as only selling and advertising. We are bombarded every day with TV commercials, catalogues, sales calls and e-mail pitches. However, selling and advertising are only the tip of the marketing iceberg.

Today, marketing must be understood not in the old sense of making a sale – 'telling and selling' – but in the new sense of *satisfying customer needs.* If the marketer understands consumer needs; develops products that provide superior customer value; and prices, distributes, and promotes them effectively, these products will sell easily. In fact, according to management guru Peter Drucker, 'The aim of marketing is to make selling unnecessary.'[3] Selling and advertising are only part of a larger 'marketing mix' – a set of marketing tools that work together to satisfy customer needs and build customer relationships.

Broadly defined, marketing is a social and managerial process by which individuals and organisations obtain what they need and want through creating and exchanging value with others. In a narrower business context, marketing involves building profitable, value-laden exchange relationships with customers. Hence, we define **marketing** as the process by which companies create value for customers and build strong customer relationships to capture value from customers in return.[4]

Marketing—The process by which companies create value for customers and build strong customer relationships to capture value from customers in return.

The marketing process

Figure 1.1 presents a simple, five-step model of the marketing process. In the first four steps, companies work to understand consumers, create customer value and build strong customer relationships. In the final step, companies reap the rewards of creating superior customer value. By creating value *for* consumers, they in turn capture value *from* consumers in the form of sales, profits, and long-term customer equity.

In this chapter and the next, we will examine the steps of this simple model of marketing. In this chapter, we review each step but focus more on the customer relationship steps – understanding customers, building customer relationships, and capturing value from customers. In Chapter 2, we look more deeply into the second and third steps – designing marketing strategies and constructing marketing programmes.

Figure 1.1 A simple model of the marketing process

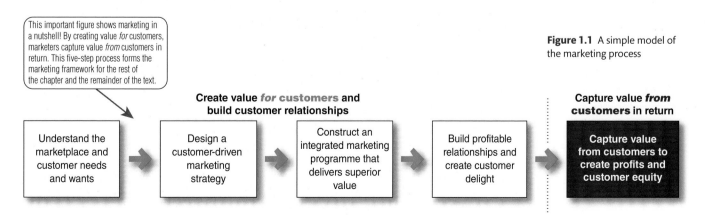

This important figure shows marketing in a nutshell! By creating value *for* customers, marketers capture value *from* customers in return. This five-step process forms the marketing framework for the rest of the chapter and the remainder of the text.

Create value *for* customers and build customer relationships

Capture value *from* customers in return

| Understand the marketplace and customer needs and wants | Design a customer-driven marketing strategy | Construct an integrated marketing programme that delivers superior value | Build profitable relationships and create customer delight | **Capture value from customers to create profits and customer equity** |

UNDERSTANDING THE MARKETPLACE AND CUSTOMER NEEDS

As a first step, marketers need to understand customer needs and wants and the marketplace in which they operate. We examine five core customer and marketplace concepts: (1) *needs, wants and demands*; (2) *market offerings (products, services and experiences)*; (3) *value and satisfaction*; (4) *exchanges and relationships*; and (5) *markets*.

Customer needs, wants and demands

Needs—States of felt deprivation.

The most basic concept underlying marketing is that of human needs. Human **needs** are states of felt deprivation. They include basic *physical* needs for food, clothing, warmth and safety; *social* needs for belonging and affection; and *individual* needs for knowledge and self-expression. Marketers did not create these needs; they are a basic part of the human makeup.

Wants—The form human needs take as they are shaped by culture and individual personality.

Wants are the form human needs take as they are shaped by culture and individual personality. A Briton *needs* food but wants cucumber sandwiches, a slice of Victoria sponge cake and a cup of milky tea. An American *needs* food but *wants* a Big Mac, french fries and a soft drink. A person in Papua New Guinea *needs* food but *wants* taro, rice, yams and pork. Wants are shaped by one's society and are described in terms of objects that will satisfy those needs. When backed by buying power, wants become **demands**. Given their wants and resources, people demand products with benefits that add up to the most value and satisfaction.

Demands—Human wants that are backed by buying power.

Outstanding marketing companies go to great lengths to learn about and understand their customers' needs, wants, and demands. They conduct consumer research and analyse mountains of customer data. Their people at all levels – including top management – stay close to customers. For example, James Averdiek, Founder and MC of Gü Chocolate Puds argues that a core tenet of any successful business is getting close to your customers by finding out what they are doing and taking part in it. At P&G, executives from the chief executive officer down spend time with customers in their homes and on shopping trips. P&G brand managers routinely spend a week or two living on the budget of low-end consumers to gain insights into what they can do to improve customers' lives.[5]

Market offerings – products, services and experiences

Market offerings—Some combination of products, services, information or experiences offered to a market to satisfy a need or want.

Consumers' needs and wants are fulfilled through **market offerings** – some combination of products, services, information, or experiences offered to a market to satisfy a need or a want. Market offerings are not limited to physical *products*. They also include *services* – activities or benefits offered for sale that are essentially intangible and do not result in the ownership of anything. Examples include banking, airline, hotel, tax preparation, and home repair services.

More broadly, market offerings also include other entities, such as *persons, places, organisations information* and *ideas*. For example, the European Travel Commission markets Europe as a tourist destination for US consumers via Facebook, emphasising history, culture and gastronomy with the tag line 'Follow Your Dreams: Visit Europe'.[6] Similarly, capitalising on recent golfing success, Tourism Ireland promotes Ireland to overseas visitors as 'The Home of Champions' where 'when your round ends the fun is only just beginning.'[7]

Many sellers make the mistake of paying more attention to the specific products they offer than to the benefits and experiences produced by these products. These sellers suffer from **marketing myopia**. They are so taken with their products that they focus only on existing wants and lose sight of underlying customer needs.[8] They forget that a product is only a tool to solve a consumer problem. A manufacturer of 8mm drill bits may think that the customer needs a drill bit. But what the customer *really* needs is a 8mm hole. These sellers will have trouble if a new product comes along that serves the customer's need better or less expensively. The customer will have the same *need* but will *want* the new product.

Smart marketers look beyond the attributes of the products and services they sell. By orchestrating several services and products, they create *brand experiences* for consumers. For example, you don't just watch a Wimbledon Tennis Tournament; you immerse yourself in the historical home of tennis. Similarly, Ferrari recognises that their cars are much more than just a combustion engine, a collection of wires and electrical components. To the owners of a Ferrari car, their Ferrari is an expression of their status, taste and style.

> **Marketing myopia**—The mistake of paying more attention to the specific products a company offers than to the benefits and experiences produced by these products.

Customer value and satisfaction

Customers usually face a broad array of products and services that might satisfy a given need. How do they choose among these many market offerings? Customers form expectations about the value and satisfaction that various market offerings will deliver and buy accordingly. Satisfied customers buy again and tell others about their good experiences. Dissatisfied customers often switch to competitors and disparage the product to others.

Marketers must be careful to set the right level of expectations. If they set expectations too low, they may satisfy those who buy but fail to attract enough buyers. If they set expectations too high, buyers will be disappointed. Customer value and customer satisfaction are key building blocks for developing and managing customer relationships. We will revisit these core concepts later in the chapter.

Exchanges and relationships

Marketing occurs when people decide to satisfy needs and wants through exchange relationships. **Exchange** is the act of obtaining a desired object from someone by offering something in return. In the broadest sense, the marketer tries to bring about a response to some market offering. The response may be more than simply buying or trading products and services. A political candidate, for instance, wants votes, a church wants membership, an orchestra wants an audience, and a social action group wants idea acceptance.

Marketing consists of actions taken to build and maintain desirable exchange *relationships* with target audiences involving a product, a service, an idea or another object. Beyond simply attracting new customers and creating transactions, companies wants to retain customers and grow their businesses. Marketers want to build strong relationships by consistently delivering superior customer value. We will expand on the important concept of managing customer relationships later in the chapter.

> **Exchange**—The act of obtaining a desired object from someone by offering something in return.

Markets

The concepts of exchange and relationships lead to the concept of a market. A **market** is the set of actual and potential buyers of a product or service. These buyers share a particular need or want that can be satisfied through exchange relationships.

Marketing means managing markets to bring about profitable customer relationships. However, creating these relationships takes work. Sellers must search for buyers, identify their needs, design good market offerings, set prices for them, promote them, and store and deliver them. Activities such as consumer research, product development, communication, distribution, pricing and service are core marketing activities.

> **Market**—The set of all actual and potential buyers of a product or service.

Figure 1.2 A modern marketing system

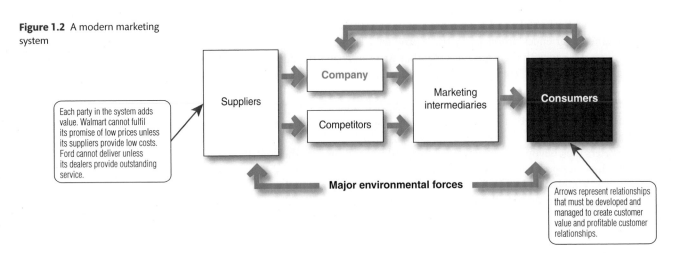

Although we normally think of marketing as being carried out by sellers, buyers also carry out marketing. Consumers market when they search for products, interact with companies to obtain information, and make their purchases. In fact, today's digital technologies, from websites and on-line social networks to mobile phones, have empowered consumers and made marketing a truly interactive affair. Thus, in addition to customer relationship management (CRM), today's market-ers must also deal effectively with *customer-managed relationships*. Marketers are no longer asking only 'How can we reach our customers?' but also 'How should our customers reach us?' and even 'How can our customers reach each other?'

Figure 1.2 shows the main elements in a marketing system. Marketing involves serving a market of final consumers in the face of competitors. The company and its competitors research the market and interact with customers to understand their needs. Then they create and send their market of-ferings and messages to customers, either directly or through marketing intermediaries. Each party in the system is affected by major environmental forces (demographic, economic, natural, techno-logical, political and social/cultural).

Each party in the system adds value for the next level. The arrows represent relationships that must be developed and managed. Thus, a company's success at building profitable relationships depends not only on its own actions but also on how well the entire system serves the needs of final consumers. Carrefour or Walmart's Asda cannot fulfil their promise of low prices unless their suppliers provide merchandise at low costs. Similarly, Citroën cannot deliver a high quality car-ownership experience unless its dealers provide outstanding sales and service.

DESIGNING A CUSTOMER-DRIVEN MARKETING STRATEGY

Marketing management—The art and science of choosing target markets and building profitable relationships with them.

Once it fully understands consumers and the marketplace, marketing management can design a customer-driven marketing strategy. We define **marketing management** as the art and science of choosing target markets and building profitable relationships with them. The marketing manager's aim is to find, attract, keep and grow target customers by creating, delivering and communicating superior customer value.

To design a winning marketing strategy, the marketing manager must answer two important questions: *What customers will we serve (what's our target market)?* and *How can we serve these cus-tomers best (what's our value proposition)?* We will discuss these marketing strategy concepts briefly here and then look at them in more detail in Chapters 2 and 7.

Selecting customers to serve

The company must first decide *who* it will serve. It does this by dividing the market into segments of customers (*market segmentation*) and selecting which segments it will go after (*target marketing*). Some people think of marketing management as finding as many customers as possible and increasing demand. But marketing managers know that they cannot serve all customers in every way. By trying to serve all customers, they may not serve any customers well. Instead, the company wants to select only customers that it can serve well and profitably. For example, Breuninger department stores in Germany and Selfridges in the United Kingdom both focus on up-market shoppers; Hema profitably targets families with more modest means.

Ultimately, marketing managers must decide which customers they want to target and the level, timing and nature of their demand. Simply put, marketing management is *customer management* and *demand management*.

Choosing a value proposition

The company must also decide how it will serve targeted customers – how it will *differentiate and position* itself in the marketplace. A brand's *value proposition* is the set of benefits or values it promises to deliver to consumers to satisfy their needs. Red Bull Energy Drink 'gives you wings' whereas with T-Mobile, family and friends can 'stick together.' Saab cars boast their engineering excellence credentials by being 'born from jets'. The diminutive Smart car suggests that you 'open your mind to the car that challenges the status quo,' whereas Infiniti 'makes luxury affordable' and BMW promises 'the ultimate driving machine'.

Such value propositions differentiate one brand from another. They answer the customer's question, 'Why should I buy your brand rather than a competitor's?' Companies must design strong value propositions that give them the greatest advantage in their target markets. For example, the Smart car is positioned as compact, yet comfortable; agile, yet economical; and safe, yet ecological. It's 'sheer automotive genius in a totally fun, efficient package. Smart thinking, indeed.'

Value propositions: in tough economic times, companies must emphasise the *value* in their value propositions. Waitrose now has an essential range that they promote as 'Waitrose quality at everyday prices.'

Source: Alamy Images/Clynt Garnham Food & Drink

AUTHOR COMMENT
Now that the company fully understands its consumers and the marketplace, it must decide which customers it will serve and how it will bring them value.

Marketing management orientations

Marketing management wants to design strategies that will build profitable relationships with target consumers. But what *philosophy* should guide these marketing strategies? What weight should be given to the interests of customers, the organisation and society? Very often, these interests conflict.

There are five alternative concepts under which organisations design and carry out their marketing strategies: *production*, *product*, *selling*, *marketing* and *societal marketing*.

The production concept

Production concept—The idea that consumers will favour products that are available and highly affordable and that the organisation should therefore focus on improving production and distribution efficiency.

The **production concept** holds that consumers will favour products that are available and highly affordable. Therefore, management should focus on improving production and distribution efficiency. This concept is one of the oldest orientations that guides sellers.

The production concept is still a useful philosophy in some situations. For example, computer maker Lenovo dominates the highly competitive, price-sensitive Chinese PC market through low labour costs, high production efficiency and mass distribution. However, although useful in some situations, the production concept can lead to marketing myopia. Companies adopting this orientation run a major risk of focusing too narrowly on their own operations and losing sight of the real objective – satisfying customer needs and building customer relationships.

The product concept

Product concept—The idea that consumers will favour products that offer the most quality, performance, and features and that the organisation should therefore devote its energy to making continuous product improvements.

The **product concept** holds that consumers will favour products that offer the most in quality, performance and innovative features. Under this concept, marketing strategy focuses on making continuous product improvements.

Product quality and improvement are important parts of most marketing strategies. However, focusing *only* on the company's products can also lead to marketing myopia. For example, some manufacturers believe that if they can 'build a better mousetrap, the world will beat a path to their doors.' But they are often rudely shocked. Buyers may be looking for a better solution to a mouse problem but not necessarily for a better mousetrap. The better solution might be a chemical spray, an exterminating service, a cat, or something else that works even better than a mousetrap. Furthermore, a better mousetrap will not sell unless the manufacturer designs, packages and prices it attractively; places it in convenient distribution channels; brings it to the attention of people who need it; and convinces buyers that it is a better product.

The selling concept

Selling concept—The idea that consumers will not buy enough of the firm's products unless it undertakes a large-scale selling and promotion effort.

Many companies follow the selling concept, which holds that consumers will not buy enough of the firm's products unless it undertakes a large-scale selling and promotion effort. The **selling concept** is typically practised with unsought goods—those that buyers do not normally think of buying, such as insurance or blood donations. These industries must be good at tracking down prospects and selling them on a product's benefits.

Such aggressive selling, however, carries high risks. It focuses on creating sales transactions rather than on building long-term, profitable customer relationships. The aim often is to sell what the company makes rather than making what the market wants. It assumes that customers who are coaxed into buying the product will like it. Or, if they don't like it, they will possibly forget their disappointment and buy it again later. These are usually poor assumptions.

The marketing concept

Marketing concept—A philosophy that holds that achieving organisational goals depends on knowing the needs and wants of target markets and delivering the desired satisfactions better than competitors do.

The **marketing concept** holds that achieving organisational goals depends on knowing the needs and wants of target markets and delivering the desired satisfactions better than competitors do. Under the marketing concept, customer focus and value are the *paths* to sales and profits. Instead of a product-centred 'make and sell' philosophy, the marketing concept is a customer-centred 'sense and respond' philosophy. The job is not to find the right customers for a product but to find the right products for your customers.

Figure 1.3 contrasts the selling concept and the marketing concept. The selling concept takes an *inside-out* perspective. It starts with the factory, focuses on the company's existing products, and calls for heavy selling and promotion to obtain profitable sales. It focuses primarily on customer conquest – getting short-term sales with little concern about who buys or why.

In contrast, the marketing concept takes an *outside-in* perspective. For example, Liverpool Football Club has a Customer Experience Department whose role is exclusively focused on improving

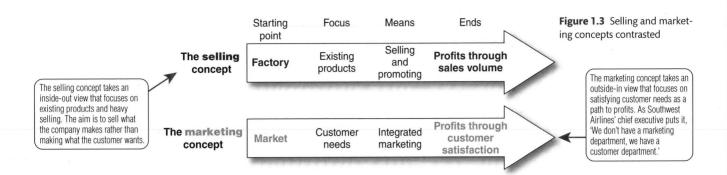

Figure 1.3 Selling and marketing concepts contrasted

The selling concept takes an inside-out view that focuses on existing products and heavy selling. The aim is to sell what the company makes rather than making what the customer wants.

The marketing concept takes an outside-in view that focuses on satisfying customer needs as a path to profits. As Southwest Airlines' chief executive puts it, 'We don't have a marketing department, we have a customer department.'

supporters' off-the-pitch experiences. The marketing concept starts with a well-defined market, focuses on customer needs, and integrates all the marketing activities that affect customers. In turn, it yields profits by creating lasting relationships with the right customers based on customer value and satisfaction.

Implementing the marketing concept often means more than simply responding to customers' stated desires and obvious needs. *Customer-driven* companies research current customers deeply to learn about their desires, gather new product and service ideas, and test proposed product improvements. Such customer-driven marketing usually works well when a clear need exists and when customers know what they want.

In many cases, however, customers *don't* know what they want or even what is possible. For example, even 20 years ago, how many consumers would have thought to ask for now-commonplace products such as notebook computers, mobile phones, digital cameras, 24-hour online buying and satellite navigation systems in their cars? Such situations call for *customer-driven* marketing – understanding customer needs even better than customers themselves do and creating products and services that meet existing and latent needs – now and in the future. As an executive at 3M puts it, 'Our goal is to lead customers where they want to go before *they* know where they want to go.'

The societal marketing concept

The **societal marketing concept** questions whether the pure marketing concept overlooks possible conflicts between consumer *short-run wants* and consumer *long-run welfare*. Is a firm that satisfies the immediate needs and wants of target markets always doing what's best for its consumers in the long run? The societal marketing concept holds that marketing strategy should deliver value to customers in a way that maintains or improves both the consumer's *and society's* well-being. It calls for *sustainable marketing*, socially and environmentally responsible marketing that meets the present needs of consumers and businesses while also preserving or enhancing the ability of future generations to meet their needs.

Consider today's bottled water industry. You may view bottled water companies as offering a convenient, tasty and healthy product. Its packaging suggests 'green' images of pristine lakes and snow-capped mountains. Yet making, filling, and shipping billions of plastic bottles generates huge amounts of carbon dioxide emissions that contribute substantially to global warming. Further more, the plastic bottles pose a substantial recycling and solid waste disposal problem. Thus, in satisfying short-term consumer wants, the bottled water industry may be causing environmental problems that run against society's long-run interests.

As Figure 1.4 shows, companies should balance three considerations in setting their marketing strategies: company profits, consumer wants, *and* society's interests. UPS does this well. Its concern for societal interests has earned it the number one or number two spot in *Fortune* magazine's Most Admired Companies for Social Responsibility rankings in four of the past five years.

Societal marketing concept— The idea that a company's marketing decisions should consider consumers' wants, the company's requirements, consumers' long-term interests, and society's long-term interests.

UPS seeks more than just short-run sales and profits. Its three-pronged corporate sustainability mission stresses *economic prosperity* (profitable growth through a customer focus), *social responsibility* (community engagement and individual well-being) and *environmental stewardship* (operating

Figure 1.4 Three considerations underlying the societal marketing concept

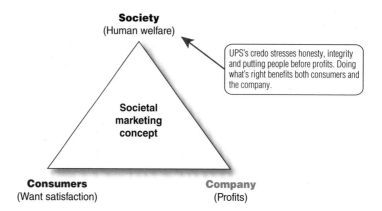

efficiently and protecting the environment). Whether it involves greening up its operations or urging employees to volunteer time in their communities, UPS proactively seeks opportunities to act responsibly. UPS knows that doing what's right benefits both consumers and the company. By operating efficiently and acting responsibly, it can 'meet the needs of the enterprise…while protecting and enhancing the human and natural resources that will be needed in the future.' Social responsibility 'isn't just good for the planet,' says the company. 'It's good for business.'[9]

AUTHOR COMMENT

The customer-driven marketing strategy discussed in the previous section outlines which customers the company will serve (the target market) and how it will serve them (the value proposition). Now, the company develops marketing plans and programmes – a marketing mix – that will actually deliver the intended customer value.

PREPARING AN INTEGRATED MARKETING PLAN AND PROGRAMME

The company's marketing strategy outlines which customers it will serve and how it will create value for these customers. Next, the marketer develops an integrated marketing programme that will actually deliver the intended value to target customers. The marketing programme builds customer relationships by transforming the marketing strategy into action. It consists of the firm's *marketing mix*, the set of marketing tools the firm uses to implement its marketing strategy.

The major marketing mix tools are classified into four broad groups, called the *four Ps* of marketing: product, price, place and promotion. To deliver on its value proposition, the firm must first create a need-satisfying market offering (product). It must decide how much it will charge for the offering (price) and how it will make the offering available to target consumers (place). Finally, it must communicate with target customers about the offering and persuade them of its merits (promotion). The firm must blend each marketing mix tool into a comprehensive *integrated marketing programme* that communicates and delivers the intended value to chosen customers. We will explore marketing programmes and the marketing mix in much more detail in later chapters.

AUTHOR COMMENT

Doing a good job with the first three steps in the marketing process sets the stage for step four, building and managing lasting customer relationships.

BUILDING CUSTOMER RELATIONSHIPS

The first three steps in the marketing process – understanding the marketplace and customer needs, designing a customer-driven marketing strategy and constructing a marketing programme – all lead up to the fourth and most important step: building profitable customer relationships.

Customer relationship management (CRM)

CRM is perhaps the most important concept of modern marketing. Some marketers define it narrowly as a customer data management activity. By this definition, it involves managing detailed information about individual customers and carefully managing customer 'touch points' to maximise customer loyalty. We will discuss this narrower CRM activity in Chapter 4 when dealing with marketing information.

Most marketers, however, give the concept of customer relationship management a broader meaning. In this broader sense, **customer relationship management (CRM)** is the overall process of building and maintaining profitable customer relationships by delivering superior customer value and satisfaction. It deals with all aspects of acquiring, keeping and growing customers.

Customer relationship management (CRM)—The overall process of building and maintaining profitable customer relationships by delivering superior customer value and satisfaction.

Relationship building blocks: customer value and satisfaction

The key to building lasting customer relationships is to create superior customer value and satisfaction. Satisfied customers are more likely to be loyal customers and give the company a larger share of their business.

Customer value

Attracting and retaining customers can be a difficult task. Customers often face a bewildering array of products and services from which to choose. A customer buys from the firm that offers the highest **customer-perceived value** – the customer's evaluation of the difference between all the benefits and all the costs of a market offering relative to those of competing offers. Importantly, customers often do not judge values and costs 'accurately' or 'objectively.' They act on *perceived* value.

Customer-perceived value—The customer's evaluation of the difference between all the benefits and all the costs of a marketing offer relative to those of competing offers.

To some consumers, value might mean sensible products at affordable prices, especially in the aftermath of the economic downturn. To other consumers, however, value might mean paying more to get more. For example, Renault Z.E. electric car owners gain a number of benefits. The most obvious benefit is fuel efficiency (especially when oil prices are rising). However, by purchasing a Renault Z.E., the owners also may receive some status and image values. Driving a Renault Z.E. makes owners feel and appear more environmentally responsible. When deciding whether to purchase a Renault Z.E., customers will weigh these and other perceived values of owning the car against the money, effort and psychic costs of acquiring it.

Customer satisfaction

Customer satisfaction depends on the product's perceived performance relative to a buyer's expectations. If the product's performance falls short of expectations, the customer is dissatisfied. If performance matches expectations, the customer is satisfied. If performance exceeds expectations, the customer is highly satisfied or delighted.

Customer satisfaction—The extent to which a product's perceived performance matches a buyer's expectations.

Outstanding marketing companies go out of their way to keep important customers satisfied. Most studies show that higher levels of customer satisfaction lead to greater customer loyalty, which in turn results in better company performance. Smart companies aim to delight customers by promising only what they can deliver and then delivering more than they promise. Delighted customers not only make repeat purchases but also become willing marketing partners and 'customer evangelists' who spread the word about their good experiences to others.[10]

Customer satisfaction: Ritz-Carlton's passion for satisfying customers is summed up in its credo, which promises a truly memorable experience – one that 'enlivens the senses, instills well-being, and fulfills even the unexpressed wishes and needs of our guests'.

Source: Getty Images/Dan Kitwood

For companies interested in delighting customers, exceptional value and service become part of the overall company culture. For example, year after year, Ritz-Carlton ranks at or near the top of the hospitality industry in terms of customer satisfaction. Its passion for satisfying customers is summed up in the company's credo, which promises that its luxury hotels will deliver a truly memorable experience – one that 'enlivens the senses, instils well-being, and fulfils even the unexpressed wishes and needs of our guests.'[11]

Check into any Ritz-Carlton hotel around the world, and you'll be amazed by the company's fervent dedication to anticipating and meeting even your slightest need. Without ever asking, they seem to know that you're allergic to peanuts and want a king-size bed, a non-allergenic pillow, the blinds open when you arrive and breakfast with decaffeinated coffee in your room. Each day, hotel staffers – from those at the front desk to those in maintenance and housekeeping – discreetly observe and record even the smallest guest preferences. Then, every morning, each hotel reviews the files of all new arrivals who have previously stayed at a Ritz-Carlton and prepares a list of suggested extra touches that might delight each guest.

Once they identify a special customer need, Ritz-Carlton employees go to legendary extremes to meet it. For example, to serve the needs of a guest with food allergies, a Ritz-Carlton chef in Bali located special eggs and milk in a small grocery store in another country and had them delivered to the hotel. In another case, when the hotel's laundry service failed to remove a stain on a guest's suit before the guest departed, the hotel manager travelled to the guest's house and personally delivered a reimbursement cheque for the cost of the suit. According to one Ritz-Carlton manager, if the chain gets hold of a picture of a guest's pet, it will make a copy, have it framed and display it in the guest's room in whatever Ritz-Carlton the guest visits. As a result of such customer service heroics, an amazing 95 per cent of departing guests report that their stay has been a truly memorable experience. More than 90 per cent of Ritz-Carlton's delighted customers return.

However, although a customer-centred firm seeks to deliver high customer satisfaction relative to competitors, it does not attempt to *maximise* customer satisfaction. A company can always increase customer satisfaction by lowering its price or increasing its services. But this may result in lower profits. Thus, the purpose of marketing is to generate customer value profitably. This requires a very delicate balance: The marketer must continue to generate more customer value and satisfaction but not 'give away the house'.

Customer relationship levels and tools

Companies can build customer relationships at many levels, depending on the nature of the target market. At one extreme, a company with many low-margin customers may seek to develop *basic relationships* with them. For example, Häagen-Dazs does not phone or call on all of its consumers to get to know them personally. Instead, Häagen-Dazs creates relationships through brand-building advertising, public relations, its newsletter, its website (**www.haagendazs .com**) and via nearly 200,000 Facebook followers. At the other extreme, in markets with few customers and high margins, sellers want to create *full partnerships* with key customers. For example, Häagen-Dazs sales representatives work closely with Tesco, Carrefour and other large retailers. In between these two extremes, other levels of customer relationships are appropriate.

Frequency marketing programmes: KLM Airways and Air France offers their Flying Blue members frequent-flyer points they can use on any seat on any KLM or Air France flight.

Source: Shutterstock.com

Beyond offering consistently high value and satisfaction, marketers can use specific marketing tools to develop stronger bonds with customers. For example, many companies offer *frequency marketing programmes* that reward customers who buy frequently or in large amounts. Airlines offer frequent-flyer programmes, hotels give room upgrades to their frequent guests, and supermarkets give patronage discounts to 'very important customers'. For example, KLM Airways and Air France offer their Flying Blue members frequent-flyer points they can use on any seat on any KLM or Air France flight. Flying Blue promises its members that 'as you travel more and more with us, we reward your loyalty by offering more and more services you can enjoy, to make every trip that much more special. By simply showing your Flying Blue card, you can access countless extra services and make your travels, or even your waiting time at the airport, smoother, easier and more pleasant.'[12]

Other companies sponsor *club marketing programmes* that offer members special benefits and create member communities. For example, BMW sponsors the BMW Car Club, which gives BMW drivers a way to share their driving passion. BMW Car Club membership benefits include a quarterly magazine, discounts on BMW servicing, parts and accessories, the club shop stocks BMW books, clothing, model cars and other BMW merchandise at discount prices. The club also organises track events and BMW festivals.

The changing nature of customer relationships

Significant changes are occurring in the ways in which companies are relating to their customers. Yesterday's big companies focused on mass marketing to all customers at arm's length. Today's companies are building deeper, more direct and lasting relationships with more carefully selected customers. Here are some important trends in the way that companies and customers are relating to one another.

Relating with more carefully selected customers

Few firms today still practise true mass marketing – selling in a standardised way to any customer who comes along. Today, most marketers realise that they don't want relationships with every customer. Instead, they target fewer, more profitable customers. 'Not all customers are worth your marketing efforts,' states one analyst. 'Some are more costly to serve than to lose.' Adds another marketing expert, 'If you can't say who your customers *aren't*, you probably can't say who your customers *are*.'[13]

Many companies now use customer profitability analysis to pass up or weed out losing customers and target winning ones for pampering. One approach is to pre-emptively screen out potentially unprofitable customers. For example, in the UK mortgage market, the Bank of China exploited the financial climate to cherry-pick lucrative clients. Xixu Sun (the Head of the Bank of China's UK Retail Operations) argued 'before the financial crises you didn't have a choice, you couldn't cherry-pick the good customers. Now you have that choice because there's a drought in terms of mortgage loans provided by banks'.[14] Similarly, the bank Lloyds TSB offers superior savings rates to 'preferred' customers, inviting them to join high-rate accounts while other savers are not offered the same exclusive deals.[15]

But what should the company do with unprofitable customers that it already has? If it can't turn them into profitable ones, it may even want to dismiss customers that are too unreasonable or that cost more to serve than they are worth. 'Like bouncers in glitzy nightspots,' says another consultant, 'executives will almost certainly have to "fire" [those] customers.' For example, most Internet Providers have a 'fair usage' policy which seems rather at odds with the 'unlimited usage' packages they also supply. Users who play too many online games, download too many movies or heavy users of peer-to-peer networks who ignore warnings may find their activities curtailed by 75 per cent caps on download speeds and even the termination of the connection altogether. American Express recently sent letters to some of its members offering them cash in exchange for paying off their balances and closing down their accounts. Reading between the lines, the credit card company was dumping unprofitable customers.

Relating more deeply and interactively

Beyond choosing customers more selectively, companies are now relating with chosen customers in deeper, more meaningful ways. Rather than relying on one-way, mass-media messages only, today's marketers are incorporating new, more interactive approaches that help build targeted, two-way customer relationships.

Two-way customer relationships

New technologies have profoundly changed the ways in which people relate to one another. New tools for relating include everything from e-mail, websites, blogs, mobile phones and video sharing to online communities and social networks, such as Facebook, YouTube and Twitter.

This changing communications environment also affects how companies and brands relate to customers. The new communications approaches let marketers create deeper customer involvement and a sense of community surrounding a brand – to make the brand a meaningful part of consumers' conversations and lives. 'Becoming part of the conversation between consumers is infinitely more powerful than handing down information via traditional advertising,' says one marketing expert. Says another, 'People today want a voice and a role in their brand experiences. They want co-creation.'[16]

However, at the same time that the new technologies create relationship-building opportunities for marketers, they also create challenges. They give consumers greater power and control. Today's consumers have more information about brands than ever before, and they have a wealth of platforms for airing and sharing their brand views with other consumers. Thus, the marketing world is now embracing not only CRM but also **customer-managed relationships**.

Greater consumer control means that, in building customer relationships, companies can no longer rely on marketing by *intrusion*. Instead, marketers must practise marketing by *attraction* – creating market offerings and messages that involve consumers rather than interrupt them. Hence, most marketers now augment their mass-media marketing efforts with a rich mix of direct marketing approaches that promote brand-consumer interaction.

For example, many brands are creating dialogues with consumers via their own or existing *online social networks*. To supplement their marketing campaigns, companies now routinely post their latest ads and made-for-the-Web videos on video-sharing sites. They join social networks. Or they launch their own blogs, online communities or consumer-generated review systems, all with the aim of engaging customers on a more personal, interactive level.

Take Twitter, for example. Organisations ranging from Tesco, Citroën, Frankfurt Airport, Greenpeace and Formula 1 to the British Monarchy have created Twitter pages and promotions. They use 'tweets' to start conversations with Twitter's more than six million registered users, address customer service issues, research customer reactions and drive traffic to relevant articles,

Customer-managed relationships—Marketing relationships in which customers, empowered by today's new digital technologies, interact with companies and with each other to shape their relationships with brands.

websites, contests, videos and other brand activities. For example, Richard Branson, Virgin Group Chairman, has 100,000 Twitter followers. He claims that 'with more than 200 Virgin companies worldwide, my days and nights are filled with exciting service launches, product announcements, parties, events, and consumer opportunities. I'm regularly asked what a day in the life of Richard Branson looks like, and Twitter helps me answer that. It also enables communication no matter where I am; thanks to Virgin America's wifi, I recently lost my Twitter interview virginity at 35,000 feet'.[17]

Similarly, almost every company has something going on Facebook these days. Nokia has nearly than four million Facebook 'fans', Nescafé has over one million followers while the British Monarchy has a mere 500,000 Facebook followers. Networks like Facebook can get consumers involved with and talking about a brand. For example, Honda's 'Everybody Knows Somebody Who Loves a Honda' Facebook page let visitors upload photos of their cars or link up with owners of their favourite old Hondas worldwide. It asks people to help prove that 'we all really can be connected through Honda love'. The campaign netted about two million Facebook friends in less than two months, more than double previous fan levels.[18]

Ikea used a simple but inspired Facebook campaign to promote the opening of a new store in Malmo, Sweden. It opened a Facebook profile for the store's manager, Gordon Gustavsson. Then it uploaded pictures of Ikea showrooms to Gustavsson's Facebook photo album and announced that whoever was first to tag a product in the pictures with their name would win it. Thousands of customers rushed to tag items. Word spread quickly to friends, and customers were soon begging for more pictures. More than just looking at an ad with Ikea furniture in it, the Facebook promotion had people poring over the pictures, examining products item by item.[19]

Most marketers are still learning how to use social media effectively. The problem is to find unobtrusive ways to enter consumers' social conversations with engaging and relevant brand messages. Simply posting a humorous video, creating a social network page, or hosting a blog isn't enough. Successful social network marketing means making relevant and genuine contributions to consumer conversations. 'Nobody wants to be friends with a brand,' says one online marketing executive. 'Your job [as a brand] is to be part of other friends' conversations.'[20]

Consumer-generated marketing

A growing part of the new customer dialogue is **consumer-generated marketing**, by which consumers themselves are playing a bigger role in shaping their own brand experiences and those of others. This might happen through uninvited consumer-to-consumer (C-to-C) exchanges in blogs, video-sharing sites, and other digital forums. But increasingly, companies are *inviting* consumers to play a more active role in shaping products and brand messages.

Some companies ask consumers for new product ideas. For example, McAfee actively seek new product ideas from existing users via their online community site.[21] Ideas regarding new products are solicited, community members are asked to comment, then vote and McAfee staff incorporate good ideas into the product range. Innocent have also generated a range of products through soliciting, listening and responding to customer ideas. For example, Innocent asked customers to send postcards with suggestions. One of the results was the hugely successful 'banana free smoothie' sold with the tag line 'you asked, we made it'. Coca-Cola's Vitaminwater brand recently created a Facebook app to obtain consumer suggestions for a new flavour, promising to manufacture and sell the winner ('Vitaminwater was our idea; the next one will be yours'.). The new flavour – Connect (black cherry and lime with vitamins and a kick of caffeine) – was a big hit. In the process, Vitaminwater doubled its Facebook fan base to more than one million.[22]

Other companies are inviting customers to play an active role in shaping ads. For example, Redrow, T-Mobile, L'Oreal, MasterCard, Unilever, H.J. Heinz, and many other companies have run contests for customer-generated commercials that have been aired on national television. T-Mobile have sponsored and filmed 'flashmob' events at Liverpool Street Station and Trafalgar Square in London that have been viewed over 35 million times online as well as aired on television. Such success inspired T-Mobile into filming a spoof Royal Wedding in 2011 during which actors playing the Royal Family (and a surprisingly funky Archbishop of Canterbury)

Consumer-generated marketing—Brand exchanges created by consumers themselves — both invited and uninvited — by which consumers are playing an increasing role in shaping their own brand experiences and those of other consumers.

literally danced down the aisle watched by over 30 million online viewers. Similarly, for the past several years, PepsiCo's Doritos brand has held a 'Crash the Super Bowl' contest in which it invites 30-second ads from customers and runs the best ones during the game. Last year, customers submitted nearly 4,000 entries. The winning fan-produced Doritos ad (called 'Underdog') was placed second in the *USA Today* Ad Meter ratings. The lowest-rated of the four customer-made ads came in 17th out of 65 Super Bowl ads.[23]

However, harnessing consumer-generated content can be a time-consuming and costly process, and companies may find it difficult to glean even a little gold from all the garbage. For example, when Heinz invited customers to submit homemade ads for its ketchup on its YouTube page, it ended up sifting through more than 8,000 entries, of which it posted nearly 4,000. Some of the amateur ads were very good – entertaining and potentially effective. Most, however, were so-so at best, and others were downright dreadful. In one ad, a contestant chugged ketchup straight from the bottle. In another, the would-be filmmaker brushed his teeth, washed his hair, and shaved his face with Heinz's product.[24]

Consumer-generated marketing, whether invited by marketers or not, has become a significant marketing force. Through a profusion of consumer-generated videos, blogs and websites, consumers are playing an increasing role in shaping their own brand experiences. Beyond creating brand conversations, customers are having an increasing say about everything from product design, usage and packaging to pricing and distribution.

AUTHOR COMMENT

Marketers can't build customer value and develop customer relationships by themselves. They must work closely with other company departments and partners outside the firm.

Partner relationship management

When it comes to creating customer value and building strong customer relationships, today's marketers know that they can't go it alone. They must work closely with a variety of marketing partners. In addition to being good at CRM, marketers must also be good at **partner relationship management**. Major changes are occurring in how marketers partner with others inside and outside the company to jointly bring more value to customers.

Partner relationship management—Working closely with partners in other company departments and outside the company to jointly bring greater value to customers.

Partners inside the company

Traditionally, marketers have been charged with understanding customers and representing customer needs to different company departments. The old thinking was that marketing is done only by marketing, sales and customer-support people. However, in today's more connected world, every functional area can interact with customers, especially electronically. The new thinking is that – no matter what your job is in a company – you must understand marketing and be customer focused. David Packard, the late co-founder of HP, wisely said, 'Marketing is far too important to be left only to the marketing department'.[25]

Today, rather than letting each department go its own way, firms are linking all departments in the cause of creating customer value. Rather than assigning only sales and marketing people to customers, they are forming cross-functional customer teams. For example, P&G assigns customer development teams to each of its major retailer accounts. These teams – consisting of sales and marketing people, operations specialists, market and financial analysts, and others – coordinate the efforts of many P&G departments toward helping the retailer be more successful.

Marketing partners outside the firm

Changes are also occurring in how marketers connect with their suppliers, channel partners and even competitors. Most companies today are networked companies, relying heavily on partnerships with other firms.

Marketing channels consist of distributors, retailers and others who connect the company to its buyers. The *supply chain* describes a longer channel, stretching from raw materials to components to final products that are carried to final buyers. For example, the supply chain for PCs consists of suppliers of computer chips and other components; the computer manufacturer; and the distributors, retailers and others who sell the computers.

Through *supply chain management*, many companies today are strengthening their connections with partners all along the supply chain. They know that their fortunes rest not just on how well they perform. Success at building customer relationships also rests on how well their entire supply chain performs against competitors' supply chains. These companies don't just treat suppliers as vendors and distributors as customers. They treat both as partners in delivering customer value. On the one hand, for example, Fiat works closely with carefully selected suppliers to improve quality and operations efficiency. On the other hand, it works with its franchise dealers to provide top-grade sales and service support that will bring customers in the door and keep them coming back.

AUTHOR COMMENT

Look back at Figure 1.1. In the first four steps of the marketing process, the company builds value *for* target customers and builds strong relationships with them. If it does that well, it can capture value *from* customers in return in the form of loyal customers who buy and continue to buy the company's brands.

CAPTURING VALUE FROM CUSTOMERS

The first four steps in the marketing process outlined in Figure 1.1 involve building customer relationships by creating and delivering superior customer value. The final step involves capturing value in return in the form of current and future sales, market share and profits. By creating superior customer value, the firm creates highly satisfied customers who stay loyal and buy more. This, in turn, means greater long-run returns for the firm. Here, we discuss the outcomes of creating customer value: customer loyalty and retention, share of market and share of customer, and customer equity.

Creating customer loyalty and retention

Good CRM creates customer delight. In turn, delighted customers remain loyal and talk favourably to others about the company and its products. Studies show big differences in the loyalty of customers who are less satisfied, somewhat satisfied and completely satisfied. Even a slight drop from complete satisfaction can create an enormous drop in loyalty. Thus, the aim of CRM is to create not only customer satisfaction but also customer delight.

The recent economic downturn put strong pressures on customer loyalty. It created a new consumer frugality that will last well into the future. One recent study in the US found that, even in an improved economy, 55 per cent of consumers say they would rather get the best price than the best brand. Nearly two-thirds say they will now shop at a different store with lower prices even if it's less convenient. It's five times cheaper to keep an old customer than acquire a new one. Thus, companies today must shape their value propositions even more carefully and treat their profitable customers well.[26]

Losing a customer means losing more than a single sale. It means losing the entire stream of purchases that the customer would make over a lifetime of patronage. In this way, our focus should be on **customer lifetime value**. Lexus, for example, estimates that a single satisfied and loyal customer is worth more than €800,000 in lifetime sales while the estimated lifetime value of a young mobile phone consumer is €34,000.[27] In fact, a company can lose money on a specific transaction but still benefit greatly from a long-term relationship. This means that companies must aim high in building customer relationships. Customer delight creates an emotional relationship with a brand, not just a rational preference. And that relationship keeps customers coming back.

Customer lifetime value—The value of the entire stream of purchases that the customer would make over a lifetime of patronage.

Growing share of customer

Beyond simply retaining good customers to capture customer lifetime value, good CRM can help marketers increase their **share of customer** – the share they get of the customer's purchasing in their product categories. Thus, banks want to increase 'share of wallet'. Supermarkets and restaurants want to get more 'share of stomach'. Car companies want to increase 'share of garage', and airlines want greater 'share of travel'.

To increase share of customer, firms can offer greater variety to current customers. Or they can create programmes to cross-sell and up-sell to market more products and services to existing customers. For example, Amazon is highly skilled at leveraging relationships with its 120 million worldwide customers to increase its share of each customer's purchases. Originally an online bookseller, Amazon now offers customers music, videos, gifts, toys, consumer electronics, office products, home improvement items, lawn and garden products, apparel and accessories, jewellery, tools and even groceries. In addition, based on each customer's purchase history, previous product searches and other data, the company recommends related products that might be of interest. This recommendation system influences up to 30 per cent of all sales.[28] In these ways, Amazon captures a greater share of each customer's spending budget.

Building customer equity

We can now see the importance of not only acquiring customers but also keeping and growing them. One marketing consultant puts it this way: 'The only value your company will ever create is the value that comes from customers – the ones you have now and the ones you will have in the future. Without customers, you don't have a business.'[29] CRM takes a long-term view. Companies want not only to create profitable customers but also 'own' them for life, earn a greater share of their purchases, and capture their customer lifetime value.

What is customer equity?

The ultimate aim of CRM is to produce high *customer equity*.[30] **Customer equity** is the total combined customer lifetime values of all of the company's current and potential customers. As such, it's a measure of the future value of the company's customer base. Clearly, the more loyal the firm's profitable customers, the higher its customer equity. Customer equity may be a better measure of a firm's performance than current sales or market share. Whereas sales and market share reflect the past, customer equity suggests the future. Consider BMW's advantage over Cadillac in the US:[31]

In the 1970s and 1980s, Cadillac had some of the most loyal customers in the industry. To an entire generation of car buyers, the name *Cadillac* defined American luxury. Cadillac's share of the luxury car market reached a whopping 51 per cent in 1976. Based on market share and sales, the brand's future looked rosy. However, measures of customer equity would have painted a bleaker picture. Cadillac customers were getting older (average age 60) and average customer lifetime value was falling. Many Cadillac buyers were on their last cars. Thus, although Cadillac's market share was good, its customer equity was not. Compare this with BMW. Its more youthful and vigorous image didn't win BMW the early market share war. However, it did win BMW younger customers with higher customer lifetime values. As a result, in the years that followed, BMW's market share and profits soared while Cadillac's fortunes eroded badly.

In recent years, Cadillac has attempted to make the Caddy cool again by targeting a younger generation of consumers. Still, the average age of its buyers remains a less-than-youthful 62 (13 years older than typical BMW owners). Says one analyst, 'no image remake can fully succeed until Cadillac comes up with more stylish models and marketing that can attract younger buyers. For now, the company's image will likely remain dinged as it continues churning out land yachts such as its DTS, which . . . appeals mainly to buyers in their 70s.' It's a real 'geezer-mobile'. As a result, the brand's fortunes continue to fall; last year was its worst sales year since 1953. The moral: marketers should care not just about current sales and market share. Customer lifetime value and customer equity are the name of the game.

Share of customer—The portion of the customer's purchasing that a company gets in its product categories.

Customer equity—The total combined customer lifetime values of all of the company's customers.

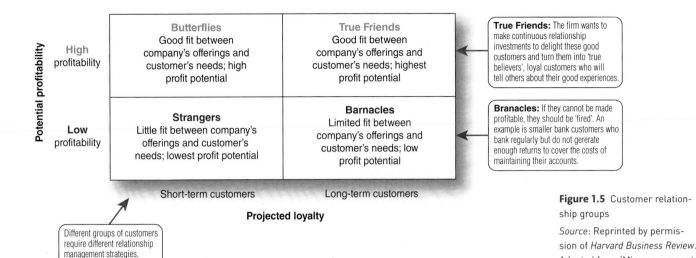

Figure 1.5 Customer relationship groups

Source: Reprinted by permission of *Harvard Business Review*. Adapted from 'Mismanagement of customer loyalty' by W. Relnartz and V. Kumar, July 2002, p. 93. Copyright © by the president and fellows of Harvard College; all rights reserved.

Building the right relationships with the right customers

Companies should manage customer equity carefully. They should view customers as assets that must be managed and maximised. But not all customers, not even all loyal customers, are good investments. Surprisingly, some loyal customers can be unprofitable, and some disloyal customers can be profitable. Which customers should the company acquire and retain?

The company can classify customers according to their potential profitability and manage its relationships with them accordingly. Figure 1.5 classifies customers into one of four relationship groups, according to their profitability and projected loyalty.[32] Each group requires a different relationship management strategy. 'Strangers' show low potential profitability and little projected loyalty. There is little fit between the company's offerings and their needs. The relationship management strategy for these customers is simple: don't invest anything in them.

'Butterflies' are potentially profitable but not loyal. There is a good fit between the company's offerings and their needs. However, like real butterflies, we can enjoy them for only a short while and then they're gone. An example is stock market investors who trade shares often and in large amounts but who enjoy hunting out the best deals without building a regular relationship with any single brokerage company. Efforts to convert butterflies into loyal customers are rarely successful. Instead, the company should enjoy the butterflies for the moment. It should create satisfying and profitable transactions with them, capturing as much of their business as possible in the short time during which they buy from the company. Then it should cease investing in them until the next time around.

'True friends' are both profitable and loyal. There is a strong fit between their needs and the company's offerings. The firm wants to make continuous relationship investments to delight these customers and nurture, retain and grow them. It wants to turn true friends into 'true believers', those who come back regularly and tell others about their good experiences with the company.

'Barnacles' are highly loyal but not very profitable. There is a limited fit between their needs and the company's offerings. An example is smaller bank customers who bank regularly but do not generate enough returns to cover the costs of maintaining their accounts. Like barnacles on the hull of a ship, they create drag. Barnacles are perhaps the most problematic customers. The company might be able to improve their profitability by selling them more, raising their fees, or reducing service to them. However, if they cannot be made profitable, they should be 'fired'.

The point here is an important one: different types of customers require different relationship management strategies. The goal is to build the *right relationships* with the *right customers*.

AUTHOR COMMENT

Marketing doesn't take place in a vacuum. Now that we've discussed the five steps in the market-ing process, let's examine how the ever-changing marketplace affects both consumers and the marketers who serve them. We'll look more deeply into these and other marketing environment factors in Chapter 3.

THE CHANGING MARKETING LANDSCAPE

Every day, dramatic changes are occurring in the marketplace. Richard Love of HP observed, 'The pace of change is so rapid that the ability to change has now become a competitive advantage'. Indeed, Rupert Murdoch notes 'the world is changing very fast. Big will not beat small anymore. It will be the fast beating the slow.' As the marketplace changes, so must those who serve it, or as Niccolo Machiavelli claims, 'whosoever desires constant success must change his conduct with the times'.

In this section, we examine the major trends and forces that are changing the marketing landscape and challenging marketing strategy. We look at five major developments: the uncertain economic environment, the digital age, rapid globalisation, the call for more ethics and social responsibility, and the growth of not-for-profit marketing.

The uncertain economic environment

The new consumer frugality: today, marketers in all industries must clearly spell out their value propositions. Even diamond marketer De Beers has adjusted its long-standing 'a diamond is forever' promise to these more frugal times.

Source: Shutterstock.com

Beginning in 2008, the world economies experienced a stunning economic meltdown, unlike anything since the Great Depression of the 1930s. The stock market plunged, and trillions of euros of market value simply evaporated. The financial crisis left shell-shocked consumers short of both money and confidence as they faced losses in income, a severe credit crunch, declining home values and rising unemployment.

The economic downturn caused many consumers to rethink their spending priorities and cut back on their buying. After a decade of overspending, 'frugality has made a comeback', says one analyst. More than just a temporary change, the new consumer buying attitudes and spending behaviour will likely remain for many years to come. 'The "new frugality", born of the Great Recession, . . . is now becoming entrenched consumer behaviour that is reshaping consumption patterns in ways that will persist even as the economy rebounds,' says another analyst.[33] Even in its aftermath, consumers are now spending more carefully.

In response, companies in all industries – from discounters such as Lidl and Aldi to luxury brands such as Lexus and Montblanc – have aligned their marketing strategies with the new economic realities. More than ever, marketers are emphasising the *value* in their value propositions. They are focusing on value-for-the-money, practicality, and durability in their product offerings and marketing pitches. 'Value is the magic word,' says a marketing executive. These days, 'people are doing the math in their heads, and they're being much more thoughtful before making purchases. Now, we're going to be even more focused on helping consumers see value.' Similarly, Whitbread customers seek 'value for money', according to the owner of Premier Inn hotels and restaurants including Brewers Fayre and Beefeater. Occupancy at their 590 budget hotels increased to 80 per cent in 2011 helped by deals such as a €35-a-night offer.[34]

Even wealthier consumers have joined the trend toward frugality. Conspicuous free spending is no longer so fashionable. As a result, even luxury brands are stressing value. Indeed, even diamond marketer De Beers has adjusted its longstanding, iconic 'a diamond is forever' promise to these more frugal times by cleverly adding 'Here's to Less'.

In adjusting to the new economy, companies were tempted to cut marketing budgets deeply and slash prices in an effort to coax cash-strapped customers into opening their wallets. However, although cutting costs and offering selected discounts can be important marketing tactics in a down economy, smart marketers understand that making cuts in the wrong places can damage long-term brand images and customer relationships. The challenge is to balance the brand's value proposition with the current times while also enhancing its long-term equity.

'A recession creates winners and losers just like a boom,' notes one economist. 'When a recession ends, when the road levels off and the world seems full of promise once more, your position in the competitive pack will depend on how skilfully you managed [during the tough times].'[35] Thus, rather than slashing prices, many marketers held the line on prices and instead explained why their brands are worth it. And rather than cutting their marketing budgets in the difficult times, companies such as Tesco, Santander, Vodafone and Ikea have maintained or actually increased their marketing spending. The goal in uncertain economic times is to build market share and strengthen customer relationships at the expense of competitors who cut back.

A troubled economy can present opportunities as well as threats. For example, the fact that 40 per cent of consumers say they are eating out less poses threats for many full-service restaurants. However, it presents opportunities for fast-food marketers. Playing on its cheap-eats value proposition, McDonald's worldwide sales grew steadily through the worst of the downturn (especially in the UK, France and Russia). Nevertheless, sandwich group Subway anointed itself the World's Biggest Restaurant Chain with 33,749 sites across the globe at the end of 2010, compared with 32,737 for McDonald's.

Similarly, the trend toward saving money by eating at home plays into the hands of name-brand food makers, who have positioned their wares as convenient and – compared with a restaurant meal – inexpensive. Rather than lowering prices, many food retailers have instead pointed out the value of their products as compared to eating out. Pizza Hut and many other restaurants offer all you can eat for €10 while supermarkets and discounters vie with each other from feeding a family of four for €10 to a two-course meal for two with wine for €10.[36]

The digital age

The recent technology boom has created a digital age. The explosive growth in computer, communications, information and other digital technologies has had a major impact on the ways companies bring value to their customers. Now, more than ever before, we are all connected to each other and information anywhere in the world. Where it once took days or weeks to receive news about important world events, we now learn about them as they are occurring via live satellite broadcasts and news websites. Where it once took weeks to correspond with others in distant places, they are now only moments away by mobile phone, e-mail or webcam. For better or worse, technology has become an indispensable part of our lives:[37]

> Francesco and Sofia Rossi of Milan, can remember simpler mornings not too long ago. They sat together and chatted as they ate breakfast and read the newspaper and competed only with the television for the attention of their two teenage sons. That was so last century. Today, Francesco wakes around 6:00 a.m. to check his work e-mail and his Facebook and Twitter accounts. The two boys, Davide and Luca, start each morning with text messages, video games and Facebook. Sofia cracks open her laptop right after breakfast. The Rossis' sons sleep with their phones next to their beds, so they start the day with text messages in place of alarm clocks. Francesco, an instructor at Milan University, sends texts to his two sons to wake them up. 'We use texting as an in-house intercom,' he says. 'I could just walk up stairs, but they always answer their texts.' This is morning in the Internet age. After six to eight hours of network deprivation – also known as sleep – people are increasingly waking up and lunging for mobile phones and laptops, sometimes even before swinging their legs to the floor and tending to more biologically current activities.

The digital age has provided marketers with exciting new ways to learn about and track customers and create products and services tailored to individual customer needs. It's helping marketers communicate with customers in large groups or one-to-one. Through Web videoconferencing, marketing researchers at a company's headquarters in Berlin can look in on focus groups in London, Paris or Lisbon without ever stepping onto a plane. With only a few clicks of a mouse button, a direct marketer can tap into online data services to learn anything from what car you drive to what you read to what flavour of ice cream you prefer. Or, using today's powerful computers, marketers can create their own detailed customer databases and use them to target individual customers with offers designed to meet their specific needs.

Digital technology has also brought a new wave of communication, advertising, and relationship building tools – ranging from online advertising, video-sharing tools and mobile phones to Web apps and online social networks. The digital shift means that marketers can no longer expect consumers to always seek them out. Nor can they always control conversations about their brands. The new digital world makes it easy for consumers to take marketing content that once lived only in advertising or on a brand website with them wherever they go and share it with friends. More than just add-ons to traditional marketing channels, the new digital media must be fully integrated into the marketer's customer-relationship-building efforts.

Internet—A vast public web of computer networks that connects users of all types all around the world to each other and an amazingly large information repository.

The most dramatic digital technology is the **Internet**. The number of Internet users worldwide now stands at more than 2 billion and will reach an estimated 3.4 billion by 2015. Over 150 million Europeans are Facebook users, they spend an average of 26 hours per month online, during which 333 million will use Google sites and 270 million Microsoft sites. Most Europeans will check their e-mails each day either via their work computer or via their mobile telephone. Indeed, by 2020, many experts believe, the Internet will be accessed primarily via a mobile device operated by voice, touch and even thought or 'mind-controlled human – computer interaction.'[38]

Whereas *Web 1.0* connected people with information, the next generation *Web 2.0* has connected people with people, employing a fast-growing set of new Web technologies such as blogs, social-networking sites and video-sharing sites. *Web 3.0*, starting now, puts all these information and people connections together in ways that will (hopefully!) make our Internet experience more relevant, useful and enjoyable.[39]

In *Web 3.0*, small, fast, customisable Internet applications, accessed through multifunction mobile devices, 'will bring you a virtual world you can carry in your pocket. We will be carrying our amusements with us – best music collections, video collections, and instant news access – all tailored to our preferences and perpetually updatable. And as this cooler stuff [evolves], we won't be connecting to this new Web so much as walking around inside it.'[40] The interactive, community-building nature of these new Web technologies makes them ideal for relating with customers.

Online marketing is now the fastest-growing form of marketing. These days, it's hard to find a company that doesn't use the Web in a significant way. In addition to the click-only dot-coms, most traditional brick-and-mortar companies have now become 'click-and-mortar' companies. They have ventured online to attract new customers and build stronger relationships with existing ones. Today, more than 60 per cent of people in Denmark, the UK, the Netherlands and Sweden and over 75 per cent of American online users use the Internet to shop.[41] Business-to-business (B-to-B) online commerce is also booming. It seems that almost every business has created shops on the Web.

Thus, the technology boom is providing exciting new opportunities for marketers. We will explore the impact of digital marketing technologies in future chapters, especially Chapter 17.

Rapid globalisation

As they are redefining their customer relationships, marketers are also taking a fresh look at the ways in which they relate with the broader world around them. In an increasingly smaller world, companies are now connected *globally* with their customers and marketing partners.

While 80% of Ikea's sales are in Europe – China and Russia are their fastest growing markets.

Source: Alamy Images/Helen Sessions

Today, almost every company, large or small, is touched in some way by global competition. A London florist buys its flowers from Dutch nurseries, and a large Italian electronics manufacturer competes in its home markets with giant Korean rivals. A fledgling Internet retailer finds itself receiving orders from all over the world at the same time that an Spanish consumer-goods producer introduces new products into emerging markets abroad.

The skilful marketing of American and Asian multinationals has challenged European firms at home. Companies such as Toyota, IBM, Chevron, and Samsung have often outperformed their European competitors. Similarly, European companies in a wide range of industries have developed truly global operations, making and selling their products worldwide. While 80 per cent of Ikea's sales are in Europe, China and Russia are their fastest – growing markets. Today, companies are not only selling more of their locally produced goods in international markets but also buying more supplies and components abroad.

Thus, managers in countries around the world are increasingly taking a global, not just local, view of the company's industry, competitors and opportunities. They are asking: What is global marketing? How does it differ from domestic marketing? How do global competitors and forces affect our business? To what extent should we 'go global'? We will discuss the global marketplace in more detail in Chapter 19.

Sustainable marketing – the call for more social responsibility

Marketers are re-examining their relationships with social values and responsibilities and the very Earth that sustains us. As worldwide consumerism and environmentalism movements mature, today's marketers are being called to develop *sustainable marketing* practices. Corporate ethics and social responsibility have become hot topics for almost every business. Few companies can ignore the renewed and very demanding environmental movement. Every company action can affect customer relationships. Today's customers expect companies to deliver value in a socially and environmentally responsible way.

The social-responsibility and environmental movements will place even stricter demands on companies in the future. Some companies resist these movements, budging only when forced by legislation or organised consumer outcries. More forward-looking companies, however, readily accept their responsibilities to the world around them. They view sustainable marketing as an opportunity to do well by doing good. They seek ways to profit by serving immediate needs and the best long-run interests of their customers and communities.

Some companies, such as Statoil, Marks & Spencer, Edison, Grupo Ferrovial and others, practise 'caring capitalism', setting themselves apart by being civic minded and responsible. They build social responsibility and action into their company value and mission statements.

> For those in the business of gold, turning green is increasingly important - that is the belief of Michael Kowalski, chief executive and chairman of Tiffany & Co. Mr Kowalski is so convinced of the need to address environmental issues that he has spent 10 years developing the company's environmental strategy. 'There is so much work to be done, so much complexity surrounding these issues of environmental responsibility, that our philosophy has always been to work quietly behind the scenes,' says Mr Kowalski. 'So we made a conscious decision to build a record of activity before we spoke out, to have a history to point to.' This is true not only for gold, but for precious gemstones – Tiffany, along with other jewellers such as Cartier, has not sold newly-mined rubies since 2002. Similarly, Tiffany stopped selling coral, after discovering that 'there is no such thing as sustainable coral farming,' says Mr Kowalski.[42] Hence, the Tiffany & Co. mission is 'to ensure the highest quality diamonds, ethical sourcing, lifetime warranty, affordable price options, and that they'll always be there for you.'[43]

We will revisit the topic of sustainable marketing in greater detail in Chapter 20.

The growth of not-for-profit marketing

In recent years, marketing also has become a major part of the strategies of many not-for-profit organisations, such as schools, hospitals, museums, zoos, symphony orchestras and even churches. The nation's not-for-profit organisations face stiff competition for support and membership. Sound marketing can help them attract membership and support.[44] Consider the marketing efforts of WaterAid:

> WaterAid's mission is to 'transform lives by improving access to safe water, hygiene and sanitation in the world's poorest communities'. They argue that this 'enables the world's poorest people to gain access to safe water and sanitation. Together with improved hygiene, these basic human rights underpin health, education and livelihoods, forming the first essential step in overcoming poverty.' To promote their work WaterAid ran emotive television advertisements but also used video blogging from a range of events including the G8 summit and the Glastonbury Music Festival. They were the first international development charity to run a 24 hour 'Australia to Zambia' 'tweetathon' that raised the profile of the charity worldwide. In this way, WaterAid is an excellent example of how charities and other not-for-profit organisations are embracing marketing in all its forms.[45]

Government agencies have also shown an increased interest in marketing. For example, the UK military has a marketing plan to attract recruits to its different services, and various government agencies are now designing *social marketing campaigns* to encourage energy conservation and concern for the environment or discourage smoking, excessive drinking and drug use. Indeed, the UK government has an annual advertising budget of more than €600 million.[46]

AUTHOR COMMENT

a Remember Figure 1.1 outlining the marketing process? Now, based on everything we've discussed in this chapter, we'll expand that figure to provide a road map for learning marketing throughout the remainder of this text.

WaterAid's mission is to 'transform lives by improving access to safe water, hygiene and sanitation in the world's poorest communities'.

Source: WaterAid

SO, WHAT IS MARKETING? PULLING IT ALL TOGETHER

At the start of this chapter, Figure 1.1 presented a simple model of the marketing process. Now that we've discussed all the steps in the process, Figure 1.6 presents an expanded model that will help you pull it all together. What is marketing? Simply put, marketing is the process of building profitable customer relationships by creating value for customers and capturing value in return.

The first four steps of the marketing process focus on creating value for customers. The company first gains a full understanding of the marketplace by researching customer needs and managing marketing information. It then designs a customer-driven marketing strategy based on the answers to two simple questions. The first question, 'What consumers will we serve?' relates to market segmentation and targeting. Good marketing companies know that they cannot serve all customers in every way. Instead, they need to focus their resources on the customers they can serve best and most profitably. The second question, 'How can we best serve targeted customers?' relates to differentiation and positioning. Here, the marketer outlines a value proposition that spells out what values the company will deliver to win target customers.

Figure 1.6 An expanded model of the marketing process

This expanded version of figure 1.1 at the beginning of the chapter provides a good road map for the rest of the text. The underlying concept of the entire text is that marketing creates value *for* customers to capture value *from* customers in return.

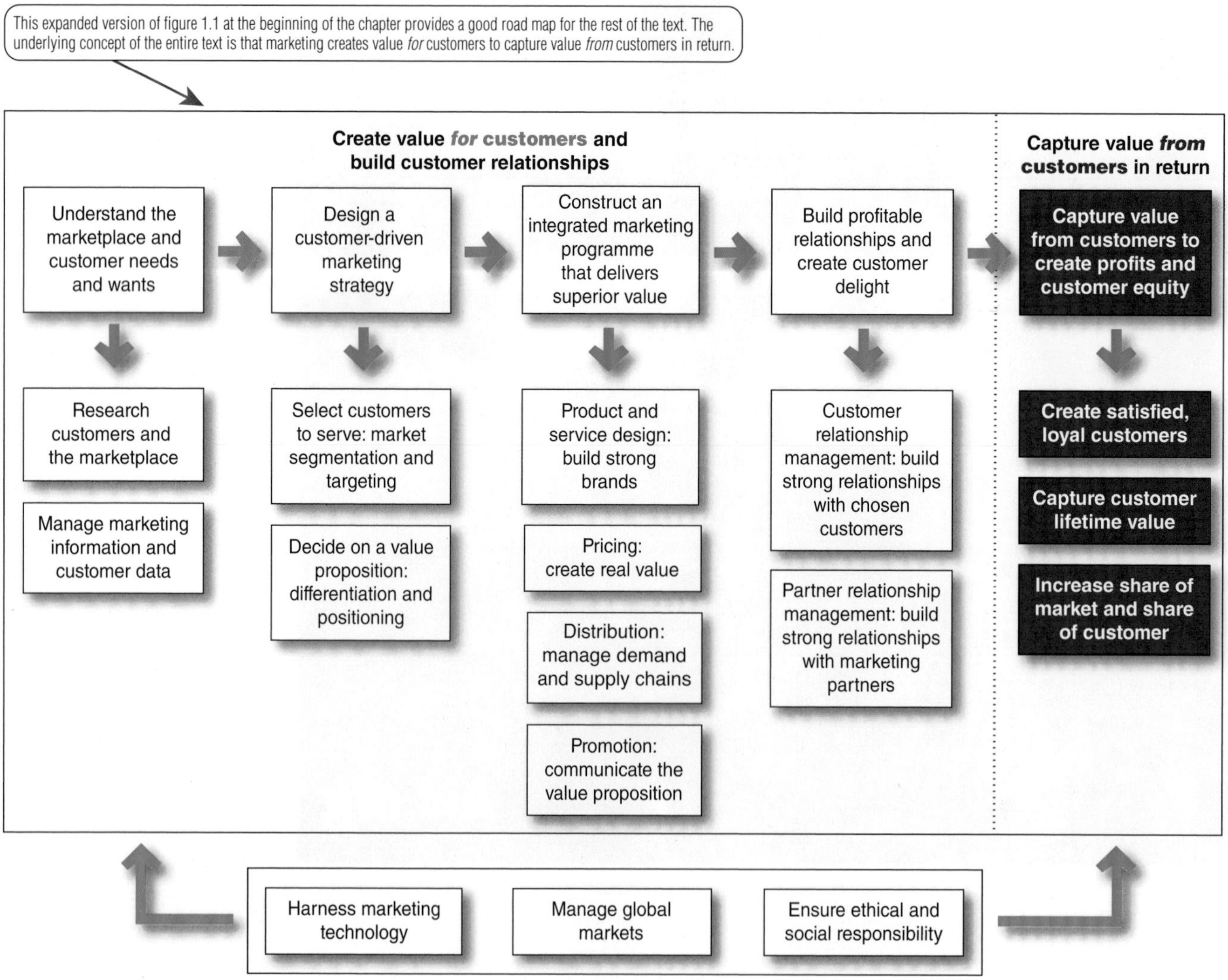

With its marketing strategy chosen, the company now constructs an integrated marketing programme – consisting of a blend of the four marketing mix elements – the four Ps – that transforms the marketing strategy into real value for customers. The company develops product offers and creates strong brand identities for them. It prices these offers to create real customer value and distributes the offers to make them available to target consumers. Finally, the company designs promotion programmes that communicate the value proposition to target customers and persuade them to act on the market offering.

Perhaps the most important step in the marketing process involves building value-laden, profitable relationships with target customers. Throughout the process, marketers practise CRM to create customer satisfaction and delight. In creating customer value and relationships, however, the company cannot go it alone. It must work closely with marketing partners both inside the company and throughout its marketing system. Thus, beyond practising good CRM, firms must also practise good partner relationship management.

The first four steps in the marketing process create value *for* customers. In the final step, the company reaps the rewards of its strong customer relationships by capturing value *from* customers. Delivering superior customer value creates highly satisfied customers who will buy more and buy again. This helps the company capture customer lifetime value and greater share of customer. The result is increased long-term customer equity for the firm.

Finally, in the face of today's changing marketing landscape, companies must take into account three additional factors. In building customer and partner relationships, they must harness marketing technology, take advantage of global opportunities, and ensure that they act in an ethical and socially responsible way.

Figure 1.6 provides a good road map to future chapters of this text. Chapters 1 and 2 introduce the marketing process, with a focus on building customer relationships and capturing value from customers. Chapters 3–6 address the first step of the marketing process – understanding the marketing environment, managing marketing information, and understanding consumer and business buyer behaviour. In Chapter 7, we look more deeply into the two major marketing strategy decisions: selecting which customers to serve (segmentation and targeting) and determining a value proposition (differentiation and positioning). Chapters 8–17 discuss the marketing mix variables, one by one. Chapter 18 sums up customer-driven marketing strategy and creating competitive advantage in the marketplace. The final two chapters examine special marketing considerations: global marketing and sustainable marketing.

REVIEWING OBJECTIVES AND KEY TERMS

Today's successful companies – whether large or small, for-profit or not-for-profit, domestic or global – share a strong customer focus and a heavy commitment to marketing. The goal of marketing is to build and manage customer relationships.

OBJECTIVE 1 Define marketing and outline the steps in the marketing process (pp. 4–5)

Marketing is the process by which companies create value for customers and build strong customer relationships in order to capture value from customers in return.

The marketing process involves five steps. The first four steps create value *for* customers. First, marketers need to understand the marketplace and customer needs and wants. Next, marketers design a customer-driven marketing strategy with the goal of getting, keeping and growing target customers. In the third step, marketers construct a marketing programme that actually delivers superior value. All of these steps form the basis for the fourth step, building profitable customer relationships and creating customer delight. In the final step, the company reaps the rewards of strong customer relationships by capturing value *from* customers.

OBJECTIVE 2 Explain the importance of understanding customers and the marketplace and identify the five core marketplace concepts (pp. 6–8)

Outstanding marketing companies go to great lengths to learn about and understand their customers' *needs*, *wants* and *demands*. This understanding helps them to design want-satisfying market offerings and build value-laden customer relationships by which they can capture *customer lifetime value* and greater *share of customer*. The result is increased long-term *customer equity* for the firm.

The core marketplace concepts are needs, wants and demands; *market offerings* (products, services, and experiences); value and satisfaction; exchange and relationships; and markets. Wants are the form taken by human needs when shaped by culture and individual personality. When backed by buying power, wants become demands. Companies address needs by putting forth a value proposition, a set of benefits that they promise to consumers to satisfy their needs. The value proposition is fulfilled through a market offering, which delivers customer value and satisfaction, resulting in long-term exchange relationships with customers.

OBJECTIVE 3 Identify the key elements of a customer-driven marketing strategy and discuss the marketing management orientations that guide marketing strategy (pp. 8–12)

To design a winning marketing strategy, the company must first decide *who* it will serve. It does this by dividing the market into segments of customers (*market segmentation*) and selecting which segments it will cultivate (*target marketing*). Next, the company must decide *how* it will serve targeted customers (how it will *differentiate and position* itself in the marketplace).

Marketing management can adopt one of five competing market orientations. The *production concept* holds that management's task is to improve production efficiency and bring down prices. The *product concept* holds that consumers favour products that offer the most in quality, performance and innovative features; thus, little promotional effort is required. The *selling concept* holds that consumers will not buy enough of an organisation's products unless it undertakes a large-scale selling and promotion effort. The *marketing concept* holds that achieving organisational goals depends on determining the needs and wants of target markets and delivering the desired satisfactions more effectively and efficiently than competitors do. The *societal marketing concept* holds that generating customer satisfaction *and* long-run societal well-being through sustainable marketing strategies is key to both achieving the company's goals and fulfilling its responsibilities.

OBJECTIVE 4 Discuss customer relationship management and identify strategies for creating value *for* customers and capturing value *from* customers in return (pp. 13–21)

Broadly defined, *customer relationship management* (CRM) is the process of building and maintaining profitable customer relationships by delivering superior customer value and satisfaction. The aim of CRM is to produce high *customer equity*, the total combined customer lifetime values of all of the company's customers. The key to building lasting relationships is the creation of superior *customer value* and *satisfaction*.

Companies want not only to acquire profitable customers but also build relationships that will keep them and grow share of customer. Different types of customers require different CRM strategies. The marketer's aim is to build the *right relationships* with the *right customers*. In return for creating value *for* targeted customers, the company captures value *from* customers in the form of profits and customer equity.

In building customer relationships, good marketers realise that they cannot go it alone. They must work closely with marketing partners inside and outside the company. In addition to being good at CRM, they must also be good at *partner relationship management*.

OBJECTIVE 5 Describe the major trends and forces that are changing the marketing landscape in this age of relationships (pp. 22–29)

Dramatic changes are occurring in the marketing arena. The recent economic downturn left many consumers short of both money and confidence, creating a new age of consumer frugality that will last well into the future. More than ever, marketers must now emphasise the *value* in their value propositions. The challenge is to balance a brand's value proposition with current times while also enhancing its long-term equity.

The boom in computer, telecommunications, information, transportation and other technologies has created exciting new ways to learn about and relate to individual customers. It has also allowed new approaches by which marketers can target consumers more selectively and build closer, two-way customer relationships in the Web 3.0 era.

In an increasingly smaller world, many marketers are now connected *globally* with their customers and marketing partners. Today, almost every company, large or small, is touched in some way by global competition. Today's marketers are also re-examining their ethical and societal responsibilities. Marketers are being called to take greater responsibility for the social and environmental impact of their actions. Finally, in recent years, marketing also has become a major part of the strategies of many not-for-profit organisations, such as schools, hospitals, museums, zoos, symphony orchestras, and even churches.

Pulling it all together, as discussed throughout the chapter, the major new developments in marketing can be summed up in a single word: *relationships*. Today, marketers of all kinds are taking advantage of new opportunities for building relationships with their customers, their marketing partners and the world around them.

NAVIGATING THE KEY TERMS

OBJECTIVE 1
Marketing (p 5)

OBJECTIVE 2
Needs (p 6)
Wants (p 6)
Demands (p 6)
Market offerings (p 6)
Marketing myopia (p 7)
Exchange (p 7)
Market (p 7)

OBJECTIVE 3
Marketing management (p 8)
Production concept (p 10)
Product concept (p 10)
Selling concept (p 10)
Marketing concept (p 10)
Societal marketing concept (p 11)

OBJECTIVE 4
Customer relationship management (p 13)
Customer-perceived value (p 13)
Customer satisfaction (p 13)
Customer-managed relationships (p 16)
Consumer-generated marketing (p 17)
Partner relationship management (p 18)
Customer lifetime value (p 19)
Share of customer (p 20)
Customer equity (p 20)

OBJECTIVE 5
Internet (p 24)

DISCUSSING AND APPLYING THE CONCEPTS

Discussing the concepts

1. Define marketing and discuss how it is more than just 'telling and selling'. (AACSB: Communication; Reflective Thinking)
2. Marketing has been criticised because it 'makes people buy things they don't really need'. Refute or support this accusation. (AACSB: Communication; Reflective Thinking)
3. Discuss the two important questions a marketing manager must answer when designing a winning marketing strategy. How should a manager approach finding answers to these questions? (AACSB: Communication; Reflective Thinking)
4. What are the five different marketing management orientations? Which orientation do you believe Apple follows when marketing products such as the iPhone and iPad? (AACSB: Communication; Reflective Thinking)
5. Explain the difference between *share of customer* and *customer equity*. Why are these concepts important to marketers? (AACSB: Communication; Reflective Thinking)
6. Discuss trends impacting marketing and the implications of these trends on how marketers deliver value to customers. (AACSB: Communication)

Applying the concepts

1. Talk to five people, varying in age from young adult to senior citizen, about their cars. Ask them what value means to them with regard to a car and how the manufacturer and dealer create such value. Write a brief report of what you learned about customer value. (AACSB: Communication; Reflective Thinking)
2. Select a retailer and calculate how much you are worth to that retailer if you continue to shop there for the rest of your life (your customer lifetime value). What factors should you consider when deriving an estimate of your lifetime value to a retailer? How can a retailer increase your lifetime value? (MCSB: Communication; Reflective Thinking; Analytic Reasoning)
3. Go online to learn about careers in marketing. Interview someone who works in one of the marketing jobs described in the appendix and ask him or her the following questions:
   (a) What does your job entail?
   (b) How did you get to this point in your career? Is this what you thought you'd be doing when you grew up? What influenced you to get into this field?
   (c) What education is necessary for this job?

(d) What advice can you give to students?

(e) Add one additional question that you create.

Write a brief report of the responses to your questions and explain why you would or would not be interested in working in this field. (AACSB: Communication; Reflective Thinking)

Focus on technology

In only a few short years, *consumer-generated marketing* has increased exponentially. It's also known as *consumer-generated media* and *consumer-generated content*. More than 100 million websites contain user-generated content. You may be a contributor yourself if you've ever posted something on a blog; reviewed a product at Amazon; uploaded a video on YouTube; or sent a video from your mobile phone to a news website, such as bbc.co.uk or www.euronews.net. This force has not gone unnoticed by marketers — and with good reason. Nielsen, the TV ratings giant, found that most consumers trust consumer opinions posted online. As a result, savvy marketers encourage consumers to generate content. For example, Nokia has more than 4 million fans on Facebook while parents can share information at Pampers Village (www.pampers.com). Apple even encourages iPhone or iPad users to develop apps for its devices. However, consumer-generated marketing is not without problems – just search 'I hate [insert company name]' in any search engine!

1. Find two examples (other than those discussed in the chapter) of marketer-supported, consumer-generated content and two examples of consumer-generated content that is not officially supported by the company whose product is involved. Provide the Web link to each and discuss how the information impacts your attitude toward the companies involved (AACSB: Communication; Reflective Thinking; Technology)

2. Discuss the advantages and disadvantages of consumer-generated marketing. (AACSB: Communication; Reflective)

Focus on ethics

Sixty years ago, about 85 per cent of British men smoked cigarettes, but now the smoking rate for the whole of Europe is around 26 per cent. This decline results from acquired knowledge on the potential health dangers of smoking and marketing restrictions for this product. However, although smoking rates are declining in most developed nations, more and more consumers in developing nations, such as Russia and China, are puffing away. Smoker rates in some countries run as high as 40 per cent. Developing nations account for more than 70 per cent of world tobacco consumption, and marketers are fuelling this growth. Most of these nations do not have the restrictions prevalent in developed nations, such as advertising bans,

warning labels and distribution restrictions. Consequently, it is predicted that one billion people worldwide will die this century from smoking-related ailments.

1. Given the extreme health risks, should marketers stop selling cigarettes even though they are legal and demanded by consumers? Should cigarette marketers continue to use marketing tactics that are restricted in one country in other countries where they are not restricted? (AACSB: Communication; Ethical Reasoning)

2. Research the history of cigarette marketing in Europe. Are there any new restrictions with respect to marketing this product? (MCSB: Communication; Reflective Thinking)

Marketing & the economy

In the run up to Christmas 2011, the Early Learning Centre (ELC) in the UK is trying hard to turn around a year that has been far from easy. Last year the ELC blamed snow disruption for poor sales figures for the festive season (although the Disney Store experienced the same snow but had a good year). This year the ELC is relying heavily on middle-class parents buying their children's Christmas gift at the educationally-oriented ELC stores. For boys, ELC has plumped for its first 'dolls' house for boys. Actually, the dolls' house is re-branded as an Emergency Centre with bedrooms and dining rooms in the three-storey house being replaced by more 'boy-friendly' features (these include a computer control centre, a gym that comes complete with a running machine and, what every Emergency Centre needs, a helipad). Gone are gentle staircases and in are more 'boyish' fireman's poles. Of course, there are basement garages for emergency vehicles. At around €120 this toy is not cheap. However, this traditional toy is educational and markedly non-electronic. Will boys be getting an Emergency Centre or an iPad for 5 year olds this Christmas? We will have to wait until Christmas morning to be sure.

1. When parents buy educational toys for their children, is this based on a need or a want?

2. Is the €120 price tag for this product too high for most frugal parents?

3. What types of customers pay more, or less, for educational toys?

Marketing by the numbers

Marketing is expensive! Do you want customers to order your product by phone? That will cost you €5–€10 per order. Do you want a sales representative calling on customers? That's about €70 per sales call, and that's if the rep doesn't have to get on an airplane and stay in a hotel, which can be very costly considering some companies have thousands of sales reps calling on thousands of customers. What about the €1 off coupon for Tropicana orange juice that you found in the Sunday newspaper? It costs

Tropicana more than €1 when you redeem it at the store. These are all examples of costs of distributing products to buyers, and the costs of all the employees working in marketing.

1. Select a publically traded company and research how much the company spent on marketing activities in the most recent year of available data. What percentage of sales do marketing expenditures represent? Have these expenditures increased or decreased over the past five years? Write

a brief report of your findings. (AACSB Communication; Analytic Reasoning)

2. Search the Internet for salary information regarding jobs in marketing. Use http://jobs.brandrepublic.com or a similar website. What is the average for five different jobs in marketing? How do the averages compare between countries? Write a brief report on your findings. (AACSB: Communication; Use of IT; Reflective Thinking)

REFERENCES

[1] This case study draws heavily on the excellent case studies and analyses (including quotes and other information) of: Liz Bolshaw, 'The UK's rich list: women on ascent' *Financial Times* (9 May 2011) http://blogs.ft.com/women-at-the-top/2011/05/09/the-uks-rich-list-women-on-ascent/#axzz1ZhZjh500, accessed October 2011; Anonymous, 'The job: mystery shopper', *Financial Times* (1 March 2011), www.ft.com/cms/s/0/239417c6-24d3-11df-8be0-00144feab49a .html#ixzz1ZhbG3ERN accessed October 2011; Rhymer Rigby, 'Identifying the right balance', *Financial Times* (31 August 2009), www.ft.com/cms/s/0/c2859952-9669-11de-84d1-00144feabdc0. html#ixzz1Zhc438R9, accessed October 2011; Bob Sherwood, 'An eye for the next opportunity', *Financial Times*, 17 September, www.ft.com/ cms /s/0/5a724d28-845f-11dd-adc7-0000779fd18c.html accessed October 2011; Andrew Cave, 'Dame Mary Perkins founded Specsavers on a table-tennis table, now she is a billionaire', *Daily Telegraph* (28 May 2011), www.telegraph.co.uk/finance/newsbysector/retailandcon sumer/8543795/Dame-Mary-Perkins-founded-Specsavers-on-a-table-tennis-table-now-she-is-a-billionaire.html, accessed October 2011. See also www.specsavers.co.uk/news-and-information/history/ and www .specsavers.co.uk/news-and-information/customer-service, accessed October 2011.

[2] See 'US Market Leaders', *Advertising Age* (21 June 2010), p. 18.

[3] As quoted in John J. Burnett, *Nonprofit Marketing Best Practices* (New York: John Wiley & Sons, 2008), p. 21.

[4] The American Marketing Association offers the following definition: 'Marketing is an organizational function and a set of processes for creating, communicating, and delivering value to customers and for managing customer relationships in ways that benefit the organization and its stakeholders.' www.marketingpower.com/_layouts/Dictionary .aspx?dLetter=M, accessed October 2011.

[5] Jeffrey M. O'Brien, 'Zappos knows how to kick it', *Fortune* (22 January 2009), accessed at http://money.cnn.com/2009/01/15/news/compa-nies/Zappos_best_companies_obrien.fortune/index.htm; and Roland T. Rust, Christine Moorman and Gaurav Bhalla, 'Rethinking Marketing', *Harvard Business Review* (January–February 2010), pp. 94–101.

[6] See www.facebook.com/visiteurope, accessed October 2011.

[7] www.discoverireland.com/gb/ireland-things-to-see-and-do/activities/ golfing/, accessed October 2011.

[8] See Theodore Levitt's classic article, 'Marketing myopia', *Harvard Business Review*, (July–August 1960), pp. 45–56. For more recent discussions, see 'What business are you in?' *Harvard Business Review* (October 2006), pp. 127–137; Lance A. Bettencourt, 'Debunking myths about

customer needs', *Marketing Management* (January/February 2009), pp. 46–51, here p. 50; and N. Craig Smith, Minette E. Drumright and Mary C. Gentile, 'The new marketing myopia', *Journal of Public Policy & Marketing*, Spring 2010, pp. 4–11.

[9] See *Sustainability* at *UPS*, www.responsibility.ups.com/community/ Static%20Files/sustainability/2008_CSR_PDF_Report.pdf, pp. 13–18; 'UPS corporate sustainability: everyone matters', www.responsibility.ups .com/Sustainability?WT.svl=Footer, accessed October 2011; 'World's Most Admired Companies', http://money.cnn.com/magazines/fortune/ mostadmired/2010/best_worst/best4.html, August 2010; and http:// sustainability.ups.com, accessed October 2011.

[10] For more on how to measure customer satisfaction, see D. Randall Brandt, 'For good measure', *Marketing Management* (January–February 2007), pp. 21–25.

[11] Based on information from Michael Bush, 'Why you should be putting on the Ritz', *Advertising Age* (21 June 2010), p. 1; Julie Barker, 'Power to the people,' *Incentive* (February 2008), p. 34; and Carmine Gallo, 'Employee motivation the Ritz-Carlton way', *BusinessWeek*, (29 February 2008), accessed at www.businessweek.com/smallbiz/content/feb2008/ sb20080229_347490.htm. Also see http://corporate.ritzcarlton.com/en/ About/Awards.htm#Hotel, accessed October 2011.

[12] See www.klm.com, accessed October 2011.

[13] Elizabeth A. Sullivan, 'Just say no', *Marketing News* (15 April 2008), p. 17; and Raymund Flandez, 'It just isn't working? Some file for customer divorce', *Wall Street Journal*, (16 November 2009), p. B7.

[14] See Anonymous, 'Bank of China to "cherry-pick" UK mortgage customers as lending drought persists', *The Telegraph* (20 August 2009), accessed at http://www.telegraph.co.uk/finance/china-business/ 6059626/Bank-of-China-to-cherry-pick-UK-mortgage-customers-as-lending-drought-persists.html.

[15] See Dan Hyde, 'Savers cherry-picked for secret accounts', *This Is Money*, (17 May 2011), accessed at www.thisismoney.co.uk/money/saving/article-1723411/Savers-cherry-picked-for-secret-accounts.html.

[16] Quotes from Andrew Walmsley, 'The year of consumer empower-ment', *Marketing* (20 December 2006), p. 9; and Jeff Heilman, 'Rules of engagement: during a recession, marketers need to have *their* keenest listening-to-customers strategy in place', *The Magazine of Branded Content* (Winter 2009), p. 7. Also see Frank's Striefler's '5 marketing princi-ples brands should embrace in 2010' *Adweek* (13 January 2010), accessed at www.adweek.com/aw/content_display/community/columns/other-columns/e3i3602f61793f3cd88ea9f341f59d8d4bf.

[17] http://images.businessweek.com/ss/09/05/0508_ceos_who_twitter/2.htm.

[18] See www.facebook.com/Honda and http://apps.facebook.com/wholovesahonda, accessed October 2011.

[19] See 'Successful Ikea Facebook campaign shows importance of offering deals to consumers on social media', *Illuminea* (27 November 2009), http://illuminea.com/social-media/ikea-facebook-social-media/; Chris Matyszczyk, 'Ikea's brilliant Facebook campaign', *CNET News*, (24 November 2009), http://news.cnet.com/8301-17852_3-10404937-71.html; and www.youtube.com/watch?v=P_K1ti4RU78&feature=player_embedded, accessed October 2011.

[20] Sullivan, 'We were right!' p. 17.

[21] See https://community.mcafee.com/docs/DOC-24899, accessed October 2011.

[22] Joel Rubenstein, 'Marketers, researchers, and your ears', *Brandweek*, (15 February 2010), p. 34.

[23] 'Doritos fan-created Super Bowl ad "underdog", created for $200, scores no. 2 on *USA Today* ad meter and $600,000 prize', 8 February 2010, http://frito-lay.com/press-release-20100208.html; Stuart Elliott, 'Do-it-yourself super ads', *New York Times* (9 February 2010); and 'USA *Today* 2010 ad meter tracks Super Bowl XLIV ads', *USA Today*, (15 February 2010), accessed at www.usatoday.com/money/advertising/admeter/2010admeter.htm.

[24] Gavin O'Malley, 'Entries pour in for Heinz ketchup commercial contest' (13 August 2007), accessed at http://publications.mediapost.com.

[25] Philip Kotler and Kevin Lane Keller, *Marketing Management*, 13th edn. (Upper Saddle River, NJ: Prentice Hall, 2009), p. 11.

[26] 'Consumer "new frugality" may be an enduring feature of post-recession economy, finds Booz & Company survey', *BusinessWire*, (24 February 2010).

[27] Graham Brown, 'Mobile youth key statistics' (28 March, 2008), www.mobileyouth.org/?s=MobileYouth+Key+Statistics. For interesting discussions on customer lifetime value, see Sunil Gupta *et al.*, 'Modeling customer lifetime value,' *Journal of Service Research* (November 2006), pp. 139-146; Nicolas Glady, Bart Baesens and Christophe Croux, 'Modeling churn using customer lifetime value,' *European Journal of Operational Research*, (16 August 2009), p. 402; and Jason Q. Zhang, Ashutosh Dixit and Roberto Friedman, 'Customer loyalty and lifetime value: an empirical investigation of consumer packaged goods', *Journal of Marketing Theory and Practice* (Spring 2010), p. 127.

[28] Heather Green, 'How Amazon aims to keep you clicking', *Business Week* (2 March 2009), pp. 34-40; and Geoffrey A. Fowler, 'Corporate news: Amazon's sales soar, lifting profit', *Wall Street Journal* (23 April 2010), p. B3.

[29] Don Peppers and Martha Rogers, 'Customers Don't Grow on Trees', *Fast Company* (July 2005), p. 26.

[30] For more discussion on customer equity, see Roland T. Rust, Valerie A. Zeithaml and Katherine A. Lemon, *Driving Customer Equity* (New York: Free Press, 2000); Rust, Lemon and Zeithaml, 'Return on marketing: using customer equity to focus marketing strategy', *Journal of Marketing* (January 2004), pp. 109-127; Dominique M. Hanssens, Daniel Thorpe and Carl Finkbeiner, 'Marketing when customer equity matters', *Harvard Business Review* (May 2008), pp. 117-124; Thorsten Wiesel, Bernd Skieram and Julián Villanueva, 'Customer equity: an integral part of financial reporting', *Journal of Marketing* (8 March 2008), pp. 1-14; and V. Kumar and Denish Shaw, 'Expanding the role of marketing: from customer equity two market capitalization', *Journal of Marketing* (November 2009), p. 119.

[31] This example is adapted from information found in Rust, Lemon and Zeithaml, 'Where should the next marketing dollar go?', *Marketing Management* (September–October 2001), pp. 24-28; and Jeff Green and David Welch, 'What Cadillac is learning from the Ritz', *Bloomberg BusinessWeek* (17 June 2010), p. 1.

[32] Werner Reinartz and V. Kumar, 'The mismanagement of customer loyalty', *Harvard Business Review* (July 2002), pp. 86-94. Also see Stanley F. Slater, Jakki J. Mohr and Sanjit Sengupta, 'Know your customer', *Marketing Management* (February 2009), pp. 37-44.

[33] Booz & Company, 'Consumer "new frugality" may be an enduring feature of post-recession economy', *Economics Week* (12 March 2010), p. 137.

[34] Rose Jacobs, 'Value demand helps boost sales at Whitbread', *Financial Times* (15 December 2010), p. 20.

[35] Emily Thornton, 'The new rules', *BusinessWeek* (19 January 2009), pp. 30-34.

[36] See for example www.marksandspencer.com/Dine-In-Offers-In-Store-MS-Food-Food-Wine/b/198933039 accessed October 2011.

[37] Adapted from information in Brad Stone, 'Breakfast can wait. Today's first stop is Online,' *New York Times* (10 August 2009), p. A1.

[38] Internet usage stats from www.internetworldstats.com/stats.htm, accessed October 2011; James Lewin, 'Pew Internet and the American life project: trend data', www.pewinternet.org/Trend-Data.aspx, accessed October 2011; and Pew/Internet, 'The future of the Internet III', 14 December 2008, accessed at www.pewinternet.org/Reports/2008/The-Future-of-the-Internet-III.aspx.

[39] For more discussion, see 'Research and markets: semantic wave report: industry roadmap to Web 3.0 and multibillion market opportunities', M2 *Presswire*, (20 January 2009); Greg Smith, 'Web 3.0: "vague, but exciting"' *Adweek*, (15 June 2009), p. 19; and Michael Baumann, 'Pew report: expert opinion divided on Web 3.0', *Information Today* (July/August 2010), p. 11.

[40] Laurie Rowell, 'In search of Web 3.0', *netWorker* (September 2008), pp. 18-24. Also see 'Research and markets: Web 3.0 manifesto', *Business Wire* (21 January 2009); and Jessi Hempel, 'Web 2.0 is so over. Welcome to Web 3.0', *Fortune* (19 January 2009), p. 36.

[41] 'Pew Internet and the American life project: trend data'.

[42] Vanessa Friedman, 'Michael Kowalski: Tiffany parades its voluntary standards', *Financial Times* (28 May 2008), accessed October 2011, www.ft.com/cms/s/0/69c21434-292e-11dd-96ce-000077b07658.html#axzz1UPifHx5H.

[43] See www.tiffany.com; accessed October 2011.

[44] For examples and for a good review of not-for-profit marketing, see Philip Kotler and Alan R. Andreasen, *Strategic Marketing for Nonprofit Organizations*, 7th edn (Upper Saddle River, NJ: Prentice Hall, 2008); Philip Kotler and Karen Fox, *Strategic Marketing for Educational Institutions* (Upper Saddle River, NJ: Prentice Hall, 1995); Philip Kotler, John Bowen, and James Makens, *Marketing for Hospitality and Tourism*, 4th edn (Upper Saddle River, NJ: Prentice Hall, 2006); and Philip Kotler and Nancy Lee, *Marketing in the Public Sector: A Roadmap for Improved Performance* (Philadelphia, PA: Wharton School Publishing, 2006).

[45] Example based on data found at www.wateraid.org/uk/about_us/vision_and_mission/default.asp; accessed October 2011.

[46] For more on social marketing, see Philip Kotler, Ned Roberto and Nancy R. Lee, *Social Marketing: Improving the Quality of Life*, 2nd edn (Thousand Oaks, CA: Sage Publications, 2002).

VIDEO CASE

Stew Leonard's   MyMarketingLab

Stew Leonard's is a little-know grocery store chain based in Connecticut. It has only four stores. But its small number of location doesn't begin to illustrate what customers experience when they visit what has been called the 'Disneyland of diary stores'. Since opening its first diary store in 1969, the company has been known for its customer-centric way of doing business. In fact, founder Stew Leonard's obsession with the concept of customer lifetime value made him determined to keep every customer who entered his store.

The video featuring Stew Leonard's shows how the retailer has delighted customers for more than 40 years. With singing animatronics farm animals, associates in costume, petting zoos and free food and drink samples, this chain serves as many as 300,000 customers per store every week and has achieved the highest sales per square foot of any single store in the USA.

After viewing the video, answer the following questions about the company.

1. What is Stew Leonard's value proposition?
2. How does Stew Leonard's build long-term customer relationships?
3. How has Stew Leonard's applied the concepts of customer equity and customer lifetime value?

Pegasus Airlines: delighting a new type of travelling customer

Until 1982, Turkish Airlines was the only airline company operating in Turkey, and it had no domestic competitors. Following deregulation and reduction of government controls across the airline industry, 29 airlines were established, with 22 finding themselves bankrupted a few years later, demonstrating the strong level of both internal and external competition and how the airline industry is affected by economic instability. Over the past 20 years, Turkey has experienced a number of financial crises, as well as political turmoil culminating in a military coup in 1980. Pegasus was created in 1989 as a charter airline partnered with Aer Lingus to create all-inclusive holidays. In 1994, the company was sold to a Turkish investment fund and in 2005 was re-sold to Ali Sabancı (of Sabancı Holding, an influential family owned business in Turkey), who changed the airline from a charter airline to a low-cost airline. In 2008, Pegasus carried a total 4.4 million passengers in Turkey, more than any other private airline. As of 2010, Pegasus has a fleet of 27 Boeing planes with a further 24 on order. Its major competitors – other than the national carrier, Turkish Airlines – are Onur Air, Fly Air, Sun Express and Atlasjet. Instead of operating from Istanbul's main airport, which is overcrowded, Pegasus Airlines flies from Istanbul's second main hub, Sabiha Gökçen International Airport. Its on-time departure rate is 93 per cent, which is well above the European average of 81 per cent, demonstrating the importance the company attaches to customer service.

TRULY CUSTOMER FOCUSED

What is the secret to the airline's success? Quite simply, it involves making sure Pegasus is continually developing to meet passenger expectations and priorities. Pegasus has put in place a yield management strategy for ticket pricing, using the strategy of Southwest Airlines of North America as an example. Supply and demand, as well as time, are taken into account in the ticket pricing strategy; for example, if customers book early (60 days) they receive further savings while those who book later pay the maximum current fare offered by competitors. The system is complemented by an electronic ticket policy whereby passengers receive their information via e-mail and SMS. Pegasus has also developed a credit/loyalty card, which offers customers a range of benefits including insurance rate reductions. Although airlines can't often control flight delays, Pegasus has developed a specific customer satisfaction guarantee policy that provides customers with (i) in the case of a delay greater than 3 hours, a refund of the ticket and (ii) in the case of a delay greater than 5 hours, a refund and a free ticket. Pegasus also offers a customer service

experience at the airport. It provides exclusive allotments for the first 72 hours of parking with a valet parking option, VIP and Business Class lounges, car rental and many hotel partners where customers can get some discount. Unlike many airlines, a one-class interior configuration is operated, but passengers can pay a small extra premium to choose their seats. This is complemented by the Pegasus Flying Café, which offers a range of refreshments and catering options for a small additional charge. Pegasus offers further customer service options, including a 10 per cent discount to passengers on international flights who order their in-flight meals 48 hours in advance. An in-plane bulletin is also available, with a mix of offers and features on certain destinations. This bulletin is free for customers but generates income via advertising. These services are supported by Pegasus' own flight crew training centre and maintenance organisation, Pegasus Technic. Both are fully licensed and are used to train new staff members. Pegasus also provides these training and technical services for other local airlines. Pegasus' innovative customer service won the company an award for 'Best Airline Business Price' in 2006. Indeed, the company regularly receives awards and recognition for, among other things, its management strategy; initiatives in website development; and its marketing strategy, which employs a new approach to advertising that includes viral marketing, flash campaigns and mobile campaigns. This strategy has succeeded in making Pegasus the most searched airline in Turkey on Google. While the industry grew at a rate of 20 per cent between 2005 and 2008, Pegasus grew at the rate of 57 per cent, which certainly indicates the success of Pegasus as a low-cost carrier. The growth rate was sustained during the most recent global recession.

MORE THAN AMENITIES

Although the tangible amenities that Pegasus offers are likely to delight most travellers, general manager Sertaç Haybat, recognises that these practices are not nearly enough to provide a sustainable competitive advantage and that Pegasus must always present its customers with the most economical flight opportunities. Here the importance of the crew training centre remains crucial. Haybat emphasises that a culture that breeds trust is the most crucial factor. It's this personal culture that gives Pegasus' customer service an edge. Indeed, taking care of customers starts as early as a customer's first encounter with the Pegasus brand and website. In 2007, Pegasus was recognised as one of Turkey's top brands, chosen from a range of 137 national and international brands operating in the country. Of the 137, only 26 were awarded the title of 'Superbrand Turkey', including Pegasus. Pegasus' employees work as a team with their goal being a common understanding of the airline's long-term objective to provide a democratic environment in which everyone shares their ideas freely. Training, as well as continuous development is provided to ensure regular career progression and high levels of motivation through a solid performance system and regular personal feedback. Early in the process, Pegasus selects the people who best exhibit these values while directing the right person to the right department at the right time. The last tenet of Pegasus' customer-service strategy lies in the regularly scheduled and innovative destinations it offers. Not only does Pegasus share planes with Air Berlin and Izair, but it also has charter and scheduled services to 70 airports in Europe and Asia. Pegasus operates regular flights to Georgia and Lebanon, providing additional destinations outside of Europe, thus maximising Turkey's short flights opportunities. These flights have prompted a strong reaction from the competition. The regular service to Tbilisi (Georgia) has been met by an announcement from Austrian Airlines of the withdrawal of its own regular flight to the same destination. This prompted speculation in the media about the changing preference of air travellers where low-cost companies are seen as a sustainable substitute to middle- and high-cost traditional carriers. Pegasus has also successfully developed its internal market with over 19 destinations within Turkey.

LOVE YOUR CUSTOMERS

Customers are the most important aspect of any service industry. Since the global recession, many airlines have seen a drop in passenger numbers, and it is a challenge to achieve and sustain profitability. In the case of Turkey, other factors provide further opportunities for the airline industry. On the one hand, the economy is growing at a faster rate than the rest of Europe, and on the other hand, as is the case in many emerging countries and in traditional industrial areas of developed economies, a substantial expatriate population exists. New migrants or integrated second- or third-generation migrants usually provide opportunities for travel due to cultural affinities and understanding. Regular holidays or business-related trips 'home' can create a good foundation in terms of overall capacity planning. In terms of weekly seat capacity, Pegasus currently ranks in the top 30 among European airlines. While most airline customers are loyal because of frequent flyer programmes, in the case of Pegasus and Turkey in general, further affinities can be developed and sustained, including a certain sense of nationalist pride or nostalgia. History can also provide potential future markets. Countries such as Azerbaijan, Turkmenistan, Uzbekistan and others around the Black Sea region are long-term trading partners of Turkey and have been growing rapidly since the breakup of the USSR in 1991. This potential is also opening up opportunities with countries such as Iran, Iraq and Syria, which have large, young markets both in terms of tourism and business. However, Pegasus customers want more in terms of social network relationships with the brand and, therefore, Pegasus aims to keep up with its customers even when they are not flying. For example, Pegasus has a Facebook page complete with a game entitling customers to win free tickets. The company also has a Twitter account, through which it offers customers special competitions. Furthermore, in association with Vodafone, a special campaign

was developed called 'mobile phone fly', whereby consumers accumulated for each SMS an award of 5 per cent toward a Pegasus ticket discount, emulating the 'shop and miles' strategy of traditional airlines. Over time, Pegasus hopes to create a sustainable relationship with its customers while leveraging the possibilities of social networks and other digital technologies. Pegasus' strong word of mouth has also been important in the airline's success and is reflected in the words of customers on a special website titled 'Pegasus Listens to You'. Sections of the website encourage customers to generate ideas for service improvement, to debate generic questions and topics relating to the airline's management and services, and to encourage customers to report problems they have encountered. Since 2005, Pegasus has shown that a low-cost airline can deliver low fares, excellent service and steady profits. It has demonstrated that even in the airline business, entry barriers can be lowered and a powerful brand can be created. Pegasus embodies success in four marketing cornerstones: (i) it ensures successful service through safety, training, and its devoted employees; (ii) it employs creative communication with its customers; (iii) it offers great destinations and easy access to international hubs; and (iv) it uses efficient management techniques, delivering low prices with a high-quality service experience. To be successful in the low-cost airline industry, great attention needs to be paid to customers' changing travel patterns and needs. Booking flights, post-purchase evaluation through regular customer relationship management, and intangible value created by a variety of details make Pegasus a formidable brand in the low-cost airline industry.

Questions for discussion

1. Give examples of the needs, wants and demands that Pegasus customers demonstrate, differentiating these three concepts. What are the implications of each for Pegasus' practices?
2. Describe in detail all the facets of Pegasus' product. What is being exchanged in a Pegasus transaction?
3. Which of the five marketing management concepts best applies to Pegasus?
4. What value does Pegasus create for its customers?
5. Is Pegasus likely to continue being successful in building customer relationships? Why or why not?

Sources: Ö. Atalik and M. Arslan, 'Wisdom of domestic customers: an empirical analysis of the Turkish private airline sector', *International Journal of Business and Management*, **4** (7), pp. 61–67; N. G. Torlak and M. Sanal 'David's strategy formulation framework in action: the example of Turkish Airlines on domestic air transportation', *I'Óstanbul Ticaret Üniversitesi Fen Bilimleri Dergisi*, **6** (12), pp. 81–114; Ralph Anker, 'Airline capacity at European airports down just 2% in early winter', Airport Business website, www.airport-business.com, accessed December 2010; 'Road block receives more than 140,000 clicks in 18 hours', Microsoft Advertising, accessed at http://advertising.microsoft.com/home, November 2006; 'Headquarters', Pegasus Airlines website, www.flypgs.com, accessed 6 September 2009.

CHAPTER TWO

Company and marketing strategy: partnering to build customer relationships

Chapter preview

In the first chapter, we explored the marketing process, the process by which companies create value for consumers to capture value from them in return. In this chapter, we dig deeper into steps two and three of that process; designing customer-driven marketing strategies and constructing marketing programmes. First, we look at the organisation's overall strategic planning, which guides marketing strategy and planning. Next, we discuss how, guided by the strategic plan, marketers partner closely with others inside and outside the firm to create value for customers. We then examine marketing strategy and planning–how marketers choose target markets, position their market offerings, develop a marketing mix and manage their marketing programmes. Finally, we look at the important step of measuring and managing return on marketing investment (marketing ROI).

First let's look at the Olympic brand. Staging an Olympics is an enormous challenge for any city or country. Not only do venues and accommodation need to be constructed for the Olympians, but also to achieve success the physical issues have to be addressed, along with the ability to market the spectacle to an ever-broadening world audience. None of this is possible unless sponsors are involved at the earliest opportunity, and they are able to see tangible benefits from their involvement.

Objective outline

➤ **Objective 1** Explain company-wide strategic planning and its four steps.
Company-wide strategic planning: defining marketing's role (pp. 40–43)

➤ **Objective 2** Discuss how to design business portfolios and develop growth strategies.
Designing the business portfolio (pp. 43–47)

➤ **Objective 3** Explain marketing's role in strategic planning and how marketing works with its partners to create and deliver customer value.
Planning marketing: partnering to build customer relationships (pp. 47–50)

➤ **Objective 4** Describe the elements of a customer-driven marketing strategy and mix and the forces that influence it.
Marketing strategy and the marketing mix (pp. 50–54)

➤ **Objective 5** List the marketing management functions, including the elements of a marketing plan, and discuss the importance of measuring and managing the return on marketing investment.
Managing the marketing effort (pp. 54–58)
Measuring and managing return on marketing investment (pp. 58–60)

The Olympics: branding on a global stage

The Olympic brand is a powerful worldwide symbol representing not only sports, but a celebration of the best in the world and an opportunity for nations to join together and compete for glory. The Beijing Olympics in 2008 was immensely popular worldwide and successful, delivering a quality experience for the athletes, spectators and millions of viewers around the world. It was also vital in rebranding and repackaging China as a modern nation. China hoped that the Olympics would help it forge business links that would propel the country forward. The massive effort to deliver the games was not without cost: billions were invested, and some of this funding came from sponsors and partners.

The London 2012 Olympic Games promised to be another tremendous spectacle, although the budget was only roughly half of what Beijing's was. Sponsors, including Coca-Cola, Samsung, Visa, BMW and Adidas were all eager to get involved and offer financial support. The purpose of the partnerships is not merely financial: it is about building customer relationships, both for the games and for the businesses.

On a slightly less grand level, the Olympics provides smaller businesses with an opportunity to be involved, to provide products and services, and to promote the fact that they have an association with the 2012 Olympics. London 2012 estimated that there will be 7,000 direct contracts with suppliers. Business engagement refers to the number of companies registered with the Olympics to provide the event with products and services. Nearly 90 per cent of the registered companies (18,000) were small-to-medium sized businesses.

The Olympic Delivery Authority (ODA) and London Organising Committee (LOCOG) estimated that in the run up to the London 2012 Games, trade amounting to more than $9 billion would involve approximately 80,000 different businesses. John Armitt, the ODA chairman, has been involved in numerous discussions with British businesses and has found that an enormous number of businesses were keen to be involved. From the outset, smaller businesses were benefiting from the Games, many being able to establish themselves as key providers for such a large-scale project. Armitt believed that this would put them in a prime position to compete with even larger contractors in the future. Armitt recognised it was a challenging project and it needed the best British businesses to keep it on track. The Organising Committee's chief executive, Paul Deighton, was suitably impressed with the British business response to the London 2012 Business Network. The London 2012 procurement team and business development partners had worked hard to encourage as many businesses as possible to become involved at some level in providing goods and services. The push continued into 2009, with increasing numbers of UK businesses registering on the Compete For system. By registering on this system, Deighton was certain that the businesses would not regret getting involved in the Games, as it represented a 'lifetime business opportunity'.

Tessa Jowell, the former Olympics Minister, said 'The fact that 70 per cent of the 650 companies that have already won work supplying the games are small- and medium-sized firms demonstrates the potential for the business benefits of London 2012 to provide a boost to the whole economy.'

New Olympics Minister, Hugh Robertson, took over the position in May 2010, against a backdrop of threatened budget cuts. Nonetheless, the venues and infrastructure were 75 per cent completed by the end of 2010. It had been the toughest period of construction and all of the main venues were on track to be completed by the summer of 2011, a year ahead of the games. Crucially, they were also on budget.

Commenting on the fact that being associated with the Olympics is a positive, beyond the value of any contract that a business might be able to secure, Lord Digby Jones, the UK's former Minister for Trade and Investment notes, 'International sporting events offer huge opportunities for UK businesses. However, size doesn't matter when it comes to British companies winning business in the 2012 London Olympic and Paralympics' Games. Hundreds of small- and medium-sized businesses have already won contracts with billions of pounds of contracts still to win. Large or small, winning that business for 2012 will provide a springboard for global growth, and an opportunity to promote our capabilities on the international stage'.

London 2012 proved a great Sporting success.

Source: Getty Images Fred Duval

Clearly, the marketing opportunities are enormous for partner businesses and suppliers to the Olympics. However, one of the key concerns is the use of the Olympic logos by businesses that have nothing to do with the event. According to intellectual property expert Tracey Huxley, 'The outstanding success of Team Great Britain in China [. . .] is likely to encourage companies to use the swell of national pride and the gathering momentum of London 2012 in their marketing, both in the immediate future and throughout the next four years.' Adidas, for example, both sponsored the Beijing Games and is a partner with London 2012. The company ran a series of advertisements with medal-winning athletes that feature the phrase: 'Impossible Is Nothing'. The British-oriented advertisements also included the UK's gold-medal winning men's cycling pursuit team with the following tagline: 'Awesome away. . . . Imagine them at home'. Likewise, LloydsTSB ran a series of advertisements featuring future Olympic hopefuls, and Visa's advertisements proudly announced 'The Journey to London 2012 Starts Now'.

However, in light of the legislation introduced primarily to stop ambush marketing as seen in previous Olympics, it is extremely easy to fall foul of the restrictions, says Huxley. Ambush marketing tends to come in two different forms – they either falsely imply that the business has an association with the Olympics, or they involve giving away branded products that will be taken into a stadium where they will be seen by viewers if the event is televised. 'In fact, the burden of proof in many cases will be reversed, so an infringement will be presumed unless the accused can prove their innocence,' Huxley adds. 'Brands must therefore be mindful of the restrictions which are already being enforced, or face the consequences. In particular those with licensees or franchisees need to ensure that they, too, are aware of the rules and don't go too far, as this may also draw the brand owner into the infringement.'[1]

AUTHOR COMMENT

The huge commercial possibilities of being associated with the Olympic brand cannot be underestimated. Businesses that either sponsor the Olympics or those that provide goods and services, or for that matter suppliers, make full use of their association with the Olympics. This consists of a full partnership approach aimed at securing and building customer relationship.

Like London 2012, outstanding marketing organisations employ strongly customer-driven marketing strategies and programmes that create customer value and relationships. These marketing strategies and programmes, however, are guided by broader company-wide strategic plans, which must also be customer focused. Thus, to understand the role of marketing, we must first understand the organisation's overall strategic planning process.

AUTHOR COMMENT

Company-wide strategic planning guides marketing strategy and planning. Like marketing strategy, the company's broad strategy must also be customer focused.

COMPANY-WIDE STRATEGIC PLANNING: DEFINING MARKETING'S ROLE

Strategic planning—The process of developing and maintaining a strategic fit between the organisation's goals and capabilities and its changing marketing opportunities.

Each company must find the game plan for long-run survival and growth that makes the most sense given its specific situation, opportunities, objectives and resources. This is the focus of **strategic planning** – the process of developing and maintaining a strategic fit between the organisation's goals and capabilities and its changing marketing opportunities.

40

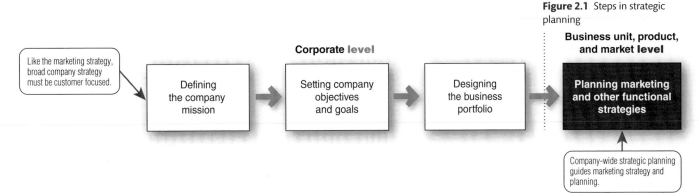

Figure 2.1 Steps in strategic planning

Corporate level

Like the marketing strategy, broad company strategy must be customer focused.

Defining the company mission

Setting company objectives and goals

Designing the business portfolio

Business unit, product, and market level

Planning marketing and other functional strategies

Company-wide strategic planning guides marketing strategy and planning.

Mission statement—A statement of the organisation's purpose – what it wants to accomplish in the larger environment.

BeQIK: Focus on quality (Q), innovation (I), customer orientation (K for the German term 'Kundenorientierung') and speed.

Source: The Advertising Archives

Strategic planning sets the stage for the rest of planning in the firm. Companies usually prepare annual plans, long-range plans and strategic plans. The annual and long-range plans deal with the company's current businesses and how to keep them going. In contrast, the strategic plan involves adapting the firm to take advantage of opportunities in its constantly changing environment.

At the corporate level, the company starts the strategic planning process by defining its overall purpose and mission (see Figure 2.1). This mission is then turned into detailed supporting objectives that guide the entire company. Next, headquarters (i.e. executive management) decide what portfolio of businesses and products is best for the company and how much support to give each one. In turn, each business and product develops detailed marketing and other departmental plans that support the company-wide plan. Thus, marketing planning occurs at the business-unit, product and market levels. It supports company strategic planning with more detailed plans for specific marketing opportunities.

Defining a market-oriented mission

An organisation exists to accomplish something, and this purpose should be clearly stated. Forging a sound mission begins with the following questions: What *is* our business? Who is the customer? What do consumers value? What *should* our business be? These simple-sounding questions are among the most difficult the company will ever have to answer. Successful companies continuously raise these questions and answer them carefully and completely.

Many organisations develop formal mission statements that answer these questions. A **mission statement** is a statement of the organisation's purpose – what it wants to accomplish in the larger environment. A clear mission statement acts as an 'invisible hand' that guides people in the organisation.

Quick. Not dirty.

As no one wants their washing to take forever, Bosch washing machines now offer express wash times on every programme – on every machine! Engineered to wash both quickly and efficiently in our shortest possible time, Bosch offer you the complete laundry solution for modern lives.
For further details call **0870 727 0446** for a free brochure, or visit www.boschappliances.co.uk

2 years manufacturer's guarantee* on all Bosch appliances

*Subject to registration

BOSCH
Excellence comes as standard

41

Table 2.1 Market-oriented business definitions

Company	Product-oriented definition	Market-oriented definition
Michelin	We make tyres.	We provide service to people and their transportation.
Royal Dutch Shell	We find, extract, refine and sell oil.	We refine and deliver energy solutions in a sustainable way.
Nestlé	We make consumer nutrition and health products.	As the world's leading nutrition, health and wellness company, we are committed to increasing the nutritional value of our products while offering better taste and more pleasure.
B & Q	We sell tools and home repair and improvement items.	We help people to create homes of which they can be proud.
eBay	We hold online auctions	We provide a global marketplace where practically anyone can trade practically anything.
Revlon	We make cosmetics.	We sell lifestyle and self-expression; success and status; memories, hopes and dreams.
Ritz-Carlton Hotels & Resorts	We rent rooms.	We create the Ritz-Carlton experience — one that enlivens the senses, instils well-being, and fulfils even the unexpressed wishes and needs of our guests.
easyJet	We sell cheap flights.	We provide our customers with safe, good value, point-to-point air services.

Some companies define their missions myopically in product or technology terms ('We make and sell furniture' or 'We are a chemical-processing firm'). But mission statements should be *market oriented* and defined in terms of satisfying basic customer needs. Products and technologies eventually become outdated, but basic market needs may last forever. Virgin Atlantic's mission statement is not just simply to sell lots of flights but is 'To grow a profitable airline where people love to fly and people love to work'. Similarly, Bosch doesn't talk about selling or making automotive parts and power tools but rather 'BeQIK': focus on quality (Q), innovation (I), customer orientation (K for the German term 'Kundenorientierung') and speed.[2] Table 2.1 provides several other examples of product-oriented versus market-oriented business definitions.

Mission statements should be meaningful and specific yet motivating. They should emphasise the company's strengths in the marketplace. Too often, mission statements are written for public relations (PR) purposes and lack specific, workable guidelines. Says marketing consultant Jack Welch:[3]

Few leaders actually get the point of forging a mission with real grit and meaning. [Mission statements] have largely devolved into fat-headed jargon. Almost no one can figure out what they mean. [So companies] sort of ignore them or gussy up a vague package deal along the lines of: 'our mission is to be the best fill-in-the-blank company in our industry'. [Instead, Welch advises, CEOs should] make a choice about how your company will win. Don't mince words! Remember Nike's old mission, 'Crush Reebok'? That's directionally correct. And Google's mission statement isn't something namby-pamby like 'To be the world's best search engine'. It's 'To organize the world's information and make it universally accessible and useful'. That's simultaneously inspirational, achievable and completely graspable.

Finally, a company's mission should not be stated as making more sales or profits; profits are only a reward for creating value for customers. Instead, the mission should focus on customers and the customer experience the company seeks to create. Thus, Ikea's mission isn't 'to be the world's best and most profitable furniture retailer'; it's 'to create a better everyday life for the many'. If Ikea accomplishes this market-focused mission, profits will follow.

Setting company objectives and goals

The company needs to turn its mission into detailed supporting objectives for each level of management. Each manager should have objectives and be responsible for reaching them. For example, Kohler makes and markets familiar kitchen and bathroom fixtures – everything from Mira showers, bathtubs and toilets to kitchen sinks. But Kohler also offers a breadth of other products and services, including furniture, tile and stone, and even small engines and backup power systems (in Italy and China). It also owns golf resorts and spas in the United States and Scotland. Kohler ties this diverse product portfolio together under the mission of 'contributing to a higher level of gracious living for those who are touched by our products and services'.

This broad mission leads to a hierarchy of objectives, including business objectives and marketing objectives. Kohler's overall objective is to build profitable customer relationships by developing efficient yet beautiful products that embrace the 'essence of gracious living' mission. It does this by investing heavily in research and design. Research is expensive and must be funded through improved profit, so improving profits becomes another major objective for Kohler. Profits can be improved by increasing sales or reducing costs. Sales can be increased by improving the company's share of domestic and international markets. These goals then become the company's current marketing objectives.

Marketing strategies and programmes must be developed to support these marketing objectives. To increase its market share, Kohler might increase its products' availability and promotion in existing markets and expand into new markets. For example, Kohler is boosting production capacity in India and China to better serve the Asian market.[4]

These are Kohler's broad marketing strategies. Each broad marketing strategy must then be defined in greater detail. For example, increasing the product's promotion may require more salespeople, advertising and PR efforts; if so, all requirements will need to be spelt out. In this way, the firm's mission is translated into a set of objectives for the current period.

Designing the business portfolio

Guided by the company's mission statement and objectives, management must now plan its **business portfolio** – the collection of businesses and products that make up the company. The best business portfolio is the one that best fits the company's strengths and weaknesses to opportunities in the environment. Business portfolio planning involves two steps: (1) The company must analyse its *current* business portfolio and determine which businesses should receive more, less, or no investment; and (2) it must shape the *future* portfolio by developing strategies for growth and downsizing.

Business portfolio—The collection of businesses and products that make up the company.

Analysing the current business portfolio

The major activity in strategic planning is business **portfolio analysis**, whereby management evaluates the products and businesses that make up the company. The company will want to put strong resources into its more profitable businesses and phase down or drop its weaker ones.

Management's first step is to identify the key businesses that make up the company, called *strategic business units* (SBUs). An SBU can be a company division, a product line within a division, or

Portfolio analysis—The process by which management evaluates the products and businesses that make up the company.

Figure 2.2 The BCG growth-
share matrix

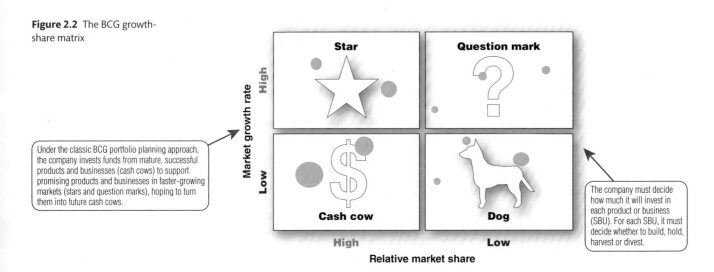

Under the classic BCG portfolio planning approach, the company invests funds from mature, successful products and businesses (cash cows) to support promising products and businesses in faster-growing markets (stars and question marks), hoping to turn them into future cash cows.

The company must decide how much it will invest in each product or business (SBU). For each SBU, it must decide whether to build, hold, harvest or divest.

sometimes a single product or brand. The company next assesses the attractiveness of its various SBUs and decides how much support each deserves. When designing a business portfolio, it's a good idea to add and support products and businesses that fit closely with the firm's core philosophy and competencies.

The purpose of strategic planning is to find ways in which the company can best use its strengths to take advantage of attractive opportunities in the environment. So most standard portfolio analysis methods evaluate SBUs on two important dimensions: the attractiveness of the SBU's market or industry and the strength of the SBU's position in that market or industry. The best-known portfolio-planning method was developed by the Boston Consulting Group, a leading management consulting firm.[5]

The Boston Consulting Group approach

Growth-share matrix—A portfolio-planning method that evaluates a company's SBUs in terms of its market growth rate and relative market share.

Using the now-classic Boston Consulting Group (BCG) approach, a company classifies all its SBUs according to the **growth-share matrix**, as shown in Figure 2.2. On the vertical axis, *market growth rate* provides a measure of market attractiveness. On the horizontal axis, *relative market share* serves as a measure of company strength in the market. The growth-share matrix defines four types of SBUs:

1. *Stars.* Stars are high-growth, high-share businesses or products. They often need heavy investments to finance their rapid growth. Eventually their growth will slow down, and they will turn into cash cows.

2. *Cash cows.* Cash cows are low-growth, high-share businesses or products. These established and successful SBUs need less investment to hold their market share. Thus, they produce a lot of the cash that the company uses to pay its bills and support other SBUs that need investment.

3. *Question marks.* Question marks are low-share business units in high-growth markets. They require a lot of cash to hold their share, let alone increase it. Management has to think hard about which question marks it should try to build into stars and which should be phased out.

4. *Dogs.* Dogs are low-growth, low-share businesses and products. They may generate enough cash to maintain themselves but do not promise to be large sources of cash.

The ten circles in the growth-share matrix represent a company that has ten current SBUs. The company has two stars, two cash cows, three question marks and three dogs. The areas of the circles are proportional to the SBU's sales. This company is in fair shape, although not in good shape. It wants to invest in the more promising question marks to make them stars and maintain the stars so that they will become cash cows as their markets mature. Fortunately, it has two good-sized cash cows. Income from these cash cows will help finance the company's question marks, stars and dogs. The company should take some decisive action concerning its dogs and its question marks.

Once it has classified its SBUs, the company must determine what role each will play in the future. It can pursue one of four strategies for each SBU. It can invest more in the business unit to *build* its share. Or it can invest just enough to *hold* the SBU's share at the current level. It can *harvest* the SBU, milking its short-term cash flow regardless of the long-term effect. Finally, it can *divest* the SBU by selling it or phasing it out and using the resources elsewhere.

As time passes, SBUs change their positions in the growth-share matrix. Many SBUs start out as question marks and move into the star category if they succeed. They later become cash cows as market growth falls and then finally die off or turn into dogs toward the end of their life cycle. The company needs to add new products and units continuously so that some of them will become stars and, eventually, cash cows that will help finance other SBUs.

Problems with matrix approaches

The BCG and other formal methods revolutionised strategic planning. However, such centralised approaches have limitations: they can be difficult, time-consuming and costly to implement. Management may find it difficult to define SBUs and measure market share and growth. In addition, these approaches focus on classifying *current* businesses but provide little advice for *future* planning.

Because of such problems, many companies have dropped formal matrix methods in favour of more customised approaches that better suit their specific situations. Moreover, unlike former strategic-planning efforts that rested mostly in the hands of senior managers at company headquarters, today's strategic planning has been decentralised. Increasingly, companies are placing responsibility for strategic planning in the hands of cross-functional teams of divisional managers who are close to their markets.

For example, consider the Walt Disney Company. Most people think of Disney as theme parks and wholesome family entertainment. But in the mid-1980s, Disney established a powerful, centralised strategic planning group to guide its direction and growth. Over the next two decades, the strategic planning group turned the Walt Disney Company into a huge and diverse collection of media and entertainment businesses. The sprawling company grew to include everything from theme resorts and film studios (Walt Disney Pictures, Touchstone Pictures, Hollywood Pictures and others) to media networks (ABC plus Disney Channel, ESPN, A&E, History Channel and half a dozen others) to consumer products and a cruise line.

The newly transformed company proved hard to manage and performed unevenly. To improve performance, Disney disbanded the centralised strategic planning unit, decentralising its functions to Disney division managers. As a result, Disney reclaimed its position at the head of the world's media conglomerates. And despite recently facing 'the weakest economy in our lifetime', Disney's sound strategic management of its broad mix of businesses has helped it fare better than rival media companies.[6]

Developing strategies for growth and downsizing

Beyond evaluating current businesses, designing the business portfolio involves finding businesses and products the company should consider in the future. Companies need growth if they are to compete more effectively, satisfy their stakeholders and attract top talent. At the same time, a firm must be careful not to make growth itself an objective. The company's objective must be to manage 'profitable growth'.

Marketing has the main responsibility for achieving profitable growth for the company. Marketing needs to identify, evaluate, and select market opportunities and establish strategies for capturing them. One useful device for identifying growth opportunities is the **product/market expansion grid**, shown in Figure 2.3.[7] We apply it here to Finnish company Vivago Oy – a healthcare technology company that develops, sells and markets automatic personal security systems that monitor and analyse users' activity levels.[8] Vivago markets the world's first system that monitors the physiological signals of wearers (including movement, skin conductivity and body temperature) and sends an alarm via the local telephone network if the health of the wearer appears to deteriorate

Product/market expansion grid—A portfolio-planning tool for identifying company growth opportunities through market penetration, market development, product development or diversification.

Figure 2.3 The product/market expansion grid

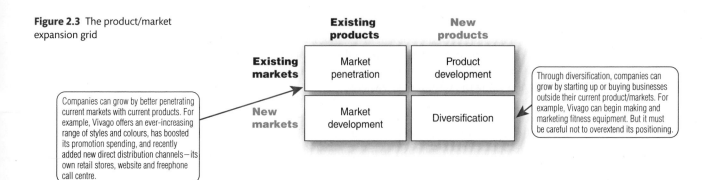

Companies can grow by better penetrating current markets with current products. For example, Vivago offers an ever-increasing range of styles and colours, has boosted its promotion spending, and recently added new direct distribution channels—its own retail stores, website and freephone call centre.

Through diversification, companies can grow by starting up or buying businesses outside their current product/markets. For example, Vivago can begin making and marketing fitness equipment. But it must be careful not to overextend its positioning.

Market penetration—
Company growth by increasing sales of current products to current market segments without changing the product.

(or if they manually trigger an alarm). Worn on a wristband that also functions as a watch, the Vivago system has won numerous international awards for innovation.

First, Vivago might consider whether the company can achieve deeper **market penetration** – making more sales without changing its original product. It can spur growth through marketing mix improvements – adjustments to its product design, advertising, pricing and distribution efforts. For example, Vivago could offer a broader range of styles, colours and designs for different users. The company could also add direct-to-consumer distribution channels, including its own retail stores, or a freephone call centre.

There are many possible options for Vivago Oy. – a healthcare technology company that develops, sells and markets automatic personal security systems monitoring and analysing users' activity levels

Source: Vivago

Second, Vivago might consider possibilities for **market development** – identifying and developing new markets for its current products. Given the ageing global population various markets could prove fruitful. Japan and the United States of America both have large, affluent, ageing populations who could prove to be a profitable long-term market.

Third, Vivago could consider **product development** – offering modified or new products to current markets. Vivago could develop and introduce other wrist- or body-worn physiological monitors for sport and fitness users. Although this would put the company into direct competition with current sports technology providers, it also offers promise for big growth.

Finally, Vivago might consider **diversification** – starting up or buying businesses beyond its current products and markets. For example, it could move into broader security and monitoring businesses. When diversifying, companies must be careful not to overextend their brands' positioning.

Companies must not only develop strategies for *growing* their business portfolios but also strategies for **downsizing** them. There are many reasons that a firm might want to abandon products or markets. The firm may have grown too fast or entered areas where it lacks experience. This can occur when a firm enters too many international markets without the proper research or when a company introduces new products that do not offer superior customer value. The market environment might change, making some products or markets less profitable. For example, in difficult economic times, many firms prune out weaker, less-profitable products and markets to focus their more limited resources on the strongest ones. Finally, some products or business units simply age and die.

When a firm finds brands or businesses that are unprofitable or that no longer fit its overall strategy, it must carefully prune, harvest or divest them. Weak businesses usually require a disproportionate amount of management attention. Managers should focus on promising growth opportunities, not fritter away energy trying to salvage fading ones.

Market development— Company growth by identifying and developing new market segments for current company products.

Product development— Company growth by offering modified or new products to current market segments.

Diversification—Company growth through starting up or acquiring businesses outside the company's current products and markets.

Downsizing—Reducing the business portfolio by eliminating products or business units that are not profitable or that no longer fit the company's overall strategy.

AUTHOR COMMENT

Marketing alone can't create superior customer value. Under the company-wide strategic plan, marketers must work closely with other departments to form an effective internal company value chain and, with other companies in the marketing system, create an overall external value delivery network that jointly serves customers.

PLANNING MARKETING: PARTNERING TO BUILD CUSTOMER RELATIONSHIPS

The company's strategic plan establishes what kinds of businesses the company will operate and its objectives for each. Then, within each business unit, more detailed planning takes place. The major functional departments in each unit – marketing, finance, accounting, purchasing, operations, information systems, human resources and others – must work together to accomplish strategic objectives.

Marketing plays a key role in the company's strategic planning in several ways. First, marketing provides a guiding *philosophy* – the marketing concept – that suggests that company strategy should revolve around building profitable relationships with important consumer groups. Second, marketing provides *inputs* to strategic planners by helping to identify attractive market opportunities and assessing the firm's potential to take advantage of them. Finally, within individual business units, marketing designs *strategies* for reaching the unit's objectives. Once the unit's objectives are set, marketing's task is to help carry them out profitably.

Customer value is the key ingredient in the marketer's formula for success. However, as we noted in Chapter 1, marketers alone cannot produce superior value for customers. Although marketing plays a leading role, it can be only a partner in attracting, keeping and growing customers. In addition to *customer relationship management*, marketers must also practise *partner relationship management*. They must work closely with partners in other company departments to form an effective internal *value chain* that serves customers. Moreover, they must partner effectively with other companies in the marketing system to form a competitively superior external *value delivery network*. We now take a closer look at the concepts of a company value chain and a value delivery network.

Partnering with other company departments

Value chain—The series of internal departments that carry out value-creating activities to design, produce, market, deliver and support a firm's products.

Each company department can be thought of as a link in the company's internal **value chain**.[9] That is, each department carries out value-creating activities to design, produce, market, deliver, and support the firm's products. The firm's success depends not only on how well each department performs its work but also on how well the various departments coordinate their activities.

For example, Aldi's goal is to create customer value and satisfaction by providing shoppers with the products they want at the lowest possible prices. Marketers at Aldi play an important role. They learn what customers need and stock the stores' shelves with the desired products at unbeatable low prices. They prepare advertising and merchandising programmes and assist shoppers with customer service. Through these and other activities, Aldi's marketers help deliver value to customers.

However, the marketing department needs help from the company's other departments. Aldi's ability to offer the right products at low prices depends on the purchasing department's skill in developing the needed suppliers and buying from them at low cost. Aldi's information technology (IT) department must provide fast and accurate information about which products are selling in each store. And its operations people must provide effective, low-cost merchandise handling.

A company's value chain is only as strong as its weakest link. Success depends on how well each department performs its work of adding customer value and the activity coordination of various departments. At Aldi, if purchasing can't obtain the lowest prices from suppliers, or if operations can't distribute merchandise at the lowest costs, then marketing can't deliver on its promise of unbeatable low prices – 'Like Aldi, Like the Price'.

Ideally, then, a company's different functions should work in harmony to produce value for consumers. But, in practice, departmental relations are full of conflicts and misunderstandings. The marketing department takes the consumer's point of view. However, when marketing tries to develop customer satisfaction, it can cause other departments to do a poorer job *in their terms*. Marketing department actions can increase purchasing costs, disrupt production schedules, increase inventories, and create budget headaches. Thus, other departments may resist the marketing department's efforts.

Yet marketers must find ways to get all departments to 'think consumer' and develop a smoothly functioning value chain. One marketing expert puts it this way: 'True market orientation does not mean becoming marketing-driven; it means that the entire company obsesses over creating value for the customer and views itself as a bundle of processes that profitably define, create, communicate, and deliver value to its target customers. . . . Everyone must do marketing regardless of function or department'.[10] Thus, whether you're an accountant, an operations manager, a financial analyst, an IT specialist or a human resources manager, you need to understand marketing and your role in creating customer value.

The value chain: Aldi aim to get customers to 'Like Aldi. Like the Price' by offering the right products at lower prices. This depends on the contributions of people in every department.

Source: Alamy Images/Image Broker

Partnering with others in the marketing system

In its quest to create customer value, the firm needs to look beyond its own internal value chain and into the value chains of its suppliers, distributors and, ultimately, its customers. Consider Ikea. People do not swarm to Ikea because they love only the chain's furniture. Consumers flock to the Ikea *network*, not only to its furniture products. Throughout the world, Ikea's finely tuned value delivery network delivers a high standard of quality, service, cleanliness and value. Ikea's is effective only to the extent that it successfully partners with its suppliers and others to create jointly 'a better everyday life' for its customers.

More companies today are partnering with other members of the supply chain – suppliers, distributors and, ultimately, customers – to improve the performance of the customer **value delivery network**. For example, cosmetics maker L'Oreal knows the importance of building close relationships with its extensive network of suppliers, who supply everything from polymers and fats to spray cans and packaging to production equipment and office supplies:[11]

Value delivery network—
The network composed of the company, its suppliers, its distributors, and, ultimately, its customers who partner with each other to improve the performance of the entire system.

L' Oréal builds long-term supplier relationships based on mutual benefit and growth. It 'wants to make L' Oréal a top performer and one of the world's most respected companies. Being respected also means being respected by our suppliers.'
Source: The Advertising Archives

L'Oreal is the world's largest cosmetics manufacturer, with 25 brands ranging from Maybelline and Kiehl's to Lancôme and Redken. The company's supplier network is crucial to its success. As a result, L'Oreal treats suppliers as respected partners. On the one hand, it expects a lot from suppliers in terms of design innovation, quality and socially responsible actions. The company carefully screens new suppliers and regularly assesses the performance of current suppliers. On the other hand, L'Oreal works closely with suppliers to help them meet its exacting standards. Whereas some companies make unreasonable demands of their suppliers and 'squeeze' them for short-term gains, L'Oreal builds long-term supplier relationships based on mutual benefit and growth. According to the company's supplier website, it treats suppliers with 'fundamental respect for their business, their culture, their growth, and the individuals who work there. Each relationship is based on . . . shared efforts aimed at promoting growth and mutual profits that make it possible for suppliers to invest, innovate, and compete.' As a result, more than 75 per cent of L'Oreal's supplier-partners have been working with the company for 10 years or more and the majority of them for several decades. Says the company's head of purchasing, 'The CEO wants to make L'Oreal a top performer and one of the world's most respected companies. Being respected also means being respected by our suppliers.'

Increasingly in today's marketplace, competition no longer takes place between individual competitors. Rather, it takes place between the entire value delivery networks created by these competitors. Thus, Citroën's performance against Ford depends on the quality of Citroën's overall value delivery network versus Ford's. Even if Citroën makes the best cars, it might lose in the marketplace if Ford's dealer network provides more customer-satisfying sales and service.

AUTHOR COMMENT

Now that we've set the context in terms of company-wide strategy, it's time to discuss customer-driven marketing strategy and programmes.

MARKETING STRATEGY AND THE MARKETING MIX

The strategic plan defines the company's overall mission and objectives. Marketing's role is shown in Figure 2.4, which summarises the major activities involved in managing a customer-driven marketing strategy and the marketing mix.

Consumers are in the centre. The goal is to create value for customers and build profitable customer relationships. Next comes **marketing strategy** – the marketing logic by which the company hopes to create this customer value and achieve these profitable relationships. The company decides which customers it will serve (segmentation and targeting) and how (differentiation and positioning). It identifies the total market and then divides it into smaller segments, selects the most promising segments, and focuses on serving and satisfying the customers in these segments.

Guided by marketing strategy, the company designs an integrated *marketing mix* composed of factors under its control – product, price, place and promotion (the four Ps). To find the best marketing strategy and mix, the company engages in marketing analysis, planning, implementation and control. Through these activities, the company watches and adapts to the actors and forces in the marketing environment. We will now look briefly at each activity. In later chapters, we will discuss each one in more depth.

Customer-driven marketing strategy

As emphasised throughout Chapter 1, companies must be customer centred to succeed in today's competitive marketplace. They must win customers from competitors and then keep and grow them by delivering greater value. But before it can satisfy customers, a company must first understand customer needs and wants. Thus, sound marketing requires careful customer analysis.

Marketing strategy—The marketing logic by which the company hopes to create customer value and achieve profitable customer relationships.

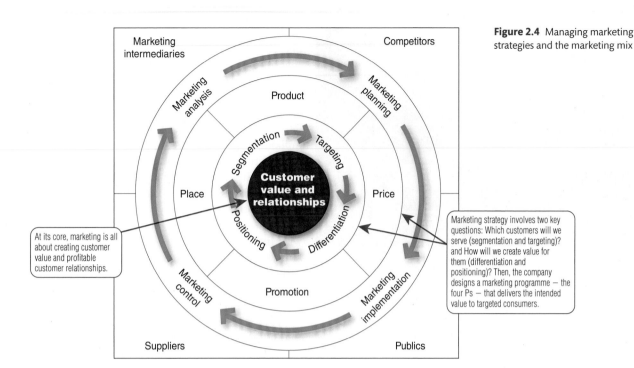

Figure 2.4 Managing marketing strategies and the marketing mix

Labels in figure:

Marketing intermediaries
Competitors
Suppliers
Publics

Marketing analysis
Marketing planning
Marketing implementation
Marketing control

Product
Price
Promotion
Place

Segmentation
Targeting
Differentiation
Positioning

Customer value and relationships

At its core, marketing is all about creating customer value and profitable customer relationships.

Marketing strategy involves two key questions: Which customers will we serve (segmentation and targeting)? and How will we create value for them (differentiation and positioning)? Then, the company designs a marketing programme — the four Ps — that delivers the intended value to targeted consumers.

Companies know that they cannot profitably serve all consumers in a given market – at least not all consumers in the same way. There are too many different kinds of consumers with too many different kinds of needs. Most companies are in a position to serve some segments better than others. Thus, each company must divide up the total market, choose the best segments, and design strategies for profitably serving chosen segments. This process involves *market segmentation, market targeting, differentiation* and *positioning*.

Market segmentation

The market consists of many types of customers, products and needs. The marketer must determine which segments offer the best opportunities. Consumers can be grouped and served in various ways based on geographic, demographic, psychographic and behavioural factors. The process of dividing a market into distinct groups of buyers who have different needs, characteristics or behaviours, and who might require separate products or marketing programmes, is called **market segmentation**.

Every market has segments, but not all ways of segmenting a market are equally useful. For example, Nurofen would gain little by distinguishing between low-income and high-income pain reliever users if both respond the same way to marketing efforts. A **market segment** consists of consumers who respond in a similar way to a given set of marketing efforts. In the car market, for example, consumers who want the biggest, most comfortable car regardless of price make up one market segment. Consumers who care mainly about price and operating economy make up another segment. It would be difficult to make one car model that was the first choice of consumers in both segments. Companies are wise to focus their efforts on meeting the distinct needs of individual market segments.

Market targeting

After a company has defined its market segments, it can enter one or many of these segments. **Market targeting** involves evaluating each market segment's attractiveness and selecting one or more segments to enter. A company should target segments in which it can profitably generate the greatest customer value and sustain it over time.

Market segmentation—Dividing a market into distinct groups of buyers who have different needs, characteristics, or behaviours, and who might require separate products or marketing programmes.

Market segment—A group of consumers who respond in a similar way to a given set of marketing efforts.

Market targeting—The process of evaluating each market segment's attractiveness and selecting one or more segments to enter.

51

Tetra GmbH manufactures aquarist and pond-related products and with their Tetramin flakes dominates the fish food market.

Source: Shutterstock.com/Vlad 61

A company with limited resources might decide to serve only one or a few special segments or market niches. Such niches specialise in serving customer segments that major competitors overlook or ignore. For example, Ferrari sells only 450 of its very high-performance cars in the United Kingdom each year but at very high prices – from an eye-opening €160,000 for its Ferrari F430 F1 Spider convertible to an astonishing more than €1.4 million for its FXX super sports car, which can be driven only on race tracks. Most niches aren't quite so exotic. Tetra GmbH manufactures aquarist and pond-related products and with their Tetramin flakes dominates the fish food market.

Alternatively, a company might choose to serve several related segments – perhaps those with different kinds of customers but with the same basic wants. Abercrombie & Fitch, for example, targets college students, teens, and kids with the same upmarket, casual clothes and accessories in different outlets: the original Abercrombie & Fitch, Hollister, Gilly Hicks and Abercrombie. Or a large company might decide to offer a complete range of products to serve all market segments. Large car companies such as BMW and Citroën do this.

Most companies enter a new market by serving a single segment, and, if this proves successful, they add more segments. For example, Nike started with innovative running shoes for serious runners. Large companies eventually seek full market coverage. Nike now makes and sells a broad range of sports products for just about anyone and everyone, with the goal of 'helping athletes at every level of ability reach their potential'.[12] It has different products designed to meet the special needs of each segment it serves.

Market differentiation and positioning

After a company has decided which market segments to enter, it must decide how it will differentiate its market offering for each targeted segment and what positions it wants to occupy in those segments. A product's *position* is the place it occupies relative to competitors' products in consumers' minds. Marketers want to develop unique market positions for their products. If a product is perceived to be exactly like others on the market, consumers would have no reason to buy it.

Positioning—Arranging for a product to occupy a clear, distinctive, and desirable place relative to competing products in the minds of target consumers.

Positioning is arranging for a product to occupy a clear, distinctive and desirable place relative to competing products in the minds of target consumers. Marketers plan positions that distinguish their products from competing brands and give them the greatest advantage in their target markets.

BMW is 'The ultimate driving machine'. Adidas promises 'Impossible is Nothing'. At Philips it is 'Sense and Simplicity'. YouTube lets you 'Broadcast Yourself'. At McDonald's you'll be saying 'I'm lovin' it', whereas at Burger King you can 'Have it your way'. Such deceptively simple statements form the backbone of a product's marketing strategy. For example, Burger King designs its entire worldwide integrated marketing campaign – from television and print commercials to its websites – around the 'Have it your way' positioning.

Differentiation—Actually differentiating the market offering to create superior customer value.

In positioning its product(s), the company first identifies possible customer value differences that provide competitive advantages on which to build the position. The company can offer greater customer value by either charging lower prices than competitors or offering more benefits to justify higher prices. But if the company *promises* greater value, it must then *deliver* that greater value. Thus, effective positioning begins with **differentiation** – actually *differentiating* the company's market offering so that it gives consumers more value. Once the company has chosen a desired position, it must take strong steps to deliver and communicate that position to target consumers. The company's entire marketing programme should support the chosen positioning strategy.

Developing an integrated marketing mix

After determining its overall marketing strategy, the company is ready to begin planning the details of the marketing mix, one of the major concepts in modern marketing. The **marketing mix** is the set of tactical marketing tools that the firm blends to produce the response it wants in the target market. The marketing mix consists of everything the firm can do to influence the demand for its product. The many possibilities can be collected into four groups of variables known as the four *P*s. Figure 2.5 shows the marketing tools under each *P*.

Marketing mix—The set of tactical marketing tools— product, price, place and promotion—that the firm blends to produce the response it wants in the target market.

- *Product* means the goods-and-services combination the company offers to the target market. Thus, an Alfa Romeo Mito consists of nuts and bolts, spark plugs, pistons, headlights and thousands of other parts. Alfa Romeo offers dozens of optional Mito features. The car comes fully serviced and with a comprehensive warranty that is as much a part of the product as the tailpipe.
- *Price* is the amount of money customers must pay to obtain the product. Alfa Romeo calculates suggested retail prices that its dealers might charge for each Mito. But Alfa Romeo dealers rarely charge the full sticker price. Instead, they negotiate the price with each customer, offering discounts, trade-in allowances and credit terms. These actions adjust prices for the current competitive and economic situations and bring them into line with the buyer's perception of the car's value.
- *Place* includes company activities that make the product available to target consumers. Alfa Romeo partners with a large body of independently owned dealerships that sell the company's many different models. Alfa Romeo selects its dealers carefully and strongly supports them. The dealers keep an inventory of Alfa Romeo cars, demonstrate them to potential buyers, negotiate prices, close sales and service the cars after the sale.
- *Promotion* means activities that communicate the merits of the product and persuade target customers to buy it. Alfa Romeo spends millions each year on advertising to tell consumers about the company and its many products. Dealership salespeople assist potential buyers and persuade them that Alfa Romeo is the best car for them. Alfa Romeo and its dealers offer special promotions – sales, cash rebates and low financing rates – as added purchase incentives.

An effective marketing programme blends each marketing mix element into an integrated marketing programme designed to achieve the company's marketing objectives by delivering value to consumers. The marketing mix constitutes the company's tactical tool kit for establishing strong positioning in target markets.

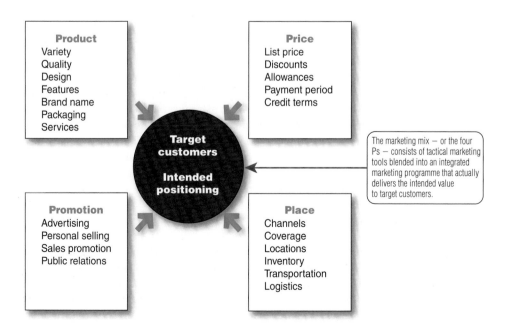

Figure 2.5 The four Ps of the marketing mix

Some critics think that the four Ps may omit or underemphasise certain important activities. For example, they ask, 'Where are services?' Just because they don't start with a *P* doesn't justify omitting them. The answer is that services, such as banking, airline and retailing services, are products too. We might call them *service products*. 'Where is packaging?' the critics might ask. Marketers would answer that they include packaging as one of many product decisions. All said, as Figure 2.5 suggests, many marketing activities that might appear to be left out of the marketing mix are subsumed under one of the four Ps. The issue is not whether there should be four, six or ten Ps so much as what framework is most helpful in designing integrated marketing programmes.

There is another concern, however, that is valid. It holds that the four Ps concept takes the seller's view of the market, not the buyer's view. From the buyer's viewpoint, in this age of customer value and relationships, the four Ps might be better described as the four Cs:[13]

4Ps	4Cs
Product	Customer solution
Price	Customer cost
Place	Convenience
Promotion	Communication

Thus, whereas marketers see themselves as selling products, customers see themselves as buying value or solutions to their problems. And customers are interested in more than just the price; they are interested in the total costs of obtaining, using and disposing of a product. Customers want the product and service to be as conveniently available as possible. Finally, they want two-way communication. Marketers would do well to think through the four Cs first and then build the four Ps on that platform.

AUTHOR COMMENT

So far we've focused on the *marketing* in marketing management. Now, let's turn to the *management*.

MANAGING THE MARKETING EFFORT

In addition to being good at the *marketing* in marketing management, companies also need to pay attention to the *management*. Managing the marketing process requires the four marketing management functions shown in Figure 2.6 – *analysis, planning, implementation* and *control*. The company first develops company-wide strategic plans and then translates them into marketing and other plans for each division, product and brand. Through implementation, the company turns the plans into actions. Control consists of measuring and evaluating the results of marketing activities and taking corrective action where needed. Finally, marketing analysis provides information and evaluations needed for all the other marketing activities.

Marketing analysis

Managing the marketing function begins with a complete analysis of the company's situation. The marketer should conduct a **SWOT analysis**, by which it evaluates the company's overall strengths (S), weaknesses (W), opportunities (O) and threats (T) (see Figure 2.7). Strengths include internal capabilities, resources and positive situational factors that may help the company serve its customers and achieve its objectives. Weaknesses include internal limitations and negative situational

SWOT analysis—An overall evaluation of the company's strengths (S), weaknesses (W), opportunities (O) and threats (T).

Figure 2.6 Managing marketing: analysis, planning, implementation and control

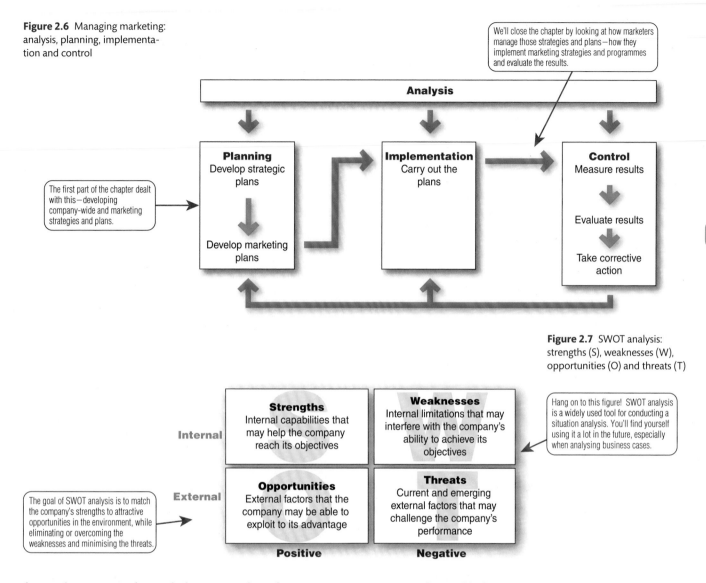

Figure 2.7 SWOT analysis: strengths (S), weaknesses (W), opportunities (O) and threats (T)

factors that may interfere with the company's performance. Opportunities are favourable factors or trends in the external environment that the company may be able to exploit to its advantage. And threats are unfavourable external factors or trends that may present challenges to performance.

The company should analyse its markets and marketing environment to find attractive opportunities and identify environmental threats. It should analyse company strengths and weaknesses as well as current and possible marketing actions to determine which opportunities it can best pursue. The goal is to match the company's strengths to attractive opportunities in the environment, while eliminating or overcoming the weaknesses and minimising the threats. Marketing analysis provides inputs to each of the other marketing management functions. We will discuss marketing analysis more fully in Chapter 3.

Marketing planning

Through strategic planning, the company decides what it wants to do with each business unit. Marketing planning involves choosing marketing strategies that will help the company attain its overall strategic objectives. A detailed marketing plan is needed for each business, product or brand. What does a marketing plan look like? Our discussion focuses on product or brand marketing plans.

Table 2.2 outlines the major sections of a typical product or brand marketing plan. (See Appendix 1 for a sample marketing plan.) The plan begins with an executive summary that quickly

Table 2.2 Contents of a marketing plan

Section	Purpose
Executive summary	Presents a brief summary of the main goals and recommendations of the plan for management review, helping top management find the plan's major points quickly. A table of contents should follow the executive summary.
Current marketing situation	Describes the target market and a company's position in it, including information about the market, product performance, competition and distribution. This section includes the following: • A *market description* that defines the market and major segments and then reviews customer needs and factors in the marketing environment that may affect customer purchasing. • A *product review* that shows sales, prices and gross margins of the major products in the product line. • A review of *competition* that identifies major competitors and assesses their market positions and strategies for product quality, pricing, distribution and promotion. • A review of *distribution* that evaluates recent sales trends and other developments in major distribution channels.
Threats and opportunities analysis	Assesses major threats and opportunities that the product might face, helping management to anticipate important positive or negative developments that might have an impact on the firm and its strategies.
Objectives and issues	States the marketing objectives that the company would like to attain during the plan's term and discusses key issues that will affect their attainment. For example, if the goal is to achieve a 15 per cent market share, this section looks at how this goal might be achieved.
Marketing strategy	Outlines the broad marketing logic by which the business unit hopes to create customer value and relationships and the specifics of target markets, positioning and marketing expenditure levels. How will the company create value for customers to capture value from customers in return? This section also outlines specific strategies for each marketing mix element and explains how each responds to the threats, opportunities and critical issues spelled out earlier in the plan.
Action programmes	Spells out how marketing strategies will be turned into specific action programmes that answer the following questions: *What* will be done? *When* will it be done? *Who* will do it? *How* much will it cost?
Budgets	Details a supporting marketing budget that is essentially a projected profit-and-loss statement. It shows expected revenues (forecasted number of units sold and the average net price) and expected costs of production, distribution and marketing. The difference is the projected profit. Once approved by higher management, the budget becomes the basis for materials buying, production scheduling, personnel planning and marketing operations.
Controls	Outlines the control that will be used to monitor progress and allow higher management to review implementation results and spot products that are not meeting their goals. It includes measures of return on marketing investment.

reviews major assessments, goals and recommendations. The main section of the plan presents a detailed SWOT analysis of the current marketing situation as well as potential threats and opportunities. The plan next states major objectives for the brand and outlines the specifics of a marketing strategy for achieving them.

A *marketing strategy* consists of specific strategies for target markets, positioning, the marketing mix and marketing expenditure levels. It outlines how the company intends to create value for target customers to capture value in return. In this section, the planner explains how each strategy responds to the threats, opportunities and critical issues spelled out earlier in the plan. Additional sections of the marketing plan lay out an action programme for implementing the marketing strategy along with the details of a supporting *marketing budget*. The last section outlines the controls that will be used to monitor progress, measure the marketing ROI and take corrective action.

Marketing implementation

Planning good strategies is only a start toward successful marketing. A brilliant marketing strategy counts for little if the company fails to implement it properly. **Marketing implementation** is the process that turns marketing *plans* into marketing *actions* to accomplish strategic marketing objectives. Whereas marketing planning addresses the *what* and *why* of marketing activities, implementation addresses the *who, where, when* and *how*.

Many managers think that 'doing things right' (implementation) is as important as, or even more important than, 'doing the right things' (strategy). The fact is that both are critical to success, and companies can gain competitive advantages through effective implementation. One firm can have essentially the same strategy as another, yet win in the marketplace through faster or better execution. Still, implementation is difficult; it is often easier to think up good marketing strategies than it is to carry them out.

In an increasingly connected world, people at all levels of the marketing system must work together to implement marketing strategies and plans. At Mercedes-Benz, for example, marketing implementation for the company's car manufacturing requires day-to-day decisions and actions by thousands of people both inside and outside the organisation. Marketing managers make decisions about target segments, branding, product development, pricing, promotion and distribution. They talk with engineering about product design, with manufacturing about production and inventory levels, and with finance about funding and cash flows. They also connect with outside people, such as advertising agencies to plan advertising campaigns and the news media to obtain publicity support. The sales force urges and supports dealers in their efforts to convince customers that choosing a Mercedes-Benz is really a choice between 'The Best or Nothing'.

Marketing department organisation

The company must design a marketing organisation that can carry out marketing strategies and plans. If the company is very small, one person might do all the research, selling, advertising, customer service and other marketing work. As the company expands, however, a marketing department emerges to plan and carry out marketing activities. In large companies, this department contains many specialists, including product and market managers, sales managers and salespeople, market researchers, advertising experts and many other specialists.

To run such large marketing organisations, many companies have now created a *chief marketing officer* position. This person runs the company's entire marketing operation and represents marketing on the company's top management team. The chief marketing officer puts marketing on an equal footing with other top-level executives, such as the chief executive officer and the chief financial officer.[14]

Modern marketing departments can be arranged in several ways. The most common form of marketing organisation is the *functional organisation*. Under this organisation, a functional specialist heads the various marketing activities – a sales manager, an advertising manager, a marketing research manager, a customer service manager or a new product manager. A company that sells across the country or internationally often uses a *geographic organisation*. Its sales and marketing people are assigned to specific countries, regions and districts. Geographic organisation allows salespeople to settle into a territory, get to know their customers, and work with a minimum of travel time and cost. Companies with many very different products or brands often create a *product*

Marketing implementation— Turning marketing strategies and plans into marketing actions to accomplish strategic marketing objectives.

management organisation. Using this approach, a product manager develops and implements a complete strategy and marketing programme for a specific product or brand.

For companies that sell one product line to many different types of markets and customers who have different needs and preferences, a *market* or *customer management organisation* might be best. A market management organisation is similar to the product management organisation. Market managers are responsible for developing marketing strategies and plans for their specific markets or customers. This system's main advantage is that the company is organised around the needs of specific customer segments. Many companies develop special organisations to manage their relationships with large customers. For example, companies such as Unilever have created large teams, or even whole divisions, to serve large customers, such as Edeka, Metro, Carrefour and Tesco.

Large companies that produce many different products flowing into many different geographic and customer markets usually employ some *combination* of the functional, geographic, product and market organisation forms.

Marketing organisation has become an increasingly important issue in recent years. More and more, companies are shifting their brand management focus toward *customer management*– moving away from managing only product or brand profitability and toward managing customer profitability and customer equity. They think of themselves not as managing portfolios of brands but as managing portfolios of customers. And rather than managing the fortunes or a brand, they see themselves as managing customer-brand experiences and relationships.

Marketing control

Marketing control—Measuring and evaluating the results of marketing strategies and plans and taking corrective action to ensure that the objectives are achieved.

Because many surprises occur during the implementation of marketing plans, marketers must practise constant **marketing control** – evaluating the results of marketing strategies and plans and taking corrective action to ensure that the objectives are attained. Marketing control involves four steps. Management first sets specific marketing goals. It then measures its performance in the marketplace and evaluates the causes of any differences between expected and actual performance. Finally, management takes corrective action to close the gaps between goals and performance. This may require changing the action programmes or even changing the goals.

Operating control involves checking ongoing performance against the annual plan and taking corrective action when necessary. Its purpose is to ensure that the company achieves the sales, profits, and other goals set out in its annual plan. It also involves determining the profitability of different products, territories, markets and channels. *Strategic control* involves looking at whether the company's basic strategies are well matched to its opportunities. Marketing strategies and programmes can quickly become outdated, and each company should periodically reassess its overall approach to the marketplace.

AUTHOR COMMENT

Measuring the marketing ROI has become a major marketing emphasis. But it can be difficult. For example, a Europe-wide ad during the Champions League Final football match reaches more than 300 million consumers but costs millions of euros. How do you measure the specific return on such an investment in terms of sales, profits, and building customer relationships? We'll look at this question again in Chapter 15.

MEASURING AND MANAGING RETURN ON MARKETING INVESTMENT

Marketing managers must ensure that their marketing euros are being well spent. In the past, many marketers spent freely on big, expensive marketing programmes, often without thinking carefully about the financial returns on their spending. They believed that marketing produces intangible creative outcomes, which do not lend themselves readily to measures of productivity or return. But in today's more constrained economy, all that is changing:[15]

> For years, corporate marketers have walked into budget meetings like neighbourhood junkies. They couldn't always justify how well they spent past handouts or what difference it all made. They just wanted more money – for flashy TV ads, big-ticket events – to get out the message and build up the brand. But those heady days of blind budget increases are fast being replaced with a new mantra: measurement and accountability. 'Marketers have been pretty unaccountable for many years,' notes one expert. 'Now they are under big pressure to estimate their impact.' Another analyst puts in more bluntly: 'Marketing needs to stop fostering' "rock star" behaviour and focus on rock-steady results.'

According to a recent study, as finances have tightened, marketers see the marketing ROI as the second biggest issue after the economy. 'Increasingly, it is important for marketers to be able to justify their expenses,' says one marketer. For every brand and marketing programme, says another, marketers need to ask themselves, 'Do I have the right combination of strategy and tactics that will generate the most return in terms of share, revenue and/or profit objectives from my investment?'[16]

In response, marketers are developing better measures of *marketing ROI*. **Return on marketing investment** (or **marketing ROI**) is the net return from a marketing investment divided by the costs of the marketing investment. It measures the profits generated by investments in marketing activities.

Marketing ROI can be difficult to measure. In measuring financial ROI, both the *R* and the *I* are uniformly measured in euros. But there is, as of yet, no consistent definition of marketing ROI. 'It's tough to measure, more so than for other business expenses,' says one analyst. 'You can imagine buying a piece of equipment . . . and then measuring the productivity gains that result from the purchase,' he says. 'But in marketing, benefits like advertising impact aren't easily put into euro returns. It takes a leap of faith to come up with a number.'[17]

A recent survey found that although two-thirds of companies have implemented marketing ROI programmes in recent years, only 22 per cent of companies report making good progress in measuring marketing ROI. Another survey of chief financial officers reported that 93 per cent of those surveyed are dissatisfied with their ability to measure marketing ROI. The major problem is figuring out what specific measures to use and obtaining good data on these measures.[18]

A company can assess marketing ROI in terms of standard marketing performance measures, such as brand awareness, sales or market share. Many companies are assembling such measures into *marketing dashboards* – meaningful sets of marketing performance measures in a single display used to monitor strategic marketing performance. Just as car dashboards present drivers with details on how their vehicles are performing, the marketing dashboard gives marketers the detailed measures they need to assess and adjust their marketing strategies.

Increasingly, however, beyond standard performance measures, marketers are using customer-centred measures of marketing impact, such as customer acquisition, customer retention, customer lifetime value and customer equity. These measures capture not only current marketing performance but also future performance resulting from stronger customer relationships. Figure 2.8 views marketing expenditures as investments that produce returns in the form of more profitable customer relationships.[19] Marketing investments

Return on marketing investment (or marketing ROI)—The net return from a marketing investment divided by the costs of the marketing investment.

Many companies are assembling marketing dashboards – meaningful sets of marketing performance measures in a single display used to set and adjust their marketing strategies.

Source: Marketing NPV Corporation

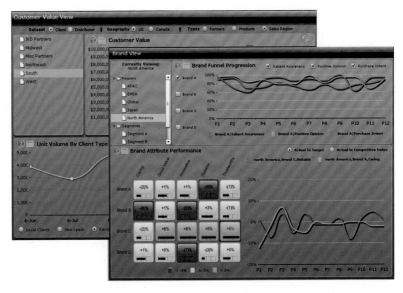

Figure 2.8 Return on marketing investment

Source: Adapted from Roland T. Rust, Katherine N. Lemon and Valerie A. Zeithaml, 'Return on marketing: using consumer equity to focus marketing strategy', *Journal of Marketing* (January 2004), p. 112.

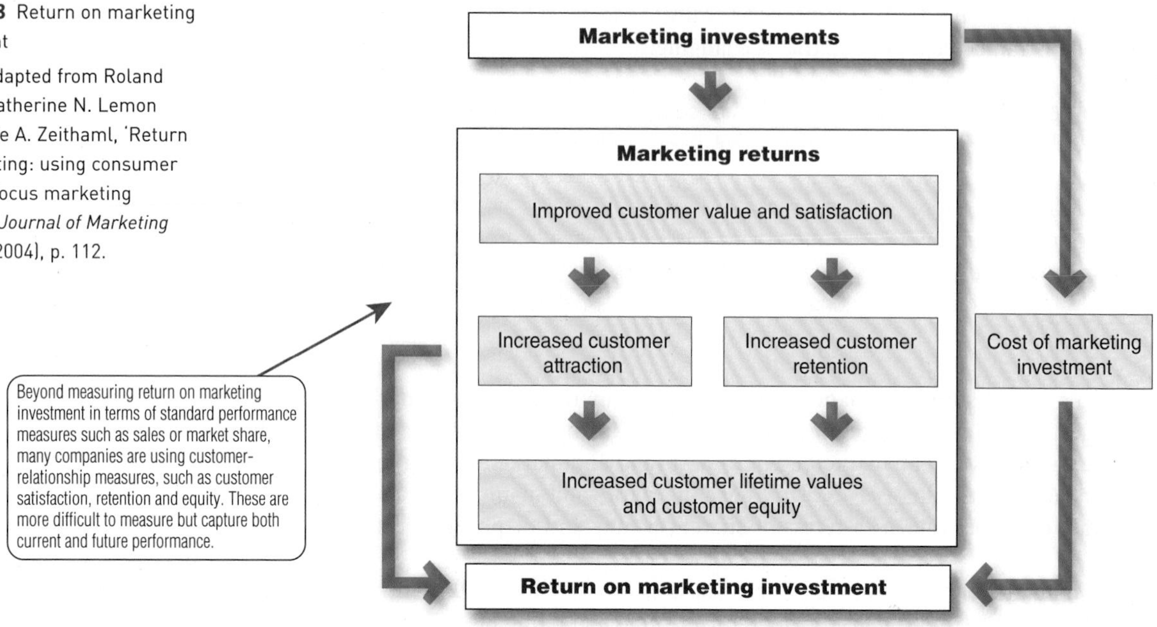

```
                        ┌─────────────────────────────┐
                        │    Marketing investments    │
                        └─────────────────────────────┘
                                      ↓
        ┌───────────────────────────────────────────────────┐
        │                 Marketing returns                  │
        │   ┌───────────────────────────────────────────┐    │
        │   │ Improved customer value and satisfaction   │    │
        │   └───────────────────────────────────────────┘    │
        │          ↓                         ↓                │
        │   ┌──────────────┐         ┌──────────────┐         │
        │   │  Increased   │         │  Increased   │         │
        │   │  customer    │         │  customer    │         │
        │   │  attraction  │         │  retention   │         │
        │   └──────────────┘         └──────────────┘         │
        │          ↓                         ↓                │
        │   ┌───────────────────────────────────────────┐    │
        │   │    Increased customer lifetime values      │    │
        │   │          and customer equity               │    │
        │   └───────────────────────────────────────────┘    │
        └───────────────────────────────────────────────────┘

                          ┌──────────────────┐
                          │ Cost of marketing│
                          │    investment    │
                          └──────────────────┘

        ┌─────────────────────────────────────────────────┐
        │        Return on marketing investment           │
        └─────────────────────────────────────────────────┘
```

Beyond measuring return on marketing investment in terms of standard performance measures such as sales or market share, many companies are using customer-relationship measures, such as customer satisfaction, retention and equity. These are more difficult to measure but capture both current and future performance.

result in improved customer value and satisfaction, which in turn increases customer attraction and retention. This increases individual customer lifetime values and the firm's overall customer equity. Increased customer equity, in relation to the cost of marketing investments, determines marketing ROI.

Regardless of how it's defined or measured, the marketing ROI concept is here to stay. 'In good times and bad, whether or not marketers are ready for it, they're going to be asked to justify their spending with financial data,' says one marketer. Adds another, 'marketers have got to know how to count.'[20]

 ## REVIEWING OBJECTIVES AND KEY TERMS

In Chapter 1, we defined *marketing* and outlined the steps in the marketing process. In this chapter, we examined company-wide strategic planning and marketing's role in the organisation. Then we looked more deeply into marketing strategy and the marketing mix and reviewed the major marketing management functions. So you've now had a pretty good overview of the fundamentals of modern marketing.

OBJECTIVE 1 Explain company-wide strategic planning and its four steps (pp. 40–43).

Strategic planning sets the stage for the rest of the company's planning. Marketing contributes to strategic planning, and the overall plan defines marketing's role in the company.

Strategic planning involves developing a strategy for long-run survival and growth. It consists of four steps: (1) defining the company's mission; (2) setting objectives and goals; (3) designing a business portfolio; and (4) developing functional plans. The company's *mission* should be market oriented, realistic, specific, motivating and consistent with the market environment. The mission is then transformed into detailed *supporting goals and objectives*, which in turn guide decisions about the business portfolio. Then each business and product unit must develop *detailed marketing plans* in line with the company-wide plan.

OBJECTIVE 2 Discuss how to design business portfolios and develop growth strategies (pp. 43–47).

Guided by the company's mission statement and objectives, management plans its *business portfolio*, or the collection of businesses and products that make up the company. The firm wants to produce a business portfolio that best fits its strengths and weaknesses to opportunities in the environment. To do this, it must analyse and adjust its *current* business portfolio and develop *growth* and *downsizing* strategies for adjusting the *future* portfolio. The company might use a formal portfolio-planning method. But many companies are now designing more-customised portfolio-planning approaches that better suit their unique situations.

OBJECTIVE 3 Explain marketing's role in strategic planning and how marketing works with its partners to create and deliver customer value (pp. 47–50).

Under the strategic plan, the major functional departments – marketing, finance, accounting, purchasing, operations, information systems, human resources and others – must work together to accomplish strategic objectives. Marketing plays a key role in the company's strategic planning by providing a *marketing concept philosophy* and *inputs* regarding attractive market opportunities. Within individual business units, marketing designs *strategies* for reaching the unit's objectives and helps to carry them out profitably.

Marketers alone cannot produce superior value for customers. Marketers must practise *partner relationship management*, working closely with partners in other departments to form an effective *value chain* that serves the customer. And they must partner effectively with other companies in the marketing system to form a competitively superior *value delivery network*.

OBJECTIVE 4 Describe the elements of a customer-driven marketing strategy and mix and the forces that influence it (pp. 50–54).

Customer value and relationships are at the centre of marketing strategy and programmes. Through market segmentation, targeting, differentiation and positioning, the company divides the total market into smaller segments, selects segments it can best serve, and decides how it wants to bring value to target consumers in the selected segments. It then designs an *integrated marketing mix* to produce the response it wants in the target market. The marketing mix consists of product, price, place and promotion decisions (the four Ps).

OBJECTIVE 5 List the marketing management functions, including the elements of a marketing plan, and discuss the importance of measuring and managing return on marketing investment (pp. 54–60).

To find the best strategy and mix and to put them into action, the company engages in marketing analysis, planning, implementation and control. The main components of a *marketing plan* are the executive summary, the current marketing situation, threats and opportunities, objectives and issues, marketing strategies, action programmes, budgets and controls. To plan good strategies is often easier than to carry them out. To be successful, companies must also be effective at *implementation* – turning marketing strategies into marketing actions.

Marketing departments can be organised in one or a combination of ways: *functional marketing organisation, geographic organisation, product management organisation* or *market management organisation*. In this age of customer relationships, more and more companies are now changing their organisational focus from product or territory management to customer relationship management. Marketing organisations carry out *marketing control*, both operating control and strategic control.

Marketing managers must ensure that their marketing euros are being well spent. In a tighter economy, today's marketers face growing pressures to show that they are adding value in line with their costs. In response, marketers are developing better measures of *marketing ROI*. Increasingly, they are using customer-centred measures of marketing impact as a key input into their strategic decision making.

 NAVIGATING THE KEY TERMS

OBJECTIVE 1
Strategic planning (p. 40)
Mission statement (p. 41)

OBJECTIVE 2
Business portfolio (p. 43)
Portfolio analysis (p. 43)
Growth-share matrix (p. 44)
Product/market expansion grid (p. 45)

Market penetration (p. 46)
Market development (p. 47)
Product development (p. 47)
Diversification (p. 47)
Downsizing (p. 47)

OBJECTIVE 3
Value chain (p. 48)
Value delivery network (p. 49)

OBJECTIVE 4
Marketing strategy (p. 50)
Market segmentation (p. 51)
Market segment (p. 51)
Market targeting (p. 51)
Positioning (p. 52)
Differentiation (p. 52)
Marketing mix (p. 53)

OBJECTIVE 5
SWOT analysis (p. 54)
Marketing implementation (p. 57)
Marketing control (p. 58)
Return on marketing investment (p. 59)

 DISCUSSING AND APPLYING THE CONCEPTS

Discussing the concepts

1. Explain what is meant by a *market-oriented* mission statement and discuss the characteristics of effective mission statements. (AACSB: Communication)

2. Define strategic planning and briefly describe the four steps that lead managers and a firm through the strategic planning process. Discuss the role marketing plays in this process. (AACSB: Communication)

3. Explain why it is important for all departments of an organisation – marketing, accounting, finance, operations management, human resources and so on-to 'think consumer'. Why is it important that even people who are not in marketing understand it? (AACSB: Communication)

4. Define *positioning* and explain how it is accomplished. Describe the positioning for the following brands: BMW's X5, Amazon, Twitter and Marks and Spencer. (AACSB: Communication; Reflective Thinking)

5. Define each of the four Ps. What insights might a firm gain by considering the four Cs rather than the four Ps? (AACSB: Communication; Reflective Thinking)

6. What is marketing ROI? Why is it difficult to measure? (AACSB: Communication; Reflective Thinking)

Applying the concepts

1. In a small group, conduct a SWOT analysis, develop objectives, and create a marketing strategy for your school, a student organisation you might be involved in or a local business. (AACSB: Communication; Reflective Thinking)

2. Explain the role of a chief marketing officer. Summarise an article that describes the importance of this position, the characteristics of an effective officer, or any issues surrounding this position. (AACSB: Communication; Reflective Thinking)

3. Marketers are increasingly held accountable for demonstrating marketing success. Research the various marketing metrics, in addition to those described in the chapter and Appendix 2, used by marketers to measure marketing performance. Write a brief report of your findings. (AACSB: Communication; Reflective Thinking)

Focus on technology

Visit the websites of several car manufacturers and you will see the technological innovations and additions offered in today's vehicles. From navigation systems to audio enhancements and DVD systems, these technologies are enhancing today's cars. Microsoft, known mostly for its computer operating systems, has been working with Fiat to develop a new 'infotainment' system known as Blue&Me. Currently offered only in limited Fiat models, the system integrates mobile phones, MP3 players and an Internet connection through controls on the steering wheel. The new technology will also contain a navigation system, weather and traffic forecasts, and anti-theft devices.

1. According to the product/market expansion grid, which strategy best describes Microsoft's expansion into automobile applications?

2. Why is Fiat an important member of Microsoft's value-delivery network?

3. Describe why this advanced technology is important to Fiat in terms of positioning its products.

Focus on ethics

With around 15 per cent obesity in the EU and less than half participating in regular physical activity, athletic shoe marketers saw an opportunity: 'toning shoes'. Marketers tout these shoes as revolutionary; you can tone your muscles, lose weight, and improve your posture just by wearing them and going about your daily business. The claims are based on shoemaker-sponsored studies, and the Podiatric Medical Association agrees that toning shoes have some health value. They purportedly perform their magic by destabilising a person's gait, making leg muscles work harder. Consumers, particularly women, are buying it.

Toning shoe sales reached an estimated €1.1 billion in 2010. Sketchers saw a 69 per cent increase in sales due to its shoe that looks like a rocking chair on the bottom. Reebok expected toning shoe sales to increase tenfold to €7.5 million in 2010. Toning shoes account for around 20 per cent of the women's performance footwear category, with prices ranging from €50 to more than €150.

However, these shoes have their critics, who claim a shoe that comes with an instruction booklet and an educational DVD to explain proper usage should wave warning flags to consumers. Some doctors claim the shoes are dangerous, causing strained Achilles tendons or worse; one wearer broke her ankle while wearing them. A recent study found no benefit in toning shoes over regular walking or other exercise. Noticeably absent from the toning shoe feeding frenzy is Nike, which thinks it's all hype and is sticking to traditional performance athletic shoes. This leader in the women's shoe market, however, is losing market share to competitors.

1. Should these shoemakers capitalise on consumers who want to be fit without doing the work to achieve that goal? Do you think that basing claims on research sponsored by the company is ethical? Explain your reasoning. (AACSB: Communication; Ethical Reasoning)

2. Should Nike have entered this product category instead of giving up market share to competitors? Explain your reasoning. (AACSB: Communication; Ethical Reasoning)

Marketing & the economy

Miller Lite

For years, Miller Lite achieved tremendous success in the USA with its 'Great Taste . . . Less Filling' campaign, which *Advertising Age* ranked as the eighth best campaign in history. But when the recent joint venture MillerCoors took over the Miller Lite brand, it decided to focus exclusively on the 'great taste' part, a positioning formula credited for 16 consecutive quarters of growth for competitor Coors Light. Unfortunately, the change in the Miller Lite branding strategy occurred as consumers began to count every penny and demand greater value in the face of new economic realities. In the new economic environment, the single-feature message didn't deliver. Miller Lite immediately began losing sales, posting its worst quarter in more than a decade. With more choices than ever in a beer market flooded with full-flavoured craft, beers, imports and microbrews, industry insiders have questioned MillerCoors' taste-only focus. To muddy the waters even further, MillerCoors halted the brand's regular pattern of price cuts and discounts. It has also increased the Miller Lite advertising budget and added some packaging innovations, such as a 'Taste-Protector Cap' and a 'Taste Activated Bottle'. Andy England, chief marketing officer of MillerCoors, is convinced that the company has Miller Lite on the right track. Given that Miller Lite's sales have yet to turn around, observers are not convinced.

1. In your opinion, which factor has had the biggest impact on Miller Lite's sagging sales?

2. Is a single product benefit enough reason to buy in a weak economy?

3. If MillerCoors had retained Miller Lite's previous brand message, would it have suffered a sales decline?

Marketing by the numbers

Appendix 2 discusses other marketing profitability metrics beyond the marketing ROI measure described in this chapter. On the next page are the profit-and-loss statements for two businesses. Review Appendix 2 and answer the following questions.

1. Calculate marketing return on sales and marketing ROI for both companies, as described in Appendix 2. (AACSB: Communication; Analytic Thinking)

2. Which company is doing better overall and with respect to marketing? Explain your answer. (AACSB: Communication; Analytic Reasoning; Reflective Thinking)

Business A		
Net sales		€800,000,000
Cost of goods sold		€375,000,000
Gross margin		€425,000,000
Marketing expenses		
Sales expenses	€70,000,000	
Promotion expenses	€30,000,000	
		€100,000,000
General and administrative expenses		
Marketing salaries and expenses	€10,000,000	
Indirect overhead	€80,000,000	
		€90,000,000
Net profit before income tax		€235,000,000

Business B		
Net sales		€900,000,000
Cost of goods sold		€400,000,000
Gross margin		€500,000,000
Marketing expenses		
Sales expenses	€90,000,000	
Promotion expenses	€50,000,000	
		€140,000,000
General and administrative expenses		
Marketing salaries and expenses	€20,000,000	
Indirect overhead	€100,000,000	
		€120,000,000
Net profit before income tax		€240,000,000

REFERENCES

1 Quotes and other information www.london2012.com, www.olympic .org, www.londonolympics2012.com, www.cocacola.com, www .britishairways.com, www.alastinglegacy.co.uk, www.culture.gov.uk, and http:// berr.gov.uk, accessed October 2011.

2 See www.bosch-career.com/en/com/bosch_worldwide_1/corporate_ culture/corporate_culture_1.html, accessed October 2011.

3 Jack and Suzy Welch, 'State your business; too many mission state- ments are loaded with fatheaded jargon. Play it straight', *BusinessWeek* (14 January 2008), p. 80. Also see Nancy Lublin, 'Do something', *Fast Company* (November 2009), p. 86; and Jack Neff, 'P&G, Walmart, Lever, General Mills are major marketers on a mission', *Advertising Age* (16 November 2009), pp. 1, 45.

4 See 'Kohler mulls second manufacturing plant in Guj', *Economic Times* (18 November 2009); and the Kohler Press Room, '2008 IBS press kit', www.us.kohler.com/pr/presskit.jsp?aid=1194383270995, accessed October 2011.

5 The following discussion is based in part on information found at www .bcg.com/documents/file13904.pdf, accessed October 2011.

6 Matthew Garrahan, 'Disney profits fall as recession hits', *Financial Times* (4 February 2009), p. 25; Richard Siklos, 'Bob Iger rocks Disney', *Fortune* (19 January 2009), pp. 80–86; and Ben Fritz, 'Company town: Disney profit increases 55%', *Los Angeles Times* (12 May 2010), p. B3.

7 H. Igor Ansoff, 'Strategies for diversification', *Harvard Business Review* (September–October 1957), pp. 113–124.

8 See www.vivago.com/en.html, accessed October 2011.

9 See Michael E. Porter, *Competitive Advantage: Creating and Sustaining Superior Performance* (New York: Free Press, 1985); and Michael E. Porter, 'What is strategy?', *Harvard Business Review* (November–December 1996), pp. 61–78. Also see 'The value chain', www.quickmba.com/ strategy/value-chain, accessed October 2011; and Philip Kotler and Kevin Lane Keller, *Marketing Management*, 13th edn (Upper Saddle River, NJ: Prentice Hall, 2009), pp. 35–36 and pp. 252–253.

10 Nirmalya Kumar, 'The CEO's marketing manifesto', *Marketing Management* (November–December 2008), pp. 24–29.

11 Rebecca Ellinor, 'Crowd pleaser', *Supply Management* (13 December 2007), pp. 26–29; and information from www.loreal.com/_en/_ww/html/ suppliers/index.aspx, accessed October 2011.

12 See www.nikebiz.com/company_overview/, accessed October 2011.

13 The four Ps classification was first suggested by E. Jerome McCarthy, *Basic Marketing: A Managerial Approach* (Homewood, IL: Irwin, 1960). For the 4Cs, other proposed classifications and more discussion, see Robert Lauterborn, 'New marketing litany: 4P's passé C-words take over', *Advertising Age* (1 October 1990), p. 26; Phillip Kotler, 'Alphabet soup', *Marketing Management* (March–April 2006), p. 51; Nirmalya Kumer, 'The CEO's marketing manifesto', *Marketing Management* (November/ December 2008), pp. 24–29; and Roy McClean, 'Marketing 101 – 4 C's versus the 4 P's of marketing', www.customfitfocus.com/marketing-1 .htm, accessed October 2011.

14 For more discussion of the chief marketing officer position, see Philip Kotler and Kevin Lane Keller, *Marketing Management*, 13th edn, pp. 11–12; Terry H. Grapentine and David Dwight, 'Lay the foundation for CMO success', *Marketing Management* (May/June 2009), pp. 24–30; and Todd Wasserman, 'The evolving CMO', *AdweekMedia* (8 June 2009), p. 13.

15 Adapted from information found in Diane Brady, 'Making marketing measure up', *BusinessWeek* (13 December 2004), pp. 112–113; Gray Hammond, 'You gotta be accountable', *Strategy* (December 2008), p. 48; and Kate Maddox, 'Optimism, accountability, social media top trends', *BtoB* (18 January 2010), p. 1.

16 See Kenneth Hein, 'CMOs pressured to show ROI', *Brandweek* (12 December 2008), p. 6; Lance Richard, 'The paradox of ROI and decreased spending in the ad industry', *American Journal of Business* (Autumn 2009), www.bsu.edu/mcobwin/majb/?p=599; and Kevin J. Clancy and Peter C. Krieg, 'Getting a grip', *Marketing Management* (Spring 2010), pp. 18–23.

[17] Mark McMaster, 'ROI: more vital than ever', *Sales & Marketing Management* (January 2002), pp. 51–52. Also see Steven H. Seggie, Erin Cavusgil and Steven Phelan, 'Measurement of return on marketing investment: a conceptual framework and the future of marketing metrics', *Industrial Marketing Management* (August 2007), pp. 834–841; and David Armano, 'The new focus group: the collective', *BusinessWeek* (8 January 2009), at www.businessweek.com/innovate/content/jan2009/id2009017_198183.htm, accessed October 2011.

[18] See Hein, 'CMOs pressured to show ROI', p. 6; Hammond, 'You gotta be accountable', p. 48; and Lawrence A. Crosby, 'Getting serious about marketing ROI', *Marketing Management* (May/June 2009), pp. 10–11.

[19] For a full discussion of this model and details on customer-centered measures of marketing ROI, see Roland T. Rust, Katherine N. Lemon and Valerie A. Zeithaml, 'Return on marketing: using customer equity to focus marketing strategy', *Journal of Marketing* (January 2004), pp. 109–127; Roland T. Rust, Katherine N. Lemon and Das Narayandas, *Customer Equity Management* (Upper Saddle River, NJ: Prentice Hall, 2005); Roland T. Rust, 'Seeking higher ROI? Base strategy on customer equity,' *Advertising Age* (10 September 2007), pp. 26–27; Thorsen Wiesel, Bernd Skiera and Julián Villanueva, 'Customer equity: an integral part of financial reporting', *Journal of Marketing* (March 2008), pp. 1–14.

[20] Elizabeth A. Sullivan, 'Measure up', *Marketing News* (30 May 2009), pp. 8–17; and 'Marketing strategy: Diageo CMO: "Workers Must Be Able to Count"', *Marketing Week* (3 June 2010), p. 5.

VIDEO CASE

Live Nation   MyMarketingLab

Live Nation may not be a household name. But if you've been to a concert in the past few years, the chances are you've purchased a Live Nation product. In fact, Live Nation has been the country's largest concert promoter for many years, promoting as many as 29,000 events annually. But through very savvy strategic planning, Live Nation is shaking up the structure of the music industry.

A recent €85 million deal with Madonna illustrates how this concert promoter is diving into other businesses as well. Under this deal, Live Nation are Madonna's record label, concert promoter, ticket vendor and merchandise agent. Similar deals have been reached with other performers such as Jay-Z and U2. But contracting with artists is only part of the picture. Live Nation is partnering with other corporations as well. A venture with Citi will expand its reach to potential customers through a leveraging of database technologies. Joining forces with ticket reseller powerhouses such as StubHub will give Live Nation a position in the thriving business of secondary ticket sales.

After viewing the video featuring Live Nation, answer the following questions about the role of strategic planning:

1. What is Live Nation's mission?

2. Based on the product/market expansion grid, provide support for the strategy that Live Nation is pursuing.

3. How does Live Nation's strategy provide better value for customers?

COMPANY CASE

Lego: one more brick in the wall?

In 1916 the founder of the Lego dynasty, Ole Kirk Kristiansen, bought a woodworking business and sold furniture to local residents and framers. By the 1930s he switched his attention to children's toys and in 1934 coined the name 'Lego' for his company. The name 'LEGO' is an abbreviation of the two Danish words 'leg' and 'godt', meaning 'play' and 'well'. Lego claim that this is more than their name; but it is ideal. The early toys made by Lego were wood-based – it wasn't until 1940 that the firm began making plastic toys that could be deconstructed and re-assembled. In 1953 Lego began producing the now epony-mous Lego interlocking bricks (actually based on an earlier UK patent by Kiddicraft that Lego spotted as full of potential and quickly bought). Today, the brand rivals Ikea, the Swedish furni-ture chain, as a symbol of Scandinavian design and values.

Since its formation to the late 1990s, Lego experienced steady (if not necessarily spectacular growth) growth. However, in 1998 the company started losing money – fast. The crisis deepened for Lego to the extent that, by 2003, sales had dropped by 26 per cent and in 2004 sales dropped a further 20 per cent. These two years represented the biggest losses in Lego history. The firm was struggling against a falling dollar, cheap Chinese imported toys and young children's growing fascination with electronic gadgetry such as MP3 players and mobile phones. But yet there was hope – 'During the crisis, people wrote letters to us saying, "Please, for God's sake, save this brand because we love it so much"', Jorgen Vig Knudstorp the current CEO recalls. 'People theorise that it's all going to be "virtual play" in future but kids are always going to want to run after a soccer ball and build things with Lego bricks'. Nevertheless, the owners and managers of the firm could see that the strategic mission of the firm was outdated, the Lego portfolio was in big trouble, key internal and external partnerships were ineffective and much of the marketing effort wasted.

In 2004, Kjeld Kirk Kristiansen the grandson of the founder of the Lego toy empire, took a brave decision and stepped down as chief executive after forecasting the largest annual loss in the history of the firm. As owner, Kjeld remained deputy chairman but relinquished control of the firm to Jorgen Vig Knudstorp, previously senior vice-president for corporate affairs. Jorgen had been poached by Lego from McKinsey Management Consultants in 2010. Aged just 36 at the time, he was handpicked by Kjeld as the first outsider to run the family owned business.

JORGEN'S CHALLENGE

With remarkable insight, Jorgen recognised that the firm needed rapid restructuring, cultural change and re-focused effort if it were to be saved from financial collapse. The company's internal focus on creativity, innovation and superior quality had created high complexity that was far from market or customer oriented. The company had a total of 12,500 stock-keeping units, with more than 100 different colours and more than 11,000 suppliers. Lego also operated one of the largest injection-moulding operations in the world, with production sites in Denmark and Switzerland, and packing and other facilities in the Czech Republic, the US and South Korea.

The process of planned change began with the company gathering a diverse group of both senior executives and (impor-tantly) outside specialists in a 'war room', where they analysed the company's portfolio, product development, sourcing, manu-facturing, marketing and logistics process. These analyses lead to a five year plan called 'Shared Vision', which by October 2004 was full approved by the board. This plan pivoted on developing and maintaining effective partnerships (both internally and externally) and was supported with a truly market – oriented mission to 'inspire and develop the builders of tomorrow', which they further explained was driven by their 'ultimate purpose to inspire and develop children to think creatively, reason system-atically and release their potential to shape their own future – experiencing the endless human possibility'.

While Jorgen is today viewed as a miracle worker in his native Denmark for saving a cherished national institution, his appoint-ment in 2004 was a huge gamble. His first challenge as chief executive was winning the support of subordinates left behind in the wake of his meteoric rise to the top of the firm. 'I told them, "I can't do this on my own, you have to work with me"', he recalls. 'Most people realised it was in their interests to help me succeed rather than prove themselves right by showing I couldn't do the job'. Jorgen could draw from what he describes as a 'very good Lego upbringing' as the son of a teacher and an engineer – the kind of middle-class northern European household that has been Lego's key market for generations. He had a deep understanding of children having spent 18 months as a trainee kindergarten teacher before finally deciding to opt for a career in business. Nevertheless, this teaching experience proved valuable to Jorgen: 'My dad says that's where I learnt everything I needed to know about leadership,' he says. 'If you can be a leader with kindergarten children, you can be a leader anywhere.'

During the development and implementation of the turna-round five-year plan, Jorgen argued that the hardest challenges for him was to get to the truth of what Lego was doing right and wrong – and crucially to avoid complacency when things were going well. 'It's so easy when you're in a leadership position to think how good you're doing based on all the nice things people say and dismiss the 1 per cent who complain,' he says. 'You have to listen extra hard to that 1 per cent because they usually represent a much bigger proportion of silent unhappiness'. Lego tries to get at the 'truth' by basing a large proportion of managers' bonuses, including Jorgen's, on customer satisfaction surveys of retailers, parents and children rather than sales figures. This approach is designed to ensure that Lego's long-term corporate health is never sacrificed for short-term financial success. 'Nobody at Lego is measured on sales because the most important thing is that kids and retailers return for more in future,' Jorgen says.

For all his empathy with Lego's heritage and the paternalism of the Kristiansen family, Jorgen did not shy away from hard decisions. He saw that harsh and fast measures were needed to turn Lego round. In the small town of Billund in the Netherlands (where Lego was founded), hundreds of workers were made redundant and some manufacturing shifted to the more cost-effective locations of Mexico and Eastern Europe. While Billund remains Lego's largest production site with its assembly plant adjoining the corporate headquarters, diversifying assembly to multiple locations has proved both efficient and effective at reducing fixed costs. This process has not affected quality; Jorgen proudly claims that 'We've never had to recall a single Lego brick', stressing the importance of quality to the brand. As part of the wider strategy the portfolio was slimmed as the company's flagship Legoland theme parks were sold (although a minority share was retained) and non-core products scrapped as part of a back-to-basics strategy focused on its classic bricks and mini-figures.

Jorgen also recognised that the family nature of the firm had created problems and strategic inertia. 'The family values had made the company too undisciplined', he recalls. Throughout the process of restructuring he tried to run Lego like a ruthless private equity firm; focusing solely on the mission of the firm. More recently, he has adopted practices from growth-orientated public companies. As a result, the embryonic family business has grown from a tiny carpentry workshop (that burned down twice) into the world's third biggest toymaker by sales. In many regards, the culture has altered from one of benevolent paternalism to that of a market-driven, professional culture. Yet, Jorgen argues that family ownership continues to hold important advantages. 'You can think long term but act very fast', he explains. 'I can talk to shareholders in the morning and have a decision by the evening'. He describes his relationship with the Kristiansen family as 'very open and trusting' but not always smooth. 'Part of getting along is that you can have conflicts and still get along. We have disagreements but they are always resolved behind closed doors'.

Possibly, and most crucially, Jorgen and his team focused on their partnerships with their suppliers, distributors and customers. In 2005, through a series of collaborations between different functions in the company, Lego cut the number of colours by half and reduced the number of stock-keeping units to 6,500 The company also decided to stick to their core functions and to outsource logistics and production. In an effort to better understand what their customers did and did not need and want, the company sought extended meetings with its top 20 clients who represented 70 per cent of Lego's total business. This process revealed one very important finding: in direct contrast to what the company had assumed, most customers did not need daily or next-day deliveries. This led to Lego's decision to solicit orders in advance and to deliver to customers just once a week.

As with all plans, implementation was not always easy. In particular, the outsourcing of logistics strained the important relationship with DHL, Lego's logistics partner. When DHL initially won the contract, it made its revenue calculations based on the existing customer service requirements (daily, which meant many more deliveries than weekly). However, after analysing the real needs of their customers, Lego required a much lower number of deliveries than DHL had originally forecast. At the same time, the new outsourced logistics facility was the biggest of its kind in Eastern Europe, thus creating huge start-up challenges for DHL. These stresses and strains inevitably caused conflicts that could have derailed the Lego turnaround. The breakthrough came when two Lego executives met secretly with their DHL counterparts in a hotel in Prague at the beginning of 2007. They took a 'four musketeers' oath – 'all for one and one for all' – not to discuss the outcome of this meeting with anyone. Instead, they undertook to change their behaviour towards one another to set a good example for the rest of their staff. It seems to have worked and relations have since flourished to genuine mutual respect.

THE OUTCOMES OF CHANGE

When Jorgen took charge in the gloomy days of 2004, Lego was so deeply in the red that it faced genuine questions over its short-term survival in an era of online computer games and ever-increasing digital gadgets. Back in 2004 industry commentators were predicting further losses and probable collapse – Lego seemed destined to become yet another crumbled edifice in the face of a virtual world. Eight years later, those doubts have been emphatically answered and the future seems bright (and slightly brick shaped). Sales are now more than a third higher than those gloomy days at around €2.25bn, with net profits of €530 million and Lego's share of the global toy market has rocketed. Between 2005 and 2008 sales increased by 35 per cent and profitability in 2008 was an all-time record. The fixed cost base has been slashed from a debilitating 75 per cent to a highly respectable 33 per cent. Furthermore, Lego is thinking more about the very long-term. Recently, Jorgen's big decisions have been positive ones about new investment. In many ways, Lego has proved relatively immune to global economic turmoil (largely because caring parents keep spending on traditional and educational toys no matter the hardship). The workforce has almost doubled in the past four years to more than 8,000 as recovery in Europe and the US is supplemented by growth in new territories such as Russia. Expansion into other emerging markets such as China, India and Brazil is still at an early stage, leaving plenty of room for growth. However, Jorgen rules out diversifying into other products, saying: 'Lego has been around 80 years and we've never made an acquisition. Companies with single brands, such as Apple and Nintendo, tend to do better than those with several.'

For customers, the outcomes were also good. While customers saw the number of product options reduced and were asked to change their ordering habits, they obtained a substantial improvement in customer service. On-time delivery rose from 62 per cent in 2005 to 92 per cent in 2008. Recently, customers rated Lego as a 'best in class' supplier and Lego won a European supply chain excellence award. Those customers were now asking their other suppliers to use Lego as the benchmark for excellence. Lego has launched an online club with over 4 million members, customers can design and order their own Lego designs, the Lego Universe MMPG has hundreds of thousands of players, the firm has well over 1 million followers on Facebook, over 550,000 videos on YouTube are tagged as 'Lego', while in 2011–2012 over 175,000 9–16 year olds took part in a Lego Robotic League.

Questions for discussion

1. Prior to 2004, was Lego focused on its products or its marketplace? Why?
2. Using the product/market expansion grid, which approach has Lego adopted under the leadership of Jorgen? Is this different to past approaches?
3. On which internal and external partners did Jorgen's approach concentrate? Why?
4. Implementing change is never easy. In implementing their plans, what did Lego do right and what did they do wrong? How would you have done things differently?

Sources: This case study draws heavily on the excellent case studies and analyses (including quotes and other information) of: Carlos Cordon, Ralf Seifert and Edwin Wellian 'Case study: Lego', *Financial Times* (24 November 2010), www.ft.com/cms/s/0/05806aa4-f819-11df-8875-00144feab49a.html#ixzz1ZnO0srvW, accessed October 2011; Clare MacCarthy, 'Lego suffers as children shun toys', *Financial Times* (7 April 2005), www.ft.com/cms/s/0/716a2a26-a701-11d9-a6df00000e2511c8.html#ixzz1ZnP1b6ce, accessed October 2011; Andrew Ward, 'A brick by brick brand revival', *Financial Times* (17 July 2011), www.ft.com/cms/s/0/0596a1f0-af27-11e0-14e00144feabdc0.html#ixzz1ZnPfOHIo, accessed October 2011; http://aboutus.lego.com/en-us/group/future.aspx, accessed October 2011; http://aboutus.lego.com/en-US/factsfigures/default.aspx (company profile), accessed October 2011. An acknowledgement should also be made to the insights generated during personal interviews and cricket matches with Lorna, Charlie and Clara Price.

PART TWO

Understanding the marketplace and consumers

CHAPTER THREE

Analysing the marketing environment

Chapter preview

In Part 1, you learned about the basic concepts of marketing and the steps in the marketing process for building profitable relationships with targeted consumers. In Part 2, we'll look deeper into the first step of the marketing process – understanding the marketplace and customer needs and wants. In this chapter, you'll see that marketing operates in a complex and changing environment. Other actors in this environment – suppliers, intermediaries, customers, competitors, publics and others – may work with or against the company. Major environmental forces – demographic, economic, natural, technological, political and cultural – shape marketing opportunities, pose threats and affect the company's ability to build customer relationships. To develop effective marketing strategies, you must first understand the environment in which marketing operates.

We start by looking at Finnish telecoms company Nokia. Nokia has been the global market leader in the mobile telephone business, but the advent of smartphones like the Apple iPhone has wrongfooted Nokia and its market share is declining. Having been slow to react to the changing characteristics of the mobile telecoms market, Nokia is now teaming up with Microsoft (which has also underperformed in the smartphones business) to try to regain lost competitive position. Many questions surround the pressure of technology convergence in this sector and how best for a company like Nokia to respond.

Objective outline

➤ **Objective 1** Describe the environmental forces that affect the company's ability to serve its customers.
The microenvironment (pp. 74–77)
The macroenvironment (p. 78)

➤ **Objective 2** Explain how changes in the demographic and economic environments affect marketing decisions.
The demographic environment (pp. 78–86)
The economic environment (pp. 86–89)

➤ **Objective 3** Identify the major trends in the firm's natural and technological environments.

The natural environment (pp. 89–91)
The technological environment (pp. 91–92)

➤ **Objective 4** Explain the key changes in the political and cultural environments.
The political and social environment (pp. 93–95)
The cultural environment (pp. 95–97)

➤ **Objective 5** Discuss how companies can react to the marketing environment.
Responding to the marketing environment (pp. 97–98)

Nokia in Telecoms: downwardly mobile

With its market leadership in smartphones on the wane, Nokia is taking a long shot in a tie-up with Microsoft, which has also struggled in the sector.

'Two turkeys do not make an Eagle.' That was the disparaging tweet from Vic Gundotra, a senior Google executive, as Nokia announced that it was to use Microsoft's software as the basis for its fightback in the rapidly growing market for Internet-enabled mobile phones.

Mr Gundotra's message referred to the Finnish company's rejection of Google's Android software for its next generation of so-called smartphones. Stephen Elop, Nokia's new chief executive, responded by comparing himself and Steve Ballmer, Microsoft's CEO, to Orville and Wilbur Wright, the American aviation pioneers. 'I think of two brothers who made bicycles in Dayton, Ohio, and one day they decided to fly,' he told the *Financial Times*, visibly irritated by the comment posted on the Twitter microblogging site.

Mr Elop has made an enormous bet that Microsoft, his own former employer, can enable Nokia – the world's largest maker of mobiles – very belatedly to strike back at Apple and Google in the $120 billon global smartphone market. His plan to use Microsoft's Windows Phone operating system to power Nokia's devices is an admission of defeat in the Finnish company's lengthy efforts to build its own software and services platform.

Since Apple released its iPhone in June 2007, Nokia's share price has fallen by more than two-thirds as it tried unsuccessfully to produce an 'iPhone killer'. But Nokia's handset leadership is in doubt not just because of its lack of sophisticated smartphones. The company is also under growing pressure from low-cost Chinese manufacturers that are eating into its sales of basic handsets in emerging markets.

Nokia's malaise also highlights Europe's waning influence in mobile phone innovation. For the first 20 years of the mobile industry, the continent set the pace in cutting-edge handsets. But the arrival of the iPhone, followed by Android in 2008, showed that the main centre of innovation had shifted from Europe to California's Silicon Valley. Apple and Android are now the pre-eminent brands in the industry.

So, will Mr Elop's strategy fly or will Nokia crash and burn? Mr Elop's choice of Microsoft's Windows Phone software – well received by technology commentators on release last year though yet to capture the consumer's attention – has given his company a chance to revive its fortunes. 'With a clear strategy, the fighting spirit of Nokia worldwide . . . has been brought to bear. As people can see, I am here to fight,' Mr Elop declared when he unveiled the partnership.

However, the odds are heavily stacked against Finland's biggest company. The edge gained by Apple and Google is starkly illustrated by the hundreds of thousands of games and other applications that software developers have produced to run on the iPhone and devices featuring Android. Just like Nokia, Microsoft also has a record of being a laggard in its responses to Apple and Google in the mobile market.

Even if Mr Elop's plan does work, the profitability of Nokia's handset unit could yet take a permanent plunge. Apple is demonstrating that earnings power in the mobile industry now resides in software and services. Nokia, by relying for these on Microsoft, will increasingly resemble a mere hardware maker. Pierre Ferragu, analyst at Bernstein, the research firm, says Nokia could suffer the same fate as Motorola, formerly the leading mobile maker. Like Nokia, Motorola missed the trend towards touchscreen smartphones, and subsequently ran up huge losses for three years from 2007. It is now trying to reinvent itself as a maker of Android-based smartphones.

In the fourth quarter of 2007, Nokia was at the peak of its power. It made four out of every 10 mobile phones sold worldwide, and its handset unit boasted an industry-leading 22.8 per cent operating profit margin. But the iPhone was about to change everything.

The edge gained by Apple over Nokia is shown starkly by the thousands of games and other applications that run on iPhone.

Source: Apple, Inc.

Nokia's long-standing strength had been in hardware – initially making basic mobiles capable of calls and text messaging, to which it added features such as cameras. The iPhone, by contrast, was a full-blown computer with touchscreen technology that turned the mobile Internet into a user-friendly experience for the first time. The apps that started appearing in 2008 enabled consumers to customise their iPhones to suit their lives.

Nokia's answers to the iPhone came slowly and the user experience was poor. Supposedly simple tasks – for instance, such as posting a picture on social networks such as Facebook – were difficult. Criticism centred on the company's clunky Symbian operating system, which became a symbol of Nokia's technological shortcomings. Critics say the failure to produce a rival to the iPhone can be partly explained by a bureaucratic structure that stifled innovation, made worse by an arrogant attitude that developed during Nokia's glory years.

Olli-Pekka Kallasvuo, who succeeded the long-serving Jorma Ollila as CEO in 2006, contributed to the company's problems, says one former senior Nokia employee. Unlike Mr Ollila, an engineer, Mr Kallasvuo was a lawyer turned finance director who did not fully understand technology, says the ex-employee. Though Mr Kallasvuo would not comment, one person close to him accepts that he does not have the technological expertise of an engineer. However, this person adds that Mr Kallasvuo's bigger problem was that he could not transform Nokia fast enough to a software and services company to compete with Apple and Google. Last September, Nokia's board ousted Mr Kallasvuo and named Mr Elop, former head of Microsoft's business unit and a software expert, as his successor.

The dire nature of the situation was apparent to all involved. The operating margin at Nokia's handset unit had fallen to 9.5 per cent in the second quarter of 2010, and Android was emerging as an even bigger threat than the iPhone. Google's platform is being used by several handset makers – including HTC, Samsung, Sony Ericsson and Motorola – and its advance is the result mainly of the fall in price of smartphones that use it.

Android is marching into Nokia's former stronghold of mid-priced smartphones. While the iPhone has a wholesale price of €450, Android smartphones now cost €150 or less. It overtook Symbian to become the most popular smartphone operating system in the fourth quarter of last year, according to Canalys, a research firm.

Against this backdrop, Mr Elop had been undertaking a no-holds-barred review of Nokia's business. He wrote a doomsday e-mail to staff in which he compared the company's predicament to that of a man standing on a 'burning' North Sea oil platform. The man faces the choice between being burnt alive on the rig or jumping into the icy waters below.

It was unsurprising, then, that Mr Elop ripped up Mr Kallasvuo's strategy of persisting with its ageing Symbian platform while developing a new operating system, MeeGo. After deciding Symbian would be phased out, he looked at the case for adopting Android, concluding the company risked a 'commoditisation' of its products. In short, according to Credit Suisse analysts, intensifying competition means all handset makers face the medium-term scenario of operating margins falling to the 5 per cent level that prevails in much of the personal computer industry. But the risk is most acute for the many brands using Android, which are likely to struggle to differentiate their products.

This left Mr Elop with little choice but to strike a deal with Mr Ballmer, his old boss, under which Nokia would use Microsoft's Windows Phone platform as its main smartphone operating system. Unveiling the tie-up, Mr Elop said the two companies were taking on Apple and Google, creating a 'three-horse race' in smartphones.

But to Mr Elop's clear frustration, his strategy has gone down badly. Nokia's stock market value has fallen about 20 per cent since the February 2011 announcement, as investors fretted that the company could suffer a further significant loss in smartphone market share as it attempts a tricky transition. The first Windows Phone models were not due until late 2011 or early 2012. But even when the transition is over, Nokia is targeting an operating margin of only '10 per cent or more' at its handset unit.

The biggest task will be persuading consumers that the Windows Phone devices are as 'sexy' as the iPhone and Android models, says Carolina Milanesi, an analyst at Gartner. Noting Mr Gundrota's 'two turkeys' tweet, she says the Nokia brand has been tarnished by its failure to produce sophisticated smart-phones; meanwhile most consumers have little or no awareness of Windows Phone.

Several analysts say the partnership is a good deal for Microsoft but a bad one for Nokia. The Finnish company, unlike handset makers operating on Android, must pay royalty fees to use Windows Phone. Microsoft, by tapping Nokia's global scale in hardware, has the opportunity to transform itself from a niche player in the mobile market. The most obvious financial benefit for Nokia is the chance to cut its research budget as it is Microsoft that will develop Windows Phone.

Nokia's best hope during its transition is that mobile operators will provide support by buying its Symbian smartphones, though it might have to cut prices to ensure significant sales. European operators, fearing a duopoly involving Apple and Google, are keen for a popular alternative to emerge. But a senior executive at one large operator said much hinged on whether the Finnish company could limit Android's advance by producing models based on Windows by early 2012. 'It's a race against time for Nokia,' said the executive.

Software developers, too, are wary of Mr Elop's plan. Jeremy Statz, a Houston developer creating animated wallpapers for Android mobiles, says he will consider working on Windows Phone only if it gains popularity. 'In the US at least, Nokia seems very much dead in the water as far as smartphones go. I know they have market share in the rest of the world but I want to work on things I know people will be interested in.'

The Nokia and Microsoft co-dependence

The word that Nokia boss Stephen Elop uses to describe the close alliance with Microsoft on which he has bet his company's future is a somewhat unfortunate one. He calls it a 'co-dependency' – which conjures up images of unhealthy mutual reliance as the two also-rans in the smartphone business cling together for support. A less-loaded description would be that tech industry catch-all, 'convergence' – in this case, between Nokia's hardware and Microsoft's Windows Phone software. If there is a way back, then these companies are betting that it lies in tying the technology pieces together more closely – an idea that has been coming into vogue in the handset world, where Apple's iPhone remains the shining example.

Hanging over all this is the question of whether the dance between Microsoft and Nokia will end in the ultimate corporate convergence. One person close to Google's board makes the case that the Finnish company is now 'in play' and that an acquisition is the best hope for redemption for Microsoft boss Steve Ballmer. Mr Elop also needs redemption: in the 16 months since he took the reins, Nokia's already-battered shares have lost another 47 per cent of their value.

Google is, of course, contemplating a degree of smartphone convergence of its own. Its acquisition of Motorola Mobility, which is still awaiting regulatory approval, is intended mainly to bring it the portfolio of patents it needs to fend off lawsuits. But with the hardware business that comes along with it, the search company will also have gained itself some options, should it eventually decide it needs a true Google Phone. The close alliance with Nokia also gives Microsoft an option. But whether a full acquisition would help in the fight with Apple and Google is debatable.

From the point of view of a Microsoft shareholder, the numbers certainly add up. Four years ago, before the financial crisis, Nokia was riding high, with a stock market value half as big as that of Microsoft. It has since lost 85 per cent of its value and, at $20 billion, could easily be handled with Microsoft's $52 billion of cash reserves, even with a sizeable premium. The fact that 85 per cent of Microsoft's cash is held outside the US only adds to the attractions, since with foreign acquisitions it avoids the tax hit that would come from repatriating the money. To complete the set, Microsoft could even think about throwing in the tax-free money to buy Canadian BlackBerry maker Research In Motion (RIM), valued at barely $8 billion, which would further extend the footprint of its Windows Phone platform.

Nokia itself has been strongly rumoured to have looked at a RIM acquisition, which might aid in its efforts to re-establish a presence in the US. However, Mr Elop played down the idea while visiting the Consumer Electronics Show in Las Vegas this week. 'I'm not sure that it would,' he said, before going on to point out that smaller acquisitions with less complexity to them were the ones that made the most sense in the tech world.

For Microsoft, though, double-dipping with both Nokia and RIM may look like a quick way to become a smartphone leader – if it could handle the angst that the loss of national tech champions would be likely to engender in both Finland and Canada. But would the tight technology convergence on which a Nokia acquisition would be predicated really answer both companies' smartphone woes?

Microsoft has tried the hardware–software combination before. Its Zune player, launched years late against the iPod, was meant to prove that there was a gadget gene embedded in its DNA. Despite good reviews, it flopped.

It is not even clear that close integration of hardware and software is the secret to world domination in smartphones, much as Microsoft and Nokia like to argue the case. The leader in smartphone operating systems is Google's Android, which has given birth to an array of devices of varying quality. Google has worked closely with hardware makers for the flagship Nexus phones it launches each year – much as Microsoft works with Nokia – but they have not been among the biggest Android successes. So either consumers don't yet appreciate the extra benefits claimed for integrated devices, or the real downside of fragmentation in the Android ecosystem has yet to reach a critical stage, says Joe Belfiore, who heads product and software design for Windows Phone.

Neither outcome is preordained. Mobile carriers and hardware makers like the extra freedom they get from Android and continue to promote it heavily. In Las Vegas, meanwhile, Nokia and Microsoft were talking up the Lumia 900, a new device they hope will reignite interest among US smartphone users. If it works, the odds will increase on their co-dependency eventually becoming a bond for life.[1]

Marketing environment—
The actors and forces outside marketing that affect marketing management's ability to build and maintain successful relationship with target customers.

A company's **marketing environment** consists of the actors and forces outside marketing that affect marketing management's ability to build and maintain successful relationships with target customers. Like Nokia and Microsoft, companies must constantly watch and adapt to the changing environment and in some cases act to completely reshape the environment – as technology changes, competitors come out with radical innovations, customer needs and preferences evolve, and other fundamental changes occur, companies must evolve and change as well or risk being left behind.

More than any other group in the company, marketers must be environmental trend trackers and opportunity seekers. Although every manager in an organisation should observe what is occurring in the outside environment, marketers have two special aptitudes. They have disciplined methods – marketing research and marketing intelligence – for collecting information about the marketing environment. They also spend more time in customer and competitor environments. By carefully studying the environment, marketers can adapt their strategies to meet new marketplace challenges and opportunities.

Microenvironment—The actors close to the company that affect its ability to serve its customers – the company, suppliers, marketing intermediaries, customer markets, competitors and publics.

Macroenvironment—The larger soccial forces that affect the microenvironment – demographic, economic, natural, technological, political and cultural forces.

The marketing environment consists of a *microenvironment* and a *macroenvironment*. The **microenvironment** consists of the actors close to the company that affect its ability to serve its customers – the company, suppliers, marketing intermediaries, customer markets, competitors and publics. The **macroenvironment** consists of the larger societal forces that affect the microenvironment– demographic, economic, natural, technological, political and cultural forces. We will look first at the company's microenvironment.

AUTHOR COMMENT

The microenvironment includes all the actors close to the company that affect, positively or negatively, its ability to create value for and relationships with its customers.

THE MICROENVIRONMENT

Marketing management's job is to build relationships with customers by creating customer value and satisfaction. However, marketing managers cannot do this alone. Figure 3.1 shows the major actors in the marketer's microenvironment. Marketing success requires building relationships with other company departments, suppliers, **marketing intermediaries**, competitors, various publics and customers, which combine to compose the company's value delivery network.

Marketing intermediaries—
Firms that help the company to promote, sell and distribute its goods to final buyers.

The company

In designing marketing plans, marketing management takes other company groups into account – groups such as top management, finance, research and development (R&D), purchasing, operations and accounting. All of these interrelated groups form the internal environment. Top management sets the company's mission, objectives, broad strategies and policies. Marketing managers make decisions within the strategies and plans created by top management.

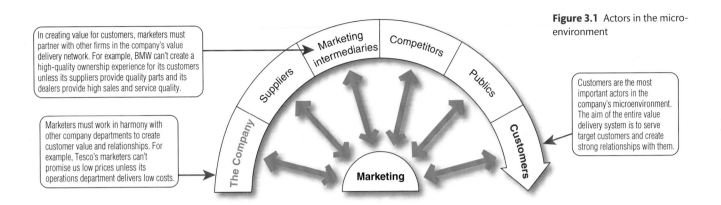

Figure 3.1 Actors in the micro-environment

In creating value for customers, marketers must partner with other firms in the company's value delivery network. For example, BMW can't create a high-quality ownership experience for its customers unless its suppliers provide quality parts and its dealers provide high sales and service quality.

Marketers must work in harmony with other company departments to create customer value and relationships. For example, Tesco's marketers can't promise us low prices unless its operations department delivers low costs.

Customers are the most important actors in the company's microenvironment. The aim of the entire value delivery system is to serve target customers and create strong relationships with them.

As we discussed in Chapter 2, marketing managers must work closely with other company departments. Other departments have an impact on the marketing department's plans and actions. And, under the marketing concept, all of these functions must 'think consumer'. According to a former chief executive officer of Xerox, the global document-management and business-process technology company, to provide a great customer experience, Xerox must 'find out what customers are facing – what their problems and opportunities are. Everyone at Xerox shares this responsibility. That includes people and departments that have not always been customer-facing, like finance, legal, and human resources.'[2]

Suppliers

Suppliers form an important link in the company's overall customer value delivery network. They provide the resources needed by the company to produce its goods and services. Supplier problems can seriously affect marketing. Marketing managers must watch supply availability and costs. Supply shortages or delays, labour strikes and other events can cost sales in the short run and damage customer satisfaction in the long run. Rising supply costs may force price increases that can harm the company's sales volume.

Most marketers today treat their suppliers as partners in creating and delivering customer value. For example, Toyota knows the importance of building close relationships with its suppliers. In fact, it even includes the phrase *achieve supplier satisfaction* in its mission statement.

Toyota's competitors often alienate suppliers through self-serving, heavy-handed dealings. According to one supplier, car manufacturers 'set annual cost-reduction targets [for the parts they buy]. To realize those targets, they'll do anything. [They've unleashed] a reign of terror, and it gets worse every year.' By contrast, rather than bullying suppliers, Toyota partners with them and helps them meet its very high expectations. Toyota learns about their businesses, conducts joint improvement activities, helps train supplier employees, gives daily performance feedback and actively seeks out supplier concerns. It even recognises top performers with annual performance awards. High supplier satisfaction means that Toyota can rely on suppliers to help it improve its own quality, reduce costs and quickly develop new products. Even after the recent massive recall following unanticipated acceleration problems

Toyota partners with suppliers and helps them meet its very high expectations.

Source: Saatchi & Saatchi

with some Toyota models, the company didn't point blame at the accelerator part supplier. Instead, Toyota took blame for a faulty part design and even issued a statement supporting the 'long-term and valued supplier'. In all, creating satisfied suppliers helps Toyota produce lower-cost, higher-quality cars, which in turn results in more satisfied customers.[3]

Marketing intermediaries

Marketing intermediaries help the company promote, sell and distribute its products to final buyers. They include resellers, physical distribution firms, marketing services agencies and financial intermediaries. *Resellers* are distribution channel firms that help the company find customers or make sales to them. These include wholesalers and retailers who buy and resell merchandise. Selecting and partnering with resellers is not easy. No longer do manufacturers have many small, independent resellers from which to choose. They now face large and growing reseller organisations, such as Tesco in the UK, Walmart in the US, and Carrefour and Metro in Europe. In the UK, for example, Tesco alone accounts for around one-third of all grocery sales, and the top three retailers dominate almost two-thirds of all food distribution.[4] These organisations frequently have enough power to dictate terms or even shut smaller manufacturers out of large markets.

Physical distribution firms help the company stock and move goods from their points of origin to their destinations. *Marketing services agencies* are the marketing research firms, advertising agencies, media firms and marketing consulting firms that help the company target and promote its products to the right markets. *Financial intermediaries* include banks, credit companies, insurance companies and other businesses that help finance transactions or insure against the risks associated with the buying and selling of goods.

Like suppliers, marketing intermediaries form an important component of the company's overall value delivery network. In its quest to create satisfying customer relationships, the company must do more than just optimise its own performance. It must partner effectively with marketing intermediaries to optimise the performance of the entire system.

Thus, today's marketers recognise the importance of working with their intermediaries as partners rather than simply as channels through which they sell their products. For example, when Coca-Cola signs on as the exclusive provider for a fast-food chain, such as global chains like McDonald's, as well as national chains, it provides much more than just soft drinks. It also pledges powerful marketing support.[5]

Coca-Cola assigns cross-functional teams dedicated to understanding the finer points of a major retail partner's business. It conducts a staggering amount of research on consumers and shares these insights with its partners. It analyses the demographics of local markets and helps partners determine which Coke brands are preferred in their areas. Coca-Cola has even studied the design of different types of menu boards to better understand which layouts, fonts, letter sizes, colours, and visuals induce consumers to order more food and drink. Based on such insights, the Coca-Cola Food Service group develops marketing programmes and merchandising tools that help its retail partners improve their soft-drink sales and profits. For example, Coca-Cola Food Service's website, www.CokeSolutions.com, provides retailers with a wealth of information, business solutions and merchandising tips. 'We know that you're passionate about delighting guests and enhancing their real experiences on every level,' says Coca-Cola to its retail partners. 'As your partner, we want to help in any way we can.' Such intense partnering efforts have given Coca-Cola competitive advantage in the soft-drink market throughout the world, notwithstanding fierce competition from other drinks suppliers.

Competitors

The marketing concept states that, to be successful, a company must provide greater customer value and satisfaction than its competitors do. Thus, marketers must do more than simply adapt to the needs of target consumers. They also must gain strategic advantage by positioning their offerings strongly against competitors' offerings in the minds of consumers.

No single competitive marketing strategy is best for all companies. Each firm should consider its own size and industry position compared to those of its competitors. Large firms with dominant positions in an industry can use certain strategies that smaller firms cannot afford. But being large is not enough. There are winning strategies for large firms, but there are also losing ones. And small firms can develop strategies that give them better rates of return than large firms enjoy.

Publics

The company's marketing environment also includes various publics. A **public** is any group that has an actual or potential interest in or impact on an organisation's ability to achieve its objectives. We can identify seven types of publics:

Public—Any group that has an actual or potential interest in or impact on an organisation's ability to achieve its objectives.

- *Financial publics.* This group influences the company's ability to obtain funds. Banks, investment analysts and shareholders are the major financial publics.
- *Media publics.* This group carries news, features and editorial opinion. It includes newspapers, magazines, television and radio stations, and blogs and other Internet media.
- *Government publics.* Management must take government developments into account. Marketers must often consult the company's lawyers on issues of product safety, truth in advertising and other matters.
- *Citizen-action publics.* Consumer organisations, environmental groups, minority groups, and others may question a company's marketing decisions. Its PR department can help it stay in touch with consumer and citizen groups.
- *Local publics.* This group includes neighbourhood residents and community organisations. Large companies usually create departments and programmes that deal with local community issues and provide community support.
- *General public.* A company needs to be concerned about the general public's attitude toward its products and activities. The public's image of the company affects its buying.
- *Internal publics.* This group includes workers, managers, volunteers and the board of directors. Large companies use newsletters and other means to inform and motivate their internal publics. When employees feel good about the companies they work for, this positive attitude spills over to the external publics.

A company can prepare marketing plans for these major publics as well as for its customer markets. Suppose the company wants a specific response from a particular public, such as goodwill, favourable word of mouth, or donations of time or money. The company would have to design an offer to this public that is attractive enough to produce the desired response.

Customers

As we've emphasised throughout, customers are the most important actors in the company's microenvironment. The aim of the entire value delivery network is to serve target customers and create strong relationships with them. The company might target any or all five types of customer markets. *Consumer markets* consist of individuals and households that buy goods and services for personal consumption. *Business markets* buy goods and services for further processing or use in their production processes, whereas *reseller markets* buy goods and services to resell at a profit. *Government markets* consist of government agencies that buy goods and services to produce public services or transfer the goods and services to others who need them. Finally, *international markets* consist of these buyers in other countries, including consumers, producers, resellers and governments. Each market type has special characteristics that call for careful study by the seller.

AUTHOR COMMENT

The macroenvironment consists of broader forces that affect the actors in the microenvironment.

THE MACROENVIRONMENT

The company and all its other actors operate in a larger macroenvironment of forces that shape opportunities and pose threats to the company. Figure 3.2 shows the six major forces in the company's macroenvironment. In the remaining sections of this chapter, we will examine these forces and show how they affect marketing plans.

The demographic environment

Demography—The study of human populations in terms of size, density, location, age, gender, face, occupational and other statistics.

Demography is the study of human populations in terms of size, density, location, age, gender, race, occupation and other statistics. The demographic environment is of major interest to marketers because it involves people, and people are the driving force for markets. The world population is growing at an explosive rate. In 2011, world population reached 7 billion and is expected to grow to more than 8 billion by the year 2030.[6] The world's large and highly diverse population poses both opportunities and challenges.

a **AUTHOR COMMENT**
Changes in demographics mean changes in markets, so they are very important to marketers. We look at some of the biggest demographic trends affecting markets.

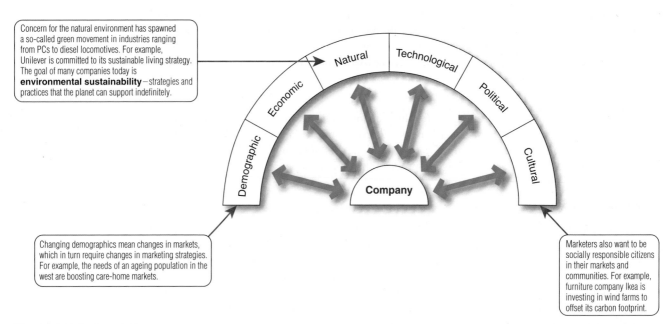

Concern for the natural environment has spawned a so-called green movement in industries ranging from PCs to diesel locomotives. For example, Unilever is committed to its sustainable living strategy. The goal of many companies today is **environmental sustainability**—strategies and practices that the planet can support indefinitely.

Changing demographics mean changes in markets, which in turn require changes in marketing strategies. For example, the needs of an ageing population in the west are boosting care-home markets.

Marketers also want to be socially responsible citizens in their markets and communities. For example, furniture company Ikea is investing in wind farms to offset its carbon footprint.

Figure 3.2 Major forces in the company's macroenviroment

Thus, marketers must keep a close eye on demographic trends and developments in their markets – both at home and abroad. They need to analyse changing age and family structures, geographic population shifts, educational characteristics and population diversity. Here, we discuss some of the most important demographic trends influencing markets and marketing throughout the world.

World population growth

World population passed the 6 billion mark in 1998 to reach 7 billion in 2011, and is likely to double again by the end of the century. The likelihood is that only a minority of the world's new inhabitants will be born into the sort of wealth and stability that most of the developed countries take for granted. More than 70 per cent of the world's population increase over the next 40 years is expected to take place outside the world's richest 20 nations.[7]

Ever more population has been supported by economic growth, while improved nutrition, sanitation and medical care has allowed people to live increasingly long lives. Life expectancy globally was around 46 years in 1950. By 2011 it had reached an average of nearly 70, and more than 80 in richer countries.[8]

The new inhabitants are likely to be urban, as millions of people across the world are being drawn from rural, agricultural areas to cities, by the promise of work and economic advancement, in the face of crippling to rural poverty. But creaking infrastructure and overcrowding means the reality of sprawling slums, in cities such as Lagos and Mumbai, makes life there challenging.

High birth rates in the world's poorer countries are in contrast to low birth rates and ageing populations in many developed countries, notably Japan, which places a severe strain on the next generation, many of whom will have to work longer to support their parents' retirement. Such is the concern at Russia's low birth rate that some fear its population could soon drop to a level that could destabilise the country.

Nonetheless, the example of some emerging markets like Brazil suggests that the correct combination of economic growth and education can bring birth rates down to levels still high enough to support the country's prospects. Meanwhile, in India, a high birth rate and booming economy are expected to propel the country past China to become the most populous nation on earth by about 2030.

The changing age structure of world population

Changes in the world demographic environment have major implications for business. Perhaps the single most important demographic trend in the world is the changing age structure of the population. For example, India has one of the youngest population profiles in the world – more than 70 per cent of the population is under 35. By 2020, the median age in India will be 28, compared to 37 in China, 38 in the United States, 45 in Western Europe and 49 in Japan.[9] If demography defines destiny, then the next century will belong to India and Africa. This is because their youthful population ensures that they will continue to enjoy a plentiful supply of young workers supporting a relatively small population of elderly people. In demographic terms, their 'dependency ratios' will be favourable. In contrast, European Union countries, the United States and China will all be carrying a growing burden because their populations are aging and their dependency ratios will be increasingly unfavourable. Countries with unfavourable age structures have concerns about a loss of dynamism and a growing burden on public finances.[10]

> Amid all the current hoopla about the emergence of China as the next global superpower, one of the commonly expressed reservations is 'China will get old, before it gets rich'. In other words, the current availability of cheap, young labour will reduce and the number of people retiring from the work force – and requiring support from their families and the state – will soar. This unfavourable situation is in large part, a perverse result of China's one-child policy, which was aimed at restricting the size of the population.[11]

There are interesting implications of the Chinese government passing regulations limiting families to one child each, around 30 years ago. One result is that China's youth born after 1980 – called 'balinghou' or the 'Me generation' by their elders – have been showered with attention and luxuries resulting in what's known as the 'little emperor' or 'little empress' syndrome. As many as six adults, two parents and four doting grandparents may be indulging the whims of each only child – all 600 million of them. Parents with only one child at home now spend about 40 per cent of their income on their cherished child.[12]

China's Me generation, now ranging in age from newborns to their early thirties, is affecting markets for everything from children's products to financial services, mobile phone services and luxury goods. For example, coffee chain Starbucks is targeting China's Me generation, positioning itself as new kind of informal but indulgent meeting place:[13]

China's one-child rule created a generation of people who have been pampered by parents and grandparents and have the means to make indulgent purchases. Instead of believing in traditional Chinese collective goals, these young people embrace individuality. 'Their view of this world is very different,' says the president of Starbucks Greater China. 'They have never gone through the hardships of our generation.' Starbucks is in sync with that, he says, given its customized drinks, personalized service, and original music compilations. 'In the US, most of Starbucks' business is takeaway,' says one analyst. 'It is the opposite in China. [Young] people go to [Starbucks] as a destination and spend hours there. They like to be seen as chic and cosmopolitan.'

Generational differences in the developed world

In the developed world, distinctions are often made between several generational groups. Here, we discuss the three largest groups – the baby boomers, Generation X and the Millennials – and their impact on today's marketing strategies.

The baby boomers

Baby boomers—The 78 million people born during years following the Second World War and lasting until 1964.

The post–Second World War **baby boomers** were born between 1946 and 1964. Over the years, the baby boomers have been one of the most powerful forces shaping the marketing environment. The youngest boomers are now in their mid-forties; the oldest are in their sixties and approaching retirement. Maturing boomers are rethinking the purpose and value of their work, responsibilities and relationships.

After years of prosperity, free spending and saving little, economic downturn and recession has hit many baby boomers hard, especially the pre-retirement boomers. A sharp decline in investment values and home values ate into their nest eggs and retirement prospects. Nonetheless, as they reach their peak earning and spending years, the boomers will continue to constitute a lucrative market for financial services, new housing and home improvements, travel and entertainment, eating out, health and fitness products, and just about everything else.

It would be a mistake to think of the older boomers as phasing out or slowing down. Today's boomers 'think young' no matter how old they are. One study showed that boomers, on average, see themselves as 12 years younger than they actually are. And rather than viewing themselves as phasing out, they see themselves as entering new life phases. The more active boomers – sometimes called zoomers, or baby boomers with zip – have no intention of abandoning their youthful lifestyles as they age.[14]

'It is time to throw out the notion that the only things marketable to [the older boomers] are chiropractic mattresses, arthritis drugs, and [staid] cruises,' says one marketer. 'Boomers have sought the fountain of youth through all stages of life and have incorporated aspects of play and fun into everything from careers to cars.'[15] Indeed, critics suggest that the baby boomers fear of mortality has created an industry worth €75 billion in the United States alone for anti-aging products and services.[16] On the other hand, new retirees, for example, are heavy spenders on consumer electronics, clothing, furniture and jewellery compared to the rest of the population: 'the last thing they want is to be told how to address a lack of dexterity. They don't want geriatric tools but cool stuff.'[17] Nonetheless, perhaps no-one is targeting the baby boomers more fervently than the financial services industry with services for retirement planning and money management.

Generation X

Generation X—The 45 million people born between 1965 and 1976 in the 'birth dearth' following the baby boom.

The baby boom was followed by a 'birth dearth' creating another generation born between 1965 and 1976. Author Douglas Coupland calls them **Generation X** because they lie in the shadow of the boomers and lack obvious distinguishing characteristics.

The Generation Xers are defined as much by their shared experiences as by their age. In the developed countries, increasing parental divorce rates and higher employment for their mothers made them the first generation of latchkey kids (children who return home from school to an empty house because both parents are at work). Although they seek success, they are less materialistic; they prize experience, not acquisition. For many of the Generation Xers who are now parents, family comes first – both children and their aging parents – and career second. From a marketing standpoint, the Generation Xers are a more sceptical bunch. They tend to research products before they consider a purchase, prefer quality to quantity, and tend to be less receptive to overt marketing pitches.

Once labelled as 'the MTV generation' and viewed as body-piercing slackers who whined about 'McJobs', the Generation Xers have grown up and are now taking over. They are increasingly displacing the lifestyles, culture and values of the baby boomers. They are moving up in their careers, and many are proud homeowners with young, growing families. They are the most educated generation to date, and they possess hefty annual purchasing power. However, like the baby boomers, the Generation Xers now face growing economic pressures. Like almost everyone else these days, they are spending more carefully.[18] Nonetheless, with so much potential, many brands and organisations are focusing on Generation Xers as a prime target segment.

Millennials

Both the baby boomers and Generation Xers will one day be passing the reins to the **Millennials** (also called Generation Y or the echo boomers). Born between 1977 and 2000, these children of the baby boomers constitute a generation dwarfing the Generation Xers and larger even than the baby boomer segment. This group includes several age cohorts: *tweens* (ages 10–12), *teens* (13–18), and *young adults* (19–33). The Millennials are a huge and attractive market in most developed countries.[19]

One thing that all the Millennials have in common is their utter fluency and comfort with digital technology. They don't just embrace technology; it's a way of life. The Millennials were the first generation to grow up in a world filled with computers, mobile phones, satellite TV, iPods and online social networks. A recent study in the US found that 91 per cent of Millennials are on the Web, making up 32 per cent of all Internet users. According to another study, 77 per cent of Millennials frequent social-networking sites, and 71 per cent use instant messaging. 'All generations are comfortable with technology, but this is the generation that's been formed by technology,' says a Yahoo! executive. For them, 'it's not something separate. It's just something they do.'[20]

Marketers of all kinds now target the Millennials segment. The Millennials are bombarded with marketing messages coming at them from all directions. Rather than having mass marketing messages pushed at them, they prefer to seek out information and engage in two-way brand conversations. Thus, reaching these message-saturated consumers effectively requires creative marketing approaches.

Millennials (or Generation Y)— The 83 million children of the baby boomers born between 1977 and 2000.

Generational marketing

Do marketers need to create separate products and marketing programmes for each generation? Some experts warn that marketers need to be careful about turning off one generation each time they craft a product or message that appeals effectively to another. Others caution that each generation spans decades of time and many socioeconomic levels. For example, marketers often split the baby boomers into three smaller groups – leading-edge boomers, core boomers and trailing-edge boomers – each with its own beliefs and behaviours. Similarly, they split the Millennials into tweens, teens and young adults.

Thus, marketers need to form more precise age-specific segments within each group. More importantly, defining people by their birth date may be less effective than segmenting them by their lifestyle, life stage or the common values they seek in the products they buy. We will discuss many other ways to segment markets in Chapter 7.

The changing family structure

The family unit is a basic structure underpinning social and economic behaviour in most societies, and yet is subject to several changes which challenge traditional assumptions.

New household formats

The traditional western household consisted of husband, wife and children (and sometimes grandparents). However, in many European countries, married couples with children represent a smaller proportion of total households, while married couples without children represent a substantial group, and single parent households another. A growing percentage are non-family households – singles living alone or adults of one or both sexes living together. More people are divorcing or separating, choosing not to marry, marrying later or marrying without intending to have children. Marketers must increasingly consider the special needs of non-traditional households because they are now growing more rapidly than traditional households. Each group has distinctive needs and buying habits.

Working women

The number of women in paid employment outside the home has also increased greatly in most European nations. Both husband and wife work in the majority of all married-couple families. Meanwhile, more men are staying home with their children, managing the household while their wives go to work. This trend has been amplified by rising male unemployment in the economic recession – economic reality has meant for many households that as men cope with unemployment, their wives head back to work.[21]

The significant number of women in the workforce has spawned the child-care business and increased the consumption of career-oriented women's clothing, financial services, and convenience foods and services. Indeed, it has been pointed out that as a market women represent a bigger opportunity than China and India combined, yet despite their dominant buying power many companies market mainly to men and fail to explore how they might meet women's needs beyond the simplistic 'make it pink' reaction.[22] Part of the challenge is that as more women balance a job with child-rearing, they struggle to find free time, so time-saving shopping and buying processes are vital.[23]

For example, British brewers have made concerted attempts to appeal to women to boost beer sales. Coors, the UK arm of Molson Coors Brewing company, established a unit called Eve to develop beer brands and marketing techniques that appeal to women – in the UK only 13 per cent of women regularly buy beer. The unit's mission is to create 'a world where women love beer as much as they love shoes'. Coor's Blue Moon beer brand is sold in London pubs served with a slice of orange to accentuate its fruity taste.[24]

Innovative gender-oriented marketing strategies are not restricted to adults. Lego, manufacturer of the famous plastic bricks for children, is building its growth strategy around selling to girls as well as boys. Female children have the same instinct for building as boys, but favour role play as well. Lego Friends introduces new colours and mini-figures and encourages children to create scenarios for storytelling, rather than just create the model pictured on the box. Lego Friends is the company's most strategic launch in decades.[25]

The youth market

One significant change in family units in many European countries has been that young people are remaining at home with their parents far longer than in the past – in the UK the proportion of 20 to 34-year-old men living at home rose to 29 per cent in 2009.[26] As a result, during the recession in the UK the 'youth pound' was robust – unburdened by mortgages, teenagers and young adults continued to shop enthusiastically. This generation has been described as the 'children of the credit revolution'.[27] Furthermore, the Internet has spawned a global youth culture sharing responses to marketing messages and purchasing behaviour across conventional geographic boundaries.[28] Nonetheless, in reality in countries like the UK, the real disposable income of people in their twenties has stagnated over the past ten years, and these younger people are unlikely to ever match their parents' living standards.[29]

In fact, demographic change suggests a decline in the size of the youth market in Europe over the coming years. Indeed, harsh economic conditions in many western countries have seen a dramatic rise of long-term unemployment among young people – the educated and jobless young. High long-term youth unemployment is associated with growing unrest in the Middle East and undermining society in Europe and the US. The continuing jobs crisis is in danger of creating a 'lost generation' of long-term unemployed across the developed world. In the UK, jobless rates among young people are escalating. Youth unemployment in Africa and the Arab world also risks exporting tensions to Europe – as an aging, relatively rich and socially conservative region acts as a magnet for young workers, many of them illegal immigrants, from across the Mediterranean.[30]

Older workers

The corollary to a declining youth market is that in the United States and many European countries, people are having to continue working beyond what was once considered retirement age. Older people may have failed to plan well, may have earned and saved little, may have suffered financial losses in the economic downturn, or longer lives may have simply depleted savings. In the United States, for example, it is expected that the number of economically active people aged 75 or over will increase dramatically as the baby boomers swell the ranks of senior citizens.[31]

Geographic shifts in population and market diversity

Migration

For a variety of reasons, the world's migrant population is rising fast. Currently, only about 3 per cent of the world's population – about 190 million people – live outside the country of their birth. Indeed, the economic recession of the late 2000s led to that number falling slightly, as poor economic growth in host countries led some migrants to head home. Nonetheless, global migrant flows look set to double by 2050.[32] Migration impacts both on the location of market demand – where people can be reached – and the nature of demand for products and services – the needs of people in new situations.

Higher migrant flows will partly be a matter of choice – fast-aging advanced economies face a looming labour shortage of potentially as many as 100 million workers by 2050, and much of that shortfall will probably be met by increased immigration. But alongside these factors, other issues will push migrants out from developing nations. For example, Africa faces particular challenges. By 2050, the continent's population will have doubled to 1.8 billion, many of whom will struggle to find economic opportunities at home. Key pressure points for migration include the following:

- *Europe.* Geographic proximity and economic pull ensures Europe will remain on the frontline of migration flows. To maintain a stable 'dependency ratio' between working and nonworking population, Europe may have to admit 1.3 billion migrants by 2050.
- *Russia and the Caucasus.* Russia is the world's second largest migrant destination with up to 15 million incomers propping up its declining population. In averting a demographic crisis, Russia has created an ethnic one, with migrants facing a nationalist backlash. As many as a third of Russia's professional class also want to leave the country.
- *China's periphery.* China's vast population, hunger for resources and willingness to deploy labour in neighbouring countries is causing disquiet around its borders. Russian nationalists fear encroachments from the south by an influx of Chinese.
- *US/Mexico border.* America's southern frontier is one of the world's most militarised borders - $8 billion has been spent on fences, sensors and surveillance drones to stop migrants from the south. Mexico suffers the consequences, with people movement, drugs and criminal violence destabilising many provinces.

- *Sub-Saharan Africa.* About 18 per cent of the world's population live in dry zones. But environmental migrants are more likely to move to poor neighbouring countries, rather than more distant advanced economies. The effect is large flows of people into the countries least able to cope, such as Somali refugees spilling over the border into Kenya.
- *UAE/Middle East.* The desert states of the Middle East top the league of nations most densely populated by migrants. Qatar and the United Arab Emirates both have populations where more than seven in 10 are foreign-born – including large, marginalised groups from south Asia.
- *Mega-cities.* Karachi in Pakistan has been dubbed the world's most dangerous city, with its 15 million residents beset by an explosive mixture of poverty, ethnic violence, crime and ineffective governance. The city offers a worrying vision of where other sprawling global mega-cities, such as Kinshasa and Lagos, may be heading.
- *Remittances.* Remittances (cash sent home by migrant workers) are an increasingly important factor in global development, providing emerging markets with vital capital flows. Some nations are increasingly dependent on these flows – in the Philippines, Moldova and Tajikistan, for example, remittances made up 48 per cent of GDP in 2008.[33]

Dramatic moves in migrants workers continue. In 2012, because of its underlying economic problems particularly in the property and construction sectors, Spain saw an exodus of workers leaving to work in other countries. As well as relocating to other European countries, large numbers of Spanish workers headed for Brazil, Africa and the United States. The Spanish exodus includes many skilled professional workers. For the first time since 1990, in 2011 more people left Spain than moved in.[34]

Ethnic diversity in markets

Certainly, population movements create interesting opportunities for marketing specialised products and services to ethnic groups within a country. For example, Mecca Cola, a pro-Muslim alternative to other colas that capitalises on anti-American sentiment, sold 300,000 litres in its first two weeks on sales in Britain.[35] Mecca Cola sells successfully to its market niche in the Arab world, many European regions and the United States and Canada.

Mecca Cola is a pro-Muslim cola that sells to its market niche in the Arab world, many European regions and the US and Canada.

Source: Corbis/Sion Touhig

More broadly, the UK is seeing the development of 'super-diverse' cities where no single ethnic group will provide the majority. This pluralism encompasses places like Leicester, Birmingham, Slough, Luton and many of the London boroughs. However, it is anticipated that immigrant and ethnic minority populations will not be dominated by the currently strong Afro-Caribbean or Asian communities, but increasing numbers will come from countries scattered across the world.[36]

It is telling that in the United States, the spending power of African American, Asian and most particularly Hispanic consumers has become pivotal for many firms. For example, Procter & Gamble is aiming to turn its Gain cleaning products range into a mega-brand, largely on the basis of the appeal of the heavier-scented products to the Hispanic consumer.[37] For multi-national brands, the challenge is transferring brand experiences and lessons about consumer preferences from Mexico and Russia to reach Hispanics in Albuquerque and Russians in Brighton Beach in the US.[38]

Similarly, in the UK, migrant workers, largely from within the European Union, are changing the consumer market rapidly and providing marketers with new opportunities. For example, the vibrant Polish immigrant community has seen a Polish radio station launched, road signs in Polish, banks like NatWest offering a dedicated account for Polish customers, supermarkets Tesco and Asda stocking a wide rangs of Polish delicacies that are advertised in the burgeoning UK-based Polish language media, and estate agents advertising properties for sales and rent in the Polish language.[39]

Recognising other aspects of diversity in markets

Diversity goes beyond ethnic heritage. For example, many major companies explicitly target gay and lesbian consumers. For example, increasing marketing attention is being paid to the role of the gay buyer in the property market. The gay community provides an attractive target of affluent buyers, often with double-income households, and high property ownership. The gay community is also one of the most enthusiastic about buying holiday homes abroad. Research suggests these trends are developing in most of the liberal western democracies. As a market segment, there are specialist media such as gay lifestyle magazines offering access to this community.[40]

Similarly, US company Hyatt Hotels & Resorts has recognised that the Web provides a route to targeting the lesbian, gay, bisexual and transgender (LGBT) market, and actually launched its own LGBT website dedicated to the travel needs of the gay community. Combining its brand image as a premium hotel with the LGBT target market, Hyatt uses gay-friendly advertising images. Hyatt also uses other travel websites and sites targeting the gay community to advertise its brand specifically to gay travellers. The attractions of this market for Hyatt are the high number of affluent frequent travellers in this community, who are often not locked into summer holiday times by childcare and school arrangements (thus generating more business in off-peak months).[41] Companies in a wide range of industries are now targeting the LGBT community with gay-specific marketing efforts.

Another interesting diversity segment is adults with disabilities. In the United States, there are nearly 60 million US adults with disabilities – comprising a market larger than African Americans or Hispanics, and representing more than $200 billion in annual spending power. Most individuals with disabilities are active consumers. For example, one study found that more than two-thirds of adults with disabilities had travelled at least once for business or pleasure during the preceding two years. Thirty-one per cent had booked at least one flight, more than half had stayed in hotels and 20 per cent had rented a car. More than 75 per cent of people with disabilities dine out at least once a week.[42]

How are companies trying to reach consumers with disabilities? Many marketers now recognise that the worlds of people with disabilities and those without disabilities are one and the same. Marketers such as McDonald's, Nike and Honda have featured people with disabilities in their mainstream advertising.

Urbanisation

In addition to flows of population between nations, there are significant movements within countries. There is, for example, a continued trend towards the movement of people from rural to urban areas. Evidence suggests that 500 million farmers will move to cities over the next 50 years, creating pressure on already teeming cities like Mumbai, Delhi, Dhaka and Shanghai (each expected to be home to more than 20 million people), as well as Kinshasa, Cairo and Lagos (each expected to contain more than 15 million people).

Indeed, within the United States, over the past two decades, the population has shifted toward the Sunbelt states. The West and South have grown, whereas the Midwest and Northeast states have lost population.[43] Such population shifts interest marketers because people in different regions buy differently. For example, people in the Midwest buy more winter clothing than people in the Southeast. On a smaller scale, regional movements of population are also observed in other developed countries.

In most developed countries, the shift in where people live has also often caused a shift in where they work. For example, the migration toward suburban areas has resulted in a rapid increase in the number of people who 'telecommute' – work at home or in a remote office and conduct their business by phone, fax, modem or the Internet. This trend, in turn, has created a booming small office/home office market. An increasing number of people are working from home with the help of electronic conveniences such as PCs, smartphones and broadband Internet access. In the US, for example, one recent study estimates that more than half of American businesses now support some kind of telecommuting programme, and 5.9 million Americans work solely from home.[44]

Many marketers are actively courting the lucrative telecommuting market. For example, WebEx, the Web-conferencing division of Cisco, helps overcome the isolation that often accompanies telecommuting. With WebEx, people can meet and collaborate online via computer or smartphone, no matter what their work location. 'All you need to run effective online meetings is a browser and a phone,' says the company. With WebEx, people working anywhere can interact with other individuals or small groups to make presentations, exchange documents, and share desktops, complete with audio and full-motion video.[45]

Interestingly, this kind of population move is no longer restricted to the developed countries. By 2012, more of the Chinese population lived in cities than in rural locations, making it a predominantly urban population for the first time in the country's history. In 1949, urban dwellers accounted for only 10 per cent of China's population, but in 2012 that proportion exceeded 50 per cent.[46]

As population changes develop, successful marketers will continue to diversify their marketing programmes to take advantage of opportunities in fast-growing segments.

AUTHOR COMMENT

The economic environment can offer both opportunities and threats. For example, the recent economic downturn took a big bite out of Apple's sales growth and stock performance. Premium products such as iPhones and iPads are often hardest hit in troubled economic times. Said Apple's CEO, 'Our stock was being buffeted by factors much larger than ourselves.'

The economic environment

Economic environment— Economic factors that affect consumer purchasing power and spending patterns.

Markets require buying power as well as people. The **economic environment** consists of economic factors that affect consumer purchasing power and spending patterns. Marketers must pay close attention to major trends and consumer spending patterns both across and within their world markets.

The changing world order

Nations vary greatly in their levels and distribution of income. Some countries have *industrial economies*, which constitute rich markets for many different kinds of goods. At the other extreme are *subsistence economies*; they consume most of their own agricultural and industrial output and may offer few immediate market opportunities. In between are *developing economies* that can offer outstanding marketing opportunities for the right kinds of products.

However, it is also important to understand that the economic world order has been subject to important and major changes in the twenty-first century, particularly regarding the impact of emerging markets like India and China. The term 'BRIC' (Brazil, Russia, India, China) is often used to describe the leading group of newly-rich and rapidly expanding countries, but in reality the group is much larger than this and their characteristics are increasingly shared by countries like South Africa, Indonesia, Mexico and others. Interestingly, the degree of change is illustrated by the fact that there are now more individuals who are dollar-billionaires in the BRIC countries than there are in Europe.[47] Nonetheless, the paradox is that while the BRIC countries will soon contribute more than half the world's growth, relative to population, they remain poor: 2014 estimates are that GDP per capita in 2014 in the BRIC countries will be €6,819, compared to €35,708 in the G7 countries.[48]

The impact of economic change at this level should not be underestimated. Recent years have seen an end to western dominance of the global economy. Statistics in 2012 from the Centre for Economics and Business Research in London show China passing Japan and poised to overtake the United States to lead the world economic league, while in sixth place Brazil has overtaken the UK on that list. The same study suggests that by 2020, no European economy will be in the world top 20. Interestingly, history repeats itself – the US reign as largest world economic power began a little before 1890, when it supplanted the previous global giant: China. Throughout the 2000s the annual real growth in China's gross domestic product averaged 10.5 per cent compared to 1.7 per cent in the US in the same period, although some economists are sceptical about China's ability to maintain this rate of growth.[49] Nonetheless, by 2010, China was exporting as much every six hours as it did in the whole of 1978.[50] Economic change of this magnitude has clear implications for consumer buying power – millions of Chinese are entering the 'consumer class' for the first time.[51]

For example, it is estimated that by 2015, the top five grocery markets in the world, in order of value, will be: China, the US, India, Russia and Brazil, with the US showing lower growth than the others. Correspondingly, the five largest worldwide grocery retailers (Walmart, Carrefour, Tesco, CostCo and Metro) – two American and three European companies – are looking for aggressive growth strategies in these high-growth, expanding markets, while defending their home market position. Nonetheless, these are fiercely competitive markets for international retailers to tackle and success in the home market does not guarantee success in these emerging markets.[52]

Economic environment: to capture India's growing middle class, Tata Motors introduced the small, affordable Tata Nano. 'Can you imagine a car within the reach of all?' asks this advertisement. 'Now you can'.

Source: Tata Motors Ltd.

The impact of economic change and new patterns of globalisation are disrupting and reshaping whole industrial sectors. For example, in the automotive sector, long dominated by US and Japanese manufacturers, Fiat from Italy holds the controlling ownership of US car giant Chrysler,[53] Volkswagen in Germany has overtaken Toyota and General Motors in vehicle sales to lead the sector[54] and the world's cheapest car is the Nano produced by Tata Motors in India, selling for around €1,560 and with ambitions to tap into the European and US markets.[55]

Changes in consumer spending

Importantly, economic factors can have a dramatic effect on consumer spending and buying behaviour. For example, until fairly recently, American and European consumers spent freely, fuelled by income growth, easily-available credit, a boom in the investment market, rapid increases in house values and other economic good fortune. They bought and bought, seemingly without caution, amassing record levels of debt. However, the free spending and high expectations of those days were dashed by the economic downturn, credit squeeze and recession of the late 2000s and early 2010s. Says one economist, 'For a generation that . . . substituted rising home equity and stock prices for personal savings, the . . . economic meltdown [was] psychologically wrenching after a quarter century of unquestioned prosperity.'[56] In contrast, having led the way in voluntary reduction of spending deficits, the UK has entered a period of extreme austerity and is looking at a prolonged period of economic near-stagnation and high unemployment numbers.[57]

As a result, as discussed in Chapter 1, consumers have now adopted a back-to-basics frugality in their lifestyles and spending patterns that is likely to persist for years to come. They are buying less and looking for greater value in the things that they do buy. In turn, *value marketing* has become the watchword for many marketers. Marketers in all industries are looking for ways to offer today's more financially cautious buyers greater value – the right combination of product quality and good service at a fair price.

Nonetheless, in many markets in the western world the new 'normal' for consumers has become one of thrift and caution in spending, and a new 'age of austerity'. Shoppers are suffering from what Bain & Co. are calling 'luxury shame', and feeling guilty about buying indulgences. Add to this a scepticism and lack of trust in business, and the potential is for long-term shifts in consumer behaviour away from consumption towards austerity.[58] The 'Great Recession' may be followed by the 'New Caution', changing spending habits and lowering future growth.[59]

Nonetheless, some companies have prospered in harsher economic conditions. Budget retailers like Aldi and Lidl in the UK and Walmart and Dollar General in the US have been successful in growing business during economic downturn, with the intention of retaining the new customers they have acquired from more expensive competitors.[60] Successful marketing strategies in this new reality will depend on a deep understanding of how economic conditions have influenced consumer choices.

Income distribution

Marketers should pay attention to *income distribution* as well as income levels. For example, key to understanding demand in emerging markets like India and China is the growth of an affluent middle class with high disposable income and the willingness to spend. Nonetheless, while growing affluence characterises the emerging markets and provides important targets, for example for luxury brands like high-end motor cars and fashion clothing, this affluence tends to be concentrated in a relatively small proportion of the population. There are also major differences between different emerging markets.

For example, China's new wealthy are an attractive target for luxury brands like Versace, LVMH, Cartier and Coach, because the country has a rapidly growing number of affluent people. Luxury property, furnishings and luxury cars dominate the spending profiles of China's new rich. Not only are their purchase priorities different to those of the wealthy in other markets, they are much younger.[61] However, China also has the largest income gap between rich and poor – it appears that with high economic growth, the rich are getting richer faster than the poor, increasing income inequality. Even so, the poor of China are substantially better off than the poor of India.[62]

China's new wealthy consumers with high disposable income and a willingness to spend are an attractive target for luxury brands.

Source: Alamy Images/ Lou Linwei

Changes in major economic variables, such as income, cost of living, interest rates, and savings and borrowing patterns, have a large impact on the marketplace. Companies watch these variables by using economic forecasting. Businesses do not have to be wiped out by an economic downturn or caught short in a boom. With adequate warning, they can take advantage of changes in the economic environment.

AUTHOR COMMENT

Today's enlightened companies are developing *environmentally sustainable* strategies in an effort to create a world economy that the planet can support indefinitely.

The natural environment

The **natural environment** involves the natural resources that are needed as inputs by marketers or that are affected by marketing activities. Environmental concerns have grown steadily over the past three decades. In many cities around the world, air and water pollution have reached dangerous levels. World concern continues to mount about the possibilities of global warming, and many environmentalists fear that we will soon be buried in our own rubbish.

Marketers should be aware of several trends in the natural environment. The first involves growing shortages of raw materials. Air and water may seem to be infinite resources, but some groups see long-term dangers. Air pollution chokes many of the world's large cities, and water shortages are already a big problem in some parts of the world. By 2030, more than one in three of the world's population will not have enough water to drink.[63] Renewable resources, such as forests and food, also have to be used wisely. Non-renewable resources, such as oil, coal and various minerals, pose a serious problem. Firms making products that require these scarce resources face large cost increases, even if the materials remain available.

Natural environment— Natural resources that are needed as inputs by marketers or that are affected by marketing activities.

89

A second environmental trend is *increased pollution*. Industry will almost always damage the quality of the natural environment. Consider the disposal of chemical and nuclear waste; the dangerous mercury levels in the ocean; the quantity of chemical pollutants in the soil and food supply; and the littering of the environment with non-biodegradable bottles, plastics and other packaging materials.

A third trend is *increased government intervention* in natural resource management. The governments of different countries vary in their concern and efforts to promote a clean environment. Some, such as the German government, vigorously pursue environmental quality policies and sanctions. Others, especially many poorer nations, do little about pollution, largely because they lack the needed funds or political will. Even richer nations lack the vast funds and political accord needed to mount a worldwide environmental effort. The general hope is that companies around the world will accept more social responsibility and that less expensive methods can be found to control and reduce pollution.

In many countries business faces increased regulation and pressure from lobby groups to behave more responsibly towards the natural environment. Instead of opposing regulation, marketers should help develop solutions to the material and energy problems facing the world.

Concern for the natural environment has spawned the so-called 'green movement'. Today, enlightened companies go beyond what government regulations dictate. They are developing strategies and practices that support **environmental sustainability** – an effort to create a world economy that the planet can support indefinitely. They are responding to consumer demands with more environmentally responsible products.

For example, GE is using its 'ecomagination' to create products for a better world – cleaner aircraft engines, cleaner locomotives, cleaner fuel technologies. And in 2005, GE launched its Evolution series locomotives, diesel engines that cut fuel consumption by 5 per cent and emissions by 40 per cent compared to locomotives built just a year earlier. Up next is a triumph of sheer coolness: a GE hybrid diesel-electric locomotive that, just like a Prius, captures energy from braking and will reduce fuel consumption by 15 per cent and emissions by as much as 50 per cent compared to most locomotives in use today.[64]

Other companies are developing recyclable or biodegradable packaging, recycled materials and components, better pollution controls, and more energy-efficient operations. For example, companies like PepsiCo and Coca-Cola are working to dramatically reduce their environmental footprints, particularly regarding water use.

> For example, PepsiCo markets hundreds of drinks and snacks products which are grown, manufactured and consumed throughout the world. Clearing, producing and distributing products like these consumes large quantities of scarce resources like water, electricity and fuel. PepsiCo set itself the goal in 2007 to reduce water use by 20 per cent, electricity consumption by 20 per cent and fuel consumption by 25 per cent, per unit of production, by 2015. In fact, the company is well on its way to achieving these goals. In one case, a solar-panel field generates the power for three quarters of the heat used in PepsiCo's plant in Modesto, California. On the other side of the world, wind turbines contribute more than two-thirds of the power needed at PepsiCo's drinks business in Mamandur, India. As far as packaging goes, the company recently introduced new half-litre bottles for many of its drinks, which it claims use 20 per cent less plastic than did the original packaging. PepsiCo boasts that its Aquafina product has trimmed the amount of plastic used in its bottles by 35 per cent since 2002, saving 50 million pounds of plastic annually.[65]

Companies today are looking to do more than just good deeds. More and more, they are recognising the link between a healthy ecology and a healthy economy. They are learning that environmentally responsible actions can also be good business.

The pivotal issue is the alignment between environmental issues and customer perceptions of value. For example, the car manufacturing business has been under pressure to respond to environmental concerns, and has done so. *Hybrid* vehicles (combining electric and conventional fuel-powered engines) like the Toyota Prius are growing in popularity to some extent but still account for less than 3 per cent of the global car market, because of their high price compared to conventional cars. *Electric* vehicles are now being developed by most large car groups – Nissan's new Leaf will be made in Sunderland from 2013 – but car manufacturers admit their limited ranges and

Environmental sustainability—Developing strategies and practices that create a world economy that the planet can support indefinitely.

higher prices will restrict sales. *Biofuels* to power cars have lost support because of environmental concerns on how the fuel is produced – though many big car manufacturers have cars that run on biofuels, and those that run on ethanol are a big market segment in sugar-rich Brazil. *Hydrogen fuel* cells have great future promise because they have zero exhaust emissions and can cover long distances – but there are environmental problems in producing the fuel and refuelling stations are expensive, limiting the number of vehicles likely to be sold. In fact, *engine downsizing* is one of the most cost-effective ways of cutting emissions, although lacking the glamour of new technologies – the UK government supported Ford's recent investment in a new generation of fuel-efficient engines to be made in Britain. Nonetheless, by 2012, sales of electric cars had been so poor, there were more charging points in the UK than there were electric cars on the road, in spite of a government scheme offering grants towards the purchase of electric cars.[66]

Marketers face the important challenge of developing and implementing environmentally responsible products and ways of doing business, while at the same time focusing on customer needs and preferences. It is important to identify the link between socially responsible business practices and the creation of superior customer value.[67]

Electric vehicles are being developed by most large car companies. The Nissan leaf starts production in Sunderland from 2013.

Source: Getty Images/AFP

AUTHOR COMMENT

Technological advances are perhaps the most dramatic forces affecting today's marketing strategies. Just think about the tremendous impact of the Web – which emerged in the mid-1990s – on marketing. You'll see examples of the fast-growing world of online marketing throughout every chapter, and we'll discuss it in detail in Chapter 17.

The technological environment

The **technological environment** is perhaps the most dramatic force now shaping our destiny. Technology has released such wonders as antibiotics, robotic surgery, miniaturised electronics, smartphones and the Internet. It also has released such horrors as nuclear missiles, chemical weapons, and assault rifles. And it has released such mixed blessings as the motor car, television and credit cards. Our attitude toward technology depends on whether we are more impressed with its wonders or its blunders.

New technologies can offer exciting opportunities for marketers. For example, what would you think about having tiny little transmitters implanted in all the products you buy, which would allow tracking of the products from their point of production through use and disposal? On the one hand, it would provide many advantages to both buyers and sellers. On the other hand, it could be a bit scary. Either way, it's already happening:

> Envision a world in which every product contains a tiny transmitter, loaded with information. As you stroll through supermarket aisles, shelf sensors detect your selections and beam ads to your shopping cart screen, offering special deals on related products. As your cart fills, scanners detect that you might be buying for a dinner party; the screen suggests a wine to go with the meal you've planned. When you leave the store, exit scanners total up your purchases and automatically charge them to your credit card. At home, readers track what goes into and out of your pantry, updating your shopping list when stocks run low. For Sunday dinner, you pop a turkey into your 'smart oven', which follows instructions from an embedded chip and cooks the meat to perfection. Seem far-fetched? Not really. In fact, it might soon become a reality, thanks to radio-frequency identification (RFID) transmitters that can be embedded in the products you buy.

Technological environment—Forces that create new technologies, creating new product and market opportunities.

RFID technology allows firms to track products through the stages of the distribution channel.

Source: Getty Images/David Hecker

Many firms are already using RFID technology to track products through various points in the distribution channel. For example, in the US, Walmart has strongly encouraged suppliers shipping products to its distribution centres to apply RFID tags to their pallets. So far, more than 600 Walmart suppliers are doing so. Clothing retailer American Apparel uses RFID to manage inventory in many of its retail stores. Every stocked item carries an RFID tag, which is scanned at the receiving docks as the item goes into inventory. American Apparel puts only one of each item on the store floor at a time. When the item is sold, a point-of-sale RFID reader alerts the inventory system and prompts employees to bring a replacement onto the floor. Another RFID reader located between the stockroom and the store floor checks to see that this was done. In all, the system creates inventory efficiencies and ensures that the right items are always on the sales floor. As a result, American Apparel stores with RFID systems average 14 per cent higher sales but 15 per cent lower stock levels than other stores. And the chain's RFID stores require 20–30 per cent fewer staff because employees don't have to spend five or more hours a day doing manual inventory checks.[68]

The technological environment changes rapidly. Think of all of today's common products that were not available until recently. Two hundred years ago, people did not know about motor cars, airplanes, radios or the electric light. A hundred years ago, no-one knew about television, aerosol cans, automatic dishwashers, air conditioners, antibiotics or computers. Seventy-five years ago, people did not know about photocopying, synthetic detergents, birth control pills, jet engines or earth satellites. Fifty years ago, people did not know about PCs, mobile phones, the Internet or Google.

New technologies create new markets and opportunities. However, every new technology replaces an older technology. Transistors hurt the vacuum-tube industry, CDs hurt conventional vinyl records, and digital photography hurt the film and camera business. When old industries fought or ignored new technologies, their businesses declined. Thus, marketers should watch the technological environment closely. Companies that do not keep up will soon find their products outdated. And they will miss new product and market opportunities.

Scientists today are researching a wide range of promising new products and services, ranging from practical solar energy, electric cars, and paint-on computer and entertainment video displays, to powerful computers that you can wear or fold into your pocket. The results are sometimes surprising – biotech GW Pharmaceuticals is in strange position of growing 20 tonnes of cannabis a year with government approval. From a plant usually known for its illicit use, GW is developing a family of medicines to treat conditions such as multiple sclerosis.[69]

Today's research usually is carried out by research teams rather than by lone inventors like Thomas Edison or Alexander Graham Bell. Many companies are adding marketing people to R&D teams to try to obtain a stronger marketing orientation. Scientists also speculate on fantasy products, such as flying cars and space colonies. The challenge in each case is not only technical but also commercial – to make *practical, affordable* versions of these products.

Naturally, as products and technology become more complex, the public needs to know that these are safe. Many countries have created agencies and complex regulations to ban potentially unsafe products, and to establish safety standards for consumer products and penalise companies that fail to meet them. This growing regulation has resulted in higher research and development costs and longer times between new product ideas and their introduction. Marketers should be aware of these regulations when applying new technologies and developing new products.

AUTHOR COMMENT

Even the most liberal free-market advocates agree that the system works best with at least some regulation. But beyond regulation, most companies *want* to be socially responsible. If you look at almost any company's website, you'll find long lists of good deeds and environmentally responsible actions. For example, check out the Nike Responsibility page (www.nikebiz.com/responsibility). We'll dig deeper into marketing and social responsibility in Chapter 20.

The political and social environment

Marketing decisions are strongly affected by developments in the political environment. The **political environment** consists of laws, government agencies and pressure groups that influence or limit various organisations and individuals in a given society.

Political environment—Laws, government agencies and pressure groups that influence and limit various organisations and individuals in a given society.

Legislation regulating business

Even the most liberal advocates of free-market economies agree that the system works best with at least some regulation. Well-conceived regulation can encourage competition and ensure fair markets for goods and services. Thus, governments develop *public policy* to guide commerce – sets of laws and regulations that limit business for the good of society as a whole – and may go further in exerting influence over business actions. Almost every marketing activity is subject to a wide range of laws, regulations and government influence.

Increasing legislation

Legislation affecting business around the world has increased steadily over the years. Many countries now have a large number of laws covering issues such as competition, fair trade practices, environmental protection, product safety, truth in advertising, consumer privacy, packaging and labelling, pricing and other important areas. For example, the European Commission has been active in establishing a new framework of laws covering competitive behaviour, product standards, product liability and commercial transactions for the nations of the European Union, in addition to those countries' own legislation.

Understanding the public policy implications of a particular marketing activity is not a simple matter. Moreover, regulations are constantly changing; what was allowed last year may now be prohibited, and what was prohibited may now be allowed. Marketers must work hard to keep up with changes in regulations and their interpretations.

Business legislation has been enacted for a number of reasons. The first is to *protect companies* from each other. Although business executives may praise competition, they sometimes try to neutralise it when it threatens them. So laws are passed to define and prevent unfair competition.

The second purpose of government regulation is to *protect consumers* from unfair business practices. Some firms, if left alone, would make shoddy products, invade consumer privacy, mislead consumers in their advertising, and deceive consumers through their packaging and pricing. Unfair business practices have been defined and regulations are enforced by various agencies.

The third purpose of government regulation is to *protect the interests of society* against unrestrained business behaviour. Profitable business activity does not always create a better quality of life. Regulation arises to ensure that firms take responsibility for the social costs of their production or products.

New laws and their enforcement will continue to increase. International marketers will encounter dozens, or even hundreds, of agencies created to enforce trade policies and regulations. Business executives must watch these developments when planning their products and marketing programmes. Marketers need to know about the major laws protecting competition, consumers and society. They need to understand these laws at national and international levels.

For example, Ikea in Sweden is keen to develop its furnishings business in India. In spite of local political controversy, after much wavering the Indian government has recently decided to allow foreign retailers to enter the country. The potential of a booming Indian market is attractive to many global retailers, including Ikea. Indeed, Mikael Ohlsson, Ikea's chief executive, told the press he had been dreaming of selling flat-pack furniture to India's rising middle class. However, in spite of New Delhi rapidly moving to open its market to foreign retailers for the first time, Ikea's strategy has stalled. The barrier is India's legal requirements for single-brand retailers to source 30 per cent of their goods from local small and medium-sized companies in India.[70]

Government influence over business

In addition to legislation, governments throughout the world frequently act to control business behaviour through influence and negotiation, and sometimes direct action.

For example, BP leads a joint venture in Russia – TNK-BP – jointly with a quartet of powerful Russian oligarchs, which accounts for a quarter of BP's worldwide oil reserves. The joint venture has been characterised by conflict, friction and a struggle for control. Disputes came to a head in 2008, when the TNK-BP CEO – Robert Dudley – had to flee Moscow and run the business from a secret location for several months, following harassment by the Russian authorities and the threat of imprisonment. Dudley misinterpreted complex Kremlin politics and underestimated the influence of his oligarch partners. Powerful figures in the Russian government appear willing to use police and intelligence services to enforce their will over business.[71]

In a completely different sector, Google pulled its Web-search engine out of China in 2010, after a very public confrontation with the Chinese government over censorship, after Google computer code was stolen by hackers and attempts were made to spy on Chinese political activists' Gmail accounts. Google took the view that it would rather pull out of the Chinese market than censor Internet-search results. Google's dilemma is that it cannot afford to miss out on the world's largest Internet market, and is trying to win over consumers with services which do not attract official censorship.[72]

International marketers, in particular, need to stay close to the ways in which foreign governments operate to control and influence business within their borders, and sometimes make hard choices.

Increased emphasis on ethics and socially responsible actions

Written regulations cannot possibly cover all potential marketing abuses, and existing laws are often difficult to enforce. However, beyond written laws and regulations, business is also governed by social codes and rules of professional ethics.

Socially responsible behaviour

Enlightened companies encourage their managers to look beyond what the regulatory system allows and simply 'do the right thing'. These socially responsible firms actively seek out ways to protect the long-run interests of their consumers and the environment.

The recent rash of business scandals and increased concerns about the environment have created fresh interest in the issues of ethics and social responsibility. Almost every aspect of marketing involves such issues. Unfortunately, because these issues usually involve conflicting interests, well-meaning people can honestly disagree about the right course of action in a given situation. Thus, many industrial and professional trade associations have suggested codes of ethics. And more companies are now developing policies, guidelines and other responses to complex social responsibility issues.

The boom in Internet marketing has created a new set of social and ethical issues. Critics worry most about online privacy issues. There has been an explosion in the amount of personal digital data available. Users, themselves, supply some of it. They voluntarily place highly private information on social-networking sites, such as Facebook or LinkedIn, or on genealogy sites that are easily searched by anyone with a computer or a smartphone.

However, much of the information is systematically developed by businesses seeking to learn more about their customers, often without consumers realising that they are under the microscope. Legitimate businesses plant cookies on consumers' PCs and collect, analyse and share digital data from every move consumers make at their websites. Critics are concerned that companies may now know *too* much and might use digital data to take unfair advantage of consumers. Although most companies fully disclose their Internet privacy policies and most work to use data to benefit their customers, abuses do occur. As a result, consumer advocates and policymakers are taking action to protect consumer privacy. In Chapter 20, we discuss these and other societal marketing issues in greater depth.

Cause-related marketing

To exercise their social responsibility and build more positive images, many companies are now linking themselves to worthwhile causes.

In fact, some companies are founded entirely on cause-related missions. Under the concept of 'value-led business' or 'caring capitalism', their mission is to use business to make the world a better place.

Cause-related marketing has become a primary form of corporate giving. It lets companies 'do well by doing good' by linking purchases of the company's products or services with fund-raising for worthwhile causes or charitable organisations. Companies now sponsor dozens of cause-related marketing campaigns each year. Many are backed by large budgets and a full complement of marketing activities.

Cause-related marketing has stirred some controversy. Critics worry that cause-related marketing is more a strategy for selling than a strategy for giving – that 'cause-related' marketing is really 'cause-exploitative' marketing. Thus, companies using cause-related marketing might find themselves walking a fine line between increased sales and an improved image and facing charges of exploitation.

However, if handled well, cause-related marketing can greatly benefit both the company and the cause. The company gains an effective marketing tool while building a more positive public image. The charitable organisation or cause gains greater visibility and important new sources of funding and support.

AUTHOR COMMENT
Cultural factors strongly affect how people think and how they consume. So marketers are keenly interested in the cultural environment.

The cultural environment

The **cultural environment** consists of institutions and other forces that affect a society's basic values, perceptions, preferences and behaviours. People grow up in a particular society that shapes their basic beliefs and values. They absorb a worldview that defines their relationships with others. The following cultural characteristics can affect marketing decision making.

*Cultural environment—
Instructions and other forces that affect society's basic values, perceptions, preference and behaviour.*

The persistence of cultural values

People in a given society hold many beliefs and values. Their core beliefs and values have a high degree of persistence. These beliefs shape more specific attitudes and behaviour found in everyday life. *Core* beliefs and values are passed on from parents to children and are reinforced by schools, churches, business and government.

Secondary beliefs and values are more open to change. Believing in marriage is a core belief; believing that people should get married early in life is a secondary belief. Marketers have some chance of changing secondary values but little chance of changing core values.

Shifts in secondary cultural values

Although core values are fairly persistent, cultural swings do take place. Consider the impact of popular music groups, film personalities, and other celebrities on young people's hairstyling and clothing norms. Marketers want to predict cultural shifts to spot new opportunities or threats. Several firms offer 'futures' forecasts in this connection. For example, the Yankelovich Monitor has tracked consumer value trends for years. Its annual State of the Consumer report analyses and interprets the forces that shape consumers' lifestyles and their marketplace interactions. The major cultural values of a society are expressed in people's views of themselves and others, as well as in their views of organisations, society, nature and the universe.

People's views of themselves

People vary in their emphasis on serving themselves versus serving others. Some people seek personal pleasure, wanting fun, change and escape. Others seek self-realisation through religion, recreation or the avid pursuit of careers or other life goals. Some people see themselves as sharers and joiners; others see themselves as individualists. People use products, brands and services as a means of self-expression, and they buy products and services that match their views of themselves. Marketers can target their products and services based on such self-views.

People's views of others

In past decades, observers have noted several shifts in people's attitudes toward others. Recently, for example, many trend trackers have seen a new wave of 'cocooning' or 'nesting'. Due in part to the uncertain economy, people are going out less with others and are staying home more. One observer calls it 'Cocooning 2.0', in which people are 'newly intent on the simple pleasures of hearth and home'. Says another, 'The instability of the economy . . . creates uncertainty for consumers, and this uncertainty tends to make them focus more on being home and finding ways to save money. It's a return to more traditional values, like home-cooked meals.'[73]

For example, the weaker economy of the past few years and increased nesting have given a boost to sales of home appliances, such as high-end coffee makers and big-screen TVs and other home entertainment products and services.

People's views of organisations

People vary in their attitudes toward corporations, government agencies, trade unions, universities and other organisations. By and large, people are willing to work for major organisations and expect them, in turn, to carry out society's work.

The past two decades have seen a sharp decrease in confidence in and loyalty toward business and political organisations and institutions in many of the developed countries. In the workplace, there has been an overall decline in organisational loyalty. Waves of company downsizings have bred cynicism and distrust. In just the last decade, rounds of redundancies resulting from the economic downturn and recession, major corporate scandals, the financial meltdown triggered by bankers' greed and incompetence, and other unsettling activities have resulted in a further loss of confidence in big business. Many people today see work not as a source of satisfaction but as a required chore to earn money to enjoy their non-work hours. This trend suggests that organisations need to find new ways to win consumer and employee confidence.

People's views of society

People vary in their attitudes toward their society; patriots defend it, reformers want to change it and malcontents want to leave it. People's orientation to their society influences their consumption patterns and attitudes toward the marketplace.

People's views of nature

People vary in their attitudes toward the natural world; some feel ruled by it, others feel in harmony with it and still others seek to master it. A long-term trend has been people's growing mastery over nature through technology and the belief that nature is bountiful. More recently, however, people have recognised that nature is finite and fragile; it can be destroyed or spoiled by human activities.

This renewed love of things natural has, for example in the United States, created a 63-million-person 'lifestyles of health and sustainability' market, consumers who seek out everything from natural, organic and nutritional products to fuel-efficient cars and alternative medicine. This segment spends nearly $300 billion annually on such products. In the green building market alone, consumers spent $100 billion in 2008 on items such as certified homes, solar systems and Energy Star appliances.[74]

Food producers have also found fast-growing markets for natural and organic products. It is interesting that even after severe economic downturn in the UK, research suggests that sales of ethical goods continue to rise – it seems British consumers refuse to sacrifice principle for price or convenience. This growth is sustained in part by the conversion of many brands like Cadbury's chocolate and Nestle's Kit Kat bars to Fair Trade – guaranteeing minimum price and conditions for producers in emerging markets.[75]

People's views of the universe

Finally, people vary in their beliefs about the origin of the universe and their place in it. Although many people are dropping out of organised religion in the west, it doesn't mean that they are abandoning their faith. Some futurists have noted a renewed interest in spirituality, perhaps as a part of a broader search for a new inner purpose. People have been moving away from materialism and dog-eat-dog ambition to seek more permanent values – family, community, Earth, faith – and a more certain grasp of right and wrong. This changing spiritualism affects consumers in everything from the television shows they watch and the books they read to the products and services they buy.

AUTHOR COMMENT
Rather than simply watching and reacting, companies should take proactive steps with respect to the marketing environment.

RESPONDING TO THE MARKETING ENVIRONMENT

Someone once observed, 'There are three kinds of companies: those who make things happen, those who watch things happen, and those who wonder what's happened.' Many companies view the marketing environment as an uncontrollable element to which they must react and adapt. They passively accept the marketing environment and do not try to change it. They analyse environmental forces and design strategies that will help the company avoid the threats and take advantage of the opportunities the environment provides.

Other companies take a *proactive* stance toward the marketing environment. 'Instead of letting the environment define their strategy,' advises one marketing expert, 'craft a strategy that defines your environment.'[76] Rather than assuming that strategic options are bounded by the current environment, these firms develop strategies to change the environment. 'Business history . . . reveals plenty of cases in which firms' strategies shape industry structure,' says the expert, 'from Ford's Model T to Nintendo's Wii.'

Even more, rather than simply watching and reacting to environmental events, these firms take aggressive actions to affect the publics and forces in their marketing environment. Such companies hire lobbyists to influence legislation affecting their industries and stage media events to gain favourable press coverage. They run 'advertorials' (ads expressing editorial points of view) to shape public opinion. They press lawsuits and file complaints with regulators to keep competitors in line, and they form contractual agreements to better control their distribution channels.

By taking action, companies can often overcome seemingly uncontrollable environmental events. For example, whereas some companies view the seemingly ceaseless online rumour mill as something over which they have no control, others work proactively to prevent or counter negative word of mouth.

Marketing management cannot always control environmental forces. In many cases, it must settle for simply watching and reacting to the environment. For example, a company would have little success trying to influence geographic population shifts, the economic environment, or major cultural values. But whenever possible, smart marketing managers will take a *proactive* rather than *reactive* approach to the marketing environment.

For example, in 2012, fast-food company McDonald's faced the wrath of critics who turned the chain's own Twitter campaign against it, unleashing a torrent of abusive tweets in an example of how social media marketing can backfire with modern consumers. McDonald's posted two 'promoted tweets' on Twitter's new advertising system to encourage happy customers to share their 'McStories' on the messaging site. The link was hijacked by less-than-satisfied diners, who used Twitter to vent claims of food-poisoning incidents and allegations of low standards of employee and animal welfare at the restaurant group. The volume of negative stories forced McDonald's to abandon the campaign. Social media campaigns have to have contingency plans for when the conversation does not go as planned.[77]

REVIEWING OBJECTIVES AND KEY TERMS

In this chapter and the next three chapters, you'll examine the environments of marketing and how companies analyse these environments to better understand the marketplace and consumers. Companies must constantly watch and manage the *marketing environment* to seek opportunities and ward off threats. The marketing environment consists of all the actors and forces influencing the company's ability to transact business effectively with its target market.

OBJECTIVE 1 Describe the environmental forces that affect the company's ability to serve its customers (pp. 74–78).

The company's *microenvironment* consists of actors close to the company that combine to form its value delivery network or that affect its ability to serve its customers. It includes the company's *internal environment* – its several departments and management levels–as it influences marketing decision making. *Marketing channel firms* – suppliers and marketing intermediaries, including resellers, physical distribution firms, marketing services agencies and financial intermediaries – cooperate to create customer value. *Competitors* vie with the company in an effort to serve customers better. Various *publics* have an actual or potential interest in or impact on the company's ability to meet its objectives. Finally, five types of customer *markets* include consumer, business, reseller, government and international markets.

The *macroenvironment* consists of larger societal forces that affect the entire microenvironment. The six forces making up the company's macroenvironment include demographic, economic, natural, technological, political/social and cultural forces. These forces shape opportunities and pose threats to the company.

OBJECTIVE 2 Explain how changes in the demographic and economic environments affect marketing decisions (pp. 78–89).

Demography is the study of the characteristics of human populations. Today's *demographic environment* shows a changing age structure, shifting family profiles, geographic population shifts, a better-educated and more white-collar population, and increasing diversity. The *economic environment* consists of factors that affect buying power and patterns. The economic environment is characterised by more frugal consumers who are seeking greater value – the right combination of good

quality and service at a fair price. The distribution of income also is shifting. The rich have grown richer, the middle class has shrunk, and the poor have remained poor, leading to a two-tiered market in many countries.

OBJECTIVE 3 Identify the major trends in the firm's natural and technological environments (pp. 89–92).

The *natural environment* shows three major trends: shortages of certain raw materials, higher pollution levels and more government intervention in natural resource management. Environmental concerns create marketing opportunities for alert companies. The *technological environment* creates both opportunities and challenges. Companies that fail to keep up with technological change will miss out on new product and marketing opportunities.

OBJECTIVE 4 Explain the key changes in the political and cultural environments (pp. 93–97).

The *political environment* consists of laws, agencies and groups that influence or limit marketing actions. The political environment has undergone three changes that affect marketing worldwide: increasing legislation regulating business, strong government agency enforcement, and greater emphasis on ethics and socially responsible actions. The *cultural environment* consists of institutions and forces that affect a society's values, perceptions, preferences and behaviors. The environment shows trends toward 'cocooning', a lessening trust of institutions, increasing patriotism, greater appreciation for nature, a changing spiritualism, and the search for more meaningful and enduring values.

OBJECTIVE 5 Discuss how companies can react to the marketing environment (pp. 97–98).

Companies can passively accept the marketing environment as an uncontrollable element to which they must adapt, avoiding threats and taking advantage of opportunities as they arise. Or they can take a *proactive* stance, working to change the environment rather than simply reacting to it. Whenever possible, companies should try to be proactive rather than reactive.

NAVIGATING THE KEY TERMS

OBJECTIVE 1
Marketing environment (p. 74)
Microenvironment (p. 74)
Macroenvironment (p. 74)
Marketing intermediaries (p. 74)
Public (p. 77)

OBJECTIVE 2
Demography (p. 78)
Baby boomers (p. 80)
Generation X (p. 80)

Millennials (or Generation Y) (p. 81)
Economic environment (p. 86)

OBJECTIVE 3
Natural environment (p. 89)
Environmental sustainability (p. 90)
Technological environment (p. 91)

OBJECTIVE 4
Political environment (p. 93)
Cultural environment (p. 95)

DISCUSSING AND APPLYING THE CONCEPTS

Discussing the concepts

1. Describe the elements of a company's marketing environment and why marketers play a critical role in tracking environmental trends and spotting opportunities. (AACSB Communication: Reflective Thinking)

2. List some of the demographic trends of interest to marketers in a country of your choice and discuss whether these trends pose opportunities or threats for marketers. (AACSB: Communication: Reflective Thinking)

3. Discuss current trends in the economic environment that marketers must be aware of and provide examples of company responses to each trend. (AACSB Communication: Reflective Thinking)

4. Discuss trends in the natural environment that marketers must be aware of and provide examples of company responses to them. (AACSB Communication)

5. Compare and contrast core beliefs/values and secondary beliefs/values. Provide an example of each and discuss the potential impact marketers have on each. (AACSB: Communication Reflective Thinking)

6. Explain how companies can take a proactive stance toward the marketing environment. (AACSB Communication)

Applying the concepts

1. China and India are emerging markets that will have a significant impact on the world in coming years. The term *Chindia* is used to describe the growing power of these two countries. In a small group, research demographic and economic trends related to Chindia's power and its impact on marketers in Europe. Write a brief report, supporting your discussion of these trends with statistics. (AACSB: Communication: Reflective Thinking)

2. In a small group, search the Internet for European population distribution maps and create a PowerPoint presentation illustrating factors such as geographical population shifts, languages spoken, age distributions and ancestry. Discuss the demographic implications for marketers. (AACSB: Communication. Use of IT; Diversity)

3. Various governmental agencies impact marketing activities. Identify three important regulatory bodies in a European country of your choice and discuss the elements of marketing that are impacted by these agencies and present a recent marketing case or issue on which each agency has focused. (AACSB: Communication; Reflective Thinking)

Focus on technology

If you really want to identify the zeitgeist, or 'spirit of the times', look at the top websites visited, the top videos watched on YouTube, the top songs downloaded or the top Twitter feeds. Trends spotters such as Faith popcorn and Tom Peters have been mainstays for marketers trying to understand cultural trends, but the Internet is now the new crystal ball for anyone wanting to predict where society is going in real time. The World Mind Network provides a clearinghouse of links to 'top' lists at www. thetopeverything.net.In just a few minutes a day, you, too, can be up on what's hot in today's culture.

1. Visit www.thetopeverything.net and review the websites identified. What can you learn about culture and cultural trends from these sources? Write a brief report on your conclusions. (MCSB Communication: Use of IT; Reflective Thinking)

2. Do you think these sources accurately reflect cultural trends? Identify other websites that might be useful in learning about cultural trends. (AACSB: Communication; Use of IT; Reflective Thinking)

Focus on ethics

You've probably heard of some specific heart procedures, such as angioplasty and stents, that are routinely performed on adults. But such heart procedures, devices and related medications are not available for infants and children, despite the fact that almost 40,000 children are born in the United States each year with heart defects that often require repair. This is a life or death situation for many young patients, yet doctors must improvise by using devices designed and tested on adults. For instance, doctors use an adult kidney balloon in an infant's heart because it is the appropriate size for a newborn's aortic valve. However, this device is not approved for the procedure. Why are specific devices and medicines developed for the huge cardiovascular market not also designed for children's health care? It's a matter of economics; this segment of young consumers is just too small. One leading cardiologist attributed the discrepancy to a 'profitability gap' between the children's market and the much more profitable adult market for treating heart disease. Although this might make good economic sense for companies, it is little comfort to the parents of these small patients.

1. Discuss the environmental forces acting on medical device and pharmaceutical companies that are preventing them from meeting the needs of the infant and child market segment. Is it wrong for these companies to not address the needs of this segment? (AACSB: Communication: Reflective Thinking, Ethical Reasoning)

2. Suggest some solutions to this problem. (AACSB: Communication: Reflective Thinking)

Marketing & the economy
Netflix

Although the recent down economy has taken its toll on the retail industry as a whole, the stars are still shining on Netflix. Business

has been so good that Netflix met its most recent new subscriber goal weeks before the deadline. In early 2009, Netflix surpassed 10 million subscribers – a remarkable feat. Eighteen months later that number had grown by 50 per cent to 15 million subscribers. Clearly all these new customers are good for the company's financials. Customers are signing up for the same reasons they always have – the convenience of renting movies without leaving home, a selection of more than 100,000 DVD titles, and low monthly fees. But the company's current good fortunes may also be the result of consumers looking for less expensive means of entertainment. They may even be the result of consumers escaping the gloom of financial l losses and economic bad news. Whatever the case Netflix appears to have a product that thrives in bad times as well as in good.

1. Visit www.netflix.com. After browsing the website and becoming more familiar with the company's offerings assess the macroenvironmental trends that have led to Netflix's success in recent years.

2. Which trends do you think have contributed most to Netflix's current growth following recent economic woes?

Marketing by the numbers

Many marketing decisions boil down to numbers. An important question is this: What is the market sales potential in a given segment? If the sales potential in a market is not large enough to warrant pursuing that market, then companies will not offer products and services to that market, even though a need may exist. Consider the market segment of infants and children discussed above in Focus on ethics. Certainly there is a need for medical products to save children's lives. Still companies are not pursuing this market.

1. Using the chain ratio method described in Appendix 2, estimate the market sales potential for heart catheterisation products to meet the needs of the infant and child segment. Assume that of the 40,000 children with heart defects each year, 60 per cent will benefit from these types of products and only 50 per cent of their families have the financial resources to obtain such treatment. Also assume the average price for a device is €1,000. (AACSB Communication; Analytical Reasoning.)

2. Research the medical devices market and compare the market potential you estimated to the sales of various devices. Are companies justified in not pursuing the infant and child segment? (AACSB: Communication; Reflective Thinking)

REFERENCES

[1] Adapted from: Andrew Parker and Andrew Ward, 'Downwardly mobile', *Financial Times* (25 February 2011), p. 13; Andrew Hill and Andrew Parker, 'Nokia prepares for drop in market share', *Financial Times* (12 April 2011), p. 17, Richard Waters, 'Nokia and Microsoft talk up benefits of co-dependence', *Financial Times* (12 January 2012), p. 23.

[2] 'Copy this advice: Xerox's CEO says "let's get personal"', *Marketing News* (15 October 2008), pp. 18–19.

[3] Quotes and other information from Jeffery K. Liker and Thomas Y. Choi, 'Building deep supplier relationships,' *Harvard Business Review*, (December 2004), pp. 104–113; Lindsay Chappell, 'Toyota aims to satisfy its suppliers,' *Automotive News* (21 February 2005), p. 10; and David Hannon, 'Automotive rebrands procurement', *Purchasing* (11 March 2010), p. 45; and www.toyotasupplier.com, accessed August 2010.

[4] Andrea Felsted, 'All lined up', *Financial Times* (6 January 2012), p. 9.

[5] Information from Robert J. Benes, Abbie Jarman and Ashley Williams, '2007 NRA sets records', at www.chefmagazine.com, accessed September 2007; and www.thecoca-colacompany.com/presscenter/presskit_fs.html and www.cokesolutions.com, accessed August 2010.

[6] World POPClock, US Census Bureau, at www.census.gov, accessed August 2010. This website provides continuously updated projections of the US and world populations.

[7] The comments in this section of based on Robert Orr, 'Growing pains' in New Demographics, *Financial Times* (18 October 2011), p. 3.

[8] Andrew Jack, 'Seven billion and counting', in New Demographics, *Financial Times* (19 October 2011), pp. 8–11.

[9] James Lamont, 'Tiger, tiger, burning bright', in New Demographics, *Financial Times* (19 October 2011), pp. 13–15.

[10] The comments in this section are based on Gideon Rachman, 'Taking the long view on success', in New Demographics, *Financial Times* (19 October 2011), pp. 6–7.

[11] Rachman, 'Taking the long view on success'.

[12] See Clay Chandler, 'Little emperors,' *Fortune* (4 October 2004), pp. 138–150; 'China's "Little Emperors"', *Financial Times* (5 May 2007), p. 1, 'Me generation finally focuses on US', Chinadaily.com.cn (27 August 2008),www.chinadaily.com.cn/china/2008-08/27/content_6972930.htm; Melinda Varley, 'China: chasing the dragon', *Brand Strategy*, (6 October 2008), p. 26; Clifford Coonan, 'New rules to enforce China's one-child policy,' *Irish Times* (14 January 2009), p. 12; and David Pilling, 'Reflections of life in China's fast Lane', *Financial Times* (19 April 2010), p. 10.

[13] Adapted from information in Janet Adamy, 'Different brew: eyeing a billion tea drinkers, Starbucks pours it on in China', *Wall Street Journal* (29 November 2006), p. A1; and Justine Lau, 'Coffee, the new tea?', *Financial Times* (2 July 2010), p. 6.

[14] See Simon Hudson, 'Wooing zoomers: marketing to the mature traveler', *Marketing Intelligence & Planning*, **28** (4), 2010, pp. 444–461.

[15] Hudson, 'Wooing zoomers: marketing to the mature traveler'.

[16] Arlene Weintraub, *Selling the Fountain of Youth: How the Anti-Aging Industry Made a Disease Out of Getting Old – And Made Billions* (New York: Basic Books, 2010).

[17] Jonathan Birchall, 'Boom time', *Financial Times* (6 December 2007), p. 13.

[18] For more discussion, see R. K. Miller and Kelli Washington, *Consumer Behavior 2009* (Atlanta, GA: Richard K. Miller & Associates, 2009), chapter 27.

[19] R. K. Miller and Kelli Washington, *Consumer Behavior 2009*, ibid; and Piet Levy, 'The quest for cool', *Marketing News* (28 February 2009), p. 6.

[20] Jessica Tsai, 'Who, what, where whey, Y', *Customer Relationship Management* (November 2008), pp. 24-28; and John Austin, 'Automakers try to reach gen Y: carmakers look for new marketing approaches, technological advances to attract millennials', *McClatchy-Tribune Business News* (1 February 2009).

[21] Diane Brady, 'The reluctant breadwinners', *Bloomberg BusinessWeek* (27 September–3 October 2010), pp. 15–26.

[22] Michael J. Silverstein and Kate Sayre, 'The female economy', *Harvard Business Review* (September 2009), pp. 46–53.

[23] Michael J. Silverstein and Kate Sayre, *Women Want More: How to Capture Your Share of the World's Largest, Fastest-Growing Market* (New York: HarperCollins, 2009).

[24] Aaron O. Patrick, 'A slice of orange with your beer, madam?', *Wall Street Journal*, (15–17 August 2008), p. 27.

[25] Brad Wieners, 'Lego is for girls', *Bloomberg BusinessWeek* (19–25 December 2011), pp. 68–73.

[26] Andrew Taylor, 'Cost forces more young men to live with parents', *Financial Times* (16 April 2009), p. 3.

[27] Samantha Pearson, 'Children of the credit revolution', *Financial Times*, (9 July 2009), p. 14 Pan Kwan Yuk, "Youth pound" shows few signs of a slowdown', *Financial Times* (19–20 June 2010), p. 13.

[28] Steve Hamm, 'Children of the Web', *BusinessWeek* (2 July 2007), pp. 50–58.

[29] Chris Giles and Sarah Neville, 'Years of struggle for a jinxed generation', *Financial Times* (17/18 March 2012), p. 1.

[30] Daniel Pimlott, 'Business wake-up call on vanishing youth', *Financial Time*,(31 May 2010), p. 3; Stanley Reed, Carol Matlack, Dexter Roberts, Diane Brady and Caroline Winter, 'A Message', *Bloomberg BusinessWeek*; (7-14 February 2011), pp. 59–65; Peter Coy, 'The lost generation', *BusinessWeek*, (19 October 2009), pp. 33–35; Gideon Rachman, 'Taking the long view on success', in New Demographics, *Financial Times* (19 October 2011).

[31] Kelly Greene and Anne Tergesen, 'More elderly Americans find they have to keep working', *Wall Street Journal* (23 January 2012), pp. 12–13.

[32] James Crabtree, 'Colliding forces', in New Demographics, *Financial Times* (19 October 2011), pp. 40–43.

[33] Crabtree, 'Colliding forces', p. 42.

[34] Richard Boudreaux and Paulo Prada, 'Exodus of European workers reverses continent's patterns', *Wall Street Journal* (16 January 2012), pp. 12–13.

[35] Jack Grimston, 'British Muslims find things go better with Mecca', *Sunday Times* (19 January 2003), S1, p. 3.

[36] Matthew Hickley, 'Where whites will be a minority', *Daily Mail*, (24 December 2007), p. 6.

[37] Andrew Edgecliffe Johnson, 'Hispanic dawn breaks for US marketers', *Financial Times* (21 October 2010), p. 29; Jonathan Birchall, 'P&G taps into popularity of heavier scents', *Financial Times* (21 October 2010), p. 29.

[38] Andrew Edgecliffe-Johnson, 'Not yet wrapped up', *Financial Times* (8 September 2010), p. 11.

[39] Robert Gray, 'World of opportunity', *The Marketer* (November 2007), pp. 28–31.

[40] Katrina Burroughs, 'The pink niche', *Financial Times Weekend* (10/11 May 2008), p. 1.

[41] Deborah L. Vence, 'Divide & conquer', *Marketing News* (15 July 2007), pp. 15–18.

[42] Andrew Adam Newman, 'Web marketing to a segment too big to be a niche', *New York Times* (30 October 2007), p. 9; Kenneth Hein, 'The invisible demographic', *Brandweek* (3 March 2008), p. 20; and Tanya Mohn, 'Smoothing the way', *New York Times* (26 April 2010), www.nytimes.com.

[43] US Census Bureau, 'Geographical mobility/migration', at www.census.gov/population/www/socdemo/migrate.html, accessed April 2010.

[44] Jennifer Schramm, 'At work in the virtual world', *HRMagazine* (June 2010), p. 152; and Marcia Heroux Pounds, '$400 billion savings could result from telework, report says', *McClatchy-Tribune Business News* (19 May 2010).

[45] See 'About WebEx', at www.webex.com/about-webex/index.html, accessed August 2010.

[46] 'Chinese living in cities outnumber rural ones', *Wall Street Journal* (18 January 2012), p. 11.

[47] Alan Rappaport, 'Bric's billionaires outnumber Europe's', *Financial Times* (10 March 2011), p. 5.

[48] Alan Beattie, 'Changing faces of power: stars shine bright but fail to transform the world', *Financial Times* (18 January 2010), p. 8.

[49] Charles Kenny, 'The case for second place', *Bloomberg BusinessWeek* (17–23 October 2011). pp. 13–15.

[50] Tim Harford, 'China's rise will change the nuts and bolts of British industry', *FT Magazine* (19/20 June 2010), p. 13.

[51] Nicky Burridge, 'A red alert over china's growth', *Daily Mail* (29 December 2011), p. 73.

[52] Andrea Felsted, 'All lined up', *Financial Times* (6 January 2012), p. 9.

[53] John Reed, 'Fiat boosts stake in Chrysler after hitting target', *Financial Times* (6 January 2012), p. 19.

[54] Chris Bryant and John Reed, 'VW overtakes Toyota with record 8m sales', *Financial Times* (20 January 2012), p. 21.

[55] Paul Beckett and Santanu Choudhury, 'Tata chairman bemoans early Nano sales efforts', *Wall Street Journal* (6–8 January 2012), p. 21.

[56] Noreen O'Leary, 'Squeeze play', *Adweek* (12 January 2009), pp. 8–9. Also see Alessandra Stanley, 'For hard times, softer sells', *New York Times* (6 February 2009); and Kenneth Hein, 'Why price isn't everything', *Brandweek* (2 March 2009), p. 6.

[57] Chris Giles and Andrew Bounds, 'Brutal for Britain', *Financial Times* (16 January 2012), p. 9; Brian Groom, 'Rocky tome ahead as joblessness near 2.7m', *Financial Times* (19 January 2012), p. 3.

[58] Nigel F. Piercy, David W. Cravens and Nikala Lane, 'Marketing out of the recession: recovery is coming, but things will never be the same again', *The Marketing Review*, **10** (1), 2010, pp. 3–23.

[59] Daniel Yergin, 'A crisis in search of a narrative', *Financial Times* (21 October 2009), p. 13.

[60] Alastair Gray, 'Budget operators seek to secure customer retention', *Financial Times* (23 August 2008), p. 16.

[61] Kathrin Hille, Justine Lau and Patti Waldmeir, 'Scramble to slake China's thirst for high-end brands', *Financial Times* (10/11October 2009), p. 6.

[62] Richard McGregor, 'China's prosperity brings income gap', *Financial Times* (9 August 2009), p. 4.

[63] Andrew Zolli, 'Business 3.0', *Fast Company* (March 2007), pp. 64–70.

[64] See www.ge.com, and www.fastcompany.com/magazine/120/50ways-to-green-your-business.html, accessed May 2012.

[65] Facts from www.pepsico.com/Purpose/Environmental-Sustainability.html, accessed April 2010.

[66] John Reed, 'Hydrogen cells move to fast lane', *Financial Times* (18 January 2012), p. 4; James Gillespie, 'Spark goes out of electric car sales', *Sunday Times* (15 January 2012), S1, p. 15.

[67] Nigel F. Piercy and Nikala Lane, 'Corporate social responsibility', *The Marketing Review*, **9** (4), 2009, pp. 335–360. Nigel F. Piercy and Nikala Lane, 'Corporate social responsibility initiatives and strategic marketing perspectives', *Social Business*, **1** (4), 2011, pp. 325–345.

[68] See David Blanchard, 'The five stages of RFID', *Industry Week* (January 2009), p. 50; Mary Hayes Weier, 'Slow and steady progress', *InformationWeek* (16 November 2009), p. 31; and information at www.autoidlabs.org, accessed August 2010.

[69] Mark Wembridge, 'GW plans cannabis offshoots', *Financial Times* (29 December 2011), p. 17.

[70] Megha Bahree and Miguel Bustillo, 'Big retailers retool India plans', *Wall Street Journal* (12 December 2011), p. 22; James Fontanella-Khan and Andrea Felsted, 'India opens up to foreigners with limited retail reforms', *Financial Times* (11 January 2012) p. 17; James Lamont, 'Ikea shelves entry to India over rules on local sourcing', *Financial Times* (23 January 2012), p. 21.

[71] Danny Fortson, 'Torments of Bob Dudley', *Sunday Times* (17 April 2011), S3, p. 5.

[72] Amir Efrati and Loretta Chao, 'Google softens stance toward China', *Wall Street Journal* (13–15 January 2012), p. 13.

[73] Karen Von Hahn, 'Plus ça change: get set for Cocooning 2.0', *Globe and Mail* (Toronto) (3 January 2008), p. L1; and Liza N. Burby, 'Tips for making your home a cozy nest, or "Hive"', *Newsday* (23 January 2009), www.newsday.com.

[74] Sarah Mahoney, 'Report: LOHAS market nears $300 billion', *Marketing Daily* (26 April 2010), www.mediapost.com/publications/?art_aid=126836&fa=Articles.showArticle; and www.lohas.com, accessed August 2010.

[75] Andrew Bounds, 'Consumers stick with principle over price', *Financial Times* (15 December 2011), p. 4.

[76] W. Chan Kim and Renée Mauborgne, 'How strategy shaped structure', *Harvard Business Review* (September 2009), pp. 73–80.

[77] Tim Bradshaw and Alan Rappaport, 'Diners hijack McDonald's Twitter ad campaign', *Financial Times* (25 January 2012), p. 17.

VIDEO CASE

TOMS Shoes MyMarketingLab

'Get involved: changing a life begins with a single step.' This sounds like a mandate from a non-profit volunteer organisation. But in fact, this is the motto of a for-profit shoe company located in Santa Monica, California. In 2006, Tom Mycoskie founded TOMS Shoes because he wanted to do something different. He wanted to run a company that would make a profit while at the same time helping the needy of the world.

Specifically, for every pair of shoes that TOMS sells, it gives a pair of shoes to a needy child somewhere in the world. So far, the company has given away tens of thousands of pairs of shoes and is on track to give away hundreds of thousands. Can TOMS succeed and thrive based on this idealistic concept? That all depends on how TOMS executes its strategy within the constantly changing marketing environment.

After viewing the video featuring TOMS Shoes, answer the following questions about the marketing environment:

1. What trends in the marketing environment have contributed to the success of TOMS Shoes?
2. Did TOMS Shoes first scan the marketing environment in creating its strategy, or did it create its strategy and fit the strategy to the environment. Does this matter?
3. Is TOMS' strategy more about serving needy childern or about creating value for customers? Explain your answer.

The era of cheap chic for Primark

The new year in 2006 started with a shower of glitter for Primark as the discount fashion chain was named by *Vogue* as one of the unlikely hits of 2005 alongside singer Pete Doherty and vital accessories such as boho skirts. But being named as one of last season's hottest items can be a backhanded compliment when it comes from fickle fashionistas, and the *Vogue* endorsement has proven a mixed blessing for the chosen few. Mr Doherty has pleaded guilty to four charges of possessing Class A drugs and is undergoing rehabilitation. Boho skirts have vanished from shop windows and the wardrobes of those in the know.

Nonetheless, Primark is faring much better than its peers. It is adding new store space with a pace and efficiency that is impressing even its rivals. Still, figures showing flat underlying sales in the six months since the endorsement by fashion's bible suggest the chain could be reaching the limits of its appeal to shoppers, who are inundated with offerings.

In fact, the chain has transformed the landscape of women's wear retailing in Britain, leading the charge of so-called fast-fashion by churning out imitations of catwalk clothing and must-have accessories in record time at unprecedented low prices. This formula has seen it grab market share from rivals at an impressive rate. In the second half of last year, it posted a 12 per cent increase in like-for-like sales.

This sales growth has come at the expense of discount rivals such as Matalan and larger chains such as Next, the mid-market clothing retailer, which has been suffering more than most. At the time in question, Next, produced its worst trading figures since 2003 and warned the City that underlying sales would be down between 3 and 6 per cent in the 2006 financial year.

But a similar sales slowdown revealed by Primark was seized on by rivals and analysts as a sign of a shift in the balance of power on the high street.

Maureen Hinton, senior analyst with Verdict Research, the retail consultancy, said: 'I think we were all surprised by the sales figures. It is quite surprising that they should have flat sales over the summer as value clothing tends to lend itself to this period, where for example vests and T-shirts sell well.' The analyst said that changing price architecture at large mid-market chains such as Marks and Spencer was challenging the value specialists. 'There is the resurgence of M&S that is selling high volumes at lower opening price points. People may be more likely to buy from M&S because of the inherent promise of quality and service. M&S is taking a lot of volume in the market so they have to be taking it from somewhere,' she says. A rejuvenated M&S was enjoying an increase in market share as customers who shunned it over the past few years are lured back in store

with the promise of faster fashion – Limited Collection is M&S's version of on-trend lines – and cheaper items.

At that time, M&S managed to increase its market share of the £40 billion-a-year clothing market for the first time in three years, taking its share of clothing and footwear market to 12.2 per cent, against 11.7 per cent in the same period last year, with women's wear rising from 11.2 per cent to 12.4 per cent.

Fashion editors who were quick to latch onto the rise of fast-fashion – advising readers to match a Chanel jacket with a Primark T-shirt – say the appeal of cheap chic has faded amid market saturation.

Vanessa Gillingham, fashion director at Condé Nast's *Glamour* magazine says: 'I think it's like with anything great, after a while it flattens off a bit. Primark was the first to get on to the designer trend and put it into their stores and it seems that others such as George at Asda, Mark One, Tesco and Sainsbury's are all cashing in on it now and may have caught up.' Moira Beningson, retail specialist, says: 'People can't keep up. We're at the point where you have to change clothes every five minutes to wear everything you can buy at these stores.'

But John Bason, Primark's finance director, was relaxed about the slowdown in underlying sales. 'We always maintained that these very high like-for-like figures were unlikely to continue,' he said, pointing out that the chain would see a huge increase in sales due to the conversion of 41 stores acquired from Littlewoods.

The retailer is already preparing for the possibility its UK growth will one day hit the buffers. It opened its first store in Madrid three months ago and, Mr Bason says, it might consider more aggressive expansion in Europe.

PRIMARK'S SLOWDOWN?

Primark has only recently suffered its first slowdown in UK sales growth for five years, raising investor concerns about the stark deterioration in overall consumer spending since the start of 2011. Until this point the value chain had shown considerable resilience to economic malaise.

The discount clothing chain has seen viral-like expansion on the high street in recent years. But in 2011, Associated British Foods (owner of Primark) said it expected sales from its Primark stores in the UK and continental Europe open at least a year to rise just 3 per cent in the six months to 5 March – sharply down from the 8 per cent increase last year. ABF cited a 'noticeable slowing down of UK consumer demand' in contrast to continental Europe, which had seen 'very encouraging' sales.

Analysts at Shore Capital estimated Primark's UK like-for-like sales growth even entered negative territory in the seven weeks from 8 January 2011, expressing concern that value chains were not immune from the malaise elsewhere on the high street. The last time Primark saw its sales growth stall was in September

2006, and it has managed impressive increases in like-for-like sales throughout the current slowdown. Shares in ABF fell nearly 6 per cent to 966½p on this trading statement.

'Primark is a best-in-class retailer and for it to be experiencing negative UK like-for-likes and volumes must send a shiver down the backbone of the trade,' said Clive Black, analyst at Shore Capital. Primark's fortunes highlight the challenging conditions on the British high street as consumers grapple with higher fuel and food prices, a rise in value added tax and concerns about unemployment ahead of expected public sector job cuts.

John Bason, finance director at ABF, said there had been a 'tipping point' for consumers since the start of year, noting that footfall on high streets had fallen since January. 'The UK consumer is feeling a little bit of a squeeze now,' he said. Mr Bason's comments follow those of Asda, the UK's second biggest grocer by market share, which said there had been a 'mindset shift' among consumers since the beginning of the year, and five weeks of lacklustre sales from John Lewis, the high street bellwether that has also been a winner during tougher times.

Primark's performance shows that younger shoppers, who have kept spending during the downturn, are starting to feel the pinch. 'For the first time for quite a number of years, we are beginning to see some impact on the younger [shopper], who has been very resilient through the recession,' said Freddie George, analyst at Seymour Pierce. Primark cautioned that its operating profit margin would be lower than the year previously, as it absorbed the rising cost of cotton.

By late 2011, the budget retailer was set to report annual sales growth half the rate of a year previously, showing that even value chains are not immune from tough conditions on the high street. Primark's like-for-like sales growth had slipped to 3 per cent in the year to 17 September, down from 6 per cent a year earlier. Although Primark's total sales are expected to be 13 per cent up on a year ago, helped by a series of European store openings, analysts calculate that like-for-like sales growth in the UK and Ireland has been as low as 1 per cent. The retailer's strategy of not passing on high cotton prices to consumers to remain the cheapest on the high street meant margins fell in the second half of the year.

Darren Shirley, retail analyst at Shore Capital, said he anticipated a 200 basis point reduction when full-year figures are announced in November. 'If you're selling T-shirts for £1, it's obviously difficult to reprice that,' he said. 'However, there's been enough downward movement in the cotton price to give us confidence in the margin [in future].'

John Bason, ABF's finance director, reiterated that sales growth at Primark's UK and Irish stores remained in positive territory for the year, although the market had got tougher. 'Other than the two bank holidays in April, it's been a tough year, and our planning assumptions are that it will continue to be tough next year,' he said. Pointing out that Primark's current fashion ranges were purchased in March, when the cotton price was at its peak, Mr Bason said he expected commodity pricing pressure to ease in 2012, which will help margins.

Noting strong growth in the group's growing European operations, he reported 'high single-digit' like-for-like sales growth in Spain and said he expected a further boost from the 350,000 sq ft (31,500m^2) of retail space in Germany that will open in the coming year.

OR MAYBE NOT SO BAD?

By 2012 it seemed that shoppers' desire for cheap clothes had kept the tills ringing at Primark, even as rival high street retailers were left reeling by consumers' thriftiness. Primark saw a 16 per cent increase in sales in the 16 weeks to 7 January. Stripping out new stores – and the group is increasing its footprint by some 10 per cent a year – like-for-like sales grew 2–3 per cent, on analysts' estimates. 'We had a slow autumn because it was warm,' said John Bason, finance director. 'But we had a really strong Christmas trading period, particularly in the UK.'

Some have attributed Primark's gain to others' pain, such as that of Barratt and Peacocks, which have collapsed into administration. But other analysts, noting that the latter's issues were more to do with debt, rather point to the retailer's value for money offerings which chime with cash-strapped consumers. The company took the hit when cotton prices soared last year, so margins could benefit now that prices have fallen sharply from the peaks. Because of this, the company has been heading towards a stronger second half.

Alicia Forry, analyst at Collins Stewart, noted that operating margins were likely to be lower in the first half as a result of cotton prices and ramped-up promotions. 'We have to wait and see if they have outpaced on the top line, but when it comes to results and profits delivered [whether] they deliver less profit than their peers,' she said. The company, like its peers, could instead opt to pass the cheaper prices directly onto consumers in order to support sales growth.

However, Ms Forry sees sales growth as sustainable given the popularity of new stores in Germany and Spain – stores outside the UK now contribute one-third of Primark's turnover – and an offering that is popular with today's thriftier consumers. At Primark, Mr Bason said that, despite the 'torrid' economic climate, Spanish shoppers were flocking to the value clothing market. The Spanish market 'is probably where the UK was 10–15 years ago,' he said.

Questions for discussion

1. What microenvironmental factors have influenced Primark's performance over the past few years?
2. What macroenvironmental factors have influenced Primark's performance during that period?
3. By focusing on low prices, has Primark pursued the best strategy? Why or why not?
4. What alternative strategy might Primark have followed in harsh economic conditions?
5. Given Primark's current position, what recommendations would you make to the chief executive for the company's future?

Sources: Eoin Callan, Lucy Killgren and Elizabeth Rigby, 'Customers feel the quality not the width', *Financial Times* (12 September 2006) p. 25; Claer Barrett and Andrea Felsted, 'Primark slowdown bodes Ill', *Financial Times* (1 March 2011) p. 19; Clare Barrett, 'Squeezed buyers halve Primark sales growth', *Financial Times* (12 September 2011); Louise Lucas, 'Strong Primark sales boost ABF', *Financial Times* (19 January 2012).

CHAPTER FOUR

Managing marketing information to gain customer insights

Chapter preview

In this chapter, we continue our exploration of how marketers gain insights into consumers and the marketplace. We look at how companies develop and manage information about four important marketplace elements: customers, competitors, products and marketing programmes. To succeed in today's marketplace, companies must know how to turn mountains of marketing information into fresh customer insights that will help them deliver greater value to customers.

Objective outline

➤ **Objective 1** Explain the importance of information in gaining insights about the marketplace and customers.
Marketing information and customer insights
(pp. 109–110)

➤ **Objective 2** Define the marketing information system and discuss its parts.
Assessing marketing information needs
(pp. 110–111)
Developing marketing information (pp. 111–113)

➤ **Objective 3** Outline the steps in the marketing research process.
Marketing research (pp. 113–128)

➤ **Objective 4** Explain how companies analyse and use marketing information.
Analysing and using marketing information
(pp. 128–130)

➤ **Objective 5** Discuss the special issues some marketing researchers face, including public policy and ethics issues.
Other marketing information considerations
(pp. 130–134)

Mu by PSA Peugeot Citroën

All around the world car manufacturers are worried. The world is in recession, oil prices are driving petrol prices ever higher and what is worse the teenagers, students and young-sters of today no longer dream of driving their first car. Frankly, they're too busy using their mobile telephones and tablets to update their Facebook accounts. Cars just aren't the status symbols they once were. The market research seems unequivocal. In a recent survey by the German industry group Bitkom, 97 per cent of people aged 14 to 29 said the one thing they could not live without was a mobile phone. What terrified car manufacturers was that this was compared unfavourably to the mere 64 per cent who said they could not imagine life without a car. 'A car is important but a mobile phone is more important,' said one 25-year-old engineering student . 'You can get by more easily without a car than without a mobile.' This apparent shift in the expressed wants and demands of young consumers poten-tially heralds a big change for car makers. While this insight may be unwelcome – car manufactures can and will respond.

The trend away from car ownership has been reinforced by a number of polls in Japan, Germany and a range of other developed markets that consistently find that 'Generation Y' consumers value mobile phones more than they do cars. While Mum and Dad continue to prize their shiny estate car, even in car-mad Germany with its speed-limitless autobahns, BMW Ultimate Driving Machines and beautiful Mercedes-Benz's, younger consumers are more interested in iPhones and Blackberrys than X5s and C classes. The rapidly cooling enthusiasm for car ownership among younger people in some developed countries was under way even before the current recession and downturn, as evidenced by falling car sales among younger people in Japan. Since then, the generational change has dovetailed with a new frugal mood and advances in mobile technology and social networking, which in turn have laid the groundwork for car sharing and partial ownership. 'If you talk to 18 to 25-year-olds, they are expressing their personality with things other than a car,' says Wolfgang Bernhart, a partner with Roland Berger Strategy Associates. 'This is a long-term trend and has nothing to do with the crisis.'

Recognition of the trend has led to car-sharing companies such as America's Zipcar (which bought Streetcar of the UK in 2011) building thriving businesses around urban consumers who want to use cars but do not want to own them outright. The consultancy Frost & Sullivan expects membership of car-sharing schemes in Europe to increase tenfold from about 500,000 today to about 5.5 million by 2016. 'The Generation Y customer doesn't want to own cars – they want personal mobility,' says Sarwant Singh,

Younger consumers simply love their mobile phones more than their cars. The solution? Mu – Peugeot's mobility solutions.

Source: Peugeot Citroen

a partner with the consultancy. The increasing demand for partial car ownership has made 'mobility' a buzzword among industry executives.

Younger consumers seem content with putting cars much further down their shopping lists than their parents do. This represents a massive threat to car manufacturers' traditional business model but also an intriguing potential opportunity. Consequently, car manufacturers faced, with a new generation of consumers weaned on mobile phones and cooling towards car ownership, are experimenting with pay-as-you-go schemes for vehicles to attract a younger market.

PSA Peugeot Citroën, the French car manufacturers, has launched a partial ownership scheme that lets customers choose their mode of transport and prepay for transport 'units' in the same way as they would for airtime on a mobile phone. Customers of the scheme, dubbed 'Mu by Peugeot', have a card and an online account allowing them to purchase 'mobility units' at €10 per 50. In 2009, Peugeot piloted the scheme in four French cities that allows customers to use the units to rent a family car, a sportscar, a scooter or even a bicycle, depending on their needs.

Peugeot devised the programme after conducting focus groups worldwide. These focus groups found that young consumers didn't want to be tied down by car ownership but instead wanted the freedom of a variety of mobility solutions. 'All over the world, car mobility is linked to new possibilities in social connection,' says Pascal Feillard, Head of Foresight and Marketing Intelligence at Peugeot. 'People want to see if they can broaden this, not necessarily by cars: they want to be able in large urban areas to shift from one mode to the other - train, metro, bicycle – quite seamlessly.' 'The main question is whether there is a real market behind these trends, and whether we as car manufacturers can make money,' said Mr Feillard.

When Mu was launched in the UK each 'mobility point' cost around €0.2. Different mobility solutions cost different amounts of points – about 25 points a day for a bicycle, 195 points for a 1250-cc scooter, 280 points for a 207 hatchback, 450 points for a 307 coupé/cabriolet and 450 points for a Boxer van. Consumers can hire a bicycle with electrical assistance for those nasty steep hills for around €14 a day or from around €359 a week, a family car, roof box and portable DVD players for the kids.

Today, the company claims to have signed up some 9,000 regular customers around Europe through 75 of its dealers. Mu mobility solutions can be found across most of Europe with particularly successful branches in Madrid, Berlin, Rome, London, and Paris. When first launched in the UK, Mu was limited to London and Bristol but now includes dealerships from Manchester to Edinburgh. That said, Peugeot accept that Mu is 'not a big deal in terms of business, but it is in terms of forming a new link with customers,' says Nadège Faul, Peugeot's spokeswoman for client mobility services. 'We are bringing into the brand new customers, 60 per cent of whom do not have a Peugeot and 25 per cent of whom have no car at all.'[1]

AUTHOR COMMENT

Focus groups found that young consumers didn't want to be tied down to owning just a single car – they want flexibility, freedom and choice – in essence, they want mobility solutions.

Good products and marketing programmes begin with good customer information. Companies also need an abundance of information on competitors, resellers and other actors and marketplace forces. But more than just gathering information, marketers must *use* the information to gain powerful *customer and market insights*.

AUTHOR COMMENT

Marketing information by itself has little value. The value is in the *customer insights* gained from the information and how these insights are used to make better marketing decisions.

MARKETING INFORMATION AND CUSTOMER INSIGHTS

To create value for customers and build meaningful relationships with them, marketers must first gain fresh, deep insights into what customers need and want. Companies use such customer insights to develop competitive advantage. 'In today's hypercompetitive world,' states a marketing expert, 'the race for competitive advantage is really a race for customer and market insights.' Such insights come from good marketing information.[2]

Key customer insights, plus a dash of Apple's design and usability magic, have made the iPod a blockbuster. It now captures more than 75 per cent of the market share and has spawned other Apple blockbusters such as the iPhone and the iPad.

Source: Getty Images/Justin Sullivan

> Consider Apple's globally successful iPod. The iPod was not the first digital music player, but Apple was the first to get it right. Apple's research uncovered a key insight about how people want to consume digital music: they want to take all their music with them, but they want personal music players to be unobtrusive. This insight led to two key design goals: make it as small as a deck of cards and build it to hold 1,000 songs. Add a dash of Apple's design and usability magic to this insight, and you have a recipe for a blockbuster. Apple's expanded iPod and iPod Touch lines now capture more than 75 per cent of the market share. And they have spawned other Apple blockbusters such as the iPhone(s) and the iPad(s).

Although customer and market insights are important for building customer value and relationships, these insights can be very difficult to obtain. Customer needs and buying motives are often anything but obvious; consumers themselves usually cannot tell you exactly what they need and why they buy. To gain good customer insights, marketers must effectively manage marketing information from a wide range of sources.

Today's marketers have ready access to plenty of marketing information. With the recent explosion of information technologies, companies can now generate information in great quantities. Moreover, consumers themselves are now generating tons of 'bottom-up' marketing information.

> Not long ago, the only way a consumer could communicate with an organisation was by mailing a handwritten letter. Then came the call centre; followed by e-mail; text messaging; instant messaging; and, indirectly, blogging, Facebook, Twitter, and so on. Each one has contributed to a growing tidal wave of 'bottom-up' information that individuals volunteer to each other and to organisations. Organisations able to . . . elicit and use such [volunteered information] will be able to gain much richer, more timely customer insights at lower cost.[3]

Far from lacking information, most marketing managers are overloaded with data and often overwhelmed by it. For example, when a company such as Carlsberg monitors online discussions about its brands by searching key words in tweets, blogs, posts and other sources, its servers take in a stunning six million public conversations a day, or more than two billion a year.[4] That is far more information than any manager can digest.

Despite this data glut, marketers frequently complain that they lack enough information of the right kind. They do not need *more* information; they need *better* information. And they need to make better *use* of the information they already have.

The real value of marketing research and marketing information lies in how it is used – in the **customer insights** that it provides. Based on such thinking, many companies are now restructuring their marketing research and information functions. They are creating 'customer insights teams', headed by a vice president of customer insights and composed of representatives from all of a firm's functional

Customer insights—
Fresh understandings of customers and the marketplace derived from marketing information that become the basis for creating customer value and relationships.

Figure 4.1 The marketing information system

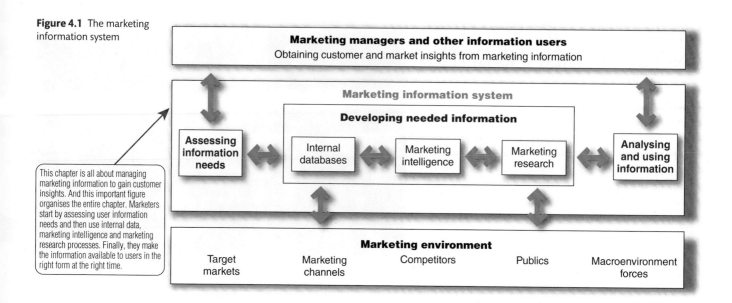

This chapter is all about managing marketing information to gain customer insights. And this important figure organises the entire chapter. Marketers start by assessing user information needs and then use internal data, marketing intelligence and marketing research processes. Finally, they make the information available to users in the right form at the right time.

Marketing information system (MIS)—People and procedures for assessing information needs, developing the needed information, and helping decision makers to use the information to generate and validate actionable customer and market insights.

areas. For example, at Unilever, marketing research is done by the Consumer and Market Insight division, which helps brand teams to harness information and turn it into customer insights. Similarly, DSG International – owner of electronics retailers Currys, PC World and Dixons has a global customer insight director while companies from Lucasfilm to MTV have directors of consumer insights.

Customer insights groups collect customer and market information from a wide variety of sources, ranging from traditional marketing research studies to mingling with and observing consumers to monitoring consumer online conversations about a company and its products. Then they *use* this information to develop important customer insights from which a company can create more value for its customers.

Thus, companies must design effective marketing information systems that give managers the right information, in the right form, at the right time and help them to use this information to create customer value and stronger customer relationships. A **marketing information system (MIS)** consists of people and procedures for assessing information needs, developing the needed information, and helping decision makers use the information to generate and validate actionable customer and market insights.

Figure 4.1 shows that the MIS begins and ends with information users – marketing managers, internal and external partners, and others who need marketing information. First, it interacts with these information users to *assess information needs*. Next, it interacts with the marketing environment to *develop needed information* through internal company databases, marketing intelligence activities, and marketing research. Finally, the MIS helps users to analyse and use the information to develop customer insights, make marketing decisions, and manage customer relationships.

AUTHOR COMMENT

The marketing information system begins and ends with users – assessing their information needs and then delivering information that meets those needs.

ASSESSING MARKETING INFORMATION NEEDS

The marketing information system primarily serves a company's marketing and other managers. However, it may also provide information to external partners, such as suppliers, resellers or marketing services agencies. For example, Tesco's Tesco Link, Sainsbury's Horizon and Walmart's

RetailLink system gives key suppliers access to information on everything from customers' buying patterns and store inventory levels to how many items they have sold in which stores in the past 24 hours.[5]

A good MIS balances the information users would *like* to have against what they really *need* and what is *feasible* to offer. A company begins by interviewing managers to find out what information they would like. Some managers will ask for whatever information they can get without thinking carefully about what they really need. Too much information can be as harmful as too little.

Other managers may omit things they ought to know, or they may not know to ask for some types of information they should have. For example, managers might need to know about surges in favourable or unfavourable consumer discussions about their brands on blogs or on-line social networks. Because they do not know about these discussions, they do not think to ask about them. The MIS must monitor the marketing environment to provide decision makers with information they should have to better understand customers and make key marketing decisions.

Sometimes a company cannot provide the needed information, either because it is not available or because of MIS limitations. For example, a brand manager might want to know how competitors will change their advertising budgets next year and how these changes will affect industry market shares. The information on planned budgets probably is not available. Even if it is, a company's MIS may not be advanced enough to forecast resulting changes in market shares.

Finally, the costs of obtaining, analysing, storing and delivering information can quickly mount. A company must decide whether the value of insights gained from additional information is worth the costs of providing it, and both value and cost are often hard to assess.

AUTHOR COMMENT

The problem is not *finding* information; the world is bursting with information from a glut of sources. The real challenge is to find the *right* information – from inside and outside sources – and turn it into customer insights.

DEVELOPING MARKETING INFORMATION

Marketers can obtain the needed information from *internal data*, *marketing intelligence* and *marketing research*.

Internal data

Many companies build extensive **internal databases**, which are electronic collections of consumer and market information obtained from data sources within a company's network. Marketing managers can readily access and work with information in the database to identify marketing opportunities and problems, plan programmes and evaluate performance. Internal data can provide a strong competitive advantage. 'Locked within your own records is a huge, largely untapped asset that no [competitor] can hope to match,' says one analyst. Companies are 'sitting on a gold mine of unrealised potential in their current customer base.'[6]

Information in the database can come from many sources. The marketing department furnishes information on customer demographics, psychographics, sales transactions and website visits. The customer service department keeps records of customer satisfaction or service problems. The accounting department prepares financial statements and keeps detailed records of sales, costs and cash flows. Operations reports on production schedules, shipments and inventories. The sales force reports on reseller reactions and competitor activities, and marketing channel partners provide data on point-of-sale transactions. Harnessing such information can provide powerful customer insights and competitive advantage.

Internal databases— Electronic collections of consumer and market information obtained from data sources within the company network.

A group of online advertising companies and publishers has launched a new code of conduct to help the industry cope with new European regulations around adverts based on tracking browsing habits. The European Advertising Standards Alliance guidelines commit to providing consumers with transparency about targeted advertising, protection for children and easier ways for consumers to complain if they feel their data have been misused. The new standards for online advertising using tracking cookies include an icon, to be appended to banners and other internet ads, linking to further information about targeting and giving consumers the opportunity to opt out of such tracking at youronlinechoices.eu. Companies committing to the system include Google, Microsoft, AOL and Yahoo, the last of which is already using a similar icon system on some of its sites. Publishers including the Guardian, the Telegraph, Yell and the Financial Times have also agreed to it. The EASA hopes that in the area of targeted advertising, its self-regulatory system will avoid the need for regular pop-ups or other clunky mechanisms to grant that permission. National industry bodies already checking that advertising does not mislead or offend, such as the UK's Advertising Standards Authority, will be enlisted to enforce the new rules. 'EASA's Best Practice Recommendation will provide European consumers with clear information and innovative ways to manage their choices concerning online behavioural advertising, as well as making available the use of the tried and tested national self-regulatory organisations if consumers wish to further complain,' said Angela Mills Wade, vice-chairman of the EASA.[7]

Internal databases usually can be accessed more quickly and cheaply than other information sources, but they also present some problems. Because internal information is often collected for other purposes, it may be incomplete or in the wrong form for making marketing decisions. Data also ages quickly; keeping the database current requires a major effort. Finally, managing the mountains of information that a large company produces requires highly sophisticated equipment and techniques.

Competitive marketing intelligence

Competitive marketing intelligence—The systematic collection and analysis of publicly available information about consumers, competitors, and developments in the marketing environment.

Competitive marketing intelligence is the systematic collection and analysis of publicly available information about consumers, competitors and developments in the marketplace. The goal of competitive marketing intelligence is to improve strategic decision making by understanding the consumer environment, assessing and tracking competitors' actions, and providing early warnings of opportunities and threats.

Marketing intelligence gathering has grown dramatically as more and more companies are now busily eavesdropping on the marketplace and snooping on their competitors. Techniques range from monitoring Internet buzz or observing consumers firsthand to quizzing a company's own employees, benchmarking competitors' products, researching the Internet, lurking around industry trade shows, and even rooting through rivals' waste bins.

Good marketing intelligence can help marketers gain insights into how consumers talk about and connect with their brands. Many companies send out teams of trained observers to mix and mingle with customers as they use and talk about a company's products. Other companies routinely monitor consumers' online chatter with the help of monitoring services such as Nielsen Online or Attentio. For example, Attentio helps companies keep track of almost any relevant online conversation:[8]

Attentio is a Belgium-based company specialising in global social media monitoring with a client list which includes Microsoft, Skype, Club Med, Johnson & Johnson, Nokia, Intel and Buenavista International/Disney. Social media has made it easier than ever for people to share – to have conversations and express their opinions, needs, ideas and complaints. And they are doing it with millions of blogs, tweets, videos, and comments daily. Marketers face the difficult task of sifting through all the noise to find the gems about their brands. Attentio provides organisations with the ability to listen, analyse and react to what is happening in the 'webosphere'. The Attentio products provide firms with clear visualisations of buzz trends, multi-language sentiment and event detection. Moreover, companies can analyse the information by topic, source, country and language. For example, Attentio recently collaborated with Naked Communications (part of the Photon Group) to understand the conversation around beer for their client Fosters. This process found that comedy was an area that Fosters could align their message with and by doing this they would have a real opportunity to differentiate in a crowded market. Fosters have subsequently invested significantly in comedy festivals (i.e. Edinburgh), programming sponsorship, and most spectacularly have contributed to the very successful re-emergence of fictional television and radio presenter Alan Partridge. This campaign can be viewed on the site fostersfunny.co.uk. 'This is an exceptionally creative way to use social media analysis to support the positioning of brands by listening to what people say and connecting that to the building of real "cultural capital" that will sustain long term positive connection between the brand and the consumer,' said Attentio CEO, Simon McDermott.

Companies also need to actively monitor competitors' activities. Firms use competitive marketing intelligence to gain early warnings of competitor moves and strategies, new product launches, new or changing markets, and potential competitive strengths and weaknesses. Much competitor intelligence can be collected from people inside a company – executives, engineers and scientists, purchasing agents and the sales force. A company can also obtain important intelligence information from suppliers, resellers and key customers. And it can get good information by observing competitors and monitoring their published information.

Competitors often reveal intelligence information through their annual reports, business publications, trade show exhibits, press releases, advertisements and Web pages. The Internet has become an invaluable source for competitive intelligence. Using Internet search engines, marketers can search specific competitor names, events or trends and see what turns up. And tracking consumer conversations about competing brands is often as revealing as tracking conversations about a company's own brands. Moreover, most competitors now place volumes of information on their websites, providing details of interest to customers, partners, suppliers, investors or franchisees. This can provide a wealth of useful information about competitors' strategies, markets, new products, facilities and other happenings.

Intelligence seekers can also pore through many thousands of online databases. Some are free. For example, the European Patent Office provides free access to 70 million patent documents and Europages is a free directory of 2.3 million European suppliers.[9] For a fee, companies can also subscribe to any of the more than 3,000 online databases and information search services, such as Kompass, Hoover's and LexisNexis. Today's marketers have an almost overwhelming amount of competitor information only a few keystrokes away.

The intelligence game goes both ways. Facing determined competitive marketing intelligence efforts by competitors, most companies are now taking steps to protect their own information. The growing use of marketing intelligence also raises a number of ethical issues. Although the preceding techniques are legal, others may involve questionable ethics. Clearly, companies should take advantage of publicly available information. However, they should not stoop to snoop. With all the legitimate intelligence sources now available, a company does not need to break the law or accepted codes of ethics to get good intelligence.

AUTHOR COMMENT

Whereas marketing intelligence involves actively scanning the general marketing environment, marketing research involves more focused studies to gain customer insights relating to specific marketing decisions.

MARKETING RESEARCH

In addition to marketing intelligence information about general consumer, competitor and marketplace happenings, marketers often need formal studies that provide customer and market insights for specific marketing situations and decisions. For example, Heineken NV and the UniCredit Group want to know what appeals will be most effective in their UEFA Champions League Football advertising. Google wants to know how Web searchers will react to a proposed redesign of its site.

This first step in the marketing research process is probably the most difficult but also the most important. It guides the entire research process. It's frustrating to reach the end of an expensive research project only to learn that you've addressed the wrong problem!

Figure 4.2 The marketing research process

Marketing research—
The systematic design, collection, analysis, and reporting of data relevant to a specific marketing situation facing an organisation.

And Aéroport de Paris wants to know how many and what kinds of people want to use airports near Paris and when they wish to do so. In such situations, marketing intelligence will not provide the detailed information needed. Managers will need marketing research.

Marketing research is the systematic design, collection, analysis and reporting of data relevant to a specific marketing situation facing an organisation. Companies use marketing research in a wide variety of situations. For example, marketing research gives marketers insights into customer motivations, purchase behaviour and satisfaction. It can help them to assess market potential and market share or measure the effectiveness of pricing, product, distribution and promotion activities.

Some large companies have their own research departments that work with marketing managers on marketing research projects. This is how P&G, Shell and many other corporate giants handle marketing research. In addition, these companies – like their smaller counterparts – frequently hire outside research specialists to consult with management on specific marketing problems and conduct marketing research studies. Sometimes firms simply purchase data collected by outside firms to aid in their decision making.

The marketing research process has four steps (see Figure 4.2): defining the problem and research objectives, developing the research plan, implementing the research plan, and interpreting and reporting the findings.

Defining the problem and research objectives

Marketing managers and researchers must work closely together to define the problem and agree on research objectives. The manager best understands the decision for which information is needed; the researcher best understands marketing research and how to obtain the information. Defining the problem and research objectives is often the hardest step in the research process. The manager may know that something is wrong, without knowing the specific causes.

Exploratory research—
Marketing research to gather preliminary information that will help define problems and suggest hypotheses.

Descriptive research—
Marketing research to better describe marketing problems, situations, or markets, such as the market potential for a product or the demographics and attitudes of consumers.

Causal research—Marketing research to test hypotheses about cause-and-effect relationships.

After the problem has been defined carefully, the manager and the researcher must set the research objectives. A marketing research project might consist of one of three types of objectives. The objective of **exploratory research** is to gather preliminary information that will help define the problem and suggest hypotheses. The objective of **descriptive research** is to describe things, such as the market potential for a product or the demographics and attitudes of consumers who buy the product. The objective of **causal research** is to test hypotheses about cause-and-effect relationships. For example, would a 10 per cent decrease in tuition fees at a private college result in an enrolment increase sufficient to offset the reduced income? Managers often start with exploratory research and later follow with descriptive or causal research.

The statement of the problem and research objectives guides the entire research process. The manager and the researcher should put the statement in writing to be certain that they agree on the purpose and expected results of the research.

Developing the research plan

Once the research problem and objectives have been defined, researchers must determine the exact information needed, develop a plan for gathering it efficiently, and present the plan to management. The research plan outlines sources of existing data and spells out the specific research approaches, contact methods, sampling plans and instruments that researchers will use to gather new data.

Research objectives must be translated into specific information needs. For example, suppose that Red Bull wants to conduct research on how consumers would react to a proposed new vitamin-enhanced water drink in several flavours sold under the Red Bull name. Red Bull currently dominates the worldwide energy drink market. However, in an effort to expand beyond its energy drink niche, the company recently introduced Red Bull Cola ('Why not?' asks the company; it is strong and natural, just like the original Red Bull energy drink). A new line of enhanced waters – akin to Glacéau's VitaminWater – might help Red Bull leverage its strong brand position even further. The proposed research might call for the following specific information:

- The demographic, economic and lifestyle characteristics of current Red Bull customers. (Do current customers also consume enhanced-water products? Are such products consistent with their lifestyles? Or would Red Bull need to target a new segment of consumers?)
- The characteristics and usage patterns of the broader population of enhanced-water users: what do they need and expect from such products, where do they buy them, when and how do they use them, and what existing brands and price points are most popular? (The new Red Bull product would need strong, relevant positioning in the crowded enhanced-water market.)
- Retailer reactions to the proposed new product line: would they stock and support it? Where would they display it? (Failure to get retailer support would hurt sales of the new drink.)
- Forecasts of sales of both the new and current Red Bull products. (Will the new enhanced waters create new sales or simply take sales away from current Red Bull products? Will the new product increase Red Bull's overall profits?)

Red Bull Energy Drink is a unique combination of Taurine, Glucuronolactone, B-vitamins and other important nutrients. It improves performance, increases endurance and concentration, improves reaction speed and stimulates the metabolism. In short, Red Bull vitalizes both body and mind.

RED BULL GIVES YOU WIIINGS.

A decision by Red Bull to add a line of enhanced waters to its already successful mix of energy and cola drinks would call for marketing research that provides lots of specific information.

Source: © Red Bull Media House

Red Bull's marketers will need these and many other types of information to decide whether and how to introduce the new product.

The research plan should be presented in a *written proposal*. A written proposal is especially important when the research project is large and complex or when an outside firm carries it out. The proposal should cover the management problems addressed, the research objectives, the information to be obtained, and how the results will help management decision making. The proposal also should include estimated research costs.

To meet a manager's information needs, the research plan can call for gathering secondary data, primary data or both. **Secondary data** consist of information that already exists somewhere, having been collected for another purpose. **Primary data** consist of information collected for the specific purpose at hand.

Secondary data—Information that already exists somewhere, having been collected for another purpose.

Primary data—Information collected for the specific purpose at hand.

Gathering secondary data

Researchers usually start by gathering secondary data. A company's internal database provides a good starting point. However, a company can also tap into a wide assortment of external information sources, including commercial data services and government sources (see Table 4.1).

Companies can buy secondary data reports from outside suppliers. For example, Nielsen sells shopper insight data from a consumer panel of more than 260,000 households in 27 countries worldwide, with measures of trial and repeat purchasing, brand loyalty and buyer demographics. Experian Consumer Research (Simmons) sells information consumer panel data on more than 8,000 brands in 450 product categories, including detailed consumer profiles that assess everything from the products consumers buy and the brands they prefer to their lifestyles, attitudes and

Table 4.1 Selected external information sources

Business data

The Nielsen Company (http://nielsen.com) provides point-of-sale scanner data on sales, market share, and retail prices; data on household purchasing; and data on television audiences.

Experian Consumer Research (Simmons) (http://smrb.com) provides detailed analysis of consumer patterns in 400 product categories in selected markets.

Information Resources, Inc. (www.infores.com) provides supermarket scanner data for tracking grocery product movement and new product purchasing data.

Arbitron (http://arbitron.com) provides local market and Internet radio audience and advertising expenditure information, among other media and ad spending data.

J.D. Power and Associates (www.jdpower.com) provides information from independent consumer surveys of product and service quality, customer satisfaction and buyer behaviour.

Dun & Bradstreet (http://dnb.com) maintains a database containing information on more than 50 million individual companies around the globe.

comScore (http://comscore.com) provides consumer behaviour information and geodemographic analysis of Internet and digital media users around the world.

Thomson Dialog (www.dialog.com) offers access to more than 900 databases containing publications, reports, newsletters and directories covering dozens of industries.

LexisNexis (www.lexisnexis.com) features articles from business, consumers and marketing publications plus tracking of firms, industries, trends and promotion techniques.

Factiva (http://factiva.com) specialises in in-depth financial, historical and operational information on public and private companies.

Hoover's, Inc. (http://hoovers.com) provides business descriptions, financial overviews and news about major companies around the world.

CNBC (http://europetv.cnbc.com) reports European business news and covers the markets and news-making companies in detail.

BBC (www.bbc.co.uk/news) reports UK and global news and covers the markets and news-making companies in detail.

World Bank Data (http://data.worldbank.org) provides a wide range of economic and social data.

Government data

European Small Business Portal (http://ec.europa. eu/small-business) features information and links for small business owners.

European Commission on Competition (http://ec.europa.eu/competition) shows regulations and decisions related to consumer protection and antitrust laws.

International Census (www.census.ac.uk/) provides detailed statistics and trends about populations.

European Patent Office (www.epo.org) provides free access to European patent documents.

European Business Directory (www.eubusiness.com/europages) a directory of European businesses.

Europages (www.europages.com) is a free directory of 2.3 million European suppliers.

Internet data
ClickZ (www.clickz.com) brings together a wealth of information about the Internet and its users, from consumers to e-commerce.
Interactive Advertising Bureau (www.iab.net) covers statistics about advertising on the Internet.
Internet World Statistics (www.internetworldstats.com) provide global Internet penetration statistics.
Forrester.com (www.forrester.com/rb/research) monitors Web traffic and ranks the most popular sites.

media preferences. The MONITOR service by Yankelovich sells information on important social and lifestyle trends. These and other firms supply high-quality data to suit a wide variety of marketing information needs.[10]

Using **commercial online databases**, marketing researchers can conduct their own searches of secondary data sources. General database services such as Dialog, ProQuest and LexisNexis put an incredible wealth of information at the keyboards of marketing decision makers. Beyond commercial websites offering information for a fee, almost every industry association, government agency, business publication and news medium offers free information to those tenacious enough to find their websites. There are so many websites offering data that finding the right ones can become an almost overwhelming task.

Internet search engines can be a big help in locating relevant secondary information sources. However, they can also be very frustrating and inefficient. For example, a Red Bull marketer searching under 'enhanced water products' would come up with some 200,000 hits! Still, well-structured, well-designed online searches can be a good starting point for any marketing research project.

Secondary data can usually be obtained more quickly and at a lower cost than primary data. Also, secondary sources can sometimes provide data an individual company cannot collect on its own – information that either is not directly available or would be too expensive to collect. For example, it would be too expensive for Red Bull's marketers to conduct a continuing retail store audit to find out about the market shares, prices and displays of competitors' brands. But it can buy the InfoScan service from Information Resources, Inc. (IRI), which provides this information based on scanner and other data from 34,000 retail stores in markets around the nation.[11]

Secondary data can also present problems. The needed information may not exist; researchers can rarely obtain all the data they need from secondary sources. For example, Red Bull will not find existing information about consumer reactions about a new enhanced-water line that it has not yet placed on the market. Even when data can be found, the information might not be very usable. A researcher must evaluate secondary information carefully to make certain it is *relevant* (fits research project needs), *accurate* (reliably collected and reported), *current* (up-to-date enough for current decisions) and *impartial* (objectively collected and reported).

> **Commercial online databases**—Collections of information available from online commercial sources or accessible via the Internet.

Primary data collection

Secondary data provide a good starting point for research and often help to define research problems and objectives. In most cases, however, a company must also collect primary data. Just as researchers must carefully evaluate the quality of secondary information, they also must take great care when collecting primary data. They need to make sure that it will be relevant, accurate, current and unbiased. Table 4.2 shows that designing a plan for primary data collection calls for a number of decisions on *research approaches, contact methods,* the *sampling plan* and *research instruments.*

Research approaches

Research approaches for gathering primary data include observation, surveys and experiments. We discuss each one in turn.

Table 4.2 Planning primary data collection

Research approaches	Contact methods	Sampling plan	Research instruments
Observation	Mail	Sampling unit	Questionnaire
Survey	Telephone	Sample size	Mechanical instruments
Experiment	Personal	Sampling procedure	
	Online		

Observational research

Observational research—
Gathering primary data by observing relevant people, actions and situations.

Observational research involves gathering primary data by observing relevant people, actions and situations. For example, a retail firm might evaluate possible new store locations by checking traffic patterns, neighbourhood conditions, and the location of competing discount retail stores.

Researchers often observe consumer behaviour to glean customer insights they cannot obtain by simply asking customers questions. For instance, Ricability is a UK charity providing consumer research and advice for older and disabled people. They use observational studies as their target customers – the elderly, infirm or disabled – often fail to notice or are unable to communicate potential health and safety hazards. Consequently, Ricability explores product experiences by observing end users operating products in their own homes rather than via direct questioning. In contrast, Fisher-Price has established an observation lab in which it can observe the reactions of younger children to new toys. The Fisher-Price Play Lab is a sunny, toy-strewn space where lucky children get to test Fisher-Price prototypes, under the watchful eyes of designers who hope to learn what will get them worked up into a new-toy frenzy.

Marketers not only observe what consumers do but also observe what consumers are saying. As discussed earlier, marketers now routinely listen in on consumer conversations on blogs, social networks and websites. Observing such naturally occurring feedback can provide inputs that simply cannot be gained through more structure and formal research approaches.

Observational research can obtain information that people are unwilling or unable to provide. In contrast, some things simply cannot be observed, such as feelings, attitudes, motives or private behaviour. Long-term or infrequent behaviour is also difficult to observe. Finally, observations can be very difficult to interpret. Because of these limitations, researchers often use observation along with other data collection methods.

Ethnographic research—
A form of observational research that involves sending trained observers to watch and interact with consumers in their 'natural environments'.

A wide range of companies now use **ethnographic research**. Ethnographic research involves sending observers to watch and interact with consumers in their 'natural environments'. The observers might be trained anthropologists and psychologists or company researchers and managers. Consider this example:[12]

Rank Group, the company behind Grosvenor casinos and Mecca bingo, has become the latest UK group to employ immersive market research to better understand its customers. Rank sends senior staff into the homes of customers to probe daily habits that would sometimes seem to have little to do with its products and services. In addition to long interviews, researchers photograph the subjects at home, travel with them on their journeys to bingo clubs or casinos' and observe them throughout their visits. Unlike other companies, however, Rank wants its top executives to take part. Ian Burke, chief executive, has already spent a day following a couple from their home to one of the company's casinos and observing them there. 'At Mecca, there are already back-to-floor initiatives [in which head office staff work at the clubs],' said Jon McPherson, Rank's group head of insight and analytics. 'But immersion with a customer is very different from seeing things through the eyes of the employee.' The push follows a year in which Rank stemmed a decline in Mecca revenues by getting customers to spend more per visit – in part through new offerings, such as food and drink table service and 'After Dark' bingo, a looser form of the game. Luring more people in is the next task – and one Mr Burke has said cannot be truly accomplished without a much better understanding of how and why people visit bingo halls. Mr McPherson hopes even to involve Rank Interactive, the group's online division. 'We have good technology for measuring how people move around a [Web] page, but we don't know if people come home, put the children in bed, make a cup of tea and then sit down at the computer.'

Beyond conducting ethnographic research in physical consumer environments, many companies now routinely conduct 'Webnography' research – observing consumers in a natural context on the Internet. Observing people as they interact online can provide useful insights into both online and off-line buying motives and behaviour.[13]

Observational and ethnographic research often yields the kinds of details that just do not emerge from traditional research questionnaires or focus groups. Whereas traditional quantitative research approaches seek to test known hypotheses and obtain answers to well-defined product or strategy questions, observational research can generate fresh customer and market insights. 'The beauty of ethnography,' says a research expert, is that it 'allows companies to zero in on their customers' unarticulated desires.' Agrees another researcher, 'Classic market research doesn't go far enough. It can't grasp what people can't imagine or articulate. Think of the Henry Ford quote: "If I had asked people what they wanted, they would have said faster horses."'[14]

Survey research

Survey research, the most widely used method for primary data collection, is the approach best suited for gathering descriptive information. A company that wants to know about people's knowledge, attitudes, preferences or buying behaviour can often find out by asking them directly.

Survey research—Gathering primary data by asking people questions about their knowledge, attitudes, preferences and buying behaviour.

The major advantage of survey research is its flexibility; it can be used to obtain many different kinds of information in many different situations. Surveys addressing almost any marketing question or decision can be conducted by phone or mail, in person or on the Web.

However, survey research also presents some problems. Sometimes people are unable to answer survey questions because they cannot remember or have never thought about what they do and why. People may be unwilling to respond to unknown interviewers or about things they consider private. Respondents may answer survey questions even when they do not know the answer just to appear cleverer or more informed. Or they may try to help the interviewer by giving pleasing answers. Finally, busy people may not take the time, or they might resent the intrusion into their privacy.

Experimental research

Whereas observation is best suited for exploratory research and surveys for descriptive research, **experimental research** is best suited for gathering causal information. Experiments involve selecting matched groups of subjects, giving them different treatments, controlling unrelated factors and checking for differences in group responses. Thus, experimental research tries to explain cause-and-effect relationships.

Experimental research—Gathering primary data by selecting matched groups of subjects, giving them different treatments, controlling related factors and checking for differences in group responses.

For example, before adding a new burger to its menu, Hard Rock Cafe might use experiments to test the effects on sales of two different prices it might charge. It could introduce the new burger at one price in one city and at another price in another city. If the cities are similar, and if all other marketing efforts for the sandwich are the same, then differences in sales in the two cities could be related to the price charged.

Contact methods

Information can be collected by mail, telephone, personal interview or online. Table 4.3 shows the strengths and weaknesses of each contact method.

Table 4.3 Strengths and weaknesses of contact methods

	Mail	Telephone	Personal	Online
Flexibility	Poor	Good	Excellent	Good
Quantity of data that can be collected	Good	Fair	Excellent	Good
Control of interviewer effects	Excellent	Fair	Poor	Fair
Control of sample	Fair	Excellent	Good	Excellent
Speed of data collection	Poor	Excellent	Good	Excellent
Response rate	Poor	Poor	Good	Good
Cost	Good	Fair	Poor	Excellent

Mail, telephone and personal interviewing

Mail questionnaires can be used to collect large amounts of information at a low cost per respondent. Respondents may give more honest answers to more personal questions on a mail questionnaire than to an unknown interviewer in person or over the phone. Also, no interviewer is involved to bias respondents' answers.

However, mail questionnaires are not very flexible; all respondents answer the same questions in a fixed order. Mail surveys usually take longer to complete, and the response rate – the number of people returning completed questionnaires – is often very low. Finally, a researcher often has little control over the mail questionnaire sample. Even with a good mailing list, it is hard to control *who* at a particular address fills out the questionnaire. As a result of the shortcomings, more and more marketers are now shifting to faster, more flexible and lower cost e-mail and online surveys.

Telephone interviewing is one of the best methods for gathering information quickly, and it provides greater flexibility than mail questionnaires. Interviewers can explain difficult questions and, depending on the answers they receive, skip some questions or probe on others. Response rates tend to be higher than with mail questionnaires, and interviewers can ask to speak to respondents with the desired characteristics or even by name.

However, with telephone interviewing, the cost per respondent is higher than with mail or online questionnaires. Also, people may not want to discuss personal questions with an interviewer. The method introduces interviewer bias – the way interviewers talk, how they ask questions and other differences that may affect respondents' answers. Finally, in this age of do-not-call lists and promotion-harassed consumers, potential survey respondents are increasingly hanging up on telephone interviewers rather than talking with them.

Personal interviewing takes two forms: individual interviewing and group interviewing. *Individual interviewing* involves talking with people in their homes or offices, on the street, or in shopping malls. Such interviewing is flexible. Trained interviewers can guide interviews, explain difficult questions and explore issues as the situation requires. They can show subjects actual products, advertisements or packages and observe reactions and behaviour. However, individual personal interviews may cost three to four times as much as telephone interviews.[15]

Clare (not her real name) has agreed to take part in a market research project launched by Mecca Bingo that seeks to draw a much more detailed picture of customers than phone surveys or analysis of cash-register figures will allow. So now every detail of Clare's life has become worth recording – not just what she says but how she has organised her house, the way she interacts with her family and where she goes when she steps outside. Photographing the sitting room is part of the drill. Immersion market research, which borrows more from anthropology and sociology than, say, the psychology that informs surveys and focus groups, has been around since the 1970s. But Ben Page, chief executive of research firm Ipsos Mori, says 'ethnology is a rapidly growing field', not least because new technologies such as GPS tracking mean 'you can spend days with people without actually being with them'. However, Rank Group, owner of Mecca Bingo, has firmly embraced one-on-one contact – a decision that has already created new business ideas. One researcher found his subject stopping off at the shops on the way to the bingo hall to pick up the sudoku books she played between rounds of bingo. He wondered –why not sell the books at the Mecca club? Another researcher thought that the company should look at modifying its bingo books after he noticed his subject setting aside time to unseal the bound pages – a task she found difficult due to her arthritis. She did not complain as she slowly laid out the pages, but he took note, asked her about the habit later and learnt that she was not alone: several of her friends at the club also required 10 to 15 minutes to prepare the books. Minutes of unfolding bingo books means minutes customers are not dropping pound coins in Mecca's table games – although Jon McPherson, group head of insight and analytics at Rank, insists that information gleaned from the immersions is not viewed quite as cynically as that. 'We want to fully understand the customer journey, especially in bingo, which has had a 10-year decline,' says Mark Jones, managing director of Mecca.

Group interviewing consists of inviting six to ten people to meet with a trained moderator to talk about a product, service or organisation. Participants normally are paid a small sum for attending. The moderator encourages free and easy discussion, hoping that group interactions will bring out actual feelings and thoughts. At the same time, the moderator 'focuses' the discussion – hence the name **focus group interviewing**.

Researchers and marketers watch the focus group discussions from behind one-way glass and record comments in writing or on video for later study. Today, focus group researchers can even use videoconferencing and Internet technology to connect marketers in distant locations with live focus group action. Using cameras and two-way sound systems, marketing executives in a far-off boardroom can look in and listen, using remote controls to zoom in on faces and pan across the focus group at will.

Along with observational research, focus group interviewing has become one of the major qualitative marketing research tools for gaining fresh insights into consumer thoughts and feelings. However, focus group studies present some challenges. They usually employ small samples to keep time and costs down, and it may be hard to generalise from the results. Moreover, consumers in focus groups are not always open and honest about their real feelings, behaviour and intentions in front of other people.

Thus, although focus groups are still widely used, many researchers are tinkering with focus group design. For example, some companies prefer 'immersion groups'–small groups of consumers who interact directly and informally with product designers without a focus group moderator present. Still other researchers are changing the environments in which they conduct focus groups. To help consumers relax and elicit more authentic responses, they use settings that are more comfortable and more relevant to the products being researched.

Thus, in recent years, many companies have been moving away from traditional, more formal and numbers-oriented research approaches and contact methods. Instead, they are employing more new ways of listening to consumers that do not involve traditional questionnaire formats. 'Long known for crunching numbers and being statistical gatekeepers of the marketing industry,' says one marketer, 'market researchers need to shift their focus toward listening and developing ideas better on the front end and away from "feeding the metrics monster"'. 'Beyond conducting surveys and tracking brand metrics, 'researchers need to employ softer skills'.[16]

Online marketing research

The growth of the Internet has had a dramatic impact on the conduct of marketing research. Increasingly, researchers are collecting primary data

Focus group interviewing– Personal interviewing that involves inviting six to ten people to gather for a few hours with a trained interviewer to talk about a good, service or organisation. The interviewer 'focuses' the group discussion on important issues.

Focus group research: using cameras and two-way sound systems, marketing executives in a far-off boardroom can look in and listen, using remote controls to zoom in on faces and pan the focus group at will.

Source: Alamy Images/Image Source

Online marketing research—
Collecting primary data online through Internet surveys, online focus groups, Web-based experiments or tracking consumers' online behaviour.

through **online marketing research**: Internet surveys, online panels, experiments, and online focus groups. By one estimate, global online research spending reached an estimated €3 billion last year and is growing at 15–20 per cent per year.[17]

Online research can take many forms. A company can use the Web as a survey medium: it can include a questionnaire on its website and offer incentives for completing it. It can use e-mail, Web links or Web pop-ups to invite people to answer questions. It can create online panels that provide regular feedback or conduct live discussions or online focus groups.

Beyond surveys, researchers can conduct experiments on the Web. They can experiment with different prices, headlines or product features on different websites or at different times to learn the relative effectiveness of their offers. Or they can set up virtual shopping environments and use them to test new products and marketing programmes. Finally, a company can learn about the behaviour of online customers by following their click streams as they visit the website and move to other sites.

The Internet is especially well suited to *quantitative* research – conducting marketing surveys and collecting data. Most Europeans now have access to the Web, making it a fertile channel for reaching a broad cross section of consumers. As response rates for traditional survey approaches decline and costs increase, the Web is quickly replacing mail and the telephone as the dominant data collection methodology. Online research now accounts for about 50 per cent of all survey research.[18]

Web-based survey research offers some real advantages over traditional phone mail and personal interviewing approaches. The most obvious advantages are speed and low costs. By going online, researchers can quickly and easily distribute Internet surveys to thousands of respondents simultaneously via e-mail or by posting them on selected websites. Responses can be almost instantaneous, and because respondents themselves enter the information, researchers can tabulate, review and share research data as they arrive.

Online research usually costs much less than research conducted through mail, phone or personal interviews. Using the Internet eliminates most of the postage, phone, interviewer and data-handling costs associated with the other approaches. As a result, Internet surveys typically cost 15–20 per cent less than mail surveys and 30 per cent less than phone surveys. Moreover, sample size has little impact on costs. Once the questionnaire is set up, there is little difference in cost between 10 respondents and 10,000 respondents on the Web.

Thus, online research is well within the reach of almost any business, large or small. In fact, with the Internet, what was once the domain of research experts is now available to almost any would-be researcher. Even smaller, less sophisticated researchers can use online survey services such as Zoomerang (www.zoomerang.com) and SurveyMonkey (www.surveymonkey.com) to create, publish and distribute their own custom surveys in minutes.

Beyond their speed and cost advantages, Web-based surveys also tend to be more interactive and engaging, easier to complete and less intrusive than traditional phone or mail surveys. As a result, they usually garner higher response rates. The Internet is an excellent medium for reaching the hard-to-reach – for example, the often-elusive teen and single, affluent and well-educated audiences. It is also good for reaching working mothers and other people who lead busy lives. Such people are well represented online, and they can respond in their own space and at their own convenience.

Just as marketing researchers have rushed to use the Internet for quantitative surveys and data collection, they are now also adopting *qualitative* Web-based research approaches, such as online depth interviews, focus groups, blogs and social networks. The Internet can provide a fast, low-cost way to gain qualitative customer insights.

Online focus groups
Gathering a small group of people online with a trained moderator to chat about a product, service or organisation and gain qualitative insights about consumer attitudes and behaviour.

A primary qualitative Web-based research approach is **online focus groups**. Such focus groups offer many advantages over traditional focus groups. Participants can log in from anywhere; all they need is a laptop and a Web connection. Thus, the Internet works well for bringing together people from different parts of the country or world, especially those in higher-income groups who cannot spare the time to travel to a central site. Also, researchers can conduct and monitor online focus groups from just about anywhere, eliminating travel, lodging and facility costs. Finally, although online focus groups require some advance scheduling, results are almost immediate.

Online focus groups can take any of several formats. Most occur in real time, in the form of online chat room discussions in which participants and a moderator sit around a virtual table exchanging comments. Alternatively, researchers might set up an online message board on which respondents interact over the course of several days or a few weeks. Participants log in daily and comment on focus group topics.

Although low in cost and easy to administer, online focus groups can lack the real-world dynamics of more personal approaches. To overcome these shortcomings, some researchers are now adding real-time audio and video to their online focus groups. For example, the online research firm Channel M2 'puts the human touch back into online research' by assembling focus group participants in people-friendly 'virtual interview rooms'.[19]

Participants are recruited using traditional methods and then sent a Web camera so that both their verbal and nonverbal reactions can be recorded. Participants receive instructions via e-mail, including a link to the Channel M2 online interviewing room and a freephone teleconference number to call. At the appointed time, when they click on the link and phone in, participants sign on and see the Channel M2 interview room, complete with live video of the other participants, text chat, screen or slide sharing, and a whiteboard. Once the focus group is underway, questions and answers occur in 'real time' in a remarkably lively setting. Participants comment spontaneously–verbally, via text messaging, or both. Researchers can 'sit in' on the focus group from anywhere, seeing and hearing every respondent. Or they can review a recorded version at a later date.

Although the use of online marketing research is growing rapidly, both quantitative and qualitative Web-based research does have some drawbacks. One major problem is controlling who is in the online sample. Without seeing respondents, it is difficult to know who they really are. To overcome such sample and context problems, many online research firms use opt-in communities and respondent panels. For example, Zoomerang offers an online consumer and business panel profiled on more than 500 attributes.[20] Alternatively, many companies are now developing their own custom social networks and using them to gain customer inputs and insights. Consider Adidas:[21]

When Adidas developed a Facebook fan page, it quickly attracted 2 million users. So did its pages on Twitter and YouTube. But monitoring and analysing postings by 2 million members in public online communities is not realistic, so the sporting goods giant created its own private online community called Adidas Insiders, inviting only the most active users on its public pages to join. Through online conversations with and among Adidas Insiders, company marketers can quickly gather real-time consumer feedback about brand perceptions, product ideas and marketing campaigns. Adidas Insiders are surprisingly willing – and even anxious – to be involved. 'It's a great help to [us] spending time with consumers that love the brand as much as we do,' says Adidas's director of digital media.

Testing strategies and concepts with the Insiders group provides fast and actionable customer insights for Adidas's product marketing teams. 'We're able to play with colours and materials and get instant feedback from these fans, which allows us to be more efficient in development and go-to-market planning', says the Adidas marketing executive. 'We've even asked about things like voiceovers for videos and received surprising feedback that's caused us to alter creative.'

Thus, in recent years, the Internet has become an important new tool for conducting research and developing customer insights. But today's marketing researchers are going even further on the Web – well beyond structured online surveys, focus groups and Web communities. Increasingly, they are listening to and watching consumers by actively mining the rich veins of unsolicited, unstructured, 'bottom-up' customer information already coursing around the Web. This might be as simple as scanning customer reviews and comments on a company's brand site or shopping sites such as Amazon, ResellerRatings.com or BestBuy.com. Or it might mean using sophisticated Web-analysis tools to deeply analyse mountains of consumer comments and messages found in blogs or on social networking sites, such as Facebook or Twitter. Listening to and watching consumers

Online customer social networks – such as Adidas Insiders – can help companies gain customer inputs and insights. Adidas Insiders are surprisingly willing – and even anxious – to be involved.

Source: Adidas

online can provide valuable insights into what consumers are saying or feeling about brands. As one information expert puts it, 'The Web knows what you want'.[22]

Perhaps the most explosive issue facing online researchers concerns consumer privacy. Some critics fear that unethical researchers will use the e-mail addresses and confidential responses gathered through surveys to sell products after the research is completed. They are concerned about the use of technologies that collect personal information online without the respondents' consent. Failure to address such privacy issues could result in angry, less-cooperative consumers and increased government intervention. Despite these concerns, most industry insiders predict continued healthy growth for online marketing research.[23]

Sampling plan

Sample—A segment of the population selected for marketing research to represent the population as a whole.

Marketing researchers usually draw conclusions about large groups of consumers by studying a small sample of the total consumer population. A **sample** is a segment of the population selected for marketing research to represent the population as a whole. Ideally, the sample should be representative so that a researcher can make accurate estimates of the thoughts and behaviours of the larger population.

Designing the sample requires three decisions. First, *who* is to be studied (what *sampling unit*)? The answer to this question is not always obvious. For example, to learn about the decision-making process for a family car purchase, should the subject be the husband, the wife, other family members, dealership salespeople or all of these? Second, *how many* people should be included (what *sample size*)? Large samples give more reliable results than small samples. However, larger samples usually cost more, and it is not necessary to sample the entire target market or even a large portion to get reliable results.

Finally, *how* should the people in the sample be *chosen* (what *sampling procedure*)? Table 4.4 describes different kinds of samples. Using *probability samples*, each population member has a known chance of being included in the sample, and researchers can calculate confidence limits for sampling error. But when probability sampling costs too much or takes too much time, marketing researchers often take *non-probability samples*, even though their sampling error cannot be

Table 4.4 Types of samples

Probability sample	
Simple random sample	Every member of the population has a known and equal chance of selection.
Stratified random sample	The population is divided into mutually exclusive groups (such as age groups) and random samples are drawn from each group.
Cluster (area) sample	The population is divided into mutually exclusive groups (such as blocks) and the researcher draws a sample of the groups to interview.
Non-probability sample	
Convenience sample	The researcher selects the easiest population members from which to obtain information.
Judgment sample	The researcher uses his or her judgment to select population members who are good prospects for accurate information.
Quota sample categories	The researcher finds and interviews a prescribed number of people in each of several categories.

measured. These varied ways of drawing samples have different costs and time limitations as well as different accuracy and statistical properties. Which method is best depends on the needs of the research project.

Research instruments

In collecting primary data, marketing researchers have a choice of two main research instruments: the *questionnaire* and *mechanical devices*.

Questionnaires

The questionnaire is by far the most common instrument, whether administered in person, by phone, by e-mail or online. Questionnaires are very flexible; there are many ways to ask questions. Closed-ended questions include all the possible answers, and subjects make choices among them. Examples include multiple-choice questions and scale questions. Open-ended questions allow respondents to answer in their own words. In a survey of airline users, Alitalia might simply ask, 'What is your opinion of Alitalia?' Or it might ask people to complete a sentence: 'When I choose an airline, the most important consideration is . . .' These and other kinds of open-ended questions often reveal more than closed-ended questions because they do not limit respondents' answers.

Open-ended questions are especially useful in exploratory research, when a researcher is trying to find out *what* people think but is not measuring *how many* people think in a certain way. Closed-ended questions, on the other hand, provide answers that are easier to interpret and tabulate.

Researchers should also use care in the *wording* and *ordering* of questions. They should use simple, direct and unbiased wording. Questions should be arranged in a logical order. The first question should create interest if possible, and difficult or personal questions should be asked last so that respondents do not become defensive.

Mechanical instruments

Although questionnaires are the most common research instrument, researchers also use mechanical instruments to monitor consumer behaviour. Nielsen Media Research attaches people meters to television sets, cable boxes and satellite systems in selected homes to record who watches which

Eyetracker use equipment that measures every movement of a shopper's eyes.

Source: Eyetracker

programmes. Retailers use checkout scanners to record shoppers' purchases. Other mechanical devices measure subjects' physical responses.[24]

Ipsos Mori, the market research firm, and its technology partner Eyetracker use equipment that measures every movement of a shopper's eyes. Encircling the head of participants is a plastic band supporting two miniature cameras wired up to a digital video recorder. One camera films everything in their field of vision. The other tracks tiny movements of their right eye to generate a visual record of every item of packaging, sign and shelf-label they looks at. This cyborg-style headgear was initially developed to give combat pilots a split-second advantage in dogfights. Nowadays, it is high-street brands that are experimenting with its possibilities as they battle for the attention of time-pressed consumers. Richard Davies, senior vice-president of consumer and market insight at Unilever, the fast-moving consumer goods group, which has an in-house eye-tracking capability, says studying how people's eyes flit about has helped the company design packs that make its shampoos and detergents more noticeable on the supermarket shelf. When participants are asked what they have just looked at during a shopping trip, most people forget details or mix them up; but their eyes tell the true story of what they looked at and what they missed, where they went into the wrong aisle and the point they gave up hunting.

Other researchers are applying 'neuromarketing', measuring brain activity to learn how consumers feel and respond. Marketing scientists using MRI scans and EEG devices have learned that tracking brain electrical activity and blood flow can provide companies with insights into what turns consumers on and off regarding their brands and marketing. 'Companies have always aimed for the customer's heart, but the head may make a better target,' suggests one neuromarketer. 'Neuromarketing is reaching consumers where the action is: the brain.'[25]

Companies ranging from Daimler AG, BMW and Honda UK to Unilever now hire neuromarketing research companies such as NeuroFocus and EmSense to help work out what people are really thinking.[26]

> Thirty men and women are studying a sporty silver test model of a next-generation Hyundai. The 15 men and 15 women are asked to stare at specific parts of the vehicle, including the bumper, the windscreen, and the tires. Electrode-studded caps on their heads capture the electrical activity in their brains as they view the car for an hour. That brainwave information is recorded in a hard drive each person wears on a belt. Hyundai believes that their brain activity will show preferences that could lead to purchasing decisions. 'We want to know what consumers think about a car before we start manufacturing thousands of them,' says Hyundai's manager of brand strategy. He expects the carmaker will tweak the exterior based on the EEG reports, which track activity in all parts of the brain.
>
> Similarly, eBay's PayPal began pitching its online payment service as 'fast' after brainwave research showed that speed turns consumers on more than security and safety, earlier themes used in eBay advertising campaigns. Recently, New Scientist approached the world's leading neurological testing company, NeuroFocus, to evaluate three different cover designs for the August issue. 'We worked with NeuroFocus to select an appealing cover design for New Scientist using their neuromarketing technology,' said Graham Lawton, deputy editor. 'This issue of the magazine achieved strong UK newsstand sales, making it the second highest selling issue of the year, which is very unusual for the normally quiet month of August. This represents a 12 per cent increase over the same issue in the previous year and is much higher than we would expect for a similar cover story at that time of year, so we would certainly say the experiment was a big success.'[27]

Although neuromarketing techniques can measure consumer involvement and emotional responses second by second, such brain responses can be difficult to interpret. Thus, neuromarketing is usually used in combination with other research approaches to gain a more complete picture of what goes on inside consumers' heads.

Implementing the research plan

The researcher next puts the marketing research plan into action. This involves collecting, processing and analysing the information. Data collection can be carried out by a company's marketing research staff or outside firms. Researchers should watch closely to make sure that the plan is implemented correctly. They must guard against problems with interacting with respondents, with the quality of participants' responses, and with interviewers who make mistakes or take shortcuts.

Researchers must also process and analyse the collected data to isolate important information and insight. They need to check data for accuracy and completeness and code it for analysis. Researchers then tabulate the results and compute statistical measures.

Interpreting and reporting the findings

The market researcher must now interpret the findings, draw conclusions and report them to management. A researcher should not try to overwhelm managers with numbers and fancy statistical techniques. Rather, a researcher should present important findings and insights that are useful in the major decisions faced by management.

However, interpretation should not be left only to researchers. They are often experts in research design and statistics, but the marketing manager knows more about the problem and the decisions that must be made. The best research means little if a manager blindly accepts faulty interpretations from a researcher. Similarly, managers may be biased; they might tend to accept research results that show what they expected and reject those that they did not expect or hope for. In many cases, findings can be interpreted in different ways, and discussions between researchers and managers will help point to the best interpretations. Thus, managers and researchers must work together closely when interpreting research results, and both must share responsibility for the research process and resulting decisions.

ANALYSING AND USING MARKETING INFORMATION

Information gathered via internal databases and through competitive marketing intelligence and marketing research usually requires additional analysis. Managers may need help applying the information to gain customer and market insights that will improve their marketing decisions. This help may include advanced statistical analysis to learn more about the relationships within a set of data. Information analysis might also involve the application of analytical models that will help marketers make better decisions.

Once the information has been processed and analysed, it must be made available to the right decision makers at the right time. In the following sections, we look deeper into analysing and using marketing information.

AUTHOR COMMENT

We have talked generally about managing customer relationships throughout the book. But here, 'customer relationship management' has a much narrower data-management meaning. It refers to capturing and using customer data from all sources to manage customer interactions and build customer relationships.

Customer relationship management

The question of how best to analyse and use individual customer data presents special problems. Most companies are awash with information about their customers. In fact, smart companies capture information at every possible customer *touch point*. These touch points include customer purchases, sales force contacts, service and support calls, website visits, satisfaction surveys, credit and payment interactions, market research studies – every contact between a customer and a company.

Unfortunately, this information is usually scattered widely across the organisation. It is buried deep in the separate databases and records of different company departments. To overcome such problems, many companies are now turning to **customer relationship management (CRM)** to manage detailed information about individual customers and carefully manage customer touch points to maximise customer loyalty.

CRM first burst onto the scene in the early 2000s. Many companies rushed in, implementing overly ambitious CRM programmes that produced disappointing results and many failures. More recently, however, companies are moving ahead more cautiously and implementing CRM systems that really work. In 2011, companies worldwide spent €4.5 billion on CRM systems from companies such as Oracle, Microsoft, Salesforce.com and SAS, up 14.2 per cent from the previous year. By 2012, they will spend an estimated €9.27 billion on CRM systems.[28]

CRM consists of sophisticated software and analytical tools that integrate customer information from all sources, analyse it in depth, and apply the results to build stronger customer relationships. CRM integrates everything that a company's sales, service and marketing teams know about individual customers, providing a 360-degree view of the customer relationship.

Customer relationship management (CRM)— Managing detailed information about individual customers and carefully managing customer touch points to maximise customer loyalty.

CRM analysts develop *data warehouses* and use sophisticated *data mining* techniques to unearth the riches hidden in customer data. A data warehouse is a company-wide electronic database of finely detailed customer information that needs to be sifted through for gems. The purpose of a data warehouse is not only to gather information but also pull it together into a central, accessible location. Then, once the data warehouse brings the data together, a company uses high-powered data mining techniques to sift through the mounds of data and dig out interesting findings about customers.

These findings often lead to marketing opportunities. For example, in grocery retailing, product demand can vary by up to 300 per cent per day depending on the weather. In the UK, Tesco have found that hotter days or days with longer sunshine hours boost sales of ready-washed salad by 19 per cent while sales of broccoli plummet.[29] Walmart's huge database provides deep insights for marketing decisions. A few years ago, as Hurricane Ivan roared toward the Florida coast, reports one observer, the giant retailer 'knew exactly what to rush onto the shelves of stores in the hurricane's path – strawberry Pop Tarts. By mining years of sales data from just prior to other hurricanes, [Walmart] figured out that shoppers would stock up on Pop Tarts – which don't require refrigeration or cooking.'[30]

> Data management might sound like a dry field, where statisticians and computer programmers haggle over terabytes and p-values. But as it becomes more sophisticated and yields ever richer portraits of customers and their behaviours, helped by social networking, it is increasingly becoming central to executive decision-making. The pioneers have reaped tremendous rewards. Sir Terry Leahy, former chief executive of Tesco, leaned so heavily on the customer portraits delivered by Dunnhumby that he ended up buying the company. Dunnhumby ploughed through the data yielded by Tesco's Clubcard programme to build ever more detailed customer profiles, to the point where, it now has 12 million unique profiles of its 15 million customers. Its work is widely credited with helping Tesco open a wide lead over its UK supermarket rivals.[31]

By using CRM to understand customers better, companies can provide higher levels of customer service and develop deeper customer relationships. They can use CRM to pinpoint high-value customers, target them more effectively, cross-sell a company's products, and create offers tailored to specific customer requirements.

CRM benefits do not come without costs or risk, either in collecting the original customer data or in maintaining and mining it. The most common mistake is to view CRM only as a technology and software solution. Yet technology alone cannot build profitable customer relationships. Companies can improve customer relationships by simply installing some new software. Instead, CRM is just one part of an effective overall *customer relationship management strategy*. 'There's lots of talk about CRM, and these days it usually has to do with a software solution,' says one analyst. But marketers should start by adhering to 'some basic tenets of actual customer relationship management – and *then* empower them with high-tech solutions.'[32] They should focus first on the *R*; it is the *relationship* that CRM is all about.

Distributing and using marketing information

Marketing information has no value until it is used to gain customer insights and make better marketing decisions. Thus, the marketing information system must make the information readily available to managers and others who need it. In some cases, this means providing managers with regular performance reports, intelligence updates and reports on the results of research studies.

But marketing managers may also need non-routine information for special situations and on-the-spot decisions. For example, a sales manager having trouble with a large customer may want a summary of the account's sales and profitability over the past year. Or a retail store manager who has run out of a best-selling product may want to know the current inventory levels in the chain's other stores. These days, therefore, information distribution involves entering information into databases and making it available in a timely, user-friendly way.

Many firms use a company *intranet* and internal CRM systems to facilitate this process. The internal information systems provide ready access to research information, customer contact information, reports, shared work documents, contact information for employees and other stakeholders, and more. For example, Cablecom, Switzerland's largest cable operator, discovered unhappy customers were most likely to quit after about nine months. So, it ran a feedback programme targeting people who had been customers for seven months. The data from the programme was analysed and more than 100 churn indicators identified – their exact nature is a closely guarded secret – but they have enabled the company to identify customers who may be about to leave. The 'customer retention team' is then activated before it's too late. In pilot studies, the technology has allowed Cablecom to reduce churn rates from 19 per cent to just 2 per cent.[33]

In addition, companies are increasingly allowing key customers and value-network members to access account, product and other data on demand through *extranets*. Suppliers, customers, resellers and select other network members may access a company's extranet to update their accounts, arrange purchases and check orders against inventories to improve customer service. For example, SkyHawke Tech Ltd produces one of the world's most popular portable golf GPS rangefinders, called the SkyCaddie. Working with Mesacom Tech Ltd of the UK, SkyHawke established an extranet for the broad range of graphic designers, media organisations and publishers involved in different campaigns which produce a huge number of files and other materials. This extranet eases the administrative burden on the firm by allowing suppliers and designers to take responsibility for updating their content.[34]

Thanks to modern technology, today's marketing managers can gain direct access to the information system at any time and from virtually any location. They can tap into the system while working at a home office, from a hotel room or from the local Starbucks through a wireless network – indeed anywhere they can turn on a laptop or BlackBerry and link up. Such systems allow managers to get the information they need directly and quickly and tailor it to their own needs.

AUTHOR COMMENT

We finish this chapter by examining three special marketing information topics.

OTHER MARKETING INFORMATION CONSIDERATIONS

This section discusses marketing information in two special contexts: marketing research in small businesses and non-profit organisations and international marketing research. Finally, we look at public policy and ethics issues in marketing research.

Marketing research in small businesses and non-profit organisations

Just like larger firms, small organisations need market information and the customer and market insights that it can provide. Managers of small businesses and non-profit organisations often think that marketing research can be done only by experts in large companies with big research budgets. True, large-scale research studies are beyond the budgets of most small businesses. However, many of the marketing research techniques discussed in this chapter also can be used by smaller organisations in a less formal manner and at little or no expense. Consider how one small-business owner conducted market research on a shoestring before even opening his doors:[35]

> After a string of bad experiences with his local dry cleaner, Robert Byerley decided to open his own dry-cleaning business. But before jumping in, he conducted plenty of market research. He needed a key customer insight: how would he make his business stand out from the others? To start, Byerley spent an entire week in the library and online, researching the dry-cleaning industry. To get input from potential customers, using a marketing firm, Byerley held focus groups on the store's name, look and brochure. He also took clothes to the 15 best competing cleaners in town and had focus group members critique their work. Based on his research, he made a list of features for his new business. First on his list: quality. His business would stand behind everything it did. Not on the list: cheap prices. Creating the perfect dry-cleaning establishment simply did not fit with a discount operation.
>
> With his research complete, Byerley opened Bibbentuckers, a high-end dry cleaner positioned on high-quality service and convenience. It featured a McDonald's-like drive-through area with curb side delivery. A computerised bar-code system read customer cleaning preferences and tracked clothes all the way through the cleaning process. Byerley added other differentiators, such as decorative awnings, TV screens, and refreshments (even 'sweets for the kids and a doggy treat for your best friend'). 'I wanted a place . . . that paired five-star service and quality with an establishment that didn't look like a dry cleaner,' he says. The market research yielded results. Today, Bibbentuckers is a thriving six-store operation.

'Too [few] small-business owners have a . . . marketing mind-set,' says a small-business consultant. 'You have to think like P&G. What would they do before launching a new product? They would find out who their customer is and who their competition is.'[36]

Thus, small businesses and not-for-profit organisations can obtain good marketing insights through observation or informal surveys using small convenience samples. Also, many associations, local media and government agencies provide special help to small organisations. For example, in the UK the Department for Business, Innovation and Skills offers dozens of free publications and a website (www.businesslink.gov.uk) that give advice on topics ranging from starting, financing and expanding a small business to ordering business cards. The European Commission supports the European Small Business portal (http://ec.europa.eu/small-business/most-of-market/human-resources/index_en.htm), which provides a wealth of helpful material and resources. Other excellent Web resources for small businesses include the European Council for Small Business and Entrepreneurship (www.ecsb.org/) and Eurostat – the Statistical Office of the European Communities (http://epp.eurostat.ec.europa.eu/portal/page/portal/eurostat/home). Finally, small businesses can collect a considerable amount of information at very little cost online. They can scour competitor and customer websites and use Internet search engines to research specific companies and issues.

In summary, secondary data collection, observation, surveys and experiments can all be used effectively by small organisations with small budgets. However, although these informal research methods are less complex and less costly, they still must be conducted with care. Managers must think carefully about the objectives of the research, formulate questions in advance, recognise the biases introduced by smaller samples and less skilled researchers, and conduct the research systematically.[37]

Small businesses and non-profit organisations can search websites and use Internet search engines to research specific companies and issues.

Source: Shutterstock.com

International marketing research

International marketing research has grown tremendously over the past decade. International researchers follow the same steps as domestic researchers, from defining the research problem and developing a research plan to interpreting and reporting the results. However, these researchers often face more and different problems. Whereas domestic researchers deal with fairly homogeneous markets within a single country, international researchers deal with diverse markets in many different countries. These markets often vary greatly in their levels of economic development, cultures and customs, and buying patterns.

In many foreign markets, the international researcher may have a difficult time finding good secondary data. Whereas marketing researchers can obtain reliable secondary data from dozens of domestic research services, many countries have almost no research services at all. Some of the largest international research services do operate in many countries. For example, the Nielsen Company (the world's largest marketing research company) has offices in more than 100 countries, from Wavre, Belgium to Oxford, UK to Nicosia, Cyprus.[38] However, most research firms operate in a relative handful of countries only. Thus, even when secondary information is available, it usually must be obtained from many different sources on a country-by-country basis, making the information difficult to combine or compare.

Because of the scarcity of good secondary data, international researchers often must collect their own primary data. For example, they may find it difficult simply to develop good samples. Researchers can use current telephone directories, e-mail lists, census tract data, and any of several sources of socioeconomic data to construct samples. However, such information is largely lacking in many countries.

Once the sample is drawn, in developed economies, the researcher usually can reach most respondents easily by telephone, by mail, on the Internet or in person. Reaching respondents is often not so easy in other parts of the world. Researchers in some parts of the world cannot rely on telephone, Internet and mail data collection; most data collection is door to door and concentrated in three or four of the largest cities. In some countries, few people have phones or personal computers. In the UK, the World Bank lists over 83 per cent of the population as having access to the Internet. In Armenia the level is about 7 per cent.[39] In some countries, the postal system is notoriously unreliable. In Brazil, for instance, an estimated 30 per cent of the mail is never delivered. In many developing countries, poor roads and transportation systems make certain areas hard to reach, making personal interviews difficult and expensive.[40]

Cultural differences from country to country cause additional problems for international researchers. Language is the most obvious obstacle. For example, questionnaires must be prepared in one language and then translated into the languages of each country researched. Responses then must be translated back into the original language for analysis and interpretation. This adds to research costs and increases the risks of error.

Translating a questionnaire from one language to another is anything but easy. Many idioms, phrases and statements mean different things in different cultures. For example, a Danish executive noted, 'Check this out by having a different translator put back into English what you've translated from English. You'll get the shock of your life. I remember [an example in which] "out of sight, out of mind" had become "'invisible things are insane"'.[41]

Consumers in different countries also vary in their attitudes toward marketing research. People in one country may be very willing to respond; in other countries, non-response can be a major problem. Customs in some countries may prohibit people from talking with strangers. In certain cultures, research questions often are considered too personal. For example, in many Muslim countries, mixed-gender focus groups are taboo, as is videotaping female-only focus groups. Even when respondents are *willing* to respond, they may not be *able* to because of high functional illiteracy rates.

Despite these problems, as global marketing grows, global companies have little choice but to conduct such international marketing research. Although the costs and problems associated with international research may be high, the costs of not doing it – in terms of missed opportunities and mistakes – might be even higher. Once recognised, many of the problems associated with international marketing research can be overcome or avoided.

Public policy and ethics in marketing research

Most marketing research benefits both the sponsoring company and its consumers. Through marketing research, companies gain insights into consumers' needs, resulting in more satisfying products and services and stronger customer relationships. However, the misuse of marketing research can also harm or annoy consumers. Two major public policy and ethics issues in marketing research are intrusions on consumer privacy and the misuse of research findings.

Intrusions on consumer privacy

Many consumers feel positive about marketing research and believe that it serves a useful purpose. Some actually enjoy being interviewed and giving their opinions. However, others strongly resent or even mistrust marketing research. They do not like being interrupted by researchers. They worry that marketers are building huge databases full of personal information about customers. Or they fear that researchers might use sophisticated techniques to probe our deepest feelings, peek over our shoulders as we shop, or eavesdrop on our conversations and then use this knowledge to manipulate our buying.

There are no easy answers when it comes to marketing research and privacy. For example, is it a good or bad thing that marketers track and analyse consumers' Web clicks and target ads to individuals based on their browsing and social networking behaviour? Similarly, should we applaud or resent companies that monitor consumer discussions on YouTube, Facebook, Twitter or other public social networks in an effort to be more responsive? For example, Skype could use Attentio's Brand Dashboard routinely to track social media conversations. Someone commenting about Skype on a popular blog might be surprised by a response from a Skype representative within only a few hours. Such monitoring is an opportunity to engage consumers in helpful two-way conversations. However, some disconcerted consumers might see it as an intrusion on their privacy.

Consumers may also have been taken in by previous 'research surveys' that actually turned out to be attempts to sell them something. Still other consumers confuse legitimate marketing research studies with promotional efforts and say 'no' before the interviewer can even begin. Most, however, simply resent the intrusion. They dislike mail, telephone or Web surveys that are too long or too personal or that interrupt them at inconvenient times.

Increasing consumer resentment has become a major problem for the marketing research industry, leading to lower survey response rates in recent years. Just as companies face the challenge of unearthing valuable but potentially sensitive consumer data while also maintaining consumer trust, consumers wrestle with the trade-offs between personalisation and privacy. Although many consumers willingly exchange personal information for free services, easy credit, discounts, upgrades and all sorts of rewards, they also worry about the growth in online identity theft.

A study by TRUSTe, an organisation that monitors the privacy practices of websites, found that more than 90 per cent of respondents view online privacy as a 'really' or 'somewhat' important issue. More than 75 per cent agreed with the statement, 'The Internet is not well regulated, and naïve users can easily be taken advantage of.' And 66 per cent of consumers do not want marketers to track their online behaviour and tailor advertisements to their interests. So it is no surprise that they are now less than willing to reveal personal information on websites.[42]

The marketing research industry is considering several options for responding to this problem. The European Federation of Associations of Market Research Organisations and ESOMAR (a global organisation that promotes market research standards) have recently jointly suggested a range of amendments to the European Commission's Directive 95/46/EC that deals with data protection. The industry also has considered adopting broad standards, perhaps based on the ESOMAR and International Chamber of Commerce worldwide code of ethical practice (the ICC/ESOMAR International Code on Market and Social Research). This code outlines researchers' responsibilities to respondents and the general public. For example, it says that researchers should make their names and addresses available to participants. It also bans companies from representing activities such as database compilation or sales and promotional pitches as research.

Most major companies – including Shell, Siemens, Deutsche Telekom, IBM and Microsoft – have now appointed a chief privacy officer (CPO), whose job is to safeguard the privacy of consumers who do business with the company. IBM's CPO claims that her job requires 'multidisciplinary thinking and attitude'. She needs to get all company departments, from technology, legal and accounting to marketing and communications working together to safeguard customer privacy.[43]

In the end, if researchers provide value in exchange for information, customers will gladly provide it. For example, Amazon's customers do not mind if the firm builds a database of products they buy as a way to provide future product recommendations. This saves time and provides value. Similarly, Bizrate users gladly complete surveys rating online seller sites because they can view the overall ratings of others when making purchase decisions. The best approach is for researchers to ask only for the information they need, use it responsibly to provide customer value, and avoid sharing information without a customer's permission.

Misuse of research findings

Research studies can be powerful persuasion tools; companies often use study results as claims in their advertising and promotion. Today, however, many research studies appear to be little more than vehicles for pitching the sponsor's products. In fact, in some cases, the research surveys appear to have been designed just to produce the intended effect. Few advertisers openly rig their research designs or blatantly misrepresent the findings; most abuses tend to be more subtle 'stretches'. For example, UK phone and broadband provider TalkTalk claimed that customers could save £140 (€160) per year. Their television advertisements exhorted customers to 'join our customers who are already saving an average of over £140 a year'. Competitors complained that such claims were misleading exaggerations as they were based on average savings of TalkTalk customers and not on the savings that could be achieved by new target customers. While TalkTalk argued that the on-screen text of their claims was surrounded by question marks (and thus was a question rather than a definitive statement), the UK Advertising Standards Authority heavily criticised TalkTalk's approach.

Recognising that surveys can be abused, several associations – including the European Society for Opinion and Market Research, the European Marketing Association, the Academy of Marketing, the American Marketing Association, the Marketing Research Association, and the Council of American Survey Research Organizations (CASRO) – have developed codes of research ethics and standards of conduct. For example, the CASRO Code of Standards and Ethics for Survey Research outlines researchers' responsibilities to respondents, including confidentiality, privacy and avoidance of harassment. It also outlines major responsibilities in reporting results to clients and the public.[44]

In the end, however, unethical or inappropriate actions cannot simply be regulated away. Each company must accept responsibility for policing the conduct and reporting of its own marketing research to protect consumers' best interests and its own.

 # REVIEWING THE CONCEPTS

To create value for customers and build meaningful relationships with them, marketers must first gain fresh, deep insights into what customers need and want. Such insights come from good marketing information. As a result of the recent explosion of marketing technology, companies can now obtain great quantities of information, sometimes even too much. The challenge is to transform today's vast volume of consumer information into actionable customer and market insights.

OBJECTIVE 1 Explain the importance of information in gaining insights about the marketplace and customers (pp. 109–110).

The marketing process starts with a complete understanding of the marketplace and consumer needs and wants. Thus, a company needs sound information to produce superior value and satisfaction for its customers. A company also requires information on competitors, resellers, and other actors and forces in the marketplace. Increasingly, marketers

CHAPTER 4 MANAGING MARKETING INFORMATION TO GAIN CUSTOMER INSIGHTS

are viewing information not only as an input for making better decisions but also as an important strategic asset and marketing tool.

OBJECTIVE 2 Define the marketing information system and discuss its parts (pp. 110–113).

The *marketing information system (MIS)* consists of people and procedures for assessing information needs, developing the needed information and helping decision makers use the information to generate and validate actionable customer and market insights. A well-designed information system begins and ends with users.

The MIS first *assesses information needs*. The MIS primarily serves a company's marketing and other managers, but it may also provide information to external partners. Then the MIS *develops information* from internal databases, marketing intelligence activities and marketing research. *Internal databases* provide information on a company's own operations and departments. Such data can be obtained quickly and cheaply but often needs to be adapted for marketing decisions. *Marketing intelligence* activities supply everyday information about developments in the external marketing environment. *Market research* consists of collecting information relevant to a specific marketing problem faced by a company. Lastly, the MIS helps users analyse and use the information to develop customer insights, make marketing decisions, and manage customer relationships.

OBJECTIVE 3 Outline the steps in the marketing research process (pp. 113–128).

The first step in the marketing research process involves *defining the problem and setting the research objectives*, which may be exploratory, descriptive or causal research. The second step consists of *developing a research plan* for collecting data from primary and secondary sources. The third step calls for *implementing the marketing research plan* by gathering, processing and analysing the information. The fourth step consists of *interpreting and reporting the findings*. Additional information analysis helps marketing managers apply the information and provides them with sophisticated statistical procedures and models from which to develop more rigorous findings.

Both *internal* and *external* secondary data sources often provide information more quickly and at a lower cost than primary data sources, and they can sometimes yield information that a company cannot collect by itself. However, needed information might not exist in secondary sources. Researchers must also evaluate secondary information to ensure that it is *relevant*, *accurate*, *current* and *impartial*.

Primary research must also be evaluated for these features. Each primary data collection method – *observational*, *survey* and *experimental* – has its own advantages and disadvantages. Similarly, each of the various research contact methods – mail, telephone, personal interview and online – also has its own advantages and drawbacks.

OBJECTIVE 4 Explain how companies analyse and use marketing information (pp. 128–130).

Information gathered in internal databases and through marketing intelligence and marketing research usually requires more analysis. To analyse individual customer data, many companies have now acquired or developed special software and analysis techniques – called *customer relationship management (CRM)* – that integrate, analyse and apply the mountains of individual customer data contained in their databases.

Marketing information has no value until it is used to make better marketing decisions. Thus, the MIS must make the information available to managers and others who make marketing decisions or deal with customers. In some cases, this means providing regular reports and updates; in other cases, it means making nonroutine information available for special situations and on-the-spot decisions. Many firms use company intranets and extranets to facilitate this process. Thanks to modern technology, today's marketing managers can gain direct access to marketing information at any time and from virtually any location.

OBJECTIVE 5 Discuss the special issues some marketing researchers face, including public policy and ethics issues (pp. 130–134).

Some marketers face special marketing research situations, such as those conducting research in small business, not-for-profit, or international situations. Marketing research can be conducted effectively by small businesses and non-profit organisations with limited budgets. International marketing researchers follow the same steps as domestic researchers but often face more and different problems. All organisations need to act responsibly to major public policy and ethical issues surrounding marketing research, including issues of intrusions on consumer privacy and misuse of research findings.

NAVIGATING THE KEY TERMS

DISCUSSING AND APPLYING THE CONCEPTS

Discussing the concepts

1. Discuss the real value of marketing research and marketing information and how that value is attained. (AACSB: Communication)

2. Discuss the sources of internal data and the advantages and disadvantages associated with this data. (AACSB: Communication)

3. Explain the role of secondary data in gaining customer insights. Where do marketers obtain secondary data, and what are the potential problems in using such data? (AACSB: Communication)

4. What are the advantages of Web-based survey research over traditional survey research? (AACSB: Communication)

5. Compare open-ended and closed-ended questions. When and for what is each type of question useful in marketing research? (AACSB: Communication; Reflective Thinking)

6. What are the similarities and differences when conducting research in another country versus the domestic market? (AACSB: Communication)

Applying the concepts

1. Perform an Internet search on 'social media monitoring' to find companies that specialise in monitoring social media. Discuss two of these companies. Then find two more sites that allow free monitoring and describe how marketers can use these to monitor their brands. Write a brief report on your findings. (AACSB: Communication; Use of IT; Reflective Thinking)

2. Summarise an article describing a marketing research study. Describe how the data were collected. Is the research objective exploratory, descriptive or causal? Explain your conclusions. (AACSB: Communication; Reflective Thinking)

3. Focus groups are commonly used during exploratory research. A focus group interview entails gathering a group of people to discuss a specific topic. In a small group, research how to conduct a focus group interview and then conduct one with six to ten other students to learn what services your university could offer to better meet student needs. Assign one person in your group to be the moderator while the others observe and interpret the responses from the focus group participants. Present a report of what you learned from this research. (AACSB: Communication; Reflective Thinking)

Focus on technology

Picture yourself with wires hooked up to your head or entering a magnetic tube that can see inside your brain. You must be undergoing some medical test, right? Think again – it's marketing research! Marketing research is becoming more like science fiction with a new field called neuromarketing, which uses technologies such as magnetic resonance imaging (MRI) to peer into consumers' brains in an attempt to understand cognitive and affective responses to marketing stimuli. One company, Thinkingcraft, uses a methodology called 'neurographix' to help marketers develop messages that fit the way customers think. The Omnicon advertising agency uses 'neuroplanning' to determine the appropriate media mix for a client. One study found that consumers preferred Pepsi over Coke in blind taste tests but preferred Coke when they could see the names of the brands tasted. Different areas of the brain were activated when they knew the brand compared to when they did not, suggesting that what marketers make us believe is more persuasive than what our own taste buds tell us.

1. Learn more about neuromarketing and discuss another example of its application. (AACSB: Communication; Technology)

2. Critics have raised concerns over the usefulness and ethics of this type of marketing research. Discuss both sides of the debate surrounding this methodology. (AACSB: Communication; Ethical Reasoning)

Focus on ethics

Marketing information helps develop insights into the needs of customers, and gathering competitive intelligence (CI) data supplies part of this information. CI has blossomed into a fully fledged industry, with most major companies establishing CI units. But not all CI gathering is ethical or legal – even at venerable Procter & Gamble. In 1943, a P&G employee bribed a Lever Brothers (now Unilever) employee to obtain bars of Swan soap, which was then under development, to improve its Ivory brand. P&G settled the case by paying Unilever almost €4 million (about €43 million in today's money) for patent infringement – a small price to pay given the market success of Ivory. In 2001, P&G once again paid a €7.5 million settlement to Unilever for a case that involved a contractor rummaging through a waste bin outside Unilever's office, an infraction that was actually reported by P&G itself.

1. Find another example of corporate espionage and write a brief report on it. Did the guilty party pay damages or serve time in prison? Discuss what punishments, if any, should be levied in cases of corporate espionage. (AACSB: Communication; Ethical Reasoning)

2. How can businesses protect themselves from corporate espionage? (AACSB: Communication; Reflective Thinking)

Marketing & the economy

Caesars Entertainment Corporation (formerly Harrah's Entertainment from 1995 to 2010) runs casinos largely in the US but also worldwide from the UK to Uruguay. Over the past decade, Caesars has honed its CRM skills to become bigger and more profitable than any other company in the gaming industry. The foundation of its success is Total Rewards, a loyalty programme that collects a mother lode of customer information and mines it to identify important customers and meet their specific needs through a personalised experience. But in recent times, Caesars has seen its flow of customers slow to a trickle. Not only are customers visiting less often, but the normally €40 gamer is now playing only €20. As a result, Caesars revenues have declined for the past two years in a row. Caesars isn't alone; the rest of the industry is also suffering as more people save their money or spend it on necessities rather than entertainment. Caesars' CRM efforts have always focused on delighting every customer. The company claims that customer spending increases 24 per cent with a happy experience. But even Caesars' uncanny ability to predict which customers will be motivated by show tickets, room upgrades or free chips has not made Caesars immune to the woes of an economic downturn.

1. Is the dip in Caesars' business unavoidable given recent economic troubles or can Caesars find new ways to connect with customers? What would you recommend?

2. In difficult economic times, is it responsible for Caesars to try to get people to spend more money on gambling?

Marketing by the numbers

Have you ever been disappointed because a television channel cancelled one of your favourite television programmes because of 'low ratings'? The channel didn't ask your opinion, did it? It probably didn't task any of your friends, either. That's because in the UK estimates of television audience sizes are based on research done by the Broadcast Audience Research Board (BARB), which uses a sample of around 5,000 households out of the more than 62 million households in the UK to determine national ratings for television programmes. That doesn't seem like enough, does it? As it turns out, statistically, it's significantly more than enough.

1. Go to www.surveysystem.com/sscalc.htm to determine the appropriate sample size for a population of 113 million households (the number for the USA). Assuming a confidence interval of 5, how large should the sample of households be if desiring a 95 per cent confidence level? How large for a 99 per cent confidence level? Briefly explain what is meant by *confidence interval* and *confidence level*. (AACSB: Communication; Use of IT; Analytical Reasoning)

2. What sample sizes are necessary at population sizes of 1 billion, 10,000 and 100 with a confidence interval of 5 and a 95 per cent confidence level? Explain the effect population size has on sample size. (AACSB: Communication; Use of IT; Analytical Reasoning)

REFERENCES

[1] This case study draws heavily on the excellent case studies and analyses (including quotes and other information) of John Reed, 'Demand is putting the mobile into automobile', *Financial Times* (7 May 2010), www.ft.com/cms/s/0/a71c37c8-597f-11df-99ba-00144feab49a.html#ixzz1aN8evMI9, accessed October 2011 John Reed , 'Carmakers tempt cellphone generation with pay-as-you-go', *Financial Times* (6 May 2010), www.ft.com/cms/s/0/8ac182d4-593b-11df-adc3-00144feab49a.html#axzz1aMTZCnRp, accessed October 2011 John Reed , 'Sharing: flexible hire is the talk of accessed October 2011 the town', *Financial Times* (12 September 2011), http://ft.com/cms/s/0/4dd389be-d7c3-11e0-a06b-00144feabdc0.html#ixzz1aN9QCPyj, accessed October 2011 Miles Brignall, 'Peugeot launches car club with a difference', *Guardian* (10 July 2010), www.guardian.co.uk/money/2010/jul/10/peugeot-car-club-mu, accessed October 2011 Andrew English, 'Credit-card motoring: Mu by Peugeot on test', *The Telegraph* (14 June 2010), www.telegraph.co.uk/motoring/green-motoring/7821496/Credit-card-motoring-Mu-by-Peugeot-on-test.html, accessed October 2010.

[2] Unless otherwise noted, quotes in this section are from the excellent, discussion of customer insights found in Mohanbir Sawhney, 'Insights into customer insight,' www.redmond.nl/hro/upload/Insights_into_Customer_Insights.pdf, accessed April 2009. The Apple iPod example is also adapted from this article. Also see 'Corporate news: demands for Macs, iPhones fuels Apple', *Wall Street Journal Asia* (27 January 2010), p. 22.

[3] Alan Mitchell, 'Consumer data gathering has changed from top to bottom', *Marketing* (12 August 2009), pp. 26–27.

[4] Carey Toane, 'Listening: the new metric', *Strategy* (September 2009), p. 45.

[5] Warren Thayer and Michael Sansolo, 'Walmart: our retailer of the year', *R&FF Retailer* (June 2009), pp. 14–20.

[6] Ian C. MacMillan and Larry Seldon, 'The incumbent's advantage', *Harvard Business Review* (October 2008), pp. 111–121.

[7] Example from Tim Bradshaw, 'Online advertisers issue tracking code', *Financial Times* (15 April 2011), www.ft.com/cms/s/0/7e9e1368-66ce-11e0-8d88-00144feab49a.html#axzz1WOopxs9y accessed October 2011.

[8] Example based on information from http://attentio.com/ and specifically regarding the Fosters Comedy Study from http://blog.attentio.com/wp-content/uploads/Adapted-case-study-NAKED-and-Attentio_Fosters2.pdf, accessed October 2011.

[9] See www.europages.com, accessed October 2011.

[10] For more on research firms that supply marketing information, see Jack Honomichl, 'Honomichl Top 50', special section, *Marketing News*, (30 June 2009). Other information from www.us.nielsen.com/products/cps.shtml; www.smrb.com/web/guest/core-solutions/national-consumer-study; and www.yankelovich.com, accessed October 2011.

[11] See http://us.infores.com/ProductsSolutions/AllProducts/AllProductsDetail/tabid/159/productid/84/Default.aspx, accessed October 2011.

[12] Example from Rose Jacobs, 'Rank sets out to discover home truths', *Financial Times* (7 February 2011), www.ft.com/cms/s/0/49bde8ca-32f9-11e0-9a61-00144feabdc0.html#axzz1UPifHx5H, accessed October 2011.

[13] See Pradeep K. Tyagi, 'Webnography: A new tool to conduct marketing research', *Journal of American Academy of Business* (March 2010), pp. 262–268.

[14] Spencer E. Ante, 'The Science of desire', *BusinessWeek* (5 June, 2006), p. 100; Rhys Blakely, 'You know when it feels like somebody's watching you . . .', *Times* (14 May 2007), p. 46; and Jack Neff, 'Marketing execs: researchers could use a softer touch', *Advertising Age* (27 January 2009), http://adage.com/article?article_id=134144.

[15] Example from Rose Jacobs, 'Mecca finds gold dust in bingogoer rituals', *Financial Times* (7 February 2011), www.ft.com/cms/s/0/676c36ac-32fd-11e0-9a61-00144feabdc0.html#axzz1UPifHx5H, accessed October 2011.

[16] Jack Neff, 'Marketing Execs: Researchers Could Use a Softer Touch', *Advertising Age*, 27 January 2009, http://adage.com/article?article_id=134144.

[17] See 'Study finds trouble for opt-in Internet surveys'; and Internet penetration statistics found at www.internetworldstats.com/stats14.htm, accessed October 2011.

[18] Ibid.

[19] Based on information found at www.channelm2.com/HowOnlineQualitativeResearch.html, accessed October 2011.

[20] See 'Online panel', www.zoomerang.com/online-panel, accessed October 2011.

[21] Adapted from Jeremy Nedelka, 'Adidas relies on insiders for insight', *1to1 Media* (9 November 2009), www.1to1media.com/view.aspx?DocID=31963&m=n.

[22] Stephen Baker, 'The Web knows what you want', *BusinessWeek* (27 July 2009), p. 48.

[23] For more on Internet privacy, see 'What would you reveal on the Internet?', *Privacy Journal* (January 2009), p. 1; Jayne O'Donnell, 'Cookies sound sweet, but they can be risky', *USA Today* (26 October 2009): and James Temple, 'All eyes on online privacy', *San Francisco Chronicle* (29 January 2010), p. D1.

[24] Example from Alicia Clegg, 'Eyes in the aisles reveal shopping secrets', *Financial Times* (17 February 2011), www.ft.com/cms/s/0/8f1665ac-3ac7-11e0-9c1a-00144feabdc0.html#axzz1UPifHx5H, accessed October 2011.

[25] Jessica Tsai, 'Are you smarter than a neuromarketer?', *Customer Relationship Management* (January 2010), pp. 19–20.

[26] This and the other neuromarketing examples are adapted from Laurie Burkitt, 'Neuromarketing: companies use neuroscience for consumer insight', *Forbes* (16 November 2009), www.forbes.com/forbes/2009/1116/marketing-hyundai-neurofocus-brain-waves-battle-for-the-brain.html, accessed October 2011.

[27] Example from Anonymous, 'Sales success shows neuromarketing moves magazines: New Scientist reports 12% increase in newsstand sales for issue featuring NeuroFocus-tested cover design', *PR Newswire Europe* (2 September 2010), www.prnewswire.com/news-releases/sales-success-shows-neuromarketing-moves-magazines-new-scientist-reports-12-increase-in-newsstand-sales-for-issue-featuring-neurofocus-tested-cover-design-102081328.htm, accessed October 2011.

[28] See Barney Beal, 'Gartner: CRM spending looking up'. *SearchCRM.com* (29 April 2008), http://searchcrm.techtarget.com/news/article/0,289142,sid11_gci1311658,00.html; David White, 'CRM Magazine announces winners of 2009 CRM service awards', *Business Wire* (1 April 2009); and 'Research and markets: global customer relationship management (CRM) sales automation software market 2008–2012', *M2 Presswire* (14 January 2010).

[29] Example from Rod Addy, 'Tesco keeps a keen eye on its fair-weather customers', *Foodmanufacture.co.uk* (26 March 2008), www.foodmanufacture.co.uk/Business-News/Tesco-keeps-a-keen-eye-on-its-fair-weather-customers, accessed October 2011.

[30] Mike Freeman, 'Data company helps Walmart, casinos, airlines analyze customers', *San Diego Union Tribune*. For another good CRM example, see 'SAS Helps 1-800-Flowers.com Grow Deep Roots with Customers', www.sas.com/success/1800flowers.html, accessed October 2011.

[31] Example from Philip Delves Broughton, 'The added value of good information', *Financial Times* (7 March 2011), www.ft.com/cms/s/0/cca74d5c-4907-11e0-af8c-00144feab49a.html#axzz1UPifHx5H, accessed October 2011.

[32] Gillian S. Ambroz, 'CRM: getting back to basics', *Folio* (January 2010), p. 97.

[33] Example from Geoff Nairn, 'System gives a warning of unhappiness', *Financial Times* (16 September 2009), www.ft.com/cms/s/0/cc18d792-a2ce-11de-ae7e-00144feabdc0.html#axzz1UPifHx5H, accessed October 2011.

[34] See www.mesacom.co.uk and specifically www.mesacom.co.uk/ProjectExtranetSoftware/Project_Extranet_CaseStudy_SkyCaddie.aspx for details of the SkyCaddie case.

[35] Adapted from information in Ann Zimmerman, 'Small business: do the research', *Wall Street Journal* (9 May 2005), p. R3; with information from John Tozzi, 'Market research on the cheap', *BusinessWeek* (9 January 2008), www.businessweek.com/smallbiz/content/jan2008/sb2008019_352779.htm; and www.bibbentuckers.com, accessed October 2011.

[36] Zimmerman, 'Small business: do the research'.

[37] For some good advice on conducting market research in a small business, see 'Marketing Research . . . Basics 101', www.sba.gov/smallbusinessplanner/index.html, accessed August 2010; and 'Researching your market', US Small Business Administration, www.sba.gov/idc/groups/public/documents/sba_homepage/pub_mt8.pdf, accessed November 2010.

[38] See http://en-us.nielsen.com/main/about/Profile, accessed October 2011.

[39] See http://data.worldbank.org/data-catalog/world-development-indicators?cid=GPD_WDI, accessed October 2011.

[40] Internet stats are from www.worldbank.org; also see www.iwcp.hpg.ig.com.br/communications.html, both accessed October 2011.

[41] Subhash C. Jain, *International Marketing Management*, 3rd edn (Boston'MA: PWS-Kent, 1990), p. 338. For more discussion on international marketing research issues and solutions, see Warren J. Keegan and Mark C. Green, *Global Marketing*, 6th edn (Upper Saddle River, NJ: Prentice Hall, 2011), pp. 170–201.

[42] See Stephanie Clifford, 'Many see privacy on the Web as big issue, survey says', *New York Times* (16 March 2009); and Mark Davis, 'Behavioral targeting of online ads is growing', *McClatchy-Tribune Business News* (19 December 2009). Also see 'Consumers encouraged to protect their privacy online', *PR Newswire* (27 January 2010).

[43] See Jaikumar Vijayan, 'Disclosure laws driving data privacy efforts, says IBM exec', *Computerworld* (8 May 2006), p. 26; 'Facebook chief privacy officer – interview', *Analyst Wire* (18 February 2009); and Rita Zeidner, 'New face in the C-cuite', *HRMagazine* (January 2010), pp. 39–41.

[44] Information at www.casro.org/codeofstandards.cfm#intro, accessed October 2011.

VIDEO CASE

Radian6   MyMarketingLab

As more and more consumers converse through digital media, companies are struggling to figure out how to 'listen in' on the conversations. Traditional marketing research methods can't sift through the seemingly infinite number of words flying around cyberspace at any given moment. But one company is helping marketers get a handle on 'word-of-Web' communication. Radian6 specialises in monitoring social media, tracking websites ranging from Facebook to Flickr. Radian6's unique software opens a door to an entirely different kind of research. Instead of using questionnaires, interviews, or focus groups, Radian6 scans online social media for whatever combination of keywords a marketer might specify. This gives companies valuable insights into what consumers are saying about their products and brands.

After watching the video featuring Radian6, answer the following questions:

1. What benefits does Radian6 provide to marketers over more traditional market research methods? What are its shortcomings?
2. Classify Radian6's software with respect to research approaches, contact methods, sampling plan and research instruments.
3. How is Radian6 helping companies develop stronger relationships with customers?

COMPANY CASE

Nestlé, L'Oréal, Britvic, SABMiller: everybody wants to get close to their customers

Fast-moving consumer good (FMCG) companies like Nestlé, L'Oréal and Britvic all want information about their customers. What is new is that, in recent years, these FMCG firms have become concerned with more than just who their customers are, where they live and how much they are likely to buy. Today, marketers want to get close and get personal and understand what makes their customers tick. It is only through this 'closeness' that companies believe that they are able to understand customer needs and position themselves as the means to satisfy them. In this sense, consistent with the marketing concept, the *raison d'être*, the Holy Grail of FMCG groups is truly to understand and fulfil customer latent needs.

A structured approach to gathering marketing information is present in most successful FMCG firms. Indeed, most FMCG companies spend between 2–3 per cent of their sales on research and development. What is different is that the business of consumer research is intensifying on virtually every level with market researchers going further afield geographically and conducting ever deeper research. In particular, new social media are increasingly being harnessed, be it through social networks or blogs.

These companies are supplementing the valuable insights that can gained via surveys, interviews and focus groups with face-to-face, up-close field work. Experts from a range of disciplines – sociologists, historians, anthropologists and semioticians – are increasingly called on to study consumers at close hand in order to understand consumers' deepest needs and wants, to analyse and predict trends, and to develop databases. The reasons for this trend are complex. In part, the spread of digital social networks drives this more sophisticated approach. However, rapidly changing market dynamics are also behind the new focus intensified by increased competition and a fragile and uncertain economy that makes it ever more important to win customers. 'Traditional research concentrated on the "what". Now we are trying to establish the "why",' says Simon Stewart, marketing director at Britvic, the beverages company. 'We are not asking what they think about products and ideas but focusing on what makes them tick.'

Fast-moving consumer good companies are devoting more resources to digital media. The increasing spread of social media gives them the perfect tool to understand consumers. Starbucks has nearly 15 million fans on Facebook, more than the British Monarchy, the Paris Tourist Board or Charlie Sheen; Coca-Cola has 13.5 million, Twix bars 2 million, Red Bull 22 million and Oreo cookies 11 million fans. In addition to sheer numbers of consumers, the social networks can provide quick feedback. Britvic, for instance, points out that teenage boys are both big Tango drinkers and heavy internet users, providing a constant source of information and feedback. Research had shown that a large percentage of Tango's target audience were avid Facebook users, so this social networking site became the natural choice for communicating directly with them. Such insight was used by the innovative social media agency Nudge who created the 'Tango Head Masher 3000' that allows Facebook users to combine their own, as well as their friends', profile pictures with random objects. Users are able to make fun of their friends by taking their photo, cropping the head and replacing it with a range of random comical objects from a cabbage to a horse's head. Nudge's commercial director, Toby Beresford, said: 'The campaign cost the same as getting 100,000 people to click on an ad and give the brand ten seconds of attention, yet 125,000 people interacted with the brand for an average of three minutes each.' Tango brand manager, Sally Symes went on to note that a staggering 37.5 per cent of users went on to buy Tango.

Consumer psychologists also use special consumer laboratories to observe and study consumers as well as technology that enables them to watch consumers in their own homes. 'It all starts with observation,' says Patricia Pineau, who oversees L'Oréal's consumer insights team, talking about the company's 'Evaluation Centres', which involve laboratories designed to look like bathrooms, as well as placing cameras in people's homes. 'Observing is necessary to decode exactly what [women] are trying to get and what they are attracted to. Sometimes it is the gesture that will reveal something that they really want to gain,' says Ms Pineau.

These gestures are the key to understanding cosmetic use. Japanese women spend a full minute massaging in lotions, patting their faces and eyelids. In Brazil, women change their nail polish every day to match their dress – and are brazenly wanton with the brush, smearing their fingers liberally along with their nails and relying on a cotton bud to mop up afterwards. Research has found that Korean women apply more potions and cosmetics to their faces than anyone else – a staggering total of more than 25 creams and cosmetics at any one time. This compares with around 20–25 in Japan, which is more than double the amount used by American or European women. Japanese women (with quite amazing patience and dedication) may apply more than 50 coatings of mascara at one time, making European women – 5 to 10 coatings – look like rather lazy amateurs (albeit ones with thinner mascara). This data is incredibly useful to L'Oréal who build such information into their targeting product offerings. Hence, Lancôme's Génifique Youth Activating Concentrate has a stickier consistency in Japan than in Europe or the US, the better to pat in. Lip gloss is lighter in Japan, the better to allow the constant reapplication beloved of Japanese women.

Sometimes, however, gestures are not enough and a deeper understanding of consumer habit, proclivities and behaviours is needed. It is then that ethnographers can help. Ethnography relies heavily on participant observation and can lead to deep, meaning and grounded insights into human behaviour. Hence Nestlé's strategy of embedding researchers in family homes, taking tea with a multigenerational Indian family or sitting cross-legged on the floor pounding pulses with a group of hijab-wearing women and their un-scarved, jeans-wearing daughters in Syria. Chandan Mukherji is a veteran of embedding. The New Delhi-based head of consumer insights at Nestlé India has in recent years watched the lifestyle of the middle classes in towns and cities seep out to the villages and countryside. Seated at the family table, he saw housewives were turning to instant noodles but that they still supplemented them with extra vegetables and garnishes. Nestlé responded by supplementing its own instant noodles with vegetables. 'It really is an eye-opener for most of the teams, because they get a real life understanding,' says Mr Mukherji. Indeed, after witnessing at first hand India's small kitchens and vulnerability to rodent infestations, the Swiss group responded to their ethnographers' insights and reduced pack sizes to great success.

Grounded insights can cause dilemmas, however. Research by Nestlé in Peru found that consumers adored the taste of lucuma (a delicious local fruit). Uncertain executives were faced with either relying on the globally favoured, well-established flavour of strawberries or trusting their grounded insights. Turning back to more conventional market research, they did the obvious (a thing that eludes many big groups) and asked sweet-toothed consumers themselves to choose between the lucuma, a local fruit, or strawberry for its popular Besos de Moza – a marshmallow and cookie confection. 'The feedback was amazing,' recalls Carlos Velasco, who heads the Peruvian operation. They chose lucuma, and Nestlé went on to sell 56 million lucuma-flavoured units in 2009 alone.

Researchers also employ social historians to understand better consumption habits and practices. For example, drinks companies take a similarly up close and broad remit – looking not just at what people like to drink but where they like to drink, how they like to drink, with whom they want to drink and when they like to drink. Take the world's second largest brewer SABMiller, the UK headquartered brewer with global operations and brands such as Grolsch, Miller Genuine Draft, Peroni Nastro Azzurro and Pilsner Urquell. SABMiller found that in the very important market of Latin America, the urge to go out to where its drinks were actually drunk – and especially to mix that favourite cocktail of beer and football – was strong but the availability of venues less so. After detailed analysis, Rob Priday, managing director of SABMiller's Peruvian operations, concluded that: 'There's a dearth of pubs in the country. In the terrorist years, people did not go out and now it is over, there are not enough pubs for on-premises drinking.' This was backed by their research which showed that consumers wanted more choice of places to drink. Today, the results of these insights by SABMiller can be can be seen across the cities, towns and streets of Colombia and Peru. The company worked with local businesses and entrepreneurs to open café-style outlets attached to football fields, where fathers can down a glass while their children play – or even have a kick-about game of soccer themselves before sinking a glass or two (of SABMiller lager of course). They have also developed bars where customers can relax and play simulated golf or a few rounds of cards with convivial company.

Semioticians can also help firms get ever closer to their customers. Semioticians study semiotics (sometimes called semiology), which is the analysis of signs and how they are constructed, used and interpreted. Greg Rowland, a semiotician based in London, advises FMCG companies on the messages they need to send to woo customers through their packaging and placing on supermarket shelves. Supermarkets, Mr Rowland says, are a battleground between puritan and hedonistic pleasures – plain fruit and veg stalls as customers first walk in, with the indulgent pleasures of alcohol and chocolate waiting to assail them further down the aisles. We instinctively want to stay on

the sober side, says Mr Rowland, so packaging of indulgent items is classily low-key. Hence the naïve, child-like smiley face on Innocent's drinks cartons or the use of white space on packaging for top-notch biscuits. Or take the heraldic devices on bottles of SABMiller lager, designed to establish the brewer's authority in the minds of drinkers. This is serious stuff, the emblems say, none of your home-made, evil-tasting 'hooch'.

While sociologists, historians, anthropologists, ethnographers and semioticians can all help in improving our understanding of consumers FMCG firms accept that this is merely part of the process. The management of marketing information to gain meaningful insights into customers' lives requires skill, time and a structured approach. Indeed, for all the time, money and expert investigation FMCG companies throw into understanding consumers, mistakes are made. During research into Japanese skincare, a L'Oréal team was surprised to see a woman supplementing her beauty routine with a tiny razor. She slid it around her nose, below her eyebrows and on the nape of her neck. The reason: she was removing almost imperceptible hairs to get a better effect when powder was applied. As a non-daily ritual, and one that required the woman to bring her own razors (which were not on offer in L'Oréal's labs), it had until then completely bypassed the ranks of researchers. Delivery can miss a step too: SABMiller, identifying a desire for a sweeter drink for women in Peru, produced the cider-like Red – which turned out to be extremely popular with the men.

In exploring some of the many innovative approaches used by Nestlé, L'Oréal, Britvic and SABMiller it is clear that genuine insights into customers' means, modes and methods of consumption can prove a crucial insights into satisfying customer needs.

Questions for discussion

1. Briefly discuss Nestle's approach of embedding researchers into people's homes compared to more traditional focus group or interview-based research (used in the Citroën Mu case study at the start of the chapter). What different insights are gained and why?

2. Describe how L'Oréal attempt to gain insight into consumers, lives. Why don't they simply use a questionnaire?

Sources: This case study draws heavily on the excellent case studies and analyses (including quotes and other information) of: Louise Lucas, 'Brands get up close and personal', *Financial Times* (13 October 2010), www.ft.com/cms/s/0/f4a691ee-d6ef-11df-aaab-00144feabdc0.html#ixzz1Zu1j4SnA, accessed October 2011; Nudge Social Media 'How Nudge helped Britvic increase sales of tango through Facebook application' (23 March 2010), www.creativematch.com/news/how-nudge-helped-britvic-increase/98508/, accessed October 2011.

CHAPTER FIVE

Consumer markets and consumer buyer behaviour

Chapter preview

In the previous chapter, you studied how marketers obtain, analyse and use information to develop customer insights and assess marketing programmes. In this chapter and the next, we continue with a closer look at the most important element of the marketplace – customers. The aim of marketing is to affect how customers think and act. To affect the *whats*, *whens* and *hows* of buyer behaviour, marketers must first understand the *whys*. In this chapter, we look at *final consumer* buying influences and processes. In the next chapter, we will study the buyer behaviour of *business customers*. You will see that understanding buyer behaviour is an essential but very difficult task.

To get a better sense of the importance of understanding consumer behaviour, we begin by first looking at Jack Wills the UK founded clothing brand. What makes Jack Wills buyers so loyal? Just what is it that makes the student-types flock to their stores, their events and parties? Partly, it's the way the clothes look and feel. But at the core, customers buy from Jack Wills because the brand itself is a part of their own self-expression and lifestyle. It's a part of what the loyal Jack Wills customer is.

Objective outline

➤ **Objective 1** Define the consumer market and construct a simple model of consumer buyer behaviour.
Model of consumer behaviour (pp. 144–145)

➤ **Objective 2** Name four major factors that influence consumer buyer behaviour.
Characteristics affecting consumer behaviour (pp. 145–159)

➤ **Objective 3** List and define the major types of buying decision behaviour and the stages in the buyer decision process.

Types of buying decision behaviour (pp. 159–160)
The buyer decision process (pp. 161–163)

➤ **Objective 4** Describe the adoption and diffusion process for new products.
The buyer decision process for new products (pp. 164–165)

Jack Wills

It's a holiday weekend and the sun is out in Rock, the Cornish resort in the south of the UK. However, the teenagers in Rock are not heading for the sand and surf but towards a newly-opened clothes shop, Jack Wills. Outside, there are bright flashes of colour – shopping bags in the Jack Wills signature colours of pink and navy blue stripes. The teenagers are all wearing branded Jack Wills clothing: denim mini-skirts worn over leggings, zip-up hoodies, and vests, shirts and shorts. To the embarrassment of their parents and the admiration of their friends, some boys are wearing their trousers 'fashionably' low, the better to display 'Jack Wills' on the elastic of their underpants.

There is something cultish about its fans' devotion to the Jack Wills brand. Visit any upmarket university, boarding school or resort town, and the teens will be there, buying Jack Wills' expensive preppy sportswear (€79 for a hooded sweatshirt and up to €22 for a pair of socks). Jack Wills ('university outfitters') isn't just on the high street. In March 2011 it hosted three nights of events for 2,000 students in Tignes, in the French Alps. It sponsors university balls (such as the Keble College, Oxford May ball) and puts on between-season 'tours' in university towns (giving away bespoke T-shirts for each town, plus mugs, underpants and other coveted trinkets).

The company is one of a number of brands, including the more well-established US label Abercrombie & Fitch, that target teenagers with money and sell them 'preppy' or 'surf-inspired' casual clothes. It prides itself on its stealth marketing and its very direct relationship with its consumers.

Jack Wills shuns advertising in favour of social media and organised events. About 220,000 Facebook and Twitter fans tune in to watch videos of its sponsored events. Among its 1,700 employees, there is a team monitoring followers' tweets and replying to questions. 'We get hundreds of mentions every day on Twitter and we reply to 90 per cent of them,' says marketing manager Freddie Wyatt. 'People ask a question and we'll tweet back an answer along with a video. It's one-to-one contact.' The firm generates buzz for its various collections by each year sending out four catalogues, or handbooks as they're known, to a 400,000-strong UK readership to coincide with U.K. school terms.

The first Jack Wills opened in Salcombe, Devon in the south of the UK, in 1999. Having just graduated, Peter Williams, then 23, became lifestyle brand obsessed. He picked the sleepy resort of Salcombe because 'I'd been once in summer and it really just registered something. When I started thinking about a premium brand I dredged up this vision of what I remembered in Salcombe. I thought, "What if you could create a brand that could bottle what being at a British university was all about and all the cool amazing stuff that goes with that?" It's such a uniquely cherished part of your life. I thought if you could create a brand that epitomised that it would be very compelling.'

He joined forces with Robert Shaw, a university friend then working at a marketing firm, and they scraped together about €50,000 of their own capital from savings, credit cards and loans. They set up Jack Wills (named after Williams' grandfather, Jack Williams) as a summer shop on Fore Street (it's still there and has expanded into the two neighbouring sites). They sold vintage-inspired T-shirts and sweaters bearing the Jack Wills lettering while sleeping above the shop.

George Wallace, head of MHE Retail, a retail consultancy, says Jack Wills has 'created a very classy lifestyle brand with a very tribal following. They've got quite a narrow position – it's very public school – but they've got that group to buy into it in a very big way. They've created something that persuades parents to pay premium prices for reasonable quality, and at very high margins. The worry is if this very fickle group falls out of love with them. It's such a volatile market. If they do, the fall could be spectacular, although I don't see that happening any time soon.'

Jack Wills also taps into the allure of 'privilege' as a selling point. Mat Bickley, founder of retail consultancy joynlondon.com, says: 'Posh is cool again, it's like the 1980s. If you look at all the celebrity endorsements, the bands, the actors and faces of Burberry even now, they're all "society" or public school educated.' There are now 46 Jack Wills shops in the UK, two in Ireland and the brand has opened several stores in the US. It is also expanding into Asia and the Middle East, with the first Jack Wills there likely to be in Dubai. In 2011, Jack Wills took a pop-up store in Terminal 5 complete with a branded Land Rover.

Williams says 'we're still very grassroots about things.' Grassroots are at the heart of everything Jack Wills is about, and its attention to its customers – its community – is what sets it apart from other shops selling to teenagers. Its tweeds, vintage hoodies and print prairie dresses are pleasant but they are not cutting-edge, individual or high fashion. Their same-ness reinforces membership of an exclusive friend-ship group.

Events in the real world make the brand, which even sounds like a friend, into a companion for the good times. The Jack Wills' Varsity Polo is the biggest event in its calendar to date. In the summer of 2011, teams from Harvard, Yale, Oxford and Cambridge universities, and the UK public schools Eton and Harrow, play against each other with 10,000 fans looking on. The company is the official sponsor. Max Reyner, insight editor at LSN Global, says: 'Events are key here and are taking over from social networking, which is still important for awareness but is seen as less cool to teens now, as parents join sites like Facebook. They used to be private spaces. With the events they have a sense of ownership. The fact that Jack Wills doesn't advertise also helps. Teens like the idea of discovery. The whole feel of Jack Wills is like you're in a club and you're shutting out the parents.'

One of Jack Wills' key innovations is its 'Seasonnaires' programme. The company recruits young good-looking people who seem cool and appear outgoing. These 'influencers' attend parties and circulate with guests, handing out free goods and merchandise. This summer a group of Seasonnaires, who are paid and given free clothing by the brand, will travel targeted locations, hosting parties on the beach and in local clubs and pubs, giving out free Jack Wills gifts.

So far Jack Wills has been able to crystallise the essence of a particular group and sell it back to them to wear at the beach and in the nightclub. And those customers seem very, very happy about it. Says Isabelle, 15, standing outside the new Jack Wills in Rock, bedecked head-to-toe in Jack Wills merchandise. 'I like that Jack Wills feels British. I get the catalogue, everyone in my school does. I love their Facebook page too.'[1]

Consumer buyer behaviour—The buying behaviour of final consumers — individuals and households that buy goods and services for personal consumption.

Consumer market—All the individuals and households that buy or acquire goods and services for personal consumption.

Buying behaviour is never simple, yet understanding it is an essential task of marketing management. **Consumer buyer behaviour** refers to the buying behaviour of final consumers – individuals and households that buy goods and services for personal consumption. All of these final consumers combine to make up the **consumer market**. The European consumer market consists of more than 500 million people who consume more €8 billion worth of goods and services each year, making it one of the most attractive consumer markets in the world. The world consumer market consists of more than 6.8 billion people who annually consume an estimated €70 trillion worth of goods and services.[2]

Consumers around the world vary tremendously in age, income, education level and tastes. They also buy an incredible variety of goods and services. How these diverse consumers relate with each other and with other elements of the world around them impacts their choices among various products, services and companies. Here we examine the fascinating array of factors that impacts upon or influences consumer behaviour.

AUTHOR COMMENT

Despite the simple-looking model in Figure 5.1, understanding the *whys* of buying behaviour is very difficult. Says one expert, 'the mind is a whirling, swirling, jumbled mass of neurons bouncing around . . .'

MODELS OF CONSUMER BEHAVIOUR

Consumers make many buying decisions every day, and the buying decision is the focal point of the marketer's effort. Most large companies research consumer buying decisions in great detail to answer questions about what consumers buy, where they buy, how and how much they buy, when

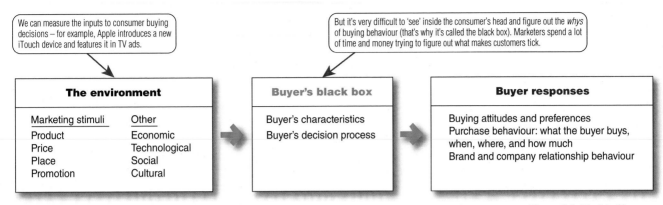

Figure 5.1 Model of buyer behaviour

they buy and why they buy. Marketers can study actual consumer purchases to find out what they buy, where and how much. But learning about the *whys* of consumer buying behaviour is not so easy; the answers are often locked deep within the consumer's mind.

Often, consumers themselves don't know exactly what influences their purchases. 'The human mind doesn't work in a linear way,' says one marketing expert. 'The idea that the mind is a computer with storage compartments where brands or logos or recognisable packages are stored in clearly marked folders that can be accessed by cleverly written ads or commercials simply doesn't exist. Instead, the mind is a whirling, swirling, jumbled mass of neurons bouncing around, colliding and continuously creating new concepts and thoughts and relationships inside every single person's brain all over the world.'[3]

The central question for marketers is : How do consumers respond to various marketing efforts the company might use? The starting point is the stimulus–response model of buyer behaviour shown in Figure 5.1. This figure shows that marketing and other stimuli enter the consumer's 'black box' and produce certain responses. Marketers must work out what is in the buyer's black box.

Marketing stimuli consist of the four Ps: product, price, place and promotion. Other stimuli include major forces and events in the buyer's environment: economic, technological, political and cultural. All these inputs enter the buyer's black box, where they are turned into a set of buyer responses: the buyer's brand and company relationship behaviour and what he or she buys, when, where and how often.

Marketers want to understand how the stimuli are changed into responses inside the consumer's black box, which has two parts. First, the buyer's characteristics influence how he or she perceives and reacts to the stimuli. Second, the buyer's decision process itself affects his or her behaviour. We look first at buyer characteristics as they affect buyer behaviour and then discuss the buyer decision process.

AUTHOR COMMENT

Many levels of factors affect our buying behaviour – from broad cultural and social influences to motivations, beliefs and attitudes lying deep within us. For example, why *did* you buy *that* specific mobile phone?

CHARACTERISTICS AFFECTING CONSUMER BEHAVIOUR

Consumer purchases are influenced strongly by cultural, social, personal and psychological characteristics, as shown in Figure 5.2. For the most part, marketers cannot control such factors, but they must take them into account.

Figure 5.2 Factors influencing consumer behaviour

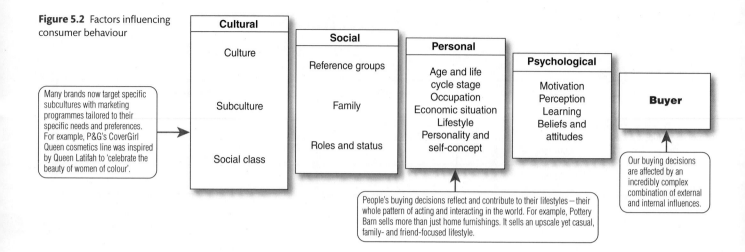

Many brands now target specific subcultures with marketing programmes tailored to their specific needs and preferences. For example, P&G's CoverGirl Queen cosmetics line was inspired by Queen Latifah to 'celebrate the beauty of women of colour'.

Cultural factors

Cultural factors exert a broad and deep influence on consumer behaviour. Marketers need to understand the role played by the buyer's *culture*, *subculture* and *social class*.

Culture

Culture—The set of basic values, perceptions, wants and behaviours learned by a member of society from family and other important institutions.

Culture is the most basic cause of a person's wants and behaviour. Human behaviour is largely learned. Growing up in a society, a child learns basic values, perceptions, wants and behaviours from his or her family and other important institutions. A European child normally learns or is exposed to the following values: achievement and success, individualism, freedom, hard work, activity and involvement, efficiency and practicality, material comfort, youthfulness, and fitness and health. Every group or society has a culture, and cultural influences on buying behaviour may vary greatly from country to country. A failure to adjust to these differences can result in ineffective marketing or embarrassing mistakes.

Marketers are always trying to spot *cultural shifts* so as to discover new products that might be wanted. For example, the cultural shift toward greater concern about health and fitness has created a huge industry for health-and-fitness services, exercise equipment and clothing, organic foods and a variety of diets. The shift toward informality has resulted in more demand for casual clothing and simpler home furnishings.

Subculture

Subculture—A group of people with shared value systems based on common life experiences and situations.

Each culture contains smaller **subcultures**, or groups of people with shared value systems based on common life experiences and situations. Subcultures include nationalities, religions, racial groups and geographic regions. Many subcultures make up important market segments, and marketers often design products and marketing programmes tailored to their needs. Across Europe many thousands of subcultures exist, from cybergoths to bodybuilders to naturists to bikers to fundamental Christians. While subcultures are distinct, they are not mutually exclusive (which suggests that somewhere there is a subculture of cybergoth bodybuilders who ride motorbikes to church in the nude). Two contrasting examples of subcultures are gamers and mature consumers.

Gamers

Originally the term 'gamer' referred to young people playing role-playing games and war-games (epitomised by players of the phenomenal successful Dungeons and Dragons dice-based,

Over 25 per cent of
Europe's population can
be considered gamers.

Source: Pearson Education
Ltd Steve Shott

role-playing game). However, today the label of gamer is attributed to anybody who enjoys playing or learning about video games – both on and offline. According to a recent study[4] over 25 per cent of Europe's population can be considered gamers (having played a video game in the last six months) with more than 95 million European adults playing video games regularly and over 253 million games sold each year (a value of over €8 billion).[5] While we might be unfairly tempted to stereotype gamers as adolescents with poor social skills and pale skin tones, recent research for the Interactive Software Federation of Europe by Game Vision Europe[6] defies such narrow-mindedness:

- 58 per cent of all gamers who are parents report playing games with their children.
- The core motivations for playing games are fun (61 per cent), relaxation (53 per cent) and a positive way to pass time (53 per cent).
- The trend is towards less dedicated patterns of play; overall 76 per cent of gamers play for less than 5 hours a week.
- 41 per cent of gamers mostly play games on handheld consoles at home, 26 per cent mostly play while travelling and 17 per cent mostly when waiting for someone.
- Gaming is most popular among the young; however, almost 30 per cent of 30–49 year olds play video games.
- 31 per cent of males and 20 per cent of females are gamers; it is therefore not the male-only preserve that it is often portrayed in the press.
- Gamers agree that games keep you mentally fit (50 per cent), allow you to spend time with the family (35 per cent) and even keep you physically fit (18 per cent).
- 71 per cent of gamers have played some form of online game in the past 3 months.
- Free online games make up a large volume of the online games played: 19 per cent of gamers are playing paid-for online games, 68 per cent of gamers are playing free online games.
- Gamers vary across Europe with gaming most popular in France (38 per cent of the population) and least popular in Italy and Poland (a mere 17 per cent).

The growth in gaming is mirrored in the intensively and increasingly competitive games consoles market.

> It has been six years since the current generation of home games consoles was launched with the unveiling of the Xbox 360, so the move to the next generation with the first sighting of the Wii U seemed long overdue. Consoles have historically been renewed in five-year cycles, but this time Microsoft and Sony are looking to get ten years out of their substantial investments in the high-definition (HD) 360 and PlayStation 3, having given them a new lease of life last year by adding their respective Kinect and Move motion-sensing controllers. Of course, they were playing catch-up on Nintendo's play-by-waving innovation, which has made it the runaway leader of this generation with more than 86 million Wiis shipped since its launch in 2006. However, the Wii's sales have been slowing in the face of the stronger competition, with the console's lower specifications and lack of HD graphics making the near-term introduction of a successor essential in its case. The Wii U – a slim white box, much deeper than it is wide – will be launched in 2012. What we do know is that this is not really about the console and its addition of HD – it is all about the controller, another startling Nintendo innovation. It is almost a console in itself, with a 6.2 inch colour touchscreen, an abundance of control buttons, camera, microphone, stylus, speakers, wireless connectivity and the same motion-sensing chips that made the Wii so easy to use for non-gamers introduced to the machine. The magic comes when a game on the TV screen can be switched by the player to the controller's screen if another family member wants to watch live television instead. Alternatively, a movie being watched on the touchscreen can be switched to the larger TV display. More important, the controller allows far more gaming possibilities – its screen revealing all manner of gaming elements to interact with the TV or showing the user a different view of the action than rival players watching the TV screen and using regular Wii remotes. The Wii U then is a literal representation of Nintendo's unique view of gaming, one that stands it in good stead as it fights to maintain its lead over Sony and Microsoft in the years to come.[7]

Mature consumers

As the population ages, mature consumers are becoming a very attractive market. By 2015, when all the baby boomers will be 50-plus, people aged 50 to 75 will account for 40 per cent of adult consumers. By 2030, adults aged 65 and older will represent nearly 20 per cent of the population. Whereas in 1960 where most European countries had three 0–14 year olds for each person over 65, by 2060 it is forecasted that each 0–14 will be matched by two people over 65. And these mature consumer segments boast the most expendable cash. The 50-plus consumer segment now accounts for nearly 50 per cent of all consumer spending, more than any current or previous generation. They have 2.5 times the discretionary buying power of those aged 18 to 34. As one marketing executive puts it, they have 'assets, not allowances'. Despite some financial setbacks resulting from the recent economic crisis, mature consumers remain an attractive market for companies in all industries, from pharmaceuticals, furniture, groceries, beauty products and clothing to consumer electronics, travel and entertainment and financial services.[8]

For decades, many marketers stereotyped mature consumers as doddering, impoverished shut-ins who are less willing to change brands. One problem: brand managers and advertising copywriters tend to be younger. 'Ask them to do an ad targeting the 50-plus demographic,' bemoans one marketer, 'and they'll default to a grey-haired senior living on a beach trailed by an aging golden retriever.' For example, in a recent survey, advertising professionals regarded the term *over the hill* as meaning people over 57. In contrast, baby boomer respondents related the term to people over age 75.[9]

As a group, however, mature consumers are anything but 'stuck in their ways'. To the contrary, a recent AARP study showed that older consumers for products such as stereos, computers and mobile phones are more willing to shop around and switch brands than their younger counterparts. For example, notes one expert, 'some 25 per cent of Apple's iPhones – the epitome of cool, cutting-edge product – have been bought by people over 50'.[10]

And in reality, people whose ages would seem to place them squarely in the 'old' category usually don't act old or see themselves that way. Thanks to advances in longevity, people are redefining what the mature life stage means. 'They're having a second middle-age before becoming elderly,' says a generational marketing expert. Marketers need to appeal to these consumers in a vibrant but authentic way.[11]

Today's mature consumers create an attractive market for travel agents and holiday firms. Indeed, mature consumers are more likely than younger consumers to take longer (and more expensive) holidays. A good example of a firm catering to this market is Solitair, who specialise in holidays for single people. Recognising the large numbers of mature consumers who are single, Solitair have developed a range of holidays exclusively for single consumers with the aim 'to rejuvenate the energy level of our travellers above 50 years during their singles holidays.' Their promotional material claims that 'we make sure that we not only cater you the best services but the adventure and fun which our over 50s travellers seek during their singles trips. With our Singles Holidays Over 50, you get to enjoy beaches, cruises and many adventurous activities like skiing holidays, scuba diving, sailing, and even mountaineering.'[12]

Social class

Almost every society has some form of social class structure. **Social classes** are society's relatively permanent and ordered divisions whose members share similar values, interests and behaviours. Social scientists have identified the seven social classes shown in Figure 5.3.

Social class is not determined by a single factor, such as income, but is measured as a combination of occupation, income, education, wealth and other variables. In some social systems, members of different classes are reared for certain roles and cannot change their social positions. In Europe, however, the lines between social classes are not fixed and rigid; people can move to a higher social class or drop into a lower one.

Marketers are interested in social class because people within a given social class tend to exhibit similar buying behaviour. Social classes show distinct product and brand preferences in areas such as clothing, home furnishings, leisure activities and cars.

Social factors

A consumer's behaviour is also influenced by social factors, such as the consumer's *small groups*, *family*, and *social roles* and *status*.

Groups and social networks

Many small **groups** influence a person's behaviour. Groups that have a direct influence and to which a person belongs are called membership groups. In contrast, reference groups serve as direct (face-to-face) or indirect points of comparison or reference in forming a person's attitudes or behaviour. People are often influenced by reference groups to which they do not belong. For example, an aspirational group is one to which the individual wishes to belong, as when a young football player hopes to someday emulate football star Cristiano Ronaldo and play in La Liga.

Marketers try to identify the reference groups of their target markets. Reference groups expose a person to new behaviours and lifestyles, influence the person's attitudes and self-concept, and create pressures to conform that may affect the person's product and brand choices. The importance of group influence varies across products and brands. It tends to be strongest when the product is visible to others whom the buyer respects.

Word-of-mouth influence and buzz marketing

Word-of-mouth influence can have a powerful impact on consumer buying behaviour. The personal words and recommendations of trusted friends, associates and other consumers tend to be

The idea that all mature consumers spend their days sitting in parks, feeding ducks is at best, dated.

Source: Press Association Images/ John Terhune.

Social class—Relatively permanent and ordered divisions in a society whose members share similar values, interests and behaviours.

Group—Two or more people who interact to accomplish individual or mutual goals.

Figure 5.3 The major social classes

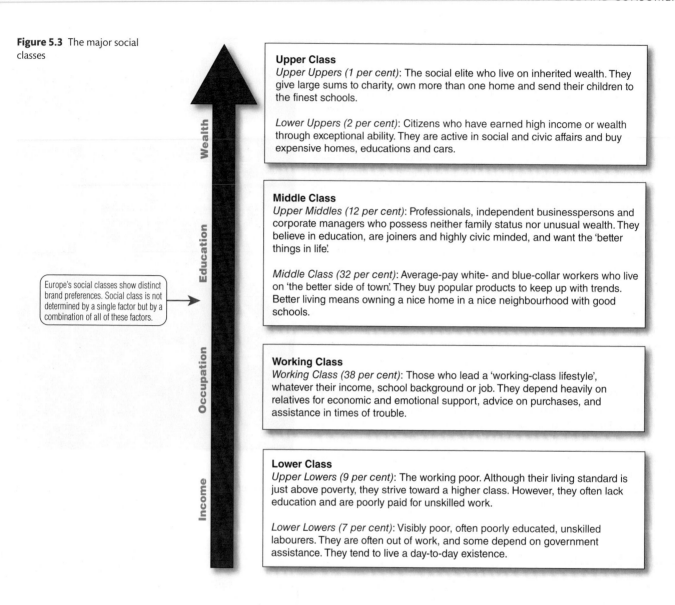

Europe's social classes show distinct brand preferences. Social class is not determined by a single factor but by a combination of all of these factors.

Upper Class

Upper Uppers (1 per cent): The social elite who live on inherited wealth. They give large sums to charity, own more than one home and send their children to the finest schools.

Lower Uppers (2 per cent): Citizens who have earned high income or wealth through exceptional ability. They are active in social and civic affairs and buy expensive homes, educations and cars.

Middle Class

Upper Middles (12 per cent): Professionals, independent businesspersons and corporate managers who possess neither family status nor unusual wealth. They believe in education, are joiners and highly civic minded, and want the 'better things in life'.

Middle Class (32 per cent): Average-pay white- and blue-collar workers who live on 'the better side of town'. They buy popular products to keep up with trends. Better living means owning a nice home in a nice neighbourhood with good schools.

Working Class

Working Class (38 per cent): Those who lead a 'working-class lifestyle', whatever their income, school background or job. They depend heavily on relatives for economic and emotional support, advice on purchases, and assistance in times of trouble.

Lower Class

Upper Lowers (9 per cent): The working poor. Although their living standard is just above poverty, they strive toward a higher class. However, they often lack education and are poorly paid for unskilled work.

Lower Lowers (7 per cent): Visibly poor, often poorly educated, unskilled labourers. They are often out of work, and some depend on government assistance. They tend to live a day-to-day existence.

more credible than those coming from commercial sources, such as advertisements or salespeople. Most word-of-mouth influence happens naturally: consumers start chatting about a brand they use or feel strongly about one way or the other. Often, however, rather than leaving it to chance, marketers can help to create positive conversations about their brands.

Opinion leader—A person within a reference group who, because of special skills, knowledge, personality or other characteristics, exerts social influence on others.

Marketers of brands subjected to strong group influence must figure out how to reach **opinion leaders** – people within a reference group who, because of special skills, knowledge, personality or other characteristics, exert social influence on others. Some experts call this group *the influentials* or *leading adopters*. When these influentials talk, consumers listen. Marketers try to identify opinion leaders for their products and direct marketing efforts toward them.

Buzz marketing involves enlisting or even creating opinion leaders to serve as 'brand ambassadors' who spread the word about a company's products. Many companies now create brand ambassador programmes in an attempt to turn influential but everyday customers into brand evangelists. A recent study found that such programmes can increase the effectiveness of word-of-mouth marketing efforts by as much as 50 per cent.[13] For example, Jeff Rubenstein, social media manager for Sony's PlayStation brand, has essentially crowdsourced his work. With a team of just three managing PlayStation's social media presence, Mr Rubenstein relies on the user community to get the company's message out. He makes images and videos of new PlayStation games open-source, and encourages fan sites to share them on their own blogs and Facebook pages. 'We want to empower smaller sites and evangelists,' he says. 'It's like putting the press kit online.' It seems to be working. PlayStation has more than 1.6 million fans on Facebook, 355,672 fans on Twitter, and posts on the PlayStation blog routinely get more than 50 comments. Every few months, a post will go viral and attract upwards of 10,000 comments. Success has meant a heavy workload for Mr Rubenstein and his team, and now, he says, it is a challenge just to keep up with his engaged community. 'We have to try not to put out too much content,' he says.[14]

Procter & Gamble has created a huge word-of-mouth marketing arm – Vocalpoint – consisting of 500,000 mums. Vocalpoint recruits 'connectors' – natural-born buzzers with vast networks of friends and a gift of the gab. They create buzz not just for P&G brands but for those of other client companies as well. P&G recently used the Vocalpoint network in the launch of its new Crest Weekly Clean toothpaste. P&G didn't pay the mums or coach them on what to say. It simply educated the Vocalpointers about the product and armed them with free samples and coupons for friends and then asked them to share their 'honest opinions with us and with other real women'. In turn, the Vocalpoint mums created hundreds of thousands of personal recommendations for the new product.[15]

Online social networks

Over the past few years, a new type of social interaction has exploded onto the scene – online social networking. **Online social networks** are online communities where people socialise or exchange information and opinions. Social networking media range from blogs (Gizmodo) and message boards (Craigslist) to social networking websites (Facebook and Twitter) and virtual worlds (Second Life). This new form of consumer-to-consumer and business-to-consumer dialogue has big implications for marketers.

Marketers are working to harness the power of these new social networks and other 'word-of-Web' opportunities to promote their products and build closer customer relationships. Instead of throwing more one-way commercial messages at consumers, they hope to use the Internet and social networks to *interact* with consumers and become a part of their conversations and lives.

For example, brands ranging from Guinness and Ikea to Real Madrid C.F. are tweeting on Twitter. H&M connects with customers via the company's Facebook and YouTube pages, has a specific H&M iPad/iPhone app and a host of enthusiast groups. Benetton sponsors 'the United Blogs of Benetton' with blogs from the Netherlands, to Portugal, Italy, Mexico and even China.[16] And during

Online social networks—Online social communities — blogs, social networking Web sites, or even virtual worlds — where people socialise or exchange information and opinions.

Benetton sponsors 'the United Blogs of Benetton'.

Source: The Advertising Archives

the 2010 winter Olympics, Visa launched a 'Go World' microsite featuring athlete videos, photos and widgets that tied into nets like Facebook. Visa customised the campaign for global markets, featuring different sets of athletes for different countries.[17]

Other companies regularly post ads or custom videos on video-sharing sites such as YouTube. For example, Cadburys posted a number of 'Glass and a Half Production' ads to market its chocolate. One of these, Cadbury Eyebrows, received some 7 million views while another of a gorilla drumming managed 5.5 million views. But marketers must be careful when tapping into online social networks. Results are difficult to measure and control. Ultimately, the users control the content, so social network marketing attempts can easily backfire. We will dig deeper into online social networks as a marketing tool in Chapter 17.

Family

Family members can strongly influence buyer behaviour. The family is the most important consumer buying organisation in society, and it has been researched extensively. Marketers are interested in the roles and influence of the husband, wife and children on the purchase of different products and services.

Husband–wife involvement varies widely by product category and by stage in the buying process. Buying roles change with evolving consumer lifestyles. In Europe, the wife traditionally has been the main purchasing agent for the family in the areas of food, household products and clothing. But with 70 per cent of women holding jobs outside the home and the willingness of husbands to do more of the family's purchasing, all this is changing. A recent study found that 65 per cent of men grocery shop regularly and prepare at least one meal a week for others in the

Family buying roles are changing. For example, 65 per cent of men grocery shop regularly while women influence 50 per cent all new technology purchases.

Source: Alamy Images/MBI

household. At the same time, women now influence 65 per cent of all new car purchases, 91 per cent of new home purchases, and 92 per cent of vacation purchases. In all, women make almost 85 per cent of all family purchases and control some 73 per cent of all household spending. Says one analyst, 'today's woman is … the designated chief operating officer of the home.'[18]

Such changes suggest that marketers in industries that have sold their products to only men or only women are now courting the opposite sex. For example, today women account for 50 per cent of all technology purchases. So consumer electronics companies are increasingly designing products that are easier to use and more appealing to female buyers:[19]

Consumer electronics engineers and designers are bringing a more feminine sensibility to products historically shaped by masculine tastes, habits and requirements. Designs are more 'feminine and softer', rather than masculine and angular. But many of the new touches are more subtle, like the wider spacing of the keys on a Sony netbook computer. It accommodates the longer fingernails that women tend to have. Some of the latest mobile phones made by LG Electronics have the cameras' automatic focus calibrated to arms' length. The company observed that young women are fond of taking pictures of themselves with a friend. This isn't the case with men. Nikon and Olympus recently introduced lines of lighter, more compact, and easy-to-use digital, single-lens reflex cameras that were designed with women in mind because they tend to be a family's primary keeper of memories.

However, marketers must be careful to avoid insensitive stereotypes. For example, last year Dell launched the Della website, geared toward women. The website emphasised colours, computer accessories and tips for counting calories and finding recipes. Many women consumers were offended, describing the site as 'slick but disconcerting' and 'condescending'. On the flip side, one stay-at-home dad and blogger ('Rebel Dad') took nappy brand Pampers to task for sending him its annual Mother's Day e-mail, with the friendly and personalised greeting: 'Happy Mother's Day, Brian!' Said Rebel Dad in a letter to Pampers, 'Every year, you blanket me (and, presumably tens of thousands of other dads) with a sweet reminder that [you] still assume that every person who wants diaper coupons is a woman. That's dumb.'[20]

Children may also have a strong influence on family buying decisions. For example, in the UK the Office for National Statistics predict that children under 16 years of age will increase to over 12 million by 2016. Between the ages of 7 and 15 these children will spend around €6,800 in pocket money and contribute €5.65 billion to the UK economy. Meanwhile each child will cost parents around €227,000 to clothe, feed and educate them to the age of 21.[21] The nation's 36 million children aged 8 to 12 wield an estimated €30 billion in disposable income. They also influence an additional €125 billion that their families spend in areas such as food, clothing, entertainment and personal care items. One study found that kids significantly influence family decisions about everything from where they take vacations to what cars and mobile phones they buy.[22]

For example, to encourage families to take their children out to eat again following the economic downturn (of 2008), casual restaurants reached out to children with everything from sophisticated children's menus and special deals to a wealth of kid-focused activities. In the UK, at Pizza Hut children eat free all day and every day over the summer with the purchase of an adult meal. To encourage parents to take holidays with their children, Forte Village in Sardinia even offer a dedicated Children's Restaurant, Children's Pool, complimentary kids clubs for children of all ages, a Chelsea Football Club Academy, rugby coaching, numerous water sports and even a special pool lagoon designed just for children.[23]

Roles and status

A person belongs to many groups – family, clubs, organisations and online communities to name a few. A person's position in each group can be defined in terms of both role and status. A role consists of the activities a person is expected to perform according to the people around them. Each role carries a status reflecting the general esteem given to it by society.

People usually choose products appropriate to their roles and status. Consider the various roles a working mother plays. In her company, she plays the role of a brand manager; in her family, she plays the role of wife and mother; at her favourite sporting events, she plays the role of avid fan. As a brand manager, she will buy the kind of clothing that reflects her role and status in her company.

Personal factors

A buyer's decisions also are influenced by personal characteristics such as the buyer's *age and life-cycle stage, occupation, economic situation, lifestyle* and *personality and self-concept.*

Age and life-cycle stage

People change the goods and services they buy over their lifetimes. Tastes in food, clothes, furniture and recreation are often age related. Buying is also shaped by the stage of the family life cycle – the stages through which families might pass as they mature over time. Life-stage changes usually result from demographics and life-changing events – marriage, having children, purchasing a home, divorce, children going to college, changes in personal income, moving out of the house and retirement. Marketers often define their target markets in terms of life-cycle stage and develop appropriate products and marketing plans for each stage.

Consumer information giant Acxiom's PersonicX life-stage segmentation system places households into distinct consumer segments and life-stage groups, based on specific consumer behaviour and demographic characteristics. PersonicX includes life-stage groups with names such as *Beginnings, Taking Hold, Cash & Careers, Jumbo Families, Transition Blues, Our Turn, Golden Years* and *Active Elders.* For example, the *Taking Hold* group consists of young, energetic, well-funded couples and young families who are busy with their careers, social lives and interests, especially fitness and active recreation. *Transition Blues* are blue-collar, less-educated, mid-income consumers who are transitioning to stable lives and talking about marriage and children.

'Consumers experience many life-stage changes during their lifetimes,' says Acxiom. 'As their life stages change, so do their behaviours and purchasing preferences. Marketers who are armed with the data to understand the timing and makeup of life-stage changes among their customers will have a distinct advantage over their competitors.'[24]

In line with today's tougher economic times, Acxiom has also developed a set of economic life-stage segments, including groups such as *Squeaking By*, *Eye on Essentials*, *Tight with a Purpose*, *It's My Life*, *Full Speed Ahead* and *Potential Rebounders*. The *Potential Rebounders* are those more likely to loosen up on spending sooner. This group appears more likely than other segments to use online research before purchasing electronics, appliances, home decor and jewellery. Thus, home improvement retailers appealing to this segment should have a strong online presence, providing pricing, features and benefits, and product availability.

Occupation

A person's occupation affects the goods and services bought. Blue-collar workers tend to buy more rugged work clothes, whereas executives buy more business suits. Marketers try to identify the occupational groups that have an above-average interest in their products and services. A company can even specialise in making products needed by a given occupational group.

> For example, Ede and Ravenscroft is a London bespoke tailor established in 1689. For over three hundred years they have produced ceremonial gowns in the UK, including the gowns for twelve royal coronations. Indeed, they are currently appointed as robe makers to Her Majesty Queen Elizabeth II, His Royal Highness The Duke of Edinburgh and His Royal Highness The Prince of Wales. However, Ede and Ravenscroft are probably best known as the dressers of the legal profession of barristers (not only in the UK but also across the world). The original Ede created the bespoke legal robes that barristers are required to wear during court appearances while Ravenscroft made the individually tailored legal wigs that barristers must wear when appearing in court.[25]

Economic situation

A person's economic situation will affect his or her store and product choices. Marketers watch trends in personal income, savings and interest rates. Following the economic downturn, most companies have taken steps to redesign, reposition and re-price their products. Take the European value clothing market, for example.

> Across Europe, retailers are facing a new reality: cash-strapped shoppers and rising costs. But it is mainly retailers that have traditionally relied on selling a high number of cheap items, from €1 T-shirts to €5 jeans, that are taking the biggest hit. 'What we are seeing is the end of the volume-driven market,' says Richard Hyman, strategic retail adviser to Deloitte. Stubbornly high inflation has been a feature of the economic downturn, exacerbated recently by rising fuel and food prices. Those with the lowest incomes are being hit hardest, as they spend a higher proportion of their money on essential items. At the same time, the costs that retailers themselves face are rising, from increases in cotton and wool prices, to rising wages in south-east Asia, although there has been some relief on cotton recently. There are also signs that younger customers, who have driven demand at companies such as the UK's ASOS, are now starting to feel the pinch. All retailers are faced with the unpalatable choice of passing higher costs on to customers, or taking a hit to their profits. Primark, owned by Associated British Foods, has decided not to pass inflation fully on to its customers in order to protect its long-term reputation for value. Also at the value end of the market, Sweden's Hennes & Mauritz has also refused to pass on higher input costs to consumers. In contrast, retailers that serve older, or more affluent customers, such as Marks and Spencer, or offer more cutting edge fashion, such as Spain's Inditex, are faring better. There is no value sector to speak of in Italy, given Italians' desire for top-end luxury. But some mid-market players, such as Gap, Banana Republic and Inditex's Zara have recently opened in the Italian market, with what are often higher prices than in their domestic markets, and are doing well. Inditex, the world's biggest

clothing retailer by sales, can ship garments from its headquarters in northern Spain to stores within two weeks, allowing it to quickly interpret emerging trends. It can react within the fashion season – responding for example to a demand for bold colours – rather than creating a collection, and placing orders, months in advance. Being on trend provides real pricing power, although Inditex has said that it is keeping its prices stable. The strategy, and Inditex's international reach, has given the group a performance that soars above the rest of the troubled Spanish clothing market.[26]

Lifestyle

People coming from the same subculture, social class and occupation may have quite different lifestyles. **Lifestyle** is a person's pattern of living as expressed in his or her psychographics. It involves measuring consumers' major AIO dimensions – activities (work, hobbies, shopping, sports, social events), interests (food, fashion, family, recreation) and opinions (about themselves, social issues, business, products). Lifestyle captures something more than the person's social class or personality. It profiles a person's whole pattern of acting and interacting in the world.

When used carefully, the lifestyle concept can help marketers understand changing consumer values and how they affect buying behaviour. Consumers don't just buy products; they buy the values and lifestyles those products represent. For example, Triumph doesn't just sell motorcycles, it sells an independent, 'Go your own way' lifestyle; Smirnoff vodka says consumers should 'Be There' and Adidas encourage consumers to 'Own the Game'. Says one marketer, 'People's product choices are becoming more and more like value choices. It's not, "I like this water, the way it tastes". It's "I feel like this car, or this show, is more reflective of who I am." '[27]

For example, retailer Jack Wills, targets young, educated middle-upper class consumers with its preppy, buzzing atmosphere, and sells a cool and casual lifestyle to which its customers aspire. (See the case study at the start of the chapter.)

Lifestyle—A person's pattern of living as expressed in his or her activities, interests and opinions.

Personality and self-concept

Each person's distinct personality influences his or her buying behaviour. **Personality** refers to the unique psychological characteristics that distinguish a person or group. Personality is usually described in terms of traits such as self-confidence, dominance, sociability, autonomy, defensiveness, adaptability and aggressiveness. Personality can be useful in analysing consumer behaviour for certain product or brand choices.

The idea is that brands also have personalities, and consumers are likely to choose brands with personalities that match their own. A *brand personality* is the specific mix of human traits that may be attributed to a particular brand. One researcher identified five brand personality traits: *sincerity* (down-to-earth, honest, wholesome and cheerful); *excitement* (daring, spirited, imaginative and up-to-date); *competence* (reliable, intelligent and successful); *sophistication* (upper class and charming); and *ruggedness* (outdoorsy and tough).[28]

Most well-known brands are strongly associated with one particular trait: Land Rover with 'ruggedness', Apple with 'excitement', BBC with 'fairness', and Dove with 'sincerity'. Hence, these brands will attract persons who are high on the same personality traits.

Many marketers use a concept related to personality – a person's *self-concept* (also called *self-image*). The idea is that people's possessions contribute to and reflect their identities – that is, 'we are what we have'. Thus, to understand consumer behaviour, marketers must first understand the relationship between consumer self-concept and possessions.

Apple applies these concepts in its long-running 'Get a Mac' commercials that characterise two people as computers: one guy plays the part of an Apple Mac, and the other plays a personal computer (PC). The two have very different personalities and self-concepts. 'Hello, I'm a Mac', says the guy on the right, who's younger and dressed in jeans. 'And I'm a PC', says the one on the left, who's wearing dweeby glasses and a jacket and tie. The two men discuss the relative advantages of Macs versus PCs, with the Mac coming out on top. The commercials present the Mac brand personality as young, laid back and cool. The PC is portrayed as buttoned down, corporate and a bit dorky. The message? If you see yourself as young and with it, you need a Mac.[29]

Personality—The unique psychological characteristics that distinguish a person or group.

Psychological factors

A person's buying choices are further influenced by four major psychological factors: *motivation, perception, learning* and *beliefs and attitudes*.

Motivation

Motive (drive)—A need that is sufficiently pressing to direct the person to seek satisfaction of the need.

A person has many needs at any given time. Some are biological, arising from states of tension such as hunger, thirst or discomfort. Others are psychological, arising from the need for recognition, esteem or belonging. A need becomes a motive when it is aroused to a sufficient level of intensity. A **motive** (or **drive**) is a need that is sufficiently pressing to direct a person to seek satisfaction. Psychologists have developed theories of human motivation. Two of the most popular – the theories of Sigmund Freud and Abraham Maslow – have quite different meanings for consumer analysis and marketing.

Sigmund Freud assumed that people are largely unconscious about the real psychological forces shaping their behaviour. He saw the person as growing up and repressing many urges. These urges are never eliminated or under perfect control; they emerge in dreams, in slips of the tongue, in neurotic and obsessive behaviour, or ultimately in psychoses.

Freud's theory suggests that a person's buying decisions are affected by subconscious motives that even a buyer may not fully understand. Thus, an ageing baby boomer who buys a sporty BMW Z4 Roadster convertible might explain that he simply likes the feel of the wind in his thinning hair. At a deeper level, he may be trying to impress others with his success. At a still deeper level, he may be buying the car to feel young and independent again.

The term *motivation research* refers to qualitative research designed to probe consumers' hidden, subconscious motivations. Consumers often don't know or can't describe why they act as they do. Thus, motivation researchers use a variety of probing techniques to uncover underlying emotions and attitudes toward brands and buying situations.

Motivation: an ageing baby boomer who buys a sporty convertible might explain that he simply likes the feel of the wind in his thinning hair. At a deeper level, he may be buying the car to feel young and independent again.

Source: Getty Images/Michelle Pedone

Many companies employ teams of psychologists, anthropologists and other social scientists to carry out motivation research. One ad agency routinely conducts one-on-one, therapy-like interviews to delve into the inner workings of consumers. Another company asks consumers to describe their favourite brands as animals or cars (say, Fiat versus Volvos) to assess the prestige associated with various brands. Still others rely on hypnosis, dream therapy or soft lights and mood music to plumb the murky depths of consumer psyches.

Such projective techniques seem goofy, and some marketers dismiss such motivation research as mumbo jumbo. But many marketers use such touchy-feely approaches, now sometimes called *interpretive consumer research*, to dig deeper into consumer psyches and develop better marketing strategies.

Abraham Maslow sought to explain why people are driven by particular needs at particular times. Why does one person spend a lot of time and energy on personal safety and another on gaining the esteem of others? Maslow's answer is that human needs are arranged in a hierarchy, as shown in Figure 5.4, from the most pressing at the bottom to the least pressing at the top.[30] They include *physiological* needs, *safety* needs, *social* needs, *esteem* needs and *self-actualisation* needs.

A person tries to satisfy the most important need first. When that need is satisfied, it will stop being a motivator and the person will then try to satisfy the next most important need. For example, starving people (physiological need) will not take an interest in the latest happenings in the art world (self-actualisation needs) nor in

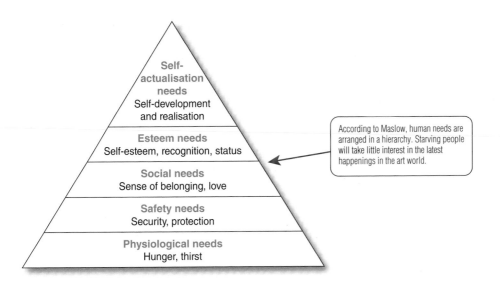

According to Maslow, human needs are arranged in a hierarchy. Starving people will take little interest in the latest happenings in the art world.

Figure 5.4 Maslow's hierarchy of needs

Perception—The process by which people select, organise, and interpret information to form a meaningful picture of the world.

This classic ad from the American Association of Advertising Agencies pokes fun at subliminal advertising. 'So-called "subliminal advertising" simply doesn't exist', says the ad. 'Overactive imaginations, however, most certainly do'.

Source: American Association of Advertising Archives

how they are seen or esteemed by others (social or esteem needs) nor even in whether they are breathing clean air (safety needs). But as each important need is satisfied, the next most important need will come into play.

Perception

A motivated person is ready to act. How the person acts is influenced by his or her own perception of the situation. All of us learn by the flow of information through our five senses: sight, hearing, smell, touch and taste. However, each of us receives, organises and interprets this sensory information in an individual way. **Perception** is the process by which people select, organise and interpret information to form a meaningful picture of the world.

People can form different perceptions of the same stimulus because of three perceptual processes: selective attention, selective distortion and selective retention. People are exposed to a large number of stimuli every day. For example, on average, people are exposed to an estimated 3,000 to 5,000 advertising messages every day. It is impossible for a person to pay attention to all these stimuli. *Selective attention* – the tendency for people to screen out most of the information to which they are exposed – means that marketers must work especially hard to attract the consumer's attention.[31]

Even noticed stimuli do not always come across in the intended way. Each person fits incoming information into an existing mind set. *Selective distortion* describes the tendency of people to interpret information in a way that will support what they already believe. People also will forget much of what they learn. They tend to retain information that supports their attitudes and beliefs. *Selective retention* means that consumers are likely to remember good points made about a brand they favour and forget good points made about competing brands. Because of selective attention, distortion and retention, marketers must work hard to get their messages through.

Interestingly, although most marketers worry about whether their offers will be perceived at all, some consumers worry that they will be affected by marketing messages without even knowing it – through *subliminal advertising*. More than 50 years ago, a researcher announced that

he had flashed the phrases 'Eat popcorn' and 'Drink Coca-Cola' on a screen in a New Jersey movie theatre every five seconds for 1/300th of a second. He reported that although viewers did not consciously recognise these messages, they absorbed them subconsciously and bought 58 per cent more popcorn and 18 per cent more Coke. Suddenly advertisers and consumer protection groups became intensely interested in subliminal perception. Although the researcher later admitted to making up the data, the issue has not died. Some consumers still fear that they are being manipulated by subliminal messages.

Numerous studies by psychologists and consumer researchers have found little or no link between subliminal messages and consumer behaviour. Recent brain wave studies have found that, in certain circumstances, our brains may register subliminal messages. However, it appears that subliminal advertising simply doesn't have the power attributed to it by its critics. Scoffs one industry insider, 'Just between us, most [advertisers] have difficulty getting a 2 per cent increase in sales with the help of $50 [€35] million in media and extremely *liminal* images of sex, money, power, and other [motivators] of human emotion. The very idea of [us] as puppeteers, cruelly pulling the strings of consumer marionettes, is almost too much to bear.'[32]

Learning

Learning—Changes in an individual's behaviour arising from experience.

When people act, they learn. **Learning** describes changes in an individual's behaviour arising from experience. Learning theorists say that most human behaviour is learned. Learning occurs through the interplay of drives, stimuli, cues, responses and reinforcement.

A *drive* is a strong internal stimulus that calls for action. A drive becomes a motive when it is directed toward a particular *stimulus object*. For example, a person's drive for self-actualisation might motivate him or her to look into buying a camera. A consumer's response to the idea of buying a camera is conditioned by the surrounding cues. *Cues* are minor stimuli that determine when, where and how a person responds. For example, a person might spot several camera brands in a shop window, hear of a special sale price or discuss cameras with a friend. These are all cues that might influence a consumer's *response* to his or her interest in buying the product.

Suppose a consumer buys a Nikon camera. If the experience is rewarding, a consumer will probably use the camera more and more, and his or her response will be *reinforced*. Then the next time he or she shops for a camera, or for binoculars or some similar product, the probability is greater that he or she will buy a Nikon product. The practical significance of learning theory for marketers is that they can build up demand for a product by associating it with strong drives, using motivating cues and providing positive reinforcement.

Beliefs and attitudes

Belief—A descriptive thought that a person holds about something.

Through doing and learning, people acquire beliefs and attitudes. These, in turn, influence their buying behaviour. A **belief** is a descriptive thought that a person has about something. Beliefs may be based on real knowledge, opinion or faith and may or may not carry an emotional charge. Marketers are interested in the beliefs that people formulate about specific products and services because these beliefs make up product and brand images that affect buying behaviour. If some of the beliefs are wrong and prevent purchase, a marketer will want to launch a campaign to correct them.

Attitude—A person's consistently favourable or unfavourable evaluations, feelings and tendencies toward an object or idea.

People have attitudes regarding religion, politics, clothes, music, food and almost everything else. **Attitude** describes a person's relatively consistent evaluations, feelings and tendencies toward an object or idea. Attitudes put people into a frame of mind of liking or disliking things, of moving toward or away from them. Our camera buyer may hold attitudes such as 'Buy the best', 'The Japanese make the best electronics products in the world', and 'Creativity and self-expression are among the most important things in life'. If so, the Nikon camera would fit well into a consumer's existing attitudes.

Attitudes are difficult to change. A person's attitudes fit into a pattern; changing one attitude may require difficult adjustments in many others. Thus, a company should usually try to fit its products into existing attitudes rather than attempt to change attitudes. For example, today's beverage marketers now cater to people's new attitudes about health and well-being with drinks that do a lot more than just taste good or quench your thirst. For example, Firefly Tonics sells a small but growing range of distinctive drinks as it rides the wave of consumer interest in natural products. Consumers can choose from six formulations – de-tox, chill-out, sharpen up, health kick, wake-up and a special-edition love potion for St Valentine's Day. The drinks contain no added sugar or preservatives.[33] By matching today's attitudes about life and healthful living, the Firefly Tonic brand has become a well-known player in the New Age beverage category.

We can now appreciate the many forces acting on consumer behaviour. A consumer's choice results from the complex interplay of cultural, social, personal and psychological factors.

AUTHOR COMMENT

Some purchases are simple and routine, even habitual. Others are far more complex – involving extensive information gathering and evaluation – and are subject to sometimes subtle influences. For example, think of everything that goes into a decision to buy a new car.

TYPES OF BUYING DECISION BEHAVIOUR

Buying behaviour differs greatly for a tube of toothpaste, an iPhone, financial services and a new car. More complex decisions usually involve more buying participants and more buyer deliberation. Figure 5.5 shows the types of consumer buying behaviour based on the degree of buyer involvement and the degree of differences among brands.

Complex buying behaviour

Consumers undertake **complex buying behaviour** when they are highly involved in a purchase and perceive significant differences among brands. Consumers may be highly involved when the product is expensive, risky, purchased infrequently and highly self-expressive. Typically, a consumer has much to learn about the product category. For example, a PC buyer may not know what attributes to consider. Many product features carry no real meaning: a '3.2GHz Intel Core i7 processor', 'WUXGA active matrix screen' or '8 GB dual-channel DDR2 SDRAM memory'.

This buyer will pass through a learning process, first developing beliefs about the product, then attitudes, and then making a thoughtful purchase choice. Marketers of high-involvement products must understand the information-gathering and evaluation behaviour of high-involvement consumers. They need to help buyers learn about product-class attributes and their relative importance. They need to differentiate their brand's features, perhaps by describing the brand's benefits using print media with long copy. They must motivate store salespeople and a buyer's acquaintances to influence the final brand choice.

Complex buying behaviour— Consumer buying behaviour characterised by high consumer involvement in a purchase and significant perceived differences among brands.

Figure 5.5 Four types of buying behaviour

Source: Adapted from Henry Assael, *Consumer Behavior and Marketing Action* (Boston, MA: Kent Publishing Company, 1987), p. 87. Copyright © 1987 by Wadsworth, Inc. Printed by permission of Kent Publishing Company, a division of Wadsworth, Inc.

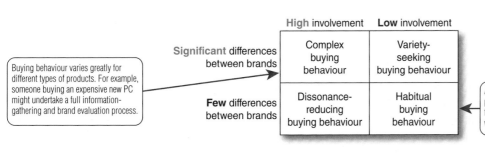

	High involvement	**Low** involvement
Significant differences between brands	Complex buying behaviour	Variety-seeking buying behaviour
Few differences between brands	Dissonance-reducing buying behaviour	Habitual buying behaviour

Buying behaviour varies greatly for different types of products. For example, someone buying an expensive new PC might undertake a full information-gathering and brand evaluation process.

At the other extreme, for low-involvement products, consumers may simply select a familiar brand out of habit. For example, what brand of salt do you buy and why?

Dissonance-reducing buying behaviour

Dissonance-reducing buying
behaviour—Consumer buying
behaviour characterised by high
involvement but few perceived
differences among brands.

Dissonance-reducing buying behaviour occurs when consumers are highly involved with an expensive, infrequent or risky purchase but see little difference among brands. For example, consumers buying carpeting may face a high-involvement decision because carpeting is expensive and self-expressive. Yet buyers may consider most carpet brands in a given price range to be the same. In this case, because perceived brand differences are not large, buyers may shop around to learn what is available but buy relatively quickly. They may respond primarily to a good price or purchase convenience.

After the purchase, consumers might experience *postpurchase dissonance* (after-sale discomfort) when they notice certain disadvantages of the purchased carpet brand or hear favourable things about brands not purchased. To counter such dissonance, a marketer's after-sale communications should provide evidence and support to help consumers feel good about their brand choices.

Habitual buying behaviour

Habitual buying behaviour—
Consumer buying behaviour
characterised by low-consumer
involvement and few significantly perceived brand
differences.

Habitual buying behaviour occurs under conditions of low-consumer involvement and little significant brand difference. For example, take table salt. Consumers have little involvement in this product category; they simply go to the store and reach for a brand. If they keep reaching for the same brand, it is out of habit rather than strong brand loyalty. Consumers appear to have low involvement with most low-cost, frequently purchased products.

In such cases, consumer behaviour does not pass through the usual belief–attitude–behaviour sequence. Consumers do not search extensively for information about the brands, evaluate brand characteristics and make weighty decisions about which brands to buy. Instead, they passively receive information as they watch television or read magazines. Ad repetition creates *brand familiarity* rather than *brand conviction*. Consumers do not form strong attitudes toward a brand; they select a brand because it is familiar. Because they are not highly involved with the product, consumers may not evaluate the choice, even after purchase. Thus, the buying process involves brand beliefs formed by passive learning, followed by purchase behaviour, which may or may not be followed by evaluation.

Because buyers are not highly committed to any brands, marketers of low-involvement products with few brand differences often use price and sales promotions to promote buying. Alternatively, they can add product features or enhancements to differentiate their brands from the rest of the pack and raise involvement. For example, to set its brand apart, Charmin toilet tissue offers Ultrastrong, Ultrasoft and Freshmate (wet) versions that are so absorbent that you can 'soften your bottom line' by using four times less than value brands. Charmin also raises brand involvement by offering a 'Sit or Squat' website and mobile phone app that helps travellers who 'Gotta go on the go!' find and rate clean public toilets.

Variety-seeking buying behaviour

Variety-seeking buying
behaviour—Consumer buying
behaviour characterised by
low consumer involvement
but significant perceived brand
differences.

Consumers undertake **variety-seeking buying behaviour** in situations characterised by low consumer involvement but significant perceived brand differences. In such cases, consumers often do a lot of brand switching. For example, when buying cookies, a consumer may hold some beliefs, choose a cookie brand without much evaluation, and then evaluate that brand during consumption. But the next time, a consumer might pick another brand out of boredom or simply to try something different. Brand switching occurs for the sake of variety rather than because of dissatisfaction.

In such product categories, the marketing strategy may differ for the market leader and minor brands. The market leader will try to encourage habitual buying behaviour by dominating shelf space, keeping shelves fully stocked and running frequent reminder advertising. Challenger firms will encourage variety seeking by offering lower prices, special deals, coupons, free samples and advertising that presents reasons for trying something new.

THE BUYER DECISION PROCESS

Now that we have looked at the influences that affect buyers, we are ready to look at how consumers make buying decisions. Figure 5.6 shows that the buyer decision process consists of five stages: *need recognition, information search, evaluation of alternatives, purchase decision* and *postpurchase behaviour*. Clearly, the buying process starts long before the actual purchase and continues long after. Marketers need to focus on the entire buying process rather than on the purchase decision only.

Figure 5.6 suggests that consumers pass through all five stages with every purchase. But in more routine purchases, consumers often skip or reverse some of these stages. A woman buying her regular brand of toothpaste would recognise the need and go right to the purchase decision, skipping information search and evaluation. However, we use the model in Figure 5.6 because it shows all the considerations that arise when a consumer faces a new and complex purchase situation.

Need recognition—The first stage of the buyer decision process in which the consumer recognises a problem or need.

Need recognition can be triggered by advertising: is it time for a snack?

Source: Campbell Soup Company

Need recognition

The buying process starts with **need recognition** – a buyer recognises a problem or a need. The need can be triggered by *internal stimuli* when one of the person's normal needs – for example, hunger or thirst – rises to a level high enough to become a drive. A need can also be triggered by *external stimuli*. For example, an advertisement or a discussion with a friend might get you thinking about buying a new car. At this stage, a marketer should research consumers to find out what kinds of needs or problems arise, what brought them about, and how they led a consumer to this particular product.

Information search

An interested consumer may or may not search for more information. If a consumer's drive is strong and a satisfying product is near

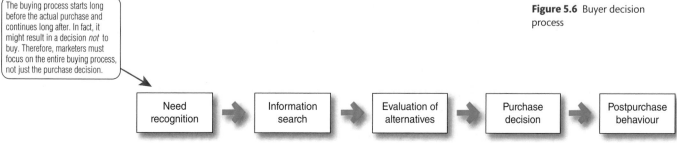

The buying process starts long before the actual purchase and continues long after. In fact, it might result in a decision *not* to buy. Therefore, marketers must focus on the entire buying process, not just the purchase decision.

Figure 5.6 Buyer decision process

| Need recognition | → | Information search | → | Evaluation of alternatives | → | Purchase decision | → | Postpurchase behaviour |

Information search—The stage of the buyer decision process in which the consumer is aroused to search for more information; the consumer may simply have heightened attention or may go into an active information search.

at hand, he or she is likely to buy it then. If not, the consumer may store the need in memory or undertake an **information search** related to the need. For example, once you've decided you need a new car, at the least, you will probably pay more attention to car ads, cars owned by friends and car conversations. Or you may actively search the Web, talk with friends and gather information in other ways.

Consumers can obtain information from any of several sources. These include *personal sources* (family, friends, neighbours, acquaintances), *commercial sources* (advertising, salespeople, dealer websites, packaging, displays), *public sources* (mass media, consumer rating organisations, Internet searches) and *experiential sources* (handling, examining, using the product). The relative influence of these information sources varies with the product and the buyer.

Generally, a consumer receives the most information about a product from commercial sources – those controlled by the marketer. The most effective sources, however, tend to be personal. Commercial sources normally *inform* a buyer, but personal sources *legitimise* or *evaluate* products for a buyer. For example, a recent study found that word of mouth is the biggest influence in people's electronics (43.7 per cent) and apparel (33.6 per cent) purchases. As one marketer states, 'It's rare that an advertising campaign can be as effective as a neighbour leaning over the fence and saying, "This is a wonderful product".' Increasingly, that 'fence' is a digital one. Another recent study revealed that consumers find sources of user-generated content – discussion forums, blogs, online review sites and social networking sites – three times more influential when making a purchase decision than conventional marketing methods such as TV advertising.[34]

As more information is obtained, a consumer's awareness and knowledge of the available brands and features increase. In your car information search, you may learn about the several brands available. The information might also help you to drop certain brands from consideration. A company must design its marketing mix to make prospective purchasers aware of and knowledgeable about its brand. It should carefully identify consumers' sources of information and the importance of each source.

Evaluation of alternatives

We have seen how consumers use information to arrive at a set of final brand choices. How does a consumer choose among alternative brands? Marketers need to know about **alternative evaluation**, that is, how a consumer processes information to arrive at brand choices. Unfortunately, consumers do not use a simple and single evaluation process in all buying situations. Instead, several evaluation processes are at work.

Alternative evaluation—The stage of the buyer decision process in which the consumer uses information to evaluate alternative brands in the choice set.

A consumer arrives at attitudes toward different brands through an evaluation procedure. How consumers go about evaluating purchase alternatives depends on the individual consumer and the specific buying situation. In some cases, consumers use careful calculations and logical thinking. At other times, the same consumers do little or no evaluating; instead they buy on impulse and rely on intuition. Sometimes consumers make buying decisions on their own; sometimes they turn to friends, online reviews or salespeople for buying advice.

Suppose you've narrowed your car choices down to three brands. And suppose that you are primarily interested in four attributes – styling, operating economy, warranty and price. By this time, you've probably formed beliefs about how each brand rates on each attribute. Clearly, if one car rated best on all the attributes, a marketer could predict that you would choose it. However, the brands will no doubt vary in appeal. You might base your buying decision on only one attribute, and your choice would be easy to predict. If you wanted styling above everything else, you would buy the car that you think has the best styling. But most buyers consider several attributes, each with different importance. If a marketer knew the importance that you assigned to each attribute, he or she could predict your car choice more reliably.

Marketers should study buyers to find out how they actually evaluate brand alternatives. If marketers know what evaluative processes go on, they can take steps to influence a buyer's decision.

Purchase decision

Purchase decision—The buyer's decision about which brand to purchase.

In the evaluation stage, a consumer ranks brands and forms purchase intentions. Generally, a consumer's **purchase decision** will be to buy the most preferred brand, but two factors can come between the purchase *intention* and the purchase *decision*. The first factor is the *attitudes of others*. If someone important to you thinks that you should buy the lowest-priced car, then the chances of you buying a more expensive car are reduced.

The second factor is *unexpected situational factors*. A consumer may form a purchase intention based on factors such as expected income, expected price and expected product benefits. However, unexpected events may change the purchase intention. For example, the economy might take a turn for the worse, a close competitor might drop its price, or a friend might report being disappointed in your preferred car. Thus, preferences and even purchase intentions do not always result in actual purchase choice.

Postpurchase behaviour

A marketer's job does not end when the product is bought. After purchasing the product, a consumer will either be satisfied or dissatisfied and will engage in **postpurchase behaviour** of interest to the marketer. What determines whether a buyer is satisfied or dissatisfied with a purchase? The answer lies in the relationship between a *consumer's expectations* and a product's *perceived performance*. If a product falls short of expectations, the consumer is disappointed; if it meets expectations, the consumer is satisfied; if it exceeds expectations, the consumer is delighted. The larger the gap between expectations and performance, the greater a consumer's dissatisfaction. This suggests that sellers should promise only what their brands can deliver so that buyers are satisfied.

Almost all major purchases, however, result in **cognitive dissonance**, or discomfort caused by postpurchase conflict. After the purchase, consumers are satisfied with the benefits of the chosen brand and are glad to avoid the drawbacks of the brands not bought. However, every purchase involves compromise. So consumers feel uneasy about acquiring the drawbacks of the chosen brand and about losing the benefits of the brands not purchased. Thus, consumers feel at least some postpurchase dissonance for every purchase.[35]

Why is it so important to satisfy the customer? Customer satisfaction is a key to building profitable relationships with consumers – to keeping and growing consumers and reaping their customer lifetime value. Satisfied customers buy a product again, talk favourably to others about the product, pay less attention to competing brands and advertising, and buy other products from the company. Many marketers go beyond merely *meeting* the expectations of customers; they aim to *delight* the customer.

A dissatisfied consumer responds differently. Bad word of mouth often travels further and faster than good word of mouth. It can quickly damage consumer attitudes about a company and its products. But companies cannot simply rely on dissatisfied customers to volunteer their complaints when they are dissatisfied. Most unhappy customers never tell the company about their problems. Therefore, a company should measure customer satisfaction regularly. It should set up systems that *encourage* customers to complain. In this way, the company can learn how well it is doing and how it can improve.

By studying the overall buyer decision process, marketers may be able to find ways to help consumers move through it. For example, if consumers are not buying a new product because they do not perceive a need for it, marketing might launch advertising messages that trigger the need and show how the product solves customers' problems. If customers know about the product but are not buying because they hold unfavourable attitudes toward it, marketers must find ways to change either the product or consumer perceptions.

Postpurchase behaviour— The stage of the buyer decision process in which consumers take further action after purchase based on their satisfaction or dissatisfaction with a purchase.

Cognitive dissonance— Buyer discomfort caused by postpurchase conflict.

AUTHOR COMMENT
Now we look at some special considerations in *new-product* buying decisions.

THE BUYER DECISION PROCESS FOR NEW PRODUCTS

We have looked at the stages buyers go through in trying to satisfy a need. Buyers may pass quickly or slowly through these stages, and some of the stages may even be reversed. Much depends on the nature of the buyer, the product and the buying situation.

New product—A good, service or idea that is perceived by some potential customers as new.

We now look at how buyers approach the purchase of new products. A **new product** is a good, service or idea that is perceived by some potential customers as new. It may have been around for a while, but our interest is in how consumers learn about products for the first time and make decisions on whether to adopt them. We define the **adoption process** as 'the mental process through which an individual passes from first learning about an innovation to final adoption', and *adoption* as the decision by an individual to become a regular user of the product.[36]

Adoption process—The mental process through which an individual passes from first hearing about an innovation to final adoption.

Stages in the adoption process

Consumers go through five stages in the process of adopting a new product:

1. *Awareness.* The consumer becomes aware of the new product but lacks information about it.
2. *Interest.* The consumer seeks information about the new product.
3. *Evaluation.* The consumer considers whether trying the new product makes sense.
4. *Trial.* The consumer tries the new product on a small scale to improve his or her estimate of its value.
5. *Adoption.* The consumer decides to make full and regular use of the new product.

This model suggests that the new-product marketer should think about how to help consumers move through these stages. For example, during the economic downturn, Hyundai developed a unique way to help customers get past evaluation and make a positive purchase decision about a new vehicle.

> Hyundai discovered many potential customers were interested in buying new cars but couldn't get past the evaluation stage of the buying process. Consumers worried that they might buy a car and then lose their jobs and subsequently their new cars and their good credit ratings. To help buyers over this hurdle, the car manufacturer offered the Hyundai Assurance Program, which promised to let buyers who financed or leased a new Hyundai vehicle return their vehicles at no cost and with no harm to their credit rating if they lost their jobs or incomes within a year. The Assurance Program, combined with a 10-year warranty and a 5-year, 24-hour roadside assistance programme, all at no extra charge, made the buying decision much easier for customers concerned about the future economy. Sales of the Hyundai Sonata surged 85 per cent in the month following the start of the Assurance campaign, and the brand's market share grew at an industry-leading pace during the following year. Hyundai continued the programme on its 2010 models, and other car manufacturers soon followed with their own assurance plans.[37]

Individual differences in innovativeness

People differ greatly in their readiness to try new products. In each product area, there are 'consumption pioneers' and early adopters. Other individuals adopt new products much later. People can be classified into the adopter categories shown in Figure 5.7. After a slow start, an increasing number of people adopt a new product. The number of adopters reaches a peak and then drops off as fewer non-adopters remain. Innovators are defined as the first 2.5 per cent of buyers to adopt a new idea (those beyond two standard deviations from mean adoption time); the early adopters are the next 13.5 per cent (between one and two standard deviations); and so forth.

The five adopter groups have differing values. *Innovators* are venturesome; they try new ideas at some risk. *Early adopters* are guided by respect; they are opinion leaders in their communities and

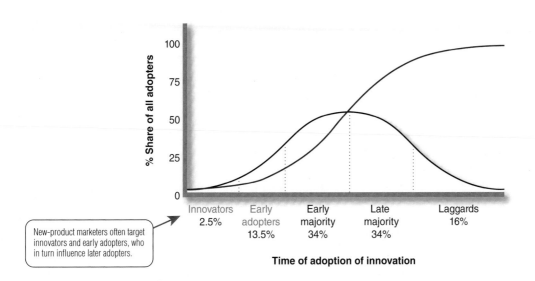

Figure 5.7 Adopter categorisation on the basis of relative time of adoption of innovations

Source: Reprinted with permission of the Free Press, a Division of Simon & Schuster, from *Diffusion of Innovations*, 5th edn, by Everett M. Rogers. Copyright © 2003 by the Free Press.

New-product marketers often target innovators and early adopters, who in turn influence later adopters.

adopt new ideas early but carefully. The *early majority* is deliberate; although they rarely are leaders, they adopt new ideas before the average person. The *late majority* is sceptical; they adopt an innovation only after a majority of people have tried it. Finally, *laggards* are tradition bound; they are suspicious of changes and adopt the innovation only when it has become something of a tradition itself.

This adopter classification suggests that an innovating firm should research the characteristics of innovators and early adopters in their product categories and direct marketing efforts toward them.

Influence of product characteristics on rate of adoption

The characteristics of the new product affect its rate of adoption. Some products catch on almost overnight; for example, both the iPod and iPhone flew off retailers' shelves at an astounding rate from the day they were first introduced. Others take a longer time to gain acceptance. For example, the first HDTVs were introduced in the 1990s, but the percentage of European households owning a high-definition set stood at only 51 per cent by 2010 with 116 million sets. By 2018 it is expected that 220 million Europeans will own an HDTV.[38]

Five characteristics are especially important in influencing an innovation's rate of adoption. For example, consider the characteristics of HDTV in relation to the rate of adoption:

- *Relative advantage* – the degree to which an innovation appears superior to existing products. HDTV offers substantially improved picture quality. This speeded up its rate of adoption.
- *Compatibility* – the degree to which an innovation fits the values and experiences of potential consumers. HDTV, for example, is highly compatible with the lifestyles of the TV-watching public. However, in the early years, HDTV was not yet compatible with programming and broadcasting systems, which slowed adoption. Now, as more and more high-definition programmes and channels have become available, the rate of HDTV adoption has increased rapidly.
- *Complexity* – the degree to which an innovation is difficult to understand or use. HDTVs are not very complex. Therefore, as more programming has become available and prices have fallen, the rate of HDTV adoption is increasing faster than that of more complex innovations.
- *Divisibility* – the degree to which an innovation may be tried on a limited basis. Early HDTVs and HD cable and satellite systems were very expensive, which slowed the rate of adoption. As prices fall, adoption rates increase.
- *Communicability* – the degree to which the results of using an innovation can be observed or described to others. Because HDTV lends itself to demonstration and description, its use will spread faster among consumers.

Other characteristics influence the rate of adoption, such as initial and ongoing costs, risk and uncertainty, and social approval. The new-product marketer must research all these factors when developing the new product and its marketing programme.

REVIEWING OBJECTIVES AND KEY TERMS

The European consumer market consists of more than 500 million people who consume more €8 billion worth of goods and services each year, making it one of the most attractive consumer markets in the world. The world consumer market consists of more than 6.8 billion people. Consumers around the world vary greatly in terms of cultural, social, personal and psychological makeup. Understanding how these differences affect *consumer buying behaviour* is one of the biggest challenges marketers face.

OBJECTIVE 1 Define the consumer market and construct a simple model of consumer buyer behaviour (pp. 144–145).

The *consumer market* consists of all the individuals and households who buy or acquire goods and services for personal consumption. The simplest model of consumer buyer behaviour is the stimulus–response model. According to this model, marketing stimuli (the four Ps) and other major forces (economic, technological, political, cultural) enter a consumer's 'black box' and produce certain responses. Once in the black box, these inputs produce observable buyer responses, such as product choice, brand choice, purchase timing and purchase amount.

OBJECTIVE 2 Name the four major factors that influence consumer buyer behaviour (pp. 145–159).

Consumer buyer behaviour is influenced by four key sets of buyer characteristics: cultural, social, personal, and psychological. Although many of these factors cannot be influenced by a marketer, they can be useful in identifying interested buyers and shaping products and appeals to serve consumer needs better. *Culture* is the most basic determinant of a person's wants and behaviour. *Subcultures* are 'cultures within cultures' that have distinct values and lifestyles and can be based on anything from age to ethnicity. Many companies focused their marketing programmes on the special needs of certain cultural and subcultural segments.

Social factors also influence a buyer's behaviour. A person's *reference groups* – family, friends, social networks, professional associations – strongly affect product and brand choices. A buyer's age, life-cycle stage, occupation, economic circumstances, personality and other *personal characteristics* influence his or her buying decisions. Consumer *lifestyles*–the whole pattern of acting and interacting in the world–are also an important influence on purchase decisions. Finally, consumer buying behaviour is influenced by four major *psychological factors*: motivation, perception, learning, and beliefs and attitudes.

Each of these factors provides a different perspective for understanding the workings of a buyer's black box.

OBJECTIVE 3 List and define the major types of buying decision behaviour and the stages in the buyer decision process (pp. 159–162).

Buying behaviour may vary greatly across different types of products and buying decisions. Consumers undertake *complex buying behaviour* when they are highly involved in a purchase and perceive significant differences among brands. *Dissonance-reducing behaviour* occurs when consumers are highly involved but see little difference among brands. *Habitual buying behaviour* occurs under conditions of low involvement and little significant brand difference. In situations characterised by low involvement but significant perceived brand differences, consumers engage in *variety-seeking buying behaviour*.

When making a purchase, a buyer goes through a decision process consisting of *need recognition, information search, evaluation of alternatives, purchase decision* and *postpurchase behaviour*. A marketer's job is to understand a buyer's behaviour at each stage and the influences that are operating. During *need recognition*, a consumer recognises a problem or a need that could be satisfied by a product or a service in the market. Once the need is recognised, a consumer is aroused to seek more information and moves into the *information search* stage. With information in hand, a consumer proceeds to *alternative evaluation*, during which the information is used to evaluate brands in the choice set. From there, a consumer makes a *purchase decision* and actually buys the product. In the final stage of the buyer decision process, *postpurchase behaviour*, a consumer takes action based on satisfaction or dissatisfaction.

OBJECTIVE 4 Describe the adoption and diffusion process for new products (pp. 164–165).

The product *adoption process* is made up of five stages: awareness, interest, evaluation, trial, and adoption. New-product marketers must think about how to help consumers move through these stages. With regard to the *diffusion process* for new products, consumers respond at different rates, depending on consumer and product characteristics. Consumers may be innovators, early adopters, early majority, late majority, or laggards. Each group may require different marketing approaches. Marketers often try to bring their new products to the attention of potential early adopters, especially those who are opinion leaders. Finally, several characteristics influence the rate of adoption: relative advantage, compatibility, complexity, divisibility, and communicability.

NAVIGATING THE KEY TERMS

OBJECTIVE 1
Consumer buyer behaviour (p. 144)
Consumer market (p. 144)

OBJECTIVE 2
Culture (p. 146)
Subculture (p. 146)
Social class (p. 149)
Group (p. 149)
Opinion leader (p. 150)
Online social networks (p. 151)
Lifestyle (p. 155)
Personality (p. 155)
Motive (drive) (p. 156)
Perception (p. 157)
Learning (p. 158)
Belief (p. 158)
Attitude (p. 158)

OBJECTIVE 3
Complex buying behaviour (p. 159)
Dissonance-reducing buying behaviour (p. 160)
Habitual buying behaviour (p. 160)
Variety-seeking buying behaviour (p. 160)
Need recognition (p. 161)
Information search (p. 162)
Alternative evaluation (p. 162)
Purchase decision (p. 162)
Postpurchase behaviour (p. 163)
Cognitive dissonance (p. 163)

OBJECTIVE 4
New product (p. 164)
Adoption process (p. 164)

DISCUSSING AND APPLYING THE CONCEPTS

Discussing the concepts

1. How do consumers respond to various marketing efforts the company might use? Which buyer characteristics that affect buyer behaviour influence you most when making a clothing purchase decision? Are these the same characteristics that would influence you when making a computer purchase? Explain. (AACSB Communication; Reflective Thinking)

2. What is an opinion leader? Describe how marketers attempt to use opinion leaders to help sell their products. (AACSB: Communication; Reflective Thinking)

3. Name and describe the types of consumer buying behaviour. Which one would most likely be involved in the purchase of a mobile phone? For choosing a frozen dinner? (AACSB: Communication; Reflective Thinking)

4. Explain the stages of the consumer buyer decision process and describe how you or your family went through this process to make a recent purchase. (AACSB: Communication; Reflective Thinking)

5. Name and describe the adopter categories and explain how a marketer of three-dimensional televisions can use this knowledge in its market targeting decision. (AACSB: Communication; Reflective Thinking)

Applying the concepts

1. Marketers often target consumers before, during or after a trigger event, an event in one's life that triggers change. For example, after having a child, new parents have an increased need for baby furniture, clothes, nappies, car seats and lots of other baby-related goods. Consumers who never paid attention to marketing efforts for certain products may now be focused on ones related to their life change. In a small group, discuss other trigger events that may provide opportunities to target the right buyer at the right time. (AACSB: Communication; Reflective Thinking)

2. Hemopure is a human blood substitute derived from cattle blood. OPK Biotechstill has this product in clinical trials, but the company has received FDA approval for a similar product, Oxyglobin, in the veterinary market. Visit http://opkbiotech.com to learn about Hemopure. Then explain how the product characteristics of relative advantage, compatibility, complexity, divisibility and communicability will influence the rate of adoption of this product once approval is attained. (AACSB: Communication; Reflective Thinking)

3. Go to the Strategic Business Insight's website and complete the VALS survey at www.strategicbusinessinsights.com/vals/

presurvey.shtml. What does VALS measure, and what is your VALS type? Does it adequately describe you? On what dimensions are the VALS types based? How can marketers use this tool to better understand consumers? (AACSB: Communication; Use of IT; Reflective Thinking)

Focus on technology

Have you noticed that some of your Facebook friends like certain advertisements? Marketers know what Facebook users like and are using that knowledge to influence users' friends. 'Social context ads' are based on data collected on the likes and friends of Facebook users. When you click on an ad indicating that you like it, you also give Facebook permission to share that preference with all your friends. Marketers like this feature because it appears as though you are endorsing the brand to your friends. Nike bought ads on users' homepages in 20 countries prior to the World Cup, and Ford uses Facebook's social context ads to its cars. Although most ads on Facebook cost as little as €1 per click for marketers, the total cost for a social context ad can be as much as €75,000.

1. Which factors are marketers advertising on Facebook using to influence consumers? Would you be influenced by an ad if you saw that your friends liked it? (AACSB: Communication; Use of IT; Reflective Thinking)

2. How would you feel about Facebook using your name in these types of ads? (AACSB: Communication; Reflective Thinking)

Focus on ethics

Vitaminwater sounds healthy, right? Although Vitaminwater has vitamins, it also has 33g of sugar – that's two heaped tablespoons – making it not much better than a soda. Vitaminwater, owned by Coca-Cola, has been under fire in the US from the Center for Science in the Public Interest (CSPI), a consumer-advocacy group that fights for safer, more nutritious foods. The CSPI filed a class-action lawsuit against Coca-Cola, claiming names for Vitaminwater flavours such as 'endurance peach mango' and 'focus kiwi strawberry' are misleading for two reasons: (1) the drinks contain zero to one per cent juice, and (2) words like *endurance, focus, defense, rescue* and *energy* imply health benefits. Coca-Cola's defence was that reasonable consumers would not be misled into believing that Vitaminwater is healthy for them.

1. Debate whether or not Coca-Cola is deliberately trying to deceive consumers into believing that Vitaminwater is a healthy alternative to soda. Which psychological factor is most affected by the product name and ad claims and might influence consumers to purchase this product? (AACSB: Communication; Ethical Reasoning)

2. Find two other examples of brands that use names, words, colours, package shapes or other elements to convey potentially deceptive meanings to consumers. (AACSB: Communication; Reflective Thinking)

Marketing & the economy

While high street retailers have all been negatively affected by the recession, distance retailers (those online or on TV shopping channels) have had a slightly better time. In a recession people go out less and spend more time at home – more often than not in front of a screen, be it a TV, laptop or smartphone. In mid-2011, Argos the UK catalogue retailer, launched its shopping channel which allows TV shoppers to choose products being demonstrated on TV and have them delivered on the same day – something no other TV retailer currently offers. Argos teamed up with Sky TV to reach new audiences, boost sales and to target the two main types of TV shopper – bargain hunters and inspiration seekers. Initial sales look good and Argos seems to be reaching a new (if more sedate) type of customer. Their typical TV viewer is 35–65, but the main items they show are toys and children's clothing.

1. Consider the buyer decision process for a shopper on the high street and one sitting watching TV at home. How do you think their decision processes differ, if at all?

2. Which factors could influence a shopper's decision to purchase via television rather than on the high street?

3. Why are Argos focusing mainly on toys and children's clothing? Would you include other types of goods and services?

Marketing by the numbers

One way consumers can evaluate alternatives is to identify important attributes and assess how purchase alternatives perform on those attributes. Consider the purchase of a notebook computer. Each attribute, such as memory, is given a weight to reflect its level of importance to that consumer. Then the consumer evaluates each alternative on each attribute. For example, in the table, memory (weighted at 0.5) is the most important computer purchase attribute for this consumer. The consumer believes that Brand C performs best on memory, rating it 7 (higher ratings indicate higher performance). Brand B rates worst on this attribute (a rating of 3). Size and price are the consumer's next most important attributes. Warranty is least important.

A score can be calculated for each brand by multiplying the importance weight for each attribute by the brand's score on that attribute. These weighted scores are then summed to determine the score for that brand. For example, Score$_{BrandA}$ = $(0.2 \times 4) + (0.5 \times 6) + (0.1 \times 5) + (0.2 \times 4) = 0.8 + 3.0 + 0.5 + 0.8 = 5.1$. This consumer will select the brand with the highest score.

	Importance	Alternative Brands		
Attributes	Weight (e)	A	B	C
Size	0.2	4	6	2
Memory	0.5	6	3	7
Warranty	0.1	5	5	4
Price	0.2	4	6	7

1. Calculate the scores for brands B and C. Which brand would this consumer be likely to choose? (AACSB: Communication; Analytic Reasoning)

2. Which brand is this consumer least likely to purchase? Discuss two ways the marketer of this brand can enhance consumer attitudes toward purchasing its brand. (AACSB: Communication; Reflective Thinking; Analytic Reasoning)

 # REFERENCES

[1] This case study draws heavily on the excellent case studies and analyses of: Lucie Green, 'Pretty, posh and profitable', *Financial Times* (13 May 2011), www.ft.com/cms/s/2/fcca7ebc-7ce4-11e0-a7c7-00144feabdc0.html#axzz1ZKhQf2fh, accessed October 2011; Clear Barrett 'High-spending tourists boost airport sales', *Financial Times* (12 September 2011) www.ft.com/cms/s/0/3ecc0056-dd57-11e0-9dac-00144feabdc0.html#axzz1ZKhQf2fh, accessed October 2011.

[2] GDP figures from *The World Fact Book* (2 April 2010), www.cia.gov/cia/publications/factbook; and 'Research and markets: evaluate the US consumer behavior 2010 market: accounting for 71% of the US gross domestic product, or over $10 Trillion', *Business Wire* (18 December 2009), Population figures from the World POPClock, US Census Bureau, www.census.gov/main/www/popclock.html, accessed May 2010. This website provides continuously updated projections of US and world populations.

[3] Don E. Schultz, 'Lines or circles', *Marketing News* (5 November 2007), p. 21; and Elizabeth A. Sullivan, 'Pick Your Brain', *Marketing News* (15 March 2009), pp. 10–13.

[4] Example and data from ISFE Consumer Survey 2010 Video Gamers in Europe 2010, Prepared for the Interactive Software Federation of Europe by Game Vision Europe, www.isfe-eu.org/index.php?oidit=T001:662b16 536388a7260921599321365911, accessed October 2011.

[5] The Software Unit Sales and Sales Value estimates are provided by Screen Digest (December 2009), in *Video Gamers in Europe 2010*, prepared for the Interactive Software Federation of Europe by Game Vision Europe, www.isfe-eu.org/index.php?oidit=T001:662b16536 388a7260921599321365911, accessed October 2011.

[6] The bullet points are selected from the fuller report detailed in The Software Unit Sales and Sales Value estimates are provided by Screen Digest (December 2009), in *Video Gamers in Europe 2010*.

[7] Example from Chris Nutall, 'Wii U kickstarts next generation of gaming', *Financial Times*, 10 June 2011, www.ft.com/cms/s/2/94aa08e2-9342-11e0-a038-00144feab49a.html#axzz1UPifHx5H, accessed October 2011.

[8] See Gene Epstein, 'Boomer Consumer', *Barron's*, (5 October 2009), http://online.barrons.com/article/SB125452437207860627.html; Stuart Elliott, 'The older audiences looking better than ever', *New York Times*, (20 April 2009); Ellen Byron, 'Seeing store shelves through senior eyes', *Wall Street Journal* (14 September 2009), p. B1; and Brent Bouchez, 'Super Bowl ads need to age gracefully', *BusinessWeek* (14 February 2010), www.businessweek.com.

[9] Elliott, 'The older audiences looking better than ever'.

[10] 'Boom time of America's new retirees feel entitled to relax – and intend to spend', *Financial Times* (6 December 2007), p. 9.

[11] Mark Dolliver, 'Marketing to today's 65-plus consumers', *Adweek*, (27 July 2009), www.adweek.com.

[12] See www.holidaysforsinglepeople.co.uk/singles-holidays-over-50.php, accessed October 2011.

[13] 'Research reveals word-of-mouth campaigns on customer networks double marketing results', *Business Wire* (27 October 2009).

[14] Example from David Gelles, 'Always online and on-message', *Financial Times* (14 July 2011), www.ft.com/cms/s/0/eee71e8a-8f8d-11df-8df0-00144feab49a.html#axzz1UPifHx5H, accessed October 2010.

[15] See www.tremor.com/revealing-case-studies/crest-weekly-clean, accessed March 2010.

[16] See http://blog.benetton.com, accessed October 2011

[17] See Brian Morrissey, 'Social rings', *Brandweek* (18 January 2010), p. 20.

[18] See Eleftheria Parpis, 'She's in charge', *Adweek* (6–13 October 2008), p. 38; Abigail Posner, 'Why package-goods companies should market to men', *Advertising Age* (9 February 2009), http://adage.com/print?article_id=134473; and Marissa Miley and Ann Mark, 'The new female consumer: the rise of the real mom', *Advertising Age*, (16 November 2009), pp. A1–A27.

[19] Adapted from Michel Marriott, 'Gadget designers take aim at women', *New York Times* (7 June 2007), p. C7. Also see Dean Takahashi, 'Philips focuses on TVs women buyers', *McClatchy-Tribune Business News*, (6 January 2008).

[20] Examples from Michael J. Silverstein and Kate Sayre, 'The female economy'; Andrea Learned and Carolyn Hadlock, 'Reaching recession dads', *Adweek* (15 June 2009), p. AM20.

[21] Example from Rebecca Smithers, 'How much does it cost to raise a child?', *Guardian* (23 February 2010), www.guardian.co.uk/news/datablog/2010/feb/23/cost-raising-child?INTCMP=SRCH, accessed October 2011 and Ryan Kisiel, 'Children have never had it so good', *Daily Mail* (21 January 2010), www.dailymail.co.uk/news/article-1241841/Children-good-Average-weekly-pocket-money-rises-6-840.html, accessed October 2011.

22 R. K. Miller and Kelli Washington, *Consumer Behavior 2009* (Atlanta, GA: Richard K. Miller & Associates, 2009), Chapter 27. Also see Michael R. Solomon, *Consumer Behavior: Buying, Having, and Being* (Upper Saddle River, NJ: Prentice Hall, 2011), pp. 439–445.

23 See www.justsardinia.co.uk/forte-village, accessed October 2011.

24 For this quote and other information on Acxiom's PersonicX segmentation system, see 'Acxiom study reveals insight on evolving consumer shopping behaviors in trying economic times', *Reuters* (13 January 2009), www.reuters.com/article/pressRelease/idUS180299+13-Jan-2009+BW20090113; 'Acxiom study offers insight into leisure travelers who still spend freely despite a down economy', *Business Wire* (18 November 2009); and 'Acxiom PersonicX' and 'Intelligent solutions for the travel industry: life-stage marketing', www.acxiom.com, accessed April 2010.

25 See www.edeandravenscroft.co.uk, accessed October 2011.

26 Example from Andrea Felsted, 'Europe's cheap chic brands feel the pinch', *Financial Times* (22 June 2011), www.ft.com/cms/s/0/ed23fef6-9cf2-11e0-8678-00144feabdc0.html#ixzz1TNHvNhkG, accessed October 2011.

27 Beth J. Harpaz, 'New book connects political and lifestyle choices', (4 November 2006), www.seattlepi.com/lifestyle/291052_lifestylevote04.html. For more on lifestyle and consumer behavior, see Solomon, *Consumer Behavior: Buying, Having, and Being*, pp. 226–233.

28 See Jennifer Aaker, 'Dimensions of measuring brand personality', *Journal of Marketing Research* (August 1997), pp. 347–356; Kevin Lane Keller, *Strategic Brand Management*, 3rd edn. (Upper Saddle River, NJ: Prentice Hall, 2008), pp. 66–67; and Vanitha Swaminathan, Karen M. Stilley and Rohini Ahluwalla, 'When brand personality matters: the moderating role of attachment styles', *Journal of Consumer Research* (April 2009), pp. 985–1002.

29 See www.apple.com/getamac/ads, accessed May 2010.

30 See Abraham. H. Maslow, 'A theory of human motivation', *Psychological Review*, **50** (1943), pp. 370–396. Also see Maslow, *Motivation and Personality*, 3rd edn. (New York: HarperCollins Publishers, 1987); and Leon G. Schiffman and Leslie Lazar Kanuk, *Consumer Behavior* (Upper Saddle River, NJ: Prentice Hall, 2010), pp. 98–106.

31 See Louise Story, 'Anywhere the eye can see, it's now likely to see an ad', *New York Times* (15 January 2007); Matthew Creamer, 'Caught in the clutter crossfire: your brand', *Advertising Age* (1 April 2007), p. 35; and Ruth Mortimer, 'Consumer awareness: getting the right attention', *Brand Strategy* (10 December 2008), p. 55.

32 See Bob Garfield, ' "Subliminal" seduction and other urban myths', *Advertising Age* (18 September 2000), pp. 4, 105; Lewis Smith, 'Subliminal advertising may work, but only if you're paying attention', *The Times* (9 March 2007); and Cahal Milmo, 'Power of the hidden message is revealed', *The Independent* (London) (28 September 2009), p. 8.

33 Example from Salamander Davoudi and Edward Blakeney, 'A business with natural energy', *Financial Times* (7 November 2007), www.ft.com/cms/s/0/b31c690a-8cd4-11dc-b887-0000779fd2ac.html#axzz1UPifHx5H and www.fireflytonics.com/our-company, accessed October 2011.

34 Quotes and information from Yubo Chen and Jinhong Xie, 'Online consumer review: word-of-mouth as a new element of marketing communication mix', *Management Science* (March 2008), pp. 477–491; 'Leo J. Shapiro & Associates: user-generated content three times more influential than TV advertising on consumer purchase decisions', *Marketing Business Weekly* (28 December 2008), p. 34; and 'Word of mouth influences most apparel purchases', *Army/Navy Store & Outdoor Merchandiser* (15 January 2010), p. 6.

35 See Leon Festinger, *A Theory of Cognitive Dissonance* (Stanford, CA: Stanford University Press, 1957); Cynthia Crossen, ' "Cognitive dissonance" became a milestone in the 1950s psychology', *Wall Street Journal* (12 December 2006), p. B1; and Anupam Bawa and Purva Kansal, 'Cognitive dissonance and the marketing of services: some issues', *Journal of Services Research* (October 2008–March 2009), p. 31.

36 The following discussion draws from the work of Everett M. Rogers. See his *Diffusion of Innovations*, 5th edn. (New York: Free Press, 2003).

37 Nick Bunkley, 'Hyundai, using a safety net, wins market share', *New York Times* (5 February 2009); Chris Woodyard and Bruce Horvitz, 'GM, Ford are latest offering help to those hit by job loss', *USA Today* (1 April 2009); and 'Hyundai assurance enhanced for 2010', *PR Newswire* (29 December 2009).

38 See www.satellitemarkets.com, accessed August 2011.

VIDEO CASE

Radian6 MyMarketingLab

Social networking has had a huge impact on society. And for marketers, online social communications are changing the way that consumers make purchase decisions. Radian6 specialises in monitoring social media. It tracks a wide array of websites at which consumers might 'chat' about companies, brands and general market offerings. Companies such as Dell and Microsoft obtain valuable insights about what consumers are saying about their products and about what factors or events are generating the discussions. But more importantly, companies are gaining a stronger understanding of how consumer online conversations are affecting purchase decisions. In this manner, Radian6 is on the cutting edge of getting a grip on the ever-expanding scope of social networking and 'word-of-Web' communication.

After watching the video featuring Radian6, answer the following questions:

1. What cultural factors have led to the explosion of social networking?
2. How has Radian6 changed the way companies understand opinion leaders and marketing?
3. How is Radian6 helping companies gain insights into the buying decision process?

Porsche: guarding the old while bringing in the new

Porsche (pronounced *Porsh*-uh) is a unique company. It has always been a niche brand that makes cars for a small and distinctive segment of automobile buyers. Top managers at Porsche spend a great deal of time thinking about customers. They want to know who their customers are, what they think and how they feel. They want to know why they buy a Porsche rather then a Jaguar, a Ferrari or a big Mercedes coupé. These are challenging questions to answer; even Porsche owners themselves don't know exactly what motivates their buying. But given Porsche's low volume and the increasingly fragmented auto market, it is imperative that management understands its customers and what gets their motors running.

THE PROFILE OF A PORSCHE OWNER

Porsche was founded in 1931 by Ferdinand Porsche, the man credited for designing the original Volkswagen Beetle – Adolf Hitler's 'people's car' and one of the most successful car designs of all time. For most of its first two decades, the company built Volkswagen Beetles for German citizens and tanks and Beetles for the military.

As Porsche AG began to sell cars under its own nameplate in the 1950s and 1960s, a few constants developed. The company sold very few models, creating an image of exclusivity. Those models had a rounded, bubble shape that had its roots in the original Beetle but evolved into something more Porsche-like with the world famous 356 and 911 models. Finally, Porsche's automobiles featured air-cooled four- and six-cylinder 'boxer' motors (cylinders in an opposed configuration) in the rear of the car. This gave the cars a unique and often dangerous characteristic – a tendency for the rear end to swing out when cornering hard. That's one of the reasons that Porsche owners were drawn to them. They were challenging to drive, which kept most people away. Since its early days, Porsche has appealed to a very narrow segment of financially successful people. These are achievers who see themselves as entrepreneurial, even if they work for a corporation.

They set very high goals for themselves and then work doggedly to meet them. And they expect no less from the clothes they wear, the restaurants they go to or the cars they drive. These individuals see themselves not as a part of the regular world but as exceptions to it. They buy Porsches because the car mirrors their self-image; it stands for the things owners like to see in themselves and their lives.

Most of us buy what Porsche executives call utility vehicles. That is, we buy cars primarily to go to work, transport children and run errands. Because we use our cars to accomplish these daily tasks, we base buying decisions on features such as price, size, fuel economy and other practical considerations. But Porsche is more than a utility car. Its owners see it as a car to be enjoyed, not just used. Most Porsche buyers are not moved by information but by feelings. A Porsche is like a piece of clothing – something the owner 'wears' and is seen in. They develop a personal relationship with their cars, one that has more to do with the way the car sounds, vibrates and feels, rather than how many cup holders it has or how much space it has in the boot. They admire their Porsche because it is a competent performance machine without being flashy or phony.

People buy Porsches because they enjoy driving. If all they needed was something to get them from point A to point B, they could find something much less expensive. And while many Porsche owners are car enthusiasts, some of them are not. One successful businesswoman and owner of a high-end Porsche said, 'When I drive this car to the high school to pick up my daughter, I end up with five youngsters in the car. If I drive any other car, I can't even find her; she doesn't want to come home.'

FROM NICHE TO NUMEROUS

For its first few decades, Porsche AG lived by the philosophy of Ferry Porsche, Ferdinand's son. Ferry created the Porsche 356 because no one else made a car like he wanted: 'We did no market research, we had no sales forecasts, no return-on-investment calculations. None of that. I very simply built my dream car and figured that there would be other people who share that dream.' So, really, Porsche AG from the beginning was very much like its customers: an achiever that set out to make the very best. But as the years rolled on, Porsche management became concerned with a significant issue: Were there enough Porsche buyers to keep the company afloat? Granted, the company never had illusions of churning out the numbers of a Chevrolet or a Toyota. But to fund innovation, even a niche manufacturer has to grow a little. And Porsche began to worry that the quirky nature of the people who buy Porsches might just run out on them.

This led Porsche to extend its brand outside the box. In the early 1970s, Porsche introduced the 914, a square-ish, mid-engine, two-seater that was much cheaper than the 911. This meant that a different class of people could afford a Porsche. It was no surprise that the 914 became Porsche's top-selling model. By the late 1970s, Porsche replaced the 914 with a hatchback coupe that had something no other regular Porsche model had ever had: an engine in the front. At less than €15,000, more than €7,500 less than the 911, the 924 and later 944 models were once again Porsche's pitch to affordability. At one point, Porsche increased its sales goal by nearly 50 per cent to 60,000 cars a year.

Although these cars were in many respects sales successes, the Porsche faithful cried foul. They considered these entry-level models to be cheap and underperforming. Most loyalists never really accepted these models as 'real' Porsches. In fact, they were not at all happy that they had to share their brand with a customer who didn't fit the Porsche owner profile. They were turned off by what they saw as a corporate strategy that had focused on *mass* over *class* marketing. This tarnished image was compounded by the fact that Nissan, Toyota, BMW and other car manufacturers had ramped up high-end sports car offerings, creating some fierce competition. In fact, both the Datsun 280-ZX and the Toyota Supra were not only cheaper than Porsche's 944 but also faster. A struggling economy threw more sand in Porsche's tank. By 1990, Porsche sales had plummeted, and the company flirted with bankruptcy.

RETURN TO ITS ROOTS?

But Porsche wasn't going down without a fight. It quickly recognised the error of its ways and halted production of the entry-level models. It rebuilt its damaged image by revamping its higher-end model lines with more race-bred technology. In an effort to regain rapport with customers, Porsche once again targeted the high end of the market in both price and performance. It set modest sales goals and decided that moderate growth with higher margins would be more profitable in the long term. Thus, the company set out to make one less Porsche than the public demanded. According to one executive, 'We're not looking for volume; we're searching for exclusivity.' Porsche's efforts had the desired effect. By the late 1990s, the brand was once again favoured by the same type of achiever who had so deeply loved the car for decades. The cars were once again exclusive. And the company was once again profitable.

But by the early 2000s, Porsche management was again asking itself a familiar question: To have a sustainable future, could Porsche rely on only the Porsche faithful? According to then CEO Wendelin Wiedeking, 'For Porsche to remain independent, it can't be dependent on the most fickle segment in the market. We don't want to become just a marketing department of some giant. We have to make sure we're profitable enough to pay for future development ourselves.'

So in 2002, Porsche did the unthinkable. It became one of the last car companies to jump into the insatiable sport utility vehicle (SUV) market. At roughly 2,500 kg, the new Porsche Cayenne was heavier than anything that Porsche had ever made, with the exception of some prototype tanks it made during the Second World War. Once again, the new model featured an engine up front. And it was the first Porsche to ever be equipped with seatbelts for five. As news spread about the car's development, howls could be heard from Porsche's customer base. But this time, Porsche did not seem too

concerned that the loyalists would be put off. Could it be that the company had already forgotten what happened the last time it deviated from the mould? After driving one of the first Cayenne's off the assembly line, one journalist stated, 'A day at the wheel of the 444 horsepower Cayenne Turbo leaves two overwhelming impressions. First, the Cayenne doesn't behave or feel like an SUV, and second, it drives like a Porsche.' This was no entry-level car. Porsche had created a two-and-a-half ton beast that could accelerate to 60 miles per hour in just over five seconds, corner like it was on rails, and hit 165 miles per hour, all while coddling five adults in sumptuous leather seats with almost no wind noise from the outside world. On top of that, it could keep up with a Land Rover when the pavement ended. Indeed, Porsche had created the Porsche of SUVs.

Recently, Porsche upped the ante one more time. It unveiled another large vehicle. But this time, it was a low-slung, five-door luxury sedan. The Porsche faithful and the automotive press again gasped in disbelief. But by the time the Panamera hit the pavement, Porsche had proven once again that Porsche customers could have their cake *and* eat it. The Panamera is almost as big as the Cayenne but can move four adults down the road at speeds of up to 188 miles per hour and accelerate from a standstill to 60 miles per hour in four seconds flat.

Although some Porsche traditionalists would never be caught dead driving a front-engine Porsche that has more than two doors, Porsche insists that two trends will sustain these new models. First, a category of Porsche buyers has moved into life stages that have them facing inescapable needs; they need to haul more people and stuff. This not only applies to certain regular Porsche buyers, but Porsche is again seeing buyers enter its dealerships that otherwise wouldn't have. Only this time, the price points of the new vehicles are drawing only the well heeled, allowing Porsche to maintain its exclusivity. These buyers also seem to fit the achiever profile of regular Porsche buyers. The second trend is the growth of emerging economies. Whereas the United States has long been the world's biggest consumer of Porsches, the company expects China to become its biggest customer before too long. Twenty years ago, the United States accounted for about 50 per cent of Porsche's worldwide sales. Now, it accounts for only about 26 per cent. In China, many people who can afford to buy a car as expensive as a Porsche also hire a chauffeur. The Cayenne and the Panamera are perfect for those who want to be driven around in style but who may also want to make a quick getaway if necessary.

The most recent economic downturn has brought down the sales of just about every maker of premium automobiles. When times are tough, buying a car like a Porsche is the ultimate deferrable purchase. But as this downturn turns back up, Porsche is better poised than it has ever been to meet the needs of its customer base. It is also in better shape than ever to maintain its brand image with the Porsche faithful and with others as well. Sure, understanding Porsche buyers is still a difficult task.

But a former CEO of Porsche summed it up this way: 'If you really want to understand our customers, you have to understand the phrase, "If I were going to be a car, I'd be a Porsche".'

Questions for discussion

1. Analyse the buyer decision process of a traditional Porsche customer.
2. Contrast the traditional Porsche customer decision process to the decision process for a Cayenne or a Panamera customer.
3. Which concepts from the chapter explain why Porsche sold so many lower-priced models in the 1970s and 1980s?

4. Explain how both positive and negative attitudes toward a brand like Porsche develop. How might Porsche change consumer attitudes toward the brand?
5. What role does the Porsche brand play in the self-concept of its buyers?

Sources: Christoph Rauwald, 'Porsche raises outlook', *Wall Street Journal* (18 June 2010), accessed at http://online.wsj.com/article/SB10001424052 748704122904575314062459444270.htm; Jonathan Welsh, 'Porsche relies increasingly on sales in China', *Wall Street Journal* (2 April 2010), accessed at http://blogs.wsj.com/drivers-seat/2010/04/02/porsche-relies-increasingly-on-sales-in-china; David Gumpert, 'Porsche on nichemanship', *Harvard Business Review* (March/April 1986), pp. 98–106; Peter Robinson, 'Porsche Cayenne – driving impression', *Car and Driver* (January 2003), accessed at www.caranddriver.com; Jens Meiners, '2010 Porsche Panamera S/4S/Turbo – first drive review', *Car and Driver* (June 2009), accessed at www.caranddriver.com.

CHAPTER SIX

Business markets and business buyer behaviour

Chapter preview

In the previous chapter, you studied *final consumer* buying behaviour and factors that influence it. In this chapter, we'll do the same for *business customers* – those that buy goods and services for use in producing their own products and services or for resale to others. As when selling to final buyers, firms marketing to business customers must build profitable relationships with business customers by creating superior customer value.

In addition to buying materials for production of goods for resale, companies in business-to-business markets have to buy equipment and maintenance services. Blancco is a Finnish company that is the global leader in providing data erasure solutions. Its customers and partners include large organisations like NASA and Dell. Selling services and products for such organisations is very different to selling PCs to consumers. Let's see how different.

Objective outline

➤ **Objective 1** Define the business market and explain how business markets differ from consumer markets.
Business markets (pp. 177–179)

➤ **Objective 2** Identify the major factors that influence business buyer behaviour.
Business buyer behaviour (pp. 180–184)

➤ **Objective 3** List and define the steps in the business buying decision process.

The business buying process (pp. 184–186)
E-procurement: buying on the Internet (pp. 186–188)

➤ **Objective 4** Compare institutional and government markets and explain how institutional and government buyers make their buying decisions.
Institutional and government Markets (pp. 188–190)

Blancco: selling to businesses – the stakes are much, much higher

Remember the last time you bought a new computer? What did you do with the old one? Left it in the corner just in case you might need it? Gave it to your little brother, or sold it to your friend? Carried it to a rubbish bin, or brought it to a recycling centre? Before you did any of these, you probably transferred the important personal data you had on your old PC to your new one and then deleted it so that any new owner of your old PC would not get their hands on your data. Did you know, however, that transferring files and documents into a computer's recycling bin and then emptying it is the same as ripping the table of contents out of a book? The information still exists, and it is easily restored. In the wrong hands, data about anybody can cause great harm. Imagine what could happen if information about thousands of people were leaked through a used computer.

Actually, something like that happened in the town of Joensuu in Finland in 1997. A student bought a used PC from a computer shop. When he switched it on he was amazed to find a record of 3,000 infarct patients who had been treated in the local hospital. Fortunately, the student was honest and handed the PC over to the police. However, the case was widely discussed in the media. The news caught the attention of another student, who a year earlier had founded an enterprise with a fellow university student. He immediately phoned his partner, who was then an exchange student in South Korea, and eagerly explained his new business idea: A 100 per cent secure data erasure tool that would be easy to use for secure wiping of hard disk drives. That was the beginning of Blancco – a Finnish company that is now the global leader in data erasure and end-of-lifecycle solutions.

While the main office is still situated in Joensuu, Blancco has affiliates and business partners in over 20 countries all over the world. International customers come from a wide range of industries, including banking, finance, government and defence, as well as refurbishing and remarketing professionals. Some of their best-known customers and partners are Dell, NASA, the Royal Air Force, the US Army, Toyota and Hewlett-Packard. Dealing with these large organisations is a lot different than dealing with individual consumers in terms of the number of people, the amount of money, and the risks involved as well as time consumed in the buying process.

When you realise that you need a new PC, you first probably start looking on the Internet and in advertisements for information about different models. You ask your friends or family for their opinion and go to different shops and seek advice from the salespeople. Then you compare the attributes and prices of different alternatives and choose the one that satisfies your needs best. This process probably takes from a couple of days to a couple of weeks, and the PC probably costs €1,000 or less. In consumer markets, sales of information technology (IT) products and services most often happen in a seller's retail store or on the Internet, and the buyer is the one who takes the initiative in the process. In business-to-business markets, the case is often the opposite: the seller is the one who makes the first move. After identifying those potential customers to whom the seller's offering would deliver value, the actual sales process may start.

In Blancco's case, the process usually starts when its selling team approaches the IT security staff of the potential customer organisation. Sometimes in this initial stage the customer has to be convinced of the importance of data erasure. Kim Väisänen, the CEO of Blancco, says that the biggest competitor in the market is ignorance. Companies do not realise the significance of data erasure or are simply not doing it. However, more companies are now aware of the risks involved in poor data leak prevention, including possible fines, lawsuits, damage to an organisation's reputation, loss in consumer confidence, bad will and, consequently, a decline in revenue. Customers do

When you no longer need your old computer, simply deleting information out of your recycling bin is not enough, information can still be restored. That's where Blancco, a global leader in data erasure, come in.

Source: Alamy Images/Oleg Shipor

not want to do business with companies who lose confidential information due to negligence. According to Väisänen, the key to successful selling in business-to business markets is to know the needs of the customer and then the best ways to satisfy them.

The initial stage of negotiations is often followed by a testing period. Because the risks are high, big companies want to make sure that the product is performing as promised. A third-party confirmation is needed. Over the years Blancco's products have been granted several international certifications and recommendations. These are vital but also difficult to obtain as the process may take several years. One of the organizations that has formally recommended Blancco products is the North Atlantic Treaty Organization (NATO). This endorsement is especially significant as the members and partners of NATO are not allowed to use products that do not have official NATO approval.

After the testing period, the process continues with further negotiations, provision of an offer, a lot of paperwork and, finally, delivery of the product to the customer. Several people from the customer's IT management and procurement sections are involved in the negotiations, and they have different tasks and roles. There are, for example, those who define the technical specifications, give their expert opinions or specify the terms of delivery. For Blancco it is important to identify the person who makes the final decision in the buyer organisation. This may not be as easy a job as it would seem, because often deals are not decided by the one who signs the contract but by someone whose expert opinion is greatly valued. The decision is based on issues such as security, trust, brand, process efficiency, customer service and, especially, international certifications. The amount of time needed from the first contact to product delivery varies from a few months to over a year, and the value of one purchase in monetary terms can be as high as a few hundred or thousands of euros.

The process does not end when the product is delivered. It is very important for Blancco to be able to provide product maintenance and updates on a regular basis. It is equally important for international customers to have access to helpdesk services and to technical support for troubleshooting. These after-sales services are crucial in creating customer relationships. Kim Väisänen says that Blancco's business is entirely built on customer relationships. Even in business-to-business relationships that are formed between individuals, Väisänen argues, 'First you have to sell yourself, then your company, and finally your products'. He continues that the main points in managing customer relationships are keeping your promises and maintaining constant contact with your customers.

Customers also are important in product development. Väisänen says that the most important steps in that area are taken after listening to customers and learning from them. The majority of Blancco's products are developed in-house, but sometimes it has cooperated with partners. For example, Blancco and Sun Microsystems have worked together to develop a global standards based solution designed to help customers manage their data centre assets. Väisänen states that in the future Blancco wants to satisfy all data erasure needs, whatever they might be. Blancco has already launched products that are suitable for smartphones since they may contain as much data as a PC.[1]

AUTHOR COMMENT

'Having relationships is the basis for doing business,' says Blancco's CEO Kim Väisänen. Consequently, to succeed in its business-to-business markets, Blancco has to create and maintain long-term customer relationships. They are based on trust, superior products, great service and constant contact.

Companies such as Unilever, Nestlé, Olivetti, Caterpillar and countless other firms sell *most* of their products to other businesses. Even large consumer-products companies, which make products used by final consumers, must first sell their products to other businesses. For example, Unilever makes many familiar consumer brands – food products (e.g. Lipton, Knorr, Bertolli and Flora), home care products (e.g. Cif, Comfort, Radiant and Omo), personal-care products (e.g. Dove, Lux, Signal and

Vaseline) and others. But to sell these products to consumers, Unilever must first sell them to its wholesale and retail customers, who in turn serve the consumer market.

Business buyer behaviour refers to the buying behaviour of organisations that buy goods and services for use in the production of other products and services that are sold, rented or supplied to others. It also includes the behaviour of retailing and wholesaling firms that acquire goods to resell or rent them to others at a profit. In the **business buying process**, business buyers determine which products and services their organisations need to purchase and then find, evaluate and choose among alternative suppliers and brands. *Business-to-business (B-to-B) marketers* must do their best to understand business markets and business buyer behaviour. Then, like businesses that sell to final buyers, they must build profitable relationships with business customers by creating superior customer value.

> **Business buyer behaviour—** The buying behaviour of organisations that buy goods and services for use in the production of other products and services that are sold, rented or supplied to others.

> **Business buying process—** The decision process by which business buyers determine which products and services their organisations need to purchase and then find, evaluate and choose among alternative suppliers and brands.

AUTHOR COMMENT

Business markets operate 'behind-the-scenes' to most consumers. Most of the things you buy involve many sets of business purchases before you ever see them.

BUSINESS MARKETS

The business market is *huge*. In fact, business markets involve far more euros and items than do consumer markets. For example, think about the large number of business transactions involved in the production and sale of a single set of Pirelli tyres. Various suppliers sell Pirelli the rubber, steel, equipment and other goods that it needs to produce tyres. Pirelli then sells the finished tyres to retailers, who in turn sell them to consumers. Thus, many sets of *business* purchases were made for only one set of *consumer* purchases. In addition, Pirelli sells tyres as original equipment to manufacturers that install them on new vehicles and as replacement tyres to companies that maintain their own fleets of company cars, trucks, buses or other vehicles.

In some ways, business markets are similar to consumer markets. Both involve people who assume buying roles and make purchase decisions to satisfy needs. However, business markets differ in many ways from consumer markets. The main differences, shown in Table 6.1, are in *market structure and demand*, the *nature of the buying unit* and the *types of decisions and the decision process* involved.

Market structure and demand

The business marketer normally deals with *far fewer but far larger buyers* than the consumer marketer does. Even in large business markets, a few buyers often account for most of the purchasing. For example, when Pirelli sells replacement tyres to final consumers, its potential market includes the owners of the millions of cars currently in use around the world. But Pirelli's fate in the business market depends on getting orders from one of only a handful of large carmakers. Similarly, Bosch sells its power tools and household appliances to tens of millions of consumers worldwide. However, it must sell these products through retail customers which combined account for a good percentage of its sales.

Furthermore, business demand is **derived demand**; it ultimately comes from (derives from) the demand for consumer goods. Olivetti and Dell buy Intel microprocessor chips to operate the computers they manufacture. If consumer demand for computers drops, so will the demand for microprocessors. Therefore, B-to-B marketers sometimes promote their products directly to final consumers to increase business demand. For example, W. L. Gore & Associates promotes its Gore-Tex fabrics directly to final consumers via a worldwide range of outlets from Prague in the Czech Republic, to Brogatan in Sweden, Amelia in Italy and Liezen in Austria.

> **Derived demand—**Business demand that ultimately comes from (derives from) the demand for consumer goods.

Table 6.1 Characteristics of business markets

Market structure and demand
Business markets contain *fewer but larger buyers*.
Business buyer demand is *derived* from final consumer demand.
Demand in many business markets is *more inelastic* – not affected as much in the short term by price changes.
Demand in business markets *fluctuates more* and more quickly.

Nature of the buying unit
Business purchases involve *more buyers*.
Business buying involves a *more professional purchasing effort*.

Types of decisions and the decision process
Business buyers usually face *more complex buying decisions*.
The business buying process is *more formalised*.
In business buying, buyers and sellers work more closely together and build close long-term *relationships*.

You can't buy anything directly from Gore, but increased demand for Gore-Tex fabrics boosts the demand for outdoor apparel and other brands made from them. So Gore advertises to consumers to educate them on the benefits of Gore-Tex in the products they buy. It also markets brands containing Gore-Tex – from Marmot, Mountain Hardware, and The North Face to Burton and L.L. Bean – directly to consumers on its own website (www.gore-tex.com/remote/Satellite/home). To deepen its relationship with outdoor enthusiasts further, Gore even sponsors an 'Experience More' online community in which members can share experiences and videos, connect with outdoor experts and catch exclusive gear offers from partner brands. As a result of these and other marketing efforts, consumers around the world have learned to look for the familiar Gore-Tex label, and both Gore and its partner brands win. No matter what brand of apparel you buy, says the label, if it's made with Gore-Text, it's 'guaranteed to keep you dry'.

Many business markets have *inelastic demand*; that is, the total demand for many business products is not dramatically affected by price changes, especially in the short run. A drop in the price of leather will not cause shoe manufacturers to buy much more leather unless it results in lower shoe prices that, in turn, will increase the consumer demand for shoes.

Finally, business markets have more *fluctuating demand*. The demand for many business goods and services tends to change more – and more quickly – than the demand for consumer goods and services does. A small percentage increase in consumer demand can cause large increases in business demand. Sometimes a rise of only 10 per cent in consumer demand can cause as much as a 200 per cent rise in business demand during the next period.

Nature of the buying unit

Compared with consumer purchases, a business purchase usually involves *more decision participants* and a *more professional purchasing effort*. Often, business buying is done by trained purchasing agents who spend their working lives learning how to buy better. The more complex the purchase, the more likely it is that several people will participate in the decision-making process. Buying committees composed of technical experts and top management are common in the buying of major goods. Beyond this, B-to-B marketers now face a new breed of higher-level, better-trained supply managers. Therefore, companies must have well-trained marketers and salespeople to deal with these well-trained buyers.

Types of decisions and the decision process

Business buyers usually face *more complex* buying decisions than do consumer buyers. Business purchases often involve large sums of money, complex technical and economic considerations, and interactions among many people at many levels of the buyer's organisation. Because the purchases are more complex, business buyers may take longer to make their decisions. The business buying process also tends to be *more formalised* than the consumer buying process. Large business purchases usually call for detailed product specifications, written purchase orders, careful supplier searches and formal approval.

Finally, in the business buying process, the buyer and seller are often much *more dependent* on each other. B-to-B marketers may roll up their sleeves and work closely with their customers during all stages of the buying process – from helping customers define problems, to finding solutions, to supporting after-sale operations. They often customise their offerings to individual customer needs.

In the short run, sales go to suppliers who meet buyers' immediate product and service needs. In the long run, however, business-to-business marketers keep a customer's sales and create customer value by meeting current needs *and* by partnering with customers to help them solve their problems. For example, Badische Anilin- und Soda-Fabrik (better known as BASF) doesn't just sell commodity plastics *to* its industrial customers; it works *with* these customers to help them succeed in their own markets.

In recent years, relationships between customers and suppliers have been changing from downright adversarial to close and chummy. In fact, many customer companies are now practising **supplier development**, systematically developing networks of supplier-partners to ensure an appropriate and dependable supply of products and materials that they will use in making their own products or resell to others. For example, Wal-Mart doesn't have a 'Purchasing Department'; it has a 'Supplier Development Department'. And giant Swedish furniture retailer Ikea doesn't just buy from its suppliers; it involves them deeply in the customer value-creation process.

Supplier development—
Systematic development of networks of supplier-partners to ensure an appropriate and dependable supply of products and materials for use in making products or reselling them to others.

Ikea, the world's largest furniture retailer, is the quintessential global cult brand. Customers from Thessaloniki in Greece to Bucharest in Romania flock to the €23 billion Scandinavian retailer's more than 300 huge stores in 38 countries, drawn by Ikea's trendy but simple and practical furniture at affordable prices. But Ikea's biggest obstacle to growth isn't opening new stores and attracting customers. Rather, it's finding enough of the right kinds of *suppliers* to help design and produce the billions of euros of affordable goods that customers will carry out of its stores. Ikea currently relies on some 1,220 suppliers in 55 countries to stock its shelves. Ikea can't just rely on spot suppliers who might be available when needed. Instead, it has systematically developed a robust network of supplier-partners that reliably provide the more than 9,500 items it stocks. Ikea's designers start with a basic customer value proposition. Then they find and work closely with key suppliers to bring that proposition to market. Thus, Ikea does more than just buy from suppliers; it also involves them deeply in the process of designing and making stylish but affordable products to keep Ikea's customers coming back.[2]

AUTHOR COMMENT
Business buying decisions can range from routine to incredibly complex, involving only a few or very many decision makers and buying influences.

Figure 6.1 A model of business buyer behaviour

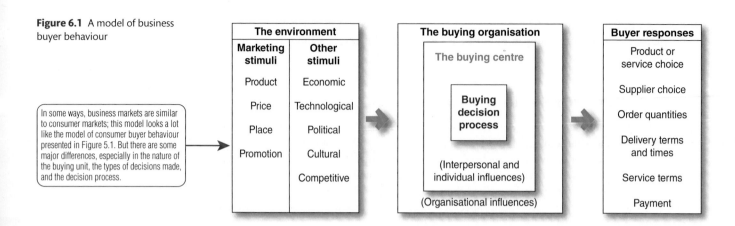

In some ways, business markets are similar to consumer markets; this model looks a lot like the model of consumer buyer behaviour presented in Figure 5.1. But there are some major differences, especially in the nature of the buying unit, the types of decisions made, and the decision process.

BUSINESS BUYER BEHAVIOUR

At the most basic level, marketers want to know how business buyers will respond to various marketing stimuli. Figure 6.1 shows a model of business buyer behaviour. In this model, marketing and other stimuli affect the buying organisation and produce certain buyer responses. These stimuli enter the organisation and are turned into buyer responses. To design good marketing strategies, marketers must understand what happens within the organisation to turn stimuli into purchase responses.

Within the organisation, buying activity consists of two major parts: the buying centre, composed of all the people involved in the buying decision, and the buying decision process. The model shows that the buying centre and the buying decision process are influenced by internal organisational, interpersonal and individual factors as well as external environmental factors.

The model in Figure 6.1 suggests four questions about business buyer behaviour: What buying decisions do business buyers make? Who participates in the buying process? What are the major influences on buyers? How do business buyers make their buying decisions?

Major types of buying situations

Straight rebuy—A business buying situation in which the buyer routinely reorders something without any modifications.

There are three major types of buying situations.[3] In a **straight rebuy**, the buyer reorders something without any modifications. It is usually handled on a routine basis by the purchasing department. To keep the business, 'in' suppliers try to maintain product and service quality. 'Out' suppliers try to find new ways to add value or exploit dissatisfaction so that the buyer will consider them.

Modified rebuy—A business buying situation in which the buyer wants to modify product specifications, prices, terms or suppliers.

In a **modified rebuy**, the buyer wants to modify product specifications, prices, terms or suppliers. The in suppliers may become nervous and feel pressured to put their best foot forward to protect an account. Out suppliers may see the modified rebuy situation as an opportunity to make a better offer and gain new business.

New task—A business buying situation in which the buyer purchases a product or service for the first time.

A company buying a product or service for the first time faces a **new task** situation. In such cases, the greater the cost or risk, the larger the number of decision participants and the greater the company's efforts to collect information. The new task situation is the marketer's greatest opportunity and challenge. The marketer not only tries to reach as many key buying influences as possible but also provides help and information. The buyer makes the fewest decisions in the straight rebuy and the most in the new task decision.

Systems selling (or solutions selling)—Buying a packaged solution to a problem from a single seller, thus avoiding all the separate decisions involved in a complex buying situation.

Many business buyers prefer to buy a complete solution to a problem from a single seller rather than separate products and services from several suppliers and putting them together. The sale often goes to the firm that provides the most complete *system* for meeting the customer's needs and solving its problems. Such **systems selling** (or **solutions selling**) is often a key business marketing strategy for winning and holding accounts.

UPS bundles a complete system of services that support the German group adidas-Salomon's footwear, apparel and accessories products supply chain in the US.

Source: Alamy Images/Mark Richardson

Thus, transportation and logistics giant UPS does more than just ship packages for its business customers; it develops entire solutions to customers' transportation and logistics problems. For example, UPS bundles a complete system of services that support the German group adidas-Salomon's footwear, apparel and accessories products supply chain in the US – including logistics, transportation, freight and customs brokerage services – into one smooth-running system.[4]

adidas America, based in Portland, hired UPS to upgrade its distribution network. There challenge was to improve the supply chain performance 'to accommodate rapid growth and efficiently meet the requirements of major retailers and team distributors'. Their solution was to 'consolidate the distribution system into a single, streamlined network, outfitted with automated inventory and order fulfilment systems to allow the company to rapidly scale its services and add enhancements to the supply chain as needed.' The result was improved order accuracy, increased delivery performance, enhanced viability and flexibility coupled with improved customer satisfaction.

Participants in the business buying process

Who does the buying of the trillions of euros' worth of goods and services needed by business organisations? The decision-making unit of a buying organisation is called its **buying centre** – all the individuals and units that play a role in the business purchase decision-making process. This group includes the actual users of the product or service, those who make the buying decision, those who influence the buying decision, those who do the actual buying, and those who control buying information.

The buying centre includes all members of the organisation who play any of five roles in the purchase decision process:[5]

- **Users** are members of an organisation who will use the product or service. In many cases, users initiate the buying proposal and help define product specifications.
- **Influencers** often help define specifications and also provide information for evaluating alternatives. Technical personnel are particularly important influencers.

Buying centre—All the individuals and units that play a role in the purchase decision-making process.

Users—Members of the buying organisation who will actually use the purchased product or service.

Influencers—People in an organisation's buying centre who affect the buying decision; they often help define specifications and also provide information for evaluating alternatives.

181

Buyers—People in an organisation's buying centre who make an actual purchase.

Deciders—People in an organisation's buying centre who have formal or informal power to select or approve the final suppliers.

Gatekeepers—People in an organisation's buying centre who control the flow of information to others.

- **Buyers** have formal authority to select the supplier and arrange terms of purchase. Buyers may help shape product specifications, but their major role is in selecting vendors and negotiating. In more complex purchases, buyers might include high-level officers participating in the negotiations.
- **Deciders** have formal or informal power to select or approve the final suppliers. In routine buying, the buyers are often the deciders, or at least the approvers.
- **Gatekeepers** control the flow of information to others. For example, purchasing agents often have authority to prevent salespersons from seeing users or deciders. Other gatekeepers include technical personnel and even personal secretaries.

The buying centre is not a fixed and formally identified unit within the buying organisation. It is a set of buying roles assumed by different people for different purchases. Within an organisation, the size and composition of the buying centre will vary for different products and for different buying situations. For some routine purchases, one person – say, a purchasing agent – may assume all the buying centre roles and serve as the only person involved in the buying decision. For more complex purchases, the buying centre may include 20 or 30 people from different levels and departments in the organisation.

The buying centre concept presents a major marketing challenge. The business marketer must learn who participates in the decision, each participant's relative influence, and what evaluation criteria each decision participant uses. This can be difficult.

For instance, 4 GASA S.L. in Spain sells disposable surgical gowns to hospitals. It identifies the hospital personnel involved in this buying decision as the vice president of purchasing, the operating room administrator and the surgeons. Each participant plays a different role. The vice president of purchasing analyses whether the hospital should buy disposable gowns or reusable gowns. If analysis favours disposable gowns, then the operating room administrator compares competing products and prices and makes a choice. This administrator considers the gowns' absorbency, antiseptic quality, design and cost and normally buys the brand that meets the requirements at the lowest cost. Finally, surgeons affect the decision later by reporting their satisfaction or dissatisfaction with the purchased brand.

The buying centre usually includes some obvious participants who are involved formally in the buying decision. For example, the decision to buy a corporate jet will probably involve the company's CEO, the chief pilot, a purchasing agent, some legal staff, a member of top management and others formally charged with the buying decision. It may also involve less obvious, informal participants, some of whom may actually make or strongly affect the buying decision. Sometimes, even the people in the buying centre are not aware of all the buying participants. For example, the decision about which corporate jet to buy may actually be made by a corporate board member who has an interest in flying and who knows a lot about aeroplanes. This board member may work behind the scenes to sway the decision. Many business buying decisions result from the complex interactions of ever-changing buying centre participants.

Buying center: 4 GASA S.L. in Spain deals with a ride range of buying influences, from purchasing executives and hospital administrators to the surgeons who actually use its products.

Source: Corbis

Major influences on business buyers

Business buyers are subject to many influences when they make their buying decisions. Some marketers assume that the major influences are economic. They think buyers will favour the supplier who offers the lowest price or the best product or the most service. They concentrate on offering strong economic benefits to buyers. Such economic factors are very important to most buyers, especially in a rough economy. However, business buyers actually respond to both economic and personal factors. Far from being cold, calculating and impersonal, business buyers are human and social as well. They react to both reason and emotion.

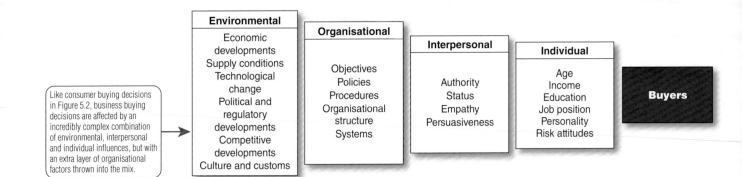

Figure 6.2 Major influences on business buyer behaviour

Today, most B-to-B marketers recognise that emotion plays an important role in business buying decisions. For example, you might expect that an advertisement promoting large trucks to corporate fleet buyers or independent owner-operators would stress objective technical, performance and economic factors. For instance, befitting today's tougher economic times, premium heavy-duty truck maker Volvo Trucks does stress performance; its dealers and website provide plenty of information about factors such as manoeuvrability, productivity, reliability, comfort, and fuel efficiency – 'Every Drop Counts'. But Volvo Trucks ads appeal to buyers' emotions as well. They show the raw beauty of the trucks, handsome drivers climb into interiors that look better than even top of the range luxury cars, the sleek black trucks are shown speeding through beautiful countryside, huge cargos are easily on and off-loaded and contemporary rock music stresses achievement and success.[6]

When suppliers' offers are very similar, business buyers have little basis for strictly rational choices. Because they can meet organisational goals with any supplier, buyers can allow personal factors to play a larger role in their decisions. However, when competing products differ greatly, business buyers are more accountable for their choices and tend to pay more attention to economic factors. Figure 6.2 lists various groups of influences on business buyers – environmental, organisational, interpersonal and individual.

Environmental factors

Business buyers are heavily influenced by factors in the current and expected *economic environment*, such as the level of primary demand, the economic outlook and the cost of money. Another environmental factor is the *supply* of key materials. Many companies now are more willing to buy and hold larger inventories of scarce materials to ensure adequate supply. Business buyers also are affected by technological, political and competitive developments in the environment. Finally, *culture and customs* can strongly influence business buyer reactions to the marketer's behaviour and strategies, especially in the international marketing environment. The business buyer must watch these factors, determine how they will affect the buyer, and try to turn these challenges into opportunities.

Organisational factors

Each buying organisation has its own objectives, strategies, structure, systems and procedures, and the business marketer must understand these factors well. Questions such as these arise: How many people are involved in the buying decision? Who are they? What are their evaluative criteria? What are the company's policies and limits on its buyers?

Interpersonal factors

The buying centre usually includes many participants who influence each other, so *interpersonal factors* also influence the business buying process. However, it is often difficult to assess such interpersonal factors and group dynamics. Buying centre participants do not wear tags that label them as 'key decision maker' or 'not influential'. Nor do buying centre participants with the highest rank always have the most influence. Participants may influence the buying decision because they control rewards and punishments, are well liked, have special expertise, or have a special relationship with other important participants. Interpersonal factors are often very subtle. Whenever possible, business marketers must try to understand these factors and design strategies that take them into account.

Individual factors

Each participant in the business buying decision process brings in personal motives, perceptions and preferences. These individual factors are affected by personal characteristics such as age, income, education, professional identification, personality and attitudes toward risk. Also, buyers have different buying styles. Some may be technical types who make in-depth analyses of competitive proposals before choosing a supplier. Other buyers may be intuitive negotiators who are adept at pitting sellers against one another for the best deal.

The business buying process

Figure 6.3 lists the eight stages of the business buying process.[7] Buyers who face a new task buying situation usually go through all stages of the buying process. Buyers making modified or straight rebuys may skip some of the stages. We will examine these steps for the typical new task buying situation.

Problem recognition

The buying process begins when someone in the company recognises a problem or need that can be met by acquiring a specific product or service. **Problem recognition** can result from internal or external stimuli. Internally, the company may decide to launch a new product that requires new production equipment and materials. Or a machine may break down and need new parts. Perhaps a purchasing manager is unhappy with a current supplier's product quality, service or prices. Externally, the buyer may get some new ideas at a trade show, see an ad, or receive a call from a salesperson who offers a better product or a lower price.

In fact, in their advertising, business marketers often alert customers to potential problems and then show how their products and services provide solutions. For example, an award-winning ad from Makino Engineering Services, a leading manufacturer of advanced machine tools, highlights a daunting customer problem: hard-to-machine parts. In the ad, the powerful visual shows a machined part that looks like a scary monster, complete with fangs. The ad's headline then offers the solution: 'Our application engineers love the scary parts'. The ad goes on to reassure customers that Makino can help them with their most difficult-to-machine parts and urges, 'Don't be afraid of the part'.

General need description

Having recognised a need, the buyer next prepares a **general need description** that describes the characteristics and quantity of the needed item. For standard items, this process presents few problems. For complex items, however, the buyer may need to work with others – engineers, users,

Problem recognition—The first stage of the business buying process in which someone in the company recognises a problem or need that can be met by acquiring a good or a service.

General need description— The stage in the business buying process in which a buyer describes the general characteristics and quantity of a needed item.

Figure 6.3 Stages of the business buying process

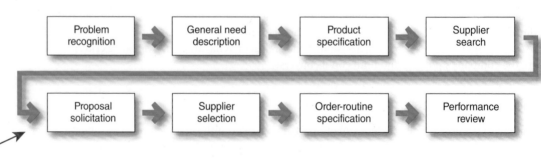

Buyers facing new, complex buying decisions usually go through all of these stages. Those making rebuys often skip some of the stages. Either way, the business buying process is usually much more complicated than this simple flow diagram suggests.

consultants – to define the item. The team may want to rank the importance of reliability, durability, price and other attributes desired in the item. In this phase, the alert business marketer can help buyers define their needs and provide information about the value of different product characteristics.

Product specification

The buying organisation next develops the item's technical **product specifications**, often with the help of a value analysis engineering team. *Product value analysis* is an approach to cost reduction in which components are studied carefully to determine if they can be redesigned, standardised or made by less costly methods of production. The team decides on the best product characteristics and specifies them accordingly. Sellers, too, can use value analysis as a tool to help secure a new account. By showing buyers a better way to make an object, outside sellers can turn straight rebuy situations into new task situations that give them a chance to obtain new business.

Product specification—The stage of the business buying process in which the buying organisation decides on and specifies the best technical product characteristics for a needed item.

Supplier search

The buyer now conducts a **supplier search** to find the best vendors. The buyer can compile a small list of qualified suppliers by reviewing trade directories, doing computer searches, or phoning other companies for recommendations. Today, more and more companies are turning to the Internet to find suppliers. For marketers, this has levelled the playing field; the Internet gives smaller suppliers many of the same advantages as larger competitors.

The newer the buying task, and the more complex and costly the item, the greater the amount of time the buyer will spend searching for suppliers. The supplier's task is to get listed in major directories and build a good reputation in the marketplace. Salespeople should watch for companies in the process of searching for suppliers and make certain that their firm is considered.

Supplier search—The stage of the business buying process in which the buyer tries to find the best vendors.

Proposal solicitation

In the **proposal solicitation** stage of the business buying process, the buyer invites qualified suppliers to submit proposals. In response, some suppliers will send only a catalogue or a salesperson. However, when the item is complex or expensive, the buyer will usually require detailed written proposals or formal presentations from each potential supplier.

Business marketers must be skilled in researching, writing and presenting proposals in response to buyer proposal solicitations. Proposals should be marketing documents, not just technical documents. Presentations should inspire confidence and make the marketer's company stand out from the competition.

Proposal solicitation—The stage of the business buying process in which the buyer invites qualified suppliers to submit proposals.

Supplier selection

The members of the buying centre now review the proposals and select a supplier or suppliers. During **supplier selection**, the buying centre often will draw up a list of the desired supplier attributes and their relative importance. Such attributes include product and service quality, reputation, on-time delivery, ethical corporate behaviour, honest communication and competitive prices. The members of the buying centre will rate suppliers against these attributes and identify the best suppliers.

Buyers may attempt to negotiate with preferred suppliers for better prices and terms before making the final selections. In the end, they may select a single supplier or a few suppliers. Many buyers prefer multiple sources of supplies to avoid being totally dependent on one supplier and allow comparisons of prices and performance of several suppliers over time. Today's supplier development managers want to develop a full network of supplier-partners that can help the company bring more value to its customers.

Supplier selection—The stage of the business buying process in which the buyer reviews proposals and selects a supplier or suppliers.

Order-routine specification—The stage of the business buying process in which the buyer writes the final order with the chosen supplier(s), listing the technical specifications, quantity needed, expected time of delivery, return policies and warranties.

Order-routine specification

The buyer now prepares an **order-routine specification**. It includes the final order with the chosen supplier or suppliers and lists items such as technical specifications, quantity needed, expected delivery time, return policies and warranties. In the case of maintenance, repair and operating items, buyers may use blanket contracts rather than periodic purchase orders. A blanket contract creates a long-term relationship in which the supplier promises to resupply the buyer as needed at agreed prices for a set time period.

Many large buyers now practise *vendor-managed inventory*, in which they turn over ordering and inventory responsibilities to their suppliers. Under such systems, buyers share sales and inventory information directly with key suppliers. The suppliers then monitor inventories and replenish stock automatically as needed. For example, most major suppliers to large retailers such as Carrefour, Tesco, Walmart and Sainsbury's assume vendor-managed inventory responsibilities.

Performance review

Performance review—The stage of the business buying process in which the buyer assesses the performance of the supplier and decides to continue, modify or drop the arrangement.

In this stage, the buyer reviews supplier performance. The buyer may contact users and ask them to rate their satisfaction. The **performance review** may lead the buyer to continue, modify or drop the arrangement. The seller's job is to monitor the same factors used by the buyer to make sure that the seller is giving the expected satisfaction.

In all, the eight-stage buying-process model shown in Figure 6.3 provides a simple view of the business buying as it might occur in a new task buying situation. However, the actual process is usually much more complex. In the modified rebuy or straight rebuy situation, some of these stages would be compressed or bypassed. Each organisation buys in its own way, and each buying situation has unique requirements.

Different buying centre participants may be involved at different stages of the process. Although certain buying-process steps usually do occur, buyers do not always follow them in the same order, and they may add other steps. Often, buyers will repeat certain stages of the process. Finally, a customer relationship might involve many different types of purchases ongoing at a given time, all in different stages of the buying process. The seller must manage the total *customer relationship*, not just individual purchases.

E-procurement—Purchasing through electronic connections between buyers and sellers — usually online.

Online buying: Cisco Systems website helps customers who want to purchase online by providing deep access to information about thousands of products. The site can also personalise the online experience for users and connect them with appropriate Cisco partner resellers.

E-procurement: buying on the Internet

Advances in information technology have changed the face of the B-to-B marketing process. Electronic purchasing, often called **e-procurement**, has grown rapidly in recent years. Virtually unknown a decade and a half ago, online purchasing is standard procedure for most companies today. E-procurement gives buyers access to new suppliers, lowers purchasing costs, and hastens order processing and delivery. In turn, business marketers can connect with customers online to share marketing information, sell products and services, provide customer support services and maintain ongoing customer relationships.

Companies can do e-procurement in any of several ways. They can conduct *reverse auctions*, in which they put their purchasing requests online and invite suppliers to bid for the business. Or they can engage in online *trading exchanges*, through which companies work collectively to facilitate the trading process. For example, Exostar is an online trading exchange that connects buyers and sellers in the aerospace and defence industries. The huge exchange has connected more than 300 procurement systems and 70,000 trading partners around the world.

Companies also can conduct e-procurement by setting up their own *company buying sites*. For example, GE operates a company trading site on which it posts its buying needs and invites bids, negotiates terms and

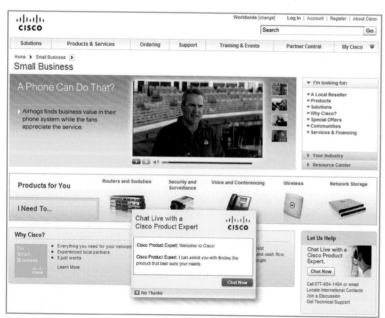

places orders. Or companies can create *extranet links* with key suppliers. For instance, they can create direct procurement accounts with suppliers such as Dell or Office Depot, through which company buyers can purchase equipment, materials and supplies directly.

B-to-B marketers can help customers who wish to purchase online by creating well-designed, easy-to-use websites. For example, *BtoB* magazine rated the site of Cisco Systems – a global market leader in Web networking hardware, software and services with offices in just about every European country – as one of its '10 great B-to-B Websites':[8]

> To spur growth, Cisco Systems recently stepped up its focus on the small and midsize business (SMB) segment. Its award-winning new SMB-specific website is simple, action-oriented and engaging but gives SMB buyers deep access. At the most basic level, customers can find and download information about thousands of Cisco products and services. Digging deeper, the site is loaded with useful video content – everything from testimonials to 'how to' videos to informational and educational on-demand Webcasts.
>
> Cisco's SMB site gets customers interacting with both the company and its partner resellers. For example, its live click-to-chat feature puts users in immediate touch with Cisco product experts. WebEx Web-conferencing software connects potential SMB customers with appropriate Cisco partner resellers, letting them share Web pages, PowerPoint slides and other documents in a collaborative online space. Finally, the Cisco SMB site can actually personalise the online experience for users. For example, if it detects that someone from the legal industry is paying attention to wireless content, it might put together relevant pieces of content to create a page for that visitor. Such personalisation really pays off. Customers visiting personalised pages stay twice as long as other visitors and go much deeper into the site.

Business-to-business e-procurement yields many benefits. First, it shaves transaction costs and results in more efficient purchasing for both buyers and suppliers. E-procurement reduces the time between order and delivery. And a Web-powered purchasing programme eliminates the paperwork associated with traditional requisition and ordering procedures and helps an organisation keep better track of all purchases. Finally, beyond the cost and time savings, e-procurement frees purchasing people from a lot of drudgery and paperwork to allow them to focus on more strategic issues, such as finding better supply sources and working with suppliers to reduce costs and develop new products.

> The predominant message from the history of e-procurement is that there has to be something in it for both buyers and suppliers. Too often, suppliers have been put off by initiatives they perceive to be 'buyer-led', and vice versa. As a result, the record of corporate e-procurement is littered with failed business models, such as the so-called 'vertical markets' of the mid to late 1990s. These third-party operators would act as aggregators of demand, then try to negotiate discounts from the supplier base. 'No supplier is going to join an initiative like that if they see their margins being cut', says Paul Clayton, a senior consultant for ProcServe, the e-procurement company set up by PA Consulting Group.
>
> The quid pro quo element that was missing in early e-procurement systems is now present, however: if suppliers are holding back in fear of losing out financially, there should now be the attraction of a bigger market, for example, to attract them. This is illustrated at the St Mary's National Health Service Trust in London, one of a group of hospital trusts introducing the Zanzibar e-procurement system. Andrew Holden, its finance director, says improved flows of information about prices should now prevent any individual health trust being 'picked off' by suppliers.
>
> On the other hand, he notes, a fully electronic system in which an online order is 'flipped over' to become an invoice means suppliers can be paid much more quickly. And while suppliers may, within a year or two, have to use Zanzibar to sell to St Mary's, those with catalogues adopted by the system can look forward to bigger markets as Zanzibar develops critical mass within buying organisations.
>
> A key lesson has been the importance of adoption by suppliers. 'The more obstacles you put in a supplier's way, the more likely it is not to join', says Mr Holden. 'Content is the core issue,' agrees Lyn Duncan, business development director at @UK PLC. 'It's terribly chicken and egg: suppliers don't want to invest time and effort into loading their content on until you can show

them orders, and buyers don't want to invest time and effort into training people how to use the system [unless sufficient content is available].' For @UK, which works with organisations to enable online procurement, the solution has been to ensure that a critical mass of a supplier's content – between 30 and 50 per cent of what the customer will need – is available on a 'plug and play' basis as soon as the site goes live.

The ordering and payment process also needs to be electronic. For buying organisations to obtain full savings from e-procurement, they must review their buy-to-pay process and 'vigorously chase out' any manual processes, says Andrew Fraser, managing director of financials at Civica, a consulting, software and services provider.[9]

The rapidly expanding use of e-procurement, however, also presents some problems. For example, at the same time that the Web makes it possible for suppliers and customers to share business data and even collaborate on product design, it can also erode decades-old customer–supplier relationships. Many buyers now use the power of the Web to pit suppliers against one another and search out better deals, products and turnaround times on a purchase-by-purchase basis.

E-procurement can also create potential security disasters. Although e-mail and home banking transactions can be protected through basic encryption, the secure environment that businesses need to carry out confidential interactions is sometimes still lacking. Companies are spending millions for research on defensive strategies to keep hackers at bay. Cisco Systems, for example, specifies the types of routers, firewalls and security procedures that its partners must use to safeguard extranet connections. In fact, the company goes even further; it sends its own security engineers to examine a partner's defences and holds the partner liable for any security breach that originates from its computers.

AUTHOR COMMENT

These two non-business organisational markets provide attractive opportunities for many companies. Because of their unique nature, we give them special attention here.

INSTITUTIONAL AND GOVERNMENT MARKETS

So far, our discussion of organisational buying has focused largely on the buying behaviour of business buyers. Much of this discussion also applies to the buying practices of institutional and government organisations. However, these two non-business markets have additional characteristics and needs. In this final section, we address the special features of institutional and government markets.

Institutional markets

Institutional market—Schools, hospitals, nursing homes, prisons and other institutions that provide goods and services to people in their care.

The **institutional market** consists of schools, hospitals, nursing homes, prisons and other institutions that provide goods and services to people in their care. Institutions differ from one another in their sponsors and their objectives. For example, in the UK Spire Healthcare runs 37 for-profit hospitals, generating €734 million in annual revenues. By contrast, the National Health Service in the UK is a huge non-profit organisation providing health care that is free at the point of delivery with 2,312 hospitals employing over 141,000 doctors and 410,000 nurses with an average net expenditure of €121 billion.

Institutional markets can be huge. Consider the massive and expanding European prison economy. Across Europe prison populations vary considerably. Norway has 66 prisoners per 100,000 citizens while England and Wales has 148. Germany, Spain, the UK, Italy and France each has prison populations over 50,000, while 39 per cent of Switzerland's prisoners are unsentenced. Although figures vary across Europe, the overall cost of the whole criminal justice system is around 2 per cent of gross domestic product (GDP) with each prisoner costing around €47,000 every year.

Many institutional markets are characterised by low budgets and captive patrons. For example, hospital patients have little choice but to eat whatever food the hospital supplies. A hospital purchasing agent has to decide on the quality of food to buy for patients. Because the food is provided as a part of a total service package, the buying objective is not profit. Nor is strict cost minimisation the goal – patients receiving poor-quality food will complain to others and damage the hospital's reputation. Thus, the hospital purchasing agent must search for institutional-food vendors whose quality meets or exceeds a certain minimum standard and whose prices are low.

Many marketers establish separate divisions to meet the special characteristics and needs of institutional buyers. For example, Nestlé produces, packages, prices and markets its broad assortment of cereals, cookies, snacks and other products to better serve the specific food service requirements of hospitals, schools, hotels and other institutional markets.

Government markets

The **government market** offers large opportunities for many companies, both big and small. In most countries, governmental organisations are major buyers of goods and services. Government buying and business buying are similar in many ways. But there are also differences that must be understood by companies that wish to sell products and services to governments. To succeed in the government market, sellers must locate key decision makers, identify the factors that affect buyer behaviour and understand the buying decision process.

Governmental organisations typically require suppliers to submit bids, and normally they award the contract to the lowest bidder. In some cases, a governmental unit will make allowances for the supplier's superior quality or reputation for completing contracts on time. Governments will also buy on a negotiated contract basis, primarily in the case of complex projects involving major research and development (R&D) costs and risks, and in cases where there is little competition.

Governmental organisations tend to favour domestic suppliers over foreign suppliers. A major complaint of multinationals operating in Europe is that each country shows favouritism toward its nationals in spite of superior offers that are made by foreign firms. The European Economic Commission is gradually removing this bias.

Like consumer and business buyers, government buyers are affected by environmental, organisational, interpersonal and individual factors. One unique thing about government buying is that it is carefully watched by outside publics, ranging from the European Commission to a variety of private groups interested in how each government spends taxpayers' money. Because their spending decisions are subject to public review, governmental organisations require considerable paperwork from suppliers, who often complain about excessive paperwork, bureaucracy, regulations, decision-making delays and frequent shifts in procurement personnel.

Given all the red tape, why would any firm want to do business with governments? The reasons are quite simple: the government are a huge buyer of products and services – in Europe, Switzerland is the only country with government spending below 30 per cent of GDP while France tops the European chart with 53 per cent.[10] For example, total government spending for hardware, software and IT services in Western Europe will increase from €39.38 billion in 2008 to €47.66 billion in 2013.[11]

Most governments provide would-be suppliers with detailed guides describing how to sell to the government. For example, the European Commission provides on its European Small Business Portal website detailed advice for small businesses seeking government contracting opportunities (http://ec.europa.eu/small-business). And the Your Europe website provided by the European Commission is loaded with information and advice on doing business in Europe and across the globe (http://ec.europa.eu/youreurope/business/index_en.htm). Most countries within Europe also have departments or centres that provide country-specific guides on the way government agencies buy, the steps that suppliers should follow, and the procurement opportunities available. Similarly, various trade magazines and associations provide information on how to reach schools, hospitals, highway departments and other governmental agencies. And almost all of these governmental organisations and associations maintain Internet sites offering up-to-date information and advice.

Non-economic criteria also play a growing role in government buying. Governmental buyers are asked to favour depressed business firms and areas; small business firms; minority-owned firms; and

Government market— Governmental units — federal, state and local — that purchase or rent goods and services for carrying out the main functions of government.

Government markets: the
Pan-**E**uropean **P**ublic **P**rocure-
ment **OnL**ine project aims to
expand market connectivity
and interoperability between
eProcurement communities
through enabling access to its
standards-based IT transport
infrastructure through access
points.

Source: PEPPOL

business firms that avoid race, gender or age discrimination. Sellers need to keep these factors in mind when deciding to seek government business.

Many companies that sell to the government have not been very marketing oriented for a number of reasons. Total government spending is determined by elected officials rather than by any marketing effort to develop this market. Government buying has emphasised price, making suppliers invest their effort in technology to bring costs down. When the product's characteristics are specified carefully, product differentiation is not a marketing factor. Nor do advertising or personal selling matter much in winning bids on an open-bid basis.

Several companies, however, have established separate government marketing departments, including Xerox, Kodak and Goodyear. These companies anticipate government needs and projects, participate in the product specification phase, gather competitive intelligence, prepare bids carefully, and produce stronger communications to describe and enhance their companies' reputations.

Other companies have established customised marketing programmes for government buyers. For example, Dell has specific business units tailored to meet the needs of federal as well as country and local government buyers. Dell offers its customers tailor-made Premier Dell.com Web pages that include special pricing, online purchasing, and service and support for each city, country and government entity.

During the past decade, a great deal of government buying has gone online. For example, in the UK the Office of Government and Commerce (now part of the Efficiency and Reform Group – a part of the Cabinet Office) has an online procurement portal. Across Europe, the European Union has established PEPPOL, the Pan-European Public Procurement OnLine project. The project involves 12 countries in the European Commission. PEPPOL aims to expand market connectivity and interoperability between eProcurement communities by enabling access to its standards-based IT transport infrastructure through access points, and provides services for eProcurement with standardised electronic document formats.[12] PEPPOL aim to generate a range of benefits, including: 'providing economic operators, in particular SMEs, with new business opportunities and increased competitiveness, while lowering costs with automated tendering solutions; saving contracting authorities significant administrative and transaction costs through standardised, speedy and streamlined procedures; and boosting the development and the capabilities of the ICT industry with increased demand for new, user-friendly IT services.'[13]

REVIEWING OBJECTIVES AND KEY TERMS

Business markets and consumer markets are alike in some key ways. For example, both include people in buying roles who make purchase decisions to satisfy needs. But business markets also differ in many ways from consumer markets. For one thing, the business market is *huge*, far larger than the consumer market. Within the United States alone, the business market includes organisations that annually purchase trillions of euros' worth of goods and services.

OBJECTIVE 1 Define the business market and explain how business markets differ from consumer markets (pp. 177–179).

The *business market* comprises all organisations that buy goods and services for use in the production of other products and services or for the purpose of reselling or renting them to others at a profit. As compared to consumer markets, business markets usually have fewer but larger buyers. Business demand is derived demand, which tends to be more inelastic and fluctuating than consumer demand. The business buying decision usually involves more, and more professional, buyers. Business buyers usually face more complex buying decisions, and the buying process tends to be more formalised. Finally, business buyers and sellers are often more dependent on each other.

OBJECTIVE 2 Identify the major factors that influence business buyer behaviour (pp. 180–184).

Business buyers make decisions that vary with the three types of *buying situations*: straight rebuys, modified rebuys and new tasks. The decision-making unit of a buying organisation – the *buying centre* – can consist of many different persons playing many different roles. The business marketer needs to know the following: Who are the major buying centre participants? In what decisions do they exercise influence and to what degree? What evaluation criteria does each decision participant use? The business marketer also needs to understand the major environmental, organisational, interpersonal and individual influences on the buying process.

OBJECTIVE 3 List and define the steps in the business buying decision process (pp. 184–188).

The *business buying decision process* itself can be quite involved, with eight basic stages: problem recognition, general need description, product specification, supplier search, proposal solicitation, supplier selection, order-routine specification and performance review. Buyers who face a new task buying situation usually go through all stages of the buying process. Buyers making modified or straight rebuys may skip some of the stages. Companies must manage the overall customer relationship, which often includes many different buying decisions in various stages of the buying decision process.

Recent advances in information technology have given birth to 'e-procurement', by which business buyers are purchasing all kinds of products and services online. The Internet gives business buyers access to new suppliers, lowers purchasing costs and hastens order processing and delivery. However, e-procurement can also erode customer–supplier relationships and create potential security problems. Still, business marketers are increasingly connecting with customers online to share marketing information, sell products and services, provide customer support services and maintain ongoing customer relationships.

OBJECTIVE 4 Compare institutional and government markets and explain how institutional and government buyers make their buying decisions (pp. 188–190).

The *institutional market* consists of schools, hospitals, prisons and other institutions that provide goods and services to people in their care. These markets are characterised by low budgets and captive patrons. The *government market*, which is vast, consists of government units that purchase or rent goods and services for carrying out the main functions of government.

Government buyers purchase products and services for defence, education, public welfare and other public needs. Government buying practices are highly specialised and specified, with open bidding or negotiated contracts characterising most of the buying. Government buyers operate under the watchful eye of the European Commission and many private watchdog groups. Hence, they tend to require more forms and signatures and respond more slowly and deliberately when placing orders.

NAVIGATING THE KEY TERMS

OBJECTIVE 1
Business buyer behaviour (p. 177)
Business buying process (p. 177)
Derived demand (p. 177)
Supplier development (p. 179)

OBJECTIVE 2
Straight rebuy (p. 180)
Modified rebuy (p. 180)
New task (p. 180)
Systems selling (or solutions selling) (p. 180)
Buying centre (p. 181)
Users (p. 181)
Influencers (p. 181)
Buyers (p. 182)
Deciders (p. 182)
Gatekeepers (p. 182)

OBJECTIVE 3
Problem recognition (p. 184)
General need description (p. 184)
Product specification (p. 185)
Supplier search (p. 185)
Proposal solicitation (p. 185)
Supplier selection (p. 185)
Order-routine specification (p. 185)
Performance review (p. 186)
E-procurement (p. 186)

OBJECTIVE 4
Institutional market (p. 188)
Government market (p. 189)

DISCUSSING AND APPLYING THE CONCEPTS

Discussing the concepts

1. Explain how the business market differs from the consumer market for a product such as cars. (AACSB: Communication; Reflective Thinking)

2. Name and describe the three types of business buying situations. (AACSB: Communication)

3. In a buying centre purchasing process, which buying centre participant is most likely to make each of the following statements? (AACSB: Communication; Reflective Thinking)

   - 'This bonding agent better be good because I have to put this product together.'

   - 'I specified this bonding agent on another job, and it worked for them.'

   - 'Without an appointment, no sales rep gets in to see Ms. Johnson.'

   - 'Okay, it's a deal; we'll buy it.'

   - 'I'll place the order first thing tomorrow.'

4. List the major influences on business buyer behaviour. Why is it important for the B-to-B marketer to understand these major influences? (MCSB: Communication; Reflective Thinking)

5. Name and briefly describe the stages of the business buying process. (AACSB: Communication)

6. Describe how electronic purchasing has changed the B-to-B marketing process and discuss the advantages and disadvantages of electronic purchasing. (AACSB: Communication)

Applying the concepts

1. Business buying occurs worldwide, so marketers need to be aware of cultural factors influencing business customers. In a small group, select a country and develop a multimedia presentation on proper business etiquette and manners, including appropriate appearance, behaviour and communication. Include a map showing the location of the country as well as a description of the country in terms of its demographics, culture and economic history. (AACSB: Communication; Multicultural and Diversity; Use of IT)

2. Interview a businessperson to learn how purchases are made in his or her organisation. Ask this person to describe a recent straight rebuy, a modified rebuy, and a new task buying situation of which he or she is aware. (If necessary, define these terms for the businessperson.) Did the buying process differ for different types of products or purchase situations? Ask the businessperson to explain his or her role in a recent purchase and discuss the factors that influenced the decision. Write a brief report of your interview, applying the concepts you learned in this chapter regarding business buyer behaviour. (AACSB: Communication; Reflective Thinking)

Focus on technology

How would you like to sell to a customer that spends billions of euros per year on contractors? If so, you need to learn how to crack the European Union government market. The EU and individual governments purchase goods ranging from toilet paper to aircraft carriers and services from janitorial supplies to high-tech IT. This is a lucrative market – especially during economic downturns. Companies such as Dataguise, a database security solutions company, and Kearney & Company, an accounting firm, focus their marketing solely on this market. How do businesses – big and small – find out about opportunities in this market? One way is to search each government's website for opportunities. A great deal of government buying is now done online.

1. Go to the European Small Business Portal (http://ec.europa.eu/small-business). Write a brief report describing the usefulness of this website for businesses desiring to sell to the government market. (AACSB: Communication; Use of IT; Reflective Thinking)

2. Search online for websites of other government buying resources. Write a brief report explaining how small businesses can use these resources. (AACSB Communication; Use of IT; Reflective Thinking)

Focus on ethics

You are the senior buyer for a growing medical products company and an avid football fan. You have just opened an invitation to attend the Champions League Final. The invitation is from a supplier company that has been trying to sell you its new line of products for the past year. The supplier will pay for everything – travel, room, meals – and you'll even get an opportunity to meet some of the players. You have read the newly released employee manual and there is no reference or rule that specifically states that an employee cannot accept a fully paid trip from a vendor, although there are some vague restrictions on lunches and dinners paid for by suppliers.

1. Do you accept or decline the invitation?

2. Just because it is not specifically mentioned in the employee manual, would you be acting ethically if you accepted?

3. Do you think the supplier will expect 'special' treatment in the next buying situation?

4. How would other company employees interpret your acceptance of this invitation?

Marketing & the economy

Caterpillar

Caterpillar had been growing for 15 years. As the largest and most geographically diverse heavy equipment maker, it was best positioned to weather a slow economy. And although Caterpillar did okay throughout 2008 while the recent economic crisis remained largely centred in the United States, it took a blow once the recession spread worldwide and institutions everywhere just stopped building things. For Caterpillar, annual revenue toppled 37 per cent (from €37 billion to €23 billion), while profits spiralled downwards by 75 per cent. Caterpillar responded by dramatically cutting costs. It has also rolled out promotional incentives similar to those offered by car manufacturers in order to spark sales. By mid-2010, as some important economic sectors began to recover, Caterpillar's sales and profits also rebounded. But like most other companies, Caterpillar is still waiting for a slower- than-expected economic turnaround to materialise.

1. Given the nature of the demand for its products, is there anything that Caterpillar could do to maintain or increase revenues in a down economy?

2. As a corporation that fuels the economy to some extent, is there anything that Caterpillar could do to facilitate a global economic recovery?

Marketing by the numbers

B-to-B marketing relies heavily on sales reps. Salespeople do more than just sell products and services; they manage relationships with customers to deliver value to both the customer and their companies. Thus, for many companies, sales reps visit customers several times per year – often for hours at a time. Sales managers must ensure that their companies have enough salespeople to adequately deliver value to customers.

1. Refer to Appendix 2 to determine the number of salespeople a company needs if it has 3,000 customers who need to be called on 10 times per year. Each sales call lasts approximately 2.5 hours, and each sales rep has approximately 1,250 hours per year to devote to customers per year. (AACSB: Communication; Analytical Reasoning)

2. If each sales rep earns a salary of €60,000 per year, what sales are necessary to break even on the sales force costs if the company has a contribution margin of 40 per cent? What effect will adding each additional sales representative have on the break-even sales? (AACSB: Communication; Analytical Reasoning)

REFERENCES

[1] Interview with Kim Väisänen, J. Lyytinen and P. Yritäedes, 32 syytä ryhtyä yrittäjäksi, Gummerous Kirjapaino Oy, Jyväskylä 2004, www.blancco.com/en, accessed December 2011.

[2] See Theresa Ooi, 'Amazing Key to Ikea Success', *Australian* (22 September 2008); Kerry Capell, 'How the Swedish retailer became a global cult brand', *BusinessWeek* (14 November 2005), p. 103; Ikea, *Hoover's Company Records* (1 April 2010), p. 42925; and information from www.ikea.com, accessed October 2011.

[3] This classic categorisation was first introduced in Patrick J. Robinson, Charles W. Faris and Yoram Wind, *Industrial Buying Behavior and Creative Marketing* (Boston, MA: Allyn & Bacon, 1967). Also see James C. Anderson and James A. Narus, *Business Market Management*, 2nd edn (Upper Saddle River, NJ: Prentice Hall, 2004), Chapter 3; and Philip Kotler and Kevin Lane Keller, *Marketing Management*, 13th edn (Upper Saddle River, NJ: Prentice Hall, 2009), Chapter 7.

[4] Example adapted from information found in 'Adidas goes for the gold in customer service', UPS case study, www.ups-scs.com/solutions/case_studies/cs_adidas.pdf, accessed October 2011.

[5] See Frederick E. Webster Jr. and Yoram Wind, *Organizational Buying Behavior* (Upper Saddle River, NJ: Prentice Hall, 1972), pp. 78–80. Also see Jorg Brinkman and Markus Voeth, 'An analysis of buying center decisions through the sales force', *Industrial Marketing Management* (October 2007), p. 998; and Philip Kotler and Kevin Lane Keller, *Marketing Management*, 13th edn, op. cit. pp. 188–191.

[6] See www.volvotrucks.com/trucks/global/en-gb/Pages/home.aspx, accessed October 2011.

[7] Robinson, Faris and Wind, *Industrial Buying Behavior*, op. cit. p. 14. Also see Philip Kotler and Kevin Lane Keller, *Marketing Management*, pp. 192–198.

[8] For this and other examples, see '10 great web sites', *BtoB Online* (15 September 2008); and 10 great web sites', *BtoB Online* (14 September 2009), both accessed at www.btobonline.com. Other information from www.cisco.com/cisco/web/solutions/small_business/index.html, accessed October 2011.

[9] Example from Andrew Baxter, 'History proves the greatest teacher', *Financial Times* (11 July 2007), www.ft.com/cms/s/0/e5038666-2f4a-11dc-b9b7-0000779fd2ac.html#ixzz1Tl2kb3Mk, accessed October 2011.

[10] See 2011 Index of Economic Freedom, http://www.heritage.org/index/explore?view=by-variables, accessed October 2011.

[11] See www.idc-gi.com/getdoc.jsp?containerId=prIT22198510, accessed October 2011.

[12] See www.peppol.eu, accessed October 2011.

[13] Ibid.

VIDEO CASE

Eaton MyMarketingLab

With nearly 60,000 employees doing business in 125 countries and sales last year of more than €8 billion, Eaton is one of the world's largest suppliers of diversified industrial goods. Eaton's products make cars more peppy, 18-wheelers safer to drive and airliners more fuel efficient. So why haven't you heard of the company? Because Eaton sells its products not to end consumers but to other businesses.

At Eaton, B-to-B marketing means working closely with customers to develop a better product. So the company partners with its sophisticated, knowledgeable clients to create total solutions that meet their needs. Along the way, Eaton maps the decision-making process to better understand the concerns and interests of decision makers. In the end, Eaton's success depends on its ability to provide high-quality, dependable customer service and product support.

Cisco Systems: solving business problems through collaboration

Perhaps you've heard of Cisco Systems. It's the company that runs those catchy 'Human Network' ads. It also produces those familiar Linksys wireless Internet routers and owns Pure Digital Technologies, the company that makes the trendy Flip video cameras. But most of what Cisco sells is not for regular consumers like you and me. Cisco is a tried and tested business-to-business (B-to-B) company. In fact, it earned honours as *BtoB* magazine's 2009 'marketer of the year'.

Three-quarters of Cisco's sales are in routers, switches and advanced network technologies – the things that keep data moving around cyberspace 24/7. But over the past decade, in addition to all that hardware, Cisco has pioneered the next generation of Internet networking tools, from cybersecurity to set-top boxes to videoconferencing.

But this story is about much more than just a tech giant that makes equipment and software that companies need to run their Internet and intranet activities. It's about a forward-thinking firm that has transitioned from a manufacturer to a leadership consultancy. To make that happen, Cisco has perfected one major concept that seems to drive both its own business and its interactions with customer organisations – collaboration. Cisco is all about collaborating with its clients in order to help those clients better collaborate employees, suppliers, partners and customers.

COLLABORATION WITHIN AND WITHOUT

John Chambers became the CEO of Cisco in 1995, when annual revenues were a mere $1.2 billion. He successfully directed the growth of Cisco as a hardware provider. But following the dotcom bust in 2000, he knew the world was a different place. In response, he engineered a massive, radical and often bumpy reorganisation of the company. Chambers turned Cisco inside out, creating a culture of 63,000 employees that truly thrives on collaboration. As such, Cisco is the perfect laboratory for developing and using the collaboration tools that it subsequently sells to external clients. Cisco not only manufactures the hardware and software that makes collaboration possible but also is the foremost expert on how to use it. All this collaboration has helped Cisco's business explode, hitting €28 billion last year.

Cisco's advertising campaign, 'Human Network Effect', illustrates the company's philosophy. The campaign highlights the benefits that come to organisations that use their people networks more effectively. According to Susan Bostrom, Cisco's chief marketing officer, the pragmatic campaign helps customers understand how Cisco's technologies can save them money, bring products to market faster, and even have an impact on the environment. At the same time it has communicated why customers need Cisco's products and services, the campaign has helped Cisco become the 14th most valuable brand in the world.

Chambers tells the story of how Cisco began its transition from hardware into services. 'Our customers literally pulled us kicking and screaming into providing consultancy,' says Chambers. Some years ago, the CEO of financial services company USAA asked Chambers to help the company figure out what to do with the Internet. Chambers replied that Cisco wasn't in the Web consulting business. But when USAA committed to giving all its networking business to Cisco if it would take the job, Chambers proclaimed, 'We are in that business!' Now Cisco has both the products and the knowledge to help other companies succeed on the Internet. Cisco itself is the best model of how to use its products to network and collaborate on the Web, so who better to help other companies do it?

A turning point for Chambers in further understanding the impact that Cisco can have on clients was the major earthquake in China in 2008.

Tae Yoo, a 19-year Cisco veteran, supervises the company's social responsibility efforts and sits on the China strategy board and the emerging-countries council. 'I had always been a believer in collaboration,' she says, but after the earthquake, 'I saw it really happen. Our local team immediately mobilized, checking in with employees, customers, and [nongovernmental organization] NGO partners. The council got people on the phone, on [video conference], to give us a complete assessment of what was happening locally. We connected West China Hospital to a specialized trauma centre in Maryland via the network.' High-level medical centres from the other side of the world were able to weigh in on diagnostics remotely. Cisco employees were on the ground helping rural areas recover and rebuild homes and schools. Within 14 days, Yoo continues, 'I walked over to the China board with a complete plan and $45 million to fund it.' That number ultimately grew to more than $100 million. 'Our business is growing 30 per cent year over year there,' Chambers says, adding that Cisco has committed to investing $16 (€12.25) billion in public–private partnerships in China. 'No one has the reach and trust that we do. No one could offer the help that we could.'

COLLABORATION BENEFITS

Cisco management knows that number one on most CEO's lists is to break down the communication barriers between a company and its customers, suppliers and partners. According to Jim Grubb, Chambers' long-time product-demo sidekick, 'If we can accelerate the productivity of scientists who are working on the next solar technology because we're hooking them together, we're doing a great thing for the world.' Doing a great thing for the world – while at the same time selling a ton of routers and switches.

But while routers and switches still account for most of Cisco's business, the really interesting stuff is far more cutting edge. Consider Cisco's involvement in what it calls the Smart Connected Communities initiative. Perhaps the best example of a smart and connected community is New Songdo City in South Korea, a city the size of Barcelona being built from scratch on an artificial island in the Yellow Sea. Cisco was hired as the technology partner for this venture and is teaming up with the construction company, architects, 3M and United Technologies as partners in the instant-city business.

Cisco's involvement goes way beyond installing routers, switches and citywide Wi-Fi. The networking giant is wiring every square inch of the city with electronic synapses. Through trunk lines under the streets, filaments will branch out through every wall and fixture like a nervous system. Cisco is intent on having this city run on information, with its control room playing the part of New Songdo's brain stem.

Not content to simply sell the hardware, Cisco will sell and operate services layered on top of its hardware. Imagine a city where every home and office is wired to Cisco's TelePresence videoconferencing screens. Engineers will listen, learn and release new Cisco-branded services for modest monthly fees. Cisco intends to bundle urban necessities – water, power, traffic, communications and entertainment – into a single, Internet-enabled utility. This isn't just big brother stuff. This Cisco system will allow New Songdo to reach new heights in environmental sustainability and efficiency. Because of these efficiencies, the cost for such services to residents will be cheaper as well.

The smart cities business is an emerging industry with a €23 billion potential. Gale International, the construction company behind New Songdo, believes that China alone could use 500 such cities, each with a capacity for one million residents. It already has established the goal to build 20 of them.

Smart cities make one of Cisco's other businesses all the more relevant. Studies show that telecommuting produces enormous benefits for companies, communities, and employees. For example, telecommuters have higher job satisfaction. For that reason, they are more productive, giving back as much as 60 per cent of their commuting time to the company. There is even evidence that people like working from home so much that they would be willing to work for less pay. An overwhelming majority of telecommuters produce work in a more timely manner with better quality. Their ability to communicate with co-workers is at least as good and in many cases better than when they work in the office. With products like Cisco Virtual Office and Cisco's expertise in running it, for example, Sun Microsystems saved €53 million. It also reduced carbon emissions by 29,000 metric tons.

Cisco has also recently unveiled a set of Web-based communication products that enhance organisations' collaborative activities. Cisco says this is all about making business more people-centric than document-centric. Along with a cloud-based e-mail system, WebEx Mail, Cisco Show and Share 'helps organizations create and manage highly secure video communities to share ideas and expertise, optimize global video collaboration, and personalize the connection between customers, employees, and students with user generated content.' Also on its way is what Cisco calls the Enterprise Collaboration Platform, a cross between a corporate directory and Facebook. These products allow the free-flow of information to increase exponentially over existing products because they exist behind an organisation's firewall with no filters, lawyers or security issues to get in the way.

Cisco's client list and product portfolio are expansive, and these examples represent just the tip of an iceberg that is growing bigger and bigger all the time. As Bostrom points out, Cisco's own products and services are helping the company itself to become even more efficient at managing the purchase process. 'I don't think I had realized how powerful the Web could be in taking a customer through the purchase journey. We can get data on an hourly basis, find out right away what's working and not working, and evolve our Web capabilities to meet those customers' expectations.'

Through its customer consultancy efforts, Cisco can share these insights and experiences to help customers do the same. That's a powerful selling proposition.

A BRIGHT FUTURE

Recently, Cisco's financial performance is down. But Chambers thinks that's only a blip in the grand scheme of things. He points out that Cisco has emerged from every economic downturn of the past two decades stronger and more flexible. During this downturn, Cisco moved quickly, seizing every opportunity to snatch up businesses and develop new products. During the 2000s, Cisco acquired 48 venture-backed companies. But last year alone, the company announced an astounding 61 new technologies, all focused on helping customers through and with collaboration. With these resources – and €27 billion in cash that it has stowed away – Cisco is now expanding into 30 different markets, each with the potential to produce $1 billion a year in revenue. Moving forward, the company has committed to adding 20 per cent more new businesses annually. And because Cisco enters a new market only when it's confident that it can gain a 40 per cent share, the chance of failure is far below normal.

The collaboration market is estimated at €27 billion, a figure that will grow substantially in years to come. Because Cisco is the leader in this emerging industry, analysts have no problem accepting John Chambers' long-term goal of 12–17 per cent revenue growth per year. Cisco has demonstrated that it has the product portfolio and the leadership structure necessary to pull it off. One thing is for sure. Cisco is no longer just a plumber, providing the gizmos and gadgets necessary to make the Web go around. It is a networking leader, a core competency that will certainly make it a force to be reckoned with for years to come.

Questions for discussion

1. Discuss the nature of the market structure and the demand for Cisco's products.
2. Given the industries in which Cisco competes, what are the implications for the major types of buying situations?
3. What specific customer benefits will likely result from the Cisco products mentioned in the case?
4. Discuss the customer buying process for one of Cisco's products. Discuss the selling process. In what ways do these processes differ from those found in buying and selling a broadband router for home use?
5. Is the relationship between Cisco's own collaborative culture and the products and services it sells something that could work for all companies? Consider this issue for a consumer products company like P&G.

Sources: Ellen McGirt, 'How Cisco's CEO John Chambers is turning the tech giant socialist', *Fast Company* (25 November 2008), accessed at www.fastcompany.com; Anya Kamenetz, 'Cisco systems', *Fast Company* (March 2010), p. 72; Greg Lindsay, 'Cisco's big bet on New Songdo: creating cities from scratch', *Fast Company* (1 February 2010), accessed at www.fastcompany.com; Ariel Schwartz, 'Cisco says telecommuting saves money, and the world', *Fast Company* (26 June 2009), accessed at www.fastcompany.com; 'Susan Bostrom, exec VP-CMO, Cisco Systems,' *BtoB* (26 October 2009), accessed at www.btobonline.com.

PART THREE

Designing a customer-driven strategy and mix

CHAPTER SEVEN

Customer-driven marketing strategy: creating value for target customers

Chapter preview

So far, you have learned what marketing is and about the importance of understanding consumers and the marketplace environment. With that as background, you're now ready to delve deeper into marketing strategy and tactics. This chapter looks further into key customer-driven marketing strategy decisions: dividing up markets into meaningful customer groups (*segmentation*), choosing which customer groups to serve (*targeting*), creating market offerings that best serve targeted customers (*differentiation*) and positioning the offerings in the minds of consumers (*positioning*). The chapters that follow explore the tactical marketing tools – the four Ps – by which marketers bring these strategies to life.

To start our discussion of the ins and outs of segmentation, targeting, differentiation and positioning, successful online fashion retailer Asos is an interesting illustration of the strength of actively marketing to a clearly defined target market and developing a business around that target. Asos segmented its market carefully and concentrates on serving its target customers better than its competitors do.

Objective outline

➤ **Objective 1** Define the major steps in designing a customer-driven marketing strategy: market segmentation, targeting, differentiation and positioning.
Customer-driven marketing strategy (pp. 203–204)

➤ **Objective 2** List and discuss the major bases for segmenting consumer and business markets.
Market segmentation (pp. 204–213)

➤ **Objective 3** Explain how companies identify attractive market segments and choose a market-targeting strategy.
Market targeting (pp. 214–221)

➤ **Objective 4** Discuss how companies differentiate and position their products for maximum competitive advantage.
Differentiation and positioning (pp. 221–227)

Asos – fast fashion for fast consumers

Online fashion retailer Asos has confounded its critics by homing in on its target market and constantly adapting its business model.

When the original Internet clothing company As Seen On Screen (ASOS) listed on London's Alternative Investment Market in 2001, it was known for its 'red carpet replicas' – selling copies of dresses worn by actresses. Fashionistas looked down on the start-up and many celebrities were uncomfortable with the idea. Ten years later, Asos has remodelled itself into a global fashion destination where celebrities are happy to shop themselves.

The business, founded by Nick Robertson with a £2 million loan from his brother, was originally conceived as a spin-off from Mr Robertson's TV product placement business. But the business took off quickly and by 2011 it was was among the UK's biggest fashion retailers, generating 11 million unique users a month. 'On a daily basis, that's around 700,000 people,' he says. 'Imagine having a shop with that many people walking through the door every day.'

Critics have consistently tried – and failed – to turn the company's growth story into something resembling the tale of the emperor's new clothes. Online fashion would never take off, they said, underestimating the net-savvy generation who make up Asos's 16 to 34-year-old core customer base. Now the company is switching its focus to international sales. In 2007, non-UK sales made up 10 per cent of the company's annual retail sales. Today, it is 44 per cent, and by September 2011 had 6.3 million registered users and 3.7 million active customers from 160 countries.

Bounding around Asos's headquarters in Camden, north London, one gets a sense of the scale of the company's operation. Everything that appears on the website is done in-house, including photo shoots – the company photographs 2,000 items a week – and catwalk videos. Spread over four floors, the 700 staff based here call it 'the fashion factory' and the open-plan floors are stuffed with shoot rails of clothes ready to be modelled and accessories. 'It's like a teenager's bedroom times 100,' jokes Mr Robertson.

Keeping the fashion and technology arms of the company under one roof – the company employs 16 designers, whose products for Asos's own label account for half of all sales, and 120 people in IT – enables both sides of the business to learn from each other. 'We are a fashion and technology business,' he says.

Everything that appears on the Asos website is done in-house, including photo shoots and catwalk videos, to create a 'fashion factory'.

Source: Alamy Images/M40S

Unusually for an office, the only phone that rings is Mr Robertson's BlackBerry. All the other employees stare at their screens and are busy blogging, tweeting or on Facebook. While many companies would discourage the use of social media at the office, Mr Robertson says this is exactly what his staff should be doing. 'They're doing what they would be doing anyway – but they're doing it for Asos,' he says. This is no coincidence. Most of Asos's staff fit the demographic of the company's customer base: young, trendy and predominantly female. Understanding exactly who its customers are is perhaps Asos's greatest strength.

Since its launch, everything Asos does has been aimed at 'the imagined 22-year-old', the median age of its shoppers. This is divided into three target groups: *Fashion Forward* – those who set the trends; *Fashion Passengers* – those who follow them; and *Functional Fashion* – the less trend-conscious. Mr Robertson believes employing the same types of people that Asos sells to means the company knows how to reach them. 'Nobody has done this before. If I had a board of seasoned retailers, they might have made decisions that were right for the retail market 10 years ago,' he says.

One result is a stealth marketing strategy built on social networking sites. Teenagers think they have 'discovered' Asos through blogs and tweets instead of feeling like they have swallowed a sales pitch. The company has also created its own sites that build on existing platforms, often before its competitors. In 2009, the company launched Asos Life, an 'online community' that is a blend of staff and shoppers who blog, chat and post on fashion forums.

In 2010, the company launched Asos Marketplace, which allows designers to set up boutique stores on its site selling their own creations and one-off vintage items. 'Like a concession in a department store, they are renting web space from us,' he says. Asos vets its traders and takes a 10–15 per cent cut of everything they sell.

In 2011, it started the Asos Facebook store, becoming one of the first retailers to launch a shop on the social networking site. Signing up automatically gives Asos the right to send you e-mails, post on your wall and view your friend lists, photographs and profile information. Much of Asos's success has, however, been built on a low-tech guarantee to customers: free returns. In the early days of internet shopping, allowing customers to send anything they did not want back was essential.

As the company shifts its focus to the global 22-year-old, it is now offering free shipping. Mr Robertson calls this 'the best marketing money can buy' and, in the US, France and Germany, returns are also free. Not everyone is convinced that this model is sustainable. 'Offering free delivery is an expensive way of getting new customers but it shows how high Asos's margins are that they can afford to do that,' notes Nick Bubb, retail analyst at Arden Partners.

Another tap on finances is the company's growing number of product lines, which have to be stored somewhere. 'They have to be a perfect 10, operationally, to achieve these ambitious growth targets,' notes a rival retailer. 'There is no margin for error. If we achieved 30 per cent sales growth, that would be fantastic from our point of view. But if Asos doesn't achieve 50 per cent, the City will lose faith in the growth story.'

At the same time, rivals are improving their own offerings. At the luxury end of the sector, this includes Net-a-Porter and My-wardrobe.com, while there is a plethora of mid-market competitors including NotOnTheHighStreet.com. Moreover, fashion brands themselves are improving their online sales outlets. Superdry, for example, makes more money through sales via its own website and has barred Asos from selling its goods in certain countries. 'It's the most profitable part of our whole business,' says Julian Dunkerton, chief executive of Supergroup, Superdry's parent company. 'If shoppers go on to Asos and find Superdry, I'm happy. But if they tap in Superdry to a search engine and it comes up with another website, that's wrong.'

Always prepared to confound his critics, Mr Robertson is about to launch Fashion Finder, a service that will publicise brands that Asos does not sell. A nod to US fashion aggregator sites Polyvore and ShopStyle, the idea is to turn Asos into a 'fashion destination' rather than just a store. 'If you work at a fashion magazine, your role in life is to guide the reader through the world of fashion and edit it for them,' he says. 'Why can't shops do that?'

A year ago, Mr Robertson said he wanted Asos to achieve £1 billion in sales, spread across five markets in five years. Four of the five target countries are the US, France, the UK and Germany – but the fifth has never been made public. Is it China? 'A big strategic market', is the most he offers. Notably, other Asos presentations have mentioned that the US and China account for 50 per cent of global internet traffic, whereas the UK represents only 3 per cent. If Asos can crack Asia, the story will enter a new dimension. So far, Mr Robertson has been able to do exactly what everyone said he could not. That management style does not seem to be going out of fashion.

In 2011, a focus on fashion-conscious and Internet-savvy young women and a global expansion programme boosted fourth-quarter year-on-year revenues more than 60 per cent at Asos. The online clothes retailer said full-year pre-tax profit before exceptional items 'would be at the top end of expecta-tions' of £24 million to £29.3 million, pushing its shares up 13 per cent.

In 2010 Asos launched websites in the US, France and Germany, and hoped to open more country-specific sites in the next financial year, hotly tipped to include China. UK sales grew 24 per cent to £44.8 million, in spite of difficult economic conditions facing consumers. For the first time, turnover from the group's international businesses overtook UK sales, and now accounts for 52 per cent of revenues.

Mr. Robertson said he expected international sales – which rose 161 per cent for the quarter year on year–to grow to more than 60 per cent of total sales 'before you can shake a stick'. Total revenues increased 63 per cent to £96.6 million in the final quarter year on year, and 53 per cent to £340 million for the full year. Asos provides free delivery and returns to many of its markets, but this initiative would knock 260 to 280 basis points from full-year gross margins, the group said.

The group's Facebook store, which it launched in February 2011, was 'performing above expectations', Mr Robertson said, while Asos's Fashion Finder service, which includes more than 50 brands that Asos does not sell, has driven web traffic. 'This is our journey from shop to destination,' Mr Robertson said. 'Customers can create outfits, build looks, tag things they like and comment on styles. It's a different way of engaging with them.'

In fact, Asos is the most expensive retailer in the sector by some margin, trading on a whopping multiple of 70 times expected 2010–2011 earnings. As the dominant online-only fashion player, it is natural that Asos should command a premium in share price.[1]

Companies today recognise that they cannot appeal to all buyers in the marketplace – or at least not to all buyers in the same way. Buyers are too numerous, widely scattered, and varied in their needs and buying practices. Moreover, the companies themselves vary widely in their abilities to serve dif-ferent segments of the market. Instead, like Asos, a company must identify the parts of the market that it can serve best and most profitably. It must design customer-driven marketing strategies that build the right relationships with the right customers.

Thus, most companies have moved away from mass marketing and toward *target marketing*: identifying market segments, selecting one or more of them, and developing products and mar-keting programmes tailored to each. Instead of scattering their marketing efforts (the 'shotgun' approach), firms are focusing on the buyers who have greater interest in the value they create best (the 'rifle' approach).

Figure 7.1 shows the four major steps in designing a customer-driven marketing strategy. In the first two steps, the company selects the customers that it will serve. **Market segmentation** involves dividing a market into smaller segments of buyers with distinct needs, characteristics or behaviours that might require separate marketing strategies or mixes. The company identifies different ways to segment the market and develops profiles of the resulting market segments. **Market targeting (or targeting)** consists of evaluating each market segment's attractiveness and selecting one or more market segments to enter.

Market segmentation— Dividing a market into smaller segments with distinct needs, characteristics or behaviour that might require separate marketing strategies or mixes.

Market targeting (targeting)—The process of evaluating each market segment's attractiveness and selecting one or more segment to enter.

Figure 7.1 Designing a customer-driven marketing strategy

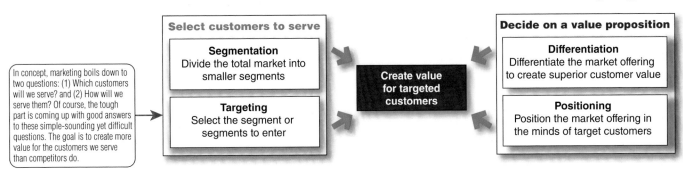

203

Differentiation—Differentiating the market offering to create superior customer value.

Positioning—Arranging for a market offering to occupy a clear, distinctive and desirable place relative to competing products in the minds of target consumers.

In the final two steps, the company decides on a value proposition – how it will create value for target customers. **Differentiation** involves actually differentiating a firm's market offering to create superior customer value. **Positioning** consists of arranging for a market offering to occupy a clear, distinctive and desirable place relative to competing products in the minds of target consumers. We discuss each of these steps in turn.

AUTHOR COMMENT

Market segmentation addresses the first simple-sounding marketing question: What customers will we serve? The answer will be different for each company. For example, the luxury hotels target the top spenders among of corporate and leisure travellers. Budget hotels target those who want to spend less because they travel for different reasons.

MARKET SEGMENTATION

Buyers in any market differ in their wants, resources, locations, buying attitudes and buying practices. Through market segmentation, companies divide large, heterogeneous markets into smaller segments that can be reached more efficiently and effectively with products and services that match their unique needs. In this section, we discuss four important segmentation topics: segmenting consumer markets, segmenting business markets, segmenting international markets and the requirements for effective segmentation.

Segmenting consumer markets

There is no single way to segment a market. A marketer has to try different segmentation variables, alone and in combination, to find the best way to view market structure. Table 7.1 outlines the major variables that might be used in segmenting consumer markets. Here we look at the major *geographic*, *demographic*, *psychographic* and *behavioural* variables.

Table 7.1   Examples of major segmentation variables for consumer markets

Geographic	
World region or country	Africa, Asia, Europe, Oceania, North America, South America, Canada, Western Europe, Middle East, Pacific Rim, England, Scotland, Wales, China, India, Brazil
Country region	England: East Midlands, East of England, Greater London, North East England, North West England, South East England, South West England, West Midlands, Yorkshire and the Humber
City or metro size (population)	Under 5,000; 5,000–20,000; 20,000–50,000; 50,000–100,000; 100,000–250,000; 250,000–500,000; 500,000–1,000,000; 1,000,000–4,000,000; over 4,000,000
Density	Urban, suburban, exurban, rural
Climatic zones	Northern, Southern, Polar, Temperate, Arid, Tropical, Mediterranean, Mountain

Demographic	
Age (years)	Under 6, 6–11, 12–19, 20–34, 35–49, 50–64, over 65
Gender	Male, female
Family size	1–2, 3–4, more than 5
Family life cycle	Young, single; married, no children; married with children; single parents; unmarried couples; older, married, no children under 18; older, single; other
Income	Under €20,000; €20,000–€30,000; €30,000–€50,000; €50,000–€100,000; €100,000–€250,000; over €250,000 and over
Occupation	A – professionals and senior managers; B – middle management executives; C1 – junior management, owners of small establishments; C2 – skilled manual workers; D – semi-skilled and unskilled manual workers; E – those dependent on long-term state benefits, unemployed, casual workers
Education	Terminal education age 16, Terminal education age 18, university graduates, those with postgraduate qualifications
Religion	Catholic, Protestant, Jewish, Muslim, Hindu, Secularised, other
Race	White, Asian, Hispanic, Black, Chinese
Generation	Baby boomer, Generation X, Millennial
Nationality	North American, South American, British, French, German, Russian, Japanese, American
Psychographic	
Social class	Underclass, Working Class (unskilled, semi-skilled, skilled), Middle Class (lower, middle, upper), Upper Class
Lifestyle	Innovators, Thinkers, Believers, Achievers, Strivers, Experiencers, Makers, Survivors
Personality	Compulsive, outgoing, authoritarian, ambitious
Behavioural	
Occasions	Regular occasion; special occasion; holiday; seasonal
Benefits	Quality, service, economy, convenience, speed
User status	Non-user, ex-user, potential user, first-time user, regular user
User rates	Light user, medium user, heavy user
Loyalty status	None, medium, strong, absolute
Readiness stage	Unaware, aware, informed, interested, desirous, intending to buy
Attitude toward product	Enthusiastic, positive, indifferent, negative, hostile

Geographic segmentation

Geographic segmentation calls for dividing the market into different geographical units, such as nations, regions, states, counties, cities or even neighbourhoods. A company may decide to operate in one or a few geographical areas or operate in all areas but pay attention to geographical differences in needs and wants.

Geographic segmentation—
Dividing a market into different geographical units, such as nations, states, regions, counties, cities or even neighbourhoods.

Many companies today are localising their products, advertising, promotion and sales efforts to fit the needs of individual regions, cities and even neighbourhoods. For example, supermarket Tesco in the UK uses the information from its Clubcard loyalty programme to examine 40 different characteristics of every item in the shopper's basket, to develop an understanding of the customer's 'DNA' and to cluster customers into different types – 'upmarket', 'price sensitive', 'green', and so on. One gain from this wealth of data and insight is the ability to create stores which reflect local demographics and purchasing patterns with great precision. In the US Walmart refers to this approach as creating the 'store of the community strategy'. It is no coincidence that Tesco stores near big universities often have a large display featuring beer and frozen pizzas, while those in residential areas place more emphasis on cooking ingredients, fresh fruit and baby products. Tesco's small-format Metro stores focus on the needs of time-pressed commuters and similar groups, depending on location.[2]

Demographic segmentation

Demographic segmentation— Dividing the market into segments based on variables such as age, gender, family size family life cycle, income, occupation, education, religion, race, generation and nationality.

Demographic segmentation divides the market into segments based on age, gender, family size, family life cycle, income, occupation, education, religion, ethnicity, generation and nationality. Demographic factors are the most popular bases for segmenting customer groups. One reason is that consumer needs, wants and usage rates often vary closely with demographic variables. Another is that demographic variables are easier to measure than most other types of variables. Even when marketers first define segments using other bases, such as benefits sought or behaviour they must know a segment's demographic characteristics to assess the size of the target market and reach it efficiently.

Age and life-cycle stage

Age and life-cycle segmentation—Dividing a market into different age and life-cycle groups.

Consumer needs and wants change with age. Some companies use **age and life-cycle segmentation**, offering different products or using different marketing approaches for different age and life-cycle groups.

For example, some companies focus on the specific age of life-stage groups. For example, Saga in the UK provides a wide range of products and services, including insurance, homecare, holidays, and a magazine, exclusively for the over 50s. In the leisure and holiday business, a cruise operator

Saga provides a range of products and services exclusively for the over-50s.

Source: Saga

might target primarily families with children – with destinations and shipboard activities designed with parents and their children in mind, trained staff on board to help younger children join in activities, teen-only spaces for older children, and individual-time options for parents and other adults. Advertising and Web pages could feature families full of smiling faces. In contrast, another cruise line might primarily target older-adult couples and singles, so there would be no children in their advertising or on the Web page. On the other hand, budget cruise operator easyCruise (now Hellenic Seaways) is aimed at younger holiday-makers travelling on a tight budget, and promotion emphasises sunshine, on-board clubbing and outstanding value-for-money.

Marketers must be careful to guard against stereotypes when using age and life-cycle segmentation. Although some 80-year-olds fit the 'doddery' stereotypes, others play tennis and run marathons. Similarly, whereas some 40-year-old couples are sending their children off to college, others are just beginning new families. Thus, age is often a poor predictor of a person's life cycle, health, work or family status, needs and buying power. Companies marketing to mature consumers usually employ positive images and appeals.

Gender

Gender segmentation has long been used in clothing, cosmetics, toiletries and magazines. For example, in the United States, P&G was among the first with Secret, a deodorant brand specially formulated for a woman's chemistry, packaged and advertised to reinforce the female image. More recently, many women's cosmetics makers have begun marketing men's lines. For example, Nivea markets Nivea for Men, a product line for men ranging from its 3-in-1 Active3 body wash, shampoo and shaving cream combination to a revitalising eye cream. According to a Nivea marketer, Active3 appeals to the male mind-set of, 'I wanted to be fast, convenient, and economical. I wanted to fit with these times.' It's 'What Men Want'.[3]

A neglected gender segment can offer new opportunities in markets ranging from consumer electronics to motorcycles. For example, struggling high-end motorcycle manufacturer Harley-Davidson has traditionally targeted its product design and marketing to a market of males between 35 and 55 years old. Women were more often just along for the ride – but no longer:[4]

> Women are now among the fastest growing customer segments in the motorcycle business. The number of female Harley-Davidson owners has tripled in the past 20 years, and female buyers now account for 12 per cent of new Harley-Davidson purchases. So the company is boosting its efforts to move more women from the back of the bike into the driver's seat. Rather than indulging in female stereotypes, however, Harley-Davidson is appealing to 'strong, independent women who enjoy taking on a challenge and a feeling of adventure,' says the company's women's outreach manager. A recent ad sports this headline: 'Not pictured: the weaker sex.' A women's Web microsite encourages women to share inspirational riding stories with one another. And to kick off Women Riders Month, Harley-Davidson recently hosted special riding events designed to 'celebrate the millions of women who have already grabbed life by the handlebars'.
>
> In marketing to women, Harley-Davidson is staying true to its tough, road-tested image. 'I don't think we're going to see any pink [Harley-Davidson motorcycles] on the road,' says an analyst. And 'they don't have to add bigger mirrors so women can do their cosmetics. . . . They want to sell Harleys to women, and they want to sell them to women who want to ride a *Harley*.'

Income

The marketers of products and services such as motor cars, clothing, cosmetics, financial services and travel have long used **income segmentation**. Many companies target affluent consumers with luxury goods and convenience services. For example, luxury hotels often provide special packages to attract the most affluent travellers. Similarly, many retailers have adapted their strategies in pursuit of the 'platinum pound' – trying to attract a broader, younger, more international group of ultra-affluent shoppers to stores in locations like London and Birmingham. Personal shopping services raise the store appeal to the 'cash-rich, time-poor' shopper. And Russian- and Chinese-speaking personal shopping assistants raise the appeal to the wealthy from those countries.[5]

Gender segmentation—
Dividing a market into different segments based on gender.

Income segmentation—
Dividing a market into different income segments.

Nivea for Men is a product line of cosmetics specifically for males, ranging from body wash and shampoo to revitalising eyes cream.

Source: The Advertising Archives

Other marketers use high-touch marketing programmes to court the well-to-do. Consider this example:

Coutts & Co. is the private bank of the British establishment. Nonetheless, the bank has forged links with high fashion to update its image and to try to attract more affluent female customers. Coutts has gone further than any other banking brand into the fashion arena in an attempt to capture the affluent female market. The goal is to convince more of the growing number of wealthy female entrepreneurs to deposit their money with the bank. Like other private banks, Coutts is also aiming to attract some of the wealthy celebrities who often act as 'ambassadors' for the brand.[6]

However, not all companies that use income segmentation target the affluent. For example, many budget retailers – such as the Poundland, Poundshop and Matalan retail chains and grocery stores Aldi and Lidl – successfully target low- and middle-income groups. The core market for such stores is represented by families with more modest incomes. With their low-income strategies, budget stores have shown impressive growth in the harsh economic conditions of recent years.

Indeed, the recent troubled economy in Europe has provided challenges for marketers targeting all income groups. Consumers at all income levels – including affluent consumers – are cutting back on their spending and seeking greater value from their purchases. In many cases, luxury marketers targeting high-income consumers have been hardest hit. Even consumers who can still afford to buy luxuries appear to be pushing the pause button. 'It's conspicuous *non*consumption,' says one economist. 'The wealthy still have the wealth, [but] it's the image you project in a bad economy of driving a nice car when your friends or colleagues may be losing their businesses.'[7]

Harley-Davidson has boosted its efforts to move women from the back of the bike onto the rider's seat.

Source: Getty Images/Bloomberg

Psychographic segmentation

Psychographic segmentation divides buyers into different segments based on social class, lifestyle or personality characteristics. People in the same demographic group can have very different psychographic characteristics.

In Chapter 5, we discussed how the products people buy reflect their *lifestyles*. As a result, marketers often segment their markets by consumer lifestyles and base their marketing strategies on lifestyle appeals. For example, car-sharing innovator Zipcar rents cars by the hour or the day, in the US and Europe. But Zipcar doesn't see itself as a car-rental company. Instead it sees itself as enhancing its customers' urban lifestyles and targets accordingly. 'It's not about cars,' says Zipcar's CEO; 'it's about urban life.'[8]

Marketers also use *personality* variables to segment markets. For example, some holiday cruise lines target adventure seekers. Royal Caribbean appeals to high-energy couples and families by providing hundreds of activities, such as rock wall climbing and ice skating. Its commercials urge travellers to 'declare your independence and become a citizen of our nation – Royal Caribbean, The Nation of Why Not'. By contrast, the Regent Seven Seas Cruise Line targets more serene and cerebral adventurers, mature couples seeking a more elegant ambience and exotic destinations, such as the Orient. Regent invites them to come along as 'luxury goes exploring'.[9]

Psychographic segmentation—Dividing a market into different segments based on social class, lifestyle or personality characteristics.

Behavioural segmentation

Behavioural segmentation divides buyers into segments based on their knowledge, attitudes, uses or responses to a product. Many marketers believe that behavioural variables are the best starting point for building market segments.

Behavioural segmentation—Dividing a market into segments based on consumer knowledge, attitudes, uses or responses to a product.

Occasions

Buyers can be grouped according to occasions when they get the idea to buy, actually make their purchase or use the purchased item. **Occasion segmentation** can help firms build up product usage. For example, most consumers who drink orange juice do so at breakfast, but orange growers are promoting drinking orange juice as a cool, healthful refresher at other times of the day.

Some holidays, such as Mother's Day and Father's Day, were originally promoted to increase the sale of chocolate, flowers, cards and other gifts. And many marketers prepare special offers and ads for these and other holiday occasions.

Occasion segmentation—Dividing the market into segments according to occasions when buyers get the idea to buy, actually make their purchase or use the purchased item.

Benefits sought

A powerful form of segmentation is grouping buyers according to the different *benefits* that they seek from a product. **Benefit segmentation** requires finding the major benefits people look for in

Benefit segmentation—Dividing the market into segments according to the different benefits that consumers seek from the product.

a product class, the kinds of people who look for each benefit, and the major brands that deliver each benefit.

International sportswear company Champion invented the hoodie, the sports bra and reversible t-shirts. In sportswear Champion segments its markets according to benefits that different consumers seek from these clothes. For example, 'Fit and Polish' consumers seek a balance between function and style; they exercise for results but want to look good doing it. 'Serious Sports Competitors' exercise heavily and live in and love their sports clothes; they seek performance and function. By contrast, 'Value-Seeking' mothers have low sports interest and low sportwear involvement; they buy for the family and seek durability and value. Thus, each segment seeks a different mix of benefits. Champion aims to target the benefit segment or segments that it can serve best and most profitably, using appeals that match each segment's benefit preferences.

User status

Markets can be segmented into non-users, ex-users, potential users, first-time users and regular users of a product. Marketers want to reinforce and retain regular users, attract targeted non-users, and reinvigorate relationships with ex-users.

Included in the potential user group are consumers facing life-stage changes – such as newly-weds and new parents – who can be turned into heavy users. For example, Ikea supplies 10 per cent of the furniture purchased in the UK – indeed, the company claims that one-in-ten Europeans were conceived in an Ikea bed. Ikea actively targets the newly-divorced. After the breakdown of a relationship, individuals face setting up new homes, often largely from scratch. Ikea's typically provocative advertising makes light of these traumatic problems and looks to turn the 'newly-single' into major buyers of Ikea's low budget home furnishings.[10]

Usage rate

Markets can also be segmented into light, medium and heavy product users. Heavy users are often a small percentage of the market but account for a high percentage of total consumption. For example, global fast-food company Burger King targets what it calls 'Super Fans' in the US. They are young (aged 18 to 34), Whopper-wolfing males and females who make up 18 per cent of the chain's customers but account for almost half of all customer visits. They eat at Burger King an average of 13 times a month. Burger King targets these Super Fans openly with ads that exalt monster burgers suitable for the biggest appetites.[11]

Loyalty status

A market can also be segmented by consumer loyalty. Consumers can be loyal to brands (e.g. Tide), stores (e.g. Waitrose) and companies (e.g. Apple). Buyers can be divided into groups according to their degree of loyalty.

Some consumers are completely loyal; they buy one brand all the time. For example, as we discussed in the previous chapter, Apple has an almost cultlike following of loyal users. Other consumers are somewhat loyal; they are loyal to two or three brands of a given product or favour one brand while sometimes buying others. Still other buyers show no loyalty to any brand; they either want something different each time they buy, or they buy whatever's on sale.

A company can learn a lot by analysing loyalty patterns in its market. It should start by studying its own loyal customers. For example, by studying Mac fanatics, Apple can better pinpoint its target market and develop marketing appeals. By studying its less-loyal buyers, the company can detect which brands are most competitive with its own. By looking at customers who are shifting away from its brand, the company can learn about its marketing weaknesses.

Using multiple segmentation bases

Marketers rarely limit their segmentation analysis to one or a few variables only. Rather, they often use multiple segmentation bases in an effort to identify smaller, better-defined target groups. Thus, a bank may not only identify a group of wealthy, retired adults but also, within that group, distinguish several segments based on their current income, assets, savings and risk preferences, housing and lifestyles.

Several business information services, such as A.C. Nielsen, TNS, GfK and Experian, provide multivariable segmentation systems that merge geographic, demographic, lifestyle and behavioural data to help companies segment their markets down to postal codes, neighbourhoods, and even households. One of the leading segmentation systems is the ACORN product provided in the UK by CACI Ltd, the UK subsidiary of CACI International in the United States.[12]

ACORN is used to understand consumers' lifestyle, behaviour and attitudes, as well as the needs of local neighbourhoods or communities. ACORN ('A Classification Of Residential Neighbourhoods') is a geodemographic segmentation of the UK's population around small neighbourhoods, postcodes or consumer households. ACORN classifies population into five categories (Wealthy Achievers, Urban Prosperity, Comfortably Off, Moderate Means and Hard-Pressed) and within these categories identifies 17 groups and 56 types. For example, Wealthy Achievers comprises around 25 per cent of the UK's population, and Affluent Greys is one group within this category, and those living in farming communities constitute one of the types within this category.

ACORN and other such systems can help marketers segment people and locations into marketable groups of like-minded consumers. Each category and group is likely to have its own pattern of likes, dislikes, lifestyles and purchase behaviours. For example, Affluent Greys living in Farming Communities have distinct demographic characteristics, but also differ from others regarding car ownership, shopping preferences, Internet activity and media usage.

Such segmentation approaches provide a powerful tool for marketers of all kinds (e.g. private and public sector). It can help companies identify and better understand key customer segments, target them more efficiently, and tailor market offerings and messages to their specific needs. It can assist public policy decision makers in identifying the needs of local communities of different kinds.

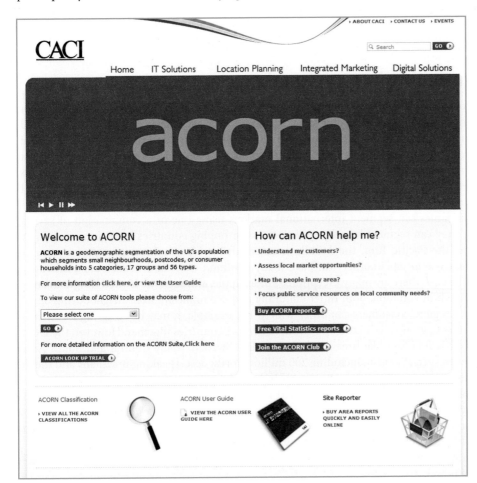

ACORN is a geodemographic segmentation system, used to understand consumers' lifestyle, behaviour and attitudes, as well as needs of local neighbourhoods or communities.

Source: CACI Limited

Segmenting business markets

Consumer and business marketers use many of the same variables to segment their markets. Business buyers can also be segmented geographically, demographically (e.g. by industry or company size), or by benefits sought, user status, usage rate and loyalty status. Yet, business marketers also use some additional variables, such as customer *operating characteristics*, *purchasing approaches*, *situational factors* and *personal characteristics*.

Almost every company serves at least some business markets. For example, globally American Express targets businesses in three segments: merchants, corporations and small businesses. It has developed distinct marketing programmes for each segment. In the merchants segment, American Express focuses on convincing new merchants to accept the card and managing relationships with those that already do. For larger corporate customers, the company offers a corporate card programme, which includes extensive employee expense and travel management services. It also offers this segment a wide range of asset management, retirement planning and financial education services. Finally, for small business customers, American Express has created a system of small business cards and financial services.[13]

Many companies establish separate systems for dealing with larger or multiple-location customers. For example, Steelcase, the global leader in the office furniture industry, provides innovative office furniture products. The company first divides customers into seven segments, including biosciences, higher education, government buyers, local government, healthcare, professional services and retail banking. Next, company salespeople work with Steelcase dealers to handle smaller or local Steelcase customers in each segment. But many national, multiple-location customers, such as ExxonMobil or IBM, have special needs that may reach beyond the scope of individual dealers. So Steelcase uses national account managers to help its dealer networks handle national accounts.

Within a given target industry and customer size, the company can segment by purchase approaches and criteria. As in consumer segmentation, many marketers believe that *buying behaviour* and *benefits* provide the best basis for segmenting business markets.

Segmenting international markets

Few companies have either the resources or the will to operate in all, or even most, of the countries that dot the globe. Although some large companies, such as Unilever, Coca-Cola or Sony, sell products in more than 200 countries, most international firms focus on a smaller set. Operating in many countries presents new challenges. Different countries, even those that are close together, can vary greatly in their economic, cultural and political makeup. Thus, just as they do within their domestic markets, international firms need to group their world markets into segments with distinct buying needs and behaviours.

Companies can segment international markets using one or a combination of several variables. They can segment by *geographic location*, grouping countries by regions such as Western Europe, the Pacific Rim, the Middle East or Africa. Geographic segmentation assumes that nations close to one another will have many common traits and behaviours. Although this is often the case, there are many exceptions. For example, although the United Kingdom and France have much in common, both differ culturally and economically from neighbouring Spain. Even within a region, consumers can differ widely. For example, it may be tempting for international marketers to group all Central and South American countries together. However, the Dominican Republic is no more like Brazil than Italy is like Sweden. Many Central and South Americans don't even speak Spanish, including 200 million Portuguese-speaking Brazilians and the millions in other countries who speak a variety of Indian dialects.

World markets can also be segmented on the basis of *economic factors*. Countries might be grouped by population income levels or by their overall level of economic development. A country's economic structure shapes its population's product and service needs and, therefore, the marketing opportunities it offers. For example, many companies are now targeting the BRIC countries – Brazil, Russia, India and China – which are fast-growing developing economies with rapidly increasing buying power.

Countries can also be segmented by *political and legal factors* such as the type and stability of government, receptivity to foreign firms, monetary regulations and amount of bureaucracy. *Cultural factors* can also be used, grouping markets according to common languages, religions, values and attitudes, customs and behavioural patterns.

Segmenting international markets based on geographic, economic, political, cultural and other factors presumes that segments consist of clusters of countries. However, as new communications technologies, such as satellite television and the Internet, connect consumers around the world, marketers can define and reach segments of like-minded consumers no matter where in the world they are. Using **intermarket segmentation** (also called **cross-market segmentation**), they form segments of consumers who have similar needs and buying behaviours even though they are located in different countries. For example, Toyota's Lexus car brand targets the world's well-to-do – the 'global elite' segment – regardless of their country. Coca-Cola creates special programmes to target teens, core consumers of its soft drinks, the world over. And Swedish furniture giant Ikea targets the aspiring global middle class; it sells good-quality furniture that ordinary people worldwide can afford.

> **Intermarket segmentation (cross-market segmentation)** —Forming segments of consumers who have similar needs and buying behaviour even though they are located in different countries.

Requirements for effective segmentation

Clearly, there are many ways to segment a market, but not all segmentations are effective. For example, buyers of table salt could be divided into blond and brunette customers. But hair colour obviously does not affect the purchase of salt. Furthermore, if all salt buyers bought the same amount of salt each month, believed that all salt is the same, and wanted to pay the same price, the company would not benefit from segmenting this market.

To be useful, market segments must be:

- *Measurable.* The size, purchasing power and profiles of the segments can be measured. Certain segmentation variables are difficult to measure. For example, around 10 per cent of the world's population of 7 billion people is left-handed. This group is larger than many countries. Yet few products are targeted toward this left-handed segment. The major problem may be that the segment is hard to identify and measure. There are no data on the demographics of lefties, and few governments keep track of left-handedness in their population surveys. Private data companies keep reams of statistics on other demographic segments but not on left-handers.
- *Accessible.* The market segments can be effectively reached and served. Suppose a fragrance company finds that heavy users of its brand are single men and women who stay out late and socialise a lot. Unless this group lives or shops at certain places and is exposed to certain media, its members will be difficult to reach.
- *Substantial.* The market segments are large or profitable enough to serve. A segment should be the largest possible homogeneous group worth pursuing with a tailored marketing programme. It would not pay, for example, for a motor manufacturer to develop cars especially for people whose height is greater than seven feet.
- *Differentiable.* The segments are conceptually distinguishable and respond differently to different marketing mix elements and programmes. If men and women respond similarly to marketing efforts for soft drinks, they do not constitute separate segments.
- *Actionable.* Effective programmes can be designed for attracting and serving the segments. For example, although one small airline identified seven market segments, its staff was too small to develop separate marketing programmes for each segment.

AUTHOR COMMENT
After dividing the market into segments, it's time to answer that first seemingly simple marketing strategy question we raised in Figure 7.1: Which customers will a company serve?

MARKET TARGETING

Market segmentation reveals a firm's market segment opportunities. A firm now has to evaluate the various segments and decide how many and which segments it can serve best. We now look at how companies evaluate and select target segments.

Evaluating market segments

In evaluating different market segments, a firm must look at three factors: segment size and growth, segment structural attractiveness, and company objectives and resources. The company must first collect and analyse data on current segment sales, growth rates and the expected profitability for various segments. It will be interested in segments that have the right size and growth characteristics.

But 'right size and growth' is a relative characteristic. The largest, fastest-growing segments are not always the most attractive ones for every company. Smaller companies may lack the skills and resources needed to serve larger segments. Or they may find these segments too competitive. Such companies may target segments that are smaller and less attractive, in an absolute sense, but some target segments are potentially more profitable for them.

The company also needs to examine major structural factors that affect long-term segment attractiveness.[14] For example, a segment is less attractive if it already contains many strong and aggressive *competitors*. The existence of many actual or potential *substitute products* may limit prices and the profits that can be earned in a segment. The relative *power of buyers* also affects segment attractiveness. Buyers with strong bargaining power relative to sellers will try to force prices down, demand more services and set competitors against one another – all at the expense of seller profitability. Finally, a segment may be less attractive if it contains *powerful suppliers* who can control prices or reduce the quality or quantity of ordered goods and services.

Even if a segment has the right size and growth and is structurally attractive, the company must consider its own objectives and resources. Some attractive segments can be dismissed quickly because they do not fit with the company's long-term objectives. Or the company may lack the skills and resources needed to succeed in an attractive segment. For example, given the current economic conditions, the economy segment of the motor car market is large and growing. But given its objectives and resources, it would make little sense for the luxury-performance car manufacturer Lexus to enter this segment. A company should enter segments only in which it can create superior customer value and gain advantages over its competitors.

Selecting target market segments

Target market—A set of buyers sharing common needs or characteristics that the company decides to serve.

After evaluating different segments, the company must decide which and how many segments it will target. A **target market** consists of a set of buyers who share common needs or characteristics that the company decides to serve. Market targeting can be carried out at several different levels. Figure 7.2 shows that companies can target very broadly (undifferentiated marketing), very narrowly (micromarketing) or somewhere in between (differentiated or concentrated marketing).

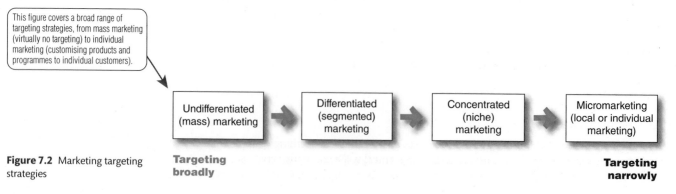

Figure 7.2 Marketing targeting strategies

Undifferentiated marketing

Using an **undifferentiated marketing** (or **mass marketing**) strategy, a firm might decide to ignore market segment differences and target the whole market with one offer. Such a strategy focuses on what is *common* in the needs of consumers rather than on what is *different*. The company designs a product and a marketing programme that will appeal to the largest number of buyers.

As noted earlier in the chapter, most modern marketers have strong doubts about this strategy. Difficulties arise in developing a product or brand that will satisfy all consumers. Moreover, mass marketers often have trouble competing with more-focused firms that do a better job of satisfying the needs of specific segments and niches.

Undifferentiated (mass) marketing—A market-coverage strategy in which a firm decides to ignore market segment differences and go after the whole market with one offer.

Differentiated marketing

Using a **differentiated marketing** (or **segmented marketing**) strategy, a firm decides to target several market segments and designs separate offers for each. Toyota Corporation produces several different brands of cars – from the Prius to Toyota to Lexus – each targeting its own segments of car buyers. In most large country markets, P&G markets multiple laundry detergent brands, which compete with each other on supermarket shelves. And US company VF Corporation offers a wardrobe full of more than 30 premium lifestyle clothing brands – the company's brands are carefully separated into five major segments – Jeanswear, Imagewear (workwear), Outdoor, Sportswear, and Contemporary Brands – which 'fit the lives of consumers the world over' in well-defined segments – 'from commuters to cowboys, surfers to soccer moms, sports fans to rock bands'.[15]

By offering product and marketing variations to segments, companies hope for higher sales and a stronger position within each market segment. Developing a stronger position within several segments creates more total sales than undifferentiated marketing across all segments. VF Corporation's combined brands give it a much greater, more stable market share than any single brand could. The four Jeanswear brands alone account for one-fourth of all jeans sold in the United States. Similarly, P&G's multiple detergent brands capture four times the market share of its nearest rival.

But differentiated marketing also increases the costs of doing business. A firm usually finds it more expensive to develop and produce, say, 10 units of 10 different products than 100 units of a single product. Developing separate marketing plans for the separate segments requires extra marketing research, forecasting, sales analysis, promotion planning and channel management. And trying to reach different market segments with different advertising campaigns increases promotion costs. Thus, the company must weigh increased sales against increased costs when deciding on a differentiated marketing strategy.

Differentiated (segmented) marketing—A market-coverage strategy in which a firm decides to target several market segments and designs separate offers for each.

Concentrated marketing

Using a **concentrated marketing** (or **niche marketing**) strategy, instead of going after a small share of a large market, a firm goes after a large share of one or a few smaller segments or niches. For example, Whole Foods Market is a niche food retailer which has become the world's largest retailer of natural and organic foods, with stores throughout North America and in the United Kingdom.[16] Whole Foods is small compared to giant rivals, such as Krogers and Walmart in the US and Tesco in the UK. Yet, over the past five years, the smaller, more upmarket retailer has grown faster than larger rivals. Whole Foods Market thrives by catering to affluent customers who the mass retailers of the world can't serve well, offering them 'organic, natural, and gourmet foods, all swaddled in Earth Day politics'. In fact, a typical Whole Foods Market customer is more likely to boycott the local mass-market supermarket than to shop at it.

Through concentrated marketing, a firm achieves a strong market position because of its greater knowledge of consumer needs in the niches it serves and the special reputation it acquires. It can market more *effectively* by fine-tuning its products, prices and programmes to the needs of carefully

Concentrated (niche) marketing—A market-coverage strategy in which a firm goes after a large share of one or a few segments or niches.

Whole Foods Market is a niche food retailer which has become the world's largest retailer of natural and organic foods.

Source: Rex Features/MCP

defined segments. It can also market more *efficiently*, targeting its products or services, channels and communications programmes toward consumers that it can serve best and most profitably.

Whereas segments are fairly large and normally attract several competitors, niches are smaller and may attract only one or a few competitors. Niching lets smaller companies focus their limited resources on serving niches that may be unimportant to or overlooked by larger competitors. Many companies start as nichers to get a foothold against larger, more-resourceful competitors and then grow into broader competitors. For example, the original low-cost airline, Southwest Airlines, began by serving intrastate, no-frills commuters in Texas but is now one of the largest airlines in the US, and its example has been followed by European airlines like easyJet and Ryanair. Enterprise Rent-A-Car began by building a network of neighbourhood offices in the US rather than competing with Hertz and Avis in airport locations, and has transferred this model across other markets.

In contrast, as markets change, some megamarketers develop niche products to create sales growth. For example, in recent years, as consumers have grown more health conscious, the demand for carbonated soft drinks has declined, and the market for energy drinks and juices has grown. With carbonated soft drink sales falling across the world, to meet this shifting demand, mainstream cola marketers PepsiCo and Coca-Cola have both developed or acquired their own niche products. PepsiCo developed Amp energy drink and purchased the SoBe and Izze brands of enhanced waters and juices. Similarly, Coca-Cola developed Vault and acquired the Vitaminwater and Odwalla brands. Says Pepsi-Cola North America's chief marketing officer, 'The era of the mass brand has been over for a long time'.[17]

Today, the low cost of setting up a shop on the Internet makes it even more profitable to serve seemingly minuscule niches. Small businesses, in particular, are realising riches from serving small niches on the Web. Consider Moonpig.com:

Moonpig.com sells personalised greeting cards online. The website was launched in July 2000, and in 2007 the company was responsible for 90 per cent of the online greeting card market in the United Kingdom. According to founder Nick Jenkins, 'Moonpig' was his nickname at school, hence the name of the brand. Customers visiting the website choose from a large selection of basic greeting card designs but then enter their own text to personalise them. As well as cards, the website offers customisable spoof magazine covers and invitations, where customers can upload their own photos for printing. The original launch of Moonpig.com coincided with the collapse of the dot-com bubble' which meant progress was difficult at first, but Jenkins raised investments from private investors and venture capital. The growth in broadband and use of digital cameras, together with news spreading by word-of-mouth, meant sales steadily increased, and the first profits were made in 2005. A television advertising campaign began in November 2006 to further build brand awareness, and in February 2008 Moonpig.com received a higher level of UK Internet traffic than any other company in the flower and gift industry. By summer 2009, the company had 2.57 million customers. The business expanded into the Australian market in 2004, and in late 2009, the business developed its offering to include a range of flowers and custom mug designs. In spring 2010, Moonpig launched in America. In July 2011, Moonpig agreed to be taken over by PhotoBox in a £120 million deal.[18]

Concentrated marketing can be highly profitable. At the same time, it involves higher-than-normal risks. Companies that rely on one or a few segments for all of their business will suffer greatly if the segment turns sour. Or larger competitors may decide to enter the same segment with greater resources. For these reasons, many companies prefer to diversify in several market segments.

Micromarketing

Differentiated and concentrated marketers tailor their offers and marketing programmes to meet the needs of various market segments and niches. At the same time, however, they do not customise their offers to each individual customer. **Micromarketing** is the practice of tailoring products and marketing programmes to suit the tastes of specific individuals and locations. Rather than seeing a customer in every individual, micromarketers see the individual in every customer. Micromarketing includes local marketing and individual marketing.

Local marketing

Local marketing involves tailoring brands and promotions to the needs and wants of local customer groups – cities, neighbourhoods and even specific stores. For example, Tesco customises its merchandise store by store to meet the needs of local shoppers. The retailer's store designers create each new store's format according to neighbourhood characteristics, based on the study of geodemographics – stores near offices, for instance, contain prominent islands featuring ready-made meals for busy workers. By using a wealth of customer data on daily sales in every store, Tesco tailors individual store merchandise with considerable precision. Different store formats – superstores, Extra, Metro, Express, One-Stop and Home-Plus – are matched to local market needs and opportunities.[19]

Advances in communications technology have given rise to a new high-tech version of location-based marketing. For example, retailers have long been intrigued by the promise of mobile phones, which live in people's pockets and send signals about shoppers' locations. The idea is to send people ads tailored to their location, like a coupon for cappuccino when passing a Starbucks. That idea is fast becoming a reality. For example, in the US, outdoor clothing retailer, the North Face, sends texts about promotions, such as a free water bottle with a purchase or seasonal merchandise arrivals:[20]

The North Face is trying a new tactic: sending people text messages as soon as they get near one of its stores. The new marketing campaign first singles out customers depending on where they are, as gleaned from their phone's GPS signal or location data provided by a phone carrier. It uses 'geo-fencing', which draws half-mile-wide virtual perimeters around selected store locations. When someone steps into a geo-fenced area, the North Face sends a text message to consumers who have opted in. Within each geo-fence, it can personalise messages to local weather and other factors. A text message might say, for example, 'TNF: The new spring running apparel has hit the

Micromarketing—Tailoring products and marketing programmes to the needs and wants of specific individuals and *local* customer segments; It includes *local marketing* and *individual marketing*.

Local marketing—Tailoring brands and promotions to the need and wants of local customer segments – cities, neighbourhoods and even specific stores.

stores! Check it out @ TNF Downtown Seattle.' But that's just for starters. Eventually, the company plans to send branded texts when people arrive at a hiking trail or mountain to alert them about weather conditions or logistics for a ski competition, for example. It also created an iPhone app called the North Face Snow Report that provides local snow conditions and trail maps. The store doesn't want to be intrusive, says the vice president of marketing. For brand fans who opt in, 'We are bringing something to the table,' he says, something that 'connects to a person's passions' – locally.

In Europe, Starbucks and L'Oréal are among leading brands developing placecasting of this kind to position localised messages direct with consumers.[21]

Local marketing has some drawbacks. It can drive up manufacturing and marketing costs by reducing the economies of scale. It can also create logistics problems as companies try to meet the varied requirements of different regional and local markets. Furthermore, a brand's overall image might be diluted if the product and message vary too much in different localities.

Still, as companies face increasingly fragmented markets, and as new supporting technologies develop, the advantages of local marketing often outweigh the drawbacks. Local marketing helps a company to market more effectively in the face of pronounced regional and local differences in demographics and lifestyles.

Individual marketing

In the extreme, micromarketing becomes **individual marketing** – tailoring products and marketing programmes to the needs and preferences of individual customers. Individual marketing has also been labelled *one-to-one marketing*, *mass customisation* and *markets-of-one marketing*.

Individual marketing—
Tailoring products and marketing programmes to the needs and preferences of individual customers – also called *one-to-one marketing, customised marketing* and *markets-of-one marketing*.

Leading brands are developing placecasting to position localised messages direct with consumers on their mobile phones.

Source: E M Clements photography

The widespread use of mass marketing has obscured the fact that for centuries consumers were served as individuals: the tailor custom-made a suit, the shoes were designed for an individual and the cabinetmaker made furniture to order. Today, however, new technologies are permitting many companies to return to customised marketing. More detailed databases, robotic production and flexible manufacturing, and interactive communication media such as mobile phones and the Internet have combined to foster 'mass customisation'. *Mass customisation* is the process through which firms interact one-to-one with masses of customers to design products and services tailor-made to individual needs.

Dell, HP and Apple create custom-configured computers. At **www.cricketbats.com**, the enthusiast can buy a cricket bat made to specific design, size, weight, handle size and shape preferences. Visitors to Nike's Nike ID website can personalise their training shoes by choosing from hundreds of colours and putting an embroidered word or phrase on the tongue.

Marketers are also finding new ways to personalise promotional messages. For example, plasma screens placed in shopping centres around the country can now analyse shoppers' faces and place ads based on an individual shopper's gender, age or ethnicity:[22]

> If you watch an ad on a video screen in a shopping centre, a health club, or a grocery store, there is a growing chance that the ad is also watching you. Small cameras can now be embedded in or around the screen, tracking who looks at the screen and for how long. With surprising accuracy, the system can determine the viewer's gender, approximate age range and, in some cases, ethnicity—and change the ads accordingly. That could mean razor ads for men, cosmetics ads for women and videogame ads for teens. Or a video screen might show a motorcycle ad for a group of men but switch to a minivan ad when women and children join them. 'This is proactive merchandising,' says a media executive. 'You're targeting people with smart ads.'

Business-to-business marketers are also finding new ways to customise their offerings. For example, in the US, John Deere manufactures farm seeding equipment that can be configured in more than two million versions to individual customer specifications. The seeders are produced one at a time, in any sequence, on a single production line. Mass customisation provides a way to stand out against competitors.

Unlike mass production, which eliminates the need for human interaction, one-to-one marketing has made relationships with customers more important than ever. Just as mass production was the marketing principle of the twentieth century, interactive marketing is becoming a marketing principle for the twenty-first century. The world appears to be coming full circle – from the good old days when customers were treated as individuals to mass marketing when nobody knew your name and then back again.

Choosing a targeting strategy

Companies need to consider many factors when choosing a market-targeting strategy. Which strategy is best depends on the company's resources. When a firm's resources are limited, concentrated marketing makes the most sense. The best strategy also depends on the degree of product variability. Undifferentiated marketing is more suited for uniform products, such as grapefruit or steel. Products that can vary in design, such as cameras and cars, are more suited to differentiation or concentration. A product's life-cycle stage also must be considered. When a firm introduces a new product, it may be practical to launch one version only, and undifferentiated marketing or concentrated marketing may make the most sense. In the mature stage of a product life cycle (PLC), however, differentiated marketing often makes more sense.

Another factor is *market variability*. If most buyers have the same tastes, buy the same amounts and react the same way to marketing efforts, undifferentiated marketing is appropriate. Finally, *competitors' marketing strategies* are important. When competitors use differentiated or concentrated marketing, undifferentiated marketing can be suicidal. Conversely, when competitors use undifferentiated marketing, a firm can gain an advantage by using differentiated or concentrated marketing, focusing on the needs of buyers in specific segments.

Socially responsible target marketing

Smart targeting helps companies become more efficient and effective by focusing on the segments that they can satisfy best and most profitably. Targeting also benefits consumers – companies serve specific groups of consumers with offers carefully tailored to their needs. However, target marketing sometimes generates controversy and concern. The biggest issues usually involve the targeting of vulnerable or disadvantaged consumers with controversial or potentially harmful products.

For example, over the years, marketers in a wide range of industries – from cereal, soft drinks, and fast food to toys and fashion – have been heavily criticised for their marketing efforts directed toward children. Critics worry that premium offers and high-powered advertising appeals presented through the mouths of lovable animated characters will overwhelm children's defences.

Other problems arise when the marketing of adult products spills over into the children's segment – intentionally or unintentionally. For example, US lingerie retailer Victoria's Secret targets its highly successful Pink line of young, hip and sexy clothing to young women from 18 to 30 years old. However, critics charge that Pink is now all the rage among girls as young as 11 years old. Responding to Victoria's Secret's designs and marketing messages, children are flocking into stores and buying Pink, with or without parental supervision. More broadly, critics worry that marketers of everything from lingerie and cosmetics to Barbie dolls are directly or indirectly targeting young girls with provocative products, promoting a premature focus on sex and appearance.[23] These concerns extend to the way in which some brands promote themselves to young people – consider the criticisms faced by trendy fashion brand Jack Wills in the UK:

> Fashionable clothing from the Jack Wills brand has become the uniform of the wealthier set in British universities and public schools. The fashion brand describes itself as 'hedonistic' and designed for the young and wealthy consumer with its preppy, rowing-inspired fashion, and sponsorship of polo events for Harrow and Eton schools. Critics believe that the brand has gone too far in using explicitly sexual imagery in its advertising. The company defended partial nudity and suggestive images in its advertising as projecting a positive, fun and flirtatious image. While aimed at 18–20 year olds, its catalogues have developed a reputation among teenagers as young as 13 for their racy imagery. Young fans even launched a Facebook page for the 'Jack Wills Nipple Appreciation Society'. In 2011, the British Advertising Standards Authority ruled that the then-current Jack Wills catalogue advertising broke advertising rules about harm and offence to children and that it should be withdrawn.[24]

With food firms accused of texting confectionery adverts to children, critics accusing companies of damaging young girls by the sexualisation of toys, clothes and cartoons, and 'junk food' firms using the Internet and social media to bypass rules that prevent them from marketing their products to children, some critics feel that more should be done and some have even called for a complete ban on advertising to children.[25]

Cigarette, beer and fast-food marketers have also generated controversy in recent years by their attempts to target inner-city minority consumers. For example, McDonald's and other chains have drawn criticism for pitching their high-fat, salt-laden fare to low-income, urban residents who are much more likely than suburbanites to be heavy consumers. Similarly, big banks and mortgage lenders have been criticised for targeting consumers in poor urban areas with attractive adjustable rate home mortgages that they can't really afford.

The growth of the Internet and other carefully targeted direct media has raised fresh concerns about potential targeting abuses. The Internet allows more precise targeting, letting the makers of questionable products or deceptive advertisers zero in on the most vulnerable audiences. Unscrupulous marketers can now send tailor-made, deceptive messages by e-mail directly to millions of unsuspecting consumers.

Not all attempts to target children, minorities or other special segments draw such criticism. In fact, most provide benefits to targeted consumers. For example, in the US, Pantene markets Relaxed and Natural hair products

Critics worry that marketers are directly or indirectly targeting young girls with provocative products.

Source: Getty Images/Boston Globe

to African American women. Samsung markets the Jitterbug, an easy-to-use phone, directly to seniors who need a simpler mobile phone that is bigger and has a louder speaker (and just makes phone calls). And Colgate makes a large selection of toothbrush shapes and toothpaste flavours for children – from Colgate Smiles toothpaste range to 'Help Dr Rabbit attack the plaque monsters' to Colgate Spiderman and Barbie character electric toothbrushes. Such products help make tooth brushing more fun and get children to brush longer and more often.[26]

Thus, in target marketing, the issue is not really *who* is targeted but rather *how* and for *what*. Controversies arise when marketers attempt to profit at the expense of targeted segments – when they unfairly target vulnerable segments or target them with questionable products or tactics. Socially responsible marketing calls for segmentation and targeting that serve not just the interests of a company but also the interests of those targeted.

AUTHOR COMMENT

At the same time that the company is answering the first simple-sounding question (Which customers will we serve?), the company must be asking the second question (How will we serve them?).

DIFFERENTIATION AND POSITIONING

Beyond deciding which segments of the market it will target, the company must decide on a *value proposition* – how it will create differentiated value for targeted segments and what positions it wants to occupy in those segments. A **product's position** is the way a product is *defined by consumers* on important attributes – the place a product occupies in consumers' minds relative to competing products. Products are made in factories, but brands happen in the minds of consumers.

Daz is positioned as a powerful, all-purpose family detergent; Fairy is positioned as the gentle detergent for fine washables and baby clothes. At Tesco, 'Every Little Helps', while Sainsbury shoppers are urged to 'Try Something New Today', and Asda customers are promised 'Always Low Prices. . . . Always'. In the car market, small Nissans and Hondas are positioned on economy, Mercedes and Lexus on luxury, and Porsche and BMW on performance. And Toyota positions its fuel-efficient, hybrid Prius as a high-tech solution to the energy shortage: 'Harmony between man, nature, and machine.'

Consumers are overloaded with information about products and services. They cannot reevaluate products every time they make a buying decision. To simplify the buying process, consumers organise products, services and companies into categories and 'position' them in their minds. A product's position is the complex set of perceptions, impressions and feelings that consumers have for the product compared with competing products.

Consumers position products with or without the help of marketers. But marketers do not want to leave their products' positions to chance. They must *plan* positions that will give their products the greatest advantage in selected target markets, and they must design marketing mixes to create these planned positions.

Positioning maps

In planning their differentiation and positioning strategies, marketers often prepare *perceptual positioning maps* that show consumer perceptions of their brands versus competing products on important buying dimensions. Figure 7.3 shows a positioning map for the US large luxury sport utility vehicle (SUV) (or four-wheel drive car – 4×4) market.[27] The position of each circle on the map indicates the brand's perceived positioning on two dimensions: price and orientation (luxury versus performance). The size of each circle indicates the brand's relative market share.

Product position—The way the product is defined by consumers on important attributes – the place the product occupies in consumers' minds relative to competing products.

Figure 7.3 Positioning map: large luxury SUVs

Source: Based on data provided by WardsAuto.com and Edmunds.com, 2010.

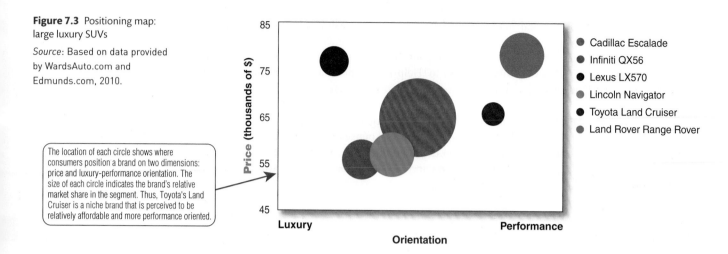

The location of each circle shows where consumers position a brand on two dimensions: price and luxury-performance orientation. The size of each circle indicates the brand's relative market share in the segment. Thus, Toyota's Land Cruiser is a niche brand that is perceived to be relatively affordable and more performance oriented.

Thus, customers view the market-leading Cadillac Escalade as a moderately priced, large, luxury 4×4 with a balance of luxury and performance. The Escalade is positioned on urban luxury, and, in its case, 'performance' probably means power and safety performance. You'll find no mention of off-road adventuring in an Escalade ad.

By contrast, the Range Rover and the Land Cruiser are positioned on luxury with nuances of off-road performance. For example, the Toyota Land Cruiser began in 1951 as a four-wheel drive, Jeep-like vehicle designed to conquer the world's most gruelling terrains and climates. In recent years, the Land Cruiser has retained this adventure and performance positioning but with luxury added. Its website brags of 'legendary off-road capability', with off-road technologies such as downhill assist control and kinetic dynamic suspension systems. 'In some parts of the world, it's an essential.' Despite its ruggedness, however, the company notes that 'its available Bluetooth hands-free technology, DVD entertainment, and a sumptuous interior have softened its edges.'

Choosing a differentiation and positioning strategy

Some firms find it easy to choose a differentiation and positioning strategy. For example, a firm well known for quality in certain segments will go for this position in a new segment if there are enough buyers seeking quality. But in many cases, two or more firms will go after the same position. Then each will have to find other ways to set itself apart. Each firm must differentiate its offer by building a unique bundle of benefits that appeals to a substantial group within the segment.

Above all else, a brand's positioning must serve the needs and preferences of well-defined target markets. For example, although both McDonalds (particularly the new McCafé format) and Starbucks are coffee shops, they offer very different product assortments and store atmospheres. Yet each succeeds because it creates just the right value proposition for its particular mix of customers.

The differentiation and positioning task consists of three steps: identifying a set of differentiating competitive advantages on which to build a position, choosing the right competitive advantages and selecting an overall positioning strategy. A company must then effectively communicate and deliver the chosen position to the market.

Identifying possible value differences and competitive advantages

To build profitable relationships with target customers, marketers must understand customer needs better than competitors do and deliver more customer value. To the extent that a company can differentiate and position itself as providing superior customer value, it gains **competitive advantage**.

But solid positions cannot be built on empty promises. If a company positions its product as *offering* the best quality and service, it must actually differentiate the product so that it *delivers* the promised quality and service. Companies must do much more than simply shout out their positions with slogans and taglines. They must first *live* the slogan. Avis' success in the car rental business is

Competitive advantage—An advantage over competitors gained by offering greater customer value, either by having lower prices or providing more benefits that justify higher prices.

pinned on its 'we try harder' slogan, but this message is deeply embedded in the way the company is run as well as in its advertising.

To find points of differentiation, marketers must think through a customer's entire experience with the company's product or service. An alert company can find ways to differentiate itself at every customer contact point. In what specific ways can a company differentiate itself or its market offer? It can differentiate along the lines of *product, services, channels, people* or *image*.

Through *product differentiation*, brands can be differentiated on features, performance, or style and design. Thus, Bose positions its speakers on their striking design and sound characteristics. Sandwich-maker Subway differentiates itself as the healthy fast-food choice. And Ecover – the biggest seller of 'eco' cleaning and laundry products in the UK – differentiates itself not so much by how its products perform but by the fact that its products are greener. Ecover products offer the eco-consumer the opportunity for 'feel good cleaning'.

Beyond differentiating its physical product, a firm can also differentiate the services that accompany the product. Some companies gain *services differentiation* through speedy, convenient or careful delivery. For example, innovative and unconventional new Metro Bank in the UK opens its branches seven days a week, including some evenings. Others differentiate their service based on high-quality customer care. In an age where customer satisfaction with airline service is in constant decline, Singapore Airlines sets itself apart through extraordinary customer care and the grace of its flight attendants. 'Everyone expects excellence from us,' says the international airline. '[So even] in the smallest details of flight, we rise to each occasion and deliver the Singapore Airlines experience.'[28]

Firms that practise *channel differentiation* gain competitive advantage through the way they design their channel's coverage, expertise and performance. Amazon.com sets itself apart with its smooth-functioning direct channel. Companies can also gain a strong competitive advantage through *people differentiation* – hiring and training better people than their competitors do. In all its global locations, Disney World people are known to be friendly and upbeat. People differentiation requires that a company select its customer-contact people carefully and train them well. For example, Disney trains its theme park people thoroughly to ensure that they are competent, courteous and friendly – from the hotel check-in staff, to the transport drivers, to the ride attendants, to the people who sweep the roads in the parks. Each employee is carefully trained to understand customers and to 'make people happy'.

Even when competing offers look the same, buyers may perceive a difference based on company or brand *image differentiation*. A company or brand image should convey a product's distinctive benefits and positioning. Developing a strong and distinctive image calls for creativity and hard work. A company cannot develop an image in the public's mind overnight by using only a few ads. If the Ritz-Carlton hotel means real quality, this image must be supported by everything the company says and does.

Symbols, such as the McDonald's golden arches, the Nike swoosh or Apple's 'bite mark' logo, can provide strong company or brand recognition and image differentiation. The company might enhance a brand around a famous person, as H&M is doing with its David Beckham underwear range. Some companies even become associated with colours, such as Virgin (red), IBM (blue) or UPS (brown). The chosen symbols, characters and other image elements must be communicated through advertising that conveys the company's or brand's personality.

Choosing the right competitive advantages

Suppose a company is fortunate enough to discover several potential differentiations that provide competitive advantages. It now must choose the ones on which it will build its positioning strategy. It must decide how many differences to promote and which ones.

How many differences to promote

Many marketers think that companies should aggressively promote only one benefit to the target market. Rosser Reeves, an advertising executive, said a company should develop a *unique selling proposition* (USP) for each brand and stick to it. Each brand should pick an attribute and tout itself as 'number one' on that attribute. Buyers tend to remember number one better, especially in this over-communicated society. Thus, Tesco promotes its 'Every Little Helps' message, and across the world Burger King promotes personal choice – 'have it your way'.

Other marketers think that companies should position themselves on more than one differentiator. This may be necessary if two or more firms are claiming to be best on the same attribute. Today, in a time when the mass market is fragmenting into many small segments, companies and brands are trying to broaden their positioning strategies to appeal to more segments. For example, whereas most laundry products marketers offer separate products for cleaning, softening and reducing static cling, Dial Corporation's Purex brand recently introduced a product that offers all three benefits in a single sheet: Purex Complete 3-in-1. 'It's like if bread came sliced, toasted, and pre-buttered', says one ad. Clearly, many buyers want these multiple benefits. The challenge is to convince them that one brand can do it all. However, as companies increase the number of claims for their brands, they risk disbelief and a loss of clear positioning.

Which differences to promote

Not all brand differences are meaningful or worthwhile; not every difference makes a good differentiator. Each difference has the potential to create company costs as well as customer benefits. A difference is worth establishing to the extent that it satisfies the following criteria:

- *Important.* The difference delivers a highly valued benefit to target buyers.
- *Distinctive.* Competitors do not offer the difference, or one company can offer it in a more distinctive way.
- *Superior.* The difference is superior to other ways that customers might obtain the same benefit.
- *Communicable.* The difference is communicable and visible to buyers.
- *Preemptive.* Competitors cannot easily copy the difference.
- *Affordable.* Buyers can afford to pay for the difference.
- *Profitable.* A company can introduce the difference profitably.

Many companies have introduced differentiations that failed one or more of these tests. When the Westin Stamford Hotel in Singapore advertised that it was the world's tallest hotel, it was a distinction that was not important to most tourists; in fact, it turned many off. Polaroid's Polarvision, which produced instantly developed home movies, bombed too. Although Polarvision was distinctive and even preemptive, it was inferior to another way of capturing motion, namely, camcorders.

Thus, choosing competitive advantages on which to position a product or service can be difficult, yet such choices may be crucial to success. Choosing the right differentiators can help a brand stand out from the pack of competitors.

Selecting an overall positioning strategy

Value proposition—The full positioning of a brand – the full mix of benefits on which it is positioned.

The full positioning of a brand is called the brand's **value proposition** – the full mix of benefits on which a brand is differentiated and positioned. It is the answer to the customer's question 'Why should I buy your brand?' Volvo's value proposition hinges on safety but also includes reliability, roominess and styling, all for a price that is higher than average but seems fair for this mix of benefits.

Figure 7.4 shows possible value propositions on which a company might position its products. In the figure, the five green cells represent winning value propositions – differentiation and positioning that gives the company competitive advantage. The red cells, however, represent losing value propositions. The centre yellow cell represents at best a marginal proposition. In the following sections, we discuss the five winning value propositions on which companies can position their products: more for more, more for the same, the same for less, less for much less, and more for less.

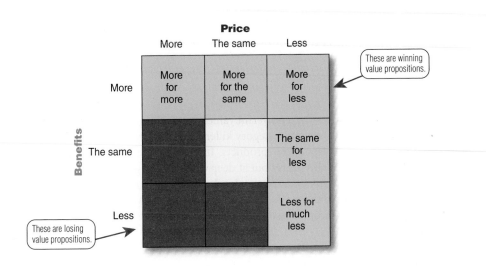

Figure 7.4 Possible value propositions

More for more

'More-for-more' positioning involves providing the most upscale product or service and charging a higher price to cover the higher costs. Rolex watches, Mercedes cars and SubZero appliances – 'A SubZero is a Refrigerator, Just Like a Diamond is a Stone' claims the advertising.[29] Each of these claims superior quality, craftsmanship, durability, performance or style and charges a price to match. Not only is the market offering high quality, but it also gives prestige to the buyer. It symbolises status and a loftier lifestyle. Often, the price difference exceeds the actual increment in quality.

Sellers offering 'only the best' can be found in every product and service category, from hotels, restaurants, food, and fashion to cars and household appliances. Consumers are sometimes surprised, even delighted, when a new competitor enters a category with an unusually high-priced brand. Starbucks coffee entered as a very expensive brand in a commodity category. Dyson's innovative carpet cleaners were priced way above conventional products in this category. When Apple premiered its iPhone, it offered higher-quality features than a traditional mobile phone, with a hefty price tag to match.

In general, companies should be on the lookout for opportunities to introduce a 'more-for-more' brand in any underdeveloped product or service category. Yet 'more-for-more' brands can be vulnerable. They often invite imitators who claim the same quality but at a lower price. For example, Starbucks now faces 'gourmet' coffee competitors ranging from Costa Coffee and Café Nero to McDonald's – McDonald's sells more coffee to consumers away from the home in the UK than any competitor. Also, luxury goods that sell well during good times may be at risk during economic downturns when buyers become more cautious in their spending. The recent gloomy economy hit premium brands, such as Starbucks, the hardest.

> Sellers offering 'only the best' can be found in every product and service category. Dyson's innovative carpet cleaners were priced way above conventional products in this category.
>
> *Source*: Rex features/Geoff Wilkinson

More for the same

Companies can attack a competitor's more-for-more positioning by introducing a brand offering comparable quality at a lower price. For example, Toyota introduced its Lexus line in the United States with a 'more-for-the-same' value proposition versus Mercedes and BMW. Its first headline read: 'Perhaps the first time in history that trading a $72,000 car for a $36,000 car could be considered trading up.' It communicated the high quality of its new Lexus through rave reviews in car magazines and a widely distributed videotape showing side-by-side comparisons of Lexus and Mercedes models. It published surveys showing that Lexus dealers were providing customers with better sales and service experiences than were Mercedes dealerships. Many Mercedes owners switched to Lexus, and the Lexus repurchase rate has been 60 per cent, twice the industry average.

The same for less

Offering 'the same for less' can be a powerful value proposition – everyone likes a good deal. Discount stores such as Poundshop and 'category killers' such as Toys R Us use this positioning. They don't claim to offer different or better products. Instead, they offer many of the same brands as department stores and speciality stores but at deep discounts based on superior purchasing power and lower-cost operations. Other companies develop imitative but lower-priced brands in an effort to lure customers away from the market leader. For example, AMD makes less-expensive versions of Intel's market-leading microprocessor chips.

Less for much less

A market almost always exists for products that offer less and therefore cost less. Few people need, want or can afford 'the very best' in everything they buy. In many cases, consumers will gladly settle for less than optimal performance or give up some of the bells and whistles in exchange for a lower price. For example, many travellers seeking overnight accommodation prefer not to pay for what they consider unnecessary extras, such as a swimming pool, an attached restaurant, or mints on the pillow. Hotel chains such as Premier Inn, Formula 1, Travelodge and Days Inn forgo some of these amenities and accordingly charge less.

'Less-for-much-less' positioning involves meeting consumers' lower performance or quality requirements at a much lower price. For example, retailers Poundland and Poundshop offer more affordable goods at very low prices. Costco membership warehouses offer less merchandise selection and consistency and much lower levels of service; as a result, they charge rock-bottom prices. Successful budget airlines easyJet and Ryanair also practise less-for-much-less positioning, based on the Southwest Airlines model from the US:

> From the start, Southwest Airlines has positioned itself firmly as *the* no-frills, low-price airline. Southwest's passengers have learned to fly without the amenities. For example, the airline provides no meals – just pretzels. It offers no first-class section, only three-across seating in all of its planes. And there's no such thing as a reserved seat on a Southwest flight. Why, then, do so many passengers love Southwest? Perhaps most importantly, Southwest excels at the basics of getting passengers where they want to go on time and with their luggage. Beyond the basics, however, Southwest offers low prices, with no extra charges for checked baggage, aisle seats or other services. No frills and low prices, however, don't mean drudgery. Southwest's cheerful employees go out of their way to amuse, surprise or somehow entertain passengers. One analyst sums up Southwest's less-for-much-less positioning this way: 'It is not luxurious, but it's cheap and it's fun.'

More for less

Of course, the winning value proposition would be to offer 'more for less'. Many companies claim to do this. And, in the short run, some companies can actually achieve such lofty positions. Yet in the long run, companies will find it very difficult to sustain such best-of-both positioning. Offering more usually costs more, making it difficult to deliver on the 'for-less' promise. Companies that try to deliver both may lose out to more focused competitors.

All said, each brand must adopt a positioning strategy designed to serve the needs and wants of its target markets. 'More for more' will draw one target market, 'less for much less' will draw another, and so on. Thus, in any market, there is usually room for many different companies, each successfully occupying different positions. The important thing is that each company must develop its own winning positioning strategy, one that makes it special to its target consumers.

Developing a positioning statement

Company and brand positioning should be summed up in a **positioning statement**. The statement should follow the form: To (target segment and need) our (brand) is (concept) that (point of difference).[30] Here is an example: 'To busy, mobile professionals who need to always be in the loop, the BlackBerry is a wireless connectivity solution that gives you an easier, more reliable way to stay connected to data, people and resources while on the go.'

Note that the positioning statement first states the product's membership in a category (wireless connectivity solution) and then shows its point of difference from other members of the category (easier, more reliable connections to data, people and resources). Placing a brand in a specific category suggests similarities that it might share with other products in the category. But the case for the brand's superiority is made on its points of difference.

Sometimes marketers put a brand in a surprisingly different category before indicating the points of difference. For example, when Nissan introduced its smallish, funky looking city car – the Cube– in the United States, it looked for a way to differentiate the brand in a market already crammed full of small-car models. So Nissan positioned the Cube not as a small *car* but as a personal *mobile device* – something that enhances young target customers' individual, mobile, connected lifestyles. Already hugely popular in Japan, the Nissan Cube was introduced in the United States as a device designed 'to bring young people together – like every mobile device they have'. It is 'a part of a fun, busy life that can be . . . personalized as easily as a cell phone ring or a Web page.' Such out-of-category positioning helps make the Cube distinctive.[31]

Communicating and delivering the chosen position

Once it has chosen a position, the company must take strong steps to deliver and communicate the desired position to its target consumers. All the company's marketing mix efforts must support the positioning strategy.

Positioning the company calls for concrete action, not just talk. If the company decides to build a position on better quality and service, it must first *deliver* that position. Designing the marketing mix – product, price, place and promotion – involves working out the tactical details of the positioning strategy. Thus, a firm that seizes on a more-for-more position knows that it must produce high-quality products, charge a high price, distribute through high-quality dealers and advertise in high-quality media. It must hire and train more service people, find retailers who have a good reputation for service, and develop sales and advertising messages that broadcast its superior service. This is the only way to build a consistent and believable more-for-more position.

Companies often find it easier to come up with a good positioning strategy than to implement it. Establishing a position or changing one usually takes a long time. In contrast, positions that have taken years to build can quickly be lost. Once a company has built the desired position, it must take care to maintain the position through consistent performance and communication. It must closely monitor and adapt the position over time to match changes in consumer needs and competitors' strategies. However, the company should avoid abrupt changes that might confuse consumers. Instead, a product's position should evolve gradually as it adapts to the ever-changing marketing environment.

Positioning statement—A statement that summarises company or brand positioning. It takes this form: *To (target segment and needs) our (brand) is (concept) that (point of difference).*

N

REVIEWING OBJECTIVES AND KEY TERMS

In this chapter, you learned about the major elements of a customer-driven marketing strategy: segmentation, targeting, differentiation and positioning. Marketers know that they cannot appeal to all buyers in their markets or at least not to all buyers in the same way. Therefore, most companies today practice *target marketing* – identifying market segments, selecting one or more of them, and developing products and marketing mixes tailored to each.

OBJECTIVE 1 Define the major steps in designing a customer-driven marketing strategy: market segmentation, targeting, differentiation and positioning (pp. 203–204).

A customer-driven marketing strategy begins with selecting which customers to serve and determining a value proposition that best serves the targeted customers. It consists of four steps. *Market segmentation* is the act of dividing a market into distinct segments of buyers with different needs, characteristics or behaviours who might require separate products or marketing mixes. Once the groups have been identified, *market targeting* evaluates each market segment's attractiveness and selects one or more segments to serve. Market targeting consists of designing strategies to build the *right relationships* with the *right customers*. *Differentiation* involves actually differentiating the market offering to create superior customer value. *Positioning* consists of positioning the market offering in the minds of target customers.

OBJECTIVE 2 List and discuss the major bases for segmenting consumer and business markets (pp. 204–213).

There is no single way to segment a market. Therefore, the marketer tries different variables to see which give the best segmentation opportunities. For consumer marketing, the major segmentation variables are geographic, demographic, psychographic and behavioural. In *geographic segmentation*, the market is divided into different geographical units, such as nations, regions, states, counties, cities or even neighbourhoods. In *demographic segmentation*, the market is divided into groups based on demographic variables, including age, gender, family size, family life cycle, income, occupation, education, religion, ethnicity, generation and nationality. In *psychographic segmentation*, the market is divided into different groups based on social class, lifestyle, or personality characteristics. In *behavioural segmentation*, the market is divided into groups based on consumers' knowledge, attitudes, uses, or responses to a product.

Business marketers use many of the same variables to segment their markets. But business markets also can be segmented by business *demographics* (industry, company size), *operating char-*

acteristics, *purchasing approaches*, *situational factors* and *personal characteristics*. The effectiveness of the segmentation analysis depends on finding segments that are *measurable*, *accessible*, *substantial*, *differentiable* and *actionable*.

OBJECTIVE 3 Explain how companies identify attractive market segments and choose a market-targeting strategy (pp. 214–221).

To target the best market segments, the company first evaluates each segment's size and growth characteristics, structural attractiveness and compatibility with company objectives and resources. It then chooses one of four market-targeting strategies–ranging from very broad to very narrow targeting. A seller can ignore segment differences and target broadly using *undifferentiated (or mass) marketing*. This involves mass producing, mass distributing and mass promoting the same product in the same way to all consumers. Or a seller can adopt *differentiated marketing* – developing different market offers for several segments. *Concentrated marketing* (or *niche marketing*) involves focusing on one or a few market segments only. Finally, *micromarketing* is the practice of tailoring products and marketing programmes to suit the tastes of specific individuals and locations. Micromarketing includes *local marketing* and *individual marketing*. Which targeting strategy is best depends on company resources, product variability, the PLC stage, market variability and competitive marketing strategies.

OBJECTIVE 4 Discuss how companies differentiate and position their products for maximum competitive advantage (pp. 221–227).

Once a company has decided which segments to enter, it must decide on its *differentiation and positioning strategy*. The differentiation and positioning task consists of three steps: identifying a set of possible differentiations that create competitive advantage, choosing advantages on which to build a position, and selecting an overall positioning strategy.

A brand's full positioning is called its *value proposition* – the full mix of benefits on which a brand is positioned. In general, companies can choose from one of five winning value propositions on which to position their products: more for more, more for the same, the same for less, less for much less, or more for less. Company and brand positioning are summarised in positioning statements that state the target segment and need, the positioning concept, and specific points of difference. The company must then effectively communicate and deliver the chosen position to the market.

NAVIGATING THE KEY TERMS

DISCUSSING AND APPLYING THE CONCEPTS

Discussing the concepts

1. Briefly describe the four major steps in designing a customer-driven marketing strategy. (AACSB: Communication)

2. Name and describe the four major sets of variables that might be used in segmenting consumer markets. Which segmenting variables does Starbucks use? (AACSB: Communication; Reflective Thinking)

3. Discuss the factors marketers consider when choosing a targeting strategy. (AACSB: Communication)

4. Explain how micromarketing differs from differentiated and concentrated marketing and discuss the two types of micromarketing. (AACSB: Communication)

5. Explain how a company differentiates its product from competitors' products. (AACSB: Communication)

6. Name and define the five winning value propositions described in the chapter. Which value proposition describes Tesco? John Lewis? Explain your answers. (AACSB: Communication; Reflective Thinking)

Applying the concepts

1. In a small group, visit a grocery store and examine the brands of breakfast cereal. Using the bases for segmenting consumer markets, identity the segmentation variables a specific brand appears to be using. Summarise the segmentation and targeting strategy for each brand. Identify brands with similar positioning strategies. (AACSB: Communication; Reflective Thinking)

2. Assume you work at a college whose traditional target market, school-leavers within your region, is shrinking. This segment is projected to decrease over the next ten years. Recommend other potential market segments and discuss the criteria you should consider to ensure that the identified segments are useful. (AACSB: Communication; Reflective Thinking)

3. Form a small group and create an idea for a new business. Using the steps described in the chapter, develop a customer-driven marketing strategy. Describe your strategy and conclude with a positioning statement for your business. (AACSB: Communication; Reflective Thinking)

Focus on technology

Most companies want customers to be *heavy* users of its products or *services*. When it comes to the Internet and wireless broadband *services, however*, that's not necessarily the case. Internet providers, such as Comcast, may block or slow down Internet traffic for some *heavy* users, such as those who watch a lot of videos on YouTube. In 2009, Comcast was banned from blocking video file sharing; this ban was overturned in 2010 by a court ruling that the government does not *have* authority to enforce its 'network neutrality' rules. Google, once a champion for unfettered Internet access for all, is changing its tune now that it can profit from favouring some customers *over* others in the burgeoning wireless broadband arena. Google and Verizon *have* teamed up to lobby for laws that allow them to *favour* some Web *services over* others.

1. Research the concept of net neutrality and write a report on the pros and cons of this principle from the viewpoint of businesses providing Internet and wireless broadband services. (AACSB: Communication; Reflective Thinking)

2. What effect does *very heavy* usage by some customers *have* on other customers of broadband *services?* What are marketers of these *services* doing to counter the effect of *heavy users*? (AACSB: Communication; Reflective Thinking)

Focus an ethics

The obesity rate among children is massive compared to what it was 30 years ago. Who's to blame? One study reported that 76 per cent of parents thought food advertising is a major contributor to childhood obesity but also found that *over* 80 per cent blamed parents, not marketers. Yet, regulators are homing their sights on marketers. Reminiscent of the 1970s. Although most regulations regarding marketing to children are limited to children ages 12 and younger, the current US guidelines include children up to 17 years old and propose restrictions on food marketing targeted to children. With €1.25 billion spent on food marketing and promotions targeted to children – €581 million of that on television in the US – more than just marketers will be affected by marketing restrictions to this market segment.

1. Are marketers to blame for increasing obesity rates among children? Should the regulators in different countries ban the advertising of food products to children aged 17 and younger? Discuss the consequences of imposing such a ban. (AACSB: Communication; Ethical Reasoning)

2. What action *have* food marketers taken to stem the threat of a ban on marketing to children? (AACSB: Communication; Reflective Thinking)

Marketing & the economy

Vanilla Bikes

In the United States, Vanilla Bicycles sells hand-built bikes with price tags ranging from €3,120 to €9,360. But last year, after only nine years in business, owner Sacha White stopped taking orders - not because business had dried up but because he had

a five-year waiting list. White and his crew of three make only 40 to 50 bikes each year. Frames are made from exotic metals, are welded with silver alloy, and weigh as little as 30 ounces. No two Vanilla bikes are the same. Each is custom fitted to the client and features intricate metal carvings and an artisan paint job. Amazingly, almost all of these high-end bicycles are sold to middle-class customers. Still, orders did not ebb during the recent economic downturn. In fact, Vanilla could have ramped up production significantly during the heart of the recession and still sold everything it made. However, White claims that ramping up would compromise the special nature of what customers consider works of art. Vanilla bikes are so special that when Portland bike couriers describe something as cool, they routinely say. 'That's, soooo Vanilla'.

1. Based on the segmentation variables discussed in the chapter construct a profile for Vanilla Bicycles' probable target market.

2. Given that most luxury products suffer in an economic downturn, why has Vanilla still succeeded?

Marketing by the numbers

When you think of hybrid or electric automobiles, you probably think don't think of the sports car. But the Fisker Karma is about to shatter that stereotype. It's been called the hybrid with sex appeal and is often compared to a Mercedes-Benz roadster. In the increasingly crowded field of new-generation electric vehicles, Fisker Automotive wants to *carve out* a niche as a high-performance eco-car with lots of style. The Fisker Karma goes from 0 to 60 miles per hour in six seconds, can go up to 125 miles per hour, and can *travel* 50 miles on electric power and 300 miles on combined electric and gasoline power. All this performance and style does not come cheap: prices range from €68,500 to €82,000 before bringing it to market. However the company needs to identify its target market and estimate the market potential in this segment.

1. Identify an appropriate market segment for this product. Discuss variables the company should consider when estimating the potential number of buyers for the high-performance Fisker Karma sports car. (AACSB: Communication; Reflective Thinking)

2. Using the chain ratio method described in Appendix 2, estimate the market potential for the Fisker Karma sports car. Search the Internet for reasonable numbers to represent the factors you identified in the previous question. Assume each buyer will purchase only one automobile and that the average price of automobiles in this market is €78,000. (AACSB: Communication; Use of IT; Analytical Reasoning)

REFERENCES

1 Sources: Claer Barrett, 'Fast fashion for fast consumers', *Financial Times*, (22 February 2011), p. 14; Mark Wembridge and Claer Bennett, 'Asos boosted by international websites', *Financial Times* (14 April 2011), p. 22.

2 Richard Fletcher, 'Tesco's success puts clubcard firm on the map', *Sunday Times* (19 September 2004), S3, p. 7; Jonathan Birchall, 'Customised shops are bringing in the customers', *Financial Times* (31 October 2005), p. 10.

3 Elaine Wong, 'P&G, Dial, Unilever target the middle man', *Brandweek* (18 May 2009), p. 8; and www.niveaformen.com, accessed March 2010.

4 Adapted from information found in Elizabeth A. Sullivan, 'H.O.G: Harley-Davidson shows brand strength as it navigates down new roads–and picks up more female riders along the way' *Marketing News* (1 November 2008), p. 8: 'Harley-Davidson hosts special rides to kick off women riders month', *PR Newswire* (23 March 2009); 'Women riders to rev for a cure at Daytona bike week', *PRNewswire* (5 February 2010), and www.harley-davidson.com/wcm/Content/Pages/women_riders/landing.jsp, accessed October 2010.

5 Bob Sherwood, 'Upmarket shops hunt "platinum pound"', *Financial Times* (22 June 2007), p. 3.

6 Vanessa Friedman, 'Coutts responds to rise of affluent women', *Financial Times* (14/15 July 2007), p. 16.

7 John Waggoner, 'Even the wealthy feel tapped out', *USA Today* (2 February 2009), p. B1; and Piet Levy, 'How to reach the new consumer', *Marketing News* (28 February 2010), pp. 16–20.

8 Elizabeth Olson, 'Car sharing reinvents the company wheels', *New York Times* (7 May 2009), p. F2.

9 Information from www.rssc.com, and http://nationofwhynot.com, accessed September 2010.

10 Andrew Ward, 'Retailer still strong on the home front', *Financial Times* (14 January 2011), p. 19; Sean Poulter, 'This flatpack nation', *Daily Mail* (7 October 2010), p. 25.

11 Blair Chancey, 'King, meet the world', *QSR Magazine* (February 2009), www.qsrmagazine.com/articles/interview/112/shaufelberger-3.phtml; and Julie Jargon, "As sales drop, Burger King draws critics for courting 'Super Fans', *Wall Street Journal* (1 February 2010), p. B1.

12 See www.caci.co.uk, accessed 5 February 2012.

13 Information from www201.americanexpress.com/business-credit-cards/home?us_nu=subtab&intlink=opennav_main, accessed August 2010; and www.americanexpress.com/uk/smallbusiness/cards/sb_default_body.shtml?uk_nu=global, accessed 5 February 2012.

14 See Michael Porter, *Competitive Advantage* (New York: Free Press, 1985), pp. 4–8, 234–236. For more recent discussions, see Stanley Slater and Eric Olson, 'A fresh look at industry and market analysis', *Business Horizons* (January-February 2002), pp. 15–22; Kenneth Sawka and Bill Fiora, 'The four analytical techniques every analyst must know: 2. Porter's five forces analysis', *Competitive Intelligence Magazine* (May–June 2003), p. 57; and Philip Kotler and Kevin Lane Keller, *Marketing Management*, 13th edn. (Upper Saddle River, NJ: Prentice Hall, 2008) pp. 342–343.

15 See Suzanne Kapner, 'How fashion's VF supercharges its brands', *Fortune* (14 April 2008), pp. 108–110; and www.vfc.com, accessed October 2010.

16 Store information found at www.wholefoodsmarket.com, accessed February 2010.

17 See Gerry Khermouch, 'Call it the Pepsi blue generation', *BusinessWeek* (3 February 2003), p. 96; Valerie Bauerlein, 'Soda-pop sales fall at faster rate', *Wall Street Journal* (31 March 2009), p. B7; and D. Gail Fleenor, 'Energetic sales?', *Progressive Grocer* (November/December 2009), pp. 80, 82.

18 Tim Bradshaw, 'Moonpig bought by Photobox for £129 m', *Financial Times* (25 July 2011). See also www.moonpig.com, accessed 6 February 2011.

19 See Darell K. Rigby and Vijay Vishwanath, 'Localization: the revolution in consumer markets', *Harvard Business Review* (April 2006), pp. 82–92. Also see Cecilie Rohwedder, 'Decoding needs and wants of shoppers', *Wall Street Journal* (24–28 December 2007), p. 4.

20 Adapted from Claire Cain Miller, 'Take a step closer for an invitation to shop', *New York Times* (23 February 2010), www.nytimes.com.

21 Jonathan Birchall, 'Codes Open New Front in Retail Wars', *Financial Times* (18 May 2010), p. 23.

22 Adapted from information found in 'When you watch these ads, the ads check you out', *New York Times* (31 January 2009), www.nytimes.com; Leonard Goh, 'Soon, billboards that know male from female' (17 June 2009), http://news.cnet.com/8301-17938_105-10266755-1.html; and www.tru-media.com, accessed March 2010.

23 Adapted from portions of Fae Goodman, 'Lingerie is luscious and lovely', *Chicago Sun-Times* (19 February 2006), p. B2; and Stacy Weiner, 'Goodbye to Girlhood', *Washington Post* (20 February 2007), p. HE01. Also see Suzanne C. Ryan and Betsy Cummings, 'Tickled pink', *Brandweek* (8 September 2008), pp. MO26-MO28; and India Knight, 'Relax: girls will be girls', *Sunday Times* (London) (21 February 2010), p. 4.

24 Sean Poulter, 'how one of Britain's trendiest brands is selling clothes to your children', *Daily Mail* (5 April 2011), p. 13.

25 Lois Rogers and Jonathan Carr-Brown, 'Food firms text sweet Ads to children', *Sunday Times* (30 May 2004), S1, p. 5; Fiona MacRae and Neil Sears, 'Sexy marketing that corrupts young lives', *Daily Mail* (21 February 2007), p. 22.

26 See www.colgate.co.uk/app/Colgate/UK/OralCare/ProductRecommender/KidsProducts.cvsp, accessed 6 February 2012.

27 SUV sales data furnished by www.WardsAuto.com, accessed March 2010. Price data from www.edmunds.com, accessed March 2010.

28 Quote from 'Singapore Airlines: company information', accessed at www.singaporeair.com, April 2010.

29 See www.westye.co.uk, accessed 7 February 2012.

30 See Bobby J. Calder and Steven J. Reagan, 'Brand Design', in Dawn Iacobucci (ed.) *Kellogg on Marketing* (New York: John Wiley & Sons, 2001), p. 61. For more discussion, see Kotler and Keller, *Marketing Management*, 13th edn, pp. 315–316.

31 See Stuart Elliott, 'With the car industry in trouble, Nissan rolls out the mobile device', *New York Times* (6 April 2009), www.nytimes.com; Dan Neil, 'Nissan's Cube is coolness in a box', *Los Angeles Times* (6 March 2009), p. 1; and www.nissanusa.com/cube, accessed November 2010.

VIDEO CASE

Meredith MyMarketingLab

The Meredith Corporation has developed an expertise in building customer relationships through segmentation, targeting and positioning. Amazingly, however, it has done this by focusing on only half of the population – the female half. Meredith has developed the largest database of any US media company and uses that database to meet the specific needs and desires of women.

Meredith is known for leading titles such as *Better Homes and Gardens*, *Family Circle* and *Ladies' Home Journal*. But that list has grown to a portfolio of 14 magazines and more than 200 special interest publications. Through these magazines alone, Meredith regularly reaches about 30 million readers. By focusing on core categories of home, family, and personal development, Meredith has developed a product mix designed to meet various needs of women. This creates multiple touch points as individual women engage with more than one magazine, as well as with speciality books and websites.

After watching the video featuring Meredith, answer the following questions about segmenting, targeting and positioning:

1. On what main variables has Meredith focused in segmenting its markets?
2. Which target marketing strategy best describes Meredith's efforts? Support your choice.
3. How does Meredith use its variety of products to build relationships with the right customers?

COMPANY CASE

Starbucks: just who is the Starbucks customer?

By now, you should be familiar with the Starbucks story. After a trip to Italy in the early 1980s, Howard Schultz was inspired to transform Starbucks — then just a handful of coffee shops in Seattle — into a chain of European-style coffeehouses. His vision wasn't based on selling only gourmet coffees, espressos, and latters, however. He wanted to provide customers with what he called a 'third place' — a place away from home and work. As CEO of Starbucks, Schultz developed what became known as the *Starbucks Experience*, built around great coffee, personal service, and an inviting ambiance.

WHAT GOES UP . . .

It wasn't long before Starbucks became a household word—a powerhouse premium brand in a category that previously consisted of only cheaper commodity products. In 20 years time, Schultz grew the company to almost 17,000 stores in dozens of countries. From 1995 to 2005, Starbucks added U.S. stores at an annual rate of 27 per cent, far faster than the 17 per cent annual growth of McDonald's in its heyday. At one point, Starbucks opened over 3,300 locations in a single year—an average of 9 per day. In one stretch of crowded Manhattan, a person could get their caffeine fix at any of five Starbucks outlets in less than a block and a half. In fact, cramming so many stores so close together caused one satirical publication to run this headline: 'A New Starbucks Opens in the Restroom of Existing Starbucks.'

For many years, new store growth was what kept Starbucks percolating. As it grew, company sales and profits rose like steam from a mug of hot java. Growth routinely averaged 20 per cent or more each year. And Starbucks made investors happy with a 25 per cent annual increase in the value of its stock for more than a decade. Schultz confidently predicted that there was no end in sight for the Starbucks boom. Just a few years ago, he announced his intentions to open 10,000 new stores in just four years and then push Starbucks to 40,000 stores.

But not long after Schultz shocked Wall Street and the industry with his projections, Starbucks' steam engine of growth started to slow. Then it started running in reverse. By the end of 2008, the 20 per cent annual growth had dropped to 10 per cent, with existing-store sales *decreasing* by 3 per cent. Total company profits dropped by a scalding by 53 per cent for the year. And for a second year in a row, Starbucks' stock value dropped by 50 per cent to around $10 a share.

The weakened economy certainly played a role. But for years, many industry observers had worried that the company was growing too fast. Revenue and traffic at Starbucks began slowing more than a year before anyone uttered the word recession. In a sign of recognising a problem, Schultz cut back on the number of new store openings. Then he did what had previously seemed unthinkable. In 2008, he announced store closures—first 600, then 300 more. in fact, as Starbucks trimmed its 2009 forecast for new store openings to 310, it projected a decrease in its number of outlets for the first time ever.

THE EVOLUTION OF THE STARBUCKS CUSTOMER

There was no shortage of armchair CEOs willing to give their opinions as to what had gone wrong that led to Starbucks' fall from perpetual growth. One issue often mentioned was that Starbucks had developed an identity crisis with respect to its target customer. In its early years, the Starbucks customer profile was clearly defined. The typical customer was wealthier, better educated, and more professional than the average American. The customer was far more likely to be female than male, predominately Caucasian, and between the ages of 24 and 44. It was this customer who fell in love with the *Starbucks Experience*. She was very loyal, often visiting a store every day or even more than once a day. She loved the fact that the barista greeted her by name when she came in and chatted with her while making her custom coffee drink, not caring if it took a while. She lounged on the comfy furniture, enjoying the perfect mix of music that always seemed to fit her mood. She met friends or just hung out by herself reading a good book.

But the more Starbucks grew, the more the *Starbucks Experience* began to change. With more stores, the place wasn't quite so special. As each location filled with more customers, baristas had more names to put with faces. as the menu expanded with more options, the number of combinations for coffee drinks grew into the hundreds, leaving baristas less time to chat with customers. As the atmosphere in each store turned to 'hustle and bustle,' it became a less attractive place to hang out.

With all these changes, Starbucks progressively appealed less to the traditional customer and more to a new customer. This customer shift was inevitable; there simply were not enough traditional customers around to fuel the kind of growth that Schultz sought. The new breed of customer was less affluent, less educated, and less professional. Not only was Starbucks drawing in different customers in places where stores already existed, but it was also putting stores in different neighbourhoods, cities, and countries.

As the customer profile evolved, the *Starbucks Experience* grew to mean something different. To the new breed of customer, it meant good coffee on the run. It was a place to meet and then move on. The more accessible Starbucks was, the better. Speed of service was more important than a barista who wanted to talk current events. This new customer came in much less frequently than the traditional customer, as seldom as once a month. As a sign of just how much this shift in customer was affecting its business, by 2007, 80 per cent of all Starbucks coffee purchased was consumed outside the store.

SOUL SEARCHING

When Starbucks' growth first started tapering off, the executives took notice. In a now famous memo to management, Schultz lamented that 'in order to achieve the growth, development, and scale necessary to go from less than 1,000 stores to 15,000 stores and beyond, Starbucks had made decisions that may have led to the watering down of the Starbucks experience. Stores no longer have the soul of the past and reflect a chain of stores versus the warm feeling of a neighborhood store.'

Starbucks management believed that efforts to recapture that soul would get the company back on track. At first, however, Starbucks was caught between the conflicting goals of reestablishing its image as the provider of a holistic experi-ence and offering better value to the cash-strapped consumer. Starbucks set out to put some water on the fire and get some of its customers back. It added labour hours and time–saving auto-mated machines to stores. It focused on the quality of its coffee with a Coffee Master training programme for its baristas and a new line of ultrapremium whole–bean coffees. It even tried free Wi-Fi service and sold its own music.

But none of these actions seemed to address the core problem: Although Starbucks still charged a premium price, it was no longer a special place. As the recession tightened its grip and more people cut back on discretionary purchases, the problem grew worse. Compounding the problem was an increase in competition. For years, if you wanted a latte, Starbucks was about the only option. Not only were Dunkin' Donuts and McDonald's selling premium coffee drinks to the masses, but just about every mini–mart in the country boasted about the quality of its coffee. All of these competitors had prices considerably lower than those of Starbucks, which made the most well known coffee bar much less justifiable to the 'grab and go' crowd. As much as Schultz denied being in direct competition with the lower–status coffee pourers, many critics seemed to be thinking the same thing: Starbucks had shifted from a warm and intimate coffeehouse to little more than a filling station, battling fast-food outlets for some of the same customer dollars.

'VALUE' TO THE RESCUE?

Throughout 2009, Schultz continued to direct activities aimed at increasing growth. Starbucks launched a campaign designed to educate consumers that Starbucks really wasn't as expensive as they thought it was. That was followed by something Schultz held back for as long as possible: price reductions. 'Breakfast pairings'—coffee cake, Oatmeal, and an egg sandwich—soon followed.

All these tactics helped. By the end of 2009, Starbucks was regaining ground. With same-store sales up 4 per cent and profits up 24 per cent for the year, Starbucks' stock price doubled versus the previous year. But Schultz made it clear that he was just getting started. 'What a difference a year makes. We're going to radically reframe Starbucks growth strategy.' He outlined a three-pronged growth strategy to illustrate that Starbucks might have a grip on defining segments of coffee customers after all. In searching for Starbucks' roots and re-creating the Starbucks' store experience, Schultz also aimed to reach customers outside the store.

The first prong of the new strategy centres on Via, an instant coffee that Starbucks introduced last year. It is available in single-serve packets at all Starbucks' stores and in grocery stores at $1 each or $9.95 for 12 packs. Via lets Starbucks promote a genuine cup of Starbucks coffee for under a buck. Promotions for the new instant have made it clear that Starbucks isn't moving downscale; instant coffee is moving upscale. At a New York taste testing, Schultz told a group of analysts, journalists, and retailers that he was ready for the critics who say, 'This is desperate, this is a Hail Mary pass, this is off-brand for Starbucks. We are going to reinvent the category. This is not your mother's instant coffee.'

Via is off to a good start, having surpassed company expecta-tions. In fact, Via accounted for more than half of the 4 per cent increase in Starbucks' 2009 same-store sales. According to Annie Young-Scrivner, global chief marketing officer for Starbucks, half of all Via serving occasions are at home, 25 percent are in the office, and 25 per cent are 'on the go.' Many Via customers aren't just out for a cheap coffee. (You can mix up a cup of Folger's for about 25 cents.) They are people who want premium coffee but are in situations where they don't have access to a store or brewing their own. An ad campaign supporting Via is the first concerted advertising push aimed at grocery customers, who are now accessible through 37,000 retail locations.

The second prong of Starbucks' strategy also focuses on the grocery business but through ground-flavoured coffees. According to NPD Group, four out of five cups of coffee are consumed at home. Starbucks a has very small share of that market. Via will certainly help. But aiming more directly at the 'brew it at home' customer, Starbucks is partnering with Kraft to launch flavoured coffees you can brew yourself. Sixty per cent of bagged coffee buyers are either drinking flavoured coffee or adding flavoured creamer. Seventy-five per cent of those customers said they would buy a flavoured product at the grocery store if Starbucks made one. So after more than two years of testing, this substan-tial segment of grocery-store buying customers can now get Starbucks Natural Fusions in vanilla, caramel and cinnamon.

The third prong of Starbucks strategy is its ace in the hole–Seattle's Best Coffee. Starbucks purchased the brand back in 2003 but is just now doing something with it. Rebranding efforts have given Seattle's Best a new look and tagline. 'Great Coffee Everywhere.' As With Via and Natural Fusions, and now with Seattle's Best, Starbucks is going after customers who don't normally buy Starbucks' coffee. It is placing Seattle's Best where Starbucks' customers aren't—in vending machines, coffee carts, fast-food restaurants (Burger King and Subway, among others), theatres, and convenience stores. These are places that Starbucks has avoided for fear of eroding its upscale image. With prices ranging from $1 to just over $2, Seattle's Best also reaches customers who perceive Starbucks as too expensive. Gap has Old Navy, BMW has Mini. Now, Seattle's Best allows Starbucks to go head-to-head with competitors like McDonald's without putting the Starbucks name in the same sentence as downscale competitors.

Michelle Gass, Seattle's Best president, clearly defines the difference versus Starbucks: 'Starbucks is a destination coffee experience and an active choice made by the customer. Seattle's Best will instead be brought to the consumer when they make other retail choices.' Gass is going to make sure that she has as many of those other retail choices covered as possible. She is taking the brand from 3,000 points of distribution in 2009 to more than 30,000 by the end of 2010.

The three-pronged strategy provides three good reasons to believe that Starbucks' growth story will return, even without opening nine stores per day. As icing on the coffee cake, only one-fifth of Starbucks' sales come from outside the United States. The company sees huge potential growth abroad. But perhaps the greatest strength in Starbucks' new strategy is that it will allow the company to go after new customer segments while also restoring the essence of the *Starbucks Experience*.

Questions for discussion

1. Using the full spectrum of segmentation variables, describe how Starbucks initially segmented and targeted the coffee market.
2. What changed first – the Starbucks customer or the *Starbucks Experience*? Explain your response by discussing the principles of market targeting.
3. Based on the segmentation variables, how is Starbucks now segmenting and targeting the coffee market?
4. Will Starbucks ever return to the revenue and profit growth that it once enjoyed? Why or why not?

Sources: Beth Kowitt, 'Can Starbucks Still Be Seattle's Best If it Grows By Hyping Seattle's Best?' *Fortune*, 25 May 2010 accessed at http://money.cnn.com/2010/05/25/news/companies/starbucks_seattles_best.fortune/index. htm; Emily Bryson York, 'Why You Are Not Drinking Nearly Enough Starbucks', *Advertising Age*, 17 May 2010, p. 1; Dan Mitchell, 'Starbucks Faces Existential Crisis in Downturn', *Washington Post*, 22 March 2009, p. G01; Bruce Horovitz, 'Starbucks perks Up with First Dividend', *USA Today*, 25 March 2010, p. 1B.

CHAPTER EIGHT

Products, services and brands: building customer value

Chapter preview

After examining customer-driven marketing strategy, we now take a deeper look at the marketing mix: the tactical tools that marketers use to implement their strategies and deliver superior customer value. In this and the next chapter, we'll study how companies develop and manage products and brands. Then, in the chapters that follow, we'll look at pricing, distribution and marketing communication tools. The product is usually the first and most basic marketing consideration. We start with a seemingly simple question: What *is* a product? As it turns out, the answer is not so simple.

Before starting the meat of this chapter, we start by looking at an interesting brand story. Marketing is all about building brands that connect deeply with customers. So, when you think about top brands, which ones pop up first? Perhaps traditional global megabrands such as Coca-Cola, Nike or McDonald's come to mind. Or maybe a trendy tech brand such as Google or Facebook. But if we asked you about air travel, you'd probably name Boeing and Airbus and numerous airlines before you thought of Rolls-Royce. But when it comes to getting aircraft into the sky and meeting the real needs of airlines and their passengers, Rolls-Royce has an interesting story to tell.

Objective outline

➤ **Objective 1** Define *product* and the major classifications of products and services.
What is a product? (pp. 238–243)

➤ **Objective 2** Describe the decisions companies make regarding their individual products and services, product lines and product mixes.
Product and service decisions (pp. 243–251)

➤ **Objective 3** Identify the four characteristics that affect the marketing of services and the additional marketing

considerations that services require.
Services marketing (pp. 251–256)

➤ **Objective 4** Discuss branding strategy – the decisions companies make in building and managing their brands.
Branding strategy: building strong brands (pp. 256–264)

Rolls-Royce service

Rolls-Royce has a history of more than 100 years as a car maker and a builder of aircraft engines. Nonetheless, the company nearly went under in the 1970s and had to be rescued by the British government, which hived off the car division. Since 2000, Rolls-Royce has worked its way up from being a small player to number two in the market for commercial airliner engines. Along with General Electric, Rolls-Royce has been selected by the two big aircraft makers to supply engines for their major new aircraft: the Boeing 787, the Airbus A380 superjumbo and the Airbus A350. Rolls has established strong partnerships with airlines in the US, and includes premier Asian carriers such as Singapore Airlines and Cathay Pacific in its customer list. In 2006, a major coup was winning the first engine order for the Boeing 787 on 50 aircraft for Japan's All Nippon Airways Co.

Driving the growth

At Rolls-Royce PLC in Derby, England, exists perhaps the world's most sophisticated help-desk. Using live satellite feeds on video screens, Rolls-Royce technicians continuously monitor the health of some 3000 aero-engines for 45 airline customers.

For example, at London Heathrow a British Airways Boeing 777 prepares for take-off. The engines power on and the aircraft lifts off on its way to a cruising altitude of 30,000 feet (9000 m), bound for New York. Back on the ground in a small office at Derby in the East Midlands, the aircraft's engines are being monitored in real-time. If at any time the engine's performance falls outside strict parameters, for example if it starts vibrating too much, it will be picked up by the expert team in Derby, who can pull up the engine's complete history, and if necessary mobilise a maintenance team to meet the aircraft on arrival in New York.

The Operations Room at Derby is a critical part of Rolls-Royce's drive to win a larger share of the engine orders for new generations of Boeing and Airbus aircraft. The key is that airlines do not just want the best aero-engine designs for their aircraft, increasingly they want elaborate service networks that extend for decades after the engine purchase.

Rolls-Royce's long-term strategy under then-CEO Sir John Rose was to expand after-sales service rather than relying solely on sales of new engines (as well as pushing into new markets). By 2009, more than half of Rolls' income was coming from servicing engines – as high as 60 per cent in civil aviation where Rolls had succeeded in persuading airlines to buy outsourcing packages in which Rolls takes over responsibility for looking after engines.

A growing fleet of aircraft throughout the world powered by Rolls-Royce engines means there is a growing market for the service and maintenance business – where estimated margins of 30 per cent are much higher than those for the original engine sales (giant aero-engines may be listed at prices of £10 million or more, but they are often sold at big discounts to win orders). For example, in 1995 Rolls-Royce had about 20,000 aero-engines in use, but that figure has since tripled.

For airlines, maintenance and fuel efficiency is becoming an increasingly important part of the game. Rolls has succeeded in persuading many of its customers to sign up to an arrangement called TotalCare, under which they pay Rolls-Royce a fee for every hour an engine is in flight. In return, Rolls assumes responsibility for the risks and costs of downtime and repairs. In this way the airline knows that Rolls is incentivised to make modifications to improve engine reliability. Rolls maintenance charges are substantially above the industry average. Nonetheless, about three-quarters of Rolls' airline customers have signed up to the TotalCare deal.

By early 2012, Rolls-Royce reported continued increases sales revenue and profits, in spite of tough economic conditions, led by its after-market sales (servicing engines). Growth was being driven by expansion in emerging market sales but also the need for airlines in Europe and the developed world to shift to more efficient engines because of high fuel prices.

The ever-present risk of reputation damage to the brand

The service strategy aligns the interests of the airline and the manufacturer and appears to have substantial benefits all round. For example, in the first four years of the operation of the Derby operations room, 'in-service events'

A growing fleet of aircraft through the world powered by Rolls-Royce engines means there is a growing market for the service and maintenance business.

Source: Alamy Images/Friedhof Foster

(maintenance incidents occurring inflight) had dropped about 25 per cent a year across the large civil engine fleet.

Nonetheless, the aerospace business relies heavily on trust and safety. In November 2010, passengers on Qantas flight QF32, one of the small fleet of Airbus A380s in the air, was forced to make an emergency landing in Singapore after an 'uncontained' failure of one of its Rolls-Royce Trent 900 engines. Pictures of a blackened, shredded Rolls-Royce engine were beamed around the world. Analysis revealed a disc component had failed allowing an excess flow of oil to the turbine, causing disintegration. The following day there was a less serious incident on a Qantas 747. Rolls share price took a 10 per cent hit after the incidents (recovering later), and the incidents cost Rolls-Royce £56 million in money paid to Qantas. Rolls tried to contain the potential reputational damage by sending out technical teams to explore and explain matters to major clients – Qantas, Singapore and Lufthansa.

Unfortunately, Rolls-Royce has been beset by a series of engine safety worries – in August 2010, a Lufthansa A380 was forced to switch off one of its Trent 900 engines as it flew over Frankfurt; in the same month, the prototype Trent 1000 engine, due to be used in Boeing's 787 Dreamliner blew up during testing. While the 2010 Qantas incident was the first uncontained failure of a Rolls engine since 1994, the fear remains that a crisis like this and the way it is handled can severely damage their corporate reputation and the strength of the brand.

The worry was that Rolls-Royce would suffer the same kind of damage to its brand as experienced by BP, after an explosion on its Deepwater Horizon platform resulted in the uncontrolled flows of oil into the Gulf of Mexico; or Toyota's product recalls due to faulty accelerator pedals in its cars; or Nestlé's baby milk scandal. Rolls believes its technical response was thorough enough to build stronger long-term relationships with its customers. Time will tell.[1]

As the Rolls-Royce example shows, in their quest to create customer relationships, marketers must build and manage products, services and brands that connect with customers and deliver superior value. This chapter begins with a deceptively simple question: *What is a product?* After addressing this question, we look at ways to classify products in consumer and business markets. Then we discuss the important decisions that marketers make regarding individual products, product lines and product mixes. Next, remembering the Rolls-Royce story at the beginning of this chapter, we examine the characteristics and marketing requirements of a special form of product – services. Finally, we look into the critically important issue of how marketers build and manage product and service brands.

AUTHOR COMMENT

As you'll see, this is a deceptively simple question with a very complex answer. For example, think back to our opening Rolls-Royce story. What is the Rolls-Royce 'product' – is it an aeroengine or the total package of engineering and service that keeps the aircraft in the sky?

WHAT IS A PRODUCT?

Product—Anything that can be offered to a market for attention, acquisition, use or consumption that might satisfy a want or need.

Service—An activity, benefit or satisfaction offered for sale that is essentially intangible and does not result in the ownership of anything.

We define a **product** as anything that can be offered to a market for attention, acquisition, use or consumption that might satisfy a want or need. Products include more than just tangible objects, such as cars, computers or mobile phones. Broadly defined, 'products' also include services, events, persons, places, organisations or ideas, or a mixture of these entities. Throughout this text, we use the term *product* broadly to include any or all of these entities. Thus, an Apple iPhone, a Jaguar XF and a Caffè Mocha at Starbucks are products. But so are a trip to Paris, E*Trade online investment services and advice from your family doctor.

Because of their importance in the world economy, we give special attention to services. **Services** are a form of product that consists of activities, benefits or satisfactions offered for sale that are essentially intangible and do not result in the ownership of anything. Examples include banking, hotel services, airline travel, retail, wireless communication and home-repair services. We will look at services more closely later in this chapter.

Products, services and experiences

Products are a key element in the overall *market offering*. Marketing-mix planning begins with building an offering that brings value to target customers. This offering becomes the basis on which the company builds profitable customer relationships.

A company's market offering often includes both tangible goods and services. At one extreme, the market offer may consist of a *pure tangible good*, such as soap, toothpaste or salt; no services accompany the product. At the other extreme are *pure services*, for which the market offer consists primarily of a service. Examples include a doctor's examination or financial services like life insurance. Between these two extremes, however, many goods-and-services combinations are possible.

Today, as products and services become more commoditised, many companies are moving to a new level in creating value for their customers. To differentiate their offers, beyond simply making products and delivering services, they are creating and managing customer *experiences* with their brands or company.

Experiences have always been an important part of marketing for some companies. Disney has long manufactured dreams and memories through its cinema films and theme parks throughout the world. And Nike has long declared, 'It's not so much the shoes but where they take you.' Today, however, all kinds of firms are recasting their traditional goods and services to create experiences. For example, BMW knows that it is selling more than a motor car, it's selling a luxury car ownership experience. This is shown to perfection in BMW's car delivery centre in Munich, called BMW Welt (BMW World):

> Designed by the Viennese architectural firm Coop Himmelb(l)au at an estimated cost of €216 million, futuristic BMW Welt is intended to create excitement when a customer gets the keys to a new car. Instead of going to the dealer where the car was purchased, the customer can stroll through exhibits, view presentations on innovation, and see the car rotate on a turntable, while illuminated by a spotlight. A recent BMW ad puts it this way: 'We realized a long time ago that what you make people feel is just as important as what you make.'[2]

Companies that market experiences realise that customers are really buying much more than just products and services. They are buying what those offers will *do* for them. 'A brand, product, or service is more than just a physical thing. Humans that connect with the brand add meaning and value to it,' says one marketing executive. 'Successfully managing the customer experience is the ultimate goal,' adds another.[3]

Levels of product and services

Product planners need to think about products and services on three levels (see Figure 8.1). Each level adds more customer value. The most basic level is the *core customer value*, which addresses the question *What is the buyer really buying?* When designing products, marketers must first define the core problem-solving benefits or services that consumers seek. A woman buying lipstick buys more than lip colour. Charles Revson of Revlon saw this early: 'In the factory, we make cosmetics; in the store, we sell hope.' And people who buy an Apple iPad are buying more than a mobile computer, an e-mail device or a personal organiser. They are buying freedom and on-the-go connectivity to people and resources.

At the second level, product planners must turn the core benefit into an *actual product*. They need to develop product and service features, design, a quality level, a brand name and packaging. For example, the iPad is an actual product. Its name, parts, styling, features, packaging and other attributes have all been carefully combined to deliver the core customer value of staying connected.

Finally, product planners must build an *augmented product* around the core benefit and actual product by offering additional consumer services and benefits. The iPad is more than just a

Figure 8.1 Three levels of product

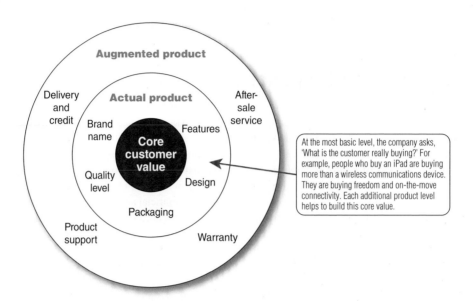

At the most basic level, the company asks, 'What is the customer really buying?' For example, people who buy an iPad are buying more than a wireless communications device. They are buying freedom and on-the-move connectivity. Each additional product level helps to build this core value.

communications device. It provides consumers with a complete solution to mobile connectivity problems. Thus, when consumers buy an iPad, the company and its dealers also might give buyers a warranty on parts and workmanship, instructions on how to use the device, quick repair services when needed, and a customer service telephone number and website to use if they have problems or questions.

Consumers see products as complex bundles of benefits that satisfy their needs. When developing products, marketers first must identify the *core customer value* that consumers seek from a product. They must then design the *actual* product and find ways to *augment* it to create this customer value and the most satisfying customer experience.

Product and service classifications

Products and services fall into two broad classes based on the types of consumers that use them: *consumer products* and *industrial products*. Broadly defined, products also include other marketable entities such as experiences, organisations, persons, places and ideas.

Consumer products

Consumer product—A product bought by final consumers for personal consumption.

Consumer products are products and services bought by final consumers for personal consumption. Marketers usually classify these products and services further based on how consumers go about buying them. Consumer products include *convenience products*, *shopping products*, *speciality products*, and *unsought products*. These products differ in the ways consumers buy them and, therefore, in how they are marketed (see Table 8.1).

Convenience product— A consumer product that customers usually buy frequently, immediately and with minimal comparison and buying effort.

Convenience products are consumer products and services that customers usually buy frequently, immediately and with minimal comparison and buying effort. Examples include laundry detergent, confectionery, magazines and fast food. Convenience products are usually low priced, and marketers place them in many locations to make them readily available when customers need or want them.

Shopping product—A consumer product that the customer, in the process of selecting and purchasing, usually compares on such attributes as suitability, quality, price and style.

Shopping products are less frequently purchased consumer products and services that customers compare carefully on suitability, quality, price and style. When buying shopping products and services, consumers spend much time and effort in gathering information and making comparisons. Examples include furniture, clothing, used cars, major appliances and hotel and airline services. Shopping products marketers usually distribute their products through fewer outlets but provide deeper sales support to help customers in their comparison efforts.

Table 8.1 Marketing considerations for consumer products

Marketing considerations	Type of consumer product			
	Convenience	Shopping	Speciality	Unsought
Customer buying behaviour	Frequent purchase; little planning, little comparison or shopping effort; low customer involvement	Less frequent purchase; much planning and shopping effort; comparison of brands on price, quality, and style	Strong brand preference and loyalty; special purchase effort; little comparison of brands; low price sensitivity	Little product awareness; knowledge (or, if aware, little or even negative interest)
Price	Low price	Higher price	High price	Varies
Distribution	Widespread distribution; convenient locations	Selective distribution in fewer outlets	Exclusive distribution in only one or a few outlets per market area	Varies
Promotion	Mass promotion by the producer	Advertising and personal selling by both the producer and resellers	More carefully targeted promotion by both the producer and resellers	Aggressive advertising and personal selling by the producer and resellers
Examples	Toothpaste, magazines, and laundry detergent	Major appliances, televisions, furniture, and clothing	Luxury goods, such as Rolex watches or fine crystal	Life insurance and Red Cross blood donations

Speciality products are consumer products and services with unique characteristics or brand identification for which a significant group of buyers is willing to make a special purchase effort. Examples include specific brands of cars, high-priced photographic equipment, designer clothes and the services of medical or legal specialists. A Lamborghini car, for example, is a speciality product because buyers are usually willing to travel great distances to buy one. Buyers normally do not compare speciality products. They invest only the time needed to reach dealers carrying the wanted products.

Unsought products are consumer products that a consumer either does not know about or knows about but does not normally consider buying. Most major new innovations are unsought until a consumer becomes aware of them through advertising. Classic examples of known but unsought products and services are life insurance, preplanned funeral services and blood donations to the National Blood Service. By their very nature, unsought products require a lot of advertising, personal selling and other marketing efforts.

Speciality product—A consumer product with unique characteristics or brand identification for which a significant group of buyers is willing to make a special purchase effort.

Unsought product—A consumer product that the consumer either does not know about or knows about but does not normally consider buying.

Industrial product—A product bought by individuals and organisations for further processing or for use in conducting a business.

Blood donations to the National Blood Services are an example of an unsought product or service.

Source: NHS Blood and Transplant

Industrial products

Industrial products are those purchased for further processing or for use in conducting a business. Thus, the distinction between a consumer product and an industrial product is based on the *purpose* for which a product is purchased. If a consumer buys a lawn mower for use around home, the lawn mower is a consumer product. If the same consumer buys the same lawn mower for use in a landscaping business, the lawn mower is an industrial product.

The three groups of industrial products and services include materials and parts, capital items, and supplies and services. *Materials and parts* include raw materials and manufactured materials and parts. Raw materials consist of farm products (e.g. wheat, cotton, livestock, fruits and vegetables) and natural products (e.g. fish, timber, crude petroleum and iron ore). Manufactured materials and parts consist of component materials (e.g. iron, yarn, cement and wires) and component parts (e.g. small motors, tyres and castings). Most manufactured materials and parts are sold directly to industrial users. Price and service are the major marketing factors; branding and advertising tend to be less important.

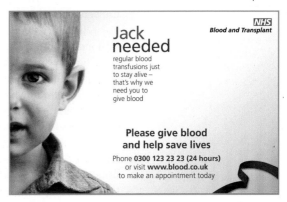

Capital items are industrial products that aid in a buyer's production or operations, including installations and accessory equipment. Installations consist of major purchases such as buildings (e.g. factories and offices) and fixed equipment (e.g. generators, drill presses, large computer systems and lifts). Accessory equipment includes portable factory equipment and tools (e.g. hand tools and lift trucks) and office equipment (e.g. computers, fax machines and desks). They have a shorter life than installations and simply aid in the production process.

The final group of industrial products is *supplies and services*. Supplies include operating supplies (e.g. lubricants, coal, paper and pencils) and repair and maintenance items (e.g. paint, nails and brooms). Supplies are the convenience products of the industrial field because they are usually purchased with a minimum of effort or comparison. Business services include maintenance and repair services (e.g. window cleaning and computer repair) and business advisory services (e.g. legal, management consulting and advertising). Such services are usually supplied under contract.

Organisations, persons, places and ideas

In addition to tangible products and services, marketers have broadened the concept of a product to include other market offerings: organisations, persons, places and ideas.

Organisations often carry out activities to 'sell' the organisation itself. *Organisation marketing* consists of activities undertaken to create, maintain or change the attitudes and behaviour of target consumers toward an organisation. Both profit and not-for-profit organisations practise organisation marketing. Business firms sponsor public relations or *corporate image advertising* campaigns to market themselves and polish their image.

For example, healthy-cereals producer Jordans promotes its Countryside Commitment to make its cereals more attractive to environmentally minded consumers:

Jordan's Countryside Commitment – We've all enjoyed our wonderful British countryside on a summer's day, however did you know that the number of herb-rich meadows has dramatically declined over the years, which, along with fewer hedgerows means there aren't enough places for wildlife to make their homes? And if they don't have homes and we lose pollinators like bees and butterflies it will heavily impact the food chain.

Hedgerow Homes – We are the only cereal company that insists the farmers who grow the grain that goes into our products, dedicate land specifically to create homes for wildlife. All the Conservation Grade farmers who grow grain for Jordans use 10% of their land just so that British wildlife, such as barn owls can have a home. Through Conservation Grade we've invested in the countryside for over 25 years and your support in buying Jordan's products has helped. But we can still do more…[4]

People can also be thought of as products. *Person marketing* consists of activities undertaken to create, maintain or change attitudes or behaviour toward particular people. People ranging from politicians, entertainers and sports figures to professionals such as doctors, lawyers and architects use person marketing to build their reputations. And businesses, charities and other organisations use well-known personalities to help sell their products or causes. For example, Nike is represented by hundreds of well-known athletes around the globe in sports ranging from tennis and basketball to ice hockey and cricket.

The skilful use of marketing can turn a person's name into a powerhouse brand. Carefully managed and well-known names adorn everything from sports clothing, housewares and magazines to book clubs and casinos. Such well-known names hold substantial branding power.

Place marketing involves activities undertaken to create, maintain or change attitudes or behaviour toward particular places. Cities, states, regions and even entire nations compete to attract tourists, new residents, conferences and conventions and company offices and factories. Slogans like 'Uniquely Singapore', 'Malaysia. Truly Asia', and 'Incredible India' vie for attention. Tourism Ireland, the agency responsible for marketing Irish tourism to the rest of the world, invites travellers to 'Go

Tourism Ireland's website offers information about the country and its attractions, a travel planner, special vacation offers and other information.

where Ireland takes you'. The agency works with the travel trade, media and other partners in key world markets, such as the United States, Canada, Australia and a dozen European countries. At its Discover Ireland website, Tourism Ireland offers information about the country and its attractions, a travel planner, special vacation offers, lists of tour operators and much more information that makes it easier to say 'yes' to visiting Ireland.[5]

Ideas can also be marketed. In one sense, all marketing is the marketing of an idea, whether it is the general idea of brushing your teeth or the specific idea that Colgate toothpastes and toothbrushes foster 'a world of oral care'. Here, however, we narrow our focus to the marketing of *social ideas*. This area has been called **social marketing**, defined by the Social Marketing Institute (SMI) as the use of commercial marketing concepts and tools in programmes designed to bring about social change.[6]

Social marketing programmes include public health campaigns to reduce smoking, drug abuse and obesity. Other social marketing efforts include campaigns to promote environmental protection, clean air and conservation. Still others address issues such as family planning, human rights and racial equality.

But social marketing involves much more than just advertising; the SMI encourages the use of a broad range of marketing tools. 'Social marketing goes well beyond the promotional "*P*" of the marketing mix to include every other element to achieve its social change objectives,' says the SMI's executive director.[7]

Social marketing—The use of commercial marketing concepts and tools in programmes designed to influence individuals' behaviour to improve their well-being and that of society.

AUTHOR COMMENT

Now that we've answered the 'What is a product?' question, we dig into the specific decisions that companies must make when designing and marketing products and services.

PRODUCT AND SERVICE DECISIONS

Marketers make product and service decisions at three levels: individual product decisions, product line decisions and product mix decisions. We discuss each in turn.

Individual product and service decisions

Figure 8.2 shows the important decisions in the development and marketing of individual products and services. We will focus on decisions about *product attributes*, *branding*, *packaging*, *labelling* and *product support services*.

Product and service attributes

Developing a product or service involves defining the benefits that it will offer. These benefits are communicated and delivered by product attributes such as *quality*, *features* and *style and design*.

Product quality

> **Product quality**—the characteristics of a product or service that bear on its ability to satisfy stated or implied customer needs.

Product quality is one of the marketer's major positioning tools. Quality has a direct impact on product or service performance; thus, it is closely linked to customer value and satisfaction. In the narrowest sense, quality can be defined as 'freedom from defects'. But most customer-centred companies go beyond this narrow definition. Instead, they define quality in terms of creating customer value and satisfaction. Quality is the characteristics of a product or service that bear on its ability to satisfy stated or implied customer needs. Similarly, Siemens defines quality this way: 'Quality is when our customers come back and our products don't'.[8]

Total quality management (TQM) is an approach in which all of the company's people are involved in constantly improving the quality of products, services and business processes. For most top companies, customer-driven quality has become a way of doing business. Today, companies are taking a 'return on quality' approach, viewing quality as an investment and holding quality efforts accountable for bottom-line results.

Product quality has two dimensions: level and consistency. In developing a product, the marketer must first choose a *quality level* that will support a product's positioning. Here, product quality means *performance quality* – the ability of a product to perform its functions. For example, a Rolls-Royce car provides higher performance quality than a Škoda Fabia: it has a smoother ride, provides more luxury and 'creature comforts', and lasts longer. Companies rarely try to offer the highest possible performance quality level; few customers want or can afford the high levels of quality offered in products such as a Rolls-Royce motor car or a Rolex watch. Instead, companies choose a quality level that matches target market needs and the quality levels of competing products.

Beyond quality level, high quality also can mean high levels of quality consistency. Here, product quality means *conformance quality* – freedom from defects and *consistency* in delivering a targeted level of performance. All companies should strive for high levels of conformance quality. In this sense, a Škoda can have just as much quality as a Rolls-Royce. Although a Škoda doesn't perform at the same level as a Rolls-Royce, it can deliver the quality that customers pay for and expect.

Product features

A product can be offered with varying features. A stripped-down model, one without any extras, is the starting point. The company can create higher-level models by adding more features. Features are a competitive tool for differentiating the company's product from competitors' products. Being the first producer to introduce a valued new feature is one of the most effective ways to compete.

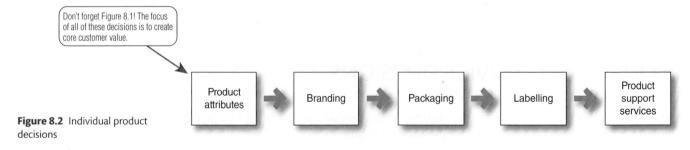

Figure 8.2 Individual product decisions

How can a company identify new features and decide which ones to add to its product? It should periodically survey buyers who have used the product and ask these questions: How do you like the product? Which specific features of the product do you like most? Which features could we add to improve the product? The answers to these questions provide the company with a rich list of feature ideas. The company can then assess each feature's *value* to customers versus its *cost* to the company. Features that customers value highly in relation to costs should be added.

Product style and design

Another way to add customer value is through distinctive *product style and design*. Design is a larger concept than style. *Style* simply describes the appearance of a product. Styles can be eye-catching or yawn producing. A sensational style may grab attention and produce pleasing aesthetics, but it does not necessarily make a product *perform* better. Unlike style, *design* is more than skin deep; it goes to the very heart of a product. Good design contributes to a product's usefulness as well as to its looks.

Good design doesn't start with brainstorming new ideas and making prototypes. Design begins with observing customers and developing a deep understanding of their needs. More than simply creating product or service attributes, it involves shaping a customer's product-use experience. Product designers should think less about product attributes and technical specifications and more about how customers will use and benefit from a product. Consider the impact of inventor James Dyson on the world of electrical appliances for the household and workplace:

> James Dyson is an inventor who started his electrical goods company in 1992, and in 2011 saw sales of products go through £1 billion for the first time. Amid economic gloom, Dyson is struggling to keep up with demand for products ranging from the bag-less cyclone carpet cleaner to the Airblade hand dryer and a bladeless cooling fan. The breakthrough was Dyson's cyclonic bag-less carpet cleaner, using centrifugal force to extract dirt from carpets. Dyson spent 14 years and produced more than 5,000 prototypes before he was satisfied he had come up with a better design. With innovative design and engineering, and a high price, Dyson's carpet cleaner has become the leading cleaner brand in the US, UK and Japan. The design aesthetics have made the Dyson cleaner a lifestyle brand not simply a way of cleaning the carpet. Dyson's principle is to find things in everyday life that do not work very well and to make a better alternative. The Dyson Airblade commercial hand dryer works with a slim jet of air moving at 400 miles an hour. Although the Dyson approach is engineering-led, the industrial design principles are impressive too – Dyson products have been put on display in a host of museums, including the Metropolitan Museum of Art in New York. In 2010, Dyson's Air Multiplier (a 'fan without blades') hit the market with a futuristic appearance and innovative air cooling technology.[9]

Branding

Perhaps the most distinctive skill of professional marketers is their ability to build and manage brands. A **brand** is a name, term, sign, symbol or design, or a combination of these, that identifies the maker or seller of a product or a service. Consumers view a brand as an important part of a product, and branding can add value to a product. Customers attach meanings to brands and develop brand relationships. Brands have meaning well beyond a product's physical attributes. For example, consider Coca-Cola as an iconic American soft drink:[10]

Brand—A name, term, sign, symbol, design or a combination of these, that identifies the products or services of one seller or group of sellers and differentiates them from those of competitors.

> In an interesting taste test of Coca-Cola versus Pepsi, 67 subjects were connected to brain-wave-monitoring machines while they consumed both products. When the soft drinks were unmarked, consumer preferences were split down the middle. But when the brands were identified, subjects choose Coke over Pepsi by a margin of 75 to 25 per cent. When drinking the identified Coke brand, the brain areas that lit up most were those associated with cognitive control and memory – a place where culture concepts are stored. That didn't happen as much when drinking Pepsi. Why? According to one brand strategist, it's because of Coca-Cola's long-established brand imagery – the almost 100-year-old contour bottle and cursive font and its association with iconic images

ranging from Mean Joe Greene and the Polar Bears to Santa Claus. Pepsi's imagery isn't quite as deeply rooted. Although people might associate Pepsi with a hot celebrity or the 'Pepsi generation' appeal, they probably don't link it to the strong and emotional American icons associated with Coke. The conclusion? Plain and simple: consumer preference isn't based on taste alone. Coke's iconic brand appears to make a difference.

Branding has become so strong that today hardly anything goes unbranded. Salt is packaged in branded containers, common nuts and bolts are packaged with a retailer's label, and car parts – spark plugs, tyres and filters – bear brand names that differ from those of the car makers. Even fruits, vegetables, dairy products and poultry are branded – Dole bananas, Florette's pre-packed salad range, Yeo Valley organic milk and Bernard Matthews turkey products.

Branding helps buyers in many ways. Brand names help consumers identify products that might benefit them. Brands also say something about product quality and consistency. Buyers who always buy the same brand know that they will get the same features, benefits and quality each time they buy. Branding also gives the seller several advantages. Brand name becomes the basis on which a whole story can be built about a product's special qualities. The seller's brand name and trademark provide legal protection for unique product features that otherwise might be copied by competitors. And branding helps the seller to segment markets. For example, Toyota Motor Corporation can offer the major Lexus and Toyota brands to European car buyers, each with numerous sub-brands – such as iQ, AYGO, Yaris, Verso, Auris, Avensis, RAV4, Land Cruiser and others – not just one general product for all consumers.

Building and managing brands are perhaps the marketer's most important tasks. We will discuss branding strategy in more detail later in the chapter.

Packaging—The activities of designing and producing the container or wrapper for a product.

Amazon.com recently launched a multi-year initiative to alleviate wrap rage by creating 'frustration free packaging'.

Source: © 2010 Amazon.com, Inc. or its affiliates

Packaging

Packaging involves designing and producing the container or wrapper for a product. Traditionally, the primary function of a package was to hold and protect a product. In recent times, however, numerous factors have made packaging an important marketing tool as well. Increased competition and clutter on retail store shelves means that packages must now perform many sales tasks – from attracting attention, to describing a product, to making the sale.

Companies are realising the power of good packaging to create immediate consumer recognition of a brand. For example, in the US an average supermarket stocks 47,000 items; the average Walmart supercentre carries 142,000 items. The typical shopper passes by some 300 items per minute, and from 40 to 70 per cent of all purchase decisions are made in stores. In this highly competitive environment, the package may be the seller's last and best chance to influence buyers. Thus, for many companies, the package itself has become an important promotional medium.[11]

Poorly designed packages can cause headaches for consumers and lost sales for the company. Think about all those hard-to-open packages, such as DVD cases sealed with impossibly sticky labels, packaging with finger-splitting wire twist-ties or sealed plastic clamshell containers that take the equivalent of the fire services' Jaws of Life to open. Such packaging causes what Amazon.com calls 'wrap rage' – the frustration we feel when

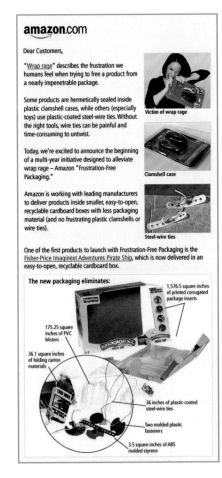

trying to free a product from a nearly impenetrable package. Amazon.com recently launched a multi-year initiative to alleviate wrap rage. It's working with companies such as Fisher-Price, Mattel, Microsoft and others to create 'frustration-free packaging' – smaller, easy-to-open recyclable packages that use less packaging material and no frustrating plastic clamshells or wire ties. These new packages not only reduce customer frustration, but they also cut down on packaging waste and energy usage. 'It will take many years,' says the company, 'but our vision is to offer our entire catalog of products in frustration-free packaging.'[12]

Innovative packaging can give a company an advantage over competitors and boost sales. Sometimes even seemingly small packaging improvements can make a big difference. For example, Heinz revolutionised the 170-year-old condiments industry by inverting the good old ketchup bottle, letting customers quickly squeeze out even the last bit of ketchup. At the same time, it adopted a 'fridge-door-fit' shape that not only slots into shelves more easily but also has a cap that is simpler for children to open. In the four months following the introduction of the new package in the US, sales jumped 12 per cent. Even more, the new package does double duty as a promotional tool. Says

Heinz revolutionised the condiments industry by inverting the ketchup bottle, letting customers squeeze out even the last bit of ketchup, and adopting a 'fridge door shape' for easier storage.

Source: Alamy Images/Ian Francis

a packaging analyst, 'When consumers see the Heinz logo on the fridge door every time they open it, it's taking marketing inside homes.'[13]

In recent years, product safety has also become a major packaging concern. We have all learned to deal with hard-to-open 'childproof' packaging. After the rash of product tampering scares in the 1980s, most drug producers and food manufacturers now put their products in tamper-resistant packages. In making packaging decisions, the company also must heed growing environmental concerns. Fortunately, many companies have gone 'green' by reducing their packaging and using environmentally responsible packaging materials.

Labelling

Labels range from simple tags attached to products to complex graphics that are part of the packaging. They perform several functions. At the very least, the label *identifies* a product or a brand, such as the Dole label on bananas. The label might also *describe* several things about a product – who made it, where it was made, when it was made, its contents, how it is to be used and how to use it safely. Finally, the label might help to *promote* a brand, support its positioning and connect with customers. For many companies, labels have become an important element in broader marketing campaigns.

Labels and brand logos can support a brand's positioning and add personality to a brand. For example, many companies are now redesigning their brand and company logos to make them more approachable, upbeat and engaging. 'The boxy, monochromatic look is out, and soft fonts, lots of colors, and natural imagery is in,' says one analyst. For instance, Kraft recently replaced its blocky red, white, and blue hexagon logo with a lowercase, multi-font, multicolour one that includes a colourful starburst and the company's new slogan, 'Make today delicious'. And Pepsi's recently updated packaging sports a new, more uplifting smiling logo. 'It feels like the same Pepsi we know and love,' says a brand expert, 'but it's more adventurous, more youthful, with a bit more personality to it.' It presents a 'spirit of optimism and youth', says a Pepsi marketer.[14]

Along with the positives, labelling also raises concerns. There has been a long history of legal concerns about packaging and labels. False, misleading or deceptive labels or packages constitute unfair competition. Labels can mislead customers, fail to describe important ingredients or fail to include needed safety warnings, and most countries have legal regulations applying to labelling standards.

Labelling has been affected in recent times by *unit pricing* (stating the price per unit of standard measure), *open dating* (stating the expected shelf life of a product) and *nutritional labelling* (stating the nutritional values in a product). As a minimum, sellers must ensure that their labels contain all information required by law.

Product support services

Customer service is another element of product strategy. A company's offer usually includes some support services, which can be a minor part or a major part of the total offering. Look back to the Rolls-Royce illustration at the beginning of this chapter. Later in this chapter, we will discuss services as products in themselves. Here, we discuss services that augment actual products.

Support services are an important part of a customer's overall brand experience. For example, Nordstrom is a famous, upscale department store retailer in the United States that knows that good marketing doesn't stop with making a sale. Keeping customers happy *after* a sale is key to building lasting relationships. Nordstrom's motto is : 'Take care of customers, no matter what it takes', before, during and after the sale.[15]

Nordstrom thrives on stories about its after-sale service heroics, such as employees dropping off orders at customers' homes or warming up cars while customers spend a little more time shopping. In one case, a sales clerk reportedly gave a customer a refund on a tyre; Nordstrom doesn't carry tyres, but the store prides itself on a no-questions-asked return policy. In another case, a Nordstrom sales clerk stopped a customer in the store and asked if the shoes she was wearing had been bought there. When a customer said yes, the clerk insisted on replacing them on the

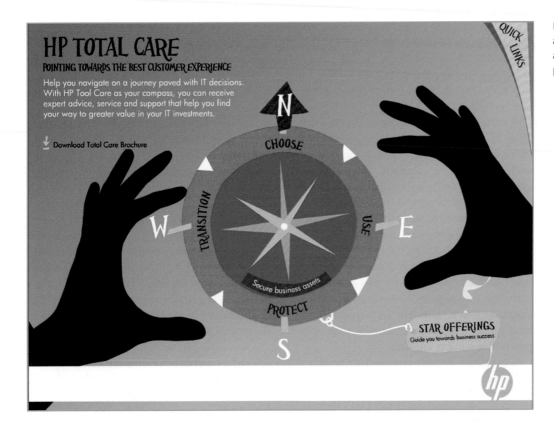

Hewlett-Packard (HP) offers a complete set of sales and after-sales services, promising 'HP Total Care'.

spot, saying that they hadn't worn as well as they should. There's even a story about a man whose wife, a loyal Nordstrom customer, died with her Nordstrom account $1,000 in arrears. Not only did Nordstrom settle the account, but it also sent flowers to the funeral. Such service heroics keep Nordstrom customers coming back again and again.

The first step in designing support services is to survey customers periodically to assess the value of current services and obtain ideas for new ones. Once the company has assessed the quality of various support services to customers, it can take steps to fix problems and add new services that will both delight customers and yield profits to the company.

Many companies are now using a sophisticated mix of phone, e-mail, fax, Internet and interactive voice and data technologies to provide support services that were not possible before. For example, in the computer business Hewlett-Packard (HP) offers a complete set of sales and after-sale services. It promises 'HP Total Care – expert help for every stage of your computer's life. From choosing it, to configuring it, to protecting it, to tuning it up – all the way to recycling it.' Customers can click on the HP Total Care service portal that offers online resources for HP products and 24/7 tech support, which can be accessed via e-mail, instant online chat and telephone.[16]

Product line decisions

Beyond decisions about individual products and services, product strategy also calls for building a product line. A **product line** is a group of products that are closely related because they function in a similar manner, are sold to the same customer groups, are marketed through the same types of outlets, or fall within given price ranges. For example, Nike produces several lines of sports shoes and clothing and Marriott offers several lines of hotels.

The major product line decision involves *product line length* – the number of items in a product line. The line is too short if a manager can increase profits by adding items; the line is too long if a manager can increase profits by dropping items. Managers need to analyse their product lines periodically to assess each item's sales and profits and understand how each item contributes to the line's overall performance.

Product line– A group of products that are closely related because they function in a similar manner, are sold to the same customer groups, are marketed through the same types of outlets or fall within given price ranges.

The product line length is influenced by company objectives and resources. For example, one objective might be to allow for upselling. Thus BMW wants to move customers up from its 1-series models to 3-, 5-, 6- and 7-series models. Another objective might be to allow cross-selling: HP sells printers as well as computers. Still another objective might be to protect against economic swings: Gap runs several clothing-store chains (Gap, Old Navy and Banana Republic) covering different price points.

A company can expand its product line in two ways: by *line filling* or *line stretching*. *Product line filling* involves adding more items within the present range of the line. There are several reasons for product line filling: reaching for extra profits, satisfying dealers, using excess capacity, being the leading full-line company and plugging holes to keep out competitors. However, line filling is overdone if it results in cannibalisation and customer confusion. The company should ensure that new items are noticeably different from existing ones.

Product line stretching occurs when a company lengthens its product line beyond its current range. The company can stretch its line downward, upward, or both ways. Companies located at the upper end of the market can stretch their lines *downward*. A company may stretch downward to plug a market hole that otherwise would attract a new competitor or respond to a competitor's attack on the upper end. Or it may add low-end products because it finds faster growth taking place in the low-end segments. Honda stretched downward for all these reasons by adding its thrifty little Honda Jazz to its line. The Jazz, economical to drive and priced around €13,600, was designed to meet increasing consumer demands for more frugal cars and to preempt competitors in the new-generation minicar segment.

Companies can also stretch their product lines *upward*. Sometimes, companies stretch upward to add prestige to their current products. Or they may be attracted by a faster growth rate or higher margins at the higher end. For example, some years ago, each of the leading Japanese car companies introduced an upmarket automobile: Honda launched Acura in its major global markets; Toyota launched Lexus; and Nissan launched Infiniti. They used entirely new names rather than their own names.

Companies in the middle range of the market may decide to stretch their lines in *both directions*. Marriott did this with its hotel product line. Along with regular Marriott hotels, it added eight new branded hotel lines to serve both the upper and lower ends of the market. For example, Renaissance Hotels & Resorts aims to attract and please top executives; Fairfield Inn by Marriott desires to attract vacationers and business travellers on a tight travel budget; and Courtyard by Marriott aims at salespeople and other 'road warriors'.[17] The major risk with this strategy is that some travellers will trade down after finding that the lower-price hotels in the Marriott chain give them pretty much everything they want. However, Marriott would rather capture its customers who move downward than lose them to competitors.

Product mix decisions

Product mix (or product portfolio)—The set of all product lines and items that a particular seller offers for sale.

An organisation with several product lines has a product mix. A **product mix** (or **product portfolio**) consists of all the product lines and items that a particular seller offers for sale. Colgate's European product mix consists of three major product lines: oral care, personal care and pet nutrition. Each product line consists of several sub-lines.[18] Each line and sub-line has many individual items. Altogether, Colgate's product mix includes dozens of items.

A company's product mix has four important dimensions: width, length, depth and consistency. Product mix *width* refers to the number of different product lines the company carries. For example, the 'Colgate World of Care' includes a fairly contained product mix, consisting of personal care products that you can 'trust to care for yourself, your home, and the ones you love.' By contrast, GE manufactures as many as 250,000 items across a broad range of categories, from light bulbs to jet engines and diesel locomotives.

The product mix *length* refers to the total number of items a company carries within its product lines. Colgate typically carries different brands within each line.

The product mix *depth* refers to the number of versions offered for each product in the line. Colgate toothpastes come in several varieties, including Colgate Total Advanced, Colgate Total

Sensitive, Colgate Max and Colgate Smiles childrens' toothpaste. Each variety comes with special forms and formulations. For example, you can buy Colgate Total in whitening, freshening and deep clean versions.

Finally, the *consistency* of a product mix refers to how closely related the various product lines are in end use, production requirements, distribution channels or some other way. Colgate product lines are consistent insofar as they are consumer products and go through the same distribution channels. The lines are less consistent insofar as they perform different functions for buyers.

These product mix dimensions provide the handles for defining the company's product strategy. The company can increase its business in four ways:

1. It can add new product lines, widening its product mix. In this way, its new lines build on the company's reputation in its other lines.

2. The company can lengthen its existing product lines to become a more full-line company.

3. It can add more versions of each product and thus deepen its product mix.

4. The company can pursue more product line consistency – or less – depending on whether it wants to have a strong reputation in a single field or in several fields.

In the face of recent economic difficulties, many companies have streamlined their product mixes to pare out marginally performing lines and models and sharpen their value propositions. Others have bolstered their product mixes by adding more affordable options. Because of the economy, 'consumers are talking about reassessing their favorite brands . . . if they think they can get a better value with the same price,' says a marketing consultant. As consumers rethink their brand preferences and priorities, marketers must do the same. They need to align their product mixes with changing customer needs and profitably create better value for customers.[19]

AUTHOR COMMENT

As noted at the start of this chapter, services are 'products' too – intangible ones. So all the product topics we've discussed so far apply to services as well as to physical products. However, in this section, we'll focus on the special characteristics and marketing needs that set services apart.

SERVICES MARKETING

Services have grown dramatically in recent years. In the developed countries, the rapidly expanding services sector is contributing more to economic growth and job creation worldwide than any other sector. The services sector accounts for some three-quarters of the gross domestic product (GDP) of the European Union countries. In addition, over three-quarters of European Union jobs are now in the services sector.[20] Services are growing quickly in the world economy, making up 64 per cent of gross world product.[21]

Service industries vary greatly. *Governments* offer services through courts, employment services, hospitals, military services, police and fire services, and schools. *Private not-for-profit organisations* offer services through museums, charities, churches, colleges, foundations and hospitals. A large number of *business organisations* offer services – airlines, banks, hotels, insurance companies, consulting firms, medical and legal practices, entertainment and telecommunications companies, property firms, retailers and others.

The nature and characteristics of a service

A company must consider four special service characteristics when designing marketing programmes: intangibility, inseparability, variability and perishability (see Figure 8.3).

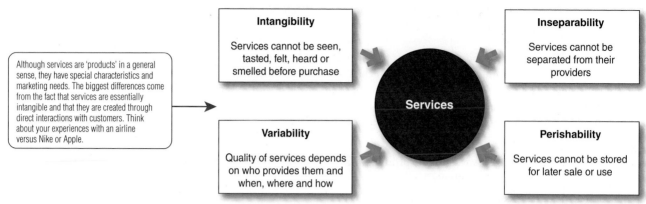

Figure 8.3 Four service characteristics

Although services are 'products' in a general sense, they have special characteristics and marketing needs. The biggest differences come from the fact that services are essentially intangible and that they are created through direct interactions with customers. Think about your experiences with an airline versus Nike or Apple.

Service intangibility—Services cannot be seen, tasted, felt, heard or smelled before they are bought.

Service intangibility means that services cannot be seen, tasted, felt, heard or smelled before they are bought. For example, people undergoing cosmetic surgery cannot see the result before the purchase. Airline passengers have nothing but a ticket and a promise that they and their luggage will arrive safely at the intended destination, hopefully at the same time. To reduce uncertainty, buyers look for 'signals' of service quality. They draw conclusions about quality from the place, people, price, equipment and communications that they can see.

Therefore, a service provider's task is to make the service tangible in one or more ways and send the right signals about quality. One analyst calls this *evidence management*, in which the service organisation presents its customers with organised, honest evidence of its capabilities. In the United States, the Mayo Clinic practises good evidence management:[22]

> When it comes to hospitals, it's very hard for the average patient to judge the quality of the 'product'. You can't try it on, you can't return it if you don't like it, and you need an advanced degree to understand it. And so, when we're considering a medical facility, most of us unconsciously turn into detectives, looking for evidence of competence, caring and integrity. The Mayo Clinic doesn't leave that evidence to chance. By carefully managing a set of visual and experiential clues, both inside and outside the clinic, the Mayo Clinic offers patients and their families concrete evidence of its strengths and values.
>
> Inside, staff are trained to act in a way that clearly signals Mayo Clinic's patient-first focus. 'My doctor calls me at home to check on how I am doing,' marvels one patient. 'She wants to work with what is best for my schedule.' The clinic's physical facilities also send the right signals. They've been carefully designed to offer a place of refuge, convey caring and respect, and signal competence. Looking for external confirmation? Go online and hear directly from those who've been to the clinic or work there. The Mayo Clinic now uses social networking – everything from blogs to Facebook and YouTube – to enhance the patient experience. For example, on the Sharing Mayo Clinic blog (http://sharing.mayoclinic.org), patients and their families retell their Mayo experiences, and Mayo employees offer behind-the-scenes views. The result? Exceptionally positive word of mouth and abiding customer loyalty have allowed the Mayo Clinic to build what is arguably the most powerful brand in health care with very little advertising. 'The quality of the [patient] experience is key,' says Dr Thoraf Sundt, a heart surgeon and chair of Mayo's marketing committee.

Service inseparability—Services are produced and consumed at the same time and cannot be separated from their providers.

Physical goods are produced, then stored, later sold, and still later consumed. In contrast, services are first sold and then produced and consumed at the same time. In services marketing, a service provider is the product. **Service inseparability** means that services cannot be separated from their providers, whether the providers are people or machines. If a service employee provides a service, then the employee becomes a part of the service. Because the customer is also present as the service is produced, *provider-customer interaction* is a special feature of services marketing. Both the provider and the customer affect the service outcome.

Service variability means that the quality of services depends on who provides them as well as when, where, and how they are provided. For example, some hotels – say, Marriott – have reputations for providing better service than others. Still, within a given Marriott hotel, one registration-counter employee may be cheerful and efficient, whereas another standing just a few feet away may be unpleasant and slow. Even the quality of a single Marriott employee's service varies according to his or her energy and frame of mind at the time of each customer encounter.

Service perishability means that services cannot be stored for later sale or use. Some private doctors and dentists charge patients for missed appointments because the service value existed only at that point and disappeared when the patient did not show up. The perishability of services is not a problem when demand is steady. However, when demand fluctuates, service firms often have difficult problems. For example, because of rush-hour demand, public transport companies have to own much more equipment than they would if demand were even throughout the day. Thus, service firms often design strategies for producing a better match between demand and supply. Hotels and holiday destinations charge lower prices in the off-season to attract more guests. And restaurants hire part-time employees to serve during peak periods.

> **Service variability**—The quality of services may vary greatly depending on who provides them and when, where and how.

> **Service perishability**—Services cannot be stored for later sale or use.

Marketing strategies for service firms

Just like manufacturing businesses, good service firms use marketing to position themselves strongly in chosen target markets. British Airways is there 'To Fly. To Serve', Tesco promises to support consumers through its 'Every Little Helps' message. Budget hotel Premier Inns offers 'Everything's premier but the price'. And Great Ormond Street Hospital for Sick Children in London puts 'The child first and always'. These and other service firms establish their positions through traditional marketing mix activities. However, because services differ from tangible products, they often require additional marketing approaches.

The service profit chain

In a service business, the customer and the front-line service employee *interact* to create the service. Effective interaction, in turn, depends on the skills of front-line service employees and on the support processes backing these employees. Thus, successful service companies focus their attention on *both* their customers and their employees. They understand the **service profit chain**, which links service firm profits with employee and customer satisfaction. This chain consists of five links:[23]

> **Service profit chain**—The chain that links service firm profits with employee and customer satisfaction.

- *Internal service quality* – superior employee selection and training, a quality work environment, and strong support for those dealing with customers, which results in . . .
- *Satisfied and productive service employees* – more satisfied, loyal and hardworking employees, which results in . . .
- *Greater service value* – more effective and efficient customer value creation and service delivery, which results in . . .
- *Satisfied and loyal customers* – satisfied customers who remain loyal, repeat purchase, and refer other customers, which results in . . .
- *Healthy service profits and growth* – superior service firm performance.

Therefore, reaching service profits and growth goals begins with taking care of those who take care of customers. Customer-service star Zappos, the online shoe, clothing and accessories retailer, knows that happy customers begin with happy, dedicated and energetic employees:[24]

> Most of Zappos' business is driven by word-of-mouth and customer interactions with company employees. So keeping *customers* happy really does require keeping *employees* happy. Zappos starts by recruiting the right people and training them thoroughly in customer-service basics. Then the Zappos culture takes over, a culture that emphasizes 'a satisfying and fulfilling job . . . and a career you can be proud of. Work hard. Play hard. All the time!' Zappos is a great place to work. The online retailer creates a relaxed, fun-loving and close-knit family atmosphere, complete with

free meals, full benefits, profit sharing, a nap room, and even a full-time life coach. The result is what one observer calls '1,550 perpetually chipper employees'. Every year, the company publishes a 'culture book', filled with unedited, often gushy testimonials from Zapponians about what it's like to work there. 'Oh my gosh,' says one employee, 'this is my home away from home. . . . It's changed my life. . . . Our culture is the best reason to work here'. Says another, 'the most surprising thing about coming to work here is that there are no limits. So pretty much anything you are passionate about is possible'. And about what are Zapponians most passionate? The company's number one core value: 'Creating WOW through service'.

Thus, service marketing requires more than just traditional external marketing using the four Ps. Figure 8.4 shows that service marketing also requires *internal marketing* and *interactive marketing*. **Internal marketing** means that a service firm must orient and motivate its customer-contact employees and supporting service people to work as a *team* to provide customer satisfaction. Marketers must get everyone in the organisation to be customer centred. In fact, internal marketing must *precede* external marketing. Service leaders start by hiring the right people and carefully orienting and inspiring them to give unparalleled customer service.

Interactive marketing means that service quality depends heavily on the quality of the buyer–seller interaction during the service encounter. In product marketing, product quality often depends little on how a product is obtained. But in services marketing, service quality depends on both the service deliverer and the quality of delivery. Service marketers, therefore, have to master interactive marketing skills. Thus, luxury hotels group Four Seasons selects only people with an innate 'passion to serve' and instructs them carefully in the fine art of interacting with customers to satisfy their every need. All new hires complete a three-month training regimen, including improvisation exercises to help them improve their customer-interaction skills.

In today's marketplace, companies must know how to deliver interactions that are not only 'high touch' but also 'high tech'. For example, retail bank customers now expect to be able to log onto their bank's website and access account information, make transactions, receive investment information and get quotations for the bank's products. This is in addition to being able to contact service representatives by phone or visit a local branch. Thus, the challenge to banks has become to master interactive marketing at all three levels – calls, clicks *and* personal visits.

Today, as competition and costs increase, and as productivity and quality decrease, more service marketing sophistication is needed. Service companies face three major marketing tasks: they want to increase their *service differentiation*, *service quality* and *service productivity*.

Managing service differentiation

In these days of intense price competition, service marketers often complain about the difficulty of differentiating their services from those of competitors. To the extent that customers view the services of different providers as similar, they care less about the provider than the price.

Internal marketing— Orienting and motivating customer contact employees and supporting service people to work as a team to provide customer satisfaction.

Interactive marketing— Training services employees in the fine art of interacting with customers to satisfy their needs.

Figure 8.4 Three types of service marketing

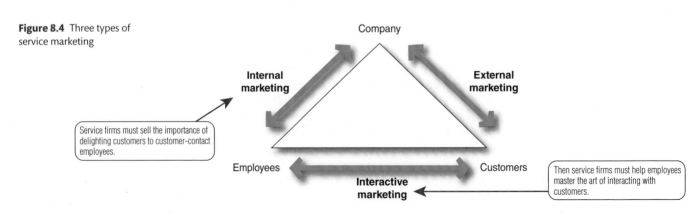

254

The solution to price competition is to develop a differentiated offer, delivery and image. The *offer* can include innovative features that set one company's offer apart from competitors' offers. Some hotels offer no-wait computerised self-registration, car-rental, banking and business-centre services in their lobbies and free high-speed Internet connections in their rooms. Some retailers differentiate themselves by offerings that take you well beyond the products they stock. For example, Pets at Home isn't your average pet shop. The stores offer pet-food, toys, bedding, medication, insurance and accessories, with the choice of ordering online for home delivery or store collection. But many locations also offer Groom Room salons for sprucing up the scruffy pet (and microchipping them as well) and links to Companion Care, veterinary surgeries. The goal is to make Pets at Home your one-stop shop for all your pet's needs.

Service companies can differentiate their service *delivery* by having more able and reliable customer-contact people, developing a superior physical environment in which the service product is delivered, or designing a superior delivery process. For example, most major grocery chains now offer online shopping and home delivery as a better way to shop than having to drive, park, wait in line and carry groceries home. And most banks allow you to access your account information from almost anywhere – from the ATM to your mobile phone or device.

Finally, service companies also can work on differentiating their *images* through symbols and branding. Online insurance and financial services company comparethemarket.com adopted the meercat as its symbol in a series of humorous TV advertisements defending their spoof website comparethemeercat.com against the real site – leading to stuffed meercat gifts for customers, screensavers and a fabricated history of meercat origins in a mythical Russia. The meercat has helped make the previously unknown insurance company memorable and approachable. Other well-known service symbols include MGM's lion and McDonald's golden arches.

Pets at Home isn't your average pet shop. Their goal is to make Pets at Home your one-stop shop for all your pet's needs.

Source: Alamy Images/Mark Mercer

Managing service quality

A service firm can differentiate itself by delivering consistently higher quality than its competitors provide. Like manufacturers before them, most service industries have now joined the customer-driven quality movement. And like product marketers, service providers need to identify what target customers expect in regard to service quality.

Unfortunately, service quality is harder to define and judge than product quality. For instance, it is harder to agree on the quality of a haircut than on the quality of a hair dryer. Customer retention is perhaps the best measure of quality; a service firm's ability to hang onto its customers depends on how consistently it delivers value to them.

Top service companies set high service-quality standards. They watch service performance closely, both their own and that of competitors. They do not settle for merely good service; they strive for 100 per cent defect-free service. Unlike product manufacturers who can adjust their machinery and inputs until everything is perfect, service quality will always vary, depending on the interactions between employees and customers. As hard as they may try, even the best companies will have an occasional late delivery, a burned steak or a grumpy employee. However, good *service recovery* can turn angry customers into loyal ones. In fact, good recovery can win more customer purchasing and loyalty than if things had gone well in the first place. Consider this example, from Southwest Airlines – the model for no-frills flying throughout the world:[25]

Bob Emig was flying home from St. Louis on Southwest Airlines when an all-too-familiar travel nightmare began to unfold. After his airplane backed away from the gate, he and his fellow passengers were told that the plane would need to be de-iced. When the aircraft was ready to fly two and a half hours later, the pilot had reached the hour limit set by the Federal Aviation Administration, and a new pilot was required. By that time, the plane had to be de-iced again. Five hours after the scheduled departure time, Emig's flight was finally ready for takeoff. A customer-service disaster, right? Not if you hear Emig tell it. Throughout the wait, the pilot walked the aisles, answering questions and offering constant updates. Flight attendants, who Emig says 'really seemed like they cared', kept up with the news on connecting flights. And within a couple of days of arriving home, Emig received a letter of apology from Southwest Airlines that included two free round-trip ticket vouchers.

Unusual? Not at all. It's the standard service-recovery procedure for Southwest Airlines. Years ago, Southwest Airlines created a high-level group headed by a senior manager – of proactive customer service communications – that carefully coordinates information sent to all frontline representatives in the event of major flight disruptions. It also sends out letters, and in many cases flight vouchers, to customers caught up in flight delays or cancellations, customer bumping incidents, baggage problems, or other travel messes – even those beyond Southwest's control. Thanks to such caring service recovery, Southwest Airlines doesn't just appease wronged customers like Bob Emig; it turns them into even more loyal customers.

Managing service productivity

With their costs rising rapidly, service firms are under great pressure to increase service productivity. They can do so in several ways. They can train current employees better or hire new ones who will work harder or more skilfully. Or they can increase the quantity of their service by giving up some quality. The provider can 'industrialise the service' by adding equipment and standardising production, as in McDonald's assembly-line approach to fast-food retailing. Finally, a service provider can harness the power of technology. Although we often think of technology's power to save time and costs in manufacturing companies, it also has great – and often untapped – potential to make service workers more productive.

However, companies must avoid pushing productivity so hard that doing so reduces quality. Attempts to industrialise a service or cut costs can make a service company more efficient in the short run. But that can also reduce its longer-run ability to innovate, maintain service quality, or respond to consumer needs and desires. For example, some airlines have learned this lesson the hard way as they attempt to economise in the face of rising costs. They stopped offering even the little things for free – such as in-flight snacks – and began charging extra for everything from luggage check-in to aisle seats. The result is a plane full of resentful customers who avoid the airline whenever they can. In their attempts to improve productivity, these airlines mangled customer service.

Thus, in attempting to improve service productivity, companies must be mindful of how they create and deliver customer value. In short, they should be careful not to take the 'service' out of service.

AUTHOR COMMENT

A brand represents everything that a product or service *means* to consumers. As such, brands are valuable assets to a company. For example, when you hear someone say 'Coca-Cola', what do you think, feel or remember? What about 'Nike'? Or 'Google'?

BRANDING STRATEGY: BUILDING STRONG BRANDS

Some analysts see brands as *the* major enduring asset of a company, outlasting its specific products and facilities. John Stewart, former CEO of Quaker Oats, once said, 'If this business were split up, I would give you the land and bricks and mortar, and I would keep the brands and trademarks, and I would fare better than you.' A former CEO of McDonald's declared, 'If every asset we own, every building, and every piece of equipment were destroyed in a terrible natural disaster, we would be able to borrow all the money to replace it very quickly because of the value of our brand . . . The brand is more valuable than the totality of all these assets.'[26]

Thus, brands are powerful assets that must be carefully developed and managed. In this section, we examine the key strategies for building and managing product and service brands.

Brand equity

Brands are more than just names and symbols. They are a key element in the company's relationships with consumers. Brands represent consumers' perceptions and feelings about a product and its performance – everything that a product or a service *means* to consumers. In the final analysis, brands exist in the heads of consumers. As one well-respected marketer once said, 'Products are created in the factory, but brands are created in the mind.' Adds Jason Kilar, CEO of the online video service Hulu, 'A brand is what people say about you when you're not in the room.'[27]

A powerful brand has high *brand equity.* **Brand equity** is the differential effect that knowing the brand name has on customer response to a product and its marketing. It's a measure of the brand's ability to capture consumer preference and loyalty. A brand has positive brand equity when consumers react more favourably to it than to a generic or unbranded version of the same product. It has negative brand equity if consumers react less favourably than to an unbranded version.

Brands vary in the amount of power and value they hold in the marketplace. Some brands – such as Coca-Cola, Nike, Disney, GE, McDonald's, Harley-Davidson and others – become larger-than-life icons that maintain their power in the market for years, even generations. Other brands create fresh consumer excitement and loyalty, brands such as Google, YouTube, Apple, eBay, Twitter and Wikipedia. These brands win in the marketplace not simply because they deliver unique benefits or reliable service. Rather, they succeed because they forge deep connections with customers.

Advertising agency Young & Rubicam's Brand Asset Valuator measures brand strength along four consumer perception dimensions: *differentiation* (what makes a brand stand out), *relevance* (how consumers feel it meets their needs), *knowledge* (how much consumers know about a brand) and *esteem* (how highly consumers regard and respect a brand). Brands with strong brand equity rate high on all four dimensions. A brand must be distinct, or consumers will have no reason to choose it over other brands. But the fact that a brand is highly differentiated doesn't necessarily mean that consumers will buy it. A brand must stand out in ways that are relevant to consumers' needs. But even a differentiated, relevant brand is far from an automatic winner. Before consumers will respond to a brand, they must first know about and understand it. And that familiarity must lead to a strong, positive consumer-brand connection.[28]

Thus, positive brand equity derives from consumer feelings about and connections with a brand. Consumers sometimes bond *very* closely with specific brands. As perhaps the ultimate expression of brand devotion, a surprising number of people – and not just Harley-Davidson fans – have their favourite brand tattooed on their bodies.

A brand with high brand equity is a very valuable asset. *Brand valuation* is the process of estimating the total financial value of a brand. Measuring such value is difficult. However, according to one estimate, the brand value of Google is a whopping €88 billion, with IBM at €66.5 billion, Apple at €64 billion and Microsoft at €59 billion. Other brands rating among the world's most valuable include Coca-Cola, McDonald's, Apple, China Mobile, GE and Nokia.[29] Many of the fastest growing brands are from emerging markets like China.

High brand equity provides a company with many competitive advantages. A powerful brand enjoys a high level of consumer brand awareness and loyalty. Because consumers expect stores to carry a particular brand, the company has more leverage in bargaining with resellers. Because a brand name carries high credibility, the company can more easily launch line and brand extensions. A powerful brand offers the company some defence against fierce price competition.

Brand equity—The differential effect that knowing the brand name has on customer response to the product or its marketing.

Perhaps the ultimate expression of brand devotion is people who have their favourite brand tattooed on their bodies.

Source: Kurtis Meyers

Above all, however, a powerful brand forms the basis for building strong and profitable customer relationships. The fundamental asset underlying brand equity is *customer equity* – the value of customer relationships that a brand creates. A powerful brand is important, but what it really represents is a profitable set of loyal customers. The proper focus of marketing is building customer equity, with brand management serving as a major marketing tool. Companies need to think of themselves not as portfolios of products but as portfolios of customers.

Building strong brands

Branding poses challenging decisions to the marketer. Figure 8.5 shows that the major brand strategy decisions involve *brand positioning*, *brand name selection*, *brand sponsorship* and *brand development*.

Brand positioning

Marketers need to position their brands clearly in target customers' minds. They can position brands at any of three levels.[30] At the lowest level, they can position a brand on *product attributes*. For example, P&G invented the disposable nappy category with its Pampers brand. Early Pampers marketing focused on attributes such as fluid absorption, fit and disposability. In general, however, attributes are the least desirable level for brand positioning. Competitors can easily copy attributes. More importantly, customers are not interested in attributes as such; they are interested in what the attributes will do for them.

A brand can be better positioned by associating its name with a desirable *benefit*. Thus, Pampers can go beyond technical product attributes and talk about the resulting containment and skin-health benefits from dryness. 'There are fewer wet bottoms in the world because of us,' says Jim Stengel, P&G's former global marketing officer. Some successful brands positioned on benefits are FedEx (guaranteed on-time delivery), Nike (performance), Lexus (quality) and Asda-Walmart (low prices).

The strongest brands go beyond attribute or benefit positioning. They are positioned on strong *beliefs and values*. These brands pack an emotional wallop. Brands such as BMW's Mini, Aston Martin, Alexander McQueen, Jack Wills and Agent Provocateur rely less on a product's tangible attributes and more on creating surprise, passion and excitement surrounding a brand – they have earned the accolade of 'cool brands'.[31] Successful brands engage customers on a deep, emotional level. According to P&G's Stengel, 'marketing inspires life, and life inspires marketing'. Thus, P&G knows that, to parents, Pampers mean much more than just containment and dryness:[32]

> If the past, we often thought of P&G's brands in terms of functional benefits. But when P&G began listening very closely to customers, they told us Pampers meant much more to them: Pampers are more about parent–child relationships and total baby care. So we started to say, 'We want to be a brand experience; we want to be there to help support parents and babies as they grow and develop.' In the beginning of this philosophical change, people thought the company was nuts.

Figure 8.5 Major brand strategy decisions

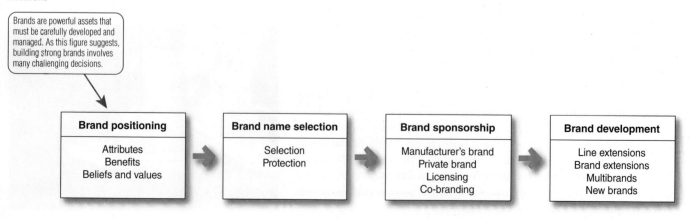

Accor's French budget hotel, formula 1, offers clean rooms, low prices and good service but does not promise expensive furnishings or large bathrooms.

How can nappies help a baby's development? But babies wear nappies 24/7 for almost three years. It actually reorients research and development (R&D) to ask a question like 'How can we help babies sleep better?' Why was P&G concerned about babies sleeping better? Because sleep is important to brain development. It helps relationship skills. Thinking like that, P&G can help improve the lives of its consumers. The equity of great brands has to be something that a consumer finds inspirational and the organisation finds inspirational. P&G's baby care business didn't start growing aggressively until Pampers was changed from being about dryness to helping a mother with her baby's development.

When positioning a brand, the marketer should establish a mission for a brand and a vision of what a brand must be and do. A brand is the company's promise to deliver a specific set of features, benefits, services and experiences consistently to buyers. The brand promise must be simple and honest. Accor's French budget hotel Formula 1, for example, offers clean rooms, low prices and good service but does not promise expensive furnishings or large bathrooms. In contrast, the Ritz-Carlton offers luxurious rooms and a truly memorable experience but does not promise low prices.

Brand name selection

A good name can add greatly to a product's success. However, finding the best brand name is a difficult task. It begins with a careful review of a product and its benefits, the target market and proposed marketing strategies. After that, naming a brand becomes part science, part art and a measure of instinct.

Desirable qualities for a brand name include the following:

1. It should suggest something about a product's benefits and qualities. Some examples include Breathe Right (nose strips) and Food Saver (sealable packaging).

2. It should be easy to pronounce, recognise and remember; examples include Daz, iPod and Jet-Blue.

3. The brand name should be distinctive, such as Rolex and UGG.

4. It should be extendable; Amazon.com began as an online bookseller but chose a name that would allow expansion into other categories.

5. The name should translate easily into foreign languages. Before changing its name to Exxon, Standard Oil of New Jersey rejected the name Enco, which it learned meant a stalled engine when pronounced in Japanese.

6. It should be capable of registration and legal protection. A brand name cannot be registered if it infringes on existing brand names.

Choosing a new brand name is hard work. After a decade of choosing quirky names (e.g Yahoo! and Google) or trademark-proof fictional names (e.g. Novartis, Aventis and Accenture), today's style is to build brands around names that have real meaning. For example, names like Blackboard (school software) are simple and make intuitive sense. But with trademark applications soaring, *available* new names can be hard to find. Try it yourself. Pick a product and see if you can come up with a better name for it. How about Moonshot? Tickle? Vanilla? Treehugger? Simplicity? If you search for them on Google, you'll find that they're already taken.

Once chosen, a brand name must be protected. Many firms try to build a brand name that will eventually become identified with a product category. Brand names such as Kleenex, Levi's, Hoover, Formica and Ziploc have succeeded in this way. However, their very success may threaten the company's rights to the name. Many originally protected brand names – such as cellophane, aspirin, nylon, kerosene, linoleum, yo-yo, trampoline, escalator, thermos and shredded wheat – are now generic names that any seller can use. To protect their brands, marketers present them carefully using the word *brand* and the registered trademark symbol, as in 'BAND-AID® Brand Adhesive Bandages'.

Brand sponsorship

A manufacturer has four sponsorship options. A product may be launched as a *national brand* (or a *manufacturer's brand*), as when Sony and Kellogg sell their output under their own brand names (Sony Bravia HDTV or Kellogg's Frosties). Or the manufacturer may sell to resellers who give a product a *private brand* (also called a *store brand, distributor brand* or an *own-label*). Although most manufacturers create their own brand names, others market *licensed brands*. Finally, two companies can join forces and *co-brand* a product. We discuss each of these options in turn.

Manufacturers' brands versus store brands

Manufacturers' brands have long dominated the retail scene. In recent times, however, an increasing number of retailers and wholesalers have created their own **store brands** (or **private brands**). Although store brands have been gaining strength for more than a decade, recent tougher economic times have created a store-brand boom. Studies show that consumers are buying more private brands, and most don't plan to return to name brands anytime soon. 'Bad times are good times for private labels,' says a brand expert. 'As consumers become more price-conscious, they also become less brand-conscious.'[33] In fact, store brands are growing much faster than national brands. A 2009 survey found that 75 per cent of Britons now opt for supermarket own-labels – triple the figure a year earlier.[34]

Many large retailers skilfully market a deep assortment of store-brand merchandise. European retailers have generally been more successful than those in the US in positioning their own-brands as successful alternatives to manufacturers' brands. For example, in the UK, at leading supermarket Tesco own-brands account for around half of all sales, and Tesco *Finest* (premium) and *Value* (low price) brands are both worth more than £1 billion in annual sales. At the other end of the grocery spectrum, upmarket Whole Foods Market offers an array of store brand products under its own label *Fresh and Wild Everyday Value* range, from organic Canadian maple syrup and frozen chicken Caesar pizza to chewy children's multivitamins and organic whole wheat pasta.[35]

In the so-called *battle of the brands* between manufacturer and private brands, retailers have many advantages. They control what products they stock, where they go on the shelf, what prices they charge and which ones they will feature in local circulars. Retailers often price their store brands lower than comparable national brands, thereby appealing to the budget-conscious shopper in all of us. Although store brands can be hard to establish and costly to stock and promote,

Store brands (or private brand)—A brand created and owned by a reseller of a product or service.

they also yield higher profit margins for the reseller. And they give resellers exclusive products that cannot be bought from competitors, resulting in greater store traffic and loyalty.

To compete with store brands, manufacturer brands must sharpen their value propositions, especially in these lean economic times. In the long term, however, leading brand marketers must invest in R&D to bring out new brands, new features, and continuous quality improvements. They must design strong advertising programmes to maintain high awareness and preference. And they must find ways to 'partner' with major distributors in a search for distribution economies and improved joint performance.

Licensing

Most manufacturers take years and spend millions to create their own brand names. However, some companies license names or symbols previously created by other manufacturers, names of well-known celebrities, or characters from popular movies and books. For a fee, any of these can provide an instant and proven brand name.

Clothing and accessories sellers pay large royalties to adorn their products – from blouses to ties and linens to luggage – with the names or initials of well-known fashion innovators such as Calvin Klein, Tommy Hilfiger, Gucci or Armani. Sellers of children's products attach an almost endless list of character names to clothing, toys, school supplies, linens, dolls, lunch boxes, cereals and other items. Licensed character names range from classics such as Sesame Street, Disney, Star Wars, the Muppets, Scooby Doo, Hello Kitty and Dr Seuss characters to the more recent Hannah Montana. And currently a number of top-selling retail toys are products based on television shows and movies.

Name and character licensing has grown rapidly in recent years. Annual retail sales of licensed products worldwide have grown from only €3 billion in 1977 to €42.5 billion in 1987 and more than €148.6 billion in 2009. Licensing can be a highly profitable business for many companies. For example, Disney, the world's biggest licensor, reported more than $30 billion in worldwide merchandise sales last year. And Nickelodeon has developed a stable full of hugely popular characters, such as Dora the Explorer; Go, Diego, Go!; iCarly; and SpongeBob SquarePants. SpongeBob alone has generated more than $8 billion in sales and licensing fees over the past decade. 'When it comes to licensing its brands for consumer products, Nickelodeon has proved that it has the Midas touch,' states a brand licensing expert.[36]

For example, Coca-Cola has a longstanding venture with Nestlé – Beverage Partners Worldwide (formerly Coca-Cola and Nestlé Refreshments), established in 2001 – to take its tea and coffee brands into global markets alongside Nestlé products. In 2007, this venture was refocused on the ready-to-drink tea market – Nestle tea brands are licensed to Coca-Cola outside the US, but Nestle and Coca-Cola compete in coffee and non-tea beverages worldwide and in the ready-to-drink tea market in the US.

Co-branding

Co-branding occurs when two established brand names of different companies are used on the same product. Co-branding offers many advantages. Because each brand dominates in a different category, the combined brands create broader consumer appeal and greater brand equity. For example, high-end shaving products brand The Art of Shaving partnered with mainstream marketer Gillette to create the Fusion Chrome Collection, featuring a power razor priced at more than £100 (€124.5) and billed as 'the world's most technologically advanced razor'. Through the partnership, The Art of Shaving gains access to Gillette's broader market; Gillette, in turn, adds high-end lustre to its shaving products line.

Co-branding can take advantage of the complementary strengths of two brands. For example, Nestlé has a very successful venture with its Nespresso operation – its Nespresso machines brew high-quality espresso coffee from expensive Nespresso coffee capsules. Nespresso capsules are sold exclusively by Nespresso but the coffee machines carry the brand names of well-known kitchen equipment manufacturers such as Krups, Magimix, Siemens and DeLonghi, Indeed, Krups and Magimix store display models of Nespresso machines are also labelled as 'Made in Switzerland'

Co-branding—The practice of using the established brand names of two different companies on the same product.

Nespresso's main business is selling the coffee capsules, but is supported by high-quality coffee machines co-branded with up-market kitchen appliance specialists.

Source: Getty Images/AFP

(noted on the bottom of the machine). Nestlé's main business is selling the coffee capsules, but this business is supported by high-quality Nespresso coffee machines co-branded with up-market kitchen appliance specialists.

Co-branding also allows a company to expand its existing brand into a category it might otherwise have difficulty entering alone. For example, Nike and Apple co-branded the Nike+iPod Sport Kit, which lets runners link their Nike shoes with their iPods to track and enhance running performance in real time. The Nike+iPod arrangement gives Apple a presence in the sports and fitness market. At the same time, it helps Nike bring new value to its customers.[37]

Co-branding can also have limitations. Such relationships usually involve complex legal contracts and licenses. Co-branding partners must carefully coordinate their advertising, sales promotion and other marketing efforts. Finally, when co-branding, each partner must trust that the other will take good care of its brand. If something damages the reputation of one brand, it can tarnish the co-brand as well.

Brand development

A company has four choices when it comes to developing brands (see Figure 8.6). It can introduce *line extensions, brand extensions, multibrands or new brands*.

Line extensions

Line extension—Extending an existing brand name to new forms, colours, sizes, ingredients or flavours of an existing product category.

Line extensions occur when a company extends existing brand names to new forms, colours, sizes, ingredients or flavours of an existing product category. Thus, the Nestlé's Cheerios line of breakfast cereals includes Honey Cheerios, Cheerio Crunchers and Oat Cheerios.

A company can introduce line extensions as a low-cost, low-risk way to introduce new products. Or it might want to meet consumer desires for variety, use excess capacity, or simply command more shelf space from resellers. However, line extensions involve some risks. An overextended brand name might lose some of its specific meaning. Or heavily extended brands can cause consumer confusion or frustration. Consider Coca-Cola's product range in the United States:

Want a Coke? Okay, but what kind? You can pick from some 20 different varieties. In no-calorie versions alone, Coca-Cola offers two sub-brands: Diet Coke and Coke Zero. Throw in flavoured and no-caffeine versions – caffeine-free Diet Coke, cherry Diet Coke, black cherry vanilla Diet Coke, Diet Coke with lemon, Diet Coke with lime, vanilla Coke Zero, cherry Coke Zero – and you come up with a head-spinning ten diet colas from Coca-Cola. And that does not count Diet Coke with Splenda, Diet Coke Plus (with vitamins B3, B6 and B12 plus minerals zinc and magnesium), or Coca-Cola C2 (half the carbohydrates, half the calories, all the great taste). Each sub-brand has its own marketing spin. But really, are we talking about choices here or just plain confusion? I mean, can you really tell the difference?

Figure 8.6 Brand development strategies

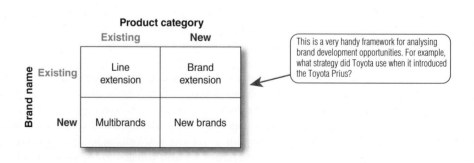

This is a very handy framework for analysing brand development opportunities. For example, what strategy did Toyota use when it introduced the Toyota Prius?

Another risk is that sales of an extension may come at the expense of other items in the line. For example, how much would yet another Diet Coke extension steal from Coca-Cola's own lines versus Pepsi's? A line extension works best when it takes sales away from competing brands, not when it 'cannibalises' a company's other items.

Brand extensions

A **brand extension** extends a current brand name to new or modified products in a new category. For example, Kellogg's has extended its Special K healthy breakfast cereal brand into a full line of cereals plus a line of biscuits, and snack and nutrition bars. Victorinox extended its venerable Swiss Army brand from multi-tool knives to products ranging from cutlery and ballpoint pens to watches, luggage and apparel.

Brand extension—Extending an existing brand name to new product categories.

A brand extension gives a new product instant recognition and faster acceptance. It also saves the high advertising costs usually required to build a new brand name. At the same time, a brand extension strategy involves some risk. The extension may confuse the image of the main brand. Brand extensions such as Heinz pet food, and Life Savers gum met early deaths. And if a brand extension fails, it may harm consumer attitudes toward other products carrying the same brand name. Furthermore, a brand name may not be appropriate to a particular new product, even if it is well made and satisfying – would you consider flying on Hooters Air or wearing an Evian water-filled padded bra (both failed)?

Each year, a survey by brand consultancy TippingSprung rates the year's best and worst brand extensions. Among the worst extensions – those that least fit a brand's core values – were Burger King men's clothing, Playboy energy drink, Kellogg's hip-hop streetwear and a cake decorating kit from Harley-Davidson. 'Marketers have come to learn that the potential harm inflicted on the brand can more than offset short-term revenue opportunities,' says TippingSprung co-founder Robert Sprung. 'But that doesn't seem to stop many from launching extensions that in retrospect seem questionable or even ludicrous.' Thus, companies that are tempted to transfer a brand name must research how well the brand's associations fit the new product.[38]

Multibrands

Companies often market many different brands in a given product category. For example, in the United States, P&G sells six brands of laundry detergent (Tide, Cheer, Gain, Era, Dreft and Ivory), five brands of shampoo (Pantene, Head & Shoulders, Aussie, Herbal Essences and Infusium 23); and four brands of dishwashing detergent (Dawn, Ivory, Joy and Cascade). *Multibranding* offers a way to establish different features that appeal to different customer segments, lock up more reseller shelf space and capture a larger market share. For example, P&G's six laundry detergent brands combined capture a whopping 62 per cent of the US laundry detergent market.

A major drawback of multibranding is that each brand might obtain only a small market share, and none may be very profitable. The company may end up spreading its resources over many brands instead of building a few brands to a highly profitable level. These companies should reduce the number of brands they sell in a given category and set up tighter screening procedures for new brands. In the early 2000s, Unilever trimmed its brand portfolio from 1,600 brand names to 400, with the goal that the money saved by the cost cutting would then be spent promoting Unilever's core, high-yield brands. The company has since focused on its core food brands (e.g. Ben & Jerry's, Lipton Teas), personal care (e.g. Dove, Lynx) and home care (e.g. Persil, Comfort).

New brands

A company might believe that the power of its existing brand name is waning, so a new brand name is needed. Or it may create a new brand name when it enters a new product category for which none of its current brand names are appropriate. For example, Toyota created the separate Lexus brand, targeted toward affluent consumers.

As with multibranding, offering too many new brands can result in a company spreading its resources too thin. And in some industries, such as consumer packaged goods, consumers and retailers have become concerned that there are already too many brands, with too few differences between them. Thus, P&G, Kraft, Unilever and other large consumer-product marketers are now pursuing *megabrand* strategies – weeding out weaker or slower-growing brands and focusing their marketing efforts on brands that can achieve the number-one or number-two market share positions with good growth prospects in their categories.

Managing brands

Companies must manage their brands carefully. First, a brand's positioning must be continuously communicated to consumers. Major brand marketers often spend huge amounts on advertising to create brand awareness and build preference and loyalty. For example, McDonald's spends more than $1.2 (€0.9) billion annually to promote its brand.[39]

Such advertising campaigns can help create name recognition, brand knowledge and perhaps even some brand preference. However, the fact is that brands are not maintained by advertising but by customers' *brand experiences*. Today, customers come to know a brand through a wide range of contacts and touch points. These include advertising but also personal experience with a brand, word of mouth, company Web pages and many others. The company must put as much care into managing these touch points as it does into producing its ads. 'Managing each customer's experience is perhaps the most important ingredient in building [brand] loyalty,' states one branding expert. 'Every memorable interaction . . . must be completed with excellence and . . . must reinforce your brand essence.' A former Disney top executive agrees: 'A brand is a living entity, and it is enriched or undermined cumulatively over time, the product of a thousand small gestures.'[40]

A brand's positioning will not take hold fully unless everyone in the company lives the brand. Therefore the company needs to train its people to be customer-centred. Even better, the company should carry on internal brand building to help employees understand and be enthusiastic about the brand promise. Many companies go even further by training and encouraging their distributors and dealers to serve their customers well.

Finally, companies need to periodically audit their brands' strengths and weaknesses.[41] They should ask: Does our brand excel at delivering benefits that consumers truly value? Is the brand properly positioned? Do all of our consumer touch points support the brand's positioning? Do the brand's managers understand what the brand means to consumers? Does the brand receive proper, sustained support? The brand audit may turn up brands that need more support, brands that need to be dropped, or brands that must be rebranded or repositioned because of changing customer preferences or new competitors.

REVIEWING OBJECTIVES AND KEY TERMS

A product is more than a simple set of tangible features. Each product or service offered to customers can be viewed on three levels. The *core customer value* consists of the core problem-solving benefits that consumers seek when they buy a product. The *actual product* exists around the core and includes the quality level, features, design, brand name and packaging. The *augmented product* is the actual product plus the various services and benefits offered with it, such as a warranty, free delivery, installation and maintenance.

OBJECTIVE 1 Define *product* and the major classifications of products and services (pp. 238–243).

Broadly defined, a *product* is anything that can be offered to a market for attention, acquisition, use or consumption that might satisfy a want or a need. Products include physical objects but also services, events, persons, places, organisations or ideas, or a mixture of these entities. *Services* are products that consist of activities, benefits or satisfactions offered for sale that are essentially intangible, such as banking, hotel, tax preparation and home-repair services.

Products and services fall into two broad classes based on the types of consumers that use them. *Consumer products* – those bought by final consumers – are usually classified according to consumer shopping habits (convenience products, shopping products, speciality products and unsought products). *Industrial products* – purchased for further processing or for use in conducting a business – include materials and parts, capital items, and supplies and services. Other marketable entities – such as organisations, persons, places and ideas – can also be thought of as products.

OBJECTIVE 2 Describe the decisions companies make regarding their individual products and services, product lines and product mixes (pp. 243–251).

Individual product decisions involve product attributes, branding, packaging, labelling and product support services. *Product attribute* decisions involve product quality, features, and style and design. *Branding* decisions include selecting a brand name and developing a brand strategy. *Packaging* provides many key benefits, such as protection, economy, convenience and promotion. Package decisions often include designing *labels*, which identify, describe and possibly promote a product. Companies also develop *product support services* that enhance customer service and satisfaction and safeguard against competitors.

Most companies produce a product line rather than a single product. A *product line* is a group of products that is related in function, customer-purchase needs or distribution channels. All product lines and items offered to customers by a particular seller make up the *product mix*. The mix can be described by four dimensions: width, length, depth and consistency. These dimensions are the tools for developing the company's product strategy.

OBJECTIVE 3 Identify the four characteristics that affect the marketing of services and the additional marketing considerations that services require (pp. 251–256).

Services are characterised by four key characteristics: they are *intangible*, *inseparable*, *variable* and *perishable*. Each characteristic poses problems and marketing requirements. Marketers work to find ways to make the service more tangible, increase the productivity of providers who are inseparable from their products, standardise quality in the face of variability, and

improve demand movements and supply capacities in the face of service perishability.

Good service companies focus attention on *both* customers and employees. They understand the *service profit chain*, which links service firm profits with employee and customer satisfaction. Services marketing strategy calls not only for external marketing but also for *internal marketing* to motivate employees and *interactive marketing* to create service delivery skills among service providers. To succeed, service marketers must create *competitive differentiation*, offer high *service quality* and find ways to increase *service productivity*.

OBJECTIVE 4 Discuss branding strategy – the decisions companies make in building and managing their brands (pp. 256–264).

Some analysts see brands as *the* major enduring asset of a company. Brands are more than just names and symbols; they embody everything that a product or a service *means* to consumers. *Brand equity* is the positive differential effect that knowing brand name has on customer response to a product or a service. A brand with strong brand equity is a very valuable asset.

In building brands, companies need to make decisions about brand positioning, brand name selection, brand sponsorship and brand development. The most powerful *brand positioning* builds around strong consumer beliefs and values. *Brand name selection* involves finding the best brand name based on a careful review of product benefits, the target market and proposed marketing strategies. A manufacturer has four *brand sponsorship* options: it can launch a *national brand* (or a manufacturer's brand), sell to resellers who use a *private brand*, market *licensed brands*, or join forces with another company to *co-brand* a product. A company also has four choices when it comes to developing brands. It can introduce *line extensions*, *brand extensions*, *multibrands* or *new brands*.

Companies must build and manage their brands carefully. A brand's positioning must be continuously communicated to consumers. Advertising can help. However, brands are not maintained by advertising but by customers' *brand experiences*. Customers come to know a brand through a wide range of contacts and interactions. The company must put as much care into managing these touch points as it does into producing its ads. Companies must periodically audit their brands' strengths and weaknesses.

NAVIGATING THE KEY TERMS

OBJECTIVE 1
Product (p. 238)
Service (p. 238)
Consumer product (p. 240)
Convenience product (p. 240)
Shopping product (p. 240)
Speciality product (p. 241)
Unsought product (p. 241)
Industrial product (p. 241)
Social marketing (p. 243)

OBJECTIVE 2
Product quality (p. 244)
Brand (p. 245)
Packaging (p. 246)
Product line (p. 249)
Product mix (product portfolio) (p. 250)

OBJECTIVE 3
Service intangibility (p. 252)
Service inseparability (p. 252)
Service variability (p. 253)
Service perishability (p. 253)
Service profit chain (p. 253)
Internal marketing (p. 254)
Interactive marketing (p. 254)

OBJECTIVE 4
Brand equity (p. 257)
Store brand (private brand) (p. 260)
Co-branding (p. 261)
Line extension (p. 262)
Brand extension (p. 263)

DISCUSSING AND APPLYING THE CONCEPTS

Discussing the concepts

1. Define *product* and the three levels of product. (AACSB: Communication)

2. Compare and contrast industrial products and consumer products. (AACSB: Communication; Reflective Thinking)

3. Explain the importance of product quality and discuss how marketers use quality to create customer value. (AACSB: Communication)

4. Compare and contrast the four brand sponsorship options available to a manufacturer and give an example of each. (AACSB: Communication Reflective Thinking)

5. Discuss the brand development strategies marketers use to develop brands. Give an example of each strategy. (AACSB: Communication; Reflective Thinking)

6. Describe the four characteristics of services that marketers must consider when designing marketing programmes. According to these characteristics, how do the services offered by a massage therapist differ from those offered by a grocery story? (AACSB: Communication; Reflective Thinking)

Applying the concepts

1. What do Betty Crocker, Pillsbury, Cheerios, and Hamburger Helper have in common? They are all familiar brands that are part of the General Mills product mix. Visit the General Mills website (www.generalmills.com) and examine its list of brands. Name and define the four dimensions of a companys product mix and describe General Mills' product mix on these dimensions. (AACSB: Communication; Reflective Thinking; Use of IT)

2. Branding is not just for products and services; the US states are getting in on the action, too, as you learned from reading about *place marketing* in the chapter. One of the most recent examples of state branding in the US comes from Michigan with its Pure Michigan 'campaign', resulting in millions of dollars of tourism revenue. Other famous place branding campaigns include 'Virginia is for Lovers', Florida – the Sunshine State, and 'What Happens in Vegas Stays in Vegas'. in a small group, develop a brand identity proposal for your local area. Present your idea to the rest of the class and explain the meaning you are trying to convey. (AACSB: Communication; Reflective thinking)

3. A product's package is often considered a 'silent salesperson'. It is the last marketing effort before consumers make a selection in the store. One model that is used to evaluate a product's package is the view model: visibility, information, emotion, and workability. Visibility refers to the package's ability to stand out among competing products on the store shelf. Information is the type and amount of information included on the package. Some packages try to simulate an emotional response to influence buyers. Finally all product packages perform the basic function of protecting and dispensing the product. Select two competing brands in a product category and evaluate each brand's packaging using these dimensions. Which brand's packaging is superior? Suggest ways to improve the other brand's packaging. (AACSB: Communication; Reflective Thinking)

Focus on technology

Who would pay €255,000 for a virtual space station? Or €77,000 for an asteroid space resort? How about €76,000 for a virtual bank licence? Players of Entropia Universe, a massive multi-player online game (MMOG), did. Those players are making money and so are the game developers. There's a new business model called 'freemium' driving the economics of these games. Under this model, users play for free but can purchase virtual goods with real money. Worldwide sales of virtual goods were €1.7 billion in 2009 and are predicted to reach €4.6 billion by 2013. The costs of virtual goods are inexpensive – costing about €0.77 – such as the tractor you can buy in *Farmville* or a weapon in *World of Warcraft*. That doesn't seem like much, but when you consider that Zynga's *Frontierville* had five million players within one month of launch we're talking real money!

1. How would you classify virtual goods – a tangible good, an experience, or a service? Discuss the technological factors enabling the growth of virtual goods. (AACSB: Communication; Reflective Thinking)

2. How do players purchase virtual goods? Identify three virtual currencies and their value in euros. (AACSB: Communication; Reflective Thinking)

Focus on ethics

'Meet us before you need us' – that's the motto of a cemetery in Denver. Facing decreasing demand as more Americans choose cremation, cemeteries across the country are marketing to the living in hopes they will become customers in the future. Although funeral homes and cemeteries have long urged customers to prepurchase funeral services before they are needed, it's the new marketing that is drawing criticism. Some activities are low-key, such as poetry workshops, art shows, and nature walks, but some are downright lively. One cemetery staged a fireworks show and skydivers. Other festivities include concerts, outdoor movies, and clowns. Cemetery directors pine for the old days when, more than a century ago, cemeteries were a place for social gatherings where families visited and picnicked near a loved one's grave. Although many of the new activities are staged in the evening, some occur during the day, so directors must use discretion to avoid interrupting a funeral.

1. What types of products are burial plots and prepurchased funeral services? Explain. (AACSB: Communication; Reflective Thinking)

2. Are these marketing activities appropriate for this product?(AACSB: Communication; Ethical Reasoning)

Marketing & the economy

Batteries Plus

Tail store that sells only batteries? That might sound like a sure-product flop in any economy. But weak economic conditions during and following the Great Recession have given a major jolt to Batteries Plus, the nation's first and largest all-battery franchise operation. Same-store sales are up a whopping 20 per cent year-to-year. What is the secret to this chain's success? Demand for products and services comes from products that retain high consumption patterns regardless of economic conditions. Specifically, no matter what the economy, people and businesses alike still use laptops, mp3 players, digital cameras, mobile phones, camcorders and even vehicles. And all these necessary items need battery power. In fact, as people hold onto their devices longer instead of replacing them, that's all the better for Batteries Plus. As older batteries lose their ability to hold a charge, consumers head to Batteries plus for replacements. This dynamic has made Batteries Plus one of the top franchise opportunities in the United States. People may cut back on luxuries, but the demand for batteries is here to stay.

1. Based on derived demand principles – as in the nature of demand for Batteries Plus's market offering – what other businesses should do well in a weak economy?

2. If Batteries Plus does nothing, it still does well in an economic downturn. What recommendations would you make to Batteries Plus to take even better advantage of such conditions and position itself an economic upturn?

Marketing by the numbers

What is a brand worth? It depends on who is measuring it. For example, in 2009, Google was valued to be worth €77 billion by one brand valuation company but only €24.7 billion by another. Although this variation is extreme, it is not uncommon to find valuation of the same brand differing by €15.5 to €23.2 billion. Interbrand and BrandZ publish global brand value rankings each year, but a comparison of these two companies' 2009 ranking reveals an overlap of only six of the top ten brands.

1. Compare and contrast the methodologies used by Interbrand (www.interbrand.com) and BrandZ (www.brandz.com) to determine brand value. Explain why there is a discrepancy

in the rankings from these two companies. (AACSB: Communication; Reflective Thinking; Analytical Reasoning)

2. In 2008 BrandZ ranked Toyota the number one car brand, valuing the brand at more than €27 billion. In 2010,

however, it valued the Toyota brand under €17 billion. Discuss some of the reasons for the drop in Toyota's brand value. (AACSB: Communication; Reflective Thinking)

REFERENCES

1 Adapted from: Diane Brady and Bruce Einhorn, 'Rolls-Royce at your service', *BusinessWeek* (14 November 2005), pp. 22 – 23; Sylvia Pfeifer, 'Rolls-Royce reaps the rewards of client care', *Financial Times* (2 June 2008), p. 22; Dominic O'Connell, 'Rolls-Royce flies high despite airlines' nosedive', *Sunday Times*, (2 August 2009), S3, p. 6; Rob Davies, 'Rolls-Royce engineers its way out of a BP moment', *Daily Mail* (9 November 2010), p. 69; Alex Brunner, 'Rose powers up the turbines', *Daily Mail* (13 November 2010), p.103; Rose Jacobs and Carola Hoya, 'Rolls-Royce plans revenue surge', *Financial Times* (10 February 2012), p. 18.

2 Alex Taylor, 'BMW Ramps Up', *Fortune* (12 November 2007), pp. 14 – 15.

3 R. K. Krishna Kumar, 'Effective marketing must begin with customer engagement', *Marketing News* (15 April 2009), p. 15.

4 www.jordanscereals.co.uk/our-story/countryside-commitment.

5 Information from www.discoverireland.com/us, accessed May 2010. Also see www.iloveny.com and www.visitcalifornia.com, accessed October 2010.

6 www.social-marketing.org/aboutus.html, accessed November 2010.

7 See Rob Gould and Karen Gutierrez, 'Social marketing has a new champion,' *Marketing News*, (7 February 2000), p. 38. Also see Alan R. Andreasen, *Social Marketing in the 21st Century* (Thousand Oaks, CA: Sage Publications, 2006); Philip Kotler and Nancy Lee, *Social Marketing: Improving the Quality of Life*, 3rd edn (Thousand Oaks, CA: Sage Publications, 2008); and www.social-marketing.org, accessed October 2010.

8 Quotes and definitions from Philip Kotler, *Kotler on Marketing* (New York: Free Press, 1999), p. 17; and www.asq.org/glossary/q.html, accessed July 2010.

9 Steve Hamm, 'the vacuum man takes on wet hands', *BusinessWeek*, (2 July 2007), pp. 84 – 86; Lucy Ballinger, 'That's cool, Mr Dyson', *Daily Mail* (17 May 2010), p. 31; 'Dyson wants recruits', *Daily Mail*, (13 February 2012), p. 63.

10 Andy Goldsmith, 'Coke vs. Pepsi: the taste they don't want you to know about,' *The 60-Second Marketer*, www.60secondmarketer.com/60SecondArticles/Branding/cokevs.pepsitast.html, accessed May 2009.

11 See 'Supermarket facts', www.fmi.org/facts_figs/?fuseaction=superfact, accessed April 2010; 'Walmart Facts', www.walmartfacts.com/StateByState/?id=2, accessed April 2010; and 'Shopper decisions made in-store by Ogilvy Action', www.wpp.com, accessed July 2010.

12 See Brennon Slattery, 'Amazon offers easy-to-open packaging', *PC World* (January 2009), p. 36; Peter Clarke, 'This holiday, help fight the dangers of wrap rage,' (23 December 2009), www.fastcompany.com/blog/peter-clarke/shaping-brandsenhancing-lives/consider-oyster-holiday-fight-dangers-wrap-rage and 'Amazon frustration-free packaging', www.amazon.com/gp/help/customer/display.html?nodeId=200285450, accessed November 2010.

13 Sonja Reyes, 'Ad blitz, bottle design fuel debate over Heinz's sales', *Brandweek* (12 February 2007), www.brandweek.com/bw/news/recent_display.jsp?vnu_content_id=1003544497.

14 Natalie Zmuda, 'What went into the updated Pepsi logo', *Advertising Age* (27 October 2008), p. 6; Natalie Zmuda, 'Pepsi, Coke tried to outdo each other with rays of sunshine', *Advertising Age* (19 January 2009), p. 6; Todd Wasserman, 'Grim times prompt more upbeat logos', *Brandweek* (23 February 2009), p. 9; and 'New Pepsi logo kicks off campaign', *McClatchy-Tribune Business News* (15 January 2010).

15 For these and other stories, see Bob Janet, 'Customers never tire of great service', *Dealerscope*, (July 2008), p. 40; and Greta Schulz, 'Nordstrom makes customer service look easy' (11 December 2009), http://amazingserviceguy.com/2370/2370.

16 See the HP Total Care site at http://h71036.www7.hp.com/hho/cache/309717-0-0-225-121.html, accessed May 2010.

17 Information at www.marriott.com/corporateinfo/glance.mi, accessed August 2010.

18 Information on Colgate's product mix from www.colgate.com/app/Colgate/US/HomePage.cvsp, accessed April 2010.

19 See Stuart Elliott, 'A strategy when times are tough: "It's New"', *New York Times* (25 March 2009), accessed at www.nytomes.com; and John A. Quelch and Katherine E. Jocz, 'How to market in a downturn', *Harvard Business Review* (April 2009), pp. 52–62.

20 http://ec.europa.eu/trade/creating-opportunities/economic-sectors/services, accessed 7 February 2012.

21 See CIA, *The World Factbook*, www.cia.gov/library/publications/the-world-factbook/geos/xx.html and www.cia.gov/library/publications/the-world-factbook/fields/2012.html, accessed August 2010; and information from the Bureau of Labor Statistics, www.bls.gov, accessed August 2010.

22 Portions adapted from information in Leonard Berry and Neeli Bendapudi, 'Clueing in customers', *Harvard Business Review* (February 2003), pp. 100–106; with additional information and quotes from Jeff Hansel, 'Mayo hits the blogosphere', *McClatchy-Tribune Business News* (22 January 2009); and www.mayoclinic.org, accessed August 2010.

23 See James L. Heskett, W. Earl Sasser Jr. and Leonard A. Schlesinger, *The Service Profit Chain: How Leading Companies Link Profit and Growth to Loyalty, Satisfaction, and Value* (New York: Free Press, 1997); Heskett, Sasser, and Schlesinger, *The Value Profit Chain: Treat Employees Like Customers and Customers Like Employees* (New York: Free Press, 2003); Christian Homburg, Jan Wieseke and Wayne D. Hoyer, 'Social identity and the service–profit chain', *Journal of Marketing* (March 2009), pp. 38–54; and Rachael W. Y. Yee et al., 'The service–profit chain: a review and extension', *Total Quality Management & Business Excellence* (2009), pp. 617–632.

24 Based on quotes and information from Pete Blackshaw, 'Zappos shows how employees can be brand-builders', *Advertising Age* (2 September 2008), http://adage.com/print?article_id=130646; Jeremy Twitchell, 'Fun counts with Web retailer', *Fort Wayne Journal-Gazette* (16 February 2009), p. C5; Jeffrey M. O'Brien, 'Zappos knows how to kick it', *Fortune*, (2 February 2009), pp. 55–60; and http://about.zappos.com/jobs, accessed August 2010.

25 Portions adapted from Jena McGregor, 'Customer service champs', *BusinessWeek*, (5 March 2007), pp. 52–64; with information from Daniel B. Honigman, '10 minutes with . . . Fred Taylor', *Marketing News* (1 May 2008), pp. 8–27.

26 See 'McAtlas shrugged', *Foreign Policy* (May–June 2001), pp. 26–37; and Philip Kotler and Kevin Lane Keller, *Marketing Management*, 13th edn (Upper Saddle River, NJ: Prentice Hall, 2009), p. 254.

27 Quotes from Jack Trout, '"Branding" Simplified' *Forbes* (19 April 2007), www.forbes.com; and a presentation by Jason Kilar at the Kenan-Flagler Business School, University of North Carolina at Chapel Hill, Autumn 2009.

28 For more on Young & Rubicam's Brand Asset Valuator, see 'Brand asset valuator', Value Based Management.net,www.valuebasedmanagement .net/methods_brand_asset_valuator.html, accessed May 2010; www .brandassetconsulting.com, accessed May 2010; and W. Ronald Lane, Karen Whitehill King and Tom Reichert, *Kleppner's Advertising Procedure*, 18th edn (Upper Saddle River, NJ: Pearson Prentice Hall, 2011), pp. 83–84.

29 *BrandZ Top 100 Most Powerful Brands 2010*, www.brandz.com/output/ brandz-top-100.aspx, accessed (14 February 2012).

30 See Scott Davis, *Brand Asset Management*, 2nd edn (San Francisco, CA: Jossey-Bass, 2002). For more on brand positioning, see Kotler and Keller, *Marketing Management*, 13th edn, chapter 10.

31 'Cool brands', *Sunday Times Supplement* (24 September 2006). Burt Helm, 'For your eyes only', *BusinessWeek* (31 July 2006), p. 66.

32 Adapted from information found in Geoff Colvin, 'Selling P&G,' *Fortune* (17 September 2007), pp. 163–169; 'For P&G, success lies in more than Merely a dryer diaper', *Advertising Age* (15 October 2007), p. 20; Jack Neff, 'Stengel discusses transition at P&G', *Advertising Age*, (21 July 2008), p. 17; and www.jimstengel.com, accessed June 2010.

33 Susan Wong, 'Foods OK, but some can't stomach more ad increases', *Brandweek* (5 January 2009), p. 7. Also see 'Brand names need to reward

consumers to keep them according to study', *PR Newswire* (23 October 2009); 'IDDBA study shows store brands spiking', *Dairy Foods* (January 2010), p. 38; and 'Consumers praise store brands,' *Adweek* (8 April 2010), www.adweek.com/aw/content_display/esearch/e3i66ddacf93da504a9d 504918bc4500715.

34 Andrea Felsted, 'Big rise in the use of own brands', *Financial Times* (4 August 2009), p. 2.

35 See information from www.wholefoodsmarket.com/products/365-everyday-value.php, accessed April 2010.

36 'Nickelodeon expands product offerings and debuts new properties for kids and teens at Licensing 2008 international show', (10 June 2008); Gary Strauss, 'Sponge Bob: a hit from square one', *USA Today* (15 July 2009); David Benady, 'Using licensing to build a megabrand', *Marketing* (3 February 2010), p. 32; and Alan Feldman and others, 'Corporate and brand licensing: year in review', *The Licensing Journal* (February 2010), pp. 1–6.

37 Quote from www.apple.com/ipod/nike, accessed August 2010.

38 The quote and the best/worst examples are from 'Tipping Sprung publishes results from fifth annual brand-extensions survey' (6 January 2009), www.tippingsprung.com/index.php?/knowledge/knowledge_ article/tippingsprung_publishes_results_from_fifth_annual_brand-extension_survey; www.brandchannel.com/papers_review.asp?sp_id=1222, accessed (8 February 2012).

39 'Leading national advertisers', *Advertising Age* (22 June 2009), p. 12.

40 Quotes from Stephen Cole, 'Value of the brand', *CA Magazine* (May 2005), pp. 39–40; and Lawrence A. Crosby and Sheree L. Johnson, 'Experience required', *Marketing Management* (July/August 2007), pp. 21–27.

41 See Kevin Lane Keller, *Strategic Brand Management* (Upper Saddle River, NJ: Prentice Hall, 2008), chapter 10.

VIDEO CASE

General Mills – GoGurt MyMarketingLab

General Mills makes a lot of food. As the sixth largest food company in the world, it sold almost €11.6 billion worth of packaged food last year. In the United States alone, General Mills markets more than 100 leading brands, such as Cheerios, Betty Crocker, Pillsbury and Green Giant. With all this experience in managing brands, it has an advantage when it comes to building equity in brands.

Such is the case of GoGurt. The GoGurt video illustrates how General Mills virtually created the category of portable yogurt. But as competitive pressures mounted and dipped

into GoGurt's market share, the brand faced many challenges. GoGurt managers needed to apply many branding and brand management concepts to turn GoGurt around and reestablish it as the dominant market leader. After viewing the video featuring GoGurt, answer the following questions about the company.

1. GoGurt is the pioneer brand in its category. Is that an advantage or a disadvantage?
2. Discuss brand equity as it relates to Gogurt.
3. How did the managers of GoGurt apply principles of branding to confront the challenges that the brand faced?

COMPANY CASE

John Lewis: middle England's retailer of choice

John Lewis is often seen as a sleepy, conservative high street department store chain with a staid, middle class customer base. But there may be more to the company than this suggests.

Julia Kuttner, an entertainment journalist from east London, seldom shops anywhere other than John Lewis. 'It's the only true department store,' she says. 'I like the fact that I can actually get what I want from John Lewis – my washing machine, my towels, my door handles, my sheepskin boots and even my lunch.' More and more Britons are coming round to Ms Kuttner's way of thinking.

The John Lewis Partnership, which started life as a small drapers shop on Oxford Street in 1864, emerged as the clear winner over Christmas 2009, taking more than £500 million in the five weeks to 2 January. The closely watched like-for-like sales measure – based on stores open at least a year – rose 12.4 per cent on 2008 and 10.4 per cent on 2007 to leave rivals in the shade. Waitrose, the food arm of the John Lewis Partnership, was the fastest-growing food retailer over the festive season. To round off its recent success, John Lewis was named Britain's favourite retailer for a third year in a row by Verdict, the retail research group. 'It's the moral face of retailing,' says one experienced retail analyst.

Indeed, part of John Lewis's winning formula is down to its unusual ownership structure. The John Lewis Partnership's 69,000 staff own John Lewis, Waitrose and the financial services arm Greenbee. Staff receive an annual bonus based on the profits of the business, and are called 'partners'. The more effort they put in, the more they get back. 'In this tough year, people have risen to that,' says Andy Street, managing director of John Lewis. The company believes that this structure – put in place by John Spedan Lewis in 1929 – fosters better customer services, lower staff turnover and higher trust among customers.

Outsiders agree the structure has played a key part in John Lewis's success, although some rivals believe the set-up, which also gives staff a say in the running of the business, can also be frustrating for managers. 'Is it the utopian business? Of course it's not. They have their flaws,' says the retail analyst. But it enables John Lewis to 'pay slightly more than the competition does, and they leverage that, to get more solid, wholesome people, who take more of a pride in what they do.'

Nonetheless, the ownership structure helps the chain to deliver strong customer service, while customers are also attracted by its long-held promise to be 'never knowingly undersold' by rivals. Mr Street says these factors have come into their own in the downturn. 'What is really special about John Lewis this year is somehow we managed to hold customers' trust as we went through the recession,' he says. 'We had a very difficult first half of the year, but customers knew we were not compromising on quality of product, on price, or on service. As a consequence, when things got a little better for customers, they wanted to shop with us.'

He adds that the structure has also enabled John Lewis to take a long-term view. 'Through the first half of the year, because we were not beholden to the City, I was not forced to do things that would damage the business, even if they promoted profit in the short term.'

But it is not just the ownership structure that has worked in the chain's favour. John Lewis carries a wide product range and in recent years has been sharpening its offer and refreshing its stores. 'Over the last 10 years or so, a group of younger, more ambitious, more dynamic managers have come through the ranks and I think they have upped the pace, both in the department stores, and in Waitrose,' says the retail analyst. Managing director Andy Street says the key is to be contemporary, without being 'bleeding-edge trendy'. In the early 2010s, the John Lewis stores have introduced high-fashion products from such names as Aspinal of London, Orla Kiely, DKNY, Guess, Gucci and Tag Heuer.

The company was able to continue its investment plan through the recession of the late-2000s to improve stores, product mix and the website operation.

John Lewis' direct Internet operation has been radically changed. The catalyst was a mocking ad from Dixons, the discount electrical chain, which in 2009 urged shoppers to: 'Step into middle England's best-loved department store, stroll through haberdashery to the audiovisual department where an awfully well brought-up man will bend over backwards to find the right television for you – and then go to dixons.co.uk and buy it.'

In fact, positioned at the other end of the market to Dixons, John Lewis has built an enviable reputation for giving the best advice to shoppers. In the run-up to Christmas 2011, its consumer electronics floors were so overrun that customer ticketing machines were put into action to manage waiting shoppers. In 1950s-style queues shoppers waited patiently for their number to come up so they could to speak to an assistant. John Lewis beat the downward trend in sales: its electricals and home technology takings increased almost 4 per cent in the first six months of 2011.

Indeed, even though it is private, the John Lewis Partnership has been prepared to tap capital markets, issuing a £275 million bond in March 2011, to fund John Lewis and Waitrose.

Over recent years, John Lewis has opened a new department store in Cardiff, and also a smaller format home furnishings outlet in Poole. Based on the success of Poole, the group plans to open up to 50 home and electrical stores. They will be key to expansion after the company was forced to scale down its ambitions to open at least half a dozen department stores, as property developers shelved regional shopping centres. Waitrose has also been pushing ahead, most notably with the launch of its first-ever value range – Essential Waitrose – which has contributed to its sales surge.

John Lewis may also have been in a sweet spot as far as customers are concerned. While unemployment has eaten into spending, those in jobs have benefited from low interest rates and energy costs.

But life is going to get tougher for some of the people who had more money to spend in the late-2000s. Middle England faces the prospect of higher VAT, potentially higher interest rates and cuts to the public sector where some shoppers may be employed. 'Next year is going to be more difficult,' says Mr Street in 2010. Indeed, sales in John Lewis stores fell 1.4 per cent in the week to 9 January, as the big freeze settled on Britain.

Given the challenging outlook, the chain is already thinking ahead. While it will continue to focus on the middle to premium market, it has already introduced a value range of homewares such as cutlery and electrical appliances. But it is not just economic headwinds that may be against John Lewis this year. According to Mr Street: 'If you have a very good season like this, everyone will be trying to work out what we have done and will be gunning for us.'

Nonetheless, John Lewis is poised for expansion into Europe, bolstering its website to attract international orders and enabling the group to gather data on which European cities could support its department stores. The company is planning its first forays into the US and Australia, and is recruiting its first partners outside the UK for a buying office in India.

RUNNING THE NATIONAL HEALTH SERVICE LIKE JOHN LEWIS?

Interestingly, John Lewis is also in the headlines for other reasons. Early in 2012, Deputy Prime Minister, Nick Clegg called for the UK to become 'more of a John Lewis economy'. The department store has become an emblem of a new capitalism for politicians, and more mutually owned businesses has been an oft-mooted ambition of all three main UK political parties.

The Partnership is even advising the British government on how its model could be applied to the public sector. In 2011, John Lewis staff gave lessons to British police officers in how to be more professional and considerate when dealing with victims and witnesses of crime.

A unique development in the history of the National Health Service is the attempt by Circle, which in 2012 became the first private company to take control of a full-service NHS hospital in the UK. A Circle hospital, founder of Circle Mr Ali Parsa says, is in part 'a solution shop, in business jargon', full of highly paid professionals called upon to use their judgment, McKinsey-style, to solve problems. Yet they must also do something 'no management consultant does, which is very precise, value-added processes' such as performing cataract surgery. 'How do you blend those two? How do you create a place where individuals feel empowered to use their intuition, professional knowledge and judgment, but also work as a highly disciplined team?' he asks. His faith is in what he calls 'distributed leadership' expressed in Circle's ownership structure. His message to hospital staff is that: 'You will all be given shares – not to get rich, but to have control.' Mr Parsa seems to want to run a hospital like a John Lewis store.

Questions for discussion

1. What do you think that the John Lewis brand means to consumers? Is this brand a strength or a weakness as the company moves forward in tough economic conditions on the high street?
2. What is John Lewis actually selling? What are loyal John Lewis customers buying? Discuss these questions in terms of the core benefit, actual product and augmented product levels.
3. What recommendations would you make to the managing director for the future of the John Lewis Partnership?
4. Can the elements of a successful service model like John Lewis really be transferred to public services? Can a hospital be like a John Lewis shop? What are the barriers likely to be?

Sources: Andrea Felsted, 'Consumer trust sees John Lewis Set retail pace', *Financial Times* (16/17 January 2010), p. 13; Jaya Narain, 'Long arm of the store', *Daily Mail* (5 January 2011), p. 3; Andrea Felsted. 'Partners hold key to John Lewis success', *Financial Times* (22/23 January 2011), p. 13; Claer Barrett, 'John Lewis to expand into Europe', *Financial Times* (14 February 2011), p. 20; Kate Walsh, 'Middle England's store bites back', *Sunday Times* (13 March 2011), S3, p. 1 & p. 8; Phillip Blond, '"John Lewis economy" talk is never knowingly undersold', *Financial Times* (17 January 2012); Sarah Neville, 'NHS tests John Lewis-style management', *Financial Times* (1 February 2012).

CHAPTER NINE

Developing new products and managing the product life cycle

Chapter preview

In the previous chapter, you learned how marketers manage and develop products and brands. In this chapter, we examine two additional product topics: developing new products and managing products through their life cycles. New products are the lifeblood of an organisation. However, new product development is risky, and many new products fail. So, the first part of this chapter lays out a process for finding and growing successful new products. Once introduced, marketers want their products to enjoy long and happy lives. In the second part of this chapter, you'll see that every product passes through several stages, and each stage poses new challenges requiring different marketing strategies and tactics. Finally, we wrap up our product discussion by looking at two additional considerations: social responsibility in product decisions and international product and services marketing.

For starters, consider Google, one of the world's most innovative companies. Google seems to come up with an almost unending flow of knock-your-eye-out new technologies and services. If it has to do with finding, refining or using information, there is probably an innovative Google solution for it. At Google, innovation is not just a process; it is in the very spirit of the place.

Objective outline

➤ **Objective 1** Explain how companies find and develop new product ideas.
New product development strategy (p. 275)

➤ **Objective 2** List and define the steps in the new product development process and the major considerations in managing this process.
The new product development process (pp. 276–283)
Managing new product development (pp. 283–286)

➤ **Objective 3** Describe the stages of the product life cycle (PLC) and how marketing strategies change during the PLC.
Product life-cycle strategies (pp. 287–291)

➤ **Objective 4** Discuss two additional product issues: socially responsible product decisions and international product and services marketing.
Additional product and service considerations (pp. 292–293)

Google

Google is wildly innovative. It recently topped *Fast Company* magazine's list of the world's most innovative companies, and it regularly ranks among everyone else's top two or three innovators. Google is also spectacularly successful. Despite formidable competition from giants like Microsoft and Yahoo!, Google's share in its core business – online search – stands at a decisive 66 per cent, 2.5 times the combined market shares of its two closest competitors. The company also captures 86 per cent of the mobile-search market and 60 per cent of all search related advertising revenues.

But Google has grown to become much more than just an Internet search and advertising company. Google's mission is 'to organise the world's information and make it universally accessible and useful'. In Google's view, information is a kind of natural resource–one to be mined and refined and universally distributed. That idea unifies what would otherwise appear to be a widely diverse set of Google projects, such as mapping the world, searching the Web on a mobile phone screen, or even providing for the early detection of flu epidemics. If it has to do with harnessing and using information, Google's got it covered in some innovative way.

Google knows how to innovate. At many companies, new product development is a cautious, step-by-step affair that might take a year or two to unfold. In contrast, Google's freewheeling new product development process moves at the speed of light. The nimble innovator implements major new services in less time than it takes competitors to refine and approve an initial idea. For example, a Google senior project manager describes the lightning-quick development of iGoogle, Google's customisable home page:

> It was clear to Google that there were two groups [of Google users]: people who loved the site's clean, classic look and people who wanted tons of information there – email, news, local weather. [For those who wanted a fuller home page] iGoogle started out with me and three engineers. I was 22, and I thought, 'This is awesome.' Six weeks later, we launched the first version in May. The happiness metrics were good, there was healthy growth, and by September, we had [iGoogle fully operational with] a link on Google.com.

Such fast-paced innovation would boggle the minds of product developers at most other companies, but at Google it is standard operating procedure. 'That's what we do,' says Google's vice president for search products and user experience. 'The hardest part about indoctrinating people into our culture is when engineers show me a prototype and I'm like, "Great, let's go!" They'll say, "Oh, no, it's not ready." I tell them, "The Googly thing is to launch it early on Google Labs [a site where users can try out experimental Google

Google is spectacularly successful and wildly innovative. Ask the people who work there and they'll tell you that innovation is more than just a process; it's in the air, in the spirit of the place.

Source: Eyevine Ltd./Eros Hoagland

applications] and then to iterate, learning what the market wants – and making it great."' Adds a Google engineering manager, 'We set an operational tempo: when in doubt, do something. If you have two paths and you're not sure which is right, take the fastest path.'

According to Google CEO Eric Schmidt, when it comes to new product development at Google, there are no two-year plans. The company's new product planning looks ahead only four to five months. Schmidt says that he would rather see projects fail quickly than a carefully planned, long drawn-out project fail.

Google's famously chaotic innovation process has unleashed a seemingly unending flurry of diverse products, ranging from an e-mail service (Gmail), a blog search engine (Google Blog Search), an online payment service (Google Checkout) and a photo-sharing service (Google Picasa) to a universal platform for mobile-phone applications (Google Android), a cloud-friendly Web browser (Chrome), projects for mapping and exploring the world (Google Maps and Google Earth) and even an early-warning system for flu outbreaks in your area (FluTrends). Google claims that FluTrends has identified outbreaks two weeks sooner than has the US Center for Disease Control and Prevention.

Google is open to new product ideas from about any source. What ties it all together is the company's passion for helping people find and use information. Innovation is the responsibility of every Google employee. Google engineers are encouraged to spend 20 per cent of their time developing their own new product ideas. And all new Google ideas are quickly tested in beta form by the ultimate judges – those who will use them. According to one observer:

> Any time you cram some 20,000 of the world's smartest people into one company, you can expect to grow a garden of unrelated ideas. Especially when you give some of those geniuses one workday a week – Google's famous '20 percent time' – to work on whatever projects fan their passions. And especially when you create Google Labs (www.googlelabs.com), a Web site where the public can kick the tires on half-baked Google creations. Some Labs projects go on to become real Google services, and others are quietly snuffed out.

In the end, at Google, innovation is more than a process; it is part of the company's DNA. 'Where does innovation happen at Google? It happens everywhere,' says a Google research scientist.

Talk to Googlers at various levels and departments, and one powerful theme emerges: whether they are designing search engines for the blind or preparing meals for their colleagues, these people feel that their work can change the world. The marvel of Google is its ability to continue to instill a sense of creative fearlessness and ambition in its employees. Prospective hires are often asked, 'If you could change the world using Google's resources, what would you build?' But here, this is not a goofy or even theoretical question: Google wants to know because thinking – and building – on that scale is what Google does. This, after all, is the company that wants to make available online every page of every book ever published. Smaller-gauge ideas die of disinterest. When it comes to innovation, Google *is* different. But the difference is not tangible. It is in the air – in the spirit of the place.[1]

AUTHOR COMMENT

Google's famously chaotic innovation process has unleashed a seemingly unending flurry of diverse new products. But at Google, innovation is more than a process. It is part of the company's DNA. 'Where does innovation happen at Google? It happens everywhere.'

As the Google story suggests, companies that excel at developing and managing new products reap big rewards. Every product seems to go through a life cycle (PLC): it is born, goes through several phases and eventually dies as newer products come along that create new or greater value for customers.

The PLC presents two major challenges: first, because all products eventually decline, a firm must be good at developing new products to replace aging ones (the challenge of *new product development*). Second, a firm must be good at adapting its marketing strategies in the face of changing tastes, technologies and competition as products pass through stages (the challenge of *PLC strategies*). We first look at the problem of finding and developing new products and then at the problem of managing them successfully over their life cycles.

AUTHOR COMMENT

New products are the lifeblood of a company. As old products mature and fade away, companies must develop new ones to take their place. For example, only eight years after it unveiled its first iPod, 51 per cent of Apple's revenues came from iPods, iPhones and iTunes.

NEW PRODUCT DEVELOPMENT STRATEGY

A firm can obtain new products in two ways. One is through *acquisition* – by buying a whole company, a patent or a licence to produce someone else's product. The other is through a firm's own **new product development** efforts. By *new products* we mean original products, product improvements, product modifications, and new brands that a firm develops through its own R&D efforts. In this chapter, we will concentrate on new product development.

New products are important – to both customers and the marketers who serve them. For customers, they bring new solutions and variety to their lives. For companies, new products are a key source of growth. Even in a down economy, companies must continue to innovate. New products provide new ways to connect with customers as they adapt their buying to changing economic times. Bad times are 'when winners and losers get created', says former Xerox CEO Anne Mulcahy. 'The ability to reinforce great marketing and great brand is extraordinarily important.' John Hayes, CEO of American Express, agrees: 'The world will pass you by if you are not constantly innovating.'[2]

Yet innovation can be very expensive and very risky. New products face tough odds. According to one estimate, 80 per cent of all new products fail or dramatically underperform. For example, in the United States each year, companies lose an estimated €15.6 billion to €23.4 billion on failed food products alone, and it is estimated that around 90 per cent of new consumer products launched in Europe fail.[3]

Why do so many new products fail? There are several reasons. Although an idea may be good, the company may overestimate market size. The actual product may be poorly designed. Or it might be incorrectly positioned, launched at the wrong time, priced too high or poorly advertised. A high-level executive might push a favourite idea despite poor marketing research findings. Sometimes the costs of product development are higher than expected, and sometimes competitors fight back harder than expected.

However, the reasons behind some new product failures seem pretty obvious. Try the following on for size. Some products fail because they simply didn't bring value to customers, while others because they attached trusted brand names to something totally out of character. Examples include: from the babyfood specialist, Gerber Singles, food for adults (perhaps the tasty pureed sweet-and-sour pork or chicken Madeira); from the motor cycle icon Harley-Davidson, cake-decorating kits, perfumes and after-shaves (to capture the smell of oil and exhaust fumes?); from toothpaste leader Colgate, a range of food products named Kitchen Entrée; Pepsi AM (a caffeine substitute for coffee at breakfast); Thirsty Cat and Thirsty Dog, bottled water for pets; and underwear from pen maker BIC. Really, what were they thinking?

New product development— The development of original products, product improvements, product modifications and new brands through the firm's own product development efforts.

AUTHOR COMMENT

Companies cannot just hope that they will stumble across good new products. Instead, they must develop a systematic new product development process.

THE NEW PRODUCT DEVELOPMENT PROCESS

Companies face a problem: they must develop new products, but the odds weigh heavily against success. To create successful new products, a company must understand its consumers, markets, and competitors and develop products that deliver superior value to customers. It must carry out strong new product planning and set up a systematic, customer-driven *new product development process* for finding and growing new products. Figure 9.1 shows the eight major steps in this process.

Idea generation

Idea generation—The systematic search for new-product ideas.

New product development starts with **idea generation** – the systematic search for new product ideas. A company typically generates hundreds of ideas, even thousands, to find a few good ones. Major sources of new product ideas include internal sources and external sources such as customers, competitors, distributors and suppliers, and others.

Internal idea sources

Using *internal sources*, a company can find new ideas through formal R&D. However, in one survey, 750 global CEOs reported that only 14 per cent of their innovation ideas came from traditional R&D. Instead, 41 per cent came from employees, and 36 per cent came from customers.[4]

Thus, beyond its internal R&D process, companies can pick the brains of its employees – from executives to scientists, engineers and manufacturing staff to salespeople. Many companies have developed successful 'intrapreneurial' programmes that encourage employees to envision and develop new product ideas. For example, the Internet networking company Cisco makes it everybody's business to come up with great ideas. It set up an internal wiki called Idea Zone or I-Zone, through which any Cisco employee can propose an idea for a new product or comment on or modify someone else's proposed idea. Since its inception, I-Zone has generated hundreds of ideas, leading to the formation of four new Cisco business units.[5]

External idea sources

Companies can also obtain good new product ideas from any of a number of external sources. For example, *distributors and suppliers* can contribute ideas. Distributors are close to the market and can pass along information about consumer problems and new product possibilities. Suppliers can tell the company about new concepts, techniques and materials that can be used to develop new products. *Competitors* are another important source. Companies watch competitors' ads to get clues about their new products. They buy competing new products, take them apart to see how they work, analyse their sales and decide whether they should bring out a new product of their own. Other idea sources include trade magazines, shows and seminars; government agencies; advertising agencies; marketing research firms; university and commercial laboratories; and inventors.

Figure 9.1 Major stages in new-product development

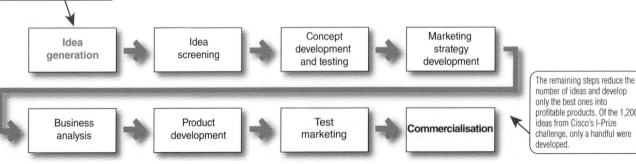

New-product development starts with good new-product ideas—*lots* of them. For example, Cisco's recent I-Prize 'crowdsourcing' challenge attracted 1,200 ideas from 2,500 innovators in 104 countries.

The remaining steps reduce the number of ideas and develop only the best ones into profitable products. Of the 1,200 ideas from Cisco's I-Prize challenge, only a handful were developed.

To harness customer new-product input, 3M has opened nearly two dozen customer innovation centres throughout the world.

Source: 3M Company

Perhaps the most important source of new product ideas is the *customers* themselves. The company can analyse customer questions and complaints to find new products that better solve consumer problems. Or it can invite customers to share suggestions and ideas. For example, Starbucks sponsors My Starbucks Idea, a website that invites customers to share, discuss and vote on new product and service ideas. 'You know better than anyone else what you want from Starbucks,' says the site. 'So tell us. What's your Starbucks idea? Revolutionary or simple – we want to hear it.'[6]

To harness customer new product input, 3M has opened nearly two dozen customer innovation centres throughout the world, including sites in the United States, Brazil, Germany, India, China and Russia. The innovation centres not only generate plenty of customer-driven new product ideas but also help 3M establish productive, long-term customer relationships.[7]

Typically located near company research facilities, the innovation centres engage 3M's corporate customers directly in the innovation process. The idea behind the centres is to gain a richer understanding of customer needs and link these needs to 3M technologies. In a typical customer visit, a customer team meets with 3M marketing and technology experts who pepper them with open-ended questions. Next, together, the customer and 3M teams visit the 'World of Innovation' showroom, where they are exposed to more than 40 3M technology platforms – core technologies in areas like optical films, reflective materials, abrasives and adhesives. This interaction often sparks novel connections and solutions to the customer's needs.

For instance, 3M and customer Visteon Corporation, an automotive supplier, have worked together in the development of a next-generation concept vehicle that incorporates 3M technologies not originally developed for automative applications. Visteon's visit to an innovation centre led to the idea of using 3M's 3D technology for navigation displays, Thinsulate materials to reduce noise and optical films to hide functional elements of the dashboard unless the driver wants them displayed.

Crowdsourcing

More broadly, many companies are now developing *crowdsourcing* or *open-innovation* new product idea programmes. **Crowdsourcing** throws the innovation doors wide open, inviting broad communities of people – customers, employees, independent scientists and researchers, and even the

Crowdsourcing—Inviting broad communities of people – customers, employees, independent scientists and researchers and even the public at large – into the new-product innovation process.

public at large – into the new product innovation process. The idea, says one analyst, is that when it comes to helping to improve 'your products, services, website, or marketing efforts . . . two heads – or 2,000 or 20,000 – are better than one'.[8]

For example, when Netflix wanted to improve the accuracy of its online recommendation system, which makes movie recommendations to customers based on their ratings of other movies they have rented, it launched a crowdsourcing effort called Netflix Prize.[9]

It was a quest that Netflix scientists and mathematicians have been working on for about a decade. Rather than hiring even more computer scientists to work on the project, Netflix decided to open it up to the world. 'We'd like to think that we have smart people bumping around the building, but we don't have anything compared to the worldwide intelligentsia,' says Netflix vice president Steve Swasey. The company created a website, NetflixPrize.com, which issued an open challenge and promised a $1 million prize to whomever submitted the best solution for improving the accuracy of the Cinematch by at least 10 per cent. Nearly three years and more than 51,000 participants later, Netflix awarded the prize to BellKors Pragmatic Chaos, a seven-member superteam consisting of engineers, statisticians and researchers from the United States, Australia, Canada and Israel. 'It was a very innovative way to generate more ideas,' says Swasey. 'If you think about it, 51,000 scientists' devoted their intelligence, creativity and man-hours to the project, all for only $1 million.

Similarly, Dell's IdeaStorm website asks consumers or anyone else for insights on how to improve the company's product offering. Users post suggestions, the community votes, and the most popular ideas rise to the top. Since its launch in 2007, the site has received more than 13,000 ideas and 713,000 votes.[10]

Crowdsourcing network InnoCentive puts its corporate clients ('seekers') in touch with its global network of more than 200,000 scientists ('solvers'). The seeker companies post 'challenges', and solvers can earn up to $1 million for providing solutions. For example, P&G wanted to create a dishwashing detergent smart enough to reveal when just the right amount of soap has been added to a sink full of dirty dishes. After seeing the problem posted on InnoCentive, an Italian chemist working from her home laboratory solved the problem by creating a new kind of dye that turns dishwater blue when a certain amount of soap is added. Her reward: $30,000. P&G estimates that more than 50 per cent of its new product innovations today have elements that originated outside the company, up from 15 per cent in 2000.[11]

Crowdsourcing can produce a flood of innovative ideas. In fact, opening the floodgates to anyone and everyone can overwhelm the company with ideas – some good and some bad. 'Even a small crowdsourcing event can generate a few hundred ideas. If I told you next year you're going to get 20,000 ideas from your customers, how would you process that?' For example, when Cisco Systems sponsored its open-innovation effort called I-Prize, soliciting ideas from external sources, it received more than 1,200 distinct ideas from more than 2,500 innovators from 104 countries. 'The evaluation process was far more labor-intensive than we'd anticipated,' says Cisco's chief technology officer. It required 'significant investments of time, energy, patience, and imagination . . . to discern the gems hidden within rough stones.' In the end, a team of six Cisco people worked full-time for three months to carve 40 semi-finalists from over 1,200 ideas.[12]

Truly innovative companies do not rely only on one source or another for new product ideas. Instead, according to one expert, they create 'extensive networks for capturing inspiration from every possible source, from employees at every walk of the company to customers to other innovators and myriad points beyond'.[13]

Idea screening

Idea screening—Screening new-product ideas to spot good ideas and drop poor ones as soon as possible.

The purpose of idea generation is to create a large number of ideas. The purpose of the succeeding stages is to *reduce* that number. The first idea-reducing stage is **idea screening**, which helps spot good ideas and drop poor ones as soon as possible. Product development costs rise greatly in later stages, so the company wants to go ahead only with those product ideas that will turn into profitable products.

Many companies require their executives to write up new product ideas in a standard format that can be reviewed by a new product committee. The write-up describes a product or a service, the proposed customer value proposition, the target market and the competition. It makes some rough estimates of market size, product price, development time and costs, manufacturing costs and rate of return. The committee then evaluates the idea against a set of general criteria.

One marketing expert proposes an R-W-W ('real, win, worth doing') product screening framework that asks three questions. First, *Is it real?* Is there a real need and desire for a particular product and will customers buy it? Is there a clear product concept and will such a product satisfy the market? Second, *Can we win?* Does a particular product offer a sustainable competitive advantage? Does the company have the resources to make such a product a success? Finally, *Is it worth doing?* Does a particular product fit the company's overall growth strategy? Does it offer sufficient profit potential? The company should be able to answer yes to all three R-W-W questions before developing a new product idea further.[14]

Concept development and testing

An attractive idea must be developed into a **product concept**. It is important to distinguish between a product idea, a product concept and a product image. A *product idea* is an idea for a possible product that the company can see itself offering to the market. A *product concept* is a detailed version of the idea stated in meaningful consumer terms. A *product image* is the way consumers perceive an actual or potential product.

Product concept—A detailed version of the new-product idea stated in meaningful consumer terms.

Concept development

Suppose a car manufacturer has developed a practical battery-powered, all-electric car. Its initial prototype is a sleek, sporty roadster convertible that sells for more than €87,000.[15] However, in the near future, it plans to introduce more-affordable, mass-market versions that will compete with today's hybrid and electric cars. This 100 per cent electric car will accelerate from 0 to 60 miles per hour in 5.6 seconds, travel more than 300 miles on a single charge, recharge in 45 minutes from a normal 120-volt electrical outlet, and cost about one penny per mile to operate.

Looking ahead, the marketer's task is to develop this new product into alternative product concepts, find out how attractive each concept is to customers, and choose the best one. It might create the following product concepts for this electric car:

- *Concept 1.* An affordably priced mid-size car designed as a second family car to be used around town for running errands and visiting friends.
- *Concept 2.* A mid-priced sporty compact appealing to young singles and couples.
- *Concept 3.* A 'green' car appealing to environmentally conscious people who want practical, low-polluting transportation.
- *Concept 4.* A high-end midsize utility vehicle appealing to those who love the space SUVs provide but lament the poor fuel mileage.

Concept testing

Concept testing calls for testing new product concepts with groups of target consumers. The concepts may be presented to consumers symbolically or physically. Here, in more detail, is concept 3:

Concept testing—Testing new-product concepts with a group of target consumers to find out if the concepts have strong consumer appeal.

An efficient, fun-to-drive, battery-powered compact car that seats four. This 100 per cent electric wonder provides practical and reliable transportation with no pollution. It goes more than 300 miles on a single charge and costs pennies per mile to operate. It is a sensible, responsible alternative to today's pollution-producing gas-guzzlers. Its fully equipped price is €25,000.

Table 9.1   Questions for battery-powered electric car concept test

1. Do you understand the concept of a battery-powered electric car?
2. Do you believe the claims about the car's performance?
3. What are the major benefits of the battery-powered electric car compared with a conventional car?
4. What are its advantages compared with a gas-electric hybrid car?
5. What improvements in the car's features would you suggest?
6. For what uses would you prefer a battery-powered electric car to a conventional car?
7. What would be a reasonable price to charge for the car?
8. Who would be involved in your decision to buy such a car? Who would drive it?
9. Would you buy such a car (definitely, probably, probably not, definitely not)?

Many firms routinely test new product concepts with consumers before attempting to turn them into actual new products. For some concept tests, a word or picture description might be sufficient. However, a more concrete and physical presentation of the concept will increase the reliability of the concept test. After being exposed to the concept, consumers then may be asked to react to it by answering questions similar to those in Table 9.1.

The answers to such questions will help the company decide which concept has the strongest appeal. For example, the last question asks about a consumer's intention to buy. Suppose 2 per cent of consumers say they 'definitely' would buy, and another 5 per cent say 'probably'. The company could project these figures to the full population in this target group to estimate sales volume. Even then, the estimate is uncertain because people do not always carry out their stated intentions.

Marketing strategy development

Marketing strategy development—Designing an initial marketing strategy for a new product based on the product concept.

Suppose the carmaker finds that concept 3 for the electric car tests best. The next step is **marketing strategy development**, designing an initial marketing strategy for introducing this car to the market.

The *marketing strategy statement* consists of three parts. The first part describes the target market; the planned value proposition; and the sales, market share and profit goals for the first few years. Thus:

> The target market is younger, well-educated, moderate- to high-income individuals, couples or small families seeking practical, environmentally responsible transportation. The car will be positioned as more fun to drive and less polluting than today's internal combustion engine or hybrid cars. The company will aim to sell 50,000 cars in the first year, at a loss of not more than €12.5 million. In the second year, the company will aim for sales of 90,000 cars and a profit of €25 million.

The second part of the marketing strategy statement outlines the product's planned price, distribution and marketing budget for the first year:

> The battery-powered electric car will be offered in three colours – red, white, and blue – and will have a full set of accessories as standard features. It will sell at a retail price of €25,000, with 15 per cent off the list price to dealers. Dealers who sell more than 10 cars per month will get an additional discount of 5 per cent on each car sold that month. A marketing budget of €44 million will be split fifty-fifty between a national media campaign and local event marketing. Advertising and the website will emphasise the car's fun spirit and low emissions. During the first year, €94,000 will be spent on marketing research to find out who is buying the car and what their satisfaction levels are.

The third part of the marketing strategy statement describes the planned long-term sales, profit goals and marketing mix strategy:

> We intend to capture a 3 per cent long-run share of the total car market and realize an after-tax return on investment of 15 per cent. To achieve this, product quality will start high and be improved over time. Price will be raised in the second and third years if competition and the economy permit. The total marketing budget will be raised each year by about 10 per cent. Marketing research will be reduced to €50,000 per year after the first year.

Business analysis

Once management has decided on its product concept and marketing strategy, it can evaluate the business attractiveness of the proposal. **Business analysis** involves a review of the sales, costs and profit projections for a new product to find out whether they satisfy the company's objectives. If they do, a product can move to the product development stage.

To estimate sales, the company might look at the sales history of similar products and conduct market surveys. It can then estimate minimum and maximum sales to assess the range of risk. After preparing a sales forecast, management can estimate the expected costs and profits for a product, including marketing, R&D, operations, accounting and finance costs. The company then uses the sales and costs figures to analyse a new product's financial attractiveness.

Business analysis—A review of the sales, costs and profit projections for a new product to find out whether these factors satisfy the company's objectives.

Product development

For many new product concepts, a product may exist only as a word description, a drawing or perhaps a crude mock-up. If a product concept passes the business test, it moves into **product development**. Here, R&D or engineering develops the product concept into a physical product. The product development step, however, now calls for a huge jump in investment. It will show whether a product idea can be turned into a workable product.

The R&D department will develop and test one or more physical versions of the product concept. R&D hopes to design a prototype that will satisfy and excite consumers and that can be produced quickly and at budgeted costs. Developing a successful prototype can take days, weeks, months or even years depending on the product and prototype methods.

Often, products undergo rigorous tests to make sure that they perform safely and effectively, or that consumers will find value in them. Companies can do their own product testing or outsource testing to other firms that specialise in testing.

Marketers often involve actual customers in product testing. For example, HP signs up consumers to evaluate prototype imaging and printing products in their homes and offices. Participants work with pre-release products for periods ranging from a few days to eight weeks and share their experiences about how the products perform in an actual use environment. The product-testing programme gives HP a chance to interact with customers and gain insights about their entire 'out-of-box experience', from product setup and operation to system compatibility. HP personnel might even visit participants' homes to directly observe installation and first usage of the product.[16]

A new product must have the required functional features and also convey the intended psychological characteristics. A battery-powered electric car, for example, should strike consumers as being well built, comfortable and safe. Management must learn what makes consumers decide that a car is well built. To some consumers, this means that the car has 'solid-sounding' doors. To others, it means that the car is able to withstand heavy impact in crash tests. Consumer tests are conducted in which consumers test-drive the car and rate its attributes.

Product development— Developing the product concept into a physical product to ensure that the product idea can be turned into a workable market offering.

Test marketing

If a product passes both the concept test and the product test, the next step is **test marketing**, the stage at which a product and its proposed marketing programme are introduced into realistic

Test marketing—The stage of new-product development in which the product and its proposed marketing programme are tested in realistic market settings.

market settings. Test marketing gives the marketer experience with marketing a product before going to the great expense of full introduction. It lets the company test a product and its entire marketing programme – targeting and positioning strategy, advertising, distribution, pricing, branding and packaging, and budget levels.

The amount of test marketing needed varies with each new product. Test marketing costs can be high, and it takes time that may allow competitors to gain advantages. When the costs of developing and introducing a product are low, or when management is already confident about a new product, the company may do little or no test marketing. In fact, test marketing by consumer-goods firms has been declining in recent years. Companies often do not test-market simple line extensions or copies of successful competitor products.

However, when introducing a new product requires a big investment, when the risks are high, or when management is not sure of a product or its marketing programme, a company may do a lot of test marketing. For instance, KFC conducted more than three years of product and market testing before rolling out its major new Kentucky Grilled Chicken product. The fast-food chain built its legacy on serving crispy, seasoned fried chicken but hopes that the new product will lure back health-conscious consumers who dropped fried chicken from their diets. 'This is transformational for our brand,' says KFC's chief food innovation officer. Given the importance of the decision, 'You might say, "what took you so long",' says the chain's president. 'I've asked that question a couple of times myself. The answer is we had to get it right."[17]

As an alternative to extensive and costly standard test markets, companies can use controlled test markets or simulated test markets. In *controlled test markets*, new products and tactics are tested among controlled groups of customers and stores. In each market, a marketing research agency can be used to measure purchases by a panel of shoppers who report all of their purchases in participating stores. Within test stores, the agency can control such factors as shelf placement, price and in-store promotions for the products being tested. The research agency can also measure television viewing in each panel household and in some situations send special commercials to panel member television sets to test their effect on shopping decisions.

By combining information on each consumer's purchases with consumer demographic and television viewing information, a skilled marketing research agency can provide store-by-store, week-by-week reports on the sales of tested products and the impact of in-store and in-home marketing efforts. Such controlled test markets usually cost much less than standard test markets and can provide accurate forecasts in as little as 12 to 24 weeks. Naturally, the choice of research agency will be important and should reflect the strength of different agencies in local markets.

Companies can also test new products using *simulated test markets*, in which researchers measure consumer responses to new products and marketing tactics in laboratory stores or simulated shopping environments. Many marketers are now using new online simulated marketing technologies to reduce the costs of test marketing and speed up the process. The Instore Marketing Institute summarises:

> The use of computer-driven store simulation technologies to conduct market research and achieve other key business objectives is fast becoming a common practice among consumer product manufacturers and retailers. If conducted properly, virtual store tests can deliver a more accurate representation of at-shelf product selection and other shopping behaviours than traditional methods of consumer research and a faster, more cost-efficient alternative to instore field tests.
>
> While startup costs can be significant, the use of virtual store simulations offers a wide variety of business benefits that practitioners say more than justify the initial expense. The strategy goes well beyond 'pure research' to encompass effective internal planning and collaboration and the fostering of stronger relationships with key retail accounts. Judged in the context of shopper marketing, virtual store simulations can be an indispensable tool for understanding in-store behaviour and designing stores and merchandising programmes that truly meet the needs of consumers.[18]

Rather than just simulating the shopping environment, Procter & Gamble recently launched an actual online store that will serve as a 'learning lab' by which the company can test new products and marketing concepts. The online store lets P&G quickly do real-time testing of marketing tactics – such as e-coupons, cross-selling efforts and advertising – and learn how they affect consumer buying. The online store probably will not boost the company's revenues or profits much. P&G is 'more interested in the data about shoppers and what works for them', says one analyst, '[new products,] product pairings, environmentally friendly pitches, and packaging options.' Says an executive associated with P&G's eStore, 'We're creating this giant sandbox for the brands to play in.'[19]

Commercialisation

Test marketing gives management the information needed to make a final decision about whether to launch the new product. If the company goes ahead with **commercialisation** – introducing a new product into the market – it will face high costs. The company may need to build or rent a manufacturing facility. And, in the case of a major new consumer product, it may spend large amounts on advertising, sales promotion, and other marketing efforts in the first year. For example, to introduce its McCafé coffee in the United States, McDonald's spent €78 million on an advertising blitz that spanned television, print, radio, outdoor, the Internet, events, public relations and sampling. Similarly, Microsoft spent €78 million or more on marketing to introduce its Bing search engine.[20]

The company launching a new product must first decide on introduction *timing*. If a manufacturer's new battery-powered electric car will eat into the sales of its other cars, the introduction may be delayed. If the car can be improved further, or if the economy is down, the company may wait until the following year to launch it. However, if competitors are ready to introduce their own battery-powered models, the company may push to introduce its car sooner.

Next, the company must decide *where* to launch the new product – in a single location, a region, the national market, or the international market. Few companies have the confidence, capital and capacity to launch new products into full national or international distribution from the start. Instead, they develop a planned *market rollout* over time.

Some companies, however, may quickly introduce new models into the full national market. Companies with international distribution systems may introduce new products through swift global rollouts. Microsoft did this with its Windows 7 operating system, using a mammoth advertising blitz to launch the operating system simultaneously in more than 30 markets worldwide.

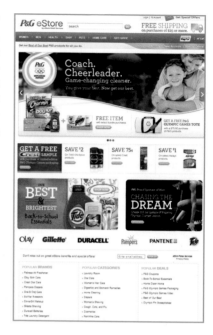

P+G's online store allows the company to do real-time testing of marketing tactics – it has created a 'giant sandbox for the brands to play in'.

Commercialisation— Introducing a new product into the market.

AUTHOR COMMENT

Above all else, new product development must focus on creating customer value. Says P&G's CEO about the company's new product development: 'We've figured out how to keep the consumer at the center of all our decisions. As a result, we don't go far wrong.'

MANAGING NEW PRODUCT DEVELOPMENT

The new product development process shown in Figure 9.1 highlights the important activities needed to find, develop and introduce new products. However, new product development involves more than just going through a set of steps. Companies must take a holistic approach to managing this process. Successful new product development requires a customer-centred, team-based and systematic effort.

Customer-centred new product development

Above all else, new product development must be customer centred. When looking for and developing new products, companies often rely too heavily on technical research in their R&D laboratories. But like everything else in marketing, successful new product development begins with a thorough understanding of what consumers need and value. **Customer-centred new product development** focuses on finding new ways to solve customer problems and create more customer-satisfying experiences.

One study found that the most successful new products are ones that are differentiated, solve major customer problems and offer a compelling customer value proposition. Another study showed that companies that directly engage their customers in the new product innovation process had twice the return on assets and triple the growth in operating income of firms that did not. Thus, customer involvement has a positive effect on the new product development process and product success.[21]

For example, whereas the consumer packaged goods industry's new product success rate is only about 15–20 per cent, P&G's success rate is over 50 per cent. According to former P&G CEO A. G. Lafley, the most important factor in this success is understanding what consumers want. In the past, says Lafley, P&G tried to push new products down to consumers rather than first understanding their needs. But now, P&G employs an immersion process it calls 'Living It', in which researchers go so far as to live with shoppers for several days at a time to envision product ideas based directly on consumer needs. P&G researchers also hang out in stores for similar insights, a process they call 'Working It'. And at its Connect + Development crowdsourcing site, P&G urges customers to submit their own ideas and suggestions for new products and services, current product design, and packaging. 'We figured out how to keep the consumer at the center of all our decisions,' says Lafley. 'As a result, we don't go far wrong.'[22]

For products ranging from consumer package goods to financial services, today's innovative companies get out of the research laboratory and mingle with customers in the search for new customer value. For example, when toy-maker Lego faced sagging sales, and losses of €234 million a year, the underlying problem was that the classic toy company had fallen out of touch with its customers. In the age of the Internet, videogames, iPods and high-tech playthings, traditional toys such as LEGO bricks had been pushed to the back of the cupboard.

> The LEGO product makeover, however, didn't start with engineers working in design laboratories. First, LEGO had to reconnect with customers. So it started by listening to customers, understanding them and including them in the new product development process. To get to know its customers better, for instance, LEGO conducted up-close-and-personal ethnographic studies – hanging out

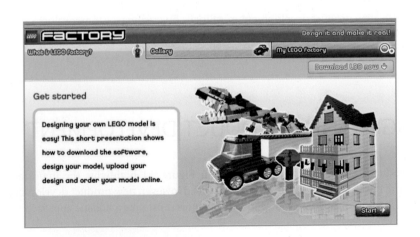

Lego's recovery is underlined by customer – centered new – product development.

Customer-centred new-product development— New-product development that focuses on finding new ways to solve customer problems and create more customer-satisfying experiences.

with and observing children aged seven to nine on their home turf. 'We thought we understood our consumers, the children of the world,' says a LEGO marketer, but it turns out that 'we didn't know them as well as we thought.' The ethnographic research produced a lot of 'Aha! moments' that shattered many of the brand's long-held traditions.

For example, LEGO had long held fast to a 'keep it simple' mantra. From the beginning, it offered only basic play sets – bricks, building bases, beams, doors, windows, wheels and slanting roof tiles – with few or no instructions. The philosophy was that giving children unstructured building sets would stimulate their imaginations and foster creativity. But that concept just wasn't cutting it in the modern world. Today's children get bored easily, and in today's fast-moving environment they are exposed to many more characters and themes. In response, LEGO shifted toward more-specialised, more-structured products.

Thanks to customer-centred new product development, LEGO is now thriving. In the past five years, even as the overall toy market has declined in a weakened economy and as competitors such as Mattel and Hasbro have struggled, LEGO's sales have soared 66 per cent, and its profits have jumped tenfold. 'Kids [including the adult variety] are ruthless,' says a senior LEGO executive. 'If they don't like the product, then at the end of the day . . . all the rest of it won't make any difference. What counts, all that counts, is that you're at the top of kids' wish lists. Thanks to all that listening and customer involvement, that's where LEGO is again.'[23]

Thus, customer-centred new product development begins and ends with understanding customers and involving them in the process. Successful innovation boils down to finding fresh ways to meet customer needs.

Team-based new product development

Good new product development also requires a total-company, cross-functional effort. Some companies organise their new product development process into the orderly sequence of steps shown in Figure 9.1, starting with idea generation and ending with commercialisation. Under this *sequential product development* approach, one company department works individually to complete its stage of the process before passing the new product along to the next department and stage. This orderly, step-by-step process can help bring control to complex and risky projects. But it can also be dangerously slow. In fast-changing, highly competitive markets, such slow-but-sure product development can result in product failures, lost sales and profits, and crumbling market positions.

To get their new products to market more quickly, many companies use a **team-based new product development** approach. Under this approach, company departments work closely together in cross-functional teams, overlapping the steps in the product development process to save time and increase effectiveness. Instead of passing a new product from department to department, the company assembles a team of people from various departments that stays with the new product from start to finish. Such teams usually include people from the marketing, finance, design, manufacturing and legal departments, and even supplier and customer companies. In the sequential process, a bottleneck at one phase can seriously slow an entire project. In the team-based approach, if one area (e.g. marketing) hits a snag, that area can work to resolve the snag while the remainder of the team moves on. Then that area can 'catch up' with the rest of the team down the road.

The team-based approach does have some limitations, however. For example, it sometimes creates more organisational tension and confusion than the more orderly sequential approach. However, in rapidly changing industries facing increasingly shorter product life cycles, the rewards of fast and flexible product development far exceed the risks. Companies that combine a customer-centred approach with team-based new product development gain a big competitive edge by getting the right new products to market faster.

Team-based new product development—An approach to developing new products in which various company departments work closely together, overlapping the steps in the product development process to save time and increase effectiveness.

Systematic new product development

Finally, the new product development process should be holistic and systematic rather than compartmentalised and haphazard. Otherwise, few new ideas will surface, and many good ideas will

RISEHOLME CAMPUS

At companies known for their new-product prowess, such as Reckitt Benckiser, the entire culture encourages, supports and rewards innovation.

Source: The Advertising Archives

sputter and die. To avoid these problems, a company can install an *innovation management system* to collect, review, evaluate and manage new product ideas.

The company can appoint a respected senior person to be the company's innovation manager. It can create Web-based idea management software and encourage all company stakeholders – employees, suppliers, distributors and dealers – to become involved in finding and developing new products. It can assign a cross-functional innovation management committee to evaluate proposed new product ideas and help bring good ideas to market. It can create recognition programmes to reward those who contribute the best ideas.

The innovation management system approach yields two favourable outcomes. First, it helps create an innovation-oriented company culture. It shows that top management supports, encourages and rewards innovation. Second, it will yield a larger number of new product ideas, among which will be found some especially good ones. The good new ideas will be more systematically developed, producing more new product successes. No longer will good ideas wither for the lack of a sounding board or a senior product advocate.

Thus, new product success requires more than simply thinking up a few good ideas, turning them into products and finding customers for them. It requires a holistic approach for finding new ways to create valued customer experiences, from generating and screening new product ideas to creating and rolling out want-satisfying products to customers.

More than this, successful new product development requires a whole-company commitment. At companies known for their new product prowess, such as Google, Apple, Reckitt Benckiser, IDEO, 3M, P&G and GE, the entire culture encourages, supports and rewards innovation.

New product development in turbulent times

When tough economic times hit, or when a company faces financial difficulties, management may be tempted to reduce spending on new product development. However, such thinking is usually shortsighted. By cutting back on new products, the company may make itself less competitive during or after the downturn. In fact, tough times might call for even greater new product development, as the company struggles to better align its market offerings with changing consumer needs and tastes. In difficult times, innovation more often helps than hurts in making the company more competitive and positioning better it for the future. Summarises one analyst:[24]

> Innovation is a messy process – hard to measure and hard to manage. When revenues and earnings decline, executives often conclude that their innovation efforts just aren't worth it. Better to focus on the tried and true than to risk money on untested ideas. The contrary view, of course, is that innovation is both a vaccine against market downturns and an elixir that rejuvenates growth. In today's economy, for example, imagine how much better off General Motors might have fared if it had matched the pace of innovation set by Honda or Toyota. Imagine how much worse off Apple would be had it not – in the midst of previously very difficult times for the company – created the iPod, iTunes, and iPhone.

Thus, rain or shine, good times or bad, a company must continue to innovate and develop new products if it wants to grow and prosper. 'The good news is . . . downturns are times of turbulence [but] are also times of incredible opportunity,' says one marketing consultant. 'Your competitors may be hunkering down, giving you more opportunities.' Another analyst notes that P&G launched two of its most successful (and highest-priced) new products, Swiffer (innovative household cleaning products) and Crest Whitestrips (tooth whitening products), during recessions.[25]

AUTHOR COMMENT

A company's products are born, grow, mature and then decline, just as living things do. To remain vital, a firm must continually develop new products and manage them effectively through their life cycles.

PRODUCT LIFE-CYCLE STRATEGIES

After launching a new product, management wants that product to enjoy a long and happy life. Although it does not expect that product to sell forever, the company wants to earn a decent profit to cover all the effort and risk that went into launching it. Management is aware that each product will have a life cycle, although its exact shape and length is not known in advance.

Figure 9.2 shows a typical **product life cycle** (PLC), the course that a product's sales and profits take over its lifetime. The PLC has five distinct stages:

1. *Product development* begins when the company finds and develops a new product idea. During product development, sales are zero, and the company's investment costs mount.

2. *Introduction* is a period of slow sales growth as a product is introduced in the market. Profits are non-existent in this stage because of the heavy expenses of product introduction.

3. *Growth* is a period of rapid market acceptance and increasing profits.

4. *Maturity* is a period of slowdown in sales growth because a product has achieved acceptance by most potential buyers. Profits level off or decline because of increased marketing outlays to defend a product against competition.

5. *Decline* is the period when sales fall off and profits drop.

Not all products follow all five stages of the PLC. Some products are introduced and die quickly; others stay in the mature stage for a long, long time. Some enter the decline stage and are then cycled back into the growth stage through strong promotion or repositioning. It seems that a well-managed brand could live forever. Venerable brands like Coca-Cola, Gillette, Budweiser, Guinness, American Express and Wells Fargo, for instance, are still going strong after more than 100 years. Guinness beer recently celebrated its 250th anniversary.

The PLC concept can describe a *product class* (petrol-powered motor cars), a *product form* (four-wheel drives or 4 × 4's) or a *brand* (the amazing BMW X5). The PLC concept applies differently in each case. Product classes have the longest life cycles; the sales of many product classes stay in the mature stage for a long time. Product forms, in contrast, tend to have the standard PLC shape. Product forms such as 'dial telephones' and 'VHS tapes' passed through a regular history of introduction, rapid growth, maturity and decline.

Product life cycle (PLC)—The course of a product's sales and profits over its lifetime. It involves five distinct stages: product development, introduction, growth, maturity and decline.

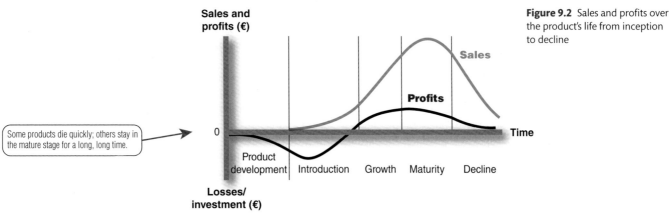

Some products die quickly; others stay in the mature stage for a long, long time.

Figure 9.2 Sales and profits over the product's life from inception to decline

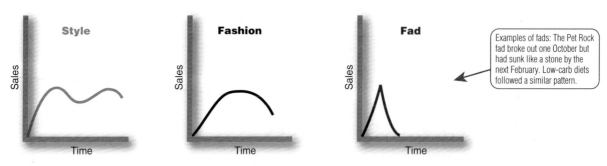

Figure 9.3 Styles, fashions and fads

A specific brand's life cycle can change quickly because of changing competitive attacks and responses. For example, although laundry soaps (product class) and powdered detergents (product form) have enjoyed fairly long life cycles, the life cycles of specific brands have tended to be much shorter. In the United States, today's leading brands of powdered laundry soap are Tide and Cheer; the leading brands almost 100 years ago were the long defunct Fels-Naptha, Octagon and Kirkman.

The PLC concept also can be applied to what are known as styles, fashions and fads. Their special life cycles are shown in Figure 9.3. A **style** is a basic and distinctive mode of expression. For example, styles appear in homes (e.g. country cottage, functional and art deco), clothing (e.g. formal and casual) and art (e.g. realist, surrealist and abstract). Once a style is invented, it may last for generations, passing in and out of vogue. A style has a cycle showing several periods of renewed interest.

A **fashion** is a currently accepted or popular style in a given field. For example, the more formal 'business attire' look of corporate dress of the 1980s and 1990s gave way to the 'business casual' look of the 2000s. Fashions tend to grow slowly, remain popular for a while, then decline slowly.

Fads are temporary periods of unusually high sales driven by consumer enthusiasm and immediate product or brand popularity.[26] A fad may be part of an otherwise normal life cycle, as in the case of recent surges in the sales of poker chips and accessories. Or a fad may comprise a brand's or product's entire life cycle. 'Pet rocks' are a classic example. Upon hearing his friends complain about how expensive it was to care for their dogs, advertising copywriter Gary Dahl joked about his pet rock. He soon wrote a spoof of a dog-training manual for it, titled 'The Care and Training of Your Pet Rock'. Soon Dahl was selling some 1.5 million ordinary beach pebbles in the US at $4 each. Yet the fad, which broke one October, had sunk like a stone by the next February. Dahl's advice to those who want to succeed with a fad: 'Enjoy it while it lasts'. Other examples of fads include the Rubik's Cube and low-carbohydrate diets.[27]

Marketers can apply the PLC concept as a useful framework for describing how products and markets work. And when used carefully, the PLC concept can help in developing good marketing strategies for its different stages. But using the PLC concept for forecasting product performance or developing marketing strategies presents some practical problems. For example, in practice, it is difficult to forecast the sales level at each PLC stage, the length of each stage and the shape of the PLC curve. Using the PLC concept to develop marketing strategy also can be difficult because strategy is both a cause and a result of the PLC. A product's current PLC position suggests the best marketing strategies, and the resulting marketing strategies affect product performance in later stages.

Moreover, marketers should not blindly push products through the traditional PLC stages. Instead, marketers often defy the 'rules' of the life cycle and position or reposition their products in unexpected ways. By doing this, they can rescue mature or declining products and return them to the growth phase of the life cycle. Or they can leapfrog obstacles to slow consumer acceptance and propel new products forward into the growth phase.

The moral of the PLC is that companies must continually innovate or else they risk extinction. No matter how successful its current product lineup, a company must skilfully manage the life cycles of existing products for future success. And to grow, it must develop a steady stream of new products that bring new value to customers.

Style—A basic and distinctive mode of expression.

Fashion—A currently accepted or popular style in a given field.

Fad—A temporary period of unusually high sales driven by consumer enthusiasm and immediate product or brand popularity.

We looked at the product development stage of the PLC in the first part of this chapter. We will now look at strategies for each of the other life-cycle stages.

Introduction stage

The **introduction stage** starts when a new product is first launched. Introduction takes time, and sales growth is apt to be slow. Well-known products such as frozen foods and HDTVs lingered for many years before they entered a stage of more rapid growth.

In this stage, as compared to other stages, profits are negative or low because of the low sales and high distribution and promotion expenses. Much money is needed to attract distributors and build their stocks. Promotion spending is relatively high to inform consumers of a new product and get them to try it. Because the market is not generally ready for product refinements at this stage, the company and its few competitors produce basic versions of a product. These firms focus their selling on those buyers who are the most ready to buy.

A company, especially a *market pioneer*, must choose a launch strategy that is consistent with the intended product positioning. It should realise that the initial strategy is just the first step in a grander marketing plan for a product's entire life cycle. If the pioneer chooses its launch strategy to make a 'killing', it may be sacrificing long-term revenue for the sake of short-term gain. As the pioneer moves through later stages of the life cycle, it must continuously formulate new pricing, promotion and other marketing strategies. It has the best chance of building and retaining market leadership if it plays its cards correctly from the start.

Introduction stage—The PLC stage in which a new product is first distributed and made available for purchase.

Growth stage

If a new product satisfies the market, it will enter a **growth stage**, in which sales will start climbing quickly. The early adopters will continue to buy, and later buyers will start following their lead, especially if they hear favourable word of mouth. Attracted by the opportunities for profit, new competitors will enter the market. They will introduce new product features, and the market will expand. The increase in competitors leads to an increase in the number of distribution outlets, and sales jump just to build reseller inventories. Prices remain where they are or decrease only slightly. Companies keep their promotion spending at the same or a slightly higher level. Educating the market remains a goal, but now the company must also meet the competition.

Profits increase during the growth stage as promotion costs are spread over a large volume and as unit manufacturing costs decrease. A firm uses several strategies to sustain rapid market growth as long as possible. It improves product quality and adds new product features and models. It enters new market segments and new distribution channels. It shifts some advertising from building product awareness to building product conviction and purchase, and it lowers prices at the right time to attract more buyers.

In the growth stage, a firm faces a trade-off between high market share and high current profit. By spending a lot of money on product improvement, promotion and distribution, the company can capture a dominant position. In doing so, however, it gives up maximum current profit, which it hopes to make up in the next stage.

Growth stage—The PLC stage in which a product's sales start climbing quickly.

Maturity stage

At some point, a product's sales growth will slow down, and it will enter the **maturity stage**. This maturity stage normally lasts longer than the previous stages, and it poses strong challenges to marketing management. Most products are in the maturity stage of the life cycle, and therefore most of marketing management deals with a mature product.

The slowdown in sales growth results in many producers with many products to sell. In turn, this overcapacity leads to greater competition. Competitors begin marking down prices, increasing their advertising and sales promotions, and upping their product development budgets to find better versions of a particular product. These steps lead to a drop in profit. Some of the weaker competitors start dropping out, and the industry eventually contains only well-established competitors.

Maturity stage—The PLC stage in which a product's sales growth slows or levels off.

Although many products in the mature stage appear to remain unchanged for long periods, most successful ones are actually evolving to meet changing consumer needs. Product managers should do more than simply ride along with or defend their mature products; a good offence is the best defence. They should consider modifying the market, product and marketing mix.

In *modifying the market*, the company tries to increase consumption by finding new users and new market segments for its brands. For example, Nintendo's Wii had a dramatic effect on the computer gaming market in spite of powerful competition from Microsoft and Sony.

When Satoru Iwata was looking for a strategy to revive Nintendo's fortunes in the computer game market, he soon realised that the Japanese company could not compete against Sony and Microsoft by attempting to woo the core market of 18–35-year-old men interested in playing violent, 'shoot-em-up' games. Instead, he went back to basics, trolling through some of Nintendo's greatest hits like Super Mario Brothers, and concluded that the company had to carve out a new market for itself by reaching out to a broader audience. Going back to basics was a huge gamble at a time when Sony's and Microsoft's consoles had the processing capacity to support hyper-realistic graphics for video games. After years of development, Nintendo launched its Wii console with the innovative motion-sensitive control, which got people up off their normal game-playing position on the couch, up on their feet, serving a virtual tennis ball or getting ready to hit an imaginary baseball off a home plate.

Both the Wii (and the smaller DS) have managed to lure women – who are now half of all users – a previously unthinkable demographic for console makers. As part of its slick marketing, Nintendo featured Nicole Kidman in a DS advertisement, playing a Brain Training Game. Nintendo has successfully broadened the computer gaming market to include children, adults and senior citizens.[28]

A manager may also look for ways to increase usage among present customers. For example, Nintendo also launched Wii Fit, a range of exercise games, and the Balance Board, on which a user can practise yoga or do push-ups. As well as offering games, the Wii brings the personal trainer into the living room, and targets those hoping to lose weight through exercise or simply to stay fit.[29]

The company might also try *modifying a product* – changing characteristics such as quality, features, style or packaging to attract new users and inspire more usage. It can improve a product's styling and attractiveness. It might improve a product's quality and performance – its durability, reliability, speed and taste. Thus, makers of consumer food and household products introduce new flavours, colours, scents, ingredients or packages to enhance performance and revitalise consumer buying. For example, Heinz Tomato Ketchup has been around since 1876, and has long been a staple in the British diet. To keep the brand young, Heinz now markets the product as: Tomato Ketchup, Tomato Ketchup with Balsamic Vinegar, Tomato Ketchup Organic, Tomato Ketchup with Reduced Salt & Sugar, Tomato Ketchup with Chilli, Tomato Ketchup blended with Indian Spices and Tomato Ketchup with Fiery Chilli.

Finally, the company can try *modifying the marketing mix* – improving sales by changing one or more marketing mix elements. The company can offer new or improved services to buyers. It can cut prices to attract new users and competitors' customers. It can launch a better advertising campaign or use aggressive sales promotions – trade deals, money-off, premiums and contests. In addition to pricing and promotion, the company can also move into new marketing channels to help serve new users.

Decline stage

The sales of most product forms and brands eventually dip. The decline may be slow, as in the cases of postage stamps and porridge for breakfast, or rapid, as in the cases of cassette and VHS tapes. Sales may plunge to zero, or they may drop to a low level where they continue for many years. This is the **decline stage**.

Sales decline for many reasons, including technological advances, shifts in consumer tastes and increased competition. As sales and profits decline, some firms withdraw from the market. Those

Heinz Tomato Ketchup has been around since 1876. To keep the brand young, Heinz markets variants like Tomato Ketchup blended with Indian Spices.

Source: H. J. Heinz Company Limited

Decline stage—the PLC stage in which a product's sales decline.

remaining may prune their product offerings. They may drop smaller market segments and marginal trade channels, or they may cut the promotion budget and reduce their prices further.

Carrying a weak product can be very costly to a firm, and not just in profit terms. There are many hidden costs. A weak product may take up too much of management's time. It often requires frequent price and inventory adjustments. It requires advertising and sales-force attention that might be better used to make 'healthy' products more profitable. A product's failing reputation can cause customer concerns about the company and its other products. The biggest cost may well lie in the future. Keeping weak products delays the search for replacements, creates a lopsided product mix, hurts current profits and weakens the company's foothold on the future.

For these reasons, companies need to pay more attention to their aging products. A firm's first task is to identify those products in the decline stage by regularly reviewing sales, market shares, costs and profit trends. Then management must decide whether to maintain, harvest or drop each of these declining products.

Management may decide to *maintain* its brand, repositioning or reinvigorating it in hopes of moving it back into the growth stage of the PLC. P&G has done this with several brands, including Mr Clean in the US and Canada and Old Spice internationally. Management may decide to *harvest* a product, which means reducing various costs (plant and equipment, maintenance, R&D, advertising, sales force), hoping that sales hold up. If successful, harvesting will increase the company's profits in the short term.

Finally, management may decide to *drop* a product from its line. It can sell it to another firm or simply liquidate it at salvage value. In recent years, P&G has sold off several lesser or declining brands, such as Folgers coffee, Crisco oil, Comet cleanser, Sure deodorant, Duncan Hines cake mixes, Jif peanut butter and most recently its last food business in the form of Pringles snacks. If the company plans to find a buyer, it will not want to run down a product through harvesting.

Table 9.2 summarises the key characteristics of each stage of the PLC. The table also lists the marketing objectives and strategies for each stage.[30]

Table 9.2 Summary of product life-cycle characteristics, objectives and strategies

	Introduction	Growth	Maturity	Decline
Characteristics				
Sales	Low sales	Rapidly rising sales	Peak sales	Declining sales
Costs	High cost per customer	Average cost per customer	Low cost per customer	Low cost per customer
Profits	Negative	Rising profits	High profits	Declining profits
Customers	Innovators	Early adopters	Middle majority	Laggards
Competitors	Few	Growing number	Stable number beginning to decline	Declining number
Marketing Objectives				
	Create product awareness and trial	Maximise market share	Maximise profit while defending market share	Reduce expenditure and milk the brand
Strategies				
Product	Offer a basic product	Offer product extensions, service, warranty	Diversify brand and models	Phase out weak items
Price	Use cost-plus	Price to penetrate market	Price to match or beat competitors	Cut price
Distribution	Build selective distribution	Build intensive distribution	Build more intensive distribution	Go selective: phase out unprofitable outlets
Advertising	Build product awareness among early adopters	Build awareness and interest in the mass market	Stress brand differences and benefits	Reduce to level needed to retain hard-core loyals
Sales promotion	Use heavy sales promotion to entice trial	Reduce to take advantage of heavy consumer demand	Increase to encourage brand switching	Reduce to minimal level

Source: Philip Kotler and Kevin Lane Keller, *Marketing Management*, 13th edn (Upper Saddle River, NJ: Prentice Hall, 2009), p. 288, © 2009. Printed and electronically reproduced by permission of Pearson Education, Inc., Upper Saddle River, New Jersey.

ADDITIONAL PRODUCT AND SERVICE CONSIDERATIONS

We wrap up our discussion of products and services with two additional considerations: social responsibility in product decisions and issues of international product and services marketing.

Product decisions and social responsibility

Marketers should carefully consider public policy issues and regulations regarding acquiring or dropping products, patent protection, product quality and safety, and product warranties.

Regarding new products, the government may prevent companies from adding products through acquisitions if the effect threatens to lessen competition. Companies dropping products must be aware that they have legal obligations, written or implied, to their suppliers, dealers and customers who have a stake in the dropped product. Companies must also obey patent and trademark laws when developing new products. A company cannot make its product illegally similar to another company's established product.

Manufacturers must comply with specific laws regarding product quality and safety. If consumers are injured by a product with a defective design, they can sue manufacturers or dealers. A recent survey of manufacturing companies found that product liability was the second-largest litigation concern, behind only labour and employment matters. Although manufacturers are found at fault in a small minority of all product liability cases, when they are found guilty, the damages awarded are often very substantial. For example, after it recalled some nine million vehicles due to problems with sudden acceleration, Toyota faced at least 89 class-action lawsuits that could end up costing the company €4.5 billion or more.[31]

This issue has resulted in huge increases in product liability insurance premiums, causing big problems in some industries. Some companies pass these higher rates along to consumers by raising prices. Others are forced to discontinue high-risk product lines. Some companies are now appointing 'product stewards', whose job is to protect consumers from harm and the company from liability by proactively ferreting out potential product problems.

Many manufacturers offer written product warranties to convince customers of their products' quality. However, growing legal requirements have led some manufacturers to switch from full to limited warranties and others to drop warranties altogether.

International product and services marketing

International product and services marketers face special challenges. First they must work out what products and services to introduce and in which countries. Then they must decide how much to standardise or adapt their products and services for world markets.

On the one hand, companies would like to standardise their offerings. Standardisation helps a company develop a consistent worldwide image. It also lowers the product design, manufacturing and marketing costs of offering a large variety of products. On the other hand, markets and consumers around the world differ widely. Companies must usually respond to these differences by adapting their product offerings. For example, Nestlé sells a variety of very popular Kit Kat flavours in Japan that might make the average western chocolate-lover's stomach turn, such as green tea, red bean and red wine. Beyond taste, Kit Kat's strong following in Japan may also be the result of some unintended cultural factors:[32]

In recent years, Kit Kat – the world's number two chocolate bar – has become very popular in Japan. Some of this popularity, no doubt, derives from the fact that the notoriously sweet-toothed Japanese love the bar's taste. But part of the bar's appeal may also be attributed to the coincidental similarity between its name and the Japanese phrase *kitto katsu*, which roughly translates in Japanese as 'You will surely win!' Spotting this opportunity, marketers for Nestlé Japan developed an innovative *Juken* (college entrance exam) Kit Kat campaign. The multimedia campaign positions the Kit Kat bar and logo as good luck charms during the highly stressful university entrance exam season. Nestlé even developed a cherry-flavoured Kit Kat bar in packaging containing the message 'May cherries blossom', wishing students luck in achieving their dreams. And it partnered with Japan's postal service to create 'Kit Kat Mail', a postcard-like product sold at the post office that could be mailed to students as an edible good-luck charm. The campaign has been such a hit in Japan that it has led to a nationwide social movement to cheer up students for *Juken*. Kit Kat has also become an even broader national good luck charm. For example, a large flag featuring the Kit Kat logo and the phrase *Kitto Katsu!* has been used by fans of professional football team Júbilo Iwata, which is sponsored by Nestlé Japan.

Packaging also presents new challenges for international marketers. Packaging issues can be subtle. For example, names, labels and colours may not translate easily from one country to another. A firm using yellow flowers in its logo might fare well in the United States but meet with disaster in Mexico, where a yellow flower symbolises death or disrespect. Similarly, although Nature's Gift might be an appealing name for gourmet mushrooms in America, it would be deadly in Germany, where *gift* means poison. Packaging may also need to be tailored to meet the physical characteristics of consumers in various parts of the world. For instance, soft drinks are sold in smaller cans in Japan to better fit the smaller Japanese hand. Thus, although product and package standardisation can produce benefits, companies must usually adapt their offerings to the unique needs of specific international markets.

Service marketers also face special challenges when going global. Some service industries have a long history of international operations. For example, the commercial banking industry was one of the first to grow internationally. Banks had to provide global services to meet the foreign exchange and credit needs of their home country clients wanting to sell overseas. In recent years, many banks have become truly global. Germany's Deutsche Bank, for example, serves more than 13 million customers through 1,981 branches in 72 countries. For its clients around the world who wish to grow globally, Deutsche Bank can raise money not only in Frankfurt but also in Zurich, London, Paris, Tokyo and Moscow.[33]

Professional and business services industries, such as accounting, management consulting and advertising, have also undertaken globalisation. The international growth of these firms followed the globalisation of the client companies they serve. For example, as more clients employ worldwide marketing and advertising strategies, advertising agencies have responded by globalising their own operations. For example, London-based WPP is the world's largest communications services group, employing 153,000 people working in 2,400 offices in 107 countries. WPP companies work with 336 of the Fortune Global 500; 29 of the Dow Jones 30; 60 of the NASDAQ 100; and 32 of the Fortune e-50. Some 640 clients are served. There are over 25 WPP team leaders assigned to focus on clients such as Bayer, Colgate, Danone, Dell, Ford, HSBC, Johnson & Johnson, Kimberly-Clark, Mazda, P&G, Shell and Vodafone.[34]

Retailers are among the latest service businesses to go global. As their home markets become saturated, retailers in mature, developed markets are expanding into faster-growing markets abroad. For example, since 1991, US mega-retailer Walmart has entered 15 countries; its international division's sales grew more than 9 per cent last year, skyrocketing to more than €77 billion. Carrefour, the world's second-largest retailer, now operates more than 15,000 stores in more than 30 countries. It is the leading retailer in Europe, Brazil and Argentina and the largest foreign retailer in China. Britain's leading retailer, Tesco, now has successful businesses in 14 countries across Asia, Europe, Malaysia, the Republic of Ireland and Thailand.[35]

The trend toward growth of global service companies will continue, especially in banking, airlines, telecommunications and professional services. Today, service firms are no longer simply following their manufacturing customers. Instead, they are taking the lead in international expansion.

REVIEWING OBJECTIVES AND KEY TERMS

A company's current products face limited life spans and must be replaced by newer products. But new products can fail; the risks of innovation are as great as the rewards. The key to successful innovation lies in a customer focus, total-company effort, strong planning and a systematic *new product development* process.

OBJECTIVE 1 Explain how companies find and develop new product ideas (p. 275).

Companies find and develop new product ideas from a variety of sources. Many new product ideas stem from *internal sources*. Companies conduct formal R&D. Or they pick the brains of their employees, urging them to envision and develop new product ideas. Other ideas come from *external sources*. Companies track *competitors'* offerings and obtain ideas from *distributors and suppliers* who are close to the market and can pass along information about consumer problems and new product possibilities.

Perhaps the most important source of new product ideas is customers themselves. Companies observe customers, invite their ideas and suggestions, or even involve customers in the new product development process. Many companies are now developing *crowdsourcing* or *open-innovation* new product idea programmes, which invite broad communities of people – customers, employees, independent scientists and researchers and even the general public – into the new product innovation process. Truly innovative companies do not rely only on one source or another for new product ideas.

OBJECTIVE 2 List and define the steps in the new product development process and the major considerations in managing this process (pp. 276–286).

The new product development process consists of eight sequential stages. The process starts with *idea generation*. Next comes *idea screening*, which reduces the number of ideas based on the company's own criteria. Ideas that pass the screening stage continue through *product concept development*, in which a detailed version of a new product idea is stated in meaningful consumer terms. In the next stage, *concept testing*, new product concepts are tested with a group of target consumers to determine whether the concepts have strong consumer appeal. Strong concepts proceed to *marketing strategy development*, in which an initial marketing strategy for a new

product is developed from a product concept. In the *business-analysis* stage, a review of the sales, costs, and profit projections for a new product is conducted to determine whether the new product is likely to satisfy the company's objectives. With positive results here, the ideas become more concrete through *product development* and *test marketing* and finally are launched during *commercialisation*.

New product development involves more than just going through a set of steps. Companies must take a systematic, holistic approach to managing this process. Successful new product development requires a customer-centred, team-based, systematic effort.

OBJECTIVE 3 Describe the stages of the product life cycle (PLC) and how marketing strategies change during the PLC (pp. 287–291).

Each product has a *life cycle* marked by a changing set of problems and opportunities. The sales of the typical product follow an S-shaped curve composed of five stages. The cycle begins with the *product development stage* in which the company finds and develops a new product idea. The *introduction stage* is marked by slow growth and low profits as a product is distributed to the market. If successful, a product enters a *growth stage*, which offers rapid sales growth and increasing profits. Next comes a *maturity stage* in which a product's sales growth slows down and profits stabilise. Finally, a product enters a *decline stage* in which sales and profits dwindle. The company's task during this stage is to recognise the decline and decide whether it should maintain, harvest, or drop a product. The different stages of the PLC require different marketing strategies and tactics.

OBJECTIVE 4 Discuss two additional product issues: socially responsible product decisions and international product and services marketing (pp. 292–293).

Marketers must consider two additional product issues. The first is *social responsibility*. This includes public policy issues and regulations involving acquiring or dropping products, patent protection, product quality and safety, and product warranties. The second involves the special challenges facing international product and services marketers. International marketers must decide how much to standardise or adapt their offerings for world markets.

NAVIGATING THE KEY TERMS

DISCUSSING AND APPLYING THE CONCEPTS

Discussing the concepts

1. Name and describe the major steps in developing a new product (AACSB: Communication)

2. Define *crowdsourcing* and describe an example not already presented in the chapter. (AACSB: Communication; Reflective Thinking)

3. Compare and contrast the terms *product idea, product concept* and *product image*. (AACSB: Communication)

4. Explain why successful new product development requires a customer-centred, team-based and systematic effort. (AACSB: Communication)

5. Why do products enter the decline stage of the product life cycle? Discuss marketers' options at this stage. (AACSB: Communication)

6. Discuss the special challenges facing international product and service marketers. (AACSB: Communication)

Applying the concepts

1. Visit http//creatingminds.org/tools/toolsideation.htm to learn about idea generation techniques. Form a small group and have each group member explain a different technique to the rest of the group. Apply one or more of the techniques to generate four new product ideas. Present your ideas to the rest of the class and explain the techniques your group applied to generate the ideas. (AACSB: Communication; Use of IT; Reflective Thinking)

2. Coca-Cola has sustained success in the maturity stage of the product life cycle for many years. Visit Coca-Cola's website (www.thecocacolacompany.com/heritage/ourheritage .html) and discuss how Coca-Cola has evolved over the years. Identify ways that Coca-Cola can continue to evolve to meet changing consumer needs and wants: (AACSB. Communication; Use of IT; Reflective Thinking)

3. To acquire new products many companies purchase other firms or buy individual brands from other companies. For example, Disney purchased Marvel Entertainment and its portfolio of more than 5,000 characters, such as Spider-Man and Captain America. Discuss two other examples of companies acquiring new products through this means. (AACSB: Communication; Reflective Thinking)

Focus on technology

Technology is speeding up new product development while also reducing its costs. What formerly took months and cost millions of dollars can now be done in seconds and for pennies. Because technology is making new product testing easy and accessible to just about any employee, from the chief executive officer to maintenance personnel, predictions are for a ground-breaking change in corporate cultures surrounding new product development – much like the Google culture described at the beginning of this chapter. An employee may come up with a great idea and test it all in a single day. This new environment may present some challenges, however. One is that managers must be prepared to give up control and empower employees.

Another is 'scaling' which means companies must be able to scale or implement new ideas rapidly and efficiently.

1. What skills would you need to function in this type of work environment? (AACSB: Communication; Reflective Thinking)

2. As described at the beginning of this chapter, Google is already ahead of this curve. Visit Google Labs (www.googlelabs.com) to learn about new products that are still in the testing stage – what Google calls the 'playground stage'. Briefly discuss two of the experiments and explain why Google hosts a site such as Google Labs. (AACSB: Communication; Reflective Thinking; Use of IT)

Focus on ethics

There is usually lots of publicity surrounding the launch of a new Apple product. The iPhone 4 was no exception. Unfortunately, much of it was negative, with some critics even labelling the introduction 'antenna-gate'. Within days of the product's release, reports surfaced of reduced signal strength and dropped calls. The problem resulted from the sleeker, slimmer phone's antenna, consisting of a metal band around the side of the phone. Apple's response was that all smartphones have signal problems. Users should hold the phone differently, and users should purchase a case for about $30 (€23) to fix the problem. It turns out that Apple engineers knew of this issue a year before the product was launched, but Steve Jobs, CEO of Apple Inc., liked the design and opted to go ahead with it. The controversy even caught the ear of a US senator, who urged Jobs to fix the problem at no cost to consumers. Contrary to typical industry practice, AT&T, the exclusive service provider, for Apple's phones was allowed to test only a disguised phone for a very limited time without touching it, so the problem was not discovered during testing. Apple later announced that all purchasers would receive a free case and reimbursed users who had already purchased one. This controversy didn't hurt sales, though; Apple sold three million of the new phones in just three weeks and could not keep up with demand.

1. Should Apple have released the iPhone 4 when engineers were aware of the antenna problem? Discuss the pros and cons of further testing before launching the product. (AACSB: Communication; Ethical Reasoning; Reflective Thinking)

2. Did Apple handle the situation effectively? Did Apple's iPhone lose brand equity from this controversy? (AACSB: Communication; Ethical Reasoning; Reflective Thinking)

Marketing & the economy

Coach, Inc.

As consumer shopping patterns began to shift during a slowing economy in late 2007, executives at Coach, Inc., were paying attention. Through ongoing research, they determined that a new 'normal' was emerging – one in which more frugal consumers shopped less and spent less when they did shop. At that time, the average price of a Coach handbag was about $330 (€254). Coach knew it had to become more innovative, relevant, and value oriented without cheapening the brand's image. Coach's managers went to work to find new sources of materials, renegotiate terms with suppliers, and develop new products. As the result of a year-long effort, Coach unveiled a new line of products called 'Poppy'. With the average price of a Poppy handbag at $260 (€200), the line is designed to be more affordable without compromising the brand's image. Unlike most luxury brands. Coach's revenue has maintained moderate but steady growth over the past four years. And although profit growth wavered somewhat, the company has remained in the black. Perhaps that's why during the most recent 18 months, its stock price is up 167 per cent. Coach really does seem to understand the new 'normal'.

1. Explain how a $260 handbag can be viewed as good value in the context of the Coach brand?

2. Is Coach safe or will the new 'normal' still catch up with the company's financial performance?

3. What suggestions would you make to Coach management for future product development?

Marketing by the numbers

Apple introduced the iPhone 4 in the US in 2010 but still continued to offer the iPhone 3G. The 16GB base version of the iPhone 4 was priced at $199 (€153), with unit variable costs equal to $187 (€144). The iPhone 3G's price had decreased to $99 (€76) by the time the iPhone 4 was introduced, and its unit variable costs were $65 (€50).

1. Refer to Appendix 2 and calculate the incremental contribution realised by adding the new iPhone 4 if sales during the first six months of launch were five million units. However, the company also estimated that 30 per cent of iPhone 4 sales came from customers who would have purchased the iPhone 3G but instead purchased the base model of the iPhone 4. (AACSB: Communication; Analytic Reasoning).

2. Apple also offered a 32GB version of the iPhone 4 at $299 (€230). Variable costs for that version were $250 (€192.5). Besides its higher price, explain why Apple would encourage customers to purchase the 32GB over the 16GB version. (AACSB: Communication; Analytic Reasoning; Reflective Reasoning)

REFERENCES

[1] Extracts and quotes from or adapted from information found in Chuck Salter, 'Google; the faces and voices of the world's most innovative company', *Fast Company* (March 2008), pp. 74–88; 'The world's most innovative companies', *Fast Company* (March 2009), p. 52; 'The world's most innovative companies', *Fast Company* (22 February 2010), p. 60; 'Google shines a light on innovation', *Computer Weekly* (9–15 September 2008), p. 3; David Pogue, 'Geniuses at play, on the job', *New York Times* (26 February 2009), p. B1; Quentin Hardy, 'When Google runs your life', *Forbes* (28 December 2009), pp. 88–93; Tom Krazit, 'Slight dip in Google's January search market share', *CNet News* (11 February 2010), http://news.cnet.com/8301-30684_3-10452235-265.html; and www.google.com and www.googlelabs.com, accessed June 2010.

[2] 'In a tough economy, innovation is king', *Marketing News* (15 April 2009), p. 14.

[3] Calvin Hodock, 'Winning the new-products game', *Advertising Age* (12 November 2007), p. 35; Neale Martin, 'Force of habit', *Brandweek* (13 October 2008), pp. 18–20; 'How P&G plans to clean up', *BusinessWeek* (13 April 2009), pp. 44–45; and 'Top 10 reasons for new-product failure', *The Marketing Fray* (7 January 2010), www.marketingfray.com/2010/01/top-10-reasons-for-new-product-failure.html. See also www.scribd.com/doc/20269401/Product-Failures-and-Their-Strategies, accessed 6 March 2012.

[4] John Peppers and Martha Rogers, 'The buzz on customer-driven innovation', *Sales & Marketing Management* (June 2007), p. 13.

[5] See Richard Martin, 'Collaboration Cisco style', *InformationWeek* (28 January 2008), p. 30; and Guido Jouret, 'Inside Cisco's search for the next big idea', *Harvard Business Review* (September 2009), pp. 43–45.

[6] See http://mystarbucksidea.force.com/ideaHome, accessed April 2010.

[7] Mary Tripsas, 'Seeing customers as partners in invention', *New York Times* (27 December 2009), www.nytimes.com.

[8] Elisabeth A. Sullivan, 'A group effort: more companies are turning to the wisdom of the crowd to find ways to innovate', *Marketing News* (28 February 2010), pp. 22–29.

[9] Adapted from Sullivan, 'A group effort', p. 26.

[10] See Brian Morrissey, 'The social sell?', *Brandweek* (14 February 2010), www.brandweek.com; and www.ideastorm.com, accessed November 2010.

[11] Jeff Howe, 'Join the crowd', *Independent* (London) (2 September 2008), p. 2; 'P&G leads 2010 Edison best new product award finalists with five nods', *PR Newswire* (11 February 2010); and 'About us', www.innocentive.com/about-us-open-innovation.php, accessed September 2010.

[12] Guido Jouret, 'Inside Cisco's search for the next big idea', *Harvard Business Review* (September 2009), pp. 43–45.

[13] Kevin O'Donnell, 'Where do the best ideas come from? The unlikeliest sources', *Advertising Age* (14 July 2008), p. 15.

[14] See George S. Day, 'Is it real? Can we win? Is it worth doing?', *Harvard Business Review* (December 2007), pp. 110–120.

[15] Information for this example obtained from www.teslamotors.com, accessed June 2010.

[16] Information from www.hpproducttest.com/index.cfm, accessed April 2010.

[17] 'KFC fires up grilled chicken' (23 March 2008), www.money.cnn.com; 'KFC serves up a second secret recipe: Kentucky grilled chicken', *PR Newswire* (14 April 2009); and Noreen O'Leary, 'KFC's grilled chicken tops most-recalled' "09 Launches", *Brandweek* (14 December 2009), p. 4.

[18] Extracted from: www.insightsinretail.com/virtual-stores/the-use-of-virtual-store-simulations-in-marketing-research-and-beyond/, accessed 15 February 2012.

[19] Dan Sewell, 'Procter & Gamble to test web sales', Associated Press (15 January 2010).

[20] See Emily Bryson York, 'McD's serves up $100m McCafé ad blitz', *Crain's Chicago Business* (4 May 2009), www.chicagobusiness.com; John Letzing, 'Bing's share rises again', *Wall Street Journal* (18 June 2009), http://online.wsj.com; and Rita Chang, 'With $100 m saturation campaign, droid will be impossible to avoid', *Advertising Age* (9 November 2009), p. 3.

[21] See Robert G. Cooper, 'Formula for success', *Marketing Management* (March-April 2006), pp. 19–23; Barry Jaruzelski and Kevin Dehoff, 'The global innovation of 1000', *Strategy + Business* (Issue 49, fourth quarter, 2007), pp. 68–83; and Shu-Hua Chien and Jyh-jye Chen, 'Supplier involvement in customer involvement effect on new product development success in the financial service industry', *The Service Industries Journal* (February 2010), p. 185.

[22] Robert Berner, 'How P&G pampers new thinking', *BusinessWeek* (14 April 2008), pp. 73–74; 'How P&G plans to clean up', *BusinessWeek* (13 April 2009), pp. 44–45; and 'Procter & Gamble Company', www.wikinvest.com/stock/Procter_&_Gamble_Company_(PG), accessed April 2010.

[23] Adapted from: 'LEGO grows by listening to customers', *Advertising Age* (9 November 2009), p. 15; Nelson D. Schwartz, 'Beyond the blocks', *The New York Times* (6 September 2009), p. BU1; Jon Henley, 'Toy story', *Guardian* (26 March 2009), p. F4; Kevin O'Donnell, 'Where do the best ideas come from? The unlikeliest sources', *Advertising Age* (14 July 2008), p. 15; Lewis Borg Cardona, 'LEGO learns a lesson', *Change Agent* (June 2008), www.synovate.com/changeagent; and www.lego.com/eng/info and http://mindstorms.lego.com/en-us/community/default.aspx, accessed April 2010.

[24] Adapted from Darrell K. Rigby, Karen Gruver and James Allen, 'Innovation in turbulent times', *Harvard Business Review* (June 2009), pp. 79–86. Also see John Hayes, 'In a tough economy, innovation is king', *Marketing News* (15 April 2009), pp. 14–17.

[25] Ibid.; and Judann Pollock, 'Now's the time to reset marketing for post-recession', *Advertising Age* (1 February 2010), p. 1.

[26] This definition is based on one found in Bryan Lilly and Tammy R. Nelson, 'Fads: segmenting the fad-buyer market', *Journal of Consumer Marketing*, **20** (3), 2003, pp. 252–265.

[27] See Katya Kazakina and Robert Johnson, 'A fad's father seeks a sequel', *New York Times* (30 May 2004), www.nytimes.com; John Schwartz, 'The joy of silly', *New York Times* (20 January 2008), p. 5; and www.crazyfads.com, accessed November 2010.

[28] Mariko Sanchanta, 'Nintendo aims to keep virtual players off the sofa', *Financial Times* (5/6 January 2008), p. 14.

[29] Suzanne Vranica, 'Nintendo targets new users with Wii Fit', *Wall Street Journal* (23 April 2008), p. 20.

[30] For a more comprehensive discussion of marketing strategies over the course of the PLC, see Philip Kotler and Kevin Lane Keller, *Marketing Management*, 13th edn (Upper Saddle River, NJ: Prentice Hall, 2009), pp. 278–290.

[31] See 'Year-by-year analysis reveals an overall compensatory award of $1,500,000 for products liability cases', *Personal Injury Verdict Reviews* (3 July 2006); Administrative Office of the US Courts, 'Judicial facts and figures: multi-year statistical compilations on the Federal Judiciary's caseload through fiscal year 2008', September 2009, www.uscourts.gov/judicialfactsfigures/2008/all2008judicialfactsfigures.pdf; and Dennis Rich, 'Toyota faces class-action suits', *McClatchy-Tribune Business News* (10 March 2010).

[32] Example based on information provided by Nestlé Japan Ltd, May 2008; with additional information from Laurel Wentz, 'Kit Kat wins Cannes media grand prix for edible postcard', *Advertising Age* (23 June 2009), http://adage.com/cannes09/article?article_id=137520; and http://en.wikipedia.org/wiki/Kit_Kat; and the Japanese Wikipedia discussion of Kit Kat at http://ja.wikipedia.org, accessed November 2010.

[33] Information accessed online at www.db.com, accessed July 2010.

[34] www.wpp.com, accessed 15 February 2012.

[35] See 'Global powers of retailing 2010', www.deloitte.com; 'Walmart Corporate International', http://walmartstores.com/AboutUs/246.aspx, February 2010; and information accessed at www.carrefour.com, accessed February 2010.

VIDEO CASE

General Mills – FiberOne

MyMarketingLab

General Mills has been mass marketing food since 1860. Today, it sells over $15 (€11.5) billion worth of packaged food each year in over 100 countries. In the United States alone, General Mills markets over 100 leading brands, such as Cheerios, Betty Crocker, Pillsbury and Green Giant. With all this experience, General Mills certainly has an advantage when it comes to introducing and managing products.

Not many years ago, FiberOne was a little-known brand without much of a footprint. The FiberOne video illustrates how General Mills grew the brand's annual sales from $35 (€27) million to more than $500 (€385) million in just five years. This growth came primarily from creating and managing new products. FiberOne was originally a line of food bars. But the FiberOne brand name is now found on numerous products, including toaster pastries, bread, yogurt, cold cereals and even cottage cheese. After watching the video featuring FiberOne, answer the following questions about the company:

1. Most new products fail. Why has General Mills had success with so many new product introductions in the FiberOne line?
2. Give an example of a FiberOne product in each phase of the product life cycle. Give evidence to support your decisions.
3. For each product identified in question 2, identify one strategy that General Mills is employing for each product that is appropriate for its life-cycle phase.

COMPANY CASE

Reckitt Benckiser: building a brand powerhouse

Reckitt Benckiser is far from being a household name, but it has become a cleaning products superstar, at times outshining P&G and Unilever with its new products and marketing prowess. Reckitt's strong suit is finding niche markets with high growth potential, instead of trying to compete in the saturated laundry detergent market. For example, Reckitt focuses on the growing segment for automatic dishwasher products, where it achieved a 40 per cent market share worldwide. By pioneering new brands, often in market niches, Reckitt has emerged as one of Europe's top performers.

Reckitt Benckiser (RB) was formed in 1999 by the merger of Dutch group Benckiser with the UK's Reckitt & Colman. In 2005, RB acquired Boots Healthcare International for £1.9 billion, expanding its presence in the over-the-counter health-care market. In 2007 the company acquired Adams Respiratory Therapeutics, allowing it to enter the US over-the-counter pharmaceuticals market. In 2010, RB made a £2.5 billion offer for SSL International, maker of Durex and Scholl products, pursuing further geographic diversification and new product areas.

RB has become a global leader in household, healthcare and personal products. The group's 19 'Powerbrands' are sold in more than 200 countries. The Powerbrands include well-known names such as Air Wick (air fresheners), Cillit Bang (household cleaners), Dettol (antiseptics), Durex (contraceptives), Gaviscon (indigestion remedies), Harpic (bleaches), Nurofen (painkillers), Strepsils (sore throat remedies) and Veet (body hair removal products). Heavy investment in the Powerbrands, focused on areas where high growth was possible, means that 16 of the Powerbrands can claim to be number one or two in their categories globally. In fact, RB markets hundreds of products, many of which are local leaders in global markets.

RB's brand strategy is captured on its website:

Innovation drives the strategy, which drives innovation

RB reinforces its brands with an exceptional rate of innovation.

Innovations must be Great Performers, Fast to Market and Cost-effective.

The innovation pipeline is built around brand strategy. So innovative cost savings improve margins and fuel growth.

And it's a full time job – RB changes a formula about every 8 hours.

Consumers are at the centre of RB innovation

Innovation starts and ends with consumers – the small ways RB can make life better. So RB builds consumers into product development, validating every idea with them.

It doesn't focus on ideas, but ideas that sell because they meet consumer needs.

This creates powerful global brands that can adapt to local preferences.

Where do those ideas come from?

Above all, from consumer insights. RB spends time with consumers in the lab and in their homes. But RB has its own technology insights too.

The RB-Idealink website sources ideas the world over. RB also keeps a close eye on technological and societal trends.

And puts all these ideas to the test.

Innovation is a team effort

Driving a global formula means reacting fast and efficiently – that takes teamwork. So innovation is integral to the business and RB creates strategic and external alliances.

All to give consumers worldwide even more reasons to buy RB products.

Product innovation is at the core of RB strategy, relying on 'value-added' products to keep customers buying during the recession. Mr Becht, the former CEO, said: 'It is even more important [during difficult times] to sort our brands apart from the cheap stuff.' The focus is on regular improvements to the Powerbrands.

In 2010, in spite of tough economic conditions, RB released Finish Quantumatic, a detergent that can be clipped to the racks of dishwashers; Airwick Aqua Mist, a 'natural' air freshener that comes in a bottle with no chemical propellants; and Vanish Oxi Action Extra Hygiene, a stain remover that claims to remove bacteria from clothes washed at low temperatures. It also brought out the Lysol No-Touch Hand Soap System, a dispenser that 'senses' the presence of hands and pumps out soap without requiring physical contact.

BECHT'S LEGACY AT BENCKEISER

In April 2011, Bart Becht stood down as CEO at Benckiser. Even then, listening to Bart Becht enthusing about the latest Reckitt Benckiser twist on air fresheners or dishwasher tablets, it was easy to imagine him checking friends' bathroom cabinets and kitchen cupboards for his group's products. His evident passion – extending even to the unpromising categories of cockroach killers and toilet cleaners – makes it hard to understand why he is quitting the group he has led since it was formed in 1999.

Mr Becht said at this time that it was a good time to announce his exit plans.

'The executive team is very strong and SSL [the maker of Durex condoms and Scholl footwear], bought last year for £2.5 billion is bedding down very well.' 'Sixteen years is a long time,' he added. 'The fact that you have passion doesn't mean you can't retire at some time.'

Mr Becht's time at the helm has transformed the merged group into a powerhouse that delivered years of great returns for shareholders. This earned him City plaudits and a great deal of money: including vested share options, his pay in 2009 totalled £92 million. During his tenure, RB shares have outperformed the FTSE by three and a half times, as well as beating the peer group: Reckitt's share have outperformed P&G's by 225 per cent and L'Oréal's by 256 per cent.

Julian Hardwick, an analyst at RBS who has covered Mr Becht's career since Benckiser's initial public offering in 1997, said: 'He is outstanding for his understanding of the business, the intensity he brings to his work and the way he has created the culture of Reckitt Benckiser'. Reckitt's success is based on zealous cost-cutting, frenetic innovation and hefty marketing spend to promote its main brands. In 2010, about 35 per cent of revenues came from products launched in the previous three years, and the group's 19 Powerbrands accounted for 69 per cent of sales.

The years immediately after the merger were marked by a lack of large acquisitions, driven by a fear of overpaying. But latterly the business was better prepared to do significant deals – notably SSL, Boots Healthcare International and Adams Respiratory Therapeutics.

Nevertheless, Mr Becht will leave the group facing strategic challenges. One relates to the drug Suboxone, which treats opiate dependency and has come off patent in the US. This drug has built to constitute 8 per cent of RB's total sales. The likelihood is the rapid emergence of generic methadone-substitute products.

The core household cleaners business is under siege from P&G, which has launched detergents and stain removers to compete directly with Reckitt's Finish and Vanish brands.

'The shares have underperformed the European Consumer Staples space over the past two years for two reasons,' Mr Hardwick said. 'The first is the huge uncertainty over what sort of generic challenge Suboxone will face. The second is that base business growth has slowed down as the company has faced weaker developed market growth and increased competition in some categories, especially from Procter & Gamble.'

Other analysts agreed about the competitive threat to niche products from the US consumer goods group. 'Reckitt's success was built on going into "shoulder" categories such as in-wash additives that were too small for the majors to touch. But P&G's need for growth is such that it is pushing into these categories now too.'

Incoming CEO Rakesh Kapoor in 2011, formerly Reckitt's marketing chief, faces the challenge of returning Reckitt to its stellar growth record after the economic downturn, after sales growth fell in 2009 and 2010.

Questions for discussion

1. How has Reckitt been able to achieve leadership positions in so many different areas?
2. Is Reckitt's product development customer-centred? Systematic?
3. Based on the PLC, what challenges does Reckitt face in managing its brand portfolio?
4. Will Reckitt be able to maintain its market position in so many areas when strong competitors enter with their own niche products? Why or why not?

Sources: Laura Cohn, 'Why it pays to reinvent the mop', *BusinessWeek* (24 January 2005), p. 23; Alison Smith, 'Succession challenge for incoming Reckitt chief', *Financial Times* (15 April 2011), p. 18; Sarah Shannon, 'The British upstart challenging P&G', *Bloomberg BusinessWeek* (2–19 August 2010), pp. 26–27; Jenny Wiggins and Adam Jones, 'Reckitt deals with burgeoning cash pile', *Financial Times* (11 February 2010), p. 19; Elizabeth Rigby, Adam Jones and Kate Burgess, 'Reckitt Benckiser chief's pay-out reaches £92m after decade of success', *Financial Times* (8 April 2010), p. 1; Paul Sonne, 'Reckitt Benckiser's CEO to step down', *Wall Street Journal* (15–22 April 2011), p. 7.

CHAPTER TEN

Pricing strategies: understanding and capturing customer value

Chapter preview

We now look at the second major marketing mix tool – pricing. If effective product development, promotion and distribution sow the seeds of business success, effective pricing is the harvest. Firms successful at creating customer value with the other marketing mix activities must still capture some of this value in the prices they earn. In this chapter, we discuss the importance of pricing, dig into three major pricing strategies, and look at internal and external considerations that affect pricing decisions. In the next chapter, we will examine some additional pricing considerations and approaches.

We begin by examining the importance of pricing in retailing. In the UK, the Waitrose chain is teaching the so called 'big four' grocery retailers a thing or two about effective pricing – and capturing market share during a recession. It appears that in this case, the big four had better watch their backs – or more accurately – their market share.

Objective outline

➤ **Objective 1** Answer the question 'What is a price?' and discuss the importance of pricing in today's fast-changing environment.
What is a price? (p. 305)

➤ **Objective 2** Identify the three major pricing strategies and discuss the importance of understanding customer-value perceptions, company costs and competitor strategies when setting prices.
Major pricing strategies (pp. 305–313)

➤ **Objective 3** Identify and define the other important external and internal factors affecting a firm's pricing decisions.
Other internal and external considerations affecting price decisions (pp. 314–318)

Waitrose

Waitrose is a UK supermarket group and part of the John Lewis chain. Waitrose generated profits of €328 million on a turnover of €9.2 billion in 2010. Waitrose's reputation has been built on quality and freshness. Coupled with this is the company's Price Commitment policy, which means Waitrose checks the prices of selected everyday items against the prices of other supermarkets. For some time, Waitrose has been running 'Outstanding Offers' where its prices are better than the competition.

Kantar World Panel, the international market research organisation, estimated that Waitrose had a 4.3 per cent market share of the grocery market in the United Kingdom in September 2011. This placed Waitrose well behind market leader Tesco (30.4 per cent), Asda (17.4 per cent), Sainsbury's (16.1 per cent) and fourth-place William Morrison (11.5 per cent). Discount supermarkets such as Lidl and Aldi had a steady market share of 6 per cent. Martin Whittingham, Director at Kantar Worldpanel explained 'the hard discounters of Aldi and Lidl continue to maintain their double digit growth' while 'Waitrose, on the other end of the price scale, has achieved growth for the fifth consecutive period in the range 8 to 9% showing that the "two nations" split remains an on-going theme'. So for the UK grocery market, the recession is proving good news for those hard discounters such as Aldi and Lidl but also surprising good news for the premium end of the market; epitomised by Waitrose.

Waitrose is considered by consumers to be at the premium end of the food retail market. Until March 2009, it had its own line of private-label products, but it decided that it would launch a brand new range of 1,400 products under the name 'Essential Waitrose' to include meat, eggs, fruit juices, milk and pasta. This was an attempt to reclaim customers that had been lost to cheaper supermarkets such as Asda, Lidl and Aldi as a result of the downturn in the UK economy.

The danger for Waitrose was that introducing a budget range could affect its public image and brand position as a premium supermarket. Rupert Thomas, Waitrose's marketing director, masterminded the strategy. He had to come up with a solution that avoided the tried and tested budget-brand phrases, such as 'value' or 'basics'. It was important to get across to consumers that although the Essential range would

Waitrose: the Essential value range.

Source: Courtesy of Waitrose Ltd.

be cheaper, quality was not being compromised. On average, prices were reduced by 10 per cent. Thomas also knew that to cover the price reductions, sales figures would have to increase by 5 per cent. By June 2010, Waitrose sales had in fact gone up 17 per cent.

Managing Director Mark Price fully supported the move by increasing the marketing budget by 20 per cent. Overall, Waitrose sales increased by 11 per cent in 2010 compared to the previous year, with the Essential range accounting for 16 per cent of all sales. In June 2010, the marketing initiative was recognised by the Marketing Society when Waitrose was awarded the Grand Prix at the annual event. In 2011 and 2012, the trend has continued and the Essential Range grows from strength to strength.

Some of the most compelling data underlining the success of the new brand was released by Waitrose in 2010. By the first anniversary of the launch of the Essential range, Waitrose were able to show that it had already achieved €585 million in sales and was on course to achieve sales of €750 million in 2011. According to Waitrose, 75 per cent of its customers were buying products belonging to the new brand.

The initiative proved undoubtedly that premium product shoppers like a bargain. Waitrose had proven that it could offer cheaper product lines without compromising either the Waitrose brand itself or without compromising sales of premium products. By the end of 2010, Waitrose had made the decision to price match the UK supermarket leaders on 1,000 branded products such as Heinz baked beans. This was a new strategy for Waitrose as it had never adopted price matching before. This was also the time when basic commodity prices for foodstuffs such as wheat had risen (up 60 per cent on July 2010) and supermarkets were absorbing the price increases and actually cutting prices on products such as loaves of bread.

In November 2010, Waitrose was awarded the Excellence in Marketing Award at the National Business Awards Gala Dinner held in London. Alex Evans, head of the judging panel, cited the fact that the Essential range and marketing campaign that supported it were stunning successes. It proved that even when consumers were more cost-conscious than ever, the Waitrose premium brand had effectively taken on the big four supermarkets.

The agency handling the campaign for Waitrose was London-based MCBD. The campaign included television, print, outdoor and digital advertising, and marketing. MCBD was also behind the new advertising campaign launched in 2010 by Waitrose, which for the first time used celebrity chefs to boost sales. The campaign, believed to be worth €12 million, featured famous chefs Delia Smith (who had previously worked with Waitrose as a consultant) and the innovatively-eccentric Heston Blumenthal (a Michelin 3-Star Chef).

It was a wise move for Waitrose, as the so-called 'Delia Effect' has had massive impacts on sales of grocery products in the past. Recipes featured on her television shows in the UK have boosted sales of products from sea salt to cranberries. The new campaign, which is set to run for three years, incorporates television, print and outdoor advertising. Richard Hodgson, Waitrose's commercial director, announced that a new television advertisement would be broadcast each week and would run for the duration of the advertising break. Each would demonstrate a new recipe; in effect, they would be miniature Delia Smith cooking shows.

Waitrose aims to retain its premium brand status with celebrity tie-ins, while trying to cater to a broader consumer market with the Essential range. While taking on market leaders with a price match promise, Waitrose is trying to reposition itself as a credible competitor at a time when supermarkets are struggling to retain their market share as consumers look for the ideal combination of price and quality.[1]

Companies today face a fierce and fast-changing pricing environment. Value-seeking customers have put increased pricing pressure on many companies. Thanks to recent economic woes, the pricing power of the Internet, and value-driven retailers such as Lidl, Aldi, Carrefour and Walmart, today's more frugal consumers are pursuing spend-less strategies. In response, it seems that almost every company is looking for ways to cut prices.

Yet, cutting prices is often not the best answer. Reducing prices unnecessarily can lead to lost profits and damaging price wars. It can cheapen a brand by signalling to customers that price is more important than the customer value a brand delivers. Yet, no matter what the state of the economy, companies should sell value, not price. In some cases, that means selling lesser products at rock-bottom prices. But in most cases, it means persuading customers that paying a higher price for the company's brand is justified by the greater value they gain.[2]

WHAT IS A PRICE?

In the narrowest sense, **price** is the amount of money charged for a product or a service. More broadly, price is the sum of all the values that customers give up to gain the benefits of having or using a product or a service. Historically, price has been the major factor affecting buyer choice. In recent decades, non-price factors have gained increasing importance. However, price still remains one of the most important elements that determines a firm's market share and profitability.

Price is the only element in the marketing mix that produces revenue; all other elements represent costs. Price is also one of the most flexible marketing mix elements. Unlike product features and channel commitments, prices can be changed quickly. At the same time, pricing is the number one problem facing many marketing executives, and many companies do not handle pricing well. Some managers view pricing as a big headache, preferring instead to focus on other marketing mix elements. However, smart managers treat pricing as a key strategic tool for creating and capturing customer value. Prices have a direct impact on a firm's bottom line. A small percentage improvement in price can generate a large percentage increase in profitability. More importantly, as part of a company's overall value proposition, price plays a key role in creating customer value and building customer relationships. 'Instead of running away from pricing,' says an expert, 'savvy marketers are embracing it.'[3]

Price—The amount of money charged for a product or a service; the sum of the values that customers exchange for the benefits of having or using the product or service.

> **AUTHOR COMMENT**
> Setting the right price is one of the marketer's most difficult tasks. A host of factors come into play. But finding and implementing the right price strategy is critical to success.

MAJOR PRICING STRATEGIES

The price the company charges will fall somewhere between one that is too high to produce any demand and one that is too low to produce a profit. Figure 10.1 summarises the major considerations in setting price. Customer perceptions of the product's value set the ceiling for prices. If customers perceive that the product's price is greater than its value, they will not buy the product. Product costs set the floor for prices. If the company prices the product below its costs, the company's profits will suffer. In setting its price between these two extremes, the company must consider several internal and external factors, including competitors' strategies and prices, the overall marketing strategy and mix, and the nature of the market and demand.

Figure 10.1 suggests three major pricing strategies: customer value-based pricing, cost-based pricing and competition-based pricing.

> **AUTHOR COMMENT**
> Like everything else in marketing, good pricing starts with *customers* and their perceptions of value.

Figure 10.1 Considerations in setting price

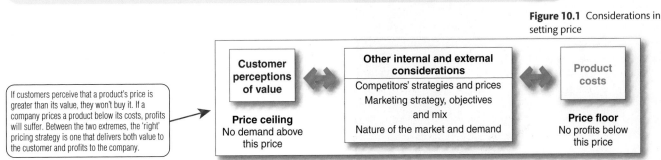

If customers perceive that a product's price is greater than its value, they won't buy it. If a company prices a product below its costs, profits will suffer. Between the two extremes, the 'right' pricing strategy is one that delivers both value to the customer and profits to the company.

Customer perceptions of value

Price ceiling
No demand above this price

Other internal and external considerations
Competitors' strategies and prices
Marketing strategy, objectives and mix
Nature of the market and demand

Product costs

Price floor
No profits below this price

Figure 10.2 Value-based pricing versus cost-based pricing

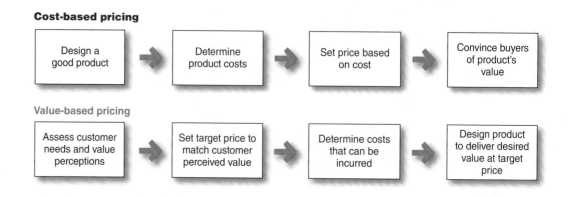

Cost-based pricing

Design a good product → Determine product costs → Set price based on cost → Convince buyers of product's value

Value-based pricing

Assess customer needs and value perceptions → Set target price to match customer perceived value → Determine costs that can be incurred → Design product to deliver desired value at target price

Customer value-based pricing

In the end, the customer will decide whether a product's price is right. Pricing decisions, like other marketing mix decisions, must start with customer value. When customers buy a product, they exchange something of value (the price) to get something of value (the benefits of having or using a particular product). Effective, customer-oriented pricing involves understanding how much value consumers place on the benefits they receive from the product and setting a price that captures this value.

Customer value-based pricing uses buyers' perceptions of value, not the seller's cost, as the key to pricing. Value-based pricing means that the marketer cannot design a product and marketing programme and then set the price. Price is considered along with all other marketing mix variables *before* the marketing programme is set.

Figure 10.2 compares value-based pricing with cost-based pricing. Although costs are an important consideration in setting prices, cost-based pricing is often product driven. The company designs what it considers to be a good product, adds up the costs of making the product and sets a price that covers costs plus a target profit. Marketing must then convince buyers that the product's value at that price justifies its purchase. If the price turns out to be too high, the company must settle for lower mark-ups or lower sales, both resulting in disappointing profits.

Value-based pricing reverses this process. The company first assesses customer needs and value perceptions. It then sets its target price based on customer perceptions of value. The targeted value and price drive decisions about what costs can be incurred and the resulting product design. As a result, pricing begins with analysing consumer needs and value perceptions, and the price is set to match perceived value.

It's important to remember that 'good value' is not the same as 'low price'. For example, a Steinway piano – any Steinway piano – costs a lot. But to those who own one, a Steinway is of great value:[4]

Customer value-based pricing—Setting price based on buyers' perceptions of value rather than on the seller's cost.

Perceived value: a Steinway piano – any Steinway piano – costs a lot. But to those who own one, a Steinway is of great value. 'A Steinway takes you places you've never been'.

Source: Courtesy of Steinway & Sons

A Steinway grand piano typically runs anywhere from €28,250 to €117,000. The most popular model sells for around €50,000. But ask anyone who owns a Steinway grand piano, and they'll tell you that, when it comes to Steinway, price is nothing; the Steinway experience is everything. Steinway makes very high quality pianos; handcrafting each Steinway grand piano requires up to one full year. But, more importantly, owners get the Steinway mystique. The Steinway name evokes images of classical concert stages and the celebrities and performers who've owned and played Steinway pianos across more than 155 years.

But Steinway pianos aren't just for world-class pianists and the wealthy. Ninety-nine percent of all Steinway buyers are amateurs who perform only in their dens. To such customers, whatever a Steinway costs, it's a small price to pay for the value of owning one. 'A Steinway takes you places you've never been,' says an ad. As one Steinway owner puts it, 'My friendship with the Steinway piano is one of the most important and beautiful things in my life.' Who can put a price on such feelings?

Companies often find it hard to measure the value customers will attach to its product. For example, calculating the cost of ingredients in a meal at a fancy restaurant is relatively easy. But assigning values to other satisfactions such as taste, environment, relaxation, conversation and status are very hard. These values are subjective; they vary both for different consumers and different situations.

Still, consumers will use these perceived values to evaluate a product's price, so the company must work to measure them. Sometimes, companies ask consumers how much they would pay for a basic product and for each benefit added to the offer. Or a company might conduct experiments to test the perceived value of different product offers. According to an old Russian proverb, there are two fools in every market: one who asks too much and one who asks too little. If the seller charges more than the buyer's perceived value, the company's sales will suffer. If the seller charges less, its products sell very well, but they produce less revenue than they would if they were priced at the level of perceived value.

We now examine two types of value-based pricing: *good-value pricing* and *value-added pricing*.

Good-value pricing

Recent economic events have caused a fundamental shift in consumer attitudes toward price and quality. In response, many companies have changed their pricing approaches to bring them in-line with changing economic conditions and consumer price perceptions. More and more, marketers have adopted **good-value pricing** strategies – offering the right combination of quality and good service at a fair price.

In many cases, this has involved introducing less-expensive versions of established, brand-name products. To meet tougher economic times and more frugal consumer spending habits, fast-food restaurants such as Quick and McDonald's offer value meals and €1 menu items. Armani offers the less-expensive, more-casual Armani Exchange fashion line. Alberto-Culver's TRESemmé hair care line promises 'A salon look and feel at a fraction of the price'. And every car company now offers small, inexpensive models better suited to the strapped consumer's budget.

In other cases, good-value pricing has involved redesigning existing brands to offer more quality for a given price or the same quality for less. Some companies even succeed by offering less value but at rock-bottom prices. For example, passengers flying the low-cost European airline Ryanair won't get much in the way of free amenities, but they'll like the airline's unbelievably low prices.[5]

Good-value pricing—Offering the right combination of quality and good service at a fair price.

Good-value pricing: Ryanair appears to have found a radical new pricing solution, one that customers are sure to love: make flying free!

Source: Ryanair

Ireland's Ryanair, Europe's most profitable airline over the past decade, appears to have found a radical pricing solution: *make flying free*! Before long, Ryanair promises, more than half of its passengers will pay nothing for their tickets. Remarkably, the airline already offers virtually free fares to one-fourth of its customers. What's their secret? Ryanair's frugal cost structure makes even the most cost-conscious competitor look like a reckless spender. In reality, however, Ryanair charges for virtually everything except the seat itself, from baggage check-in to seat-back advertising space. Once in the air, flight attendants hawk everything from scratch-card games to perfume and digital cameras to their captive audience. After arriving

307

at some out-of-the-way airport, Ryanair will sell you a bus or train ticket into town. The airline even gets commissions from the leases of Hertz rental cars and the sales of hotel rooms, ski packages and travel insurance. Despite Ryanair's sometimes pushy efforts to extract more revenue from each traveller, customers aren't complaining. Most of the additional purchases are discretionary, and you just can't beat those outrageously low prices.

An important type of good-value pricing at the retail level is *everyday low pricing* (EDLP). EDLP involves charging a constant, everyday low price with few or no temporary price discounts. Retailers such as Costco and the furniture seller Room & Board practise EDLP. The king of EDLP is Walmart, which practically defined the concept. Except for a few sale items every month, Walmart promises everyday low prices on everything it sells. In contrast, *high–low pricing* involves charging higher prices on an everyday basis but running frequent promotions to lower prices temporarily on selected items. Department stores such as Debenhams and Marks & Spencer practise high – low pricing by having frequent sales days, early-bird savings and bonus earnings for store credit-card holders.

Value-added pricing

Value-added pricing—
Attaching value-added features and services to differentiate a company's offers and charging higher prices.

Value-based pricing doesn't mean simply charging what customers want to pay or setting low prices to meet competition. Instead, many companies adopt **value-added pricing** strategies. Rather than cutting prices to match competitors, they attach value-added features and services to differentiate their offers and thus support higher prices.

When the monsoon season in Mumbai, India starts, the locals know that for three solid months it will rain almost without a break. What's more, we're talking about monsoon rain that comes down in a solid wall of water making the British drizzle of London seem like a pleasant memory. For over 150 years the majority of Mubaikars have used the sturdy Stag umbrella, sold by the venerable Ebrahim Currim & Sons. The basic Stag umbrella was cheap, durable and available in any colour as long as you like black. Fashionable it wasn't but it's durability and quality outsold all others. However, by the late twentieth century, the Stag was under threat from cheap and cheerful imports from China. Under-pressure managers responded to these threats with knee-jerk price cuts and reductions in product quality. The results were predictable; for the first time in half a century, the brand started losing money.

Thankfully, wiser counsels prevailed and company saw the errors of its cost-cutting, quality-reducing strategy. Recognising that a price war was unwinnable the company came out fighting through innovation. Designer umbrellas were made in the bright colours so-much loved by Indian consumers. Funky colours and cool designs attracted fashion-conscious teenagers and young adults. For the thousands of Mumbaikars who commute along unlit roads, umbrellas were made with built-in troches and even pre-recorded tunes for music fans. Women consumers walking secluded streets were sold umbrellas with glare lights, alarms and emergency blinkers. Such innovations found that consumers would pay twice as much for a umbrella tailored to their needs. Using this value-added strategy the Stag brand is now firmly profitable and clearly positioned. Indeed, classic black Stags have been reappeared – although consumers are now prepared to pay a 15% premium for this retro-chic design.[6]

The Stag example illustrates once again that customers are motivated not by price but by what they get for what they pay. 'If consumers thought the best deal was simply a question of money saved, we'd all be shopping in one big discount store,' says one pricing expert. 'Customers want value and are willing to pay for it. Savvy marketers price their products accordingly.'[7]

AUTHOR COMMENT

Costs set the floor for price, but the goal isn't always to *minimise* costs. In fact, many firms invest in higher costs so that they can claim higher prices and margins (think about Steinway pianos). The key is to manage the *spread* between costs and prices – how much the company makes for the customer value it delivers.

Cost-based pricing

Whereas customer-value perceptions set the price ceiling, costs set the floor for the price that the company can charge. **Cost-based pricing** involves setting prices based on the costs for producing, distributing and selling the product plus a fair rate of return for its effort and risk. A company's costs may be an important element in its pricing strategy.

Some companies, such as Ryanair and Walmart, work to become the 'low-cost producers' in their industries. Companies with lower costs can set lower prices that result in smaller margins but greater sales and profits. However, other companies – such as Apple, BMW and Steinway – intentionally generate higher costs so that they can claim higher prices and margins. For example, it costs more to make a 'handcrafted' Steinway piano than a Yamaha production model. But the higher costs result in higher quality, justifying that eye-popping €50,000 price. The key is to manage the spread between costs and prices – how much the company makes for the customer value it delivers.

> **Cost-based pricing**—Setting prices based on the costs for producing, distributing, and selling the product plus a fair rate of return for effort and risk.

Types of costs

A company's costs take two forms: fixed and variable. **Fixed costs** (also known as **overheads**) are costs that do not vary with production or sales level. For example, a company must pay each month's bills for rent, heat, interest and executive salaries – whatever the company's output. **Variable costs** vary directly with the level of production. Each PC produced by HP involves a cost of computer chips, wires, plastic, packaging and other inputs. Although these costs tend to be the same for each unit produced, they are called variable costs because the total varies with the number of units produced. **Total costs** are the sum of the fixed and variable costs for any given level of production. Management wants to charge a price that will at least cover the total production costs at a given level of production.

The company must watch its costs carefully. If it costs the company more than its competitors to produce and sell a similar product, the company will need to charge a higher price or make less profit, putting it at a competitive disadvantage.

> **Fixed costs (overhead)**—Costs that do not vary with production or sales level.
>
> **Variable costs**—Costs that vary directly with the level of production.
>
> **Total costs**—The sum of the fixed and variable costs for any given level of production.

Costs at different levels of production

To price wisely, management needs to know how its costs vary with different levels of production. For example, suppose Nokia built a plant to produce 1,000 mobile phones per day. Figure 10.3(a) shows the typical short-run average cost curve (SRAC). It shows that the cost per mobile phone is high if Nokia's factory produces only a few per day. But as production moves up to 1,000 mobile phones per day, the average cost per unit decreases. This is because fixed costs are spread over more units, with each one bearing a smaller share of the fixed cost. Nokia can try to produce more than 1,000 mobile phones per day, but average costs will increase because the plant becomes inefficient. Workers have to wait for machines, the machines break down more often and workers get in each other's way.

> **Figure 10.3** Cost per unit at different levels of production per period

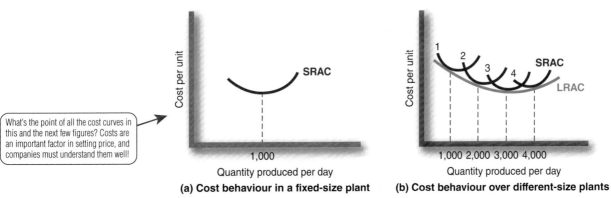

> What's the point of all the cost curves in this and the next few figures? Costs are an important factor in setting price, and companies must understand them well!

(a) Cost behaviour in a fixed-size plant   (b) Cost behaviour over different-size plants

If Nokia believed it could sell 2,000 mobile phones a day, it should consider building a larger plant. The plant would use more efficient machinery and work arrangements. Also, the unit cost of producing 2,000 mobile phones per day would be lower than the unit cost of producing 1,000 units per day, as shown in the long-run average cost (LRAC) curve (Figure 10.3(b)). In fact, a 3,000-capacity plant would be even more efficient, according to Figure 10.3(b). But a 4,000-daily production plant would be less efficient because of increasing diseconomies of scale – too many workers to manage, paperwork slowing things down, and so on. Figure 10.3(b) shows that a 3,000-daily production plant is the best size to build if demand is strong enough to support this level of production.

Costs as a function of production experience

Suppose Nokia operates a plant that produces 3,000 mobile phones per day. As Nokia gains experience in producing mobile phones, it learns how to do it better. Workers learn shortcuts and become more familiar with their equipment. With practice, the work becomes better organised, and Nokia finds better equipment and production processes. With higher volumes, Nokia becomes more efficient and gains economies of scale. As a result, the average cost tends to decrease with accumulated production experience. This is shown in Figure 10.4.[8] Thus, the average cost of producing the first 100,000 mobile phones is €10 per phone. When the company has produced the first 200,000 mobile phones, the average cost has fallen to €8.50. After its accumulated production experience doubles again to 400,000, the average cost is €7. This drop in the average cost with accumulated production experience is called the **experience curve** (or the **learning curve**).

If a downward-sloping experience curve exists, this is highly significant for the company. Not only will the company's unit production cost decrease, but it will decrease faster if the company makes and sells more during a given time period. But the market has to stand ready to buy the higher output. And to take advantage of the experience curve, Nokia must get a large market share early in the product's life cycle. This suggests the following pricing strategy: Nokia should price its mobile phones low; its sales will then increase and its costs will decrease through gaining more experience – and then it can lower its prices further.

Some companies have built successful strategies around the experience curve. However, a single-minded focus on reducing costs and exploiting the experience curve will not always work. Experience-curve pricing carries some major risks. The aggressive pricing might give the product a cheap image. The strategy also assumes that competitors are weak and not willing to fight it out by meeting the company's price cuts. Finally, while the company is building volume under one technology, a competitor may find a lower-cost technology that lets it start at prices lower than those of the market leader, who still operates on the old experience curve.

Cost-plus pricing

The simplest pricing method is **cost-plus pricing** (or **mark-up pricing**) – adding a standard mark-up to the cost of the product. Construction companies, for example, submit job bids by estimating the total project cost and adding a standard mark-up for profit. Lawyers, accountants and other professionals typically price by adding a standard mark-up to their costs. Some sellers tell their

Experience curve (learning curve)—The drop in the average per-unit production cost that comes with accumulated production experience.

Cost-plus pricing (mark-up pricing)—Adding a standard markup to the cost of the product.

Figure 10.4 Cost per unit as a function of accumulated production: the experience curve

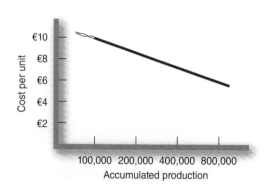

customers they will charge cost plus a specified mark-up; for example, aerospace companies often price this way to governments.

To illustrate mark-up pricing, suppose a toaster manufacturer had the following costs and expected sales:

Variable cost	€10
Fixed costs	€300,000
Expected unit sales	50,000

Then the manufacturer's cost per toaster is given by the following:

$$\text{Unit cost} = \text{Variable cost} + \frac{\text{Fixed costs}}{\text{Unit sales}} = €10 + \frac{€300,000}{50,000} = €16$$

Now suppose the manufacturer wants to earn a 20 per cent mark-up on sales. The manufacturer's mark-up price is given by the following:[9]

$$\text{Markup price} = \frac{\text{Unit cost}}{(1 - \text{Desired return on sales})} = \frac{€16}{1 - 0.2} = €20$$

The manufacturer would charge dealers €20 per toaster and make a profit of €4 per unit. The dealers, in turn, will mark up the toaster. If dealers want to earn 50 per cent on the sales price, they will mark up the toaster to €40 (€20 + 50% of €40). This number is equivalent to a *mark-up on cost* of 100 per cent (€20/€20).

Does using standard mark-ups to set prices make sense? Generally, no. Any pricing method that ignores demand and competitor prices is not likely to lead to the best price. Still, mark-up pricing remains popular for many reasons. First, sellers are more certain about costs than about demand. By tying the price to cost, sellers simplify pricing; they do not need to make frequent adjustments as demand changes. Second, when all firms in the industry use this pricing method, prices tend to be similar, so price competition is minimised. Third, many people feel that cost-plus pricing is fairer to both buyers and sellers. Sellers earn a fair return on their investment but do not take advantage of buyers when buyers' demand becomes great.

Break-even analysis and target profit pricing

Another cost-oriented pricing approach is **break-even pricing** (or a variation called **target return pricing**) (see Figure 10.5). The firm tries to determine the price at which it will break even or make the target return it is seeking.

Target return pricing uses the concept of a *break-even chart*, which shows the total cost and total revenue expected at different sales volume levels. Figure 10.5 shows a break-even chart for the toaster manufacturer discussed above. Fixed costs are €300,000 regardless of sales volume. Variable costs are added to fixed costs to form total costs, which rise with volume. The total revenue curve starts at zero and rises with each unit sold. The slope of the total revenue curve reflects the price of €20 per unit.

The total revenue and total cost curves cross at 30,000 units. This is the *break-even volume*. At €20, the company must sell at least 30,000 units to break even, that is, for total revenue to cover total cost. Break-even volume can be calculated using the following formula:

$$\text{Break-even volume} = \frac{\text{Fixed cost}}{\text{Price} - \text{Variable cost}} = \frac{€300,000}{€20 - €10} = 30,000$$

Break-even pricing (target return pricing)—Setting price to break even on the costs of making and marketing a product or setting price to make a target return.

Figure 10.5 Break-even chart for determining target-return price and break-even volume

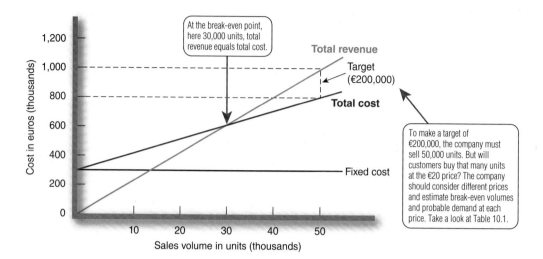

If the company wants to make a profit, it must sell more than 30,000 units at €20 each. Suppose the toaster manufacturer has invested €1,000,000 in the business and wants to set a price to earn a 20 per cent return, or €200,000. In that case, it must sell at least 50,000 units at €20 each. If the company charges a higher price, it will not need to sell as many toasters to achieve its target return. But the market may not buy even this lower volume at the higher price. Much depends on price elasticity and competitors' prices.

The manufacturer should consider different prices and estimate break-even volumes, probable demand and profits for each. This is done in Table 10.1. The table shows that as price increases, the break-even volume drops (column 2). But as price increases, the demand for toasters also decreases (column 3). At the €14 price, because the manufacturer clears only €4 per toaster (€14 less €10 in variable costs), it must sell a very high volume to break even. Even though the low price attracts many buyers, demand still falls below the high break-even point, and the manufacturer loses money. At the other extreme, with a €22 price, the manufacturer clears €12 per toaster and must sell only 25,000 units to break even. But at this high price, consumers buy too few toasters, and profits are negative. The table shows that a price of €18 yields the highest profits. Note that none of the prices produce the manufacturer's target return of €200,000. To achieve

Table 10.1 Break-even volume and profits at different prices

(1) Price	(2) Unit demand needed to break even	(3) Expected unit demand at given price	(4) Total revenue (1) × (3)	(5) Total costs	(6) Profit (4)–(5)
€14	75,000	71,000	€994,000	€1,010,000	−€16,000
16	50,000	67,000	1,072,000	970,000	102,000
18	37,500	60,000	1,080,000	900,000	180,000
20	30,000	42,000	840,000	720,000	120,000
22	25,000	23,000	506,000	530,000	−€24,000

*Assumes fixed costs of €300,000 and constant unit variable costs of €10.

this return, the manufacturer will have to search for ways to lower the fixed or variable costs, thus lowering the break-even volume.

> **AUTHOR COMMENT**
>
> In setting prices, the company must also consider competitors' prices. No matter what price it charges – high, low or in-between – the company must be certain to give customers superior value for that price.

Competition-based pricing

Competition-based pricing involves setting prices based on competitors' strategies, costs, prices and market offerings. Consumers will base their judgments of a product's value on the prices that competitors charge for similar products.

In assessing competitors' pricing strategies, the company should ask several questions. First, how does the company's market offering compare with competitors' offerings in terms of customer value? If consumers perceive that the company's product or service provides greater value, then such a company can charge a higher price. If consumers perceive less value relative to competing products, the company must either charge a lower price or change customer perceptions to justify a higher price.

Next, how strong are current competitors, and what are their current pricing strategies? If the company faces a host of smaller competitors charging high prices relative to the value they deliver, it might charge lower prices to drive weaker competitors from the market. If the market is dominated by larger, low-price competitors, the company may decide to target unserved market niches with value-added products at higher prices.

For example, Daunt Books, an independent bookseller in London, UK, isn't likely to win a price war against Amazon or Barnes & Noble; it doesn't even try. Instead, the shop relies on its personal approach, cosy atmosphere and friendly and knowledgeable staff to turn local book lovers into loyal patrons, even if they have to pay a little more.

> James Daunt, 46, is the founder of Daunt Books, the independent book-shop based in London's Marylebone High Street, with branches in Belsize Park, Hampstead, Holland Park and Chelsea. The shops are known for their old-fashioned interiors and organisation of books by country instead of subject. The shops are original Edwardian bookshops with beautiful, long oak galleries and graceful skylights. The interiors whisper old-fashioned charm, tradition and conservative geniality. No loud music blares, no crass assistants atone 'Have a nice day'; instead the aged old floors and relaxed atmosphere generates a feeling of tranquillity and calm.[10]

What principle should guide decisions about what price to charge relative to those of competitors? The answer is simple in concept but often difficult in practice: no matter what price you charge – high, low or in-between – be certain to give customers superior value for that price.

Competition-based pricing— Setting prices based on competitors' strategies, prices, costs and market offerings.

Pricing against larger, low-price competitors: independent bookstore Daunt Books isn't likely to win a price war against Amazon.com or Barnes & Noble. Instead, it relies on outstanding customer service and a cosy atmosphere to turn book-lovers into loyal customers.

Source: Alamy Images/Alex Segre

> **AUTHOR COMMENT**
>
> Now that we've looked at the three general pricing approaches – value-, cost- and competitor-based pricing – let's dig into some of the many other factors that affect pricing decisions.

OTHER INTERNAL AND EXTERNAL CONSIDERATIONS AFFECTING PRICE DECISIONS

Beyond customer value perceptions, costs and competitor strategies, the company must consider several additional internal and external factors. Internal factors affecting pricing include the company's overall marketing strategy, objectives and marketing mix, as well as other organisational considerations. External factors include the nature of the market and demand and other environmental factors.

Overall marketing strategy, objectives and mix

Price is only one element of the company's broader marketing strategy. Thus, before setting price, the company must decide on its overall marketing strategy for the product or service. If the company has selected its target market and positioning carefully, then its marketing mix strategy, including price, will be fairly straightforward. For example, when Honda developed its Acura brand to compete with European luxury-performance cars in the higher-income segment, this required charging a high price. In contrast, when it introduced the Honda Fit model – billed as 'a pint-sized fuel miser with feisty giddy up' – this positioning required charging a low price. Thus, pricing strategy is largely determined by decisions on market positioning.

Pricing may play an important role in helping to accomplish company objectives at many levels. A firm can set prices to attract new customers or profitably retain existing ones. It can set prices low to prevent competition from entering the market or set prices at competitors' levels to stabilise the market. It can price to keep the loyalty and support of resellers or avoid government intervention. Prices can be reduced temporarily to create excitement for a brand. Or one product may be priced to help the sales of other products in the company's line.

Price is only one of the marketing mix tools that a company uses to achieve its marketing objectives. Price decisions must be coordinated with product design, distribution and promotion decisions to form a consistent and effective integrated marketing programme. Decisions made for other marketing mix variables may affect pricing decisions. For example, a decision to position the product on high-performance quality will mean that the seller must charge a higher price to cover higher costs. And producers whose resellers are expected to support and promote their products may have to build larger reseller margins into their prices.

Companies often position their products on price and then tailor other marketing mix decisions to the prices they want to charge. Here, price is a crucial product-positioning factor that defines the product's market, competition and design. Many firms support such price-positioning strategies with a technique called **target costing**. Target costing reverses the usual process of first designing a new product, determining its cost and then asking, 'Can we sell it for that?' Instead, it starts with an ideal selling price based on customer-value considerations and then targets costs that will ensure that the price is met. For example, when Honda set out to design the Fit, it began with a €10,800 starting price point and an operating efficiency of 33 miles per gallon firmly in mind. It then designed a stylish, peppy little car with costs that allowed it to give target customers those values.

Other companies deemphasise price and use other marketing mix tools to create *non-price* positions. Often, the best strategy is not to charge the lowest price but rather differentiate the marketing offer to make it worth a higher price. For example, Bang & Olufsen (B&O) – known for its cutting-edge consumer electronics – builds more value into its products and charges sky-high prices. A B&O 50-inch BeoVision 4 HDTV will cost you around €5,300, a 65-inch model costs €9,500, and a 103-inch model goes for €67,000. A complete B&O entertainment system? Well, you don't really want to know the price. But target customers recognise B&O's very high quality and are willing to pay more to get it.

Some marketers even position their products on *high* prices, featuring high prices as part of their product's allure. For example, Grand Marnier offers a €160 bottle of Cuvée du Cent Cinquantenaire liqueur that's marketed with the tagline 'Hard to find, impossible to pronounce, and prohibitively expensive'. And Stella Artois's famous advertising campaign which proudly informed consumers that the premium lager was 'Reassuringly expensive' and the height of sophisticated European modernity.

Target costing—Pricing that starts with an ideal selling price and then targets costs that will ensure that the price is met.

Thus, marketers must consider the total marketing strategy and mix when setting prices. But again, even when featuring price, marketers need to remember that customers rarely buy on price alone. Instead, they seek products that give them the best value in terms of benefits received for the prices paid.

Organisational considerations

Management must decide who within the organisation should set prices. Companies handle pricing in a variety of ways. In small companies, prices are often set by top management rather than by the marketing or sales departments. In large companies, pricing is typically handled by divisional or product line managers. In industrial markets, salespeople may be allowed to negotiate with customers within certain price ranges. Even so, top management sets the pricing objectives and policies, and it often approves the prices proposed by lower-level management or salespeople.

In industries in which pricing is a key factor (airlines, aerospace, steel, railways and oil companies), companies often have pricing departments to set the best prices or help others in setting them. These departments report to the marketing department or top management. Others who have an influence on pricing include sales managers, production managers, finance managers and accountants.

The market and demand

As noted earlier, good pricing starts with an understanding of how customers' perceptions of value affect the prices they are willing to pay. Both consumer and industrial buyers balance the price of a product or service against the benefits of owning it. Thus, before setting prices, the marketer must understand the relationship between price and demand for the company's product. In this section, we take a deeper look at the price–demand relationship and how it varies for different types of markets. We then discuss methods for analysing the price–demand relationship.

Pricing in different types of markets

The seller's pricing freedom varies with different types of markets. Economists recognise four types of markets, each presenting a different pricing challenge.

Under *pure competition*, the market consists of many buyers and sellers trading in a uniform commodity, such as wheat, copper or financial securities. No single buyer or seller has much effect on the going market price. In a purely competitive market, marketing research, product development, pricing, advertising and sales promotion play little or no role. Thus, sellers in these markets do not spend much time on marketing strategy.

Under *monopolistic competition*, the market consists of many buyers and sellers who trade over a range of prices rather than a single market price. A range of prices occurs because sellers can differentiate their offers to buyers. Sellers try to develop differentiated offers for different customer segments and, in addition to price, freely use branding, advertising and personal selling to set their offers apart. Thus, Toyota sets its Prius brand apart through strong branding and advertising, reducing the impact of price. It promotes that the third-generation Prius as taking you from 'zero to sixty in 70 percent fewer emissions'. Because there are many competitors in such markets, each firm is less affected by competitors' pricing strategies than in oligopolistic markets.

Under *oligopolistic competition*, the market consists of a few sellers who are highly sensitive to each other's pricing and marketing strategies. Because there are few sellers, each seller is alert and responsive to competitors' pricing strategies and moves.

In a *pure monopoly*, the market consists of one seller. The seller may be a government monopoly (e.g. the UK's Royal Mail), a private regulated monopoly (e.g. a power company) or a private non-regulated monopoly (e.g. DuPont when it introduced nylon). Pricing is handled differently in each case.

Analysing the price–demand relationship

Each price the company might charge will lead to a different level of demand. The relationship between the price charged and the resulting demand level is shown in the **demand curve** in

Demand curve—A curve that shows the number of units the market will buy in a given time period, at different prices that might be charged.

Figure 10.6 Demand curves

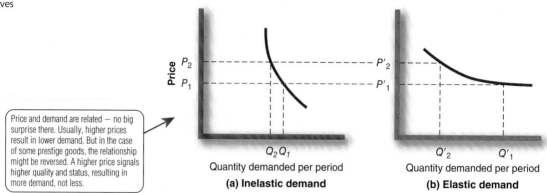

Price and demand are related — no big surprise there. Usually, higher prices result in lower demand. But in the case of some prestige goods, the relationship might be reversed. A higher price signals higher quality and status, resulting in more demand, not less.

(a) Inelastic demand

(b) Elastic demand

Figure 10.6. The demand curve shows the number of units the market will buy in a given time period at different prices that might be charged. In the normal case, demand and price are inversely related – that is, the higher the price, the lower the demand. Thus, the company would sell less if it raised its price from P_1 to P_2. In short, consumers with limited budgets probably will buy less of something if its price is too high.

The overall strategy of the French food conglomerate, Danone is reliant on a clear understanding of the consumer's willingness to pay. To Danone, volume is more important than sales growth and careful pricing is needed to maintain volume.[11]

Franck Riboud is the executive chairman of Danone. He has shifted Danone's strategy to volume growth rather than sales growth. His view appears to be that setting a high sales target in the current economic environment would put undue pressure on managers, risking mistakes and short-cuts to achieve the growth. Much better to cut prices and increase volumes than to shut factories, he has said. The company sells its products – including Activia yoghurt and Actimel yoghurt drink, as well as Evian, Badoit and baby food, including Milupa, to 700 million people worldwide. It aims to achieve its mission to 'bring health through food to the largest number of people' by selling to 1 billion people by the end of 2011. Although its international sales are expanding, it still relies on Western Europe for 48 per cent of its sales. For Danone, the shift towards volume rather than sales growth means targeting and expanding sales in emerging markets. But because people in these countries are less wealthy than in more prosperous countries, the company cannot expect to generate the same profit margins. Its cheapest yoghurt is sold in Bangladesh at 6 euro cents in an 80 g cup. In France, plain Activia yoghurt sells for 26 euro cents for 125 g.

Most companies try to measure their demand curves by estimating demand at different prices. The type of market makes a difference. In a monopoly, the demand curve shows the total market demand resulting from different prices. If the company faces competition, its demand at different prices will depend on whether competitors' prices stay constant or change with the company's own prices.

Price elasticity of demand

Price elasticity—A measure of the sensitivity of demand to changes in price.

Consider the two demand curves in Figure 10.6. In Figure 10.6(a), a price increase from P_1 to P_2 leads to a relatively small drop in demand from Q_1 to Q_2. In Figure 10.6(b), however, the same price increase leads to a large drop in demand from Q'_1 to Q'_2. If demand hardly changes with a small change in price, we say the demand is *inelastic*. If demand changes greatly, we say the demand is *elastic*. The **price elasticity of demand** is given by the following formula:

$$\text{Price elasticity of demand} = \frac{\% \text{ change in quantity demanded}}{\% \text{ change in price}}$$

Suppose demand falls by 10 per cent when a seller raises its price by 2 per cent. The price elasticity of demand is therefore −5 (the minus sign confirms the inverse relation between price and demand), and demand is elastic. If demand falls by 2 per cent with a 2 per cent increase in price, then elasticity is −1. In this case, the seller's total revenue stays the same: the seller sells fewer items but at a higher price that preserves the same total revenue. If demand falls by 1 percent when price is increased by 2 per cent, then elasticity is −1/2, and demand is inelastic. The less elastic the demand, the more it pays for the seller to raise the price.

What determines the price elasticity of demand? Buyers are less price sensitive when the product they are buying is unique or when it is high in quality, prestige or exclusiveness; substitute products are hard to find or when they cannot easily compare the quality of substitutes; and the total expenditure for a product is low relative to their income or when the cost is shared by another party.[12]

If demand is elastic rather than inelastic, sellers will consider lowering their prices. A lower price will produce more total revenue. This practice makes sense as long as the extra costs of producing and selling more do not exceed the extra revenue. At the same time, most firms want to avoid pricing that turns their products into commodities. In recent years, forces such as dips in the economy, deregulation and the instant price comparisons afforded by the Internet and other technologies have increased consumer price sensitivity, turning products ranging from telephones and computers to new cars into commodities in some consumers' eyes.

Marketers need to work harder than ever to differentiate their offerings when a dozen competitors are selling virtually the same product at a comparable or lower price. More than ever, companies need to understand the price sensitivity of their customers and the trade-offs that people are willing to make between price and product characteristics.

The economy

Economic conditions can have a strong impact on the firm's pricing strategies. Economic factors such as a boom or recession, inflation and interest rates affect pricing decisions because they affect consumer spending, consumer perceptions of the product's price and value, and the company's costs of producing and selling a product.

In the aftermath of the recent economic downturn, consumers have rethought the price–value equation. Many consumers have tightened their belts and become more value conscious. In the new, more-frugal economy, bemoans one marketer, 'The frill is gone'. Even more, consumers are likely to continue their thrifty ways well beyond any economic recovery. As a result, many marketers have increased their emphasis on value-for-money pricing strategies. 'Value is the magic word', says a P&G marketer. 'In these economic times, people are … being much more thoughtful before making purchases… . Now, we're going to be even more focused on helping consumers see value.'[13]

The most obvious response to the new economic realities is to cut prices and offer deep discounts. And thousands of companies have done just that. Lower prices make products more affordable and help spur short-term sales. However, such price cuts can have undesirable long-term consequences. Lower prices mean lower margins. Deep discounts may cheapen a brand in consumers' eyes. And once a company cuts prices, it's difficult to raise them again when the economy recovers. Consider companies such as Starbucks, Tiffany's or Veuve-Clicquot, which have spent years successfully positioning themselves on premium products at premium prices. In adapting to the new pricing environment, such firms face the difficult task of realigning their value propositions while staying true to their longer-term 'more-for-more' positioning.

Rather than cutting prices, many companies are instead shifting their marketing focus to more affordable items in their product mixes. For example, whereas its previous promotions emphasised high-end products and pricey concepts such as creating dream kitchens, OBI's (Europe's second largest DIY retailer) more recent advertising emphasises value and

Companies such as Veuve-Clicquot have spent years successfully positioning themselves on premium products at premium prices.

Source: Getty Images/Michael Loccisano

financial savings compared to expensive workers. Other companies are holding prices but redefining the 'value' in their value propositions. For instance, Unilever has repositioned its higher-end Bertolli frozen meals as an eat-at-home brand that's more affordable than eating out. And Kraft's Velveeta cheese ads tell shoppers to 'forget the cheddar, Velveeta is better', claiming that a package of Velveeta is 'twice the size of cheddar, for the same price'.[14]

Remember, even in tough economic times, consumers do not buy based on prices alone. They balance the price they pay against the value they receive. For example, according to a recent survey, despite selling its shoes for as much as €360 a pair (the Nike Mercurial Superfly III), Nike commands the highest consumer loyalty of any brand in the footwear segment.[15] Customers perceive the value of Nike's products and the Nike ownership experience to be well worth the price. Thus, no matter what price they charge – low or high – companies need to offer great *value for money*.

Other external factors

Beyond the market and the economy, the company must consider several other factors in its external environment when setting prices. It must know what impact its prices will have on other parties in its environment. How will *resellers* react to various prices? The company should set prices that give resellers a fair profit, encourage their support and help them to sell the product effectively. The *government* is another important external influence on pricing decisions. Finally, *social concerns* may need to be taken into account. In setting prices, a company's short-term sales, market share and profit goals may need to be tempered by broader societal considerations. We will examine public policy issues in pricing at the end of Chapter 11.

 REVIEWING OBJECTIVES AND KEY TERMS

Companies today face a fierce and fast-changing pricing environment. Firms successful at creating customer value with the other marketing mix activities must still capture some of this value in the prices they earn. This chapter examined the importance of pricing, general pricing strategies, and the internal and external considerations that affect pricing decisions.

OBJECTIVE 1 Answer the question 'What is a price?' and discuss the importance of pricing in today's fast-changing environment (p. 305).

Price can be defined narrowly as the amount of money charged for a good or service. Or it can be defined more broadly as the sum of the values that consumers exchange for the benefits of having and using the product or service. The pricing challenge is to find the price that will let the company make a fair profit by getting paid for the customer value it creates.

Despite the increased role of non-price factors in the modern marketing process, price remains an important element in the marketing mix. It is the only marketing mix element that produces revenue; all other elements represent costs. More importantly, as a part of a company's overall value proposition, price plays a key role in creating customer value and building customer relationships. Smart managers treat pricing as a key strategic tool for creating and capturing customer value.

OBJECTIVE 2 Identify the three major pricing strategies and discuss the importance of understanding customer-value perceptions, company costs and competitor strategies when setting prices (pp. 305–313).

Companies can choose from three major pricing strategies: customer value-based pricing, cost-based pricing and competition-based pricing. *Customer value-based pricing* uses buyers' perceptions of value as the basis for setting price. Good pricing begins with a complete understanding of the value that a product or service creates for customers and setting a price that captures that value. Customer perceptions of the product's value set the ceiling for prices. If customers perceive that a product's price is greater than its value, they will not buy the product.

Companies can pursue either of two types of value-based pricing. *Good-value pricing* involves offering just the right combination of quality and good service at a fair price. EDLP is an example of this strategy. *Value-added pricing* involves attaching value-added features and services to differentiate the company's offers and support charging higher prices.

Cost-based pricing involves setting prices based on the costs for producing, distributing and selling products plus a fair rate of return for effort and risk. Company and product costs are an important consideration in setting prices. Whereas customer value perceptions set the price ceiling, costs set the floor for pricing. However, cost-based pricing is product driven rather than customer driven. The company designs what it considers to be a good product and sets a price that covers costs plus a target profit. If the price turns out to be too high, the company must settle for lower mark-ups or lower sales, both resulting in disappointing profits. If the company prices the product below its costs, its profits will also suffer. Cost-based pricing approaches include *cost-plus pricing* and *break-even pricing* (or target profit pricing).

Competition-based pricing involves setting prices based on competitors' strategies, costs, prices and market offerings. Consumers base their judgments of a product's value on the prices that competitors charge for similar products. If consumers perceive that the company's product or service provides greater value, the company can charge a higher price. If consumers perceive less value relative to competing products, the company must either charge a lower price or change customer perceptions to justify a higher price.

OBJECTIVE 3 Identify and define the other important internal and external factors affecting a firm's pricing decisions (pp. 314–318).

Other *internal* factors that influence pricing decisions include the company's overall marketing strategy, objectives and marketing mix, as well as organisational considerations. Price is only one element of the company's broader marketing strategy. If the company has selected its target market and positioning carefully, then its marketing mix strategy, including price, will be fairly straightforward. Some companies position their products on price and then tailor other marketing mix decisions to the prices they want to charge. Other companies deemphasise price and use other marketing mix tools to create *non-price* positions.

Other *external* pricing considerations include the nature of the market and demand and environmental factors such as the economy, reseller needs and government actions. The seller's pricing freedom varies with different types of markets. Ultimately, the customer decides whether the company has set the right price. The customer weighs price against the perceived values of using the product: if the price exceeds the sum of the values, consumers will not buy. So the company must understand concepts such as demand curves (the price–demand relationship) and price elasticity (consumer sensitivity to prices).

Economic conditions can also have a major impact on pricing decisions. The economic downturn caused consumers to rethink the price–value equation. Marketers have responded by increasing their emphasis on value-for-money pricing strategies. Even in tough economic times, however, consumers do not buy based on prices alone. Thus, no matter what price they charge – low or high – companies need to offer superior value for money.

 # NAVIGATING THE KEY TERMS

OBJECTIVE 1
Price (p. 305)

OBJECTIVE 2
Customer value-based pricing (p. 306)
Good-value pricing (p. 307)
Value-added pricing (p. 308)

OBJECTIVE 3
Cost-based pricing (p. 309)
Fixed costs (overheads) (p. 309)

Variable costs (p. 309)
Total costs (p. 309)
Experience curve (learning curve) (p. 310)
Cost-plus pricing (mark-up pricing) (p. 310)
Break-even pricing (target return pricing) (p. 311)
Competition-based pricing (p. 313)
Target costing (p. 314)
Demand curve (p. 315)
Price elasticity (p. 316)

DISCUSSING AND APPLYING THE CONCEPTS

Discussing the concepts

1. What factors must marketers consider when setting prices? (AACSB Communication).

2. Name and describe the two types of value-based pricing methods. (AACSB: Communication)

3. Describe the types of cost-based pricing and the methods of implementing each. (AACSB: Communication)

4. What is *target costing* and how is it different from the usual process of setting prices? (AACSB: Communication)

5. Discuss the impact of the economy on a company's pricing strategies. (AACSB: Communication)

6. Name and describe the four types of markets recognised by economists and discuss the pricing challenges posed by each. (AACSB: Communication)

Applying the concepts

1. In a small group, discuss your perceptions of value and how much you are willing to pay for the following products: cars, frozen dinners, jeans and athletic shoes. Are there differences among members of your group? Explain why those differences exist. Discuss some examples of brands of these products that are positioned to deliver different value to consumers. (AACSB: Communication; Reflective Thinking)

2. Find estimates of price elasticity for a variety of consumer goods and *services*. Explain what price elasticities of 0.5 and 2.4 mean. (*Note:* These are absolute values, as price elasticity is usually negative.) (AACSB: Communication; Reflective Thinking)

3. In a small group, determine the costs associated with offering an online MBA degree in addition to a traditional MBA degree at a university. Which costs are fixed and which are variable)? Determine the tuition fee (that is, price) to charge for a year core module in this degree programme. Which pricing method is your group using to determine the price? (AACSB: Communication; Reflective Thinking)

Focus on technology

Would you shop around for the best price on a medical procedure? Most patients do not know the price of a medical procedure, and many might not care because they think insurance or their government will cover it. But that is not always the case. Many patients are paying out of their own pockets for their health care. However, health-care costs and doctors'

prices are now more transparent thanks to the Internet. Several websites arm patients with cost information, and others allow them to make price comparisons in their areas. They might even get a coupon for a price reduction from a participating provider.

1. Search online (for example, www.bodiesbeautiful.co.uk) for abdominoplasty (tummy tuck) surgery prices in different countries. What is the most and least expensive place to have this surgery? Why are there differences or similarities in the range of prices? (AACSB: Communication; Use of IT; Reflective Thinking)

2. Health-care providers offer price deals through these types of websites. Debate the likelihood of consumers taking advantage of Internet price discounts for medical care. (AACSB: Communication; Reflective Thinking)

Focus on ethics

In airline pricing, €5 here and €10 there – it all starts to add up. Airlines are adding 'extra' costs for flyers right and left, except that there are more zeros after the fives and tens! Add-on fees contributed more than €5 billion in airline revenue in 2009. Change your flight – that will cost upward of €150. Check-in a bag – add another €10 to €25 and perhaps €50 for a second bag if travelling long haul. Some airlines *even* charge for carry-on bags! Taking a pet along? That's another €50 to €100. Hungry? €10 or more, please. For €10 to €30, you can jump to the front of the check-in and security lines and board before other passengers. These fees are in addition to all the other taxes and fees imposed on flyers. A recent report, however, raises concerns over the disclosure of fees. Airlines are required to disclose only checked in hold baggage fees, making it harder for consumers to compare total costs when booking flights.

1. Go to www.ryanair.com and determine what it would cost to fly from Dublin to Stockholm for a one-week round trip next month. What additional fees would you have to pay to change your flight, check-in one bag, bring your dog with you and eat lunch while flying? (AACSB; Communication; Reflective Thinking)

2. How easy was it to determine the total cost of your flight? Should airlines be required to disclose all fees through an easier method? (AACSB: Communication; Ethical Reasoning)

Marketing & the economy

Colgate-Palmolive

As the uncertain economy has made people more aware of their spending, many companies *have* slashed prices on their goods and services. Still other companies successfully held prices steady, selling as much or more than they did before the economic bottom fell out. But Colgate-Palmolive is one of the fortunate few that has actually been able to *increase* prices during this more frugal era and reap benefits from doing so. Think about it – how grim would your budget *have* to get before you'd stop brushing your teeth or taking a shower? Economic conditions *have* relatively little impact on people's basic personal care habits, and brand preferences are deeply ingrained for these necessities. Based on an accurate evaluation of customer buying habits, Colgate-Palmolive raised prices by an average of 7.5 per cent without experiencing any dip in sales. Higher prices and stable volumes equal cha-ching higher profits. Indeed, Colgate-Palmolive saw its profits rise for 2008, 2009 and 2010, during the heart of the recent recession. It seems as though looking and smelling clean might just be recession-proof concepts.

1. Does the success of Colgate-Palmolive's price increases have anything to do with the economy?

2. In the longer term, as the economy recovers, what should Colgate-Palmolive anticipate in the wake of its price increases?

Marketing by the numbers

One external factor that manufacturers must consider when setting prices is reseller margins. Manufacturers do not have the final say concerning the price to consumers; retailers do. So manufacturers must start with their suggested retail prices and work back, subtracting the mark-ups required by resellers that sell the product to consumers. Once that is considered, manufacturers know at what price to sell their products to resellers, and they can determine what volume they must sell to *break even* at that price and cost combination. To answer the following questions, refer to Appendix 2.

1. A consumer purchases a computer for €800 from a retailer. If the retailer's mark-up is 30 per cent and the wholesaler's mark-up is 10 per cent, both based on their respective selling prices, at what price does the manufacturer sell the product to the wholesaler? (AACSB: Communication; Analytical Reasoning)

2. If the unit variable cost for each computer is €350 and the manufacturer has fixed costs totalling €2 million, how many computers must this manufacturer sell to break *even*? How many must it sell to realise a profit of €50 million? (AACSB: Communication; Analytical Reasoning)

 REFERENCES

[1] This case study draws heavily on the excellent case studies and analyses (including quotes and other information) of: www.kantar.com, accessed October 2011; www.marketing-society.org.uk, accessed October 2011; www.waitrose.com. accessed October 2011. Thanks must also be given to the excellent insights of Penguin and Crocs Associates.

[2] See Allen Adamson, 'Marketers: expect a return to core brand value – and values – in 2010', *Forbes* (4 January 2010), www.forbes.com; and 'Consumer "New Frugality" may be an enduring feature of post-recession economy, finds Booz & Company survey', *Business Wire* (24 February 2010).

[3] For more on the importance of sound pricing strategy, see Thomas T. Nagle, John Hogan and Joseph Zale, *The Strategy and Tactics of Pricing: A Guide to Growing More Profitably* (Upper Saddle River, NJ: Prentice Hall, 2011), chapter 1.

[4] Based on information from Anne Marie Chaker, 'For a Steinway, I did it my way', *Wall Street Journal* (22 May 2008); and www.steinway.com/steinway and www.steinway.com/steinway/quotes.shtml, accessed October 2011.

[5] See Kevin Done, 'Runway success–Ryanair', *Financial Times* (20 March 2009), www.ft.com/home/us; Matthew Maier, 'A radical fix for airlines: make flying free', *Business 2.0* (April 2006), pp. 32–34; 'Ryanair lures 14% more passengers with price cuts', *Western Mail* (2 February 2010); and www.ryanair.com/en, accessed October 2011.

[6] Example adapted from Anupam Mukerji, 'Monsoon marketing', *Fast Company* (April 2007), p. 22. Also see www.stagumbrellas.com, accessed October 2011.

[7] Elizabeth A. Sullivan, 'Value pricing: smart marketers know cost-plus can be costly', *Marketing News* (15 January 2008), p. 8. Also see Peter J. Williamson and Ming Zeng, 'Value-for-money strategies', *Harvard Business Review* (March 2009), pp. 66–74.

[8] Accumulated production is drawn on a semi-log scale so that equal distances represent the same percentage increase in output.

[9] The arithmetic of markups and margins is discussed in Appendix 2, Marketing by the numbers.

[10] Example from Natalie Graham, 'My first million: James Daunt', *Financial Times* (19 February 2010), accessed October 2011, www.ft.com/cms/s/2/798781da-1d81-11df-a893-00144feab49a.html#axzz1UPifHx5H and www.dauntbooks.co.uk.

[11] Example from Scheherazade Daneshkhu and Jenny Wiggins, 'Food group shifts strategy to volume growth', *Financial Times* (10 January 2010), www.ft.com/cms/s/0/3181527e-fe11-11de-9340-00144feab49a. html#ixzz1UQpXzTG4, accessed October 2011.

[12] See Nagle, Hogan and Zale, *The Strategy and Tactics of Pricing*, chapter 7.

[13] Susan Mires, 'The new economy of frugality: cost-seating skills going up in value', *McClatchy-Tribune Business News* (19 March 2009); Laura Petrecca, 'Marketers try to promote value without cheapening image', *USA Today* (17 November 2008), p. B1; Adamson, 'Marketers: expect a return to core brand value – and values – in 2010'.

[14] Petrecca, 'Marketers try to promote value without cheapening image', D'Innocenzio, 'Butter, Kool-Aid in limelight in advertising shift' (21 April 2009), www.azcentral.com/business/articles/2009/04/21/20090421biz-NewFrugality0421.html; and Judann Pollack, 'Now's the time to reset marketing for post-recession', *Advertising Age* (1 February 2010), p. 1.

[15] Kenneth Hein, 'Study: value trumps price among shoppers', *Brandweek* (2 March 2009), p. 6.

VIDEO CASE

Ikea MyMarketingLab

Lots of companies have idealistic missions. But Ikea's *vision,* 'To create a better *everyday* life for the many people', seems somewhat implausible. How can a company that makes furniture improve *everyday* life for the masses? Interestingly, the most important part of that strategy is price. For every product that it designs, from leather sofas to plastic mugs, Ikea starts with a target price. The target price is one that's deemed affordable, making the product accessible to the masses.

Only then does Ikea begin the gruelling process of creating a high-quality, stylish and *innovative* product that can be delivered to the customer for that target price. As Ikea points out, anyone can make high-quality goods for a high price or poor-quality goods for a low price. The real challenge is making high-quality products at a low price. To do so requires a relentless focus on costs combined with a thirst for innovation. That has been Ikea's quest for more than 65 years. After watching the video featuring Ikea, answer the following questions about the company's pricing strategy:

1. What is Ikea's promise of value?
2. Referring to the Klippan sofa, illustrate how Ikea delivers its promise of value to consumers.
3. Based on the concepts from the text, does Ikea employ a value-based pricing approach or a cost-based pricing approach? Support your answer.

COMPANY CASE

Tesco: every little (pricing strategy) helps?

Kate L. Daunt (*Cardiff Business School*)

Founded in 1919 by Jack Cohen, Tesco has grown to become a dominant player in both domestic and global markets. Tesco holds the position of third largest retailer in the world, while one in every ten pounds spent in the UK is spent at Tesco. Cohen started operations with a market stall selling surplus groceries in London's East End. On his first day of trade Cohen made £1 profit from just £4 of sales. With growing profits, in 1929 Cohen opened his first Tesco store in Burn Oak, North London. Driven by the motto 'pile it high and sell it cheap', Cohen aimed to sell large amounts of produce at low prices, earning him the nickname Jack 'the Slasher' Cohen. The 'pile it high' strategy was founded on what Cohen deemed a virtuous cycle. Here, selling products at cheaper prices enabled the brand to sell a greater volume of produce, which in turn facilitated the organisation to grow bigger, which in turn fuelled cheaper prices and so forth. Driven by this motto, Tesco embarked on an organic and takeover-driven strategy of growth. In addition to a flurry of new store openings stemming from the 1930s to the current day, during the 1950s to the 1980s Tesco bought out a number of existing supermarket brands. This move granted Tesco overnight access to areas in the United Kingdom previously unserved by Tesco stores.

As Tesco grew, new store varieties were introduced. In addition to the original Tesco superstore and compact store formats, in 1992, Tesco opened the first of many 'Metro' stores in London's Covent Garden. These smaller stores aimed to access and serve busy high street shoppers in inner city areas. Following the opening of the 'Express' store format in 1994, targeted at serving neighbourhood locations, in 1997 Tesco opened its first 'Extra' store. In addition to serving the inner city and surrounding suburban markets, Tesco were now utilising out-of-town space to build enormous stores averaging over 1000 m² in size. The availability of such floor space, in part, enabled Tesco to widen its product offering beyond a portfolio characterized by branded grocery goods to also trading non-grocery products and own-branded goods.

DIVERSIFICATION

Based on Tesco's core strategy of low prices = greater volume of sales = growth = lower prices, Tesco saw an opportunity in the marketplace to offer customers products that were not traditionally sold in supermarkets at prices lower than those on the high street. This approach saw Tesco diversify its product offering to include, garden furniture, cosmetics, books, CDs, DVDs, electrical items and clothing. Overwhelmingly, this strategy has been successful. In 2010, one in every six microwaves and one in every four small televisions sold in the UK was purchased from a Tesco store. However, while many customers and suppliers welcomed a greater variety of products on offer in store, not all parties were impressed. In 2002, five years after it was first instigated, Tesco lost a landmark legal battle against Levi Strauss Jeans. As a promotional tool, Tesco had sold Levi's 501 jeans as a loss leader at £27.99 each, nearly half the recommended Levi retail price. Levi complained that the low price and supermarket environment was harmful to its brand image, a complaint that was upheld by the court. The High Court ruled that Tesco was not allowed to source Levi jeans from outside Europe and sell them at low prices without the brand's prior consent. Joe Middleton, Levi's president, said of the ruling 'For 130 years the Levi's name has been a promise of outstanding quality and value . . . this decision allows us to carry on keeping that promise'. Offering an alternative perspective, Phil Evans a policy adviser for the Consumer's Association stated 'Tesco may have lost their legal battle against Levi's – but the real loser is the consumer'.

Unrestrained by big brand pricing and distribution strategies, during the 1990s Tesco began to develop its own branded grocery and non-grocery products. Recognising different market segments and customer needs, Tesco introduced a portfolio of own-brands characterized by differences in price architecture. Reflecting the recessionary times and penny – pinching agendas of consumers in the early 1990s, in 1992 Tesco launched the slogan 'Every Little Helps' followed by its successful Value range of produce the following year. The Tesco Value brand offered shoppers basic grocery items including bread, baked beans and orange juice at prices significantly lower than those of their branded competitors. In addition to the introduction of Tesco's own branded organic produce, healthy living and kids ranges of groceries, in 1998 Tesco brought its range of Finest produce to the marketplace. Designed to respond to UK consumers' changing lifestyles and increasing affluence, products sold under the Finest label offered premium quality and prices. Not only did this strategy assist Tesco in gaining market share and securing a greater percentage of consumers' spend, own branded goods also facilitated Tesco in achieving higher profit margins on their products compared to those earned from the sale of branded goods purchased from external suppliers. Tim Danaher, former editor of *Retail Week*, commented that in creating the Value and Finest ranges, Tesco sent a message 'that everyone is welcome'. The success of the Tesco 'welcome' and diversification strategy is seen both in and out of store. Numerous non-food goods and services are sold under the Tesco brand including banking and insurance services, telecommunications, weight loss programmes and electrical goods. Tesco's own brand of televisions 'Technika' is among the top five selling brands in the UK. In 2003, Tesco Chairman, David Reid commented 'we have the same strategy for non-foods as on grocery: if we can be 15% to 20% cheaper than the expensive British high street, customers will come to you'.

COMPETITIVE FORCES

Tesco operates in a fiercely competitive oligopolistic market. Viewed as the market leader of the 'Big Five', Tesco competes with Asda, Sainsburys, Morrisons and Waitrose for the majority share of UK consumer's expenditure. Oligopolistic markets are often characterised by copy-cat competitive moves and the supermarket industry is no different. Tesco's four main competitors all offer own branded goods at different price points. Sainsburys distinguishes between its 'basics', 'be good', 'so organic' and 'taste the difference' ranges, while Asda trades its no frills range under the label 'smart price' and premium offerings using the mark 'extra special'. Asda also sells its own label television sets under the brand name Luxor. Because the Big Five supermarket brands all sell similar products, price-led promotional tactics are a key means of increasing market share and fostering customer loyalty. Tesco's mission is 'to create value for our customers to earn their lifetime loyalty'. Consequently, in 1995, Tesco was the first of the Big Five to introduce a loyalty card. In return for allowing Tesco previously unprecedented access to record where, when, what, how much and at what price consumers purchased goods from Tesco, the 'Clubcard' rewards participants with money off coupons (earned via points for every pound spent at Tesco) and tailored price promotions. Thus, allowing Tesco to build detailed profiles of their consumers' purchase habits and price sensitivities. At the end of the 2011 financial year Tesco had in excess of 15 million registered Clubcard holders.

As a competitive mechanism to increase customer footfall in stores and maintain and build customer loyalty, Tesco and its four main rivals have engaged in numerous price-based promotions and 'wars'. These include price cuts on individual items, 'two for £x' promotions, 'x% free' offers and 'buy one get one free' (BOGOF) discounts. Yet, while many customers welcome such 'more for less' promotional activities, in light of statistics that show each year the UK fills the equivalent of 4,700 Olympic swimming pools with wasted food and drink, environmental lobbyists have labelled such promotions as 'irresponsible'. In response to such criticism in 2010, Tesco introduced 'Buy One Get One Free Next Week' deals. Tesco's Lucy Neville-Rolfe commented that 'customers really like our Buy One Get One Free deals but feedback shows smaller households sometimes can't use the free product before its use-by date . . . now we're giving customers the flexibility by

claiming their free product the following week instead, as well as giving our customers a flexible new offer, we're helping them to cut food waste'.

With the UK economy entering recessionary conditions in 2008 and statistics showing that more than 40 per cent of products that go through supermarket tills are 'on promotion', Tesco and its main rivals turned to price war tactics to win custom. In the autumn of 2011, Tesco announced its biggest price-driven promotional campaign to date, termed 'The Big Price Drop'. Costing Tesco over £500 million, funded in part by slashing Clubcard points and one-off promotions, the Price Drop campaign promised consumers price cuts on over 3,000 essential items across their stores making the cost of customers' shopping baskets cheaper. A price war soon ensued with Asda launching its Price Guarantee scheme offering a £5 voucher to spend on the next £40 shop and a promise that the firm is 10 per cent cheaper than rivals or they will refund the difference. Similarly, Sainsbury's introduced its 'Brand Match' campaign that checked competitors' prices at the till point and immediately printed customers a money-off voucher to match any savings. Like Asda and Sainsburys, Morrisons also engaged in coupon-based promotional activities. The end result of such activities? Reduced grocery costs for customers but increasingly small margins for the supermarkets. Following this round of promotional activity, in early 2012 Tesco announced its first profit warning in over 20 years. It appeared that Tesco's price reductions had not been offset by customers making additional purchases. Rather, savvy, money–conscious consumers were going from supermarket to supermarket looking for the best deals, so in total they handed Tesco less money for the goods in their baskets than they would have done prior. Philip Clarke, Tesco's CEO admitted that Tesco's 'immediate error was not to match the money-off coupons that were being offered by the main rivals in the run up to Christmas'. In the 2012 Christmas and New Year trading statement Cohen further explained 'we delivered a very good Christmas shopping experience for our customers, but in a highly promotional market, the volume response to our increased investment into lowering prices did not offset the deflation it has driven'.

Highlighting an inherent flaw to the Big Five's price-based promotional activities, Bryan Roberts, director of retail research at Kantar Retail stated that the supermarkets are engaged in a 'Mexican standoff . . . they have all got a gun to each other's head. The number of promotions has been increasing year on year, quarter on quarter. There is no longer any reason for customers to buy key things like cheddar cheese and dishwasher tablets when they are full price.' The authenticity of Tesco's Big Price Drop campaign has also been questioned by consumer sources. BBC's investigative *Panorama* programme termed Tesco's Big Price Drop a sales ploy rather than genuine price promotions. Investigators for the documentary argued that Tesco's price deals were often not as customer-friendly as they initially seemed – illustrated by the withdrawal of 16 'misleading' Tesco price comparison-based advertisements in the past five years by the Advertising Standards Authority. Panorama also highlighted the existence of multibuy deals that offered no savings (e.g. two products sold on offer for £2 that are priced individually at £1) and confusing price-establishing strategies. Although legal in the UK, price-establishing strategies are often frowned on by consumer groups and commentators. Tesco was reported to have sold products at one price for a long period of time before raising the price and then lowering it to the original price again under the guise of the Big Price Drop. John Bridgeman CBE, a former director of the General Office of Fair Trading, commented 'It's confusing, its volatile, there is the illusion of value . . . the customer is being confused'.

In light of the unsuccessful Big Price Drop promotion, in January 2012, Tesco introduced a £5 off a £40 shop voucher with the tagline 'it's just our way of saying "thanks"', in a move to revive its fortunes. Asda labelled the move an 'imitation . . . and nothing more than a short-term gimmick'. Cliona Lynch, a retail analyst, remarked that it was no surprise that Tesco have turned to coupons 'because other retailers drowned out the message of Tesco's Price Drop with their discounting and coupons'. Looking ahead, Lynch comments 'I think Tesco will look to move away from price deals and focus on the quality and range of its products in the future'.

Questions for discussion

1. Does Tesco's promotional pricing campaign, The Big Price Drop, deviate from Cohen's original motto of 'pile them high and sell them cheap'? If so, how?
2. How has Tesco used pricing to segment the food market and position its offering? Why are customers willing to pay different prices for the same category of food (e.g. a tin of baked beans, a chicken or a hand wash)?
3. How can Tesco's Clubcard assist managers in developing pricing strategies?
4. Since 1919, which major pricing strategies have Tesco demonstrated evidence of adopting?
5. Cliona Lynch predicts that Tesco will move away from price deals and focus on the quality and range of its products in the future. Why do you think this is so? Do you believe that price deals should play a role in Tesco's future promotional strategies?

Sources: BBC *Panorama*, 'The truth about supermarket "Bargains"' (5 December 2011), http://news.bbc.co.uk/panorama/hi/front_page/newsid_9652000/9652944.stm; Philip Clarke, 'Christmas and New Year trading statement: determined to move faster, Tesco', www.tescoplc.com/news/news-releases/2012/christmas-new-year-trading-statement; Coriolos Research, 'Tesco: a case study in supermarket excellence' (July); Richard Cree, 'Sir Terry Leahy, CEO, Tesco', *Director Magazine* (February 2011), www.director.co.uk/magazine/2011/2_Feb/terry-leahy_64_06.html; Datamonitor, 'Tesco PLC: company profile', www.datamonitor.com (2011); Andrea Felsted, Tesco in voucher move to revive fortunes', *Financial Times* (18 January 2012), www.ft.com/cms/s/0/d8615e66-41f5-11e1-a1bf-00144feab49a.html#axzz1jtx4tlqv; Mark King, 'Tesco attempts to win back customers', *Guardian* (18 January 2012), www.guardian.co.uk/money/2012/jan/18/tesco-attempts-win-back-customers; Robert Peston, 'Is this the end of Tesco's UK growth?', *BBC News* (12 January 2012), www.bbc.co.uk/news/business-16527080?print=true; Sean Poulter, 'Buy one, get one free next week . . . Tesco launch new deal in bid to cut waste', *Daily Mail* (21 January 2010), www.dailymail.co.uk/news/article-1244863/Tesco-launch-new-deal-bid-cut-waste.html; 'Tesco defeated in cheap jeans battle', *BBC News* (31 July 2002), http://news.bbc.co.uk/1/hi/business/2163561.stm; Tesco PLC, www.tescoplc.com/about-tesco/our-history; Zoe Wood, 'Tesco's price war threat sends supermarket shares plunging', *Guardian* (21 September 2011), www.guardian.co.uk/business/2011/sep/21/tesco-price-war-threatens-supermarkets?INTCMP=ILCNETTXT3487.

CHAPTER ELEVEN

Additional pricing considerations

Chapter preview

In the previous chapter, you learned that price is an important marketing mix tool for both creating and capturing customer value. You explored the three main pricing strategies – customer value-based, cost-based and competition-based pricing – and the many internal and external factors that affect a firm's pricing decisions. In this chapter, we'll look at some additional pricing considerations: new product pricing, product mix pricing, price adjustments and initiating and reacting to price changes. We close the chapter with a discussion of public policy and pricing.

We start by looking at GlaxoSmithKline (GSK), who need to recover huge research and development costs while avoiding allegations of unfair profit-making. GSK do this through ensuring that their pricing strategies are clear and their profits are balanced by several initiatives to make drugs available to those who need but can't afford them. Globally, GSK employs tiered-pricing; that is, selling its medicines in different countries at varying prices based on the ability to pay in each country. While this is sometimes controversial, GSK believes that this ethical approach is best.

Objective outline

▶ **Objective 1** Describe the major strategies for pricing new products.
New product pricing (pp. 329–330)

▶ **Objective 2** Explain how companies find a set of prices that maximises the profits from the total product mix.
Product mix pricing (pp. 330–332)

▶ **Objective 3** Discuss how companies adjust their prices to take into account different types of customers and situations.
Price-adjustment (pp. 332–338)

▶ **Objective 4** Discuss the key issues related to initiating and responding to price changes.
Price changes (pp. 338–341)

▶ **Objective 5** Discuss the social and legal issues that affect pricing decisions.
Public policy and pricing (pp. 342–343)

GlaxoSmithKline

The pharmaceutical industry has historically been one of Europe's most profitable industries. Annual revenues have grown at a growth rate that few industries can match. As the world's second-largest pharmaceutical company, London headquartered GlaxoSmithKline has played a large role in the industry's success. It produces a medicine cabinet full of well-known prescription drugs that combat infections, depression, adverse skin conditions, asthma, heart and circulatory disease and cancer. It also makes dozens of familiar over-the-counter remedies, from Contac, Panadol, Nicorette, Aquafresh and Sensodyne to Tagamet and Tums.

GSK is doing very well in a high-performing industry. In most situations, we applaud companies for such strong performance. However, when it comes to pharmaceutical firms, critics claim, healthy sales and profits may not be so healthy for consumers. Learning that companies like GSK are reaping big profits leaves a bad taste in the mouths of many consumers. It's like learning that the oil companies are profiting when gas prices rocket upward. Although most consumers appreciate the steady stream of beneficial drugs produced by pharmaceutical companies, they worry that the industry's huge success may be coming at their own expense – literally.

Europeans spend more than €180 billion a year on prescription medications. Across Europe prescription prices have risen rapidly over the years, and healthcare costs continue to jump. Last year, while many other industries were cutting prices and many recession-weary consumers struggled just to make ends meet, the pharmaceutical industry raised wholesale prices for brand name prescription drugs by 9 per cent, adding up to €7.36 billion to its revenues.

The critics claim that competitive forces don't operate well in the pharmaceutical market, allowing GSK and other companies to charge excessive prices. Unlike purchases of other consumer products, drug purchases cannot be postponed. And consumers don't usually shop for the best deals on medicines – they simply take what the doctor orders. Because physicians who write the prescriptions don't pay for the medicines they recommend, they have little incentive to be price conscious. Finally, because of patents, the European Medicines Agency and other national-level approval bodies, few competing brands exist to force lower prices, and existing brands don't go on sale.

The critics claim that these market factors leave pharmaceutical companies free to practice monopoly pricing, resulting in unfair practices and price gouging. To add insult to injury, the critics say, drug companies pour more than €2.95 billion a year into direct-to-consumer advertising and another €13.25 billion into sampling. These marketing efforts dictate higher prices at the same time that they build demand for more expensive remedies. Thus, the severest critics say, GSK and the other big drug companies may be profiting unfairly – even at the expense of human life – by promoting and pricing products beyond the reach of many people who need them.

But there's another side to the drug-pricing issue. Industry proponents point out that, over the years, the drug companies have developed a steady stream of medicines that transform people's lives. Developing such new drugs is a risky and expensive endeavour, involving legions of scientists, expensive technology and years of effort with no certainty of success. The pharmaceutical industry invests nearly €37 billion a year in R&D; GSK alone invested nearly €4 billion last year. GSK now has 134 drug projects under development. On average, each new drug takes 12–15 years to develop and typically costs €625 million. Seventy per cent of new drugs never generate enough revenue to recover the cost of development. Although the prices of prescription drugs seem high, they're needed to fund the development of important future drugs. Additionally, a publically held company like GSK has a *bona fide* responsibility to return a profit to shareholders.

A recent GSK advertisement notes that it took 15 years to complete all the tests and find the exact right compound for a new heart medicine, at a cost of more than the price of a space shuttle mission. Profits from the heart drug will help to fund critical research on diseases such as multiple sclerosis and Alzheimer's. The ad concludes: 'Inventing new medicines isn't easy, but it's worth it. . . . Today's medicines finance tomorrow's miracles.'

As for all that expensive prescription drug advertising, the industry argues that the ads have strong information value: they help educate people about

Responsible pricing: most consumers understand that they'll *have* to pay the price for beneficial drugs. They just want to be treated fairly in the process.

Source: Shutterstock.com

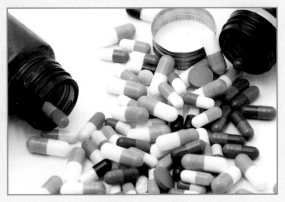

treatments and encourage them to get help for conditions of which they might not otherwise have been aware.

And so the controversy continues. As drug prices climb, GSK and the industry are facing pressures from government, insurance companies, managed-care providers and consumer groups to exercise restraint in setting prices. Rather than waiting for tougher legislation on prices – or simply because it's the right thing to do – GSK has undertaken several initiatives to make drugs available to those who need but can't afford them.

For example, internationally, GSK employs tiered-pricing – selling its medicines in different countries at varying prices based on the ability to pay in each country. People in the poorest countries pay the least, typically one-fifth (or less) the price in industrialised countries. GSK sells its malaria vaccine, sold almost exclusively in developing countries, at little or no profit to keep prices as low as possible. The company also reinvests 20 per cent of the profits from selling drugs in lesser-developed countries (LDCs) to strengthen healthcare infrastructure in those countries. And GSK regularly donates free medicines in response to disaster relief efforts around the globe. 'I want GSK to be a very successful company but not at the expense of leaving the population of Africa behind,' says GSK's CEO.

Tiered pricing is an admirable solution, but it's fraught with challenges. For one thing, it requires that consumers in industrialised countries foot the massive bill for medications to LDCs – for example, 80 per cent of GSK's vaccines go to LDCs. Tiered pricing also overlooks the fact that there are many poor people in even the wealthiest countries who can't afford to pay for prescription drugs. That's why, in some developed countries, GSK sponsors patient assistance programmes and discount cards that provide prescription medicines to low-income, uninsured patients free or at minimal cost.

In all, pharmaceuticals pricing is no easy issue. For GSK, it's more than a matter of sales and profits. In setting prices, short-term financial goals must be tempered by broader societal considerations. GSK's heartfelt mission is 'to improve the quality of human life by enabling people to do more, feel better, and live longer'. Accomplishing this mission won't come cheap. Most consumers understand that. One way or another, they know, they'll have to pay the price. All they really ask is that they be treated fairly in the process.[1]

AUTHOR COMMENT

Pharmaceutical pricing is not easy – a balance is needed between 'acceptable profits' and ethical responsibility.

As we learned in the previous chapter, pricing decisions are subject to a complex array of company, environmental and competitive forces. To make things even more complex, a company does not set a single price but rather a *pricing structure* that covers different items in its line. This pricing structure changes over time as products move through their life cycles. The company adjusts its prices to reflect changes in costs and demand and account for variations in buyers and situations. As the competitive environment changes, the company considers when to initiate price changes and when to respond to them.

This chapter examines additional pricing approaches used in special pricing situations and adjusting prices to meet changing situations. We will look at *new product pricing* for products in the introductory stage of the PLC, *product mix pricing* for related products in the product mix, *price adjustment tactics* that account for customer differences and changing situations and strategies for initiating and responding to *price changes.*[2]

AUTHOR COMMENT

Pricing new products can be especially challenging. Just think about all the things you need to consider in pricing a new mobile phone, say the first Apple iPhone. Even more, you need to start thinking about the price – along with many other marketing considerations – at the very beginning of the design process.

NEW PRODUCT PRICING

Pricing strategies usually change as a product passes through its life cycle. The introductory stage is especially challenging. Companies bringing out a new product face the challenge of setting prices for the first time. They can choose between two broad strategies: *market-skimming pricing* and *market-penetration pricing*.

Market-skimming pricing

Many companies that invent new products set high initial prices to 'skim' revenues layer by layer from the market. Apple frequently uses this strategy, called **market-skimming pricing (or price skimming)**. When Apple first introduced the iPhone, its initial price was as much as €417 per phone. The phones were purchased only by customers who really wanted the sleek new gadget and could afford to pay a high price for it. Six months later, Apple dropped the price to €278 for an 8 GB model and €348 for the 16 GB model to attract new buyers. Within a year, it dropped prices again to €138 and €208, respectively, and you can now buy an 8 GB model for €69. In this way, Apple skimmed the maximum amount of revenue from the various segments of the market.

Market skimming makes sense only under certain conditions. First, the product's quality and image must support its higher price, and enough buyers must want the product at that price. Second, the costs of producing a smaller volume cannot be so high that they cancel out the advantage of charging more. Finally, competitors should not be able to enter the market easily and undercut the high price.

> **Market-skimming pricing (price skimming)**—Setting a high price for a new product to skim maximum revenues layer by layer from the segments willing to pay the high price; the company makes fewer but more profitable sales.

Market-penetration pricing

Rather than setting a high initial price to skim off small but profitable market segments, some companies use **market-penetration pricing**. Companies set a low initial price to *penetrate* the market quickly and deeply – to attract a large number of buyers quickly and win a large market share.

> **Market-penetration pricing**—Setting a low price for a new product to attract a large number of buyers and a large market share.

> Penetration pricing: to lure famously frugal Chinese customers, Ikea slashed its prices. The strategy worked. Weekend crowds at its cavernous Beijing store are so big that employees need to use megaphones to keep them under control.
>
> *Source*: Alamy Images/Lou Linwei

The high sales volume results in falling costs, allowing companies to cut their prices even further. For example, the giant Swedish retailer Ikea used penetration pricing to boost its success in the Chinese market:[3]

> When Ikea first opened stores in China in 2002, people crowded in but not to buy home furnishings. Instead, they came to take advantage of the freebies – air conditioning, clean toilets and even decorating ideas. Chinese consumers are famously frugal. When it came time to actually buy, they shopped instead at local stores just down the street that offered knockoffs of Ikea's designs at a fraction of the price. So to lure the finicky Chinese customers, Ikea slashed its prices in China to the lowest in the world, the opposite approach of many western retailers there. By increasingly stocking its Chinese stores with China-made products, the retailer pushed prices on some items as low as 70 per cent below prices in Ikea's outlets outside China. The penetration pricing strategy worked. Ikea now captures a 43 per cent market share of China's fast-growing home wares market alone, and the sales of its seven mammoth Chinese stores surged 25 per cent last year. The cavernous Beijing store draws nearly six million visitors annually. Weekend crowds are so big that employees need to use megaphones to keep them under control.

Several conditions must be met for this low-price strategy to work. First, the market must be highly price sensitive so that a low price produces more market growth. Second, production and distribution costs must decrease as sales volume increases. Finally, the low price must help keep out the competition, and the penetration pricer must maintain its low-price position, otherwise the price advantage may be only temporary.

AUTHOR COMMENT

Most individual products are part of a broader product mix and must be priced accordingly. For example, Gillette prices its Fusion razors low. But once you buy the razor, you're a captive customer for its higher-margin replacement cartridges.

PRODUCT MIX PRICING

The strategy for setting a product's price often has to be changed when the product is part of a product mix. In this case, the firm looks for a set of prices that maximises its profits on the total product mix. Pricing is difficult because the various products have related demand and costs and face different degrees of competition. We now take a closer look at the five product mix pricing situations summarised in Table 11.1: *product line pricing, optional product pricing, captive product pricing, by-product pricing* and *product bundle pricing*.

Table 11.1 Product mix pricing

Pricing situation	Description
Product line pricing	Setting prices across an entire product line
Optional product pricing	Pricing optional or accessory products sold with the main product
Captive product pricing	Pricing products that must be used with the main product
By-product pricing	Pricing low-value by-products to get rid of them
Product bundle pricing	Pricing bundles of products sold together

Product line pricing

Companies usually develop product lines rather than single products. For example, Rossignol offers seven different collections of alpine skis of all designs and sizes, at prices that range from €100 for its junior skis, such as Fun Girl, to more than €800 for a pair from its Radical racing collection. It also offers lines of Nordic and cross-country skis, snowboards and ski-related apparel. In **product line pricing**, management must determine the price steps to set between the various products in a line.

The price steps should take into account cost differences between products in the line. More importantly, they should account for differences in customer perceptions of the value of different features. For example, Sage offers an entire line of financial management software, including Sage One Accounts, Instant Accounts, Instant Accounts Plus, 50 Accounts and 50 Accounts Plus versions, priced at around €14, €170, €275, €775 and €1,116, respectively. Although it costs Sage no more to produce the CD containing the 50 Accounts Plus version than the CD containing the Sage One version, many buyers happily pay more to obtain additional features. Sage's task is to establish the perceived value differences that support the price differences.

> **Product line pricing**—Setting the price steps between various products in a product line based on cost differences between the products, customer evaluations of different features and competitors' prices.

Optional product pricing

Many companies use **optional product pricing** – offering to sell optional or accessory products along with the main product. For example, a car buyer may choose to order a global positioning system (GPS) and Bluetooth wireless communication. Refrigerators come with optional ice makers. And when you order a new PC, you can select from a bewildering array of processors, hard drives, docking systems, software options and service plans. Pricing these options is a sticky problem. Companies must decide which items to include in the base price and which to offer as options.

> **Optional product pricing**—The pricing of optional or accessory products along with a main product.

Captive product pricing

Companies that make products that must be used along with a main product are using **captive product pricing**. Examples of captive products are razor blade cartridges, computer games and printer cartridges. Producers of the main products (razors, computer games consoles and printers) often price them low and set high mark-ups on the supplies. For example, when Sony first introduced its PlayStation3 (PS3) computer games console, priced at €347 and €417 for the regular and premium versions, respectively, it lost as much as €213 per unit sold. Sony hoped to recoup the losses through the sales of more lucrative PS3 games.

However, companies that use captive product pricing must be careful. Finding the right balance between the main product and captive product prices can be tricky. For example, despite industry-leading PS3 computer game sales, Sony has yet to earn back its losses on the PS3 console. Even more, consumers trapped into buying expensive captive products may come to resent the brand that ensnared them.

In the case of services, captive product pricing is called *two-part pricing*. The price of the service is broken into a *fixed fee* plus a *variable usage rate*. Thus, at Aqualand in the South of France and other amusement parks, you pay a daily ticket or season pass charge plus additional fees for food and other in-park features.

> **Captive product pricing**—Setting a price for products that must be used along with a main product, such as blades for a razor and games for a computer games console.

By-product pricing

Producing products and services often generates by-products. If the by-products have no value and if getting rid of them is costly, this will affect pricing of the main product. Using **by-product pricing**, the company seeks a market for these by-products to help offset the costs of disposing of them and help make the price of the main product more competitive.

The by-products themselves can even turn out to be profitable – turning trash into cash. For example, whisky can fuel you in more than one way:[4]

> **By-product pricing**—Setting a price for by-products to make the main product's price more competitive.

Viobutanol is a biofuel made from whisky by-products. It can be used in ordinary cars, and is predicted to be the next generation of biofuel, which they estimate gives 30 per cent more output power than ethanol. They were provided with samples of whisky distilling by-products from Diageo's Glenkinchie distillery in East Lothian, which makes The Edinburgh Malt. It uses the two main by-products of whisky production – pot ale, the liquid from the copper stills, and draff, the spent grains, as the basis for producing the butanol that can then be used as fuel. The local scientists at a biofuel research centre have filed for a patent and intend to create a spin-off company to take the new fuel to market. With 1.6 million litres of pot ale and 187,000 tonnes of draff produced by the malt whisky industry annually, the scientists believe there is real potential for biofuel to be available at local garage forecourts alongside traditional fuels. Unlike ethanol, the nature of the innovative biofuel means that ordinary cars could use the more powerful fuel, instead of traditional petrol, without modification. The product can also be used to make other green renewable biochemicals, such as acetone.

By-product pricing: you can make biofuel from whisky by-products.

Source: Glenkinchie Distillery

Product bundle pricing— Combining several products and offering the bundle at a reduced price.

Product bundle pricing

Using **product bundle pricing**, sellers often combine several products and offer the bundle at a reduced price. For example, fast-food restaurants bundle a burger, fries and a soft drink at a 'combo' price. Body Shop with 2,400 stores in 61 countries is offering 'three-fer' deals on its soaps and lotions (such as buy three lotions and save €5 or buy three save €10). And Sky, France Telecom, Virgin, Deutsche Telecom, British Telecom and other telecommunications companies bundle TV, telephone and high-speed Internet connections at a low combined price. Price bundling can promote the sales of products consumers might not otherwise buy, but the combined price must be low enough to get them to buy the bundle.

AUTHOR COMMENT

Setting the base price for a product is only the start. The company must then adjust the price to account for customer and situational differences. When was the last time you paid the full suggested retail price for something?

PRICE ADJUSTMENTS

Companies usually adjust their basic prices to account for various customer differences and changing situations. Here we examine the seven price adjustment strategies summarised in Table 11.2: *discount and allowance pricing, segmented pricing, psychological pricing, promotional pricing, geographical pricing, dynamic pricing* and *international pricing*.

Discount and allowance pricing

Most companies adjust their basic price to reward customers for certain responses, such as the early payment of bills, volume purchases and off-season buying. These price adjustments – called *discounts* and *allowances* – can take many forms.

Discount—A straight reduction in price on purchases during a stated period of time or of larger quantities.

The many forms of **discounts** include a *cash discount*, a price reduction to buyers who pay their bills promptly. A typical example is '2/10, net 30', which means that although payment is due within 30 days, the buyer can deduct 2 per cent if the bill is paid within 10 days. A *quantity discount* is a price reduction to buyers who buy large volumes. A seller offers a *functional discount* (also called a *trade discount*) to trade-channel members who perform certain functions, such as selling, storing and record keeping. A *seasonal discount* is a price reduction to buyers who buy merchandise or services out of season.

Table 11.2 Price adjustments

Strategy	Description
Discount and allowance pricing	Reducing prices to reward customer responses such as paying early or promoting the product
Segmented pricing	Adjusting prices to allow for differences in customers, products or locations
Psychological pricing	Adjusting prices for psychological effect
Promotional pricing	Temporarily reducing prices to increase short-run sales
Geographical pricing	Adjusting prices to account for the geographic location of customers
Dynamic pricing	Adjusting prices continually to meet the characteristics and needs of individual customers and situations
International pricing	Adjusting prices for international markets

Allowances are another type of reduction from the list price. For example, *trade-in allowances* are price reductions given for turning in an old item when buying a new one. Trade-in allowances are most common in the car industry but are also given for other durable goods. *Promotional allowances* are payments or price reductions to reward dealers for participating in advertising and sales support programmes.

Segmented pricing

Companies will often adjust their basic prices to allow for differences in customers, products and locations. In **segmented pricing,** the company sells a product or service at two or more prices, even though the difference in prices is not based on differences in costs.

Segmented pricing takes several forms. Under *customer-segment* pricing, different customers pay different prices for the same product or service. Museums and movie theatres, for example, may charge a lower admission for students and senior citizens. Under *product-form pricing*, different versions of the product are priced differently but not according to differences in their costs. For instance, a one-litre bottle of Evian mineral water may cost €1 at your local supermarket. But a 150ml aerosol can of Evian Brumisateur Mineral Water Spray sells for a suggested retail price of €8 at beauty boutiques and spas. The water is all from the same source in the French Alps, and the aerosol packaging costs little more than the plastic bottles. Yet you pay about €1 a litre for one form and €53.3 a litre for the other.

Using *location-based pricing*, a company charges different prices for different locations, even though the cost of offering each location is the same. For instance, in the US, state universities charge higher tuition fees for out-of-state students, and theatres vary their seat prices because of audience preferences for certain locations. Tickets for a Monday night performance of Les Misérables in London's West End cost €23 for a seat in the upper circle, whereas seats in the stalls go for €94. Finally, using *time-based pricing*, a firm varies its price by the season, the month, the day and even the hour. Movie theatres charge matinee pricing during the daytime. Resorts give weekend and seasonal discounts.

For segmented pricing to be an effective strategy, certain conditions must exist. The market must be segmentable, and segments must show

Allowance—Promotional money paid by manufacturers to retailers in return for an agreement to feature the manufacturer's products in some way.

Segmented pricing—Selling a product or service at two or more prices, where the difference in prices is not based on differences in costs.

Product-form pricing: Evian water in a one-litre bottle might cost you €0.03 an ounce at your local supermarket, whereas the same water might run to €1.60 an ounce when sold in five-ounce aerosol cans as Evian Brumisateur Mineral Water Spray moisturiser.

Source: Jim Whitmer

different degrees of demand. The costs of segmenting and reaching the market cannot exceed the extra revenue obtained from the price difference. Of course, the segmented pricing must also be legal.

Most importantly, segmented prices should reflect real differences in customers' perceived value. Consumers in higher price tiers must feel that they're getting their extra money's worth for the higher prices paid. By the same token, companies must be careful not to treat customers in lower price tiers as second-class citizens. Otherwise, in the long run, the practice will lead to customer resentment and ill will. For example, in recent years, the airlines have incurred the wrath of frustrated customers at both ends of the aeroplane. Passengers paying full fare for business or first class seats often feel that they are being gouged. At the same time, passengers in lower-priced coach seats feel that they're being ignored or treated poorly.

Psychological pricing

Price says something about the product. For example, many consumers use price to judge quality. A €100 bottle of perfume may contain only €3 worth of scent, but some people are willing to pay the €100 because this price indicates something special.

Psychological pricing—
Pricing that considers the psychology of prices, not simply the economics; the price says something about the product.

In using **psychological pricing**, sellers consider the psychology of prices, not simply the economics. For example, consumers usually perceive higher-priced products as having higher quality. When they can judge the quality of a product by examining it or by calling on past experience with it, they use price less to judge quality. But when they cannot judge quality because they lack the information or skill, price becomes an important quality signal. For example, who's the better lawyer – one who charges €50 per hour or one who charges €500 per hour? You'd have to do a lot of digging into the respective lawyers' credentials to answer this question objectively; even then, you might not be able to judge accurately. Most of us would simply assume that the higher-priced lawyer is better.

Reference prices—Prices that buyers carry in their minds and refer to when they look at a given product.

Another aspect of psychological pricing is **reference prices** – prices that buyers carry in their minds and refer to when looking at a given product. The reference price might be formed by noting current prices, remembering past prices, or assessing the buying situation. Sellers can influence or use these consumers' reference prices when setting price. For example, a grocery retailer might place its store brand of bran flakes and raisins cereal priced at €1.32 next to Kellogg's Raisin Bran priced at €2.24. Or a company might offer more expensive models that don't sell very well to make their less expensive but still-high-priced models look more affordable by comparison.[5]

> In the midst of the economic downturn, Ralph Lauren was selling a 'Ricky' alligator bag for €10,000, making its Tiffin Bag a steal at just €1,800. And Williams-Sonoma once offered a fancy bread maker for €190. Then it added a €340 model. The costly model flopped, but sales of the cheaper one doubled.

For most purchases, consumers don't have all the skill or information they need to work out whether they are paying a good price. They don't have the time, ability or inclination to research different brands or stores, compare prices, and get the best deals. Instead, they may rely on certain cues that signal whether a price is high or low. Interestingly, such pricing cues are often provided by sellers, in the form of sales signs, price-matching guarantees, loss-leader pricing and other helpful hints.[6]

Even small differences in price can signal product differences. For example, in a recent American study, people were asked how likely they were to choose among LASIK eye surgery providers based only on the prices they charged: $299 or $300 (around €211). The actual price difference was only $1 (€0.81), but the study found that the psychological difference was much greater. Preference ratings for the providers charging $300 were much higher. Subjects perceived the $299 price as significantly less, but it also raised stronger concerns about quality and risk.[7] Some psychologists even argue that each digit has symbolic and visual qualities that should be considered in pricing. Thus, eight is round and even and creates a soothing effect, whereas seven is angular and creates a jarring effect.

Promotional pricing

With **promotional pricing**, companies will temporarily price their products below list price and sometimes even below cost to create buying excitement and urgency. Promotional pricing takes several forms. A seller may simply offer *discounts* from normal prices to increase sales and reduce inventories. Sellers also use *special-event pricing* in certain seasons to draw more customers. Thus, large-screen TVs and other consumer electronics are promotionally priced in November and December to attract holiday shoppers into the stores.

Manufacturers sometimes offer *cash rebates* to consumers who buy the product from dealers within a specified time; the manufacturer sends the rebate directly to the customer. Rebates have been popular with car manufacturers and producers of mobile phones and small appliances, but they are also used with consumer packaged goods. Some manufacturers offer *low-interest financing*, *longer warranties* or *free maintenance* to reduce the consumer's 'price'. This practice has become another favourite of the car industry.

Promotional pricing, however, can have adverse effects. Used too frequently and copied by competitors, price promotions can create 'deal-prone' customers who wait until brands go on sale before buying them. Or, constantly reduced prices can erode a brand's value in the eyes of customers. Marketers sometimes become addicted to promotional pricing, especially in difficult economic times. They use price promotions as a quick fix instead of sweating through the difficult process of developing effective longer-term strategies for building their brands. But companies must be careful to balance short-term sales incentives against long-term brand building. One analyst advises.[8]

> When times are tough, there's a tendency to panic. One of the first and most prevalent tactics that many companies try is an aggressive price cut. Price trumps all. At least, that's how it feels these days: 20 per cent off; 30 per cent off; 50 per cent off; buy one, get one free. Whatever it is you're selling, you're offering it at a discount just to get customers in the door. But aggressive pricing strategies can be risky business. Companies should be very wary of risking their brands' perceived quality by resorting to deep and frequent price cuts. Some discounting is unavoidable in a tough economy, and consumers have come to expect it. But marketers have to find ways to shore up their brand identity and brand equity during times of discount mayhem.

The point is that promotional pricing can be an effective means of generating sales for some companies in certain circumstances. But it can be damaging for other companies or if taken as a steady diet.

Geographical pricing

A company also must decide how to price its products for customers located in different parts of Europe or the world. Should the company risk losing the business of more-distant customers by charging them higher prices to cover the higher shipping costs? Or should the company charge all customers the same prices regardless of location? We will look at five **geographical pricing** strategies for the following hypothetical situation:

> The Peerless Paper Company is located in Madrid, Spain, and sells paper products to customers all over Europe. The cost of freight is high and affects the companies from whom customers buy their paper. Peerless wants to establish a geographical pricing policy. It is trying to determine how to price a €10,000 order to three specific customers: Customer A (Lisbon, Portugal), Customer B (Florence, Italy) and Customer C (Riga, Latvia).

Promotional pricing— Temporarily pricing products below the list price, and sometimes even below cost, to increase short-run sales.

Geographical pricing—Setting prices for customers located in different parts of the country or world.

FOB-origin pricing—A geographical pricing strategy in which goods are placed free on board a carrier; the customer pays the freight from the factory to the destination.

One option is for Peerless to ask each customer to pay the shipping cost from the Madrid factory to the customer's location. All three customers would pay the same factory price of €10,000, with Customer A paying, say, €100 for shipping; Customer B, €150; and Customer C, €250. Called **FOB-origin pricing**, this practice means that the goods are placed *free on board* (hence, *FOB*) a carrier. At that point the title and responsibility pass to the customer, who pays the freight from the factory to the destination. Because each customer picks up its own cost, supporters of FOB pricing feel that this is the fairest way to assess freight charges. The disadvantage, however, is that Peerless will be a high-cost firm to distant customers.

Uniform-delivered pricing—A geographical pricing strategy in which the company charges the same price plus freight to all customers, regardless of their location.

Uniform-delivered pricing is the opposite of FOB pricing. Here, the company charges the same price plus freight to all customers, regardless of their location. The freight charge is set at the average freight cost. Suppose this is €150. Uniform-delivered pricing therefore results in a higher charge to the Lisbon customer (who pays €150 freight instead of €100) and a lower charge to the Riga customer (who pays €150 instead of €250). Although the Lisbon customer would prefer to buy paper from another local paper company that uses FOB-origin pricing, Peerless has a better chance of winning over the Latvian customer in Riga.

Zone pricing—A geographical pricing strategy in which the company sets up two or more zones. All customers within a zone pay the same total price; the more distant the zone, the higher the price.

Zone pricing falls between FOB-origin pricing and uniform-delivered pricing. The company sets up two or more zones. All customers within a given zone pay a single total price – the more distant the zone, the higher the price. For example, Peerless might set up a West-Europe Zone and charge €100 freight to all customers in this zone, a Mid-Europe Zone in which it charges €150 and an East-Europe Zone in which it charges €250. In this way, the customers within a given price zone receive no price advantage from the company. For example, customers in Lisbon and Madrid pay the same total price to Peerless. The complaint, however, is that the Lisbon customer is paying part of the Madrid customer's freight cost.

Base-point pricing—A geographical pricing strategy in which the seller designates some city as a base point and charges all customers the freight cost from that city to the customer.

Using **base-point pricing**, the seller selects a given city as a 'base point' and charges all customers the freight cost from that city to the customer's location, regardless of the city from which the goods are actually shipped. For example, Peerless might set Paris as the base point and charge all customers €10,000 plus the freight from Paris to their respective locations. This means that a Madrid customer pays the freight cost from Paris to Madrid, even though the goods may be shipped from Madrid. If all sellers used the same base-point city, delivered prices would be the same for all customers, and price competition would be eliminated.

Freight-absorption pricing—A geographical pricing strategy in which the seller absorbs all or part of the freight charges to get the desired business.

Finally, the seller who is anxious to do business with a certain customer or geographical area might use **freight-absorption pricing**. Using this strategy, the seller absorbs all or part of the actual freight charges to get the desired business. The seller might reason that if it can get more business, its average costs will decrease and more than compensate for its extra freight cost. Freight-absorption pricing is used for market penetration and to hold on to increasingly competitive markets.

Dynamic pricing

Throughout most of history, prices were set by negotiation between buyers and sellers. *Fixed price policies* – setting one price for all buyers – is a relatively modern idea that arose with the development of large-scale retailing at the end of the nineteenth century. Today, most prices are set this way. However, some companies are now reversing the fixed pricing trend. They are using **dynamic pricing** – adjusting prices continually to meet the characteristics and needs of individual customers and situations.

Dynamic pricing—Adjusting prices continually to meet the characteristics and needs of individual customers and situations.

For example, think about how the Internet has affected pricing. From the mostly fixed pricing practices of the past century, the Internet seems to be taking us back into a new age of fluid pricing. The flexibility of the Internet allows Web sellers to instantly and constantly adjust prices on a wide range of goods based on demand dynamics (sometimes called *real-time pricing*). In other cases, customers control pricing by bidding on auction sites such as eBay or negotiating on sites such as Priceline.

CarTrawler, uses innovative technology to link airlines, hotel chains and other travel industry customers with 500 multinational and independent car rental companies. Annual turnover is around €100 million. CarTrawler is based in Dublin but has 85 employees and offices in the US and Alicante in Spain, the main European market for car hire. The CarTrawler platform is installed in a number of international airlines, such as Malaysia Airlines and Virgin Blue, and the booking service is available to about 200 million airline passengers worldwide. The platform, which can be installed directly into a hotel or airline's own booking software, acts like a car rental exchange, pricing the product in real time to match the market and maximise the returns. An airline might no longer have an exclusive deal with one rental car supplier but can use the CarTrawler system to get the best deal from all available operators.

Dynamic pricing offers many advantages for marketers. For example, Internet sellers such as Amazon can mine their databases to gauge a specific shopper's desires, measure his or her means, instantaneously tailor products to fit that shopper's behaviour, and price products accordingly. Catalogue retailers such as Argos or Gratton in the UK can change prices on the fly according to changes in demand or costs, changing prices for specific items on a day-by-day or even hour-by-hour basis. And many direct marketers monitor inventories, costs and demand at any given moment and adjust prices instantly. Consumers also benefit from the Internet and dynamic pricing. A wealth of price comparison sites – such as Pricerunner and Kelkoo – offer instant product and price comparisons from thousands of vendors.

In addition, consumers can negotiate prices at online auction sites and exchanges. Suddenly the centuries-old art of haggling is back in vogue. Want to sell that antique pickle jar that's been collecting dust for generations? Post it on eBay, the world's biggest online flea market. Want to name your own price for a hotel room or rental car? Visit Priceline or another reverse auction site. Want to bid on a ticket to a Coldplay show? Check out Ticketmaster, which now offers an online auction service for concert tickets.

Dynamic pricing makes sense in many contexts; it adjusts prices according to market forces, and it often works to the benefit of the customer. But marketers need to be careful not to use dynamic pricing to take advantage of certain customer groups, damaging important customer relationships.

Dynamic pricing: CarTrawler uses innovative technology to link airlines, hotel chains and other travel industry customers with 500 multinational and independent car rental companies.

Source: CarTrawler.com

International pricing

Companies that market their products internationally must decide what prices to charge in the different countries in which they operate. In some cases, a company can set a uniform worldwide price. For example, Airbus sells its jetliners at about the same price everywhere, whether in the United States, Europe or a third-world country. However, most companies adjust their prices to reflect local market conditions and cost considerations.

The price that a company should charge in a specific country depends on many factors, including economic conditions, competitive situations, laws and regulations, and the development of the wholesaling and retailing system. Consumer perceptions and preferences also may vary from country to country, calling for different prices. Or the company may have different marketing objectives in various world markets, which require changes in pricing strategy. For example, Samsung might introduce a new product into mature markets in highly developed countries with the goal of quickly gaining mass-market share; this would call for a penetration-pricing strategy. In contrast, it might enter a less-developed market by targeting smaller, less price-sensitive segments; in this case, market-skimming pricing makes sense.

Costs play an important role in setting international prices. Travellers abroad are often surprised to find that goods that are relatively inexpensive at home may carry outrageously higher price tags in other countries. A pair of Levi's selling for €30 in the United States might go for €63 in Tokyo and €88 in Paris. A McDonald's Big Mac selling for a modest €3.57 in the United States might cost €5.29 in Norway, and an Oral-B toothbrush selling for €2.49 in Europe may cost €10 in China. Conversely, a Gucci handbag going for only €140 in Milan, Italy, might fetch €240 in the United States. In some cases, such *price escalation* may result from differences in selling strategies or market conditions. In most instances, however, it is simply a result of the higher costs of selling in another country – the additional costs of operations, product modifications, shipping and insurance, import tariffs and taxes, exchange-rate fluctuations and physical distribution.

Price has become a key element in the international marketing strategies of companies attempting to enter emerging markets, such as China, India and Brazil. Consider Unilever's pricing strategy for developing countries:

> There used to be one way to sell a product in developing markets, if you bothered to sell there at all: slap on a local label and market at premium prices to the elite. Unilever – the maker of such brands as Dove, Lipton and Vaseline – changed that. Instead, it built a following among the world's poorest consumers by shrinking packages to set a price even consumers living on €3 a day could afford. The strategy was forged about 25 years ago when Unilever's Indian subsidiary found that its products were out of reach for millions of Indians. To lower the price while making a profit, Unilever developed single-use packets for everything from shampoo to laundry detergent, costing just pennies a pack. The small, affordable packages put the company's premier brands within reach of the world's poor. Today, Unilever continues to woo cash-strapped customers with great success. For example, its approachable pricing helps explain why Unilever now captures 70 per cent of the Brazil detergent market.[9]

Thus, international pricing presents some special problems and complexities. We will discuss international pricing issues in more detail in Chapter 19.

AUTHOR COMMENT

When and how should a company change its price? What if costs rise, putting the squeeze on profits? What if the economy sags and customers become more price-sensitive? Or what if a major competitor raises or drops its prices? As Figure 11.1 suggests, companies face many price-changing options.

PRICE CHANGES

After developing their pricing structures and strategies, companies often face situations in which they must initiate price changes or respond to price changes by competitors.

Figure 11.1 Assessing and responding to competitor price changes

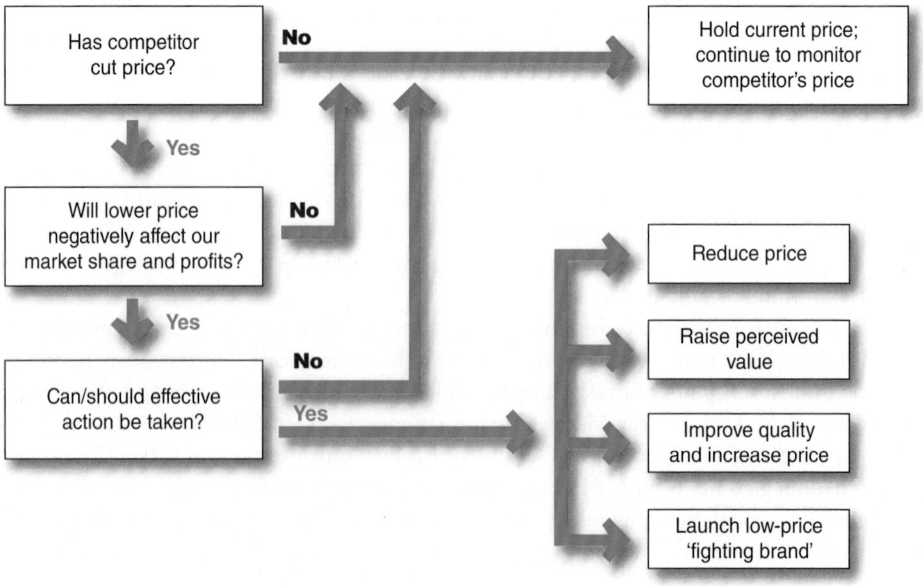

When a competitor cuts prices, a company's first reaction may be to drop its prices as well. But that is often the wrong response. Instead, the firm may want to emphasise the 'value' side of the price—value equation.

Has competitor cut price? — No → Hold current price; continue to monitor competitor's price

Yes ↓

Will lower price negatively affect our market share and profits? — No

Yes ↓

Can/should effective action be taken? — No / Yes → Reduce price / Raise perceived value / Improve quality and increase price / Launch low-price 'fighting brand'

Initiating price changes

In some cases, the company may find it desirable to initiate either a price cut or a price increase. In both cases, it must anticipate possible buyer and competitor reactions.

Initiating price cuts

Several situations may lead a firm to consider cutting its price. One such circumstance is excess capacity. Another is falling demand in the face of strong price competition or a weakened economy. In such cases, the firm may aggressively cut prices to boost sales and market share. But as the airline, fast-food, car and other industries have learned in recent years, cutting prices in an industry loaded with excess capacity may lead to price wars as competitors try to hold on to market share.

A company may also cut prices in a drive to dominate the market through lower costs. Either the company starts with lower costs than its competitors, or it cuts prices in the hope of gaining market share that will further cut costs through larger volume. Lenovo uses an aggressive low-cost, low-price strategy to increase its market share of the PC market in developing countries.

Initiating price increases

A successful price increase can greatly improve profits. For example, if the company's profit margin is 3 per cent of sales, a 1 per cent price increase will boost profits by 33 per cent if the sales volume is unaffected. A major factor in price increases is cost inflation. Rising costs squeeze profit margins and lead companies to pass cost increases on to customers. Another factor leading to price increases is over demand: when a company cannot supply all that its customers need, it may raise its prices, ration products to customers, or both. Consider today's worldwide oil and gas industry.

When raising prices, the company must avoid being perceived as a *price gouger*. For example, when petrol prices rise rapidly, angry customers often accuse the major oil companies of enriching themselves at the expense of consumers. Customers have long memories, and they will eventually turn away from companies or even whole industries that they perceive as charging excessive prices. In the extreme, claims of price gouging may even bring about increased government regulation.

Initiating price increases: when petrol or diesel prices rise rapidly, angry consumers often accuse the major oil companies of enriching themselves by gouging customers.

Source: Press Association Images/ Paul Sakuma

There are some techniques for avoiding these problems. One is to maintain a sense of fairness surrounding any price increase. Price increases should be supported by company communications telling customers why prices are being raised.

Wherever possible, the company should consider ways to meet higher costs or demand without raising prices. For example, it can consider more cost-effective ways to produce or distribute its products. It can shrink the product or substitute less-expensive ingredients instead of raising the price. For example, Imperial Leather soap recently reduced the size of its bars from 125 g to 100 g while Cadbury's Dairy Milk bars shrank from 140 g to 120 g (that's two whole chunks!) while the price remained unchanged.[10] Or it can 'unbundle' its market offering, removing features, packaging or services, and separately pricing elements that were formerly part of the offer.

Buyer reactions to price changes

Customers do not always interpret price changes in a straightforward way. A price *increase*, which would normally lower sales, may have some positive meanings for buyers. For example, what would you think if Rolex *raised* the price of its latest watch model? On the one hand, you might think that the watch is even more exclusive or better made. On the other hand, you might think that Rolex is simply being greedy by charging what the market will bear.

Similarly, consumers may view a price *cut* in several ways. For example, what would you think if Rolex were to suddenly cut its prices? You might think that you are getting a better deal on an exclusive product. More likely, however, you'd think that quality had been reduced, and the brand's luxury image might be tarnished.

A brand's price and image are often closely linked. A price change, especially a drop in price, can adversely affect how consumers view the brand. Tiffany found this out when it attempted to broaden its appeal by offering a line of more affordable jewellery:[11]

Tiffany is all about luxury and the cachet of its blue boxes. However, in the late 1990s, the high-end jeweller responded to the 'affordable luxuries' craze with a new 'Return to Tiffany' line of less-expensive silver jewelry. The 'Return to Tiffany' silver charm bracelet quickly became a must-have item, as teens jammed Tiffany's hushed stores clamouring for the €78 silver bauble. Sales skyrocketed. But despite this early success, the bracelet fad appeared to alienate the firm's older, wealthier and more conservative clientele, damaging Tiffany's reputation for luxury. So, in 2002, the firm began reemphasizing its pricier jewelry collections. Although high-end jewelry has once again replaced silver as Tiffany's fastest-growing business, the company has yet to fully regain its exclusivity. Says one well-heeled customer: 'You used to aspire to be able to buy something at Tiffany, but now it's not that special anymore.'

Competitor reactions to price changes

A firm considering a price change must worry about the reactions of its competitors as well as those of its customers. Competitors are most likely to react when the number of firms involved is small, when the product is uniform, and when the buyers are well informed about products and prices.

How can the firm anticipate the likely reactions of its competitors? The problem is complex because, like the customer, the competitor can interpret a company price cut in many ways. It might think the company is trying to grab a larger market share or that it's doing poorly and trying to boost its sales. Or it might think that the company wants the whole industry to cut prices to increase total demand.

The company must guess each competitor's likely reaction. If all competitors behave alike, this amounts to analysing only a typical competitor. In contrast, if the competitors do not behave alike – perhaps because of differences in size, market shares or policies – then separate analyses are necessary. However, if some competitors will match the price change, there is good reason to expect that the rest will also match it.

Responding to price changes

Here we reverse the question and ask how a firm should respond to a price change by a competitor. The firm needs to consider several issues: Why did the competitor change the price? Is the price change temporary or permanent? What will happen to the company's market share and profits if it does not respond? Are other competitors going to respond? Besides these issues, the company must also consider its own situation and strategy and possible customer reactions to price changes.

Figure 11.1 shows the ways a company might assess and respond to a competitor's price cut. Suppose the company learns that a competitor has cut its price and decides that this price cut is likely to harm its sales and profits. It might simply decide to hold its current price and profit margin. The company might believe that it will not lose too much market share, or that it would lose too much profit if it reduced its own price. Or it might decide that it should wait and respond when it has more information on the effects of the competitor's price change. However, waiting too long to act might let the competitor get stronger and more confident as its sales increase.

If the company decides that effective action can and should be taken, it might make any of four responses. First, it could *reduce its price* to match the competitor's price. It may decide that the market is price sensitive and that it would lose too much market share to the lower-priced competitor. Cutting the price will reduce the company's profits in the short run. Some companies might also reduce their product quality, services and marketing communications to retain profit margins, but this will ultimately hurt their long-term market share. The company should try to maintain its quality as it cuts prices.

Alternatively, the company might maintain its price but *raise the perceived value* of its offer. It could improve its communications, stressing the relative value of its product over that of the lower-price competitor. The firm may find it cheaper to maintain price and spend money to improve its perceived value than to cut price and operate at a lower margin. Or, the company might *improve quality and increase price*, moving its brand into a higher price-value position. The higher quality creates greater customer value, which justifies the higher price. In turn, the higher price preserves the company's higher margins.

Finally, the company might *launch a low-price 'fighter brand'* – adding a lower-price item to the line or creating a separate lower-price brand. This is necessary if the particular market segment being lost is price sensitive and will not respond to arguments of higher quality. For example, France Telecom, Vivendi's SFR and Bouygues Telecom have all reacted to the entry of a new rival Iliad into France's €40 billion-a-year telecoms market. Of that €40 billion market, €7 billion comes from broadband, €2 billion from fixed lines, €6 billion from business-to-business services and €25 billion from mobile services. In order to protect its share of the mobile market and to protect its Orange brand, France Telecom launched 'Sosh' a new low-cost brand to compete with Iliad's 'Free'.[12] Another example is Bosch's fighter brand 'Viva'. While Bosch white goods competed well at the higher end of the market, their white goods were at a major disadvantage when competing in the low-price category. Consequently, Bosch launched the Viva brand to compete with white good price-discounters in the low-price market while protecting its brand reputation, image and premium position for Bosch branded white goods in the premium market.

Fighter brands: in order to protect its share of the mobile market and to protect its Orange brand, France Telecom launched 'Sosh' a new low-cost brand to compete with Iliad's 'Free'.

Source: Getty Images

AUTHOR COMMENT

Pricing decisions are often constrained by social and legal issues. For example, think about the pharmaceutical industry. Are rapidly rising prescription prices justified? Or are the drug companies unfairly lining their pockets by gouging consumers who have few alternatives? Should the government step in?

PUBLIC POLICY AND PRICING

Price competition is a core element of our free-market economy. In setting prices, companies usually are not free to charge whatever prices they wish. In the US, for example, many federal, state and even local laws govern the rules of fair play in pricing. In addition, companies must consider broader societal pricing concerns. In setting their prices, for example, pharmaceutical firms must balance their development costs and profit objectives against the sometimes life-and-death needs of drug consumers.

Across Europe there are many different statutory provisions governing pricing and competition. For example, in the European Union, Article 82(c) of the European Commission Treaty deals with abuses of dominant positions. In addition, member states of the European Union seek to protect consumers and firms through national-level laws and organisations such as the UK's Office of Fair Trading.

Figure 11.2 shows the major public policy issues in pricing. These include potentially damaging pricing practices within a given level of the channel (price-fixing and predatory pricing) and across levels of the channel (retail price maintenance, discriminatory pricing and deceptive pricing).[13]

Pricing within channel levels

Federal legislation on *price-fixing* states that sellers must set prices without talking to competitors. Otherwise, price collusion is suspected. Price-fixing is illegal per se – that is, the government does not accept any excuses for price-fixing. Companies found guilty of such practices can receive heavy fines. Recently, governments at state and EU levels have been aggressively enforcing price-fixing regulations in industries ranging from petrol, insurance and concrete to credit cards, CDs and computer chips.

Sellers are also prohibited from using *predatory pricing* – selling below cost with the intention of punishing a competitor or gaining higher long-term profits by putting competitors out of business. This protects small sellers from larger ones who might sell items below cost temporarily or in a specific locale to drive them out of business. The biggest problem is determining just what constitutes predatory pricing behaviour. Selling below cost to unload excess inventory is not considered predatory; selling below cost to drive out competitors is. Thus, the same action may or may not be predatory depending on intent, and intent can be very difficult to determine or prove.

In recent years, Amazon has been repeatedly accused of practising predatory pricing. For example, the American Booksellers Association, which represents small independent US booksellers, wrote to the Department of Justice asking it to investigate what it called 'predatory pricing' by Amazon, Walmart and Target. All three offer new hardback best-sellers for about €8, compared

Figure 11.2 Public policy issues in pricing

Source: Adapted from Dhruv Grewal and Larry D. Compeau, 'Pricing and public policy: a research agenda and overview of the special issue,' *Journal of Public Policy and Marketing* (Spring 1999), pp. 3–10.

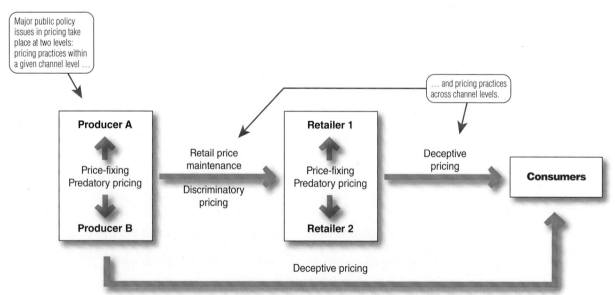

with list prices of above €20.[14] Earlier, Amazon challenged French law by refusing to eliminate its free shipping on books offer. The action, brought by the French Booksellers' Union (Syndicat de la Librairie Française) argued that Amazon offered illegal discounts. Amazon said it would pay the €1,000 per day fine rather than abide with a French High Court ruling.[15]

Pricing across channel levels

As in the US, the European Union also seeks to prevent unfair *price discrimination* by ensuring that sellers offer the same price terms to customers at a given level of trade. For example, every retailer is entitled to the same price terms from a given manufacturer, whether the retailer is Halfords or your local bicycle shop. However, price discrimination is allowed if the seller can prove that its costs are different when selling to different retailers – for example, that it costs less per unit to sell a large volume of bicycles to Halfords than to sell a few bicycles to the local dealer.

The seller can also discriminate in its pricing if the seller manufactures different qualities of the same product for different retailers. The seller has to prove that these differences are proportional. Price differentials may also be used to match competition in good faith, provided the price discrimination is temporary, localised and defensive rather than offensive.

Laws also prohibit *retail (or resale) price maintenance* – a manufacturer cannot require dealers to charge a specified retail price for its product. Although the seller can propose a manufacturer's *suggested* retail price to dealers, it cannot refuse to sell to a dealer that takes independent pricing action nor can it punish the dealer by shipping late or denying advertising allowances.

Deceptive pricing occurs when a seller states prices or price savings that mislead consumers or are not actually available to consumers. This might involve bogus reference or comparison prices, as when a retailer sets artificially high 'regular' prices and then announces 'sale' prices close to its previous everyday prices. For example, in the US, Overstock.com recently came under scrutiny for inaccurately listing manufacturers' suggested retail prices, often quoting them higher than the actual price. Such comparison pricing is widespread.

Other deceptive pricing issues include *scanner fraud* and price confusion. The widespread use of scanner-based computer checkouts has led to increasing complaints of retailers overcharging their customers. Most of these overcharges result from poor management – from a failure to enter current or sale prices into the system. Other cases, however, involve intentional overcharges.

Many federal and state statutes regulate against deceptive pricing practices. For example, the European Union has recently addressed the issue of extra credit card charges for online purchases:[16]

Hefty credit card charges when paying online for goods or services – such as airline tickets – could soon be a thing of the past after European Union lawmakers passed rules on consumer rights in Europe. Buried in the myriad of new rules is a provision which states: 'Member states shall prohibit traders from charging consumers, in respect of a given means of payment, fees that exceed the cost borne by the trader for the use of such means.' 'This law will put an end to growing unfair business practices – like, when buying flights, consumers will not be charged unjustified fees just to use their credit card,' said Monique Goyens, director-general of Beuc, the European consumers' organisation. Consumer advocates say a common source of complaint in this area relates to budget airlines, which are apt to charge travellers significant additional sums depending merely on what type of card they use for the purchase. For example, a €32.15 Aberdeen–London ticket with easyJet could cost €47.02 if purchased with a credit card, €41.33 with a debit card and incur no premium if purchased with Visa Electron. EasyJet says its fees 'stand comparison with any other airline – which is why people choose to fly with us'. The aim of the legislation is to provide consumers across the EU with harmonised minimum rights, and although that intention has been watered down to some extent during long and difficult negotiations, consumers will now have a 14-day, EU-wide 'cooling off' period when shopping online, during which they can change their minds about purchases.

However, reputable sellers go beyond what is required by law. Treating customers fairly and making certain that they fully understand prices and pricing terms is an important part of building strong and lasting customer relationships.

REVIEWING OBJECTIVES AND KEY TERMS

In this chapter, we examined some additional pricing considerations – new product pricing, product mix pricing, price adjustments, and initiating and reacting to prices changes. A company sets not a single price but rather a *pricing structure* that covers its entire mix of products. This pricing structure changes over time as products move through their life cycles. The company adjusts product prices to reflect changes in costs and demand and account for variations in buyers and situations. As the competitive environment changes, the company considers when to initiate price changes and when to respond to them.

OBJECTIVE 1 Describe the major strategies for pricing new products (pp. 329–330).

Pricing is a dynamic process, and pricing strategies usually change as the product passes through its life cycle. The introductory stage – setting prices for the first time – is especially challenging. The company can decide on one of several strategies for pricing innovative new products: it can use *market-skimming pricing* by initially setting high prices to 'skim' the maximum amount of revenue from various segments of the market. Or it can use *market-penetrating pricing* by setting a low initial price to penetrate the market deeply and win a large market share. Several conditions must be set for either new product pricing strategy to work.

OBJECTIVE 2 Explain how companies find a set of prices that maximises the profits from the total product mix (pp. 330–332).

When the product is part of a product mix, the firm searches for a set of prices that will maximise the profits from the total mix. In *product line pricing*, the company determines the price steps for the entire product line it offers. In addition, the company must set prices for *optional products* (optional or accessory products included with the main product), *captive products* (products that are required for using the main product), *by-products* (waste or residual products produced when making the main product) and *product bundles* (combinations of products at a reduced price).

OBJECTIVE 3 Discuss how companies adjust their prices to take into account different types of customers and situations (pp. 332–338).

Companies apply a variety of *price adjustment strategies* to account for differences in consumer segments and situations. One is *discount and allowance pricing*, whereby the company establishes cash, quantity, functional or seasonal discounts, or varying types of allowances. A second strategy is *segmented*

pricing, where the company sells a product at two or more prices to accommodate different customers, product forms, locations or times. Sometimes companies consider more than economics in their pricing decisions, using *psychological pricing* to better communicate a product's intended position. In *promotional pricing*, a company offers discounts or temporarily sells a product below list price as a special event, sometimes even selling below cost as a loss leader. Another approach is *geographical pricing*, whereby the company decides how to price to distant customers, choosing from such alternatives as *FOB-origin pricing*, *uniform-delivered pricing*, *zone pricing*, *base-point pricing* and *freight-absorption pricing*. Finally, *international pricing* means that the company adjusts its price to meet different conditions and expectations in different world markets.

OBJECTIVE 4 Discuss the key issues related to initiating and responding to price changes (pp. 338–341).

When a firm considers initiating a *price change*, it must consider customers' and competitors' reactions. There are different implications to *initiating price cuts* and *initiating price increases*. Buyer reactions to price changes are influenced by the meaning customers see in the price change. Competitors' reactions flow from a set reaction policy or a fresh analysis of each situation.

There are also many factors to consider in responding to a competitor's price changes. The company that faces a price change initiated by a competitor must try to understand the competitor's intent as well as the likely duration and impact of the change. If a swift reaction is desirable, the firm should pre-plan its reactions to different possible price actions by competitors. When facing a competitor's price change, the company might sit tight, reduce its own price, raise perceived quality, improve quality and raise price, or launch a fighting brand.

OBJECTIVE 5 Discuss the social and legal issues that affect pricing decisions (pp. 342–343).

Many federal, state and even local laws govern the rules of fair pricing. Also, companies must consider broader societal pricing concerns. The major public policy issues in pricing include potentially damaging pricing practices *within* a given level of the channel, such as price-fixing and predatory pricing. They also include pricing practices *across* channel levels, such as retail price maintenance, discriminatory pricing and deceptive pricing. Although many federal and state statutes regulate pricing practices, reputable sellers go beyond what is required by law. Treating customers fairly is an important part of building strong and lasting customer relationships.

NAVIGATING THE KEY TERMS

OBJECTIVE 1
Market-skimming pricing (p. 329)
Market-penetration pricing (p. 329)

OBJECTIVE 2
Product line pricing (p. 331)
Optional product pricing (p. 331)
Captive product pricing (p. 331)
By-product pricing (p. 331)
Product bundle pricing (p. 332)

OBJECTIVE 3
Discount (p. 332)
Allowance (p. 333)

Segmented pricing (p. 333)
Psychological pricing (p. 334)
Reference prices (p. 334)
Promotional pricing (p. 335)
Geographical pricing (p. 335)
FOB-origin pricing (p. 336)
Uniform-delivered pricing (p. 336)
Zone pricing (p. 336)
Base-point pricing (p. 336)
Freight-absorption pricing (p. 336)
Dynamic pricing (p. 336)

DISCUSSING AND APPLYING THE CONCEPTS

Discussing the concepts

1. Compare and contrast market-skimming and market-penetration pricing strategies and discuss the conditions under which each is appropriate. (AACSB: Communication; Reflective Thinking)

2. Name and briefly describe the five product mix pricing decisions. (AACSB: Communication)

3. Explain how discounts and allowances differ from promotional pricing. (AACSB: Communication; Reflective Thinking)

4. Compare and contrast the geographic pricing strategies that companies use for customers located in different parts of the country or the world. Which strategy is best? (AACSB: Communication; Reflective Thinking)

5. What factors influence the prices a company charges in different countries? (AACSB: Communication)

6. Why would a company consider increasing its price? What precautions must be taken to avoid being perceived as a price gouger? (AACSB: Communication)

Applying the concepts

1. Identify three price-comparison shopping websites and shop for a specific model of a digital camera on all three sites. Compare the price ranges given at each site. Based on your search, determine a fair price for the camera. (AACSB: Communication; Use of IT)

2. Convert €1.00 to the currencies of five other countries. (You can do this at www.xe.com.) What implications do currency exchange rates hold for setting prices in other countries? (AACSB: Communication; Use of IT; Reflective Thinking)

3. One psychological pricing tactic is just-below pricing. It is also called '9-ending' pricing because prices usually end in the number 9 (or 99). In a small group, have each member select five different products and visit a store to find the price of those items. Is there a variation among the items and stores with regard to 9-ending pricing? Why do marketers use this pricing tactic? (AACSB: Communication; Reflective Thinking)

Focus on technology

The Internet is great for selling products and services. But don't make a pricing mistake online! Intercontinental Hotels mistakenly priced rooms at one of its four-star hotels near Venice, Italy, for €1 per night instead of the actual price of €150 per night. Internet users booked 1,400 nights before the mistake was realised. Intercontinental Hotels honoured the reservations at a cost of €90,000 to the company. In Taiwan, an eight-hour online pricing snafu on Dell's website created tremendous problems for the company, such as 40,000 orders for a laptop computer priced at about one-quarter of the intended price. Unlike Intercontinental Hotels, however, Dell refused to honour the erroneous price and offered a discount instead. The Taiwanese government disagreed, ordered Dell to honour orders for erroneously priced products, and fined the company.

1. Find two other examples of online pricing mistakes. How did the companies handle the problems resulting from the pricing errors? (AACSB: Communication; Reflective Thinking)

2. Research ways in which marketers protect against the consequences of online pricing errors and write a brief report summarising what you learn. (AACSB: Communication; Reflective Thinking)

Focus on ethics

You'd think that the further you fly, the more expensive your airfare would be. According to easily accessible data, however, that's not the case. For example, one study compared five US and EU city-pairs (Los Angeles–San Francisco, New York–Boston, Chicago–Detroit, Denver–Las Vegas, Miami–Orlando versus London–Edinburgh, Paris–Nice, Milan–Rome, Dusseldorf–Berlin, Barcelona–Madrid). The total distance of all five US-based flights is a total (return) distance of 3,172 miles while for the five European flights the total distance travelled would be slightly more at 3,338 miles. Yet the European flights are about half of the cost of those in the US at around €276 versus €527! That's the average cost; fliers sitting next to each other are likely to have paid different prices. Many factors influence the pricing of airfares; distance has minor impact, even though two major expenses – fuel and labour – increase the longer the flight. Airlines claim they are just charging what the market will bear.

1. Should airlines be required to charge standard prices based on distance and equal airfares for passengers seated in the same class (such as standard or business class) on the same flight? What will likely happen to prices if the government requires airlines to base fares only on distance and passenger class? (AACSB: Communication; Ethical Reasoning; Reflective Thinking)

2. What factors account for the variation in airfares? Should airlines be permitted to get as much as they can for a seat? (AACSB: Communication; Reflective Thinking)

Marketing & the economy

Pizza Hut

Restaurants of all kinds have scrambled to keep customers coming in during recent difficult economic times. Pizza Hut is in an unusual spot. It isn't exactly fast food, but it isn't quite

full-service fare either. Pizza Hut has never been perceived as being on the low end of pizza prices. As the economy sagged, all these factors cooled down business for the red-roofed purveyor of pies. So Pizza Hut did what many companies did – it cut prices. At first, it shocked the pizza category with its '€10 any' promotion – any pizza, any size, any crust, any toppings, for just €10. Customers responded enthusiastically to the limited time offer. But as soon as the price deal ended, Pizza Hut's incremental promotional revenues disappeared. So the company has made more permanent adjustments to the new frugality reality. To increase customer loyalty, it has introduced everyday low prices. Most medium pizzas cost €8, most large pizzas cost €10 and most speciality pizzas cost €12; these price cuts represent up to 50 per cent reductions from previous pricing. Under this new pricing, Pizza Hut expects that revenues will increase significantly. But the new pricing mechanism will require some time before it proves itself.

1. What are the implications of Pizza Hut's big price cuts for its brand image?

2. Can customer loyalty be generated through low prices?

3. Can Pizza Hut sustain such dramatically lower prices and still remain profitable?

Marketing by the numbers

The recently weak economy caused many consumers to switch to lower-priced products. Although P&G had sales of €56 billion in 2009 and €58 billion in 2010, many of its relatively expensive brands, such as Tide detergent and Secret deodorant, were stranded on store shelves. So, in 2010, P&G did the unthinkable – it slashed prices on many of its products, such as batteries (13.3 per cent), liquid laundry detergents (5.1 per cent), shampoos (5.4 per cent) and conditioners (6.6 per cent). The price cuts come at a cost, however, and sales must increase considerably just to break even or make the price cuts profitable.

1. P&G's average contribution margin before the price cuts was 20 per cent. Refer to Appendix 2 and calculate the new contribution margin if prices are reduced 10 per cent. (AACSB: Communication; Analytical Reasoning)

2. What level of total sales must P&G capture at the new price levels to maintain the same level of total contribution before the price reduction (that is, total contribution = €11.2 billion, which is 20 per cent of €56 billion in sales)? (AACSB: Communication; Analytic Reasoning)

REFERENCES

1 This case study draws heavily on the excellent case studies and analyses (including quotes and other information) of: Linda A. Johnson, 'Drugmakers boost consumer ad spending 2 percent in '09', (2 March 2010), http://abcnews.go.comlBusinesslwireStory?id=10024145; Andrew Jack, 'GSK gives price pledge on malaria vaccine', *Financial Times* (21 January 2010); Duff Wilson, 'Drug makers raise prices in face of health care reform', *New York Times* (15 November 2009); Congressional Budget Office, 'Promotional spending for prescription drugs', *Economic and Budget Issue Brief* (2 December 2009); 'Drug company reaches out to poor', *Financial Chronicle*, (10 February 2010), www.mydigitalk.comlnews/ drug-company-reaches-outpoor-589; and information from www .gsk.com, accessed October 2011. The authors acknowledge the assistance of Millie and Tabitha in preparing this case study.

2 For comprehensive discussions of pricing strategies, see Thomas T. Nagle, John E. Hogan and Joseph Zale, *The Strategy and Tactics of Pricing*, 5th edn. (Upper Saddle River, NJ: Prentice Hall, 2011).

3 Adapted from information found in Mei Fong, 'Ikea hits home in China: the Swedish design giant, unlike other retailers, slashes prices for the Chinese', *Wall Street Journal* (3 March 2006), p. B1; 'Beijing loves Ikea – but not for shopping', *Los Angeles Times*, http://articles.latimes .com/2009/aug/25/business/fi-china-ikea25; and www.ikea.com/ms/ en_US/about_ikea/facts_and_figures/index.html, accessed October 2011.

4 Example from Andrew Bolger, 'Scottish scientists develop whisky biofuel', *Financial Times* (17 August 2010), www.ft.com/cms/s/0/62e0f67a-aa0b-11df-8eb1-00144feabdc0.html#ixzz1UWPinXkk, accessed October 2011.

5 Peter Coy, 'Why the price is rarely right', *Bloomberg BusinessWeek* (1/7 February 2010), pp. 77–78.

6 See Eric Anderson and Duncan Simester, 'Mind your pricing cues', *Harvard Business Review* (September 2003), pp. 96–103; and Peter J. Boyle and E. Scott Lathrop, 'Are consumers' perceptions of price-quality relationships well calibrated?', *International Journal of Consumer Studies* (January 2009), p. 58.

7 Anthony Allred, E. K. Valentin and Goutam Chakraborty, 'Pricing risky services: preference and quality considerations', *The Journal of Product and Brand Management*, **19** (1), 2010, p. 54. Also see Kenneth C. Manning and David E. Sprott, 'Price endings, left-digit effects, and choice', *Journal of Consumer Research* (August 2009), pp. 328–336.

8 Adapted from information found in Elizabeth A. Sullivan, 'Stay on course', *Marketing News* (15 February 2009), pp. 11–13. Also see Stuart Elliott, 'Never mind what it costs. Can i get it 70 percent off?', *New York Times* (27 April 2009), www.nytimes.com/2009/04/28/ business/media/28adco.html?_r=1&scp=1&sq=Never%20Mind%20 What%20It%20Costs&st=cse; and 'Consumer' "new frugality" may be an enduring feature of post-recession economy, finds Booz & Company survey', *Business Wire* (24 February 2010).

9 Based on information found in 'the world's most influential companies: Unilever', *BusinessWeek* (22 December 2008), p. 47; and www.unilever .com/sustainability, accessed October 2011.

10 See www.bbc.co.uk/news/magazine-13725050, accessed October 2011.

11 Example adapted from information found in Ellen Byron, 'fashion victim: to refurbish its image, Tiffany risks profits', *Wall Street Journal* (10 January 2007), p. A1; and Aliza Rosenbaum and John Christy, 'Financial insight: Tiffany's boutique risk: by breaking mall fast, high-end exclusivity may gain touch of common', *Wall Street Journal* (20 October 2007), p. B14. Also see Brian Burnsed, 'Where discounting can be dangerous', *BusinessWeek* (3 August 2009), p. 49.

12 Example from James Boxell, 'France Telecom earmarks disposals', *Financial Times* (28 July 2011), www.ft.com/cms/s/0/263d5932-b8ee-11e0-bd87-00144feabdc0.html#axzz1UPifHx5H, accessed October 2011; and Ross Tieman, 'France's free is wired for telecoms success', *Financial Times* (17 March 2011), www.ft.com/cms/s/0/9e2bfb0e-440b-11e0-8f20-00144feab49a.html#axzz1TD6Um28m, accessed October 2011.

13 For discussions of these issues, see Dhruv Grewel and Larry D. Compeau, 'Pricing and public policy: a research agenda and overview of the special issue', *Journal of Public Policy and Marketing* (Spring 1999), pp. 3–10; Michael V. Marn, Eric V. Roegner and Craig C. Zawada, *The Price Advantage* (Hoboken, NJ: John Wiley & Sons, 2004), appendix 2; and Nagle, Hogan and Zale, *The Strategy and Tactics of Pricing*, 5th edn, op.cit.

14 Example from Jonathan Birchall, 'Amazon net profit rises 68%', *Financial Times* (23 October 2009), www.ft.com/cms/s/0/dbb2bace-bf6b-11de-a696-00144feab49a.html#ixzz1UWGxJSMa, accessed October 2011.

15 Example from Victoria Shannon, 'Amazon.com is challenging French competition law', *New York Times* (14 January 2008), www.nytimes .com/2008/01/14/technology/14iht-amazon.4.9204272.html, accessed October 2011.

16 Example from Nikki Tait, 'Brussels targets online credit card fees', *Financial Times* (23 June 2011) , www.ft.com/cms/s/0/3ed2e7e4-9dd4-11e0-b30c-00144feabdc0.html#ixzz1UWarBS2y, accessed October 2011.

VIDEO CASE

Land Rover MyMarketingLab

Like Hummer and Jeep, Land Rover is a car manufacturer whose roots are in off-road utility vehicles rather than passenger cars. For a long while, Land Rover only made their pioneering, multi-purpose, all-terrain vehicle, but in 1970 their completely radical all-terrain luxury Range Rover created the sports utility vehicle (SUV). When launched in the US, it proved so popular among the rich and wealthy that it became known as the 'Hollywood Jeep'. However, the company's narrow focus on large 4 × 4 vehicles now seems ill-fitting to a world of high fuel prices and concerns for global warming.

Nevertheless, Land Rover remains profitable and successful, partly because Land Rover 4 × 4s are real all-terrain vehicles, which maintains the products' cult status with magazines and off-the-road enthusiasts dedicated to the brand.

After watching the Land Rover video, answer the following questions about the company:

1. How and why does the company position the Land Rover brand across different markets such as North America, Africa and countries like China?
2. What is the company doing in response to the challenges of globalisation and environmental sustainability?

COMPANY CASE

Radiohead: pricing strategy and the music industry

In 2010 the average price of a music CD fell below €8.75 for the first time in the history of the industry. This all-time-low highlighted the challenges faced by artists and record companies that have already seen revenues undermined by significantly cheaper digital downloads and widespread online piracy. In the past decade the average price of a CD has fallen by 28 per cent, or about €3.60, from €12.75 in 2000 to €9.15 in 2009, according to figures from the BPI, an influential music industry trade body. 'The falling price of CDs just adds to the woes of record companies,' said James Bates, media partner at the consultancy Deloitte. 'The cost of producing the music is still approximately the same, so the slide in prices puts a lot of pressure on margins.' Mr Bates pointed to supermarkets that often sold CDs at a loss to boost footfall as one factor in the downward pressure on prices. So, is the music industry in terminal decline? Some industry insiders think so. As far back as 1994, Thom Yorke, the lead singer of Radiohead, an English band from Abingdon in Oxfordshire warned apocalyptically of its being 'simply a matter of time – months rather than years – before the music business establishment completely folds'. His advice to young bands: 'Don't tie yourself to the sinking ship, because believe me, it's sinking.' Later, in October 2007, Radiohead shook the industry to the core with their radically innovative pricing strategy. Radiohead, an internationally critically renowned band, took the unusual step of telling fans that they could pay as much or as little as they liked for the band's new album *In Rainbows*. In a break from well-established industry tradition the UK band (famous for hits such as 'Creep', 'Paranoid Android' and 'Karma Police') told its fans 'it's your choice' and that they could pay what they wanted to download the album. This wasn't the first time that a band had opted to charge nothing for a download, but the move was significant because Radiohead are one of the world's biggest bands. Downloading fans could choose to pay as little as €0.50 (the credit card handling fee) or as much as they liked. However, the band also offered a €60 package, which included two CDs, two 'old-fashioned' vinyl albums and an artwork-filled booklet. The boxed set was sold only on its website, allowing the band to control its price. Bryce Edge (one of the band's trio of managers) admitted, 'We can't control how much Tesco will sell [a typical CD] for, nor can the record companies.'

Radiohead was free to sell its album directly from its official website because it is no longer tied to a record label. The previous six releases by the band had been through the traditional tie-up with a record company. After 16 years with EMI, however, Radiohead split with the record company shortly after it was taken over by the private equity group Terra Firma.

Initially, official sales figures were not released by the band. However, news filtered out that 1.2 million downloads occurred on the day of the release of *In Rainbows*. Industry insiders also responded with widespread reports that Guy Hands, chairman of Terra Firma, had met the management team of Radiohead to discuss bringing the group back to EMI Music. Furthermore, although Radiohead's decision to sell direct to fans was seen as a blow to the traditional music industry, it quickly emerged that the Radiohead management team were in discussions with the four large record companies – Universal Music, Sony BMG, Warner Music and EMI – for help with the traditional CD release. Subsequently, in late 2007 in Europe and early 2008 in North America, *In Rainbows* was released as a traditional CD and reached the number one slot on both sides of the Atlantic. The CD went on to sell over 3 million copies worldwide.

The success of this initial 'pay-as-you-choose' or premium payment for the box set followed by traditionally priced formal CD release pricing strategy was widely acknowledged. Indeed, the decision to release *In Rainbows* online and to allow buyers to pay as little as they like was lauded by some analysts as a ground-breaking model for an industry struggling to compete with free illegal downloads. While some predicted that only the most fanatical of music fans would choose to buy a CD when the download was (almost) free, Radiohead's management were confident that music buyers would recognise the value of both forms of release. 'If we didn't believe that when people hear the music they will want to buy the CD, then we wouldn't do what we are doing,' Bryce Edge told *Music Week*, the UK's industry magazine. Speaking shortly after the online launch, Mr Edge argued that as many as half of those who registered for the download had paid more than the minimum €0.50 transaction fee, but he described the initiative as 'a solution for Radiohead, not the industry', and defended the superior quality of CD recordings. 'You can't listen to a Radiohead record on MP3 [the digital music file standard] and hear the detail; it's impossible,' Mr Edge said. 'We can't understand why record companies don't go on the offensive and say what a great piece of kit CDs are. CDs are undervalued and sold too cheaply.'

Indeed, others in the music industry were less than happy with this new pricing business model. 'While the band, its fans and artists alike are celebrating what looks like a success for Radiohead's bold move in releasing their new album using the "pay what you'd like" model, I think everybody has overlooked one very important aspect of this, and it doesn't bode well for the future of the music industry,' said Michael Laskow,

349

CEO of TAXI, the world's leading independent A&R (Artist and Repertoire) company. 'Radiohead has been bankrolled by their former label for the last 15 years. They've built a fan base in the millions with their label, and now they're able to cash in on that fan base with none of the income or profit going to the label this time around. That's great for the band and for fans who paid less than they would under the old school model. But at some point in the not too distant future, the music industry will run out of artists who have had major label support in helping them build a huge fan base. The question is: how will *new* artists be able to use this model in the future if they haven't built a fan base in the millions in the years leading up to the release of their album under the pay what you'd like model?'

In 2007, the year of its release, global revenues in recorded music were €14.27 billion. Three years on, Radiohead were back in the studio. In the meantime the music industry's problems have worsened. In 2009, global recorded music revenues dropped to €12.5 billion, while by 2011, global recorded music revenues fell by 8.4 per cent, about €1 billion, to €11.69 billion according to the annual Recording Industry in Numbers report by international music industry body the IFPI. Overall physical sales, the term used in the industry for sales of products such as CDs, fell by 14.2 per cent year on year to €7.65 billion. Digital revenues grew by 5.3 per cent year on year to €3.38 billion to account for 29 per cent of all recorded music revenues. However, the rate of digital revenue growth has halved year on year as the industry continues to struggle with piracy and winning consumers over to legal download models.

On Valentine's Day (14 February) 2011, Radiohead announced the release of their eighth album *The King of Limbs* (named after a 1,000-year-old oak tree in the Savernake Forest in the UK). Four days later the album was released via their website. However, this time around, the management of Radiohead tweaked their pricing strategy. Rather than allowing fans to set their own price for digital downloads, this time, the album download was only available for a fixed price. While the download pricing undercut the typical price for a new album from a big artist on digital services such as Apple's iTunes, the band shied away from the 'honesty box' payment system of 2007. In part this decision was based on clear statistical facts. One month after the launch of the 'pay-as-you-choose' album in 2007, comScore.Inc (a leading firm in measuring the digital world) published a report that found that while *In Rainbows* did sell millions of albums and proved that established acts could survive without record labels, three out of five people downloading the album had not paid anything for it. Specifically, of the 1.2 million people who downloaded the album in the first month of release, 62 per cent did not pay anything. According to comScore, downloaders from the US paid on average €4.41, a full euro more than non-US downloaders (who paid on average €3.41). Seventeen per cent of downloading fans paid under €2.94 while only 4 per cent of downloaders paid more than €8.82. Nevertheless, Radiohead stuck with the release of traditional CD and 12-inch vinyl six

weeks later and a special 'newspaper', premium-priced deluxe package with two vinyl records, a CD and numerous sheets of variously sized artwork (at around €35). This prompted Ed O'Brien (guitar and backing vocals) in 2011 to claim that this approach meant that 'We sell less records, but we make more money'.

Talking of Radiohead's pricing strategy, Cliff Fluet, lawyer at Lewis Silkin, said: 'What they are doing is having tiered pricing points and creating new products for fans and evangelists. It's a very smart move.' Gregor Pryor, lawyer at Reed Smith, said: '*In Rainbows* was a trial. The album was released at a time when people were still uncertain what consumers would pay for music.' 'Radiohead simply conducted an experiment but consumers are now used to paying with a range of retail pricing so there isn't that need anymore.'

Excluded record labels are responding to this threat to their income stream in a variety of ways. Take, for example, the Kaiser Chiefs, the British indie rock stalwarts, who in the summer of 2011 invited fans to create a bespoke version of their new album – choosing tracklisting and cover design. The band, which has enjoyed success with songs such as 'I Predict a Riot' and the chart-topping album *Yours Truly, Angry Mob*, released its new album *The Future is Medieval* not via iTunes but through their own website. The launch is a collaboration between Universal Music and the advertising agency Wieden + Kennedy, which has managed the development of the website and the viral launch, keeping much of the music industry in the dark.

On the website, kaiserchiefs.com, fans are able to select 10 tracks from 20 new songs and create their own version of the album by choosing the playlist and designing the cover. They can download the album for around €8.62. However, the band has also given fans the opportunity to post their versions of the album on Facebook and Twitter – and make money in the process. For every copy of their own version of the album fans sell, they receive €1.15. All sales take place via the band's website using the online payment system PayPal. Only eight sales are required for a fan to start making a profit. Ricky Wilson, the band's lead singer who came up with the idea, says: 'I'd been looking at how people buy music and I thought "Well if that's what you want, we'll give it to you". If people want to buy tracks, let them buy tracks. If people don't want to buy the album you've put together but just buy the tracks they like, all right.' 'You've got to embrace being digital, but the only problem with being digital is that it's not very tactile, there's no ownership over it,' says Wilson. 'It's not just that you get your own artwork and your own tracklisting, it's the experience. The experience of making the album does make the untangible tangible.'

'I think it's really important that we as record labels help bring the value back to music,' says Jim Chancellor, head of Fiction Records, a subsidiary of Universal Music Group, who has been working on the Kaiser Chiefs launch. 'It's becoming harder and harder. It's not just the general perception, its retailers trying to push prices down.'

Questions for discussion

1. Is the Radiohead pricing strategy market-skimming or market penetrating or both? Why?
2. Describe the Radiohead pricing structure in terms of product line pricing. How could they extend the approach?
3. Both the management of Radiohead and the Kaiser Chiefs seem less than happy with retailers' pricing strategies. Why?
4. If you were the management of Radiohead, what would your pricing strategy for the next album look like?

Sources: This case study draws heavily on the excellent case studies and analyses (including quotes and other information) of: Carl Wilkinson, "Kaisers" predict riot of interest in bespoke album 'financial Times', (2 June 2011) www.ft.com/cms/s/2/a6eac7ec-8d45-11e0-bf23-00144feab49a. html#ixzz1aTVDBQgR, accessed October 2011 Ludovic Hunter-Tilney, 'The music industry's new business model', *Financial Times* (10 September 2011) http://www.ft.com/cms/s/2/92d98d1c-bae9-11df-9e1d-00144feab49a.html#ixzz1aTVb8Vxa, accessed October 2011; Esther Bintliff, 'CD price fall adds to music industry's blues' (12 May 2011), www.ft.com/ cms/s/0/6f20d9fe-5d2c-11df-8373-00144feab49a.html#ixzz1aTVgsLd7, accessed October 2011; Andrew Edgecliffe-Johnson, 'Radiohead MP3 release a tactic to lift CD sales', *Financial Times* (11 October 2007), www.ft.com/cms/s/0/0a9c779a-7797-11dc-9de8-0000779fd2ac .html#ixzz1aTVnQwbO, accessed October 2011; Salamander Davoudi, 'Radiohead ditches "honesty box" principle' (18 February 2011), www.ft.com/ cms/s/0/efe1016a-3b55-11e0-9970-00144feabdc0.html#ixzz1aTW5T9E3 accessed October 2011; Angela Monaghan, 'Radiohead challenges labels with free album', *Daily Telegraph* (October 2007); David Byrne, 'David Byrne and Thom Yorke on the real value of music', *Wired* (18 November 2007), www.wired.com/entertainment/music/magazine/16-01/ ff_yorke?currentPage=all; Lars Brandle, 'Radiohead returning to the road in 2008', *Billboard.com* (18 October 2007), http://web.archive.org/ web/20080208234628 http://www.billboard.com/bbcom/news/article_display.jsp?vnu_content_id=1003660154, accessed October 2011; *The Colbert Report*, Comedy Central, New York City (26 September 2011); Mark Sweeney, 'Global recorded' music sales fall almost $1.5bn amid increased piracy', *Guardian* (28 March 2011), www.guardian.co.uk/business/2011/ mar/28/global-recorded-music-sales-fall. Larry Fitzmaurice, 'Radiohead newspaper album revealed', *Pitchfork* (27 April 2011), http://pitchfork .com/news/42343-radiohead-newspaper-album-revealed/.comScore Press Release, 'For Radiohead fans, does "free" + "download" = "freeload"?', (5 November 2007), www.comscore.com/Press_Events/Press _Releases/2007/11/Radiohead_Downloads, accessed October 2011.

CHAPTER TWELVE

Marketing channels: delivering customer value

Chapter preview

We now arrive at the third marketing mix tool – distribution. Firms rarely work alone in creating value for customers and building profitable customer relationships. Instead, most are only a single link in a larger supply chain and marketing channel. As such, an individual firm's success depends not only on how well *it* performs but also on how well its *entire marketing channel* competes with competitors' channels. To be good at customer relationship management, a company must also be good at partner relationship management. The first part of this chapter explores the nature of marketing channels and the marketer's channel design and management decisions. We then examine physical distribution – or logistics – an area that is growing dramatically in importance and sophistication. In the next chapter, we'll look more closely at two major channel intermediaries: retailers and wholesalers.

We start by looking at a company whose groundbreaking, customer-centred distribution strategy took it to the top of its industry.

Objective outline

➤ **Objective 1** Explain why companies use marketing channels and discuss the functions these channels perform.
Supply chains and the value delivery network (pp. 354–355)
The nature and importance of marketing channels (pp. 355–358)

➤ **Objective 2** Discuss how channel members interact and how they organise to perform the work of the channel.
Channel behaviour and organisation (pp. 358–363)

➤ **Objective 3** Identify the major channel alternatives open to a company.
Channel design decisions (pp. 364–367)

➤ **Objective 4** Explain how companies select, motivate and evaluate channel members.
Channel management decisions (pp. 367–369)
Public policy and distribution decisions (p. 369)

➤ **Objective 5** Discuss the nature and importance of marketing logistics and integrated supply chain management.
Marketing logistics and supply chain management (pp. 370–377)

Zara: fast fashions — *really* fast

Fashion retailer Zara is on a tear. It sells 'cheap chic' — stylish designs that resemble those of big-name fashion houses but at moderate prices. Zara is the prototype for a new breed of 'fast-fashion' retailer, companies that recognise and respond to the latest fashion trends quickly and nimbly. While competing retailers are still working out their designs, Zara has already put the latest fashion into its stores and is moving on to the next big thing.

Zara has attracted a near cultlike clientele in recent years. Following the recent economic slide, even upscale shoppers are swarming to buy Zara's stylish but affordable offerings. Thanks to Zara's torrid growth, the sales, profits, and store presence of its parent company, Spain–based Inditex, have more than quadrupled since 2000. Despite the poor economy, Inditex opened 450 stores last year, while other big retailers such as Gap closed stores. Despite the poor economy, Inditex's sales grew 9 per cent last year. By comparison, Gap's sales *fell*. As a result, Inditex has now sprinted past Gap to become the world's largest clothing retailer. Inditex's 4,670 stores in 74 countries sewed up $14.9 billion in sales last year.

Zara dearly sells the right goods for these times. But it's amazing success comes not just from *what* it sells. Perhaps more important, success comes from how and how fast Zara's cutting-edge distribution system *delivers* what it sells to eagerly awaiting customers. Zara delivers fast fashion — *really* fast fashion. Through vertical integration, Zara controls all phases of the fashion process, from design and manufacturing to distribution through its own managed stores. The company's integrated supply system makes Zara faster, more flexible, and more efficient than international competitors such as Gap, Benetton, and H&M. Zara can take a new fashion concept through design, manufacturing, and store-shelf placement in as little as two weeks, whereas competitors often take six months or more. And the resulting low costs let Zara offer the very latest midmarket chic at downmarket prices.

The whole process starts with input about what consumers want. Zara store managers act as trend spotters. They patrol store aisles using handheld computers, reporting in real time what's selling and what's not selling. They talk with customers to learn what they're looking for but not yet finding. At the same time, Zara trend seekers roam fashion shows in Pairs and concerts in Tokyo, looking for young people who might be wearing something new or different. Then they're on the phone to company headquarters in tiny La Coruña, Spain, reporting on what they've seen and heard. Back home, based on this and other feedback, the company's team of 300 designers, 200 specifically for Zara, conjures up a prolific flow of hot new fashions.

Once the designers have done their work, production begins. But rather than relying on a hodgepodge of slow-moving suppliers in Asia, as most competitors do, Zara makes 40 per cent of its own fabrics and produces more than half of its own clothes. Even farmed-out manufacturing goes primarily to local contractors. Almost all clothes sold in Zara's stores worldwide are made quickly and efficiently at or near company headquarters in a remote corner of northwest Spain.

Finished goods then feed into Zara's modern distribution centres, which ship them immediately and directly to stores around the world, saving time, eliminating the need for warehouses, and keeping inventories low. The highly automated centres can sort, pack, label, and allocate up to 80,000 items per hour.

Again, the key word describing Zara's distribution system is *fast*. The time between receiving an order at the distribution centre to the delivery of goods to a store averages 24 hours for European stores and a maximum of 48 hours for American or Asian stores. Zara stores receive small shipments of new merchandise two to three times each week, compared with competing chains' outlets, which get large shipments seasonally, usually just four to six times per year.

Speedy design and distribution allows Zara to introduce a copious supply of new fashions — some 30,000 items last year, compared with a competitor average of less than 10,000. The combination of a large number of new fashions delivered in frequent small batches gives Zara stores a continually updated merchandise mix that brings customers back more often. Zara customers visit the store an average of 17 times per year, compared to less than five customer visits at competing stores. Fast turnover also results in less outdated and discounted merchandise.

Zara store managers act as trend spotters. They patrol store aisles reporting in real time on what's selling and what's not.

Source: Copyright © Inditex

Because Zara makes what consumers already want or are now wearing, it doesn't have to guess what will be hot six months in the future.

In all, Zara's carefully integrated design and distribution process gives the fast-moving retailer a tremendous competitive advantage. Its turbocharged system gets out the goods customers what, when they want them – perhaps even before:

A few summers ago, Zara managed to latch onto one of the season's hottest trends in just four weeks. The process started when trend spotters spread the word back to headquarters: White eyelet – cotton with tiny holes in it – was set to become white-hot. A quick telephone survey of Zara store managers confirmed that the fabric could be a winner, so in-house designers got down to work. They zapped patterns electronically to Zara's factory across the street, and the fabric was cut. Local subcontractors stitched white-eyelet V-neck belted dresses – think Jackie Kennedy, circa 1960 – and finished them in less than a week. The $129 dresses were inspected, tagged and transported through a tunnel under the street to a distribution centre. From there, they were quickly dispatched to Zara stores from New York to Tokyo – where they were flying off the racks just two days later.[1]

As the Zara story shows, innovative distribution strategies can contribute strongly to customer value and create competitive advantage for a firm. But firms cannot bring value to customers by themselves. Instead, they must work closely with other firms in a larger value delivery network.

AUTHOR COMMENT

These are pretty hefty terms for a really simple concept: a company can't go it alone in creating customer value. It must work within an entire network of partners to accomplish this task. Individual companies and brands don't compete; their entire value delivery networks compete.

SUPPLY CHAINS AND THE VALUE DELIVERY NETWORK

Producing a product or a service and making it available to buyers requires building relationships not only with customers but also with key suppliers and resellers in the company's *supply chain*. This supply chain consists of upstream and downstream partners. Upstream from the company is the set of firms that supply the raw materials, components, parts, information, finances and expertise needed to create a product or a service. Marketers, however, have traditionally focused on the downstream side of the supply chain – on the *marketing channels* (or *distribution channels*) that look toward the customer. Downstream marketing channel partners, such as wholesalers and retailers, form a vital connection between the firm and its customers.

The term *supply chain* may be too limited; it takes a *make-and-sell* view of the business. It suggests that raw materials, productive inputs and factory capacity should serve as the starting point for market planning. A better term would be *demand chain* because it suggests a *sense-and-respond* view of the market. Under this view, planning starts by identifying the needs of the target customers, to which the company responds by organising a chain of resources and activities with the goal of creating customer value.

Yet, even a demand chain view of a business may be too limited because it takes a step-by-step, linear view of purchase, production and consumption activities. With the advent of the Internet and other technologies, however, companies are now forming more numerous and complex relationships with other firms. For example, Ford manages many supply chains – think about all the parts it takes to create a vehicle, from radios to catalytic converters to tyres to transistors. Ford also sponsors or transacts on many B-to-B websites and online purchasing exchanges as needs arise. Like Ford, most large companies today are engaged in building and managing a complex, continuously evolving *value delivery network.*

As defined in Chapter 2, a **value delivery network** is composed of the company, suppliers, distributors and, ultimately, customers who 'partner' with each other to improve the performance of the entire system. For example, in making and marketing one of its many models for the global market, such as the Ford Escape hybrid (soon to be the Ford Kuga), Ford manages a huge network of people within Ford plus thousands of suppliers and dealers outside the company who work together effectively to give final customers 'the most fuel-efficient SUV on the market'.

This chapter focuses on marketing channels – on the downstream side of the value delivery network. We examine four major questions concerning marketing channels: What is the nature of marketing channels and why are they important? How do channel firms interact and organise to do the work of the channel? What problems do companies face in designing and managing their channels? What role do physical distribution and supply chain management play in attracting and satisfying customers? In Chapter 13, we will look at marketing channel issues from the viewpoint of retailers and wholesalers.

Ford manages a huge network of people within Ford plus thousands of suppliers and dealers outside the company, to make the Ford Kuga 'the most fuel-efficient SUV on the market'.

Source: Press Association Images

AUTHOR COMMENT

In this section, we look at the downstream side of the value delivery network – the marketing channel organisations that connect the company and its customers. To understand their value, imagine life without retailers – say, without grocery stores or department stores.

THE NATURE AND IMPORTANCE OF MARKETING CHANNELS

Few producers sell their goods directly to final users. Instead, most use intermediaries to bring their products to market. They try to forge a **marketing channel** (or **distribution channel**) – a set of interdependent organisations that help make a product or a service available for use or consumption by the consumer or business user.

A company's channel decisions directly affect every other marketing decision. Pricing depends on whether the company works with discount chains, uses high-quality speciality stores or sells directly to consumers via the Internet. The firm's sales force and communications decisions depend on how much persuasion, training, motivation and support its channel partners need. Whether a company develops or acquires certain new products may depend on how well those products fit the capabilities of its channel members. For example, Kodak initially sold its EasyShare printers only in major retail electronics stores because of the retailers' on-the-floor sales staff and their ability to educate buyers on the economics of paying a higher initial printer price but lower prices on the long-term consumables – ink cartridges.

Companies often pay too little attention to their distribution channels – sometimes with damaging results. In contrast, many companies have used imaginative distribution systems to gain a competitive advantage. Enterprise revolutionised the car-rental business by establishing off-airport rental offices. Apple turned the retail music business on its head by selling music for the iPod via the Internet on iTunes. And FedEx's creative and imposing distribution system made it a leader in express delivery.

Value delivery network—
A network composed of the company, suppliers, distributors and, ultimately, customers who 'partner' with each other to improve the perfomance of the entire system in delivering customer value.

Marketing channel (distribution channel)—A set of interdependent organisations that help make a product or service available for use or consumption by the consumer or business user.

Distribution channel decisions often involve long-term commitments to other firms. For example, companies such as Ford, McDonald's or HP can easily change their advertising, pricing or promotion programmes. They can scrap old products and introduce new ones as market tastes demand. But when they set up distribution channels through contracts with franchisees, independent dealers or large retailers, they cannot readily replace these channels with company-owned stores or websites if the conditions change. Therefore, management must design its channels carefully, with an eye on both tomorrow's likely selling environment and today's environment.

How channel members add value

Why do producers give some of the selling job to channel partners? After all, doing so means giving up some control over how and to whom they sell their products. Producers use intermediaries because they create greater efficiency in making goods available to target markets. Through their contacts, experience, specialisation and scale of operation, intermediaries usually offer the firm more than it can achieve on its own.

Figure 12.1 shows how using intermediaries can provide economies. Figure 12.1a shows three manufacturers, each using direct marketing to reach three customers. This system requires nine different contacts. Figure 12.1b shows the three manufacturers working through one distributor, which contacts the three customers. This system requires only six contacts. In this way, intermediaries reduce the amount of work that must be done by both producers and consumers.

From the economic system's point of view, the role of marketing intermediaries is to transform the variety of products made by producers into the specific products wanted by consumers. Producers make narrow ranges of products in large quantities, but consumers want broad ranges of products in small quantities. Marketing channel members buy large quantities from many producers and break them down into the smaller quantities and broader ranges desired by consumers.

For example, Unilever makes millions of bars of hand soap each week, but you want to buy only a few bars at a time. So big food, pharmaceuticals and discount retailers, such as Tesco, Boots and Superdrug, buy Unilever's soaps by the truckload and stock it on their stores' shelves. In turn, you can buy a single bar of soap, along with a shopping basket full of small quantities of toothpaste, shampoo and other related products as you need them. Thus, intermediaries play an important role in matching supply and demand.

In making products and services available to consumers, channel members add value by bridging the major time, place and possession gaps that separate goods and services from those who use them. Members of the marketing channel perform many key functions. Some help to complete transactions:

- *Information* – gathering and distributing marketing research and intelligence information about actors and forces in the marketing environment needed for planning and aiding exchange.
- *Promotion* – developing and spreading persuasive communications about an offer.

Figure 12.1 How adding a distributor reduces the number of channel transactions

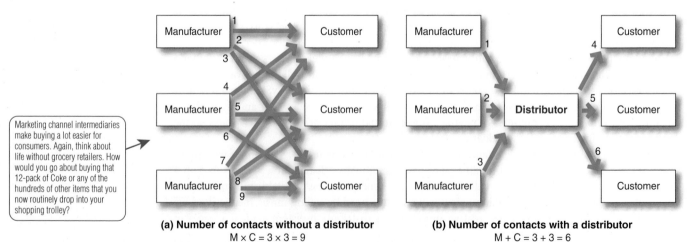

Marketing channel intermediaries make buying a lot easier for consumers. Again, think about life without grocery retailers. How would you go about buying that 12-pack of Coke or any of the hundreds of other items that you now routinely drop into your shopping trolley?

(a) Number of contacts without a distributor
M × C = 3 × 3 = 9

(b) Number of contacts with a distributor
M + C = 3 + 3 = 6

- *Contact* – finding and communicating with prospective buyers.
- *Matching* – shaping and fitting the offer to the buyer's needs, including activities such as manufacturing, grading, assembling and packaging.
- *Negotiation* – reaching an agreement on price and other terms of the offer so that ownership or possession can be transferred.

Others help to fulfil the completed transactions:

- *Physical distribution* – transporting and storing goods.
- *Financing* – acquiring and using funds to cover the costs of the channel work.
- *Risk taking* – assuming the risks of carrying out the channel work.

The question is not *whether* these functions need to be performed – they must be – but rather *who* will perform them. To the extent that the manufacturer performs these functions, its costs go up, and, therefore, its prices must be higher. When some of these functions are shifted to intermediaries, the producer's costs and prices may be lower, but the intermediaries must charge more to cover the costs of their work. In dividing the work of the channel, the various functions should be assigned to the channel members who can add the most value for the cost.

Number of channel levels

Companies can design their distribution channels to make products and services available to customers in different ways. Each layer of marketing intermediaries that performs some work in bringing the product and its ownership closer to the final buyer is a **channel level**. Because both the producer and the final consumer perform some work, they are part of every channel.

The *number of intermediary levels* indicates the *length* of a channel. Figure 12.2a shows several consumer distribution channels of different lengths. Channel 1, called a **direct marketing channel**, has no intermediary levels; the company sells directly to consumers. For example, companies like Avon Cosmetics sell their products door-to-door, through home and office sales parties, and on the Internet. Another example is Amway, with a sales force of more than 3 million people, Amway markets and sells health, beauty, durables and homecare and personal care products to consumers in more than 90 countries and

Channel level—A layer of intermediaries that performs some work in bringing the product and its ownership closer to the final buyer.

Direct marketing channel—A marketing channel that has no intermediary levels.

Figure 12.2 Consumer and business marketing channels

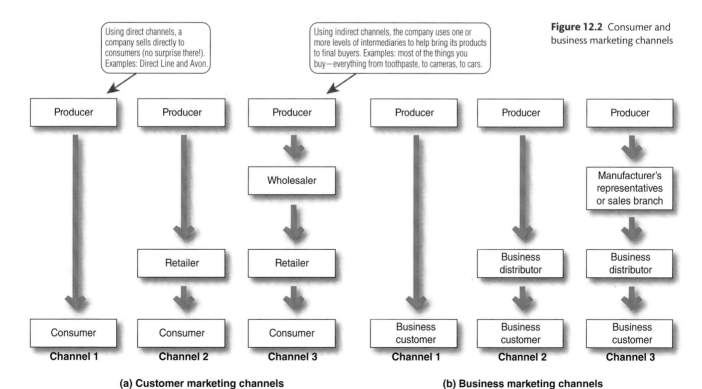

(a) Customer marketing channels   **(b) Business marketing channels**

Indirect marketing channel—
Channel containing one or more intermediary levels.

territories worldwide. Direct Line sells insurance direct via the telephone and the Internet. The remaining channels in Figure 12.2a are **indirect marketing channels**, containing one or more intermediaries.

Figure 12.2b shows some common business distribution channels. The business marketer can use its own sales force to sell directly to business customers. Or it can sell to various types of intermediaries, who in turn sell to these customers. Consumer and business marketing channels with even more levels can sometimes be found, but these are uncommon. From the producer's point of view, a greater number of levels means less control and greater channel complexity. Moreover, all the institutions in the channel are connected by several types of *flows*. These include the *physical flow* of products, the *flow of ownership*, the *payment flow*, the *information flow* and the *promotion flow*. These flows can make channels with only one or a few levels very complex.

AUTHOR COMMENT

Channels are composed of more than just boxes and arrows on paper. They are behavioural systems composed of real companies and people who interact to accomplish their individual and collective goals. Like groups of people, sometimes they work well together and sometimes they don't work well together.

CHANNEL BEHAVIOUR AND ORGANISATION

Distribution channels are more than simple collections of firms tied together by various flows. They are complex behavioural systems in which people and companies interact to accomplish individual, company and channel goals. Some channel systems consist of only informal interactions among loosely organised firms. Others consist of formal interactions guided by strong organisational structures. Moreover, channel systems do not stand still – new types of intermediaries emerge, and whole new channel systems evolve. Here we look at channel behaviour and how members organise to do the work of the channel.

Channel behaviour

A marketing channel consists of firms that have partnered for their common good. Each channel member depends on the others. For example, a Ford dealer depends on Ford to design cars that meet customer needs. In turn, Ford depends on the dealer to attract customers, persuade them to buy Ford cars, and service the cars after the sale. Each Ford dealer also depends on other dealers to provide good sales and service that will uphold the brand's reputation. In fact, the success of individual Ford dealers depends on how well the entire Ford marketing channel competes with the channels of other car manufacturers.

Each channel member plays a specialised role in the channel. For example, the role of consumer electronics maker Samsung is to produce electronics products that consumers will like and create demand through national advertising. The retailer's role is to display these Samsung products in convenient locations, answer buyers' questions and complete sales. The channel will be most effective when each member assumes the tasks it can do best.

Ideally, because the success of individual channel members depends on overall channel success, all channel firms should work together smoothly. They should understand and accept their roles, coordinate their activities and cooperate to attain overall channel goals. However, individual channel members rarely take such a broad view. Cooperating to achieve overall channel goals sometimes means giving up individual company goals. Although channel members depend on one another, they often act alone in their own short-term best interests. They often disagree on who should do what and for what rewards. Such disagreements over goals, roles and rewards generate **channel conflict**.

Channel conflict—
Disagreement among marketing channel members on goals, roles and rewards – who should do what and for what rewards.

Horizontal conflict occurs among firms at the same level of the channel. For instance, some Ford dealers in a particular location might complain that other dealers in the same location steal sales from them by pricing too low or advertising outside their assigned territories. Or Holiday Inn franchisees might complain about other Holiday Inn operators overcharging guests or giving poor service, hurting the overall Holiday Inn image.

Vertical conflict, conflicts between different levels of the same channel, is even more common. In recent years, for example, Burger King has had a steady stream of conflicts with its franchised dealers over everything from increased advertising spending and offensive ads to the prices it charges for cheeseburgers. At issue is the chain's right to dictate policies to franchisees.[2]

> The price of a double cheeseburger has generated a lot of heat among Burger King franchisees. In an ongoing dispute in the US, the burger chain insisted that the burger be sold for no more than $1– in line with other items on its 'Value Menu'. Burger King saw the value price as key to competing effectively in the current economic environment. But the company's franchisees claimed that they would lose money at that price. To resolve the dispute, angry franchisees filed a lawsuit (only one of several over the years) asserting that Burger King's franchise agreements don't allow it to dictate prices. (The company had won a separate case in 2008 requiring franchisees to offer the Value Menu, which is core to its efforts to attract price-conscious consumers.) After months of public wrangling, Burger King finally let franchisees have it their way. It introduced a $1 double-patty burger with just one slice of cheese, instead of two, cutting the cost of ingredients. The regular quarter-pound double cheeseburger with two pieces of cheese remained on the Value Menu but was priced at $1.19.

Some conflict in the channel takes the form of healthy competition. Such competition can be good for the channel – without it, the channel could become passive and non-innovative. For example, Burger King's conflict with its franchisees might represent normal give-and-take over the respective rights of the channel partners. But severe or prolonged conflict can disrupt channel effectiveness and cause lasting harm to channel relationships. Burger King should manage the channel conflict carefully to keep it from getting out of hand.

Vertical marketing systems

For the channel as a whole to perform well, each channel member's role must be specified, and channel conflict must be managed. The channel will perform better if it includes a firm, agency or mechanism that provides leadership and has the power to assign roles and manage conflict.

Historically, *conventional distribution channels* have lacked such leadership and power, often resulting in damaging conflict and poor performance. One of the biggest channel developments over the years, particularly in the huge US market, has been the emergence of *vertical marketing systems* that provide channel leadership. Figure 12.3 contrasts the two types of channel arrangements.

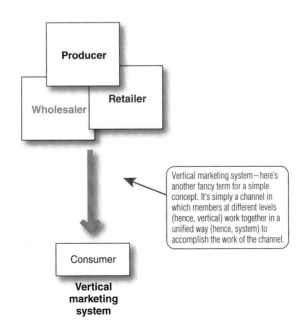

Figure 12.3 Comparison of conventional distribution channel with vertical marketing system

Vertical marketing system—here's another fancy term for a simple concept. It's simply a channel in which members at different levels (hence, vertical) work together in a unified way (hence, system) to accomplish the work of the channel.

Conventional marketing channel

Vertical marketing system

Conventional distribution channel—A channel consisting of one or more independent producers, wholesalers and retailers, each a separate business seeking to maximise its own profits, even at the expense of profits for the system as a whole.

Luxottica sells many famous eyewear brands through its owned store chains.

Source: Getty Images/Rebecca Sapp

Vertical marketing system (VMS)—A distribution channel structure in which producers, wholesalers and retailers act as a unified system. One channel member owns the others, has contracts with them, or wields so much power that they all cooperate.

Corporate VMS—A vertical marketing system that combines successive stages of production and distribution under single ownership – channel leadership is established through common ownership.

Contractual VMS—A vertical marketing system in which independent firms at different levels of production and distribution join together through contracts.

Franchise organisation— A contractual vertical marketing system in which a channel member, called a franchisor, links several stages in the production-distribution process.

A **conventional distribution channel** consists of one or more independent producers, wholesalers and retailers. Each is a separate business seeking to maximise its own profits, perhaps even at the expense of the system as a whole. No channel member has much control over the other members, and no formal means exists for assigning roles and resolving channel conflict.

In contrast, a **vertical marketing system (VMS)** consists of producers, wholesalers and retailers acting as a unified system. One channel member owns the others, has contracts with them, or wields so much power that they must all cooperate. The VMS can be dominated by the producer, the wholesaler or the retailer.

We look now at three major types of VMSs: *corporate*, *contractual* and *administered*. Each uses a different means for setting up leadership and power in the channel.

Corporate VMS

A **corporate VMS** integrates successive stages of production and distribution under single ownership. Coordination and conflict management are attained through regular organisational channels. For example, little-known Italian eyewear maker Luxottica produces many famous eyewear brands – including its own Ray-Ban and Oakley brands and licensed brands such as Burberry, Chanel, Polo Ralph Lauren, Dolce & Gabbana, Donna Karan, Prada, Versace and Bulgari. It then sells these brands through some of the world's largest optical chains – LensCrafters, Pearle Vision and Sunglass Hut – that it also owns.[3] As we saw at the beginning of the chapter, controlling the entire distribution chain has turned Spanish clothing chain Zara into the world's fastest-growing fashion retailer.

Contractual VMS

A **contractual VMS** consists of independent firms at different levels of production and distribution who join together through contracts to obtain more economies or sales impact than each could achieve alone. Channel members coordinate their activities and manage conflict through contractual agreements.

The **franchise organisation** is the most common type of contractual relationship. A channel member called a *franchisor* links several stages in the production-distribution process. In Europe, even though American brands are still hugely popular, many franchises originating in European countries have also become big names across the continent and beyond. Some of the most successful European franchises include: Tecnocasa, an Italian estate agency franchise founded in 1980, that has 3,760 units in eight countries; Jean Louis David, a French health & beauty company established in 1960, which now has 1,200 units in nine countries; Foto Quelle, a German franchise focused on framing for photos and art, which was started in 1957 and has 1,000 units in four countries; and, Fornetti, a food distribution business from Hungary, that began franchising in 1997 and has grown to 655 units in six countries.

A 2005 survey by the European Franchise Federation (www.eff-franchise.com) found that there are 6,500 distinct franchised brands operating in different countries including: Austria, Belgium, the Czech Republic, Denmark, Finland, France, Germany, Greece, Hungary, Italy, the Netherlands, Portugal, Slovenia, Spain, Sweden, Switzerland, Poland and Russia. A survey conducted by the International Franchise Association in the 2000s indicated that franchise brands accounted for 56 per cent of quick service restaurants, 18 per cent of lodging establishments, 14 per cent of retail food businesses and 13 per cent of table/full service restaurants. Franchises employed almost 10 million people, with direct output close to $625 billion and a payroll of $230 billion.[4] Almost every kind of business has been franchised – from hotels and fast-food restaurants to dental centres and dating services, from wedding consultants and cleaning services to fitness centres and funeral homes.

There are three types of franchises. The first type is the *manufacturer-sponsored retailer franchise system*. Ford and its network of independent franchised dealers is an example of a manufacturer-sponsored system. The second type is the *manufacturer-sponsored wholesaler franchise system*. For example, Coca-Cola licenses bottlers (wholesalers) in various markets who buy Coca-Cola syrup concentrate and then bottle and sell the finished product to retailers in local markets. The third type is the *service-firm-sponsored retailer franchise system*. Burger King and its nearly 10,500 franchisee-operated restaurants around the world is an example of a service-firm-sponsored system. Other examples can be found in everything from car rentals (e.g. Hertz and Avis), clothing retailers (e.g. The Athlete's Foot and Laura Ashley) and hotels (e.g. Holiday Inn and Ramada Inn) to estate agencies (e.g. Century 21) and personal services (e.g. Mr Handyman and Molly Maid).

The fact that most consumers cannot tell the difference between contractual and corporate VMSs shows how successfully the contractual organisations compete with corporate chains. Chapter 13 presents a fuller discussion of the various contractual VMSs.

Administered VMS

In an **administered VMS**, leadership is assumed not through common ownership or contractual ties but through the size and power of one or a few dominant channel members. Manufacturers of a top brand can obtain strong trade cooperation and support from resellers. For example, GE, P&G and Kraft can command unusual cooperation from resellers regarding displays, shelf space, promotions and price policies. In turn, large retailers such as Walmart, Carrefour, Metro and Tesco can exert strong influence on the many manufacturers that supply the products they sell.

Administered VMS—A vertical marketing system that coordinates successive stages of production and distribution, through the size and power of one of the parties.

Horizontal marketing systems

Another channel development is the **horizontal marketing system**, in which two or more companies at one level join together to follow a new marketing opportunity. By working together, companies can combine their financial, production or marketing resources to accomplish more than any one company could alone.

Horizontal marketing system—A channel arrangement in which two or more companies at one level join together to follow a new marketing opportunity.

Companies might join forces with competitors or non-competitors. They might work with each other on a temporary or a permanent basis, or they may create a separate company. For example, Domino's Pizza is trialling take-away pizza units in Tesco stores in the UK. The aim is that Domino's benefits from Tesco's heavy store traffic, and Tesco keeps hungry shoppers happy.

Competitors Microsoft and Yahoo! joined forces to create a horizontal Internet search alliance. For the next decade, Microsoft's Bing will be the search engine on Yahoo! websites, serving up the same search results listings available directly through Bing. In turn, Yahoo! will focus on creating a richer search experience by integrating strong Yahoo! content and providing tools to tailor the Yahoo! user experience. Although they haven't been able to do it individually, together Microsoft and Yahoo! might yet become a strong challenger to search leader Google.[5]

Multichannel distribution systems

In the past, many companies used a single channel to sell to a single market or market segment. Today, with the proliferation of customer segments and channel possibilities, more and more companies have adopted **multi-channel distribution systems**. Such multi-channel marketing occurs when a single firm sets up two or more marketing channels to reach one or more customer segments. The use of multi-channel systems has increased greatly in recent years.

Multi-channel distribution system—A distribution system in which a single firm sets up two or more marketing channels to reach one or more customer segments.

Figure 12.4 shows a multi-channel marketing system. In the figure, the producer sells directly to consumer segment 1 using catalogues, telemarketing and the Internet, and reaches consumer segment 2 through retailers. It sells indirectly to business segment 1 through distributors and dealers and to business segment 2 through its own sales force.

These days, almost every large company and many small ones distribute through multiple channels. For example, Dell Inc. built its worldwide business around a direct business model – selling direct from the Web to corporate customers and consumers. However, changing competitive conditions and market requirements have driven Dell to use multiple channels as well as the direct model. The first step in building an indirect channel network was a deal in 2007 to sell

Figure 12.4 Multi-channel distribution system

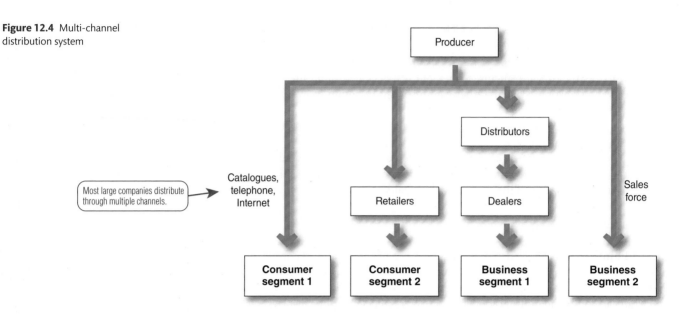

Dell computers in Walmart in the US, through Carphone Warehouse and Tesco in the UK, Bic Camera outlets in Japan and Carrefour in Europe, with plans for its own retail stores in Budapest and Moscow. Dell now operates a small number of retail stores but also hundreds of kiosks in shopping malls in the US. At the same time, Dell began to retail through stores in Mexico, and to sell to much of the rest of Latin America through travelling shows. In China, Dell's products are sold through Gome, the Chinese electronics retailer, to meet the requirements of a market where a high value is placed on face-to-face contact in commercial transactions. The goal of Dell's retail strategy is to tap into a pool of new customers less comfortable with making such a life style purchase over the telephone or Internet, where they do not have the same opportunity to see and feel the machine before making a purchase. Dell has been pushed towards multichannel distribution through competitive necessity.[6]

Multi-channel distribution systems offer many advantages to companies facing large and complex markets. With each new channel, the company expands its sales and market coverage and gains opportunities to tailor its products and services to the specific needs of diverse customer segments. But such multi-channel systems are harder to control, and they generate conflict as more channels compete for customers and sales. For example, in moving from a direct model to a multi-channel distribution approach, Dell faces the challenge of managing the competing demands of third-party computer resellers, independent retailers and its own retail operations, and balancing those demands with its direct selling and Internet operation.

Complex channels bring additional risks of conflict. For example, in 2012, major book retailer Barnes & Noble and others refused to stock books from the publishing arm of the online retailer Amazon. The move was retaliation for Amazon's aggressive moves to gain a foothold in publishing, and particularly the online company's push to sign exclusive deals with authors that prevent other retailers selling digital versions of their books. In reality, Amazon's push into publishing is an attempt to cut out the intermediaries between producers and consumers, i.e. other book stores, so conflict is perhaps inevitable.[7]

Changing channel organisation

Disintermediation—The cutting out of marketing channel intermediaries by product or service producers or the displacement of traditional resellers by radical new types of intermediaries.

Changes in technology and the explosive growth of direct and online marketing are having a profound impact on the nature and design of marketing channels. One major trend is toward **disintermediation** – a big term with a clear message and important consequences. Disintermediation occurs when product or service producers cut out intermediaries and go directly to final buyers or when radically new types of channel intermediaries displace traditional ones.

Thus, in many industries, traditional intermediaries are dropping by the wayside. For example, no-frills airlines like Ryanair in Europe and Southwest Airlines and JetBlue in the US, sell their tickets direct to final buyers, cutting travel agents from their marketing channels altogether. In other cases, new forms of resellers are displacing traditional intermediaries. For example, online marketers have taken business from traditional brick-and-mortar retailers. Consumers can buy hotel rooms and airline tickets from Expedia.com and Travelocity.com; electronics from Sonystyle.com; clothes and accessories from Asos.com; and books, videos, toys, jewellery, sports, consumer electronics, home and garden items, and almost anything else from Amazon.com – all without ever stepping into a traditional retail store. Online music download services such as iTunes and Amazon.com are threatening the existence of traditional music-store retailers. In fact, many once-dominant music retailers such as Tower Records have declared bankruptcy and closed their doors for good.

Disintermediation presents both opportunities and problems for producers and resellers. Channel innovators who find new ways to add value in the channel can sweep aside traditional resellers and reap the rewards. In turn, traditional intermediaries must continue to innovate to avoid being swept aside. For example, when Netflix pioneered online video rentals, it sent traditional brick-and-mortar video stores such as Blockbuster reeling. To meet the threat, Blockbuster developed its own online DVD rental service. Now, both Netflix and Blockbuster face disintermediation threats from an even hotter channel – digital video downloads and video on demand. But instead of simply watching digital video distribution developments, Netflix intends to lead them:[8]

> Netflix has already added a 'Watch Instantly' feature to its website that allows subscribers to instantly stream near-DVD quality video for a growing list of movie titles and TV programmes. And it recently announced that it will soon let users stream movies to selected mobile phones. 'Our intention,' says Netflix founder and CEO Reed Hastings, 'is to get [our Watch Instantly] service to every Internet-connected screen, from cell phones to laptops to Wi-Fi-enabled plasma screens.' In this way, Netflix plans to disintermediate its own distribution model before others can do it. To Hastings, the key to the future is all in how Netflix defines itself. 'If [you] think of Netflix as a DVD rental business, [you are] right to be scared,' he says. But 'if [you] think of Netflix as an online movie service with multiple different delivery models, then [you are] a lot less scared. We're only now starting to deliver that second vision.'

Fender's online marketing provides information about its guitars and amps but then refers customers to resellers' websites and stores.

Source: Alamy Images/Pictorial Press

Similarly, to remain competitive, product and service producers must develop new channel opportunities, such as the Internet and other direct channels. However, developing these new channels often brings them into direct competition with their established channels, resulting in conflict.

To ease this problem, companies often look for ways to make going direct a plus for the entire channel. For example, guitar and amp maker Fender knows that many customers would prefer to buy its guitars, amps and accessories online. But selling directly through its website would create conflicts with retail partners, from large chains stocking the instruments to small shops scattered throughout the world, such as Hollywood Music in Milton Keynes in the UK or Freddy for Music in Amman, Jordan. So Fender's website provides detailed information about the company's products, but you can't buy a new Fender Stratocaster or Acoustasonic guitar there. Instead, the Fender website refers you to resellers' websites and stores. Thus, Fender's direct marketing helps both the company and its channel partners.

AUTHOR COMMENT

Like everything else in marketing, good channel design begins with analysing customer needs. Remember, marketing channels are really *customer-value delivery networks*.

CHANNEL DESIGN DECISIONS

We now look at several channel decisions manufacturers face. In designing marketing channels, manufacturers struggle between what is ideal and what is practical. A new firm with limited capital usually starts by selling in a limited market area. Deciding on the best channels might not be a problem: the problem might simply be how to convince one or a few good intermediaries to handle the line.

If successful, the new firm can branch out to new markets through existing intermediaries. In smaller markets, the firm might sell directly to retailers; in larger markets, it might sell through distributors. In one part of the country, it might grant exclusive franchises; in another, it might sell through all available outlets. Then it might add a Web store that sells directly to hard-to-reach customers. In this way, channel systems often evolve to meet market opportunities and conditions.

For maximum effectiveness, however, channel analysis and decision making should be more purposeful. **Marketing channel design** calls for analysing consumer needs, setting channel objectives, identifying major channel alternatives and evaluating those alternatives.

Marketing channel design— Designing effective marketing channels by analysing customer needs, setting channel objectives, identifying major channel alternatives and evaluating those alternatives.

Analysing consumer needs

As noted previously, marketing channels are part of the overall *customer-value delivery network*. Each channel member and level adds value for the customer. Thus, designing the marketing channel starts with finding out what target consumers want from the channel. Do consumers want to buy from nearby locations or are they willing to travel to more distant and centralised locations? Would customers rather buy in person, by phone, or online? Do they value breadth of product availability or do they prefer specialisation? Do consumers want many add-on services (e.g. delivery, installation and repairs) or will they obtain these services elsewhere? The faster the delivery, the greater the breadth provided, and the more add-on services supplied, the greater the channel's service level.

Providing the fastest delivery, the greatest variety and the most services may not be possible or practical. The company and its channel members may not have the resources or skills needed to provide all the desired services. Also, providing higher levels of service results in higher costs for the channel and higher prices for consumers. For example, your local hardware store probably provides more personalised service, a more convenient location and less shopping hassle than the nearest huge B&Q or OBI store. But it may also charge higher prices. The company must balance consumer needs not only against the feasibility and costs of meeting these needs but also against customer price preferences. The success of discount retailing shows that consumers will often accept lower service levels in exchange for lower prices.

Setting channel objectives

Companies should state their marketing channel objectives in terms of targeted levels of customer service. Usually, a company can identify several segments wanting different levels of service. The company should decide which segments to serve and the best channels to use in each case. In each segment, the company wants to minimise the total channel cost of meeting customer-service requirements.

The company's channel objectives are also influenced by the nature of the company, its products, its marketing intermediaries, its competitors and the environment. For example, the company's size and financial situation determine which marketing functions it can handle itself and which it must give to intermediaries. Companies selling perishable products may require more direct marketing to avoid delays and too much handling.

In some cases, a company may want to compete in or near the same outlets that carry competitors' products. For example, top-of-the market Maytag and Amana want their designer kitchen appliances displayed alongside competing brands to facilitate comparison shopping. In other cases, companies may avoid the channels used by competitors. Avon Cosmetics, for example, sells directly to consumers through its corps of more than six and a half million representatives worldwide, and has generally avoided going head-to-head with other cosmetics makers for scarce positions in retail stores.[9] Direct Line primarily markets car and homeowner's insurance directly to consumers via the telephone and the Internet rather than through insurance agents or price comparison websites.

Finally, environmental factors such as economic conditions and legal constraints may affect channel objectives and design. For example, in a depressed economy, producers want to distribute their goods in the most economical way, using shorter channels and dropping unneeded services that add to the final price of the goods.

Identifying major alternatives

When the company has defined its channel objectives, it should next identify its major channel alternatives in terms of the *types* of intermediaries, the *number* of intermediaries and the *responsibilities* of each channel member.

Types of intermediaries

A firm should identify the types of channel members available to carry out its channel work. Most companies face many channel member choices. For example, until recently, Dell sold directly to final consumers and business buyers only through its sophisticated phone and Internet marketing channel. It also sold directly to large corporate, institutional and government buyers using its direct sales force. However, to reach more consumers and match competitors such as HP, Dell now sells indirectly through retailers such as Walmart, Tesco, Carphone Warehouse and Carrefour. It also sells indirectly through value-added resellers, independent distributors and dealers who develop computer systems and applications tailored to the special needs of small and medium-sized business customers.

Using many types of resellers in a channel provides both benefits and drawbacks. For example, by selling through retailers and value-added resellers in addition to its own direct channels, Dell can reach more and different kinds of buyers. However, the new channels will be more difficult to manage and control. And the direct and indirect channels will compete with each other for many of the same customers, causing potential conflict. In fact, Dell often finds itself 'stuck in the middle', with its direct sales reps complaining about competition from retail stores, while its value-added resellers complain that the direct sales reps are undercutting their business.

Number of marketing intermediaries

Companies must also determine the number of channel members to use at each level. Three strategies are available: intensive distribution, exclusive distribution and selective distribution. Producers of convenience products and common raw materials typically seek **intensive distribution** – a strategy in which they stock their products in as many outlets as possible. These products must be available where and when consumers want them. For example, toothpaste, confectionery and other similar items are sold in millions of outlets to provide maximum brand exposure and consumer convenience. Many fast-moving consumer goods companies like Kraft, Coca-Cola, Kimberly-Clark and Unilever distribute their products in this way.

By contrast, some producers purposely limit the number of intermediaries handling their products. The extreme form of this practice is **exclusive distribution**, in which the producer gives only a limited number of dealers the exclusive right to distribute its products in their territories. Exclusive distribution is often found in the distribution of luxury brands. For example, exclusive Bentley cars are typically sold by

Intensive distribution—Stocking the product in as many outlets as possible.

Exclusive distribution—Giving a limited number of dealers the exclusive right to distribute the company's products in their territories.

Exclusive Bentley cars are typically sold by only a handful of exclusive dealers.

Source: Bentley Houston

only a handful of authorised dealers in any given market area. By granting exclusive distribution, Bentley gains stronger dealer selling support and more control over dealer prices, promotion and services. Exclusive distribution also enhances the brand's image and allows for higher markups.

Between intensive and exclusive distribution lies **selective distribution** – the use of more than one but fewer than all the intermediaries who are willing to carry a company's products. Most television, furniture and home appliance brands are distributed in this manner. For example, Hotpoint and Dyson sell their major appliances through dealer networks and selected large retailers. By using selective distribution, they can develop good working relationships with selected channel members and expect a better-than-average selling effort. Selective distribution gives producers good market coverage with more control and less cost than does intensive distribution.

Selective distribution—The use of more than one but fewer than all the intermediaries who are willing to carry the company's products.

Responsibilities of channel members

The producer and the intermediaries need to agree on the terms and responsibilities of each channel member. They should agree on price policies, conditions of sale, territory rights and the specific services to be performed by each party. The producer should establish a list price and a fair set of discounts for the intermediaries. It must define each channel member's territory, and it should be careful about where it places new resellers.

Mutual services and duties need to be spelled out carefully, especially in franchise and exclusive distribution channels. For example, McDonald's provides franchisees with promotional support, a record-keeping system, training at Hamburger University and general management assistance. In turn, franchisees must meet company standards for physical facilities and food quality, cooperate with new promotion programmes, provide requested information and buy specified food products.

Evaluating the major alternatives

Suppose a company has identified several channel alternatives and wants to select the one that will best satisfy its long-term objectives. Each alternative should be evaluated against economic, control and adaptability criteria.

Using *economic criteria*, a company compares the likely sales, costs and profitability of different channel alternatives. What will be the investment required by each channel alternative, and what returns will result? The company must also consider *control issues*. Using intermediaries usually means giving them some control over the marketing of the product, and some intermediaries take more control than others. Other things being equal, the company prefers to keep as much control as possible. Finally, the company must apply *adaptability criteria*. Channels often involve long-term commitments, yet the company wants to keep the channel flexible so that it can adapt to environmental changes. Thus, to be considered, a channel involving long-term commitments should be greatly superior on economic and control grounds.

Designing international distribution channels

International marketers face many additional complexities in designing their channels. Each country has its own unique distribution system that has evolved over time and changes very slowly. These channel systems can vary widely from country to country. Thus, global marketers must usually adapt their channel strategies to the existing structures within each country.

In some markets, the distribution system is complex and hard to penetrate, consisting of many layers and large numbers of intermediaries. For example, many western companies find Japan's distribution system difficult to navigate. It's steeped in tradition and very complex, with many distributors touching a product before it makes it to the store shelf.

At the other extreme, distribution systems in developing countries may be scattered, inefficient or altogether lacking. For example, China and India are huge markets – each with a population of well over one billion people. However, because of inadequate distribution systems, most companies can profitably access only a small portion of the population located in each country's most affluent cities. 'China is a very decentralized market,' notes a China trade expert. '[It is] made up of two dozen distinct markets sprawling across 2,000 cities. Each has its own culture. . . . It's like operating in an asteroid belt.' China's distribution system is so fragmented that logistics costs to wrap, bundle, load, unload, sort, reload and transport goods amount to more than 22 per cent of the nation's GDP, far higher than in most other countries. (In the US logistics costs account for just over 10 per cent of the nation's GDP.) After years of effort, global retailers continue to struggle with the challenge of assembling efficient supply chains in China.[10]

Sometimes customs or government regulation can greatly restrict how a company distributes products in global markets. For example, an inefficient distribution structure wasn't the cause of problems for Avon in China; the cause was restrictive government regulation. Fearing the growth of multi-level marketing schemes, the Chinese government banned door-to-door selling altogether in 1998, forcing Avon to abandon its traditional direct marketing approach and sell through retail shops. In 2006, the Chinese government gave Avon and other direct sellers permission to sell door-to-door again, but that permission is tangled in a web of restrictions. Fortunately for Avon, its earlier focus on store sales is helping it weather the restrictions better than most other direct sellers. In fact, through a combination of direct and retail sales, Avon's sales in China are now booming.[11]

Indeed, complications from government policies and local customs affecting marketing and distribution also occur in Europe. For example, in France, the government still regulates the setting of retail prices and sets minimum prices that retailers must pay suppliers. In Germany it took years of debate to eliminate laws that prohibited haggling and put limits on bonus schemes like store-loyalty cards – designed to protect small shopkeepers from large stores. For decades, European retailers could cut prices only during certain periods set by the government and winter sales were in the new year, not at Christmas. In many European countries, the hours stores are open is also regulated by local and central government – even in Britain, one of the most deregulated European states, stores can only open six hours on Sundays. Some retailers in Europe like Galeries Lafayette in Paris and Harrods in London still stick to a full-priced Christmas, on the grounds it makes little sense to discount when people are desperate to buy.[12]

International marketers face a wide range of channel alternatives. Designing efficient and effective channel systems between and within various country markets poses a difficult challenge. We discuss international distribution decisions further in Chapter 19.

Galeries Lafayette in Paris still sticks to a full-priced Christmas, reasoning that it makes little sense to discount when people are desperate to buy.

Source: Alamy Images/David Pearson

AUTHOR COMMENT

Now it's time to implement the chosen channel design and work with selected channel members to manage and motivate them.

CHANNEL MANAGEMENT DECISIONS

Once the company has reviewed its channel alternatives and determined the best channel design, it must implement and manage the chosen channel. **Marketing channel management** calls for selecting, managing and motivating individual channel members and evaluating their performance over time.

Marketing channel management—Selecting managing and motivating individual channel members and evaluating their perfomance over time.

Selecting channel members

Producers vary in their ability to attract qualified marketing intermediaries. Some producers have no trouble signing up channel members. For example, when Toyota first introduced its luxury Lexus line into the United States, it had no trouble attracting new dealers. In fact, it had to turn down many would-be resellers.

At the other extreme are producers who have to work hard to line up enough qualified intermediaries. For example, when Timex first tried to sell its inexpensive watches through regular jewellery stores, most refused to carry them. The company then managed to get its watches into mass-merchandise outlets. This turned out to be a wise decision because of the rapid growth of mass merchandising.

Even established brands may have difficulty gaining and keeping desired distribution, especially when dealing with powerful resellers. Major retailers like Walmart, Tesco, CostCo, Metro and Carrefour are renowned for their tough policies in regularly streamlining product assortments and favouring their own-brands over manufacturer brands.

When selecting intermediaries, the company should determine what characteristics distinguish the better ones. It will want to evaluate each channel member's years in business, other lines carried, growth and profit record, cooperativeness and reputation. If the intermediaries are sales agents, the company will want to evaluate the number and character of other lines carried and the size and quality of the sales force. If the intermediary is a retail store that wants exclusive or selective distribution, the company will want to evaluate the store's customers, location and future growth potential.

Managing and motivating channel members

Once selected, channel members must be continuously managed and motivated to do their best. The company must sell not only *through* the intermediaries but also *to* and *with* them. Most companies see their intermediaries as first-line customers and partners. They practise strong *partner relationship management* (PRM) to forge long-term partnerships with channel members. This creates a value delivery system that meets the needs of both the company *and* its marketing partners.

In managing its channels, a company must convince distributors that they can succeed better by working together as a part of a cohesive value delivery system. Thus, P&G works closely with its major retailer customers across the world to create superior value for final consumers, jointly planning merchandising goals and strategies, stocking levels and advertising and promotion programmes.

Similarly, heavy-equipment manufacturer Caterpillar and its worldwide network of independent dealers work in close harmony to find better ways to bring value to customers.[13]

One-hundred-year-old Caterpillar produces innovative, high-quality products. Yet the most important reason for Caterpillar's dominance is its distribution network of 220 outstanding independent dealers worldwide. Caterpillar and its dealers work as partners. According to a former Caterpillar CEO: 'After the product leaves our door, the dealers take over. They are the ones on the front line. They're the ones who live with the product for its lifetime. They're the ones customers see.' When a big piece of Caterpillar equipment breaks down, customers know that they can count on Caterpillar and its outstanding dealer network for support. Dealers play a vital role in almost every aspect of Caterpillar's operations, from product design and delivery to product service and support.

Caterpillar really knows its dealers and cares about their success. It closely monitors each dealership's sales, market position, service capability and financial situation. When it sees a problem, it jumps in to help. In addition to more formal business ties, Caterpillar forms close personal ties with dealers in a kind of family relationship. Caterpillar and its dealers feel a deep pride in what they are accomplishing together. As the former CEO puts it, 'There's a camaraderie among our dealers around the world that really makes it more than just a financial arrangement. They feel that what they're doing is good for the world because they are part of an organization that makes, sells, and tends to the machines that make the world work.'

As a result of its partnership with dealers, Caterpillar dominates the world's markets for heavy construction, mining and logging equipment. Its familiar yellow tractors, crawlers, loaders, bulldozers and trucks capture some 40 per cent of the worldwide heavy-equipment business, twice that of number-two Komatsu.

Many companies are now installing integrated high-tech PRM systems to coordinate their whole-channel marketing efforts. Just as they use CRM software systems to help manage relationships with important customers, companies can now use PRM and supply chain management (SCM) software to help recruit, train, organise, manage, motivate and evaluate relationships with channel partners.

Evaluating channel members

The company must regularly check channel member performance against standards such as sales quotas, average inventory levels, customer delivery time, treatment of damaged and lost goods, cooperation in company promotion and training programmes, and services to the customer. The company should recognise and reward intermediaries who are performing well and adding good value for consumers. Those who are performing poorly should be assisted or, as a last resort, replaced.

Finally, companies need to be sensitive to their channel partners. Those who treat their partners poorly risk not only losing their support but also causing some legal problems. The next section describes various rights and duties pertaining to companies and other channel members.

PUBLIC POLICY AND DISTRIBUTION DECISIONS

For the most part, companies are legally free to develop whatever channel arrangements suit them. In fact, the laws affecting channels seek to prevent the exclusionary tactics of some companies that might keep another company from using a desired channel. Most legal requirements influencing distribution channels deal with the mutual rights and duties of channel members once they have formed a relationship.

Many producers and wholesalers like to develop exclusive channels for their products. When the seller allows only certain outlets to carry its products, this strategy is called *exclusive distribution*. When the seller requires that these dealers not handle competitors' products, its strategy is called *exclusive dealing*. Both parties can benefit from exclusive arrangements: the seller obtains more loyal and dependable outlets, and the dealers obtain a steady source of supply and stronger seller support. But exclusive arrangements also exclude other producers from selling to these dealers. In most countries, exclusive arrangements are legal as long as they do not substantially lessen competition or tend to create a monopoly and as long as both parties enter into the agreement voluntarily.

Exclusive dealing often includes *exclusive territorial agreements*. The producer may agree not to sell to other dealers in a given area, or the buyer may agree to sell only in its own territory. The first practice is normal under franchise systems as a way to increase dealer enthusiasm and commitment. Usually, this is also perfectly legal; a seller has no legal obligation to sell through more outlets than it wishes. The second practice, whereby the producer tries to keep a dealer from selling outside its territory, may be more likely to conflict with local laws.

Producers of a strong brand sometimes sell it to dealers only if the dealers will take some or all the rest of the line. This is called full-line forcing. Such *tying agreements* are not necessarily illegal, but may be questionable under some countries' legal frameworks if they tend to lessen competition substantially. The practice may prevent consumers from freely choosing among competing suppliers of these other brands.

Finally, producers are free to select their dealers, but their right to terminate dealers is somewhat restricted in some countries. In general, sellers can drop dealers for a justifiable reason. However, they usually cannot drop dealers if, for example, the dealers refuse to cooperate in a doubtful legal arrangement, such as exclusive dealing or tying agreements.

AUTHOR COMMENT
Marketers used to call this plain old 'physical distribution'. But as these titles suggest, the topic has grown in importance, complexity and sophistication.

MARKETING LOGISTICS AND SUPPLY CHAIN MANAGEMENT

In today's global marketplace, selling a product is sometimes easier than getting it to customers. Companies must decide on the best way to store, handle and move their products and services so that they are available to customers in the right variety, at the right time, and in the right place. Logistics effectiveness has a major impact on both customer satisfaction and company costs. Here we consider the nature and importance of logistics management in the supply chain, the goals of the logistics system, major logistics functions and the need for integrated supply chain management.

Nature and importance of marketing logistics

Marketing logistics (physical distribution)—Planning, implementing and controlling the physical flow of materials, final goods and related information from points of origin to points of consumption to meet customer requirements at a profit.

To some managers, marketing logistics means only lorries and warehouses. But modern logistics is much more than this. **Marketing logistics** – also called **physical distribution** – involves planning, implementing and controlling the physical flow of goods, services and related information from points of origin to points of consumption to meet customer requirements at a profit. In short, it involves getting the right product to the right customer in the right place at the right time.

In the past, physical distribution planners typically started with products at the plant and then tried to find low-cost solutions to get them to customers. However, today's marketers prefer *customer-centred* logistics thinking, which starts with the marketplace and works backward to the factory or even to sources of supply. Marketing logistics involves not only *outbound distribution* (moving products from the factory to resellers and ultimately to customers) but also *inbound distribution* (moving products and materials from suppliers to the factory) and *reverse distribution* (moving broken, unwanted or excess products returned by consumers or resellers). That is, it involves entire **supply chain management** – managing upstream and downstream value-added flows of materials, final goods and related information among suppliers, the company, resellers and final consumers, as shown in Figure 12.5.

Supply chain management— Managing upstream and downstream value-added flows of materials, final goods and related information among suppliers, the company, resellers and final consumers.

The logistics manager's task is to coordinate the activities of suppliers, purchasing managers, marketers, channel members and customers. These activities include forecasting, information systems, purchasing, production planning, order processing, inventory, warehousing and transportation planning.

Companies today are placing greater emphasis on logistics for several reasons. First, companies can gain a powerful competitive advantage by using improved logistics to give customers better service or lower prices. Second, improved logistics can yield tremendous cost savings to both a company and its customers. As much as 20 per cent of an average product's price is accounted for by shipping and transport alone. This far exceeds the cost of advertising and many other marketing costs. Even more, as fuel and other costs rise, so do logistics costs. For example, the cost of shipping one 40-foot container from Shanghai to the United States rose from €2,340 in 2000 to more than €6,240 in 2009.[14]

Figure 12.5 Supply chain management

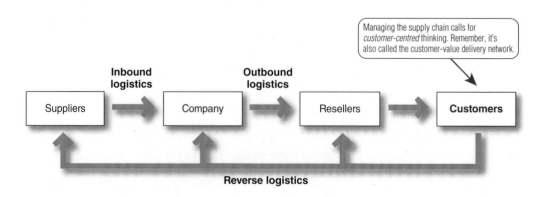

Managing the supply chain calls for *customer-centred* thinking. Remember, it's also called the customer-value delivery network.

Shaving off even a small fraction of logistics costs can mean substantial savings. For example, the world's largest retailer Walmart recently undertook a programme of logistics improvements through more efficient sourcing, better inventory management and greater supply chain productivity that will reduce supply chain costs by 5–15 per cent over the next five years – that's a whopping €3.1 billion to €9.4 billion.[15] Many of the world's top retailers are looking for similar supply chain efficiencies.

Third, the explosion in product variety has created a need for improved logistics management. For example, in 1911 the typical local grocery store carried only about 270 items. The store manager could keep track of this inventory on about 10 pages of notebook paper stuffed in a shirt pocket. Today, the average local store carries a bewildering stock of more than 25,000 items. At the other extreme, superstores run by companies like Tesco, Carrefour, CostCo and Walmart, can carry more than 100,000 products.[16] Ordering, shipping, stocking and controlling such a variety of products presents a sizeable logistics challenge.

Improvements in information technology have also created opportunities for major gains in distribution efficiency. Today's companies are using sophisticated SCM software, Web-based logistics systems, point-of-sale scanners, RFID tags, satellite tracking and electronic transfer of order and payment data. Such technology lets them quickly and efficiently manage the flow of goods, information and finances through the supply chain.

Finally, more than almost any other marketing function, logistics affects the environment and a firm's environmental sustainability efforts. Transportation, warehousing, packaging and other logistics functions are typically the biggest supply chain contributors to the company's environmental footprint. At the same time, they also provide one of the most fertile areas for cost savings. So developing a *green supply chain* is not only environmentally responsible but also profitable. But sustainability is not simply about meeting government goals for environmental protection and lower carbon footprints, says one supply chain expert. 'This is a lot about money, about reducing costs.'[17]

Goals of the logistics system

Some companies state their logistics objective as providing maximum customer service at the least cost. Unfortunately, as nice as this sounds, no logistics system can *both* maximise customer service *and* minimise distribution costs. Maximum customer service implies rapid delivery, large stocks, flexible product variety, liberal returns policies and other services – all of which raise distribution costs. In contrast, minimum distribution costs imply slower delivery, smaller stocks in reserve and larger shipping lots – which represent a lower level of overall customer service.

The goal of marketing logistics should be to provide a *targeted* level of customer service at the least cost. A company must first research the importance of various distribution services to customers and then set desired service levels for each segment. The objective is to maximise *profits*, not sales. Therefore, the company must weigh the benefits of providing higher levels of service against the costs. Some companies offer less service than their competitors and charge a lower price. Other companies offer more service and charge higher prices to cover higher costs.

Major logistics functions

Given a set of logistics objectives, the company is ready to design a logistics system that will minimise the cost of attaining these objectives. The major logistics functions include *warehousing, stock management, transportation* and *logistics information management.*

Warehousing

Production and consumption cycles rarely match, so most companies must store their goods while they wait to be sold. For example, manufacturers producing products such as lawn mowers with seasonal demand are likely to want to run their factories all year long and so need to store up products for the heavy spring and summer buying seasons. The storage function overcomes differences in needed quantities and timing, ensuring that products are available when customers are ready to buy them.

A company must decide on *how many* and *what types* of warehouses it needs and *where* they will be located. The company might use either *storage warehouses* or *distribution centres*. Storage warehouses store goods for moderate to long periods. **Distribution centres** are designed to move goods rather than just store them. They are large and highly automated warehouses designed to receive goods from various plants and suppliers, take orders, fill them efficiently and deliver goods to customers as quickly as possible.

For example, Amazon.com is the world's most successful Internet business platform, but obviously still faces the physical challenge of getting products to customers. For this reason, Amazon's business is supported by a group of huge, highly automated fulfilment centres operating in the US, Europe and Asia, supported by a network of smaller distribution centres. For example, at Marston Gate, Milton Keynes in the UK, Amazon's fulfilment centre is half a mile long and stocks everything from cuddly toys to saucepans. At peak times such as holidays, thousands of casual workers pick and pack customer orders. Amazon places considerable emphasis on environmental impact – recycling packaging, avoiding packaging waste, reducing transport and energy saving – in its distribution network.

Like almost everything else these days, warehousing has seen dramatic changes in technology in recent years. Outdated materials-handling methods are steadily being replaced by newer, computer-controlled systems requiring few employees. Computers and scanners read orders and direct fork-lift trucks, electric hoists or robots to gather goods, move them to loading docks and issue invoices. For example, in the US, office supplies retailer Staples now employs 'a team of super-retrievers – in day-glo orange – that keep its warehouse humming'.[18]

For example, in Chambersburg, Pennsylvania in the US, every day, Staples' huge distribution centre receives thousands of customer orders, each requesting a wide assortment of office supply items. Clearly, having human beings running around a warehouse looking for those items is expensive and slow, especially when Staples has promised to delight customers by delivering orders the next day. However, robotics is dramatically changing the way Staples delivers notepads, pens and paper clips to its customers. On the distribution centre floor, 150 robots are working. When the customer orders arrive, a centralised computer tells the robots where to find racks with the appropriate items. The robots find the products and carry them to picking stations, then wait patiently as humans pull the correct products and place them in boxes. When orders are filled, the robots neatly park the racks back among the rest. When they run low on power, the robots head off to battery-charging terminals. The robots now run 50 per cent of Staples' Chambersburg distribution centre, where average daily output is up 60 per cent since they arrived on the scene.

Stock management

The management of stock also affects customer satisfaction. Here, managers must maintain the delicate balance between carrying too little stock and carrying too much. With too little stock, the firm risks not having products when customers want to buy. To remedy this, the firm may need costly emergency shipments or production. Carrying too much stock results in higher-than-necessary stock-carrying costs and stock obsolescence. Thus, in managing stock levels, firms must balance the costs of carrying larger stocks against resulting sales and profits.

Many companies have greatly reduced their stock levels and related costs through *just-in-time* logistics systems. With such systems, producers and retailers carry only small stocks of parts or merchandise, often enough for only a few days of operations. New stock arrives exactly when needed, rather than being stored until being used. Just-in-time systems require accurate forecasting along with fast, frequent and flexible delivery so that new supplies will be available when needed. However, these systems result in substantial savings in stock-carrying and handling costs.

Marketers are always looking for new ways to make stock management more efficient. In the not-too-distant future, handling stock might even become fully automated. For example, in Chapter 3 we discussed RFID or 'smart tag' technology, by which small transmitter chips are embedded in or

Distribution centre—A large, highly automated warehouse designed to receive goods from various plants and suppliers, take orders, fill them efficiently and deliver goods to customers as quickly as possible.

placed on products and packaging on everything from flowers and razors to tyres. 'Smart' products could make the entire supply chain – which often accounts for as much as 75 per cent of a product's cost – intelligent and automated.

Companies using RFID would know, at any time, exactly where a product is located physically within the supply chain. 'Smart shelves' would not only tell them when it's time to reorder but also place the order automatically with their suppliers. Such exciting new information technology applications will revolutionise distribution as we know it. Many large and resourceful marketing companies, such as Tesco, P&G, Kraft, IBM, HP and major retail groups, are investing heavily to make the full use of RFID technology a reality.[19]

Transportation

The choice of transportation carriers affects the pricing of products, delivery performance and the condition of goods when they arrive – all of which will affect customer satisfaction. In shipping goods to its warehouses, dealers and customers, depending on the country in question, the company can choose among five main transportation modes: road, rail, water, pipeline and air, along with an alternative mode for digital products – the Internet.

Across the European Union countries, road transport dominates the inland freight market, accounting for 78 per cent of all freight. Rail transport comprises around 7 per cent of freighting, while 5–6 per cent is carried by inland waterways. International freighting out of Europe in 2010 involved 14.2 million tonnes of air freight and 3,445 million tonnes of seaborne freight.[20]

Road transport has generally increased its share of transportation steadily, in spite of the controversial environmental impact associated with this mode of freighting. Lorries are highly flexible in their routing and time schedules, and they can usually offer faster service than railways. They are efficient for short hauls of high-value merchandise. Trucking firms have evolved in recent years to become full-service providers of global transportation services. For example, large trucking firms now offer everything from satellite tracking, Web-based shipment management and logistics planning software to cross-border shipping operations.

Railways are one of the most cost-effective modes for shipping large amounts of bulk products – coal, sand, minerals and farm and forest products – over long distances. In recent years, railways have increased their customer services by designing new equipment to handle special categories of goods, and providing in-transit services such as the diversion of shipped goods to other destinations en route and the processing of goods en route.

Waterways can transport large amounts of goods by ships and barges. Although the cost of water transportation is very low for shipping bulky, low-value, non-perishable products such as sand, coal, grain, oil and metallic ores, water transportation is the slowest mode and may be affected by the weather. *Pipelines* are a specialised means of shipping petroleum, natural gas and chemicals from sources to markets. Most pipelines are used by their owners to ship their own products.

Although *air* carriers transport a small proportion of all goods, they are an important transportation mode. Airfreight rates are much higher than railway or road rates, but airfreight is ideal when speed is needed or distant markets have to be reached. Among the most frequently airfreighted products are perishables (e.g. fresh fish and cut flowers) and high-value, low-bulk items (e.g. technical instruments and jewellery). Companies find that airfreight also reduces stock levels, packaging costs and the number of warehouses needed.

The *Internet* carries digital products from producer to customer via satellite, cable or phone wire. Software firms, the media, music and video companies, and education all make use of the Internet to transport digital products. Although these firms primarily use traditional transportation to distribute DVDs, newspapers and more, the Internet holds the potential for lower product distribution costs. Whereas planes, trucks and trains move freight and packages, digital technology moves information bits.

Road transport has generally increased its share of transportation, in spite of the controversial environmental impact.

Source: Alamy Images/Justin Kase

Intermodal transportation—
Combining two or more modes
of transportation.

Shippers also use **intermodal transportation** – combining two or more modes of transportation. *Piggyback* can describe the use of rail and trucks; *fishyback* usually refers to water and trucks; *trainship* denotes water and rail; and *airtruck* refers to air and trucks. Combining modes provides advantages that no single mode can deliver. Each combination offers advantages to the shipper. For example, not only is it combining modes of transport often cheaper than one form of transport on its own but it may also provide greater flexibility and convenience.

In choosing a transportation mode for a product, shippers must balance many considerations: speed, dependability, availability, cost and others. Thus, if a shipper needs speed, air and road are the prime choices. If the goal is low cost, then water or rail might be best. The environmental impact of the transportation mode chosen is a growing concern because of the impact on customer perceptions of companies and their products.

Logistics information management

Companies manage their supply chains through information. Channel partners often link up to share information and make better joint logistics decisions. From a logistics perspective, flows of information, such as customer transactions, billing, shipment and stock levels, and even customer data, are closely linked to channel performance. Companies need simple, accessible, fast and accurate processes for capturing, processing and sharing channel information.

Information can be shared and managed in many ways, but most sharing takes place through traditional or Internet-based *electronic data interchange* (EDI), the computerised exchange of data between organisations, which primarily is transmitted via the Internet. Major retailers such as Tesco and Carrefour in Europe and Walmart in the US, for example, require EDI links with their suppliers. If new suppliers don't have EDI capability, the retailers will work with the supplier to find and implement the needed software. 'EDI has proven to be the most efficient way of conducting business with our product suppliers,' says Walmart. 'This system of exchanging information . . . allows us to improve customer service, lower expenses, and increase productivity.'[21]

In some cases, suppliers might actually be asked to generate orders and arrange deliveries for their customers. Many large retailers – such as Tesco, Carrefour and B&Q – work closely with major suppliers such as P&G or Black & Decker to set up *vendor-managed inventory* (VMI) systems or *continuous inventory replenishment* systems. Using VMI, the customer shares real-time data on sales and current stock levels with the supplier. The supplier then takes full responsibility for managing stocks and deliveries. Some retailers even go so far as to shift stocking and delivery costs to the supplier. Such systems require close cooperation between the buyer and seller.

Integrated logistics management

Integrated logistics
management—The logistics
concept that emphasises teamwork - both inside the company
and among all the marketing
channel organisations – to
maximise the performance of
the entire distribution system.

Today, more and more companies are adopting the concept of **integrated logistics management**. This concept recognises that providing better customer service and trimming distribution costs require *teamwork*, both inside the company and among all the marketing channel organisations. Inside, the company's various departments must work closely together to maximise its own logistics performance. Outside, the company must integrate its logistics system with those of its suppliers and customers to maximise the performance of the entire distribution network.

Cross-functional teamwork inside the company

Most companies assign responsibility for various logistics activities to many different departments – marketing, sales, finance, operations and purchasing. Too often, each function tries to optimise its own logistics performance without regard for the activities of the other functions. However, transportation, stockholding, warehousing and information management activities interact, often in an inverse way. Lower stock levels reduce stock-carrying costs. But they may also reduce customer service and increase costs from stock-outs, back orders, special production runs and costly fast-freight shipments. Because distribution activities involve strong trade-offs, decisions by different functions must be coordinated to achieve better overall logistics performance.

The goal of integrated SCM is to harmonise all of the company's logistics decisions. Close working relationships among departments can be achieved in several ways. Some companies have created permanent logistics committees composed of managers responsible for different physical distribution activities. Companies can also create supply chain manager positions that link the logistics activities of functional areas. For example, P&G has created product supply managers who manage all the supply chain activities for each product category. Many companies have a director of logistics with cross-functional authority.

Finally, companies can employ sophisticated, system-wide SCM software, now available from a wide range of software enterprises large and small, from SAP and Oracle to Infor and Logility. The worldwide market for SCM software topped €5 billion in 2009 and will reach an estimated €9 billion by 2013.[22] The important thing is that the company must coordinate its logistics and marketing activities to create high market satisfaction at a reasonable cost.

Building logistics partnerships

Companies must do more than improve their own logistics. They must also work with other channel partners to improve whole-channel distribution. The members of a marketing channel are linked closely in creating customer value and building customer relationships. One company's distribution system is another company's supply system. The success of each channel member depends on the performance of the entire supply chain. For example, Ikea can create its stylish but affordable furniture and deliver the 'Ikea lifestyle' only if its entire supply chain – consisting of thousands of merchandise designers and suppliers, transport companies, warehouses and service providers – operates at maximum efficiency and customer-focused effectiveness.

Smart companies coordinate their logistics strategies and forge strong partnerships with suppliers and customers to improve customer service and reduce channel costs. Many companies have created *cross-functional, cross-company teams*. For example, P&G has a team of more than 200 people working in Bentonville, Arkansas, home of Walmart. The P&G personnel work jointly with their counterparts at Walmart to find ways to squeeze costs out of their distribution system. Working together benefits not only P&G and Walmart but also their shared, final consumers.

Other companies partner through *shared projects*. For example, many large retailers conduct joint in-store programmes with suppliers, in some cases allowing key suppliers to use their stores as a testing ground for new merchandising programmes. The suppliers can spend time in stores watching how their product sells and how customers relate to it. They then create programmes specially tailored to the retailer and its customers. Clearly, both the supplier and the customer can benefit from such partnerships. The point is that all supply chain members must work together in the cause of bringing value to final consumers.

Third-party logistics

Most big companies love to make and sell their products. But many loathe the associated logistics 'grunt work'. They detest the bundling, loading, unloading, sorting, storing, reloading, transporting, customs clearing and tracking required to supply their factories and get products to their customers. They hate it so much that a growing number of firms now outsource some or all of their logistics to **third-party logistics (3PL) providers**. Consider the following example of Whirlpool Corporation in the US which is the world's largest home appliance manufacturer:[23]

> Whirlpool's ultimate goal is to create loyal customers who continue to buy its brands over their lifetimes. One key loyalty factor is good repair service, which in turn depends on fast and reliable parts distribution. Only a few years ago, however, Whirlpool's replacement parts distribution

Third-party logistics (3PL) provider— An independent logistics provider that performs any or all of the functions required to get a client's product to market.

system was fragmented and ineffective, often causing frustrating customer service delays. 'Whirlpool is the world's largest manufacturer and marketer of appliances, but we're not necessarily experts in parts warehousing and distribution,' says Whirlpool's national director of parts operations. So to help fix the problem, Whirlpool turned the entire job over to 3PL provider Ryder, which quickly streamlined Whirlpool's service parts distribution system. Ryder now provides order fulfillment and worldwide distribution of Whirlpool's service parts across six continents to hundreds of customers that include, in addition to end consumers, the Sears service network, authorised repair centers and independent parts distributors that in turn ship parts out to a network of service companies and technicians. 'Through our partnership with Ryder, we are now operating at our highest service level ever,' says the Whirlpool executive. 'We've . . . dramatically reduced [our parts distribution] costs. Our order cycle time has improved, and our customers are getting their parts more quickly.'

A group of around 25 third-party logistics providers (3PLs) increasingly dominate logistics outsourcing around the world, as they have taken on an increasingly important role for multinational manufacturers and retailers. Manufacturers need absolutely reliable sources of supply. Retailers need flexible links to suppliers with low-cost production. But these suppliers are often in remote regions. At the same time, retailers need rapid delivery channels for an ever-expanding distribution network of consumers. These global 3PLs provide transportation, consolidation, forwarding and customs brokerage, warehousing, fulfilment, distribution and virtually any logistics and trade-related services that their international customers need. On the list of leading global 3PLs, UK-based Exel holds the top spot on the list with revenues of €6.5 billion. The number two and three spots go to Swiss-based Kuehne & Nagel and German-based

Third party logistics providers (3 PLs) increasingly dominate logistics outsourcing around the world.

Schenker. These two companies, along with Panalpina and DHL's Danzas Air & Ocean operations, have been leading forwarders and transportation management 3PLs in Europe for several decades.[24]

Companies use 3PL providers for several reasons. First, because getting the product to market is their main focus, these providers can often do it more efficiently and at lower cost. Outsourcing typically results in cost savings of 15–30 per cent. Second, outsourcing logistics frees a company to focus more intensely on its core business. Finally, integrated logistics companies understand increasingly complex logistics environments.

3PL partners can be especially helpful to companies attempting to expand their global market coverage. For example, companies distributing their products across Europe face a bewildering array of environmental restrictions that affect logistics, including packaging standards, truck size and weight limits, and noise and emissions pollution controls. By outsourcing its logistics, a company can gain a complete pan-European distribution system without incurring the costs, delays and risks associated with setting up its own system.

REVIEWING OBJECTIVES AND KEY TERMS

Some companies pay too little attention to their distribution channels, but others have used imaginative distribution systems to gain competitive advantage. A company's channel decisions directly affect every other marketing decision. Management must make channel decisions carefully, incorporating today's needs with tomorrow's likely selling environment.

OBJECTIVE 1 Explain why companies use marketing channels and discuss the functions these channels perform (pp. 354–358).

In creating customer value, a company can't go it alone. It must work within an entire network of partners – a value delivery network – to accomplish this task. Individual companies and brands don't compete; their entire value delivery networks compete.

Most producers use intermediaries to bring their products to market. They forge a *marketing channel* (or *distribution channel*) – a set of interdependent organisations involved in the process of making a product or service available for use or consumption by the consumer or business user. Through their contacts, experience, specialisation and scale of operation, intermediaries usually offer the firm more than it can achieve on its own.

Marketing channels perform many key functions. Some help *complete* transactions by gathering and distributing *information* needed for planning and aiding exchange, developing and spreading persuasive *communications* about an offer, performing *contact* work (finding and communicating with prospective

buyers), *matching* (shaping and fitting the offer to the buyer's needs) and entering into *negotiation* to reach an agreement on price and other terms of the offer so that ownership can be transferred. Other functions help to *fulfill* the completed transactions by offering *physical distribution* (transporting and storing goods), *financing* (acquiring and using funds to cover the costs of the channel work) and *risk taking* (assuming the risks of carrying out the channel work).

OBJECTIVE 2 Discuss how channel members interact and how they organise to perform the work of the channel (pp. 358–363).

The channel will be most effective when each member assumes the tasks it can do best. Ideally, because the success of individual channel members depends on overall channel success, all channel firms should work together smoothly. They should understand and accept their roles, coordinate their goals and activities, and cooperate to attain overall channel goals. By cooperating, they can more effectively sense, serve and satisfy the target market.

In a large company, the formal organisation structure assigns roles and provides needed leadership. But in a distribution channel composed of independent firms, leadership and power are not formally set. Traditionally, distribution channels have lacked the leadership needed to assign roles and manage conflict. In recent years, however, new types of channel organisations have appeared that provide stronger leadership and improved performance.

OBJECTIVE 3 Identify the major channel alternatives open to a company (pp. 364–367).

Channel alternatives vary from direct selling to using one, two, three or more intermediary *channel levels*. Marketing channels face continuous and sometimes dramatic change. Three of the most important trends are the growth of *vertical, horizontal* and *multichannel marketing systems*. These trends affect channel cooperation, conflict and competition.

Channel design begins with assessing customer channel service needs and company channel objectives and constraints. The company then identifies the major channel alternatives in terms of the *types* of intermediaries, the *number* of intermediaries and the *channel responsibilities* of each. Each channel alternative must be evaluated according to economic, control and adaptive criteria. *Channel management* calls for selecting qualified intermediaries and motivating them. Individual channel members must be evaluated regularly.

OBJECTIVE 4 Explain how companies select, motivate and evaluate channel members (pp. 367–369).

Producers vary in their ability to attract qualified marketing intermediaries. Some producers have no trouble signing up channel members. Others have to work hard to line up enough qualified intermediaries. When selecting intermediaries, the company should evaluate each channel member's qualifications and select those that best fit its channel objectives.

Once selected, channel members must be continuously motivated to do their best. The company must sell not only *through* the intermediaries but also *with* them. It should forge strong partnerships with channel members to create a marketing system that meets the needs of both the manufacturer *and* the partners.

OBJECTIVE 5 Discuss the nature and importance of marketing logistics and integrated supply chain management (pp. 370–377).

Marketing logistics (or *physical distribution*) is an area of potentially high cost savings and improved customer satisfaction. Marketing logistics addresses not only *outbound distribution* but also *inbound distribution* and *reverse distribution*. That is, it involves the entire *supply chain management* – managing value-added flows between suppliers, the company, resellers and final users. No logistics system can both maximise customer service and minimise distribution costs. Instead, the goal of logistics management is to provide a *targeted* level of service at the least cost. The major logistics functions include *warehousing, stock management, transportation* and *logistics information management*.

The *integrated supply chain management concept* recognises that improved logistics requires teamwork in the form of close working relationships across functional areas inside the company and across various organizations in the supply chain. Companies can achieve logistics harmony among functions by creating cross-functional logistics teams, integrative supply manager positions and senior-level logistics executives with cross-functional authority. Channel partnerships can take the form of cross-company teams, shared projects and information-sharing systems. Today, some companies are outsourcing their logistics functions to 3PL providers to save costs, increase efficiency and gain faster and more effective access to global markets.

 NAVIGATING THE KEY TERMS

OBJECTIVE 1
Value delivery network (p. 355)
Marketing channel (distribution channel) (p. 355)
Channel level (p. 357)
Direct marketing channel (p. 357)
Indirect marketing channel (p. 358)

OBJECTIVE 2
Channel conflict (p. 358)
Conventional distribution channel (p. 360)
Vertical marketing system (VMS) p. 360)
Corporate VMS p. 360)
Contractual VMS (p. 360)
Franchise organisation (p. 360)
Administered VMS (p. 361)
Horizontal marketing system (p. 361)
Multi-channel distribution system (p. 361)
Disintermediation (p. 362)

OBJECTIVE 3
Marketing channel design (p. 364)
Intensive distribution (p. 365)
Exclusive distribution (p. 365)
Selective distribution (p. 366)

OBJECTIVE 4
Marketing channel management (p. 367)

OBJECTIVE 5
Marketing logistics (physical distribution) (p. 370)
Supply chain management (p. 370)
Distribution centre (p. 372)
Intermodal transportation (p. 374)
Integrated logistics management (p. 374)
Third-party logistics (3PL) provider (p. 375)

DISCUSSING AND APPLYING THE CONCEPTS

Discussing the concepts

1. Describe the key functions performed by marketing channel members. (AACSB: Communication)

2. Compare and contrast direct and indirect marketing channels and discuss the types of *flows* in a distribution channel. (AACSB: Communication)

3. What is franchise organisation? Discuss the types of franchise organisation and give an example of each. (AACSB: Communication; Reflective Thinking)

4. Describe the three strategies available regarding the number of intermediaries and discuss the types of products for which each is appropriate. (AACSB: Communication Reflective Thinking)

5. Discuss the complexities international marketers face when designing channels in other countries. (AACSB: Communication)

6. List and briefly describe the major logistics functions. Give an example of a decision a logistics manager would make for each major function. (AACSB: Communication; Reflective Thinking)

Applying the concepts

1. In a small group, debate whether or not the Internet will result in disintermediation of the following retail stores: (1) video rental stores, (2) music stores, and (3) clothing stores. (AACSB: Communication; Reflective Thinking)

2. Consumer packaged goods manufacturers typically distribute products to retailers through wholesalers. However, Walmart deals directly with manufacturers, many having offices in Bentonville, Arkansas, and catering just to Walmart. Discuss the consequence of manufacturers, such as Kraft and P&G, distributing products directly to one or more large retailers while distributing the same products indirectly to smaller retailers through wholesalers. (AACSB: Communication; Reflective Thinking)

3. Visit www.youtube.com/watch?v=eob532iEpqk and watch the 'The Future Market' video. What impact will RFID tags have on each major logistical function? What are the biggest current obstacles in adopting this technology? (AACSB: Communication; Use of IT; Reflective Thinking)

Focus on technology

Brewing craft beer (real ales or artisan beers often produced in microbreweries) is both an art and a science, and Sonia Collin,

a Belgian researcher, is trying to devise a way for this highly perishable beer to have a longer shelf life. If successful, brewers can ship more beer longer distances. Hoping to boost exports of homegrown products, the Belgian government is investing $7 million for research, with $1.7 million of that allocated to Ms Collin's research. A $250,000 tasting machine in her laboratory identifies the chemical compounds in a sample of beer, which allows researchers to recommend using organic ingredients, adjust the oxygen and yeast levels, and reduce the time the beer is at high temperatures in the brewing process. Although pasteurisation and bottling methods allow giants such as Heineken and Anheuser to export their brews, aficionados prefer the more delicate flavour of craft beers. But craft brews don't travel well – time and sunlight are its worst enemies – so they are limited to local distribution. Most craft beers lose flavour in less than three months.

1. Describe the channel of distribution for a craft beer from Belgium to your city or town. How many channel levels will be involved? (AACSB: Communication; Reflective Thinking)

2. The craft beer movement in the US has seen significant growth in recent years. Discuss the options facing Belgian craft brewers desiring to sell their products in the United States if researchers cannot discover a way to sufficiently extend the shelf life of craft beers. (AACSB: Communication; Reflective Thinking)

Focus on ethics

Tension is escalating between clothing retailers and suppliers during the economic recovery. Retailers previously placed orders almost a year in advance and suppliers produced high volumes cheaply. Now many retailers are placing small initial orders, and if styles take off with consumers, they quickly reorder – a tactic known as 'chasing'. Teen retailer Aeropostale has been buying conservatively and chasing for items that are hot with buyers. Appropriate inventory levels in the clothing industry have always been difficult to predict, but it appears that retailers are pushing this worry back to suppliers.

1. Discuss the concerns of suppliers (i.e garment makers) and clothing retailers in the channel of distribution. Is it fair that retailers should expect suppliers to respond so quickly? Is it fair that suppliers should demand long lead times? (AACSB; Communication; Ethical Reasoning; Reflective Thinking)

2. What type of channel conflict does this represent? Are there any benefits from this conflict? (AACSB: Communication; Reflective Thinking)

Marketing & the economy

Expedia.com

When the travel business takes a hit, so do travel agents. As individuals and businesses have cut back their travel budgets over the past few years, websites in general faced financial difficulties. With Priceline.com returning to its 'name your own price' roots, competition is becoming tougher than ever. Even Expedia, the market leader, has had to drastically reformulate its strategy to survive. To keep customers from bypassing travel sites and booking directly with airlines, Expedia permanently eliminated its $10 booking fee. Most recently, it has engaged in a new branding campaign called 'Where you book matters' which targets frequent leisure travellers and seek to earn their loyalty. Compared to Priceline's singular focus on price, Expedia is aiming higher up on the food chain. It wants to establish itself as the generic place to shop for all things travel, highlighting its full range of services. In a market driven by frugality, this approach might seem risky. But as travel now shows signs of renewed life, Expedia might be turning things around quicker than the rest. Its recent US bookings are up 20 per cent, compared to a 16 per cent increase for Priceline.

1. As an intermediary, does Expedia have power to spur demand when the travel industry suffers?

2. Is Expedia taking the right approach with its branding and promotional strategy?

3. If the economy doesn't recover as quickly as hoped, will Expedia be in good shape?

Marketing by the numbers

Consumers typically buy products such as toiletries, food and clothing from retailers rather than directly from the manufacturer. Likewise, retailers buy from wholesalers. Resellers perform functions for the manufacturer and the consumer and mark up the price to reflect the value. Refer to Appendix 2 and answer the following questions.

1. If a manufacturer sells its laundry detergent to a wholesaler for $2.50, at what price will the wholesaler sell it to a retailer if the wholesaler wants a 15 per cent margin based on the selling price? (AACSB: Communication, Analytical Reasoning)

2. If a retailer wants a 20 per cent margin based on the selling price, at what price will the retailer sell the product to consumers? (AACSB: Communication; Analytical Reasoning)

REFERENCES

[1] Sources: Emaille Marsh, 'Zara Help Lift Inditex 4th-Qtr Net' *WWD*, 18 March 2010, p 11; Cecilie Rohwedder, 'Zara Grows as Retail Rivals Struggle,' *Wall Street Journal*, 26 March 2009, p B1; Kerry Capell, 'Fashion Conquistador', *BusinessWeek*, 4 September 2006, pp. 38–39; Rohwedder, 'Supply Chain May Speed Zara Past Gap as Top Clothing Retailer,' *Globe and Mail*, 26 March 2009, p B12; www.gap.com, accessed April 2010; and information from the Inditex Press Dossier, www. inditex.com/en/press/information/press_kit, accessed October 2010.

[2] Example adapted from Richard Gibson, 'Burger King franchisees can't have it *their* own way', *Wall Street Journal* (21 January 2010), p. B1; with additional information from Emily Bryson York, 'BK swears off sex in ads to quell franchisee freak Out', *Advertising Age* (13 July 2009), p. 1; and York, 'Burger King, franchisees start making Nice', *Advertising Age* (17 February 2010), http://adage.com/article?article_id=142158.

[3] Information accessed at www.luxottica.com/en/company/quick_view, accessed October 2010.

[4] Information accessed at www.franchiseeurope.com/top500/article/europeanfranchisingtrendsanddevelopments/1 and www.eff-franchise.com, accessed (15 February 2012).

[5] Brent Kendall and Scott Morrison, 'regulators clear Microsoft–Yahoo alliance', *Wall Street Journal* (19 February 2010), p. B5.

[6] Kevin Allison and Chris Nuttall, 'Dell to sell computers at Walmart', *Financial Times* (25 May 2007), p. 24; Steve Hamm, 'The back roads to IT growth', *BusinessWeek* (6 August 2007), p. 78; Kevin Allison and Robin Kwong, 'China chapter of Dell's retail adventure opens', *Financial Times* (24 September 2007), p. 24.

[7] Barney Jopson, 'Retailers refuse to sell Amazon books', *Financial Times* (13 February 2012), p. 20.

[8] Quotes and other information from Matthew Boyle, 'Reed Hastings', *Fortune* (28 May 2007), p. 30; 'Nick Wingfield, 'Netflix vs. naysayers', *Wall Street Journal* (27 March 2007), p. B1; Michael V. Copeland, 'Netflix lives!' *Fortune* (28 April 2008), p. 40; Terrence O'Brien, 'Netflix to let users, "Watch Instantly" on Windows Phone 7 series' (15 March 2010), www.switched.com; and www.netflix.com, accessed June 2010.

[9] Andrew Davidson, 'The Avon lady with a calling', *Sunday Times* (17 October 2010), S3, p. 9.

[10] Quotes and information from Normandy Madden, 'Two Chinas', *Advertising Age* (16 August 2004), pp. 1, 22; Russell Flannery, 'China: the slow boat', *Forbes* (12 April 2004), p. 76; Jeff Berman, 'U.S. providers say logistics in China on the right track', *Logistics Management* (March 2007), p. 22; Jamie Bolton, 'China: the infrastructure imperative', *Logistics Management* (July 2007), p. 63; and China trade facts from http://cscmp.org/press/fastfacts.asp, accessed March 2010.

[11] Nanette Byrnes, 'Avon Calls. China opens the door', *BusinessWeek Online* (28 February 2006), p. 19; Mei Fong, 'Avon's calling, but China opens door only a crack', *Wall Street Journal* (26 February 2007), p. B1; 'Cosmetic changes in China market' (11 October 2007), www.chinadaily.com.cn; and David Barboza, 'Direct selling flourishes in China', *New York Times* (26 December 2009), p. B1.

[12] Cecilie Rohwedder, 'European shoppers enjoy novelty: Christmas Sales', *Wall Street Journal* (24–26 December 2007), pp. 1–2.

[13] Quotes and other information from Alex Taylor III, 'Caterpillar', *Fortune* (20 August 2007), pp. 48–54; Donald V. Fites, 'Make your dealers your partners', *Harvard Business Review* (March – April 1996), pp. 84–95; and information at www.cat.com, accessed August 2010.

[14] John D. Schultz, 'Logistics news: U.S. logistics costs drop for the first time in six years', *Supply Chain Management Review* (18 June 2009); Larry Rohter, 'Shipping costs start to crimp globalization', *New York Times* (3 August 2008), p. A1; and supply chain facts from http://cscmp.org/press/fastfacts.asp, accessed June 2010.

[15] William B. Cassidy, 'Walmart squeezes costs from supply chain', *Journal of Commerce* (5 January 2010).

[16] Shlomo Maital, 'The last frontier of cost reduction', *Across the Board* (February 1994), pp. 51–52; and information from http://walmartstores.com//default.aspx, accessed June 2010.

[17] Bill Mongrelluzzo, 'Supply chain expert sees profits in sustainability', *Journal of Commerce* (11 March 2010).

[18] Example adapted from Evan West, 'These robots play fetch', *Fast Company* (July/August 2007), pp. 49–50. See also John Teresko, 'Getting lean with armless robots', *Industry Week* (September 2008), p. 26; and www.kivasystems.com/video.htm, accessed February 2010.

[19] See 'A worldwide look at RFID', *Supply Chain Management Review* (April 2007), pp. 48–55; 'Walmart says use RFID tags or pay up', *Logistics Today* (March 2008), p. 4; David Blanchard, 'The five stages of RFID', *Industry Week* (1 January 2009), p. 50; and Maaida Napolitano, 'RFID revisited', *Modern Materials Handling* (February 2010), p. 45.

[20] http://epp.eurostat.ec.europa.eu/statistics_explained/index.php/Freight_transport_statistics, accessed February 17 2012.

[21] See Walmart's supplier requirements at http://walmartstores.com/Suppliers/248.aspx, accessed June 2010. Also see Sriram Narayanan, Ann S. Marucheck and Robert B. Handfield, 'Electronic data interchange: research review and future directions', *Decision Sciences* (February 2009), p. 121.

[22] See Bob Trebilcock, 'Top 20 supply chain management software suppliers', *Modern Material Handling* (12 August 2009), www.logistic-smgmt.com/article/331247-Top-20-supply-chain_management_software_suppliers_2009.php; and 'The 2009 Supply & Demand Chain Executive 100', *Supply & Demand Chain Executive* (June–July 2009), www.sdcexec.com.

[23] 'Whirlpool: outsourcing its national service parts operation provides immediate benefits', www.ryder.com/pdf/MCC633_Whirlpool_single.pdf, accessed October 2010.

[24] www.supplychainbrain.com/content/nc/sponsored-channels/kenco-logistic-services-third-party-logistics/single-article-page/article/top-25-third-party-logistics-providers-extend-their-global-reach, accessed (17 February 2012).

VIDEO CASE

Progressive MyMarketingLab

Progressive has attained top-tier status in the insurance industry by focusing on innovation. Progressive was the first company to offer drive-in claims services, installment payment of premiums and 24/7 customer service. But some of Progressive's most innovative moves involve its channels of distribution. Whereas most insurance companies distribute their products to consumers via intermediary agents or direct-to-consumer methods, Progressive was one of the first companies to recognise the value in doing both. In the late 1980s, it augmented its agency distribution with a direct 800-number channel.

In 1995, Progressive moved into the future by becoming the first major insurer in the world to launch a website. In 1997, customers could buy car insurance policies online in real time. Today, at Progressive's website, customers can do everything from managing their own account information to reporting claims directly. Progressive even offers a one-stop concierge claim service.

After watching the Progressive video, answer the following questions about marketing channels:

1. Apply the concept of the supply chain to Progressive.
2. Using the model of consumer and business channels found in the chapter, sketch out as many channels for Progressive as you can. How does each of these channels meet distinct customer needs?
3. Discuss the various ways that Progressive has had an impact on the insurance industry.

COMPANY CASE

Netflix: disintermediator or disintermediated?

Baseball great Yogi Berra, known more for his mangled phrasing than for his baseball prowess, once said, 'the future ain't what it used to be.' For Netflix, the world's largest online movie-rental service, no matter how you say it, figuring out the future is challenging and a bit scary. Netflix faces dramatic changes in how movies and other entertainment content will be distributed. So, will Netflix be among the disintermediators or among the disintermediated?

Less than a decade ago, if you wanted to watch a movie in the comfort of your own home, your only choice was to roust yourself out of your recliner and trot down to the local Blockbuster or other neighbourhood movie-rental store. Blockbuster is still the world's largest store-rental chain with over 9,000 stores in 25 countries and $4.1 billion in annual sales. But it revenues have been flat or in decline for the past few years. To make matters worse, it has lost money in all but one of the last 13 years – over $550 billion in 2009 alone! Blockbuster's stock price has plummeted to mere $0.28 a share while the company teeters on the brink of bankruptcy. This riches-to-rags story underscores the fact that the old model for distributing movies is simply not working anymore.

One thing about the future is certain. The business of distributing home video is full of disruption and confusion. Things are really changing, and the dust is far from settling. HBO offers its classic subscription services as well as its new premium service, HBO On Demand. Then there's Redbox, the Coinstar Company that rents DVDs for a dollar a day through vending machines in more than 25,000 convenience stores, supermarkets, and fast-food restaurants. That's from a company that no one had even heard of just a few years ago. Adding even more chaos to the mix, Hulu leads the army of start-ups and veterans that show full-length movies, TV shows, and clips for free, as long as you're willing to watch some ads.

THE NETFLIX REVOLUTION

But amid the chaos, Netflix has carved out its own successful niche. Netflix CEO Reed Hastings remains focused on a well-defined strategy with unwavering commitment. That strategy outlines not only what Netflix will do but also what it won't do. The company won't distribute content in brick-and-mortar stores, through vending machines, as pay-per-view, or in ad-supported format. 'Commercial-free subscription is where we can compete. It's our best shot'.

Netflix is demonstrating how its model can flexibly reach millions of viewers through various channels. In the late 1990s,

Netflix pioneered a new way to rent movies—via the Web and direct mail. For a monthly subscription fee, members could create a movie wish list online. The company would then send out a set of DVDs from that list via the USPS. One of Netflix's main selling points was that members could keep the DVDs as long as they wanted. When they were done with them, they simply returned the DVDs in the mail with a prepaid return envelope. Netflix then automatically sent the next set of DVDs from the member's list.

The Netflix DVD-by-mail model was quickly favoured by hundreds of thousands of viewers, then by millions. It's easy to see why. As Netflix's clever ad campaign has been pointing out, there is no hassle or cost from those trips to the video store. There is no worry about late fees. The selection from more than 100,000 DVD titles dwarfs anything that a brick-and-mortar store could hold. Finding rare, old, documentary, or independent films is easy. And the cost of renting—set by members based on how many DVDs they can check out at one time—is always the same and as little as $5 month.

NOTHING LASTS FOREVER

As much as this Netflix model revolutionised the movie rental business, Hastings quickly points out that it will not last forever. In fact, he predicts that the Netflix core business model will be in decline in as little as three years. What Netflix has in store offers a rare case of how a company manages a still-hot business as it watches the clock tick down. Rather than clinging to an entrenched business model, Netflix is determined to out-innovate its competitors. In fact, in a true sign of forward thinking, Hastings avoided naming the company something catchy like 'Movies-by-Mail' when he founded it. He knew that such branding would be far too limiting to allow dynamic change.

Netflix's innovation really took off just a little more than three years ago when it launched Instant Watch, a feature that allowed members to stream videos instantly via their computers as part of their monthly membership fee. At first, the selection was slim—only a few thousand movies available for streaming—and the quality wasn't all that great. But Netflix has been hard at work expanding its library of streaming videos. That library now stands at more than 17,000 films and TV shows and is growing rapidly. And with technology advancements, viewers can watch movies in beautiful high-definition, full-screen splendour.

As media touchpoints exploded, Hastings knew that Netflix's growth would be limited if it streamed only to computers and laptops. So Hastings assembled a team to develop a prototype set-top box that would access the Web through a viewer's broadband connection, allowing members to stream movies remotely to their TVs from the comfort of their couches. Barry

McCarthy, Netflix's chief financial officer, recalls that Hastings was so infatuated with the plan that it could be described only as 'Apple lust.' But just as Netflix neared a public unveiling of the set-top box, Netflix executives had an epiphany. 'Are we out of our [minds]?' McCarthy recalls thinking. 'We don't even know what we don't know about this business.' The Netflix-only set-top box is now available, but Netflix turned it over to Roku, a small electronics company.

At that critical turning point, Hastings and his team realised that they had to move into other distribution points. They decided that it made much more sense to partner with experts who already market popular devices. Netflix moved quickly. Now, every xBox, PlayStation, and Wii has become a home theatre, allowing members full access to Netflix's streaming library. The same access can be had through Blu-ray DVD players and TiVo DVRs.

Hastings also sees a future with Web-enabled TVs. He believes that in five to ten years, viewers will interact with the big screen in the same way they now interact with the small screen. 'We'll be calling up movies and channels and Web sites with a click of a button or just a spoken word: "Wizard of Oz." Or "ESPN." Or "Netflix."' In small measure, it's already happening. Instant Watch is available on TVs from Sony, LG, and Vizio. Netflix's streaming service is available only through US-based Web addresses for now. But with a projected 500 million Web-connected devices worldwide by 2013, Netflix plans to expand internationally.

Along with TVs, DVD players, and gaming platforms, Netflix is also moving into mobile devices. It now offers an Instant Watch app for Windows Phone 7 and Apple's iPad and iPhone. Other mobile platforms will follow soon, including Google's Android.

FOCUS ON THE CUSTOMER

As Blockbuster's financial performance has plummeted, Netflix's has skyrocketed. With more than 12 million members and 2.5 billion movie views under its belt, annual revenue has increased 70 per cent in the past three years to $1.7 billion. Profits have climbed 130 per cent. And in less than two years, Netflix stock has risen from $20 a share to $118. That's a return on investment of more than 500 per cent for those savvy enough to have bought in at the right time. Such performance is even

more amazing when you consider that it happened in the midst of a global economic meltdown. 'We were growing at 25 percent when the economy was growing. We're growing at 25 percent now,' says Hastings.

Hastings has no intention of slowing down. And it isn't just about distribution points. The dynamic Hastings is on a crusade to improve the viewing experience of its members. 'For most people, they watch one or two movies a week. Only maybe once a month do they get a movie that's like, "Wow. I loved that movie!" It really is a hard problem to figure out which ones to watch with your valuable time. We're trying to get it to where every other movie that you watch from Netflix is "Wow. I loved that movie!" As we get closer to achieving that, we increase human happiness with movies.'

Netflix has its work cut out for it. The various delivery models being pursued by its competitors and the complexities of dealing with content producers don't make it any easier. But with unlimited DVDs by mail and unlimited instant streaming to computers, TVs, and other Web-enabled devices for a flat $8.99 a month, the future looks bright for Netflix.

Questions for discussion

1. As completely as possible, sketch the value chain for Netflix from the production of content to viewer.
2. How do horizontal and vertical conflict impact Netflix?
3. How does Netflix add value for customers through distribution functions?
4. What threats does Netflix face in the future?
5. Will Netflix be successful in the long term? Why or why not?

Sources: Patricia Sellers, 'Netflix CEO Focuses on the Future', *Fortune*, 22 July 2009, accessed at http://postcards.blogs.fortune.cnn.com/2009/07/22/Netflix-CEO-focuses-on-the-future; Chuck Salter, 'The World's 50 Most Innovative Companies: #12 Netflix', *Fast Company*, 17 February 2010, p. 68; Nick Wingfield, 'Netflix Boss Plots Life after the DVD,' *Wall Street Journal*, 23 June 2009, p. A1; Beth Snyder Builk, 'How Netflix Stays Ahead of Shifting Consumer Behaviour,' *Advertising Age*, 22 February 2010, p. 28.

CHAPTER THIRTEEN

Retailing and wholesaling

Chapter preview

In the previous chapter, you learned the basics of delivering customer value through good distribution channel design and management. Now, we'll look more deeply into the two major intermediary channel functions: retailing and wholesaling. You already know something about retailing; retailers of all shapes and sizes serve you everyday. However, you probably know much less about the horde of wholesalers that work behind the scenes. In this chapter, we will examine the characteristics of different kinds of retailers and wholesalers, the marketing decisions they make, and trends for the future.

Retailing is a highly changeable business. Although we always think first of the mega-companies like Walmart, Carrefour, CostCo, Metro and Tesco, there are other 'movers and shakers' as well, with a big impact on the global retail scene. Consider how relatively-unknown discount supermarket Aldi is achieving high impact not simply in its German home market, but also globally. What Aldi shares with other successful retailers is an unrelenting focus on bringing value to its customers.

Objective outline

➤ **Objective 1** Explain the role of retailers in the distribution channel and describe the major types of retailers.
Retailing (pp. 386–392)

➤ **Objective 2** Describe the major retailer marketing decisions.
Retailer marketing decisions (pp. 392–397)

➤ **Objective 3** Discuss the major trends and developments in retailing.
Retailing trends and developments (pp. 397–403)

➤ **Objective 4** Explain the major types of wholesalers and their marketing decisions.
Wholesaling (pp. 404–409)

Aldi

Aldi is not a household name in the way that Tesco, Walmart and Carrefour can claim, but its performance has been remarkable. The essence of the business is low prices through store-brand goods, sold in no-frills stores. The original Aldi shops had bare neon lights, the goods were stacked on pallets, there was no refrigerated produce and there were few staff. Now, the Aldi group operates more than 8,000 individual stores worldwide, including Trader Joe's in the US.

Aldi has been able to grow quickly under the radar because it is so private. The group does not report results, but consultancy Planet Retail estimates sales of €53 billion in 2009, and Aldi is one of the fastest-growing retailers in the world. Aldi has pioneered a distinct brand of pile-it-high, sell-it-cheap shopping that has transformed retailing in Germany and much of Europe. Aldi buys in bulk from suppliers and commissions them to make its store-brand groceries cheaper than those of its rivals. The thing is that although the stores are no-frills to the extreme, Aldi is so cheap that even the mighty Walmart closed its stores in Germany, partly because shoppers found the US giant too expensive in comparison with Aldi.

Aldi, short for 'Albrecht Discount', is a discount supermarket chain based in Germany. The chain is made up of two separate groups, Aldi Nord, headquartered in Essen, and Aldi Süd, headquartered in Mülheim an der Ruhr, which operate independently from each other within specific market boundaries. The individual groups were originally owned and managed by brothers Karl and Theo Albrecht; Karl has since retired and is Germany's richest man. Theo was Germany's second richest man until his death in July 2010. The brothers were always secretive and reclusive, and many senior Aldi executives spent their whole careers at the company without ever seeing one of the brothers.

Aldi's German operations currently consist of Aldi Nord's 35 individual regional companies with about 2,500 stores in western, northern and eastern Germany, and Aldi Süd's 31 regional companies with 1,600 stores in western and southern Germany. According to a survey conducted in 2002 by the German market research institute Forsa, 95 per cent of blue-collar workers, 88 per cent of white-collar workers, 84 per cent of public servants and 80 per cent of self-employed Germans shop at Aldi. Aldi and the other deep discounters account for 40 per cent of all grocery sales in Germany. Internationally, Aldi Nord operates in Denmark, France, the Benelux countries, the Iberian peninsula and Poland, while Aldi Süd operates in countries including Ireland, the United Kingdom, Hungary, Greece, Switzerland, Austria, Slovenia (operating as Hofer in Austria and Slovenia) and Australia. In the United States, Aldi Nord is the parent company of the Trader Joe's niche food stores, while Aldi Süd operates the regular Aldi stores in the country.

In 2009, in the UK, having struggled to make inroads after first arriving in the UK in the early 1990s, Aldi became of the few retail winners in the economic downturn, with sales rising 25 per cent in a single year. The momentum of the brand was fuelled by a customer base increasingly made up of the wealthier sections of society – half the customer base is now made up of more affluent ABC1 consumers. But with only 3 per cent of the UK groceries market, Aldi believes it has plenty of scope for further growth. Some estimates suggest that discount supermarkets' share of UK groceries could rise from less than 5 per cent to more than 20 per cent.

Certainly, in 2010, when consumer group *Which?* surveyed consumers regarding store quality, staff attitude and range of products and prices, discounters Aldi (and its smaller German rival Lidl) both came out ahead of the 'big four' (Tesco, Sainsbury's, Asda and Morrisons) in consumer satisfaction. Tesco is so worried it has built a mock-up of an Aldi store at its headquarters, where its executives, marketers and product buyers can study the tactics being used by the enemy. Tesco has already had to respond to the discounters by introducing its own discount brand range.

In the harsh economic conditions of the late-2000s, the no-frills discount supermarkets (mainly Aldi but also Lidl) were attracting droves of new shoppers as unemployment figures rocketed and the credit crunch forced households to slash spending. Offering high-quality products on a limited number of lines at low prices, the discounters were luring shoppers away from Tesco, Sainsbury, Asda and Morrisons, as the British middle classes tightened their belts in the face of soaring energy and food bills.

Aldi prices were running around one-third cheaper than its competitors. Product choice is restricted, but that keeps costs lower than rivals – while Aldi

Aldi is not a household name. The essence of the business is low prices through store-brand goods, sold in no-frills stores.

Source: Shutterstock.com

stocks one variety of tomato ketchup, Tesco stocks about 24 varieties. Lower costs meant that Aldi could sell a £7.99 bottle of Chateau-Neuf-du-Pape to go with a £4.99 Canadian lobster from Lidl. Paul Foley, Aldi's UK chief says 'If you offer the consumer the lowest prices and the highest quality, then you shouldn't be surprised that we take market share'.

Aldi's 2012 advertising campaign uses quirky, slightly bizarre, consumers making direct comparisons between expensive branded products and the much cheaper Aldi own-label, emphasising the equivalence of the competing offers in quality, linked by the slogan suggesting that Aldi is 'Like Brands. Only Cheaper'.

The US arm of Aldi is expanding on Walmart's home turf in America, looking to seize on the economic downturn to lure consumers to its spartan stores and cheap groceries. The company is counting on the global downturn to break through a traditional barrier – that US grocery shoppers tend to be loyal to big-name brands. According to Nielsen Co, store-brand goods generally make up about 22 per cent of US sales (it is closer to 30 per cent in Europe), but at Aldi 95 per cent of the goods on sale are the retailer's own-brands. In the US Midwest Aldi prices are between 15 and 20 per cent less than Walmart and 30 to 40 per cent cheaper than regional chains. In fact, Aldi has been in the US since 1976, and has more than 1,000 stores. The issue is whether the tough economy and Aldi's big push will make an impact.

At the same time, Aldi has upgraded its German retailing by improving food ranges and offering more upscale non-food promotions to bring in middle-class shoppers with more disposable income. At one time in the US and UK, Aldi located unattractive stores in low-income areas and sold very few products and little fresh food. Store designs have been improved and grocery ranges enhanced. In the US, Aldi is locating new stores near Walmart Supercenters to draw customers. The test is whether Aldi can repeat its UK success by moving up the market in the huge US market.[1]

The Aldi story sets the stage for examining the fast-changing world of today's resellers. This chapter looks at *retailing* and *wholesaling*. In the first section, we will look at the nature and importance of retailing, the major types of store and non-store retailers, the decisions retailers make and the future of retailing. In the second section, we will discuss these same topics as they apply to wholesalers.

AUTHOR COMMENT

You already know a lot about retailers. You deal with them every day – store retailers, service retailers, online retailers and others.

RETAILING

Retailing—All the activities involved in selling goods or services directly to final consumers for their personal, non-business use.

Retailers—A business whose sales come *primarily* from retailing.

What is retailing? We all know that Costco, B&Q, Boots the Chemist, PC World and Carphone Warehouse are retailers, but so are Avon representatives, Amazon, the local Holiday Inn and a doctor seeing patients. **Retailing** includes all the activities involved in selling products or services directly to final consumers for their personal, non-business use. Many institutions – manufacturers, wholesalers and retailers – do retailing. But most retailing is done by **retailers**, businesses whose sales come *primarily* from retailing.

Retailing plays a very important role in most marketing channels. They connect brands to consumers in what OgilvyAction, a marketing agency, calls 'the last mile' – the final stop in the consumer's path to purchase. It's the 'distance a consumer travels between an attitude and an action,' explains OgilvyAction's CEO. Some 40 per cent of all consumer decisions are made in or near the store. Thus, retailers 'reach consumers at key moments of truth, ultimately [influencing] their actions at the point of purchase'.[2]

In fact, many marketers are now embracing the concept of **shopper marketing**, using in-store promotions and advertising to extend brand equity to 'the last mile' and encourage favourable in-store purchase decisions. Shopper marketing recognises that the retail store itself is an important marketing medium. Thus, marketing must drive shoppers to action at the store level. For example, P&G follows a 'store back' concept, in which all marketing ideas need to be effective at the store-shelf level and work back from there. 'We are now brand-building from the eyes of the consumer toward us,' says a P&G executive.[3]

In fact, point-of-sale marketing inside a large retail store chain can produce the same kinds of numbers as advertising on a hit TV show. For example, while several million people may watch an average episode of a popular TV show, even bigger crowds attack the aisles of large retailers. What's more, unlike TV advertising's remote impact, point-of-sale promotions hit consumers when they are actually making purchase decisions.[4]

Shopper marketing involves focusing the entire marketing process – from product and brand development to logistics, promotion and merchandising – toward turning shoppers into buyers at the point of sale. Of course, every well-designed marketing effort focuses on customer buying behaviour. But the concept of shopper marketing suggests that these efforts should be coordinated around the shopping process itself. 'By starting with the store and working backward, you design an integrated programme that make sense to the consumer.'[5]

Although most retailing is done in retail stores, in recent years *non-store retailing* has been growing much faster than store retailing. Non-store retailing includes selling to final consumers via the Internet, direct mail, catalogues, the landline and mobile telephone, and other direct-selling approaches. We will discuss such direct-marketing approaches in detail in Chapter 17. In this chapter, we focus on store retailing.

> **Shopper marketing**—Using in-store promotions and advertising to extend brand equity to 'the last mile' and encourage favourable hi-store purchase decisions.

Types of retailers

Retail stores come in all shapes and sizes – from your local hairdressing salon or family-owned restaurant to national speciality chain retailers, such as JD Sports or Lakeland, to mega-retailers such as Costco or Carrefour. The most important types of retail stores are described in Table 13.1 and discussed in the following sections. They can be classified in terms of several characteristics, including the *amount of service* they offer, the breadth and depth of their *product lines*, the *relative prices* they charge and how they are *organised*.

Amount of service

Different types of customers and products require different amounts of service. To meet these varying service needs, retailers may offer one of three service levels: self-service, limited service and full service.

Self-service retailers serve customers who are willing to perform their own 'locate-compare-select' process to save time or money, and increasingly also operate self-service checkouts. Self-service is the basis of all discount operations and is typically used by retailers selling convenience goods (such as supermarkets) and nationally branded, fast-moving shopping goods (such as Tesco or Auchan). *Limited-service retailers*, such as PC World or Comet (electrical goods), provide more sales assistance because they carry more shopping goods about which customers need information. Their increased operating costs may result in higher prices.

In *full-service retailers*, such as high-end speciality stores (for example, up-market jewellery stores or specialists in products like expensive kitchenware) and first-class department stores (such as Harrods and John Lewis in the UK), salespeople assist customers in every phase of the shopping process. Full-service stores usually carry more speciality goods for which customers need or want assistance or advice. They provide more services resulting in much higher operating costs, which are passed along to customers as higher prices.

Table 13.1 Major store retailer types

Type	Description	Examples
Speciality stores	A store that carries a narrow product line with a deep assortment, such as clothing apparel stores, sporting-goods stores, furniture stores, florists and bookshops. A clothing store would be a *single-line* store, a men's clothing store would be a *limited-line* store, and a men's custom-shirt store would be a *super-speciality* store.	Charles Tyrwhitt (men's clothes), JD Sports (sporting goods), Lakeland (special-ised kitchenware)
Department stores	A store that carries several product lines – typically clothing, home furnishings and household goods – with each line operated as a separate department managed by specialist buyers or merchandisers.	House of Fraser (UK), Le Bon Marché (France), Karstadt (Germany)
Supermarkets	A relatively large, low-cost, low-margin, high-volume, self-service operation designed to serve the consumer's total needs for grocery and household products.	Tesco, Sainsbury's (UK), Auchan, Carrefour (France), Aldi, Metro, Lidl (Germany)
Convenience stores	Relatively small stores located near residential areas, open long hours seven days a week, and carrying a limited line of high-turnover convenience products at slightly higher prices.	Tesco Express (UK), Spar (throughout Europe), Albert Heijn To Go (Netherland)
Discount stores	A store that carries standard merchandise sold at lower prices with lower margins and higher volumes.	Poundworld (UK), Dia (Carrefour's hard discount stores across Europe)
Off-price retailers	A store that sells merchandise bought at less-than-regular wholesale prices and sold at less than retail, often leftover goods, overruns, and irregulars obtained at reduced prices from manufacturers or other retailers. These include *factory outlets* owned and operated by manufacturers. *independent off-price retailers* owned and run by entrepreneurs or by divisions of larger retail corporations; and *warehouse (or wholesale) clubs* selling a limited selection of brand-name groceries, appliances, clothing, and other goods at deep discounts to consumers who pay membership fees.	Superdrug (UK and Ireland), Costco, Sam's Club, BJ's Wholesale Club (warehouse clubs in US and UK), TJ Maxx (UK and Europe), Gap Outlet (UK and Europe)
Superstores	Very large stores traditionally aimed at meeting con-sumers' total needs for routinely purchased food and nonfood items. This category includes supercentres, combined supermarket and discount stores, and *category killers*, which carry a deep assortment in a particular category and have a knowledgeable staff.	Tesco Superstores (UK), Auchan and Carrefour hypermarkets (Europe), Staples (UK and Europe), Toys R Us (category killers)

Product line

Speciality store—A retail store that carries a narrow product line with a deep assortment within that line.

Department store—A retail organisation that carries a wide variety of product lines – each line is operated as a separate department managed by specialist buyers or merchandisers.

Retailers can also be classified by the length and breadth of their product assortments. Some retailers, such as **speciality stores**, carry narrow product lines with deep assortments within those lines. In many cases, speciality stores are flourishing. The increasing use of market segmentation, market targeting and product specialisation has resulted in a greater need for stores that focus on specific products and segments.

In contrast, **department stores** carry a wide variety of product lines. In recent years, department stores have been squeezed between more focused and flexible speciality stores on the one hand and more efficient, lower-priced discounters on the other. In response, many have added promotional pricing to meet the discount threat. Others have stepped up the use of store brands and single-brand 'designer shops' to compete with speciality stores. Still others are trying catalogue, telephone and Web selling. Service remains the key differentiating factor. High-end department stores do well by emphasising exclusive merchandise and high-quality service.

Supermarkets are the most frequently shopped at type of retail store. However, even in the grocery business they face an increase in competition from discount supercentres (Tesco, Carrefour) and speciality food stores (e.g. Whole Foods Market and local delicatessens). In the harsh economic conditions of the late-2000s, supermarkets regained ground in some countries through heavy price discounting to attract consumers.

In the battle for 'share of stomachs', some supermarkets have moved upmarket, providing improved store environments and higher-quality food offerings, such as bakeries, gourmet deli counters, natural foods and fresh seafood departments. Others, however, are attempting to compete head-on with food discounters such as Tesco, Auchan, Aldi and Carrefour, by cutting costs, establishing more-efficient operations and lowering prices. For example, in the UK Waitrose (a division of the John Lewis Partnership), has successfully rebuilt its market position in tough economic conditions:

> While its major competitors have their own segments – research agency Experian says Sainsbury appeals to younger, well-educated shoppers with cosmopolitan tastes, compared to the broader appeal of Tesco to the price-conscious, and Asda aims at more down-to-earth types – Waitrose is frequented by career professionals and the well-educated. Some call it the posh peoples' supermarket, which is famed for its emphasis on quality. In spite of the economic downturn, 2010 saw new customers flocking to Waitrose stores, and the company was expanding faster than its bigger competitors, and was the UK's fastest growing grocery retailer. The company benefited from expanding its 'Essential Waitrose' range of value items (to counter perceptions that Waitrose was more expensive than rivals on everyday items), as well as by expanding the high-end Duchy Originals ranges (natural, organic, food and other high-quality products made to traditional methods, associated with the Prince of Wales' estates and his well-known environmental proselytising). Advertising campaigns featured designer chef Heston Blumenthal and the well-known British chef Delia Smith to promote upmarket recipes and products. Waitrose has been successfully persuading customers to do more of their everyday shopping at the store, rather than regarding Waitrose as a shop only for the special occasion. They have been attracting customers from both the mainstream rivals like Tesco and Sainsbury but also from the hard discounters like Aldi.[6]

Convenience stores are small stores that carry a limited line of high-turnover convenience goods. For example, Tesco Express and Sainsbury Local are chains of convenience stores operated by the major supermarket companies, with the aim of allowing consumers to do local 'top-up' shopping as well as the main shop at a supermarket or superstore. The big companies have purchased small chains of local convenience outlets and rebranded them, as well as opening new sites and locating at petrol stations. Other convenience stores are operated as independent ventures or as small regional chains.

Superstores are much larger than regular supermarkets and offer a large assortment of routinely purchased food products, non-food items and services. These discount retailers offer *supercentres*, very large combination food and discount stores. Recent years have also seen the explosive growth of superstores that are actually giant speciality stores, the so-called **category killers** (e.g. B&Q and Toys R Us). They feature huge stores that carry a very deep assortment of a particular line with a knowledgeable staff. Category killers are prevalent in a wide range of categories, including electronics, home-improvement products, books, baby products, toys and sporting goods.

Finally, for many retailers, the product line is actually a service. **Service retailers** include hotels, banks, airlines, colleges, hospitals, cinemas, sports and fitness clubs, restaurants, repair services, hairdressers and dry cleaners. In many countries, service retailers are growing faster than product retailers.

Supermarket—A large, low-cost, low-margin, high-volume, self-service store that carries a wide variety of grocery and household products.

Convenience store—A small store, located near a residential area. That is open long hours seven days a week and carries a limited line of high-turnover convenience goods.

Superstore—A store much larger than a regular supermarket that offers a large assortment of routinely purchased food products, non-food items and services.

Category killer—A giant speciality store that carries a very deep assortment of a particular line and is staffed by knowledgeable employees.

Service retailer—A retailer whose product line is actually a service, including hotels, airlines, banks, colleges and many others.

Relative prices

Retailers can also be classified according to the prices they charge (see Table 13.1). Most retailers charge regular prices and offer normal-quality goods and customer service. Others offer higher-quality goods and service at higher prices. Retailers that feature low prices are discount stores and 'off-price' retailers.

Discount stores

Discount store—A retail operation that sells standard merchandise at lower prices by accepting lower margins and selling at higher volume.

A **discount store** sells standard merchandise at lower prices by accepting lower margins and selling in higher volume. The early discount stores cut expenses by offering few services and operating in warehouse-like facilities in low-rent, high traffic areas.

Poundland is Europe's biggest single-price discount store (all items in its UK stores sell for £1).

Source: Getty Images/Bloomberg

Today's discounters have improved their store environments and increased their services, while at the same time keeping prices low through lean, efficient operations. Leading 'big-box' discounters, such as Walmart, Costco and Target, dominate the retail scene in the US although that dominance by this type of retailer is much less pronounced in Europe. However, even 'small-box' discounters are thriving in the current economic environment. For example, Poundland is Europe's biggest single-price discount store (all items in its UK stores sell for £1), has done well during the recession and has moved from its low-income consumer base to move into mainstream shopping centres and attract a broader market. Poundland is expanding its non-UK business as DEALZ, although not using the single-price policy. The Poundland slogan is 'Amazing Value Every Day'.

Off-price retailers

Off-price retailer—A retailer that buys at less-than-regular wholesale price and sells at less than retail. Example are factory outlets, independents and warehouse clubs.

As the major discount stores have tended to trade up, a new wave of **off-price retailers** moved in to fill the ultralow-price, high-volume gap. Ordinary discounters buy at regular wholesale prices and accept lower margins to keep prices down. In contrast, off-price retailers buy at less-than-regular wholesale prices and charge consumers less than retail. Off-price retailers can be found in all areas, from food, clothing and electronics to no-frills banking and discount brokerages.

Independent off-price retailer—An off-price retailer that is either independently owned and run or is a division of a larger retail corporation.

The three main types of off-price retailers are *independents, factory outlets* and *warehouse clubs*. **Independent off-price retailers** either are independently owned and run or are divisions of larger retail corporations. Although many off-price operations are run by smaller independents, most large off-price retailer operations are owned by bigger retail chains. Examples include Web sellers such as Overstock.com.

Factory outlet—An off-price retailing operation that is owned and operated by a manufacturer and normally carries the manufacturer's surplus discontinued or irregular goods.

Factory outlets – manufacturer-owned and operated stores by firms such as Gap, Levi Strauss and others – sometimes group together in *factory outlet malls* and *value-retail centres*, where dozens of outlet stores offer prices as much as 50 per cent below retail on a wide range of mostly surplus, discounted or irregular goods. Whereas outlet malls consist primarily of manufacturers' outlets, value-retail centres combine manufacturers' outlets with off-price retail stores and department store clearance outlets. Factory outlet malls have become one of the hottest growth areas in retailing in the United States, and are growing in popularity in some European countries.

The malls in general are now moving upmarket – and even dropping 'factory' from their descriptions. A growing number of outlet malls now feature luxury brands such as Coach, Polo Ralph Lauren, Dolce&Gabbana, Giorgio Armani, Burberry and Versace. As consumers become more value-minded, even upper-end retailers are accelerating their factory outlet strategies, placing more emphasis on these outlets. Many companies now regard outlets not simply as a way of disposing of problem merchandise but as an additional way of gaining business for fresh merchandise. The combination of highbrow brands and lowbrow prices found at outlets provides powerful shopper appeal, especially in a tighter economy.[7]

Warehouse club—An off-price retailer that sells a limited selection of brand name grocery items, appliances, clothing and a hodgepodge of other goods at deep discounts to members who pay annual membership fees.

Warehouse clubs (or *wholesale clubs* or *membership warehouses*), such as Costco, operate in huge, drafty, warehouse-like facilities and offer few frills. However, they offer ultralow prices and surprise deals on selected branded merchandise. Warehouse clubs have grown rapidly in recent years. These retailers appeal not only to low-income consumers seeking bargains on bare-bones products but also all kinds of customers shopping for a wide range of goods, from necessities to extravagances.

Consider Costco, now the third-largest retailer in the United States, behind only Walmart and Kroger, and with stores in the UK, the Asia-Pacific region and Latin America. Low price is an important part of Costco's equation, but what really sets Costco apart is the products it carries and the sense of urgency that it builds into the Costco shopper's store experience. Consider the typical Costco US store:[8]

> Costco brings flair to an otherwise dreary setting. Alongside the gallon jars of peanut butter and 2,250-count packs of Q-Tips, Costco offers an ever-changing assortment of high-quality products – even luxuries – all at tantalisingly low margins. As one industry analyst puts it, 'Costco is a retail treasure hunt, where one's shopping cart could contain a $50,000 diamond ring resting on top of a vat of mayonnaise.' It's the place where high-end products meet deep-discount prices. In just one year, Costco sold 91 million hot dog and soda combinations (still only $1.50 as they have been for more than 25 years). At the same time, it sold more than 96,000 carats of diamonds at up to $100,000 per item. It's the nation's biggest baster of poultry (77,000 rotisserie chickens a day at $4.99) but also the country's biggest seller of fine wines (including the likes of a Chateau Cheval Blanc Premier Grand Cru Classe at $1,750 a bottle). It once even offered a Pablo Picasso drawing at Costco.com for only $129,999.99!
>
> Each Costco store is a theatre of retail that creates buying urgency and excitement for customers. Mixed in with its regular stock of staples, Costco features a glittering, constantly shifting array of one-time specials, such as discounted Prada bags, Calloway golf clubs or Kenneth Cole bags – deals you just won't find anywhere else. In fact, of the 4,000 items that Costco carries, 1,000 are designated as 'treasure items' (Costco's words). The changing assortment and great prices keep people coming back, wallets in hand. There was a time when only the great, unwashed masses shopped at off-price retailers, but Costco has changed all that. Even people who don't have to pinch pennies shop there.

Organisational approach

Although many retail stores are independently owned, others band together under some form of corporate or contractual organisation. The major types of retail organisations – *corporate chains, voluntary chains, retailer cooperatives* and *franchise organisations* are described in Table 13.2.

Chain stores are two or more outlets that are commonly owned and controlled. They have many advantages over independents. Their size allows them to buy in large quantities at lower prices and

Chain stores—Two or more outlets that are commonly owned and controlled.

Table 13.2 Major types of retail organisations

Type	Description	Examples
Corporate chain store	Two or more outlets that are commonly owned and controlled. Corporate chains appear in all types of retailing, but they are strongest in department stores, discount stores, food stores, pharmacies and restaurants.	John Lewis (UK department stores), Tesco (UK discount stores), Sainsbury (UK grocery stores), Boots the Chemists (UK pharmacies)
Voluntary chain	Wholesaler-sponsored group of independent retailers engaged in group buying and merchandising.	Spar (European voluntary chain)
Retailer cooperative	Group of independent retailers who jointly establish a central buying organisation and conduct joint promotion efforts.	The Cooperative Group (UK consumer cooperative)
Franchise organisation	Contractual association between a franchisor (a manufacturer, wholesaler or service organisation) and franchisees (independent businesspeople who buy the right to own and operate one or more units in the franchise system).	McDonald's, Subway, Pizza Hut

gain promotional economies. They can hire specialists to deal with areas such as pricing, promotion, merchandising, inventory control and sales forecasting.

The great success of corporate chains caused many independent retailers to band together in one of two forms of contractual associations. One is the *voluntary chain*: a wholesaler-sponsored group of independent retailers that engages in group buying and common merchandising. The other type of contractual association is the *retailer cooperative*: a group of independent retailers that bands together to set up a jointly owned, central wholesale operation and conduct joint merchandising and promotion efforts. Founded in the Netherlands in 1932, Spar is the world's largest independent voluntary retail trading chain, trading from approximately 12,500 stores in 34 countries worldwide. These organisations give independents the buying and promotion economies they need to meet the prices of corporate chains.

Another form of contractual retail organisation is a **franchise**. The main difference between franchise organisations and other contractual systems (voluntary chains and retail cooperatives) is that franchise systems are normally based on some unique product or service; a method of doing business; or the trade name, goodwill or patent that the franchisor has developed. Franchising has been prominent in fast-food restaurants, hotels, health and fitness centres, motor car sales and service, and estate agency.

But franchising covers a lot more than just burger joints and fitness centres. Franchises have sprung up to meet just about any need. For example, Mad Science Group franchisees put on science programmes for schools, children's clubs and birthday parties. And Mr Handyman provides repair services for homeowners, while Merry Maids tidies up their houses.

Once considered upstarts among independent businesses, the International Franchise Association estimates that franchised brands account for 56 per cent of quick service restaurants, 18 per cent of lodging establishments, 14 per cent of retail food businesses and 13 per cent of table/full service restaurants. In this study franchises were found to employ almost 10 million people, with direct output close to €488 billion and a payroll of €180 billion.[9] Certainly, franchises now command 40 per cent of all retail sales in the United States. These days, it's nearly impossible to stroll down a high street without seeing a McDonald's, Subway or Holiday Inn. One of the best-known and most successful franchisers, McDonald's, now has 32,000 stores in 118 countries, including almost 14,000 in the United States. It serves 58 million customers a day and racks up more than €42 billion in annual system-wide sales. Nearly 80 per cent of McDonald's restaurants worldwide are owned and operated by franchisees. Now a larger business than McDonald's, Subway is one of the fastest-growing franchises, with more than 32,000 shops in 91 countries, including more than 23,000 in the United States.[10]

Franchise—A contractual association between a manufacturer, wholesaler or service organisation (a franchisor) and independent businesspeople (franchisees) who buy the right to own and operate one or more units in the franchise system.

Franchised brands are estimated to account for 56 per cent of quick service restaurants.

Source: Eyevine Ltd (top)

Retailer marketing decisions

Retailers are always searching for new marketing strategies to attract and hold customers. In the past, retailers attracted customers with unique product assortments and more or better services. Today, retail assortments and services are looking more and more alike. Many manufacturers, in their drive for volume, have placed their brands almost everywhere. You can find most consumer brands not only in department stores but also in mass-merchandise discount stores, off-price discount stores and all over the Web. Thus, it's now more difficult for any one retailer to offer exclusive merchandise.

Service differentiation among retailers has also eroded. Many department stores have trimmed their services, whereas discounters have increased theirs. Customers have become smarter and more price sensitive. They see no reason to pay more for identical brands, especially when service differences are shrinking. For all these reasons, many retailers today are rethinking their marketing strategies.

As shown in Figure 13.1, retailers face major marketing decisions about *segmentation and targeting, store differentiation and positioning*, and the *retail marketing mix*.

Figure 13.1 Retailer marketing strategy

Segmentation, targeting, differentiation and positioning decisions

Retailers must first segment and define their target markets and then decide how they will differentiate and position themselves in these markets. Should the store focus on upmarket, middle-market or down-market shoppers? Do target shoppers want variety, depth of assortment, convenience or low prices? Until they define and profile their markets, retailers cannot make consistent decisions about product assortment, services, pricing, advertising, store décor or any of the other decisions that must support their positions.

Too many retailers, even big ones, fail to clearly define their target markets and positions. For example, what market does the global clothing chain Gap target? What is its value proposition and positioning? If you're having trouble answering those questions, you're not alone – so is Gap's management.[11]

Gap was founded in San Francisco in 1969 by Doris and Don Fisher with the intent to make it easier to find a pair of jeans. By its heyday in the late 1980s and early 1990s, Gap was solidly positioned on the then-fashionable preppy look. But as its core customers aged and moved on, Gap stores didn't. In the past five years, as the chain has struggled unsuccessfully to define new positioning that works with today's younger shoppers, Gap store sales have slipped more than 22 per cent. Says one industry expert, 'Gap is in danger of death by a thousand cuts. Abercrombie & Fitch does the authentic preppy look. Uniqlo sells staples such as cashmere [sweaters] and scarves for a penny apiece. Primark, Topshop and Zara offer access to high-end fashion cheaply, so what is left?' Agrees another expert, 'Right now, Gap could be anything. It hasn't got a story.' The answer? Gap needs to 'define who the brand's core customers are and be exceptional to them; make distinctive and desirable clothes; and be noticed.'

In contrast, successful retailers define their target markets well and position themselves strongly. For example, Tesco positions itself strongly on low prices and what those always low prices mean to its customers. It consistently promises customers that 'Every little helps'.

But if giant Tesco, with roughly a third of the UK grocery market, dominates the low-price position, how can other retailers hope to compete? Again, the answer is good targeting and positioning. For example, Waitrose has fewer than 250 stores in the UK and slightly more than 4 per cent of the market versus Tesco's global network of stores in multiple trading formats and 30 per cent of the UK market. How does this small grocery chain compete with Tesco? Waitrose succeeds by carefully positioning itself *away* from Tesco. It targets a select group of upmarket customers and offers them high quality products with outstanding provenance. In fact, not only is Waitrose growing much faster than Tesco, some devoted Waitrose customers are more likely to boycott the local Tesco than to shop at it.

Waitrose can't match Tesco's massive economies of scale, incredible volume purchasing power, ultra-efficient logistics, wide selection and hard-to-beat prices. But then again, it doesn't generally try. By positioning itself strongly away from Tesco and other discounters, Waitrose has grown rapidly, even in tighter economic times.

Product assortment and services decision

Retailers must decide on three major product variables: *product assortment*, *services mix* and *store atmosphere*.

The retailer's *product assortment* should differentiate the retailer while matching target shoppers' expectations. One strategy is to offer merchandise that no other competitor carries, such as store brands, or manufacturer brands on which it holds exclusives. For example, a department store like John Lewis may get exclusive rights to carry a well-known designer's labels, and also offer its own private-label lines.

For example, fresh produce is currently the battleground for competitive wars between the supermarkets in the UK. Morrisons is upgrading its 'Market Street' concept, which offers instore fishmongers, butchers and bakers. Morrisons is Britain's fourth largest supermarket by market share. The chain already produces half the fresh food it sells itself rather than using suppliers and in 2012 bought a fish factory with the intention of producing 10,000 tonnes of seafood a year for its stores, including salmon, cod and surimi. Morrisons aims at a distinctive advantage in fresh food by controlling supplies.[12]

Another strategy is to feature blockbuster merchandising events. In the US, department store Bloomingdale's is known for running spectacular shows featuring goods from a certain country, such as India or China. Or the retailer can offer surprise merchandise, as when Aldi and Lidl or Poundland offers surprise assortments of seconds, overstocks and closeouts (products no longer manufactured). Finally, the retailer can differentiate itself by offering a highly targeted product assortment: High & Mighty carries extra-large clothing sizes; Gadget Shop offers an unusual

In the UK, Morrisons is upgrading its 'Market Street' concept, which offers in-store fishmongers, butchers and bakers.

Source: Morrisons

assortment of gadgets and gifts; and Accessorize offers almost every kind of hair decoration and cheap jewellery imaginable.

The *services mix* can also help set one retailer apart from another. For example, some retailers invite customers to ask questions or consult service representatives in person or via phone or keyboard. The John Lewis Partnership promises 'The Partnership aims to deal honestly with its customers and secure their loyalty and trust by providing outstanding choice, value and service'; do-it-yourself home improvement giant B&Q Home Depot offers a diverse mix of services for do-it-yourselfers, from 'how-to' guides and advice to inspire.

The *store's atmosphere* is another important element in the reseller's product arsenal. Retailers desire to create a unique store experience, one that suits the target market and moves customers to buy. Many retailers practise 'experiential retailing'. For example, at several REI stores (Recreational Equipment Inc.) in the US, consumers can get hands-on experience with merchandise, before buying it, via the store's mountain bike test trail, gear-testing stations, a huge rock climbing wall or an in-store simulated rain shower.

Today's successful retailers carefully orchestrate virtually every aspect of the consumer store experience. The next time you step into a retail store – whether it sells consumer electronics, hardware or high fashion – stop and carefully consider your surroundings. Think about the store's layout and displays. Listen to the background sounds. Smell the smells. Chances are good that everything in the store, from the layout and lighting to the music and even the smells, has been carefully orchestrated to help shape the customer's shopping experience – and open their wallets. At a Sony Style store, for instance, the environment is designed to encourage touch, from the silk wallpaper to the smooth maple wood cabinets, to the etched-glass countertops. Products are displayed like museum pieces and are set up to be touched and tried.

Perhaps the hottest store environment frontier these days is scent – that's right, the way the store smells. Most large retailers are developing 'signature scents' that you smell only in their stores:[13]

> Luxury shirtmaker Thomas Pink pipes the smell of clean, pressed shirts into its stores – its signature 'line-dried linen' scent. Bloomingdale's uses different essences in different departments: the soft scent of baby powder in the baby store, coconut in the swimsuit area, lilacs in intimate apparel, and sugar cookies and evergreen scent during the holiday season. At a Sony Style store, the subtle fragrance of vanilla and mandarin orange – designed exclusively for Sony – wafts down on shoppers, relaxing them and helping them believe that this is a very nice place to be. Such scents can increase customer 'dwell times' and, in turn, buying. Says the founder of ScentAir, a company that produces such scents, 'Developing a signature fragrance is much like [developing] a message in print or radio: What do you want to communicate to consumers and how often?'

Such 'experiential retailing' confirms that retail stores are much more than simply assortments of goods. They are environments to be experienced by the people who shop in them. Store atmospheres offer a powerful tool by which retailers can differentiate their stores from those of competitors.

In fact, retail establishments sometimes become small communities in themselves – places where people get together. These places include coffee shops and cafés, shopping malls, bookshops, children's play areas, superstores and urban greenmarkets. For example, today's bookshops have become part bookshop, part library, part living room and part coffee-house. On an early evening at your local Waterstones, for example, you are likely to find school students with school bags doing their homework with friends in the coffee bar. Nearby, retired people sit in comfortable chairs thumbing through travel or gardening books, while parents read aloud to their small children. Waterstones tries to sell more than just books; it sells comfort, relaxation and community.

Price decision

A retailer's price policy must fit its target market and positioning, product and service assortment, the competition and economic factors. All retailers would like to charge high markups and achieve high volume, but the two seldom go together. Most retailers seek *either* high markups on lower volume (most speciality stores) *or* low markups on higher volume (mass merchandisers and discount stores).

Thus, Harvey Nichols, founded in 1813, caters to the upper crust by selling clothing, shoes and jewellery created by designers such as Chanel, Prada and Hermes. The upmarket retailer pampers its customers with services such as a personal shopper and in-store showings of the upcoming season's trends with cocktails and hors d'oeuvres. By contrast, T.K. Maxx sells brand-name clothing at discount prices aimed at the budget-conscious. Stocking new products each week, the discounter provides a treasure hunt for bargain shoppers.

Retailers must also decide on the extent to which they will use sales and other price promotions. Some retailers use no price promotions at all, competing instead on product and service quality rather than on price. For example, it's difficult to imagine Harvey Nichols holding a two-for-the-price-of-one sale on Chanel handbags, even in a down economy. Other retailers – such as Asda, Costco and Poundland – practise EDLP, charging constant, everyday low prices with few sales or discounts.

Still other retailers practise '*high–low*' *pricing* – charging higher prices on an everyday basis, coupled with frequent sales and other price promotions to increase store traffic, create a low-price image, or attract customers who will buy other goods at full prices. The recent economic downturn has caused a rash of high–low pricing, as retailers pour on price cuts and promotions to coax bargain-hunting customers into their stores. Which pricing strategy is best depends on the retailer's overall marketing strategy, the pricing approaches of its competitors and the economic environment.

Promotion decision

Retailers use any or all of the five promotion tools – advertising, personal selling, sales promotion, public relations (PR) and direct marketing – to reach consumers. They advertise in newspapers and magazines and on the radio, television and the Internet. Advertising may be supported by newspaper inserts and catalogues. Store salespeople greet customers, meet their needs and build relationships. Sales promotions may include in-store demonstrations, displays, sales and loyalty programmes. PR activities, such as store openings, special events, newsletters and blogs, store magazines and public service activities, are always available to retailers. Most retailers have also created websites, offering customers information and other features and selling merchandise directly.

Place decision

Retailers often point to three critical factors in retailing success: *location, location* and *location*! It's very important that retailers select locations that are accessible to the target market in areas that are consistent with the retailer's positioning. For example, Apple locates its stores in high-end shopping centres and trendy shopping districts. Small retailers may have to settle for whatever locations they can find or afford. Large retailers, however, usually employ specialists who use advanced methods to select store locations.

Most stores today cluster together to increase their customer pulling power and give consumers the convenience of one-stop shopping. In the US and most European countries, *city centres* were the main form of retail cluster until the 1950s. Every large city and town had a central area with department stores, speciality stores, banks and cinemas. When people began to move to the suburbs, however, city centres, with their traffic, parking and crime problems, began to lose business. In recent years, many cities have joined with retailers to try to revive city centre shopping areas, generally with only mixed success.

Shopping centre—A group of retail businesses built on a site that is planned, developed, owned and managed as a unit.

A **shopping centre** is a group of retail businesses built on a site that is planned, developed, owned and managed as a unit. The most complex differentiation between different levels and types of shopping centres is shown in America. Here a *regional shopping centre*, or *regional shopping mall*, the largest and most dramatic shopping centre, can have from 50 to more than 100 stores, including 2 or more full-line department stores. It is like a covered mini-downtown and attracts customers from a wide area. A *community shopping centre* contains between 15 and 50 retail stores. It normally contains a branch of a department store or variety store, a supermarket, speciality stores, professional offices and sometimes a bank. Most shopping centres are *neighbourhood shopping centres* or *strip malls* that generally contain between 5 and 15 stores. They are close and convenient for consumers. They usually contain a small supermarket, perhaps a discount store, and several service stores – dry cleaner, chemist, video-rental store, hardware store, local restaurant or other stores.[14]

In Europe, while there has been considerable development of more attractive central shopping malls throughout the UK, like the giant Bluewater out-of-town shopping centre in Kent, and the new Westfield shopping centre, market size limits the potential more than is the case in the United States.

In fact, with more 100,000 shopping centres in the United States, many experts suggest that the country is now 'overmalled'. During the 1990s, shopping centre space grew at about twice the rate of population growth. However, more recently, several factors have caused hard times for American shopping malls. First, consumer spending cutbacks following the recession have forced many retailers – small and large – out of business, increasing mall vacancy rates. Second, shopping centres face increased competition – everything from the rapid growth of online shopping to ever-growing sales by the mega-retailers. As a result, increased numbers of traditional shopping centres are going under.

A shopping centre is a group of retail businesses built on a site that is planned, developed and managed as a unit.

Source: Getty Images/David Goddard

Although some traditional shopping centres are dying in the US, other types of centres are still being constructed. The current trend is toward the so-called power centres. *Power centres* are huge unenclosed shopping centres consisting of a long strip of retail stores, including large, freestanding anchor shops. Each store has its own entrance with parking directly in front for shoppers who wish to visit only one store. Power centres have increased rapidly over the past few years and challenge traditional indoor malls.

In contrast, *lifestyle centres* are smaller, open-air malls with upmarket stores, convenient locations, and non-retail activities, such as a playground, skating rink, hotel, dining establishments and a movie theatre. They are usually located near affluent residential neighbourhoods and cater to the retail needs of consumers in their areas. In fact, the original power centre and lifestyle centre concepts are now morphing into hybrid lifestyle–power centres. 'The idea is to combine the hominess and community of an old-time village square with the cachet of fashionable urban stores; the smell and feel of a neighbourhood park with the brute convenience of a strip center.' In all, today's centres are more about 'creating places to be rather than just places to buy'.[15]

Bear in mind that the 'mall' is an American icon, as in 'hanging out at the mall' as a prime leisure activity. However, in the UK and Europe, the intensity of large shopping centres is generally less, although the situation varies across the different countries involved. While the American shopping centre types are of interest, the European picture is complicated by the smaller geographical area of most individual countries, a longer history of urbanisation, longer established city centres and cultural differences that are reflected in consumer shopping preferences and attitudes towards shopping. You should not expect to find a direct replication of the American model in any European country, although there will be examples of each shopping centre type in each country, varying from local shopping areas to major regional centres and malls. It is not feasible to generalise about shopping centre types and developments Europe-wide, and marketers need to look closely at differences between countries of interest regarding retail developments. Retail structures vary considerably across the countries in Europe.

Retailing trends and developments

Retailers operate in a harsh and fast-changing environment, which offers threats as well as opportunities. For example, in some countries, the retail industry suffers from chronic overcapacity (too many shops), resulting in fierce competition for customer expenditure, especially in tough economic times. This is especially the case in the United States. Customer demographics, lifestyles and spending patterns are changing rapidly, as are retailing technologies. To be successful, retailers need to choose target segments carefully and position themselves strongly. They need to take the following retailing developments into account as they plan and execute their competitive strategies.

A slowed economy and tighter consumer spending

Following many years of good economic times for retailers, economic downturn and recession turned many retailers' fortunes from boom to bust. According to one American observer:[16]

> It was great to be in retailing during the past 15 years. Inflated home values, freely available credit, and low interest rates fueled unprecedented levels of consumer spending. Retailers responded by aggressively adding new stores, launching new concepts, building an online presence, and expanding internationally. While the U.S. economy grew 5 per cent annually from 1996 to 2006, . . . the retail sector grew at more than double that rate – an eye-popping 12 per cent. Revenues rose sharply, profits ballooned, and share prices soared. But that's all gone now. [Since the recent recession,] same-store sales . . . have dropped by double digits for many chains, store closures have accelerated, store openings are slowed, and shareholder-value destruction has been massive.

To a greater or lesser extent, these comments hold true for most of the developed economies in Europe. Nonetheless, some retailers actually benefit from economic downturn. For example, as consumers cut back and look for ways to spend less on what they buy, big discounters scoop up new business from bargain-hungry shoppers. Think of retailers like Aldi and Poundland in the UK. Similarly, lower-priced fast-food chains, such as McDonald's, have taken business from their pricier eating-out competitors.

For most retailers, however, a sluggish economy means tough times. Some large and familiar retailers have declared bankruptcy and closed their doors completely over recent years – for example, in the UK this includes household names such as Woolworths, Past Times, La Senza, Focus DIY, Oddbins and Borders, to name a few, and others remain at risk. Other retailers have laid off employees, cut their costs, and offered deep price discounts and promotions aimed at luring cash-strapped customers back into their stores – one estimate is that Britain's multiple retailers closed 14 stores a day on average across the country in 2011. Beyond cost-cutting and price promotions, many retailers have also added new value pitches to their positioning.

When reacting to economic difficulties, retailers must be careful that their short-term actions don't damage their long-term images and positions. Drastic price discounting is 'a sign of panic', says a retail strategist. 'Anyone can sell product by dropping their prices, but it does not breed loyalty.'[17] Instead of relying on cost-cutting and price reductions, retailers should focus on building greater customer value within their long-term store positioning strategies. For example, in the long term, a retailer like Waitrose cannot afford to abandon the quality, innovation and service that differentiate it from Tesco and other discounters.

New retail forms, shortening retail life cycles, and retail convergence

New retail forms continue to emerge to meet new situations and consumer needs, but the life cycle of new retail forms is getting shorter. Department stores took about 100 years to reach the mature stage of the life cycle; more recent forms, such as warehouse stores, reached maturity in about 10 years. In such an environment, seemingly solid retail positions can crumble quickly. For example, in the US of the top 10 discount retailers in 1962 (the year that Walmart and Kmart began), not one exists today. Even the most successful retailers can't sit back with a winning formula. To remain successful, they must keep adapting.

Wheel-of-retailing concept—
A concept that states that new types of retailers usually begin as low-margin, low-price, low-status operations but later evolve into higher priced, higher-service operations, eventually becoming like the conventional retailers they replaced.

Many retailing innovations are partially explained by the **wheel-of-retailing concept**. According to this concept, many new types of retailing forms begin as low-margin, low-price and low-status operations. They challenge established retailers that have become 'fat' by letting their costs and margins increase. The new retailers' success leads them to upgrade their facilities and offer more services. In turn, their costs increase, forcing them to increase their prices. Eventually, the new retailers become like the conventional retailers they replaced. The cycle begins again when still newer types of retailers evolve with lower costs and prices. The wheel of-retailing concept seems to explain the initial success and later troubles of department stores, supermarkets and discount stores, and the recent success of off-price retailers.

Although new retail forms are always emerging, today's forms appear to be converging. Increasingly, different types of retailers now sell the same products at the same prices to the same consumers. For example, you can buy brand-name home appliances at department stores, discount stores, home improvement stores, off-price retailers, electronics specialists, supermarkets and a slew of websites that all compete for the same customers. So if you can't find the microwave oven you want at Comet, step across the street and find one for a better price at Tesco or Aldi – or just order one online from Amazon or a more specialised home appliance website. This merging of consumers, products, prices and retailers is called *retail convergence*. Such convergence means greater competition for retailers and greater difficulty in differentiating the product assortments of different types of retailers.

The rise of mega-retailers

The rise of huge mass merchandisers and speciality superstores, the formation of vertical marketing systems, and a rash of retail mergers and acquisitions have created a core of superpower mega-retailers, usually operating globally. Through their superior information systems and buying power, these giant retailers can offer better merchandise selections, good service and strong price savings to consumers. As a result, they grow even larger by squeezing out their smaller, weaker competitors.

The mega-retailers have shifted the balance of power between retailers and producers. A small handful of retailers now control access to enormous numbers of consumers, giving them the upper hand in their dealings with manufacturers. For example, you may never have heard of speciality coatings and sealants manufacturer RPM International, but you've probably used one or more of its many familiar do-it-yourself brands – such as Rust-Oleum paints, Plastic Wood and Dap fillers, and Testors hobby cements and paints – all of which you can buy at your local hardware store or hobby shop. However, a dominant hardware retailer like Home Depot in the US is a very important customer to RPM, accounting for a significant share of its consumer sales. But, Home Depot's sales of €51.5 billion are close to 20 times RPM's sales of €2.7 billion. As a result, the giant retailer can, and often does, use this power to wring concessions from RPM and thousands of other smaller suppliers.[18]

Growth of non-store retailing

Many of us still make most of our purchases the old-fashioned way: we go to the store, find what we want, wait patiently in line to plunk down our cash or credit card, and bring home the goods. However, consumers now have a broad array of non-store alternatives, including mail order, mobile phone and online shopping. Consumers everywhere are increasingly avoiding the hassles and crowds at shops by doing more of their buying by phone or computer. As we'll discuss in Chapter 17, direct and online marketing are currently the fastest-growing forms of distribution.

Today, thanks to advanced technologies, easier-to-use and enticing websites, improved online service and the increasing sophistication of search technologies, online retailing is thriving. In the United States, online retailing still accounts for less than 4 per cent of total US retail sales. However, in the UK, online retail sales increased by 14 per cent in 2011 to more than £50 billion, with predictions that the growth will continue to hit high streets. Predictions are a similar increase in online spending in 2012 and beyond – well above the expected 3–4 per cent rise in total UK retail sales. British online shoppers spent an average of just under £1,500 each on 39 items in 2011, with Internet retail trade accounting for 12 per cent of total UK retail spending, the highest proportion in Europe. Other European countries with high online retail market shares included Germany (9 per cent), Switzerland (8.7 per cent) and Norway (8.1 per cent), while the lowest were in Poland (3.1 per cent) and Italy (1.3 per cent).[19]

Retailer online sites also influence a large amount of in-store buying. Here are some surprising statistics from the US: 80 per cent of shoppers

Direct and online marketing are currently the fastest-growing forms of distribution.

Source: Alamy Images/Pixellover RM5

research products online before going to a store to make a purchase; 62 per cent say that they spend at least 30 minutes online every week to help them decide whether and what to buy.[20] So it's no longer a matter of customers deciding to shop in the store *or* shop online. Increasingly, customers are merging store and online outlets into a single shopping process. In fact, the Internet has spawned a whole new breed of shopper and way of shopping:[21]

> Many people just can't buy anything unless they first look it up online and get the lowdown. In a recent survey, 78 per cent of shoppers said that ads no longer have enough information. So many buyers search online for virtually everything. Window shoppers have become 'windows' shoppers. A whopping 92 per cent said they had more confidence in information they sought online than anything coming from a salesclerk or other source. As a result, shoppers are devoting time and energy to ferreting out detailed information before they buy. Whether it's cars, homes, PCs or medical care, nearly four in five shoppers say they gather information on their own from the Web before buying. 'Do-it-yourself doctors' (that is, info-seeking patients) show up at their doctor's office with the Web-derived diagnosis in hand and a list of the medicines they need prescribed. Customers appear at the car dealership with the wholesale price and the model already picked out. Now this trend is spreading down the product chain. In the survey, 24 per cent of shoppers said they are even doing online research before buying shampoo. And they have questions: How does this shampoo work on different hair types, thicknesses and colours? Are the bottles recyclable? Has the product been tested on animals?

All types of retailers now employ direct and online channels. The online sales of large bricks-and-mortar retailers, such as Tesco, John Lewis, Staples and Carphone Warehouse, are increasing rapidly. Several large online-only retailers – Amazon, Zappos.com, online travel companies such as Travelocity.com and Expedia.com, and others – are now making it big on the Internet. At the other extreme, hordes of niche marketers are using the Internet to reach new markets and expand their sales.

Still, much of the anticipated growth in online sales will go to multi-channel retailers – the clicks-and-bricks marketers who can successfully merge the virtual and physical worlds. In a recent ranking of the top 500 online retail sites in America, 58 per cent were multi-channel retailers.[22] For example, John Lewis' enhanced website complements its stores around the UK. Although many John Lewis customers make purchases online, the site offers a range of features designed to build loyalty to the Partnership and pull customers into stores. Like many retailers, John Lewis has discovered that its best customers shop both online and offline. Similarly, in the US at department store chain Macy's: 'When our customers shop [both] online and in stores they spend 20 per cent more in stores than the average in-store shopper and 60 percent more online than the average online shopper at Macys.com,' says the chairperson. But the website aims to do more than just sell products online. 'We see Macys.com as far more than a selling site. We see it as the online hub of the Macy's brand.'[23] What is more, through its international website and electronic commerce partner FiftyOne, Macy's entire offering is also available online to European countries.

Growing importance of retail technology

Retail technologies have become critically important as competitive tools. Progressive retailers are using advanced IT and software systems to produce better forecasts, control inventory costs, interact electronically with suppliers, send information between stores and even sell to customers within stores. They have adopted sophisticated systems for checkout scanning, RFID stock tracking, merchandise handling, information sharing and interacting with customers.

Perhaps the most startling advances in retail technology concern the ways in which retailers are connecting with consumers. Today's customers have become used to the speed and convenience of buying online and to the control that the Internet gives them over the buying process. The Web lets consumers shop when and where they like, with instant access to huge storehouses of information about competing products and prices. No real-world store can do all that.

Increasingly, however, retailers are attempting to meet these new consumer expectations by bringing Web-style technologies into their stores. Many retailers now routinely use technologies ranging from touch-screen kiosks, mobile handheld shopping assistants and customer-loyalty cards to self-scanning checkout systems and in-store access to store inventory databases.

Green retailing

Today's retailers are increasingly adopting environmentally sustainable practices. They are 'greening' their stores and operations, promoting more environmentally responsible products, launching programmes to help customers be more responsible and working with channel partners to reduce their environmental impact.

At the most basic level, most large retailers are making their stores more environmentally friendly through sustainable building design, construction and operations. For example, new retail stores commonly employ extensive recycling and compost programmes, wind energy and solar panels for power, and locally sourced sustainable building materials. Similarly, even McDonald's Golden Arches are now going green. Its new eco-friendly restaurants are designed from the bottom up with a whole new eco-attitude.[24]

New 'green' McDonald's restaurants are built and furnished mostly with reclaimed building materials. The car parks are made with permeable surfaces, which absorb and clean storm water and filter it back into the water table. Exterior and interior lighting uses energy-efficient LEDs, which consume as much as 78 per cent less energy and last 10 to 20 times longer than traditional lighting. The restaurants are landscaped with hearty, drought-resistant native plants, which require less water. Then, what little water they do need comes from rainwater channelled from the roof and condensation from the super-high-efficiency HVAC system. Inside the restaurant, solar-tube skylights bring in natural light and reduce energy use. A sophisticated lighting system adjusts indoor illumination based on light entering through the skylights. The dining room is filled with materials made from recycled content (recycled floor tiles, for example, and counters made from recycled glass and concrete), and paints and cleaning chemicals are chosen for their low environmental impact. Other green features include high-efficiency kitchen equipment and water-saving, low-flow water taps and toilets. Some new restaurants even offer electric vehicle charging stations for customers.

Retailers are also greening up their product assortments and in some cases different approaches to niche retailing have developed. For example, Green Baby was set up by Canadian mother Jill Barker in the UK. Green Baby provides organic products, washable nappies, wooden toys, toiletries and maternity wear from four London stores and a mail-order business. Their Merino knitwear is produced by a Women's Fair Trade cooperative in Uruguay. They use luxurious natural merino fibres sourced via MANOS, who economise on water use and other resources and avoid using harmful chemicals during the kettle dyeing process. More generally, greener product assortments can both boost sales and lift a retailer's image as a responsible company. 'More than ever, our consumers are aware of the choices and behaviors that affect the world around us,' says a Safeway marketing executive. 'We want to simplify "choosing green".'[25]

Many large retailers have also launched programmes that help consumers make more environmentally responsible decisions. For example, global office products retailer Staples' EcoEasy programme helps customers identify green products sold in its stores and makes it easy to recycle printer cartridges, mobile phones, computers and other office technology products. As one of the world's leading ink sellers, Staples was one of the first international retailers to offer an in-store technology recycling programme. As a result, Staples recycled more than 50 million ink and toner cartridges in 2009 and collected more than 7.8 million pounds of technology waste for responsible recycling through its retail technology recycling programme. Staples has recycled more than 100,000 mobile phones and PDAs since 2005 through its partnership with Collective Good, which recycles and refurbishes small electronics.[26]

Finally, many large retailers are joining forces with suppliers and distributors to create more sustainable products, packaging and distribution systems. For example, Amazon works closely with the producers of many of the products it sells to reduce and simplify their packaging. And beyond their own substantial sustainability initiatives, mega-retailers like Walmart in the US and Tesco and Carrefour in the UK and Europe wield their huge buying power to urge their armies of suppliers to improve their environmental impact and practices.

Green retailing yields both top- and bottom-line benefits. Sustainable practices lift a retailer's top line by attracting consumers looking to support environmentally friendly sellers and products. They also help the bottom line by reducing costs. For example, Amazon's reduced-packaging efforts increase customer convenience and eliminate 'wrap rage' while at the same time save packaging costs. And an earth-friendly McDonald's restaurant not only appeals to customers and helps save the planet but costs less to operate. 'Green retailing has recently become another legitimate differentiator in the [retail] brand equation, and it creates significant quick-hit ROI opportunities, as well,' concludes a retail analyst.[27]

Global expansion of major retailers

Retailers with unique formats and strong brand positioning are increasingly developing international expansion strategies. Many are expanding globally to escape mature and saturated home markets. Over the years, some giant retail operations, such as McDonald's and KFC, have become globally prominent as a result of their marketing prowess. The world's largest retailer, US-based Walmart, is rapidly establishing a global presence. Walmart, which now operates more than 4,000 stores in 14 countries outside the US, sees exciting global potential. Its international division alone last year racked up sales of more than €78 billion, over 50 per cent more than US rival Target's *total* sales of €49 billion.[28]

However, in fact most US retailers are still significantly behind Europe and Asia when it comes to global expansion. Ten of the world's top 20 retailers are US companies; but only four of these retailers have established stores outside North America (Walmart, Home Depot, Sears and Costco). Of the 10 non-US retailers in the world's top 20, seven have stores in at least 10 countries. Among non-US retailers that have gone global are France's Carrefour and Auchan chains, Germany's Metro and Aldi chains, Hong Kong's pan-Asian Dairy Farm operation and Britain's Tesco. Generally, global expansion by European and Asian retailers has been more successful than that of US retailers.[29]

For example, French discount retailer Carrefour, the world's second-largest retailer, has embarked on an aggressive mission to extend its role as a leading international retailer:

> The Carrefour Group has an interest in more than 15,400 stores in over 30 countries in Europe, Asia and the Americas, including over 1,000 hypermarkets (supercentres). It leads Europe in supermarkets and the world in hypermarkets. Carrefour is outpacing Walmart in several emerging markets, including South America, China and the Pacific Rim. It's the leading retailer in Brazil and Argentina, where it operates more than 1,000 stores, compared to Walmart's 477 units in those two countries. Carrefour is the largest foreign retailer in China, where it operates more than 443 stores versus Walmart's 279. In short, although Walmart has more than three times Carrefour's overall sales, Carrefour is forging ahead of Walmart in most markets outside North America. The big question is, can the French retailer hold its lead? Although no one retailer can safely claim to be in the same league with Walmart as an overall retail presence, Carrefour stands a better chance than most to hold its own in global retailing.[30]

Perhaps the biggest challenge for international retailers in their globalisation is how to succeed in emerging markets like India and China, where local trading conditions and regulatory

French discount retailer Carrefour, the world's second – largest retailer, has embarked on an aggressive mission to extend its international rule.

Source: Getty Images/AFP

environments are very different to those in the west. It is also worth bearing in mind that globalisation means exactly that – for example, leading Asian retailers such as Aeon, Dairy Farm and Seiyu are extending their operations across the Asia-Pacific region, possibly with ambitions beyond those confines including the European and American marketplaces. Don't forget – companies who have developed ways of doing business that are effective in some of the world's toughest markets (the emerging markets) may see considerable prospects for their ways of doing business in the austerity-dominated European and American markets.

AUTHOR COMMENT

Whereas retailers primarily sell goods and services directly to final consumers for personal use, wholesalers sell primarily to those buying for resale or business use. Because wholesalers operate behind the scenes, they are largely unknown to final consumers. But they are very important to their business customers.

WHOLESALING

Wholesaling—All the activities involved in selling goods and services to those buying for resale or business use.

Wholesaler—A firm engaged *primarily* in wholesaling activities.

Wholesaling includes all the activities involved in selling goods and services to those buying for resale or business use. Firms engaged *primarily* in wholesaling activities are called **wholesalers**.

Wholesalers buy mostly from producers and sell mostly to retailers, industrial consumers and other wholesalers. As a result, many of the largest and most important wholesalers are largely unknown to final consumers. In Britain, the Institute of Grocery Distribution estimates that sales through the grocery and food-service wholesaling sector in 2011 reached £26.6 billion, in a grocery market worth around £150 billion at the retail level. Surprisingly, there are approximately 92,000 grocery stores in the UK, and hypermarkets, supermarkets and superstores account for less than 10 per cent of this number. Convenience and traditional grocery retailers get their supplies mainly from wholesalers.[31] For example, while Boots the Chemist is familiar to British consumers as a high street retailer, consumers are generally less aware of the Alliance Boots International wholesale business or the importance of wholesalers in supplying small pharmacies throughout the country:

> Pharmaceutical distributors provide 90 per cent of Britain's medicines, covering all of the UK's population. Full-service wholesalers act as a one stop shop for almost all pharmaceutical products and services, playing a key role in the cost-effective and safe distribution of a diverse and comprehensive range of healthcare products, all to exact orders on a same-day basis. The National Health Service relies on the efficient and effective service they provide – delivering to pharmacists, doctors, hospitals, sometimes even to individual patients across the whole country.
>
> Boots the Chemist is one of Britain's best-known high street retailers. But Boots UK is a member of Alliance Boots, an international pharmacy-led health and beauty group. Alliance Boots is a pharmaceutical wholesale business, which together with associates and joint ventures, supplies medicines, other healthcare products and related services to over 160,000 pharmacies, doctors, health centres and hospitals from over 370 distribution centres in 21 countries. The business provides high service levels to pharmacists in terms of frequency of delivery, product availability, delivery accuracy, timeliness and reliability at competitive prices. Retail customers are offered innovative added-value services which help pharmacists develop their own businesses. In addition to the wholesaling of medicines and other healthcare products, Alliance Boots provides services to pharmaceutical manufacturers who are increasingly seeking to gain greater control over their product distribution. These services include pre-wholesale and contract logistics, direct deliveries to pharmacies, and specialised medicine delivery including related home healthcare. Alliance Boots is the largest pharmaceutical wholesaler/distributor in Europe.[32]

Why are wholesalers important to sellers? For example, why would a producer use wholesalers rather than selling directly to retailers or consumers? Simply put, wholesalers add value by performing one or more of the following channel functions:

- *Selling and promoting.* Wholesalers' sales forces help manufacturers reach many small customers at a low cost. The wholesaler has more contacts and is often more trusted by the buyer than the distant manufacturer.
- *Buying and assortment building.* Wholesalers can select items and build assortments needed by their customers, thereby saving much work.
- *Bulk breaking.* Wholesalers save their customers money by buying in large lots and breaking bulk (breaking large lots into small quantities).
- *Warehousing.* Wholesalers hold stocks, thereby reducing the stocking costs and risks of suppliers and customers.
- *Transportation.* Wholesalers can provide quicker delivery to buyers because they are closer to buyers than are producers.
- *Financing.* Wholesalers finance their customers by giving credit, and they finance their suppliers by ordering early and paying bills on time.
- *Risk bearing.* Wholesalers absorb risk by taking title and bearing the cost of theft, damage, spoilage and obsolescence.

- *Market information.* Wholesalers give information to suppliers and customers about competitors, new products and price developments.
- *Management services and advice.* Wholesalers often help retailers train their sales staff, improve store layouts and displays, and set up accounting and stock control systems.

Types of wholesalers

Wholesalers fall into three major groups (see Table 13.3): *merchant wholesalers, agents and brokers* and *manufacturers' sales branches and offices*. **Merchant wholesalers** are generally the largest single group of wholesalers in a trade. Merchant wholesalers include two broad types: full-service wholesalers and limited-service wholesalers. *Full-service wholesalers* provide a full set of services, whereas the various *limited-service wholesalers* offer fewer services to their suppliers and customers. The different types of limited-service wholesalers perform varied specialised functions in the distribution channel.

Merchant wholesaler—An independently owned wholesale business that takes title to the merchandise it handles.

Table 13.3   Major types of wholesalers

Type	Description
Merchant wholesalers	Independently owned businesses that take title to all merchandise they handle. They include *full-service wholesalers* and *limited-service wholesalers*.
Full-service wholesalers	Provide a full line of services: carrying stock, maintaining a sales force, offering credit, making deliveries and providing management assistance. Full-service wholesalers include wholesale merchants and industrial distributors.
Wholesale merchants	Sell primarily to retailers and provide a full range of services. *General merchandise wholesalers* carry several merchandise lines, whereas *general line wholesalers* carry one or two lines in great depth. *Speciality wholesalers* specialise in carrying only part of a line.
Industrial distributors	Sell to manufacturers rather than to retailers. Provide several services, such as carrying stock, offering credit, and providing delivery. May carry a broad range of merchandise, a general line, or a speciality line.
Limited-service wholesalers	Offer fewer services than full-service wholesalers. There are many types of limited-service wholesalers, including cash-and-carry wholesalers, truck wholesalers, drop shippers, rack jobbers, producers' cooperatives and mail-order or Web wholesalers.
Cash-and-carry wholesalers	Carry a limited line of fast-moving goods and sell to small retailers for cash. Normally do not deliver.
Truck wholesalers (or truck jobbers)	Perform primarily a selling and delivery function. Carry a limited a line of semi-perishable merchandise (such as milk, bread, snack foods), which is sold for cash. Deliveries are made to supermarkets, small grocery stores, hospitals, restaurants, factory cafeterias and hotels.
Drop shippers	Do not carry stock or handle the product. On receiving an order, drop shippers select a manufacturer, who then ships the merchandise directly to the customer. Drop shippers operate in bulk industries, such as coal, timber and heavy equipment.
Rack jobbers	Serve grocery and pharmaceutical retailers, mostly in non-food items. Rack jobbers send delivery trucks to stores, where the delivery people set up toys, paperbacks, hardware items, health and beauty aids, or other items. Rack jobbers price the goods, keep them fresh, set up point-of-purchase displays and keep stock records.

405

Table 13.3 *Continued*

Producers' cooperatives	Farmer-owned members that assemble farm produce for sale in local markets. Producers' cooperatives often attempt to improve product quality and promote a co-op brand name, such as Sun-Maid raisins, Sunkist oranges or Diamond walnuts.
Mail-order or Web wholesalers	Send catalogues to or maintain websites for retail, industrial and institutional customers featuring jewellery, cosmetics, speciality foods and other small items. Main primary customers are small businesses.
Brokers and agents	Do not take title to goods. Main function is to facilitate buying and selling, for which they earn a commission on the selling price. Generally specialise by product line or customer type.
Brokers	Bringing buyers and sellers together and assisting in negotiation. Brokers are paid by the party who hired them and do not carry stock, get involved in financing or assume risk. Examples include food brokers, property brokers, insurance brokers and security brokers.
Agents	Represent either buyers or sellers on a more permanent basis than do brokers. There are several four types of agents: manufacturers' agents, selling agents, purchasing agents and commission merchants.
Manufacturers' agents	Represent two or more manufacturers of complementary lines. Often used in such lines as clothing, furniture and electrical goods. A manufacturer's agent is hired by small manufacturers who cannot afford their own field sales forces and by large manufacturers who use agents to open new territories or to cover territories that cannot support full-time salespeople.
Selling agents	Have contractual authority to sell a manufacturer's entire output. The selling agent serves as a sales department and has significant influence over prices, terms and conditions of sale. Found in product areas such as textiles, industrial machinery and equipment, coal and coke, chemicals and metals.
Purchasing agents	Generally have a long-term relationship with buyers and make purchases for them, often receiving, inspecting, warehousing and shipping the merchandise to the buyers. Purchasing agents help clients obtain the best goods and prices available.
Commission merchants	Take physical possession of products and negotiate sales. Used most often in agricultural marketing by farmers who do not want to sell their own output. A commission merchant may take a truckload of commodities to a central market, sell it for the best price, deduct a commission and expenses, and remit the balance to the producers.
Manufacturers' and retailers' braches and offices	Wholesaling operations conducted by sellers or buyers themselves rather than through independent wholesalers. Separate branches and offices can be dedicated to either sales or purchasing.
Sales branches and offices	Established by manufacturers to improve stock control, selling and promotion. *Sales branches* carry stock and are found in industries such as timber and automotive equipment and parts. *Sales offices* do not carry stock and are most prominent in industries like the clothing, accessories and dry goods industries.
Purchasing officers	Perform a role similar to that of brokers or agents but are part of the buyer's organisation. Many retailers establish purchasing offices in major market centres, such as London, New York, Paris and Frankfurt.

Brokers and *agents* differ from merchant wholesalers in two ways: they do not take title to goods, and they perform only a few functions. Like merchant wholesalers, they generally specialise by product line or customer type. A **broker** brings buyers and sellers together and assists in negotiation. **Agents** represent buyers or sellers on a more permanent basis. *Manufacturers' agents* (also called *manufacturers' representatives*) are the most common type of agent wholesaler. The third major type of wholesaling is that done in **manufacturers' sales branches and offices** by sellers themselves rather than through independent wholesalers.

Wholesaler marketing decisions

Wholesalers now face growing competitive pressures, more-demanding customers, new technologies, and more direct-buying programmes on the part of large industrial, institutional and retail buyers. As a result, they have taken a fresh look at their marketing strategies. As with retailers, their marketing decisions include choices of segmentation and targeting, differentiation and positioning, and the marketing mix – product and service assortments, price, promotion, and distribution (see Figure 13.2).

Segmentation, targeting, differentiation and positioning decisions

Like retailers, wholesalers must segment and define their target markets and differentiate and position themselves effectively; they cannot serve everyone. They can choose a target group by size of customer (small retailers only), type of customer (convenience stores only), the need for service (customers who need credit) or other factors. Within the target group, they can identify the more profitable customers, design stronger offers and build better relationships with them. They can propose automatic reordering systems, establish management-training and advisory systems, or even sponsor a voluntary chain. They can discourage less-profitable customers by requiring larger orders or adding service charges to smaller ones.

Marketing mix decisions

Like retailers, wholesalers must decide on product and service assortments, prices, promotion and place. Wholesalers add customer value through the *products and services* they offer. They are often under great pressure to carry a full line and stock enough for immediate delivery. But this practice can damage profits. Wholesalers today are cutting down on the number of lines they carry, choosing to carry only the more-profitable ones. They are also rethinking which services count most in

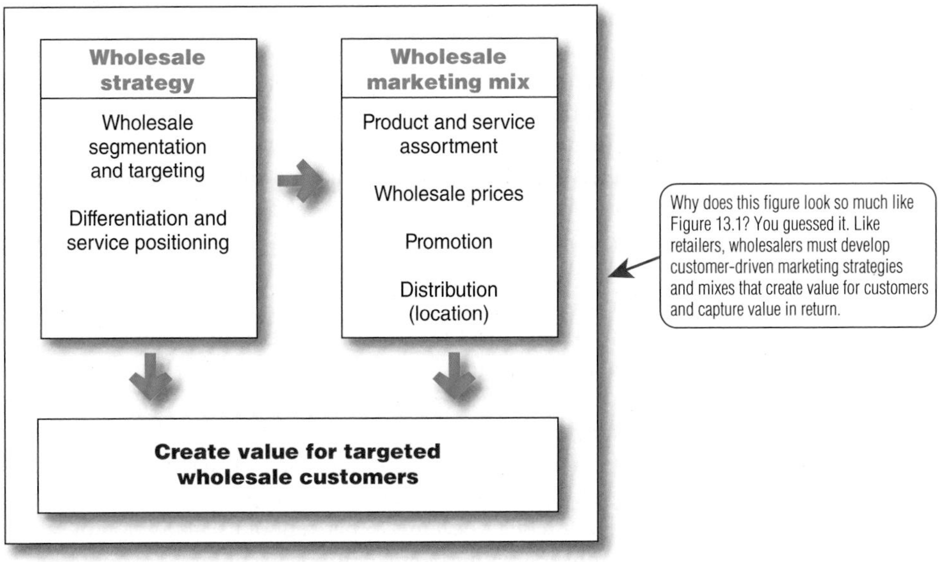

Broker—A wholesaler who does not take title to goods and whose function is to bring buyers and sellers together and assist in negotiation.

Agent—A wholesaler who represents buyers or sellers on a relatively permanent basis, performs only a few functions and does not take title to goods.

Manufacturers' sales branches and offices—Wholesaling by seller or buyers themselves rather than through independent wholesalers.

Figure 13.2 Wholesaler marketing strategy

building strong customer relationships and which should be dropped or paid for by the customer. The key is to find the mix of services most valued by their target customers.

Price is also an important wholesaler decision. Wholesalers usually mark up the cost of goods by a standard percentage – say, 20 per cent. Expenses may consume 17 per cent of the gross margin, leaving a profit margin of 3 per cent. In grocery wholesaling, the average profit margin is often less than 2 per cent. Wholesalers are trying new pricing approaches. The recent economic downturn put heavy pressure on wholesalers to cut their costs and prices. As their retail and industrial customers face sales and margin declines, these customers turn to wholesalers looking for lower prices. Wholesalers may cut their margins on some lines to keep important customers. They may ask suppliers for special price breaks, when they can turn them into an increase in the supplier's sales.

Although *promotion* can be critical to wholesaler success, most wholesalers are not promotion minded. They often use largely scattered and unplanned trade advertising, sales promotion, personal selling and PR. Many are behind the times in personal selling – they still see selling as a single salesperson talking to a single customer instead of as a team effort to sell, build and service major accounts. Wholesalers also need to adopt some of the non-personal promotion techniques used by retailers. They need to develop an overall promotion strategy and make greater use of supplier promotion materials and programmes.

Finally, *distribution* (location) is important. Wholesalers must choose their physical locations, facilities and Web locations carefully. There was a time when wholesalers could locate in low-rent, low-tax areas and invest little money in their buildings, equipment and systems. Today, however, as technology zooms forward, such behaviour results in outdated systems for material handling, order processing and delivery.

Instead, today's large and progressive wholesalers have reacted to rising costs by investing in automated warehouses and IT systems. Orders are fed from the retailer's information system directly into the wholesaler's, and the items are picked up by mechanical devices and automatically taken to a shipping platform where they are assembled. Most large wholesalers use technology to carry out accounting, billing, stock control and forecasting. Modern wholesalers are adapting their services to the needs of target customers and finding cost-reducing methods of doing business. They are also transacting more business online.

Trends in wholesaling

Today's wholesalers face considerable challenges. The industry remains vulnerable to one of its most enduring trends – the need for ever-greater efficiency. Recent economic conditions have led to demands for even lower prices and the winnowing out of suppliers who are not adding value based on cost and quality. Progressive wholesalers constantly watch for better ways to meet the changing needs of their suppliers and target customers. They recognise that their only reason for existence comes from adding value by increasing the efficiency and effectiveness of the entire marketing channel. As with other types of marketers, the goal is to build value-adding customer relationships.

The distinction between large retailers and large wholesalers continues to blur. Many retailers now operate formats such as supercentres that perform many wholesale functions. One of the greatest strengths of the large retailer is to integrate wholesale and retail operations under direct control. Companies like Tesco, Carrefour and Walmart make relatively little use of independent wholesalers, often dealing direct with manufacturers and managing their own logistics operations for greater efficiency. Retailers like these maintain buying functions actively seeking products direct from manufacturers across the world.

Although it is relatively unusual to date, there is also the potential for wholesale businesses to enter the retail market. For example, in the United States until recently, SuperValu was classified as a food wholesaler, with a majority of its business derived from supplying grocery products to independent grocery retailers. However, over the past decade, SuperValu has started or acquired several retail food chains of its own – for example, Albertsons – to become America's third-largest food retailer (behind Walmart and Kroger). Thus, even though it remains the largest food wholesaler in the US, SuperValu is now classified as a retailer because 75 per cent of its $44 billion in sales come from retailing.[33] Nonetheless, such moves are unusual in a European context.

Independent wholesalers are likely to continue to increase the services they provide to retailers – retail pricing, cooperative advertising, marketing and management information reports, accounting services, online transactions and so on. The weak economy, the growing power of large retailers who deal direct with manufacturers, and the demand for increased services from smaller customers are putting the squeeze on wholesaler profits. Wholesalers who do not find efficient ways to deliver value to their customers will soon drop by the wayside. However, the increased use of computerised, automated and Web-based systems will help wholesalers contain the costs of ordering, shipping and stock holding, thus boosting their productivity in some markets.

REVIEWING OBJECTIVES AND KEY TERMS

Retailing and wholesaling consist of many organisations bringing goods and services from the point of production to the point of use. In this chapter, we examined the nature and importance of retailing, the major types of retailers, the decisions retailers make and the future of retailing. We then examined these same topics for wholesalers.

OBJECTIVE 1 Explain the role of retailers in the distribution channel and describe the major types of retailers (pp. 386–392).

Retailing includes all the activities involved in selling goods or services directly to final consumers for their personal, non-business use. Retail stores come in all shapes and sizes, and new retail types keep emerging. Store retailers can be classified by the *amount of service* they provide (self-service, limited service or full service), *product line sold* (speciality stores, department stores, supermarkets, convenience stores, superstores and service businesses) and *relative prices* (discount stores and off-price retailers). Today, many retailers are banding together in corporate and contractual *retail organisations* (corporate chains, voluntary chains, retailer cooperatives and franchise organisations).

OBJECTIVE 2 Describe the major retailer marketing decisions (pp. 392–397).

Retailers are always searching for new marketing strategies to attract and hold customers. They face major marketing decisions about segmentation and targeting, store differentiation and positioning, and the retail marketing mix.

Retailers must first segment and define their target markets and then decide how they will differentiate and position themselves in these markets. Those that try to offer 'something for everyone' end up satisfying no market well. In contrast, successful retailers define their target markets well and position themselves strongly.

Guided by strong targeting and positioning, retailers must decide on a retail marketing mix – product and services assortment, price, promotion and place. Retail stores are much more than simply an assortment of goods. Beyond the products and services they offer, today's successful retailers carefully orchestrate virtually every aspect of the consumer store experience. A retailer's price policy must fit its target market and positioning, products and services assortment, and competition. Retailers use any or all of the five promotion tools – advertising, personal selling, sales promotion, PR and direct marketing – to reach consumers. Finally, it's very important that retailers select locations that are accessible to the target market in areas that are consistent with a retailer's positioning.

OBJECTIVE 3 Discuss the major trends and developments in retailing (pp. 397–403).

Retailers operate in a harsh and fast-changing environment, which offers threats as well as opportunities. Following years of good economic times for retailers, the economic downturn turned many retailers' fortunes from boom to bust. New retail forms continue to emerge. At the same time, however, different types of retailers are increasingly serving similar customers with the same products and prices (retail convergence), making differentiation more difficult. Other trends in retailing include the rise of mega-retailers, the rapid growth of non-store retailing, the growing importance of retail technology, a surge in green retailing and the global expansion of major retailers.

OBJECTIVE 4 Explain the major types of wholesalers and their marketing decisions (pp. 404–409).

Wholesaling includes all the activities involved in selling goods or services to those who are buying for the purpose of resale or business use. Wholesalers fall into three groups.

First, *merchant wholesalers* take possession of the goods. They include *full-service wholesalers* (wholesale merchants and industrial distributors) and *limited-service wholesalers* (cash-and-carry wholesalers, truck wholesalers, drop shippers, rack jobbers, producers' cooperatives and mail-order wholesalers). Second, *brokers* and *agents* do not take possession of the goods but are paid a commission for aiding buying and selling. Finally, *manufacturers' sales branches and offices* are wholesaling operations conducted by non-wholesalers to bypass the wholesalers.

Like retailers, wholesalers must target carefully and position themselves strongly. And, like retailers, wholesalers must decide on product and service assortments, prices, promotion and place. Progressive wholesalers constantly watch for better ways to meet the changing needs of their suppliers and target customers. They recognise that, in the long run, their only reason for existence comes from adding value by increasing the efficiency and effectiveness of the entire marketing channel. As with other types of marketers, the goal is to build value-adding customer relationships

NAVIGATING THE KEY TERMS

OBJECTIVE 1
Retailing (p. 386)
Retailers (p. 386)
Shopper marketing (p. 387)
Speciality store (p. 388)
Department store (p. 388)
Supermarket (p. 389)
Convenience store (p. 389)
Superstore (p. 389)
Category killer (p. 389)
Service retailer (p. 389)
Discount store (p. 390)
Off-price retailer (p. 390)
Independent off-price retailer (p. 390)
Factory outlet (p. 390)
Warehouse club (p. 390)

Chain stores (p. 391)
Franchise (p. 392)

OBJECTIVE 2
Shopping centre (p. 396)

OBJECTIVE 3
Wheel-of-retailing concept (p. 398)

OBJECTIVE 4
Wholesaling (p. 404)
Wholesaler (p. 404)
Merchant wholesaler (p. 405)
Broker (p. 407)
Agent (p. 407)
Manufacturers' sales branches and offices (p. 407)

DISCUSSING AND APPLYING THE CONCEPTS

Discussing the concepts

1. Discuss how retailers and wholesalers add value to the marketing system. Explain why marketers are embracing the concept of *shopper marketing*. (AACSB: Communication; Reflective Thinking)

2. Discuss the factors used to classify retail establishments and list the types within each classification. (AACSB: Communication)

3. List and briefly discuss the trends impacting the future of retailing. (AACSB: Communication)

4. Suppose you are a manufacturer's agent for three lines of complementary women's clothing. Discuss the types of marketing mix decisions you will make. (AACSB: Communication; Reflective Thinking)

5. Discuss the different organisational approaches for retailers and provide an example of each. (AACSB: Communication; Reflective Thinking)

6. What is retail convergence? Has it helped or harmed small retailers? (AACSB: Communication; Reflective Thinking)

Applying the concepts

1. The atmosphere in a retail store is carefully crafted to influence shoppers. Select a retailer with both a physical store and an online store. Describe the elements of the physical store's atmosphere, such as colouring, lighting, music, scents, and décor. What image is the store's atmosphere projecting? Is the atmosphere appropriate given the store's merchandise assortment and target market? Which elements of the physical store's atmosphere are in the online store's atmosphere? Does the retailer integrate the physical store's atmosphere with its online presence? Explain. (AACSB: Communication; Use of IT; Reflective Thinking)

2. Shop for a product of your choice on Amazon. Do consumer reviews influence your perception of a product or brand offered? (AACSB: Communication; Use of IT; Reflective Thinking)

3. Determining the target market and the positioning for a retail store are very important marketing decisions. In a small group, develop the concept for a new retail store. Who is the target market for your store? How is your store positioned? What retail atmospherics will enhance this positioning effectively to attract and satisfy your target market? (AACSB: Communication; Reflective Thinking)

Focus on technology

'Mirror, mirror on the wall, who's the fairest of them all?' This is no fairy tale feature anymore and can be found online or at a retailer near you. EZFace, a virtual mirror using augmented reality, is changing the cosmetics aisle in some stores. A shopper stands in front of the magical mirror, swipes the bar code of the cosmetic she is interested in, and virtually tries it on without opening the package. No more regrets about buying the wrong shade of lipstick! Self-service retailers are interested in this technology because it can reduce damaged inventory from consumers opening a package and then not buying it. This is just one of the interactive digital technologies that retailers are experimenting with; keep an eye out for many more!

1. Visit www.ezface.com or www.ray-ban.com/usa/science/virtual-mirror and use the virtual mirror to try on makeup or sunglasses. Does this technology help you select an appropriate product for your face? (AACSB: Communication; Use of IT; Reflective Thinking)

2. Find other examples of how retailers are using digital technologies, such as digital signage and mobile technologies, to better serve customers. (AACSB: Communication; Use of IT; Reflective Thinking)

Focus on ethics

In the United States, paying for purchases with a credit card is old news. That's not so in much of Asia. The United States leads the world in credit cards per capita – 2.01, which is much higher than many Asian countries, such as China with 0.15 cards per capita or India with 0.02. But that's changing dramatically. Between 2004 and 2009, Asian card transactions grew 158 per cent, approaching one-fourth of the global transaction volume. Asian governments are encouraging this growth because it stimulates the economy and brings in more tax revenue. Retailers embrace it because consumers spend more when using cards as compared to cash. This trend is not without critics, however, given the historical aversion to debt exhibited by Asians.

1. What are the ethical implications of encouraging electronic payment methods compared to cash payments in Asian countries? (AACSB: Communication; Ethical Reasoning; Reflective Thinking)

2. Most stores have eliminated layaway options for consumers and encourage credit purchases. Should retailers encourage customers to rely heavily on credit? (AACSB: Communication; Reflective Thinking)

Marketing & the economy

Walmart

In tough economic times, low-price leaders generally do well. They keep existing customers and gain new ones who are trading down. That was the case for Walmart throughout most of the recent economic downturn. But more recently, Walmart has seen a changing dynamic. By late 2010, traffic and same-store sales at US stores had been declining for a year. This is puzzling, especially given that the retailer had been aggressively discounting its already low prices during that period. There are two possible reasons for Walmart's declining numbers. First, Walmart's core shoppers have lower average incomes than typical Target shoppers and have felt little relief from the economic recovery. Already at the ends of their budgets, they are not ready to increase spending, even when something enticing goes on sale. Second, better-off customers who traded down to Walmart are now feeling more relaxed about spending. But rather than spending at Walmart, those customers are returning to other stores they frequented prior to the economic downturn. With a bleak forecast for job growth, Walmart's revenue trend is not expected to change anytime soon.

1. Are there any other options for Walmart other than waiting out the recovering economy?

2. What needs to change in the external environment before Walmart sees stronger growth?

REFERENCES

[1] Sources: Cecilie Rohwedder and Davod Kesmodel, 'German discounter Aldi invades Wal-Mart's turf', *Wall Street Journal* (14 January 2009), p. 5; Elizabeth Rigby, 'Aldi sales rise 25% as it lures wealthy', *Financial Times* (13 January 2009), p. 19; Michael Woohead, 'Secretive lives of the aldi founders', *Sunday Times* (4 January 2009), S1, p.7; 'Aldi and Lidl beat the big boys for happy customers', *Daily Mail* (29 January 2010), p. 35; Etain Lavelle, 'Superstores go to war against Aldi and Lidl', *Daily Mail* (17 September 2008), p. 74; Neil Craven, 'Belt-tightening shoppers are defecting to, discounter Aldi', *Mail on Sunday* (8 June 2008), p. 53; Neil Craven, 'Germans' cut-price lobster puts the squeeze on Tesco in the battle over middle britain', *Mail on Sunday* (17 February 2008), p. 57; Sean Poulter, 'Cut-price stores cash in as families feel the squeeze', *Daily Mail* (24 January 2008), p. 34.

[2] Quotes and other information on OgilvyAction from Katy Bachman, 'Suit your shelf', *AdweekMedia* (19 January 2009), pp. 10–12; 'OgilvyAction takes regional marketers to the last mile' (23 January 2008), accessed at www.entrepreneur.com/tradejournals/article/173710015.html; and Jack Neff, 'Trouble in store for shopper marketing', *Advertising Age* (2 March 2009), pp. 3–4. Retail sales statistics from 'Monthly and annual retail trade', US Census Bureau, www.census.gov/retail, accessed February 2010.

[3] Jack Neff, 'P&G pushes design in brand-building strategy' (12 April 2010), accessed at http://adage.com/print?article_id=143211.

[4] Store shopping statistics from Bachman, 'Suit your shelf', p. 10. For more on shopper marketing, see Grocery Manufacturers Association and Deloitte Consulting, *Delivering the Promise of Shopper Marketing: Mastering Execution of Competitive Advantage*, 2008, accessed at www.deloitte.com/view/en_US/us/Services/consulting/Strategy-Operations/finance-consulting/8d3aa0be83ffd110VgnVCM100000ba42f00aRCRD.htm; Ken Featherstone, '"The Last Mile" of Marketing', *AdweekMedia* (4 May 2009), p. 17; and 'Where to for shopper marketing?', *Retail World* (1 February 2010), p. 20.

[5] Richard Westlund, 'Bringing brands to life: the power of in-store marketing', *Brandweek* (18 January 2010), pp. IS1–IS2.

[6] Illustration based on David Wilkes, 'Supermarket snobs', *Daily Mail* (10 October 2007), p. 25; Rupert Steiner, 'Waitrose prospers despite friction with John Lewis', *Daily Mail* (13 November 2010), p. 101; Andrea Felsted, 'Waitrose upsurge signals revival', *Financial Times* (19 August 2009), p. 16; Andrea Felsted, 'Value range boosts Waitrose', *Financial Times* (22 June 2009), p. 1.

[7] Extract adapted from information found in Sandra M. Jones, 'Outlets proved promising for high-end retailers: luxury goods for less attract shoppers', *McClatchy-Tribune Business News* (11 April 2009). Also see Karen Talley, 'Bloomingdale's to open outlet stores', *Wall Street Journal* (21 January 2010); and David Moin, 'VCs considering outlets', *WWD* (22 January 2010), p. 2.

[8] Quotes and other information from 'Costco outshines the rest', *Consumer Reports* (May 2009), p. 8; Matthew Boyle, 'Why Costco is so addictive', *Fortune* (25 October 2006), pp. 126–132; Andrew Bary, 'Everybody's store', *Barron's* (12 February 2007), pp. 29–32; Jeff Chu and Kate Rockwood, 'Thinking outside the big box', *Fast Company* (November 2008), pp. 128–131; 'Top 10 U.S. retailers', *RIS News* (15 December 2009), accessed at www.risnews.com; and www.costco.com, accessed September 2010.

[9] see www.franchiseeurope.com/top500/article/europeanfranchisingtrendsanddevelopments/1, accessed (21 February 2012).

[10] Company information from www.aboutmcdonalds.com/mcd and www.subway.com/subwayroot/AboutSubway/index.aspx, accessed June 2010.

[11] 'Ten brands, ten challenges', *Chain Store Age* (August 2008), p. 6A; and Jeremy Lee, 'Gap', *Marketing* (27 August 2008), p. 19; Marianne Wilson, 'Talking retail', *Chain Store Age* (May 2009), p. 14; and www.gapinc.com/public/Investors/inv_financials.shtml, accessed June 2010.

[12] 'Grocer lands fresh catch', *Sunday Times* (4 March 2012), S3, p.2; Andrea Felsted, 'Fresh produce is new battleground in supermarket war', *Financial Times* (3/4 March 2012), p. 19.

[13] See Sandy Smith 'Scents and sellability', *Stores* (July 2009), www.stores.org/Marketing/2009/07/Edit06.asp; and www.scentair.com, accessed March 2010.

[14] For definitions of these and other types of shopping centres, see 'Dictionary', American Marketing Association, www.marketingpower.com/_layouts/Dictionary.aspx, accessed December 2010.

[15] Paul Grimaldi, 'Shopping for a new look: lifestyle centers are replacing enclosed malls', *Providence Journal* (*Rhode Island*) (29 April 2007), p. F10; Neil Nisperos, 'Lifestyle centers offer more than fresh air', *Inland Valley Daily Bulletin* (5 January 2009); and Courtenay Edelhart, 'Malls can't take customers for granted as new outdoor centers pop up', *McClatchy-Tribune Business News* (16 January 2010).

[16] Ken Favaro, Tim Romberger and David Meer, 'Five rules for retailing in a recession', *Harvard Business Review* (April 2009), pp. 64–72.

[17] Kenneth Hein, 'Target tries first price point driven TV ads', *Brandweek* (14 January 2009), www.brandweek.com.

[18] See www.rpminc.com/consumer.asp, accessed April 2010.

[19] US Census Bureau News, 'Quarterly retail e-commerce sales, 4th quarter 2009' (16 February 2010), accessed at www.census.gov/retail/mrts/www/data/html/09Q4.html. See also www.guardian.co.uk/money/2012/jan/19/online-retail-sales-hit-50bn, accessed 22 February 2012.

[20] Mark Penn, 'New info shoppers', *Wall Street Journal* (8 January 2009), accessed at http://online.wsj.com/article/SB123144483005365353.html.

[21] The online shopper statistics and extract example are from or adapted from Penn, 'New info shoppers'.

[22] 'Facts about America's top 500 e-retailers', *Internet Retailer*, www.internetretailer.com/top500/facts.asp, accessed September 2010.

[23] See Don Davis, 'M is for multi-channel', *Internet Retailer* (June 2007), www.internetretailer.com/2007/06/01/m-is-for-multi-channel; Macy's, Inc., 'online selling sites enhance integration with bricks-and-mortar stores', *Business Wire* (8 December 2008); and information from www.macys.com, accessed June 2010.

[24] See Jordan Cooke, 'McDonald's eco-friendly seal', *McClatchy-Tribune Business News* (13 January 2010); 'The golden arches go green: McDonald's first LEED certified restaurant' (11 December 2008), accessed at www.greenbeanchicago.com/leed-certified-permeable-pavers-led-lighting-recyclinggolden-arches-green-mcdonalds-leed-certified-restaurant/; 'McDonald's green prototype uses 25 percent less energy', *Environmental Leader* (8 April 2009), accessed at www.environmental-leader.com/2009/04/08/mcdonalds-green-restaurant-uses-25-percent-less-energy; and D. Gail Fleenor, 'Green light', *Stores* (October 2009), p. 52.

[25] Quotes and other information from Peter Berlinski, 'Green keeps growing', *Private Label Magazine*, www.privatelabelmag.com/feature.cfm, accessed (31 March 2010), p. 1; and www.jcpenney.com/jcp/default.aspx, accessed April 2010. See also www.greenbaby.co.uk, accessed (22 February 2012).

[26] See Alan Wolf, 'Chains embrace eco strategies', *Twice* (30 March 2009), p. 1; and information from www.staples.com; www.bestbuy.com, accessed April 2010; and www.ecoeasy.eu/en/europe_ecoeasy_initiatives, accessed (22 February 2012).

[27] Berlinski, 'Green keeps growing'. Also see Kee-hung Lai, T.C.E. Cheng and Ailie K.Y. Tang, 'Green retailing: factors for success', *California Management Review* (Winter 2010), pp. 6+.

[28] 'Walmart: international data sheet', http://walmartstores.com/pressroom/news/9705.aspx, accessed February 2010; and http://investors.target.com/phoenix.zhtml?c=65828&p=irol-IRHome, accessed April 2010.

[29] See 'Emerging from the downturn: global powers of retailing 2010', *Stores* (January 2010), accessed at www.deloitte.com/assets/Dcom-Global/Local%20Assets/Documents/Consumer%20Business/dtt_globalpowersofretailing2010.pdf.

[30] Information from http://walmartstores.com//default.aspx and www.carrefour.com, accessed June 2010.

[31] See www.igd.com/index.asp?id=1&fid=1&sid=7&tid=26&cid=1451, accessed 22 February 2012 and www.igd.com/index.asp?id=1&fid=1&sid=7&tid=26&cid=94, accessed 22 February 2012.

[32] See www.bapw.net, accessed 22 February 2012; www.boots-uk.com, accessed (22 February 2012).

[33] Facts from www.supervalu.com/sv-webapp, accessed June 2010.

VIDEO CASE

Zappos. com MyMarketingLab

These days, online retailers are a dime a dozen. But in less than 10 years, Zappos.com has become a billion dollar company. How did it hit the dot-com jackpot? By providing some of the best service available anywhere. Zappos customers are showered with such perks as free shipping both ways, surprise upgrades to overnight service, a 365-day return policy, and a call centre that is always open. Customers are also delighted by employees who are empowered to spontaneously hand out rewards based on unique needs. It's no surprise that Zappos.com has an almost cult-like following of repeat customers. After viewing the video featuring Zappos.com, answer the following questions.

1. How has Zappos.com differentiated itself from other retailers through each element of the retail marketing mix?
2. What is the relationship between how Zappos.com treats its employees and how it treats its customers?
3. Why did Amazon.com buy Zappos.com, given that it already sells what Zappos.com sells?

COMPANY CASE

Auchan – maybe Walmart is not unbeatable after all?

Auchan is sometimes called the French Walmart. It is a mega-retailer with a powerful patriarch, and a goal of expansion, headquartered in Croix, France. Auchan is France's second-largest supermarket group after Carrefour. In fact, Gérard Mulliez is the plain-speaking, small-town entrepreneur who has built a sprawling retail empire from a single store. Mulliez leads a secretive family that controls one of the world's biggest retail operations with more than 7,000 stores and sales of around €74 billion.

The Mulliez family runs more than two dozen companies, including Auchan (a big-box retailer similar to Wallmart), Decathlon (the world's biggest sporting goods retailer) and the European and Latin American operations of the US Midas car exhaust replacement chain. Auchan is gaining ground against competitors, especially in emerging markets. The major Auchan businesses are shown in the table below.

The Mulliez family has an estimated €17 billion fortune, making them one of France's wealthiest families, but also one that goes to extreme lengths to avoid publicity. Even most French people do not realise the extent of the family's holdings.

Auchan is the only Mulliez business to publish an annual report. Economist Benoît Boussemart's investigation of the Auchan empire suggests it is very strong with most of the companies nearly debt-free. The network that binds the Mulliez businesses together is strong but invisible. While legally separate, the Mulliez businesses are controlled by an extended family of about 550 people. Although Gérard Mulliez retired in 2006, his son, cousins, nephews and nieces hold top positions in nearly all the businesses. All the companies are privately-held. A family agreement allows the family to trade shares to each other, but not to outsiders.

While Auchan's roughly €74 billion sales means it is smaller than global leaders Walmart and Carrefour, it is on a par with Tesco and Germany's Metro. Auchan has been a particularly fast mover in emerging markets like China and Russia, where it has performed better than global peers Walmart, Tesco and Carrefour.

Indeed, Auchan's China operations have outperformed its rivals from the start. While close competitor Carrefour designed its China stores to mimic raucous street markets, Auchan's stores are designed to appeal to upwardly mobile and more refined shoppers. Consultancy Planet Retail estimates that Auchan's 145 China stores average €35 million in annual sales, compared to around €20 million for Walmart's mainland outlets.

In fact, Walmart's emphasis in China on very low prices seems to have backfired. It seems that Chinese consumers often assume that cheaper goods are counterfeit or dangerous. The affluent, modern Chinese consumer has very little taste for fakes and low-quality products, or even perhaps for undiluted western-style retailing.

For example, RT-Mart, the best-performing foreign big-box retailer in China, is also one of the most local of the foreign-owned retailers. It is owned by Sun Art, a joint venture of Taiwan's Ruentex Group and Auchan, and it listed on the Hong Kong stock exchange last year. RT-Mart's per-store sales are nearly double those of its main foreign competitors, according to Kantar Retail. On a weekday evening at its flagship store in Beijing, RT-Mart's blend of western-style efficiency and Chinese touches is on display. The vegetable section resembles that of any modern supermarket but for the burly female employee who stands in the aisle barking out bargains. The feel is more

Brand	2008 sales ($ billion)	Business	Outlets
Auchan	58.7	Hypermarkets	1,245 in 13 countries
Leroy Merlin	14.8	Home improvement	452 in 9 countries
Decathlon	7.4	Sporting goods	424 in 14 countries
3 Suisses*	5.5	Catalogue/online	Websites for 24 countries
Midas**	1.9	Car repairs	1,100 in 11 countries

* 44% owned by Mulliez family ** Only in Europe and Latin America
Source: Carol Matlack, *Bloomberg BusinessWeek* (21 December 2008), p. 64.

akin to the street markets the locals know so well, than to the sterility of big-box stores.

The Mulliez operations are growing rapidly in Russia as well, and 'Russia is poised to become the largest consumer market in Europe,' says Per Hong, Moscow-based partner at management consultancy AT Kearney. After the economic downturn of the late-2000s, Russia now has a new middle class that likes to shop. Seven years after opening its first Moscow outlet, Auchan has become Russia's top foreign hypermarket business, with 34 stores and around $6 billion in sales in 2009. By contrast, Walmart and Tesco are not in Russia and Carrefour has pulled out. Decathlon and the family's Leroy Merlin home improvement chain are piling into Russia. Support comes from property group Immochan, yet another Mulliez business, which acquires properties for the other family companies.

In 2012, Auchan, seen by local commentators as the most aggressive rival to Walmart globally, held talks with the Landmark Group for a possible India entry, reported by *The Times of India*. The discussions centred around a potential joint venture, but the final agreement will depend on whether India moves ahead with plans for foreign direct investment (FDI) in multi-brand retailing, which is politically sensitive in India. The stores which will be opened in India, if the agreement is signed between the two groups, may operate with the Auchan brand name, although the finer details are still to be worked out.

Nonetheless, in spite of its global success, Auchan has not prospered in the US or the UK. Auchan and Decathlon tried stores in America in the 1980s and 1990s but pulled out. The family bought Britain's Allied Carpets in 1999, but then sold it on after sales slumped.

Questions for discussion

1. Describe Auchan according to the different types of retailers discussed in this chapter.
2. As a retail brand, assess the Auchan retail strategy with respect to segmentation, targeting, differentiation and positioning.
3. What are Auchan's long term prospects and what threats does the company face in its dependence on emerging markets?
4. What recommendations would you make to Auchan's management for the future of their global business?

Sources: Carol Matlack, 'A French Wal-Mart's global blitz', *Bloomberg BusinessWeek* (21 December 2009), pp. 64–65; Laurie Burkitt, 'Chinese shoppers lose taste for fakes', *Wall Street Journal* (14 February 2012), p. 17; Simon Rabinovitch, 'China growth paradox baffles Walmart', *Financial Times* (14 February 2012); Paul Gould, 'Consumers: a new middle class that likes to shop', *Financial Times* (3 October 2011); Samidha Sharma and Boby Kurian 'French company Auchan eyes landmark joint venture', *The Times of India* (13 February 2012).

CHAPTER FOURTEEN

Communicating customer value: integrated marketing communications strategy

Chapter preview

In this and the next four chapters, we'll examine the last of the marketing mix tools – promotion. Companies must do more than just create customer value; they must also use promotion to clearly and persuasively communicate that value. Promotion is not a single tool but, rather, a mix of several tools. Under the concept of integrated marketing communications (IMC), the company must carefully coordinate these promotion tools to deliver a clear, consistent and compelling message about its organisation and its brands.

We begin by introducing the various promotion mix tools. Next, we examine the rapidly changing communications environment and the need for IMC. Finally, we discuss the steps in developing marketing communications and the promotion budgeting process. In the next three chapters, we will present the specific marketing communications tools.

Let's start by looking at a good IMC campaign – the 'Häagen-Dazs loves honeybees' campaign. From TV and print ads and an engaging website to public affairs and grassroots community events, the campaign employs a rich mix of promotional elements that work harmoniously to communicate Häagen-Dazs' unique message and positioning.

Objective outline

➤ **Objective 1** Define the five promotion mix tools for communicating customer value.
The promotion mix (pp. 418–419)

➤ **Objective 2** Discuss the changing communications landscape and the need for integrated marketing communications.
Integrated marketing communications (419–422)

➤ **Objective 3** Outline the communication process and the steps in developing effective marketing communications.

A view of the communication process (pp. 422–424)
Steps in developing effective marketing communication (pp. 424–429)

➤ **Objective 4** Explain the methods for setting the promotion budget and factors that affect the design of the promotion mix.
Setting the total promotion budget and mix (pp. 430–434)
Socially responsible marketing communication (pp. 434–435)

Häagen-Dazs

Häagen-Dazs is one of today's top-selling super premium ice cream brands. But only a few years ago, the brand teetered on the verge of commodity status. A glut of top ice cream brands had turned to beating each other up on price in an increasingly frugal marketplace. Häagen-Dazs needed to find a way to strengthen its emotional connection to consumers – to stand out from the crowd of competing brands. 'We needed a socially relevant idea . . . linked to the brand's core essence,' says Katty Pien, brand director for Häagen-Dazs.

In response, the brand launched its 'Häagen-Dazs loves honey bees' campaign. The campaign centred on an issue that's important to both the brand and its customers – a mysterious colony-collapse disorder threatening the honey bee population. Honey bees pollinate one-third of all the natural products we eat and up to 40 per cent of the natural flavours used in Häagen-Dazs ice cream. Yet, honey bee populations are disappearing at an alarming rate. The 'Häagen-Dazs loves honey bees' ('HD loves HB') message is a natural one for the brand. 'We want to keep these little heroes buzzing,' says the company.

Perhaps even more important than the 'help the honey bees' message itself is the way that Häagen-Dazs communicates that message. More than just running a few ads and a website, Häagen-Dazs has created a fully fledged, beautiful IMC campaign, using a wide range of media and PR elements that work harmoniously for the cause. At the heart of the campaign is a website, www.helpthehoneybees.com, a kind of honey bee central where customers can learn about the problem and find out how they can help.

The campaign began with creative broadcast and print ads that were designed to drive traffic to the website. The first TV ad was a beautifully staged mini-opera that poignantly outlined the plight of the honey bee. 'Honey bees are dying, and we rely on them for many of our natural ingredients,' said the ad. 'Help us save them.' An early print ad introduced Häagen-Dazs' vanilla honey bee flavour ice cream and implored, 'Honey, please don't go. Nature needs honey bees. We all do.'

Once at the website, which is carefully integrated with other campaign elements, the emotional connections really blossom. With the sounds of birds chirping and bees buzzing, the site greets visitors with the headline 'Imagine a world without honey bees' and explains the colony-collapse disorder problem. 'Get involved,' the site suggests. 'Donate now! Buy a carton, save a bee. Plant a bee-friendly garden.' At the site, visitors can read more about the bee crisis and what Häagen-Dazs is doing, tap into a news feed called *The Buzz*, turn on Bee TV, purchase Bee-Ts with phrases like 'Long live the queen' and 'Bee a hero', create their own animated honeybee and 'Bee-mail' it to friends, or make a direct donation to support honeybee research.

At the grass roots level, to create even more bee buzz, Häagen-Dazs hands out samples of Vanilla Honey bee ice cream and wildflower seeds at local farmers markets across the country. It sponsors projects and fund-raisers by local community groups and schools. It also donates a portion of the sales of

The Häagen-Dazs loves honeybees IMC campaign uses a rich, well-coordinated blend of promotion elements to successfully deliver Häagen-Dazs' unique message.

Source: Häagen-Dazs

417

all bee-dependent flavours (including all of the proceeds from vanilla honey bee) to fund pollination and colony-collapse disorder research at two major universities.

From the start, the 'HD loves HB' communications campaign has been a resounding success. Initially, Häagen-Dazs wanted to achieve 125 million media impressions within a year. 'We were blown away to see that we reached that goal in the first two weeks,' says Pien. Moreover, the campaign helped boost Häagen-Dazs' sales by 16 per cent during a recessionary year. And brand advocacy among consumers for Häagen-Dazs hit 69 per cent, the highest among nineteen brands tracked in one study.

Beyond traditional advertising media and the www.helpthehoneybee.com website, the 'HD loves HB' campaign has begun integrating social networking into the communications mix. For example, during a recent one-week period, Häagen-Dazs used Twitter's social-cause portal, TwitCause, to encourage people to spread the message, donating $1 per tweet to honey bee research. The brand has also leveraged the substantial public affairs potential of the honeybee crisis by lobbying Congress. The public affairs campaign included ice cream socials, media outreach efforts, and even testimony by Pien before the US Congress to save the honey bee. The burst of media attention from the public affairs efforts added new momentum. 'We originally thought this was one small part of the integrated campaign,' says Pien. 'But it has breathed new life into our consumer campaign.'

Thus, the 'HD loves HB' IMC campaign uses a rich, well-coordinated blend of communications elements to successfully deliver Häagen-Dazs' unique message and positioning. Only a few years ago, Häagen-Dazs was just a brand of ice cream. But now, thanks to the 'HD loves HB' campaign, the premium ice cream brand also stands out as one of the nation's premium social marketers. It's 'a brand with a heart and a soul,' says Pien. 'We're not only raising brand awareness,' she says, 'but making a difference in the world.'[1]

AUTHOR COMMENT

The beautiful 'Häagen-Dazs loves honey bees' IMC campaign has helped make Häagen-Dazs more than just another premium ice cream brand. It is now 'a brand with a heart and a soul'.

AUTHOR COMMENT

The promotion mix is the marketer's bag of tools for communicating with customers and other stakeholders. To deliver a clear and compelling message, each tool must be carefully coordinated under the concept of *integrated marketing communications*.

Building good customer relationships calls for more than just developing a good product, pricing it attractively, and making it available to target customers. Companies must also *communicate* their value propositions to customers, and what they communicate should not be left to chance. All communications must be planned and blended into carefully integrated programmes. Just as good communication is important in building and maintaining any kind of relationship, it is a crucial element in a company's efforts to build profitable customer relationships.

THE PROMOTION MIX

Promotion mix (or marketing communications mix)—The specific blend of promotion tools that the company uses to persuasively communicate customer value and build customer relationships.

A company's total **promotion mix** – also called its **marketing communications mix** – consists of the specific blend of advertising, public relations, personal selling, sales promotion and direct-marketing tools that the company uses to persuasively communicate customer value and build customer relationships. The five major promotion tools are defined as follows:[2]

- *Advertising*. Any paid form of non-personal presentation and promotion of ideas, goods or services by an identified sponsor.
- *Sales promotion*. Short-term incentives to encourage the purchase or sale of a product or a service.

. Personal presentation by the firm's sales force for the purpose of making
ng customer relationships.

Building good relations with the company's various publics by obtaining
favourable publicity; building up a good corporate image; and handling or heading off
unfavourable rumours, stories and events.

- *Direct marketing*. Direct connections with carefully targeted individual consumers to both
obtain an immediate response and cultivate lasting customer relationships.

Each category involves specific promotional tools used to communicate with customers. For example, **advertising** includes broadcast, print, Internet, outdoor and other forms. **Sales promotion** includes discounts, coupons, displays and demonstrations. **Personal selling** includes sales presentations, trade shows and incentive programmes. **Public relations** (**PR**) includes press releases, sponsorships, special events and Web pages. And **direct marketing** includes catalogues, telephone marketing, kiosks, the Internet, mobile marketing and more.

At the same time, marketing communication goes beyond these specific promotion tools. The product's design, its price, the shape and colour of its package, and the stores that sell it – *all* communicate something to buyers. Thus, although the promotion mix is the company's primary communications activity, the entire marketing mix – promotion *and* product, price *and* place – must be coordinated for greatest impact.

AUTHOR COMMENT

This is a really hot marketing topic these days. Perhaps no other area of marketing is changing so quickly and profoundly as marketing communications.

INTEGRATED MARKETING COMMUNICATIONS

In past decades, marketers perfected the art of mass marketing: selling highly standardised products to masses of customers. In the process, they developed effective mass-media communications techniques to support these strategies. Large companies now routinely invest millions or even billions of dollars in television, magazine or other mass-media advertising, reaching tens of millions of customers with a single ad. Today, however, marketing managers face some new marketing communications realities. Perhaps no other area of marketing is changing so profoundly as marketing communications, creating both exciting and anxious times for marketing communicators.

The new marketing communications model

Several major factors are changing the face of today's marketing communications. First, *consumers* are changing. In this digital, wireless age, they are better informed and more communications empowered. Rather than relying on marketer-supplied information, they can use the Internet and other technologies to find information on their own. They can connect more easily with other consumers to exchange brand-related information or even create their own marketing messages.

Second, *marketing strategies* are changing. As mass markets have fragmented, marketers are shifting away from mass marketing. More and more, they are developing focused marketing programmes designed to build closer relationships with customers in more narrowly defined micro-markets.

Finally, sweeping advances in *communications technology* are causing remarkable changes in the ways in which companies and customers communicate with each other. The digital age has spawned a host of new information and communication tools – from smartphones and iPods to satellite and cable television systems to the many faces of the Internet (e-mail, social networks, blogs, brand websites and so much more). These explosive developments have had a dramatic impact on marketing communications. Just as mass marketing once gave rise to a new generation of mass-media communications, the new digital media have given birth to a new marketing communications model.

Advertising—Any paid form of non-personal presentation and promotion of ideas, goods or services by an identified sponsor.

Sales promotion—Short-term incentives to encourage the purchase or sale of a product or a service.

Personal selling—Personal presentation by the firm's sales force for the purpose of making sales and building customer relationships.

Public relations—Building good relations with the company's various publics by obtaining favourable publicity; building up a good corporate image; and handling or heading off unfavourable rumours, stories and events.

Direct marketing—Direct connections with carefully targeted individual consumers to both obtain an immediate response and cultivate lasting customer relationships.

RISEHOLME CAMPUS

Although television, magazines, newspapers and other mass media remain very important, their dominance is declining. In their place, advertisers are now adding a broad selection of more-specialised and highly targeted media to reach smaller customer segments with more personalised, interactive messages. The new media range from speciality cable television channels and made-for-the-Web videos to Internet catalogues, e-mail, blogs, mobile phone content and online social networks. In all, companies are doing less *broadcasting* and more *narrowcasting*.

Some advertising industry experts even predict that the old mass-media communications model will soon be obsolete. Mass media costs are rising, audiences are shrinking, ad clutter is increasing and viewers are gaining control of message exposure through technologies such as video streaming or digital video recorders (DVRs) that let them skip past disruptive television commercials. As a result, they suggest, marketers are shifting ever-larger portions of their marketing budgets away from old-media mainstays such as 30-second TV commercials and glossy magazine ads to digital and other new-age media. For example, one study forecasts that whereas TV advertising spending will grow by only 4 per cent per year over the next five years, ad spending on the Internet and other digital media will surge by 17 per cent a year.[3]

When Kellogg's recently launched its Crunchy Nut Cornflakes in the US (after many years of success in Europe), for instance, it skipped national TV advertising altogether – something once unthinkable in the consumer products industry. Instead, it targeted 18–35 single males who were mostly college students through a 24-hour, day-long launch in a six-storey tall cuckoo clock, websites, SMS messages, Facebook, live video streams, e-mail and in-store promotions. Similarly, when Microsoft recently relaunched its Zune Pass online music service, it used 30-second spots but placed them online only, allowing more precise targeting. By using ads on many smaller sites, Zune Pass reached as many of its targeted young, male consumers as it did using national TV ads the previous year but in a more relevant way and at half the cost.[4]

In the new marketing communications world, rather than old approaches that interrupt customers and force-feed them mass messages, new media formats let marketers reach smaller groups of consumers in more interactive, engaging ways. For example, think about television viewing these days. Consumers can now watch their favourite programmes on just about anything with a screen – on standard televisions but also laptops, mobile phones or tablets. And they can choose to watch programmes whenever and wherever they wish, often with or without commercials. Increasingly, some programmes, ads and videos are being produced only for Internet viewing.

Despite the shift toward new digital media, however, traditional mass media still capture the lion's share of the promotion budgets of most major marketing firms, a fact that probably won't change quickly. For example, in the UK, the total advertising market was around €4 billion, of which around €1 billion was via social media. This means that one in every four euros spent on advertising was through social media.[5] At a broader level, although some may question the future of the 30-second TV spot, it's still very much in use today. Some 99 per cent of video watching is still done via traditional TV, and average viewership is up 20 per cent from 10 years ago. So, says one media expert, 'Traditional TV [is] still king.'[6]

Thus, rather than the old media model rapidly collapsing, most industry insiders see a more gradual blending of new and traditional media. The new marketing communications model will consist of a shifting mix of both traditional mass media and a wide array of exciting, new, more-targeted and more-personalised media. The challenge is to bridge the 'media divide' that too often separates traditional creative and media approaches from new interactive and digital ones. Many advertisers and ad agencies are now grappling with this transition. In the end, however, regardless of whether it's traditional or digital, the key is to find the mix of media that best communicates the brand message and enhances the customer's brand experience.

The need for integrated marketing communications

The shift toward a richer mix of media and communication approaches poses a problem for marketers. Consumers today are bombarded by commercial messages from a broad range of sources. But consumers don't distinguish between message sources the way marketers do. In the consumer's mind, messages from different media and promotional approaches all become part of a single

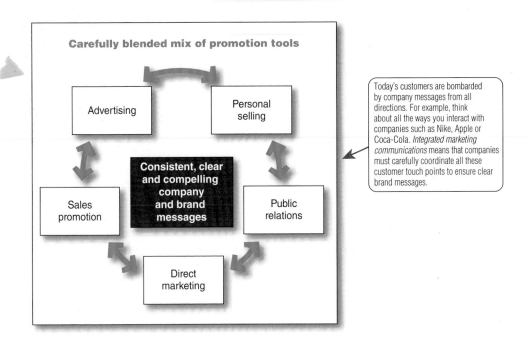

Figure 14.1 Integrated marketing communications

Carefully blended mix of promotion tools

Advertising

Personal selling

Consistent, clear and compelling company and brand messages

Sales promotion

Public relations

Direct marketing

Today's customers are bombarded by company messages from all directions. For example, think about all the ways you interact with companies such as Nike, Apple or Coca-Cola. *Integrated marketing communications* means that companies must carefully coordinate all these customer touch points to ensure clear brand messages.

message about the company. Conflicting messages from these different sources can result in confused company images, brand positions and customer relationships.

All too often, companies fail to integrate their various communications channels. The result is a hodgepodge of communications to consumers. Mass-media advertisements say one thing, while an in-store promotion sends a different signal, and company sales literature creates still another message. And a company's website, e-mails, Facebook page or videos posted on YouTube say something altogether different.

The problem is that these communications often come from different parts of the company. Advertising messages are planned and implemented by the advertising department or an ad agency. Personal selling communications are developed by sales management. Other company specialists are responsible for PR, sales promotion events, Internet or social network efforts, and other forms of marketing communications. However, whereas these companies have separated their communications tools, customers don't. Mixed communications from these sources result in blurred brand perceptions by consumers.

Today, more companies are adopting the concept of **integrated marketing communications (IMC)**. Under this concept, as illustrated in Figure 14.1, the company carefully integrates its many communications channels to deliver a clear, consistent and compelling message about its organisation and its brands.

IMC calls for recognising all touchpoints where the customer may encounter the company and its brands. Each *brand contact* will deliver a message – whether good, bad or indifferent. The company's goal should be to deliver a consistent and positive message to each contact. IMC leads to a total marketing communications strategy aimed at building strong customer relationships by showing how the company and its products can help customers solve their problems.

IMC ties together all of the company's messages and images. Its television and print ads have the same message, look and feel as its e-mail and personal selling communications. And its PR materials project the same image as its website or social network presence. Often, different media play unique roles in attracting, informing and persuading consumers; these roles must be carefully coordinated under the overall marketing communications plan.

Integrated marketing communications—Carefully integrating and coordinating the company's many communications channels to deliver a clear, consistent and compelling message about an organisation and its products.

IMC: Dinosaurs Unleashed is a richly integrated, multipronged campaign, which employed a broad range of marketing techniques and media.

Source: Rex Features/1096104 am

A great example of the power of a well-integrated marketing communications effort is the 'Häagen-Dazs loves honey bees' campaign.[7] Another is the Dinosaurs Unleashed campaign:

> Dinosaurs Unleashed is the largest life-size dinosaur adventure in the UK that gives feature 25 life-size dinosaurs, a CGI prehistoric aquarium, holographic video presentations, real and replica fossils and more than 40 interactive educational interpretation panels. The exhibition hired the UK agency The Think Tank with the remit to launch and to market the dinosaur exhibition within the very competitive London market. Accordingly, The Think Tank developed a well-integrated marketing communications strategy to launch Dinosaurs Unleashed at the huge O2 arena in central London. The Think Tank combined a broad range of marketing techniques and media. The launch included significant media activity with television coverage on a wide range of popular television shows and articles across the national press. A media launch event attracted more than 400 journalists and celebrities. The press activity was supported by innovative poster campaign across the London Tube network, supported by advertising in specialist press and given the education merit of the exhibition; schools were also targeted through direct marketing. The firms also employed social media to widen the reach with an interesting dinosaur blog to discuss dinosaur discoveries. As a result, visitors to the Dinosaurs Unleashed exhibition were over 33 per cent more than expected – a remarkable achievement.[8]

In the past, no one person or department was responsible for thinking through the communication roles of the various promotion tools and coordinating the promotion mix. To help implement IMC, some companies have appointed a marketing communications director who has overall responsibility for the company's communications efforts. This helps to produce better communications consistency and greater sales impact. It places the responsibility in someone's hands – where none existed before – to unify the company's image as it is shaped by thousands of company activities.

AUTHOR COMMENT

To develop effective marketing communications, you must first understand the general communication process.

A VIEW OF THE COMMUNICATION PROCESS

IMC involves identifying the target audience and shaping a well-coordinated promotional programme to obtain the desired audience response. Too often, marketing communications focus on immediate awareness, image or preference goals in the target market. But this approach to communication is too short-sighted. Today, marketers are moving toward viewing communications as *managing the customer relationship over time.*

Because customers differ, communications programmes need to be developed for specific segments, niches and even individuals. And, given the new interactive communications technologies, companies must ask not only 'How can we reach our customers?' but also 'How can we let our customers reach us?'

Thus, the communications process should start with an audit of all the potential touchpoints that target customers may have with the company and its brands. For example, someone purchasing a new mobile phone plan may talk to others; see television ads; read articles and ads in newspapers and magazines; visit various websites for prices and reviews; and check out plans at local retailers, or a wireless provider's kiosk or store at the mall. The marketer needs to assess what influence each communication experience will have at different stages of the buying process. This understanding helps marketers allocate their communication spend more efficiently and effectively.

To communicate effectively, marketers need to understand how communication works. Communication involves the nine elements shown in Figure 14.2. Two of these elements are the major parties in a communication: the *sender* and the *receiver*. Another two are the major communication

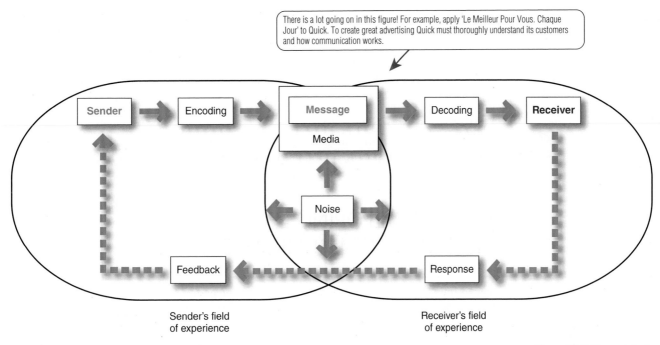

There is a lot going on in this figure! For example, apply 'Le Meilleur Pour Vous. Chaque Jour' to Quick. To create great advertising Quick must thoroughly understand its customers and how communication works.

Figure 14.2 Elements in the communication process

tools: the *message* and the *media*. Four more are major communication functions: *encoding*, *decoding*, *response* and *feedback*. The last element is *noise* in the system. Definitions of these elements follow and are applied to a Quick (the pan-Europe burger chain) 'Le Meilleur Pour Vous. Chaque Jour' (The Best for You. Every Day) television commercial:

- *Sender*. The *party sending the message* to another party – here, Quick.
- *Encoding*. The process of *putting thought into symbolic form* – for example, Quick's ad agency assembles words, sounds and illustrations into an ad that will convey the intended message.
- *Message*. The *set of symbols* that the sender transmits – the actual Quick ad.
- *Media*. The *communication channels* through which the message moves from the sender to the receiver – in this case, television and the specific television programmes that Quick selects.
- *Decoding*. The process by which the receiver *assigns meaning to the symbols* encoded by the sender – a consumer watches the Quick commercial and interprets the words and images it contains.
- *Receiver*. The *party receiving the message* sent by another party – the customer who watches the Quick ad.
- *Response*. The *reactions of the receiver* after being exposed to the message – any of hundreds of possible responses, such as the consumer likes Quick better, is more likely to eat at Quick next time, hums the 'Best for You' jingle or does nothing.
- *Feedback*. The part of the *receiver's response communicated back to the sender* – Quick's research shows that consumers are either struck by and remember the ad or they write or call Quick, praising or criticising the ad or its products.
- *Noise*. The *unplanned static or distortion* during the communication process, which results in the receiver getting a different message than the one the sender sent – the consumer is distracted while watching the commercial and misses its key points.

For a message to be effective, the sender's encoding process must mesh with the receiver's decoding process. The best messages consist of words and other symbols that are familiar to the receiver. The more the sender's field of experience overlaps with that of the receiver, the more effective the message is likely to be. Marketing communicators may not always *share* their customer's field of experience. For example, an ad copywriter from one socioeconomic level might create ads for customers from another level – say, wealthy business owners. However, to communicate effectively, the marketing communicator must *understand* the customer's field of experience.

This model points out several key factors in good communication. Senders need to know what audiences they wish to reach and what responses they want. They must be good at encoding messages that take into account how the target audience decodes them. They must send messages through media that reach target audiences, and they must develop feedback channels so that they can assess an audience's response to the message.

AUTHOR COMMENT

Now that we understand how communication works, it's time to turn all of those promotion mix elements into an actual marketing communications programme.

STEPS IN DEVELOPING EFFECTIVE MARKETING COMMUNICATION

We now examine the steps in developing an effective integrated communications and promotion programme. Marketers must identify the target audience, determine the communication objectives, design a message, choose the media through which to send the message, select the message source and collect feedback.

Identifying the target audience

A marketing communicator starts with a clear target audience in mind. The audience may be current users or potential buyers, those who make the buying decision or those who influence it. The audience may be individuals, groups, special publics or the general public. The target audience will heavily affect the communicator's decisions on *what* will be said, *how* it will be said, *when* it will be said, *where* it will be said and *who* will say it.

Determining the communication objectives

Buyer-readiness stages—The stages consumers normally pass through on their way to a purchase, including awareness, knowledge, liking, preference, conviction and, finally, the actual purchase.

Figure 14.3 Buyer-readiness stages

Once the target audience has been defined, marketers must determine the desired response. Of course, in many cases, they will seek a *purchase* response. But purchase may result only after a lengthy consumer decision-making process. The marketing communicator needs to know where the target audience now stands and to what stage it needs to be moved. The target audience may be in any of six **buyer-readiness stages**, the stages consumers normally pass through on their way to making a purchase. These stages include *awareness, knowledge, liking, preference, conviction* and, finally, the actual *purchase* (see Figure 14.3).

The marketing communicator's target market may be totally unaware of the product, know only its name, or know only a few things about it. Thus, the communicator must first build *awareness* and *knowledge*. This can be both domestically and internationally. For example, Standard Life sponsored the shirts worn by the players of English Premier League Club Liverpool to raise brand awareness in Asian, African and Middle East markets.

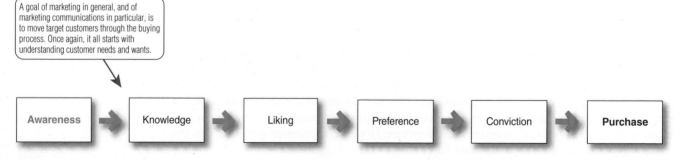

A goal of marketing in general, and of marketing communications in particular, is to move target customers through the buying process. Once again, it all starts with understanding customer needs and wants.

| Awareness | Knowledge | Liking | Preference | Conviction | **Purchase** |

Standard Chartered Bank joined the roll call of companies paying large sums to put their names on the shirts of leading European football clubs by agreeing a four-year sponsorship deal with Liverpool worth up to €94 million. It is putting its money into the English Football Association, which gives it sponsorship access to the England national team, Wembley stadium and the FA Cup. StanChart expects the deal to increase brand awareness in Asia, Africa and the Middle East. 'Liverpool will do that in a cost-effective way,' StanChart said. 'We are in growth markets. Now is the time to have a step change in brand recognition.'[9]

In contrast, after a series of takeovers in the UK, Santander sponsored a Formula 1 team (in part) to raise brand awareness within the UK.

The podium at the Bahrain Grand Prix must have been a welcome spectacle for executives at Santander – beneath the spray of champagne the Spanish bank's logo was emblazoned across the jumpsuits of all three of the winning racing drivers. For the millions of UK viewers of the race, the red-and-white flame is a familiar sight. The logo now adorns 1,000 UK branches after the Spanish group's predatory buying spree has seen it snap up three of the best-known brands in British banking in five years. Santander's presence on the Formula 1 circuit has been key to its UK expansion. When it acquired Abbey National at the end of 2004, the vast majority of the former building society's customers had little idea who the Spanish bank was and little faith that it could rejuvenate the struggling brand. The hugely expensive sponsorship of motor racing was a way of raising brand awareness in its coveted UK banking market. Five years later, Santander has the fifth largest branch network in the UK and is rapidly stealing market share from rivals.[10]

Assuming that target consumers *know* about a particular product, how do they *feel* about it? Once potential buyers know about a product, marketers then want to move them through successively stronger stages of feelings toward the product. These stages include *liking* (feeling favourable about the product), *preference* (preferring the product to other) and *conviction* (believing that the product is the best for them). Failure to respond to changing consumer preferences can be problematic.

David Wild, the Chief Executive of Halfords, the UK retailer of bicycles and car maintenance services recently reported that 'we had a tough summer on bikes relative to where we were this time last year'. 'The bike business last year was up by 20 per cent in the first half, and this year it was down by about 1 per cent.' He acknowledged that the group did not respond quickly enough to a change in consumer preference away from mountain bikes, designed to be used off-road, and toward town bikes, which are designed for city cycling. In essence, they failed to keep track with shifting consumer preferences.[11]

Finally, some members of the target market might be convinced about the product but not quite get around to making the *purchase*. Potential buyers might decide to wait for more information or for the economy to improve. The communicator must lead these consumers to take the final step. Actions might include offering special promotional prices, rebates or premiums. Dealers might call, write or e-mail selected customers, inviting them to visit the showroom or outlet. Of course, marketing communications alone cannot create positive feelings and purchases for products. The product itself must provide superior value for the customer. In fact, outstanding marketing communications can actually speed the demise of a poor product. The more quickly potential buyers learn about a poor product, the more quickly they become aware of its faults. Thus, good marketing communications call for 'good deeds followed by good words'.

Designing a message

Having defined the desired audience response, the communicator then turns to developing an effective message. Ideally, the message should get *attention*, hold *interest*, arouse *desire* and obtain *action* (a framework known as the AIDA model). In practice, few messages take the consumer all the way from awareness to purchase, but the AIDA framework suggests the desirable qualities of a good message.

When putting a message together, the marketing communicator must decide what to say (*message content*) and how to say it (*message structure* and *format*).

Message content

The marketer has to figure out an appeal or theme that will produce the desired response. There are three types of appeals: rational, emotional and moral. *Rational appeals* relate to the audience's self-interest. They show that the product will produce the desired benefits. Examples are messages showing a product's quality, economy, value or performance. Thus, in one ad, Virgin Atlantic simply states, 'Fly Virgin Atlantic Upper Class and get your own suite' or try 'Quaker Instant Oatmeal. A warm, yummy way to help lower your cholesterol.' And a Weight Watchers' ad states this simple fact: 'The diet secret to end all diet secrets is that there is no diet secret.'

Emotional appeals attempt to stir up either negative or positive emotions that can motivate purchase. Communicators may use emotional appeals ranging from love, joy and humour to fear and guilt. Advocates of emotional messages claim that they attract more attention and create more belief

Emotional appeal: Michelin sells tyres using mild fear appeals, showing families riding in cars and telling parents that Michelin tyres are the very safest.

Source: Michelin, North America, Inc.

in the sponsor and the brand. The idea is that consumers often feel before they think, and persuasion is emotional in nature. Thus, Michelin sells tyres using mild fear appeals, showing families riding in cars and telling parents 'Michelin: because so much is riding on your tyres.' And De Beers uses emotional ads showing silhouettes of men surprising the women they love with diamond jewellery. One recent ad concludes 'Celebrate your loving marriage. A diamond is forever.'[12]

Moral appeals are directed to an audience's sense of what is 'right' and 'proper'. They are often used to urge people to support social causes, such as a cleaner environment or aid to the disadvantaged. For example, the Red Cross urges people to donate money to help people in emergencies and to save and rebuild lives. In the recent East Africa Food Crisis Appeal the Red Cross argued that 'famine, drought and conflict have left millions of people needing food, water and healthcare' and presented the morally appealing story of Amina, who plaintively asked 'What if my children don't get food?'[13]

These days, it seems as if every company is using humour in its advertising. Properly used, humour can capture attention, make people feel good and give a brand personality. However, advertisers must be careful when using humour. Used poorly, it can detract from comprehension, wear out its welcome fast, overshadow the product and even irritate consumers.

Many brands manage to be sporadically funny but those that successfully build themselves around humour are far more unusual. The UK soft drink brand Tango did it from the mid-1990s with a series of advertisements. The most popular featured an orange blobby man who slapped drinkers with the catchphrase 'You've been Tangoed', a slogan that passed into common usage. A more recent example is Comparethemarket.com, the insurance comparison site whose brand identity centres on a Russian meerkat called Aleksandr Orlov and the fact that comparethemarket.com is easily confused with comparethemeerkat.com. 'In 2008, we'd been going for a year and research suggested we had a big issue with name recognition,' says Kal Atwal, the website's managing director. All the comparison sites 'had "compare" in their names.' The campaign had a tangible impact: monthly site visits went up from 50,000 to 2 million. The meerkat has proved so popular that a number of spin-off products were launched, including an 'autobiography' of Orlov that was published in time for Christmas. 'Even the Russians seem to like him,' says Ms Atwal. 'Russian TV covered the book launch.' Humour can also reinvigorate older brands. Old Spice has found a new audience with its 'Smell like a man, man' ads. Iain Tait of Wieden+Kennedy, the agency behind the campaign, says that because a lot of men's toiletries are bought for them by women, 'we needed to create a character who was adored by ladies but who men don't find threatening'. The answer was a character who combines extreme handsomeness with being funny. 'It's a very knowing kind of humour that comes from the character playing it straight,' says Mr Tait. Why don't more brands take the plunge? Mr Prior says companies worry that being amusing makes people question their credibility. But, he argues, 'consumers are more sophisticated than that. If you take an airline, passengers know that airlines take safety very seriously.' '[The Old Spice ads don't] send up the product and he doesn't make fun of himself,' explains Mr Tait. 'You need to treat the audience with a bit of respect and credit them with intelligence. When you try and spoon-feed them the gag, that's when it becomes embarrassing.'[14]

Message structure

Marketers must also decide how to handle three message structure issues. The first is whether to draw a conclusion or leave it to the audience. Research suggests that, in many cases, rather than drawing a conclusion, the advertiser is better off asking questions and letting buyers come to their own conclusions.

The second message structure issue is whether to present the strongest arguments first or last. Presenting them first gets strong attention but may lead to an anticlimactic ending.

The third message structure issue is whether to present a one-sided argument (mentioning only the product's strengths) or a two-sided argument (touting the product's strengths while also admitting its shortcomings). Usually, a one-sided argument is more effective in sales presentations – except when audiences are highly educated or likely to hear opposing claims or when the communicator has a negative association to overcome. In this spirit, Marmite (the yeast extract spread) ran the 'You either Love it or Hate it' campaign with the follow-up of 'Show Your Love'. Heinz ran the message 'Heinz Ketchup is slow good', and Listerine ran the message 'Listerine tastes bad twice a day'. In such cases, two-sided messages can enhance an advertiser's credibility and make buyers more resistant to competitor attacks.

Message format

The marketing communicator also needs a strong *format* for the message. In a print ad, the communicator has to make decisions related to the headline, the copy, the use of illustrations and the use of colour. To attract attention, advertisers can use novelty and contrast; eye-catching pictures and headlines; distinctive formats; message size and position; and colour, shape and movement. If a message is to be carried over the radio, the communicator has to choose words, sounds and voices. The 'sound' of an ad promoting banking services should be different from one promoting an iPod.

IMC: colour increases brand recognition by up to 80 per cent.

Source: Alamy/Ian Francis

If a message is to be carried on television or in person, then all these elements plus body language must be planned. Presenters plan every detail – facial expressions, gestures, dress, posture and even hairstyles. If a message is carried on a product or its package, the communicator must watch texture, scent, colour, size and shape. For example, colour alone can enhance message recognition for a brand. One study suggests that colour increases brand recognition by up to 80 per cent – for example, Veuve Clicquot's (trademark orange), KitKat's (red and white), Ecover's (blue and green), Quick Burger Restaurant's (red and white), Dove's (predominately white with blue text) or UPS (brown). Thus, in designing effective marketing communications, marketers must consider colour and other seemingly unimportant details carefully.[15]

Choosing media

The communicator must now select the *channels of communication*. There are two broad types of communication channels: *personal* and *non-personal*.

Personal communication channels

In **personal communication channels**, two or more people communicate directly with each other. They might communicate face to face, on the phone, via mail or e-mail, or even through an Internet 'chat'. Personal communication channels are effective because they allow for personal addressing and feedback.

Personal communication channels—Channels through which two or more people communicate directly with each other, including face to face, on the phone, via mail or e-mail, or even through an Internet 'chat'.

Word-of-mouth influence— Personal communications about a product between target buyers and neighbours, friends, family members and associates.

Some personal communication channels are controlled directly by the company. For example, company salespeople contact business buyers. But other personal communications about the product may reach buyers through channels not directly controlled by the company. These channels might include independent experts – consumer advocates, online buying guides and others – making statements to buyers. Or they might be neighbours, friends, family members and associates talking to target buyers. This last channel, **word-of-mouth influence**, has considerable effect in many product areas.

Personal influence carries great weight for products that are expensive, risky or highly visible. Consider the power of simple customer reviews on Amazon:[16]

> It doesn't matter how loud or often you tell consumers your 'truth', few today are buying a big-ticket item before they know what existing users have to say about the product. This is a low-trust world. That's why 'a recommendation by a relative or a friend' comes out on top in just about every survey of purchasing influences. One study found that 90 per cent of customers trust recommendations from people they know and 70 per cent trust consumer opinions posted online, whereas the trust in ads runs from a high of about 62 per cent to less than 24 per cent, depending on the medium. Customer reviews are also a major reason for Amazon's success in growing sales per customer. Who hasn't made an Amazon purchase based on another customer's review or the 'Customers who bought this also bought . . .' section? And it explains what a recent Shop.org survey found that 96 per cent of retailers find ratings and reviews to be an effective tactic in lifting online sales.

Buzz marketing—Cultivating opinion leaders and getting them to spread information about a product or a service to others in their communities.

Companies can take steps to put personal communication channels to work for them. For example, as we discussed in Chapter 5, they can create *opinion leaders* for their brands – people whose opinions are sought by others – by supplying influencers with the product on attractive terms or by educating them so that they can inform others. **Buzz marketing** involves cultivating opinion leaders and getting them to spread information about a product or a service to others in their communities.

This can be done on a large or more modest scale. For example, P&G has created a huge word-of-mouth marketing arm – Vocalpoint – consisting of 500,000 mums. Vocalpoint recruits 'connectors' – natural-born buzzers with vast networks of friends and a gift for the gab. They create buzz not only for P&G brands. P&G doesn't pay the mums or coach them on what to say. It simply educated the Vocalpointers about the product, armed them with free samples and coupons for friends, and then asked them to share their 'honest opinions with us and with other real women'.[17] On a smaller scale, the Premier Foods brand Hovis used a similar approach to support its Hearty Oats bread. Their campaign recruited 8,000 advocates to support the launch of the cholesterol beneficial bread. Targeting mums over 35 as brand champions, the launch was highly successful and supported by a Heart Oats community website that now has over 16,000 members.[18]

Non-personal communication channels

Non-personal communication channels—Media that carry messages without personal contact or feedback, including major media, atmospheres and events.

Non-personal communication channels are media that carry messages without personal contact or feedback. They include major media, atmospheres and events. Major *media* include print media (newspapers, magazines and direct-mail), broadcast media (television and radio), display media (billboards, signs and posters) and online media (e-mail, company websites and online social and sharing networks). *Atmospheres* are designed environments that create or reinforce the buyer's leanings toward buying a product. Thus, lawyers' offices and banks are designed to communicate confidence and other qualities that might be valued by clients. *Events* are staged occurrences that communicate messages to target audiences. For example, PR departments arrange grand openings, shows and exhibits, public tours and other events.

Non-personal communication affects buyers directly. In addition, using mass media often affects buyers indirectly by causing more personal communication. For example, communications might first flow from television, magazines and other mass media to opinion leaders and then from these opinion leaders to others. Thus, opinion leaders step between the mass media and their audiences and carry messages to people who are less exposed to media. Interestingly, marketers often use non-personal communications channels to replace or stimulate personal communications by embedding consumer endorsements or word-of-mouth testimonials in their ads and other promotions.

Selecting the message source

In either personal or non-personal communication, the message's impact also depends on how the target audience views the communicator. Messages delivered by highly credible sources are more persuasive. Thus, many food companies promote to doctors, dentists and other health-care providers to motivate these professionals to recommend specific food products to their patients. And marketers hire celebrity endorsers – well-known athletes, actors, musicians and even cartoon characters – to deliver their messages. Premier League football star Wayne Rooney lends his image to brands such as Nike and EA. Sports, Sarah Jessica Parker speaks for Garnier, Keith Richards endorses Louis Vuitton and the end of every Formula 1 race finds drivers scrabbling to put on their latest endorsed watches and caps.[19]

But companies must be careful when selecting celebrities to represent their brands. Picking the wrong spokesperson can result in embarrassment and a tarnished image. For example, Coca-Cola dismissed English and Manchester United footballer Wayne Rooney after he was caught swearing into a television camera after scoring a hat-trick of goals. And more than a dozen big brands faced embarrassment when golfer Tiger Woods' personal problems were publically exposed, tarnishing his previously pristine image. Gatorade, AT&T and Accenture abruptly ended their associations with Woods; Nike, Gillette, EA Sports and others stayed with the troubled golf superstar in hopes that the public would forgive his indiscretions. 'Arranged marriages between brands and celebrities are inherently risky,' notes one expert. 'Ninety-nine percent of celebrities do a strong job for their brand partners,' says another, 'and 1 percent goes off the rails.'[20]

Collecting feedback

After sending the message, the communicator must research its effect on the target audience. This involves asking the target audience members whether they remember the message, how many times they saw it, what points they recall, how they felt about the message, and their past and present attitudes toward a particular product and its manufacturer. The communicator would also like to measure behaviour resulting from the message – how many people bought the product, talked to others about it or visited the store.

Feedback on marketing communications may suggest changes in the promotion programme or in the product offer itself. For example, Marks & Spencer uses television and newspaper advertising to inform area consumers about its stores, services and merchandising events. Suppose feedback research shows that 80 per cent of all shoppers in an area recall seeing the store's ads and are aware of its merchandise and sales. Sixty per cent of these aware shoppers have visited a Marks & Spencer store in the past month, but only 20 per cent of those who visited were satisfied with the shopping experience. These results suggest that although promotion is creating *awareness*, Marks & Spencer stores aren't giving consumers the *satisfaction* they expect. Therefore, Marks & Spencer needs to improve the shopping experience while staying with the successful communications programme. In contrast, suppose research shows that only 40 per cent of area consumers are aware of the store's merchandise and events, only 30 per cent of those aware have shopped recently, but 80 per cent of those who have shopped expect to return soon to shop again. In this case, Marks & Spencer needs to strengthen its promotion programme to take advantage of its power to create customer satisfaction.

Celebrity endorsers can be risky: Tag Heuer and a dozen other big brands faced embarrassment when golfer Tiger Woods' personal problems were publicly exposed, tarnishing his previously pristine image.

Source: Getty Images: David Mc New

AUTHOR COMMENT

In this section, we'll look at the promotion budget-setting process and how marketers blend the various marketing communication tools into a smooth-functioning integrated promotion mix.

SETTING THE TOTAL PROMOTION BUDGET AND MIX

We have looked at the steps in planning and sending communications to a target audience. But how does the company determine its total *promotion budget* and the division among the major promotional tools to create the *promotion mix*? By what process does it blend the tools to create IMC? We now look at these questions.

Setting the total promotion budget

One of the hardest marketing decisions facing a company is how much to spend on promotion. John Wanamaker, the department store magnate, once said, 'I know that half of my advertising is wasted, but I don't know which half. I spent $2 [€1.4] million for advertising, and I don't know if that is half enough or twice too much.' Thus, it is not surprising that industries and companies vary widely in how much they spend on promotion. Promotion spending may be 10–12 per cent of sales for consumer packaged goods, 14 per cent for cosmetics and only 1 per cent for industrial machinery products. Within a given industry, both low and high spenders can be found.[21]

How does a company determine its promotion budget? Here, we look at four common methods used to set the total budget for advertising: the *affordable method*, the *percentage-of-sales method*, the *competitive-parity method* and the *objective-and-task method*.[22]

Affordable method

Affordable method—Setting the promotion budget at the level management thinks the company can afford.

Some companies use the **affordable method**: they set the promotion budget at the level they think the company can afford. Small businesses often use this method, reasoning that the company cannot spend more on advertising than it has. They start with total revenues, deduct operating expenses and capital outlays, and then devote some portion of the remaining funds to advertising.

Unfortunately, this method of setting budgets completely ignores the effects of promotion on sales. It tends to place promotion last among spending priorities, even in situations in which advertising is critical to the firm's success. It leads to an uncertain annual promotion budget, which makes long-range market planning difficult. Although the affordable method can result in overspending on advertising, it more often results in underspending.

Percentage-of-sales method

Percentage-of-sales method—Setting the promotion budget at a certain percentage of current or forecasted sales or as a percentage of the unit sales price.

Other companies use the **percentage-of-sales method**, setting their promotion budget at a certain percentage of current or forecasted sales. Or they budget a percentage of the unit sales price. The percentage-of-sales method is simple to use and helps management think about the relationship between promotion spending, selling price and profit per unit.

Despite these claimed advantages, however, the percentage-of-sales method has little to justify it. It wrongly views sales as the *cause* of promotion rather than as the *result*. Although studies have found a positive correlation between promotional spending and brand strength, this relationship often turns out to be effect and cause, not cause and effect. Stronger brands with higher sales can afford the biggest ad budgets.

Thus, the percentage-of-sales budget is based on the availability of funds rather than on opportunities. It may prevent the increased spending sometimes needed to turn around falling sales. Because the budget varies with year-to-year sales, long-range planning is difficult. Finally, the method does not provide any basis for choosing a *specific* percentage, except what has been done in the past or what competitors are doing.

Competitive-parity method

Competitive-parity method—Setting the promotion budget to match competitors' outlays.

Still other companies use the **competitive-parity method**, setting their promotion budgets to match competitors' outlays. They monitor competitors' advertising or get industry promotion spending estimates from publications or trade associations and then set their budgets based on the industry average.

Two arguments support this method. First, competitors' budgets represent the collective wisdom of the industry. Second, spending what competitors spend helps prevent promotion wars. Unfortunately, neither argument is valid. There are no grounds for believing that the competition has a better idea of what a company should be spending on promotion than does the company itself. Companies differ greatly, and each has its own special promotion needs. Finally, there is no evidence that budgets based on competitive parity prevent promotion wars.

Objective-and-task method

The most logical budget-setting method is the **objective-and-task method**, whereby the company sets its promotion budget based on what it wants to accomplish with promotion. This budgeting method entails (1) defining specific promotion objectives, (2) determining the tasks needed to achieve these objectives, and (3) estimating the costs of performing these tasks. The sum of these costs is the proposed promotion budget.

The advantage of the objective-and-task method is that it forces management to spell out its assumptions about the relationship between euros spent and promotion results. But it is also the most difficult method to use. Often, it is hard to work out which specific tasks will achieve the stated objectives. For example, suppose Canon Europe wants a 95 per cent awareness for its latest camcorder model during a six-month introductory period. What specific advertising messages and media schedules should Canon use to attain this objective? How much would these messages and media schedules cost? Canon's management must consider such questions, even though they are hard to answer.

Objective-and-task method—
Developing the promotion budget by (1) defining specific promotion objectives, (2) determining the tasks needed to achieve these objectives, and (3) estimating the costs of performing these tasks. The sum of these costs is the proposed promotion budget.

Shaping the overall promotion mix

The IMC concept suggests that the company must blend the promotion tools carefully into a coordinated *promotion mix*. But how does it determine what mix of promotion tools to use? Companies within the same industry differ greatly in the design of their promotion mixes. For example, Mary Kay spends most of its promotion funds on personal selling and direct marketing, whereas competitor CoverGirl spends heavily on consumer advertising. We now look at factors that influence the marketer's choice of promotion tools.

The nature of each promotion tool

Each promotion tool has unique characteristics and costs. Marketers must understand these characteristics in shaping the promotion mix.

Advertising

Advertising can reach masses of geographically dispersed buyers at a low cost per exposure, and it enables the seller to repeat a message many times. For example, television advertising can reach huge audiences. An estimated 300 million people worldwide watched the 2011 Champions League Final, about 56 million people watched at least part of the 2011 French Open Tennis Championship at Roland Garros and 10 million fans regularly tune in for Germany's most popular reality television show 'Wetten, dass . . . ?' ('Wanna Bet?'). For companies that want to reach a mass audience, TV is the place to be.

Beyond its reach, large-scale advertising says something positive about a seller's size, popularity and success. Because of advertising's public nature, consumers tend to view advertised products as more legitimate. Advertising is also very expressive; it allows the company to dramatise its products through the artful use of visuals, print, sound and colour. On the one hand, advertising can be used to build up a long-term image for a product (such as for Volkswagen Golf). On the other hand, advertising can trigger quick sales (as when Play.com advertises weekend specials).

Advertising also has some shortcomings. Although it reaches many people quickly, advertising is impersonal and cannot be as directly persuasive as can company salespeople. For the most part, advertising can carry on only a one-way communication with an audience, and the audience does not feel that it has to pay attention or respond. In addition, advertising can be very costly. Although some advertising forms, such as newspaper and radio advertising, can be done on smaller budgets, other forms, such as network TV advertising, require very large budgets.

Personal selling

Personal selling is the most effective tool at certain stages of the buying process, particularly in building up buyers' preferences, convictions and actions. It involves personal interaction between two or more people, so each person can observe the other's needs and characteristics and make quick adjustments. Personal selling also allows all kinds of customer relationships to spring up, ranging from matter-of-fact selling relationships to personal friendships. An effective salesperson keeps the customer's interests at heart to build a long-term relationship by solving a customer's problems. Finally, with personal selling, the buyer usually feels a greater need to listen and respond, even if the response is a polite 'No thank-you'.

These unique qualities come at a cost, however. A sales force requires a longer-term commitment than does advertising; advertising can be turned up or down, but the size of a sales force is harder to change. Personal selling is also the company's most expensive promotion tool, costing companies on average €250 or more per sales call, depending on the industry.[23] Firms can spend up to three times as much on personal selling as they do on advertising.

Sales promotion

Sales promotion includes a wide assortment of tools – coupons, contests, money-off deals, premiums and others – all of which have many unique qualities. They attract consumer attention, offer strong incentives to purchase and can be used to dramatise product offers and boost sagging sales. Sales promotions invite and reward quick response. Whereas advertising says, 'Buy our product', sales promotion says, 'Buy it now'. Sales promotion effects are often short lived, however, and often are not as effective as advertising or personal selling in building long-term brand preference and customer relationships.

Public relations

Public relations (PR) is very believable – news stories, features, sponsorships and events seem more real and believable to readers than ads do. PR can also reach many prospects who avoid salespeople and advertisements; the message gets to buyers as 'news' rather than as a sales-directed communication. And, as with advertising, PR can dramatise a company or product. Marketers tend to under-use PR or use it as an afterthought. Yet a well-thought-out PR campaign used with other promotion mix elements can be very effective and economical.

Direct marketing

Although there are many forms of direct marketing – direct mail and catalogues, online marketing, telephone marketing and others – they all share four distinctive characteristics. Direct marketing is less public: the message is normally directed to a specific person. Direct marketing is immediate and customised: messages can be prepared very quickly and can be tailored to appeal to specific consumers. Finally, direct marketing is interactive: it allows a dialogue between the marketing team and the consumer, and messages can be altered depending on the consumer's response. Thus, direct marketing is well suited to highly targeted marketing efforts and building one-to-one customer relationships.

Promotion mix strategies

Push strategy—A promotion strategy that calls for using the sales force and trade promotion to push a product through channels. A producer promotes a particular product to channel members, who in turn promote it to final consumers.

Marketers can choose from two basic promotion mix strategies: *push* promotion or *pull* promotion. Figure 14.4 contrasts the two strategies. The relative emphasis given to specific promotion tools differs for push and pull strategies. A **push strategy** involves 'pushing' the product through marketing channels to final consumers. The producer directs its marketing activities (primarily personal selling and trade promotion) toward channel members to induce them to carry the product and

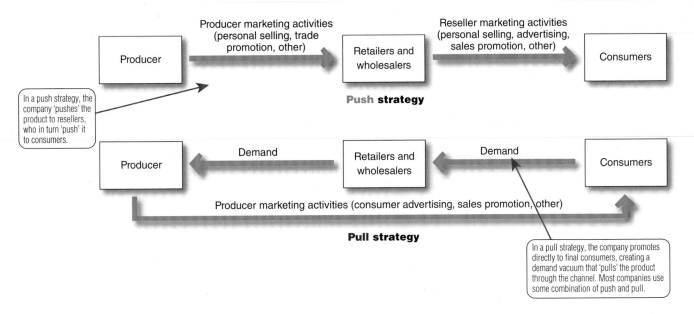

In a push strategy, the company 'pushes' the product to resellers, who in turn 'push' it to consumers.

In a pull strategy, the company promotes directly to final consumers, creating a demand vacuum that 'pulls' the product through the channel. Most companies use some combination of push and pull.

Figure 14.4 Push versus pull promotion strategy

promote it to final consumers. For example, Husqvarna (the originally Swedish but now truly global firm) does very little promoting of its outdoor products to final consumers. Instead, Husqvarna's sales force works with national-level retailers, independent dealers and other channel members, who in turn push Husqvarna's products to final consumers.

Using a **pull strategy**, a producer directs its marketing activities (primarily advertising and consumer promotion) toward final consumers to induce them to buy a particular product. For example, Unilever promotes its Axe grooming products directly to its young male target market using TV and print ads, a brand website, its YouTube channel and other channels. If the pull strategy is effective, consumers will then demand the brand from retailers, such as Carrefour, Tesco or Walmart, who will in turn demand it from Unilever. Thus, under a pull strategy, consumer demand 'pulls' the product through the channels.

Some industrial-goods companies use only push strategies; some direct-marketing companies use only pull strategies. However, most large companies use some combination of both. For example, Unilever spends €5.6 billion on worldwide media advertising and consumer sales promotions to create brand preference and pull customers into stores that carry its products. At the same time, it uses its own and distributors' sales forces and trade promotions to push its brands through the channels, so that they will be available on store shelves when consumers come calling. In recent years, facing a tight economy and slumping sales, many consumer-goods companies have been decreasing the brand-building pull portions of their mixes in favour of more push. This has caused concern that they may be driving short-run sales at the expense of long-term brand equity.

Companies consider many factors when designing their promotion mix strategies, including the *type of product/market* and the *PLC stage*. For example, the importance of different promotion tools varies between consumer and business markets. Business-to-consumer (B-to-C) companies usually pull more, putting more of their funds into advertising, followed by sales promotion, personal selling and then PR. In contrast, B-to-B marketers tend to push more, putting more of their funds into personal selling, followed by sales promotion, advertising and PR. In general, personal selling is used more heavily with expensive and risky goods and in markets with fewer and larger sellers.

The effects of different promotion tools also vary with PLC stages. In the introduction stage, advertising and PR are good for producing high awareness, and sales promotion is useful in promoting early trial. Personal selling must be used to get the trade to carry the product. In the growth stage, advertising and PR continue to be powerful influences, whereas sales promotion can be

Pull strategy—A promotion strategy that calls for spending a lot on consumer advertising and promotion to induce final consumers to buy a particular product, creating a demand vacuum that 'pulls' a product through the channel.

reduced because fewer incentives are needed. In the mature stage, sales promotion again becomes important relative to advertising. Buyers know the brands, and advertising is needed only to remind them of a particular product. In the decline stage, advertising is kept at a reminder level, PR is dropped and salespeople give a particular product only scant attention. Sales promotion, however, might continue to be strong.

Integrating the promotion mix

Having set the promotion budget and mix, the company must now take steps to see that each promotion mix element is smoothly integrated. Guided by its overall communications strategy, the various promotion elements should work together to carry the firm's unique brand messages and selling points. Integrating the promotion mix starts with customers. Whether it's advertising, personal selling, sales promotion, PR or direct marketing, communications at each customer touch-point must deliver consistent messages and positioning. An integrated promotion mix ensures that communications efforts occur when, where and how *customers* need them.

To achieve an integrated promotion mix, all of the firm's functions must cooperate to plan jointly communications efforts. Many companies even include customers, suppliers and other stakeholders at various stages of communications planning. Scattered or disjointed promotional activities across the company can result in diluted marketing communications impact and confused positioning. By contrast, an integrated promotion mix maximises the combined effects of all a firm's promotional efforts.

SOCIALLY RESPONSIBLE MARKETING COMMUNICATION

In shaping its promotion mix, a company must be aware of the large body of legal and ethical issues surrounding marketing communications. Most marketers work hard to communicate openly and honestly with consumers and resellers. Still, abuses may occur, and public policy makers have developed a substantial body of laws and regulations to govern advertising, sales promotion, personal selling and direct marketing. In this section, we discuss issues regarding advertising, sales promotion and personal selling. We will discuss issues regarding direct marketing in Chapter 17.

Advertising and sales promotion

By law, companies must avoid false or deceptive advertising. Advertisers must not make false claims, such as suggesting that a product cures something when it does not. They must avoid ads that have the capacity to deceive, even though no one actually may be deceived. A car cannot be advertised as getting 32 miles per gallon unless it does so under typical conditions, and a diet bread cannot be advertised as having fewer calories simply because its slices are thinner.

Sellers must avoid bait-and-switch advertising that attracts buyers under false pretences. For example, a large retailer advertised a sewing machine at €150. However, when consumers tried to buy the advertised machine, the seller downplayed its features, placed faulty machines on showroom floors, understated the machine's performance, and took other actions in an attempt to switch buyers to a more expensive machine. Such actions are both unethical and illegal.

A company's trade promotion activities also are closely regulated. For example, under the EU Unfair Commercial Practices Directives sellers cannot undertake misleading or aggressive practices that disadvantage customers.

Beyond simply avoiding legal pitfalls, such as deceptive or bait-and-switch advertising, companies can use advertising and other forms of promotion to encourage and promote socially responsible programmes and actions. Ecover, the Belgium-based manufacturer and distributor of domestic cleaning products, has the mission the 'to offer efficient and sustainable solutions for the hygienic needs of people today and of future generations', with a vision 'to contribute the process of creating economical, ecological and social change within our society to build a sustainable future for everyone'[24] The Ecover company slogan is 'Powered by Nature'. A recent print ad for Ecover washing up liquid simply states 'protect our future. Begin with the Washing Up'![25]

The Ecover company slogan is 'Powered by Nature'.

Source: Alamy Images/Shiny Pix

Personal selling

A company's salespeople must follow the rules of 'fair competition'. Most states have enacted deceptive sales acts that spell out what is not allowed. For example, salespeople may not lie to consumers or mislead them about the advantages of buying a particular product. To avoid bait-and-switch practices, salespeople's statements must match advertising claims.

Different rules apply to consumers who are called on at home or who buy at a location that is not the seller's permanent place of business versus those who go to a store in search of a product. Because people who are called on may be taken by surprise and may be especially vulnerable to high-pressure selling techniques, the EU Distance Selling Directive is most commonly interpreted as allowing a *seven-day cooling-off rule* to give special protection to customers who are not seeking products. Under this rule, customers who agree to sales via mail order, the Internet, digital TV or telephone have a week in which to cancel a contract or return merchandise and get their money back – no questions asked.

Much personal selling involves B-to-B trade. In selling to businesses, salespeople may not offer bribes to purchasing agents or others who can influence a sale. They may not obtain or use technical or trade secrets of competitors through bribery or industrial espionage. Finally, salespeople must not disparage competitors or competing products by suggesting things that are not true.[26]

REVIEWING OBJECTIVES AND KEY TERMS

In this chapter, you learned how companies use IMC to communicate customer value. Modern marketing calls for more than just creating customer value by developing a good product, pricing it attractively, and making it available to target customers. Companies also must clearly and persuasively *communicate* that value to current and prospective customers. To do this, they must blend five promotion mix tools, guided by a well-designed and implemented IMC strategy.

OBJECTIVE 1 Define the five promotion mix tools for communicating customer value (pp. 418–419).

A company's total *promotion mix* – also called its *marketing communications mix* – consists of a specific blend of *advertising, personal selling, sales promotion, PR* and *direct-marketing* tools that a company uses to persuasively communicate customer value and build customer relationships. Advertising includes any paid form of non-personal presentation and promotion of ideas, goods or services by an identified sponsor. In contrast, PR focuses on building good relations with the company's various publics by obtaining favourable, unpaid publicity.

Personal selling is any form of personal presentation by the firm's sales force for the purpose of making sales and building customer relationships. Firms use sales promotion to provide short-term incentives to encourage the purchase or sale of a product or a service. Finally, firms seeking immediate response from targeted individual customers use non-personal direct-marketing tools to communicate with customers and cultivate relationships with them.

OBJECTIVE 2 Discuss the changing communications landscape and the need for integrated marketing communications (pp. 419–422).

Recent shifts toward targeted or one-to-one marketing, coupled with advances in information and communications technology, have had a dramatic impact on marketing communications. As marketing communicators adopt richer but more fragmented media and promotion mixes to reach their diverse markets, they risk creating a communications hodgepodge for consumers. To prevent this, more companies are adopting the concept of *integrated marketing communications* (IMC). Guided by an overall IMC strategy, the company works out the roles that the various promotional tools will play and the extent to which each will be used. It carefully coordinates the promotional activities and the timing of when major campaigns take place. Finally, to help implement its integrated marketing strategy, the company can appoint a marketing communications director who has overall responsibility for the company's communications efforts.

OBJECTIVE 3 Outline the communication process and the steps in developing effective marketing communications (pp. 422–429).

The communication process involves nine elements: two major parties (sender and receiver), two communication tools (message and media), four communication functions (encoding, decoding, response and feedback) , and noise. To communicate effectively, marketers must understand how these elements combine to communicate value to target customers.

In preparing marketing communications, the communicator's first task is to *identify the target audience* and its characteristics. Next, the communicator has to determine the *communication objectives* and define the response sought, whether it be *awareness, knowledge, liking, preference, conviction* or *purchase*. Then a *message* should be constructed with an effective content and structure. *Media* must be selected, both for personal and non-personal communication. The communicator must find highly credible sources to deliver messages. Finally, the communicator must collect *feedback* by watching how much of the market becomes aware, tries the product and is satisfied in the process.

OBJECTIVE 4 Explain the methods for setting the promotion budget and factors that affect the design of the promotion mix (pp. 430–435).

The company must determine how much to spend for promotion. The most popular approaches are to spend what the company can afford, use a percentage of sales, base promotion on competitors' spending, or base it on an analysis and costing of the communication objectives and tasks. The company has to divide the *promotion budget* among the major tools to create the *promotion mix*. Companies can pursue a *push* or a *pull* promotional strategy – or a combination of the two. The best specific blend of promotion tools depends on the type of product/market, the buyer's readiness stage and the PLC stage. People at all levels of an organisation must be aware of the many legal and ethical issues surrounding marketing communications. Companies must work hard and proactively at communicating openly, honestly and agreeably with their customers and resellers.

NAVIGATING THE KEY TERMS

OBJECTIVE 1
Promotion mix (marketing communications mix) (p. 418)
Advertising (p. 419)
Sales promotion (419)
Personal selling (p. 419)
Public relations (PR; p. 419)
Direct marketing (p. 419)

OBJECTIVE 2
Integrated marketing communications (IMC) p. 421)

OBJECTIVE 3
Buyer-readiness stages (p. 424)
Personal communication channels (p. 427)
Word-of-mouth influence (p. 428)
Buzz marketing (p. 428)
Non-personal communication channels (p. 428)

OBJECTIVE 4
Affordable method (p. 430)
Percentage-of-sales method (p. 430)

DISCUSSING AND APPLYING THE CONCEPTS

Discussing the concepts

1. List and briefly describe the five major promotion mix tools. (MSCB: Communication)

2. Define IMC and discuss how marketers implement it. (AACSB: Communication)

3. Name and briefly describe the nine elements of the communications process. Why do marketers need to understand these elements? (AACSB: Communication; Reflective Thinking)

4. Name and describe the six buyer-readiness stages. Discuss why it is important for a marketing communicator to know where the target audience stands and to what stage it needs to be moved. (AACSB: Communication)

5. Discuss the factors to consider with regard to message structure when designing a message. (AACSB: Communication)

6. Compare and contrast personal and non-personal communication channels. (AACSB: Communication.)

Applying the concepts

1. Describe the three types of appeals used in marketing communications messages and develop three different ads for the same brand of a product of your choice, each using a different appeal. (AACSB: Communication; Reflective Thinking)

2. Discuss the two basic promotion mix strategies. Form a small group and recommend a promotion mix for a brand of peanut butter implementing primarily a push promotion strategy. Then recommend a promotion mix for the same brand implementing primarily a pull promotion strategy. Explain how your two recommendations differ. (AACSB Communication; Reflective Thinking)

3. Brands are now starring in movies, television game shows, and books. Select three different television programmes and identify the brands shown or mentioned in each programme. What product categories seem to be prevalent? How were the brands presented? Write a report on what you find. (AACSB: Communication; Reflective Thinking)

Focus on technology

Small businesses account for well over 90 per cent of all companies in Europe, and many do not have resources to spare for promoting their businesses. Newspaper, radio and the yellow pages have been the mainstay mediums for local businesses, but they can be expensive. As a result, many businesses are turning to the Internet. One survey found that over half of small businesses using the Internet are creating or maintaining a social-networking presence on sites such as Facebook, Twitter and Foursquare. However, social-networking media can be daunting to a small business owner, so MerchantCircle offers a network that brings customers and local businesses together. Founded in 2005 in the US, MerchantCircle is now the largest on-line network of local business owners, with well over 1.3 million members. In 2010 it expanded to the UK, and elsewhere. Consumers can go to the site to search for local businesses or ask questions and get input from any of MerchantCircle's business members.

1. Visit www.UK.MerchantCircle.com/corporate and search for a pizza in your city or some other city. What information was provided? Are any jewellers in your city members of MerchantCircle? Search for other products and services and describe the benefits this network provides to the customer (AACSB: Communication; Use of IT; Reflective Thinking).

2. Explore the MerchantCircle website to learn the benefits and costs for local businesses. Write a brief report about what you learn. (AACSB: Communication; Use of IT; Reflective Thinking)

Focus on ethics

Purchase a television, computer or other electronic device and you are bound to be asked whether you would like to purchase a service contract. Most large electronics retailers carefully train their salespeople and cashiers to ask this important question. In fact, some retailers urge their salespeople to exert strong sales pressure to sell these contracts. It's no wonder, because service contracts provide extremely high profits for the retailers, several times the profit margins realised from the equipment you are purchasing. But do you know when to say yes and when to pass on a contract? Most consumers are confused and will buy the contract because the price seems low in comparison to the price of that new plasma television. Experts, such as those at Consumer Reports, generally recommend that buyers pass on these contracts. With increased product reliability and decreasing prices that make replacement more reasonable, such contracts are rarely worth the price. If most consumers do not need them, should retailers continue to offer and promote them?

1. Is it ethical for retailers to offer and strongly promote service contracts?

2. When should you purchase a service contract?

3. Why do retailers continue to offer these contracts, even under criticism from customer advocacy groups?

Marketing & the economy

Towards the end of 2011, Jeff Bezos, Amazon's zany-geeky founder and Chief Executive announced the launch of the Kindle Fire. At less than half the price of Apple's cheapest iPad, the Kindle Fire has a colour touchscreen and a new higher-speed browser optimised for accessing online content. Amazon's growing music and video libraries are easily accessible. With a smaller screen, the Fire is intended to take on and beat the iPad and the iPad2 as an easier-to-hold, more compact and even better designed media consumption device. The middle of a recession may seem like a strange time to pick a fight with the mighty (and previously unperturbed) Apple but Bezos seems certain that this the best way forward for Amazon. Amazon has long been positioning itself as the online equivalent of Walmart, in that the firm has consistently attempted to operate at mass scale with wafer-thin margins which drive out smaller, higher-margin competitors. But this time, the main competitor is big, strong and well-entrenched.

1. In terms of the Product/Market Expansion Grid, which growth strategy does Amazon appear to be adopting. Is this wise?

2. Undertake a SWOT analysis for Amazon and for Apple. Which corporation look best positioned to win this fight? Why?

Marketing by the numbers

Using the percentage of sales method, an advertiser sets its budget at a certain percentage of current or forecasted sales. However, determining what percentage to use is not always clear. Many marketers look at industry averages and competitor spending for comparisons. Websites and trade publications, such as *Advertising Age*, publish data about industry averages and advertising-to-sales ratios for top advertisers.

1. Using information regarding industry advertising-to-sales ratios (see http://company.news-record.com/advertising/advertising/ratio.html), recommend percentages of sales that advertisers in the following industries should use to set next year's advertising budget: a grocery store, a physician, a cosmetic brand and a brewer. (MCSB: Communication; Use of IT)

2. Explain why there is variation in the percentage of sales spent on advertising among the four industries in the previous question. (AACSB: Communication; Reflective Thinking)

 REFERENCES

[1] See 'Integrated campaigns: Häagen-Dazs', *Communication Arts Advertising Annual 2009*, pp. 158–159; Tiffany Meyers, 'Marketing 50: Häagen-Dazs, Katty Pien', *Advertising Age* (17 November 2008), p. S15; Barbara Lippert, 'Häagen-Dazs tries beekeeping', *Adweek* (5 May 2008), accessed at www.adweek.com/aw/content_display/creative/critique/e3i26f1bfd408799a2088db93460922ea3f; Ted McKenna, 'The right message', *PR Week* (28 July 2008), p. 17; Karen Egolf, 'Häagen-Dazs extends social media effort', *Advertising Age* (10 November 2009), accessed at http://adage.com/goodworks/post?article_id=140412; 'Häagen-Dazs loves honey bees' (28 April 2010), a summary video accessed at http://limeshot.com/2010/haagen-dazs-loves-honey-bees-titanium-silver-lion-cannes-2009; and information from www.helpthehoneybees.com, accessed October 2011.

[2] For other definitions, see www.marketingpower.com/_layouts/Dictionary.aspx, accessed October 2011.

[3] Piet Levy, 'Touching the dial', *Marketing News* (3 March 2010), pp. 16–18. Also see Bob Garfield, *The Chaos Scenario* (Franklin, TN: Stielstra Publishing, 2009); Garfield, 'Future may be brighter but it's apocalypse now', *Advertising Age* (23 March 2009), pp. 1, 14; and James Othmer,

'When I knew advertising had completely changed', *Advertising Age* (4 January 2010), pp. 4, 23.

[4] Burt Helm, 'TV commercials: who needs them', *BusinessWeek* (25 May 2009), p. 24; and Elizabeth A. Sullivan, 'Targeting to the extreme', *Marketing News* (15 June 2009), pp. 17–19.

[5] Example from Mark Sweney, 'Facebook effect lifts UK online advertising past £4bn', *The Guardian* (29 March 2011), www.guardian.co.uk/media/2011/mar/29/facebook-online-advertising-social-media, accessed October 2011.

[6] Television advertising stats accessed at http://adage.com/datacenter/article?article_id=127791, accessed October 2011. Quote from Michael Schneider, 'Nielsen: traditional TV still king', *Variety* (7 December 2009).

[7] See www.helpthehoneybees.com/, accessed October 2011.

[8] See www.thinktank.org.uk/du_at_the_o2.php, accessed October 2011.

[9] Example from Roger Blitz, 'StanChart puts its sponsor's shirt on Liverpool', *Financial Times* (15 September 2009), www.ft.com/cms/s/0/ec0f311e-a18d-11de-a88d-00144feabdc0.html#axzz1UPifHx5H, accessed October 2011.

10 Example from Sharlene Goff, 'Santander drives on to next set of challenges', *Financial Times* (7 May 2010), www.ft.com/cms/s/0/a743ca30-5980-11df-99ba-00144feab49a.html#axzz1UPifHx5H, accessed October 2011.

11 Example from John O'Doherty, 'Halfords slips a gear as cycle sales back-pedal', *Financial Times* (7 October 2010), www.ft.com/cms/s/0/5d64773e-d22f-11df-8fbe-00144feabdc0.html#ixzz1Twz5aBqY, accessed October 2011.

12 De Beers Commercial (2009), see www.popisms.com/TelevisionCommercial/4544/De-Beers-Commercial-2009.aspx, accessed October 2011.

13 See www.redcross.org.uk/ and www.redcross.org.uk/What-we-do/Emergency-response/Current-emergency-appeals/East-Africa-Food-Crisis-Appeal/Aminas-story.

14 Example from Rhymer Rigby, 'Brands that laugh all the way to the bank', *Financial Times* (6 January 2011), www.ft.com/cms/s/0/cd02d8c4-19c4-11e0-b921-00144feab49a.html#ixzz1Trdnoyod, accessed October 2011.

15 See 'Brand design: cracking the colour code', *Marketing Week* (11 October 2007), p. 28; and Joe Tradii, 'Available for your brand: burnt umber! Any takers?', *Brandweek* (17 November 2009), accessed at www.brandweek.com/bw/content_display/esearch/e3i45e1bc-c0b65a294f442520efa2d3b051.

16 Jonah Bloom, 'The truth is: consumers trust fellow buyers before marketers', *Advertising Age* (13 February 2006), p 25; and 'Global advertising: consumers trust real friends and virtual strangers the most', *Nielsen Wire* (7 July 2009).

17 See www.tremor.com/revealing-case-studies/crest-weekly-clean, accessed June 2010.

18 John Reynolds, 'Hovis embarks on first "buzz marketing" drive', *Marketing* (2 June 2010), p. 3; and www.hovisheartyoats.co.uk/, accessed October 2010.

19 See Lacey Rose, 'The 10 most trusted celebrities', *Forbes* (25 January 2010), accessed at www.forbes.com/2010/01/25/most-trusted-celebrities-business-entertainment-trust.html; Robert Klara, 'I'm with the celebrity, get me out of here!' *Brandweek* (8 March 2010), p. 13; and 'Which athletes can lift brands?', *Mediaweek* (19 April 2010), p. 23.

20 T. L. Stanley, 'Dancing with the stars', *Brandweek* (8 March 2010), pp. 10–12.

21 For more on advertising spending by company and industry, see http://adage.com/datacenter/datapopup.php?article_id=119881, accessed September 2010.

22 For more on setting promotion budgets, see W. Ronald Lane, Karen Whitehill King and J. Thomas Russell, *Kleppner's Advertising Procedure*, 18th edn (Upper Saddle River, NJ: Prentice Hall, 2011), chapter 6.

23 Susan Greco, 'How to reduce your cost of sales', Inc. (5 March 2010), accessed at www.inc.com/guide/reducing-cost-of-sales.html#.

24 See www.ecover.com.

25 See www.visit4infor.com/advert/Ecover-protect-Our-Future-Ecover/47656.

26 For more on the legal aspects of promotion, see Lane, King and Russell, *Kleppner's Advertising Procedure*, chapter 25; and William L. Cron and Thomas E. DeCarlo, *Dalrymple's Sales Management*, 10th edn (New York: Wiley, 2009), chapter 10.

VIDEO CASE

CP+B MyMarketingLab

Crispin Porter + Bogusky (Crispin) may not be the oldest advertising agency in the world. It isn't the biggest either. But it has been working overtime to prove that it is the most innovative firm at integrating marketing promotions. In fact, Crispin relies very little on the king of all advertising channels, broadcast TV. Instead, Crispin has worked miracles for companies such as Virgin Atlantic Airways, BMWs Mini Cooper and Burger King by employing non-traditional campaigns on limited budgets.

Crispin attributes its success to the fact that it redefined what an advertisement is. Customer appropriate messages, Crispin discovered, could be delivered in many different ways.

So its realm of ad space includes things as obscure as the side of a postbox or an oversized phone booth in an airport. By communicating a message in many different ways, Crispin has developed a reputation for truly integrating marketing communications.

After watching the video featuring Crispin, answer the following questions about advertising and promotions:

1. Alex Bogusky once said, 'Anything and everything is an ad'. What does this mean? How is Crispin demonstrating this mantra?
2. In what ways has Crispin differentiated itself from other advertising agencies?
3. Give some examples as to how Crispin balances strategy with creativity.

COMPANY CASE

TELE2: the Baltic success

Tomas Palaima (Warwick Business School)

THE COMPANY

In 1970, as the mobile telecommunications market started to take off, the Swedish company Industriförvaltnings AB Kinnevik began to invest in the telecoms market. In 1986, when the demand for mobile telephony was increasing TELE2 was founded by Industriförvaltnings AB Kinnevik. As the interest in mobile telephony continued to grow followed by the development of, at this time, the advanced GSM technology, the company was awarded a GSM license in 1988. Finally, the government monopoly started to dissolve in 1991 while the Internet emerged as an interesting communications channel. TELE2 was the first company to offer Internet access to the Swedish market and was also granted a license to conduct fixed telephony operations. International expansion started with the company's launch of operations in the Netherlands (1996) and Norway (1997). TELE2 continued to implement a rigorous expansion strategy, which has resulted in successful operations and good performance indicators across numerous countries: Austria, Croatia, Estonia, Germany, Latvia, Lithuania, the Netherlands, Norway, Russia and Sweden. Today, the company serves over 31 million customers, generating an annual turnover and profit of approximately €4.5 and €1.07 billion (EBITDA) respectively. Although the economic environment is challenging, TELE2 has focused on growth and manages to expand at a profit. Indeed, it was the first company in Europe to offer 4G smartphones, enabling customers to enjoy download speeds up to an exciting 80 megabits per second.

THE BALTIC SUCCESS

As the building of profitable customer relationships across different European markets would not have been possible without taking an holistic approach to the communication of value propositions, this case study will explore the success story of TELE2 focusing in particular on the management of integrated marketing communications in Lithuania.

The Lithuanian market deserves special attention. Although the country has a population of just over three million, the mobile penetration rate is the third highest in the European Union: 147.16 mobile subscriptions per 100 inhabitants. Furthermore, the country has the fastest broadband in the world (according to *The Wall Street Journal*), equalling the average download speed of 31.89 Mbps with 99.6 per cent of actual speed as promised by Internet providers. Besides that, customers can enjoy an almost fully functioning 4G network. Finally, the mobile market comprises three mobile operators competing fiercely for every individual client and business. Nevertheless, TELE2 has reported an annual income and profit of €139.51 and €49.78 million respectively. Although the company was the last to enter the Lithuanian market while fighting with powerful companies backed by substantial Scandinavian capital, market research has demonstrated that it is perceived as the most reliable and honest telecommunication company. Furthermore, the analysis of the total market income across all segments demonstrated that the market share of TELE2 has been increasing by leaps and bounds. Having reached a market share of 32 per cent in 2010, the company is now the second largest mobile operator in the country.

THE PATHWAY TO SUCCESS

Having set the scene about the company and its performance in the Lithuanian market, we will look at the start of its pathway to success. As the identification of strengths, weaknesses, threats and opportunities is an essential part of any marketing strategy, we will first look at the environment before and at the moment of market entry.

Lithuania regained its independence from the Soviet Union in 1990. In 1992 the state founded the national company Lithuanian Telecom. While the country underwent the immense transformation associated with moving from a planned to a market economy, the process of privatisation began. Unfortunately, the process was not very smooth and the Lithuanian government made some crucial mistakes. Lithuanian Telecom was sold in 1998 to the consortium Amber Teleholding A/S comprising the two Scandinavian companies: Swedish Telia and Finish Sonera. As the company was the only player in the landline and Internet markets, this decision resulted in the creation of a powerful monopoly, which immediately started to jeopardise the wallets of its customers, offering poor services and even worse, dial-up Internet working at a snail's pace. Although the image of the company started to deteriorate by leaps and bounds, substitution was impossible: the mobile market was an oligopoly which comprised two other players offering even more expensive services: Omnitel and Bite? GSM. Hence, the new monopoly continued its opportunism without thinking about its image, reputation and relationships. However, in 1999, Swedish company TELE2 decided to enter the Lithuanian market. When the company began to build its network infrastructure in the Lithuanian capital city Vilnius, nobody took it seriously at first. Opportunism continued to flourish in the form of unfair tariffs, rude contact personnel and deceitful contract conditions provided in small print. Although there were two fully functioning GSM networks operating at a substantial profit, the mobile penetration rate of 9.8 per cent was one of the lowest in Europe, indicating 9.8 mobile cellular subscriptions per 100 inhabitants. On the other hand, the penetration rate of landlines was much higher, at 32.6.

THE ENTRY TO THE MARKET

TELE2 initially faced many problems. The huge investment in network infrastructure increased costs while expansion of network coverage was slow and effective competition on price was difficult to achieve. Moreover, the biggest competitor launched a simple, but very successful, advertising campaign: 'enjoy cheaper conversations between the members of the biggest network', shouted the chorus of happy faces in the media again and again while creating relevant, distinctive and believable points-of-difference. Although TELE2 tried to respond by being the first company to offer almost free handsets and substantially cheaper services, the brands of competitors managed to break even in those areas. Unfortunately, the fragile points-of-difference were successfully negated, at least for a while. Nevertheless, as the GSM network of TELE2 increased, the situation started to change dramatically with each launch of a new mobile station. Indeed, the competitors lost their main competitive advantage and started to focus instead on emotional appeals to stir up positive emotions to motivate purchase. Thus, Omnitel introduced the advertising campaign 'You have a reliable friend', in which a young, handsome and stylish man walked through the streets with a black panther, which protected him in every situation, while attracting the attention of beautiful women. Commentators agreed that the ad is appealing. Nevertheless, some experts deemed it an irresponsible waste of client's money organised by advertising creative types. Although the target audience enjoyed the ad, the process of switching continued. Indeed, the big black cat was a symbol of good luck for competitors: 'this campaign allowed us to take our breath again while enjoying the rising numbers of sales', stated the executive of one of the competing companies.

Instead of looking for a more unique position, the second biggest competitor, Bite? GSM, followed the emotional ideas of Omnitel and launched the campaign 'For better life' which said nothing to the target audience. Finally, the communications started to disintegrate by leaps and bounds: consumers were bombarded by conflicting messages from different sources. Instead of thinking about a systematic development of unique points-of-difference, the competitors of TELE2 focused on short-term tactics. The scenarios and quality of advertising were often poor and contradictive. Furthermore, the companies focused too much on the short term effects of sales promotion. Hence, poor marketing communication resulted in confused company images and brand positions and deteriorating customer relationships.

DEVELOPMENT OF STRATEGY

While Omnitel and Bite? GSM were involved in tactical wars of sales promotion and competed for immediate awareness, TELE2 focused instead on the development of a rigorous strategy and decided to invade the market segment-by-segment. As the landline segment had suffered from the monopoly of Lithuanian Telecom for a long time, TELE2 saw many opportunities. Indeed, Lithuanian Telecom had a reputation for poor management of customer relationships, an even worse image and no committed costumers. Furthermore, the landline segment comprised older customers, pensioners and people with slightly lower income, and thus was not seen as the most attractive by the mobile services providers. Hence, the two competing companies, Omnitel and Bit? GSM, targeted people with higher income and business customers. As the segment looked strategically attractive, TELE2 started to define the target audience and shape a well-coordinated programme to obtain the desired audience response.

Having defined the demographic and psychographic characteristics of the target audience and determined the communication objectives, the company proceeded to design a message. The initial research demonstrated that the target segment enjoyed watching Mexican soap operas. Indeed, the era of Mexican TV series began with the legendary *Rich People Also Cry*. As the economy faced many problems, lots of people dreamed about a better life and enjoyed the exotic intrigues portrayed by the Mexican stars in an environment of sparkling luxury. Surprisingly, pensioners often called each other to discuss the latest episodes but the immense increase in landline prices was an obstacle. Having analysed lots of scenarios and message content alternatives, TELE2 decided to produce a humorous ad campaign 'Rich People Also Save' in the style of the Mexican TV series. Interestingly, the story still continues and the sympathetic characters are always played by the same actors. Although the style of communication is always very consistent, the scenario is often adapted to different occasions: Easter, Mothering Sunday, Christmas and New Year. On the one hand, the emotional appeal in the form of sarcasm and humour captures the audience's attention, makes people feel good during the hard times of economic crisis and gives the brand a personality. On the other hand, the rational appeal relates to the audience's self-interest: 'Why pay more?' the rich people ask at the end of the ad. Gradually the characters of the TV series appeared everywhere. A well-coordinated blend of broadcasting, print, the Internet, outdoor advertising, electronic screens and even radio delivered the same message. Although at first sight radio looks incompatible with the scenario and unable to deliver the message, the company used it to announce the release of a new episode. The text of advertising was intermingled creatively with a dose of good humour and thus sounded very appealing. Marketing research demonstrated that the TV series is the country's second most recalled ad campaign – second only to the other brand of TELE2, which will be discussed shortly. Finally, the successful communications reflected in the numbers of sales: clients of both landline and mobile services started to switch to the new service. Surprisingly, even the older and most conservative customers forgot about landlines and began using mobile services.

Having invaded the segment successfully, TELE2 decided to target a different group of customers – young people and students. As the previous TV series was a great success, the company took the same approach. Instead of bombarding the target customers with conflicting messages, as did the competitors, the company introduced the advertising campaign 'Chatting builds friendships', which mimicked the popular TV series *Friends*. The company advertised cheap and simple pay-as-you-go services designed for young people. As in the previous case, the TV series still continues and the six characters are always portrayed by the same actors. On the one hand, the series captures its audience's attention by using humour. On the other hand, it reminds customers about the new opportunities to foster friendships cheaply and sometimes even for free. Although TELE2 followed quite a similar approach in designing the two campaigns, the demographic and psychographic features of the second segment resulted in some important differences. As young people are involved in the Internet, the company decided to exploit the advantages of social media. TELE2 organised a talent competition and invited participants aged from 8 to 19. First, prospective candidates were asked to submit evidence of talent on a Facebook site. Second, the candidates were short-listed using SMS voting. Finally, the candidates underwent many creative trials suggested by the Facebook fans. As social media offers instant feedback and comments, they were the criteria to identify the winner who received a fascinating prize – the new role in the advertising TV series 'Chatting builds friendships'. Market research has demonstrated that the advertising campaign is the most recalled in the country. Furthermore, the brand remains the most popular mobile service in the country: 27.4 per cent of respondents indicated that they use this service.

Questions for discussion

1. In designing the message, how did TELE2 employ the AIDA model?
2. Using the nine steps of the communication process, how did TELE2 achieve the integration of its marketing communications?
3. Using the nine steps the of communication process, how did TELE2 employ the Internet to improve communication?
4. Implementing strategy is never easy. What did the competitors of TELE2 do right and what did they do wrong? How would you have done things differently?

Sources: Carl Bialik, 'Internet providers hit a speed trap', *The Wall Street Journal* (10 December 2011),http://online.wsj.com/article/SB10001424 052970203413304577088332871541336.html, accessed February 2012; http://db1.stat.gov.lt/statbank/SelectVarVal/Define.asp?Maintable=M708 0303&PLanguage=1 (public fixed and mobile telephone networks at the end of the year by year), accessed February 2012; www.ad-research.lt/naujienos?story=1 (the results of advertising research), accessed February 2012; www.itu.int/ITU-D/ict/statistics/material/excel/2010/MobileCellular Subscriptions_00-10.xls (mobile cellular subscriptions), accessed February 2012; www.rrt.lt/download/15548/report%202011%20q3.pdf (report on the electronic communications sector), accessed February 2012; www.tele2.com/meet-our-company/get-the-facts/history.html (company history), accessed February 2012; http://www.tele2.com/meet-our-company/get-the-facts/markets.html (markets), accessed February 2012; www.tele2.lt/apie_TELE2.html (company profile), accessed February 2012; www.tele2.lt/files/RAIT_report_TELE2_2007.10.25_lt.pdf (the usage of mobile services in Lithuania), accessed February 2012; www.tele2.lt/svedijos_tele2_klientai_pirmieji_europoje_gali_isigyti_4g_telefona.html; www.teo.lt/en/node/1440 (historical facts), accessed February 2012.

CHAPTER FIFTEEN

Advertising and public relations

Chapter preview

After an analysis of overall IMC planning, we dig more deeply into the specific marketing communications tools. In this chapter, we explore advertising and public relations (PR). Advertising involves communicating the company's or brand's value proposition by using paid media to inform, persuade and remind consumers. PR involves building good relations with various company publics – from consumers and the general public to the media, investor, donor and government publics. As with all the promotion mix tools, advertising and PR must be blended into the overall IMC programme. In Chapters 16 and 17, we will discuss the remaining promotion mix tools: personal selling, sales promotion and direct marketing.

Let's start with a question: Does advertising really make a difference? Microsoft and Apple certainly must think so. Each spends more than half a billion dollars a year on it. Here, we examine the long-running advertising battle between the two computer industry giants. As you read, think about the impact of advertising on each brand's fortunes.

Objective outline

- ➤ **Objective 1** Define the role of advertising in the promotion mix.
  Advertising (p. 447)

- ➤ **Objective 2** Describe the major decisions involved in developing an advertising programme.
  Setting advertising objectives (pp. 447–449)
  Setting the advertising budget (pp. 449–450)
  Developing advertising strategy (pp. 450–458)
  Evaluating advertising effectiveness and the return on advertising investment (pp. 458–459)
  Other advertising considerations (pp. 459–461)

- ➤ **Objective 3** Define the role of PR in the promotion mix.
  Public relations (pp. 461–462)
  The role and impact of PR (pp. 462–463)

- ➤ **Objective 4** Explain how companies use PR to communicate with their publics.
  Major PR tools (p. 463)

Apple and Microsoft

In 2006, Apple launched its now-famous 'Get a Mac' ad campaign, featuring two characters – 'Mac' and 'PC' – sparring over the advantages of the Apple Mac versus a Microsoft Windows-based PC. The ads portrayed Mac as a young, hip, laid-back guy in a hoodie, whereas PC was a stodgy, befuddled, error-prone, middle-aged nerd in baggie khakis, a brown sports coat and unfashionable glasses. Not surprisingly, adroit and modern Mac always got the best of outdated and inflexible PC. Over the years, Apple unleashed a nonstop barrage of Mac vs. PC ads that bashed Windows-based machines – and their owners – as outmoded and dysfunctional.

The 'Get a Mac' campaign produced results. When the campaign began, Mac held only a 2 – 3 per cent share of the US computer market. Less than two years later, its share had more than doubled to 6–8 per cent and was still growing. The cool campaign also helped boost customer value perceptions of Apple computers. Even though its computers were widely viewed as more expensive, at one point, Apple scored a whopping 70 on the BrandIndex (which tracks daily consumer perceptions of brand value on a scale of –100 to 100). Microsoft, meanwhile, floundered below zero.

Good advertising wasn't the only thing contributing to Apple's success. The popularity of its iPod, iPhone and other new products was also converting customers to Mac computers. But the smug ads were consistently hitting their mark. Microsoft needed to do something dramatic to turn the advertising tide. So, two years after the Apple 'Get a Mac' onslaught began, conservative Microsoft hired the anything-but-conservative ad agency Crispin Porter + Bogusky, known for its award-winning but cheeky and irreverent campaigns for clients such as Burger King and Coke Zero. Microsoft and Crispin made for an odd mix of corporate personalities. Even Rob Reilly, executive creative director for Crispin, worried a bit about the partnership. After all, Crispin itself was a Mac shop through and through. Still, Reilly was enthused about creating a campaign to blunt Apple's attacks and restore Microsoft's image as an innovative industry leader.

To break from the past, Microsoft and Crispin first launched a set of 'teaser ads' designed to 'get the conversation going'. In the ads, comedian Jerry Seinfeld and Microsoft founder Bill Gates spent time together, shopping for shoes, eating ice cream and exchanging irrelevant banter, all with little or no mention of Microsoft Windows. Although they made few selling points, the humorous, well-received ads put a more human face on the giant software company.

A few weeks later, Microsoft replaced the teaser commercials with a direct counterpunch to Apple's 'Get a Mac' ads. It launched its own 'I'm a PC' campaign, featuring a dead-on look-alike of Apple's PC character. In the first ad, dressed in PC's dorky outfit, Microsoft's character opened with the line, 'I'm a PC. And I've been made into a stereotype.' He was followed by a parade of everyday PC users – from environmentalists, political bloggers, mixed martial arts fighters and mash-up disk jockeys to budget-conscious laptop shoppers and remarkably tech-savvy preschoolers – each proclaiming, 'I'm a PC'.

The Microsoft 'I'm a PC' campaign struck a chord with Windows users. They no longer had to sit back and take Apple's jibes like the clueless drones they were made out to be. 'That's where the whole notion of "I'm a PC" and putting a face on our users came about,' said Reilly. Identifying real PC people 'was important to do on behalf of our users, who really aren't like that [Mac vs. PC] guy,' says a Microsoft brand marketer.

Off to a successful start, Microsoft and Crispin soon extended the 'I'm a PC' campaign with a new pitch, one that was more in tune with the then-troubled economy. Part advertising and part reality TV, the new campaign – called 'Laptop Hunters' – tagged along with real consumers as they shopped for new computers. The first ad featured an energetic young redhead named Lauren, who wanted a laptop with 'comfortable keys and a 17-inch screen' for under $1,000 Stopping first at a Mac store, she learned that Apple offered only one laptop at $1,000, but it had only a 13-inch screen. To get what she wanted from Apple, she figured, 'I'd have to double my budget, which isn't feasible. I guess I'm just not cool enough to be a Mac person.' Instead, Lauren giddily buys an HP Pavilion laptop for less than $700. 'I'm a PC,' she concludes, 'only I got just what I wanted.'

In the long-running advertising battle between Microsoft and Apple, Microsoft's innovative 'I'm a PC' has given PC fans everywhere a boost.

Source: Microsoft Limited

If previous 'I'm a PC' ads started a shift in perceptions, the 'Laptop Hunters' series really moved the needle. The ads spoke volumes in a difficult economy, portraying Apple as too expensive, 'too cool', and out of touch with mainstream consumers. The provocative ads, in tandem with the nation's economic woes, bumped Microsoft's BrandIndex score from near zero to 46.2, while Apple's score dropped from its previous high of 70 to only 12.4. In a sure sign that Microsoft's revitalised advertising was striking a nerve, Apple's lawyers called Microsoft chief operating officer B. Kevin Turner, demanding that he change the ads because Apple was lowering its prices and the ads were no longer accurate. It was 'the greatest single phone call' he'd ever taken, said Turner. 'I did cartwheels down the hallway.'

To maintain momentum, Microsoft and Crispin launched yet another iteration of the 'I'm a PC' campaign – this one introducing Microsoft's new Windows 7 operating system. Consistent with the 'I'm a PC' theme, the campaign featured testimonials from everyday folks telling how specific Windows 7 features reflected ideas they'd passed along to Microsoft in an eight million-person beta test of the software. At the end of each ad, customers gloated, 'I'm a PC, and Windows 7 was my idea.'

Once again, Apple responded. It struck back directly with one of its most negative Mac vs. PC ads yet. Called 'Broken Promises', it featured a gloating PC telling Mac that Windows 7 wouldn't have any of the problems associated with the old Window's versions. A bewildered Mac notes that he'd heard such claims before, with each previous Windows generation. In the end, PC says, 'Trust me'. Many analysts felt that the biting tone of the ad suggested that Apple was feeling the heat and getting defensive. Uncharacteristically, Mac seemed to be losing his cool.

By mid-2010, both companies appeared to be turning down the competitive advertising heat. Apple retired its 'Get a Mac' campaign in favour of a more straightforward 'Why You'll Love a Mac' campaign, which listed the reasons for choosing a Mac rather than a PC. Microsoft had long since ditched its 'Laptop Hunter' attack ads. Both companies appeared to be focusing more positively on what their products could do, rather than on what the competition couldn't do.

Thanks to the 'I'm a PC' campaign, Microsoft has now put itself on an equal advertising footing with Apple – perhaps a better footing. Consumer value perceptions for Microsoft and Apple are now running pretty much neck and neck. And the campaign has given PC fans everywhere a real boost. 'I've never seen more pride at Microsoft,' says one Microsoft employee. 'You walk through the campus, and you see people's laptops that have "I'm a PC" stickers on them. I walk in the company store, and there are these huge banners that say "I'm a PC" and shirts and ties and mugs.' Crispin's Rob Reilly now owns not one but two PC laptops and is thrilled with the impact of his agency's efforts. 'You are not so embarrassed to take your PC out of the bag on a plane anymore,' he says. 'It's actually kind of cool that you do. I know this [campaign] is working.'[1]

AUTHOR COMMENT

After years of PC bashing by Apple's classic 'Get a Mac' campaign, Microsoft is now on an equal – perhaps better – footing in the heated advertising battle waged by the two computer industry giants. Microsoft's 'I'm a PC' campaign is really working.

As we discussed in the previous chapter, companies must do more than simply create customer value. They must also clearly and persuasively communicate that value to target customers. In this chapter, we take a closer look at two marketing communications tools: *advertising* and *PR*.

AUTHOR COMMENT

You already know a lot about advertising; you are exposed to it every day. But here we'll look behind the scenes at how companies make advertising decisions.

ADVERTISING

Advertising can be traced back to the very beginnings of recorded history. Archaeologists working in countries around the Mediterranean Sea have dug up signs announcing various events and offers. The Romans painted walls to announce gladiator fights, and the Phoenicians painted pictures on large rocks to promote their wares along parade routes. During the golden age in Greece, town criers announced the sale of cattle, crafted items and even cosmetics. An early 'singing commercial' went as follows: 'For eyes that are shining, for cheeks like the dawn / For beauty that lasts after girlhood is gone / For prices in reason, the woman who knows / Will buy her cosmetics from Aesclyptos.'

Modern advertising, however, is a far cry from these early efforts. Global advertising expenditure in 2011 was around €360 billion. US advertisers now run up an estimated annual bill of more than $155 (€120) billion on measured advertising media, with the next largest advertising markets: Japan (€35 billion), China (€23 billion), Germany (€19 billion), UK (€14 billion).[2] Procter & Gamble, the world's largest advertiser, on its own spends around $5 (€4) billion on US advertising and €8 billion worldwide.[3]

Although advertising is employed mostly by business firms, a wide range of not-for-profit organisations, professionals and social agencies also employ advertising to promote their causes to various target publics. In fact, in most countries one of the largest advertising spenders is a not-for-profit organisation – the government. In the US federal agency spending on advertising was $945 (€737) million in 2010. The UK government spent £113 (€141) million on advertising in 2010, down from £227 (€284) million in 2009, when major campaigns included the 'Catch It, Bin It, Kill It' swine flu adverts and the Change4Life anti-obesity campaign.[4] It seems that as 'nanny states' in Europe claim the right to dictate behaviour to their citizens and invade their freedoms (don't smoke, don't drink, don't eat, and so on), media owners become richer through government advertising expenditure. Advertising is a good way to inform and persuade, whether the purpose is to sell Coca-Cola worldwide or get people in a developing nation to use birth control.

Marketing management must make four important decisions when developing an advertising programme (see Figure 15.1): *setting advertising objectives*, *setting the advertising budget*, *developing advertising strategy* (*message decisions* and *media decisions*) and *evaluating ad campaigns*.

Advertising—Any paid form of non-personal presentation and promotion of ideas, goods or services by an identified sponsor.

Setting advertising objectives

The first step is to set *advertising objectives*. These objectives should be based on past decisions about the target market, positioning and the marketing mix, which define the job that advertising must

Figure 15.1 Major advertising decisions

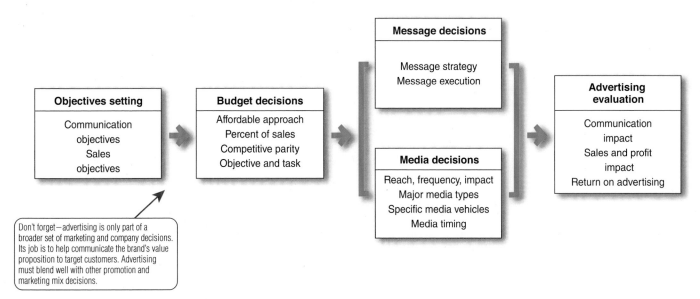

do in the total marketing programme. The overall advertising objective is to help build customer relationships by communicating customer value. Here, we discuss specific advertising objectives.

An **advertising objective** is a specific communication *task* to be accomplished with a specific *target* audience during a specific period of *time*. Advertising objectives can be classified by their primary purpose – to *inform*, *persuade* or *remind*. Table 15.1 lists examples of each of these specific objectives.

Informative advertising is used heavily when introducing a new product category. In this case, the objective is to build primary demand. Thus, early producers of DVD players first had to inform consumers of the image quality and convenience benefits of the new product.

Persuasive advertising becomes more important as competition increases. Here, the company's objective is to build selective demand. For example, once DVD players became established, Sony began trying to persuade consumers that *its* brand offered the best quality for their money.

Some persuasive advertising has become *comparative advertising* (or *attack advertising*), in which a company directly or indirectly compares its brand with one or more other brands. You see examples of comparative advertising in many product categories, ranging from sports drinks, coffee, and soup to computers, car rentals and credit cards. For example, Unilever ran into trouble in 2011 with the UK's Advertising Standards Authority (ASA) for adverts promoting its Knorr gravy granules, which contained headlines that said 'unbeatable taste vs. Bisto'. The ads contained further text that said Knorr's gravy had recorded 'unbeatable scores for taste, appearance, consistency and aroma' in testing. One of the adverts claimed Knorr gravy recorded 'unbeatable scores' over 'main competitors'. Premier Goods Group who owns Bisto took some exception to this advertising and the ASA agreed.[5] Meanwhile in the US, Dunkin' Donuts ran a TV and Web campaign comparing the chain's coffee to Starbuck's brews. 'In a recent national blind taste test,' proclaimed the ads, 'more Americans preferred the taste of Dunkin' Donuts coffee over Starbucks. It's just more proof it's all about the coffee (not the couches or music).'

Advertisers should use comparative advertising with caution. All too often, such ads invite competitor responses, resulting in an advertising war that neither competitor can win. Upset competitors might decide to take more drastic action, such as filing complaints with the regulatory

Advertising objective—A specific communication *task* to be accomplished with a specific *target* audience during a specific period of *time*.

Table 15.1 Possible advertising objectives

Informative advertising	
Communicating customer value	Suggesting new uses for a product
Bulding a brand and company image	Informing the market of a price change
Telling the market about a new product	Describing avaliable services and support
Explaining how a product works	Correction false impressions
Persuasive Advertising	
Building brand preference	Persuading customers to purchase now
Encouraging switching to a brand	Persuading customers to receive a sales call
Changing customer perception of product value	Convincing customers to tell others about the brand
Reminder Advertising	
Maintaining customer relationships	Reminding consumers where to buy the product
Reminding consumers that the product may be needed in the near future	Keeping the brand in a customer's mind during off-seasons

authorities (e.g. the ASA in the UK and the National Advertising Division of the Council of Better Business Bureaus in the US) or even filing false-advertising lawsuits. Unilever's Knorr advertising mentioned above was, for example, banned by the ASA.[6]

Reminder advertising is important for mature products as it helps to maintain customer relationships and keep consumers thinking about the product. Expensive Coca-Cola television ads primarily build and maintain the Coca-Cola brand relationship rather than inform or persuade customers to buy it in the short term.

Advertising's goal is to help move consumers through the buying process. Some advertising is designed to move people to immediate action. For example, a direct-response television ad by Weight Watchers urges consumers to pick up the phone and sign up right away, and a PC World newspaper insert for a weekend sale encourages immediate store visits. However, many ads focus on building or strengthening long-term customer relationships. For example, a Nike television ad in which well-known athletes work through extreme challenges in their Nike gear never directly asks for a sale. Instead, the goal is to somehow change the way the customers think or feel about the brand.

Setting the advertising budget

After determining its advertising objectives, a company next sets its **advertising budget** for each product. Four commonly used methods for setting promotion budgets were discussed in Chapter 14. Here we discuss some specific factors that should be considered when setting the advertising budget.

A brand's advertising budget often depends on its *stage in the product life cycle*. For example, new products typically need relatively large advertising budgets to build awareness and gain consumer trial. In contrast, mature brands usually require lower budgets as a ratio to sales. *Market share* also impacts the amount of advertising needed: because building market share or taking market share from competitors requires larger advertising spending than does simply maintaining current share, low-share brands usually need more advertising spending as a percentage of sales. Also, brands in a market with many competitors and high advertising clutter must be advertised more heavily to be noticed above the noise in the marketplace. Undifferentiated brands – those that closely resemble other brands in their product class (e.g. soft drinks and laundry detergents) – may require heavy advertising to set them apart. When one product differs greatly from competing products, advertising can be used to point out the differences to consumers.

No matter what method is used, setting the advertising budget is no easy task. How does a company know if it is spending the right amount? Some critics charge that large consumer packaged-goods firms tend to spend too much on advertising and that B-to-B marketers generally underspend on advertising. They claim that, on the one hand, large consumer companies use lots of image advertising without really knowing its effects. They overspend as a form of 'insurance' against not spending enough. On the other hand, business advertisers tend to rely too heavily on their sales forces to bring in orders. They underestimate the power of company image and product image in pre-selling to industrial customers. Thus, they do not spend enough on advertising to build customer awareness and knowledge.

Companies such as Coca-Cola, Unilever and Kraft have built sophisticated statistical models to determine the relationship between promotional spending and brand sales, which helps determine the 'optimal investment' across various media. Still, because so many factors affect advertising effectiveness, some controllable and others not, measuring the results of advertising spending remains an inexact science. In most cases, managers must rely on large doses of judgment along with more quantitative analysis when setting advertising budgets.[7]

As a result, advertising is one of the easiest budget items to cut when economic times get tough. Cuts in brand-building advertising appear to do little short-term harm to sales. For example, in the wake of the economic downturn and recession, US advertising expenditures plummeted 12 per cent from the previous year. In the early-2010s economic turmoil in the Eurozone and the rest of Western Europe looks likely to encourage companies to reduce advertising expenditures. However, slashing ad spending risks long-term damage to a brand's image and market share. In fact, companies that can maintain or even increase their advertising spending while competitors are decreasing theirs can gain competitive advantage. Consider the carmaker Audi:[8]

Advertising budget—The money and other resources allocated to a product or a company advertising programme.

Although Audi's sales slipped during the recession, they fell far less than those of competitors amid a calamitous year for the motor car industry. Even more, Audi's brand awareness and buyer consideration are up substantially, with gains outstripping those of BMW, Mercedes and Lexus. In short: Audi might be the hottest car brand on the market right now. And it's strongly positioned for the future as the economy recovers. What is Audi's advantage? The brand spent heavily on advertising and marketing at a time when rivals were retrenching. During the past three years, despite the harsh economy, Audi increased its ad spending fourfold. Audi 'has kept its foot on the pedal while everyone else [was] pulling back,' says an Audi ad executive. 'Why would we go backwards now when the industry [was] generally locking the brakes and cutting spending?' adds Audi's chief marketing executive.

Developing advertising strategy

Advertising strategy—The strategy by which the company accomplishes its advertising objectives. It consists of two major elements: creating advertising messages and selecting advertising media.

Advertising strategy consists of two major elements: creating advertising *messages* and selecting advertising *media*. In the past, companies often viewed media planning as secondary to the message-creation process. The creative department first created good ads; then the media department selected and purchased the best media for carrying those ads to desired target audiences. This often caused friction between creatives and media planners.

Today, however, soaring media costs, more focused target marketing strategies and the blizzard of new digital and interactive media have promoted the importance of the media planning function. The decision about which media to use for an ad campaign – television, newspapers, magazines, mobile phones, website or online network, or e-mail – is now sometimes more critical than the creative elements of the campaign. As a result, more and more advertisers are orchestrating a closer harmony between their messages and the media that deliver them. In fact, in a really good ad campaign, you often have to ask 'Is that a media idea or a creative idea?'

Creating the advertising message

No matter how big the budget, advertising can succeed only if ads gain attention and communicate well. Good ad messages are especially important in today's costly and cluttered advertising environment. In 1950, the average US household received only three network television channels and a handful of major national magazines. Today, the average American household receives more than 118 channels, and consumers have more than 20,000 magazines from which to choose.[9] Add in the countless radio stations and a continuous barrage of catalogues, direct mail, e-mail and online ads and out-of-home media, and consumers are being bombarded with ads at home, work and all points in between. As a result, American consumers are exposed to as many as 3,000 to 5,000 commercial messages every day.[10] Though less extreme in European countries, the same phenomenon is occurring here.

Breaking through the clutter

If all this advertising clutter bothers some consumers, it also causes huge headaches for advertisers. Take the situation facing network television advertisers in the US. They pay an average of $302,000 (€235,500) to make a single 30-second commercial. Then, each time they show it, they pay an average of $122,000 (€95,000) for 30 seconds of advertising time during a popular prime-time programme. They pay even more if it's an especially popular programme, such as *American Idol* ($642,000), *Sunday Night Football* ($340,000), *Grey's Anatomy* ($240,000), *Two and a Half Men* ($227,000) or a mega-event such as the Super Bowl (nearly $3 million per 30 seconds!).[11]

Then their ads are sandwiched in with a clutter of other commercials, announcements and network promotions, totalling nearly 20 minutes of non-programme material per prime-time hour with commercial breaks coming every six minutes on average. Such clutter in television and other ad media has created an increasingly hostile advertising environment. According to one recent study, more than 70 per cent of Americans think there are too many ads on TV, and 62 per cent of national advertisers believe that TV ads have become less effective, citing clutter as the main culprit.[12] Media costs are lower outside the US, but European advertisers are experiencing exactly the same pressures as those in America to stand out from the crowd in busy and increasingly fragmented advertising media.

Until recently, television viewers were essentially a captive audience for advertisers. But today's digital wizardry has given consumers a rich new set of information and entertainment choices. With the growth in cable and satellite TV, the Internet, video on demand (VOD), video downloads and DVD rentals, today's viewers have many more options.

Digital technology has also armed consumers with an arsenal of weapons for choosing what they watch or don't watch. Increasingly, thanks to the growth of digital video recorder (DVR) systems, consumers are choosing *not* to watch ads. More than 33 per cent of American households now have DVRs, and an estimated 44 per cent will have them by 2014. One ad agency executive calls these DVR systems 'electronic weedwhackers'. Research shows that DVR owners view only about 40 per cent of the commercials aired. At the same time, VOD and video downloads are exploding, allowing viewers to watch programming on their own time terms – with or without commercials.[13] The globalisation of the world technology market underlines the rapid spread of this technology across the world.

Thus, advertisers can no longer force-feed the same old conventional ad messages to captive consumers through traditional media. Just to gain and hold attention, today's advertising messages must be better planned, more imaginative, more entertaining and more emotionally engaging. Simply interrupting or disrupting consumers no longer works. Instead, unless ads provide information that is interesting, useful or entertaining, many consumers will simply skip by them.

Advertising clutter: today's consumers, armed with an arsenal of weapons, can choose what they watch and don't watch. Increasingly, they are choosing not to watch ads.
Source: Alamy Images/Gallo Images

Merging advertising and entertainment

To break through the clutter, many marketers are now subscribing to a new merging of advertising and entertainment, dubbed '**Madison & Vine**'. in the US. You've probably heard of Madison Avenue. It's the New York City street that houses the headquarters of many of America's largest advertising agencies. You may also have heard of Hollywood & Vine, the intersection of Hollywood Avenue and Vine Street in Hollywood, California, long the symbolic heart of the US entertainment industry. Now, Madison Avenue and Hollywood & Vine are coming together to form a new intersection – Madison & Vine – that represents the merging of advertising and entertainment in an effort to create new avenues for reaching customers with more engaging messages.

This merging of advertising and entertainment takes one of two forms: advertainment or branded entertainment. The aim of *advertainment* is to make ads themselves so entertaining, or so useful, that people *want* to watch them. There's no chance that you'd watch ads on purpose, you say? Think again. Consider the impact of comparethemarket.com's meerkat advertising described in the Company Case at the end of this chapter, and the loyal fans of the meerkats on the website, Facebook and Twitter.

In fact, DVR systems can actually *improve* viewership of a really good ad. Rather than zipping past the ads, people can skip back to watch them again and again – but only if they are really entertaining and amusing. Consumers with a DVR, may watch favourite ads several times, and share them with others.

Beyond making their regular ads more entertaining, advertisers are also creating new advertising forms that look less like ads and more like short films or shows. For example, Dove's famous 'Evolution' video wasn't technically an ad, but it drew more – and more meaningful – views than many TV ads do, and the views were initiated by consumers. [14] A range of new brand messaging platforms – from Webisodes and blogs to viral videos – are now blurring the line between ads and entertainment.

Branded entertainment (or *brand integrations*) involves making the brand an inseparable part of some other form of entertainment. The most common form of branded entertainment is product

Madison & Vine—A term that has come to represent the merging of advertising and entertainment in an effort to break through the clutter and create new avenues for reaching consumers with more engaging messages.

placements – embedding brands as props within other programming. This technique is so highly developed in the US, it is almost compulsory for programme makers. It might be a brief glimpse of the latest LG phone on *Grey's Anatomy*. It could be worked into the show's overall storyline, as it is on *The Big Bang Theory*, whose character Penny works at the Cheesecake Factory restaurant. The product placement might even be scripted into an episode. For example, one entire episode of US comedy programme *Modern Family* centres around finding geeky father character Phil Dunphy the recently released, hard-to-find Apple iPad he covets as his special birthday present. And in one episode of *30 Rock*, network boss Jack Donaghy blatantly extols the virtues of his Verizon Wireless service. Liz Lemon agrees: 'Well sure, that Verizon Wireless service is just unbeatable.' She then turns to the camera and deadpans, 'Can we have our money now?'[15]

Originally created with TV in mind, branded entertainment has spread quickly into other sectors of the entertainment industry. It's widely used in films (remember all those GM vehicles in the *Transformers* series; the prominence of Purina Puppy Chow in *Marley & Me*, and the appearance of brands ranging from Audi and Oracle to LG in *Iron Man 2*?). If you look carefully, you'll also see product placements in video games, comic books, Broadway musicals and even pop music. For example, there's a sandwich-making scene featuring Wonder Bread and Miracle Whip in the middle of Lady Gaga's 10-minute 'Telephone' video (which captured more than 50 million YouTube views in less than a month).

In all, US advertisers shelled out an estimated $4 (€3) billion on product placements in 2009, half the global spend. In the first three months of the year alone, America's top 11 TV channels produced a massive 117,976 product placements. By itself, Fox's *American Idol* shoehorned in more than 3,000 placements. Old Navy dressed the contestants while Clairol did their hair, Ford supplied the winners with new cars, and Coca-Cola refreshed the judges.[16]

Many mainstream brands rely on product placement, from enterprise companies such as data storage company EMC, which featured its wares on TV show *24*, to Apple, the most prolific brand, which saw its products appear in more than a third of all number one films at the US box office in the past decade.

While at its most developed and sophisticated in the US media, product placement and related communication activities are rapidly spreading to Europe. In France, Spain and Germany, companies have embraced product placement since the relaxation of strict European Union laws in 2007. The new EU rules bring Europe broadly into line with the US on product placement regulation. In 2011, the new rules allowed product placement for the first time in the UK. Nonetheless, in the UK an onscreen 'P' logo must be displayed at the start and end of programmes and between ad breaks to warn viewers when shows contain product placement, and Ofcom the UK regulator enforces more stringent rules and restrictions than most countries (childrens' and religious programming are exempt and some products like gambling and alcohol are excluded). While global product placement spending totalled €4.9 billion in 2009, it is on track for double-digit growth across European media from 2010 to 2014.[17]

So, there is a new meeting place for the advertising and entertainment industries. The goal is for brand messages to become a part of the entertainment rather than interrupting it. As JWT, an ad agency, puts it, 'We believe advertising needs to stop interrupting what people are interested in and be what people are interested in.' However, advertisers must be careful that the new intersection itself doesn't become too congested. With all the new ad formats and product placements, Madison & Vine threatens to create even more of the very clutter that it was designed to break through. At that point, consumers might decide to take yet a different route.

Message strategy

The first step in creating effective advertising messages is to plan a *message strategy* – the general message that will be communicated to consumers. The purpose of advertising is to get consumers to think about or react to the product or company in a certain way. People will react only if they believe they will benefit from doing so. Thus, developing an effective message strategy begins with identifying customer *benefits* that can be used as advertising appeals.

Ideally, the message strategy will follow directly from the company's broader positioning and customer value strategies. Message strategy statements tend to be plain, straightforward outlines of benefits and positioning points that an advertiser wants to stress. The advertiser must next develop a compelling **creative concept** – or 'big idea' – that will bring the message strategy to life in a distinctive and memorable way. At this stage, simple message ideas become great ad campaigns. Usually, a copywriter and an art director will team up to generate many creative concepts, hoping that one of these concepts will turn out to be the big idea. The creative concept may emerge as a visualisation, a phrase or a combination of the two.

The creative concept will guide the choice of specific appeals to be used in an ad campaign. *Advertising appeals* should have three characteristics. First, they should be *meaningful*, pointing out benefits that make the product more desirable or interesting to consumers. Second, appeals must be *believable*. Consumers must believe that the product or service will deliver the promised benefits.

However, the most meaningful and believable benefits may not be the best ones to feature. Appeals should also be *distinctive*. They should tell how one product is better than its competing brands. For example, the most meaningful benefit of owning a wristwatch is that it keeps accurate time, yet few watch ads feature this benefit. Instead, based on the distinctive benefits they offer, watch advertisers might select any of a number of advertising themes. For years, Timex has been the affordable watch. Last Father's Day in the US, for example, Timex ads suggested 'Tell Dad more than time this Father's Day. Tell him that you've learned the value of a dollar.' Similarly, Rolex ads never talk about keeping time. Instead, they talk about the brand's 'obsession with perfection' and the fact that 'Rolex has been the preeminent symbol of performance and prestige for more than a century'.

For example, consider the massive impact of Cadbury's gorilla advertising in 2007 (you can see the ad at www.youtube.com/watch?v=TnzFRV1LwIo):

> Publicis creative agency Fallon Worldwide designed an advertising campaign for Cadbury's Dairy Milk chocolate which started with an ad showing a man in a gorilla suit smiling while playing the drums to Phil Collins, 'In the Air Tonight', and showing the bar of chocolate only in the fade-out shot at the end with the slogan 'A glass and a half full of joy'. Fallon is renowned for persuading large advertisers to make unconventional ads. The ad was first shown during the final of the programme *Big Brother*, then a major hit. Importantly, after the 90-second ad appeared on British television it quickly became an Internet hit and was downloaded seven million times on YouTube as well as generating dozens of imitative spoofs and its own Wikipedia page.
>
> Almost as soon as the ad aired the questions began. Did it feature a real or fake gorilla playing the drums? Was it Phil Collins, the rock drummer who wrote the original song, in a costume? How could this help a staid confectionery brand regain its traditional hold on Britain's chocoholic youth? The secret to its success was the benefit of free 'viral' distribution of the advert as consumers e-mailed, blogged, created and posted spoof versions. This, in turn, provided free editorial coverage in mainstream media, including an uninterrupted full showing of the ad on Australian TV news where the ad itself is not even on the air.
>
> CEO, Todd Stitzer, went on record as saying that the campaign worked because it communicated the joy of eating a chocolate bar 'without being obvious about it'. Cadbury Dairy Milk chocolate sales rose 9 per cent in the two months after the ad was aired, stealing market share from rival Mars. Internal company e-mails refer to 'the gorilla phenomenon'. Cadbury has since been bought by Kraft Foods.[18]

Message execution

The advertiser now must turn the big idea into an actual ad execution that will capture the target market's attention and interest. The creative team must find the best approach, style, tone, words and format for executing a message. A message can be presented in various **execution styles**, such as the following:

- *Slice of life*. This style shows one or more 'typical' people using a particular product in a normal setting. Dairylea cheese triangles are shown being consumed by children in various settings to underline the taste and healthy dimensions of the product.
- *Lifestyle*. This style shows how a product fits in with a particular lifestyle. For example, an ad for Gap's Athleta women's active wear shows a woman in a complex yoga pose and states 'If your body is your temple, build it one piece at a time'.

Creative concept—The compelling 'big idea' that will bring the advertising message strategy to life in a distinctive and memorable way.

Execution style—The approach style, tone, words and format used for executing an advertising message.

- *Fantasy.* This style creates a fantasy around the product or its use. For example, insurance company More Than shows its representative in improbable situations linked to insurance, speaking with Morgan Freeman's voice, signing off with the line 'I'm More Than Freeman…' Dreamies luxury cat biscuits shows a cat repeatedly diving through a wall, and leaving an endearing cat-size hole, in response to the rattle of the biscuits.
- *Mood or image.* This style builds a mood or image around the product or service, such as beauty, love, intrigue or serenity. Few claims are made about the product or service except through suggestion. For example, staple British bread brand Hovis' advertising showcases over 100 years of British history through a boy's eyes to celebrate the 122 years since Hovis was established.
- *Musical.* This style shows people or cartoon characters singing about the product. For example, UK comparison website Gocompare.com tells its story exclusively through a series of singing advertisements, where Gio Compario, an 'Italian' tenor sings the 'Go Compare' message in a number of unlikely situations.
- *Personality symbol.* This style creates a character that represents the product. The character might be animated (e.g. Alexsandr Orlov the meerkat, Mr Clean or Tony the Tiger) or real (e.g. Ronald McDonald or MoreThan Freeman).
- *Technical expertise.* This style shows the company's expertise in making the product. Thus, Kenco Coffee shows the care with which coffee beans are selected for its brands.
- *Scientific evidence.* This style presents survey or scientific evidence that the brand is better or better liked than one or more other brands. For years, P&G's Crest toothpaste (Blend-A-Med in some European markets) has used scientific evidence to convince buyers that the brand is better than others at fighting tooth decay.
- *Testimonial evidence or endorsement.* This style features a highly believable or likeable source endorsing the product. It could be ordinary people saying how much they like a given product. For example, in the US Subway uses spokesman Jared, a customer who lost 245 pounds (110 kg) on a diet of Subway sandwiches. Or it might be a celebrity presenting the product. Olympic gold medal swimmer Michael Phelps also speaks for Subway.

Staple British brand Hovis showcases historical scenes and moods.

Source: The History of Advertising Trust

The advertiser also must choose a *tone* for the ad. P&G always uses a positive tone: its ads say something very positive about its products. Other advertisers now use edgy humour to break through the commercial clutter. The advertiser must use memorable and attention-getting *words* in the ad.

Finally, *format* elements make a difference in an ad's impact as well as in its cost. A small change in an ad design can make a big difference in its effect. In a print ad, the *illustration* is the first thing the reader notices; it must be strong enough to draw attention. Next, the *headline* must effectively entice the right people to read the copy. Finally, the *copy* – the main block of text in the ad – must be simple but strong and convincing. Moreover, these three elements must effectively work *together* to persuasively present customer value.

Consumer-generated messages

Taking advantage of today's interactive technologies, many companies are now tapping consumers for message ideas or actual ads. They are searching existing video sites, setting up their own sites and sponsoring ad-creation contests and other promotions. Sometimes the results are outstanding; sometimes they are forgettable. If done well, however, user-generated content can incorporate the voice of the customer into brand messages and generate greater consumer brand involvement. The dramatic growth of social networking sites like Facebook and MySpace is encouraging advertisers to step up their experiments with user-generated Internet content. Many brands develop brand websites or hold contests that invite consumers to submit ad message ideas and videos.

For example, for the past several years, in the US PepsiCo's Doritos brand has held its annual 'Crash the Super Bowl Challenge' contest that invites consumers to create their own video ads about the tasty triangular corn chips. The consumer-generated Doritos ads have been a success. At the other end of the spectrum, international online crafts marketplace/community Etsy.com – 'Your best place to buy and sell all things handmade' – ran a contest inviting consumers to tell the Etsy.com story in 30-second videos. The results were what one well-known former advertising critic called 'positively remarkable'.[19]

> The ten semifinalists are, as a group, better thought-out and realised than any ten random commercials running on TV anywhere in the world. The best user-created Etsy ad features a simple, sad, animated robot, consigned to a life of soul-crushing assembly-line production. 'See, there's a lot of robots out there', says the voice of the unseen Etsy craftswomen who crafted him. 'A lot of these robots are sad, because they're stuck making these boring, mass-produced things. Me, I really can believe all that great stuff about how it helps the environment and microeconomics and feeling special about getting something handmade by someone else. But the real reason I make handmade goods is because every time somebody buys something handmade, a robot gets its wings.' The user-made ad 'is simply magnificent,' concludes the ad critic, 'in a way that the agency business had better take note of'.

Not all consumer-generated advertising efforts, however, are so successful. As many big companies have learned, ads made by amateurs can be . . . well, pretty amateurish. Done well, however, consumer-generated advertising efforts can produce new creative ideas and fresh perspectives on the brand from consumers who actually experience it. Such campaigns can boost consumer involvement and get consumers talking and thinking about a brand and its value to them.[20]

Selecting advertising media

The major steps in **advertising media** selection are (1) defining *reach*, *frequency* and *impact*; (2) choosing among major *media types*; (3) selecting specific *media vehicles*; and (4) choosing *media timing*.

Defining reach, frequency and impact

To select media, an advertiser must determine the reach and frequency needed to achieve the advertising objectives. *Reach* is a measure of the *percentage* of people in the target market who are exposed to an ad campaign during a given period of time. For example, an advertiser might try to reach 70 per cent of the target market during the first three months of the campaign. *Frequency* is a measure of how many *times* the average person in the target market is exposed to a message. For example, an advertiser might want an average exposure frequency of three.

But advertisers want to do more than just reach a given number of consumers a specific number of times. An advertiser also must determine the desired *media impact* – the *qualitative value* of message exposure through a given medium. For example, the same message in one magazine (say, *The Economist*) may be more believable than in another (say, *Hello!*). For products that need to be demonstrated, messages on television may have more impact than messages on radio because television uses sight *and* sound. Products for which consumers provide input on design or features might be better promoted at an interactive website than in a direct mailing.

More generally, an advertiser wants to choose media that will *engage* consumers rather than simply reach them. For example, for television advertising, how relevant an ad is for its audience is often much more important than how many people it reaches. For example, in an effort to make every advertising penny count, in the US Ford has recently been selecting TV programmes based on viewer engagement ratings:[21]

> Ford had little reason to advertise on the Discovery Channel's *Dirty Jobs* series, which stars Mike Rowe. The show delivers puny Nielsen ratings. But when engagement metrics were applied to the programme, the viewers most deeply absorbed in the show turned out to be truck-buying men

Advertising media—The vehicles through which advertising messages are delivered to their intended audiences.

between the ages of 18 and 49 – a ripe demographic for Ford. That pr⬚⬚⬚⬚⬚⬚⬚⬚vertise heavily and hire Rowe to appear in highly successful Web vide⬚⬚⬚⬚⬚⬚⬚⬚⬚ility of the F-Series pickup.

Although Nielsen is beginning to measure the levels of television *media engagement*, such measures are hard to come by for most media. Current media measures are things such as ratings, readership, listenership and click-through rates for websites. However, engagement happens inside the consumer. Notes one expert, 'Just measuring the number of eyeballs in front of a television set is hard enough without trying to measure the intensity of those eyeballs doing the viewing.'[22] Still, marketers need to know how customers connect with an ad and brand idea as a part of the broader brand relationship.

Choosing among major media types

Media planners have to know the reach, frequency and impact of each major media type. As summarised in Table 15.2, the major media types are television, newspapers, the Internet, direct mail, magazines, radio and outdoor. Advertisers can also choose from a wide array of new digital media, such as mobile phones and other digital devices, which reach consumers directly. Each medium has its advantages and its limitations. Media planners consider many factors when making their media choices. They want to choose media that will effectively and efficiently present the advertising message to target customers. Thus, they must consider each medium's impact, message effectiveness and cost.

Typically, it's not a question of which one medium to use. Rather, an advertiser selects a mix of media and blends them into an IMC campaign. Each medium plays a specific role.

The mix of media must be re-examined regularly. For a long time, television and magazines dominated the media mixes of major, consumer goods advertisers, with other media often neglected.

Table 15.2 Profiles of major media types

Medium	Advantages	Limitations
Television	Good mass-marketing coverage; low cost per exposure; combines sight, sound and motions; appealing to the sences	High absolute costs; high clutter; fleeting exposure; less audience selectivity
Newspapers	Flexbility; timeliness; good local market coverage; broad acceptability; high believability	Short life; poor reproduction quality; small pass-along audience
The Internet	High selectivity; low cost; immediacy; interactive capabilites	Potentially low impact; the audience controls exposure
Direct mail	High audience selectivity; flexibility; no ad competition within the same medium; allows personalisation	Relatively high cost per exposure; 'junk mail' image
Magazines	High geographic and demographic selectivity; credibility and prestige; high-quality reproduction; long life and good pass-along readership	Long ad purchase lead time; high cost; no guarantee of position
Radio	Good local acceptance; high geographic and demographic selectivity; low cost	Audio only; fleeting exposure; low attention ('the half-heard' medium); fragmented audiences
Outdoor	Flexibility; high repeat eposure; low cost; low message competition; good positional selectivity	Little audience selectivity; creative limitations

However, as discussed previously, the media mix appears to be shifting. As mass-media costs rise, audiences shrink and exciting new digital and interactive media emerge, many advertisers are finding new ways to reach consumers. They are supplementing the traditional mass media with more specialised and highly targeted media that cost less, target more effectively and engage customers more fully.

For example, in addition to the explosion of online media, cable and satellite television systems are booming. Such systems allow narrow programming formats, such as all sports, all news, arts, home improvement and gardening, cooking, travel, history, finance and others that target select groups. Cable TV operators are even testing systems that will let them target specific types of ads to specific neighbourhoods or individually to specific types of customers. For example, ads for a Polish-language channel would run in only Polish neighbourhoods, or only pet owners would see ads from pet food companies.

Advertisers can take advantage of such 'narrowcasting' to 'rifle in' on special market segments rather than use the 'shotgun' approach offered by network broadcasting. Cable and satellite television media seem to make good sense. But, increasingly, ads are popping up in far less likely places. In their efforts to find less costly and more highly targeted ways to reach customers, advertisers have discovered a dazzling collection of 'alternative media'. These days, no matter where you go or what you do, you will probably run into some new form of advertising. This search for new media opportunities is at its most extreme in the United States:

> Tiny billboards attached to shopping trolleys and advertising decals on supermarket floors urge you to buy JELL-O Pudding Pops or Pampers, while ads roll by on the store's checkout conveyor touting your local Volvo dealer. Step outside and there goes a rubbish truck sporting an ad for Glad rubbish bags. A nearby fire hydrant is emblazoned with advertising for KFC's 'fiery' chicken wings. You escape to the ballpark, only to find billboard-size video screens running Budweiser ads while a blimp with an electronic message board circles lazily overhead. How about a quiet trip in the country? Sorry – you might find an enterprising farmer using his milk cows as four-legged billboards mounted with ads for Ben & Jerry's ice cream.
>
> These days, you're likely to find ads – well – anywhere. Taxi cabs sport electronic messaging signs tied to GPS location sensors that can pitch local stores and restaurants wherever they roam. Ad space is being sold on DVD cases, parking tickets, airline boarding passes, subway turnstiles, golf scorecards, ATMs, litter bins, and even police cars, doctors' examining tables and church bulletins. One agency even leases space on the shaved heads of college students for temporary advertising tattoos ('cranial advertising'). And the group meeting at the office water cooler has a new member – a 'coolertising' ad sitting on top of the water cooler jug trying to start up a conversation about the latest episode of *American Idol*.

Such alternative media seem a bit far-fetched, and they sometimes irritate consumers who resent it all as 'ad nauseam'. But for many marketers, these media can save money and provide a way to hit selected consumers where they live, shop, work and play. Of course, all this may leave you wondering if there are any commercial-free havens remaining for ad-weary consumers. Public elevators, perhaps, or stalls in a public lavatory? Forget it! Innovative marketers have already invaded them.

For example, Cambridge graduates have launched a business selling advertisers their faces (and those of thousands of like-minded volunteers) as advertising hoardings, sold through their website Buymyface.com. While seemingly bizarre, advertisers have already included Airfix model kits, Paddy Power the bookmakers and Ernst & Young the accountants.[23]

Another important trend affecting media selection is the rapid growth in the number of 'media multitaskers', people who absorb more than one medium at a time. One survey found that three-quarters of US TV viewers read the newspaper while they watch TV, and two-thirds of them go online during their viewing time. According to another study, Americans between

Cambridge graduates have launched a business selling their faces as advertising hoardings.

Source: BuyMyFace.com

457

the ages of eight and 18 are managing to cram an average 10.75 hours of media consumption into 7.5 hours.[24] These days it is not uncommon to find a teenage boy chasing down photos of Megan Fox on Google, becoming a fan of a group on Facebook, watching a film online and texting a friend on his mobile phone – all while trying to complete an essay he's got open in a Word file a few layers down on his desktop. Media planners need to take such media interactions into account when selecting the types of media they will use.

Selecting specific media vehicles

Media planners must also choose the best *media vehicles* – specific media within each general media type. For example, television programmes ot specific magazines.

Media planners must compute the cost per thousand persons reached by a vehicle. For example, if a full-page, four-colour advertisement in a monthly business magazine cost €165,000 and its readership is 1.5 million people, the cost of reaching each group of thousand persons is about €110. The same advertisement in a regional trade magazine may cost only €115,600 but reach only 900,000 people – at a cost per thousand of about €128. The media planner ranks each magazine by cost per thousand and favours those magazines with the lower cost per thousand for reaching target customers.[25]

Media planners must also consider the costs of producing ads for different media. Whereas newspaper ads may cost very little to produce, flashy television ads can be very costly. Many online ads cost little to produce, but costs can climb when producing made-for-the-Web videos and ad series.

In selecting specific media vehicles, media planners must balance media costs against several media effectiveness factors. First, the planner should evaluate the media vehicle's *audience quality*. For a Huggies disposable nappies advertisement, for example, *Mother & Baby* magazine would have a high exposure value; *GQ* magazine would have a low-exposure value. Second, the media planner should consider *audience engagement*. Readers of *Vogue*, for example, typically pay more attention to ads than do *Economist* readers. Third, the planner should assess the vehicle's *editorial quality*. *The Economist* and the *Financial Times* are more believable and prestigious than the *Sun* or the *National Enquirer*.

Choosing media timing

An advertiser must also decide how to schedule the advertising over the course of a year. Suppose sales of a product peak in December and drop in March (for winter sports gear, for instance). The firm can vary its advertising to follow the seasonal pattern, oppose the seasonal pattern or be the same all year. Most firms do some seasonal advertising. For example, confectionery manufacturers run special ads for their sweets for almost every holiday and 'season', from Christmas, to Easter to Halloween. Moonpig.com, the online customised greetings card producer is likely to advertise more heavily before major holidays, such as Christmas, Easter, Mother's Day, Father's Day and Valentine's Day. Some marketers do *only* seasonal advertising. For instance, P&G advertises its cold remedies only during the annual cold and flu season.

Finally, an advertiser must choose the pattern of the ads. *Continuity* means scheduling ads evenly within a given period. *Pulsing* means scheduling ads unevenly over a given time period. Thus, 52 ads could either be scheduled at one per week during the year or pulsed in several bursts. The idea behind pulsing is to advertise heavily for a short period to build awareness that carries over to the next advertising period. Those who favour pulsing feel that it can be used to achieve the same impact as a steady schedule but at a much lower cost. However, some media planners believe that although pulsing achieves minimal awareness, it sacrifices depth of advertising communications.

Evaluating advertising effectiveness and the return on advertising investment

Return on advertising investment—The net return on advertising investment divided by the costs of the advertising investment.

Measuring advertising effectiveness and the **return on advertising investment** has become a hot issue for most companies, especially in the tight economic environment. A less friendly economy 'has obligated us all to pinch pennies all the more tightly and squeeze blood from a rock,' says one advertising executive.[26] That leaves top management at many companies asking their marketing managers, 'How do we know that we're spending the right amount on advertising?' and 'What return are we getting on our advertising investment?'

Advertisers should regularly evaluate two types of advertising results: the communication effects, and the sales and profit effects. Measuring the *communication effects* of an ad or ad campaign tells whether the media are communicating the ad message well. Individual ads can be tested before or after they are run. Before an ad is placed, an advertiser can show it to consumers, ask how they like it, and measure message recall or attitude changes resulting from it. After an ad is run, an advertiser can measure how the ad affected consumer recall or product awareness, knowledge and preference. Pre- and post-evaluations of communication effects can be made for entire ad campaigns as well.

Advertisers are generally quite good at measuring the communication effects of their ads and ad campaigns. However, *sales and profit* effects of advertising are often much harder to measure. For example, what sales and profits are produced by an ad campaign that increases brand awareness by 20 per cent and brand preference by 10 per cent? Sales and profits are affected by many factors other than advertising – such as product features, price and availability.

One way to measure the sales and profit effects of advertising is to compare past sales and profits with past advertising expenditures. Another way is through experiments. For example, to test the effects of different advertising spending levels, Coca-Cola could vary the amount it spends on advertising in different market areas and measure the differences in the resulting sales and profit levels. More complex experiments could be designed to include other variables, such as differences in the ads or media used.

However, because so many factors affect advertising effectiveness, some controllable and others not, measuring the results of advertising spending remains an inexact science. For example, dozens of advertisers spend lavishly on high-profile ads around major sporting events each year. Although they sense that the returns are worth the sizeable investment, few can actually measure or prove it. A study by the Association of National Advertisers in the US asked advertising managers if they would be able to 'forecast the impact on sales' of a 10 per cent cut in advertising spending. Sixty-three per cent said no. Another recent survey found that more than one-third of the surveyed firms have made no effort at all to measure marketing ROI, and another one-third have been working on it for less than two years.[27]

'Marketers are tracking all kinds of data and they still can't answer basic questions' about advertising accountability, says a marketing analyst, 'because they don't have real models and metrics by which to make sense of it.' Advertisers are measuring 'everything they can, and that ranges from how many people respond to an ad to how many sales are closed and then trying to hook up those two end pieces,' says another analyst. 'The tough part is, my goodness, we've got so much data. How do we sift through it?'[28] Thus, although the situation is improving as marketers seek more answers, managers often must rely on large doses of judgment along with quantitative analysis when assessing advertising performance.

Other advertising considerations

In developing advertising strategies and programmes, the company must address two additional questions. First, how will the company organise its advertising function? Who will perform which advertising tasks? Second, how will the company adapt its advertising strategies and programmes to the complexities of international markets?

Organising for advertising

Different companies organise in different ways to handle advertising. In small companies, advertising might be handled by someone in the sales department. Large companies have advertising departments whose job it is to set the advertising budget, work with the ad agency, and handle other advertising not done by the agency. Most large companies use outside advertising agencies because they offer several advantages.

Advertising agency—A marketing services firm that assists companies in planning, preparing, implementing and evaluating all or portions of their advertising programmes.

How does an **advertising agency** work? Advertising agencies were originated in the mid- to late-1800s by salespeople and brokers who worked for the media and received a commission for selling advertising space to companies. As time passed, the salespeople began to help customers prepare their ads. Eventually, they formed agencies and grew closer to the advertisers than to the media.

Today's agencies employ specialists who can often perform advertising tasks better than the company's own staff can. Agencies also bring an outside point of view to solving the company's problems, along with lots of experience from working with different clients and situations. So, today, even companies with strong advertising departments of their own use advertising agencies.

Some ad agencies are huge. In recent years, many agencies have grown by gobbling up other agencies, thus creating huge agency holding companies. The largest of these 'megagroups' in the world, London-based WPP, includes several large advertising, PR and promotion agencies with combined worldwide revenues of €10.6 billion. WPP is closely followed by the Paris-based Publicis Groupe, which has global revenues of €6.1 billion in 2011 from its global network.[29] Most large advertising agencies have the staff and resources to handle all phases of an ad campaign for their clients, from creating a marketing plan to developing ad campaigns and preparing, placing and evaluating ads. Smaller advertising agencies tend to specialise in particular countries or types of communications, such as online.

International advertising decisions

International advertisers face many complexities not encountered by domestic advertisers. The most basic issue concerns the degree to which global advertising should be adapted to the unique characteristics of various country markets. Some large advertisers have attempted to support their global brands with highly standardised worldwide advertising, with campaigns that work as well in Bangkok as they do in Baltimore. For example, McDonald's unifies its creative elements and brand presentation under the familiar 'I'm lovin' it' theme in all its 100-plus markets worldwide. Coca-Cola pulls advertising together for its flagship brand under the theme, 'Open Happiness'. And Visa coordinates worldwide advertising for its debit and credit cards under the 'more people go with Visa' creative platform, which works as well in Korea as it does in the United States or Europe.

In recent years, the increased popularity of online social networks and video sharing has boosted the need for advertising standardisation for global brands. Most big marketing and ad campaigns include a large online presence. Connected consumers can now zip easily across borders via the Internet, making it difficult for advertisers to roll out adapted campaigns in a controlled, orderly fashion. As a result, at the very least, most global consumer brands coordinate their websites internationally. For example, visit the McDonald's websites from Germany to Jordan to China. You'll find the golden arches logo, the 'I'm lovin it' logo and jingle, a Big Mac equivalent, and maybe even Ronald McDonald himself.

Standardisation produces many benefits – lower advertising costs, greater global advertising coordination, and a more consistent worldwide image. But it also has drawbacks. Most importantly, it ignores the fact that country markets differ greatly in their cultures, demographics and economic conditions. Thus, most international advertisers 'think globally but act locally'. They develop global advertising *strategies* that make their worldwide efforts more efficient and consistent. Then they adapt their *programmes* to make them more responsive to consumer needs and expectations within local markets. For example, although Visa employs its 'more people go with Visa' theme globally, ads in specific locales employ local language and inspiring local imagery that make the theme relevant to the local markets in which they appear.

Global advertisers face several special problems. For instance, advertising media costs and availability differ vastly from country to country. Countries also differ in the extent to which they regulate ad practices. Many countries have extensive systems of laws restricting how much a company can spend on advertising, the media used, the nature of advertising claims and other aspects of the programme. Such restrictions often require advertisers to adapt their campaigns from country to country.

For example, alcohol products cannot be advertised in India or in Muslim countries. In many countries, such as Sweden and Canada, junk food ads are banned from children's television programming. To play it safe, McDonald's advertises itself as a family restaurant in Sweden. Comparative ads, although acceptable and even common in the United States and Canada, are less commonly used in the United Kingdom and are actually illegal in India and Brazil. China bans sending e-mails for advertising purposes to people without their permission, and all advertising e-mails that are sent must be titled 'advertisement'.

China also has restrictive censorship rules for TV and radio advertising; for example, the words *the best* are banned, as are ads that 'violate social customs' or present women in 'improper ways'. McDonald's once avoided government sanctions in China by publicly apologising for an ad that crossed cultural norms by showing a customer begging for a discount. Similarly, Coca-Cola's Indian subsidiary was forced to end a promotion that offered prizes, such as a trip to Hollywood, because it violated India's established trade practices by encouraging customers to buy to 'gamble'.

Thus, although advertisers may develop global strategies to guide their overall advertising efforts, specific programmes must usually be adapted to meet local cultures and customs, media characteristics and regulations.

AUTHOR COMMENT

Not long ago, PR was considered a marketing stepchild because of its limited marketing use. That situation is changing fast, however, as more marketers recognise PR's brand-building power.

PUBLIC RELATIONS

Another major mass-promotion tool is **public relations** (**PR**) – building good relationships with the company's various publics by obtaining favourable publicity; building up a good corporate image; and handling or heading off unfavourable rumours, stories and events. PR specialists may perform any or all of the following functions:[30]

Public relations (PR)— Building good relations with the company's various publics by obtaining favourable publicity, building up a good corporate image, and heading off unfavourable rumours, stories and events.

- *Press relations or press agency.* Creating and placing newsworthy information in the news media to attract attention to a person, product or service.
- *Product publicity.* Publicising specific products.
- *Public affairs.* Building and maintaining national or local community relationships.
- *Lobbying.* Building and maintaining relationships with law-makers and government departments to influence regulation and public policy.
- *Investor relations.* Maintaining relationships with shareholders and others in the financial community.
- *Development.* Working with donors or members of not-for-profit organisations to gain financial or volunteer support.

PR is used to promote products, people, places, ideas, activities, organisations and even nations. Companies use PR to build good relationships with consumers, investors, the media and their communities. Trade associations have used PR to rebuild interest in declining commodities, such as eggs, apples, potatoes and milk. Even government organisations use PR to build awareness. For example, in the United States the National Heart, Lung, and Blood Institute (NHLBI) of the National Institutes of Health sponsors a long-running PR campaign that builds awareness of heart disease in women:[31]

Heart disease is the number one killer of women; it kills more women each year than all forms of cancer combined. But a 2000 survey by the NHLBI showed that only 34 per cent of women knew this, and that most people thought of heart disease as a problem mostly affecting men.

So with the help of Ogilvy Public Relations Worldwide, the NHLBI set out to 'create a personal and urgent wake up call to American women'. In 2002, it launched a national PR campaign – 'The Heart Truth' – to raise awareness of heart disease among women and get women to discuss the issue with their doctors.

The centrepiece of the campaign is the Red Dress, now the national symbol for women and heart disease awareness. The campaign creates awareness through an interactive website, mass media placements and campaign materials – everything from brochures, DVDs and posters to speaker's kits and airport dioramas. It also sponsors several major national events, such as the National Wear Red Day, an annual Red Dress Collection Fashion Show and The Heart Truth Road Show, featuring heart disease risk factor screenings in major US cities. Finally, the campaign works with more than three-dozen corporate sponsors, such as Diet Coke, St. Joseph aspirin, Tylenol, Cheerios, CVS Pharmacy, Swarovski and Bobbi Brown Cosmetics. So far, some 2.65 billion product packages have carried the Red Dress symbol. The results are impressive: awareness among American women of heart disease as the number one killer of women has increased to 57 per cent, and the number of heart disease deaths in women has declined steadily from one in three women to one in four. The American Heart Association has also adopted the Red Dress symbol and introduced its own complementary campaign.

Through PR alone, Apple's iPad launch generated unbounded consumer excitement.

Source: Getty Images/AFP

The role and impact of PR

PR can have a strong impact on public awareness at a much lower cost than advertising can. The company does not pay for the space or time in the media. Rather, it pays for a staff to develop and circulate information and manage events. If the company develops an interesting story or event, it could be picked up by several different media, having the same effect as advertising that would cost much more. And it would have more credibility than advertising.

PR results can sometimes be spectacular. Consider the launch of Apple's iPad:[32]

Apple's iPad was one of the most successful new product launches in history. And here's the funny thing: whereas most big product launches are accompanied by huge pre-launch ad campaigns, Apple pulled this one off with no advertising. None at all. Instead, it simply fed the PR fire. It built buzz months in advance by distributing iPads for early reviews, feeding the offline and online press with tempting tidbits, and offering fans an early online peek at thousands of new iPad apps that would be available. At launch time, it fanned the flames with a cameo on the television sitcom *Modern Family*, a flurry of launch-day appearances on TV talk shows, and other launch-day events. In the process, through PR alone, the iPad launch generated unbounded consumer excitement, a media frenzy and long lines outside retail stores on launch day. Apple sold more than 300,000 of the sleek gadgets on the first day alone and more than two million in the first two months – even as demand outstripped supply.

Despite its potential strengths, PR is sometimes described as a marketing stepchild because of its often limited and scattered use. If there is a PR department, it is often located at corporate headquarters or PR may be handled by a third-party agency. Its staff is so busy dealing with various publics – stockholders, employees, legislators and the press – that PR programmes to support product marketing objectives may be ignored. Moreover, marketing managers and PR practitioners do not always speak the same language. Whereas many PR practitioners see their jobs as simply communicating, marketing managers tend to be much more interested in how advertising and PR affect brand building, sales and profits, and customer relationships.

This situation is changing, however. Although PR still captures only a small portion of the overall marketing budgets of most firms, PR can be a powerful brand-building tool. And in this digital age, the lines between advertising and PR are becoming more and more blurred. For example, are brand websites, blogs, online social networks and viral brand videos advertising efforts or PR efforts? All are both. 'Blurriness can be good,' says one PR executive. 'When you have more overlap between PR and other marketing disciplines, it's easier to promote the same message.' The point is that advertising and PR should work hand in hand within an IMC programme to build brands and customer relationships.[33]

Major PR tools

PR encompasses several tools. One of the major tools is *news*. PR professionals find or create favourable news stories about the company and its products or people. Sometimes news stories occur naturally; sometimes the PR person can suggest events or activities that would create news. *Speeches* can also create product and company publicity. Increasingly, company executives must field questions from the media or give talks at trade associations or sales meetings, and these events can either build or hurt the company's image. Another common PR tool is *special events*, ranging from news conferences, press tours, grand openings and fireworks displays to laser light shows, hot air balloon releases, multimedia presentations or educational programmes designed to reach and interest target publics.

PR people also prepare *written materials* to reach and influence their target markets. These materials include annual reports, brochures, articles and company newsletters and magazines. *Audiovisual materials*, such as slide-and-sound programmes, DVDs and online videos are being used increasingly as communication tools. *Corporate identity materials* can also help create a corporate identity that the public immediately recognises. Logos, stationery, brochures, signs, business forms, business cards, buildings, uniforms and company cars and trucks all become marketing tools when they are attractive, distinctive and memorable. Finally, companies can improve public goodwill by contributing money and time to *public service activities*.

As discussed above, the Web is also an increasingly important PR channel. Websites, blogs, and social networks such as YouTube, Facebook and Twitter are providing interesting new ways to reach more people. 'The core strengths of public relations – the ability to tell a story and spark conversation – play well into the nature of such social media,' says a PR expert.

By itself, a company's website is an important PR vehicle. Consumers and other publics often visit websites for information or entertainment. Websites can also be ideal for handling crisis situations. For example, when several bottles of Odwalla apple juice sold on the West Coast of the United States were found to contain *E. coli* bacteria, Odwalla initiated a massive product recall. Within only three hours, it posted a website laden with information about the crisis and Odwalla's response. Company staffers also combed the Internet looking for newsgroups discussing Odwalla and posted links to the site. In this age where 'it's easier to disseminate information through e-mail marketing, blogs, and online chat,' notes an analyst, 'public relations is becoming a valuable part of doing business in a digital world.'[34] The Odwalla response to crisis was impressive compared to the Toyota products recall in 2010 and BP's handling of the Deepwater oil spill crisis.

As with the other promotion tools, in considering when and how to use product PR, management should set PR objectives, choose the PR messages and vehicles, implement the PR plan and evaluate the results. The firm's PR should be blended smoothly with other promotion activities within the company's overall IMC effort.

REVIEWING OBJECTIVES AND KEY TERMS

Companies must do more than make good products; they have to inform consumers about product benefits and carefully position products in consumers' minds. To do this, they must master *advertising* and *PR*.

OBJECTIVE 1 Define the role of advertising in the promotion mix (p. 447).

Advertising – the use of paid media by a seller to inform, persuade and remind buyers about its products or its organisation – is an important promotion tool for communicating the value that marketers create for their customers. American marketers spend more than $163 (€127) billion each year on advertising, and worldwide spending exceeds €350 billion. Advertising takes many forms and has many uses. Although advertising is employed mostly by business firms, a wide range of not-for-profit organisations, professionals and social agencies also employ advertising to promote their causes to various target publics. *PR* – gaining favourable publicity and creating a favourable company image – is the least used of the major promotion tools, although it has great potential for building consumer awareness and preference.

OBJECTIVE 2 Describe the major decisions involved in developing an advertising programme (pp. 447–461).

Advertising decision making involves making decisions about the advertising objectives, budget, message and media, and, finally, culminates with an evaluation of the results. Advertisers should set clear target, task and timing *objectives*, whether the aim is to inform, persuade or remind buyers. Advertising's goal is to move consumers through the buyer-readiness stages discussed in Chapter 14. Some advertising is designed to move people to immediate action. However, many of the ads you see today focus on building or strengthening long-term customer relationships. The advertising *budget* depends on many factors. No matter what method is used, setting the advertising budget is no easy task.

Advertising strategy consists of two major elements: creating advertising *messages* and selecting advertising *media*. The *message decision* calls for planning a message strategy and executing it effectively. Good messages are especially important in today's costly and cluttered advertising environment. Just to gain and hold attention, today's messages must be better planned, more imaginative, more entertaining, and more rewarding to consumers. In fact, many marketers are now subscribing to a new merging of advertising and entertainment, dubbed *Madison & Vine*. The *media decision* involves defining reach, frequency and impact goals; choosing major media types; selecting media vehicles; and choosing media timing. Message and media decisions must be closely coordinated for maximum campaign effectiveness.

Finally, *evaluation* calls for evaluating the communication and sales effects of advertising before, during and after ads are placed. Advertising accountability has become a hot issue for most companies. Increasingly, top management is asking: 'What return are we getting on our advertising investment?' and 'How do we know that we're spending the right amount?' Other important advertising issues involve *organising* for advertising and dealing with the complexities of international advertising.

OBJECTIVE 3 Define the role of PR in the promotion mix (pp. 461–463).

PR is used to promote products, people, places, ideas, activities, organisations and even nations. Companies use PR to build good relationships with consumers, investors, the media and their communities. PR can have a strong impact on public awareness at a much lower cost than advertising can, and PR results can sometimes be spectacular. Although PR still captures only a small portion of the overall marketing budgets of most firms, PR is playing an increasingly important brand-building role. In the digital age, the lines between advertising and PR are becoming more and more blurred.

OBJECTIVE 4 Explain how companies use PR to communicate with their publics (p. 463).

Companies use PR to communicate with their publics by setting PR objectives, choosing PR messages and vehicles, implementing the PR plan and evaluating PR results. To accomplish these goals, PR professionals use several tools, such as *news*, *speeches* and *special events*. They also prepare *written*, *audiovisual* and *corporate identity materials* and contribute money and time to *public service activities*. The Web has also become an increasingly important PR channel, as websites, blogs and social networks are providing interesting new ways to reach more people.

NAVIGATING THE KEY TERMS

OBJECTIVE 1
Advertising (p. 447)

OBJECTIVE 2
Advertising objective (p. 448)
Advertising budget (p. 449)
Advertising strategy (p. 450)
Madison & Vine (p. 451)

Creative concept (p. 453)
Execution style (p. 453)
Advertising media (p. 455)
Return on advertising investment (p. 458)
Advertising agency (p. 460)

OBJECTIVE 3
Public relations (p. 461)

DISCUSSING AND APPLYING THE CONCEPTS

Discussing the concepts

1. List the primary types of advertising objectives and discuss the kinds of advertising used to achieve each type. (AASCB: Communication)

2. Why is it important that the advertising media and creative departments work closely together? (AACSB: Communication)

3. Name and describe five of the many execution styles advertisers use when developing ads. For each execution style, describe a recent television commercial using that style. (AACSB: Communication: Reflective Thinking)

4. How should a company measure the effectiveness of its advertising? (AACSB: Communication)

5. What are the role and functions of public relations within an organisation? (AACSB: Communication)

6. Discuss the tools used by public relations professionals. (AACSB: Communication)

Applying the concepts

1. Select two print ads (such as magazine ads). Based on the three characteristics advertising appeals should possess evaluate the appeals used in each ad. (AACSB: Communication: Reflective Thinking)

2. Marketers are developing branded Web series to get consumers involved with their brands. One successful series is 'Real Women of Philadelphia' from Kraft (www. realwomenofphiladelphia.com). Fans can watch videos of professionals making delicious, simple recipes with one common ingredient – Philadelphia Cream Cheese, of course! The site features a recipe contest and entrants even get training on how to photograph their entries to make them look as yummy as possible. Visit this website and find two other branded Web series. Critique the sites and describe how viewers interact with the websites. (AACSB: Communication: Use of IT: Reflective Thinking)

3. In a small group discuss the major public relations tools and develop three public relations items for each of the following: a hospital, a restaurant and any brand of your choice. (AACSB Communication: Reflective Thinking)

Focus on technology

The Internet can pose a public relations nightmare for companies. Venerable P&G found this out firsthand after launching its revolutionary Dry Max technology for its best-selling Pampers nappies. Touted as its most significant innovation in 25 years, the new nappies are 20 per cent smaller but much more absorbent than competitive brands because a more-absorbent chemical gel replaced the cottony fluff pulp. Not long after the new product's release, however, customer complaints of severe nappy rash or chemical burns surfaced on the Internet. Angry parents spouted off on P&G's websites and several Facebook pages: 'Recall Pampers Dry Max', 'Boycott New Pampers Dry Max,' and 'Bring Back the Old Cruisers/Swaddlers.' Mainstream media picked up the discontent and started spreading the news. Almost 5,000 consumer complaints were received, 85 per cent occurring within the first few months of the product launch. There seems to be no link between severe nappy rash and Pampers Dry Max but that did not stop some parents from continuing to use the Internet to call for boycotts or lawyers to solicit lawsuits.

1. Research P&G's problems with its Pampers Dry Max brand. How has P&G responded to this crisis? Write a report on what you learn. (AACSB: Communication; Reflective Thinking)

2. Find examples of other online rumours and discuss how companies can combat negative publicity spread on the Internet. (AACSB: Communication: Reflective Thinking)

Focus on ethics

The Federal Drug Administration in the US is enlisting doctors in its battle against misleading and deceptive prescription drug ads targeted toward consumers (called direct-to-consumer or DTC ads) and other promotional activities directed at medical professionals. You've seen television commercials for Viagra, Lipitor, Chantix and other prescription drugs. Since the FDA relaxed the rules regarding broadcast prescription drug advertising in the late 1990s, DTC advertising has increased more than 300 per cent, with $4.5 billion spent in 2009. That's actually down from the peak of $5.5 billion in 2006 because of the recession. It's difficult for the FDA to monitor DTC ads and other promotional activity aimed at medical professionals, so it created the 'Bad Ad Programme' and spent most of 2010 educating doctors about this programme.

1. Visit www.fda.gov and search for 'Bad Ad Programme' to learn more about it. What is the FDA asking medical professionals to look for in DTC ads and other promotional activities directed toward them? How might this programme be abused by the pharmaceutical industry? (AACSB: Communication: Ethical Reasoning; Reflective Thinking)

2. Many US consumers are not aware of the FDA's regulations regarding DTC advertising. The agency has a parallel programme – called EthicAd – to educate consumers and encourage them to report violations. Search the FDA's website for this programme, look at examples of correct and incorrect ads, and evaluate two prescription drug advertisements using these guidelines. (AACSB: Communication; Ethical Reasoning; Reflective Thinking)

Marketing & the economy

McDonald's

Despite a down economy – or perhaps because of it – McDonald's has been beating competitors badly in recent years. In fact, the fast-food giant pretty much owns the value menu. But, surprisingly. McDonald's current financial good fortunes are not being driven by its low-price items but rather by its higher-price, higher-margin items. Throughout tough economic times, McDonald's advertising strategy focused on its traditional, full-priced specialities. One month it pushed Big Macs, the next month Chicken McNuggets and then Quarter Pounders. But McDonald's hasn't forsaken its value menu. Instead, it has increased promotional support for its flagship specialities. It's all part of an effort to grab business from diners who are trading down from higher-priced eateries. McDonald's has gambled that people would view the old favourites as comfort food. Add to this promotional strategy the Burger

King's migration into a full beverage menu that includes lattes and all-fruit smoothies, and you have a real one-two punch. The company's overall revenues and profits continue to rise, even as the percentage of revenues generated from lower-price items falls. Its promotional pricing and product strategies are attracting new customers while also encouraging existing value menu customers to trade up. All this has both executives and franchisees singing 'I'm lovin it'.

1. What was McDonald's advertising objective with this promotional campaign?

2. In communicating value during hard times, what elements of McDonald's advertising strategy contributed to its success?

Marketing by the numbers

Nielsen ratings are very important to both advertisers and television programmers because the cost of television advertising time is based on this rating. A show's *rating* is the number of households in Nielsen's sample tuned to that programme divided by the number of television-owning households – 15 million in the United States. A show's *share* of the viewing audience is the number of households watching that show divided by the number of households using TV at that time. That is, ratings consider all TV-owning households, whereas share considers only those households that actually have the television on at the time. Ratings and share are usually given together. For example, during one evening hour on 9 September 2010, the following ratings/shares were reported for the major broadcast networks:

Network	Programme	Rating/Share
NBC	*Sunday Night Football* (played on Thursday)	13.6/22
CBS	*Big Brother 12*	4.6/8
ABC	*Wipeout*	3.1/5
Fox	*Bones*	2.9/5
The CW	*The Vampire Diaries*	2.0/3

1. If one rating point represents 1 per cent of TV households, how many households were watching football that evening? How many households were tuned to *The Vampire Diaries*? (AACSB: Communication; Analytical Reasoning)

2. What total share of the viewing audience was captured by all five networks? Explain why share is higher than the rating for a given programme. (AACSB: Communication; Analytical Reasoning; Reflective Thinking)

REFERENCES

1 See Devin Leonard, 'Hey, PC, who taught you to fight back?' *New York Times* (30 August 2009), p. BU1; Eleftheria Parpis, 'Microsoft fetes Windows 7 'creators', *Adweek* (22 October 2009), accessed at www.adweek.com/aw/content_display/esearch/e3i92ec830f3865d5c0c7438cad8708e49e; Noreen O'Leary, 'Amid transition, rivals are descending on Apple', *Brandweek* (7 November 2009), p. 4; Abbey Klaassen, 'In Mac vs. PC battle, Microsoft winning in value perception', *Advertising Age* (18 May 2009), accessed at http://adage.com/digital/article?article_id=136731; Rupal Parekh, 'Microsoft vs. Apple fight enters new round', *Advertising Age* (18 September 2008), accessed at http://adage.com/article?article_id=131102; and Josh Smith, 'Apple ends 'Get a Mac' ads: goodbye Mac, goodbye PC' (26 May 2010), accessed at www.walletpop.com/blog/2010/05/26/apple-ends-get-a-mac-ads-goodbye-mac-goodbye-pc.

2 Figures extracted from http://zenithoptimedia.blogspot.com/2011/12/quadrennial-events-to-help-ad-market.html, accessed 24 February 2012.

3 Data on US and global advertising spending obtained at 'Leading national advertiser's,' *Advertising Age* (22 June 2009), pp. 12–13; 'Top 50 global marketers', *Advertising Age* (28 December 2009); and Emily Steel, 'Forecasters predict ad stabilization in 2010', *Wall Street Journal* (7 December 2009), accessed at http://online.wsj.com/article/SB10001424052748704825504574582310496271156.html; and http://adage.com/datacenter/#top_marketers;_adspend_stats, accessed June 2010.

4 See http://2010.census.gov/mediacenter/paid-ad-campaign/new-ads/index.php?v,n11, accessed June 2010; www.fas.org/sgp/crs/misc/R41681.pdf, accessed 24 February 2012; www.telegraph.co.uk/finance/newsbysector/mediatechnologyandtelecoms/media/8232075/UK-Government-halves-advertising-spend.html, accessed 24 February 2012.

5 See www.out-law.com/page-11979, accessed 24 February 2012.

6 For these and other examples of comparative advertising, see Emily Bryson York and Natalie Zmuda, 'So sue me: why big brands are taking claims to court', *Advertising Age* (4 January 2010), pp. 1, 23; 'AT&T ends Verizon ad lawsuit', *Techweb* (2 December 2009); 'Pepsi suing Coca-Cola over Powerade ads', *New York Times* (13 April 2009), accessed at www.nyt.com; Emily Bryson York, 'Book of tens: nasty comparative campaigns of 2009', *Advertising Age* (14 December 2009), accessed at http://adage.com/print?article_id=141025; and Isabella Soscia, Simona Girolamo and Bruno Busacca, 'The effect of comparison advertising on consumer perceptions: similarity or differentiation?', *Journal of Business and Psychology* (March 2010), pp. 109–118.

7 For more on advertising budgets, see Ronald Lane, Karen King and Thomas Russell, *Kleppner's Advertising Procedure*, 18th edn (Upper Saddle River, NJ: Prentice Hall, 2011), chapter 6.

8 Example adapted from Jean Halliday, 'Thinking big takes Audi from obscure to awesome', *Advertising Age* (2 February 2009), accessed at http://adage.com/print?article_id=134234. Also see Jack Neff, 'Study: cutting spending hurts brands in long-term: following boom/bust cycle flirts with danger', *Advertising Age* (6 April 2009), accessed at http://adage.com/print?article_id135790; and Nat Ives, 'Ad spending dropped 12% in 2009, but things are looking up', *Advertising Age* (17 March 2010), accessed at http://adage.com/print?article_id=142832.

9 'Average US home now receives a record 118.6 TV channels, according to Nielsen' (6 June 2008), http://en-us.nielsen.com/content/nielsen/en_us/news/news_releases/2008/june/average_u_s_home.html; and 'Number of magazines by category', www.magazine.org/asme/editorial%5Ftrends, accessed August 2010.

10 Louise Story, 'Anywhere the eye can see, it's likely to see an ad', *New York Times*, (15 January 2007), p. A12; and James Othmer, 'Persuasion gives way to engagement', *Vancouver Sun* (20 August 2009), p. A13.

11 See Bill Carter, 'An "idol" ratings loss, but not in its pocketbook', *New York Times* (6 April 2010); 'Executive summary of the 4A's television production cost survey', (15 December 2009), www.aaaa.org/news/bulletins/Documents/2008TVPCSExecSumcosts.pdf; Bill Gorman, 'Fox's average ad price in Q4 2009: $122,000', (16 March 2010), www.tvbytheNumbers.com; Brian Steinberg, 'Sunday Night Football' remains costliest TV show', *Advertising Age* (26 October 2009), p. 8; and "Sluggish economy pinches Super Bowl ad prices', *Associated Press*, (11 January 2010).

12 'Advertising in the US: Synovate global survey shows internet, innovation and online privacy a must' (3 December 2009), accessed at www.synovate.com/news/article/2009/12/advertising-in-the-us-synovate-global-survey-shows-internet-innovation-and-online-privacy-a-must.html; and Katy Bachman, 'Survey: clutter causing TV ads to lack effectiveness', *MediaWeek* (8 February 2010).

13 'Report: ad execs stymied by DVR ad skipping', *Mediaweek* (29 June 2009), accessed at www.mediaweek.com/publications; Nielsen, *How DVRs Are Changing the Television Landscape* (April 2009), http://blog.nielsen.com/nielsenwire/wp-content/uploads/2009/04/dvr_tvlandscape_043009.pdf; Bill Carter, 'DVR, once TVs mortal foe, helps ratings', *New York Times* (2 November 2009); and Andrew O'Connell, 'Advertisers: learn to love the DVR', *Harvard Business Review* (April 2010), p. 22.

14 See www.youtube.com/watch?v=hibyAJOSW8U, accessed 24 February 2012.

15 See Alessandra Stanley, 'Commercials you can't zap', *New York Times* (7 June 2009), p. MT1; Sam Schechner and Suzanne Vranica, 'IPad gets star turn in television comedy', *Wall Street Journal* (2 April 2010), p. B8; and Rupal Parekh, 'Why long-form ads are the wave of the future', *Advertising Age* (3 May 2010), accessed at http://adage.com/madisonandvine/article?article_id=143603.

16 For more on product placements, see Randee Dawn and Alex Ben Block, 'Brands take "American Idol" Stage', *Adweek* (12 May 2009), accessed at www.adweek.com/aw/content_display/news/strategy/e3if21dd856cf-b9103e5d9128faa8ed6740; Richard Huff, 'Product placement outsells ads', *Daily News* (27 December 2007), p. 73; Ravi Somaiya, 'Chloe, it's Kac. Who does our phones?', *Guardian* (16 June 2008), accessed at www.guardian.com; Stanley, 'Commercials you can't zap'; and T. L. Stanley, 'A Place for Everything', *Brandweek*, 1 March 2010, pp. 12–4 key.

17 David Gelles and Tim Bradshaw, 'When props pay for production', *Financial Times* (1 March 2011), p. 16.

18 Aaron O. Patrick, 'Fallon in London hones an unconventional edge', *Wall Street Journal* (11 December 2007), p. 6; Jenny Wiggins and Maggie Urry, 'Cadbury benefits from gorilla tactics', *Financial Times* (12 December 2007), p. 23; Carlos Grande, 'Aping of ad helps to drum up chocolate brand interest', *Financial Times* (12 December 2007), p. 23.

19 Adapted from information found in Bob Garfield, 'How Etsy made us rethink consumer-generated ads', *Advertising Age* (21 September 2009), p. 4.

20 For more on consumer-generated advertising, see Emma Hall, 'Most winning creative work involves consumer participation'', *Advertising Age* (6 January 2010), accessed at http://adage.com/print?article_id=141329; Stuart Elliott, 'Do-it-yourself super ads', *New York Times* (8 February 2010); Michael Learmonth, 'Brands team up for user-generated-Ad contests',

Advertising Age (23 March 2009), p. 8; and Rich Thomaselli, 'If consumer is your agency, it's time for review', *Advertising Age* (17 May 2010), p. 2.

[21] See David Kiley, 'Paying for viewers who pay attention', *BusinessWeek*, (18 May 2009), p. 56.

[22] Brian Steinberg, 'Viewer-engagement rankings signal change for TV industry', *Advertising Age* (10 May 2010), p. 12.

[23] Jack Grimston, 'We're no mugs, we've sold our faces', *Sunday Times* (4 March 2012), S1, p. 11.

[24] See Claudia Wallis, 'The multitasking generation', *Time* (27 March 2006), accessed at www.time.com/time/magazine/article/0,9171,1174696,00.html; Tanya Irwin, 'Study: kids are master multitaskers on TV, Web, mobile', *MediaPost Publications* (10 March 2008), accessed at www.mediapostpublications.com; Jon Lafayette, 'Integrated campaigns worth overcoming hurdles', (29 April 2009), accessed at www.tvweek.com/news/2009/04/integrated_campaigns_worth_ove.php; and Henry J. Kaiser Family Foundation, *Generation M2: Media in the Lives of 8- to 18-year-olds* (20 January 2010), accessed at www.kff.org/entmedia/mh012010pkg.cfm.

[25] *Newsweek* and *BusinessWeek* cost and circulation data online at http://mediakit.businessweek.com and www.newsweekmediakit.com, accessed August 2010.

[26] Kate Maddox, 'Optimism, accountability, social media top trends', *BtoB*, (18 January 2010), p. 1.

[27] See Lawrence A. Crosby, 'Getting serious about marketing ROI', *Marketing Management*, (May/June 2009), pp. 10–17.

[28] Elliott, 'How effective is this ad, in real numbers? Beats me', p. C8; and 'Taking measure of which metrics matter', *BtoB* (5 May 2008).

[29] Information on advertising agency revenues from 'Agency Report 2010', *Advertising Age* (26 April 2010), pp. 22.

[30] Adapted from Scott Cutlip, Allen Center and Glen Broom, *Effective Public Relations*, 10th edn (Upper Saddle River, NJ: Prentice Hall, 2009), chapter 1.

[31] Information from 'The heart truth: making healthy hearts fashionable', Ogilvy Public Relations Worldwide, accessed at www.ogilvypr.com/en/case-study/heart-truth?page=0, accessed June 2010; and www.nhlbi.nih.gov/educational/hearttruth/about/index.htm, accessed June 2010.

[32] See Geoffrey Fowler and Ben Worthen, 'Buzz powers iPad launch', *Wall Street Journal* (2 April 2010); 'Apple iPad sales top 2 million since launch', *Tribune-Review* (Pittsburgh) (2 June 2010); and 'PR pros must be Apple's iPad as a true game-changer', *PRweek* (May 2010), p. 23.

[33] Matthew Schwartz, 'New influence', *Advertising Age* (26 October 2009), p. S4.

[34] Paul Holmes, 'Senior marketers are sharply divided about the role of PR in the overall mix', *Advertising Age* (24 January 2005), pp. C1–C2. For another example, see Jack Neff, 'How Pampers battled diaper debacle', *Advertising Age* (10 May 2010), accessed at http://adage.com/article?article_id=143777.

VIDEO CASE

E*Trade MyMarketingLab

Super Bowl XXXIV, the first of the new millennium, was known as the Dot-com Bowl for the glut of Internet companies that plopped down an average of $2.2 million per 30-second spot ad. Today, most of the companies that defined the dot-com glory days are gone. But one darling of the dot-com era, E*TRADE, remains one of the few survivors. Although E*Trade has experienced challenges since the turn of the century, it has also turned profits.

Advertising on the big game hasn't worked out well for everyone. But for E*TRADE, Super Bowl ads have been part of a larger advertising effort that played a role in its survival. In this video, E*TRADE reports on its advertising strategy as well as the advantages and disadvantages of Super Bowl advertising.

After watching the video featuring E*TRADE, answer the following questions about advertising and promotions:

1. What makes E*TRADE different from now-defunct dot-coms?
2. What has been the role of advertising at E*TRADE?
3. Discuss the factors in E*TRADE's decision to advertise during the Super Bowl.

COMPANY CASE

The mighty meercats – simples!

Aleksandr Orlov is a talking meerkat, with heavily-accented and barely passable English, who stars in television ads for compare-themarket.com, the insurance and credit card website. Usually appearing in a threadbare smoking jacket or velvet dressing gown that has seen better days, Alexsandr urges people to compare meerkats on his website – comparethemeerkats.com. The bane of his life appears to be consumers who confuse the two websites, visiting the meerkat site when in fact looking for cheap car insurance.

In fact, there are those who would say that Sergei, Alexandr's stooge and quieter companion meerkat is the star of the ads. The storyline is based on the supposed confusion among consumers between comparethemarket.com and the fictional comparethemeerkat.com, and the meerkats' pleas to consumers to go to the right website to avoid overloading the meerkat's own page and causing Sergei excessive work. The story has expanded to include the great historical meerkat battles with their mongoose enemies, their experience as émigrés from Russia, and the danger that Sergei may have worms and moult excessively.

The fascination of the public with Alexsandr and Sergei has seen the establishment of an actual compare-the-meerkat website, www.comparethemeerkat.com, offering fans the opportunity to delve further into the complexity of meerkat 'history' and Meerkova, the meerkat village, as well as download ads and other treats.

Christmas 2010 saw the autobiography of the furry Alexandr outselling the life stories of stars such as Michael McIntyre and Keith Richards, and sitting at the top of the *Sunday Times* nonfiction bestseller list. The royalties were not destined for a good cause because Alexsandr, the little furry author, said 'I am hope to remarble roof on Orlov family mansion. Please enjoyment.' Rival author, comedian Paul O'Grady fumed: 'Now we have the life and times of a meerkat – a piece of stuffed vermin who flogs insurance. What next? Churchill, the life of a dog?'

Alexsandr's ornate family life detailed in *A Simples Life* includes ancestors struggling through the Kalahari, the meerkat–mongoose war of 1728 and the ancient village of Meerkova. The underlying joke is that Alexsandr, an eccentric Russian billionare living in faded grandeur, is annoyed with the British public for confusing his business–comparethemeerkat.com–with the insurance website. The TV ads are apparently Alexsandr's way of explaining the obvious difference – leading to his cry of 'Simples!' at the end.

A master of social media, Alexsandr has 770,000 friends on Facebook, 700,000 subscribers to his iPhone app (iSimples) and more than 44,000 followers on Twitter. A limited-edition replica meerkat toy in Alexsandr's image sold through Harrods and became an immediate collectible. Undoubtedly, Alexsandr Orlov is heading towards advertising immortality as the star of one of the UK's most acclaimed ad campaigns. For some months in 2009, traffic to the fictional meerkat site exceeded that to comparethemarket.com itself.

But this was all created by advertising agency VCCP in 2009 to help a flagging insurance site sell more quotes.

The campaign has transformed the fortunes of the client. The first year of the meerkat campaign saw very strong growth of comparethemarket.com of 189 per cent. In 2010, BGL Group, who own comparethemarket.com, saw a 6 per cent rise in revenue in a tough trading environment, and a jump in pre-tax profit to £62.3 (€77.9) million.

In a category with no functional differentiation between the competitors and a once-a-year relationship with customers, the campaign has pulled off the neat trick of creating a marketing conversation that has nothing to do with the product, but links the name with something people like. Moreover, the creatives have once again seen off the risk of overkill by continuing to keep it fresh.

Early in 2009, comparethemarket.com had been languishing at fourth place in its sector, and trading conditions were difficult. The advertising challenge was to make an essentially boring product something which was fun and to put some life into the comparethemarket.com brand. In fact, within days of the first ad hitting TV screens, it achieved the most modern of accolades: it was a YouTube sensation. In the first nine weeks of the campaign, quotes on the insurance site increased by 80 per cent and awareness of the brand tripled.

Other comparison websites like Confused.com and Go Compare have slipped down the rankings since the arrival of the meerkats on the scene.

Aleksandr is one of the more prominent examples of the trend for animated characters or puppets to act as brand ambassadors. US consumers have long been charmed by the frogs that feature in Budweiser's advertising or the cockney gecko that stars in Geico's campaigns. Meanwhile, Domo, the saw-toothed mascot for Japanese broadcaster NHK, has gone on to appear in video games and comics, and spread virally online.

But the proliferation and popularity of these creations and the merchandising they have spawned raises questions for both brand owners and advertising agencies hoping to capitalise on the value of the intellectual property.

For brand owners, the appeal of creating characters is that they are cheaper and more reliable than the celebrities often enlisted to star in campaigns. 'Quite often celebrities do things outside of your advertising campaign which can reflect badly back on your brand,' says Charlie Herbert, director of e-commerce and marketing at Travelodge, the budget UK hotel chain that has just launched a campaign featuring Mr Sleep and the Zzz Squad, a group of gangster teddy bears with a vendetta against night-time noise. 'With puppets, you can control your iconography.'

The Zzz Squad was developed by London-based agency Mother, which insists on sharing profits from future merchandising with the client. 'In these last few years, the consideration of how we retain IP on our characters has been at the forefront when we create them,' says Stuart Outhwaite, a creative director at the agency. Mother's stance follows its experience with Monkey, a cuddly character it created in 2001 for the UK broadcaster ITV Digital. When ITV Digital went into administration, a row erupted over who controlled the intellectual property rights to Monkey. After a legal battle, the rights to the character were donated to the charity Comic Relief. In 2007, Monkey was revived for Unilever's PG Tips brand of tea under licence from the charity, working with Mother as part of the deal.

In spite of not holding the rights, Mr Outhwaite says the agency remains Monkey's legal 'carers' and 'creative guardians'. 'Monkey and Mother are intrinsically linked,' he says. 'As a creative property, he has been fantastic. Beyond any significant financial gain, he has won us two or three awards and brought in enough business. He's earned his fair share over the years.' Nonetheless, proceeds from Monkey merchandise – from toys to babywear – go to Comic Relief.

By contrast, VCCP, the agency behind Aleksandr and Sergei, does not receive any direct proceeds from meerkat merchandise. Kal Atwal, managing director of comparethemarket.com, argues that the absence of revenue-sharing arrangements is fair because, as the client, her company has taken the bigger risk by investing in it. 'There were a number of pitches and the brief was quite specific,' she says. 'You work in partnership.'

Chris Satterthwaite, chief executive of Chime Communications, VCCP's parent company, points out that a successful campaign creates more work for that client and attracts new ones. 'Lots of agencies have talked about creating their own IP and I really haven't seen any who have succeeded in doing it,' he says. 'They are in the services business. You produce it to a brief and [the IP] belongs to the client.'

But with the advertising industry's traditional business model under pressure from moves towards time-based remuneration, sharing in the upside of creative work through IP ownership could unlock a new form of revenue for agencies.

Moreover, the guarantee of a ten-year royalty stream would be very welcome for agencies as long-term retainers become scarcer.

Some agencies have set up dedicated brand licensing units in response to the new challenges. M&C Saatchi established one such division earlier this year. 'Traditional advertising is becoming less important, new ways of communicating are growing, yet no one was really doing licensing,' says Matthew Conrad, a former IP lawyer who leads the unit. 'The way we look at licensing, it's a response to a specific marketing challenge. By doing that you'll mitigate the huge risk of brand [dilution].' He also hopes to incorporate licensing into more agency contracts for traditional marketing work to avoid missing out on meerkat-like opportunities.

Another unit has been set up by BBH, the agency behind Flat Eric, the orange puppet who shot to fame ten years ago in adverts for Levi's Sta-Prest jeans. As well as T-shirts, toys and other merchandising, Flat Eric even topped the charts with the techno anthem 'Flat Beat'. But BBH shared in little of the upside, prompting it to create Zag, its own brand invention business.

'It's a challenging model that requires a long-term commitment but if you get it right it will be game-changing for you as a business,' says Neil Munn, who runs the unit.

But for all the valuable merchandising opportunities they generate, the main purpose of all these cute and cuddly characters remains to promote the brand. 'I almost don't see it as brand extension,' says comparethemarket.com's Ms Atwal. 'It's more about how we've broadened the communications platform that we have.'

In spite of all the spin-off merchandising, Kal Atwal, managing director of comparethemarket.com, denies that the meerkat franchise is becoming overextended. 'If we wanted to, we could do a lot more on merchandising,' she says. 'But we have this asset that we need to protect and we don't want to have overexposure.' Ms Atwal also insists that any tie-ins are meant to promote the car insurance site, not generate revenue themselves. 'We have been strict at focusing on elements that are important to the campaign,' she says. 'It would be too short term from our perspective to do it as a revenue driver.'

Questions for discussion

1. How does the meerkat advertising fit with the advertising objectives of informing, persuading and reminding?
2. If the primary purpose of advertising is actually to sell things, how do the message execution techniques in the meerkat advertising fit with this purpose?
3. To what extent is there a danger that highly creative advertising actually promotes the adverts more than the product itself?

4. Do you agree or disagree with the premise that the primary function of advertising is to sell? Give examples of advertising campaigns to support your position.

5. Should advertising create secondary income streams from merchandising, and if so, who should benefit – the agency or the client?

Sources: 'Meerkat makes millions', *Sunday Times* (17 October 2010), S3, p. 1; Giles Hattersley, 'How to hit the jackpot: simples!', *Sunday Times* (5 December 2010), S1, p. 24; Richard Gold 'The public image: Comparethemarket.com', *Financial Times* (11 January 2010), www.ft.com, accessed 22 February 2012; Tim Bradshaw, 'Cute, cuddly and commercial', *Financial Times* (22 June 2010), www.ft.com, accessed 22 February 2012.

CHAPTER SIXTEEN

Personal selling and sales promotion

Chapter preview

In the previous two chapters, you learned about communicating customer value through IMC and two elements of the promotion mix: advertising and public relations. In this chapter, we examine two more IMC elements: personal selling and sales promotion. Personal selling is the interpersonal arm of marketing communications, in which the sales force interacts with customers and prospects to build relationships and make sales. Sales promotion consists of short-term incentives to encourage the purchase or sale of a product or a service. As you read, remember that although this chapter presents personal selling and sales promotion as separate tools, they must be carefully integrated with the other elements of the promotion mix.

First, what is your first reaction when you think of a salesperson or a sales force? Perhaps you think of pushy retail sales assistants, aggressive salespeople in television advertising or the stereotypical untrustworthy and insincere 'used-car salesman'. But such stereotypes simply don't fit the reality of most of today's salespeople – sales professionals who succeed not by taking advantage of customers but by listening to their needs and helping to forge solutions. For most companies, personal selling plays an important role in building profitable customer relationships. Consider P&G, whose customer-focused sales force has long been considered one of the most effective in the world.

Objective outline

➤ **Objective 1** Discuss the role of a company's salespeople in creating value for customers and building customer relationships.
Personal selling (pp. 474– 477)

➤ **Objective 2** Identify and explain the six major sales force management steps.
Managing the sales force (pp. 477–487)

➤ **Objective 3** Discuss the personal selling process, distinguishing between transaction-oriented marketing and relationship marketing.
The personal selling process (pp. 487–490)

➤ **Objective 4** Explain how sales promotion campaigns are developed and implemented.
Sales promotion (pp. 491–496)

Procter & Gamble

For decades, P&G has been at the top of almost every expert's A-list of outstanding marketing companies. The experts point to P&G's stable of top-selling consumer brands, or that, year in and year out, P&G is the world's largest advertiser. Consumers seem to agree. You will find least one of P&G's blockbuster brands in 99 per cent of all American households; in many homes, there will be a dozen or more familiar P&G products. But P&G is also highly respected for something else – its top-notch, customer-focused sales force.

P&G's sales force has long been an icon for selling at its very best. When it comes to selecting, training and managing salespeople, P&G sets the gold standard. The company employs a massive sales force of more than 5,000 salespeople worldwide. At P&G, however, the company rarely calls it 'sales'. Instead, it's 'Customer Business Development' (CBD). And P&G sales reps aren't 'salespeople'; they are 'CBD managers' or 'CBD account executives'. All this might seem like 'corp-speak', but at P&G the distinction goes to the very core of how selling works.

P&G understands that if its customers don't do well, neither will the company. To grow its own business, therefore, P&G must first grow the business of the retailers that sell its brands to final consumers. And at P&G, the primary responsibility for helping customers grow falls to the sales force. Rather than just selling *to* its retail and wholesale customers, CBD managers partner strategically *with* customers to help develop their business in P&G's product categories. 'We depend on them as much as they depend on us', says one CBD manager. By partnering with each other, P&G and its customers create 'win-win' relationships that help both to prosper.

Most P&G customers are huge and complex businesses – such as Walgreens, Walmart or Dollar General – with thousands of stores and billions of dollars in revenues. Working with and selling to such customers can be a very complex undertaking, more than any single salesperson or sales team could accomplish. Instead, P&G assigns a full CBD team to every large customer account. Each CBD team contains not only salespeople but also a full complement of specialists in every aspect of selling P&G's consumer brands at the retail level.

CBD teams vary in size depending on the customer. For example, P&G's largest customer, Walmart, which accounts for an amazing 20 per cent of the company's sales, commands a 350-person CBD team. By contrast, the P&G Dollar General team consists of about 30 people. Regardless of size, every CBD team constitutes a complete, multifunctional customer-service unit. Each team includes a CBD manager and several CBD account executives (each responsible for a specific P&G product category), supported by specialists in marketing strategy, product development, operations, information systems, logistics, finance and human resources.

To deal effectively with large accounts, P&G salespeople must be smart, well trained and strategically grounded. They deal daily with high-level retail category buyers who may purchase hundreds of millions of dollars worth of P&G and competing brands annually. It takes a lot more than a friendly smile and a firm handshake to interact with such buyers. Yet, individual P&G salespeople can't know everything, and thanks to the CBD sales structure, they don't have to. Instead, as members of a full CBD team, P&G salespeople have at hand all the resources they need to resolve even the most challenging customer problems. 'I have everything I need right here', says a household care account executive. 'If my customer needs help from us with in-store promotions, I can go right down the hall and talk with someone on my team in marketing about doing some kind of promotional deal. It's that simple'.

CBD involves partnering with customers to jointly identify strategies that create shopper value and satisfaction and drive profitable sales at the store level. When it comes to profitably moving Tide, Pampers, Gillette or other P&G brands off store shelves and into consumers' shopping carts, P&G reps and their teams often know more than the retail buyers they advise. In fact, P&G's retail partners often rely on CBD teams to help them manage not only the P&G brands on their shelves but also entire product categories, including competing brands.

Wait a minute. Does it make sense to let P&G advise on the stocking and placement of competitors' brands as well as its own? Would a P&G CBD rep ever tell a retail buyer to stock fewer P&G products and more of a competing brand? Believe it or not, it happens all the time. The CBD team's primary goal is to help the customer win in each product category. Sometimes, analysis shows that the best solution for the customer is 'more of the other guy's product'. For P&G, that's okay. It knows that creating the best situation for the retailer ultimately pulls in more customer traffic, which in turn will likely lead to increased sales for other P&G products in the same category. Because most of P&G's brands are market share leaders, it stands to benefit more from the increased traffic than competitors do. Again, what's good for the customer is good for P&G; it's a win-win situation.

Honest and open dealings also help to build long-term customer relationships. P&G salespeople become trusted advisors to their retailer-partners, a status they work hard to maintain. 'It took me four years to build the trust I now have with my buyer', says a veteran CBD account executive. 'If I talk her into buying P&G products that she can't sell or out of stocking competing brands that she should be selling, I could lose that trust in a heartbeat.'

Finally, collaboration is usually a two-way street: P&G gives and customers give back in return. 'We'll help customers run a set of commercials or do some merchandising events, but there's usually a return-on-investment', explains another CBD manager. 'Maybe it's helping us with distribution of a new product or increasing space for fabric care. We're very willing if the effort creates value for us as well as for the customer and the final consumer'.

According to P&G, 'Customer Business Development is selling and a whole lot more. It's a P&G-specific approach [that lets us] grow business by working as a "strategic partner" with our accounts, focusing on mutually beneficial business building opportunities. All customers want to improve their business; it's [our] role to help them identify the biggest opportunities'.

Thus, P&G salespeople aren't the stereotypical untrustworthy and insincere 'glad-handlers' that some people have come to expect when they think of selling. In fact, they aren't even called 'salespeople'. They are CBD managers – talented, well-educated, well-trained sales professionals who do all they can to help customers succeed. They know that good selling involves working with customers to solve their problems for mutual gain. They know that if customers succeed, they succeed.[1]

AUTHOR COMMENT

P&G's sales force has long been an icon for selling at its very best. But at P&G, the company rarely calls it 'sales'. Instead, it's 'Customer Business Development'.

In this chapter, we examine two more promotion mix tools: *personal selling* and *sales promotion*. Personal selling consists of interpersonal interactions with customers and prospects to make sales and maintain customer relationships. Sales promotion involves using short-term incentives to encourage customer purchasing, reseller support and sales force efforts.

AUTHOR COMMENT

Personal selling is the interpersonal arm of the promotion mix. A company's sales force creates and communicates customer value through personal interactions with customers.

PERSONAL SELLING

Robert Louis Stevenson once noted, 'Everyone lives by selling something'. Companies around the world use sales forces to sell products and services to business customers and final consumers. But sales forces are also found in many other kinds of organisations. For example, universities use recruiters to attract new students, and churches use membership committees to attract new members. Museums and fine arts organisations use fund-raisers to contact donors and raise money.

Even public sector organisations use sales forces. The Royal Mail Group, for instance, uses a sales force to sell Parcelforce Worldwide and other services to corporate customers. In the first part of this chapter, we examine personal selling's role in the organisation, sales force management decisions and the personal selling process.

The nature of personal selling

Personal selling is one of the oldest professions in the world. The people who do the selling go by many names, including salespeople, sales representatives, agents, district managers, account executives, sales consultants and sales engineers.

People hold many stereotypes of salespeople – including some unfavourable ones. 'Salesman' may bring to mind the image of Arthur Miller's pitiable Willy Loman in *Death of a Salesman* or Chris Finch, the brashly confident, openly sexist, rasping-voiced, bullying Wernham Hogg paper salesman from the TV comedy programme *The Office*. And then there are the real-life aggressive salespeople, who hawk everything from 'buy one, get one free' replacement windows to cleaning products in TV commercials. However, the majority of salespeople are a far cry from these unfortunate stereotypes.

As the opening P&G story shows, most salespeople are well-educated and well-trained professionals who add value for customers and maintain long-term customer relationships. They listen to their customers, assess customer needs and organise the company's efforts to solve customer problems.[2]

> Some assumptions about what makes someone a good salesperson are dead wrong. There's this idea that the classic sales personality is overbearing, pushy and outgoing – the kind of people who walk in and suck all the air out of the room. But the best salespeople are good at one-on-one contact. They create loyalty and customers because people trust them and want to work with them. It's a matter of putting the client's interests first, which is the antithesis of how most people view salespeople. The most successful salespeople are successful for one simple reason: they know how to build relationships. You can go in with a big personality and convince people to do what you want them to do, but that really isn't selling; it's manipulation, and it only works in the short term. A good salesperson can read customer emotions without exploiting them because the bottom line is that he or she wants what's best for the customer.

Consider Siemens' electric locomotive business. It takes more than fast talk and a warm smile to sell a batch of high-tech locomotives, at a multi-million price tag per locomotive. A single big sale can easily run into the hundreds of millions of euros. Seventy locos sold to Amtrak in the US in 2010 were worth €388 million. Siemens' sales engineers are at the forefront of an extensive team of company specialists – all dedicated to finding ways to satisfy the needs of large customers. The selling process can take years from the first sales presentation to the day the sale is announced. The real challenge is to win a buyer's business by building partnerships with them – day-in, day-out, year-in, year-out – based on superior products and close collaboration.

The term **salesperson** covers a wide range of positions. At one extreme, a salesperson might be largely an *order taker*, such as the department store salesperson standing behind the counter. At the other extreme are *order getters*, whose positions demand *creative selling* and *relationship building* for products and services ranging from appliances, industrial equipment and locomotives to insurance and IT services.[3] Here, we focus on the more creative types of selling and the process of building and managing an effective sales force.

The role of the sales force

Personal selling is the interpersonal arm of the promotion mix. Advertising consists largely of non-personal communication with large groups of consumers. By contrast, personal selling involves interpersonal interactions between salespeople and individual customers – whether face-to-face, by telephone, via e-mail, through video or Web conferences, or by other means. Personal selling

Personal selling—Personal presentations by the firm's sales force for the purpose of making sales and building customer relationships.

Salesperson—An individual representing a company to customers by performing one or more of the following activities: prospecting, communicating, selling, services, information gathering and relationship building.

can be more effective than advertising in more complex selling situations. Salespeople can probe customers to learn more about their problems and then adjust the marketing offer and presentation to fit the special needs of each customer.

The role of personal selling varies from company to company. Some firms have no salespeople at all – for example, companies that sell only online or through catalogues, or companies that sell through manufacturers' reps, sales agents or brokers. In most firms, however, the sales force plays a major role. In companies that sell business products and services, such as IBM, BP or Airbus, salespeople work directly with customers. In consumer product companies such as P&G and Nestlé, the sales force plays an important behind-the-scenes role. It works with wholesalers and retailers to gain their support and help them be more effective in selling the company's products.

Linking the company with its customers

Salespeople link the company to its customers. To many customers, the salesperson *is* the company.

Source: Shutterstock.com

The sales force serves as a critical link between a company and its customers. In many cases, salespeople serve two masters: the seller and the buyer. First, they *represent the company to customers*. They find and develop new customers and communicate information about the company's products and services. They sell products by approaching customers, presenting their offerings, answering objections, negotiating prices and terms and closing sales. In addition, salespeople provide customer service and carry out market research and intelligence work.

At the same time, salespeople *represent customers to a particular company*, acting inside the firm as 'champions' of customers' interests and managing the buyer–seller relationship. Salespeople relay customer concerns about company products and actions back inside to those who can handle them. They learn about customer needs and work with other marketing and non-marketing people in the company to develop greater customer value.

In fact, to many customers, the salesperson *is* the company – the only tangible manifestation of the company that they see. Hence, customers may become loyal to salespeople as well as to the companies and products they represent. This concept of 'salesperson-owned loyalty' lends even more importance to the salesperson's customer relationship building abilities. Strong relationships with the salesperson will result in strong relationships with the company and its products. Conversely, poor relationships will probably result in poor company and product relationships.

Given its role in linking the company with its customers, the sales force must be strongly customer-solutions focused. In fact, such a customer-solutions focus is a must not only for the sales force but also for the entire organisation. Anne Mulcahy, successful former CEO and chairperson of Xerox, who started her career in sales, says that a strong customer-service focus 'has to be the center of your universe, the heartland of how you run your company':

Today, for most companies, personal selling plays an important role in building profitable customer relationships. In turn, those relationships contribute greatly to overall company success. Just ask Anne Mulcahy, recently retired CEO and current chairperson of the board at Xerox. She took the reins of the then-nearly-bankrupt copier company in early 2001 and transformed it into a successful, modern-day, digital technology and services enterprise. She began her career in 1976 as a Xerox sales rep in Boston. From there, she worked her way up the sales ladder to become Xerox's vice president of global sales in the late 1990s. Then, 25 years after first knocking on customer doors, she was appointed CEO of Xerox.

As CEO, Mulcahy brought with her a sales and marketing mentality that now permeates the entire Xerox organisation, with a new focus solving customer problems. Looking back, Mulcahy recalls, Xerox had lost touch with its markets. 'Sales helps you understand what drives the business and that customers are a critical part of the business,' Mulcahy says. 'This will be important in any business function, but you learn it [best] in sales management where it is critical, the jewel in the crown.' Implementing this customer-first sales philosophy, one of Mulcahy's first actions as CEO was to put on her old sales hat and hit the road to visit customers. Mulcahy knows that putting customers first isn't just a sales force responsibility; it's an emphasis for everyone in the company. To stress that point at all levels, she quickly set up a rotating 'customer officer of the day' programme at Xerox, which requires a top executive to answer customer calls that come to corporate head-quarters. As the customer officer of the day, the executive has three responsibilities: listen to the customer, resolve the problem and take responsibility for fixing the underlying cause. That sounds a lot like sales. So if you're still thinking of salespeople as fast-talking, ever-smiling peddlers who foist their wares on reluctant customers, you're probably working with an out-of-date stereotype. Good salespeople succeed not by taking customers in but by helping them out – by assessing customer needs and solving customer problems. In fact, that isn't just good sales thinking; it applies to the entire organisation.[4]

Coordinating marketing and sales

Ideally, the sales force and other marketing functions (marketing planners, brand managers and researchers) should work together closely to jointly create value for customers. Unfortunately, however, some companies still treat sales and marketing as separate functions. When this happens, the separate sales and marketing groups may not get along well. When things go wrong, marketers blame the sales force for its poor execution of what they see as an otherwise splendid strategy. In turn, the sales team blames the marketers for being out of touch with what's really going on with customers. Neither group fully values the other's contributions. If not repaired, such disconnects between marketing and sales can damage customer relationships and company performance.

A company can take several actions to help bring its marketing and sales functions closer together. At the most basic level, it can increase communications between the two groups by arranging joint meetings and spelling out communications channels. It can create opportunities for salespeople and marketers to work together. Brand managers and researchers can occasionally go along on sales calls or sit in on sales planning sessions. In turn, salespeople can sit in on marketing planning sessions and share their firsthand customer knowledge.

A company can also create joint objectives and reward systems for sales and marketing teams or appoint marketing-sales liaisons – people from marketing who 'live with the sales force' and help coordinate marketing and sales force programmes and efforts. Finally, it can appoint a high-level marketing executive to oversee both marketing and sales. Such a person can help infuse marketing and sales with the common goal of creating value for customers to capture value in return.[5]

> **AUTHOR COMMENT**
>
> Here's another definition of sales force management: 'Planning, organising, leading and control-ling personal contact programmes designed to achieve profitable customer relationships.' Once again, the goal of every marketing activity is to create customer value and build customer relation-ships.

MANAGING THE SALES FORCE

We define **sales force management** as analysing, planning, implementing and controlling sales force activities. It includes designing the sales force strategy and structure and recruiting, selecting, training, compensating, supervising and evaluating the firm's salespeople. These major sales force management decisions are shown in Figure 16.1 and are discussed in the following sections.

Sales force management—
Analysing, planning, imple-menting and controlling sales force activities.

Designing the sales force strategy and structure

Marketing managers face several sales force strategy and design questions. How should salespeople and their tasks be structured? How big should the sales force be? Should salespeople sell alone or

Figure 16.1 Major steps in sales force management

The goal of this process? You guessed it! The company wants to build a skilled and motivated sales team that will help to create customer value and build strong customer relationships.

| Designing sales force strategy and structure | → | Recruiting and selecting salespeople | → | Training salespeople | → | Compensating salespeople | → | Supervising salespeople | → | Evaluating salespeople |

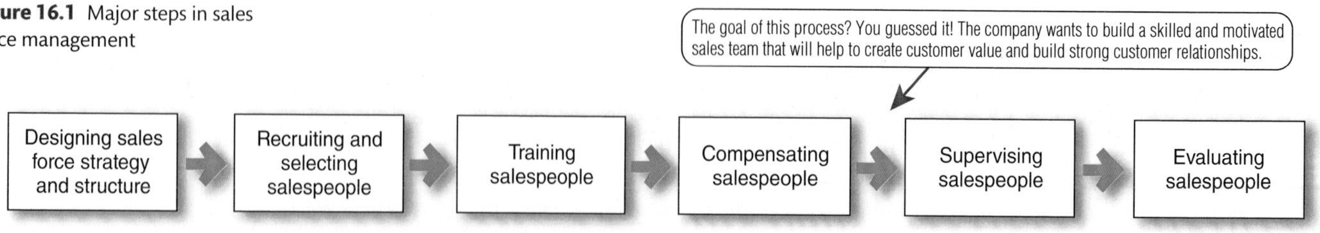

work in teams with other people in the company? Should they sell in the field, by telephone or on the Web? We address these issues next.

The sales force structure

A company can divide sales responsibilities along any of several lines. The structure decision is simple if the company sells only one product line to one industry with customers in many locations. In that case the company would use a *territorial sales force structure*. This remains the commonest sales force structure in Europe. However, if the company sells many products to many types of customers, it might need a *product sales force structure*, a *customer sales force structure*, or a combination of the two.

Territorial sales force structure

Territorial sales force structure—A sales force organisation that assigns each salesperson to an exclusive geographic territory in which that salesperson sells the company's full line.

In the **territorial sales force structure**, each salesperson is assigned to an exclusive geographic area and sells the company's full line of products or services to all customers in that territory. This organisation clearly defines each salesperson's job and fixes accountability. It also increases the salesperson's desire to build local customer relationships that, in turn, improve selling effectiveness. Finally, because each salesperson travels within a limited geographic area, travel expenses are relatively small.

A territorial sales organisation is often supported by many levels of sales management positions. For example, global tools and security products company Stanley Black & Decker uses a territorial structure in which each salesperson is responsible for selling all of the company's products – from hand tools to lawn and garden equipment to security systems – in assigned territories. In the large US market, starting at the bottom of the organisation are entry-level *territory sales representatives* who report to *territory managers*. Territory sales representatives cover smaller areas, such as Eastern North Carolina, and territory managers cover larger areas such as the Carolinas and Virginia. Territory managers, in turn, report to *regional managers*, who cover regions such as the Southeast or West Coast. Regional managers, in turn, report to a *director of sales*. In smaller European and other markets fewer sales force management levels are more usual.

Product sales force structure

Product sales force structure—A sales force organisation in which sales-person specialise in selling only a portion of the company's products or lines.

Salespeople must know their products, especially when the products are numerous and complex. This need, together with the growth of product management, has led many companies to adopt a **product sales force structure**, in which the sales force sells along product lines. For example, GE employs different sales forces within different product and service divisions of its major businesses. Within GE Infrastructure, for instance, the company has separate sales forces for aviation, energy, transportation and water processing products and technologies. Within GE Healthcare, it employs different sales forces for diagnostic imaging, life sciences and integrated IT products and services. In all, a company as large and complex as GE might have dozens of separate sales forces serving its diverse product and service portfolio across its global markets.

The product structure can lead to problems, however, if a single large customer buys many different company products. For example, several different GE salespeople might end up calling on the same large healthcare customer in a given period. This means that they travel over the same routes and wait to see the same customer's purchasing agents. These extra costs must be compared with the benefits of better product knowledge and attention to individual products.

Customer sales force structure

More and more companies are now using a **customer (or market) sales force structure**, in which they organise the sales force along customer or industry lines. Separate sales forces may be created for different industries, serving current customers versus finding new ones, and serving major accounts versus regular accounts. Many companies even have special sales forces to handle the needs of individual large customers. For example, above its territory structure, Stanley Black & Decker has a sales organisation specifically focused on individual mass-retailer customers. Many companies have developed sales and account structures around the needs of their most important customers.[6]

Organising the sales force around customers can help a company build closer relationships with important customers. Consider Hill-Rom, a global supplier of medical equipment, including hospital beds, stretchers and nurse communication systems, which recently restructured its product-based US sales force into a customer-based one:[7]

> Hill-Rom divided its sales force into two customer-based teams. One sales force focuses on 'key' customers – large accounts that purchase high-end equipment and demand high levels of sales force collaboration. The second sales force focuses on 'prime' customers – smaller accounts that are generally more concerned about getting the features and functions they need for the best possible price. Assigning the separate sales forces helps Hill-Rom better understand what the different types of customers need. It also lets the company track how much attention the sales force devotes to each customer group.
>
> For example, prior to restructuring its sales force, Hill-Rom had been treating both key and prime customers the same way. As a result, it was trying to sell smaller prime customers a level of service and innovation that they did not value or could not afford. So the cost of sales for prime customers was four to five times higher than for key customers. Now, a single account manager and team focus intensely on all the areas of each key customer's business, working together to find product and service solutions. Such intensive collaboration would have been difficult under the old product-based sales structure, in which multiple Hill-Rom sales reps serviced the different specialty areas within a single key account. In the two years following the sales force redesign, Hill-Rom's sales growth doubled.

Complex sales force structures

When a company sells a wide variety of products to many types of customers over a broad geographic area, it often combines several types of sales force structures. Salespeople can be specialised by customer and territory; product and territory; product and customer; or territory, product and customer. For example, Stanley Black & Decker specialises its sales force by customer (with different sales forces calling on mass-merchandisers like B&Q and Bauhaus, and smaller independent retailers) *and* by territory for each key customer group (territory representatives, territory managers and so on). No single structure is best for all companies and situations. Each company should select a sales force structure that best serves the needs of its customers and fits its overall marketing strategy.

A good sales structure can mean the difference between success and failure. Over time, sales force structures can grow complex, inefficient and unresponsive to customers' needs.

Companies should periodically review their sales force organisations to be certain that they serve the needs of the company and its customers – see the HP Company Case at the end of the chapter for an illustrative example.

Sales force size

Once the company has established its structure, it is ready to consider *sales force size*. Sales forces may range in size from only a few salespeople to tens of thousands. Some sales forces are huge: for example, PepsiCo employs 36,000 salespeople; American Express, 23,400; GE, 16,400; and Xerox, 15,000.[8] Salespeople constitute one of the company's most productive – and most expensive – assets. Therefore, increasing their numbers will increase both sales and costs. Nonetheless, tough economic times in Europe have seen sales force downsizing in some companies.

Customer (or market) sales force structure—A sales force organisation in which salespeople specialise in selling only to certain customers or industries.

Many companies use some form of *workload approach* to establish sales force size. Using this approach, a company first groups accounts into different classes according to size, account status, or other factors related to the amount of effort required to maintain the account. It then determines the number of salespeople needed to call on each class of accounts the desired number of times.

The company might reason as follows. Suppose a company has 1,000 A-level accounts and 2,000 B-level accounts. A-level accounts require 36 calls per year, and B-level accounts require 12 calls per year. In this case, the sales force's *workload* – the number of calls it must make per year – is 60,000 calls [(1,000 × 36) + (2,000 × 12) = 36,000 + 24,000 = 60,000]. Suppose the average salesperson can make 1,000 calls a year. Thus, the company needs 60 salespeople (60,000 ÷ 1,000).[9]

Other sales force strategy and structure issues

Sales management must also determine who will be involved in the selling effort and how various sales and sales support people will work together.

Outside and inside sales forces

Outside sales force (or field sales force)—Salespeople who travel to call on customers in the field.

Inside sales force—Salespeople who conduct business from their offices via telephone, the Internet or visits from prospective buyers.

Inside salespeople conduct business from their offices, via telephone, the Internet, or visits from buyers.

Source: Climax Portable Machine Tools

The company may have an **outside sales force (or field sales force)**, an **inside sales force** or both. Outside salespeople travel to call on customers in the field. Inside salespeople conduct business from their offices via telephone, the Internet, or visits from buyers.

Some inside salespeople provide support for the outside sales force, freeing them to spend more time selling to major accounts and finding new prospects. For example, *technical sales support people* provide technical information and answers to customers' questions. *Sales assistants* provide administrative backup for outside salespeople. They call ahead and confirm appointments, follow up on deliveries and answer customers' questions when outside salespeople cannot be reached. Using such combinations of inside and outside salespeople can help serve important customers better. The inside rep provides daily access and support; the outside rep provides face-to-face collaboration and relationship building.

Other inside salespeople do more than just provide support. *Telemarketers* and *Web sellers* use the phone and Internet to find new leads and qualify prospects or sell and service accounts directly. Telemarketing and Web selling can be very effective, less costly ways to sell to smaller, harder-to-reach customers. Depending on the complexity of the product, a telemarketer can make from 20 to 33 decision-maker contacts a day, compared to the average of four that an outside salesperson can make. And whereas an average B-to-B field sales call can cost £250 or more, a routine industrial telemarketing call costs only about £3–5 and a complex call about £15.[10]

Although the government regulators in many countries have developed 'opt-out' schemes, which have put a dent in telephone sales to consumers, telemarketing remains a vital tool for many B-to-B marketers. For some smaller companies, telephone and Web selling may be the primary sales approaches. However, larger companies also use these tactics, either to sell directly to small and midsize customers or help out with larger ones. Especially in the leaner times following the recession, many companies reduced their in-person customer visits in favour of more telephone, e-mail and Internet selling.

For many types of products and selling situations, phone or Web selling can be as effective as a personal sales call. Climax Portable Machine Tools is an American company with a base in the north of England, as well as a worldwide distributor network.

Climax Portable Machine Tools, which manufactures portable maintenance tools for the metal cutting industry, has proven in its US business that telemarketing can save money and still lavish attention on buyers. Under the old system, Climax sales engineers spent one-third of their time on the road, training distributor salespeople and accompanying them on calls. They could make about four contacts a day. Now, each of five sales engineers on Climax's inside sales team calls

480

about 30 prospects a day, following up on leads generated by ads and e-mails. Because it takes about five calls to close a sale, the sales engineers update a prospect's profile after each contact, noting the degree of commitment, requirements, next call date and personal comments. 'If anyone mentions he's going on a fishing trip, our sales engineer enters that in the sales information system and uses it to personalize the next phone call', says Climax's president, noting that this is one way to build good relations.

Another is that the first direct contact with a prospect includes the sales engineer's business card with his or her picture on it. Climax's customer information system also gives inside reps instant access to customer information entered by the outside sales force and service people. Armed with all the information, inside reps can build surprisingly strong and personal customer relationships. Of course, it takes more than friendliness to sell $15,000 machine tools over the phone (special orders may run $200,000), but the telemarketing approach works well. When Climax customers were asked, 'Do you see the sales engineer often enough?' the response was overwhelmingly positive. Obviously, many people didn't realise that the only contact they had with Climax had been on the phone.[11]

Team selling

As products become more complex, and as customers grow larger and more demanding, a single salesperson simply can't handle all of a large customer's needs. Instead, most companies now use **team selling** to service large, complex accounts. Sales teams can unearth problems, solutions and sales opportunities that no individual salesperson could do. Such teams might include experts from any area or level of the selling firm – sales, marketing, technical and support services, R&D, engineering, operations, finance and others.

In many cases, the move to team selling mirrors similar changes in customers' buying organisations. 'Buyers implementing team-based purchasing decisions have necessitated the equal and opposite creation of team-based selling – a completely new way of doing business for many independent, self-motivated salespeople,' says a sales force analyst. 'Today, we're calling on teams of buying people, and that requires more firepower on our side', agrees one sales vice president. 'One salesperson just can't do it all – can't be an expert in everything we're bringing to the customer. We have strategic account teams, led by customer business managers, who basically are our quarterbacks.'[12]

Some companies, such as IBM, Xerox and P&G, have used teams for a long time. In the chapter-opening story, we learned that P&G sales reps are organised into CBD teams. Each CBD team is assigned to a major P&G retailer customer. The CBD organisation places the focus on serving the complete needs of each major customer. It lets P&G 'grow business by working as a "strategic partner" with our accounts,' not just as a supplier.[13]

Team selling does have some pitfalls. For example, salespeople are by nature competitive and have often been trained and rewarded for outstanding individual performance. Salespeople who are used to having customers all to themselves may have trouble learning to work with and trust others on a team. In addition, selling teams can confuse or overwhelm customers who are used to working with only one salesperson. Finally, difficulties in evaluating individual contributions to the team selling effort can create some sticky compensation issues.

Recruiting and selecting salespeople

At the heart of any successful sales force operation is the recruitment and selection of good salespeople. The performance difference between an average salesperson and a top salesperson can be substantial. In a typical sales force, the top 30 per cent of the salespeople might bring in 60 per cent of the sales. Thus, careful salesperson selection can greatly increase overall sales force performance. Beyond the differences in sales performance, poor selection results in costly turnover. When a salesperson quits, the costs of finding and training a new salesperson – plus the costs of lost sales – can be very high. Also, a sales force with many new people is less productive, and turnover disrupts important customer relationships.

Team selling—Using team of people from sales, marketing, engineering, finance, technical support and even upper management to service large, complex accounts.

What sets great salespeople apart from all the rest? In an effort to profile top sales performers, Gallup Consulting, a division of the well-known Gallup polling organisation in the US interviewed hundreds of thousands of salespeople. Its research suggested that the best salespeople possess four key talents: intrinsic motivation, a disciplined work style, the ability to close a sale and perhaps most important, the ability to build relationships with customers.[14]

Super salespeople are motivated from within; they have an unrelenting drive to excel. Some salespeople are driven by money, a desire for recognition, or the satisfaction of competing and winning. Others are driven by the desire to provide service and build relationships. The best salespeople possess some or each of these motivations. They also have a disciplined work style. They lay out detailed, organised plans and then follow through in a timely way.

But motivation and discipline mean little unless they result in closing more sales and building better customer relationships. Super salespeople build the skills and knowledge they need to get the job done. Perhaps most important, top salespeople are excellent customer problem solvers and relationship builders. They understand their customers' needs. Talk to sales executives and they'll describe top performers in these terms: good listeners, empathetic, patient, caring and responsive. Top performers can put themselves on the buyer's side of the desk and see the world through their customers' eyes. They don't want just to be liked; they want to add value for their customers.

When recruiting, a company should analyse the sales job itself and the characteristics of its most successful salespeople to identify the traits needed by a successful salesperson in their industry. Then it must recruit the right salespeople. The human resources department looks for applicants by getting names from current salespeople, using employment agencies, searching the Web, placing classified ads, and working through school and university placement services. Another source is to attract top salespeople from other companies. Proven salespeople need less training and can be productive immediately.

Recruiting will attract many applicants from which a company must select the best. The selection procedure can vary from a single informal interview to lengthy testing and interviewing. Many companies give formal tests to sales applicants. Tests typically measure sales aptitude, analytical and organisational skills, personality traits and other characteristics. But test scores provide only one piece of the information pie that includes personal characteristics, references, past employment history and interviewer reactions.

Training salespeople

New salespeople may spend anywhere from a few weeks or months to a year or more in training. Then, most companies provide continuing sales training via seminars, sales meetings and Web e-learning throughout the salesperson's career. Across the world, companies spend huge sums annually on training salespeople, and sales training typical captures the largest share of the training budget. For example, US technology companies invest 29 per cent of their training budgets on sales training. Although training can be expensive, it can also yield dramatic returns. For instance, one recent study showed that sales training conducted by ADP, an administrative services firm operating internationally, resulted in an ROI of nearly 338 per cent in only 90 days.[15]

Training programmes have several goals. First, salespeople need to know about customers and how to build relationships with them. So the training programme must teach them about different types of customers and their needs, buying motives and buying habits. It must also teach them how to sell effectively and train them in the basics of the selling process. Salespeople also need to know and identify with the company – its products and its competitors. So an effective training programme teaches them about the company's objectives, organisation, products and the strategies of major competitors.

Today, many companies are adding e-learning to their sales training programmes. Online training may range from simple text-based product training and Internet-based sales exercises that build sales skills, to sophisticated simulations that recreate the dynamics of real-life sales calls. Training online instead of on-site can cut travel and other training costs, and it takes up less of a salesperson's selling time. It also makes on-demand training available to salespeople, letting them train as little or as much as needed, whenever and wherever needed. Most e-learning is Web-based, but many companies now offer on-demand training via smartphones and even iPod-type devices.

Many companies are now using imaginative and sophisticated e-learning techniques to make sales training more efficient – and sometimes even more fun. For example, Bayer HealthCare Pharmaceuticals (an international business with divisions based in the US and Germany) worked with Concentric RX, a healthcare marketing agency in America, to create a role-playing simulation video game to train its sales force on a new drug marketing programme:[16]

> Most people don't usually associate fast-paced rock music and flashy graphics with online sales training tools. But Concentric Rx's innovative role-playing video game – Rep Race: The Battle for Office Supremacy – has all that and a lot more. Rep Race gives Bayer sales reps far more entertainment than the staid old multiple-choice skills tests it replaces. The game was created to help breathe new life into a mature Bayer product – Betaseron, a 17-year-old multiple sclerosis therapy treatment. The aim was to find a fresh, more active way to help Bayer sales reps apply the in-depth information they learned about Betaseron to actual selling and objections-handling situations. Bayer also wanted to increase rep engagement through interactive learning and feedback through real-time results. Bayer reps liked Rep Race from the start. According to Bayer, when the game was first launched, reps played it as many as 30 times. In addition to its educational and motivational value, Rep Race allowed Bayer to measure sales reps' individual and collective performance. In the end, Bayer calculated that the Rep Race simulation helped improve the Betaseron sales team's effectiveness by 20 per cent.

Compensating salespeople

To attract good salespeople, a company must have an appealing compensation plan. Compensation consists of four elements: a fixed amount, a variable amount, expenses and fringe benefits. The fixed amount, usually a salary, gives the salesperson some stable income. The variable amount, which might be commission or bonuses based on sales performance, rewards the salesperson for greater effort and success.

Management must determine what *mix* of these compensation elements makes the most sense for each sales job. Different combinations of fixed and variable compensation give rise to four basic types of compensation plans: straight salary, straight commission, salary plus bonus and salary plus commission. According to one study of sales force compensation, 18 per cent of companies pay straight salary, 19 per cent pay straight commission and 63 per cent pay a combination of salary plus incentives. A study showed that the average salesperson's pay consists of about 67 per cent salary and 33 per cent incentive pay.[17]

A sales force compensation plan can both motivate salespeople and direct their activities. Compensation should direct salespeople toward activities that are consistent with overall sales force and marketing objectives. For example, if the strategy is to acquire new business, grow rapidly and gain market share, the compensation plan might include a larger commission component, coupled with a new-account bonus to encourage high sales performance and new account development. In contrast, if the goal is to maximise current account profitability, the compensation plan might contain a larger base-salary component with additional incentives for current account sales or customer satisfaction.

In fact, more and more companies are moving away from high commission plans that may drive salespeople to make short-term grabs for business. They worry that a salesperson who is pushing too hard to close a deal may ruin the customer relationship. Instead, companies are designing compensation plans that reward salespeople for building customer relationships and growing the long-term value of each customer.

When the times get tough economically, some companies are tempted to cut costs by reducing sales compensation. However, although some cost-cutting measures make sense when business is sluggish, cutting sales force compensation across the board is usually a 'don't-go-there, last-of-the-last-resorts' action, says one sales compensation expert. 'Keep in mind that if you burn the salesperson, you might burn the customer relationship.' If a company must reduce its compensation expenses, says the expert, a better strategy than across-the-board cuts is to 'keep the pay up for top performers and turn the [low performers] loose'.[18]

Supervising and motivating salespeople

New salespeople need more than a territory, compensation and training – they need supervision and motivation. The goal of *supervision* is to help salespeople 'work smart' by doing the right things in the right ways. The goal of *motivation* is to encourage salespeople to 'work hard' and energetically toward sales force goals. If salespeople work smart and work hard, they will realise their full potential – to their own and the company's benefit.

Supervising salespeople

Companies vary in how closely they supervise their salespeople. Many help salespeople identify target customers and establish call objectives. Some may also specify how much time the sales force should spend prospecting for new accounts and set other time management priorities. One tool is the weekly, monthly or annual *call plan* that shows which customers and prospects to call on and which activities to carry out. Another tool is *time-and-duty analysis*. In addition to time spent selling, the salesperson spends time travelling, waiting, taking breaks and doing administrative chores.

Figure 16.2 shows how salespeople spend their time. On average, active selling time accounts for only 10 per cent of total working time! If selling time could be raised from 10 per cent to 30 per cent, this would triple the time spent selling.[19] Companies are always looking for ways to save time – simplifying administrative duties; developing better sales-call and routing plans; supplying more and better customer information; and using phone, e-mail or video conferencing instead of travelling. Consider the changes GE made to increase its sales force's face-to-face selling time.[20]

When Jeff Immelt became GE's new chairman, he was dismayed to find that members of the sales team were spending far more time on deskbound administrative chores than in face-to-face meetings with customers and prospects. 'He said we needed to turn that around,' recalls Venki Rao, an IT leader in global sales and marketing at GE Power Systems, a division focused on energy systems and products. '[We need] to spend four days a week in front of the customer and one day for all the admin stuff'. GE Power's salespeople spent much of their time at their desks because they had to go to many sources for the information needed to sell multimillion-dollar turbines, turbine parts and services to energy companies worldwide. To fix the problem, GE created a new sales portal, a kind of 'one-stop shop' that connects the vast array of GE databases, providing salespeople with everything from sales tracking and customer data to parts pricing and information on planned outages. GE also added external data, such as news feeds. 'Before, you were randomly searching for things', says Bill Snook, a GE sales manager. Now, he says, 'I have the sales portal as my home page, and I use it as the gateway to all the applications that I have'. The sales portal has freed Snook and 2,500 other users around the globe from once time-consuming administrative tasks, greatly increasing their face time with customers.

Figure 16.2 How salespeople spend their time

Source: Proudfoot Consulting. Data used with permission.

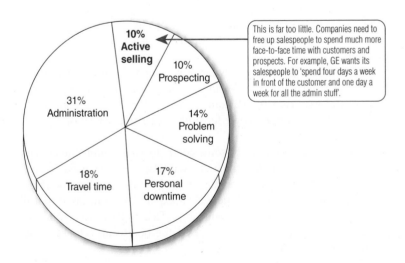

Many firms have adopted *sales force automation systems*: computerised, digitised sales force operations that let salespeople work more effectively anytime, anywhere. Companies now routinely equip their salespeople with technologies such as laptops, smartphones, wireless Web connections, webcams for videoconferencing, and customer-contact and relationship management software. Armed with these technologies, salespeople can more effectively and efficiently profile customers and prospects, analyse and forecast sales, schedule sales calls, make presentations, prepare sales and expense reports and manage account relationships. The result is better time management, improved customer service, lower sales costs and higher sales performance.[21]

Selling and the Internet

Perhaps the fastest-growing sales technology tool is the Internet. The Internet offers explosive potential for conducting sales operations and interacting with and serving customers. Sales organisations are now both enhancing their effectiveness and saving time and money by using a host of Internet approaches to train sales reps, hold sales meetings, service accounts and even conduct live sales meetings with customers. Some call it **Sales 2.0**, the merging of innovative sales practices with Web 2.0 technologies to improve sales force effectiveness and efficiency:[22]

Sales 2.0—The merging of innovative sales practices with Web 2.0 technologies to improve sales force effectiveness and efficiency.

> Web 2.0 enables a way of interacting, collaborating and information sharing. With the Internet as a new business platform, now all stakeholders – prospects, customers, salespeople and marketers – can connect, learn, plan, analyze, engage, collaborate and conduct business together in ways that were not even imaginable a few years ago. Sales 2.0 brings together customer-focused methodologies and productivity-enhancing technologies that transform selling from an art to an interactive science. Sales 2.0 has forever changed the process by which people buy and companies sell. Will all this new sales technology reduce the role of face-to-face selling? The good news is that Sales 2.0 will not make salespeople obsolete. It will make them a lot more productive and effective.

Web-based technologies can produce big organisational benefits for sales forces. They help conserve salespeople's valuable time, save travel expenses and give salespeople a new vehicle for selling and servicing accounts. Over the past decade, the buying patterns of customers have changed. In today's Web 2.0 world, customers often know almost as much about a company's products as their salespeople do. This gives customers more control over the sales process than they had in the days when brochures and pricing were only available from a sales rep. Sales 2.0 recognises and takes advantage of these buying process changes, creating new avenues for connecting with customers in the Internet age.

For example, sales organisations can now generate lists of prospective customers from online databases and networking sites, such as Hoovers and LinkedIn. They create conversations when prospective customers visit their websites through live chats with the sales team. They can use Web conferencing tools such as WebEx or GoToMeeting to talk live with customers about products and services. Other Sales 2.0 tools allow salespeople to monitor Internet interactions between customers about how they would like to buy, how they feel about a vendor and what it would take to make a sale.

Today's sales forces are also ramping up their use of social networking media, from proprietary online customer communities to webinars and even Twitter, Facebook and YouTube applications. A recent survey of business-to-business marketers found that, whereas they have recently cut back on traditional media and event spending, 68 per cent are investing more in social media. Consider Makino, a global manufacturer of metal cutting and machining technology:[23]

> Makino complements its sales force efforts through a wide variety of social media initiatives that inform customers and enhance customer relationships. For example, it hosts an ongoing series of industry-specific 'webinars' that position the company as an industry thought leader. Makino produces about three webinars each month and has archived more than 100 on topics ranging from how to get the most out of your machine tools to how metal-cutting processes are done. Webinar content is tailored to specific industries, such as aerospace or medical, and

is promoted through carefully targeted banner ads and e-mail invitations. The webinars help to build Makino's customer database, generate leads, build customer relationships, and prepare the way for salespeople by serving up relevant information and educating customers online. Makino even uses Twitter, Facebook and YouTube to inform customers and prospects about the latest Makino innovations and events and dramatically demonstrate the company's machines in action. 'We've shifted dramatically into the electronic marketing area', says Makino's marketing manager. 'It speeds up the sales cycle and makes it more efficient – for both the company and the customer. The results have been "outstanding".'

Ultimately, 'Sales 2.0 technologies are delivering instant information that builds relationships and enables sales to be more efficient and cost-effective and more productive', says one sales technology analyst. 'Think of it as . . . doing what the best reps always did but doing it better, faster, and cheaper', says another.[24]

But the technologies also have some drawbacks. For starters, they're not cheap. And such systems can intimidate low-tech salespeople or clients. Even more, there are some things you just can't present or teach via the Web – things that require personal interactions. For these reasons, some high-tech experts recommend that sales executives use Web technologies to supplement training, sales meetings and preliminary client sales presentations but resort to old-fashioned, face-to-face meetings when the time draws near to close the deal.

Motivating salespeople

Beyond directing salespeople, sales managers must also motivate them. Some salespeople will do their best without any special urging from management. To them, selling may be the most fascinating job in the world. But selling can also be frustrating. Salespeople often work alone, and they must sometimes travel away from home. They may face aggressive competing salespeople and difficult customers. Therefore, salespeople often need special encouragement to do their best.

Management can boost sales force morale and performance through its organisational climate, sales quotas and positive incentives. *Organisational climate* describes the feeling that salespeople have about their opportunities, value and rewards for a good performance. Some companies treat salespeople as if they are not very important, so performance suffers accordingly. Other companies treat their salespeople as valued contributors and allow virtually unlimited opportunity for income and promotion. Not surprisingly, these companies enjoy higher sales force performance and less personnel turnover.

Many companies motivate their salespeople by setting **sales quotas**: standards stating the amount they should sell and how sales should be divided among the company's products. Compensation is often related to how well salespeople meet their quotas. Companies also use various *positive incentives* to increase the sales force effort. *Sales meetings* provide social occasions, breaks from the routine, opportunities to meet and talk with 'company brass', and opportunities to air feelings and identify with a larger group. Companies also sponsor *sales contests* to spur the sales force to make a selling effort above and beyond what is normally expected. Other incentives include honours, merchandise and cash awards, trips and profit-sharing plans.

Sales quota—A standard that states the amount a salesperson should sell and how sales should be divided among the company's products.

Evaluating salespeople and sales force performance

We have thus far described how management communicates what salespeople should be doing and how it motivates them to do it. This process requires good feedback. And good feedback means getting regular information about salespeople to evaluate their performance.

Management gets information about its salespeople in several ways. The most important source is, of course, *sales reports*, including weekly or monthly work plans and longer-term territory marketing plans. Salespeople also write up their completed activities on *call reports* and turn in *expense reports* for which they are partly or wholly reimbursed. The company can also monitor the sales and profit performance data in the salesperson's territory. Additional information comes from personal observation, customer surveys and discussions with other salespeople.

Using various sales force reports and other information, sales management evaluates the members of the sales force. It evaluates salespeople on their ability to 'plan their work and work their plan'. Formal evaluation forces management to develop and communicate clear standards for judging performance. It also provides salespeople with constructive feedback and motivates them to perform well.

On a broader level, management should evaluate the performance of the sales force as a whole. Is the sales force accomplishing its customer relationship, sales and profit objectives? Is it working well with other areas of the marketing and company organisation? Are sales force costs in line with outcomes? As with other marketing activities, the company wants to measure its *return on sales investment*.

> **AUTHOR COMMENT**
>
> So far, we've examined how sales management develops and implements overall sales force strategies and programmes. In this section, we'll look at how individual salespeople and sales teams sell to customers and build relationships with them.

THE PERSONAL SELLING PROCESS

We now turn from designing and managing a sales force to the personal selling process. The **selling process** consists of several steps that salespeople must master. These steps focus on the goal of getting new customers and obtaining orders from them. However, most salespeople spend much of their time maintaining existing accounts and building long-term customer *relationships*. We discuss the relationship aspect of the personal selling process in a later section.

Selling process—The steps that salespeople follow when selling, which include prospecting and qualifying, pre-approaching, presenting and demonstrating, handling objections, closing and following up.

Steps in the selling process

As shown in Figure 16.3, the selling process consists of seven steps: prospecting and qualifying, pre-approaching, approaching, presenting and demonstrating, handling objections, closing and following up.

Prospecting and qualifying

The first step in the selling process is **prospecting** – identifying qualified potential customers. Approaching the right potential customers is crucial to the selling success. As one sales expert puts it, 'If the sales force starts chasing anyone who is breathing and seems to have a budget, you risk accumulating a roster of expensive-to-serve, hard-to-satisfy customers who never respond to whatever value proposition you have'. He continues, 'The solution to this isn't rocket science. [You must]

Prospecting—A salesperson or company identifies qualified potential customers.

Figure 16.3 Steps in the selling process

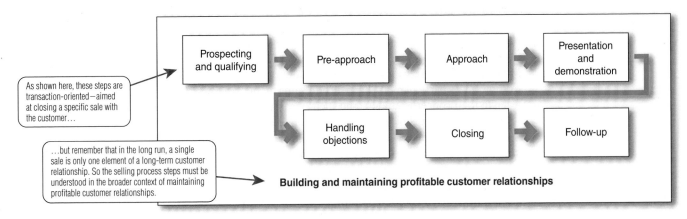

train salespeople to actively scout the right prospects.' Another expert concludes, 'Increasing your prospecting effectiveness is the fastest single way to boost your sales.'[25]

The salesperson must often approach many prospects to get only a few sales. Although the company will often supply some leads, salespeople need skill in finding their own. The best source is referrals. Salespeople can ask current customers for referrals and cultivate other referral sources, such as suppliers, dealers, non-competing salespeople and Web or other social networks. They can also search for prospects in directories or on the Web and track down leads using telephone and e-mail. Or they can drop in unannounced on various offices (a practice known as *cold calling*).

Salespeople also need to know how to *qualify* leads – that is, how to identify the good ones and screen out the poor ones. Prospects can be qualified by looking at their financial ability, volume of business, special needs, location and possibilities for growth.

Pre-approaching

Pre-approaching—A salesperson learns as much as possible about a prospective customer before making a sales call.

Before calling on a prospect, the salesperson should learn as much as possible about an organisation (what it needs, who is involved in the buying) and its buyers (their characteristics and buying styles). This step is known as **pre-approaching**. 'Revving up your sales starts with your preparation,' says one sales consultant. 'A successful sale begins long before you set foot in the prospect's office.' Pre-approaching begins with good research. The salesperson can consult standard industry and online sources, acquaintances and others to learn about the company. Then that salesperson must apply the research to develop a customer strategy. 'Being able to recite the prospect's product line in your sleep isn't enough,' says the consultant. 'You need to translate the data into something useful for your client.'[26]

The salesperson should set *call objectives*, which may be to qualify the prospect, gather information or make an immediate sale. Another task is to determine the best approach, which might be a personal visit, a phone call, a letter or an e-mail. The best timing should be considered carefully because many prospects are busiest at certain times of the year. Finally, the salesperson should give thought to an overall sales strategy for the account.

Approaching

Approaching—A salesperson meets the customer for the first time.

In **approaching** a potential customer, the salesperson should know how to meet and greet the buyer and get the relationship off to a good start. This step involves the salesperson's appearance, opening lines and follow-up remarks. The opening lines should be positive to build goodwill from the outset. This opening might be followed by some key questions to learn more about the customer's needs or by showing a display or sample to attract the buyer's attention and curiosity. As in all stages of the selling process, listening to the customer is crucial.

Presenting and demonstrating

Presenting—A salesperson tells the 'value story' to the buyers, showing how the company's offer solves the customer's problems.

When **presenting**, the salesperson tells the 'value story' to the buyer, showing how the company's offer would solve the customer's problems. The *customer-solution approach* fits better with today's relationship marketing focus than does a hard sell or insincere approach. 'Stop selling and start helping', advises one sales consultant. 'Your goal should be to sell your customers exactly what will benefit them most,' says another.[27] Buyers today want answers, not smiles; results, not razzle-dazzle. Moreover, they don't want just products. More than ever in today's economic climate, buyers want to know how a particular product will add value to their businesses. They want salespeople who will listen to their concerns, understand their needs and respond with the right products and services.

But before salespeople can *present* customer solutions, they must *develop* solutions to present. The solutions approach calls for good listening and problem-solving skills. The qualities that buyers *dislike most* in salespeople include being pushy, late, deceitful, unprepared, disorganised or overly talkative. The qualities they *value most* include good listening, empathy, honesty, dependability, thoroughness and follow-through. Great salespeople know how to sell, but more importantly they know how to listen and build strong customer relationships. Says one professional, 'You have two ears and one mouth. Use them proportionally.' Says another, 'Everything starts with listening. I think the magic of these days is we've got so many more ways to listen.'[28] A classic ad from office products maker Boise Cascade makes the listening point. It shows a Boise salesperson with huge ears drawn on. 'With Boise, you'll notice a difference right away, especially with our sales force,' says the ad. 'At Boise . . . our account representatives have the unique ability to listen to your needs.'

Finally, salespeople must also plan their presentation methods. Good interpersonal communication skills count when it comes to making effective sales presentations. However, today's media-rich and cluttered communications environment presents many new challenges for sales presenters. Today's information-overloaded customers demand richer presentation experiences. And presenters now face multiple distractions during presentations from mobile phones, text messages and mobile Internet devices. Salespeople must deliver their messages in more engaging and compelling ways.

Thus, today's salespeople are employing advanced presentation technologies that allow for full multimedia presentations to only one or a few people. The venerable old flip chart has been replaced with sophisticated presentation software, online presentation technologies, interactive whiteboards and handheld computers and projectors.

Handling objections

Customers almost always have objections during the presentation or when asked to place an order. The problem can be either logical or psychological, and objections are often unspoken. In **handling objections**, the salesperson should use a positive approach, seek out hidden objections, ask the buyer to clarify any objections, take objections as opportunities to provide more information and turn the objections into reasons for buying. Every salesperson needs training in the skill of handling objections.

Handling objections—A salesperson seeks out, clarifies and overcomes any customer objections to buying.

Closing

After handling the prospect's objections, the salesperson now tries to close the sale. Some salespeople do not get around to **closing** or handle it well. They may lack confidence, feel guilty about asking for the order or fail to recognise the right moment to close the sale. Salespeople should know how to recognise closing signals from the buyer, including physical actions, comments and questions. For example, the customer might sit forward and nod approvingly or ask about prices and credit terms.

Closing—A salesperson asks the customer for an order.

Salespeople can use one of several closing techniques. They can ask for an order, review points of agreement, offer to help write up an order, ask whether the buyer wants this model or that one, or note that the buyer will lose out if an order is not placed now. The salesperson may offer the buyer special reasons to close, such as a lower price or an extra quantity at no charge.

Following up

The last step in the selling process – **following up** – is necessary if the salesperson wants to ensure customer satisfaction and repeat business. Right after closing, the salesperson should complete any details on delivery time, purchase terms and other matters. The salesperson then should schedule a follow-up call immediately after the buyer receives the initial order to make sure proper installation, instruction and servicing occur. This visit would reveal any problems, assure the buyer of the salesperson's interest, and reduce any buyer concerns that might have arisen since the sale.

Following up—A salesperson follows up after the sale to ensure customer satisfaction and repeat business.

Personal selling and managing customer relationships

The steps in the selling process as just described are *transaction oriented*; their aim is to help salespeople close a specific sale with a customer. But in most cases, the company is not simply seeking a sale. Rather, it wants to serve the customer over the long haul in a mutually profitable *relationship*. The sales force usually plays an important role in customer relationship building.

Thus, as shown in Figure 16.3, the selling process must be understood in the context of building and maintaining profitable customer relationships.

Today's large customers favour suppliers who can work with them over time to deliver a coordinated set of products and services to many locations. For these customers, the first sale is only the beginning of the relationship. Unfortunately, some companies ignore these relationship realities. They sell their products through separate sales forces, each working independently to close sales. Their technical people may not be willing to lend time to educate a customer. Their engineering, design and manufacturing people may have the attitude that 'it's our job to make good products and the salesperson's to sell them to customers'. Their salespeople focus on pushing products toward customers rather than listening to customers and providing solutions.

Other companies, however, recognise that winning and keeping accounts requires more than making good products and directing the sales force to close lots of sales. If the company wishes only to close sales and capture short-term business, it can do this by simply slashing its prices to meet or beat those of competitors. Instead, most companies want their salespeople to practise *value selling* – demonstrating and delivering superior customer value and capturing a return on that value that is fair for both the customer and the company.

Unfortunately, in the heat of closing sales – especially in a tough economy – salespeople too often take the easy way out by cutting prices rather than selling value. Thus, the challenge of sales management is to transform salespeople from customer advocates for price cuts into company advocates for value. Here's how Rockwell Automation – a global provider of industrial automation, power, control and information solutions and regularly named One of the World's Most Ethical Companies – sells value and relationships rather than price:[29]

Facing pressure . . . to lower its prices, a condiment producer hastily summoned several competing supplier representatives – including Rockwell Automation sales rep Jeff Policicchio – who were given full access to the plant for one day and asked to find ways to dramatically reduce the customer's operating costs. Policicchio quickly learned that a major problem stemmed from lost production and down time due to poorly performing pumps on 32 huge condiment tanks. Policicchio gathered relevant cost and usage data and then used a Rockwell Automation laptop value-assessment tool to construct the best pump solution for the customer.

The next day, Policicchio and the competing reps presented their solutions to plant management. Policicchio's value proposition was as follows: 'With this Rockwell Automation pump solution, through less downtime, reduced administrative costs in procurement, and lower spending on repair parts, your company will save at least $16,268 per pump – on up to 32 pumps – relative to our best competitor's solution'. It turns out the Policicchio was the only rep to demonstrate tangible cost savings for his proposed solution. Everyone else made fuzzy promises about possible benefits or offered to save the customer money by simply shaving their prices.

The plant managers were so impressed with Policicchio's value proposition that – despite its higher initial price – they immediately purchased one Rockwell Automation pump solution for a trial. When the actual savings were even better than predicted, they placed orders for the remaining pumps. Thus, Policicchio's value-selling approach rather than price-cutting approach not only landed the initial sale but also provided the basis for a profitable long-term relationship with the customer.

Value selling requires listening to customers, understanding their needs and carefully coordinating the whole company's efforts to create lasting relationships based on customer value.[30]

AUTHOR COMMENT
Sales promotion has the shortest term of the promotion mix tools. Whereas advertising or personal selling says 'buy', sales promotions say 'buy now'.

SALES PROMOTION

Personal selling and advertising often work closely with another promotion tool, sales promotion. **Sales promotion** consists of short-term incentives to encourage the purchase or sales of a product or service. Whereas advertising offers reasons to buy a product or service, sales promotion offers reasons to buy *now*.

Examples of sales promotions are found everywhere. A freestanding insert in the local paper or posted through the letterbox contains a coupon offering money off new cat treats. An ad in your favourite magazine offers 20 per cent off your next purchase of clothing. The end-of-the-aisle display in the local supermarket tempts impulse buyers with a wall of Cola cans – four 8-packs for €10. An executive buys a new laptop and gets a free memory upgrade. A hardware store receives a 10 per cent discount on selected lawn and garden tools if it agrees to advertise them in local newspapers. Sales promotion includes a wide variety of promotion tools designed to stimulate earlier or stronger market response.

> **Sales promotion**—Short-term incentives to encourage the purchase or sale of a product or a service.

The rapid growth of sales promotion

Sales promotion tools are used by most organisations, including manufacturers, distributors, retailers and not-for-profit institutions. They are targeted toward final buyers (*consumer promotions*), retailers and wholesalers (*trade promotions*), business customers (*business promotions*) and members of the sales force (*sales force promotions*). Today, in the average American consumer packaged-goods company, sales promotion accounts for 74 per cent of all marketing expenditures.[31] In Europe, overall companies probably spend at least as much on sales promotion as they do on higher-profile media advertising.

Several factors have contributed to the rapid growth of sales promotion, particularly in consumer markets. First, inside the company, product managers face greater pressures to increase current sales, and they view promotion as an effective short-term sales tool. Second, externally, the company faces more competition, and competing brands are less differentiated. Increasingly, competitors are using sales promotion to help differentiate their offers. Third, advertising efficiency has declined because of rising costs, media clutter and legal restraints. Finally, consumers have become more deal oriented, particularly as a result of economic downturn and recession across Europe. In the current economy, consumers are demanding lower prices and better deals.[32] Sales promotions can help attract today's more thrift-oriented consumers.

The growing use of sales promotion has resulted in *promotion clutter*, similar to advertising clutter. A given promotion runs the risk of being lost in a sea of other promotions, weakening its ability to trigger an immediate purchase. Manufacturers are now searching for ways to rise above the clutter, such as offering larger value deals, creating more dramatic point-of-purchase displays or delivering promotions through new interactive media – such as the Internet or mobile phones.

In developing a sales promotion programme, a company must first set sales promotion objectives and then select the best tools for accomplishing these objectives.

Sales promotion objectives

Sales promotion objectives vary widely. Sellers may use *consumer promotions* to urge short-term customer buying or enhance customer brand involvement. Objectives for *trade promotions* include getting retailers to carry new items and stock more product, buy ahead, or promote the company's products and give them more shelf space. For the *sales force*, objectives include getting more sales force support for current or new products or getting salespeople to sign up new accounts.

Sales promotions are usually used together with advertising, personal selling, direct marketing or other promotion mix tools. Consumer promotions must usually be advertised and can add excitement and pulling power to ads. Trade and sales force promotions support the firm's personal selling process.

When the economy sours and sales lag, it's tempting to offer deep promotional discounts to spur consumer spending. In general, however, rather than creating short-term sales or temporary brand switching, sales promotions should help to reinforce the product's position and build long-term *customer relationships*. If properly designed, every sales promotion tool has the potential to build both short-term excitement and long-term consumer relationships. Marketers should avoid 'quick fix', price-only promotions in favour of promotions that are designed to build brand equity. Examples include the various loyalty cards that have mushroomed in recent years. Most hotels, supermarkets and airlines offer frequent-guest/buyer/flyer programmes that give rewards to regular customers to keep them coming back. All kinds of companies now offer rewards programmes. Such promotional programmes can build loyalty through added value rather than discounted prices.

For example, Starbucks suffered sales setbacks resulting from the recent economic downturn, coupled with the introduction of cheaper gourmet coffees by a host of fast-food competitors. Starbucks could have lowered its prices or offered promotional discounts. But deep discounts might have damaged the chain's long-term premium positioning. So instead, Starbucks dropped its prices only slightly and ran ads telling customers why its coffee was worth a higher price. With headlines such as 'Beware of a cheaper cup of coffee. It comes with a price', the ads laid out what separates Starbucks from the competition, such as its practices of buying fair-trade beans and providing health care for employees who work more than 20 hours a week. At the same time, to build loyalty, Starbucks promoted its Starbucks Card Rewards programme.[33]

Major sales promotion tools

Many tools can be used to accomplish sales promotion objectives. Descriptions of the main consumer, trade and business promotion tools follow.

Consumer promotions

Consumer promotions—Sales promotion tools used to boost short-term customer buying and involvement or enhance long-term customer relationships.

Consumer promotions include a wide range of tools – from samples, coupons, refunds, premiums and point-of-purchase displays to contests, sweepstakes and event sponsorships.

Samples are offers of a trial amount of a product. Sampling is the most effective – but most expensive – way to introduce a new product or create new excitement for an existing one. Some samples are free; for others, the company will charge a small amount to offset its cost. The sample might be sent by mail, handed out in a store or at a kiosk, attached to another product or featured in an ad or an e-mail. Sometimes, samples are combined into sample packs, which can then be used to promote other products and services. Sampling can be a powerful promotional tool.

Coupons are savings certificates for buyers when they purchase specified products. Many consumers love coupons, although it is a tradition better established in the US than Europe. In Europe, couponing is more frequently associated with the rewards paid out by retailer loyalty cards like Tesco Clubcard and Marks & Spencer's credit card. For example, Nielsen research reports that while 38 per cent of European consumers they surveyed indicate they use coupons to save, there is wide variation within the Continent. At least half of consumers reported coupon use in several western and southern European countries, such as Belgium and Portugal (63 per cent each), Greece (55 per cent), France (53 per cent) and Spain (50 per cent), yet in other markets, particularly in northern and eastern Europe, reported coupon use is much less prevalent. In countries such as Germany and the Netherlands, coupon use is very marginal. Reported coupon use is also less common as a saving strategy in Latin America (25 per cent) and the Middle East/Africa (18 per cent).[34]

Nonetheless, US package-goods companies distributed more than 367 billion coupons last year with an average face value of $1.44 (€1.12). Consumers redeemed more than 3.3 billion of them for total savings of about $3.5 billion (€2.7 billion).[35] While European retailers are frequently reluctant to use coupons, coupons can promote early trial of a new brand or stimulate sales of a mature brand. However, in the US as a result of coupon clutter, redemption rates have been declining in recent years. Thus, most major consumer-goods companies are issuing fewer coupons and targeting them more carefully.

The Groupon website

Marketers are also cultivating new outlets for distributing coupons, such as supermarket shelf dispensers, electronic point-of-sale coupon printers and online and mobile phone coupon programmes. According to a recent study, digital coupons now outpace printed newspaper coupons by 10 to 1. Already, almost one-third of all US coupon users are digital coupon users who get coupons only online or by mobile phone via sites such as Coupons.com and Groupon. This trend is also apparent in Europe:

> The total number of people using coupon sites in Europe in a month grew 162 per cent to 34.9 million visitors in December 2010 when compared to the prior year. The sizeable growth can largely be attributed to the emergence of Groupon, which was not a significant player in Europe in 2009. Groupon, buoyed by its acquisition of its leading competitor in Europe, was able to establish a presence in more than one hundred European cities in the past year and now reaches more than 12 million visitors a month, approximately one-third of the total coupon market.[36]

Cash refunds (or *rebates* or *cashback*) are like coupons except that the price reduction occurs after the purchase rather than at the retail outlet. The customer sends a 'proof of purchase' to the manufacturer, which then refunds part of the purchase price by mail. For example, global company Lowrance is the world leader in the design, manufacture and marketing of high-quality sportfishing sonar and global positioning system mapping instruments. In this specialised market, the company's carefully timed Spring Rebate scheme in Europe offers customers cash back per product purchased, which then qualifies the customer for additional extra cashback on further purchases. The timing is aimed to attract users before the new season starts.

Price packs (also called *money-off deals*) offer consumers savings off the regular price of a product. The producer marks the reduced prices directly on the label or package. Price packs can be single packages sold at a reduced price (such as two for the price of one) or two related products banded together (such as a toothbrush and toothpaste). Price packs are very effective – even more so than coupons – in stimulating short-term sales. One of the commonest forms of this promotion in Europe is 'BOGOF' offers (buy one, get one free).

Premiums are goods offered either free or at low cost as an incentive to buy a product, ranging from toys included with children's products to phone cards and DVDs. A premium may come inside the package (in-pack), outside the package (on-pack) or through the mail. For example, over the years, McDonalds has offered a variety of premiums in its Happy Meals and, in 2012, McDonald's aimed to cash in on the popularity of the launch of blockbuster film *War Horse*, by striking a deal to give away millions of children's books by author Michael Morpurgo as part of a campaign for its Happy Meal product. The McDonald's giveaway coincided with the launch of Steven Spielberg's big-screen adaptation of Morpurgo's 1982 children's book. The giveaway was backed by a major TV campaign, with McDonald's claiming the initiative was about increasing literacy and creativity among children.[37]

Advertising specialities, also called *promotional products*, are useful articles imprinted with an advertiser's name, logo, or message that are given as gifts to consumers. Typical items include T-shirts and other clothing, pens, coffee mugs, calendars, key rings, mouse pads, matches, sports bags, memory sticks, golf balls and caps. US marketers spent more than €14 billion on advertising specialities last year and UK expenditure is estimated as around €1 billion.[38] Such items can be very effective. The 'best of them stick around for months, subtly burning a brand name into a user's brain,' notes a promotional products expert.[39]

Point-of-sales (POS) *promotions* include displays and demonstrations that take place at the point of sale. Think of your last visit to your local supermarket. Chances are good that you were tripping over aisle displays, promotional signs, 'shelf talkers', or demonstrators offering free tastes of featured food products. Unfortunately, many retailers do not like to handle the hundreds of displays, signs and posters they receive from manufacturers each year, and in Europe some refuse to have these materials in their stores at all, because they believe it undermines the image of the store. Manufacturers have responded by offering better POS materials; offering to set them up; and tying them in with television, print or online messages.

Contests, *sweepstakes* and *games* give consumers the chance to win something, such as cash, trips or goods, by luck or through extra effort. A *contest* calls for consumers to submit an entry – a jingle, guess or suggestion, for example – to be judged by a panel that will select the best entries. A *sweepstake* calls for consumers to submit their names for a draw. A *game* presents consumers with something – for example, bingo numbers or missing letters – every time they buy, which may or may not help them win a prize. Such promotions can create considerable brand attention and consumer involvement. Nonetheless, most European countries have strict laws regarding running lotteries (contests where no skill is required of participants) and illegal gaming, so some care is needed in designing consumer contests which remain within the law.

Events like competitions require very careful planning and management. Consider the following example of how things can go wrong:

> In 2011 the UK's largest fresh soup brand – New Covent Garden Soup Co – ran a competition offering the winner £500,000 (€625,000) to buy a small farm of their own. More than 260,000 people took part in the competition. But whoever had the pack with the winning number apparently discarded it without checking, so no-one won the prize, and the competition was closed. As a result, Facebook and consumer websites were inundated with complaints from disgruntled competition participants, and the company got adverse media attention nationally. The company promised to review how future promotions should be run, but there was no escape from the negative impact on loyal consumers.[40]

Event marketing (or event sponsorships)—Creating a brand-marketing event or serving as a sole or participating sponsor of events created by others.

Finally, marketers can promote their brands through **event marketing** (or **event sponsorships**). They can create their own brand-marketing events or serve as sole or participating sponsors of events created by others. The events might include anything from mobile brand tours to festivals, reunions, marathons, concerts or other sponsored gatherings. Event marketing is huge, and it may be the fastest-growing area of promotion, especially in tough economic times.

Event marketing can provide a less costly alternative to expensive TV commercials. When it comes to event marketing, sports are in a league of their own. Marketers spend large sums to associate their brands with sporting events and clubs. For example, Manchester United football club attracts multiple corporate sponsorships, including: AON (insurance and outsourcing) as official sponsor; DHL as official logistics partner; Betfair as official betting partner; Casillero del Diablo as official wine partner; Hublot as official time-keeper; Smirnoff as official responsible drinking partner; Mister Potato as official snack partner; Nike as official kit manufacturer; Audi as official car supplier; Singha as official beer; Thomas Cook as official travel partner; Turkish Airlines as official airline partner; Epson as official office products supplier; STC as official integrated telecommunications partner; plus some 14 more companies partnering in some form.[41] All these companies hope that sponsorship will connect their brands with major audiences throughout the world through the matches the club plays and the strength of its sporting brand – Manchester United has an estimated worldwide following of 333 million people with 92 million in Asia, and a uniquely strong brand in football. Manchester United sponsorship agreements are worth in excess of €162 million, including a recent ground-breaking €50 million deal with logistics firm DHL to sponsor the club's training kit.

In the United States, P&G creates numerous events for its major brands. Consider this example:

> For the past few years, P&G has sponsored a holiday event promotion for its Charmin brand in New York's Times Square, where it can be very difficult to find a public restroom. P&G sets up 20 free, sparkling clean Charmin-themed mini-bathrooms, each with its own sink and a bountiful supply of Charmin. The event is the ultimate in experiential marketing – touching people in places advertising wouldn't dare go. Over the past three holiday seasons, the event has been flushed with success. More than one million people have gratefully used the facilities.[42]

Trade promotions

Manufacturers direct more sales promotion expenditure toward retailers and wholesalers (81 per cent in one US estimate) than to final consumers (19 per cent).[43] **Trade promotions** can persuade resellers to carry a brand, give it shelf space, promote it in advertising and push it to consumers. Shelf space is so scarce these days that manufacturers often have to offer price-offs, allowances, buy-back guarantees or free goods to retailers and wholesalers to get products on the shelf and, once there, to keep them on it.

Manufacturers use several trade promotion tools. Many of the tools used for consumer promotions – such as contests, premiums and displays – can also be used as trade promotions. Or the manufacturer may offer a straight *discount* off the list price on each case purchased during a stated period of time (also called a *price-off*, *off-invoice* or *off-list*). Manufacturers also may offer an *allowance* (usually so much off per case) in return for the retailer's agreement to feature the manufacturer's products in some way. An advertising allowance compensates retailers for advertising the product. A display allowance compensates them for using special displays. Powerful retailers in Europe like Tesco and Carrefour sometimes require suppliers to make large cash payments for access to their stores or special displays in-store.

Manufacturers may offer *free goods*, which are extra cases of merchandise, to resellers who buy a certain quantity or who feature a certain flavour or size. They may offer *push money* – cash or gifts to dealers or their sales forces to 'push' the manufacturer's goods. Manufacturers may give retailers free *speciality advertising items* that carry the company's name, such as pens, pencils, calendars, paperweights, matchbooks, memo pads and other attractive free gifts. However, in the UK and Europe suppliers have to be very careful not to breach strict anti-bribery laws in European countries – both local and EU-wide. Under new laws in the UK, even minor gifts or payments to individuals are liable to be seen as bribes, with severe penalties for the donors.

Business promotions

Companies spend huge amounts each year on promotion to industrial customers. **Business promotions** are used to generate business leads, stimulate purchases, reward customers and motivate salespeople. Business promotions include many of the same tools used for consumer or trade promotions. Here, we focus on two additional major business promotion tools: conventions and trade shows and sales contests.

Many companies and trade associations organise *conferences, exhibitions and trade shows* to promote their products. Firms selling to a particular industry show their products at an industrial

Trade promotions—Sales promotion tools used to persuade resellers to carry a brand, give it shelf space, promote it in advertising and push it to consumers.

Business promotions—Sales promotion tools used to generate business leads, stimulate purchases, reward customers and motivate salespeople.

Trade shows help companies reach many prospects not reached through their sales forces.

Source: Consumer Electronics Association (CEA)

trade show. Sellers receive many benefits, such as opportunities to find new sales leads, contact customers, introduce new products, meet new customers, sell more to present customers and educate customers with publications and audiovisual materials. Trade shows also help companies reach many prospects not reached through their sales forces.

Some trade shows are huge. For example, at the 2012 International Consumer Electronics Show, 3,000 exhibitors attracted some 150,000 professional visitors. Even more impressive, at the 2010 BAUMA mining and construction equipment trade show in Munich, Germany, more than 3,100 exhibitors from 53 countries presented their latest product innovations to more than 415,000 attendees from more than 200 countries. Total exhibition space equalled about 5.9 million square feet.[44]

A *sales contest* is a contest for salespeople or dealers to motivate them to increase their sales performance over a given period. Sales contests motivate and recognise good company performers, who may receive travel, cash prizes or other gifts. Some companies award points for performance, which a receiver can cash in for any of a variety of prizes. Sales contests work best when they are tied to measurable and achievable sales objectives (such as finding new accounts, reviving old accounts or increasing account profitability).

Developing the sales promotion programme

Beyond selecting the types of promotions to use, marketers must make several other decisions in designing the full sales promotion programme. First, they must determine the *size of the incentive*. A certain minimum incentive is necessary if the promotion is to succeed; a larger incentive will produce more sales response. The marketer also must establish *conditions for participation*. Incentives might be offered to everyone or only to select groups.

Marketers must determine how to *promote and distribute the promotion* programme itself. A money-off coupon could be given out in a package, at the store, via the Internet or in an advertisement. Each distribution method involves a different level of reach and cost. Increasingly, marketers are blending several media into a total campaign concept. The *length of the promotion* is also important. If the sales promotion period is too short, many prospects (who may not be buying during that time) will miss it. If the promotion runs too long, the deal will lose some of its 'act now' force.

Evaluation is also very important. Many companies fail to evaluate their sales promotion programmes, and others evaluate them only superficially. Yet marketers should work to measure the returns on their sales promotion investments, just as they should seek to assess the returns on other marketing activities. The most common evaluation method is to compare sales before, during, and after a promotion. Marketers should ask: Did the promotion attract new customers or more purchasing from current customers? Can we hold onto these new customers and purchases? Will the long-term customer relationship and sales gains from the promotion justify its costs?

Clearly, sales promotion plays an important role in the total promotion mix. To use it well, the marketer must define the sales promotion objectives, select the best tools, design the sales promotion programme, implement the programme and evaluate the results. Moreover, sales promotion must be coordinated carefully with other promotion mix elements within the overall IMC programme.

REVIEWING OBJECTIVES AND KEY TERMS

This chapter is the second of three chapters covering the final marketing mix element–promotion. The previous chapter dealt with IMC, advertising and public relations. This one investigated personal selling and sales promotion. Personal selling is the interpersonal arm of the communications mix. Sales promotion consists of short-term incentives to encourage the purchase or sale of a product or service.

OBJECTIVE 1 **Discuss the role of a company's salespeople in creating value for customers and building customer relationships (pp. 474–477).**

Most companies use salespeople, and many companies assign them an important role in the marketing mix. For companies selling business products, the firm's sales force works directly with customers. Often, the sales force is the customer's only direct contact with the company and therefore may be viewed by customers as representing the company itself. In contrast, for consumer-product companies that sell through intermediaries, consumers usually do not meet salespeople or even know about them. The sales force works behind the scenes, dealing with wholesalers and retailers to obtain their support and helping them become more effective in selling the firm's products.

As an element of the promotion mix, the sales force is very effective in achieving certain marketing objectives and carrying out such activities as prospecting, communicating, selling and servicing and information gathering. But with companies becoming more market oriented, a customer-focused sales force also works to produce both customer satisfaction and company profit. The sales force plays a key role in developing and managing profitable customer relationships.

OBJECTIVE 2 **Identify and explain the six major sales force management steps (pp. 477–487).**

High sales force costs necessitate an effective sales management process consisting of six steps: designing sales force strategy and structure, recruiting and selecting, training, compensating, supervising, and evaluating salespeople and sales force performance.

In designing a sales force strategy, sales management must address various issues, including what type of sales force structure will work best (territorial, product, customer or complex structure), how large the sales force should be, who will be involved in the selling effort, and how its various salespeople and sales-support people will work together (inside or outside sales forces and team selling).

To hold down the high costs of hiring the wrong people, salespeople must be recruited and selected carefully. In recruiting salespeople, a company may look to the job duties and the characteristics of its most successful salespeople to suggest the traits it wants in its salespeople. It must then look for applicants through recommendations of current salespeople, employment agencies, classified ads, the Internet and university recruitment/placement centres. In the selection process, the procedure may vary from a single informal interview to lengthy testing and interviewing. After the selection process is complete, training programmes familiarise new salespeople not only with the art of selling but also with the company's history, its products and policies, and the characteristics of its market and competitors.

The sales force compensation system helps to reward, motivate and direct salespeople. In compensating salespeople, companies try to have an appealing plan, usually close to the going rate for the type of sales job and needed skills. In addition to compensation, all salespeople need supervision, and many need continuous encouragement because they must make many decisions and face many frustrations. Periodically, the company must evaluate their performance to help them do a better job. In evaluating salespeople, the company relies on getting regular information gathered through sales reports, personal observations, customers' letters and complaints, customer surveys and conversations with other salespeople.

OBJECTIVE 3 **Discuss the personal selling process, distinguishing between transaction-oriented marketing and relationship marketing (pp. 487–490).**

The art of selling involves a seven-step selling process: prospecting and qualifying, pre-approaching, approaching, presenting and demonstrating, handling objections, closing and following up. These steps help marketers close a specific sale and, as such, are transaction oriented. However, a seller's dealings with customers should be guided by the larger concept of relationship marketing. The company's sales force should help to orchestrate a whole-company effort to develop profitable long-term relationships with key customers based on superior customer value and satisfaction.

OBJECTIVE 4 **Explain how sales promotion campaigns are developed and implemented (pp. 491–496).**

Sales promotion campaigns call for setting sales promotions objectives (in general, sales promotions should be *consumer relationship building*); selecting tools; and developing and implementing the sales promotion programme by using *consumer promotion tools* (coupons, refunds, premium and point-of-sales promotions, and contests, sweepstakes and events), *trade promotion tools* (discounts, allowances, free goods and push money), and *business promotion tools* (conferences, exhibitions, trade shows and sales contests), as well as determining such things as the size of the incentive, the conditions for participation, how to promote and distribute the promotion package, and the length of the promotion. After this process is completed, the company must evaluate its sales promotion results.

NAVIGATING THE KEY TERMS

OBJECTIVE 1
Personal selling (p. 475)
Salesperson (p. 475)

OBJECTIVE 2
Sales force management (p. 477)
Territorial sales force structure (p. 478)
Product sales force structure (p. 478)
Customer (or market) sales force structure (p. 479)
Outside sales force (or field sales force) (p. 480)
Inside sales force (p. 480)
Team selling (p. 481)
Sales 2.0 (p. 485)
Sales quota (p. 486)

OBJECTIVE 3
Selling process (p. 487)
Prospecting (p. 487)

Pre-approaching (p. 488)
Approaching (p. 488)
Presenting (p. 488)
Handling objections (p. 489)
Closing (p. 489)
Following up (p. 489)

OBJECTIVE 4
Sales promotion (p. 491)
Consumer promotions (p. 492)
Event marketing (or event sponsorship), (p. 494)
Trade promotions (p. 495)
Business promotions (p. 495)

DISCUSSING AND APPLYING THE CONCEPTS

Discussing the concepts

1. Discuss the role of personal selling in the promotion mix. In what situations is it more effective than advertising? (AACSB: Communication; Reflective Thinking)

2. Compare and contrast the three sales force structures outlined in the chapter. Which structure is most effective? (AACSB: Communication; Reflective Thinking)

3. What role does an inside sales force play in an organisation? (AACSB: Communication)

4. Define *sales promotion* and discuss its objectives. (AACSB: Communication)

5. Name and describe the types of consumer promotions. (AACSB: Communication; Reflective Thinking)

6. Name and describe the types of trade sales promotions. (AACSB: Communication)

Applying the concepts

1. Although many manufacturers maintain their own sales forces, many use the services of sales agents in the channel of distribution. Discuss the pros and cons of using sales agents compared to a company sales force. Who will best fulfil the channel functions for the manufacturer? (AACSB: Communication; Reflective Thinking)

2. Select a product or service and role-play a sales call – from the approach to the close – with another student. Have one member of the team act as the salesperson with the other member acting as the customer, raising at least three objections. Select another product or service and perform this exercise again with your roles reversed. (AACSB: Communication; Reflective Thinking)

3. Design a sales promotion campaign for your local animal shelter with the goal of increasing pet adoption. Use at least three types of consumer promotions and explain the decisions regarding this campaign. (AACSB: Communication; Reflective Thinking)

Focus on technology

Want to improve your business's operations? Hold a contest and get some of the best and brightest minds in the world working on it! That's what Netflix did – and it wasn't your everyday contest, either. Netflix, the video streaming and DVD rental company, held a three-year, $1 million contest with the goal of improving its movie-recommendation system by 1 per cent. The company wanted to improve its system for predicting what customers might like based on their ratings of previous movies rented or *viewed*. The contest garnered more than 51,000 contestants from almost 200 countries. The contest attracted entries from scientists, researchers and engineers, and the winning team consisted of first time competitors who joined forces to submit the best solution within a few minutes of the contest's deadline. The sequel – Netflix prize 2 – aimed to improve the movie-recommendation system for Netflix customers who do not regularly rate movies on Netflix, but this contest hit a legal roadblock and was discontinued.

1. Using Google, search for 'Netflix Prize' to learn about this contest and the subsequent troubles Netflix experienced with Netflix Prize 2. Write a brief report on what you find and argue for or against cancellation of the second contest. (AACSB: Communication; Use of IT; Reflective Thinking)

2. What other contests or sweepstakes has Netflix sponsored? Discuss the rules of the promotion and winners, if the promotion is complete. (AACSB: Communication; Reflective Thinking)

Focus on ethics

Hank is a sales representative for a CRM software company and makes *several* cold calls each day prospecting for customers. He usually starts his call to a technology professional in a company by introducing himself and asking the person if he or she would take a few moments to participate in a survey on technology needs in companies. After a few questions, however, it becomes obvious that Hank is trying to sell software solutions to the potential customer.

1. Is Hank being ethical? Discuss other sales tactics that might be unethical. (AACSB: Communication; Ethical Reasoning; Reflective Thinking)

2. What traits and behaviours should an ethical salesperson possess? What role does the sales manager play in ethical selling behaviour? (AACSB: Communication; Ethical Reasoning; Reflective Thinking)

Marketing & the economy

Procter & Gamble

Historically, consumer goods companies fare well during hard economic times. Such items are relatively inexpensive to begin with, brand loyalty is strong, and no one wants to give up clean clothes and healthy teeth. But as the sluggish economy has lasted longer than anticipated, the rules are changing. Consumers remain more price sensitive, *even* on small purchases. For P&G, that means that *even* brands such as Tide and Crest are experiencing fallout. To keep *volume* up, P&G has cut prices on existing products *and* introduced cheaper items. Although this may protect sales *volume*, both tactics result in thinner margins and lower profits – as much as 18 per cent lower. And the new cheaper-item strategy may cause customers to trade down, eroding profits *even* more. P&G had plans to raise prices in 2011. But the price cutting cycle may be hard to stop. Not only do consumers get used to lower prices, but retailers also get into the habit of awarding shelf space to manufacturers who provide lower wholesale prices. There are always likely to be manufacturers willing to meet such retailer demands, adding pressure on P&G to continue offering its premium brands at cheaper prices.

1. What can a P&G sales rep do, apart from product and pricing strategies, to boost sales?

2. What should P&G do to boost profits in these and future economic times?

Marketing by the numbers

FireStop Inc, is a manufacturer of drop-in household fireplaces sold primarily in the eastern United States. The company has its own sales force that does more than just sell products and services; it manages relationships with retail customers to enable them to better meet consumers' needs. FireStop's sales reps visit customers serveral times per year – often for hours at a time. Thus, sales managers must ensure that they *have* enough salespeople to adequately deliver value to customers. Refer to Appendix 2 to answer the following questions.

1. Determine the number of salespeople FireStop needs if it has 1,000 retail customer accounts that need to be called on *five* times per year. Each sales call lasts approximately 2.5 hours, and each sales rep has approximately 1,250 hours per year to devote to customers. (AACSB: Communication; Analytical Reasoning)

2. FireStop wants to expand to the Midwest and western United states and intends to hire ten new sales representatives to secure distribution for its products. Each sales rep earns a salary of $50,000 plus commission. Each retailer generates an average $50,000 in revenue for FireStop. If FireStop's contribution margin is 40 per cent, what increase in sales will it need to break even on the increase in fixed costs to hire the new sales reps? How many new retail accounts must the company acquire to break even on this tactic? What average number of accounts must each new rep acquire? (AACSB: Communication; Analytical Reasoning)

REFERENCES

1 Based on information from numerous P&G managers; with information from '500 largest sales forces in America', *Selling Power* (October 2009), pp. 43–60; and www.pg.com/jobs/jobs_us/cac/f_cbd_home.shtml, accessed May 2010.

2 Adapted from information in Kim Wright Wiley, 'For the love of sales', *Selling Power* (October 2008), pp. 70–73.

3 See, for example: Nigel F. Piercy and Nikala Lane, *Strategic Customer Management: Strategizing the Sales Organization* (Oxford: Oxford University Press, 2009).

4 Sources for this illustration: Henry Canaday, 'Sales rep to CEO: Anne Mulcahy and the Xerox revolution', *Selling Power* (November/December 2008), pp. 53–57; '2008 chief executive of the year', *Chief Executive* (September/October 2008), p. 68; Andrea Deckert, 'Mulcahy describes the keys to Xerox turnaround' (2 November 2007), p. 3; 'Women CEOs, Xerox', *Financial Times* (31 December 2008), p. 10; and 'Anne Mulcahy to retire as Xerox CEO', *Wireless News* (27 May 2009).

5 See Philip Kotler, Neil Rackham and Suj Krishnaswamy, 'Ending the war between sales and marketing', *Harvard Business Review* (July–August 2006), pp. 68–78; Christian Homburg, Ove Jensen and Harley Krohmer, 'Configurations of marketing and sales: A taxonomy', *Journal of Marketing* (March 2008), pp. 133–154; and Paul Greenberg, 'The shotgun marriage of sales and marketing', *Customer Relationship Management* (February 2010), pp. 30–36.

6 Piercy and Lane, *Strategic Customer Management*.

7 Example based on Ernest Waaser and others, 'How you slice it: smarter segmentation for your sales force', *Harvard Business Review* (March 2004), pp. 105–111.

8 'Selling Power 500: the largest sales force in America', www.sellingpower.com/content/article.php?a=7823, accessed October 2009.

9 For more on this and other methods for determining sales force size, see Mark W. Johnston and Greg W. Marshall, *Sales Force Management*, 9th edn (Boston, MA: McGraw-Hill Irwin, 2009), pp. 152–156.

10 Susan Greco, 'How to reduce your cost of sales', *Inc.* (5 March 2010), accessed at www.inc.com/guide/reducing-cost-of-sales.html#.

11 See 'Case study: Climax Portable Machine Tools', www.selltis.com/products.aspx?menuid=13, accessed August 2010.

12 Jennifer J. Salopek, 'Bye, bye, used car guy', *T+D* (April 2007), pp. 22–25; William F. Kendy, 'No more lone rangers', *Selling Power* (April 2004), pp. 70–74; Michelle Nichols, 'Pull together–or fall apart', *BusinessWeek* (2 December 2005), accessed at www.businessweek.com/smallbiz/content/may2005/sb20050513_6167.htm; and John Boe, 'Cross-selling takes teamwork', *American Salesman* (March 2009), pp. 14–16.

13 'Customer business development', www.pg.com/jobs/jobs_us/cac/f_cbd_home.shtml, accessed June 2010.

14 For this and more information and discussion, see www.gallup.com/consulting/1477/Sales-Force-Effectiveness.aspx, accessed October 2009; Benson Smith, *Discover Your Strengths: How the World's Greatest Salespeople Develop Winning Careers* (New York: Warner Business Books, 2003); Tom Reilly, 'Planning for success', *Industrial Distribution* (May 2007), p. 25; Dave Kahle, 'The four characteristics of successful salespeople', *Industrial Distribution* (April 2008), p. 54; and 'The 10 skills of super salespeople', www.businesspartnerships.ca/articles/the_10_skills_of_super_salespeople.phtml, accessed May 2010.

15 '2008 corporate learning factbook values US training at $58.5B', *Business Wire* (29 January 2008); and 'ADP case study', Corporate Visions, Inc., www.corporatevisions.com/client_result.html, accessed August 2010.

16 Based on information found in Sara Donnelly, 'Staying in the game', *Pharmaceutical Executive* (May 2008), pp. 158–159; 'Improving sales force effectiveness: Bayer's experiment with new technology', Bayer Healthcare Pharmaceuticals, Inc., 2008, www.icmrindia.org/casestudies/catalogue/Marketing/MKTG200.htm; and Tanya Lewis, 'Concentric', *Medical Marketing and Media* (July 2008), p. 59. For more on e-learning, see 'Logging on for sale school', *CustomRetailer* (November 2009), p. 30; and Sarah Boehle, 'Global sales training's balancing act', *Training* (January 2010), p. 29.

17 See Joseph Kornak, ''07 compensation survey: what's it all worth?' *Sales & Marketing Management* (May 2007), pp. 28–39; and William L. Cron and Thomas E. DeCarlo, *Dalrymple's Sales Management*, 10th edn (New York: John Wiley & Sons, 2009), p. 303.

18 Greco, 'How to reduce your cost of sales'.

19 See Henry Canady, 'How to increase the times reps spend selling', *Selling Power* (March 2005), p. 112; David J. Cichelli, 'Plugging sales "time leaks"', *Sales & Marketing Management* (April 2006), p. 23; and Rebecca Aronauer, 'Time well spent', *Sales & Marketing Management* (January–February 2007), p. 7.

20 See Gary H. Anthes, 'Portal powers GE sales', *Computerworld* (2 June 2003), pp. 31–32. Also see Henry Canaday, 'How to boost sales productivity and save valuable time', *Agency Sales* (November 2007), p. 20; and 'According to IDC, one-third of potential selling time is wasted due to poor sales enhancement', *Business Wire* (13 November 2008).

21 For extensive discussions of sales force automation, see the May 2005 issue of *Industrial Marketing Management*, which is devoted to the subject; Anupam Agarwal, 'Bringing science to sales', *Customer Relationship Management* (March 2008), p. 16; and Robert M. Barker, Stephen F. Gohmann, Jian Guan and David J. Faulds, 'Why is my sales force automation system failing?' *Harvard Business Review* (May/June 2009), p. 233.

22 Adapted from information found in Pelin Wood Thorogood, 'Sales 2.0: how soon will it improve your business?' *Selling Power* (November/December 2008), pp. 58–61; and Gerhard Gschwandtner, 'What is sales 2.0, and why should you care?' *Selling Power* (March/April 2010), p. 9.

23 Adapted from information in Elizabeth A. Sullivan, 'B-to-B marketers: one-to-one marketing', *Marketing News* (15 May 2009), pp. 11–13. Also see 'Social media to lead growth in online B2B marketing', *MIN's B2B* (8 February 2010), accessed at www.minonline.com/b2b/13441.html; and 'Eye on advertising: social media taps its way into B2B marketing plans', *MIN's B2B* (1 February 2010), accessed at www.minonline.com/b2b/13378.html.

24 Quotes from David Thompson, 'Embracing the future: a step by step overview of sales 2.0', *Sales and Marketing Management* (July/August 2008), p. 21; and 'Ahead of the curve: how sales 2.0 will affect your Sales process–for the Better', *Selling Power* (March/April 2010), pp. 14–17.

25 Quotes from Bob Donath, 'Delivering value starts with proper prospecting', *Marketing News* (10 November 1997), p. 5; and Bill Brooks, 'Power-packed prospecting pointers', *Agency Sales* (March 2004), p. 37. Also see Maureen Hrehocik, 'Why prospecting gets no respect', *Sales & Marketing Management* (October 2007), p. 7; and 'Referrals', *Partner's Report* (January 2009), p. 8.

26 Quotes in this paragraph from Lain Ehmann, 'Prepare to win', *Selling Power* (April 2008), pp. 27–29.

27 John Graham, 'Salespeople under siege: the profession redefined', *Agency Sales* (January 2010), pp. 20–25; and Rick Phillips, 'Don't pressure, persuade', *Selling Power* (January/February 2010), p. 22.

28 'For B-to-B, engagement, retention are key', *Marketing News* (15 April 2009), p. 9; and Nancy Peretsman, 'Stop talking and start listening', *Fortune* (9 November 2009), p. 24.

29 Example based on information from James C. Anderson, Nirmalya Kumar and James A. Narus, 'Be a value merchant', *Sales & Marketing Management* (6 May 2008); and 'Business market value merchants', *Marketing Management* (March/April 2008), pp. 31. Also see John A. Quelch and Katherine E. Jocz, 'How to market in a downturn', *Harvard Business Review* (April 2009), pp. 52–62.

30 See, for example: Piercy and Lane, *Strategic Customer Management*.

31 *Shopper-Centric Trade: The Future of Trade Promotion* (Wilton, CT: Cannondale Associates, May 2010), p. 15.

32 Nigel F. Piercy, David W. Cravens and Nikala Lane, 'Marketing out of the recession: recovery is coming, but things will never be the same again', *The Marketing Review*, **10** (1), (2010), pp. 3–23.

33 Based on information and quotes from Richard H. Levey, 'A slip between cup and lip', *Direct* (1 May 2008), http://directmag.com/roi/0508-starbucks-loyalty-programme/index.html; Emily Bryson York, 'Starbucks: don't be seduced by lower prices', *Advertising Age* (30 April 2009), accessed at http://adage.com/print?article_id=136389; and Emily Bryson York, 'Starbucks gets its business brewing again with social media', *Advertising Age* (22 February 2010), p. 34.

34 See www.nielsen.com/us/en/insights/press-room/2011/good-value-trumps-low-prices–even-in-tough-economy.html.

35 See 'Coupon use skyrocketed in 2009', *Promo* (27 January 2010).

36 See www.comscoredatamine.com/2011/02/groupon-contributes-to-significant-growth-for-coupon-sites-in-europe.

37 See www.guardian.co.uk/media/2012/jan/11/mcdonalds-war-horse, accessed 26 February 2012.

38 See www.bpma-sourcing.co.uk, accessed 26 February 2012.

39 See '2010 promotion products fact sheet', www.ppa.org/NR/rdonlyres/35235FB0-A367-4498-B0AF-E88085C3A60B/0/PPAIProProFactSheet.pdf, accessed April 2010.

40 Sean Poulter, 'Win-a-farm competition where everyone is a loser', *Daily Mail* (22 February 2012), p. 7.

41 See www.manutd.com/en/Club/Sponsors.aspx.

42 'The Charmin restrooms return to Times Square this holiday season to help consumers really "Enjoy the Go"', *PR Newswire* (23 November 2009); and http://www.charmin.com/en_US/enjoy-the-go-nyc-restrooms.php, accessed March 2010.

43 *Shopper-Centric Trade: The Future of Trade Promotion*, p. 15.

44 See Erica Ogg, 'CES attendance bounces back', *Circuit Breaker – CNET News* (11 January 2010), accessed at http://news.cnet.com/8301-31021_3-10432369-260.html; and the Bauma website, www.bauma.de, accessed October 2010.

VIDEO CASE

Nestlé Waters MyMarketingLab

Who sells more bottled water than any other company? It isn't Coca-Cola with its Dasani line. it isn't PepsiCo with its Aquafina line. Surprisingly, it's Nestlé. With brands like Arrowhead, Poland Spring, Ice Mountain and Nestlé Pure Life, Nestlé Waters easily outsells its top competitors.

Nestlé Waters hasn't achieved market leadership simply by advertising to consumers. In fact, it does very little advertising. Nestlé Waters understands that for a product like bottled water, success is all about shelf space. The Nestlé Waters video illustrates how the brand's managers developed a sales force strategy that focuses on maximising relationships with major retailers. Nestlé Waters has a unique approach to personal selling that has solidified its presence in the marketplace. After watching the video featuring Nestlé Waters, answer the following questions about the company:

1. How is the sales force at Nestlé Waters structured?
2. Discuss Nestlé Waters' unique approach to personal selling. How does this affect the manner in which the company carries out each step of the selling process?
3. How has Nestlé Waters' unique approach enabled it to maintain customer relationships?

COMPANY CASE

HP: overhauling a vast corporate sales force

Imagine this scenario: You need a new digital camera. You're not sure which one to buy or even what features you need. So you visit your nearest electronics superstore to talk with a salesperson. You walk through the camera section but can't find anyone to help you. When you finally find a salesperson, he yawns and tells you that he's responsible for selling all the products in the store, so he doesn't really know all that much about cameras. Then he reads some information from the box of one of the models that you ask about, as if he is telling something that you can't figure out for yourself. He then suggests that you should talk to someone else. You finally find a camera-savvy salesperson. However, after answering a few questions, she disappears to handle some other task, handing you off to someone new. And the new salesperson seems to contradict what the first salesperson said, even quoting different prices on a couple of models you like.

That imaginary situation may actually have happened to you. If so, then you can understand what many business buyers face when attempting to buy from a large corporate supplier. This was the case with business customers of technology giant Hewlett-Packard before Mark Hurd took over as HP's CEO a few years ago. Prior to Hurd assuming command, HP's revenues and profits had flattened, and its stock price had plummeted. To find out why, Hurd first talked directly with 400 corporate customers. Mostly what he heard were gripes about HP's corporate sales force.

Customers complained that they had to deal with too many salespeople, and HP's confusing management layers made it hard to figure out whom to call. They had trouble tracking down HP sales representatives. And once found, the reps often came across as apathetic, leaving the customer to take the initative. HP reps were responsible for a broad range of complex products, so they sometimes lacked the needed depth of knowledge on any subset of them. Customers grumbled that they received varying price quotes from different sales reps, and it often took weeks for reps to respond to seemingly simple requests. In all, HP's corporate customers were frustrated, not a happy circumstance for a company that gets more than 70 per cent of its revenues from businesses.

But customers weren't the only ones frustrated by HP's unwiedly and unresponsive sales force structure. HP was organised into three main product divisions: the Personal Systems Group (PSG), the Technology Solutions Group (TSG), and the Image and Printing Group (IPG). However, HP's corporate sales force was housed in a fourth division, the Customer Sales Group (CSG). All salespeople reported directly to the CSG and were responsible for selling products from all three product divisions. To make matters worse, the CSG was bloated and underperforming. According to one reporter, 'of the 17,000 people working in HP's corporate sales, only around 10,000 sold directly to customers. The rest were support staff or in management.' HP division executives were frustrated by the CSG structure. They complained that they had little or no direct control over the salespeople who sold their products. And multiple layers of management slowed sales force decision making and customer responsiveness.

Finally, salespeople themselves were frustrated by the structure. They weren't being given the time and support they needed to serve their customers well. Burdened with administrative tasks and bureaucratic red tape, they were spending less than one-third of their time with customers. And they had to work through multiple layers of bureaucracy to get price quotes and sample products for customers. 'The customers focus was lacking,' says an HP sales vice president. 'Trying to navigate HP was difficult. It was unacceptable.'

As Hurd peeled back the layers, it became apparent that HP's organisational problems went deeper than the sales force. The entire company had become so centralised, with so many layers of management, that it was unresponsive and out of touch with customers. Hurd had come to HP with a reputation for cost-cutting and ruthless efficiency. Prior to his new position, he spent 25 years at NCR, where he ultimately headed the company. Although it was a considerably smaller company than HP, Hurd had it running like a well-oiled machine. Nothing bothered him more than the discoveries he made about HP's inefficient structure.

Thus began what one observer called 'one of Hurd's biggest management challenges: overhauling HP's vast corporate sales force.' For starters, Hurd eliminated the CSG division, instead assigning salespeople directly to the three product divisions. He also did away with three layers of management and cut hundreds of unproductive sales workers. This move gave divisional marketing and sales executives direct control over a leaner, more efficient sale process, resulting in speedier sales decisions and quicker market response.

Hurd also took steps to reduce salesperson and customer frustrations. Eliminating the CSG meant that each salesperson was responsible for selling a smaller number of products and was able to devlop expertise in a specific product area. Hurd urged sales managers to cut back on salesperson administrative requirements and improve sales support so that salespeople could spend more quality time with customers. As a result, salespeople now spend more than 40 per cent of their time with customers, up from just 30 per cent before. And HP salespeople are noticing big changes in the sales support they receive:

Salesman Richard Ditucci began noticing some of the changes late last year. At the time, Ditucci was trying to sell computer servers to Staples. As part of the process, Staples had asked him to provide a sample server for the company to evaluate. In the past, such requests typically took two three weeks to fulfil because of HP's bureaucracy. This time, Ditucci got the server he needed within three days. The quick turnaround helped him win the contract, valued at several million dollars.

To ensure that important customers are carefully tended, HP assigned each salesperson three or fewer accounts. The top 2,000 accounts were assigned just one salesperson – 'so they'll always know whom to contact.' Customers are noticing differences in the attention that they get from HP salespeople:

James Farris, a senior technology executive at Staples, says HP has freed up his salesman to drop by Staples at least twice a month instead of about once a month before. The extra face time enabled the HP salesman to create more valuable interactions, such as arranging a workshop recently for Staples to explain HP's technology to the retailer's executives. As a result, Farris says he is planning to send more business HP's way. Similarly, Keith Morrow, chief information officer of convenience-store chain 7-Eleven, says his HP sales representative is now 'here all the time' and has been more knowledgeable in pitching products tailored to his business. As a result, last October, 7-Eleven began deploying in its US stores 10,000 HP pen pads — a mobile device that helps 7-Eleven workers on the sales floor.

A SALESMAN AT HEART

Once the new sales force started to take shape, Hurd began to focus on the role of the client in the sales process. The fact that HP refers to its business buyers as 'partners' says a lot about its philosophy. 'We heavily rely on [our partners]. We look at them as an extension of the HP sales force, 'Hurd said. To strengthen the relationship between HP and its partners, HP and its partners, HP has partners participating in account planning and strategy development, an activity that teams the partners with HP sales reps and its top executive team.

Because Hurd wants the sales force to have strong relationships with its partners, he practises what he preaches. He spends up to 60 per cent of the year on the road with various channel partners and *their* customers. Part of his time is funnelled through HP's Executive Connections programme, roundtable meetings that take place worldwide. But many of Hurd's interactions with HP partners take place outside that programme as well. This demonstration of customer commitment at the highest level has created some fierce customer loyalty toward HP.

'I've probably met Mark Hurd more times in the last three or four years than all the CEOs of our other vendors combined,' said Simon Palmer, president of California-based STA, one of HP's fastest growing solution provider partners. 'There's no other CEO of any company that size that's even close. He's such a down-to-earth guy. He presents the HP story in very simple-to-understand terms.' 'Mark Sarazin, executive vice president of AdvizeX Technologies, an HP partner for 25 years, sings similar praises. 'He spent

two-and-a-half hours with our customers. He talked in terms they could relate with, about his own relationship with HP IT. He knocked the ball out of the park with our 25-plus CIOs who were in the room. One said it was the best event he'd been to in his career.'

In the four years since Hurd took over as CEO, HP's revenues, profits and stock price have increased by 44 per cent, 123 per cent, and 50 per cent, respectively. Still, with HP's markets as volatile as they've been, Hurd has taken HP into new equipment markets as well as gaining a substantial presence in service solutions. Each time the company enters a new market and faces new competitors, the HP sales force is at the centre of the activity. In an effort to capture market share from Dell, Cisco and Lexmark in the server market, HP opened a new sales operation in New Mexico called the SMB Exchange. It combines a call centre, inside sales and channel sales teams. Observers have noted that whereas HP's sales force was known for being more passive in the past, it is now much more aggressive – like Cisco's.

Hurd knows that because of HP's enormous size, it walks a fine line. In fact, he refers to the company' size, as a 'strange friend'. On the one hand, it allows the company to offer a tremendous portfolio of products and services with support from a massive sales force. On the other hand, multiple organisational layers can make it more difficult to create solutions for partners and customers. Hurd is doing everything he can to make HP leaner and meaner so that it can operate with the nimbleness and energy of a much smaller company.

The changes that have taken place at HP have made most everyone more satisfied. And happier salespeople are more productive, resulting in happier customers. That should mean a bright future for HP. Hurd knows that there's still much more work to be done. But with a continued focus on the sales force and the sales process, HP is creating a structure that creates better value for its business customers. Now, if your local electronics superstore could only do the same for you . . . .

Questions for discussion

1. Which of the sales force structures described in the text best describes HP's structure?
2. What are the positive and negative aspects of HP's new sales force structure?
3. Describe some of the differences in the selling process that an HP sales rep might face in selling to a long-term established customer versus a prospective customer.
4. Given that Hurd has an effective sales force, does he really need to meet with HP partners as much as he does?
5. Is it possible for HP to function like a smaller company? Why or why not?

Sources: Quotes and adapted examples from Pui-Wing Tam, 'System Reboot: Hurd's Big Challenge at HP: Overhauling Corporate Sales,' *Wall Street Journal*, 3 April 2006, A1; Christopher Hosford, 'Rebooting Hewlett-Packard,' *Sales & Marketing Management*, july – August 2006, pp. 32–35; Steven Burke, 'HP vs Ciscoe: It's Personal,' *Computer Reseller News*, 1 November, 2009, p. 8; Damon Poeter, 'Never Enough,' *Computer Reseller News*, 1 April 2010, p. 24.

CHAPTER SEVENTEEN

Direct and online marketing: building direct customer relationships

Chapter preview

In the previous three chapters, you learned about communicating customer value through IMC and about four elements of the marketing communications mix: advertising, public relations, personal selling and sales promotion. In this chapter, we examine direct marketing and online marketing, the fastest-growing form of direct marketing. Actually, direct marketing can be viewed as more than just a communications tool. In many ways it constitutes an overall marketing approach – a blend of communication and distribution channels all rolled into one. As you read this chapter, remember that although direct marketing is presented as a separate tool, it must be carefully integrated with the other elements of the promotion mix.

Amazon.com is great example of online marketing. In only about 15 years, Amazon has blossomed from an obscure dot-com upstart into one of the best-known names on the Internet throughout the world. According to one estimate, 52 per cent of people who shop on the Internet start at Amazon. How has it become such an incredibly successful direct and online marketer? It's all about creating direct, personal and satisfying online customer experiences. Few direct marketers do that as well as Amazon.com.

Objective outline

➤ **Objective 1** Define direct marketing and discuss its benefits to customers and companies.
The new direct-marketing model (p. 507)
Growth and benefits of direct marketing (pp. 507–509)
Customer databases and direct marketing (pp. 509–510)

➤ **Objective 2** Identify and discuss the major forms of direct marketing.
Forms of direct marketing (pp. 510–517)

➤ **Objective 3** Explain how companies have responded to the Internet and other powerful new technologies

with online marketing strategies.
Online marketing (pp. 517–521)

➤ **Objective 4** Discuss how companies go about conducting online marketing to profitably deliver more value to customers.
Establishing an online marketing presence (pp. 522–526)

➤ **Objective 5** Overview the public policy and ethical issues presented by direct marketing.
Public policy issues in direct marketing (pp. 527–529)

Amazon

When you think of shopping on the Web, there's a good chance that you will think first of Amazon. The online pioneer first opened its virtual doors in 1995, selling books out of founder Jeff Bezos's garage in suburban Seattle. Amazon still sells books – *lots and lots* of books. But it now sells just about everything else as well, from music, videos, electronics, tools, housewares, apparel, moible phones and groceries to loose diamonds and Maine lobsters. Many analysts view Amazon.com as *the* model for direct marketing in the digital age.

From the start, Amazon has grown explosively. Its annual sales have rocketed from a modest €117 million in 1997 to more than €22 billion today. In the past five years, despite the shaky economy, its sales have more than tripled. Although it took the company eight years to turn its first full-year profit in 2003, Amazon's profits have since surged more than 25-fold. In 2009, sales grew 28 per cent; profits popped nearly 40 per cent. In the 2009 holiday season, at one point, the online store's more than 88 million active customers worldwide were purchasing 110 items per second.

What has made Amazon one of the world's premier direct marketers? To its core, the company is relentlessly customer driven. 'The thing that drives everything is creating genuine value for customers,' says Bezos. The company starts with the customer and works backward. 'Rather than ask what are we good at and what else can we do with that skill,' says Bezos, 'we ask, who are our customers? What do they need? And then [we] learn those skills.'

For example, when Amazon saw an opportunity to serve its book-buying customers better through access to e-books and other e-content, it developed its own product for the first time ever – the innovative Kindle, a wireless reading device for downloading books, blogs, magazines, newspapers and other matter. The Kindle took more than four years and a whole new set of skills to develop. But Amazon's start-with-the-customer thinking paid off handsomely. The Kindle is now the company's number-one selling product, accounting for 2 per cent of total sales; e-books account for another 1.5 per cent of sales. The Kindle Store now offers more than 550,000 e-books, including new releases and bestsellers, at $11.99 or less in the US and €15.99 in the European Kindle Store. Various Kindle apps let customers enjoy e-books on devices ranging from BlackBerrys and Droids to iPhones and iPads.

Perhaps more important than *what* Amazon sells is *how* it sells. The company wants to do much more than just sell books or DVDs or digital cameras. It wants to deliver a special *experience* to every customer. 'The customer experience really matters,' says Bezos. 'We've focused on just having a better store, where it's easier to shop, where you can learn more about the products, where you have a bigger selection, and where you have the lowest prices. You combine all of that stuff together and people say, "Hey, these guys really get it."'

And customers get it, too. Most Amazon regulars feel a surprisingly strong relationship with the company, especially given the almost complete lack of actual human interaction. Amazon obsesses over making each customer's experience uniquely personal. For example, the website greets customers with their very own personalised home pages, and its 'Recommendations for You' feature offers personalised product recommendations. Amazon was first to use 'collaborative filtering' technology, which sifts through each customer's past purchases and the purchasing patterns of customers with similar profiles to come up with personalised site content. 'We want Amazon.com to be the right store for you as an individual,' says Bezos. 'If we have 88 million customers, we should have 88 million stores.'

Visitors to Amazon.com receive a unique blend of benefits: huge selection, good value and convenience. But it's the 'discovery' factor that makes the buying experience really special. Once on the website, you're compelled to stay for a while – looking, learning and discovering. Amazon.com has become a kind of online community in which

In only about 15 years, Amazon has blossomed from an obscure dot.com upstart into one of the best known business on the Internet throughout the world.

Source: Press Association Limited

customers can browse for products, research purchase alternatives, share opinions and reviews with other visitors, and chat online with authors and experts. In this way, Amazon does much more than just sell goods on the Web. It creates direct, personalised customer relationships and satisfying online experiences. Year after year, Amazon comes in number one or number two on the American Customer Satisfaction Index, regardless of industry.

To create even greater selection and discovery for customers, Amazon.com allows competing retailers – from home-based operations to Marks & Spencer – to offer their products on Amazon.com, creating a virtual shopping mall of incredible proportions. It even encourages customers to sell used items on the site. The broader selection attracts more customers, and everyone benefits. 'We are becoming increasingly important in the lives of our customers,' says an Amazon marketing executive.

Based on its powerful growth, many have speculated that Amazon.com will become the Walmart of the Web. In fact, some argue, it already is. As pointed out in Chapter 10, although Walmart's total sales of more than €312 billion dwarf Amazon's €22 billion in sales, Amazon's Internet sales are 12 times greater than Walmart's. So it's Walmart that's chasing Amazon on the Web. Put another way, Walmart wants to become the Amazon of the Web, not the other way around. However, despite its mammoth proportions, to catch Amazon online, Walmart will have to match the superb Amazon customer experience, and that won't be easy.

Whatever the eventual outcome, Amazon has changed the face of online marketing forever. Most importantly, the innovative direct retailer has set a very high bar for the online customer experience. 'The reason I'm so obsessed with . . . the customer experience is that I believe [our success] has been driven exclusively by that experience,' says Bezos. 'We are not great advertisers. So we start with customers, figure out what they want, and figure out how to get it to them.'[1]

AUTHOR COMMENT

Amazon.com excels at creating direct, personalised customer relationships and satisfying online experiences. Many analysts view Amazon as *the* model for direct marketing in the digital age.

Many of the marketing and promotion tools that we have examined in previous chapters were developed in the context of *mass marketing*: targeting broad markets with standardised messages and offers distributed through intermediaries. Today, however, with the trend toward narrower targeting and the surge in digital technology, many companies are adopting *direct marketing*, either as a primary marketing approach, as in Amazon's case, or as a supplement to other approaches. In this section, we explore the exploding world of direct marketing.

Direct marketing consists of connecting directly with carefully targeted consumers, often on a one-to-one, interactive basis. Using detailed databases, companies tailor their marketing offers and communications to the needs of narrowly defined segments or individual buyers.

Beyond brand and relationship building, direct marketers usually seek a direct, immediate and measurable consumer response. For example, as we learned in the opening vignette, Amazon interacts directly with customers on its website to help them discover and buy almost anything and everything on the Internet. Similarly, Dell interacts directly with customers – by telephone; through its website; or even on its Facebook, Twitter or YouTube pages – to build individual customer relationships with the Dell brand, give technical advice and assistance, sell products and services, or service customer accounts.

Direct marketing—
Connecting directly with carefully targeted segments of individul consumers, often on a one-to-one, interactive basis.

AUTHOR COMMENT

For most companies, direct marketing is a supplemental channel or medium. But for many other companies today – such as Amazon, Dell or eBay – direct marketing is a complete way of doing business.

THE NEW DIRECT–MARKETING MODEL

Early direct marketers – catalogue companies, direct mailers and telemarketers – gathered customer names and sold goods mainly by mail and telephone. Today, however, spurred by rapid advances in database technologies and new marketing media – especially the Internet – direct marketing has undergone a dramatic transformation.

In previous chapters, we discussed direct marketing as direct distribution – as marketing channels that contain no intermediaries. We also include direct marketing as one element of the promotion mix – as an approach for communicating directly with consumers. In fact, direct marketing is both of these things and more.

Most companies still use direct marketing as a supplementary channel or medium. Thus, Toyota's Lexus car markets mostly through mass-media advertising and its high-quality dealer network but also supplements these channels with direct marketing. Its direct marketing includes promotional DVDs and other materials mailed directly to prospective buyers and Web pages (for example, www.lexus.com and www.lexus.co.uk) that provide customers with information about various models, competitive comparisons, financing and distributor locations. Similarly, many department stores, such as Debenhams or John Lewis, sell the majority of their merchandise off their store shelves, but they also sell through direct mail and online catalogues.

For many companies today, direct marketing is more than just a supplementary channel or advertising medium; it constitutes a complete model for doing business. Firms employing this new *direct model* use it as the *only* approach. Companies such as Amazon, Dell and eBay have built their entire approach to the marketplace around direct marketing.

AUTHOR COMMENT

Direct marketing – especially online marketing – is growing explosively. It's at the heart of the trend toward building closer, more interactive customer relationships.

GROWTH AND BENEFITS OF DIRECT MARKETING

In many countries, direct marketing has become the fastest-growing form of marketing. For example, in the United States, according to the Direct Marketing Association (DMA), US companies spent €116.5 billion on direct marketing in 2009, 54 per cent of the total dollars spent on advertising. This means that an investment of €1 in direct-marketing advertising expenditures returned, on average, an estimated €11.65 in incremental revenue across all industries. Put another way, these expenditures generated an estimated €0.9 trillion in direct-marketing sales, which is about 8 per cent of total sales in the US economy. The DMA estimates that direct marketing sales will grow by 5.3 per cent annually to 2013, compared with a projected 4.1 per cent annual growth for total US sales.[2]

Similar patterns exist in most European markets, though there are some national differences and the continuing negative impact of the economic downturn on advertising expenditure generally should also be taken into account. But this is a dynamic and fast-changing area of marketing just about everywhere. For example, in emerging markets shops are few and transport is rudimentary, which makes direct selling an attractive option for companies. So, in Mexico direct sales account for a quarter of sales of cosmetics, fragrances and toiletries, while the same figure for Brazil is around one-third of sales.[3]

Also, direct marketing continues to become more Web-oriented, and Internet marketing is claiming a fast-growing share of marketing spending and sales. Global online advertising spending was estimated to be €48 billion in 2011, according to research by market research firm eMarketer. The research also predicted that online ad spending would rise to €75.5 billion by 2014, growing at a 12 per cent compound annual rate. The Internet's share of total global ad spending will also increase from 12 per cent in 2009 to 17 per cent in 2014, according to eMarketer. North America and Western Europe accounted for 72 per cent of the world's advertising spending online in 2009. However, their combined share will drop to 66 per cent by 2014, as Asia-Pacific, Eastern Europe and Latin America experience more rapid growth.[4]

Benefits to buyers

For buyers, direct marketing is convenient, easy and private. Direct marketers never close their doors, and customers don't have to trek to and through stores to find products. From their homes, offices or almost anywhere else, customers can shop on the Web at any time of the day or night. Business buyers can learn about products and services without tying up time with salespeople.

Direct marketing gives buyers ready access to a wealth of products. Direct marketers can offer an almost unlimited selection to customers almost anywhere in the world. Just compare the huge selections offered by many Web merchants to the more meagre assortments of their brick-and-mortar counterparts. For instance, direct retailer Zappos.com stocks more than 2.7 million shoes, handbags, clothing items and accessories from more than 1,300 brands. No physical store could offer handy access to such vast selections.

Direct-marketing channels also give buyers access to a wealth of comparative information about companies, products and competitors. Good catalogues or websites often provide more information in more useful forms than even the most helpful retail salesperson can provide. For example, Amazon.com offers more information than most of us can digest, ranging from top-10 product lists, extensive product descriptions, and expert and user product reviews to recommendations based on customers' previous purchases. Catalogues from retailers often provide a treasure trove of information about the store's products and services. In fact, in some cases, you probably wouldn't think it strange to see a retail salesperson referring to a catalogue in the store for more detailed product information while trying to advise a customer.

Finally, direct marketing is immediate and interactive: buyers can interact with sellers by phone or on the seller's website to create exactly the configuration of information, products or services they desire and then order them on the spot. Moreover, direct marketing gives consumers a greater measure of control. Consumers decide which catalogues they will browse and which websites they will visit.

Benefits to sellers

For sellers, direct marketing is a powerful tool for building customer relationships. Today's direct marketers can target small groups or individual customers. Because of the one-to-one nature of direct marketing, companies can interact with customers by phone or online, learn more about their needs, and personalise products and services to specific customer tastes. In turn, customers can ask questions and volunteer feedback.

Direct marketing also offers sellers a low-cost, efficient, speedy alternative for reaching their markets. Direct marketing has grown rapidly in B-to-B marketing, partly in response to the ever-increasing costs of marketing through the sales force. When personal sales calls cost an average of €300 or more per contact, they should be made only when necessary and to high-potential customers and prospects.[5] Lower-cost-per-contact media – such as B-to-B telemarketing, direct mail and company websites – often prove more cost effective.

Similarly, online direct marketing results in lower costs, improved efficiencies and speedier handling of channel and logistics functions, such as order processing, handling stocks and delivery. Direct marketers such as Amazon or Netflix also avoid the expense of maintaining a store and the related costs of rent, insurance and utilities, passing the savings along to customers.

Direct marketing can also offer greater flexibility. It allows marketers to make ongoing adjustments to prices and programmes or make immediate, timely and personal announcements and offers. For example, in the United States in its signature folksy manner, Southwest Airlines uses techie direct-marketing tools – including a widget (DING!) and a blog (Nuts about Southwest) – to inject itself directly into customers' everyday lives, at their invitation:[6]

> DING! is an application that consumers can download to their computer desktops. Whenever exclusive discount fares are offered, the programme emits the familiar in-flight seatbelt-light bell dinging sound. The deep discounts last only 6 to 12 hours and can be accessed only online by clicking on the application. Also available as an iPhone app, DING! lets Southwest Airlines bypass the reservations system and pass bargain fares directly to interested customers. Eventually, DING! may even allow Southwest Airlines to customise fare offers based on each customer's unique characteristics and travel preferences. In its first two years, the DING! application was downloaded by about two million consumers and generated more than $150 million (€117 million) in ticket sales.

Finally, direct marketing gives sellers access to buyers that they could not reach through other channels. Smaller firms can mail catalogues to customers outside their local markets and post free telephone numbers to handle orders and inquiries. Internet marketing is a truly global medium that allows buyers and sellers to click from one country to another in seconds. A Web user from Paris or Istanbul can access an online Gap catalogue as easily as someone living in San Francisco, which is the retailer's hometown. Even small marketers find that they have ready access to global markets. For example, global e-commerce company FiftyOne provides a technology and services platform that enables many US retailers with international ambitions to transact with consumers in more than 90 countries worldwide. Gap, Macy's and Nordstrom in the US partner with FiftyOne to reach consumers in Europe and other non-US, markets direct.

AUTHOR COMMENT

Direct marketing begins with a good customer database. A company is no better than what it knows about its customers.

CUSTOMER DATABASES AND DIRECT MARKETING

Effective direct marketing begins with a good customer database. A **customer database** is an organised collection of comprehensive data about individual customers or prospects. A good customer database can be a potent relationship-building tool. The database gives companies a 360-degree view of their customers and how they behave. A company is no better than what it knows about its customers.

In consumer marketing, the customer database might contain a customer's geographic data (e.g. address, region), demographic data (e.g. age, income, family members, birthdays), psychographic data (e.g. activities, interests and opinions) and buying behaviour (buying preferences and the recency, frequency and monetary value [RFM] of past purchases). In B-to-B marketing, the customer profile might contain the products and services the customer has bought, past volumes and prices, key contacts, competing suppliers, the status of current contracts, estimated future spending, and competitive strengths and weaknesses in selling and servicing the account.

Some of these databases are huge. For example, leading supermarket Tesco has leaned heavily on the customer portraits delivered by research agency Dunnhumby, to establish an advantage over its rivals. Tesco now has 12 million unique profiles of its 15 million customers. The Internet adds massively to the ability of companies to gather data, build databases and use them:

> Through its iTunes, App Store and iBooks retail platforms, Apple has 200 million customers with Apple ID accounts, linked to credit cards and one-click purchase access. And this is not the kind of data Apple is going to give up easily. It is now battling publishers who sell content through Apple for control of customer information.
>
> Facebook's arsenal of personal information allows it to create highly detailed pictures of individuals and groups of consumers. It can tell who is related to whom, what they like to buy, search for and vote for, and how they react to new products or ideas. Facebook continues to look for ways to make commercial use of its greatest asset, its user data, without seeming too creepy.[7]

Customer database—An organised collection of comprehensive data about individual customers or prospects, including geographic, demographic, psychographic and behavioural data.

509

Companies use their databases in many ways. They use databases to locate good potential customers and generate sales leads. They mine their databases to learn about customers in detail and then fine-tune their market offerings and communications to the special preferences and behaviours of target segments or individuals. In all, a company's database can be an important tool for building stronger long-term customer relationships.

For example, in providing its world-famous outstanding level of customer service, American financial services provider USAA uses its database to find ways to serve the long-term needs of customers, regardless of immediate sales impact, creating an incredibly loyal customer base:

> USAA provides financial services to US military personnel and their families, largely through direct marketing via the telephone and the Internet. It maintains a customer database built from customer purchasing histories and information collected directly through customer surveys, transaction data, and browsing behaviour at its website. USAA uses the database to tailor direct marketing offers to the specific needs of individual customers. For example, for customers looking toward retirement, it sends information on estate planning. If the family has college-age children, USAA sends those children information on how to manage their credit cards. If the family has younger children, it sends booklets on things such as financing a child's education.
>
> One delighted reporter, a USAA customer, recounted how USAA even helped him teach his 16-year-old daughter to drive. Just before her birthday, but before she received her driving licence, USAA mailed a 'package of materials, backed by research, to help me teach my daughter how to drive, help her practice, and help us find ways to agree on what constitutes safe driving later on, when she gets her license.' What's more, marvels the reporter, 'USAA didn't try to sell me a thing. My take-away: that USAA is investing in me for the long term, that it defines profitability not just by what it sells today.'
>
> Through such skillful use of its database, USAA serves each customer uniquely, resulting in high customer loyalty. The $18 billion (€14 billion) company retains 98 per cent of its customers. For the past four years, *Bloomberg BusinessWeek* magazine has ranked USAA among its top two 'Customer Service Champs', highlighting its legendary customer service. And last year, MSN Money ranked USAA number one on its Customer Service Hall of Fame list.[8]

Like many other marketing tools, database marketing requires a special investment. Companies must invest in computer hardware, database software, analytical programmes, communication links and skilled personnel. The database system must be user-friendly and available to various marketing groups, including those in product and brand management, new product development, advertising and promotion, direct mail, telemarketing, Web marketing, field sales, order fulfilment and customer service. However, a well-managed database usually results in sales and customer-relationship gains that more than cover these costs.

AUTHOR COMMENT

Direct marketing is rich in tools, from traditional old favourites such as direct mail, catalogues and telemarketing to the Internet and other new digital approaches.

FORMS OF DIRECT MARKETING

The major forms of direct marketing – as shown in Figure 17.1 – include personal selling, direct-mail marketing, catalogue marketing, telephone marketing, direct-response television (DRTV) marketing, kiosk marketing, new digital direct-marketing technologies and online marketing. We examined personal selling in depth in Chapter 16. Here, we examine the other forms of direct marketing.

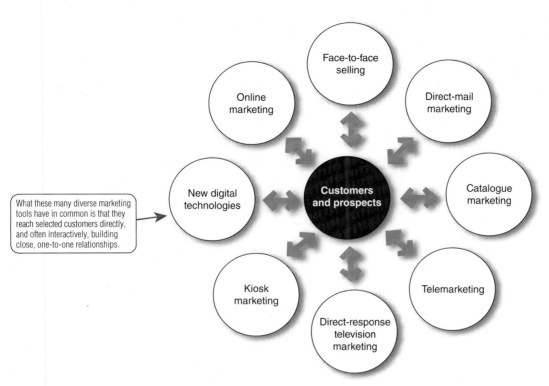

Figure 17.1 Forms of direct marketing

What these many diverse marketing tools have in common is that they reach selected customers directly, and often interactively, building close, one-to-one relationships.

Direct-mail marketing

Direct-mail marketing involves sending an offer, announcement, reminder or other item to a person at a particular physical or virtual address. Using highly selective mailing lists, direct marketers send out millions of mail pieces each year – letters, catalogues, ads, brochures, samples, DVDs and other 'salespeople with wings'. Direct mail is by far the largest direct-marketing medium. For example, the DMA reports that US marketers spent €34.6 billion on direct mail last year (including both catalogue and non-catalogue mail), which accounted for 32 per cent of all direct-marketing spending.[9] In 2011 UK expenditure on direct mail was the fastest growing type of advertising – Germany, the UK and France are the largest direct mail markets in Europe.[10] In Britain, notwithstanding the growth in electronic communications, the number of direct mail items dispatched by organisations jumped to a record level of 1.7 billion items in 2011.[11]

Direct mail is well suited to direct, one-to-one communication. It permits high target-market selectivity, can be personalised, is flexible and allows the easy measurement of results. Although direct mail costs more per thousand people reached than mass media such as television or magazines, the people it reaches are much better prospects. Direct mail has proved successful in promoting all kinds of products, from books, DVDs, insurance, gift items, gourmet foods, clothing and other consumer goods to industrial products of all kinds. Charities also use direct mail heavily to raise funds.

Some analysts predict a decline in the use of traditional forms of direct mail in coming years, as marketers switch to newer digital forms, such as e-mail and mobile marketing. E-mail, mobile and other newer forms of direct mail deliver direct messages at incredible speeds and lower costs compared to the post office's 'snail mail' pace. We will discuss e-mail and mobile marketing in more detail later in the chapter.

However, even though the new digital forms of direct mail are gaining popularity, the traditional form is still by far the most widely used, though this is likely to change – in some countries e-mail has already overtaken print as the main way of delivering marketing offers. Mail marketing offers some distinct advantages over digital forms. It provides something tangible for people to hold and

Direct-mail marketing— Direct marketing by sending an offer, announcement, reminder or other item to a person at a particular physical or virtual address.

keep. E-mail is easily screened or trashed. '[With] spam filters and spam folders to keep our messaging away from consumers' inboxes,' says one direct marketer, 'sometimes you have to lick a few stamps.'[12]

Traditional direct mail can be used effectively in combination with other media, such as company websites. For example, some marketers now send out direct mail featuring personalised URLs (PURLs) – Web addresses such as www.intel.com/JohnSmith – that invite intrigued prospects to individualised websites. Consider this example describing developments at global supply chain solutions company JDA Software:[13]

> For companies that had their heads in the clouds when it came time to upgrade their computers, JDA Software Group decided it was time for some skywriting. It teamed with HP and Intel to send out personalised direct mail pieces that featured a man with his arms spread upward, experiencing an epiphany in the form of fluffy words forming above his head: 'Bruce Schwartz, The Moment Has Arrived'. In reality, the direct mail piece didn't come from out of the blue. Based on customers' upgrade schedules, JDA targeted carefully selected decision makers who were considering buying $500,000 to $1.5 million software suites. These high-value prospects received personalised direct mailings and e-mails with PURLs that led them to individualised Web pages. Once there, prospects learned all about how hardware from HP and Intel would support software from JDA. Customers revealed more information about themselves each time they visited the PURL, which allowed JDA, HP and Intel to work with them throughout the buying process. The result? The $50,000 campaign yielded a 9.2 per cent response rate and $13 million in sales. 'Sending specific [information] to specific people does make a huge difference,' says Intel's strategic relationships manager.

Direct mail, whether traditional or digital, may be resented as 'junk mail' or spam if sent to people who have no interest in it. For this reason, smart marketers are targeting their direct mail carefully so as not to waste their money and recipients' time. They are designing permission-based programmes, sending mail, e-mail and mobile ads only to those who want to receive them and have indicated this.

Catalogue marketing

Catalogue marketing—Direct marketing through print, video or digital catalogues that are mailed to select customers, made available in stores, or presented online.

Advances in technology, along with the move toward personalised, one-to-one marketing, have resulted in exciting changes in **catalogue marketing**. In the US home of catalogue marketing, *Catalog Age* magazine formerly defined a *catalogue* as 'a printed, bound piece of at least eight pages, selling multiple products, and offering a direct ordering mechanism'. But things are changing fast.

With the stampede to the Internet, more and more catalogues are going digital. A variety of Web-only cataloguers have emerged, and most print cataloguers have added Web-based catalogues to their marketing mixes. Web-based catalogues eliminate printing and mailing costs. And whereas space is limited in a print catalogue, online catalogues can offer an almost unlimited amount of merchandise. Finally, online catalogues allow real-time merchandising; products and features can be added or removed as needed, and prices can be adjusted instantly to match demand.

However, despite the advantages of Web-based catalogues, as your overstuffed mailbox may suggest, printed catalogues are still thriving. For example, US direct marketers mailed out more than 17 billion catalogues last year, which amounts to about 56 for every American. In the UK, catalogue shopping was worth around €6.25 billion in 2009, with 70 per cent of home shoppers using a physical print catalogue. Britons shopping from home catalogues are a key driver of online sales – two-thirds of them use a catalogue to inform a purchase or to actually buy.[14]

This may explain why companies aren't ditching their old-fashioned paper catalogues in the new digital era. For one thing, paper catalogues create emotional connections with customers that Web-based sales spaces simply can't. 'Glossy catalog pages still entice buyers in a way that computer images don't,' says an analyst. 'Among retailers who rely mainly on direct sales, 62 per cent say their biggest revenue generator is a paper catalog.'[15]

In addition, printed catalogues are one of the best ways to drive online sales, making them more important than ever in the digital era. According to a recent study, 70 per cent of Web purchases are driven by catalogues. Another study found that consumers who received catalogues from the retailer spent 28 per cent more on that retailer's website than those who didn't get a catalogue. Thus, even dedicated online-only retailers, such as Zappos.com, have started producing catalogues with the hopes of driving online sales.[16]

Telephone marketing

Telephone marketing involves using the telephone to sell directly to consumers and business customers. Last year, telephone marketing accounted for more than 19 per cent of all direct-marketing - driven sales. We're all familiar with telephone marketing directed toward consumers, but B-to-B marketers also use telephone marketing extensively, accounting for more than 55 per cent of all telephone marketing sales.[17] Marketers use *outbound* telephone marketing to sell directly to consumers and businesses. They use *inbound* freephone numbers to receive orders from television and print ads, direct mail or catalogues.

Properly designed and targeted telemarketing provides many benefits, including purchasing convenience and increased product and service information. However, the explosion in unsolicited outbound telephone marketing over the years has annoyed many consumers, who object to the almost daily 'junk phone calls'. For this reason, an increasing number of countries have laws and voluntary agreements allowing people to opt out of receiving commercial messages over the phone if they do not want to receive them. Automated redial systems for calling back are generally not allowed either in most European states. The penalties for companies breaching these legal and regulatory restrictions vary by country.

Do-not-call rules have hurt the telemarketing industry. But two major forms of telemarketing – inbound consumer telemarketing and outbound B-to-B telemarketing – remain strong and growing. Telemarketing also remains a major fund-raising tool for non-profit and political groups. In fact, do-not-call regulations appear to be helping most direct marketers more than it's hurting them. Rather than making unwanted calls, many of these marketers are developing 'opt-in' calling systems, in which they provide useful information and offers to customers who have invited the company to contact them by phone or e-mail. The opt-in model provides better returns for marketers than the formerly invasive one.

Meanwhile, marketers who violate do-not-call regulations have themselves increasingly become the targets of crusading consumer activist groups, who return the favour by flooding the violating company's phone system and website with return calls and messages.[18]

Direct-response television marketing

Direct-response television (DRTV) marketing takes one of two major forms. The first is *DRTV advertising*. Direct marketers air television spots, often 60 or 120 seconds in length, which persuasively describe a product and give customers a phone number or a website for ordering. In some countries, television viewers also often encounter full 30-minute or longer advertising programmes, called *infomercials*, for a single product. The widest use of infomercials is in the United States. In other countries, such as the UK, there are stringent compliance procedures, which make it more difficult to use this approach.

The US experience is that successful DRTV campaigns can result in big sales. For example, Bowflex (home gyms and training equipment) has grossed more than €1 billion in infomercial sales. And little-known infomercial maker Guthy-Renker has helped propel Proactiv Solution acne treatment into a power brand that pulls in €647 million in sales annually to five million active customers (compare that to about €117 million in annual drugstore sales of acne products in the United States).[19]

DRTV ads are often associated with somewhat loud or questionable pitches for cleaners, stain removers, kitchen gadgets and nifty ways to stay in shape without working very hard at it. In recent years, however, a number of large companies – from P&G, Disney, Revlon, Apple and Kodak to Coca-Cola, Anheuser-Busch and even the US armed forces – have begun using infomercials to sell their wares, refer customers to retailers, recruit members or attract buyers to their websites.

Telephone marketing—Using the telephone to sell directly to customers.

Direct-response television (DRTV) marketing—Direct marketing via television, including direct-response television advertising (or infomercials) and home shopping channels.

Home-shopping channels, another form of DRTV marketing, are television programmes or entire channels dedicated to selling goods and services. Some home-shopping channels, such as the Quality Value Channel (QVC), Home Shopping Network (HSN) and ShopNBC, broadcast 24 hours a day in the US. In addition to local providers like HSE24 in Germany, QVC brings home shopping services to European markets like the UK, Italy and Germany. Programme hosts chat with viewers by phone and offer products ranging from jewellery, lamps, collectible dolls and clothing to power tools and consumer electronics. Viewers call a phone number or go online to order goods. With widespread distribution on cable and satellite television, the top three shopping networks combined now reach 248 million homes worldwide.

Despite their lowbrow images, home-shopping channels have evolved into highly sophisticated, very successful marketing operations. For example, HSN has upgraded both its products and its pitches, and its TV operations now work hand in hand with sophisticated Web marketing to build close customer relationships.

> HSN now has hosts not so pushy and goods not so schlocky. It has replaced the cheesy baubles and generic electronics once featured with mainstream brands like Sephora cosmetics and 7 for All Mankind jeans. Celebrities and entrepreneurs, including Wolfgang Puck, Tori Spelling and Joy Mangano, inventor of HSN's curiously popular Huggable Hangers, often get as much airtime as HSN's TV and Web hosts. They chitchat with shoppers who call in to rave about products more often than they push merchandise. HSN wants to be its female audience's 'best girlfriend', says HSN's CEO and continues: 'It's not just a transactional relationship. It becomes an emotional relationship.'[20]

In the UK, a visit to Boots the Chemists provides kiosk access to photo printing technology.

Source: Courtesy of Boots

Kiosk marketing

As consumers become more and more comfortable with digital and touch-screen technologies, many companies are placing information and ordering machines – called *kiosks* (similar to good old-fashioned vending machines but so much more) – in shops, airports, hotels, college and university campuses, and other locations. Kiosks are everywhere these days, from self-service hotel and airline check-in devices to in-store ordering devices that let you order merchandise not carried in the store. 'Flashy and futuristic, souped-up machines are popping up everywhere,' says one analyst. 'They have touch screens instead of buttons, facades that glow and pulse . . . [they] bridge the gap between old-fashioned stores and online shopping.'[21]

In-store Kodak, Fuji and HP kiosks let customers transfer pictures from memory sticks, mobile phones and other digital storage devices, edit them and make high-quality colour prints. In the UK, a visit to Boots the Chemists on most high streets provides access to this photo printing technology. Kiosks in Hilton hotel lobbies let guests view their reservations, get room keys, view pre-arrival messages, check in and out, and even change seat assignments and print boarding passes for flights on a selection of airlines. At budget airline JetBlue's Terminal Five at New York's John F. Kennedy airport, more than 200 screens throughout the terminal allow travellers to order food and drinks to be delivered to their respective gate. And in the US a company called Redbox operates more than 24,000 DVD rental kiosks in McDonald's, Walmart and other retail outlets. Customers make their selections on a touch screen, then swipe a credit or debit card to rent DVDs. Customers can even pre-reserve DVDs online to ensure that their trip to the kiosk will not be a wasted one. Thanks to an ailing economy, even as DVD sales slid last year, wallet-friendly Redbox's sales doubled.[22]

New digital direct-marketing technologies

Today, thanks to a wealth of new digital technologies, direct marketers can reach and interact with consumers just about anywhere, at anytime, about almost anything. Here, we look into several exciting new digital direct-marketing technologies: mobile phone marketing, podcasts and vodcasts, and interactive TV (iTV).

Mobile phone marketing

The rapid diffusion of smartphones (e.g. Blackberry, iPhone) and pad devices (e.g. iPad) provides a growing method of gaining direct access to targeted individuals. It is estimated that there are 6 billion mobile phone and device users in the world (around 87 per cent of world population), with growth led mainly by India and China, which together account for 30 per cent of world mobile subscriptions. Mobile subscribers in each country are rapidly approaching 1 billion, dwarfing the number of subscribers in third place US. Interestingly, South Korea and Japan are the leading countries for mobile broadband penetration, with the UK and US ranked 21st and 24th in the world, respectively, for mobile broadband penetration.[23]

Access to mobile users emphasises texting and instant messaging as well as e-mail. There are now 1.2 billion mobile Web users worldwide, based on the latest statistics for active mobile broadband subscriptions worldwide, and Asia is the top region. South Korea and Japan have mobile broadband penetration of 91 and 88 per cent respectively. Mobile technology is quickly developing payment and banking systems, as well as several ticketing and couponing approaches. It is likely that expanding ownership of mobile devices will encourage further developments.

For example, placecasting is a growing way of making direct contact with consumers through their mobile phones:

> Starbucks and L'Oréal are among leading brands developing placecasting to position their marketing and product messages direct with European consumers. Placecasting involves consumers receiving offers and discounts over their mobile phones by text message and uses a 'geofencing' system that directs text messages to consumers' mobile phones, when they are in the proximity of stores.
>
> The system uses technology developed by Placecast, a private US company, which has used brand-specific geofencing susyems in the US for North Face, the outdoor clothing brand, and American Eagle, the youth clothing brand. Several major retailers in the United States, including Best Buy, Macy's and Target, are trialling Shopkick, a system that uses a non-audible audio signal to send promotions to selected participating customers' mobile phones when they enter the store.
>
> Also in the US, supermarkets like Kroger and discounter Target, have begun issuing 'digital coupons' on the Internet that can be downloaded to mobile phones, and scanned against purchases at the store checkout. Quick Response codes can be scanned by a smartphone camera to link the device to a retailer's mobile website. Youth-oriented cosmetics retailer, Sephora, uses this to link customers' phones to its Tarina Tarantino website and also has a mobile phone link for customer-generated product reviews, which can be uploaded to Facebook.[24]

In another interesting application, for example, Fresh Encounter, a Findlay, Ohio, grocery store, uses text messaging to help customers plan their meals:[25]

> Like many food retailers, Fresh Encounter tries to help shoppers resolve their daily dilemma: What to have for dinner? But this 32-store chain has come up with a unique strategy: texting suggestions to the mobile phones of shoppers who have opted into its Text-N-Save mobile advertising program. Last month, for example, Fresh Encounter sent text messages at 2 pm on a Thursday and Friday offering a deal on a whole rotisserie chickens to shoppers who came in after 5 pm on those days. 'We asked them, "What's for dinner?" and if they don't know, then how about this for $3.99?,' says Fresh Encounter executive Eric Anderson.
>
> Shoppers in the programme receive new text offers each Sunday, ranging from free items (such as milk and soft drinks) to 5 per cent off a total purchase of $50 or more. The offers can be customized by store. To cash in, shoppers present their mobile phone to the cashier, showing a PLU number in the text message. The redemption rates are 'unbelievable', Anderson says – 20 per cent or more. Takers inevitably buy complementary items as well. When Fresh Encounter sends out a more urgent same-day offer, as in the chicken promotion, redemptions can exceed 30 per cent.

Gartner predicts that mobile advertising revenue will be €2.6 billion in 2011, and this will increase to €16.1 billion in 2015, more than doubling each year. In 2011, this ad expenditure was divided as follows: North America (€546 million), Western Europe (€444.6 million), Asia Pacific/Japan (€1.271 million) and the rest of the world (€312 million). Asia is expected to continue to dominate global mobile advertising spending, but to a lessening degree from 49 per cent of mobile ad revenue in 2011 to 34 per cent in 2015.[26] In the US, Google is the main recipient of mobile advertising revenues, estimated at €780 million in 2011.[27] Leading US retailers including Walmart, Sears and Gap, as well as companies like John Lewis in the UK, have launched mobile versions of their websites, together with shopping and browsing applications for iPhones and Blackberrys. Other retailers, such as JC Penney and Sephora, are participating in Facebook's initiative to allow users to populate their Facebook pages with product, information, images and reviews, accessed through their mobile devices, even when in the store.[28]

As with other forms of direct marketing, however, companies must use mobile marketing responsibly or risk angering already ad-weary consumers. 'If you were interrupted every two minutes by advertising, not many people want that,' says a mobile marketing expert. 'The industry needs to work out smart and clever ways to engage people on mobiles.' The key is to provide genuinely useful information and offers that will make consumers want to opt in or call in. One study found that 42 per cent of mobile phone users are open to mobile advertising if it's relevant.[29]

Podcasts and vodcasts

Podcasting and vodcasting are on-the-go, on-demand technologies. The name *podcast* derives from Apple's now-everywhere iPod. With podcasting, consumers can download audio files (podcasts) or video files (vodcasts) via the Internet to a handheld device and then listen to or view them whenever and wherever they wish. These days, you can download podcasts or vodcasts on an exploding array of topics, everything from your favourite news programme, a recent sitcom episode, or current sports features to the latest music video or commercial for an interesting product.

Disney offers prodcasts on a mix of topics around the theme of 'Inside the Magic'.

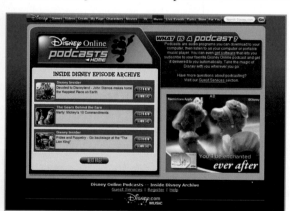

In America, an estimated 25 per cent of the US population has listened to or viewed at least one podcast. A recent study predicts that the US podcast audience will reach 38 million by 2013, up from six million in 2005.[30] The podcast audience outside the US is underlined by the fact that some podcasts of programming from the BBC have been downloaded more than a billion times, and the UK podcast audience is growing at 30 per cent a year.[31] As a result, this medium is drawing much attention from marketers. Many are now integrating podcasts and vodcasts into their direct-marketing programmes in the form of ad-supported podcasts, downloadable ads and informational features, and other promotions.

For example, Disney offers weekly podcasts on a mix of topics, including behind-the-scenes tours, interviews, upcoming events and news about new attractions, around the theme of 'Inside the Magic', available throughout the world. Nestlé's Purina petcare business publishes a multimedia library of 'petcasts' on cat and dog training and behavioural issues. And HP publishes vodcasts that highlight new business technologies as wells as pertinent information for investors.[32]

Interactive TV (iTV)

Interactive TV lets viewers interact with television programming and advertising using their remote controls. In the past, iTV has been slow to catch on. However, the technology now appears poised to take off as a direct-marketing medium. Research shows that the level of viewer engagement with iTV is much higher than with 30-second spots. A recent poll indicated that 66 per cent of viewers would be 'very interested' in interacting with commercials that piqued their interest. In the US broadcasting systems such as DIRECTV, EchoStar and Time Warner are now offering iTV capabilities.[33] In the UK, there are three different digital transmission platforms that carry interactive television. Digital satellite is provided by BSkyB, digital cable from Virgin Media, and there are now the 60 or so free-to-air digital terrestrial channels provided by Freeview – a consortium consisting of the BBC, Crown Castle International and BSkyB. Use of iTV is poised to expand rapidly in Europe. In particular, it is likely that increased access to digital television will lead to more purchases being made through interactive systems. TV shopping has not really taken off in the UK to date, although several newer channels have been launched and share Britain's digital screens with QVC and Ideal World. With the UK switching to digital TV, growth is likely in this area. Supermarket chain Asda, for example, has already experimented with taking customers' orders via interactive TV.[34]

Interactive TV gives marketers an opportunity to reach targeted audiences in an interactive, more involving way. For example, QVC Active is an interactive television service made accessible using the red button on QVC UK's cable, Sky and digital terrestrial services.

The most advanced applications so far are in the United States. For example, New York area cable provider Cablevision offers an iTV service by which advertisers can run interactive 30-second spots.[35]

> During the ads, a bar at the bottom of the screen lets viewers use their remotes to choose additional content and offers, such as on-demand free product samples, brand channels or video showcases. For example, a Gillette ad offered to send free samples of their body wash product, Benjamin Moore offered coupons for paint colour samples, and Century 21 offered $10 gift cards. Advertisers such as Mattel Barbie and the US Navy invited viewers to select their branded Cablevision channels for optional information and entertainment. So far, response rates for the interactive content have been impressive. For example, in an early test in 2009, the Disney Travel Channel allowed subscribers to browse information about Disney theme parks and then request a call from an agent. The booking rate for people requesting a call was 25 per cent. More broadly, iTV ads slated to run for two weeks apiece had to be shortened, on average, by a week because marketers ran out of materials. For instance, Gillette pulled its on-demand samples offer a week early after maxing out the promotion at 30,000 samples.

Mobile phone marketing, podcasts and vodcasts, and iTV offer exciting direct-marketing opportunities. But marketers must be careful to use these new direct-marketing approaches wisely. As with other direct-marketing forms, marketers who use them risk backlash from consumers who may resent such marketing as an invasion of their privacy. Marketers must target their direct-marketing offers carefully, bringing real value to customers rather than making unwanted intrusions into their lives.

AUTHOR COMMENT

Online direct marketing is growing at a blistering pace. By one estimate, the Internet now influences a staggering 50 per cent of total retail sales.

ONLINE MARKETING

As noted earlier, **online marketing** is the fastest-growing form of direct marketing. Widespread use of the Internet is having a dramatic impact on both buyers and the marketers who serve them. In this section, we examine how marketing strategy and practice are changing to take advantage of today's Internet technologies.

Online marketing—Efforts to market products and services and build customer relationships over the Internet.

Marketing and the Internet

Much of the world's business today is carried out over digital networks that connect people and companies. The **Internet**, a vast public web of computer networks, connects users of all types all around the world to each other and an amazingly large information repository. The Internet has fundamentally changed customers' notions of convenience, speed, price, product information and service. As a result, it has given marketers a whole new way to create value for customers and build relationships with them.

Internet usage and impact continues to grow steadily. Worldwide, more than 1.8 billion people now have Internet access. In Europe, around 58 per cent of the population are Internet users.

Internet—A vast public web of computer networks that connects users of all types around the world to each other and an amazingly large information repository.

In some European countries Internet use is much higher: UK (82 per cent), Germany (80 per cent), France (70 per cent), the Netherlands (88 per cent), rising to as high as 94 per cent in Norway. Use rates are much lower in the newer European states, which were formerly Eastern Europe.[36] Last year, 74 per cent of the US population had access to the Internet. The average US Internet user spends some 60 hours a month surfing the Web and for the first time in the United States residents are devoting as much time to online activities as they are watching TV.[37]

According to an IBM survey of consumer digital media and entertainment habits, audiences have more control and are increasingly wised up about filtering marketing messages, with serious repercussions for marketers, ad agencies, broadcasters and publishers. The IBM Institute for Business Value survey of more than 2,400 households in the United States, the United Kingdom, Germany, Japan and Australia covered global usage and adoption of new multimedia devices and media and entertainment consumption on PCs, mobile phones, portable media players and more. According to IBM, the global findings overwhelmingly suggest personal Internet time rivals TV time: among consumer respondents, 19 per cent reported spending six hours or more per day on personal Internet usage, versus 9 per cent of respondents who reported the same levels of TV viewing; 66 per cent reported viewing 1–4 hours of TV per day, versus 60 per cent who reported the same levels of personal Internet usage.[38]

All kinds of companies now market online. **Click-only companies** operate on the Internet only. They include a wide array of firms, from *e-tailers* such as Amazon.com and Expedia.com that sell products and services directly to final buyers via the Internet to *search engines and portals* (such as Yahoo!, Google and MSN), *transaction sites* (e.g. eBay and Craigslist) and *content sites* (e.g. the *Financial Times* on the Web, bbc.co.uk and *Encyclopædia Britannica*). Many click-only dot-coms are now prospering in today's online marketplace.

The success of the dot-coms has caused existing *brick-and-mortar* manufacturers and retailers to re-examine how they serve their markets. Now, almost all of these traditional companies have created their own online sales and communications channels, becoming **click-and-mortar companies**. It's hard to find a company today that doesn't have a substantial Web presence.

In fact, many click-and-mortar companies are now having more online success than their click-only competitors. A recent ranking of the world's ten largest online retail sites contained only one click-only retailer (Amazon.com, which was ranked number one). All the others were multichannel retailers.[39] For example, number two on the list is Staples, a €18.7 billion office supply retailer. Staples operates more than 2,240 superstores worldwide. But you might be surprised to learn that more than half of Staples' North American sales and profits come from its online and direct-marketing operations. In fact, whereas Staples' brick-and-mortar store sales in North America have been flat or declining over the past two years, online and direct sales have soared 46 per cent.[40]

> Selling on the Web lets Staples build deeper, more personalised relationships with customers large and small. A large customer, such as GE or P&G, can create lists of approved office products at discount prices and then let company departments or even individuals do their own online purchasing. This reduces ordering costs, cuts through the red tape and speeds up the ordering process for customers. At the same time, it encourages companies to use Staples as a sole source for office supplies. Even the smallest companies find 24-hour-a-day online ordering easier and more efficient. In addition, Staple's Web operations complement store sales. The Staples.com site builds store traffic by helping customers find a local store and check stock and prices. In return, the local store promotes the website through in-store kiosks. If customers don't find what they need on the shelves, they can quickly order it via the kiosk. Thus, Staples offers a full range of contact points and delivery modes – online, catalogues, phone or fax, and in the store. No click-only or brick-only seller can match that kind of the call, click or visit convenience and support.

Online marketing domains

The four major online marketing domains are shown in Figure 17.2. They include B-to-C, B-to-B, consumer-to-consumer (C-to-C) and consumer-to-business (C-to-B).

Click-only companies—The so-called dot-coms, which operate online only and have no brick-and-mortar market presence.

Click-and-mortar companies—Traditional brick-and-mortar companies that have added online marketing to their operations.

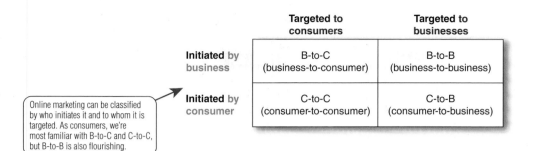

Online marketing can be classified by who initiates it and to whom it is targeted. As consumers, we're most familiar with B-to-C and C-to-C, but B-to-B is also flourishing.

Figure 17.2 Online marketing domains

Business-to-consumer

The popular press has paid the most attention to **business-to-consumer (B-to-C) online marketing** – businesses selling goods and services online to final consumers. Today's consumers can buy almost anything online – from clothing, kitchen gadgets and airline tickets to computers and cars. Even following the economic downturn and recession, online consumer buying continues to grow at a healthy rate. Online sales in Western Europe grew more than 13 per cent to €92 billion in 2011, after growing 18 per cent to €81 billion in 2010. According to Forrester, online sales will increase 10 per cent year-on-year from now until 2015, matching the growth rate of online retail in the US. The consumer electronics category will lead the expansion, increasing its share of the e-commerce market from 25 per cent to 28 per cent by 2015; shoes will grow 13 per cent year-on-year and clothing, the second-largest category, will generate €21 billion in online sales in 2015. The total number of online buyers in Europe, which includes the EU-17 (Austria, Belgium, Denmark, Finland, France, Germany, Greece, Ireland, Italy, Luxembourg, the Netherlands, Norway, Portugal, Spain, Sweden, Switzerland and the UK), grew by 18 per cent from 2009 to 2010, and is expected to grow from 157 million to 205 million. Currently, 57 per cent of European adults buy online, up 13.4 million (9 per cent) from 2009.[41]

More than half of all US households now regularly shop online. In some European countries this figure is higher: in the UK it is 72 per cent, in the Netherlands 70 per cent and in Germany 66 per cent, though dropping to 34 per cent for Italy and Spain. Current US online retail sales of an estimated €217.6 billion are expected to grow at better than 11 per cent a year over the next five years, compared with a growth rate of 2.5 per cent in total retail sales.[42]

Perhaps even more important, the Internet now influences an estimated 42 per cent of total retail sales – sales transacted online plus those carried out offline but encouraged by online research. Some 97 percent of Web-goers now use the Internet to research products before making purchases. By one estimate, the Internet influences a staggering 50 per cent of total retail sales.[43] Thus, smart marketers are employing integrated multi-channel strategies that use the Web to drive sales to other marketing channels.

Internet buyers differ from traditional offline consumers in their approaches to buying and their responses to marketing. In the Internet exchange process, customers initiate and control the contact. Traditional marketing targets a somewhat passive audience. In contrast, online marketing targets people who actively select which websites they will visit and what marketing information they will receive about which products and under what conditions. Thus, online marketing requires new marketing approaches.

People now go online to order a wide range of goods – clothing from Gap or Marks & Spencers, books or electronics or just about anything else from Amazon, major appliances from Comet or John Lewis, home mortgages from if.com, or even a will from onlinewill.co.uk or a divorce from quickdivorce.com. Where else but the Web could you find a place that specialises in anything and everything about just about any special interest you may have?

Business-to-business

Although the popular press has given the most attention to B-to-C websites, **business-to-business (B-to-B) online marketing** is also flourishing. B-to-B marketers use websites, e-mail, online

Business-to-consumer (B-to-C) online marketing—Businesses selling goods and services online to final consumers.

Business-to-business (B-to-B) online marketing—Businesses using online marketing to reach new business customers, serve current customers more effectively and obtain buying efficiencies and better prices.

product catalogues, online trading networks and other online resources to reach new business customers, serve current customers more effectively and obtain buying efficiencies and better prices.

Most major B-to-B marketers now offer product information, customer purchasing and customer-support services online. For example, corporate buyers can visit networking equipment and software maker Cisco Systems' website (www.cisco.com), select detailed descriptions of Cisco's products and service solutions, request sales and service information, attend events and training seminars, watch videos on a wide range of topics, have live chats with Cisco staff and place orders. Some major companies conduct almost all of their business on the Web. Cisco Systems, for example, takes more than 80 per cent of its orders over the Internet.

Beyond simply selling their products and services online, companies can use the Internet to build stronger relationships with important business customers. For example, Dell has created customised websites for more than 100,000 business and institutional customers worldwide. These individualised Premier.Dell.com sites help business customers more efficiently manage all phases of their Dell computer buying, ownership and end-of-life recycling of equipment. Each customer's Premier.Dell.com website includes a customised online computer store, purchasing and asset management reports and tools, system-specific technical information, links to useful information throughout Dell's extensive website, and more. The site makes all the information a customer needs to do business with Dell available in one place, 24/7.[44]

Consumer-to-consumer

Consumer-to-consumer (C-to-C) online marketing—Online exchanges of goods and information between final consumers.

Much **consumer-to-consumer (C-to-C) online marketing** and communication occurs on the Web between interested parties over a wide range of products and subjects. In some cases, the Internet provides an excellent means by which consumers can buy or exchange goods or information directly with one another. For example, eBay, and other auction sites offer popular market spaces for displaying and selling almost anything, from art and antiques, coins and stamps, and jewellery to computers and consumer electronics.

eBay's C-to-C online trading community of more than 90 million active users worldwide (that's more than the total populations of Britain, Egypt or Turkey) transacted some €46.8 billion in trades last year. At any given time, the company's website lists more than 113 million items up for auction in more than 50,000 categories. Such C-to-C sites give people access to much larger audiences than the local market or newspaper classifieds (which, by the way, have also gone online at websites such as eBay Classifieds). Interestingly, based on its huge success in the C-to-C market, eBay has now attracted more than 500,000 B-to-C sellers, ranging from small businesses peddling their regular wares to large businesses liquidating excess inventory at auction.[45]

In other cases, C-to-C involves interchanges of information through Internet forums that appeal to specific special-interest groups. Such activities may be organised for commercial or non–commercial purposes. Web logs, or **blogs**, are online journals where people post their thoughts, usually on a narrowly defined topic. Blogs can be about anything, from politics or baseball to haiku, car repair or the latest television series. Since 2002, Twitter accounts aside, more 133 million blogs have been 'keyed' in 81 different languages. Currently, 77 per cent of online consumers actively read them. Such numbers give blogs – especially those with large and devoted followings – substantial influence.[46]

Blogs—Online journals where people post their thoughts, usually on a narrowly defined topic.

Many marketers are now tapping into the blogosphere as a medium for reaching carefully targeted consumers. For example, some companies have created their own blogs. Sports footwear maker Vans has created several blogs – from 'Off the Wall' to 'Vans Girls' – at which customers can read up on Van's-related news and views about fashion, art, sports and music. In 2011, General Motors and Ford in the US between them invited more than 120 bloggers and Facebook enthusiasts to attend the Detroit car show, from as far afield as New Zealand and South Africa. The carmakers are relying on their guests to spread news from the car show through their blogging.[47] The downside is, of course, the potential for negative blogs that damage a brand. In 2010, Nestlé faced a deluge of negative cyber-comments regarding its continued promotion of powdered baby milk to developing countries, where the water may be too dirty and unsafe for children. The company struggled to engage with its online critics to deny the criticisms.[48]

Companies can also advertise on existing blogs or influence content there. For example, they might encourage 'sponsored conversations' by influential bloggers:[49]

> As part of its 'Living in High Definition' push, Panasonic wanted to build buzz about its brand at the Consumer Electronics Show (CES). But rather than relying on the usual tech journalists attending the show, Panasonic recruited five influential bloggers – including popular Internet figures Chris Brogan and Steve Garfield – to travel to the CES at its expense. It footed the bill for their travel and passes to the event while also loaning them digital video and still cameras. In return, the bloggers agreed to share their impressions of the show, including Panasonic product previews, with their own powerful distribution networks, in the form of blog posts, Twitter updates and YouTube videos. The catch: Panasonic had no say on what their guests posted. To maintain credibility, Panasonic kept its distance, and the bloggers fully disclosed the brand's sponsorship. Still, even though Panasonic didn't dictate content – and didn't want to – the 'sponsored conversations' allowed the brand to tap into the groundswell of Internet buzz. 'When you give [bloggers] equipment and they love it, just like any other consumer they'll evangelize it,' says a Panasonic spokesperson. 'We're not looking for them to hit message points and in effect shill.' Panasonic just wants to be a catalyst for conversations about its brand.

As a marketing tool, blogs offer some advantages. They can offer a fresh, original, personal and cheap way to enter into consumer Web conversations. However, the blogosphere is cluttered and difficult to control. Blogs remain largely a C-to-C medium. Although companies can sometimes leverage blogs to engage in meaningful customer relationships, consumers remain largely in control.

Companies need to be very careful about how they intervene in blogs. Coca-Cola, for example has issued its own set of social media guidelines for its employees, to encourage common sense and transparency when discussing the brand online. Fake blogs and spamming are not welcomed by users.[50]

Whether or not they actively participate in the blogosphere, companies should show up, monitor, and listen to them. For example, Starbucks sponsors its own blog (http://mystarbucksidea.force.com) but also closely follows consumer dialogue on the 30 or more other third-party online sites devoted to the brand. It then uses the customer insights it gains from all these proprietary and third-party blogs to adjust its marketing programmes.[51]

In all, C-to-C means that online buyers don't just consume product information – increasingly, they create it. As a result, 'word of Web' is joining 'word of mouth' as an important buying influence.

Consumer to business

The final online marketing domain is **consumer-to-business (C-to-B) online marketing**. Thanks to the Internet, today's consumers are finding it easier to communicate with companies. Most companies now invite prospects and customers to send in suggestions and questions via company websites. Beyond this, rather than waiting for an invitation, consumers can search out sellers on the Web, learn about their offers, initiate purchases and give feedback. Using the Web, consumers can even drive transactions with businesses, rather than the other way around. For example, using Priceline.com, would-be buyers can bid for airline tickets, hotel rooms, rental cars, cruises and vacation packages, leaving the sellers to decide whether to accept their offers.

In the US, for example, consumers can also use websites such as GetSatisfaction.com, Complaints.com and PlanetFeedback.com to ask questions, offer suggestions, lodge complaints or deliver compliments to companies. GetSatisfaction.com provides 'people-powered customer service' by creating a user-driven customer service community. The site provides forums where customers discuss problems they're having with the products and services of 35,000 companies – from Microsoft and P&G to Google and Zappos.com – whether the company participates or not. GetSatisfaction.com also provides tools by which companies can adopt GetSatisfaction.com as an official customer service resource.[52] Nonetheless, sites like tripadvisor.co.uk in the UK have attracted considerable controversy because of their hostile consumer reviews of hotels and restaurants.

Consumer-to-business (C-to-B) online marketing— Online exchanges in which consumers search out sellers, learn about their offers and initiate purchases, sometimes even driving transaction terms.

Establishing an online marketing presence

In one way or another, most companies have now moved online. Companies conduct online marketing in any of the four ways shown in Figure 17.3: creating a website, placing ads and promotions online, establishing or participating in online social networks or using e-mail.

Creating a website

For most companies, the first step in conducting online marketing is to create a website. However, beyond simply creating a website, marketers must design an attractive site and find ways to get consumers to visit the site, stay around and come back often.

Websites vary greatly in purpose and content. The most basic type is a **corporate** (or **brand**) **website**. These sites are designed to build customer goodwill, collect customer feedback and supplement other sales channels rather than sell the company's products directly. They typically offer a rich variety of information and other features in an effort to answer customer questions, build closer customer relationships and generate excitement about the company or brand.

For example, you can't buy anything at P&G's Old Spice brand site, but you can learn about the different Old Spice products, watch recent ads, enter the latest contest and post comments on the Old Spice blog. Similarly, GE's corporate website serves as a global public face for the huge company. It presents a massive amount of product, service and company information to a diverse audience of customers, investors, journalists and employees. It's both a B-to-B site and a portal for consumers, whether it's a US consumer researching a microwave, an Indonesian business buyer checking out eco-friendly locomotives or a German investor looking for shareholder information.

Other companies create a **marketing website**. These sites engage consumers in an interaction that will move them closer to a direct purchase or other marketing outcome. For example, BMW operates a marketing website for its trendy Mini car range at www.mini.co.uk. Once a potential customer clicks in, the manufacturer wastes no time trying to turn the inquiry into a sale and then into a long-term relationship. The site offers a garage full of useful information and interactive selling features, including detailed and fun descriptions of current Mini models, tools for designing your very own Mini, information on dealer locations and services and even tools for tracking your new Mini from factory to delivery.

Creating a website is one thing; getting people to *visit* the site is another. To attract visitors, companies aggressively promote their websites in offline print and broadcast advertising and through ads and links on other sites. But today's Web users are quick to abandon any website that doesn't measure up. The key is to create enough value and excitement to get consumers who come to the site to stick around and come back again. At the very least, a website should be easy to use, professional looking and physically attractive. Ultimately, however, websites must also be *useful*. When it comes to Web browsing and shopping, most people prefer substance over style and function over flash. Thus, effective websites contain deep and useful information, interactive tools that help buyers find and evaluate products of interest, links to other related sites, changing promotional offers and entertaining features that lend relevant excitement.

Corporate (brand) website—A website designed to build customer goodwill, collect customer feedback and supplement other sales channels rather than sell the company's products directly.

Marketing website—A website that engages consumers in interactions that will move them closer to a direct purchase or other marketing outcome.

Figure 17.3 Setting up for online marketing

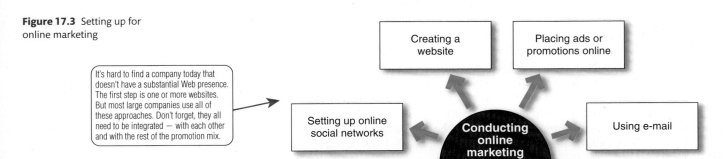

Placing ads and promotions online

As consumers spend more and more time on the Internet, companies are shifting more of their marketing expenditure to **online advertising** to build their brands or attract visitors to their websites. Online advertising has become a major medium. The advertising industry throughout the world is in the midst of a digital revolution as clients follow their customers and shift resources to the Web and new forms of advertising. The global Internet advertising market was worth around €42 billion in 2009, and the US was the largest market. Internet advertising is now ranked second only to television when compared to all ad-supported media (including newspapers and magazines). Online advertising already represents about 15 per cent of total media spend in the US, and 27 per cent in the UK.[53] Here, we discuss forms of online advertising and promotion and their future.

The major forms of online advertising include search-related ads, display ads and online classifieds. Online display ads might appear anywhere on an Internet user's screen and are often related to the information being viewed. For instance, while browsing vacation packages on Expedia.com, you might encounter a display ad offering a free upgrade on a rental car from Avis. Or while visiting the Yahoo! Finance site, a flashing E*TRADE ad might promise a free BlackBerry smartphone when you open a new account. Internet display ads have come a long way in recent years in terms of attracting and holding consumer attention. New *rich media* ads now incorporate animation, video, sound and interactivity.

The largest form of online advertising is *search-related ads* (or *contextual advertising*), which accounts for more than 48 per cent of all online advertising spending.[54] In search advertising, text-based ads and links appear alongside search engine results on sites such as Google and Yahoo! For example, search Google for 'LCD TVs'. At the top and side of the resulting search list, you'll see inconspicuous ads for ten or more advertisers, ranging from Samsung and Dell to Comet, Sainsburys, Argos and Amazon.com. Nearly all of Google's €18.4 billion in revenues come from ad sales. Search is an always-on kind of medium. And in today's tight economy, the results are easily measured. Search-related advertising accounts for nearly two-thirds of all Internet advertising expenditure, and Google dominates this field.

A search advertiser buys search terms from the search site and pays only if consumers click through to its site. For instance, type 'Coke' or 'Coca-Cola' or even just 'soft drinks' or 'rewards' into your Google or Yahoo! search engine and almost without fail 'My Coke Rewards' comes up as one of the top options. This is no coincidence. Coca-Cola supports its popular online loyalty programme largely through search buys (for example, see www.cokezone.co.uk). The global soft drink giant started first with traditional TV and print advertising but quickly learned that search was the most effective way to attract consumers. Now, any of dozens of purchased search terms will return Coke rewards at or near the top of the search list.[55]

Other forms of online promotions include content sponsorships and viral advertising. Using *content sponsorships*, companies gain name exposure on the Internet by sponsoring special content on various websites, such as news or financial information or special interest topics. For example, international hotel group Marriott sponsors a 'Summer to the Rescue!' microsite at Travelocity.com. Sponsorships are best placed in carefully targeted sites where they can offer relevant information or service to the audience.

Finally, online marketers use **viral marketing**, the Internet version of word-of-mouth marketing. Viral marketing involves creating a website plus a video, e-mail mobile phone message, advertisement or other marketing event that is so infectious that customers will want to pass it along to their friends. Because customers pass the message or promotion along to others, viral marketing can be very inexpensive. And when the information comes from a friend, the recipient is much more likely to view or read it.

Sometimes a well-made regular ad can go viral with little help from its sponsoring company. For example, the clever 'Gimme back the Filet-O-Fish' ad from McDonald's, featuring a mechanised singing fish mounted on a wall, grabbed 780,000 YouTube views and a five-star rating in little more than three months. It also inspired a rash of consumer-generated spots posted on YouTube featuring people singing the song while ordering. However, leaving viral efforts to chance rarely works. 'It's one of those things you never really know until it's out there,' says a McDonald's marketer.[56]

Online advertising— Advertising that appears while consumers are browsing the Web, including display ads, search-related ads, online classifieds and other forms.

Viral marketing—The Internet version of word-of-mouth marketing: websites, videos, e-mail messages or other marketing events that are so infectious that customers will want to pass them along to friends.

Although marketers usually have little control over where their viral messages end up, a well-concocted viral campaign can gain vast exposure. Consider T-Mobile's 'Life's for Sharing' flash mob viral video 'Dance'. The nearly three-minute video features a seemingly 'spontaneous' outburst of dancing among hundreds of passengers at London's crowded Liverpool Street railway station. It took months of logistical planning but landed more than 21 million views on YouTube. T-Mobile credits the video for a 29 per cent jump in sales in the United Kingdom.[57]

Creating or participating in online social networks

Online social networks— Online social communities – blogs, social networking websites or even virtual worlds – where people socialise or exchange information and opinions.

As we discussed in Chapters 1 and 5, the popularity of the Internet has resulted in a rash of **online social networks** or *Web communities*. Countless independent and commercial websites have arisen that give consumers online places to congregate, socialise and exchange views and information. These days, it seems, almost everyone is buddying up on Facebook, checking in with Twitter, tuning into the day's hottest videos at YouTube or checking out photos on Flickr. And, of course, wherever consumers congregate, marketers will surely follow. More and more marketers are now riding the huge social networking wave.

Marketers can engage in online communities in two ways: they can participate in existing Web communities or they can establish their own. Joining existing networks seems the easiest. Thus, many major brands – from Intel and Harley-Davidson to Volkswagen and Victoria's Secret – have created branded YouTube channels. GM and other companies have posted visual content on Flickr. Coca-Cola's Facebook page has 5.4 million fans.

Some of the major social networks are huge. The largest social network – Facebook – by itself commands 70 per cent of all social network traffic. Forty-seven per cent of the online population visits Facebook every day. That rivals the 55 per cent who watch any TV channel and trounces the percentage listening to radio (37 per cent) and reading newspapers (22 per cent) daily. In only a few years, Facebook has signed up more than 400 million members. That's 30 per cent greater than the entire US population. And Facebook is adding new members at a rate of five million every week. The massive online network aims to reach one billion members by 2012.[58]

Although large online social networks such as Facebook, YouTube and Twitter have grabbed most of the headlines, a new breed of more focused niche networks has also emerged. These more focused networks cater to the needs of smaller communities of like-minded people, making them ideal vehicles for marketers who want to target special interest groups:

It is worth noting that while the giant social networks like Facebook and Twitter and very high proifle, smaller more specialised social networks, built around interests as obscure as knitting or bird watching, can also present marketers with strong targeting opportunities. For example, ASmallWorld.net is an exclusive social-networking website reserved for the affluent that has attracted the attention of advertisers. This invitation-only site, with 300,000 selected members, has become a magnet for companies making luxury goods and trying to reach people who can afford them. The biggest advertisers on the site include Burberry, Cartier and Land Rover. Cognac maker Remy Martin last month threw a tasting party for the site's elite members, at which its premium drinks flowed freely.

In fact thousands of social-networking sites have emerged catering for specific interests, backgrounds, professions and age groups. In the US, nightclub revellers can meet at DontStayIn.com; wine connoisseurs can connect at Snooth.com, and people going through divorce can commiserate with each other and plot revenge at Divorce360.com.

Research by the Pew Research Center in the US suggests 73 per cent of teenagers, 72 per cent of young adults, and 40 per cent of adults over 30 have an account with at least one social network. A running tally of emerging social networks, now beyond 7,000 by one estimate, suggests an exploding market. This provides both a golden opportunity and a colossal dilemma for brands trying to identify the best new network for their campaigns.

Although niche sites have far fewer members than huge sites like Facebook, they contain dedicated communities of like-minded people. This can make niche sites ideal vehicles for marketers who want to target special interest groups of this kind. Niche sites often provide a better marketing message environment than mass market sites. Because members of niche social networks share common interests and experiences, they tend to spend more time on the site and contribute more. On the bigger sites, members tend to be less involved and for that reason they are less attractive to advertisers. An online consultant notes, 'the bigger sites have become so cluttered and overrun with advertisers that members are used to tuning stuff out, even personalized ads . . . But on networking sites that have a self-selecting demographic, [people tend to trust the content, including ads.'

However, not all niche networks welcome marketers. Sermo.com – a social-networking site at which some 112,000 doctors consult with colleagues specialising in areas ranging from dermatology to psychiatry – allows no marketing. Nonetheless, for a fee, companies can gain acess to Sermo.com data and member discussions. 'They can monitor online discussions, with the doctors' names omitted, or see a tally of topics being discussed at the site to determine what's rising or falling in popularity,' notes a health-care industry analyst.

The more focused audiences offered by niche networks are increasingly popular with brands because 'relevance', says the consultant, 'trumps size'.[59]

But participating successfully in existing online social networks presents challenges. First, most companies are still experimenting with how to use them effectively, and results are hard to measure. Second, such online networks are largely user controlled. The company's goal is to make the brand a part of consumers' conversations and their lives. However, marketers can't simply muscle their way into consumers' online interactions; they need to earn the right to be there. 'You're talking about conversations between groups of friends,' says one analyst. 'And in those conversations a brand has no right to be there, unless the conversation is already about that brand.' Rather than intruding, marketers must learn to become a valued part of the online experience.[60]

To avoid the mysteries and challenges of building a presence on existing online social networks, many companies are now launching their own targeted Web communities. For example, Finnish scrapbooking and crafting tools and supplies maker Fiskars created Fiskateers, an exclusive, global online network of crafters. More than creating sales, the Fiskateers community creates a relationship between the brand and important customers. Similarly, on Nike's Nike Plus website, more than 500,000 runners upload, track and compare their performances. More than half visit the site at least four times a week, and Nike plans eventually to have 15 per cent or more of the world's 100 million runners actively participating in the Nike Plus online community.

Finnish crafting tools and supplies makers Fiskars created Fiskateers, an exclusive, global network of crafters.

Source: Fiskars Group

Using e-mail

E-mail is an important and growing online marketing tool. A recent study by the DMA found that 79 per cent of all direct–marketing campaigns employ e-mail. US companies now spend about €450 million a year on e-mail marketing, and spending will reach an estimated €1.6 billion by 2014.[61] Similarly, in the UK, e-mail has overtaken print direct mail as companies exploit the low cost and other benefits of electronic campaigns.[62]

When used properly, e-mail can be the ultimate direct-marketing medium. Most blue-chip marketers use it regularly and with great success. E-mail lets these marketers send highly targeted, tightly personalised, relationship-building messages. For example, global entertainment brand Cirque du Soleil's e-mail team sends six to eight campaigns per week with exceptional response rates. With dozens of activities going on constantly (permanent shows in Las Vegas and Florida, touring shows on four continents, TV specials, new CDs and DVDs, etc.), Cirque du Soleil faces the challenge of sending fans only the most relevant news. This challenge is met by asking fans to opt-in to what sort of e-mail they want to get, including: cities where people prefer to attend shows; whether people wanted news on any particular permanent-location shows; and English vs. French language preferences. Club members respond to emails at an unusually high rate. For show tours, the customised fan e-mails have a very high conversion rate to ticket sales. [63]

But there's a dark side to the growing use of e-mail marketing. The explosion of **spam** – unsolicited, unwanted commercial e-mail messages that clog up our e-mailboxes – has produced consumer irritation and frustration. According to one research company, spam now accounts for almost 90 per cent of all e-mail sent.[64] E-mail marketers walk a fine line between adding value for consumers and being intrusive.

To address these concerns, most legitimate marketers now practise *permission-based e-mail marketing*, sending e-mail pitches only to customers who 'opt in'. Many companies use configurable e-mail systems that let customers choose what they want to get. Amazon.com targets opt-in customers with a limited number of helpful 'we thought you'd like to know' messages based on their expressed preferences and previous purchases. Few customers object and many actually welcome such promotional messages. Similarly, Cirque du Soleil designed its e-mail system to make certain that its e-mails go only to fans who actually *want* to receive them.

Given its targeting effectiveness and low costs, e-mail can be an outstanding marketing investment. According to the DMA, e-mail marketing produces the greatest ROI of all direct-marketing media.[65]

In all, online marketing continues to offer both great promise and many challenges for the future. Its most ardent apostles still envision a time when the Internet and online marketing will replace magazines, newspapers and even stores as sources for information and buying. Most marketers, however, hold a more realistic view. Certainly, online marketing has become a successful business model for some companies – Internet firms such as Amazon.com and Google and many direct-marketing companies such as Direct Line. However, for most companies, online marketing will remain as one important approach to the marketplace that works alongside other approaches in a fully integrated marketing mix.

Spam—Unsolicited, unwanted commercial e-mail messages.

The explosion of spam has produced consumer irritation and frustration.

Source: Alamy Images/Incamerastock(l)/istockphoto(r)

AUTHOR COMMENT
Although we mostly benefit from direct marketing, like most other things in life, it has its dark side as well. Marketers and customers alike must guard against irritating or harmful direct-marketing practices.

PUBLIC POLICY ISSUES IN DIRECT MARKETING

Direct marketers and their customers usually enjoy mutually rewarding relationships. Occasionally, however, a darker side emerges. The aggressive and sometimes shady tactics of a few direct marketers can bother or harm consumers, giving the entire industry a black eye. Abuses range from simple excesses that irritate consumers to instances of unfair practices or even outright deception and fraud. The direct-marketing industry has also faced growing invasion-of-privacy concerns, and online marketers must deal with Internet security issues.

Irritation, unfairness, deception and fraud

Direct-marketing excesses sometimes annoy or offend consumers. Most of us dislike television commercials that are too loud, long and insistent. Our letter boxes fill up with unwanted junk mail, our e-mailboxes bulge with unwanted spam and our computer screens flash with unwanted display or pop-up ads.

Beyond irritating consumers, some direct marketers have been accused of taking unfair advantage of impulsive or less-sophisticated buyers. In the US in particular, television shopping channels and programme-long infomercials targeting television-addicted shoppers seem to be the worst culprits. They feature smooth-talking hosts, elaborately staged demonstrations, claims of drastic price reductions, 'while they last' time limitations and unequalled ease of purchase to inflame buyers who have low sales resistance. Worse yet, so-called heat merchants design mailers and write copy intended to mislead buyers.

Fraudulent schemes, such as investment scams or phoney collections for charity, have also multiplied in recent years. *Internet fraud*, including identity theft and financial scams, has become a serious problem. In the United States, in 2009 alone, the Federal Bureau of Investigation's Internet Crime Complaint Center (IC3) received more than 336,650 complaints related to Internet fraud involving monetary loss, with a total loss of $560 million (€436.8 million).[66] Comparable figures are not available for Europe, although the global Internet fraud industry is worth a potential €5.5 billion according to Symantec, the world's largest maker of security software.[67]

One common form of Internet fraud is *phishing*, a type of identity theft that uses deceptive e-mails and fraudulent websites to fool users into divulging their personal data. For example, consumers may receive an e-mail, supposedly from their bank or credit card company, saying that their account's security has been compromised. The sender asks them to log onto a provided Web address and confirm their account number, password and perhaps even other personal details. If they follow the instructions, they are actually turning this sensitive information over to criminals. Although many consumers are now aware of such schemes, phishing can be extremely costly to those caught in the net. It also damages the brand identities of legitimate online marketers who have worked to build user confidence in Web and e-mail transactions.

Many consumers also worry about *online security*. They fear that unscrupulous snoopers will eavesdrop on their online transactions, picking up personal information or intercepting credit and debit card numbers. Although online shopping has grown rapidly, in one survey, 75 per cent of participants said they still do not like sending personal or credit card information over the Internet.[68] Internet shoppers are also concerned about contracting annoying or harmful viruses, spyware and other malware (malicious software).

Another Internet marketing concern is that of *access by vulnerable or unauthorised groups*. For example, marketers of adult-oriented materials and sites have found it difficult to restrict access by minors. In a recent survey, for instance, one in four children ages 8 to 12 admitted to having an account on a social network site such as Facebook or MySpace, which supposedly do not allow children under 13 to have a profile. The survey also found that 17 per cent of their parents did not know they had a social network account.[69]

Invasion of privacy

Invasion of privacy is perhaps the toughest public policy issue now confronting the direct-marketing industry. Consumers often benefit from database marketing; they receive more offers that are closely matched to their interests. However, many critics worry that marketers may know *too* much about consumers' lives and that they may use this knowledge to take unfair advantage of consumers. At some point, they claim, the extensive use of databases intrudes on consumer privacy.

These days, it seems that almost every time consumers enter a competition, apply for a credit card, visit a website or order products by mail, telephone or the Internet, their names are entered into some company's already bulging database. Using sophisticated computer technologies, direct marketers can use these databases to 'microtarget' their selling efforts. *Online privacy* causes special concerns. Most online marketers have become highly skilled at collecting and analysing detailed consumer information. As Web tracking technology grows in sophistication, digital privacy experts worry that some marketers will use such information to take unfair advantage of unknowing customers:[70]

> The problem is what economists call 'information asymmetry'. In simple terms, on one side of your screen is grandmother searching for arthritis treatments or a birthday gift for her granddaughter, and on the other side of the screen is a black-belt quant-jock working for a data-mining start-up. The consumer can't be expected to understand – and follow – all that happens with his or her data. In the realm of online data collection, the notion of 'consumer empowerment' tends to ring hollow.

Some consumers and policy makers worry that the ready availability of information may leave consumers open to abuse. For example, they ask, should Web sellers be allowed to plant cookies in the browsers of consumers who visit their sites and use tracking information to target ads and other marketing efforts? Should credit card companies be allowed to make data on their millions of cardholders worldwide available to retailers who accept their cards? Or is it right for government agencies to sell the names and addresses of driving licence holders, along with their personal information, to allow them to be targeted by sellers?

A need for action

To curb direct marketing excesses, various government agencies in several countries are investigating not only do-not-call lists but also 'do-not-mail' lists, 'do-not-track' lists and 'Can Spam' legislation. In response to online privacy and security concerns, many national governments are considering numerous legislative actions to regulate how Web operators obtain and use consumer information. New laws promise to give consumers more control over how Web information is used, and to allow regulators to take a more active role in policing online privacy. Regulators have several times taken action in Europe and the US to curb what they regard as unwarranted invasion of consumer privacy.

For example, in addition to the Privacy and Electronic Communications Regulations introduced in the EU in 2003, in 2012 the EU Privacy and Electronic Communications Directive came into force, apparently heralding a new era of regulation for digital business models. The new directive is designed to protect users' privacy if they do not wish their browsing habits to be tracked. The regulations have been driven by complaints from privacy campaigners concerned about cookies tracking details of Web use to allow targeted advertising based on the Web user's behaviour online. The directive introduces an 'opt-in' regime where users have to agree to cookies being used. However, it is clear that different European countries are taking different views on how to interpret and apply the new regulations, and the EU Information Commissioner faces a considerable challenge in enforcing them.[71]

In addition, regulators struggle to control the actions of powerful global organisations like Facebook and Google. In early 2012 Google rolled out a new privacy policy which makes it possible for Google to take what it has learnt about a consumer from one of its services, such as search or Gmail, and use it to tailor what the user sees on other services. The content of emails sent on Gmail could, for example, be used to influence what advertising is shown to that person on YouTube. Google made these changes in spite of repeated requests from regulators to delay, and warnings that the policy might not be lawful in the European Union.[72]

Particular concern relating to privacy issues relates to Google and Facebook. The ability of Google to use its records of individuals' Internet searches to identify them as targets for advertising and marketing offers on the basis of their search interests is a major worry for privacy advocates. The capacity of Facebook to track online behaviour and connections of users of its social network provides a unique database relating to peoples' behaviour and preferences, often collected without their explicit permission. The argument about whether these companies breach peoples' rights continues.

All of this calls for strong actions by marketers to prevent privacy abuses before legislators and regulators step in to do it for them. For example, in the United States, to head off increased government regulation, four advertiser groups – the American Association of Advertising Agencies, the Association of National Advertisers, the Direct Marketing Association and the Interactive Advertising Bureau – recently issued new guidelines for websites. Among other measures, the guidelines call for Web marketers to alert consumers if their activities are being tracked. The ad industry has agreed on a standard icon – a little 'i' – that it will add to most behaviourally targeted online ads to tell consumers 'Why do I get this ad?'[73]

Of special concern are the privacy rights of children. With the advent of online social networks, mobile phones and other new technologies, and high levels of use by young people in particular, the main concern is the amount of data mined by third parties from social networks as well as the social networks' own hazy privacy policies. In the United States, 2000 saw the Children's Online Privacy Protection Act (COPPA), which requires website operators targeting children to post privacy policies on their sites. They must also notify parents about any information they're gathering and obtain parental consent before collecting personal information from children under age 13. Privacy groups are now urging the US Senate to extend COPPA to include both the new technologies and teenagers.[74] However, while there is a comparable European legal framework surrounding online privacy issues, there are significant differences between the EU data protection and US data privacy laws. Critics on both sides of the Atlantic fear that legal protections for individuals are inadequate.

Many companies have responded to consumer privacy and security concerns with actions of their own. Still others are taking an industry-wide approach. For example, TRUSTe, a non-profit self-regulatory organisation operating worldwide, works with many large corporate sponsors, including Microsoft, Yahoo!, AT&T, Facebook, Disney and Apple, to audit privacy and security measures and help consumers navigate the Web safely. According to the company's website, 'TRUSTe believes that an environment of mutual trust and openness will help make and keep the Internet a free, comfortable, and richly diverse community for everyone.' To reassure consumers, the company lends its TRUSTe privacy seal to websites that meet its privacy and security standards.[75] However, the TRUSTe seal does not indicate that a website complies with any specific set of privacy rules, such as the European Union's Data Protection Directive, but only that the site has self-certified as complying with the site's own privacy statement.

The direct-marketing industry as a whole is also addressing public policy issues. Professional bodies like the DMA in the US make efforts to build consumer confidence in shopping direct through their explicit privacy promises.

Direct marketers know that, left untended, such direct marketing abuses will lead to increasingly negative consumer attitudes, lower response rates and calls for more restrictive legal controls. Most direct marketers want the same things that consumers want: honest and well-designed marketing offers targeted only toward consumers who will appreciate and respond to them. Direct marketing is just too expensive to waste on consumers who don't want it.

REVIEWING OBJECTIVES AND KEY TERMS

This chapter is the last of three chapters covering the final marketing mix element – promotion. The previous chapters dealt with advertising, public relations, personal selling and sales promotion. This one investigated the burgeoning field of direct and online marketing.

OBJECTIVE 1 Define direct marketing and discuss its benefits to customers and companies (pp. 507–510).

Direct marketing consists of direct connections with carefully targeted segments or individual consumers. Beyond brand and relationship building, direct marketers usually seek a direct, immediate and measurable consumer response. Using detailed databases, direct marketers tailor their offers and communications to the needs of narrowly defined segments or even individual buyers.

For buyers, direct marketing is convenient, easy to use, and private. It gives buyers ready access to a wealth of products and information, at home and around the globe. Direct marketing is also immediate and interactive, allowing buyers to create exactly the configuration of information, products or services they desire and then order them on the spot. For sellers, direct marketing is a powerful tool for building customer relationships. Using database marketing, today's marketers can target small groups or individual customers, tailor offers to individual needs and promote these offers through personalised communications. It also offers them a low-cost, efficient alternative for reaching their markets. As a result of these advantages to both buyers and sellers, direct marketing has become the fastest-growing form of marketing.

OBJECTIVE 2 Identify and discuss the major forms of direct marketing (pp. 510–517).

The main forms of direct marketing include *personal selling*, *direct-mail marketing*, *catalogue marketing*, *telephone marketing*, *DRTV marketing*, kiosk marketing and *online marketing*. We discussed personal selling in the previous chapter.

Direct-mail marketing, the largest form of direct marketing, consists of the company sending an offer, announcement, reminder or other item to a person at a specific address. Recently, new forms of mail delivery have become popular, such as e-mail and mobile marketing. Some marketers rely on catalogue marketing – selling through catalogues mailed to a select list of customers, made available in stores or accessed on the Web. Telephone marketing consists of using the telephone to sell directly to consumers. DRTV marketing has two forms: direct-

response advertising (or infomercials) and home shopping channels. Kiosks are information and ordering machines that direct marketers place in stores, airports, hotels and other locations. In recent years, a number of new digital direct-marketing technologies have emerged, including mobile marketing, podcasts and vodcasts and interactive TV (iTV). Online marketing involves online channels that digitally link sellers with consumers.

OBJECTIVE 3 Explain how companies have responded to the Internet and other powerful new technologies with online marketing strategies (pp. 517–521).

Online marketing is the fastest-growing form of direct marketing. The *Internet* enables consumers and companies to access and share huge amounts of information with just a few mouse clicks. In turn, the Internet has given marketers a whole new way to create value for customers and build customer relationships. It's hard to find a company today that doesn't have a substantial Web marketing presence.

Online consumer buying continues to grow at a healthy rate. Most online users now use the Internet to shop. Perhaps more importantly, the Internet influences offline shopping. Thus, smart marketers are employing integrated multichannel strategies that use the Web to drive sales to other marketing channels.

OBJECTIVE 4 Discuss how companies go about conducting online marketing to profitably deliver more value to customers (pp. 522–526).

Companies of all types are now engaged in online marketing. The Internet gave birth to the *click-only companies* that operate online only. In addition, many traditional brick-and-mortar companies have added online marketing operations, transforming themselves into *click-and-mortar companies*. Many click-and-mortar companies are now having more online success than their click-only companies.

Companies can conduct online marketing in any of the four ways: creating a website, placing ads and promotions online, establishing or participating in Web communities and online social networks or using e-mail. The first step typically is to create a website. Beyond simply creating a site, however, companies must make their sites engaging, easy to use and useful to attract visitors, hold them and bring them back again.

Online marketers can use various forms of online advertising and promotion to build their Internet brands or attract visitors to their websites. Forms of online promotion include online display advertising, search-related advertising, content sponsorships and *viral marketing*, the Internet version of word-of-mouth marketing. Online marketers can also participate in online social networks and other Web communities, which take advantage of the *C-to-C* properties of the Web. Finally, e-mail marketing has become a fast-growing tool for both *B-to-C* and *B-to-B* marketers. Whatever direct-marketing tools they use, marketers must work hard to integrate them into a cohesive marketing effort.

OBJECTIVE 5 Overview the public policy and ethical issues presented by direct marketing (pp. 527–529).

Direct marketers and their customers usually enjoy mutually rewarding relationships. Sometimes, however, direct marketing presents a darker side. The aggressive and sometimes shady tactics of a few direct marketers can bother or harm consumers, giving the entire industry a black eye. Abuses range from simple excesses that irritate consumers to instances of unfair practices or even outright deception and fraud. The direct-marketing industry has also faced growing concerns about invasion-of-privacy and Internet security issues. Such concerns call for strong action by marketers and public policy makers to curb direct marketing abuses. In the end, most direct marketers want the same things that consumers want: honest and well-designed marketing offers targeted only toward consumers who will appreciate and respond to them.

NAVIGATING THE KEY TERMS

OBJECTIVE 1
Direct marketing (p. 506)
Customer database (p. 509)

OBJECTIVE 2
Direct-mail marketing (p. 511)
Catalogue marketing (p. 512)
Telephone marketing (p. 513)
Direct-response television (DRTV) marketing (p. 513)

OBJECTIVE 3
Online marketing (p. 517)
Internet (p. 517)
Click-only companies (p. 518)

Click-and-mortar companies (p. 518)
Business-to-consumer (B-to-C) online marketing (p. 519)
Business-to business (B-to-B) online marketing (p. 519)
Consumer-to-consumer (C-to-C) online marketing (p. 520)
Blogs (p. 520)
Consumer-to-business (C-to-B) online marketing (p. 521)

OBJECTIVE 4
Corporate (brand) website (p. 522)
Marketing website (p. 522)
Online advertising (p.523)
Viral marketing (p. 523)
Online social networks (p. 524)
Spam (p. 526)

DISCUSSING AND APPLYING THE CONCEPTS

Discussing the concepts

1. Discuss the importance of customer databases in direct marketing. (AACSB: Communication)

2. Describe the four major online marketing domains and give an example of each. (AACSB: Communication)

3. Name and describe the major forms of direct marketing. (AACSB: Communication)

4. Explain the ways in which companies can establish an online marketing presence. (AACSB: Communication)

5. Compare and contrast the different forms of online advertising. What factors should a company consider in deciding among these different forms? (AACSB: Communication)

6. What is *phishing*? How does it harm consumers and marketers? (AACSB: Communication; Reflective Thinking)

Applying the concepts

1. In a small group, design a viral marketing campaign targeted at teens for a brand of soft drink, Discuss the challenges marketers

might encounter when implementing this viral campaign. (AACSB: Communication; Use of IT; Reflective Thinking)

2. Visit Nike's website at http://nikeid.nike.com/nikeid/index.jsp and design your own shoe. Print out your shoe design and bring it to class. Do you think the price is appropriate for the value received from being able to customise your shoe? Identify and describe two other websites that allow buyers to customise products. (AACSB: Communication; Use of IT; Reflective Thinking)

3. Find news articles about two recent data security breaches. How did the breaches occur? Who was potentially affected by them? (AACSB: Communication; Reflective Thinking)

Focus on technology

The Internet opened the door for explosive growth in direct marketing, and much of that growth is through applications for mobile devices. For example, for $12.99 per month, Schlage, a lock manufacturer, now offers a wireless, keyless door lock system integrated with mobile phones. And Zipcar, a car-sharing service, launched an app for the iPhone enabling customers to not only reserve and locate a car but also unlock it and drive it away – all without contacting a customer service representative. Honking the virtual horn on an iPhone triggers the horn on the reserved car so the member can locate it in the Zipcar lot. The app even looks like a key fob, prompting the user to push the button to unlock the door. Once in the car, swiping a membership card allows access to the keys in the car.

1. What key benefits do these forms of direct marketing offer for consumers and for marketers? (AACSB: Communication; Use of IT; Reflective Thinking)

2. Find or conceive of other applications in which the Internet and mobile devices create direct marketing opportunities. (AACSB: Communication; Reflective Thinking)

Focus on ethics

The World Wide Web is often referred to as the Wild West. Unlike advertising, which openly identifies the sponsor, much product and brand information seen on the Internet does not reveal sponsorship. You might read about a product in a blog, see it in a YouTube video or follow it in Twitter, often unaware that the person was paid or provided free merchandise or goodies to say positive things. These undercover company shills are difficult to detect. Sony Pictures, HP, and other marketers use companies like IZEA to develop sponsored conversations using its network of bloggers. Sponsored conversations generated by IZEA disclose sponsorships, but many others do not. However, that could be changing soon. Endorsement guidelines in the US require bloggers to disclose sponsorships. Violators could be slapped with an $11,000 fine per Violation, but with almost 30 million bloggers out there – 80 per cent of whom occasionally or frequently post product or brand reviews – it will be difficult, if not impossible, to enforce this rule. Even with the new rules, sponsored conversations grew almost 14 per cent to $46 million in 2009.

1. Find examples of product information posted in blogs. Did the blogger indicate in the post that he or she was paid or provided free products? Should the government enact laws to require bloggers and others on the Internet to disclose sponsorship from marketers? Explain. (AACSB: Communication; Ethical Reasoning)

2. Review the revised US guidelines on endorsements and testimonials in advertising (www.ftc.gov/os/2009/10/091005revisedendorsementguides.pdf) and visit the Word of Mouth Marketing Association's website (http//womma.org/main) and the website of a social marketing company, such as (http://izea.com). Write a report on how marketers can effectively use sponsored conversations within the guidelines. (AACSB: Communication; Reflective Thinking)

Marketing & the economy

Dell

Not long ago, Dell was the PC industry darling, turning the industry upside down with its direct marketing approach. At one point, it was the world's leading PC maker. But in recent years, Dell has been hit hard by a combination of factors. One is competition: HP took Dell's 'top-seller' status away by providing a better one-stop shop for equipment and services to businesses, where Dell gets three-quarters of its sales. At the same time, Taiwanese competitor Acer took a bite out of Dell's low-cost advantage. By selling cheaper machines, Acer bumped Dell out of the number-two market share spot. The final blow came from the weak economic environment, which has made consumers and businesses more reluctant to upgrade to newer, faster models. Dell's PC sales fell by 13 per cent in 2010, and its net profits fell by 44 per cent. The company has cut costs and is also looking to its other businesses to shore up sagging PC sales. But for the most part, Dell appears to just be hanging on while waiting for an improved economy and a predicted powerful PC replacement cycle to reboot the industry.

1. What is wrong with Dell's strategy to increase PC sales?

2. How can Dell overcome this problem, particularly as consumer frugality persists? What would you recommend?

Marketing by the numbers

Many companies are realising the efficiency of telemarketing in the face of soaring sales force costs. Whereas the average cost of a B-to-B sales call by an outside salesperson costs more than €230, the cost of a telemarketing sales call can be as little as €4 to €15. In addition, telemarketers can make up to 33 decision maker contacts per day compared to a salesperson's four per day. This has got the attention of many B-to-B marketers, where telemarketing can be very effective.

1. Refer to Appendix 2 to determine the marketing return on sales (marketing ROS) and marketing ROI for each company in the chart below. Which company is performing better? Explain. (AACSB: Communication; Analytical Reasoning; Reflective Thinking)

	Company A (sales force only)	Company B (telemarketing only)
Net sales	€2,000,000	€1,000,000
Cost of goods sold	€800,000	€500,000
Sales expenses	€700,000	€200,000

2. Should all companies consider reducing their sales forces in favour of telemarketing? Discuss the pros and cons of this action. (AACSB: Communication; Reflective Thinking)

REFERENCES

1 See Daniel Lyons, 'The customer is always right', *Newsweek* (4 January 2010), p. 85; Brad Stone, 'Can Amazon be the Walmart of the web?' *New York Times* (20 September 2009), p. BU1; Heather Green, 'How Amazon aims to keep you clicking', *BusinessWeek* (2 March 2009) pp. 34-40; Joe Nocera, 'Putting buyers first? What a concept', *New York Times* (5 January 2008); Brian Morrissey, 'Marketer of the year: Jeff Bezos', *Brandweek* (14 September 2009), p. 30; Geoffrey A. Fowler, 'Corporate news: Amazon's sales soar, lifting profit', *Wall Street Journal* (23 April 2010), p. B3; and annual reports and other information found at www.amazon.com, accessed July 2010.

2 For these and other direct-marketing statistics in this section, see Direct Marketing Association, *The DMA 2010 Statistical Fact Book, 32nd edition* February 2010; and Direct Marketing Association, *The Power of Direct Marketing: 2008–2009 Edition* June 2009; 'DMA's power to direct marketing report finds DM ad expenditures climb to over 54% of all advertising expenditures' (19 October 2009), accessed at www.the-dma.org/cgi/dispannouncements?article=1335; and a wealth of other information at www.the-dma.org, accessed November 2010.

3 Louise Lucas, 'Moving on from door-to-door', *Financial Times* (21 February 2012), p. 14.

4 See www.dmnews.com/online-ad-spending-to-hit-618b-for-2010-emarketer/article/175745/, accessed (26 February 2012).

5 Susan Greco, 'How to reduce your cost of sales', *Inc.* (5 March 2010), accessed at www.inc.com/guide/reducing-cost-of-sales.html.

6 Portions adapted from Mike Beirne, 'A wing – and a ding', *Brandweek* (23 October 2006), p. 22; and Jason Voight, 'Southwest keeps fans from straying', *Adweek* (20 August 2007), accessed at www.adweek.com/aw/esearch/article_display.jsp?vnu_content_id=1003627839. Other information from 'Southwest Airlines celebrates anniversary of DING!', *PR Newswire* (28 February 2008); Bob Garfield, 'What's the big deal with widgets?', *Advertising Age* (1 December 2008), p. 1; www.blogsouthwest.com and 'What Is DING!?', www.southwest.com/ding, accessed December 2010.

7 Philip Delves Broughton, 'The value of information', *Financial Times* (8 March 2011), p. 16.

8 See Scott Horstein, 'Use care with that database', *Sales & Marketing Management* (May 2006), p. 22; 'USAA announces mobile RDC app for Android phones', *TechWeb* (27 January 2010); 'USAA', *Hoover's Company Records* (15 June 2010); Jean McGregor, 'Customer service champs: USAA's battle plan', *Bloomberg Businessweek* (1 March 2010), pp. 40-43; 'Largest US corporations', *Fortune*, (3 May 2010), p. F7; and www.usaa.com, accessed August 2010.

9 See DMA, *The Power of Direct Marketing, 2009-2010 Edition*; and 'Mail spend to rise', *Deliver Magazine* (7 January 2010), www.delivermagazine.com/the-magazine/2010/01/07/mail-spend-to-rise.

10 See www.marketingweek.co.uk/ad-spend-growth-to-slow-to-29-in-2011/3024809.article and www.acton.com/index.php?option=com_content&view=article&id=48&Itemid=130&lang=en, accessed February 26, 2012.

11 See Trevor Clawson, 'How to revive your direct mail marketing', *The Marketer* (March/April 2012), pp. 38 – 41.

12 Julie Liesse, 'When times are hard, mail works', *Advertising Age*, (30 March 2009), p. 14; and Sarah O'Leary, 'Thanks to spam, it's not junk mail anymore', *Huffington Post* (19 April 2010). For counterpoints, see Gavin O'malley, 'Direct-mail doomed, long live e-mail', *MediaPost News*, (20 May 2009), accessed at www.mediapost.com/publications.

13 Based on information from 'JDA, HP, and Intel team up with Mahoney to yield outstanding quantifiable results', The Mahoney Company, www.mahoneyprint.com/caseStudies/jda.pdf; and Heather Fletcher, 'PURLs of Wisdom', *Target Marketing* (January 2009), pp. 27–29.

14 See www.royalmail.com/sites/default/files/docs/pdf/trend.pdf, accessed (26 February 2012).

15 Jeffrey Ball, 'Power shift: in digital era, marketers still prefer a paper trail', *Wall Street Journal* (16 October 2009), p. A3.

16 Ibid.; and 'report: catalogs increasingly drive online sales', *RetailCustomer Experience.com* (17 March 2010), www.retailcustomerexperience.com/article/21521/Report-Catalogs-increasingly-drive-online-sales.

17 DMA, *The Power of Direct Marketing, 2009–2010 Edition*.

[18] Geoffrey A. Fowler, 'Peeved at auto warranty calls, a Web posse strikes back', *Wall Street Journal* (15 May 2009), A1.

[19] See Brian Steinberg, 'Read this now!; But wait! There's more! The infomercial king explains', *Wall Street Journal* (9 March 2005), p. 1; Rachel Brown, 'Perry, Fischer, Lavigne Tapped for Proactiv', *WWD* (13 January 2010), p. 3; and www.proactiv.com, accessed May 2010.

[20] Adapted from Allison Fass, 'Extreme makeover', *Forbes* (1 September 2008), pp. 64–66. Also see Richard Mullins, 'TV, Web sales have HSN clicking', *Tampa Tribune* (6 May 2010), p. 8.

[21] Stephanie Rosenbloom, 'The new touch-face of vending machines', *New York Times* (25 May 2010), accessed at www.nytimes.com/2010/05/26/business/26vending.html.

[22] Beth Snyder Bulik, 'redbox rakes in green in tough times', *Advertising Age* (23 February 2009), p. 6; Jessica Mintz, 'Redbox's machines take on Netflix's red envelopes', *USA Today* (22 June 2009), accessed at www.usatoday.com/tech/news/2009-06-22-redbox_N.htm; Brad Tuttle, 'Movies for Cheap', *Time* (8 March 2010), p. 50; and www.redbox.com, accessed August 2010.

[23] Statistics extracted from: http://mobithinking.com/mobile-marketing-tools/latest-mobile-stats, accessed (26 February 2012).

[24] Jonathan Birchall, 'Codes open new frontiers in retail wars', *Financial Times* (18 May 2010), p. 23. Jonathan Birchall, 'Placecast signals change for shop offers', *Financial Times* (15 October 2010), p. 23.

[25] Adapted from Michael Garry, 'Going mobile', *Supermarket News* (12 January 2009), p. 65.

[26] Statistics extracted from: http://mobithinking.com/mobile-marketing-tools/latest-mobile-stats, accessed (26 February 2012).

[27] MobiThinking, 'Global mobile statistics 2011', www.mobithinking.com/mobile-marketing-tools/latest-mobile-stats, accessed (22 August 2011).

[28] Jonathan Birchall, 'Codes open new front in retail wars', op.cit.

[29] See Emily Burg, 'Acceptance of mobile ads on the rise', *MediaPost Publications* (16 March 2007), accessed at www.mediapost.com/publications; Steve Miller and Mike Beirne, 'The iPhone Effect', *Adweek.com*, (28 April 2008), www.adweek.com/aw/content_display/news/digital/e3ibcf1ad2007731abae868def5f67da804; Altmeyer, 'Smart phones, social networks to boost mobile advertising', (29 June 2009); and Richard Westlund, 'Mobile on Fast Forward', *Brandweek* (15 March 2010), pp. M1–M5.

[30] Arbitron/Edison Internet and Multimedia Study, 'The podcast consumer revealed 2009', accessed at www.edisonresearch.com/home/archives/2009/05/the_podcast_consumer_2009.php; and 'Marketing News' digital handbook', *Marketing News* (3 April 2009), pp. 9–18.

[31] See www.telegraph.co.uk/technology/news/8946965/BBC-podcasts-hit-1-billion-downloads.html, accessed (28 February 2012); and www.littlevoicemedia.com/podcast-statistics, accessed (28 February 2012).

[32] 'Disney online podcasts', http://disney.go.com/music/podcasts/today/index.html, accessed December 2010; 'HP audio and video podcasts', www.hp.com/hpinfo/podcasts.html, accessed December 2010; and 'Take these shows on the Road', www.purina.com/downloads/Podcasts/Index.aspx, accessed December 2010.

[33] Shahnaz Mahmud, 'Survey: viewers crave TV ad fusion', *Adweek.com*, (25 January 2008), www.adweek.com/aw/content_display/news/media/e3i9c26dcb46eda7449d1197b0419feb7a1; Andrew Hampp, 'Addressable ads are here; who's ready?', *Advertising Age* (13 April 2009), p. 9; and Hampp, 'Scorecard: were we wrong or almost right on ITV?', *Advertising Age* (12 April 2010).

[34] See www.prospects.ac.uk/industries_retail_future_trends.htm, accessed (28 February 2012).

[35] Adapted from information in Zachary Rodgers, 'Cablevision's interactive TV ads pay off for Gillette', *ClickZ* (21 October 2009), accessed at www.clickz.com/3635413/print; and David Goetzl, 'Interactive ads pay off for cablevision', *MediaPost News* (12 January 2010), accessed at www.mediapost.com/publications.

[36] See http://www.internetworldstats.com/stats4.htm. accessed 28 February 2012.

[37] For these and other statistics on Internet usage, see 'Nielsen online reports topline U.S. web data for February 2010', *Nielsen Online* (15 March 2009), accessed at http://blog.nielsen.com/nielsenwire/online_mobile/nielsen-provides-topline-u-s-web-data-for-february-2010; and www.internetworldstats.com, accessed July 2010. See alsohttp://gosolo.org/internet-versus-tv/, accessed 28 February 2012.

[38] See www.marketingcharts.com/television/ibm-consumer-study-internet-rivals-declining-tv-as-primary-media-source-1340/ibm-media-entertainment-internet-vs-televisionjpg, accessed 28 February 2012.

[39] See 'Internet retailer: top 500 guide', www.internetretailer.com/top500/list, accessed July 2010.

[40] Staples data from annual reports and other information found at www.staples.com, accessed July 2010.

[41] See http://mashable.com/2011/02/28/forrester-online-sales-europe, accessed 28 February 2012.

[42] See 'U.S. web retail sales to reach $249 billion by 14 – Study', *Reuters* (8 March 2010), accessed at www.reuters.com/article/idUSN0825407420100308; and 'Retail and travel spending', *Advertising Age's Digital Marketing Facts 2010* section, (22 February 2010). See also http://mashable.com/2011/02/28/forrester-online-sales-europe, accessed February 28 2012.

[43] Erick Schonfeld, 'Forrester forecast: online retail sales will grow to $250 billion by 2014', *Tech Crunch.com*, (8 March 2010), accessed at http://techcrunch.com/2010/03/08/forrester-forecast-online-retail-sales-will-grow-to-250-billion-by-2014/; and Anna Johnson, 'Local marketing: 97 percent of consumers use online media for local shopping', *Kikabink News* (17 March 2010), accessed at www.kikabink.com/news/local-marketing-97-percent-of-consumers-use-online-media-for-local-shopping.

[44] Information for this example at www.dell.com/content/topics/topic.aspx/global/premier/login/signin?c=us&l=en, accessed August 2010.

[45] See 'eBay Inc.', *Hoover's Company Records* (19 April 2009), p. 56307; and facts from eBay annual reports and other information at www.ebayinc.com, accessed July 2010.

[46] Nigel Hollis, 'Going global? Better think local instead', *Brandweek* (1 December 2008), p. 14; Jeff Vandam, 'Blogs find favor as buying guides', *New York Times* (22 December 2008), p. B3; and 'State of the blogosphere 2009', *Technorati* (May 2009), accessed at http://technorati.com/blogging/feature/state-of-the-blogosphere-2009.

[47] Bernard Simon, 'Bloggers spread word on car show', *Financial Times* (12 January 2011), p. 21.

[48] Neil Craven, 'Nestlé in battle of the cyber boycotts', *Daily Mail* (7 February 2010), p. 79.

[49] Adapted from information found in Brian Morrissey, 'Brands tap into web elite for advertorial 2.0: well-connected bloggers are creating content on behalf of sponsors thirsty for buzz', *Adweek* (12 January 2009), p. 9. Also see Elizabeth A. Sullivan, 'Blog savvy', *Marketing News*

(15 November 2009), p. 8; and Michael Bush, 'All marketers use online influencers to boost branding efforts', *Advertising Age* (21 December 2009), accessed at http://adage.com/digital/article?article_id=141147.

50 David Gelles, 'Blogs that spin a web of deception', *Financial Times* (12 February 2009), p. 14.

51 See Michael Bush, 'Starbucks gets Web 2.0 religion, but can it convert nonbelievers?' *Advertising Age* (24 March 2008), p. 1; and B. L. Bachman, 'Starbucks social media monitoring & community help it survive brand attack', *WhatNextBlog.com*, (3 June 2009), accessed at www.whatsnextblog.com/archives/2009/06/starbucks_social_media_community_helps_it_survive_brand_attack.asp.

52 See 'Get satisfaction connects customer support and the social web', *PRNewswire*, (21 April 2010); and www.getsatisfaction.com, accessed July 2010.

53 See www.econsultancy.com, accessed 1 March 2012. Ben Fenton, 'Online advertising retakes top slot', *Financial Times* (5 October 2011), www.ft.com; Paul Taylor, 'Advertising: a marlet in transition', *Financial Times*, (19 December 2011), www.ft.com.

54 'U.S. online advertising forecast by format', *Advertising Age's Digital Marketing Facts* 2010 section (22 February 2010); and Internet Advertising Bureau, *IAB Internet Advertising Revenue Report* (7 April 2010).

55 See Elaine Wong, 'Coke, ConAgra, Kellogg cozy up with search buys', *Brandweek* (12 October 2008), accessed at www.brandweek.com/bw/content_display/esearch/e3ib51a5e93dda16ab7f3a8e4e09f1c789f.

56 Leftheria Parpis, 'Behind McD's flashy new spot: mounted musical mouthpiece makes a splash on the net', *Adweek* (10 March 2009), accessed at www.adweek.com.

57 Noreen O'Leary, 'Does viral pay?', *Adweek* (29 March 2010); and www.youtube.com/watch?v=VQ3d3KigPQM, accessed May 2010.

58 Brian Morrissey, 'social media use becomes pervasive', *Adweek* (15 April 2010), accessed at www.adweek.com/aw/content_display/news/digital/e3iceae27f23a68f24b217e45338fb39727.

59 These illustrations are adapted from Betsey Cummings, 'Why marketers love small social networks', *Brandweek* (27 April 2008), accessed at www.brandweek.com/bw/esearch/article_display.jsp?vnu_content_id=1003794853; with adapted extracts, quotes and other information from Kim Hart, 'Online networking goes small, and sponsors follow', *Washington Post* (29 December 2007), p. D1; Brian Morrissey, 'Social media use becomes pervasive', *Adweek* (15 April 2010), accessed at www.adweek.com/aw/content_display/news/digital/e3iceae27f23a68f24b217e45338fb39727; Amanda Lenhardt and others, 'Social media and young adults', Pew Research Center (3 February 2010), www.pewinternet.org/Reports/2010/Social-Media-and-Young-Adults.aspx; and www.sermo.com, accessed July 2010.

60 Chaddus Bruce, 'Big biz buddies up to gen Y', *Wired* (20 December 2006), accessed at www.wired.com; and Brian Morrissey, 'Kraft gives Facebook users reason to share', *Adweek* (30 December 2008), accessed at www.adweek.com/aw/content_display/news/digital/e3ied80d20-a4b4691a426764ce2ce16daf6.

61 See Ken Magill, 'E-mail ROI still stunning, still slipping: DMA', *Direct Magazine* (20 October 2009), accessed at http://directmag.com/magilla/1020-e-mail-roi-still-slipping; 'E-Mail', *Advertising Age's Digital Marketing Facts 2010* section (22 February 2010); and 'success stories in e-mail marketing', *Brandweek*, (1 February 2010), pp. EM2–EM6.

62 Carlos Grande, 'E-mail overtakes print for marketing offerings', *Financial Times* (13 August 2007), p. 2.

63 See www.marketingsherpa.com/article.php?ident=27496#, accessed 1 March 2012.

64 Symantec, *The State of Spam and Phishing: Home of the Monthly Report – April 2010*, accessed at www.symantec.com/business/theme.jsp?themeid=state_of_spam.

65 Carroll Trosclair, 'Direct marketing, advertising and ROI: commercial e-mail delivers highest DM return on investment', Suite101.com (2 April 2010), http://advertising.suite101.com/article.cfm/direct-marketing-advertising-and-roi.

66 See Internet Crime Complaint Center, 'IC3 2009 annual report on internet crime released' (12 March 2010), accessed at www.ic3.gov/media/2010/100312.aspx.

67 Philip Stafford, 'Internet fraud's business model is crunch-proof', *Financial Times* (24 November 2008), www.ft.com, accessed 1 March 2012.

68 See Greg Sterling, 'Pew: Americans increasingly shop online but still fear identity theft', *SearchEngineLand.com* (14 February 2008), accessed at http://searchengineland.com/pew-americans-increasingly-shop-online-but-still-fear-identity-theft-13366. See also http://www.ftc.gov/bcp/edu/microsites/idtheft, accessed June 2010.

69 See 'A quarter of Internet users aged 8–12 say they have under-age social networking profiles', Ofcom (26 March 2010), www.ofcom.org.uk/media/news/2010/03/nr_20100326a.

70 Steve Lohr, 'Privacy concerns limit online ads, study says', *New York Times* (30 April 2010).

71 Muireann Bolger, 'Cookie monster', *The Marketer* (March/April 2012), pp. 34–37.

72 Maija Palmer, Tim Bradshaw and Alex Barker, 'Google rolls out privacy policy in defiance of EU legality warnings', *Financial Times* (2 March 2012), p. 1; Tim Bradshaw, 'Google's privacy policy given airing', *Financial Times* (3/4 March 2012), p. 17.

73 Emily Steel, 'Web privacy efforts targeted – facing rules, ad firms to give consumers more control', *Wall Street Journal* (26 June 2009), B10; Michael Learmonth, 'Since incoming regulation, online ad groups unite', *Advertising Age* (13 January 2009), accessed at http://adage.com/print?article_id=133730; and Stephanie Clifford, 'A little "i" to teach about online privacy', *New York Times* (26 January 2010).

74 See Mark Rotenberg, 'An examination of children's privacy: new technologies and the Children's Online Privacy Protection Act (COPPA)', (29 April 2010), http://epic.org/privacy/kids/EPIC_COPPA_Testimony_042910.pdf; and 'FTC to study Children's Online Privacy Protection Act' (21 April 2010), accessed at www.aaaa.org/advocacy/gov/news/Pages/042110_children.aspx.

75 Information on TRUSTe at www.truste.com, accessed October 2010.

VIDEO CASE

Zappos.com   MyMarketingLab

Zappos.com spends almost no money on advertising – it doesn't have to. Customers are so enamoured with the company, they keep coming back. And they keep telling their friends. Instead of mass media advertising, Zappos.com focuses on strengthening customer relationships through marketing directly to customers. Like its impeccable customer service, the company's unique promotional methods are valued by customers. When Zappos.com sends out an e-mail or Tweet, customers listen. Its strength

in direct marketing, combined with user-friendly Web design, have made Zappos one of the strongest retailers anywhere.

After watching the video featuring Zappos, answer the following questions:

1. What benefits has Zappos.com gained by marketing directly to customers rather than engaging heavily in mass-market advertising?
2. What role does database technology play in Zappos.com's ability to connect with its customers?
3. Discuss Zappos.com's website in terms of effective Web design. What are its strengths and weaknesses?

COMPANY CASE

Ocado – taking on the Internet giants direct

The online grocery market is one of the fastest-growing, most competitive retail markets in the UK. Worth £3.6 billion (€4.5 billion) in 2007, it is forecast to grow to at least £12 billion (€15 billion) in 2012. Institute of Grocery Distribution research suggests that the online grocery business was growing six times faster than in-store sales even in the tough conditions of the late 2000s.

Ocado is an upmarket British-based online grocery retailer, mainly selling Waitrose products (Waitrose is the supermarket division of the John Lewis Partnership in the UK – the country's 'posh' department store group). Sales are running at around £450 million (€562.5 million) and Ocado has around 1.6 million registered users.

The founders of Ocado were Tim Steiner, an investment banker, Jonathan Faiman, a friend of Steiner's since nursery school and also previously an investment banker, and Jason Gissing. In 2000, the John Lewis Partnership struck a deal to take a 40 per cent stake in Ocado and for its Waitrose business to act as Ocado's supplier (though Ocado has developed its own branded fresh food ranges as well). Intriguingly, in 2008 P&G took a stake in Ocado despite its loss-making status at that time, in its first-ever retailer investment.

Sir Terry Leahy, the respected Tesco boss, made no secret of his doubts about an upstart business set up by inexperienced youngsters in the early 2000s, when the dot-com boom was at its height, compared to his own Tesco Direct operation. The upstarts at Ocado retaliated with the claim that Teco's direct model was not profitable, with its results an artefact of misleading internal cost allocations – an accusation that Tesco vehemently rejects. Sir Terry's swipe at Ocado's business model, which he said was not viable, escalated the ferocity of competition in the online grocery business. Bitter rivalry emerged between Tesco and Ocado, as Ocado began to corner the online market within the M25, where it now controls an estimated 50 per cent of grocery delivery sales. Price wars ensued with Ocado targeting price parity with Tesco on its top 100 lines.

Ocado has pioneered its own approach to online grocery shopping and won awards for its customer service. Like the Boden 'posh' clothing catalogue, Pilates classes and honey-blonde highlights, the weekly Ocado delivery has become a 'must-have' for the affluent, urban tribe of yummy mummies. Ocado's fans are an emblem of middle–class aspirations. Its affluent customers, half of them inside the M25, love Ocado's emphasis on service. The company has cultivated an image of selling high-class food, while caring for the environment because customers don't need to drive to a store.

By 2010, the UK online grocery retailing market was divided as follows: Tesco (52 per cent), Asda (16 per cent), Sainsburys (16 per cent), Ocado (14 per cent) and Waitrose (2 per cent). Interestingly, most of Ocado's new customers were not acquired from Waitrose – 85 per cent were won from Tesco and Asda.

From the outset, Ocado's unique concept was to pick orders and despatch them direct to consumers from a huge, semi-automated, low-cost warehouse in Hertfordshire. The warehouse has the space of ten football pitches, with a 15 km network of conveyor belts handling as many as 7,200 grocery crates an hour, ready for despatch to customers. This is a much faster and more accurate way of picking orders. Direct distribution means Ocado can boast that every fresh item it delivers will have a shelf life of at least six days, and that its food waste is the lowest in the industry at 0.3 per cent of sales. By contrast, rivals such as Tesco began their Internet operations by picking goods from store shelves, meaning that some items would be out of stock and others towards the end of their shelf life (and stores were disrupted for regular shoppers by the order pickers with their giant shopping trolleys). Tesco is now getting its act together with Ocado-style warehouses. Indeed, 2010 saw Tesco and Asda opening 'ghost stores' in London, closed to customers, from which to pick online orders, to try and challenge Ocado's strong position in this important market.

Nonetheless, the floatation of the company in July 2010 saw Ocado's shares fall within weeks from the offer price of 180p to 135p. Ocado lost a quarter of its market value in its first month as a public company. Since then the shares have seen a slow and erratic recovery.

Ocado's critics doubted whether the business would ever gain enough scale to make a profit. One worry was Waitrose's plans to ramp up its own Internet operation (basically selling the same products as Ocado in much the same areas). Waitrose occupies the dual role of supplier and competitor to Ocado, and in 2011 Waitrose invested £6.5 million in its own online grocery business and rolling out its new website. Indeed, with John Lewis holding shares in Ocado, there is an ownership role as well. Nonetheless, in 2010, Ocado signed a further exclusive ten-year supply deal with Waitrose

There are also concerns that, as the online grocery market matures, latecomers like Marks & Spencer and Morrisons will enter at the same time that Waitrose expands, all threatening Ocado's current strong position.

In fact, some analysts, such as Morgan Stanley, believe that the online market is already mature and its relatively small share of the total grocery business is because over half of Britain's households have tried online and have gone back to shopping in-store, because they find it just as convenient as online. This suggests that the relatively low penetration of online grocery shopping is because the proposition simply is not attractive for most consumers.

Early in 2011, Ocado defied its critics by posting its first quarterly profit, after a tough year in which its shares tanked following the controversial stock market debut. At this time Ocado's chief executive, Tim Steiner, said the business would step up its challenge to industry heavyweights like Tesco by selling more and cheaper groceries. Ocado expects more British shoppers to switch to shopping online using mobile phones.

At the same time, Ocado warned that customer demand has exceeded the capacity of its Hatfield depot. The company has rented warehouses in Bristol and Wimbledon, increasing its coverage by 1 million households to over 70 per cent of UK households, and allowing the firm to break into South Wales for the first time.

Questions for discussion

1. How would you describe the competitive advantage in Ocado's business, compared to its larger rivals?

2. Can Ocado maintain its current strong position in this market?

3. Is online grocery shopping really likely to become a bigger part of Britain's food shopping, or has the market reached its maximum potential? What does your evaluation suggest for Ocado's future?

4. Is Ocado doing the right thing by sticking to its current strategy? What changes or new developments would you recommend to the company?

Sources: Neil Craven, 'Supermarket giants in online price war', *Mail on Sunday* (24 February 2008), pp. 53–54; Elizabeth Rigby, 'P&G takes stake in lossmaking Ocado in boost to online retailer', *Financial Times* (27 November 2008), p. 19; Jenny Davey, 'For sale: Loss-making delivery firm. Price: £1bn', *Sunday Times* (2 February 2010), S3, p. 9; Jenny Davey, 'Waitrose looks to take on its rivals with online drive', *Sunday Times* (8 February 2009), S1, p. 33; Andrew Davidson, 'Ocado retailer stands on the brink of delivering', *Sunday Times* (27 June 2010), S3, p. 6; Andrea Felsted and Elizabeth Rigby, 'Ocado extends exclusive Waitrose deal to 2010', *Financial Times* (27 May 2010), p. 19; Kate Walsh, 'Web pioneers fashion future of retailing', *Sunday Times* (22 August 2010), S3, p. 8; Ian Lyall, 'Can Ocado deliver on the city's demanding targets?', *Daily Mail* (18 September 2010), p. 108; 'Ocado shares hit highs on maiden profit', *Daily Mail* (2 February 2011), p. 64; Ruth Sutherland, 'How tycoons made a mint from Ocado', *Daily mail* (9 March 2011), p. 72; Rupert Steiner, 'Ocado set to deliver maiden annual profit despite gloom', *Daily Mail* (5 March 2011), p. 93.

CHAPTER EIGHTEEN

Creating competitive advantage

Chapter preview

In previous chapters, you explored the basics of marketing. You learned that the aim of marketing is to create value *for* customers and capture value *from* them in return. Good marketing companies win, keep and grow customers by understanding customer needs, designing customer-driven marketing strategies, constructing value-delivering marketing programmes, and building customer and marketing partner relationships. In the final three chapters, we'll extend this concept to three special areas: creating competitive advantage, global marketing, and social and environmental marketing sustainability.

In this chapter, we pull all the marketing basics together. Understanding customers is an important first step in developing profitable customer relationships, but it's not enough. To gain competitive advantage, companies must use this understanding to design marketing offers that deliver more value than the offers of competitors seeking to win the same customers. In this chapter, we look first at competitor analysis – the process companies use to identify and analyse competitors. Then we examine competitive marketing strategies by which companies position themselves against competitors to gain the greatest possible competitive advantage.

Let's look again at Asos the online retailer (see also Chapter 7, p. 201). Asos has grown from nothing to a position where it is challenging the market leader. In ten years it has gone from a small UK start-up to a firm that has customers in over 160 countries and a click-fall of around 700,000 customers a day. While others have failed the competitive challenge, Asos has thrived and has carved a unique competitive position. Is the success of Asos mere luck? Or is Asos the result of astute strategic manoeuvring?

Objective outline

➤ **Objective 1** Discuss the need to understand competitors as well as customers through competitor analysis.
Competitor analysis (pp. 543–549)

➤ **Objective 2** Explain the fundamentals of competitive marketing strategies based on creating value for customers.

Competitive strategies (pp. 549–557)

➤ **Objective 3** Illustrate the need for balancing customer and competitor orientations in becoming a truly market-centred organisation.
Balancing customer and competitor orientations (p. 558)

PART FOUR

Extending marketing

Asos – As Seen on Screen have
come a long way to challenge
the market leader.

Source: Alamy Images/1 Exposure

ASOS

As alluded to in Chapter 7, why do some companies thrive while others go under? What separates, in fashion retail, for example, the wildly successful Asos (As Seen on Screen) from a notorious flop like Boo.com, which motored its way through almost £91 million before failing? Pets.com and eToys.com are two other high-profile flame-outs of the past decade. Even Ocado, a relatively successful company that sells Waitrose supermarket food online, has only recently posted a small pre-tax profit after nine years of trading.

When Internet clothing company Asos was listed on London's Alternative Investment Market in 2001, it was known for its 'red carpet replicas' – that is, selling copies of dresses worn by models and actresses. Aloof 'fashionistas' looked down their long patrician noses at the start-up and many celebrities were uncomfortable with the idea. Ten years later, Asos has grown beyond any expectations and has remodelled itself into a global fashion destination where, even previously snobby, celebrities are happy to shop themselves.

The business, founded by chief executive Nick Robertson with a £2 million loan from his brother, was originally conceived as a spin-off from Mr Robertson's TV product placement business. However, the business took off quickly and is now among the UK's biggest fashion retailers, generating well over 11 million unique users a month. 'On a daily basis, that's around 700,000 people,' he says. 'Imagine having a shop with that many people walking through the door every day.' Asos sales have risen from £285,000 in 2001 to £387 million in the year to March 2011. The growth has been so fast that the retailer has been forced to move warehouses five times in seven years to cope.

Critics have consistently attempted – and failed – to present the company's growth story as something resembling the tale of the emperor's new clothes (that is, an artificial façade which disguised deep-rooted strategic failures). Online fashion would never take off, they said (hugely underestimating the net-savvy generation who make up Asos's 16 to 34-year-old core customer base). Others argued that companies such as Asos wouldn't stand a chance against the market leader Next (the fashion and homeware group). Next had spent years building a successful directory division which they switched online at just the right time to capture a distinct market leader position in the online fashion category.

However, in 2010 Asos' annual report featured a banner with the message: 'Winning the online fashion race'. It was a bold and cheeky claim – especially as Asos was only the UK's second most popular fashion retail website, having trailed Next for the previous three years, according to Experian Hitwise. 'To win it [is] the point,' says Nick Robertson 'The reason Next are ahead is that they've been around forever but also that they've transferred their Directory business onto the internet. The race is still to be won.'

As a clear main market challenger to Next, Asos has astutely adopted a range of strategies to erode the position of the market leader in the UK, while expanding its own total market and market share.

First, international expansion has been rigorously pursued. Last year Asos launched websites in the US, France and Germany, and hopes to open at least five country-specific sites in 2012, hotly tipped to include the massive market of China. In 2010–2011, turnover from the group's international wings overtook UK sales, and now accounts for 52 per cent of revenues (with Singapore, Russia and Australia among the fastest-growing markets). Nick Robertson said he expected international sales – which rose 161 per cent for the quarter year on year – to grow to more than 60 per cent of total sales 'before you can shake a stick'. 'We've got a goal. Let's get to a billion pounds [in sales] in five years, in five markets,' Mr Robertson says. Asos also intends to make free global shipping a permanent part of its business model, after such promising international sales growth. 'Free global shipping is working, and it is our intention to bake it into the plan, and make it permanent', said Mr Robertson.

Second, to protect its market share back in the UK, Asos has cleverly balanced customer ad competitive orientations. For its demanding customers it has adopted a delivery loyalty scheme, while Asos Premier, similar to Amazon's Prime service, is to protect market share. Customers pay an annual fee of €28.50 to gain unlimited next-day delivery, encouraging them to increase the frequency of orders while giving them a loyalty incentive. In the UK, as a tactical swipe towards its competitors, the cut-off time for next-day delivery has been extended to midnight – in an explicit attempt to beat the 9 pm cut-off for online orders from arch-rivals Next. 'Between 9 pm and 10 pm is our biggest hour in terms of orders, so this could be a real game changer,' Mr Robertson said. To boost sales during quite periods, Asos also periodically uses e-mail promotions offering free next-day delivery to customers.

Third, Asos's approach has striven for constant innovation, particularly with social media (reflecting their customers' habits and age-profile). The group's Facebook store, which it launched in 2011, has performed above expectations with over 1.1 million linked customers within a few months and around 300,000 involved in the monthly app-based Asos competition. Asos's Fashion Finder service, which includes more than 50 brands that Asos does not sell, has also increased Web traffic. 'This is our journey from shop to destination,' Mr Robertson said. 'Customers can create outfits, build looks, tag things they like and comment on styles. It's a different way of engaging with them.' Trying to recreate the social aspect of shopping for the armchair consumer is logical, says Robin Goad, research director at Experian Hitwise, which monitors internet traffic. 'Social networks account for around one in every five page views in the UK,' he says. 'If people are spending a lot of time on Facebook or Twitter, retailers should be aiming to pick up traffic through them.'

Asos also encourages its consumers to use their customer-preferred forms of media to connect to the company. James Hart, Asos's e-commerce director claims that around 8 per cent of visitors to Asos arrive 'via non-traditional sources' such as mobile devices. 'And that number is going to grow exponentially, starting this year, with the proliferation of tablets and cheap smartphones; connected TVs may even gain some momentum this year. In emerging territories there are people accessing the internet for the first time via mobile who may never even use a PC.'

Whether Asos become market leader in the UK or continue their push strategically to challenge, time alone will time. As it stands, it is clear that the management of Asos will not simply allow the firm to drift. Asos will evolve and proactively seek competitive advantage where it can.[1]

AUTHOR COMMENT

Asos have gone from a relatively small scale start-up to market challenger in a decade. Is market leadership their destiny? If so, how are they going to do it?

Today's companies face their toughest competition ever. In previous chapters, we argued that to succeed in today's fiercely competitive marketplace, companies must move from a product-and-selling philosophy to a customer-and-marketing philosophy.

This chapter spells out in more detail how companies can go about outperforming competitors to win, keep and grow their customers. To win in today's marketplace, companies must become adept not only in managing products but also in managing customer relationships in the face of determined competition and a difficult economic environment. Understanding customers is crucial, but it's not enough. Building profitable customer relationships and gaining **competitive advantage** requires delivering more value and satisfaction to target customers than competitors do. Customers will see competitive advantages as *customer advantages*, giving the company an edge over its competitors.

In this chapter, we examine competitive marketing strategies – how companies analyse their competitors and develop successful, customer value-based strategies for building and maintaining profitable customer relationships. The first step is **competitor analysis**, the process of identifying, assessing and selecting key competitors. The second step is developing **competitive marketing strategies** that strongly position the company against competitors and give it the greatest possible competitive advantage.

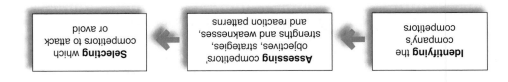

AUTHOR COMMENT

Creating competitive advantage begins with a thorough understanding of competitors' strategies. But before a company can analyse its competitors, it must first identify them – a task that's not as simple as it seems.

COMPETITOR ANALYSIS

To plan effective marketing strategies, the company needs to find out all it can about its competitors. It must constantly compare its marketing strategies, products, prices, channels and promotions with those of close competitors. In this way, the company can find areas of potential competitive advantage and disadvantage. As shown in Figure 18.1, competitor analysis involves first identifying and assessing competitors and then selecting which competitors to attack or avoid.

Identifying competitors

Normally, identifying competitors would seem to be a simple task. At the narrowest level, a company can define its competitors as other companies offering similar products and services to the same customers at similar prices. Thus, El Corte Inglés in Spain might see French discount operators such as Carrefour and Auchan as competitors, but Debenhams or Marks & Spencer would not be a competitor. Ritz-Carlton might see Four Seasons as a major competitor, but Holiday Inn, Ibis or any of the thousands of bed-and-breakfasts that dot the nation would not be competitors.

However, companies actually face a much wider range of competitors. The company might define its competitors as all firms with the same product or class of products. Thus, in these circumstances Ritz-Carlton would see itself as competing against all other hotels. Even more broadly, competitors might include all companies making products that supply the same service. Here Ritz-Carlton would see itself competing not only against other hotels but also against anyone who supplies rooms for weary travellers. Finally, and still more broadly, competitors might include all companies that compete for the same consumer euros. Here Ritz-Carlton

Competitive advantage—An advantage over competitors gained by offering consumers greater value than competitors do.

Competitor analysis—The process of identifying key competitors; assessing their objectives, strategies, strengths and weaknesses, and reaction patterns; and selecting which competitors to attack or avoid.

Competitive marketing strategies—Strategies that strongly position the company against competitors and give the company the strongest possible strategic advantage.

Identifying the company's competitors → **Assessing** competitors' objectives, strategies, strengths and weaknesses, and reaction patterns → **Selecting** which competitors to attack or avoid

Figure 18.1 Steps in analysing competitors

543

would see itself competing with travel and leisure services, from cruises and summer homes to vacations abroad.

Companies must avoid 'competitor myopia'. A company is more likely to be 'buried' by its latent competitors than its current ones. For example, it wasn't direct competitors that put an end to British Telecom's telegram business after 153 years; it was mobile phones and the Internet. Music superstores Our Price and Tower Records didn't go bankrupt at the hands of other traditional music stores; they fell victim to unexpected competitors such as supermarkets, online retailers and iTunes and other digital download services. Another classic example of competitor myopia is the Royal Mail of the UK:[2]

> The Royal Mail is currently losing money at a rapid rate – millions of euros per year. But it's not direct competitors such as FedEx or UPS that are the problem. Instead, it's a competitor that the Royal Mail could hardly have even imagined a decade and a half ago – the soaring use of personal and business e-mail and online transactions. Last year they experienced a 4 per cent fall in core mail volumes. In the future, the Royal Mail expects more declines of about 5 per cent a year as customers switch to e-mail and other forms of electronic communication. The response of the Royal Mail is increases in postage stamp prices and a reduction in delivery time, moves that will almost certainly reduce mail volume further. The solution? When I figure it out, I'll e-mail you!

Companies can identify their competitors from an *industry* point of view. They might see themselves as being in the oil industry, the pharmaceutical industry or the beverage industry. A company must understand the competitive patterns in its industry if it hopes to be an effective player in that industry. Companies can also identify competitors from a *market* point of view. Here they define competitors as companies that are trying to satisfy the same customer need or build relationships with the same customer group.

From an industry point of view, Pepsi might see its competition as Coca-Cola, Orangina, Fanta, 7UP and the makers of other soft drink brands. From a market point of view, however, the customer really wants 'thirst quenching' – a need that can be satisfied by bottled water, energy drinks, fruit juice, iced tea and many other fluids. Similarly, the maker of Crayola crayons might define its competitors as other makers of crayons and children's drawing supplies. But from a market point of view, it would include all firms making recreational and educational products for children. In general, the market concept of competition opens the company's eyes to a broader set of actual and potential competitors.

Assessing competitors

Having identified the main competitors, marketing management now asks: What are the competitors' objectives? What does each seek in the marketplace? What is each competitor's strategy? What are various competitors' strengths and weaknesses, and how will each react to actions the company might take?

Determining competitors' objectives

Each competitor has a mix of objectives. The company wants to know the relative importance that a competitor places on current profitability, market share growth, cash flow, technological leadership, service leadership and other goals. Knowing a competitor's mix of objectives reveals whether the competitor is satisfied with its current situation and how it might react to different competitive actions. For example, a company that pursues low-cost leadership will react much more strongly to a competitor's cost-reducing manufacturing breakthrough than to the same competitor's advertising increase.

A company also must monitor its competitors' objectives for various segments. If the company finds that a competitor has discovered a new segment, this might be an opportunity. If it finds that competitors plan new moves into segments now served by the company, it will be forewarned and, hopefully, forearmed.

Identifying competitors' strategies

The more that one firm's strategy resembles another firm's strategy, the more the two firms compete. In most industries, the competitors can be sorted into groups that pursue different strategies. A **strategic group** is a group of firms in an industry following the same or a similar strategy in a given target market. For example, in the major appliance industry, Bosch and Zanussi belong to the same strategic group. Each produces a full line of medium-price appliances supported by good service. In contrast, Smeg and Miele belong to a different strategic group. They produce a narrower line of higher-quality appliances, offer a higher level of service and charge a premium price.

Some important insights emerge from identifying strategic groups. For example, if a company enters a strategic group, the members of that group become its key competitors. Thus, if the company enters a group containing Bosch and Zanussi, it can succeed only if it develops strategic advantages over these two companies.

Although competition is most intense within a strategic group, there is also rivalry among groups. First, some strategic groups may appeal to overlapping customer segments. For example, no matter what their strategy, all major appliance manufacturers will go after the apartment and homebuilders segment. Second, customers may not see much difference in the offers of different groups; they may see little difference in quality between Bosch and Zanussi. Finally, members of one strategic group might expand into new strategy segments. Thus, Bosch's Logixx Premium Range of appliances compete in the premium-quality, premium-price line with Smeg and Miele.

The company needs to look at all the dimensions that identify strategic groups within the industry. It must understand how each competitor delivers value to its customers. It needs to know each competitor's product quality, features and mix; customer services; pricing policy; distribution coverage; sales force strategy; and advertising and sales promotion programmes. And it must study the details of each competitor's R&D, manufacturing, purchasing, financial and other strategies.

Assessing competitors' strengths and weaknesses

Marketers need carefully to assess each competitor's strengths and weaknesses to answer a critical question: What *can* our competitors do? As a first step, companies can gather data on each competitor's goals, strategies and performance over the past few years. Admittedly, some of this information will be hard to obtain. For example, B-to-B marketers find it hard to estimate competitors' market shares because they do not have the same syndicated data services that are available to consumer packaged-goods companies.

Companies normally learn about their competitors' strengths and weaknesses through secondary data, personal experience and word of mouth. They can also conduct primary marketing research with customers, suppliers and dealers. Or they can **benchmark** themselves against other firms, comparing one company's products and processes to those of competitors or leading firms in other industries to identify best practices and find ways to improve quality and performance. Benchmarking has become a powerful tool for increasing a company's competitiveness.

Estimating competitors' reactions

Next, the company wants to know: What *will* our competitors do? A competitor's objectives, strategies, strengths and weaknesses go a long way toward explaining its likely actions. They also suggest its likely reactions to company moves, such as price cuts, promotion increases or new product introductions. In addition, each competitor has a certain philosophy of doing business, a certain internal culture and guiding beliefs. Marketing managers need a deep understanding of a given competitor's mentality if they want to anticipate how the competitor will act or react.

Each competitor reacts differently. Some do not react quickly or strongly to a competitor's move. They may feel their customers are loyal, they may be slow in noticing the move, or they may lack the funds to react. Some competitors react only to certain types of moves and not to others. Other competitors react swiftly and strongly to any action. Thus, Unilever does not allow a competitor's

Strategic group—A group of firms in an industry following the same or a similar strategy.

Benchmarking—The process of comparing one company's products and processes to those of competitors or leading firms in other industries to identify best practices and find ways to improve quality and performance.

new detergent to come easily into the market. Many firms avoid direct competition with Unilever and look for easier prey, knowing that Unilever will react fiercely if it is challenged.

In some industries, competitors live in relative harmony; in others, they fight constantly. Knowing how major competitors react gives the company clues on how best to attack competitors or how best to defend its current positions.

Selecting competitors to attack and avoid

A company has already largely selected its major competitors through prior decisions on customer targets, distribution channels and its marketing-mix strategy. Management now must decide which competitors to compete against most vigorously.

Strong or weak competitors

The company can focus on one of several classes of competitors. Most companies prefer to compete against weak competitors. This requires fewer resources and less time. But in the process, the firm may gain little. You could argue that the firm should also compete with strong competitors to sharpen its abilities. Moreover, even strong competitors have some weaknesses, and succeeding against them often provides greater returns.

Customer value analysis—An analysis conducted to determine what benefits target customers value and how they rate the relative value of various competitors' offers.

A useful tool for assessing competitor strengths and weaknesses is the **customer value analysis**. The aim of customer value analysis is to determine the benefits that target customers value and how customers rate the relative value of various competitors' offers. In conducting a customer value analysis, the company first identifies the major attributes that customers value and the importance customers place on these attributes. Next, it assesses its performance and the performance of its competitors on those valued attributes.

The key to gaining competitive advantage is to take each customer segment and examine how the company's offer compares to that of its major competitors. As shown in Figure 18.2, the company wants to find the 'strategic sweet spot' – the place where it meets customers' needs in a way that rivals can't. If the company's offer delivers greater value by exceeding the competitor's offer on important attributes, the company can charge a higher price and earn higher profits, or it can charge the same price and gain more market share. But if the company is seen as performing at a lower level than its major competitors on some important attributes, it must invest in strengthening those attributes or finding other important attributes where it can build a lead on its competitors.

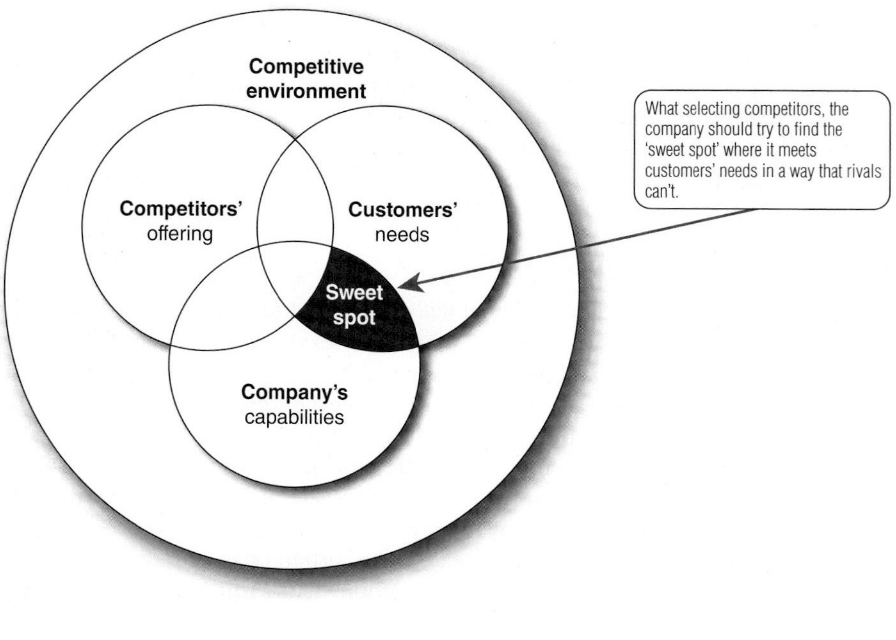
Competitive environment
Competitors' offering
Customers' needs
Sweet spot
Company's capabilities
What selecting competitors, the company should try to find the 'sweet spot' where it meets customers' needs in a way that rivals can't.

Figure 18.2 Strategic sweet spot versus competitors

Source: Adapted from David J. Collins and Michael G. Rukstad, 'Can You Say What Your Strategy Is?' *Harvard Business Review*, April 2008, p. 89. Copyright © 2008 by the President and Fellows of Harvard College; all rights reserved.

Close or distant competitors

Most companies will compete with close competitors – those that resemble them most – rather than distant competitors. Thus, Nike competes more against adidas than against Timberland or Keen. And Target competes against Walmart rather than Neiman Marcus or Nordstrom.

At the same time, the company may want to avoid trying to 'destroy' a close competitor. For example, in the late 1970s, Bausch & Lomb moved aggressively against other soft lens manufacturers with great success. However, this forced weak competitors to sell out to larger firms such as Johnson & Johnson (J&J). As a result, Bausch & Lomb then faced much larger competitors – and it suffered the consequences. J&J acquired Vistakon, a small nicher with only €25 million in annual sales. Backed by J&J's deep pockets, the small but nimble Vistakon developed and introduced its innovative Acuvue disposable lenses. With Vistakon leading the way, J&J is now the dominant contact lens maker, while Bausch & Lomb lags in third place. In this case, success in hurting a close rival brought in tougher competitors.[3]

Good or bad competitors

A company really needs and benefits from competitors. The existence of competitors results in several strategic benefits. Competitors may share the costs of market and product development and help legitimise new technologies. They may serve less-attractive segments or lead to more product differentiation. Finally, competitors may help increase total demand. For example, you might think that an independent coffeehouse surrounded by Starbucks stores might have trouble staying in business. But that's often not the case:[4]

> Coffee shop owners around the country have discovered that the corporate steamroller known as Starbucks is actually good for their business. It turns out that when a Starbucks comes to the neighbourhood, the result is new converts to the latte-drinking fold. When all those converts overrun the local Starbucks, the independents are there to catch the spillover. In fact, some independent storeowners now actually try to open their stores near a Starbucks if they can. That's certainly not how the coffee behemoth planned it. 'Starbucks is actually *trying* to be ruthless,' says the owner of a small coffeehouse chain. But 'in its predatory store-placement strategy, Starbucks has been about as lethal a killer as a fluffy bunny rabbit.'

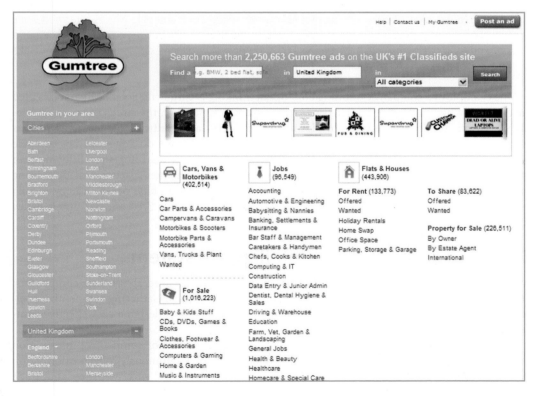

Bad competitors: Gumtree.com offers consumers a network of online classified advertisements and local/community websites. Such sites have helped to drive many traditional newspapers into bankruptcy in recent years.

However, a company may not view all its competitors as beneficial. An industry often contains *good competitors* and *bad competitors*. Good competitors play by the rules of the industry. Bad competitors, in contrast, break the rules. They try to buy share rather than earn it, take large risks, and play by their own rules.

For example, traditional newspapers face a lot of bad competitors these days. Digital services that overlap with traditional newspaper content are bad competitors because they offer for free real-time content that subscription-based newspapers printed once a day can't match. An example is Craigslist, the online community that lets local users post largely free classified ads. Started as a hobby about 15 years ago by Craig Newmark, Craigslist has never cared all that much about profit margins, and that's about as bad as the competitor can get. Another example is Gumtree.com, which is owned by Kijiji, eBay's internal classifieds group. Gumtree.com is popular across the UK, Ireland and Poland and has Kijiji affiliates across the rest of Europe. Essentially similar to Craigslist, Gumtree.com offers consumers a network of online classifieds advertisements and local/community websites. Consumers can browse local classified ads or post free or paid ads (depending on what they are advertising).

Finding uncontested market spaces

Rather than competing head to head with established competitors, many companies seek out unoccupied positions in uncontested market spaces. They try to create products and services for which there are no direct competitors. Called a 'blue ocean strategy', the goal is to make competition irrelevant:[5]

Companies have long engaged in head-to-head competition in search of profitable growth. They have flocked for competitive advantage, battled over market share, and struggled for differentiation. Yet in today's overcrowded industries, competing head-on results in nothing but a bloody 'red ocean' of rivals fighting over a shrinking profit pool. In their book *Blue Ocean Strategy: Uncontested Market Space and Make Competition Irrelevant*, two marketing professors contend that although most companies compete within such red oceans, the strategy isn't likely to create profitable growth in the future. Tomorrow's leading companies will succeed not by battling competitors but by creating 'blue oceans' of uncontested market space. Such strategic moves – termed *value innovation* – create powerful leaps in value for both the firm and its buyers, creating new demand and rendering rivals obsolete. By creating and capturing blue oceans, companies can largely take rivals out of the picture.

One example of a company exhibiting blue-ocean thinking is Cirque du Soleil, which reinvented the circus as a higher form of modern entertainment. At a time when the circus industry was declining, Cirque du Soleil innovated by eliminating high cost and controversial elements such as animal acts and instead focused on the theatrical experience. Cirque du Soleil did not compete with the then market leader Ringling Bros. and Barnum & Bailey; it was altogether different from anything that preceded it. Instead, it created an uncontested new market space that made existing competitors irrelevant. The results have been spectacular. Thanks to its blue-ocean strategy, in only its first 20 years, Cirque du Soleil achieved more revenues than Ringling Bros. and Barnum & Bailey achieved in its first 100 years.

Designing a competitive intelligence system

We have described the main types of information that companies need about their competitors. This information must be collected, interpreted, distributed and used. Gathering competitive intelligence can cost considerable money and time, so the company must design a cost-effective competitive intelligence system.

The competitive intelligence system first identifies the vital types of competitive information needed and the best sources of this information. Then, the system continuously collects information from the field (sales force, channels, suppliers, market research firms, websites and trade associations) and published data (government publications, speeches and online databases). Next the system checks the information for validity and reliability, interprets it and organises it in an appropriate way. Finally, it sends key information to relevant decision makers and responds to inquiries from managers about competitors.

With this system, company managers receive timely intelligence information about competitors in the form of reports, phone calls, e-mails, bulletins and newsletters. Managers can also connect with the system when they need to interpret a competitor's sudden move, when they want to know a competitor's weaknesses and strengths, or when they need to know how a competitor will respond to a planned company move.

Smaller companies that cannot afford to create formal competitive intelligence offices can assign specific executives to watch specific competitors. Thus, a manager who used to work for a competitor might follow that competitor closely; he or she would be the 'in-house expert' on that competitor. Any manager needing to know the thinking of a given competitor could contact the assigned in-house expert.

AUTHOR COMMENT

Now that we've identified competitors and know all about them, it's time to design a strategy for gaining competitive advantage.

COMPETITIVE STRATEGIES

Having identified and evaluated its major competitors, the company now must design broad competitive marketing strategies by which it can gain competitive advantage through superior customer value. But what broad marketing strategies might the company use? Which ones are best for a particular company or for the company's different divisions and products?

Approaches to marketing strategy

No one strategy is best for all companies. Each company must determine what makes the most sense given its position in its industry and its objectives, opportunities and resources. Even within a company, different strategies may be required for different businesses or products. Swiss-based pharmaceutical giant Novartis uses one marketing strategy for its leading brands in stable consumer markets, such as Nicotinell, and a different marketing strategy to medical professionals when marketing Glivec – a drug used to treat a range of cancers that generates revenue of €2.2 billion, potentially costing €70,000 per patient per year.

Companies also differ in how they approach the strategy-planning process. Many large firms develop formal competitive marketing strategies and implement them religiously. However, other companies develop strategy in a less formal and orderly fashion. Some companies, such as Harley-Davidson, Virgin Atlantic Airways and BMW's Mini Cooper unit, succeed by breaking many of the rules of marketing strategy. Such companies don't operate large marketing departments, conduct expensive marketing research, spell out elaborate competitive strategies and spend huge sums on advertising. Instead, they sketch out strategies on the fly, stretch their limited resources, live close to their customers and create more satisfying solutions to customer needs. They form buyer's clubs, use buzz marketing and focus on winning customer loyalty. It seems that not all marketing must follow in the footsteps of marketing giants such as Nestlé and Unilever.

In fact, approaches to marketing strategy and practice often pass through three stages: entrepreneurial marketing, formulated marketing and intrepreneurial marketing.

● *Entrepreneurial marketing.* Most companies are started by individuals who live by their wits. For example, Jamie Murray-Wells, founder of online spectacles business Glasses

549

Direct, launched Glasses Direct nine years ago. Mr Murray-Wells has a provocative style of marketing that shook up a sleepy industry. He also had a disruptive business model: selling cheap glasses online using prescriptions provided to customers by high street opticians as loss leaders for their own spectacle sales. In the start up phase of the company, Glasses Direct took a characteristically direct approach to competition by targeting the optician chain Specsavers. Glass Direct launched their Specspensive campaign that saw people wearing sheep outfits wandering around city centres handing out flyers that advised the public 'Don't get fleeced by Specsavers'. Accompanied by billboard ads, radio and other events the campaign proved newsworthy and great publicity for the fledgling firm.[6]

- *Formulated marketing.* As small companies achieve success, they inevitably move toward more formulated marketing. They develop formal marketing strategies and adhere to them closely. As brands grow, companies adopt a more formal approach to their marketing efforts. In the case of Glasses Direct, branding was improved, PR companies hired, sales promotion introduced, social media integrated and a number of other initiatives. Although Glasses Direct will no doubt remain less formal in its marketing than the Specsavers of the marketing world, as it grows it will adopt more developed marketing tools.

- *Intrepreneurial marketing.* Many large and mature companies get stuck in formulated marketing. They pore over the latest Nielsen numbers, scan market research reports, and try to fine-tune their competitive strategies and programmes. These companies sometimes lose the marketing creativity and passion they had at the start. They now need to re-establish within their companies the entrepreneurial spirit and actions that made them successful in the first place. They need to encourage more initiative and 'intrepreneurship' at the local level. They need to refresh their marketing strategies and try new approaches. Their brand and product managers need to get out of the office, start living with their customers, and visualise new and creative ways to add value to their customers' lives.

The bottom line is that there are many approaches to developing effective competitive marketing strategy. There will be a constant tension between the formulated side of marketing and the creative side. It is easier to learn the formulated side of marketing, which has occupied most of our attention in this book. But we have also seen how marketing creativity and passion in the strategies of many of the companies studied – whether small or large, new or mature – have helped to build and maintain success in the marketplace. With this in mind, we will now look at the broad competitive marketing strategies that companies can use.

Basic competitive strategies

Three decades ago, Michael Porter suggested four basic competitive positioning strategies that companies can follow – three winning strategies and one losing one.[7] The three winning strategies are as follows:

- *Overall cost leadership.* Here the company works hard to achieve the lowest production and distribution costs. Low costs let it price lower than its competitors and win a large market share. Carrefour and Walmart are leading practitioners of this strategy.
- *Differentiation.* Here the company concentrates on creating a highly differentiated product line and marketing programme so that it comes across as the class leader in the industry. Most customers would prefer to own this brand if its price is not too high. Mercedes cars and Bang & Olufsen follow this strategy in the car and audio goods markets, respectively.
- *Focus.* Here the company focuses its effort on serving a few market segments well rather than going after the whole market. For example, Ritz-Carlton focuses on the top 5 per cent of corporate and leisure travellers. Tetra Food supplies 80 per cent of pet tropical fish food. Similarly, Hohner owns a stunning 85 per cent of the harmonica market.

Companies that pursue a clear strategy – one of the above – are likely to perform well. The firm that carries out that strategy best will make the most profits. But firms that do not pursue a clear strategy – *middle-of-the-roaders* – do the worst. Ibis and Holiday Inn encountered difficult times because they did not stand out as the lowest in cost, highest in perceived value, or best in serving some market segment. Middle-of-the-roaders try to be good on all strategic counts but end up being not very good at anything.

Two marketing consultants, Michael Treacy and Fred Wiersema, offer a more customer-centred classification of competitive marketing strategies.[8] They suggest that companies gain leadership positions by delivering superior value to their customers. Companies can pursue any of three strategies – called *value disciplines* – for delivering superior customer value. These are:

- *Operational excellence.* The company provides superior value by leading its industry in price and convenience. It works to reduce costs and create a lean and efficient value-delivery system. It serves customers who want reliable, good-quality products or services cheaply and easily. Examples include Walmart, Ikea and Tesco.

- *Customer intimacy.* The company provides superior value by precisely segmenting its markets and tailoring its products or services to exactly match the needs of targeted customers. It specialises in satisfying unique customer needs through a close relationship with and intimate knowledge of the customer. It builds detailed customer databases for segmenting and targeting and empowers its marketing people to respond quickly to customer needs. Customer-intimate companies serve customers who are willing to pay a premium to get precisely what they want. They will do almost anything to build long-term customer loyalty and capture lifetime customer value. Examples include Lexus, British Airways, Visa and Ritz-Carlton.

- *Product leadership.* The company provides superior value by offering a continuous stream of leading-edge products or services. It aims to make its own and competing products obsolete. Product leaders are open to new ideas, relentlessly pursue new solutions and work to get new products to market quickly. They serve customers who want state-of-the-art products and services, regardless of the costs in terms of price or inconvenience. Examples include Apple, and Rolls Royce aero-engines.

Some companies successfully pursue more than one value discipline at the same time. For example, FedEx excels at both operational excellence and customer intimacy. However, such companies are rare – few firms can be the best at more than one of these disciplines. By trying to be good at all value disciplines, a company usually ends up being best at none.

Treacy and Wiersema found that leading companies focus and excel on a single value discipline, while meeting industry standards on the other two. Such companies design their entire value delivery network to single-mindedly support the chosen discipline. For example, Carrefour knows that customer intimacy and product leadership are important. Compared with other discounters, it offers very good customer service and an excellent product assortment. Still, it purposely offers less customer service and less product depth than other supermarkets which pursue customer intimacy. Instead, Carrefour focuses obsessively on operational excellence – on reducing costs and streamlining its order-to-delivery process to make it convenient for customers to buy just the right products at the lowest prices. By the same token, Ritz-Carlton wants to be efficient and employ the latest technologies. But what really sets the luxury hotel chain apart is its customer intimacy – Ritz-Carlton creates custom-designed experiences to coddle its customers.

Classifying competitive strategies as value disciplines is appealing. It defines marketing strategy in terms of the single-minded pursuit of delivering superior value to customers. Each value discipline defines a specific way to build lasting customer relationships.

Carrefour focuses obsessively on operational excellence – on reducing costs and streamlining its order-to-delivery process to make it convenient for customers to buy just the right products at the lowest prices.

Source: Alamy Images/Mike Finn-Kelcey

Competitive positions

Market leader—The firm in an industry with the largest market share.

Market challenger—A runner-up firm that is fighting hard to increase its market share in an industry.

Market follower—A runner-up firm that wants to hold its share in an industry without rocking the boat.

Market nicher—A firm that serves small segments that the other firms in an industry overlook or ignore.

Firms competing in a given target market, at any point in time, differ in their objectives and resources. Some firms are large, others small. Some have many resources, others are strapped for funds. Some are mature and established, others new and fresh. Some strive for rapid market share growth, others for long-term profits. And all these firms occupy different competitive positions in the target market.

We now examine competitive strategies based on the roles firms play in the target market – leader, challenger, follower or nicher. Suppose that an industry contains the firms shown in Figure 18.3. Forty per cent of the market is in the hands of the **market leader**, the firm with the largest market share. Another 30 per cent is in the hands of **market challengers**, runner-up firms that are fighting hard to increase their market share. Another 20 per cent is in the hands of **market followers**, other runner-up firms that want to hold their share without rocking the boat. The remaining 10 per cent is in the hands of **market nichers**, firms that serve small segments not being pursued by other firms.

Table 18.1 shows specific marketing strategies that are available to market leaders, challengers, followers and nichers.[9] Remember, however, that these classifications often do not apply to a whole company but only to its position in a specific industry. Large companies such as Unilever, Nestlé, GE, Microsoft or Disney might be leaders in some markets and nichers in others. For example, Unilever leads in many segments, such as hand soaps, but challenges P&G in other segments, such as laundry detergents and shampoo, and Kimberly-Clark in facial tissues. Such companies often use different strategies for different business units or products, depending on the competitive situations of each.

Market leader strategies

Most industries contain an acknowledged market leader. The leader has the largest market share and usually leads the other firms in price changes, new product introductions, distribution coverage and promotion spending. The leader may or may not be admired or respected, but other firms concede its dominance. Competitors focus on the leader as the company to challenge,

Table 18.1 Strategies for market leaders, challengers, followers and nichers

Market leader strategies	Market challenger strategies	Market follower strategies	Market nicher strategies
Expand total market	Full frontal attack	Follow closely	By customer, market, quality-price, service
Protect market share	Indirect attack	Follow at a distance	Multiple niching
Expand market share			

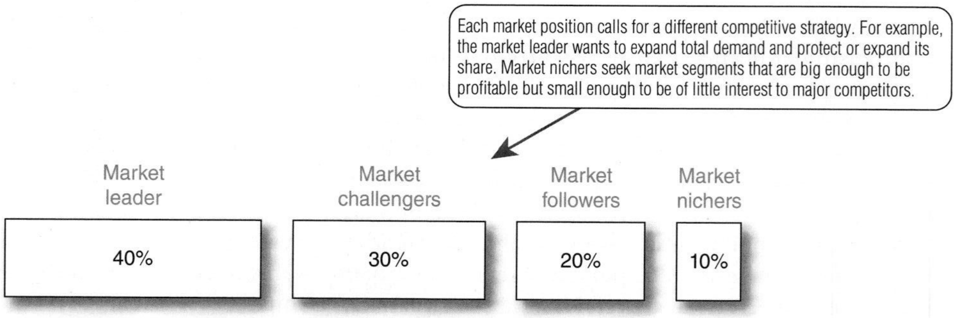

> Each market position calls for a different competitive strategy. For example, the market leader wants to expand total demand and protect or expand its share. Market nichers seek market segments that are big enough to be profitable but small enough to be of little interest to major competitors.

Market leader	Market challengers	Market followers	Market nichers
40%	30%	20%	10%

Figure 18.3 Competitive market positions and roles

imitate, or avoid. Some of the best-known market leaders are Facebook (social networking), L'Oreal (cosmetics), McDonald's (fast food), Amazon (online books), Coca-Cola (beverages), Microsoft (computer software), Caterpillar (earth-moving equipment) and Google (Internet search services).

A leader's life is not easy. It must maintain a constant watch. Other firms keep challenging its strengths or trying to take advantage of its weaknesses. The market leader can easily miss a turn in the market and plunge into second or third place. A product innovation may come along and hurt the leader (as when Apple developed the iPod and took the market lead from Sony's Walkman portable audio devices). The leader might grow arrogant or complacent and misjudge the competition (as when Sainsburys lost its lead of the UK grocery market to Tesco). Or the leader might look old-fashioned against new and peppier rivals (as when the Sony Walkman lost serious ground to the funky, stylish Apple iPods).

To remain number one, leading firms can take any of three actions: (1) they can find ways to expand total demand; (2) they can protect their current market share through good defensive and offensive actions; and (3) they can try to expand their market share further, even if market size remains constant.

Expanding total demand

The leading firm normally gains the most when the total market expands. If Europeans eat more fast food, McDonald's stands to gain the most because it holds more than three times the fast-food market share of its nearest competitors: Subway and Burger King. If McDonald's can convince more Europeans that fast food is the best eating-out choice in these value-oriented times, it will benefit more than its competitors.

Market leaders can expand the market by developing new users, new uses and more usage of its products. They usually can find new users or untapped market segments in many places. For example, Issey Miyake or Jean Paul Gaultier could both sell more perfume to men if they could convince men in existing markets who don't use perfume (disguised as aftershave) to use their products or sell their perfume in markets where the wearing of male fragrances is less popular.

Marketers can expand markets by discovering and promoting new uses for the product. For example, Nintendo is now expanding into classrooms with its popular handheld Nintendo DS game system:[10]

A giggly class of 32 seventh graders uses plastic pens to spell words like 'hamburger' and 'cola' on the touch screen – the key feature of the Nintendo DS – following an electronic voice from the handheld console. It's a sort of high-tech spelling test. When the student gets the spelling right, the word *good* pops up on the screen, and the student proceeds to the next exercise. 'It's fun,' says a 12-year-old student. The instructor acknowledges that she has never before seen the kind of enthusiastic concentration the DS classes have inspired in her students.

Nintendo, never content to create gaming products that are simply for gaming, is taking its portable DS system to school. Using a PC, teachers can interact with students with Wi-Fi, beaming questions, visual aids and other information to a special DS Classroom cartridge in students' hand-held devices. Teachers can receive responses from students in real time, instantly monitoring which students answered correctly and which are falling behind. The system can even help grade tests as they are happening, letting students see their performance immediately after finishing a test. Creating classroom uses substantially expands the market for market leader Nintendo's gaming products.

Finally, market leaders can encourage *more usage* by convincing people to use the product more often or use more per occasion. For example, Nestlé urges people to eat Carnation branded desserts and milk products more often by running ads containing new recipes. It also offers a tailored web-site (www.carnation.co.uk) that lets visitors search for or exchange recipes, sign up for a newsletter, and even watch podcasts (rather predictably listed as 'pud casts') of famous chefs and celebrities making Carnation-based puddings and snacks.

Protecting market share

While trying to expand total market size, the leading firm also must protect its current business against competitors' attacks. BMW versus Lexus; Caterpillar against Komatsu; and BA against Virgin Atlantic.

What can the market leader do to protect its position? First, it must prevent or fix weaknesses that provide opportunities for competitors. It must always fulfil its value promise. Its prices must remain consistent with the value that customers see in the brand. It must work tirelessly to keep strong relationships with valued customers. The leader should 'plug holes' so that competitors do not jump in.

But attack is the best form of defence and the best response is *continuous innovation*. The market leader refuses to be content with the way things are and leads the industry in new products, customer services, distribution effectiveness, promotion and cost cutting. It keeps increasing its competitive effectiveness and value to customers. And when attacked by challengers, the market leader reacts decisively. For example, in the laundry products category, Unilever faced huge problems breaking into the US market because of the decisive actions of the US market leader P&G.

In one of the most fabled marketing battles of the past century, P&G won the laundry war because it was bigger, better, more focused and more aggressive than challenger Unilever. Entering this millennium, even though its US laundry detergent market share was well over 50 per cent, P&G kept raining blows on Unilever and all other comers with stepped-up product launches. By 2007, P&G was outgunning Unilever on US media spending for laundry brands by €153 million to €17 million. New products such as Tide with Downey, Tide Coldwater and the scent-focused Simple Pleasures line-up for Tide and Downey helped P&G steadily gain a share point or two per year, so that by 2008, it owned a 62.5 per cent share of the €2.6 billion laundry-detergent market to Unilever's 12.9 per cent (including Unilever's All, Wisk and Surf brands). It had an even bigger lead in fabric softeners – 66 per cent to Unilever's 8.4 per cent (Unilever's Snuggle brand). Globally, P&G went from being the number-two laundry player in the early 1990s to a dominant market leader, with a global market share of 34 per cent to Unilever's 17 per cent. In the face of P&G's relentless assault, in mid-2008, Unilever finally threw in the towel and sold its North American detergents business.[11]

Expanding market share

Market leaders also can grow by increasing their market shares further. In many markets, small market share increases mean very large sales increases. For example, in the European beer market, a 1 per cent increase in market share is worth €2 billion; in the spirits market it is worth €1 billion.

Studies have shown that, on average, profitability rises with increasing market share. Because of these findings, many companies have sought expanded market shares to improve profitability. GE, for example, declared that it wants to be at least number one or two in each of its markets or else get out. GE shed its computer, air-conditioning, small appliances and television businesses because it could not achieve top-dog position in those industries.

However, some studies have found that many industries contain one or a few highly profitable large firms, several profitable and more focused firms, and a large number of medium-sized firms with poorer profit performance. It appears that profitability increases as a business gains share relative to competitors in its *served market*. For example, Lexus holds only a small share of the total car market, but it earns a high profit because it is the leading brand in the luxury-performance car segment. And it has achieved this high share in its served market because it does other things right, such as producing high-quality products, creating good service experiences and building close customer relationships.

Companies must not think, however, that gaining increased market share will automatically improve profitability. Much depends on their strategy for gaining increased share. There are many high-share companies with low profitability and many low-share companies with high profitability.

The cost of buying higher market share may far exceed the returns. Higher shares tend to produce higher profits only when unit costs fall with increased market share or when the company offers a superior-quality product and charges a premium price that more than covers the cost of offering higher quality.

Market challenger strategies

Firms that are second, third or lower in an industry are sometimes quite large, such as Royal Dutch Shell, Peugeot, Quick Restaurants, Samsung and Hertz. These runner-up firms can adopt one of two competitive strategies: they can challenge the market leader and other competitors in an aggressive bid for more market share (market challengers), or they can play along with competitors and not rock the boat (market followers).

A market challenger must first define which competitors to challenge and its strategic objective. The challenger can attack the market leader, a high-risk but potentially high-gain strategy. Its goal might be to take over market leadership. Or the challenger's objective may simply be to wrest more market share.

Although it might seem that the market leader has the most going for it, challengers often have what some strategists call a 'second-mover advantage'. The challenger observes what has made the market leader successful and improves on it. For example, BookStacks or books.com, founded by Charles Stack in 1991 and launched online in 1992, is credited as being the first online book store. However, in 1994, Jeff Bezos founded Amazon and subsequently launched online in 1995. After rapidly expanding the product line (to, for example, DVDs and CDs), the second-mover advantage of Amazon is reflected in their turnover which is about three times that of Stacks Inc.

In fact, challengers often become market leaders by imitating and improving on the ideas of pioneering processors. For example, Chrysler invented the modern minivan and led in that market for more than a decade. However, then-followers Honda and Toyota improved on the concept and now dominate the minivan market. Similarly, McDonald's first imitated and then mastered the fast-food system first pioneered by White Castle. And founder Sam Walton admitted that Walmart borrowed most of its practices from discount pioneer Sol Price's FedMart and Price Club chains and then perfected them to become today's dominant retailer.[12]

Alternatively, the challenger can avoid the leader and instead challenge firms its own size or smaller local and regional firms. These smaller firms may be underfinanced and not serving their customers well. Several of the major beer companies grew to their present size not by challenging large competitors but by gobbling up small local or regional competitors. If the challenger goes after a small local company, its objective may be to put that company out of business. The important point remains: the challenger must choose its opponents carefully and have a clearly defined and attainable objective.

How can the market challenger best attack the chosen competitor and achieve its strategic objective? It may launch a full *frontal attack*, matching the competitor's product, advertising, price and distribution efforts. It attacks the competitor's strengths rather than its weaknesses. The outcome depends on who has the greater strength and endurance. PepsiCo challenges Coca-Cola in this way.

If the market challenger has fewer resources than the competitor, however, a frontal attack makes little sense. Thus, many new market entrants avoid frontal attacks, knowing that market leaders can head them off with ad blitzes, price wars and other retaliations. Rather than challenging head-on, the challenger can make an *indirect attack* on the competitor's weaknesses or on gaps in the competitor's market coverage. It can carve out toeholds using tactics that established leaders have trouble responding to or choose to ignore. For example, compare the vastly different strategies of two different European challengers – Virgin Drinks and Red Bull – when they entered the US soft drink market in the late 1990s against market leaders Coca-Cola and PepsiCo.[13]

Virgin Drinks took on the leaders head-on, launching its own cola, advertising heavily and trying to get into all the same retail outlets that stocked the leading brands. At Virgin Cola's launch,

Virgin CEO Richard Branson even drove a tank through a wall of rivals' cans in New York's Times Square to symbolise the war he wished to wage on the big, established rivals. However, Coca-Cola's and PepsiCo's vicelike grip on US shelf space proved impossible for Virgin Drinks to break. Although Virgin Drinks is still around, it has never gained more than a 1 per cent share of the US cola market.

Red Bull, by contrast, tackled the leaders indirectly. It entered the US soft drink market with a niche product: a carbonated energy drink retailing at about twice what you would pay for a Coke or Pepsi. It started by selling Red Bull through unconventional outlets not dominated by the market leaders, such as bars and nightclubs, where 20-somethings gulped down the caffeine-rich drink so they could dance all night. After gaining a loyal following, Red Bull used the pull of high margins to elbow its way into the corner store, where it now sits in refrigerated bins within arm's length of Coke and Pepsi. Despite rapidly intensifying competition in the United States, Red Bull captures a 33 per cent share of the energy drink market.

Market follower strategies

Not all runner-up companies want to challenge the market leader. The leader never takes challenges lightly. If the challenger's lure is lower prices, improved service or additional product features, the market leader can quickly match these to defuse the attack. The leader probably has more staying power in an all-out battle for customers. For example, a few years ago, when Walmart/Asda in the UK renewed its low-price 'Saving you Money Everyday' campaign, directly challenging Tesco, the latter immediately responded with its own cut-price campaign. Thus, many firms (even if they are market dominant elsewhere – as Walmart is in the US) prefer to follow rather than challenge the market leader.

A follower can gain many advantages. The market leader often bears the huge expenses of developing new products and markets, expanding distribution and educating the market. By contrast, as with challengers, the market follower can learn from the market leader's experience. It can copy or improve on the leader's products and programmes, usually with much less investment.

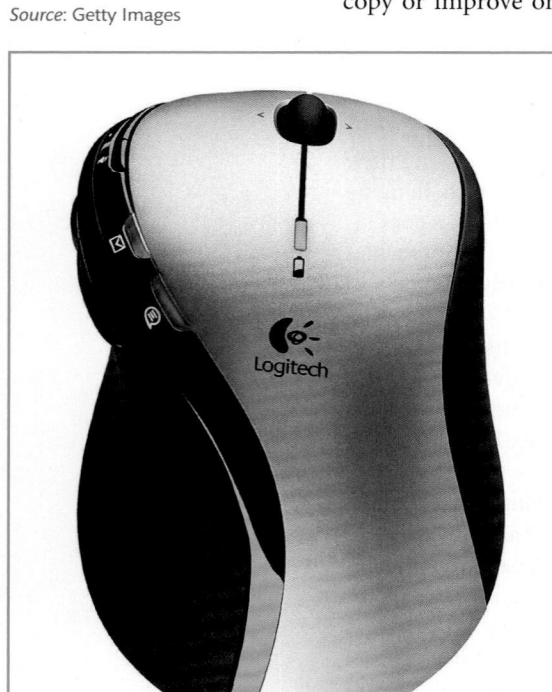

Nichers: Logitech is only a fraction the size of giant Microsoft. Yet, through skilful niching, it dominates the PC mouse market, with Microsoft as its runner-up.

Source: Getty Images

Although the follower will probably not overtake the leader, it often can be as profitable.

Following is not the same as being passive or a carbon copy of the market leader. A follower must know how to hold current customers and win a fair share of new ones. It must find the right balance between following closely enough to win customers from the market leader but following at enough of a distance to avoid retaliation. Each follower tries to bring distinctive advantages to its target market – location, services, financing. A follower is often a major target of attack by challengers. Therefore, the market follower must keep its manufacturing costs and prices low or its product quality and services high. It must also enter new markets as they open up.

Market nicher strategies

Almost every industry includes firms that specialise in serving market niches. Instead of pursuing the whole market or even large segments, these firms target sub-segments. Nichers are often smaller firms with limited resources. But smaller divisions of larger firms also may pursue niching strategies. Firms with low shares of the total market can be highly successful and profitable through smart niching.

Why is niching profitable? The main reason is that the market nicher ends up knowing the target customer group so well that it meets their needs better than other firms that casually sell to that niche. As a result, the nicher can charge a substantial mark-up over costs because of the added value. Whereas the mass marketer achieves high volume, the nicher achieves high margins.

Nichers try to find one or more market niches that are safe and profitable. An ideal market niche is big enough to be profitable and has growth potential. It is one that the firm can serve effectively. Perhaps most importantly, the niche is of little interest to major competitors. A firm can build the skills and customer goodwill to defend itself against a major competitor as the niche grows and becomes more attractive. For example, computer mouse and interface device maker Logitech is only a fraction the size of giant Microsoft. Yet, through skilful niching, it dominates the PC mouse market, with Microsoft as its runner-up. Another example is Sence Copenhagen, the niche jewellery makers:

Marnix Etterna and Christian Priess are the Dutch and Danish founders of Sence Copenhagen – the tiny Switzerland-based costume jewellery maker. Costume jewellery may seem an odd choice for two men, nearing middle age, lacking a design or fashion background. 'We'd considered various things, including consumer and industrial products, but decided jewellery was best,' says Mr Priess. Their decision-making was assisted by his wife's design background, helping them identify a niche. 'It's a sector with great fundamentals, but no dominant players. There are dozens of small and often extremely creative players, but sometimes lacking business skills,' says Mr Priess. 'Plus, the financial costs of entry were relatively low . . . But we knew we wouldn't make any money in the first two years.' Sales, which started in Switzerland and Denmark, have expanded to Germany and the Benelux countries. 'We thought we'd start with Switzerland as it's our base and it's relatively small. We reckoned if we couldn't make it here, we shouldn't try anywhere else,' says Mr Priess. Sence Copenhagen is targeting a niche its founders call 'designer jewellery,' far from the diamond-studded rings in the windows of branded jewellery, but equally distinct from the cheap trinkets popularly known as 'costume jewellery.' 'We felt there was a space between "real jewellery" – meaning solid gold rings and precious stones and the "costume jewellery" sold in women's fashion shops,' explains Mr Priess. Sence's jewellery retails in Switzerland for (€30 – €100) and uses tin, bronze or zinc, which is then gold or rhodium plated. While some 'stones' are acrylic, the company has aimed for a higher-quality feel by using glass and, occasionally, semi-precious stones. 'We like to think we've invented a new marketing term, covering a niche just below "real" jewellery,' says Mr Etterna. The target is younger, fashion-conscious women, seeking something classy and contemporary to wear with their more conventional jewellery. Obvious, and much bigger, rivals are the jewellery collections of brands such as Guess, or specialists such as Dyberg/Kern and Pilgrim, two similar, but much larger, Danish brands.[14]

The key idea in niching is specialisation. A market nicher can specialise along any of several market, customer, product or marketing mix lines. For example, it can specialise in serving one type of *end user*, as when a law firm specialises in the criminal, civil or business law markets. The nicher can specialise in serving a given *customer-size group*. Many nichers specialise in serving small and midsize customers who are neglected by the majors.

Some nichers focus on one or a few *specific customers*, selling their entire output to a single company, such as Unilever or Nestlé. Still other nichers specialise by *geographic market*, selling only in a certain locality, region or area of the world. *Quality-price* nichers operate at the low or high end of the market. For example, HP specialises in the high-quality, high-price end of the hand-calculator market. Finally, *service nichers* offer services not available from other firms. For example, Friends Reunited is an online social networking site that specialises in selling user access to user-generated data which aims to reunite people with a common past school, college, university or job.

Niching carries some major risks. For example, the market niche may dry up, or it might grow to the point that it attracts larger competitors. That is why many companies practise *multiple niching*. By developing two or more niches, a company increases its chances for survival. Even some large firms prefer a multiple niche strategy to serving the total market.

BALANCING CUSTOMER AND COMPETITOR ORIENTATIONS

Competitor-centred company—A company whose moves are mainly based on competitors' actions and reactions.

Whether a company is a market leader, challenger, follower or nicher, it must watch its competitors closely and find the competitive marketing strategy that positions it most effectively. And it must continually adapt its strategies to the fast-changing competitive environment. This question now arises: Can the company spend *too* much time and energy tracking competitors, damaging its customer orientation? The answer is yes. A company can become so competitor centred that it loses its even more important focus on maintaining profitable customer relationships.

A **competitor-centred company** is one that spends most of its time tracking competitors' moves and market shares and trying to find strategies to counter them. This approach has some pluses and minuses. On the positive side, the company develops a fighter orientation, watches for weaknesses in its own position and searches out competitors' weaknesses. On the negative side, the company becomes too reactive. Rather than carrying out its own customer relationship strategy, it bases its own moves on competitors' moves. As a result, it may end up simply matching or extending industry practices rather than seeking innovative new ways to create more value for customers.

Customer-centred company—A company that focuses on customer developments in designing its marketing strategies.

A **customer-centred company**, by contrast, focuses more on customer developments in designing its strategies. Clearly, the customer-centred company is in a better position to identify new opportunities and set long-run strategies that make sense. By watching customer needs evolve, it can decide what customer groups and what emerging needs are the most important to serve. Then it can concentrate its resources on delivering superior value to target customers.

Market-centred company—A company that pays balanced attention to both customers and competitors in designing its marketing strategies.

In practice, today's companies must be **market-centred companies**, watching both their customers and their competitors. But they must not let competitor watching blind them to customer focusing.

Figure 18.4 shows that companies might have any of four orientations. First, they might be product oriented, paying little attention to either customers or competitors. Next, they might be customer oriented, paying attention to customers. In the third orientation, when a company starts to pay attention to competitors, it becomes competitor oriented. Today, however, companies need to be market oriented, paying balanced attention to both customers and competitors. Rather than simply watching competitors and trying to beat them on current ways of doing business, they need to watch customers and find innovative ways to build profitable customer relationships by delivering more customer value than competitors do.

Market-centred companies understand both customers and competitors. They build profitable customer relationships by delivering more customer value than competitors do.

Figure 18.4 Evolving company orientation

REVIEWING OBJECTIVES AND KEY TERMS

Today's companies face their toughest competition ever. Understanding customers is an important first step in developing strong customer relationships, but it's not enough. To gain competitive advantage, companies must use this understanding to design market offers that deliver more value than the offers of *competitors* seeking to win over the same customers. This chapter examined how firms analyse their competitors and design effective competitive marketing strategies.

OBJECTIVE 1 Discuss the need to understand competitors as well as customers through competitor analysis (pp. 543–549).

To prepare an effective marketing strategy, a company must consider its competitors as well as its customers. Building profitable customer relationships requires satisfying target consumer needs better than competitors *do*. A company must continuously analyse competitors and develop competitive marketing strategies that position it effectively against competitors and give it the strongest possible competitive advantage.

Competitor analysis first involves identifying the company's major competitors, using both an industry-based and a market-based analysis. The company then gathers information on competitors' objectives, strategies, strengths and weaknesses, and reaction patterns. With this information in hand, it can select competitors to attack or avoid. Competitive intelligence must be collected, interpreted and distributed continuously. Company marketing managers should be able to obtain full and reliable information about any competitor affecting their decisions.

OBJECTIVE 2 Explain the fundamentals of competitive marketing strategies based on creating value for customers (pp. 549–557).

Which competitive marketing strategy makes the most sense depends on the company's industry and on whether it is a market leader, challenger, follower or nicher. The *market leader* has to mount strategies to expand the total market, protect market share and expand its market share. A *market challenger* is a firm that tries aggressively to expand its market share by attacking the leader, other runner-up companies or smaller firms in the industry. The challenger can select from a variety of direct or indirect attack strategies.

A *market follower* is a runner-up firm that chooses not to rock the boat, usually from fear that it stands to lose more than it might gain. But the follower is not without a strategy and seeks to use its particular skills to gain market growth. Some followers enjoy a higher rate of return than the leaders in their industry. A *market nicher* is a smaller firm that is unlikely to attract the attention of larger firms. Market nichers often become specialists in some end use, customer size, specific customer, geographic area or service.

OBJECTIVE 3 Illustrate the need for balancing customer and competitor orientations in becoming a truly market-centred organisation (p. 558).

A competitive orientation is important in today's markets, but companies should not overdo their focus on competitors. Companies are more likely to be hurt by emerging consumer needs and new competitors than by existing competitors. *Market-centred companies* that balance customer and competitor considerations are practicing a true market orientation.

NAVIGATING THE KEY TERMS

Discussing the concepts

1. Which point of view is best for identifying competitors – industry or market? (AACSB: Communication)
2. Explain how having strong competitors can benefit a company. (AACSB: Communication; Reflective Thinking)
3. Name and describe the three basic winning competitive strategies espoused by Michael Porter. (AACSB: Communication)
4. Describe the three value disciplines for delivering superior customer value and explain why classifying competitive strategies in this way is appealing. (AACSB: Communication)
5. Discuss the advantages of being a market follower and the factors to consider when pursuing this strategy. (AACSB: Communication)
6. Compare and contrast product-oriented, competitor-centred, customer-centred and market-centred companies.

Applying the concepts

1. Form a small group and discuss the differences between increasing market share and increasing customer share. What factors should a company consider when deciding on which to focus? (AACSB: Communication; Reflective Thinking)
2. Research 'blue ocean strategy' and discuss examples of companies that have succeeded in pursuing this strategy. Do companies developing uncontested marketspaces necessarily have to be innovative upstarts? (AACSB: Communication; Reflective Thinking)
3. Identify a company following a market niche strategy in each of the following industries: higher education, apparel, soft drinks and rental cars. (AACSB: Communication; Reflective Thinking)

Focus on technology

Apple has hit three home runs in less than ten years – the iPod, iPhone and iPad. Apple sold three million iPads within 80 days of its release, and there were 25,000 iPad-specific apps in Apple's App Store within six months. Like iPhone apps, many iPad apps are free because they display ads that produce revenues for developers. So far, Apple is not taking a cut on the ad revenues, and developers keep 70 per cent of the money that they take in from paid-for consumer applications. Publishers in Apple's iBook app keep 70 per cent of the money they take in. Consequently, Barnes and Noble's Nook and Amazon's Kindle increased the percentage of revenue publishers earn to 70 per cent as well. Forecasters are predicting that iPad sales in 2011 will reach 20 to 30 million, which has competitors worried.

1. Who are Apple's iPad competitors? What is Apple's competitive position in this industry? (AACSB: Communication; Reflective Thinking)
2. Why is Apple virtually giving away this platform to third-party applications developers? Wouldn't it be more profitable for Apple to generate more revenue from its App Store? (AACSB: Communication; Reflective Thinking)

Focus on ethics

Deconstruction experts eagerly anticipated the release of Apple's iPad. Some like Luke Soules wanted to be the first to get his hands on the device so that he could take it apart and analyse it – called 'teardowns' in the industry. He even spread video of his purchase and teardown on the Internet and bragged about feeding intimate information about the device's innards to folks before stores even opened. Although Soules' company, iFixit, makes teardown information public, most deconstruction firms provide data only to paying clients. Apple's gadgets are particularly tricky to crack; there are no screws. The tool of choice for prying open the iPhone was a dental pick. Apple is very secretive about the components that make up its gadgets and some components carry the Apple name rather than the manufacturer's name. However, experts armed with X-ray machines and scanning electron microscopes, with a little bit of sleuthing mixed in, are often able to determine the origins and cost of parts.

1. Using Google, search for 'iPad teardown' to find what information is available on the iPad. Is it ethical to teardown a product and share that information publicly or sell it to other firms? (AACSB: Communication; Ethical Reasoning; Reflective Thinking)
2. iFixit used the iPad teardown as a publicity stunt to promote its repair business. Apple is a 'closed company' and doesn't want users repairing its products. In fact, users cannot replace a battery on an iPad; they have to return it to Apple and purchase a refurbished device for around £73 plus shipping. Replacing a battery is not as simple as popping in a new one because the batteries are soldered in. Is it right for Apple to be so restrictive regarding what customers can do with the product? (AACSB: Communication; Ethical Reasoning; Reflective Thinking)

Marketing & the economy

British Airways

British Airways offers airline services in all segments. Yet a significant portion of its business targets first-class and business-class travellers. Private 'demi-cabins' are available on its 747s, each with comfortable beds, an LCD widescreen for in-flight entertainment and power outlets. Recently, British Airways launched a business-class only service between New York and London City, with planes configured with only 32 roomy seats that spread fully flat.

The travel industry has suffered amidst a weak economy. Low-fare airlines have struggled, and premium services have felt significant air travel reductions. British Airways has seen first- and business-classes seats decline as a percentage of overall tickets sold. Passengers flying premium services have opted to pay less and settle for non-refundable tickets. As a result, British Airways endured an 11 per cent sales decline in 2009 and a net loss of over £584 million, which was its worst performance since it went public in 1987. Things looked a little better in 2010 as IAG (now the parent company of British Airways) posted profits of around £21 million. In this regard, the travel industry is seeing signs of renewed life, which has flyers returning to premium services to some extent.

1. How should British Airways handle a decline in premium air travel?

2. After such an extended economic downturn, when the economy does recover, will air travellers fully return to their pre-recession travel spending habits?

3. Should British Airways be content with signs that the airline industry is recovering? What could it do to better position itself for similar cycles in the future?

Marketing by the numbers

The base Wi-Fi 16 GB iPad2 was introduced at around £570, but like all electronic products, Apple is likely to lower the price within a year or two of introduction. The 16 GB iPad's cost of goods sold is £250. Refer to Appendix 2 to answer the following questions:

1. Calculate Apple's gross margin per unit and gross margin as a percentage of sales for the 16 GB iPad2. What is Apple's gross margin if the company sells 10 million iPads? (AACSB: Communication; Analytical Reasoning)

2. What will happen to the gross margin generated by the iPad if Apple reduces the price by £100? (AACSB: Communication; Analytical Reasoning)

REFERENCES

1 This case study draws heavily on the excellent case studies and analyses (including quotes and other information) of Claer Barrett, 'Fast fashion for fast consumers', *Financial Times* (21 February 2011), www.ft.com/cms/s/0/8c81c140-3de9-11e0-99ac-00144feabdc0.html#ixzz1abOgIc5i, accessed October 2011; Claer Barrett, 'Global growth drives Asos sales', *Financial Times* (14 July 2011), www.ft.com/cms/s/0/b3c82d3e-ae2d-11e0-8752-00144feabdc0.html#ixzz1aawE9FfZ, accessed October 2011; Esther Bintliff, 'Asos aims to wrest the web crown from Next', *Financial Times* (12 March 2010), www.ft.com/cms/s/0/0bd29f9e-2e02-11df-b85c-00144feabdc0.html#ixzz1aayqB0Pc, accessed October 2011; Hugo Greenhalgh, 'Beauty in the eye of the web browser', *Financial Times* (1 August 2011), www.ft.com/cms/s/0/f9767e06-b464-11e0-9eb8-00144feabdc0.html#ixzz1aaxTS170, accessed October 2011; Fiona Harkin, 'Trying on the future', *Financial Times* (23 September 2011), www.ft.com/cms/s/0/f8b8dc94-e547-11e0-85ze-00144feabdc0.html#ixzz1aawK7Jae, accessed October 2011; Mark Wembridge and Claer Barrett, 'International expansion boosts Asos', *Financial Times* (13 April 2011), www.ft.com/cms/s/0/90d6de4-65ae-11e0-baee-00144feab49a.html#ixzz1aaw3D5K6, accessed October 2011.

2 Example adapted from information found in Frank James 'Postal service quarterly losses surge; Internet gets blamed' (5 August 2009), www.NPR.org/blogs/thetwoway/2009/08/postal_service_quarterly_losse.html, accessed October 2011; and 'Postal facts: facts and figures about your postal service'; and Brian Groom, Royal Mail losses cast doubt on sell-off, *Financial Times* (14 June 2011), www.ft.com/cms/s/0/a64898b6-9682-11e0-afc5-00144feab49a.html#ixzz1U4bQykWD, accessed October 2011.

3 See 'Bausch & Lomb', www.wikinvest.com/wiki/Bausch_&_Lomb, accessed October 2011.

4 Adapted from Taylor Clark, 'Who's afraid of the big bad Starbucks?', *The Week* (18 January 2008), p. 46.

5 Adapted from information found in 'Blue ocean strategy: making the competition irrelevant', accessed at www.blueoceanstrategy.com, accessed June 2010; and W. Chan Kim and Renée Mauborgne, *Blue Ocean Strategy: How to Create Uncontested Market Space and Make Competition Irrelevant* (Boston, MA: Harvard Business Press, 2005). For other discussion and examples, see Kim and Mauborgne, 'How strategy shapes structure', *Harvard Business Review* (September 2009), pp. 72-90; and Mieke Mallaro, 'Is HME retailing a blue ocean? Could be', *HME News* (March 2010), p. 57.

6 Example from Jonathan Guthrie, 'The young ones, older and wiser', *Financial Times* (16 November 2010), www.ft.com/cms/s/0/192f198c-f1b2-11df-b55a-00144feab49a.html#ixzz1USFWbrs and see www.glassesdirect.co.uk/about/story, accessed October 2011.

7 Michael E. Porter, *Competitive Strategy: Techniques for Analyzing Industries and Competitors* (New York: Free Press, 1980), chapter 2; and Porter, 'What is strategy?', *Harvard Business Review* (November-December 1996), pp. 61-78. Also see Stefan Stern, 'May the force be with you and your plans for 2008', *Financial Times* (8 January 2008), p. 14; and 'Porter's generic strategies', www.quickmba.com/strategy/generic.shtml, accessed October 2011.

8 See Michael Treacy and Fred Wiersema, 'Customer intimacy and other value disciplines', *Harvard Business Review* (January–February 1993), pp. 84-93; Treacy and Wiersema, *The Discipline of Market Leaders: Choose Your Customers, Narrow Your Focus, Dominate Your Market* (New York: Perseus Press, 1997); Wiersema, *Customer Intimacy: Pick Your Partners, Shape Your Culture, Win Together* (Santa Monica, CA: Knowledge

VIDEO CASE

Umpqua Bank   MyMarketingLab

The retail banking industry has become very competitive. And with a few powerhouses dominating the market, how is a small bank to thrive? By differentiating itself through a competitive advantage that the big guys can't touch.

That's exactly what Umpqua has done. Step inside a branch of this Oregon-based community bank and you'll see immediately that this is not your typical Christmas club savings account/free toaster bank. Umpqua's business model has transformed banking from retail drudgery into a holistic experience. Umpqua has created an environment in which people just love to hang

out. It not only has its own music download service featuring local artists, it even has its own blend of coffee.

But beneath all these bells and whistles lies the core of what makes Umpqua so different – a rigorous service culture where every branch and employee gets measured on how well they serve customers. That's why every customer feels like they get the help and attention they need from employees.

After viewing the video featuring Umpqua Bank, answer the following questions about creating competitive advantage:

1. With what companies does Umpqua compete?
2. What is Umpqua's competitive advantage?
3. Will Umpqua be able to maintain this advantage in the long run? Why or why not?

---

[9] For more discussion, see Philip Kotler and Kevin Lane Keller, *Marketing Management*, 13th edn. (Upper Saddle River, NJ: Prentice Hall, 2009), chapter 11.

[10] Adapted from information found in Clay Dillow, 'Nintendo goes to school: DS classroom turns handheld console into teaching tool', *Fast Company* (12 June 2009), accessed at www.fastcompany.com/blog/clay-dillow/culture-buffet/nintendo-goes-school-ds-classroom-turns-handheld-console-teaching-to; Yuri Kageyama, 'In Tokyo school, Nintendo DS is an English teacher', *USA Today* (27 June 2008); Matt Peckham, 'The great Nintendo DS invasion', *PC World* (19 March 2010); and Raphael G. Slatter, 'Nintendo aims to get consoles in schools', *Associated Press* (19 March 2010), www.msnbc.msn.com/id/35952226/ns/technology_and_science-games.

[11] Adapted from information found in Jack Neff, 'Why Unilever lost the laundry war', *Advertising Age* (6 August 2007), pp. 1, 25; 'Bidders eye Unilever's US detergent arm', *Financial Times* (9 April 2008), p. 24; 'Unilever sells North American detergents unit', (28 July 2008), accessed at www.msnbc.msn.com/id/25884712.

[12] See Oded Shenkar, 'Defend your research: imitation is more valuable than innovation', *Harvard Business Review* (April 2010), pp. 28–29.

[13] Adapted from David J. Bryce and Jeffrey H. Dyer, 'Strategies to crack well-guarded markets', *Harvard Business Review* (May 2007), pp. 84–91; with information from Matthew Futterman, 'Red Bull's latest buzz: new soccer stadium', *Wall Street Journal* (18 March 2010).

[14] Example from Haig Simonian, 'Entrepreneurs with designs on a shining career', *Financial Times*, (31 May 2010), www.ft.com/cms/s/0/2d675cda-6c4b-11df-86c5-00144feab49a.html#ixzz1U4q4G0fJ, accessed October 2011.

Amazon's Kindle Fire versus Apple's iPad: let battle commence!

When Steve Jobs, the inspirational co-founder and visionary passed away in October 2011, the battle lines had already been drawn, the troops mobilised and the opening shots fired – Amazon had declared at war on Apple. While Steve Jobs had spent the last few years of his life fighting to secure the long-term position of the company he led, the rapidly changing world of mobile telephones, tablet computers and linked technology provides no guarantees of stability. That said, Apple begins the post-jobs era in a strong position, largely down to the drive and insight of Mr Jobs. The firm holds a truly massive war chest of £55 billion in net cash and equivalents on its balance sheet. Somewhat ironically, this is more than enough to buy the two top PC makers by revenue, Hewlett-Packard (HP) and Dell, outright.

These companies are among those scrambling to come up with a plausible rival to the iPad. This is a tough challenge given that the iPad tablet that has sold over 30 million units in less than two years and that Léo Apotheker, the outgoing chief executive of HP, admitted was transforming the world of personal computing. Already the Samsung Galaxy Tab is taking enough market share that Apple has accelerated a defence of its intellectual property in the courts. In the summer of 2011, Apple won a preliminary injunction barring Samsung from selling its Galaxy Tab in every European Union member nation (bar the Netherlands) – the most significant victory so far in an escalating legal clash between the two technology powerhouses. Samsung responded by threatening to seek injunctions against European sales of the iPhone 4S (launched the day before the death of Mr Jobs). Similar legal spats are occurring worldwide.

However, notwithstanding these irritating distractions, Apple's real competitor in the tablet market seems to be Amazon's Kindle Fire. Priced at a wafer-thin margin, near cost, of about £145, Amazon intends to demonstrate that a clever, persistent, well-planned and deep-pocketed competitor is able and willing to spend in the entire chain of distribution: not merely in term of content – music, video and books – but also via the devices on which they are consumed. Central to Amazon's technology approach is a stripped-down (literally and metaphorically) piece of hardware that is designed to fit neatly into the new world of 'cloud computing'. This modern view of technology sets it apart from a raft of other tablets, most of which have tried – and (largely) failed – to match the explicitly high-end iPad in design, looks, innovativeness and capabilities while lacking the enormous economies of scale that Apple has benefited from as the first-mover in the new tablet market.

After numerous rumours, denials, general malarkey and much shenanigans, Jeff Bezos, Amazon's founder and chief executive announced the launch of the Kindle Fire in the Autumn of 2011 (the actual product launch was two months later in time for Christmas sales). Mr Bezos's presentation was beautiful to watch – even hardened Apple fans found his arguments persuasive. As he strolled confidently through his presentation unveiling the Kindle Fire tablet computer, the target whose name hung unspoken in the air was 'Apple'. At one point, a surprisingly deadpan Mr Bezos pulled up a huge image of a dangling and ostentatiously white USB cable (a cable that millions of consumers have used to send content between their laptops and Apple's iPods and iPads). The media present audibly chuckled because they guessed what back-handed dig was coming. 'Syncing should be done invisibly, in the background, wirelessly – and it should actually work,' Mr Bezos said.

Commentators noted that Mr Bezos couldn't resist a little smirk as he announced the £145 price of his new competitor to the Apple iPad – and to the entire ecosystem of films, music, magazines and books that can appear on Apple's device: 'This is unbelievable value. We are building premium products at non-premium prices. We are determined to do that, and we are doing it.' This seems to sum-up Amazon's approach – their new business mantra and business model is simply *premium products at non-premium prices*. For Apple this seems to be a deliberate statement that Amazon intends to market devices that compete with Apple's and have similarly sophisticated technology but are much, much cheaper.

In many regards, Amazon has long been positioning itself as the online equivalent of Walmart, in that the firm has consistently attempted to operate at mass scale with wafer-thin margins which drive out smaller, higher-margin competitors. In some senses, Amazon's business model for their Kindle e-readers can be viewed as a strategic pilot test. That strategy of driving down prices to exert market power was evident in the updated Kindle e-readers, which now sell for around £99 each (or less). Traditional book shops and book publishers will be feeling even more threatened by Amazon than before. The Nook e-reader produced by Barnes & Noble (B&N) is already seen by many industry commentators as out-classed by the Kindle reader. Indeed, 17 years after Mr Bezos founded Amazon, taking on the then mighty US bookstore chain B&N, his company long ago left its detractors behind (most of which predicted Amazon's demise and B&N's continued dominance). Amazon is now worth £73 billion – 100 times the value of B&N, whose shares dropped

After a year littered with failed attempts to match the iPad, from the HP TouchPad to the BlackBerry PlayBook, it might seem rash (or, at least, ill-timed) for yet another pretender to kick sand in the face of the mighty Apple. This time, though, things feel different. With a technology architecture and business strategy that differ markedly from the earlier flops, according to tech industry analysts, Amazon has positioned itself to become the first true challenger to the iPad. Which company will win? Well time will tell. But it will be fun to watch . . . via a tablet, of course.

Questions for discussion

1. What advantage does Apple's iPad have over the Kindle Fire?
2. Conversely, what advantages has Amazon's new entrant Kindle Fire over the more elderly Apple iPad?
3. Why have other products fared so badly when competing with the iPad?
4. Which strategy is Amazon pursuing in its attack on Apple? Will it work? Why?

Sources: This case study draws heavily on the excellent case studies and analyses (including quotes and other information) of: John Gapper, 'Jeff Bezos of Amazon takes aim at Apple', *Financial Times* (28 September 2011), http://blogs.ft.com/businessblog/2011/09/jeff-bezos-of-amazon-takes-aim-at-apple/#ixzz1aYEijlqM, accessed October 2011; John Gapper and Barney Jopson, 'An inventor with Fire in his belly and Jobs in his sights', *Financial Times* (30 September 2011), www.ft.com/cms/s/0/4ada7e06-ea98-11e0-b0f5-00144feab49a.html#ixzz1aYVqzXB3, accessed October 2011; David Gelles and Andrew Edgecliffe-Johnson, 'High expectations for Amazon's tablet', *Financial Times* (27 September 2011), www.ft.com/cms/s/2/92a4e0fa-e90d-11e0-ac9c-00144feab49a.html#ixzz1aYFNQPHN, accessed October 2011; Lex Column, 'Amazon: under Fire over financials', *Financial Times* (28 September 2011), www.ft.com/cms/s/3/6ba92fb6-e9e8-11e0-a149-00144feab49a.html#ixzz1aYG3UYus, accessed October 2011; Joseph Menn, Richard Waters and Alan Rappeport, 'Amazon opens app store for Android devices', *Financial Times* (22 March 2011), http://cachef.ft.com/cms/s/0/5b571de8-54b6-11e0-b1ed-00144feab49a.html#ixzz1aYGpvj2c, accessed October 2011;Joseph Menn, 'No guarantees in the era after Jobs', *Financial Times* (6 October; 2011), www.ft.com/cms/s/2/12349726-f033-11e0-977b-00144feab49a.html#ixzz1aYHttsyb, accessed October 2011; Joseph Menn, 'Apple wins EU victory against Samsung', *Financial Times* (10 August 2011), http://www.ft.com/cms/s/2/7173f850-c2d2-11e0-8cc7-00144feabdc0.html#ixzz1aYMmUGJa, accessed October 2011; Richard Waters, Barney Jopson and David Gelles, 'Amazon tablet fires its ambitions', *Financial Times* (29 September 2011), www.ft.com/cms/s/2/ce7860cc-ea14-11e0-b997-00144feab49a.html#ixzz1aYEAbU4C, accessed October 2011.

CHAPTER NINETEEN

The global marketplace

Chapter preview

You have learned the fundamentals of how companies develop competitive marketing strategies to create customer value and build lasting customer relationships. In this chapter, we extend these fundamentals to global marketing. Although we discussed global topics in each previous chapter – it's difficult to find an area of marketing that doesn't contain at least some international applications – here we'll focus on special considerations that companies face when they market their brands globally. Advances in communication, transportation and other technologies have made the world a much smaller place. Today, almost every firm, large or small, faces international marketing issues. In this chapter, we will examine six major decisions marketers make in going global.

To start our exploration of global marketing, let's look again at Google. Google is a truly global operation. It's accessible just about anywhere in the world and in hundreds of different languages. But just as international markets provide opportunities, they sometimes present daunting challenges. Here, we examine Google's odyssey into China – and back out again.

Objective outline

Google: into China and back out again

Google's mission is 'to organize the world's information and make it universally accessible and useful'. Almost by definition, this suggests that Google needs to operate internationally. What's more, international markets are a key to the Google's expansion, as growth slows in domestic search advertising, Google's strongest business.

True to its mission and growth model, Google has, in fact, gone global. International markets now make up more than one-half of the company's revenues. Whereas Google controls 60 per cent of the US Internet search market, it controls an even more impressive 80 per cent of the European market. Google is available in hundreds of languages – from Korean to Arabic to Zulu – almost anywhere in the world. Anywhere, that is, except China. After a long-running feud with the Chinese government over censorship and other issues, Google has shut down – at least for now – its operations in China and its Google.cn search engine.

Google's experiences in China vividly illustrate the prospects and perils of going global. The world's most populous country and third-largest economy, China represents a huge potential market for Google. Although only 23 per cent of Chinese now use the Internet, the number of Internet users in China reached 330 million last year, more than the entire population of the United States. The Internet in China, espe-cially for young people, offers an outlet for enormous pent-up demand for entertainment, amusement and social interaction. More than 70 per cent of Chinese Internet users are under 30 years old. Moreover, online advertising in China generates an estimated €2.3 billion in annual revenues.

To access all that potential, however, Google has had to run against a gauntlet of local competitors and government restrictions. Google began in early 2000 by building a Chinese language version of its search engine, one that mirrored the English language content on Google.com. In 2002, however, the Chinese government shut down Google's site in China, claiming that people were using it to access forbidden content. To the disappointment of many, Google revised the site to self-censor content deemed taboo by the Chinese government. It argued that it was blocking only a small proportion of the sites that Chinese users visit. Users still would be able to get uncensored information on most important topics.

By early 2006, Google had received Chinese government approval to launch Google.cn. The company wanted to locate its own servers in China – inside the so-called 'Great Firewall of China', the government's system of censoring electronic information that enters or leaves the country. Although Chinese Internet users could access Google.com, having servers inside the country would help Google to compete more effectively with Chinese-owned market leader Baidu and with Yahoo and Microsoft's MSN, which had already established local Chinese operations.

Google was especially interested in providing services for the potentially lucrative Chinese mobile phone market. China has more than 500 million mobile-phone users – more than the United States, Japan, Germany and the United Kingdom combined. The Chinese use their phones to buy ringtones, pictures and other content from Internet portals such as KongZhong and TOM Online. Although such downloads sell for only a few cents each, when multiplied by hundreds of millions, the revenues add up quickly. Mobile users also like to play online multiplayer games, providing substantial subscription and accessories revenues.

With Google.cn established, Google began a bruising competitive battle for the hearts, minds and wallets of Chinese consumers. Its most formidable rival was Baidu, which successfully targeted less-educated, lower-income users, the fastest-growing Chinese subscriber segment. Baidu had a six-year head start on Google in China. As a local company, Baidu had a better understanding of the nuances of the Chinese market and language. Mandarin Chinese is a character-based language in which characters can have multiple meanings. Google had to learn how to 'talk' to users – how to interpret the correct meaning of characters in search requests. Still, by late 2009, Google's share of the China search market had increased to 35.6 per cent, while Baidu's share had fallen to 58 per cent.

Despite this success, however, Google was growing increasingly uncomfortable with China's censorship restrictions. Chinese law banned the spread of 'content subverting State power, undermining national unity, infringing upon national honour and interest, inciting ethnic hatred and secession', or supporting pornography or terrorism. By 2010, the Chinese government was enforcing strict interpretations of these laws on foreign IT companies operating in China. But knuckling under to government censorship just didn't fit well with Google's culture of free and open expression. To top things off, while Google was

GLOBAL MARKETING TODAY

The world is shrinking rapidly with the advent of faster communication, transportation and financial flows. Products developed in one country – Gucci purses, Sony electronics, McDonald's hamburgers, Japanese sushi, German BMWs – have found enthusiastic acceptance in other countries. It is not surprising to hear about a German businessman wearing an Italian suit meeting

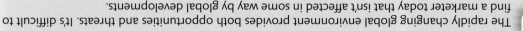

AUTHOR COMMENT

The rapidly changing global environment provides both opportunities and threats. It's difficult to find a marketer today that isn't affected in some way by global developments.

In the past, European companies paid little attention to international trade. If they could pick up some extra sales via exports, that was fine. But the big market was at home, and it teemed with opportunities. The home market was also much safer. Managers did not need to learn other languages, deal with strange and changing currencies, face political and legal uncertainties or adapt their products to different customer needs and expectations. Today, however, the situation is much different. Organisations of all kinds, from BASF, Google, Fiat and BMW to Michelin and even Champions League Football, have gone global.

AUTHOR COMMENT

Google's odyssey into China - and back out again - vividly illustrates the prospects and perils of going global.

struggling with self-censorship issues, it suffered what it called a 'highly sophisticated' cyber attack by Chinese hackers who stole some proprietary code and infiltrated the Google e-mail accounts of Chinese human-rights activists.

In early 2010, Google had seen enough of what it saw as the Chinese government's heavy-handed tactics. It announced that it would move its servers out of mainland China and route users to an uncensored version of its site in Hong Kong, which is not subject to the restrictions.

In pulling its search operations out of China, Google doesn't lose all that much current business: analysts estimated that Google earned only 1–2 per cent of its global revenue from China – between £195 and €230 million. And about 30–40 per cent of that revenue comes from Chinese companies that place ads on Google sites outside China, which is likely to continue. However, leaving mainland China cedes the country's huge search advertising potential to competitors. It also threatens Google's mobile phone business in China. Thus, many analysts think that Google will eventually resolve its feud with the Chinese government and once again enter this important market.

For now, however, Google's China pullout has won praise on moral grounds. Beyond its mission to make the world's information universally accessible, Google was founded on a simple code of conduct: 'Don't be evil.' According to Google founders Larry Page and Sergey Brin, that means 'we believe strongly that in the long term, we will be better served - as shareholders and in all other ways - by a company that does good things for the world, even if we forego some short term gains'. In the eyes of many Google fans - even those in China - the company's strong stand against censorship is simply the right thing to do. Says one prominent Chinese blogger, it was 'high time to change [Google's policy in China] back to the right track.'

Many European companies have now made the world their market.

Source: Getty Images/Bloomberg

an English friend at a Japanese restaurant who later returns home to drink Russian vodka and watch *Strictly Come Dancing* on TV.

International trade has boomed over the past three decades. Since 1990, the number of multinational corporations in the world has grown from 30,000 to more than 63,000. Some of these multinationals are true giants. In fact, of the largest 150 economies in the world, only 81 are countries. The remaining 69 are multinational corporations. Walmart, the world's largest company, has annual revenues greater than the GDP of all but the world's 21 largest countries.[2]

Between 2000 and 2008, total world trade grew more than 7 per cent per year, easily outstripping GDP output, which was about 3 per cent. Despite a dip in world trade caused by the recent worldwide recession, the world trade of products and services last year was valued at more than €8.5 trillion, about 17 per cent of worldwide GDP[3]

Many European companies have long been successful at international marketing: BMW, Nestlé, Ikea, Siemens and dozens of other European firms have made the world their market. However, non-European firms have also become well-established with such names such as McDonald's, Coca-Cola, Starbucks, GE, IBM, Colgate, Caterpillar and Boeing. Other products and services that appear to be European are, in fact, produced or owned by foreign companies, such as Campbell's Soup, Asda (now owned by US giant Walmart), Cadbury (the quintessential British chocolate maker), Mulberry (the British lifestyle brand is owned by Singaporean business tycoon Christina Ong), Laura Ashley, Lanvin, Crabtree and Evelyn (all owned by Asian companies), Michelin, the oh-so-French tyre manufacturer, now does 34 per cent of its business in North America. And America's own Caterpillar belongs more to the wider world, with 61 per cent of its sales coming from outside the United States.[4]

But as global trade grows, global competition is also intensifying. Foreign firms are expanding aggressively into new international markets, and home markets are no longer as rich in opportunity. Few industries are now safe from foreign competition. If companies delay taking steps toward internationalising, they risk being shut out of growing markets in North America, South America, China and the Pacific Rim, Russia, India and elsewhere. Firms that stay at home to play it safe might not only lose their chances to enter other markets but also risk losing their home markets. Domestic companies that never thought about foreign competitors suddenly find these competitors in their own backyards.

Ironically, although the need for companies to go abroad is greater today than in the past, so are the risks. Companies that go global may face highly unstable governments and currencies, restrictive government policies and regulations, and high trade barriers. The recently dampened global economic environment has also created big global challenges. And corruption is an increasing problem – officials in several countries often award business not to the best bidder but to the highest briber.

A **global firm** is one that, by operating in more than one country, gains marketing, production, R&D and financial advantages that are not available to purely domestic competitors.

The global company sees the world as one market. It minimises the importance of national boundaries and develops global brands. It raises capital, obtains materials and components, and manufactures and markets its goods wherever it can do the best job. For example, Otis Elevator, the world's largest elevator maker, achieves 80 per cent of its sales from outside the United States. It gets its elevator door systems from France, small geared parts from Spain, electronics from Germany and special motor drives from Japan. It uses the United States only for systems integration.[5] Many of today's global corporations – both large and small – have become truly borderless.

This does not mean that small and medium-sized firms must operate in a dozen countries to succeed. These firms can practise global niching. But the world is becoming smaller, and every company operating in a global industry – whether large or small – must assess and establish its place in world markets.

The rapid move toward globalisation means that all companies will have to answer some basic questions: What market position should we try to establish in our country, in our economic region and globally? Who will our global competitors be and what are their strategies and resources? Where should we produce or source our products? What strategic alliances should we form with other firms around the world?

As shown in Figure 19.1, a company faces six major decisions in international marketing. We will discuss each decision in detail in this chapter.

Global firm—A firm that, by operating in more than one country, gains R&D, production, marketing, and financial advantages in its costs and reputation that are not available to purely domestic competitors.

AUTHOR COMMENT

As if operating within a company's own borders wasn't difficult enough, going global adds many layers of complexities. For example, Coca-Cola markets its products in hundreds of countries around the globe. It must understand the varying trade, economic, cultural and political environments in each market.

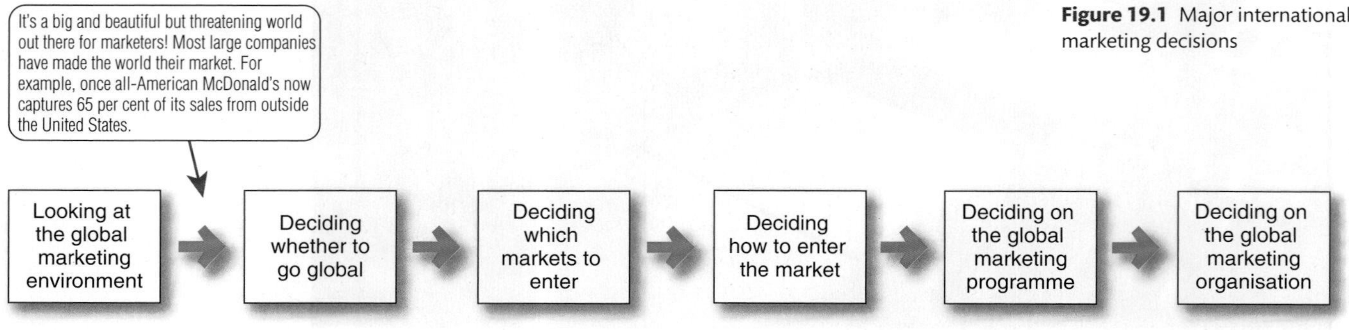

Figure 19.1 Major international marketing decisions

It's a big and beautiful world out there for marketers! Most large companies have made the world their market. For example, once all-American McDonald's now captures 65 per cent of its sales from outside the United States.

| Looking at the global marketing environment | → | Deciding whether to go global | → | Deciding which markets to enter | → | Deciding how to enter the market | → | Deciding on the global marketing programme | → | Deciding on the global marketing organisation |

LOOKING AT THE GLOBAL MARKETING ENVIRONMENT

Before deciding whether to operate internationally, a company must understand the international marketing environment. That environment has changed a great deal in the past two decades, creating both new opportunities and new problems.

The international trade system

Companies looking abroad must start by understanding the international trade system. When selling to another country, a firm may face restrictions on trade between nations. Governments may charge tariffs, taxes on certain imported products designed to raise revenue or protect domestic firms. Tariffs are often used to force favourable trade behaviours from other nations. For example, the United States recently threatened high tariffs on – of all things – Roquefort cheese in retaliation for a European Union (EU) ban on US hormone-treated beef.[6]

Roquefort cheese and some other popular European food imports could have disappeared from US gourmet shops and fancy food departments thanks to a threatened 100 – 300 per cent import tax. The imports were hostages in a long-running trans-Atlantic food fight over the EU's French-led refusal to import hormone-treated US beef. By the tit-for-tat logic of playground and world trade disputes, if the EU didn't lift its 20-year beef ban, the United States would impose punishing World Trade Organization (WTO)-sanctioned tariffs on selected products that EU members sold in the United States. No one would have starved as a result, but the 300 per cent duty on Roquefort would have driven its price into the unheard-of, demand-stifling range of $60 a pound (£21 per kg). Although Roquefort was the most harshly attacked, other US tariffs would have doubled the retail prices of 34 items, ranging from Italian mineral water to Irish oatmeal, French chestnuts and other regional foodie delights from 26 EU countries. In the end, it was hard to tell who won this battle. The United States dropped the threatened tariff increases after the EU agreed to quadruple its US non-hormone-treated beef imports over the next four years. But the EU still bans US hormone-treated beef.

Countries may set quotas, limits on the amount of foreign imports that they will accept in certain product categories. The purpose of a quota is to conserve on foreign exchange and protect local industry and employment. Firms may also face exchange controls, which limit the amount of foreign exchange and the exchange rate against other currencies.

A company also may face non-tariff trade barriers, such as biases against its bids, restrictive product standards or excessive host-country regulations. For example, non-Chinese companies trying to crack the huge and fast-growing Chinese life insurance market have found the going tough. Domestic companies, such as China Life, Ping An and others, enjoy tremendous name recognition. But they also benefit from protectionist regulations. For instance, whereas domestic firms can obtain nationwide licences, foreign firms need separate permissions for every new city or province in which they want to do business – a daunting hurdle. 'There is clearly an uneven playing field,' says an American insurance executive.[7]

At the same time, certain other forces can help trade between nations. Examples include the General Agreement on Tariffs and Trade (GATT) and various regional free-trade agreements.

The WTO and GATT

GATT is a 65-year-old treaty designed to promote world trade by reducing tariffs and other international trade barriers. Since the treaty's inception in 1947, member nations (currently numbering 153) have met in eight rounds of negotiations to reassess trade barriers and establish new rules for international trade. The first seven rounds of negotiations reduced the average worldwide tariffs on manufactured goods from 45 per cent to just 5 per cent.[8]

The most recently completed negotiations, dubbed the Uruguay Round, dragged on for seven long years before concluding in 1994. The benefits of the Uruguay Round will be felt for many years as the accord promotes long-term global trade growth. It reduced the world's remaining merchandise tariffs by 30 per cent. The agreement also extended GATT to cover trade in agriculture and a wide range of services, and it toughened the international protection of copyrights, patents, trademarks and other intellectual property. Although the financial impact of such an agreement is difficult to measure, research suggests that cutting agriculture, manufacturing and services trade barriers by one-third would boost the world economy by €433 billion, the equivalent of adding another Poland to the world economy.[9]

Beyond reducing trade barriers and setting global standards for trade, the Uruguay Round created the World Trade Organization (WTO) to enforce GATT rules. In general, the WTO acts as an umbrella organisation, overseeing GATT, mediating global disputes, helping developing countries build trade capacity and imposing trade sanctions. The previous GATT organisation never possessed such authority. A new round of negotiations, the Doha round, began in Doha, Qatar, in late 2001 and was set to conclude in 2005, but the discussions still continue.[10]

Regional free-trade zones

Certain countries have formed *free-trade zones* or **economic communities**. These are groups of nations organised to work toward common goals in the regulation of international trade. One such community is the European Union (EU). Formed in 1957, the EU (formerly EEC) set out to create a single European market by reducing barriers to the free flow of products, services, finances and labour among member countries and developing policies on trade with non-member nations. Today, the EU represents one of the world's largest single markets. Currently, it has 27 member countries containing close to half a billion consumers and accounting for more than 20 per cent of the world's exports.[11]

European unification offers tremendous trade opportunities for non-European firms. However, it also poses threats. As a result of increased unification, European companies have grown bigger and more competitive. Perhaps an even greater concern, however, is that lower barriers *inside* Europe will create only thicker *outside* walls. Some observers envision a 'Fortress Europe' that heaps favours on firms from EU countries but hinders outsiders by imposing obstacles.

Progress toward European unification has been slow. In recent years, however, 16 member nations have taken a significant step toward unification by adopting the euro as a common currency. Many other countries are expected to follow within the next few years. Widespread adoption of the euro will, in theory, decrease much of the currency risk associated with doing business in Europe, making member countries with previously weak currencies potentially more attractive markets.[12]

However, even with the adoption of the euro, it is unlikely that the EU will ever go against 2,000 years of tradition and become the 'United States of Europe'. A community with more than two dozen different languages and cultures will always have difficulty coming together and acting as a single entity. Still, with a combined annual GDP of more than €11.4 trillion, the EU has become a potent economic force.[13]

In 1994, NAFTA established a free-trade zone among the United States, Mexico and Canada. The agreement created a single market of 452 million people who produce and consume almost €12 trillion worth of goods and services annually. Over the past 15 years, NAFTA has eliminated trade barriers and investment restrictions among the three countries. According to the International Monetary Fund (IMF), total trade among the three countries has more than doubled from €216 billion in 1993 to €450 billion in 2009.[14]

Following the apparent success of NAFTA, in 2005 the Central American Free Trade Agreement (CAFTA-DR) established a free-trade zone between the United States and Costa Rica, the Dominican Republic, El Salvador, Guatemala, Honduras and Nicaragua. Other free-trade areas

Source: European Union 2010

Economic communities: the EU represents one of the world's single largest markets. It's current member countries contain more than half a billion consumers and account for 20 per cent of the world's exports.

Economic community—A group of nations organised to work toward common goals in the regulation of international trade.

have formed in Latin America and South America. For example, the Union of South American Nations (UNASUR), modelled after the EU, was formed in 2004 and formalised by a constitutional treaty in 2008. Consisting of 12 countries, UNASUR makes up the largest trading bloc after NAFTA and the EU, with a population of 361 million, a combined economy of more than €688 billion and exports worth €127 billion. Similar to NAFTA and the EU, UNASUR aims to eliminate all tariffs between nations by 2019.[15]

Each nation has unique features that must be understood. A nation's readiness for different products and services and its attractiveness as a market to foreign firms depend on its economic, political–legal and cultural environments.

Economic environment

The international marketer must study each country's economy. Two economic factors reflect the country's attractiveness as a market: its industrial structure and its income distribution.

The country's *industrial structure* shapes its product and service needs, income levels and employment levels. The four types of industrial structures are as follows:

- *Subsistence economies.* In a subsistence economy, the vast majority of people engage in simple agriculture. They consume most of their output and barter the rest for simple goods and services. They offer few market opportunities.

- *Raw material exporting economies.* These economies are rich in one or more natural resources but poor in other ways. Much of their revenue comes from exporting these resources. Some examples are Chile (tin and copper), the Democratic Republic of the Congo (copper, cobalt and coffee) and Saudi Arabia (oil). These countries are good markets for large equipment, tools and supplies, and trucks. If there are many foreign residents and a wealthy upper class, they are also a market for luxury goods.

- *Emerging economies (industrialising economies).* In an emerging economy, fast growth in manufacturing results in rapid overall economic growth. Examples include the BRIC countries – Brazil, Russia, India and China. As manufacturing increases, the country needs more imports of raw textile materials, steel and heavy machinery, and fewer imports of finished textiles, paper products and cars. Industrialisation typically creates a new rich class and a small but growing middle class, both demanding new types of imported goods.

- *Industrial economies.* Industrial economies are major exporters of manufactured goods, services and investment funds. They trade goods among themselves and also export them to other types of economies for raw materials and semi-finished goods. The varied manufacturing activities of these industrial nations and their large middle classes make them rich markets for all sorts of goods. Examples include the United States, most of Europe, Japan and Norway.

The second economic factor is the country's *income distribution*. Industrialised nations may have low-, medium- and high-income households. In contrast, countries with subsistence economies consist mostly of households with very low family incomes. Still other countries may have households with only either very low or very high incomes. Even poor or emerging economies may be attractive markets for all kinds of goods. These days, companies in a wide range of industries – from cars to computers to confectionery – are increasingly targeting even low- and middle-income consumers in emerging economies. For example, in India, Ford recently introduced a new model targeted at consumers who are now able to afford their first car:[16]

In an effort to boost its presence in Asia's third-largest auto market behind Japan and China, Ford introduced the Figo, a €5,444 hatchback design for a hypothetical 20-something Indian named Sandeep. He works in IT, finance or another service industry and travels around on a motorcycle. But now that he's enjoying the first fruits of affluence, Sandeep wants four wheels. 'There are huge numbers of people wanting to move off their motorbikes,' says Ford's India general manager. Some 70 per cent of cars sold in India are in the Figo's size and price range. In fact, GM beat Ford to the punch by two months with its new €5,375 Chevy Beat, which is so popular in India that there's now a two-month waiting list.

Political–legal environment

Nations differ greatly in their political–legal environments. In considering whether to do business in a given country, a company should consider a country's attitudes toward international buying, government bureaucracy, political stability and monetary regulations.

Some nations are very receptive to foreign firms, but others are less accommodating. For example, India has tended to bother foreign businesses with import quotas, currency restrictions and other limitations that make operating there a challenge. In contrast, neighbouring Asian countries, such as Singapore and Thailand, court foreign investors and shower them with incentives and favourable operating conditions. Political and regulatory stability is another issue. For example, Venezuela's government is notoriously volatile – due to economic factors such as inflation and steep public spending – which increases the risk of doing business there. Although most international marketers still find the Venezuelan market attractive, the unstable political and regulatory situation will affect how they handle business and financial matters.[17]

Companies must also consider a country's monetary regulations. Sellers want to take their profits in a currency of value to them. Ideally, the buyer can pay in the seller's currency or in other world currencies. Short of this, sellers might accept a blocked currency – one whose removal from the country is restricted by the buyer's government – if they can buy other goods in that country that they need themselves or can sell elsewhere for a needed currency. In addition to currency limits, a changing exchange rate also creates high risks for the seller.

Most international trade involves cash transactions. Yet many nations have too little hard currency to pay for their purchases from other countries. They may want to pay with other items instead of cash. For example, *barter* involves the direct exchange of goods or services: China recently agreed to help the Democratic Republic of Congo develop €4.25 billion of desperately needed infrastructure – 2,400 miles of roads, 2,000 miles of railways, 32 hospitals, 145 health centres and 2 universities – in exchange for natural resources needed to feed China's booming industries – 10 million tonnes of copper and 400,000 tons of cobalt.[18]

Cultural environment

Every country has its own folklore, norms and taboos. When designing global marketing strategies, companies must understand how culture affects consumer reactions in each of its world markets. In turn, they must also understand how their strategies affect local cultures.

The impact of culture on marketing strategy

Sellers must understand the ways that consumers in different countries think about and use certain products before planning a marketing programme. There are often surprises. For example, the average French man uses almost twice as many cosmetics and grooming aids as his wife. The Germans and the French eat more packaged, branded spaghetti than Italians do. Some 49 per cent of Chinese eat on the way to work. Most American women let down their hair and take off makeup at bedtime, whereas 15 per cent of Chinese women style their hair at bedtime and 11 per cent put *on* makeup.[19]

Companies that ignore cultural norms and differences can make some very expensive and embarrassing mistakes. Here are two examples:

Nike inadvertently offended Chinese officials when it ran an ad featuring LeBron James crushing a number of culturally revered Chinese figures in a kung fu-themed television ad. The Chinese government found that the ad violated regulations to uphold national dignity and respect the 'motherland's culture' and yanked the multimillion-dollar campaign. With egg on its face, Nike released a formal apology.

Burger King made a similar mistake when it created in-store ads in Spain showing Hindu goddess Lakshmi atop a ham sandwich with the caption 'a snack that is sacred'. Cultural and religious groups worldwide objected strenuously because Hindus are vegetarian. Burger King apologised and pulled the ads.[20]

Business norms and behaviour also vary from country to country. For example, American executives like to get right down to business and engage in fast and tough face-to-face bargaining. However, Japanese and other Asian businesspeople often find this behaviour offensive. They prefer to start with polite conversation, and they rarely say no in face-to-face conversations. As another example, South Americans like to sit or stand very close to each other when they talk business – in fact, almost nose-to-nose. An American business executive tends to keep backing away as the South American moves closer. Both may end up being offended. Business executives need to understand these kinds of cultural nuances before conducting business in another country.

By the same token, companies that understand cultural nuances can use them to their advantage when positioning products and preparing campaigns internationally. Consider LG Electronics, the €15.55 billion South Korean electronics, telecommunications and appliance powerhouse. LG now operates in more than 60 countries and captures 87 per cent of its sales from markets outside its home country. LG's global success rests on understanding and catering to the unique characteristics of each local market through in-country research, manufacturing and marketing.[21]

Have you ever smelled kimchi? Well, if you had you'd remember it! In Korea, kimchi is a firm favourite and is served with most meals. Kimchi is made from fermented cabbage that has been liberally seasoned with chilli and garlic. Storing kimchi is a big problem. Putting it in a conventional refrigerator rapidly leads to everything in that fridge smelling of the pungent, distinctive kimchi. While Koreans love their kimchi – kimchi flavoured butter and milk is an experience most consumers avoid! This is why, over twenty years ago, LG launched their kimchi refrigerator that contains a dedicated kimchi compartment that isolates the malodorous cabbage from other foodstuffs. LG is now the top-selling manufacturer of kimchi refrigerators in Korea and over 65% of Korean homes are now fitted with a kimchi refrigerator.

The success of LG's kimchi refrigerators reflects their mission to make products that seamlessly fit-in their customer's lives and solve their needs in a culturally sensitive way. In contrast to their European refrigerators, in India, LG designed and sell units with a much larger capacity to store fresh vegetables and cool water while being surge-resistant to cope with the vagaries of the Indian power grid. The European love of white and chrome is also rejected in favour of the bright colours of India – red

Overlooking cultural differences can result in embarrassing mistakes. China imposed a nationwide ban on this 'blasphemous' kung fu–themed television ad featuring LeBron James crushing a number of culturally revered Chinese figures.

Source: Getty Images/AFP

being preferred in the south and green in Kashmir. In India, microwaves are made with brown inte-riors to hide stains from spicy food while in Iran; LG offers microwave ovens with a special pre-set button for reheating, much loved, shish kebabs. In the opulence-loving and ostentatious Middle East, LG recently unveiled a 71-inch television that is gold-plated (for a mere €60,000). Somewhat less opulent was LG's karaoke phone for the Russian market. Designed to entertain bored Russians during their long winter evenings, the phone could be loaded with the top 100 Russian songs, complete with scrolling lyrics. This seamless fit saw LG sell 220,000 handsets in the first year alone.

Thus, understanding cultural traditions, preferences and behaviours can help companies not only avoid embarrassing mistakes but also take advantage of cross-cultural opportunities.

The impact of marketing strategy on cultures

Whereas marketers worry about the impact of culture on their global marketing strategies, others may worry about the impact of marketing strategies on global cultures. For example, social critics con-tend that large American multinationals such as McDonald's, Coca-Cola, Starbucks, Nike, Microsoft, Disney and MTV, aren't just 'globalising' their brands, they are 'Americanising' the world's cultures.[22]

There are now as many people studying English in China (or playing basketball, for that matter) as there are people in the United States. Seven of the ten most watched TV shows around the world are American. *Avatar* is the top-grossing film of all time in China, and the world is as fixated on US brands as ever, which is why US multinationals from McDonald's to Nike earn more than half their revenues overseas. If you bring together teenagers from Nigeria, Sweden, South Korea and Argentina – to pick a random foursome – what binds these kids together in some kind of community is American culture – music, Hollywood fare, electronic games, Google and American consumer brands. The only thing they are likely to have in common that doesn't revolve around the United States is an interest in soccer. The . . . rest of the world is becoming [evermore] like America – in ways good and bad.

'Today, globalization often wears Mickey Mouse ears, eats Big Macs, drinks Coke or Pepsi, and does its computing with Windows', says Thomas Friedman, in his book *The Lexus and the Olive Tree: Understanding Globalization*.[23] Critics worry that, under such 'McDomination', countries around the globe are losing their individual cultural identities. Teens in India watch MTV and ask their parents for more westernised clothes and other symbols of American pop culture and values. Grand-mothers in small European villas no longer spend each morning visiting local meat, bread and produce markets to gather the ingredients for dinner. Instead, they now shop at Walmart Supercenters. Women in Saudi Arabia see American films and question their societal roles. In China, most people didn't drink coffee before Starbucks entered the market. Now Chinese consumers rush to Starbucks stores 'because it's a symbol of a new kind of lifestyle'. Similarly, in China, where McDonald's operates more than 80 restaurants in Beijing alone, nearly half of all children identify the chain as a domestic brand. Such concerns have sometimes led to a backlash against American globalisation. Well-known US brands have become the targets of boycotts and protests in some international markets. As symbols of American capitalism, companies such as Coca-Cola, McDonald's, Nike and KFC have been singled out by anti-globalisation protestors in hot spots around the world, especially when anti-American sentiment peaks.

Despite such problems, defenders of globalisation argue that concerns of 'Americanisation' and the potential damage to American brands are overblown. US brands are doing very well inter-nationally. In the most recent Millward Brown Optimor brand value survey of global consumer brands, 16 of the top 20 brands were American owned, including megabrands such as Google, IBM, Apple, Microsoft, Coca-Cola, McDonald's, GE, Amazon.com and Walmart.[24] Many iconic Ameri-can brands are prospering globally, even in some of the most unlikely places:[25]

Despite such problems, defenders of globalization argue that concerns of Americanization and the potential damage to American brands are overblown. US. brands are doing very well inter nationally. In the most recent Millward Brown Optimor brand value survey of global consumer brands, 16 of the top 20 brands were American owned, including megabrands such as Google, IBM, Apple, Microsoft, Coca-Cola, McDonald's, GE, Amazon.com, and Walmart.[26] Many iconic American brands are prospering globally, even in some of the most unlikely places.

For example, it is possible to meet elegant Iranian women in the suburbs of Tehran, wearing Western designer clothes and accessories, chatting in French, English and Farsi, where the only sign that they are not in London or Paris is the expensive Hermès scarves covering their hair, in deference to local traditions. Their drink of preference in alcohol-free Iran is likely to be Coca-Cola. Though some zealots want Iranians to avoid 'Great Satan' brands like Coke and Pepsi, those brands have taken around half national soft drink sales in Iran, one of the biggest Middle East drinks markets.[27]

More fundamentally, the cultural exchange goes both ways: America gets as well as gives cultural influence. True, Hollywood dominates the global movie market, but British TV gives as much as it gets in dishing out competition to US shows, spawning such hits as *The Office*, *American Idol* and *Dancing with the Stars*. Although Chinese and Russian youth are donning NBA superstar jerseys, American kids are similarly wearing the football strips of Barcelona, Liverpool and Inter Milan. Even American childhood has been increasingly influenced by European and Asian cultural imports. Most kids know all about Hello Kitty, the Bakugan Battle Brawler, or any of a host of Nintendo or Sega game characters. And J. K. Rowling's so-very-British Harry Potter books have shaped the thinking of a generation of youngsters across the globe, not to mention the millions of adults who've fallen under their spell as well. For the moment, English remains the dominant language of the Internet, and having Web access often means that third-world youth have greater exposure to American popular culture. Yet these same technologies let Eastern European students studying in the United States hear Webcast news and music from Poland, Romania or Belarus.

Thus, globalisation is a two-way street. If globalisation has Mickey Mouse ears, it is also wearing a French beret, talking on a Nokia mobile phone, buying furniture at Ikea, driving a Toyota Camry and watching England play cricket on a Samsung plasma TV.

DECIDING WHETHER TO GO GLOBAL

Not all companies need to venture into international markets to survive. For example, most local businesses need to market well only in their local marketplace. Operating domestically is easier and safer. Managers don't need to learn another country's language and laws. They don't have to deal with unstable currencies, face political and legal uncertainties, or redesign their products to suit different customer expectations. However, companies that operate in global industries, where their strategic positions in specific markets are affected strongly by their overall global positions, must compete on a regional or worldwide basis to succeed.

Any of several factors might draw a company into the international arena. Global competitors might attack the company's home market by offering better products or lower prices. The company might want to counterattack these competitors in their home markets to tie up their resources. The company's customers might be expanding abroad and require international servicing. Or, most likely, international markets might simply provide better opportunities for growth. For example, Coca-Cola has emphasised international growth in recent years to offset stagnant or declining US soft drink sales. 'It's been apparent that Coke's signature cola can't grow much on its home turf anymore,' states an industry analyst. Today, about 80 per cent of Coke's profits come from outside North America.[26]

Before going abroad, the company must weigh several risks and answer many questions about its ability to operate globally. Can the company learn to understand the preferences and buyer behaviour of consumers in other countries? Can it offer competitively attractive products? Will it be able to adapt to other countries' business cultures and deal effectively with foreign nationals? Do the company's managers have the necessary international experience? Has management considered the impact of regulations and the political environments of other countries?

DECIDING WHICH MARKETS TO ENTER

P&G's decision to enter the Chinese toothpaste market with Crest is a no-brainer: China is the world's largest toothpaste market. But P&G must still question whether market size alone is reason enough for investing heavily in China.

Source: Press Association Images/ Xu Ruiping

Before going abroad, the company should try to define its international *marketing objectives and policies*. It should decide what *volume* of foreign sales it wants. Most companies start small when they go abroad. Some plan to stay small, seeing international sales as a small part of their business. Other companies have bigger plans, seeing international business as equal to or even more important than their domestic business.

The company also needs to choose *how many* countries it wants to market. Companies must be careful not to spread themselves too thin or expand beyond their capabilities by operating in too many countries too soon. Next, the company needs to decide on the *types* of countries to enter. A country's attractiveness depends on the product, geographical factors, income and population, political climate and other factors. The seller may prefer certain country groups or parts of the world. In recent years, many major new markets have emerged, offering both substantial opportunities and daunting challenges.

After listing possible international markets, the company must carefully evaluate each one. It must consider many factors. For example, Unilever's and P&G's decision to compete in the Chinese toothpaste market was a no-brainer: China's huge population makes it the world's largest toothpaste market. And given that only 20 per cent of China's rural dwellers currently brush daily, this already huge market can grow even larger. Unilever produces Zhonghua toothpaste through a licensing agreement which began in the late 1990s. Yet P&G still had to ask themselves whether market size *alone* was enough reason for investing heavily in China.

P&G had to ask some important questions: Can Crest compete effectively with dozens of local competitors, Colgate, and the state-owned brand managed by Unilever? Will the Chinese government remain stable and supportive? Does China provide for the needed production and distribution technologies? Can the company master China's vastly different cultural and buying differences? Crest's current success in China suggests that it could answer yes to every question.[27]

'Just 10 years ago, P&G's Crest brand was unknown to China's population, most of whom seldom – if ever – brushed their teeth,' says one analyst. 'Now P&G . . . sells more tubes of toothpaste there than it does in America, where Crest has been on store shelves for 52 years.' P&G achieved this by sending researchers to get a feel for what urban and rural Chinese were willing to spend and what flavours they preferred. These researchers discovered that urban Chinese are happy to pay more than €1 for tubes of Crest with exotic flavours such as Icy Mountain Spring and Morning Lotus Fragrance. But rural Chinese prefer the 50-cent Crest Salt White because many rural Chinese believe that salt whitens teeth. Armed with such insights, Crest now leads all competitors in China with a 25 per cent market share. Some users even believe it's a Chinese brand. P&G hopes to find similar success in other emerging markets across its entire product mix. Such markets now account for 30 per cent of the company's total sales.

Possible global markets should be ranked on several factors, including market size, market growth, the cost of doing business, competitive advantage and risk level. The goal is to determine the potential of each market, using indicators such as those shown in Table 19.1. Then the marketer must decide which markets offer the greatest long-run ROI.

AUTHOR COMMENT

A company has many options for entering an international market, from simply exporting its products to working jointly with foreign companies to holding its own foreign-based operations.

Table 19.1 Indicators of market potential

Demographic characteristics	Sociocultural factors
Education Population size and growth Population age composition	Consumer lifestyles, beliefs and values Business norms and approaches Cultural and social norms Languages
Geographic characteristics	**Political and legal factors**
Climate Country size Population density – urban, rural Transportation structure and market accessibility	National priorities Political stability Government attitudes toward global trade Government bureaucracy Monetary and trade regulations
Economic factors	
GDP size and growth Income distribution Industrial infrastructure Natural resources Financial and human resources	

DECIDING HOW TO ENTER THE MARKET

Once a company has decided to sell in a foreign country, it must determine the best mode of entry. Its choices are *exporting*, *joint venturing* and *direct investment*. Figure 19.2 shows three market entry strategies, along with the options each one offers. As the figure shows, each succeeding strategy involves more commitment and risk but also more control and potential profits.

Exporting

The simplest way to enter a foreign market is through **exporting**. The company may passively export its surpluses from time to time, or it may make an active commitment to expand exports to a particular market. In either case, such a company produces all its goods in its home country. It may or may not modify them for the export market. Exporting involves the least change in the company's product lines, organisation, investments or mission.

Exporting—Entering a foreign market by selling goods produced in a company's home country, often with little modification.

Figure 19.2 Market entry strategies

Direct investment — owning your own foreign-based operation — affords greater control and profit potential, but it's often riskier.

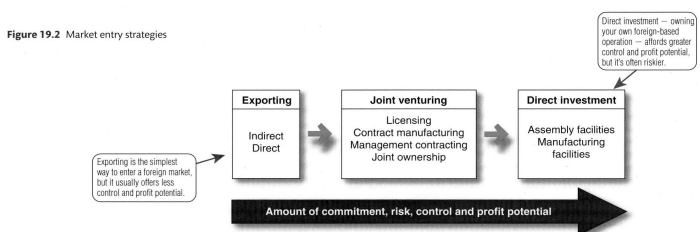

Exporting is the simplest way to enter a foreign market, but it usually offers less control and profit potential.

Exporting	Joint venturing	Direct investment
Indirect Direct	Licensing Contract manufacturing Management contracting Joint ownership	Assembly facilities Manufacturing facilities

Amount of commitment, risk, control and profit potential

Companies typically start with *indirect exporting*, working through independent international marketing intermediaries. Indirect exporting involves less investment because the firm does not require an overseas marketing organisation or network. It also involves less risk. International marketing intermediaries bring know-how and services to the relationship, so the seller normally makes fewer mistakes. Sellers may eventually move into *direct exporting*, whereby they handle their own exports. The investment and risk are somewhat greater in this strategy, but so is the potential return.

Joint venturing

Joint venturing—Entering foreign markets by joining with foreign companies to produce or market a product or a service.

A second method of entering a foreign market is by **joint venturing** – joining with foreign companies to produce or market products or services. Joint venturing differs from exporting in that the company joins with a host country partner to sell or market abroad. It differs from direct investment in that an association is formed with someone in the foreign country. There are four types of joint ventures: licensing, contract manufacturing, management contracting and joint ownership.

Licensing

Licensing—A method of entering a foreign market in which a company enters into an agreement with a licensee in a foreign market.

Licensing is a simple way for a manufacturer to enter international marketing. The company enters into an agreement with a licensee in the foreign market. For a fee or royalty payments, the licensee buys the right to use the company's manufacturing process, trademark, patent, trade secret or other item of value. The company thus gains entry into a foreign market at little risk; the licensee gains production expertise or a well-known product or name without having to start from scratch.

In Japan, Budweiser beer flows from Kirin breweries, and Moringa Milk Company produces Sunkist fruit juice, drinks and dessert items. Coca-Cola markets internationally by licensing bottlers around the world and supplying them with the syrup needed to produce the product. Its global bottling partners range from the Coca-Cola Bottling Company of Saudi Arabia to Europe-based Coca-Cola Hellenic, which bottles and markets Coca-Cola products to 560 million people in 28 countries, from Italy and Greece to Nigeria and Russia.

Licensing has potential disadvantages, however. The firm has less control over the licensee than it would over its own operations. Furthermore, if the licensee is very successful, the firm has given up these profits; if the contract should end, the firm may find it has created a competitor.

Contract manufacturing

Contract manufacturing—A joint venture in which a company contracts with manufacturers in a foreign market to produce a product or provide a service.

Another option is **contract manufacturing** – the company contracts with manufacturers in the foreign market to produce its product or provide its service. Sears used this method in opening up department stores in Mexico and Spain, where it found qualified local manufacturers to produce many of the products it sells. The drawbacks of contract manufacturing are decreased control over the manufacturing process and loss of potential profits on manufacturing. The benefits are the chance to start faster, with less risk, and the later opportunity either to form a partnership with or buy out the local manufacturer.

Management contracting

Management contracting—A joint venture in which a domestic firm supplies the management know-how to a foreign company that supplies the capital; the domestic firm exports management services rather than products.

Under **management contracting**, the domestic firm supplies management know-how to a foreign company that supplies the capital. The domestic firm exports management services rather than products. Hilton uses this arrangement in managing hotels around the world. For example, the hotel chain recently announced the opening of a Doubletree by Hilton in Oradea, Romania. The property is locally owned, but Hilton manages the hotel with its world-renowned hospitality expertise.[28]

Management contracting is a low-risk method of getting into a foreign market, and it yields income from the beginning. The arrangement is even more attractive if the contracting firm has an option to buy some share in the managed company later on. The arrangement is not sensible, however, if the company can put its scarce management talent to better uses or if it can make greater profits by undertaking the whole venture. Management contracting also prevents the company from setting up its own operations for a period of time.

Joint ownership

Joint ownership ventures consist of one company joining forces with foreign investors to create a local business in which they share joint ownership and control. A company may buy an interest in a local firm, or the two parties may form a new business venture. Joint ownership may be needed for economic or political reasons. The firm may lack the financial, physical or managerial resources to undertake the venture alone. Or a foreign government may require joint ownership as a condition for entry.

Best Buy recently formed a 50/50 joint venture with UK-based Carphone Warehouse to open its first European Best Buy stores, starting in Britain:[29]

> A new Best Buy store in Britain is exactly like its American counterpart. Even the carpets and the fittings have been imported from the United States. But the management team and senior employees are from the United Kingdom. To learn the Best Buy way of retailing, the locals receive nine weeks of training at Best Buy's 'Blue Shirt Academy' in the United States. Best Buy is betting that this combination of its proven superstore concept with Carphone's local market savvy will differentiate Best Buy from the largely price-driven UK competition. Whereas other US retail chains, such as Walmart, have struggled in the United Kingdom, partnering with Carphone will help. 'Best Buy has a much better chance of being successful in Europe by partnering with Carphone than it would opening stores there all by itself,' says a retailing analyst. 'Having a management team that already has experience and connections in Europe is a huge, huge benefit.'

Joint ownership has certain drawbacks, however. The partners may disagree over investment, marketing, or other policies. Whereas many European firms like to reinvest earnings for growth, local firms often prefer to take out these earnings; whereas European firms emphasise the role of marketing, local investors may rely on selling.

Direct investment

The biggest involvement in a foreign market comes through **direct investment** – the development of foreign-based assembly or manufacturing facilities. For example, Daimler has recently injected €200 million into its South African plant. The factory in the Eastern Cape province was one of four chosen to produce the new Mercedes-Benz C-Class, scheduled for launch in 2014, alongside plants in China, Germany and the US. Hansgeorg Niefer, chief executive of Mercedes-Benz South Africa, said that the investment would add capacity at the plant from 45,000 to 65,000 units a year with about 70 per cent of the factory's output being exported to Asia.[30]

If a company has gained experience in exporting and if the foreign market is large enough, foreign production facilities offer many advantages. The firm may have lower costs in the form of cheaper labour or raw materials, foreign government investment incentives and freight savings. The firm may improve its image in the host country because it creates jobs. Generally, a firm develops a deeper relationship with the government, customers, local suppliers and distributors, allowing it to adapt its products to the local market better. Finally, the firm keeps full control over the investment and therefore can develop manufacturing and marketing policies that serve its long-term international objectives.

The main disadvantage of direct investment is that the firm faces many risks, such as restricted or devalued currencies, falling markets or government changes. In some cases, a firm has no choice but to accept these risks if it wants to operate in the host country.

Joint ownership—A joint venture in which a company joins investors in a foreign market to create a local business in which a company shares joint ownership and control.

Direct investment—Entering a foreign market by developing foreign-based assembly or manufacturing facilities.

AUTHOR COMMENT

The major global marketing decision usually boils down to this: How much, if at all, should a company adapt its marketing strategy and programmes to local markets? How might the answer differ for Boeing versus McDonald's?

DECIDING ON THE GLOBAL MARKETING PROGRAMME

Companies that operate in one or more foreign markets must decide how much, if at all, to adapt their marketing strategies and programmes to local conditions. At one extreme are global companies that use **standardised global marketing**, essentially using the same marketing strategy approaches and marketing mix worldwide. At the other extreme is **adapted global marketing**. In this case, the producer adjusts the marketing strategy and mix elements to each target market, bearing more costs but hoping for a larger market share and return.

The question of whether to adapt or standardise the marketing strategy and programme has been much debated over the years. On the one hand, some global marketers believe that technology is making the world a smaller place, and consumer needs around the world are becoming more similar. This paves the way for 'global brands' and standardised global marketing. Global branding and standardisation, in turn, result in greater brand power and reduced costs from economies of scale.

On the other hand, the marketing concept holds that marketing programmes will be more effective if tailored to the unique needs of each targeted customer group. If this concept applies within a country, it should apply even more across international markets. Despite global convergence, consumers in different countries still have widely varied cultural backgrounds. They still differ significantly in their needs and wants, spending power, product preferences and shopping patterns. Because these differences are hard to change, most marketers today adapt their products, prices, channels and promotions to fit consumer desires in each country.

However, global standardisation is not an all-or-nothing proposition. It's a matter of degree. Most international marketers suggest that companies should 'think globally but act locally' – that is, they should seek a balance between standardisation and adaptation. The company's overall strategy should provide global strategic direction. Then regional or local units should focus on adapting the strategy to specific local markets.

Collectively, local brands still account for the overwhelming majority of consumers' purchases. 'The vast majority of people still lead very local lives,' says a global analyst. 'By all means go global, but the first thing you have to do is win on the ground. You have to go local.' Another analyst agrees: 'You need to respect local culture and become part of it.' A global brand must 'engage with consumers in a way that feels local to them.' Simon Clift, head of marketing for global consumer-goods giant Unilever, puts it this way: 'We're trying to strike a balance between being mindlessly global and hopelessly local.'[31]

McDonald's operates this way: it uses the same basic fast-food look, layout and operating model in its restaurants around the world but adapts its menu to local tastes. In Japan, it offers Ebi Filet-O-Shrimp burgers and fancy Salad Macs salad plates. In Korea it sells the Bulgogi Burger, a grilled pork patty on a bun with a garlicky soy sauce. In India, where cows are considered sacred, McDonald's serves McChicken, Filet-O-Fish, McVeggie (a vegetable burger), Pizza McPuffs, McAloo Tikki (a spiced-potato burger) and the Maharaja Mac – two all-chicken patties, special sauce, lettuce, cheese, pickles and onions in a sesame-seed bun. In all, McDonald's serves local markets with a global brand.

Product

Five strategies allow for adapting product and marketing communication strategies to a global market (see Figure 19.3).[32] We first discuss the three product strategies and then turn to the two communication strategies.

Straight product extension means marketing a product in a foreign market without any change. Top management tells its marketing people, 'Take the product as is and find customers for it'. The first step, however, should be to find out whether foreign consumers use that product and what form they prefer.

Straight extension has been successful in some cases and disastrous in others. Apple iPads, Gillette razors and Bosch tools are all sold successfully in about the same form around the world.

Standardised global marketing—An international marketing strategy that basically uses the same marketing strategy and mix in all of a company's international markets.

Adapted global marketing—An international marketing strategy that adjusts the marketing strategy and mix elements to each international target market, bearing more costs but hoping for a larger market share and return.

Straight product extension—Marketing a product in a foreign market without any change.

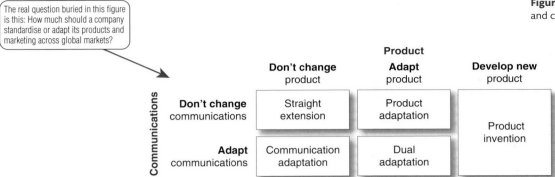

Figure 19.3 Five global product and communications strategies

The real question buried in this figure is this: How much should a company standardise or adapt its products and marketing across global markets?

But when General Foods introduced its standard powdered JELL-O in the British market, it discovered that British consumers preferred a solid wafer or cake form. Likewise, Philips began to make a profit in Japan only after it reduced the size of its coffee makers to fit into smaller Japanese kitchens and its shavers to fit smaller Japanese hands. Straight extension is tempting because it involves no additional product development costs, manufacturing changes or new promotion. But it can be costly in the long run if products fail to satisfy consumers in specific global markets.

Product adaptation involves changing the product to meet local conditions or wants. For example, Finnish cell phone maker Nokia customises its mobile phones for every major market. To meet the needs of less-affluent consumers in large developing countries such as India, China and Kenya, the company has created full-featured but rugged and low-cost phones especially designed for harsher living conditions. For instance, it developed dustproof keypads – crucial in dry, hot countries with many unpaved roads. Some phones have built-in radio antennas for areas where radio is the main source of entertainment. Thanks to such adaptation, Nokia commands a whopping 62.3 per cent share of the market in Africa and the Middle East, 48.5 per cent in Eastern Europe and 41.8 per cent in Asia.[33]

Campbell found out the hard way that it couldn't just slap new labels on its products and peddle them abroad:[34]

> In its first foray into China in the early 1990s, Campbell essentially slapped a Chinese label on its classic condensed soups. They sold well for a while, but when the novelty wore off, sales fell and Campbell withdrew. The company returned to China in 2007, but only after two years of thorough research with Chinese consumers. It found that in China, as well as Russia, there's a cultural disposition to cooking soup from scratch. In both countries, about 98 per cent of soup is homemade. So, in both countries, Campbell has now introduced products that reduce the time to make home-made soup from 2.5 hours to about 45 minutes. Getting the product right is important. Consumers in each country typically eat soup four to five times per week and Campbell estimates that if it could capture just 3 per cent of the soup market in the two countries combined, it would create a business as big as their domestic soup market.

Product invention consists of creating something new to meet the needs of consumers in a given country. For example, companies ranging from computer and carmakers to candy producers have developed products that meet the special purchasing needs of low-income consumers in developing economies such as India and China. Ford developed the economical, low-priced Figo model especially for entry-level consumers in India. And Cadbury, long known for its premium chocolates, is now developing products for less-affluent consumers in India and other developing economies:[35]

> As more Indians begin to treat themselves to little luxuries, Cadbury hopes to capture millions of new customers with chocolates that sell for only a few pennies. The candy maker has been in India for more than 60 years and dominates the chocolate market there with a 70 per cent market share. For years, however, Cadbury was considered a luxury brand purchased only by

Product adaptation—Adapting a product to meet local conditions or wants in foreign markets.

Product invention—Creating new products or services for foreign markets.

the elite. But now Cadbury is taking aim at India's huge population of lower-income consumers by offering cheaper products. India constitutes a vast untapped market – less than half of India's 1.1 billion people have ever tasted chocolate. The premium candy maker's latest product for the low end of the Indian market is Cadbury Dairy Milk Shots – pea-sized chocolate balls sold for just two rupees, or about four US cents, for a package of two. Cadbury has also developed other small, low-cost candies, such as Eclair caramels, which cost about two euro cents each. Last year, emerging markets accounted for 35 per cent of Cadbury's sales and about 60 per cent of its sales growth.

Promotion

Companies can either adopt the same communication strategy they use in the home market or change it for each local market. Consider advertising messages. Some global companies use a standardised advertising theme around the world. For example, Apple sold millions of iPods with a single global campaign featuring silhouetted figures dancing against a colourful background. And

Even highly standardised global ad campaigns must be adapted to meet cultural differences. In Western markets, Dove's Campaign for Real Beauty featured images of everyday women in their underwear. But in the Middle East, where attitudes toward nudity are more conservative, the ads were modified to simply reveal the face behind a woman's veil.

Source: Ogilvy.com

other than for language, the Apple website looks about the same for any of the more than 70 countries in which Apple markets its products, from Australia to Senegal to the Czech Republic.

Of course, even in highly standardised communications campaigns, some adjustments might be required for language and cultural differences. For example, in western markets, Dove's high-impact Campaign for Real Beauty campaign featured images of everyday women in their underwear. In the Middle East, however, where attitudes toward nudity are more conservative, the campaign was modified to simply reveal the face behind a woman's veil.[36]

Global companies often have difficulty crossing the language barrier, with results ranging from mild embarrassment to outright failure. Seemingly innocuous brand names and advertising phrases can take on unintended or hidden meanings when translated into other languages. For example, an Italian company's Traficante mineral water received an interesting reception in Spain, where the name translates as 'drug dealer'. Ikea marketed a children's workbench named 'Fartfull' (the word means 'speedy' in Swedish); it soon discontinued the product. And Motorola's Hellomoto ring tone sounds like 'Hello, Fatty' in India.

Communication adaptation— A global communication strategy of fully adapting advertising messages to local markets.

Other companies follow a strategy of **communication adaptation**, fully adapting their advertising messages to local markets. Kellogg's ads in the United States promote the taste and nutrition of Kellogg's cereals versus competitors' brands. In France, where consumers drink little milk and eat little for breakfast, Kellogg's ads must convince consumers that cereals are a tasty and healthful breakfast. In India, where many consumers eat heavy, fried breakfasts, Kellogg's advertising convinces buyers to switch to a lighter, more nutritious breakfast diet.

Similarly, Coca-Cola sells its low-calorie beverage as Diet Coke in North America, the United Kingdom and the Middle and Far East, but as Coke Light elsewhere. According to Diet Coke's global brand manager, in Spanish-speaking countries Coke Light ads 'position the soft drink as an object of desire, rather than as a way to feel good about yourself, as Diet Coke is positioned in the United States'. This 'desire positioning' plays off research showing that 'Coca-Cola Light is seen in other parts of the world as a vibrant brand that exudes a sexy confidence'. (Check out this ad and others on YouTube: www.youtube.com/watch?v=Tu5dku6YkHA.)[37]

Media also need to be adapted internationally because media availability and regulations vary from country to country. TV advertising time is very limited in Europe, for instance, ranging from four hours a day in France to none in Scandinavian countries. Advertisers must buy time months in advance, and they have little control over airtimes. However, mobile phone ads are much more widely accepted in Europe and Asia than in the United States. Magazines also vary in effectiveness. For example, magazines are a major medium in Italy but a minor one in Austria. Newspapers are national in the United Kingdom but only local in Spain.[38]

Price

Companies also face many considerations in setting their international prices. For example, how might Bosch price its tools globally? It could set a uniform price globally, but this amount would be too high a price in poor countries and not high enough in rich ones. It could charge what consumers in each country would bear, but this strategy ignores differences in the actual costs from country to country. Finally, the company could use a standard mark-up of its costs everywhere, but this approach might price Bosch out of the market in some countries where costs are high.

Regardless of how companies go about pricing their products, their foreign prices probably will be higher than their domestic prices for comparable products. An Apple iPad that sells for €425 in the United States goes for €575 in the United Kingdom. Why? Apple faces a *price escalation* problem. It must add the cost of transportation, tariffs, importer margin, wholesaler margin and retailer margin to its factory price. Depending on these added costs, the product may have to sell for two to five times as much in another country to make the same profit.

To overcome this problem when selling to less-affluent consumers in developing countries, many companies make simpler or smaller versions of their products that can be sold at lower prices. For example, in China and other emerging markets, Dell sells its simplified Vostro PC for €282, and Unilever and P&G sell consumer goods – everything from shampoo to toothpaste – in less-costly formulations and smaller packages at more affordable prices.

Another problem involves setting a price for goods that a company ships to its foreign subsidiaries. If the company charges its foreign subsidiary too much, it may end up paying higher tariff duties even while paying lower income taxes in that country. If the company charges its subsidiary too little, it can be charged with *dumping*. Dumping occurs when a company either charges less than its costs or less than it charges in its home market.

For example, the United States has been slapping duties on a growing list of Chinese products – from tyres to chickens – found to be unfairly priced. One such product is pipes used in oil and gas wells. It might not sound glamorous, but it's an €7.77 billion market, with Chinese imports accounting for about 10 per cent. When a group of companies complained that Chinese firms were pricing these goods below market value, the European Union and the US Commerce Department agreed and imposed duties as high as 99 per cent on oil field pipe imports from China.[39] Various governments are always watching for dumping abuses, and they often force companies to set the price charged by other competitors for the same or similar products.

Recent economic and technological forces have had an impact on global pricing. For example, the Internet is making global price differences more obvious. When firms sell their wares over the Internet, customers can see how much products sell for in different countries. They can even order a given product directly from the company location or dealer offering the lowest price. This is forcing companies toward more standardised international pricing.

Distribution channels

An international company must take a **whole-channel view** of the problem of distributing products to final consumers. Figure 19.4 shows the two major links between the seller and the final buyer.

Whole-channel view—Designing international channels that take into account the entire global supply chain and marketing channel, forging an effective global value delivery network.

Figure 19.4 Whole-channel concept for international marketing

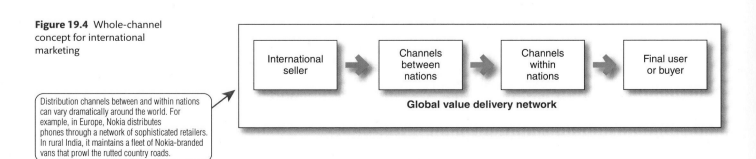

Distribution channels between and within nations can vary dramatically around the world. For example, in Europe, Nokia distributes phones through a network of sophisticated retailers. In rural India, it maintains a fleet of Nokia-branded vans that prowl the rutted country roads.

International seller → Channels between nations → Channels within nations → Final user or buyer

Global value delivery network

Distribution channels vary greatly from nation to nation. In its efforts to sell rugged, affordable phones to Indian consumers, Nokia forged its own distribution structure, including a fleet of distinctive blue Nokia-branded vans that prowl rutted country roads to visit remote villages.

Source: Getty Images/India Today Group

The first link, *channels between nations*, moves company products from points of production to the borders of countries within which they are sold. The second link, *channels within nations*, moves products from their market entry points to the final consumers. The whole-channel view takes into account the entire global supply chain and marketing channel. It recognises that to compete well internationally, the company must effectively design and manage an entire *global value delivery network*.

Channels of distribution within countries vary greatly from nation to nation. There are large differences in the numbers and types of intermediaries serving each country market and in the transportation infrastructure serving these intermediaries. For example, whereas large-scale retail chains dominate Europe, most of the retailing in other countries occurs with small, independent retailers. In India, millions of retailers operate tiny shops or sell in open markets. Thus, in its efforts to sell those rugged, affordable phones discussed earlier to Indian consumers, Nokia has had to forge its own distribution structure.[40]

In India, Nokia has a presence in almost 90 per cent of retail outlets selling mobile phones. It estimates there are 90,000 points-of-sale for its phones, ranging from modern stores to makeshift kiosks. That makes it difficult to control how products are displayed and pitched to consumers. 'You have to understand where people live, what the shopping patterns are,' says a Nokia executive. 'You have to work with local means to reach people – even bicycles or rickshaws.' To reach rural India, Nokia has outfitted its own fleet of distinctive blue Nokia-branded vans that prowl the rutted country roads. Employees park these advertisements-on-wheels in villages, often on market or festival days. There, with crowds clustering around, Nokia reps explain the basics of how the phones work and how to buy them. Nokia has extended the concept to minivans, which can reach even more remote places. Thanks to smart product development and innovative channels, Nokia now owns an astounding 50 per cent share of India's mobile device market.

Similarly, Coca-Cola adapts its distribution methods to meet local challenges in global markets. For example, in Montevideo, Uruguay, where larger vehicles are challenged by traffic, parking and pollution difficulties, Coca-Cola purchased 30 small, efficient three-wheeled ZAP alternative transportation trucks. The little trucks average about one-fifth the fuel consumption and scoot around congested city streets with greater ease. In rural areas, Coca-Cola uses a manual delivery process. In China, an army of more than 10,000 Coca-Cola sales reps make regular visits to small retailers, often on foot or bicycle. To reach the most isolated spots, the company even relies on teams of delivery donkeys. In Tanzania, 93 per cent of Coca-Cola's products are manually delivered via pushcarts and bicycles.[41]

AUTHOR COMMENT

Many large companies, regardless of their 'home country', now think of themselves as truly *global* organisations. They view the entire world as a single borderless market. For example, although headquartered in Chicago, Boeing is as comfortable selling planes to Lufthansa or Air China as to American Airlines.

DECIDING ON THE GLOBAL MARKETING ORGANISATION

Companies manage their international marketing activities in at least three different ways. Most companies first organise an export department, then create an international division and finally become a global organisation.

A firm normally gets into international marketing by simply shipping out its goods. If its international sales expand, the company will establish an *export department* with a sales manager and a few assistants. As sales increase, the export department can expand to include various marketing services so that it can actively go after business. If the firm moves into joint ventures or direct investment, the export department will no longer be adequate.

Many companies get involved in several international markets and ventures. A company may export to one country, license to another, have a joint ownership venture in a third and own a subsidiary in a fourth. Sooner or later it will create *international divisions* or subsidiaries to handle all its international activity.

International divisions are organised in a variety of ways. An international division's corporate staff consists of marketing, manufacturing, research, finance, planning and personnel specialists. It plans for and provides services to various operating units, which can be organised in one of three ways. They can be *geographical organisations*, with country managers who are responsible for salespeople, sales branches, distributors and licensees in their respective countries. Or the operating units can be *world product groups*, each responsible for worldwide sales of different product groups. Finally, operating units can be *international subsidiaries*, each responsible for their own sales and profits.

Many firms have passed beyond the international division stage and are truly *global organisations*. For example, consider Reckitt Benckiser (RB), a €7.7 billion European producer of household products and consumer goods with a stable full of familiar brands (Air Wick, Lysol, Woolite, Calgon, Mucinex, Clearasil, French's and many others):[42]

> RB has operations in more than 60 countries. Its top 400 managers represent 53 different nationalities. Although headquartered in the United Kingdom, an Italian runs its UK business, an American runs the German business and a Dutchman runs the US business. An Indian runs the Chinese business, a Belgian the Brazilian business and a Frenchman the Russian business. 'Most of our top managers . . . view themselves as global citizens rather than as citizens of any given nation,' says RB's chief executive officer.
>
> The company has spent the past decade building a culture of global mobility because it thinks that's one of the best ways to generate new ideas and create global entrepreneurs. And it has paid off. Products launched in the past three years – all the result of global cross-fertilisation – account for 35–40 per cent of net revenue. Over the past few years, even during the economic downturn, the company has outperformed its rivals – P&G, Unilever and Colgate – in growth.

Global organisations don't think of themselves as national marketers who sell abroad but think of themselves as global marketers. The top corporate management and staff plan worldwide manufacturing facilities, marketing policies, financial flows and logistical systems. The global operating units report directly to the chief executive officer or the executive committee of the organisation, not to the head of an international division. Executives are trained in worldwide operations, not just domestic *or* international operations. Global companies recruit management from many countries, buy components and supplies where they cost the least, and invest where the expected returns are greatest.

Today, major companies must become more global if they hope to compete. As foreign companies successfully invade their domestic markets, companies must move more aggressively into foreign markets. They will have to change from companies that treat their international operations as secondary to companies that view the entire world as a single borderless market.

REVIEWING OBJECTIVES AND KEY TERMS

Companies today can no longer afford to pay attention only to their domestic market, regardless of its size. Many industries are global industries, and firms that operate globally achieve lower costs and higher brand awareness. At the same time, global marketing is risky because of variable exchange rates, unstable governments, protectionist tariffs and trade barriers, and several other factors. Given the potential gains and risks of international marketing, companies need a systematic way to make their global marketing decisions.

OBJECTIVE 1 Discuss how the international trade system and the economic, political – legal and cultural environments affect a company's international marketing decisions (pp. 568–578).

A company must understand the *global marketing environment*, especially the international trade system. It must assess each foreign market's *economic*, *political – legal* and *cultural characteristics*. The company must then decide whether it wants to go abroad and consider the potential risks and benefits. It must decide on the volume of international sales it wants, how many countries it wants to market in, and which specific markets it wants to enter. These decisions call for weighing the probable ROI rate against the level of risk.

OBJECTIVE 2 Describe three key approaches to entering international markets (pp. 579–581).

The company must decide how to enter each chosen market – whether through *exporting*, *joint venturing* or *direct investment*. Many companies start as exporters, move to joint ventures and finally make a direct investment in foreign markets. In *exporting*, the company enters a foreign market by sending and selling products through international marketing intermediaries

(indirect exporting) or the company's own department, branch, or sales representative or agents (direct exporting). When establishing a *joint venture*, a company enters foreign markets by joining with foreign companies to produce or market a product or service. In *licensing*, the company enters a foreign market by contracting with a licensee in the foreign market, offering the right to use a manufacturing process, trademark, patent, trade secret or other item of value for a fee or royalty.

OBJECTIVE 3 Explain how companies adapt their marketing mixes for international markets (pp. 582–586).

Companies must also decide how much their products, promotion, price and channels should be adapted for each foreign market. At one extreme, global companies use *standardised global marketing* worldwide. Others use *adapted global marketing*, in which they adjust the marketing strategy and mix to each target market, bearing more costs but hoping for a larger market share and return. However, global standardisation is not an all-or-nothing proposition. It's a matter of degree. Most international marketers suggest that companies should 'think globally but act locally' – that is, they should seek a balance between globally standardized strategies and locally adapted marketing mix tactics.

OBJECTIVE 4 Identify the three major forms of international marketing organisation (pp. 586–587).

The company must develop an effective organization for international marketing. Most firms start with an *export department* and graduate to an *international division*. A few become *global organizations*, with worldwide marketing planned and managed by the top officers of the company. Global organisations view the entire world as a single, borderless market.

NAVIGATING THE KEY TERMS

OBJECTIVE 1
Global firm (p. 570)
Economic community (p. 572)

OBJECTIVE 2
Exporting (p. 579)

Joint venturing (p. 580)
Licensing (p. 580)
Contract manufacturing (p. 580)
Management contracting (p. 580)
Joint ownership (p. 581)
Direct investment (p. 581)

OBJECTIVE 3
Standardised global marketing (p. 582)
Adapted global marketing (p. 582)
Straight product extension (p. 582)

Product adaptation (p. 583)
Product invention (p. 583)
Communication adaptation (p. 584)
Whole-channel view (p. 585)

 ## DISCUSSING AND APPLYING THE CONCEPTS

Discussing the concepts

1. Explain what is meant by the term *global firm* and list the six major decisions involved in international marketing. (AACSB: Communication)

2. Discuss the types of restrictions governments might impose on trade between nations. (AACSB: Communication)

3. Name and define the four types of country industrial structures. (AACSB: Communication)

4. What factors do companies consider when deciding on possible global markets to enter? (AACSB: Communication; Reflective Thinking)

5. Discuss the three ways to enter foreign markets. Which is the best? (AACSB: Communication; Reflective Thinking)

6. Discuss how global distribution channels differ from domestic channels. (AACSB: Communication)

Applying the concepts

1. Visit www.transparency.org and click on 'corruption perception index'. What is the most recent Corruption Perceptions Index (CPI) for the following countries: Denmark, Jamaica, Malaysia, Myanmar, New Zealand, Somalia and the United States? What are the implications of this index for European companies doing business in these countries? (AACSB: Communication; Use of IT; Reflective Thinking)

2. Visit the Central Intelligence Agency's World Factbook at www.cia.gov/library/publications/the-world-factbook. In a small group, select a country and describe the information provided about that country on this site. How is this information useful to marketers? (AACSB: Communication; Use of IT; Reflective Thinking)

Focus on technology

'Reverse innovation', 'innovation blowback', and 'trickle-up innovation' are terms used to describe the process by which innovations developed to meet the needs of emerging markets make their way into developed markets. Traditionally, innovations are birthed in developed countries, with older models later offered in lower-income markets, such as India and China. Although many 'bottom of the pyramid' emerging markets are low on the economic food chain, they are large in numbers, providing opportunities for businesses that meet growing needs at an affordable price. GE, the dominant maker of expensive electrocardiograph (ECG) machines sold to hospitals, developed a lower-priced, small, battery-powered ECG machine for use in India and China. GE then marketed this product to primary care doctors, visiting nurses, and rural hospitals and clinics across Europe. Reverse innovation is not limited to technological products; it can apply to products as basic as yogurt.

1. Learn more about how GE used reverse innovation to capitalise on opportunities. Find two other examples of reverse innovation for technological products. (AACSB: Communication; Reflective Thinking)

2. Discuss two examples of reverse innovation for non-technology products. (AACSB: Communication; Reflective Thinking)

Focus on ethics

Imagine Ford building a passenger van in Turkey, shipping it to the United States, and then ripping out the back windows and seats to convert it into a delivery van. The fabric and foam from the seats are shredded and become landfill cover, while the steel and glass are recycled in other ways. Seems like a waste, doesn't it? Well, that's actually cheaper than paying the 25 per cent tariff Ford would have to pay to import its own delivery vans. The windows and seats are there just to get around an on-going trade spat with Europe, known as the 'chicken tax'. In the 1960s, Europe imposed high tariffs on imported chicken due to increased US poultry sales to West Germany. In retaliation, US President Johnson imposed a tax on imports of foreign-made trucks and commercial vans – specifically targeting German-made Volkswagens. The chicken tax has long pestered vehicle manufacturers. Even US automobile companies such as Ford must pay the tariff, which is ironic because US trade rules have protected the US vehicle manufacturers' truck market for years. However, converting the vehicle into a delivery truck after reaching the US represents costs of 2.5 per cent, significantly lower than the 25 per cent tariff if the vehicle came into the country that way.

1. Should US companies be penalised for importing their own products from other countries? (AACSB: Communication; Ethical Reasoning)
2. Although Ford is complying 'with the letter of the law', are Ford's actions proper? (AACSB: Communication; Ethical Reasoning)

Marketing & the economy

SPAM

For decades, SPAM (the Hormel canned meat product, not unwanted e-mail) has been the brunt of bad jokes. But it's all in good fun, as consumers all around the world gobble up hundreds of millions of euros worth of the pork concoction every year. In the United Kingdom, deep-fried SPAM slices – known as SPAM fritters – adorn menus at fish and chips shops. In Japan, it's an ingredient in a popular stir-fry dish. South Koreans eat the meat with rice or wrap it up in sushi rolls. In Hawaii, even McDonald's and Burger King sell SPAM specialties.

But here's one of the most interesting things about SPAM: the 'SPAM Index'. Over the years, SPAM sales have been very strongly and inversely correlated with economic indicators that some analysts consider the canned meat's revenues themselves as an index of economic conditions. The Great Recession was no exception. SPAM experienced double-digit increases in sales after economists officially announced the beginning of the recession. Hormel responded by launching SPAM's first major advertising campaign in five years. Radio, TV and print ads carry a 'Break the Monotony' message, showing how SPAM can breathe new life into home-cooked meals. The Hormel website boasts 350 new SPAM recipes, including Cheesy Country SPAM Puff, SPAMaroni and SPAM Lettuce Wraps. A little bit of SPAM goes a long way.

1. Why does SPAM have such universal appeal to global consumers?
2. What recommendations would you make to Hormel to keep SPAM sales high when the economy is once again strong?

Marketing by the numbers

A country's import/export activity is revealed in its balance-of-payments statement. This statement includes three accounts: the current account, the capital account and the reserves account. The current account is most relevant to marketing because it is a record of all merchandise exported from and imported into a country. The latter two accounts record financial transactions. The Eurostat Key Indicators provides yearly and monthly figures on the country's trade in goods and services.

1. Visit http://epp.eurostat.ec.europa.eu/portal/page/portal/eurostat/home and find the international trade in goods and services for Europe for the most recent year available. What does that number mean? (AACSB: Communication; Use of IT; Reflective Thinking)
2. Search the Internet for China's balance of trade information for the same year. How does it compare to that of Europe? (AACSB: Communication; Use of IT; Reflective Thinking)

 REFERENCES

[1] Quotes and other information from Matthew Fomey and Arthur Kroeber, 'Google's business reason for leaving China,' *Wall Street Journal* (6 April 2010), p. 15; Aaron Back and Loretta Chao, 'Google weaves a tangled Chinese web', *Wall Street Journal* (25 March 2010); Jessica E. Vascellaro, 'Brin drove Google's pullback', *Wall Street Journal* (25 March 2010), p. A1; Normandy Madden, 'Whether it stays or goes, Google wasn't winning in China anyway', *Advertising Age* (18 January 2010), p. 2; Bruce Einhorn, 'Google in China: a win for liberty – and strategy', *Bloomberg Businessweek* (25 January 2010), p. 35; and Renjie, 'Multinationals "Should respect laws in china"', *Global News Wire* (16 June 2010).

[2] Data from Michael V. Copeland, 'The mighty micro-multinational', *Business 2.0* (28 July 2006), accessed at http://money.cnn.com/magazines/business2/business2_archive/2006/07/01/8380230/index.htm; 'List of countries by GDP: list by the CIA World Factbook', www.cia.gov/library/publications/the-world-factbook/fields/2195.html)?>http://en.wikipedia.org/wiki/List_of_countries_by_GDP_(nominal), accessed July 2010; and 'Fortune 500', *Fortune* (3 May 2010), pp. F1-F26.

[3] 'Global economic prospects 2010: crisis, finance, and growth', *World Bank* (21 January 2010), accessed at http://tinyurl.com/2bfgrd6; and 'Trade to Expand by 9.5% in 2010 after a dismal 2009, WTO reports', *World Trade Organization* (26 March 2010), accessed at www.wto.org/english/news_e/pres10_e/pr598_e.htm.

[4] Information from www.michelin.com/corporate/front/templates/affich.jsp?codeRubrique=1&lang=FR, www.jnj.com/connect, and www.mcdonalds.com/us/en/home.html, accessed October 2011; and Huang Lijie, 'European brands shine in Asian hands', *The Straits Times* (4 April 2011), http://www.asianewsnet.net/home/news.php?id=18287, accessed October 2011.

[5] See 'Otis Elevator Company', *Hoover's Company Records* (15 June 2010), p. 56332; and www.otisworldwide.com, accessed October 2011.

[6] Frank Greve, 'International food fight could spell end to Roquefort dressing', *McClatchy-Tribune Business News* (9 April 2009); James Hagengruber, 'A victory for cheese eaters?', *Christian Science Monitor* (7 May 2009).

[7] Frederik Balfour, 'A slog in China for foreign insurers', *Businessweek* (23 November 2009), p. 24; and 'Research and markets: analyzing China's insurance industry – comprehensive report', *Business Wire* (19 April 2010).

[8] 'What is the WTO?', www.wto.org/english/thewto_e/whatis_e/whatis_e. htm, accessed September 2010.

[9] See *WTO Annual Report 2009*, www.wto.org/english/res_e/publications_ e/anrep09_e.htm, accessed September 2010; and World Trade Organization, '10 benefits of the WTO trading system', www.wto.org/english/thewto_e/ whatis_e/10ben_e/10b00_e.htm, accessed September 2010.

[10] Pascal Lamy, 'Europe and recovery: now is the time to conclude Doha', *Wall Street Journal* (Europe edition) (11 February 2009), p. 13; and Tim Colebatch, 'No sign of giving ground in Doha trade talks', *Age* (Melbourne, Australia) (4 March 2010), p. B4.

[11] 'The EU at a glance', http://europa.eu/abc/index_en.htm, accessed September 2010.

[12] 'Economic and monetary affairs', http://europa.eu/pol/emu/index_ en.htm, accessed September 2010.

[13] CIA, *The World Factbook*, www.cia.gov/library/publications/the-world-factbook, accessed October 2011.

[14] Statistics and other information from CIA, *The World Factbook*, op. cit., accessed June 2010; 'NAFTA analysis 2007' and 'North American FTA', Office of the US Trade Representative, www.ustr.gov/Trade_Agreements/ Regional/NAFTA/Section_Index.html, October 2011; and Thomas L. Gallagher, 'NAFTA trade dropped 23 percent in 2009', *Journal of Commerce* (18 March 2010), www.joc.com/logistics-economy/nafta-trade-dropped-historic-23-percent-2009.

[15] See CIA, *The World Factbook*, op.cit., accessed June 2010; and www .comunidadandina.org/ingles/sudamerican.htm, October 2011.

[16] Adapted from information found in Bruce Einhorn, 'Alan Mulally's Asian sales call', *Bloomberg Businessweek* (12 April 2010), pp. 41-43.

[17] See Leticia Lozano, 'Trade disputes roil South American nations', *Journal of Commerce* (18 January 2010); and 'Welcome to the US commercial service Venezuela', www.buyusa.gov/venezuela/en/, accessed July 2010.

[18] '$9 billion barter deal', *BarterNews.com* (19 April 2008), accessed at www.barternews.com/9_billion_dollar_barter_deal.htm; and David Pilling, 'Africa builds as Beijing scrambles to invest', *Financial Times* (10 December 2009), p. 11.

[19] For these and other examples, see Emma Hall, 'Do you know your rites? BBDO does', *Advertising Age* (21 May 2007), p. 22.

[20] Jamie Bryan, 'The Mintz dynasty', *Fast Company* (April 2006), pp. 56-61; Viji Sundaram, 'Offensive Durga display dropped', *India-West* (February 2006), p. A1; and Emily Bryson York and Rupal Parekh, 'Burger King's MO: offend, earn media, apologize, repeat', *Advertising Age* (8 July 2009), accessed at http://adage.com/print?article_id=137801.

[21] See Elizabeth Esfahani, 'Thinking locally, succeeding globally', *Business 2.0* (December 2005), pp. 96–98; Evan Ramstas, 'LG Electronics' net surges 91 percent as cell phone margins improve', *Wall Street Journal* (25 January 2006), p. B2; and www.lg.com/us/index.jsp, accessed October 2011.

[22] Andres Martinez, 'The next American century', *Time* (22 March 2010), p. 1.

[23] Thomas L. Friedman, *The Lexus and the Olive Tree: Understanding Globalization* (New York: Anchor Books, 2000).

[24] 'Top 100 most valuable global brands 2010', Millward Brown Optimor, accessed at www.millwardbrown.com/Libraries/Optimor_BrandZ_Files/ 2010_BrandZ_Top100_Chart.sflb.ashx.

[25] Eric Ellis, 'Iran's cola war', *Fortune* (5 March 2007), pp. 35–38; and 'Iran pressures firm over Coca-Cola links', (19 January 2009), *World News Network*, accessed at www.google.com/hostednews/afp/article/ ALeqM5i0vWNjBSFX67GiiSk01zDDUwtY1w.

[26] Betsy McKay, 'Coke bets on Russia for sales even as economy falls flat', *Wall Street Journal* (28 January 2009), p. A1; and William Neuman, 'Coke profit edges up; American sales stall', *New York Times* (21 October 2009), p. B2.

[27] See Noreen O'Leary, 'Bright lights, big challenge', *Adweek* (15 January 2007), pp. 22-28; Dexter Roberts, 'Scrambling to bring crest to the masses', *Businessweek* (25 June 2007), p. 72; Jonathan Birchall, 'P&G set to expand in emerging markets', *Financial Times* (12 December 2008), p. 22; and Jonathan Birchall, 'P&G set to regain market share', *Financial Times* (29 January 2010), p. 17.

[28] See www.etravelblackboard.us/showarticle.asp?id=92363 and http:// doubletree.hilton.com/en/dt/promotions/dt_new_hotels/index.jhtml, accessed October 2011.

[29] Alex Armitage, 'Best Buy acquires stake in carphone warehouse', *Bloomberg.com* (8 May 2008); and Jenny Davey and James Ashton, 'American invader aims to topple Comet and Currys', *Sunday Times* (London) (28 February 2010), p. 7.

[30] Example from Simon Mundy, 'Daimler invests in S African plans', *Financial Times* (8 December 2010), www.ft.com/cms/s/0/42bba152-02b6-11e0-a07e-00144feabdc0.html#ixzz1UPvkHyUb, accessed October 2011.

[31] Quotes from Andrew McMains, 'To compete globally, brands must adapt', *Adweek* (25 September 2008), accessed at www.adweek.com/ aw/content_display/special-reports/other-reports/e3i382d62ad1770e 9ed08b537b94a343337?pn=2; Pankaj Ghemawat, 'Regional strategies for global leadership', *Harvard Business Review* (December 2005), pp. 97–108; Eric Pfanner, 'The myth of the global brand', *New York Times* (11 January 2009), www.nytimes.com/2009/01/11/technology/11iht-ad12.3.19251743.htm. Also see Pankej Ghemawat, 'Finding your strategy in the new landscape', *Harvard Business Review* (March 2010), pp. 54-60.

[32] See Warren J. Keegan and Mark C. Green, *Global Marketing*, 6th edn. (Upper Saddle River, NJ: Prentice Hall, 2011), pp. 314–321.

[33] See Jack Ewing, 'First mover in mobile: how it's selling cell phones to the developing world', *Businessweek* (14 May 2007), p. 60; and Nelson D. Schwartz, 'Can Nokia recapture its glory days?', *New York Times* (12 December 2009), accessed at www.nytimes.com/2009/12/13/ business/13nokia.html?pagewanted=1&_r=2.

[34] Mike Hughlett, 'Packaged food is taking off in emerging markets', *Charleston Gazette* (23 March 2010), p. A10.

[35] Adapted from information found in Sonya Misquitta, 'Cadbury redefines cheap luxury – marketing to India's poor, candy makers sells small bites for pennies', *Wall Street Journal* (8 June 2009), p. B4.

[36] See McMains, 'To compete globally, brands must adapt.', op. cit.

[37] Kate MacArthur, 'Coca-Cola light employs local edge', *Advertising Age* (21 August 2000), pp. 18–19; 'Case studies: Coke light hottest guy', MSN India, accessed at http://in.msn.com, (15 March 2004); and www .youtube.com/watch?v=Tu5dku6YkHA, accessed July 2010.

[38] See George E. Belch and Michael A. Belch, *Advertising and Promotion: An Integrated Marketing Communications Perspective*, 7th edn. (New York: McGraw Hill, 2007), Chapter 20; Shintero Okazaki and Charles R. Taylor, 'What is SMS advertising and why Do multinationals adopt it?',

Journal of Business Research (January 2008), pp. 4–12; and. Keegan and Green, *Global Marketing*, op. cit. pp. 413–415.

[39] Jonathan Stearns, 'EU hits China with tariffs on steel pipes', *Trade News - wire* (29 June 2011), www.tradenewswire.net/2011/eu-hits-china-with-tariffs-on-steel-pipes, accessed October 2011; and Howard Schneider, 'US sets tariff on Chinese oil field pipes of up to 99%', *Washington Post* (11 April 2010), p. A10.

[40] Adapted from Ewing, 'First mover in mobile: how it's selling cell phones to the developing world; op. cit. with information from Anshul Gupta, 'Mobile handsets: hand set growth to be flat in 2009', (9 March 2009), accessed at www.expresscomputeronline.com/20090309/2009anniversary14.shtml.

[41] See 'Coca-Cola rolls out new distribution model with ZAP', *ZAP* (23 January 2008), www.zapworld.com/zap-coca-cola-truck; and Jane Nelson, Eriko Ishikawa and Alexis Geaneotes, 'Developing inclusive business models: a review of Coca-Cola's manual distribution centers in Ethiopia and Tanzania', Harvard Kennedy School (2009), accessed at www.hks.harvard.edu/m-rcbg/CSRI/publications/other_10_MDC_report.pdf. For some interesting photos of Coca-Cola distribution methods in third-world and emerging markets, see www.flickr.com/photos/73509998@N00/sets/72157594299144032, accessed October 2011.

[42] Adapted from information found in Bart Becht, 'Building a company without borders', *Harvard Business Review* (April 2010), pp. 103–106.

VIDEO CASE

Monster MyMarketingLab

In 1994, Monster Worldwide pioneered job recruiting on the Internet. Today, it is the only online recruitment provider that can service job seekers and job posters on a truly global basis. With a presence in 50 countries around the world, Monster has unparalleled international reach. Although global economic woes have hindered the growth of corporations everywhere, Monster is investing heavily with plans to become even bigger worldwide. Most recently, Monster's international expansion has included the purchase of ChinaHR.com giving it a strong presence in the world's largest country. Monster already gets about 45 per cent of its annual revenue of €1 billion from outside the United States. But it expects to become even more global in the coming years. To back that geographic expansion, Monster is also inventing heavily in search technologies and Web design in order to appeal to clients everywhere.

After watching the video featuring Monster Worldwide, answer the following questions about the company and the global marketplace:

1. Which of the five strategies for adapting products and promotion for global markets does Monster employ?
2. Which factors in the global marketing environment have challenged Monster's global marketing activities most? How has Monster met those challenges?

COMPANY CASE

Nokia: envisioning a connected world

What brand of mobile phone do you own? If you're living in the United States, chances are it isn't a Nokia. But if you're living anywhere else in the world, it probably is. The Finnish electronics company grabs only a single-digit slice of the US mobile phone pie, but it dominates the global mobile phone market with close to a 40 per cent share. Few companies lead their industries the way that Nokia does. Half of the world's population holds an active mobile phone, and more than one in three of those phones is a Nokia. That's over one billion people holding a cell phone with a Nokia logo. Perhaps even more amazing, the company sells about half that many again – i.e. half a billion – phones every year. In fact, Nokia sells more cell phones each year than its three closest rivals – Samsung, Motorola and Sony-Ericsson – combined!

You might think that Nokia has accomplished this feat by being the product leader, always introducing the latest cutting-edge gadget. But Nokia has actually been slow to take advantage of design trends, such as clamshell phones, 'candy-bar' phones that slide open and closed, and ultrathin, blingy, multi-function phones. Rather, Nokia has risen to global dominance based on a simple, age-old strategy: sell basic products at low prices. Although Nokia markets a huge variety of mobile phone models, it is best known for its trademarked easy-to-use block handset. Nokia mass-produces this basic reliable hardware cheaply and ships it in huge volumes to all parts of the world.

GAINING STRENGTH AS THE VOLUME LEADER

Based in Finland, Nokia's single most profit- and revenue-generating region is Europe. But the company's global strategy has been likened to that of Honda decades ago. Honda started by focusing on developing markets with small motorbikes. As the economies of such countries emerged and people could afford cars, they were already loyal to Honda.

Nokia has followed that same model. It sells phones in more than 150 countries, and in most of those countries it is the market leader. Nokia has a real knack for forging regional strategies based on the overall needs of its consumers. But Nokia has filled its coffers by understanding the growth dynamics of specific emerging markets. Soren Peterson, Nokia's senior vice president of mobile phones, understands that concept more than anyone. He spends a great deal of his time studying the needs of consumers in emerging markets. And for the most part, these consumers need cheap phones.

To that end, Petersen has led Nokia on a crusade to bring down costs and make its phones even less expensive. Petersen cites an example of one cost-cutting tactic that sparked a chain of events at Nokia. While on a visit to Kenya, he stopped by an 'excessively rural storefront', where he noticed that all the products were displayed in plastic bags. When he asked the merchant where the boxes and manuals had gone, the man replied, 'Make good fire'. Petersen quickly realised that packaging for many areas of the world barely needed to 'last the journey'. Packaging changes resulted in a savings of €115 million a year.

Among other notable discoveries for emerging markets, Nokia developed an icon-based interface to replace text, a welcome innovation for many people in the world who don't know how to read. Nokia also added multiple phonebooks to its devices, based on the fact that many people in less-developed countries share their phones with up to a half-dozen other people. Nokia has even developed an inexpensive charging kit for bicycles with a dynamo that attaches to the wheel and a phone holder for the handlebars. At 7.5 miles per hour, it charges as fast as a traditional wall charger.

CAPITALISING ON MARKET LEADERSHIP

Just as Honda used strength gained from selling motorbikes in emerging countries to establish itself as a manufacturer of virtually every kind of passenger vehicle, Nokia aims to do the same in the mobile industry. Although Nokia remains committed to the entry-level market and emerging nations, it has developed a comprehensive global strategy. According to Nokia's vision statement, that strategy has three facets: growing the number of people using Nokia devices, transforming the devices people use and building new businesses.

For the first part of this plan, Nokia projects that global mobile phone usage will reach five billion users by 2015. That means Nokia can significantly increase the number of phones it sells, even if it doesn't increase its market share. In fact, if Nokia simply holds its current share of the market, that means that approximately 1.7 billion people will be holding Nokia phones, 67 per cent more than today. That's good news for Nokia. According to one analyst, given the number of players in the global market, it will be almost impossible for Nokia to maintain a 40 per cent share.

As for transforming the devices that people use, Nokia is aiming to become more than just an entry-level phone provider. Of its 123,000 employees, almost one-third work in R&D, whose expenses account for approximately 10 per cent of net sales. Nokia invests heavily in developing more cutting-edge devices in hopes that as its customers in developing nations gain the resources, they will trade-up and stay with Nokia. Nokia may have an advantage here. Beyond selling lots of phones, Nokia is also one of the most trusted brands in the world. With a brand value of €27 billion, it's the fifth-most-valuable brand in the world. 'The trust is so high, it has less trouble than other brands getting a customer back who may have tried out a competing brand,' says a branding expert.

Nokia also recognises that the biggest trends in mobile devices are music, navigation and gaming. Focusing on these activities, it is collaborating with the best minds in the business to find ways to add value for the consumer. Nokia appears poised to take advantage of the convergence of the Internet, media and the mobile phone. Last year, Nokia sold more than 200 million camera phones (far more cameras than Canon) and more than 140 million music phones (Apple only sold 52 million iPods). Thus, through its mobile handsets, Nokia can claim to sell more computers, portable music players and cameras than any other company. However, it has yet to find a way to secure a steady income stream from its devices once they are in place.

This creates a logical transition to the third leg of Nokia's strategy – building new businesses. In an effort to gain income from existing devices, Nokia has opened its 'Ovi Store'. The goal is to accomplish something that has eluded many mobile network operators – building a profitable business in mobile services. The Ovi Store is a one-stop shop that connects consumers with content providers through their Nokia phones. Users can access apps, games, videos, widgets, podcasts, location-based services and personalised content. Nokia customers all over the planet now download more than one million apps per day; that's not close to the 30 million apps downloaded from Apple's iTunes store, but it's a start.

Nokia continues to develop a host of mobile services, including Point & Find (a service that lets users gain relevant Internet content by simply pointing a camera phone at a real-world object), Nokia Home Control Center (lets users interact with home appliances and devices) and various satellite location services. Not only has the mobile phone giant invested a great deal of money in these projects, it is has also lured executives from Yahoo!, Microsoft, eBay and IBM and is collaborating with numerous other corporations to help build these business ventures.

STORM ON THE HORIZON

Regardless of the fact that Nokia dominates the mobile phone market, it seems that the latest wares from smaller competitors have been the darlings of the press. In an attempt to downplay the initial success of Apple's iPhone after it sold four million units its first year out, one Nokia vice president was heard to say, 'We've done that since we've had dinner last Friday'. That statement was meant to draw attention to the fact that Apple has only 4 per cent of the global mobile phone market. But given

the shifting tides of consumer preference, it is now apparent that Nokia has a serious threat on its hands.

Growth in smartphones is fast outpacing the growth of the overall market. Although global sales of mobile handsets surged 17 per cent in the first quarter of 2010, most of that was due to the increasing hunger for smartphones, which grew by a whopping 40 per cent, the strongest annual increase for the category since 2006. Despite Nokia's R&D efforts to expand its portfolio of high-end devices, the company still lags in that area. Smartphones are the only phones that Apple makes, so it is poised to enjoy the lion's share of market growth. For example, Apple sold 83 per cent more iPhones in 2009 than it did the year before, a bigger iump than any other company. In terms of market share, that translates to a jump from 3 per cent of the global smartphone market to more than 13 per cent.

Nokia stills hold the title not only for the most phones sold but also for the most smartphones, with a 39 per cent share. But Apple has hit another home run with its new iPhone4. On the first day of preorders, the company sold 600,000 units (a company record) despite the fact that higher than expected volume crashed the servers at both Apple's online store and AT&T. Close on the heels of Apple's new 'must have', Samsung's Galaxy S and Sony Ericsson's Xperia X10 will also be on the market. And Google's open-platform Android now boasts the fourth most widely used mobile-operating system.

Falling behind in this rapidly growing market segment is taking its toll on Nokia's financial performance. Halfway through 2010, the Finnish giant announced that its market share by volume would be flat for the year. Given that smartphones have higher prices and higher margins, this means that Nokia's share of the market by revenue would actually drop. Nokia dropped another bomb on investors by admitting that its profits would also be lower than previously forecasted.

But Nokia is determined to stay in the battle. Months following the release of the latest gadgets by its competitors, Nokia will launch it's impressive new N8, complete with a 12-megapixel camera, high-definition video and streaming TV services. But given its competitors' head start, many analysts question just how much of a splash Nokia's top-end model will make.

Questions for discussion

1. Does Nokia have a truly global strategy or just a series of regional strategies? Explain.
2. Consider the different global marketing environments discussed in the text. How do these environments differ in developing versus developed countries?
3. Discuss Nokia's global strategy in terms of the five global product and communications strategies.

4. Can competitors easily replicate Nokia's global strategy? Why or why not?

5. Based on the most recent competitive threats, what do you predict for Nokia in the coming years?

Sources: Kit Eaton, 'Nokia profit warning: it's been outmaneuvered by Apple', *Fast Company* (16 June 2010), accessed at www.fastcompany .com/1660601/nokia-cellphones-business-collapse-iphone-smartphones-profits-market-share; Ruth Bender, 'Apple, RIM gain ground in handset market', *Wall Street Journal* (20 May 2010), accessed at http://online.wsj .com/article/SB10001424052748703691804575253862699771880.html; Matt Kapko, 'Nokia world: strategies for the US, emerging markets', *RCR Wireless News* (17 December 2007), p. 16; James Ashton, 'Emerging markets help Nokia to win race for mobile supremacy', *The Sunday Times* (*London*) (27 January 2008), p. 11.

CHAPTER TWENTY

Sustainable marketing: social responsibility and ethics

Chapter preview

In this final chapter, we'll examine the concepts of sustainable marketing: meeting the needs of consumers, businesses and society – now and in the future – through socially and environmentally responsible marketing actions. We'll start by defining sustainable marketing and then look at some common criticisms of marketing as it impacts on individual consumers and public actions that promote sustainable marketing. Finally, we'll see how companies themselves can benefit from proactively pursuing sustainable marketing practices that bring value to not only individual customers but also society as a whole. Sustainable marketing actions are more than just the right thing to do; they're also good for business.

First, let's visit the concept of social and environmental sustainability in business. Perhaps no one gets more fired up about corporate social responsibility than Paul Polman, CEO of Anglo-Dutch consumer goods company Unilever. He's on a mission to use the resources of his company to combat the world's social ills. But he knows that to do this, his company must also be profitable. Polman firmly believes that companies actually can do both – that they can do well by doing good, and Unilever's performance suggests that may well be true.

Objective outline

➤ **Objective 1** Define sustainable marketing and discuss its importance.
Sustainable marketing (pp. 599–600)

➤ **Objective 2** Identify the major social criticisms of marketing.
Social criticisms of marketing (pp. 600–608)

➤ **Objective 3** Define consumerism and environmentalism and explain how they affect marketing strategies.

Consumer actions to promote sustainable marketing (pp. 609–613)

➤ **Objective 4** Describe the principles of sustainable marketing.
Business actions toward sustainable marketing (pp. 614–617)

➤ **Objective 5** Explain the role of ethics in marketing.
Marketing ethics (pp. 617–622)
The sustainable company (pp. 622)

Unilever – a prototype for tomorrow's company?

Unilever, the Anglo-Dutch consumer goods company, is a leading player in putting sustainability at the top of the corporate agenda.

In November 2010, Paul Polman, chief executive of Unilever, outlined his company's 'sustainable living plan' to city analysts in London. Anyone who has followed corporate pronouncements in recent years should be fluent in sustainability. His opening phrases were about customers demanding that their goods be ethically sourced and that companies help preserve the environment. Sustainability requires that companies reduce their use of water, energy and packaging. This cuts costs and boosts profitability, so shareholders win too.

So, the Unilever briefing began in familiar fashion. Consumers were increasingly turning to socially responsible brands, such as the company's Small & Mighty concentrated laundry detergent, which washes at lower temperatures. By 2020, Unilever's transport carbon dioxide emissions would be at or below current levels in spite of significantly higher volumes. Unilever would achieve this by reducing truck miles, using lower-emission vehicles and relying more on rail and ships.

But where were the figures on cost savings? Where were the promises about savings flowing to the bottom line? Someone asked: What will investors make of this? Mr Polman gave an unusual answer:

> 'Unilever has been around for 100-plus years. We want to be around for several hundred more years. So if you buy into this long-term value-creation model, which is equitable, which is shared, which is sustainable, then come and invest with us. If you don't buy into this, I respect you as a human being, but don't put your money in our company.'

But Unilever's tough stance on ethical behaviour and sustainability as a core social responsibility is more than promises, it turns into practical actions throughout its operations.

For a start, Unilever management believes there is a 'fortune at the bottom of the pyramid' – that companies can profit by selling cheap products to the poorest people in the world. Half of Unilever's sales are in emerging markets. For example, so notable is the drive to find adaptable products for the Indian mass market that it has a name, 'Indovation'. Recently, Unilever showed off Pureit, its low-cost water purifier. (At his London presentation Mr Polman had hoped to drink imported Mumbai water after putting it though the device. UK customs vetoed this, so he downed purified Thames water instead.)

Earlier, in Unilever's London headquarters, Gavin Neath, the consumer goods group's head of sustainability, took a plastic contraption out of its cardboard box and placed it on a table. It looks like a small and semi-transparent version of the vending machines that dispense drinks to office workers. The device is called a Pureit – and it is a drinks dispensing machine of sorts. Developed by Hindustan Unilever, the company's Indian subsidiary, the Pureit provides drinking water from any source, however polluted, purifying it with a series of meshes, parasite and pesticide traps and a germ-killing battery kit, without the need for boiling and without the use of mains electricity.

The Pureit is an illustration of how multinationals like Unilever are trying to get to grips with the notion of sustainability. In the US and Western Europe, the priorities are reducing the amount of packaging, cutting fuel consumption and providing for consumers who want to be sure that their purchases have been produced in an ethical or environmentally friendly fashion.

But in emerging markets, priorities are different. One high priority is to kill the harmful germs that can lead to water-borne diseases such as cholera and typhoid. In developing the market for Pureit, Hindustan Unilever had to come up with a product capable of competing with the usual method of purifying water

Unilever's Small + Mighty concentrated laundry detergent saves energy by washing at lower temperatures.

Source: Alamy Images/Stewart Goldstein

for drinking – boiling it. Unilever's study of how to provide India with clean drinking water resulted in the production of Pureit. The cost of boiling water means that one rupee buys 2.5 litres. For those who can afford bottled water, one rupee buys 0.3 litres. The up-front cost of a Pureit is Rs1,800 (€28), while the germ-killing battery has to be replaced at a cost of Rs300 (€5.60) after producing 1,500 litres of purified water. One rupee buys 3.5 litres of Pureit water, including the initial cost. The potential market for a low-cost machine providing drinkable water is huge, and not just in India. 'China has appalling water problems,' Mr Neath points out.

And companies like Unilever say that focusing on sustainability also helps them develop new markets. A study by Unilever on how clothes are washed in India revealed that far more water was used in rinsing than in the washing itself. The result was Surf Excel, an 'easy rinse' detergent.

But there is far more to Unilever's approach to social responsibility strategy. Today, in the developing world, 3.5million children under five die from diarrhoea and respiratory infections. Teaching children to wash their hands is a way of reducing this toll. The company sees opportunities to save lives and sell soap.

Not long ago, in south-west Uganda, the residents of Muko stood transfixed yet suspicious, arms crossed and frowning, as the strangers who arrived that morning danced on a stage they had erected from the back of a truck. With the aid of a sound system – rare enough to draw a crowd of 150 – three easygoing young visitors pumped out music and tried to strike up casual conversations with the villagers.

'How many people ate breakfast this morning?' one asks the audience, composed of women in kalei-doscopic shawls, men in sports shirts and children in blue school sweaters. The majority of hands are raised, but not all. 'And how many people washed their hands before eating?, About 30 people signal they did. And then: 'How many people used soap?' Two.

The result is familiar, which is why Unilever looks increasingly to emerging markets to drive sales growth, but finds antibacterial soaps a hard sell in parts of Africa. That is why its staff helped to write songs and skits for the show in Muko, which is delivering a message that washing hands with soap can eliminate the bugs that cause diarrhoea and respiratory infections – the two biggest killers of children in Africa after malaria. The event is a pilot for a government–backed country-wide campaign in which performers, decked out in 'Hands touch everywhere' T–shirts, will promote handwashing in 11 languages. But two aspects of Unilever's involvement make it unusual.

First, the company does not coat it in the do-goody mantra of 'corporate social responsibility'. It states openly that it wants to make washing hands with soap a habit – especially after going to the toilet and before eating – in order to sell more bars of its Lifebuoy soap. Unilever sells around €875,000 of soap in Uganda each year and is third in the market behind local manufacturers Mukwano and Bidco. But a survey by the Steadman research group found that only 14 per cent of Ugandan adults used soap to wash their hands after going to the toilet. 'Imagine if we change behaviour, if every household starts to wash hands with soap,' says George Inholo, Unilever's head in Uganda. 'We'll be smiling all the way to the bank.'

The second novel feature of the campaign in Africa is that Unilever has gained several unlikely bedfellows: Unicef, USAid, the London School of Hygiene and Tropical Medicine, the Bill and Melinda Gates Foundation and several non-governmental organisations. The institutions have formed a public–private partnership that is coordinated by the World Bank and replicated in Kenya, Tanzania, Senegal and Benin, where a total of €3.5million will be spent on handwashing.

But even for Unilever, it is not always easy maintaining the high moral ground.

Unilever built Dove into a multibillion pound brand with ads promoting women's Self–esteem, emphasising the gentle, caring and accepting nature of the brand. But environmental activists at Greenpeace made parodies of the Unilever ads, which were big hits on YouTube, accusing the company of destroying Indonesian rainforests for palm oil, a key ingredient in its products. Greenpeace demonstrators, some dressed as orangutans, climbed on to balconies at Unilever's London headquarters and other company sites to protest at the alleged destruction of Indonesia's rainforests for palm oil. Unilever's response was not to fight with Greenpeace, but instead to reverse its purchasing policy to buy palm oil only from suppliers who can demonstrate they do not cut down forests. Unilever's smart response to this pressure was important to protect its credibility on wider environmental issues.[1]

Responsible marketers discover what consumers want and respond with market offerings that create value for buyers to capture value in return. The *marketing concept* is a philosophy of customer value and mutual gain. Its practice leads the economy by an invisible hand to satisfy the many and changing needs of millions of consumers.

Not all marketers follow the marketing concept, however. In fact, some companies use questionable marketing practices that serve their own rather than consumers' interests. Moreover, even well-intentioned marketing actions that meet the current needs of some consumers may cause immediate or future harm to other consumers or the larger society. Responsible marketers must consider whether their actions are sustainable in the longer run.

Consider the sale of four-wheel drive cars (4 × 4s). These large vehicles meet the immediate needs of many drivers in terms of capacity, power and utility, and are great to drive – in fact a heck of a lot of fun to drive! However, to some, four-wheel drive vehicle sales involve larger questions of consumer safety and environmental responsibility. For example, environmental critics suggest that, in accidents, four-wheel drive vehicles are more likely to kill both their own occupants and the occupants of other vehicles. Their research claims that four-wheel drive vehicle occupants are three times more likely to die from their vehicle rolling, than are occupants of other cars. Moreover, environmentalists say that gas-guzzling 4 × 4s use more than their fair share of the world's energy and other resources and contribute disproportionately to pollution and congestion problems, creating costs that must be borne by both current and future generations. Of course, it may also be that environmentalists just don't like car drivers having fun.[2]

This chapter examines sustainable marketing and the social and environmental effects of private marketing practices. First, we address the question: What is sustainable marketing and why is it important?

AUTHOR COMMENT

Marketers must think beyond immediate customer satisfaction and business performance toward strategies that preserve the world for future generations.

SUSTAINABLE MARKETING

Sustainable marketing calls for socially and environmentally responsible actions that meet the present needs of consumers and businesses while also preserving or enhancing the ability of future generations to meet their needs. Figure 20.1 compares the sustainable marketing concept with marketing concepts we studied in earlier chapters.

The *marketing concept* recognises that organisations thrive from day to day by determining the current needs and wants of target group customers and fulfilling those needs and wants more effectively and efficiently than competitors do. It focuses on meeting the company's short-term sales, growth and profit needs by giving customers what they want now. However, satisfying consumers' immediate needs and desires doesn't always serve the future best interests of either customers or the business.

Sustainable marketing— Socially and environmentally responsible marketing that meets the present needs of consumers and business while also preserving or enhancing the ability of future generations to meet their needs.

Figure 20.1 Sustainable marketing

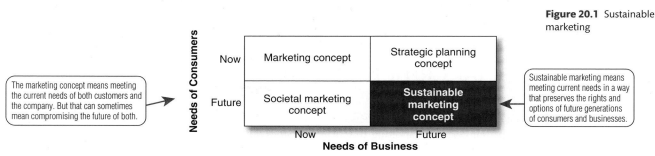

For example, fast-food giant McDonald's early decisions to market tasty but fat- and salt-laden fast foods created immediate satisfaction for customers and sales and profits for the company. However, critics assert that McDonald's and other fast-food chains have contributed to a longer-term international obesity epidemic, damaging consumer health and burdening national health systems. In response, many consumers have begun looking for healthier eating options, causing a slump in the sales and profits of the fast-food industry. Beyond issues of ethical behaviour and social welfare, McDonald's was also criticised for the sizeable environmental footprint of its vast global operations, everything from wasteful packaging and solid waste creation to inefficient energy use in its stores. Thus, McDonald's strategy was not sustainable in terms of either consumer or company benefit.

Whereas the *societal marketing concept* identified in Figure 20.1 considers the future welfare of consumers and the *strategic planning concept* considers future company needs, the *sustainable marketing concept* considers both. Sustainable marketing calls for socially and environmentally responsible actions that meet both the immediate and future needs of customers and the company.

For example, as we discussed in Chapter 2, in recent years, McDonald's has responded with a more sustainable 'Plan to Win' strategy of diversifying into salads, fruits, grilled chicken, low-fat milk and other healthy food and drinks. After a seven-year search for healthier cooking oil, McDonald's phased out traditional artery-clogging transfats without compromising the taste of its french fries. And the company launched a major multifaceted education campaign – called 'It's what I eat and what I do … I'm lovin' it' – to help consumers better understand the keys to living balanced, active lifestyles.

The McDonald's 'Plan to Win' strategy also addresses environmental issues. For example, it calls for food-supply sustainability, reduced and environmentally sustainable packaging, re-use and recycling, and more responsible store designs. McDonald's has even developed an environmental scorecard that rates its suppliers' performance in areas such as water use, energy use and solid waste management.

McDonald's more sustainable strategy is benefiting the company as well as its customers. Since announcing its 'Plan to Win' strategy, McDonald's sales have increased by more than 50 per cent, and profits have more than quadrupled. And for the past five years, the company has been included in the Dow Jones Sustainability Index, recognising its commitment to sustainable economic, environmental and social performance. Thus, McDonald's is well positioned for a sustainably profitable future.[3]

Truly sustainable marketing requires a smooth-functioning marketing system in which consumers, companies, public policy makers and others work together to ensure socially and environmentally responsible marketing actions. Unfortunately, however, the marketing system doesn't always work smoothly. The following sections examine several sustainability questions: What are the most frequent social criticisms of marketing? What steps have private citizens taken to curb marketing ills? What steps have legislators and government agencies taken to promote sustainable marketing? What steps have enlightened companies taken to carry out socially responsible and ethical marketing that creates sustainable value for both individual customers and society as a whole?[4]

AUTHOR COMMENT

In most ways, we all benefit greatly from marketing activities. However, like most other human endeavours, marketing has its flaws. Here we present both sides of some of the most common criticisms of marketing.

SOCIAL CRITICISMS OF MARKETING

Marketing receives much criticism. Some of this criticism is justified; much is not. Social critics claim that certain marketing practices hurt individual consumers, society as a whole and other business firms.

Marketing's impact on individual consumers

Consumers have many concerns about how well the marketing system serves their interests. Surveys usually show that consumers hold mixed or even slightly unfavourable attitudes toward marketing practices. Consumer advocates, government agencies and other critics have accused marketing of harming consumers through high prices, deceptive practices, high-pressure selling, shoddy or unsafe products, planned obsolescence and poor service to disadvantaged consumers. Such questionable marketing practices are not sustainable in terms of long-term consumer or business welfare.

High prices

Many critics charge that marketing causes prices to be higher than they would be under more 'sensible' systems. Such high prices are hard to swallow, especially when the economy takes a downturn. Critics point to three factors – *high costs of distribution, high advertising and promotion costs* and *excessive mark-ups*.

High costs of distribution

A long-standing charge is that greedy channel intermediaries mark up prices beyond the value of their services. Critics charge that there are too many intermediaries, which are also inefficient and/or provide unnecessary or duplicate services. As a result, distribution costs too much, and consumers pay for these excessive costs in the form of higher prices.

How do resellers answer these charges? They argue that intermediaries do work that would otherwise have to be done by manufacturers or consumers. Mark-ups reflect services that consumers themselves want – more convenience, larger stores and assortments, more service, longer store hours, returns policies and others. In fact, they argue, retail competition is so intense that margins are actually quite low. If some resellers try to charge too much relative to the value they add, other resellers will step in with lower prices. Low-price stores such as Walmart, Tesco, Carrefour, Costco and other discounters pressure their competitors to operate efficiently and keep their prices down. In fact, in the wake of economic downturn and recession, only the most efficient retailers have survived profitably.

High advertising and promotion costs

Modern marketing is also accused of pushing up prices to finance heavy advertising and sales promotion. For example, a few dozen tablets of a heavily promoted brand of pain reliever sell for the same price as 100 tablets of less-promoted brands. Differentiated products – cosmetics, detergents, toiletries – include promotion and packaging costs that can amount to 40 per cent or more of the manufacturer's price to the retailer. Critics charge that much of the packaging and promotion adds only psychological, not functional, value to the product.

Marketers respond that although advertising adds to product costs, it also adds value by informing potential buyers of the availability and merits of a brand. Brand name products may cost more, but branding gives buyers assurances of consistent quality. Moreover, consumers can usually buy functional versions of products at lower prices. However, they *want* and are willing to pay more for products that also provide psychological benefits – that make them feel wealthy, attractive or special. Also, heavy advertising and promotion may be necessary for a firm to match competitors' efforts; the business would lose 'share of mind' if it did not match competitive spending.

At the same time, companies are cost conscious about promotion and try to spend their funds wisely. Today's increasingly more frugal consumers are demanding genuine value for the prices they pay. The continuing shift toward buying retailer own-brands and generics suggests that when it comes to value, consumers want action, not just talk.

Excessive mark-ups

Critics also charge that some companies mark up goods excessively. They point to the drug industry, where a pill costing 5 cents to make may cost the consumer €2 to buy. They point to the pricing

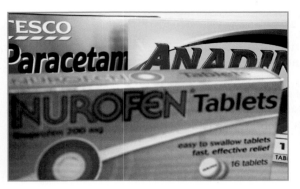

Pharmaceutical product mark-up must cover the costs of purchasing, promoting and distributing existing medicines plus the high R & D costs of formulating and testing new medicines.

Source: Alamy Images/Lynne Sutherland

tactics of funeral homes that prey on the confused emotions of bereaved relatives, and the high charges for car repairs and other services.

Marketers respond that most businesses try to deal fairly with consumers because they want to build customer relationships and repeat business, and that most consumer abuses are unintentional. Marketers also respond that consumers often don't understand the reasons for high mark-ups. For example, pharmaceutical mark-ups must cover the costs of purchasing, promoting and distributing existing medicines plus the high R&D costs of formulating and testing new medicines. As pharmaceuticals company GlaxoSmithKline states in its ads, 'Today's medicines finance tomorrow's miracles.'

Deceptive practices

Marketers are sometimes accused of deceptive practices that lead consumers to believe they will get more value than they actually do. Deceptive practices fall into three groups: pricing, promotion and packaging. *Deceptive pricing* includes practices such as falsely advertising 'factory' or 'wholesale' prices or a large price reduction from a falsely high retail list price. *Deceptive promotion* includes practices such as misrepresenting the product's features or performance or luring customers to the store for a bargain that is out of stock. *Deceptive packaging* includes exaggerating package contents through subtle design, using misleading labelling or describing size in misleading terms.

Deceptive practices have led to legislation and other consumer protection actions. Despite laws and regulations, some critics argue that deceptive claims are still the norm. Consider the glut of 'environmental responsibility' claims some marketers are now making, which some call 'greenwashing'. Biodegradable, eco-friendly, recycled, green, carbon neutral, carbon offsets, made from sustainable resources – such phrases are popping up more and more on products worldwide, leading many to question their validity. Last year, Canadian environmental conultancy TerraChoice Environmental Marketing, which advises companies on green positioning, reviewed claims companies made about 2,219 widely sold goods. TerraChoice concluded that 98 per cent of the products committed 'at least one of the sins of greenwashing.' 'There is a lot going on there that just isn't right,' says one environmental trend-watcher. 'If truly green products have a hard time differentiating themselves from fake ones, then this whole notion of a green market will fall apart,' says a TerraChoice executive.[5]

The toughest problem is defining what is 'deceptive.' For instance, an advertiser's claim that its chewing gum will 'rock your world' isn't intended to be taken literally. Instead, the advertiser might claim, it is 'puffery' – innocent exaggeration for effect. However, others claim that puffery and alluring imagery can harm consumers in subtle ways. Think about the popular and long-running MasterCard priceless commercials that painted pictures of consumers fulfilling their priceless dreams despite the costs. The ads suggested that your credit card can make it happen. But critics charge that such imagery by credit card companies encouraged a spend-now-pay-later attitude that caused many consumers to *over*use their cards. They point to statistics showing that consumers in the developed countries took on record amounts of credit card debt – often more than they could repay – contributing heavily to the international financial crisis of the early 2010s.

Marketers argue that most companies avoid deceptive practices. Because such practices harm a company's business in the long run, they simply aren't sustainable. Profitable customer relationships are built on a foundation of value and trust. If consumers do not get what they expect, they will switch to more reliable products. In addition, consumers usually protect themselves from deception. Most consumers recognise a marketer's selling intent and are careful when they buy, sometimes even to the point of not believing completely true product claims.

High-pressure selling

Salespeople are sometimes accused of high-pressure selling that persuades people to buy goods they had no intention of buying. It is often said that insurance, property and used cars are *sold*, not *bought*. Salespeople are trained to deliver smooth, canned talks to entice purchase. They sell hard because sales contests promise big prizes to those who sell the most. Similarly, TV infomercial pitchmen use 'yell and sell' presentations that create a sense of consumer urgency that only those with the strongest willpower can resist.

But in most cases, marketers have little to gain from high-pressure selling. Such tactics may work in one-off selling situations for short-term gain. However, most selling involves building long-term relationships with valued customers. High-pressure or deceptive selling can seriously damage such relationships. For example, imagine a P&G account manager trying to pressure a Tesco buyer or an IBM salesperson trying to browbeat an IT manager at GE. It simply wouldn't work.

Shoddy, harmful or unsafe products

Another criticism concerns poor product quality or function. One common complaint is that products/services are not made well and do not perform adequately. A second complaint concerns product safety. Product safety has been a problem for several reasons, including company indifference, increased product complexity and poor quality control. A third complaint is that many products deliver little benefit or that they might even be harmful.

For example, think again about the fast-food industry. Many critics blame the plentiful supply of fat-laden, high calorie, fast-foods for the rapidly growing global obesity epidemic. According to the World Health Organization, obesity is one of the greatest public health challenges of the twenty-first century and its prevalence has tripled in many European countries since the 1980s. The numbers of those affected continue to rise at an alarming rate, particularly among children. Obesity is already responsible for 2–8 per cent of health-care costs and 10–13 per cent of deaths in different parts of Europe. Within Europe, the UK has the highest level of obesity in Europe – and the West Midlands was the fattest region in the European Union, with 29 per cent of adults classed as obese. The level was double that of the EU average of 14 per cent. Similarly, studies show that some 34 per cent of American adults are obese, with another 34 per cent considered overweight. Some 32 per cent of American children are obese. The obesity epidemic continues to spread despite numerous medical studies showing that excess weight brings increased risks for heart disease, diabetes and other maladies, even cancer.[6]

Critics are quick to fault what they see as greedy food marketers, who are cashing in on vulnerable consumers, producing generations of overeaters. Some food marketers are looking pretty much guilty as charged. Take Hardee's, for example – the number-five fast-food restaurant in the United States. At a time when other fast-food chains, such as McDonald's and Subway, have been pushing healthier meals, Hardee's has launched one artery-clogging burger after another – gifts to consumers fed up with 'healthy', low-fat menu items. Its Monster Thickburger contains two-thirds of a pound of Angus beef, four strips of bacon and three slices of American cheese, all nestled in a buttered sesame-seed bun slathered with mayonnaise. The blockbuster burger weighs in at an eye-popping 1,320 calories and 95 grams of fat, far greater than the government's recommended fat intake for an entire day (65 grams). Hardee's appears to be bucking the trend: since introducing the mouth-watering Thickburger line, Hardee's has experienced healthy sales increases and even fatter profits.

Is Hardee's being socially irresponsible by aggressively promoting overindulgence to ill-informed or unwary consumers? Or is it simply practising good marketing, creating more value for its customers by offering big juicy burgers that stimulate their taste buds and let them make their own eating choices? Hardee's claims the latter. It says that its target consumers – young men between the ages of 18 and 34 – are capable of making their own decisions about health and well-being.

And Hardee's certainly doesn't hide the nutritional facts; they are clearly posted on the company's website. The site describes the Monster Thickburger as 'a monument to decadence – the only thing that can slay the hunger of a young guy on the move'. And the chief executive officer of CKE, Hardee's parent company, notes that the chain has salads and low-carb burgers on its menus, but 'we sell very few of them'. So, is Hardee's being irresponsible or simply responsive? As in many matters of social responsibility, what's right and what's wrong may be a matter of opinion.

However, most manufacturers *want* to produce quality goods. The way a company deals with product quality and safety problems can damage or help its reputation. Companies selling poor-quality or unsafe products risk damaging conflicts with consumer groups and regulators. Unsafe products can result in product liability suits and large awards for damages. More fundamentally, consumers who are unhappy with a firm's products may avoid future purchases and talk other consumers into doing the same. Thus, quality missteps are not consistent with sustainable marketing. Today's marketers know that good quality results in customer value and satisfaction, which in turn creates sustainable customer relationships.

Planned obsolescence

Critics also have charged that some companies practise *planned obsolescence*, causing their products to become obsolete before they actually should need replacement. They accuse some producers of using materials and components that will break, wear, rust or rot sooner than they should. And if the products themselves don't wear out fast enough, other companies are charged with *perceived obsolescence* – continually changing consumer concepts of acceptable styles to encourage more and earlier buying.[7] An obvious example is constantly changing clothing fashions.

Still others are accused of introducing planned streams of new products that make older models obsolete. Critics claim that this occurs all the time in the consumer electronics and computer industries. If you're like most people, you probably have a drawer full of yesterday's hottest technological gadgets – from mobile phones and cameras to iPods and flash drives – now reduced to the status of fossils. It seems that anything more than a year or two old is hopelessly out of date. For example, here's one critic's tongue-in-cheek take on Apple's methods for getting customers to ditch the old iPod and buy the latest and greatest version:[8]

> Apple has probably already developed iPods that double as jetpacks that allow you to orbit the moon. But you won't see those anytime soon. And when they come out, they'll first just have iPods that can fly you to your neighbour's house. Then a few months later they'll introduce ones that can fly you across the country. And that'll seem pretty amazing compared to the ones that could only go down the street, but they won't be amazing three months later, when the iPod Sputnik hits the market.

Marketers respond that consumers *like* style changes; they get tired of the old goods and want a new look in fashion. Or they *want* the latest high-tech innovations, even if older models still work. No one has to buy the new product, and if too few people like it, it will simply fail. Finally, most companies do not design their products to break down earlier because they do not want to lose customers to other brands. Instead, they seek constant improvement to ensure that products will consistently meet or exceed customer expectations. Much of the so-called planned obsolescence is the working of the competitive and technological forces in a free society – forces that lead to ever-improving goods and services.

Poor service to disadvantaged consumers

Finally, the marketing system has been accused of poorly serving disadvantaged consumers. For example, critics in the US claim that the urban poor of that country often have to shop in smaller stores that carry inferior goods and charge higher prices. The presence of large national chain stores in low-income neighbourhoods would help to keep prices down. However, the critics accuse major chain retailers of 'redlining', drawing a red line around disadvantaged neighbourhoods and avoiding placing stores there creating 'food deserts'.

Interestingly, the food desert concept was first introduced in the UK in the early 1990s to examine disparities in food pricing, and to describe geographical areas with limited access to retail grocery stores. Food deserts can be found in rural as well as urban areas, but are most prevalent in low-socioeconomic minority communities in the inner cities of Europe. They are associated with a variety of diet-related health problems, and with a shortage of supermarkets.[9]

Similarly, in the US, poor areas have 30 per cent fewer supermarkets than affluent areas do. As a result, many low-income consumers find themselves in 'food deserts', which are awash with small markets offering fast-food, confectionery and Cokes, but where fruits and vegetables or fresh fish or chicken are out of reach. 'In low-income areas, you can go for miles without being able to find a fresh apple or a piece of broccoli,' says the executive director of the Food Trust, a group that's trying to tackle the US problem. In turn, the lack of access to healthy, affordable fresh foods has a negative impact on the health of under-served consumers in these areas.

Similar redlining charges have been levelled at the insurance, consumer lending, banking and health-care industries Most recently, however, consumer advocates charged that banks and mortgage lenders were practising 'reverse-redlining'. Instead of staying away from people in poor urban areas, they targeted and exploited them by offering them risky subprime mortgages rather than safer mortgages with better terms. These subprime mortgages often featured adjustable interest rates that started out very low but quickly increased. When interest rates went up, many house owners around the world could no longer afford their mortgage payments. And as housing prices dropped, these owners were trapped in debt and owed more than their houses were worth, leading to bankruptcies, repossessions and the subprime mortgage crisis.

Clearly, better marketing systems must be built to service disadvantaged consumers. In fact, many marketers profitably target such consumers with legitimate goods and services that create real value. In cases in which marketers do not step in to fill the void, it is likely governments will force them. There is also the growing potential for emerging market companies to bring their ways of doing business – successful with the poorest consumers in the world – to bear in Europe and the US and shut existing companies out from this market.

Marketing's impact on society as a whole

The marketing system has been accused of adding to several 'evils' in society at large, such as creating too much materialism, too few social goods, and a glut of cultural pollution.

False wants and too much materialism

Critics have charged that the marketing system urges too much interest in material possessions, and the consumer's love affair with worldly possessions is not sustainable. Too often, people are judged by what they *own* rather than by who they *are*. The critics do not view this interest in material things as a natural state of mind but rather as a matter of false wants created by marketing. Marketers, they claim, stimulate people's desires for goods and create materialistic models of the good life. Thus, marketers have created an endless cycle of mass consumption based on a distorted interpretation of the human priorities.

One sociologist attributes consumer overspending to a growing 'aspiration gap' – the gap between what we have and what we want, between the lifestyles we can afford and those to which we aspire. This aspiration gap results at least partly from a barrage of marketing that encourages people to focus on the acquisition and consumption of goods. Advertising encourages consumers to aspire to celebrity lifestyles, to keep up with the Joneses by acquiring more stuff. Some marketing-frenzied consumers will let nothing stand between them and their acquisitions. Recently, rumours of half-price clothes caused a riot among shoppers at Primark's new flagship store in London. A security guard was injured as eager shoppers surged into the Oxford Street store shoving other shoppers to the ground. It was reported that mounted police and the store security guards struggled to get control of the hundreds of shoppers who were shouting and screaming. As the doors were opened the bargain-hunters, some of whom had been queuing for several hours, surged forward and the doors collapsed. The scenes of mayhem continued inside as shoppers were seen stripping down to their underwear to try on clothes. Staff at Primark said although they were prepared for a large number of customers even they were amazed by the chaotic scenes.[10]

Thus, marketing is seen as creating false wants that benefit industry more than consumers. 'In the world of consumerism, marketing is there to promote consumption,' says one marketing critic. It is 'inevitable that marketing will promote over-consumption, and from this, a psychologically, as well as ecologically, unsustainable world.' Says another critic: 'For most of us, our basic material needs are satisfied, so we seek in ever-growing consumption the satisfaction of wants, which consumption cannot possibly deliver. More is not always better; it is often worse.'[11]

Some critics have taken their concerns to the public, via the Web or even straight to the streets. For example, consumer activist Annie Leonard founded the Story of Stuff project with a 20-minute Web video about the social and environmental consequences of the consumerist society's love affair with stuff; the video has been viewed more than 10 million times online and in thousands of schools and community centres around the world (see www.storyofstuff.org).[12]

Marketers respond that such criticisms overstate the power of business to create needs. People have strong defences against advertising and other marketing tools. Marketers are most effective when they appeal to existing wants rather than when they attempt to create new ones. Furthermore, people seek information when making important purchases and often do not rely on single sources. Even minor purchases that may be affected by advertising messages lead to repeat purchases only if the product delivers the promised customer value. Finally, the high failure rate of new products shows that companies are not able to control demand.

On a deeper level, our wants and values are influenced not only by marketers but also by family, peer groups, religion, cultural background and education. If Europeans and Americans are highly materialistic, these values arose out of basic socialisation processes that go much deeper than business and mass media could produce alone.

Moreover, consumption patterns and attitudes are also subject to larger forces, such as the economy. As discussed in Chapter 1, the economic downturn and recession put a damper on materialism and conspicuous spending. In one consumer survey, 75 per cent of respondents agreed that 'the downturn is encouraging me to evaluate what is really important in life'. Many observers predict a new age of consumer thrift. Says one observer, shoppers 'now are taking pride in their newfound financial discipline'. As a result, far from encouraging today's more frugal consumers to overspend their means, marketers are working to help them find greater value with less.[13]

Too few social goods

Business has been accused of overselling private goods at the expense of public goods. As private goods increase, they require more public services that are usually not forthcoming. For example, an increase in car ownership (private good) requires more roads, traffic control, parking spaces and police services (public goods). The overselling of private goods results in 'social costs'. For cars, some of the social costs include traffic congestion, fuel shortages and air pollution. Traffic congestion costs the European Union more than one per cent of gross domestic product – or over €100 billion per year.[14] In the United States, American travellers lose, on average, 36 hours a year in traffic jams, costing the country more than $87 billion a year, and in the process, they waste 2.8 billion gallons of fuel and emit millions of tons of greenhouse gases.[15]

A way must be found to restore a balance between private and public goods. One option is to make producers bear the full social costs of their operations. For example, many governments are requiring car manufacturers to build vehicles with more efficient engines and better pollution-control systems. Carmakers will then raise their prices to cover the extra costs. If buyers find the price of some cars too high, however, the producers of these cars will disappear, or the models will be discontinued. Demand will then move to those producers that can support the sum of the private and social costs.

A second option is to make consumers pay the social costs. For example, many cities around the world are now charging 'congestion tolls' in an effort to reduce traffic congestion. To unclog its streets, the city of London levies a congestion charge of £10 per day per car to drive in an eight-square-mile area of the city. The charge has not only reduced traffic congestion within the zone by 21 per cent (70,000 fewer vehicles per day) and increased bicycling by 43 per cent but also raises money to help pay for London's public transport system.[16]

Cultural pollution

Critics charge the marketing system with creating *cultural pollution*. Our senses are being constantly assaulted by marketing and advertising. Frequent commercials interrupt serious programmes; pages of ads obscure magazines; advertising inserts cascade from newspapers and magazines; advertising hoardings mar beautiful scenery; spam fills our e-mail inboxes. These interruptions continually pollute people's minds with messages of materialism, sex, power or status. Research suggests that most consumers think there are too many TV ads, and some critics call for sweeping changes.[17]

Marketers answer the charges of 'commercial noise' with these arguments. First, they hope that their ads primarily reach the target audience. But because of mass-communication channels, some ads are bound to reach people who have no interest in the product and are therefore bored or annoyed. People who buy magazines addressed to their interests – such as *Vogue* or *Fortune* – rarely complain about the ads because the magazines advertise products of interest.

Second, ads make much of commercial television and radio free to users and keep down the costs of magazines and newspapers. Many people think commercials are a small price to pay for these benefits. Consumers find many television commercials entertaining and seek them out; for example, by viewing them on YouTube and sharing with friends. Finally, today's consumers have alternatives. For example, they can zip or zap TV commercials on recorded programmes or avoid them altogether on many paid cable or satellite channels. Thus, to hold consumer attention, advertisers are making their ads more entertaining and informative.

Balancing private and public goods: in response to lane-clogging traffic congestion, London now levies a congestion charge.

Source: Alamy Images/Finnbarr Webster

Marketing's impact on other businesses

Critics also charge that a company's marketing practices can harm other companies and reduce competition. Three problems are involved: acquisition of competitors, marketing practices that create barriers to entry, and unfair competitive marketing practices.

Critics claim that firms are harmed and competition reduced when companies expand by acquiring competitors rather than by developing their own new products. The large number of acquisitions and the rapid pace of industry consolidation over the past several decades have caused concern that vigorous young competitors will be absorbed, so competition will be reduced. In virtually every major industry – retailing, entertainment, financial services, public utilities, transport, automotive, telecommunications, health care – the number of major competitors is shrinking.

Acquisition is a complex subject. Acquisitions can sometimes be good for society. The acquiring company may gain economies of scale that lead to lower costs and lower prices. A well-managed company may take over a poorly managed company and improve its efficiency. An industry that was not very competitive might become more competitive after the acquisition. But acquisitions can also be harmful and, therefore, are closely regulated by government.

Critics have also charged that marketing practices bar new companies from entering an industry. Large marketing companies can use patents and heavy promotion spending or tie up suppliers or dealers to keep out or drive out competitors. Those concerned with anti-monopoly regulation recognise that some barriers are the natural result of the economic advantages of doing business on a large scale. Existing and new laws can challenge other barriers. For example, some critics have proposed a progressive tax on advertising spending to reduce the role of selling costs as a major barrier to entry.

Finally, some firms have, in fact, used unfair competitive marketing practices with the intention of hurting or destroying other firms. They may set their prices below costs, threaten to cut off

Critics of Tesco's dominant position have subverted Tesco's 'Every little helps' slogan to 'Every little hurts' on their website.

business with suppliers, or discourage the buying of a competitor's products. Various laws work to prevent such predatory competition. It is difficult, however, to prove that the intent or action was really predatory.

> For example, in the UK over recent years, Tesco has been accused of trying to build a 'Tescopoly' or monopoly on British towns and cities. The retailer is accused of using predatory pricing and sheer market power in selected towns to drive smaller retailers out of business. Tesco has become a lightning rod for protests by people in many towns who worry that the dominant UK retailer's unfair practices will choke out local businesses – protestors have subverted Tesco's 'Every little helps' slogan into 'Every little hurts' on their website (see www.everylittlehurts.co.uk/web). However, whereas critics charge that Tesco's actions are predatory and an abuse of market power, others assert that its actions are just the healthy competition of a more efficient company against less efficient ones.

Interestingly, in the US, when mass retailer Walmart began a programme to sell generic drugs at \$4(€3) a prescription, local pharmacists complained of predatory pricing. They charged that at those low prices, Walmart must be selling under cost to drive them out of business. But Walmart claimed that, given its substantial buying power and efficient operations, it could make a profit at those prices. The \$4 pricing programme, the retailer claimed, was not aimed at putting competitors out of business. Rather, it was simply a good competitive move that served customers better and brought more of them in the door. Moreover, Walmart's programme drove down prescription prices at the pharmacies of other supermarkets and discount stores, again to the benefit of customers. Currently more than 300 prescription drugs are available for \$4 at the various chains.[18]

AUTHOR COMMENT

Sustainable marketing isn't the province of businesses and governments only. Through consumerism and environmentalism, consumers themselves can play an important role.

CONSUMER ACTIONS TO PROMOTE SUSTAINABLE MARKETING

Sustainable marketing calls for more responsible actions by both businesses and consumers. Because some people view business as the cause of many economic and social ills, grassroots movements have arisen from time to time to keep companies in line. Two major movements have been *consumerism* and *environmentalism*.

Consumerism

Consumerism is an organised movement of citizens and government agencies to improve the rights and power of buyers in relation to sellers. Traditional *sellers' rights* include the following:

- The right to introduce any product in any size and style, provided it is not hazardous to personal health or safety, or, if it is, to include proper warnings and controls.
- The right to charge any price for the product, provided no discrimination exists among similar kinds of buyers.
- The right to spend any amount to promote the product, provided it is not defined as unfair competition.
- The right to use any product message, provided it is not misleading or dishonest in content or execution.
- The right to use buying incentive programmes, provided they are not unfair or misleading.

Traditional *buyers' rights* include the following:

- The right not to buy a product that is offered for sale.
- The right to expect the product to be safe.
- The right to expect the product to perform as claimed.

Comparing these rights, many believe that the balance of power lies on the seller's side. True, the buyer can refuse to buy. But critics feel that the buyer has too little information, education and protection to make wise decisions when facing sophisticated sellers, even though this view is somewhat patronising. Consumer advocates call for the following additional consumer rights:

- The right to be well informed about important aspects of the product.
- The right to be protected against questionable products and marketing practices.
- The right to influence products and marketing practices in ways that will improve 'quality of life'.
- The right to consume now in a way that will preserve the world for future generations of consumers.

Each proposed right has led to more specific proposals by consumerists and consumer protection actions by government. The right to be informed includes the right to know the true interest on a loan (truth in lending), the true cost per unit of a brand (unit pricing), the ingredients in a product (ingredient labelling), the nutritional value of foods (nutritional labelling), product freshness (sell-by dating) and the true benefits of a product (truth in advertising). Proposals related to consumer protection include strengthening consumer rights in cases of business fraud, requiring greater product safety, ensuring information privacy and giving more power to government agencies. Proposals relating to quality of life include controlling the ingredients that go into certain products and packaging and reducing the level of advertising 'noise'. Proposals for preserving the world for future consumption include promoting the use of sustainable ingredients, recycling and reducing solid wastes, and managing energy consumption.

Sustainable marketing applies not only to consumers but also to businesses and governments. Consumers have not only the *right* but also the *responsibility* to protect themselves instead of leaving this function to the government or someone else. Consumers who believe they got a bad deal

Consumerism—An organised movement of citizens and government agencies to improve the rights and power of buyers in relation to sellers.

have several remedies available, including contacting the company or the media contacting compliance and enforcement authorities and going to small-claims courts. Consumers should also make good consumption choices, rewarding companies that act responsibly while punishing those that don't. Ultimately, the move from irresponsible consumption to sustainable consumption is in the hands of consumers.

Environmentalism

Environmentalism—An organised movement of concerned citizens and government agencies to protect and improve people's current and future living environment.

Whereas consumerists consider whether the marketing system is efficiently serving consumer wants, environmentalists are concerned with marketing's effects on the environment and the environmental costs of serving consumer needs and wants. **Environmentalism** is an organised movement of concerned citizens, businesses and government agencies to protect and improve people's current and future living environment.

Most environmentalists are not against marketing and consumption (though some are); they usually just want people and organisations to operate with more care for the environment. 'Too often the environment is seen as one small piece of the economy,' says one activist. 'But it's not just one little thing, it's what every single thing in our life depends upon.'[19] The marketing system's goal, as asserted by environmentalists, should not be to maximise consumption, consumer choice or consumer satisfaction but rather maximise life quality. 'Life quality' means not only the quantity and quality of consumer goods and services but also the quality of the environment.

The first wave of modern environmentalism was driven by environmental groups and concerned consumers in the 1960s and 1970s. They were concerned with damage to the ecosystem caused by mining, forest depletion, acid rain, global warming, toxic and solid wastes, and litter. They were also concerned with the loss of recreational areas and the increase in health problems caused by bad air, polluted water and chemically treated food.

The second environmentalism wave was driven by governments in most countries responding to the growing 'green lobby', which passed laws and regulations during the 1970s and 1980s governing industrial practices impacting the environment. Although varying between different countries, this wave hit some industries hard. Steel companies and utilities had to invest massive amounts in pollution control equipment and cleaner but more expensive fuels. The motor industry had to introduce expensive emissions controls in cars. The packaging industry had to find ways to improve recyclability and reduce solid wastes. These industries and others have often resented and resisted environmental regulations, especially when they have been imposed too rapidly to allow companies to make proper adjustments. Many of these companies claim they have had to absorb large costs that have made them less competitive.

Environmental sustainability—A management approach that involves developing strategies that both sustain the environment and produce profits for the company.

The first two environmentalism waves have now merged into a third and stronger wave in which companies are accepting more responsibility for doing no harm to the environment. They are shifting from protest to prevention, from regulation to responsibility. More and more companies are adopting policies of **environmental sustainability**. Simply put, environmental sustainability is about generating profits while helping to save the planet. Environmental sustainability is a crucial but difficult societal goal.

Some companies have responded to consumer environmental concerns by doing only what is required to avert new regulations or keep environmentalists quiet. Enlightened companies, however, are taking action not because someone is forcing them to or to reap short-term profits, but because it's the right thing to do – for both the company and the planet's environmental future.

Figure 20.2 shows a grid that companies can use to gauge their progress toward environmental sustainability. In includes both internal and external 'greening' activities that will pay off for the firm and environment in the short term and 'beyond greening' activities that will pay off in the longer term. At the most basic level, a company can practise *pollution prevention*. This involves more than pollution control – cleaning up waste after it has been created. Pollution prevention means eliminating or minimising waste before it is created. Companies emphasising prevention have responded with internal 'green marketing' programmes – designing and developing ecologically safer products, recyclable and biodegradable packaging, better pollution controls and more energy-efficient operations.

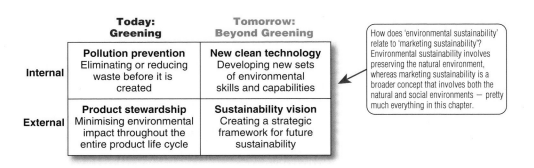

	Today: Greening	**Tomorrow:** Beyond Greening
Internal	**Pollution prevention** Eliminating or reducing waste before it is created	**New clean technology** Developing new sets of environmental skills and capabilities
External	**Product stewardship** Minimising environmental impact throughout the entire product life cycle	**Sustainability vision** Creating a strategic framework for future sustainability

How does 'environmental sustainability' relate to 'marketing sustainability'? Environmental sustainability involves preserving the natural environment, whereas marketing sustainability is a broader concept that involves both the natural and social environments — pretty much everything in this chapter.

Figure 20.2 The environmental sustainability portfolio

Sources: Stuart L. Hart, 'Innovation, Creative Destruction and Surtainability', *Research Technology Management*, September–October 2005, pp. 21–27.

For example, Burger King stopped using its Indonesian palm oil suppliers, because of concerns about environmental damage following Greenpeace allegations of rainforest destruction. Unilever, Nestlé and Kraft have broken off relationships with the same suppliers for the same reason. Swedish furniture company Ikea has bought German wind farms as part of its efforts to reduce the carbon footprint of its worldwide chain of flat-pack furniture stores, following a similar deal in France. In the UK, retailers are changing the practice of centralised buying to stock more local produce – Tesco is looking at sales of locally-sourced goods reaching €1.25 billion, and Asda is achieving a 25 per cent annual growth in sales of local produce – supporting local farmers and reducing transport costs. Some of the world's largest clothing and footwear manufacturers and retailers are launching an eco-label to allow shirts, trousers and shoes sold globally to be labelled with tags so consumers can see how much the items' production and use impacts on the environment – participants include Gap, Levi Strauss, Marks & Spencer, H&M and Li & Fung (a major textile supplier).[20]

The intensity of media and consumer scrutiny of these promises is more searching than ever before. If you do not make information about your products and supplies public, the chances are increasing that consumers will do it for you. For example, GoodGuide is an online database of information about the health, environmental and social impact of 65,000 common products, which consumers can access to trace the provenance of their products.[21] Nonetheless, sometimes companies get it wrong and suffer the consequences:

> Shoppers buying Polo mints at Poundworld's discount store in York might have expected them to come from the Nestlé factory a mile up the road. In fact, the mints have travelled 7,300 miles from Indonesia where Poundworld buys them at a cheaper price than they can get from the factory in York. Nestlé does not appear to think this is a problem. In 2011, supermarket Tesco was accused of stocking Britain's least sustainable tinned tuna after a study found that hundreds of thousands of sharks, turtles, dolphins and other creatures were killed each year by its suppliers. The retailer quickly announced its intention to end all links with these fisheries. Ginster's factory making pasties is next to a Tesco store in Cornwall, yet its pasties make a 250 mile road trip to a distribution depot before returning to the store next to the factory – and neither company appeared to think there might be anything wrong with this regarding environmental impact.[22]

At the next level, companies can practise *product stewardship* – minimising not only pollution from production and product design but also all environmental impacts throughout the full product life cycle, while at the same time reducing costs. Many companies are adopting *design for environment* (DFE) and *cradle-to-cradle* practices. This involves thinking ahead to design products that are easier to recover, reuse, recycle or safely return to nature after usage, becoming part of the ecological cycle. Design for environment and cradle-to-cradle practices not only help to sustain the environment, they can also be highly profitable for the company.

For example, more than a decade ago, IBM started a business designed to reuse and recycle parts from its mainframe computers returned from lease. Today, IBM takes in 40,000 pieces of used IBM and other equipment per week, strips them down to their chips, and recovers valuable metals. 'We find uses for more than 99 per cent of what we take in, and have a return-to-landfill rate of [less than 1 per cent],' says an IBM spokesperson. What started out as an environmental effort has now grown into a €1.5 billion IBM business that profitably recycles electronic equipment at 22 sites worldwide.[23]

Today's 'greening' activities focus on improving what companies already do to protect the environment. The 'beyond greening' activities identified in Figure 20.2 look to the future. First, internally, companies can plan for *new clean technology*. Many organisations that have made good sustainability headway are still limited by existing technologies. To create fully sustainable strategies, they will need to develop innovative new technologies. For example, Coca-Cola is investing heavily in research addressing many sustainability issues:[24]

> From a sustainability viewpoint for Coca-Cola, an aluminum can is an ideal package. Aluminum can be recycled indefinitely. Put a Coke can in a recycling bin, and the aluminum finds its way back to a store shelf in about six weeks. The trouble is, people prefer clear plastic bottles with screw-on tops. Plastic bottles account for nearly 50 per cent of Coke's global volume, three times more than aluminum cans. And they are not currently sustainable. They're made from oil, which is a finite resource. Most wind up in landfills or, worse, as roadside rubbish. They can't be recycled indefinitely because the plastic discolours. To attack this waste problem, Coca-Cola is investing more than $60 million (€46.8 million) to build the world's largest state-of-the-art plastic-bottle-to-bottle recycling plant. The new recycling plant will produce approximately 100 million pounds of PET plastic for reuse each year.
>
> As a more permanent solution, Coke is also investing in new clean technologies that address these and other environmental issues. For example, it's researching and testing new bottles made from aluminium, corn or bioplastics. It's also designing more eco-friendly distribution alternatives. Currently, some ten million vending machines and refrigerated coolers gobble up energy and use potent greenhouse gases called hydrofluorocarbons (HFCs) to keep Cokes cold. To eliminate them, the company invested $40 million (€31.2 million) in research and recently began installing sleek new HFC-free coolers that use 30 to 40 per cent less energy. Coca-Cola also aims to become 'water neutral' by researching ways to help its bottlers waste less water and protect or replenish watersheds around the world.

Coca cola is researching and testing new bottles made from aluminium, corn and bioplastics.

Source: Getty Images

Finally, companies can develop a *sustainability vision*, which serves as a guide to the future. It shows how the company's products and services, processes and policies must evolve and what new technologies must be developed to get there. This vision of sustainability provides a framework for pollution control, product stewardship and new environmental technology for the company and others to follow.

Most companies today focus on the upper-left quadrant of the grid in Figure 20.2, investing most heavily in pollution prevention. Some forward-looking companies practise product stewardship and are developing new environmental technologies. Few companies have well-defined sustainability visions. However, emphasising only one or two quadrants in the environmental sustainability grid can be shortsighted. Investing only in the left half of the grid puts a company in a good position today but leaves it vulnerable in the future. In contrast, a heavy emphasis on the right half suggests that a company has good environmental vision but lacks the skills needed to implement it. Thus, companies should work at developing all four dimensions of environmental sustainability.

We saw in the case opening this chapter that Unilever is setting a high sustainability standard. For six years running it has been named one of the most sustainable corporations in the annual 'Global 100 Most Sustainable Corporations in the World' ranking:[25]

> Unilever has multiple programmes in place to manage the environmental impacts of its own operations. But that's only the start. 'The world faces enormous environmental pressures,' says the company. 'Our aim is to make our activities more sustainable and also encourage our customers, suppliers, and others to do the same.' On the 'upstream side', more than two-thirds

of Unilever's raw materials come from agriculture, so the company helps suppliers develop sustainable farming practices that meet its own high expectations for environmental and social impacts. The long-term goal is to source all key raw materials sustainably by 2015. On the 'downstream side' – when consumers use its products – Unilever reduces the environmental impacts of its products during use through innovative product development and consumer education. For example, almost one-third of households worldwide use Unilever laundry products to do their washing – approximately 125 billion washes every year. So the company launched the Cleaner Planet Plan project, which aims to reduce the impact of laundry on the environment by designing sustainable products and manufacturing them efficiently. But up to 70 per cent of the total greenhouse gas footprint and 95 per cent of the water footprint of Unilever's laundry products occur during consumer use. So the Cleaner Planet Plan also engages consumers directly to educate them on better laundry habits to reduce their environmental impact. Thus, Unilever leads the entire value chain – from suppliers to consumers – in the cause of saving the environment.

Environmentalism creates some special challenges for global marketers. As international trade barriers come down and global markets expand, environmental issues are having an ever-greater impact on international trade. Countries in North America, the European Union and other developed regions are generating strict environmental standards. For example, over the past 30 years the EU has adopted a substantial and diverse range of environmental measures aimed at improving the quality of the environment for European Union citizens and providing them with a high quality of life. The European Union Forum of Judges for the Environment contributes to promote the enforcement of national, European Union and international environmental law. To support the implementation and enforcement of environmental legislation, the EU has adopted the directive on environmental liability, the recommendation providing for minimum criteria for environmental inspections, and the directive on the protection of the environment through criminal law. In addition, the EU's Eco-Management and Audit Scheme (EMAS) provides guidelines for environmental self-regulation.[26]

However, environmental policies still vary widely from country to country. Countries such as Denmark, Germany, Japan and the United States have fully developed environmental policies and high public expectations. But major developing countries like the BRICs are only in the early stages of developing such policies. Moreover, environmental factors that motivate consumers in one country may have no impact on consumers in another. For example, PVC soft-drink bottles cannot be used in Switzerland or Germany. However, they are preferred in France, which has an extensive recycling process for them. Thus, international companies have found it difficult to develop standard environmental practices that work globally. Instead, they are creating general policies and then translating these policies into tailored programmes that meet local regulations and expectations.

Public actions to regulate marketing

Citizen concerns about marketing practices will usually lead to public attention and legislative proposals. Many of the laws that affect marketing were identified in Chapter 3. The task is to translate these laws into a language that marketing executives understand as they make decisions about competitive relations, products, price, promotion and distribution channels. Figure 20.3 illustrates the major legal issues facing marketing management.

AUTHOR COMMENT

In the end, marketers themselves must take responsibility for sustainable marketing. That means operating in a responsible and ethical way to bring both immediate and future value to customers.

Figure 20.3 Major marketing decision areas that may be called into question under the law

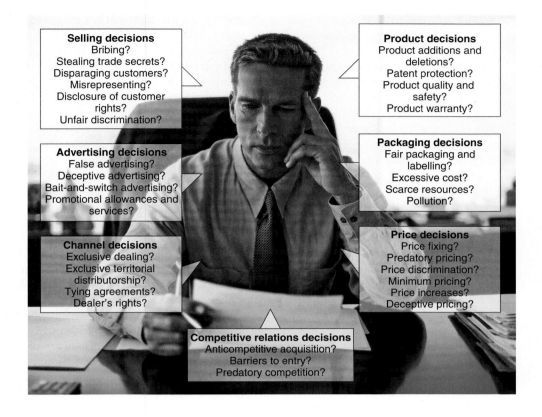

Selling decisions
Bribing?
Stealing trade secrets?
Disparaging customers?
Misrepresenting?
Disclosure of customer rights?
Unfair discrimination?

Product decisions
Product additions and deletions?
Patent protection?
Product quality and safety?
Product warranty?

Advertising decisions
False advertising?
Deceptive advertising?
Bait-and-switch advertising?
Promotional allowances and services?

Packaging decisions
Fair packaging and labelling?
Excessive cost?
Scarce resources?
Pollution?

Channel decisions
Exclusive dealing?
Exclusive territorial distributorship?
Tying agreements?
Dealer's rights?

Price decisions
Price fixing?
Predatory pricing?
Price discrimination?
Minimum pricing?
Price increases?
Deceptive pricing?

Competitive relations decisions
Anticompetitive acquisition?
Barriers to entry?
Predatory competition?

BUSINESS ACTIONS TOWARD SUSTAINABLE MARKETING

At first, many companies opposed consumerism, environmentalism and other elements of sustainable marketing. They thought the criticisms were either unfair or unimportant. But by now, most companies have grown to embrace sustainability marketing principles as a way to create greater immediate and future customer value and strengthen customer relationships.

Sustainable marketing principles

Under the sustainable marketing concept, a company's marketing should support the best long-term performance of the marketing system. It should be guided by five sustainable marketing principles: *consumer-oriented marketing, customer-value marketing, innovative marketing, sense-of-mission marketing* and *societal marketing*.

Consumer-oriented marketing

Consumer-oriented marketing—A principle of sustainable marketing that holds a company should view and organise its marketing activities from the consumer's point of view.

Consumer-oriented marketing means that the company should view and organise its marketing activities from the consumer's point of view. It should work hard to sense, serve and satisfy the needs of a defined group of customers – both now and in the future. The good marketing companies that we've discussed in this text have had this in common: an all-consuming passion for delivering superior value to carefully chosen customers. Only by seeing the world through its customers' eyes can the company build lasting and profitable customer relationships.

Customer-value marketing

According to the principle of **customer-value marketing**, the company should put most of its resources into customer-value-building marketing investments. Many things marketers do – one-shot sales promotions, cosmetic packaging changes, direct-response advertising – may raise sales in the short term but add less *value* than would actual improvements in the product's quality, features or convenience. Enlightened marketing calls for building long-term consumer loyalty and relationships by continually improving the value consumers receive from the firm's market offering. By creating value *for* consumers, the company can capture value *from* consumers in return.[27]

Customer-value marketing— A principle of sustainable marketing that holds a company should put most of its resources into consumer-value-building marketing investments.

Innovative marketing

The principle of **innovative marketing** requires that the company continuously seek real product and marketing improvements. The company that overlooks new and better ways to do things will eventually lose customers to another company that has found a better way. An excellent example of an innovative marketer is Samsung:

Innovative marketing— A principle of sustainable marketing that requires a company to seek real product and marketing improvements.

> Not too many years ago, Samsung was a copycat consumer electronics brand you bought if you couldn't afford Sony. But today, the brand holds a high-end, cutting-edge aura. In 1996, Samsung Electronics turned its back on making cheap knock-offs and set out to overtake rival Sony, not just in size but also in style and innovation. It hired a crop of fresh, young designers who unleashed a torrent of sleek, bold and beautiful new products targeted to high-end users. Samsung called them 'lifestyle works of art' – from brightly coloured mobile phones to flatscreen TVs that hang on walls like paintings. Every new product has to pass the 'Wow!' test: If it doesn't get a 'Wow!' reaction during market testing, it goes straight back to the design studio. Thanks to its strategy of innovation, the company quickly surpassed its lofty goals – and more. Samsung Electronics is now, by far, the world's largest consumer electronics company, with 50 percent greater sales than Sony. It's the world's largest TV manufacturer and second-largest mobile phone producer. And its designs are coveted by consumers. Samsung recently bagged eight awards at the IDEA; design darling Apple took home only seven awards. Says a Samsung designer, 'We are not el cheapo anymore.'[28]

Sense-of-mission marketing

Sense-of-mission marketing means that the company should define its mission in broad *social* terms rather than narrow *product* terms. When a company defines a social mission, employees feel better about their work and have a clearer sense of direction. Brands linked with broader missions can serve the best long-term interests of both the brand and consumers.

Sense-of-mission marketing—A principle of sustainable marketing that holds a company should define its mission in broad social terms rather than narrow products terms.

> For example, Pedigree makes good dog food, but that's not what the brand is really all about. Instead, the brand came up with the tagline 'Dogs rule'. The tagline 'is the perfect encapsulation of everything we stand for,' says a Pedigree marketer. 'Everything that we do is because we love dogs, because dogs rule. It's just so simple.' This mission-focused positioning drives everything the brand does – internally and externally. One look at a Pedigree ad or a visit to the Pedigree.com or UK.Pedigree.com website confirms that the people behind the Pedigree brand really do believe the 'Dogs rule' mission. An internal manifesto called 'Dogma' even encourages employees to take their dogs to work and on sales calls. To further fulfil the 'Dogs rule' brand promise, the company created the Pedigree Adoption Drive Foundation, which has raised millions of dollars for helping 'shelter dogs' find good homes. Sense-of-mission marketing has made Pedigree the world's number one dog food brand.[29]

Some companies define their overall corporate missions in broad societal terms. For example, defined in narrow product terms, the mission of well-known US outdoor gear and apparel maker Patagonia might be 'to sell clothes and outdoor equipment'. However, Patagonia states its mission more broadly, as one of producing the highest quality products while doing the least harm to the environment. From the start, Patagonia has pursued a passionately held social responsibility mission:[30]

> For the people at Patagonia, 'a love of wild and beautiful places demands participation in the fight to save them, and to help reverse the steep decline in the overall environmental health of our planet.' Their reason for being is to 'build the best product, cause no unnecessary harm, use business to inspire and implement solutions to the environmental crisis.' Yet they remain keenly aware that everything they do as a business – or have done as a company – leaves its mark on the environment. As yet, there is no such thing as a sustainable business, but every day they take steps to lighten their footprint and do less harm.
>
> Each year since 1985, the company has given away 10 per cent of its pretax profits to support environmental causes. Today Patagonia says, 'we donate our time, services and at least 1% of sales to hundreds of grassroots environmental groups all over the world who work to help reverse the environmental tide.'

However, having a 'double bottom line' of values and profits isn't easy. Over the years, companies such as Patagonia, Ben & Jerry's and the Body Shop – all known and respected for putting 'principles before profits' – have at times struggled with less-than-stellar financial returns. In recent years, however, a new generation of social entrepreneurs has emerged, well-trained business managers who know that to 'do good', they must first 'do well' in terms of profitable business operations. For example, Timberland CEO Jeff Swartz refers to this as the beautiful – and profitable – nexus between 'commerce and justice'. Timberland's mission is to make profits while at the same time making a difference in the world. Moreover, today, socially responsible business is no longer the sole province of small, socially conscious entrepreneurs. Many large, established companies and brands have adopted substantial social and environmental responsibility missions.

For example, Starbucks has created CAFE Practices (Coffee and Farmer Equity) – guidelines for achieving product quality, economic accountability, social responsibility and environmental leadership. Similarly, Nike supports a broad social and environmental responsibility agenda, everything from eco-friendly product designs and manufacturing processes to improving conditions for the nearly 800,000 workers in its global supply chain to programmes that engage the world's youth in the fight against AIDS in Africa. Nike states 'We can use the power of our brand, the energy and passion of our people, and the scale of our business to create meaningful change.' Says one Nike manager, 'Our customers expect this from us. It's not about two or three green shoes – it's about changing the way our company does things in general.'[31] But the Ben & Jerry's story underlines how tough it can be to survive with a 'double bottom-line':

> The classic 'do good' pioneer is Ben & Jerry's. Ben Cohen and Jerry Greenfield founded the company in 1978 as a firm that cared deeply about its social and environmental responsibilities. Ben & Jerry's bought only hormone-free milk and cream and used only organic fruits and nuts to make its ice cream, which it sold in environmentally friendly containers. It went to great lengths to buy from minority and disadvantaged suppliers. From its early Rainforest Crunch to its more recent Chocolate Macadamia (made with sustainable, sourced macadamias and fair trade certified cocoa and vanilla), Ben & Jerry's championed a host of social and environmental causes over the years. From the start, Ben & Jerry's donated a whopping 7.5 per cent of pretax profits to support projects that exhibited 'creative problem solving and hopefulness … relating to children and families, disadvantaged groups, and the environment'. By the mid-1990s, Ben & Jerry's had become America's number-two super-premium ice cream brand. However, as competitors not shackled by Ben & Jerry's 'principles before profits' mission invaded its markets, growth and profits flattened. After several years of lacklustre financial returns, Ben & Jerry's was acquired by consumer goods giant Unilever.[32]

Societal marketing—A principle of sustainable marketing that holds a company should make marketing decisions by considering consumers' wants, the company's requirements, consumers' long-term interests and society's long-term interests.

Societal marketing

Following the principle of **societal marketing**, a company makes marketing decisions by considering consumers' wants and interests, the company's requirements and society's long-term inter-

Figure 20.4 Societal classification of products

ests. Companies should be aware that neglecting consumer and societal long-term interests is a disservice to consumers and society. Alert companies view societal problems as opportunities.

Sustainable marketing calls for products that are not only pleasing but also beneficial. The difference is shown in Figure 20.4. Products can be classified according to their degree of immediate consumer satisfaction and long-term consumer benefit.

Deficient products, such as bad-tasting and ineffective medicine, have neither immediate appeal nor long-term benefits. **Pleasing products** give high immediate satisfaction but may hurt consumers in the long term. Examples include cigarettes and junk food. **Salutary products** have low immediate appeal but may benefit consumers in the long term; for instance, bicycle helmets or some insurance products. **Desirable products** give both high immediate satisfaction and high long-term benefits, such as a tasty *and* nutritious breakfast food.

Examples of desirable products abound. GE's Energy Smart compact fluorescent lightbulb provides good lighting at the same time that it gives long life and energy savings. Maytag's front-loading Neptune washing machine provides superior cleaning along with water savings and energy efficiency. And Haworth's German-designed Zody office chair is not only attractive and functional but also environmentally responsible. It's made without PVC, chlorofluorocarbons (CFCs), chrome or any other toxic materials. Ninety-eight per cent of the chair can be recycled; some 50 per cent of it already has been. The energy used in the manufacturing process is completely offset by wind-power credits. When the chair is ready to be retired, the company will take it back and reuse its components.[33]

Companies should try to turn all of their products into desirable products. The challenge posed by pleasing products is that they sell very well but may end up hurting the consumer. The product opportunity, therefore, is to add long-term benefits without reducing the product's pleasing qualities. The challenge posed by salutary products is to add some pleasing qualities so that they will become more desirable in consumers' minds.

For example, PepsiCo recently hired a team of 'idealistic scientists', headed by a former director of the World Health Organization, to help the company create attractive new healthy product options while 'making the bad stuff less bad'.[34] The group of medical doctors, PhDs and other health advocates, under the direction of PepsiCo's vice president for global health policy, looks for healthier ingredients that can go into multiple products. For example, their efforts led to an all-natural zero-calorie sweetener now featured in several new PepsiCo brands, including the €100-million Trop50 brand, a Tropicana orange juice variation that contains no artificial sweeteners and half the sugar and calories.

Deficient products—Products that have neither immediate appeal nor long-term benefits.

Pleasing products—Products that give high immediate satisfaction but may hurt consumers in the long term.

Salutary products—Products that have low appeal but may benefit consumers in the long-term.

Desirable products—Products that give both high immediate satisfaction and high long-term benefits.

MARKETING ETHICS

Good ethics are a cornerstone of sustainable marketing. In the long term, unethical marketing harms customers and society as a whole. Furthermore, it eventually damages a company's reputation and effectiveness, jeopardising its very survival. Thus, the sustainable marketing goals of long-term consumer and business welfare can be achieved only through ethical marketing conduct.

Conscientious marketers face many moral dilemmas. The best thing to do is often unclear. Because not all managers have fine moral sensitivity, companies need to develop *corporate marketing ethics policies* – broad guidelines that everyone in the organisation must follow. These policies should cover distributor relations, advertising standards, customer service, pricing, product development and general ethical standards.

The finest guidelines cannot resolve all the difficult ethical situations the marketer faces. Table 20.1 lists some difficult ethical issues marketers could face during their careers. If marketers choose immediate sales-producing actions in all these cases, their marketing behaviour might well be described as immoral or even amoral. If they refuse to go along with *any* of the actions, they might be ineffective as marketing managers and unhappy because of the constant moral tension. Managers need a set of principles that will help them figure out the moral importance of each situation and decide how far they can go in good conscience.

But *what* principle should guide companies and marketing managers on issues of ethics and social responsibility? One philosophy is that the free market and the legal system should decide such issues. Under this principle, companies and their managers are not responsible for making moral judgments. Companies can in good conscience do whatever the market and legal systems allow.

A second philosophy puts responsibility not on the system but in the hands of individual companies and managers. This more enlightened philosophy suggests that a company should have a 'social conscience'. Companies and managers should apply high standards of ethics and morality when making corporate decisions, regardless of 'what the system allows'. History provides an endless list of examples of company actions that were legal but highly irresponsible.

Each company and marketing manager must work out a philosophy of socially responsible and ethical behaviour. Under the societal marketing concept, each manager must look beyond what is

Table 20.1   Some morally difficult situations in marketing

Your R&D department has slightly changed one of your company's products. It is not really 'new and improved', but you know that putting this statement on the package and in advertising will increase sales. What would you do?

You have been asked to add a stripped-down model to your line that could be advertised to pull customers into the store. The product won't be very good, but salespeople will be able to switch buyers up to higher-priced units. You are asked to give the green light for the stripped-down version. What would you do?

You are thinking of hiring a product manager who has just left a competitor's company. She would be more than happy to tell you all the competitor's plans for the coming year. What would you do?

One of your top dealers in an important territory recently has had family troubles, and his sales have slipped. It looks like it will take him a while to straighten out his family trouble. Meanwhile you are losing many sales. Legally, on performance grounds, you can terminate the dealer's franchise and replace him. What would you do?

You have a chance to win a big account that will mean a lot to you and your company. The purchasing agent hints that a 'gift' would influence the decision. Your assistant recommends sending a large-screen television to the buyer's home. What would you do?

You have heard that a competitor has a new product feature that will make a big difference in sales. The competitor will demonstrate the feature in a private dealer meeting at the annual trade show. You can easily send a spy to this meeting to learn about the new feature. What would you do?

You have to choose between three advertising campaigns outlined by your agency. The first (a) is a soft-sell, honest, straight information campaign. The second (b) uses sex-loaded emotional appeals and exaggerates the product's benefits. The third (c) involves a noisy, somewhat irritating commercial that is sure to gain audience attention. Pretests show that the campaigns are effective in the following order: c, b, and a. What would you do?

You are interviewing a capable female applicant for a job as salesperson. She is better qualified than the men who have been interviewed. Nevertheless, you know that in your industry some important customers prefer dealing with men, and you will lose some sales if you hire her. What would you do?

legal and allowed and develop standards based on personal integrity, corporate conscience and long-term consumer welfare.

Dealing with issues of ethics and social responsibility in an open and forthright way helps to build strong customer relationships based on honesty and trust. In fact, many companies now routinely include consumers in the social responsibility process. Consider toy maker Mattel:[35]

When the discovery of lead paint on several of its best-selling products forced Mattel to recall millions of toys worldwide, the company's forthright response helped it maintain consumer confidence.

Source: Getty Images/Film Magic

In the autumn of 2007, the discovery of lead paint on several of its best-selling products forced Mattel to make worldwide recalls on millions of toys. Threatening as this was, rather than hesitating or hiding the incident, the company's brand advisors were up to the challenge. Their quick, decisive response helped to maintain consumer confidence in the Mattel brand, even contributing to a 6 per cent sales increase over the same period from the year before. Just who were these masterful 'brand advisors'? They were the 400 mothers with kids aged three to ten who are the Playground Community, a private online network launched by Mattel's worldwide consumer insights department in June 2007 to 'listen to and gain insight'. Throughout the crisis, Playground Community members kept in touch with Mattel regarding the product recalls and the company's forthright response plan, even helping to shape the promotional strategy for one of the recalled product lines. Even in times of crisis, 'brands that engage in a two-way conversation with their customers create stronger, more trusting relationships,' says a Mattel executive.

As with environmentalism, the issue of ethics presents special challenges for international marketers. Business standards and practices vary immensely from one country to the next. Countries like the UK and the US have stringent and actively enforced laws prohibiting bribery. For example, the 2011 Bribery Act in the UK created a new offence of failure to prevent bribery by people working on behalf of a business, in addition to the existing criminal offence to give, promise or offer a bribe at home or abroad. Penalties for bribery were increased to ten years' imprisonment and an unlimited fine. British anti-corruption law is now more sweeping than its American counterpart.[36] Similarly, bribes and kickbacks are illegal for US firms. In addition, a variety of treaties against bribery and corruption have been signed and ratified by more than 60 countries. Yet these are still standard business practices in many countries.

Transparency International, a Berlin-based anti-corruption watchdog, cites Greece as a problem area for Europe. Greece is not alone, however, The Middle East, sub-Saharan Africa and the former Soviet bloc all struggle with corruption. Indeed, in 2009, Britain sank to a new low in Transparency International's annual ranking of the world's most corrupt countries, in the wake of the politicians' expenses scandal. Transparency International reports from its global survey of business executives that two in five have been asked to pay a bribe when dealing with business institutions. Politicians and officials in the emerging markets are estimated to receive bribes of between €16 billion and €31 billion annually. The Bribe Payers index is headed by Russia, China, Mexico and India. The least corrupt countries are Denmark, New Zealand and Sweden.[37]

The question arises as to whether a company must lower its ethical standards to compete effectively in countries with lower standards. The answer is no. Companies should make a commitment to a common set of shared standards worldwide. Consider the long-term risks in not doing so:

BAE is Britain's biggest defence contractor, and is one of the UK's biggest employers. The company is top of the global arms league. BAE has achieved outstanding success in the US market – which accounts for 54 per cent of the global €725 billion spent on defence each year. BAE is the biggest foreign supplier to the Pentagon.

BAE's stellar global performance has been surrounded by a media-storm of criticism relating to accusations of corrupt business practices in overseas markets. Accusations include: *Saudi Arabia* – bribing Saudi officials for lucrative arms contracts to supply Tornedo fighter jets; *South Africa* – claims of bribes for warplanes, leading to inflated prices; *Tanzania* – Tanzania's top corruption investigator plans criminal charges relating to BAE's sale of a €35 million radar system for air traffic control; *Czech Republic* – a planes deal; *Chile* – another planes order; *Romania* – refurbishment of two frigates; *Australia* – paying 'hush money' to two Australian airlines to silence them about toxic fumes escaping into the cabins of BAE 146 jets.

Less susceptible to Saudi pressure than the British, in June 2007, US authorities launched their own probe into the Saudi deal, and requested legal assistance from the UK. A major concern is that investigations into bribery corruptions by US authorities will destroy future relationships with the Pentagon, even if no action is taken against the company, and further acquisitions in the US may be blocked by the Department of Justice. A deal done by BAE with the Serious Fraud Office has been overturned, so the company faces further investigations in the UK as well.[38]

Many industrial and professional associations have suggested codes of ethics, and many companies are now adopting their own codes. One of the longest-established and widely accepted codes is the one produced by the American Marketing Association, the international association of marketing managers and scholars. This code of ethics is shown in Table 20.2. Companies are also developing programme to teach managers about important ethical issues and help them find the proper responses. They hold ethics workshops and seminars and create ethics committees. Furthermore, most major US companies have appointed high-level ethics officers to champion ethical issues and help resolve ethics problems and concerns facing employees.

PricewaterhouseCoopers (PwC) is a good example. In 2002, PwC established a global ethics office and comprehensive ethics programme, headed by a high-level global ethics officer. The ethics programme begins with a code of conduct, called 'The Way We Do Business'. PwC employees learn about the code of conduct and about how to handle thorny ethics issues in comprehensive ethics training programmes, which start when the employee joins the company and continue throughout the employee's career. The programme also includes an ethics help line and regular communications at all levels. 'It is obviously not enough to distribute a document,' says PwC's former CEO, Samuel DiPiazza. 'Ethics is in everything we say and do.'[39]

Table 20.2   **American Marketing Association Code of Ethics**

Ethical norms and values for marketers
Preamble
The American Marketing Association commits itself to promoting the highest standard of professional ethical norms and values for its members. Norms are established standards of conduct that are expected and maintained by society and/or professional organizations. Values represent the collective conception of what communities find desirable, important and morally proper. Values also serve as the criteria for evaluating our own personal actions, and the actions of others. As marketers we recognize that we not only serve our organizations but also act as stewards of society in creating, facilitating and executing the transactions that are part of the greater economy. In this role, marketers are expected to embrace the highest professional ethical norms and the ethical values implied by our responsibility toward multiple stakeholders (e.g., customers, employees, investors, peers, channel members, regulators and the host community).
Ethical norms
As Marketers, we must: 1. **Do no harm**. This means consciously avoiding harmful actions or omissions by embodying high ethical standards and adhering to all applicable laws and regulations in the choices we make. 2. **Foster trust in the marketing system**. This means striving for good faith and fair dealing so as to contribute toward the efficacy of the exchange process as well as avoiding deception in product design, pricing, communication, and delivery of distribution. 3. **Embrace ethical values**. This means building relationships and enhancing consumer confidence in the integrity of marketing by affirming these core values: honesty, responsibility, fairness, respect, transparency and citizenship.

Ethical values

Honesty – to be forthright in dealings with customers and stakeholders. To this end, we will.

* Strive to be truthful in all situations and at all times.
* Offer products of value that do what we claim in our communications.
* Stand behind our products if they fail to deliver their claimed benefits.
* Honor our explicit and implicit commitments and promises.

Responsibility – to accept the consequences of our marketing decisions and strategies. To this end, we will:

* Strive to serve the needs of customers.
* Avoid using coercion with all stakeholders.
* Acknowledge the social obligations to stakeholders that come with increased marketing and economic power.
* Recognize our special commitments to vulnerable market segments such as children, seniors, the economically impoverished, market illiterates and others who may be substantially disadvantaged.
* Consider environmental stewardship in our decision-making.

Fairness – to balance justly the needs of the buyer with the interests of the seller. To this end, we will:

* Represent products in a clear way in selling, advertising and other forms of communication; this includes the avoidance of false, misleading and deceptive promotion.
* Reject manipulations and sales tactics that harm customer trust.
* Refuse to engage in price fixing, predatory pricing, price gouging or 'bait-and-switch' tactics.
* Avoid knowing participation in conflicts of interest.
* Seek to protect the private information of customers, employees and partners.

Respect – to acknowledge the basic human dignity of all stakeholders. To this end, we will:

* Value individual differences and avoid stereotyping customers or depicting demographic groups (e.g., gender, race, sexual orientation) in a negative or dehumanizing way.
* Listen to the needs of customers and make all reasonable efforts to monitor and improve their satisfaction on an ongoing basis.
* Make every effort to understand and respectfully treat buyers, suppliers, intermediaries and distributors from all cultures.
* Acknowledge the contributions of others, such as consultants, employees and coworkers, to marketing endeavors.
* Treat everyone, including our competitors, as we would wish to be treated.

Transparency – to create a spirit of openness in marketing operations. To this end, we will:

* Strive to communicate clearly with all constituencies.
* Accept constructive criticism from customers and other stakeholders.
* Explain and take appropriate action regarding significant product or service risks, component substitutions or other foreseeable eventualities that could affect customers or their perception of the purchase decision.
* Disclose list prices and terms of financing as well as available price deals and adjustments.

Citizenship – to fulfill the economic, legal, philanthropic, and societal responsibilities that serve stakeholders. To this end, we will:

* Strive to protect the ecological environment in the execution of marketing campaigns.
* Give back to the community through volunteerism and charitable donations.
* Contribute to the overall betterment of marketing and its reputation.
* Urge supply chain members to ensure that trade is fair for all participants, including producers in developing countries.

Implementation

We expect AMA members to be courageous and proactive in leading and/or aiding their organizations in the fulfillment of the explicit and implicit promises made to those stakeholders. We recognize that every industry sector and marketing sub-discipline (e.g. marketing research, e-commerce, Internet selling, direct marketing, and advertising) has its own specific ethical issues that require policies and commentary. An array of such codes can be accessed through links on the AMA Web site. Consistent with the principle of subsidiarity (solving issues at the level where the expertise resides), we encourage all such groups to develop and/or refine their industry and discipline-specific codes of ethics to supplement these guiding ethical norms and values.

Source: Reprinted with permission of the American Marketing Association, www.marketingpower.com/AboutAMA/Pages/Statement%20of%20Ethics.aspx#.

Still, written codes and ethics programmes do not ensure ethical behaviour. Ethics and social responsibility require a total corporate commitment. They must be a component of the overall corporate culture. According to DiPiazza, 'I see ethics as a mission-critical issue . . . deeply embedded in who we are and what we do. It's just as important as our product development cycle or our distribution system . . . It's about creating a culture based on integrity and respect, not a culture based on dealing with the crisis of the day . . . We ask ourselves every day, "Are we doing the right things?" '[40]

THE SUSTAINABLE COMPANY

At the foundation of marketing is the belief that companies that fulfil the needs and wants of customers will thrive. Companies that fail to meet customer needs or that intentionally or unintentionally harm customers, others in society or future generations will decline. Says one observer, 'Sustainability is an emerging business megatrend, like electrification and mass production, that will profoundly affect companies' competitiveness and even their survival.'[41]

Sustainable companies are those that create value for customers through socially, environmentally and ethically responsible actions. Sustainable marketing goes beyond caring for the needs and wants of today's customers. It means having concern for tomorrow's customers in assuring the survival and success of the business, shareholders, employees and the broader world in which they all live. Sustainable marketing provides the context in which companies can build profitable customer relationships by creating value *for* customers to capture value *from* customers in return – now and in the future.

 ## REVIEWING OBJECTIVES AND KEY TERMS

In this chapter, we addressed many of the important *sustainable marketing* concepts related to marketing's sweeping impact on individual consumers, other businesses and society as a whole. Sustainable marketing requires socially, environmentally and ethically responsible actions that bring value to not only present-day consumers and businesses but also future generations and society as a whole. Sustainable companies are those that act responsibly to create value for customers to capture value from customers in return – now and in the future.

ability of future generations to meet their needs. Whereas the marketing concept recognises that companies thrive by fulfilling the day-to-day needs of customers, sustainable marketing calls for socially and environmentally responsible actions that meet both the immediate and future needs of customers and the company. Truly sustainable marketing requires a smooth-functioning marketing system in which consumers, companies, public policymakers and others work together to ensure responsible marketing actions.

OBJECTIVE 1 Define sustainable marketing and discuss its importance (pp. 599–600).

Sustainable marketing calls for meeting the present needs of consumers and businesses while preserving or enhancing the

OBJECTIVE 2 Identify the major social criticisms of marketing (pp. 600–608).

Marketing's *impact on individual consumer welfare* has been criticized for high prices, deceptive practices, high-pressure selling, shoddy or unsafe products, planned obsolescence and poor service to disadvantaged consumers. Marketing's *impact on society* has been criticised for creating false wants and too much materialism, too few social goods and cultural pollution. Critics have also denounced marketing's *impact on other businesses* for harming competitors and reducing competition through acquisitions, practices that create barriers to entry, and unfair competitive marketing practices. Some of these concerns are justified; some are not.

OBJECTIVE 3 **Define consumerism and environmentalism and explain how they affect marketing strategies (pp. 609–613).**

Concerns about the marketing system have led to *citizen action movements. Consumerism* is an organized social movement intended to strengthen the rights and power of consumers relative to sellers. Alert marketers view it as an opportunity to serve consumers better by providing more consumer information, education, and protection. *Environmentalism* is an organised social movement seeking to minimize the harm done to the environment and quality of life by marketing practices. The first wave of modern environmentalism was driven by environmental groups and concerned consumers; the second wave was driven by the federal government, which passed laws and regulations governing industrial practices impacting the environment. The first two environmentalism waves are now merging into a third and stronger wave, in which companies are accepting responsibility for doing no environmental harm. Companies now are adopting policies of *environmental sustainability* – developing strategies that both sustain the environment and produce profits for the company. Both consumerism and environmentalism are important components of sustainable marketing.

OBJECTIVE 4 **Describe the principles of sustainable marketing (pp. 614–617).**

Many companies originally resisted these social movements and laws, but most now recognise a need for positive consumer information, education, and protection. Under the sustainable marketing concept, a company's marketing should support the best long-term performance of the marketing system. It should be guided by five sustainable marketing principles: *consumer-oriented marketing, customer-value marketing, innovative marketing, sense-of-mission marketing* and *societal marketing*.

OBJECTIVE 5 **Explain the role of ethics in marketing (pp. 617–622).**

Increasingly, companies are responding to the need to provide company policies and guidelines to help their managers deal with questions of *marketing ethics*. Of course, even the best guidelines cannot resolve all the difficult ethical decisions that individuals and firms must make. But there are some principles from which marketers can choose. One principle states that the free market and the legal system should decide such issues. A second and more enlightened principle puts responsibility not on the system but in the hands of individual companies and managers. Each firm and marketing manager must work out a philosophy of socially responsible and ethical behaviour. Under the sustainable marketing concept, managers must look beyond what is legal and allowable and develop standards based on personal integrity, corporate conscience and long-term consumer welfare.

 ## NAVIGATING THE KEY TERMS

DISCUSSING AND APPLYING THE CONCEPTS

Discussing the concepts

1. What is sustainable marketing? Explain how the sustainable marketing concepts differs form the marketing concept and the social marketing concept. (AACSB: Communication)

2. Discuss the issues relevant to marketing's impact on society as a whole and how marketers respond to these criticisms. (AACSB: Communication)

3. Discuss the types of harmful impact that marketing practices can have on competition and the associated problems. (AACSB: Communication)

4. What is consumerism? Describe the rights of sellers and buyers. (AACSB: Communication)

5. Describe the five sustainable marketing principles and explain how companies benefit from adhering to them. (AACSB: Communication)

6. Describe the two philosophies regarding what principle should guide companies and marketing managers on issues of ethics and social responsibility. (AACSB: Communication)

Applying the concepts

1. Visit www.causemarketingsfourm.com and learn about the Halo Awards for outstanding cause-related marketing programmes. Describe an award-winning case that exemplifies the sustainable marketing concept. (AACSB: Communication; Use Of IT Reflective Thinking)

2. In a small group, discuss each of the morally difficult situations in marketing presented in Table 20.1. Which philosophy is guiding your decision in each situation? (AACSB: Communication; Ethical Reasoning)

3. KGOY stands for 'kids getting older younger', and marketers are getting much of blame, especially for young girls. Critics describe clothing designed for young girls ages 8–11 as floozy and sexual, with department stores selling thongs for youngsters and T-shirts that say 'Naughty Girl'. Although Barbie's sexuality has never been subtle, she was originally targeted at girls 9–12 years old. Now, Barbie dolls target primarily 3–7-years-old girls. In a small group, discuss other examples of the phenomenon and debate whether marketers are to blame. Are any companies countering this trend by offering age-appropriate products for children? (AACSB: Communication; Reflective Thinking)

Focus on technology

Marketers are hungry for customer information, and the electronic tracking industry is answering the call by gathering consumer Internet behaviour data. A recent investigation by the

Wall Street Journal found that the 50 most popular US websites installed more than 3,000 tracking files on the computers used in the study. The total was even higher – 4,123 tracking files – for the top 50 sites popular with children and teens. Many sites installed more than 100 tracking tools each during the tests. Tracking tools include files placed on users' computers and on websites. You probably know about the cookies, smell information files that are placed on your computer. Newer technology such as Web beacons (also known as Web bugs, tracking bugs, pixel tags and clear GIFs) are invisible graphic files placed on websites and in e-mails that, when combined with cookies, can tell a lot about the user. For example, beacons can tell a marketer if a page was viewed and for how long and can even tell if you read the e-mail sent to you.

Such tracking has become aggressive to the point where keystrokes can be analysed for clues about a person, and 'flash cookies' can reappear after a user deletes them. Although the date does not identify users by name, data-gathering companies can construct consumer profiles that include demographic, geographic and lifestyle information. Marketers use this information to target online ads.

1. Critics claim that Internet tracking infringes consumer privacy rights. Should marketers have access to such information? Discuss the advantages and disadvantages of this activity for marketers and consumers. (AACSB: Communication; Ethical Reasoning)

2. Discuss the position of the government on this activity. Is it right to track a computer user's online search behaviour? (AACSB: Communication; Ethical Reasoning)

Foucs on ethics

Many companies, such as Timberland, take sustainable marketing seriously. Consumers might soon be able to use the Outdoor Industry Association's (OIA) Eco Index to help them identify such companies. The OIA has guided brand manufacturers and retailers, such as Nike, Strauss, Timberland, Target, Patagonia and many others in developing a software tool to measure the eco-impact of their products. A product as simple as a pair of jeans has considerable environmental impact. A pair of Levis jeans moves from cotton grown in Louisiana; to fabric woven in North Carolina; to jeans cut in the Dominican Republic, sewn in Haiti, and finished in Jamaica; to the final product distributed in the store where you purchase them. And that's just for jeans sold in the United States; Levi's are sold all over the world. The Eco Index takes all this into account and more. It factors in other environmental things, such as washing methods, the amount of water used in the life of the jeans, and the disposal of the product. The holdup on the Eco Index, however, is that all the information is self-reported, and manufacturers have to obtain information from their suppliers as well.

1. Learn more about this initiative by visiting the OIA's website at www.outdoorindustry.org. If implemented, will this index help marketers who score well on it develop a sustainable competitive advantage? Would you be more willing to purchase a product from a company that scores well on this index? (AACSB: Communication; Use of IT; Reflective Thinking)

2. The Eco Index is an industry-led initiative; all information is self-reported with no proof required. Is there a potential to abuse the system and possibly deceive consumers? Explain. (AACSB: Communication; Ethical Reasoning; Reflective Thinking)

Marketing & the economy

Charity shops

It makes sense that as unemployment rates rise and incomes weaken, more middle-class shoppers turn to charity shops in search of bargains. But in recent times, charity shops have benefited from more than just a new consumer frugality. The negative stigma of shopping at musty, second-hand shops has diminished. For fashonistas everywhere the line between 'thrift' and 'vintage' has grown razor thin. Today people aren't just buying any old rags at charity shops. They're finding treasures in some top-name brands. Goodwill Industries in the US is taking advantage of this trend. It promotes its wares to hipster trendsetters through fashion shows and apparel blogs and by offering store credit for apparel donations.

Goodwill's overall sales have gone up by about 7 per cent in the face of a weaker economy. Other charity shops report increases of up to 35 per cent. But the industry's good fortunes present a unique dilemma. The same forces that are driving charity shops sales up are driving donations down. People are keeping their old stuff longer. And rather than donating old

clothing, people are selling it elsewhere for cash. As a result, the two-bag donor is now bringing in only one bag. And the goods that are donated tend to be lower in quality. This unusual dynamic could make it difficult for thrift stores to stock their shelves in the future.

1. In what ways does the charity shop industry present solutions to the common social criticisms of marketing outlined in the text?

2. How might the charity shop industry overcome its supply problems in the current environment of more frugal consumers?

Marketing by the numbers

One element of sustainability is organic farming. But if you've priced organic foods, you know they are more expensive. For example a dozen conventionally farmed eggs costs consumers €1.20 whereas a dozen organic eggs costs €2.20. Organic farming costs much more than conventional farming, and those costs are passed onto consumers. However, if prices get too high, consumers will not purchase the organic eggs. Suppose that the average fixed costs per year for conventionally farmed eggs are €780,000, but they are twice that amount for organic eggs. Organic farmers' variable costs per dozen are twice as much as well – €1.40 per dozen. Refer to Appendix 2 to answer the following questions.

1. Most large egg farmers sell eggs directly to retailers. What is the farmer's price per dozen to the retailer for conventional and organic eggs if the retailer's margin is 20 per cent based on the retail price? (AACSB: Communication; Analytical Reasoning)

2. How many dozen eggs does a conventional farmer need to sell to break even? How many does an organic farmer need to sell to break even? (AACSB: Communication; Analytical Reasoning)

 REFERENCES

[1] Sources: Barney Jopson, 'Unilever looks to clean up in Africa', *Financial Times* (15 November 2007), p. 20; Aaron O. Patrick, 'Turnabout at Unilever', *Wall Street Journal* (2–4 May 2008), p. 6; Michael Skapinker, 'Virtue's reward? Companies make the business case for ethical initiatives', *Financial Times* (27 April 2008), www.ft.com; Michael Skapinker, 'Long-term corporate plans may be lost in translation', *Financial Times* (23 November 2010), p. 15; James Lamont, 'Indian innovators target nation's high demand', *Financial Times* (19 January 2010), www.ft.com.

[2] For lots of information on SUV safety and environmental performance, see www.citizen.org/autosafety/suvsafety, accessed September 2010.

[3] McDonald's financial information and other facts from www.aboutmc-donalds.com/mcd/investors.html and www.aboutmcdonalds.com/mcd, accessed July 2010. Also see 'Dow Jones sustainability world 80 index', (May 2010), accessed at www.sustainability-index.com/djsi_pdf/publications/Factsheets/SAM_IndexesMonthly_DJSIWorld80.pdf.

[4] See, for example: Nigel F. Piercy and Nikala Lane, 'Corporate social responsibility: impacts on marketing and customer value', *The Marketing Review* (2009), **9** (4) (2009), pp. 335–360; Nigel F. Piercy and Nikala Lane, 'Corporate social responsibility initiatives and strategic marketing imperatives', *Social Business*, **1** (Winter 2011), pp. 325–345.

5 Heather Green, 'How green is that gizmo?' *Businessweek* (31 December 2007), p. 36; Tom Wright, 'False 'Green' ads draw global scrutiny', *Wall Street Journal* (30 January 2008), p. B4; Benjamin Heath, 'FTC updating green guides', GlobalClimateLaw.com (7 April 2009), www.globalclimatelaw.com/2009/04/articles/environmental/ftc-updating-green-guides-which-govern-environmental-building-claims; and http://sinsofgreenwashing.org and www.terrachoice.com http://sinsofgreenwashing.org and www.terrachoice.com, accessed July 2010.

6 See www.euro.who.int/en/what-we-do/health-topics/noncommunicable-diseases/obesity, accessed (1 March 2012). See www.independent.co.uk/life-style/health-and-families/health-news/uk-has-highest-level-of-obesity-in-europe-2160047.html, accessed (1 March 2012). See Jennifer Corbett Dooren, 'One-third of American adults are obese, but rate Slows', *Wall Street Journal* (8 February 2010); and 'Overweight and Obesity', Centers for Disease Control and Prevention, www.cdc.gov/nccdphp/dnpa/obesity/trend/index.htm, accessed July 2010.

7 For more on perceived obsolescence, see Annie Leonard, *The Story of Stuff* (New York: Free Press, 2010), pp. 162–163; and www.storyofstuff.com, accessed April 2010.

8 Dan Pashman, 'Planned obsolescence-induced insanity (or: damn you Steve Jobs! Why must you torment me?!)', *National Public Radio* (6 September 2007), www.npr.org/blogs/bryantpark/2007/09/planned_obsolescenceinduced_in_1.html. For more discussion, see Joseph Guiltinan, 'Creative destruction and destructive creations: environmental ethics and planned obsolescence', *Journal of Business Ethics* (May 2009), pp. 19–28; and 'American dream of home ownership morphs into nightmare', *Irish Times* (7 November 2009), p. 11.

9 See Karen Auge, 'Planting seed in food deserts: neighborhood gardens, produce in corner stores', *Denver Post* (18 April 2010), p. 1; and 'Supermarket campaign: improving access to supermarkets in underserved communities', *The Food Trust* www.thefoodtrust.org/php/programmes/super.market.campaign.php, accessed July 2010.

10 Leonard Stern, 'Aspiration gap behind Downward Cycle in US', *Calgary Herald* (Canada) (9 November 2008), p. A11. See 'Riot at new london primark store', *Metro* www.metro.co.uk/news/44366-riot-at-new-london-primark-store#ixzz1nt5ze01L, accessed (1 March 2012).

11 Oliver James, 'It's more than enough to make you sick', *Marketing* (23 January 2008), pp. 26–28; and Richard J. Varey, 'Marketing means and ends for a sustainable society: a welfare agenda for transformative change,' *Journal of Macromarketing* (June 2010), pp. 112–126.

12 See 'Overconsumption is costing us the Earth and human happiness', *Guardian* (21 June 2010), accessed at www.guardian.co.uk/environment/2010/jun/21/overconsumption-environment-relationships-annie-leonard; and *The Story of Stuff*, www.storyofstuff.com, accessed July 2010.

13 Conor Dougherty and Elizabeth Holmes, 'Consumer spending perks up economy', *Wall Street Journal* (13 March 2010), p. A1.

14 See www-07.ibm.com/innovation/my/exhibit/documents/pdf/2_The_Case_For_Smarter_Transportation.pdf, accessed (1 March 2012).

15 See 'Traffic congestion and urban mobility', *Texas Transportation Institute* http://tti.tamu.edu/infofor/media/topics/congestion_mobility.htm, accessed July 2010.

16 See www.tfl.gov.uk/roadusers/congestioncharging/6710.aspx, accessed July 2010.

17 See 'Advertising in the US: Synovate global survey shows Internet, innovation and online privacy a must', (3 December 2009), accessed at www.synovate.com/news/article/2009/12/advertising-in-the-us-synovate-global-survey-shows-internet-innovation-and-online-privacy-a-must.html; and Katy Bachman, 'Survey: clutter causing TV ads to lack effectiveness', *MediaWeek* (8 February 2010), www.mediaweek.com/mw/content_display/esearch/e3ief7f94880dc0982ebfa130c698f8d2e8?src=bchallenge.

18 See Martin Sipkoff, 'Four-dollar pricing considered boom or bust', *Drug Topics* (August 2008), p. 4S; and Sarah Bruyn Jones, 'Economic survival guide: drug discounts common now', *McClatchy-Tribune Business News* (23 February 2009).

19 'Overconsumption is costing us the Earth and human happiness'. *Guardian* (21 June 2010).

20 Examples taken from Anthony Deutsch, 'Burger King axes palm oil supplier', *Financial Times* (4/5 September 2010), p. 17; Andrew Ward and Mark Mulligan, 'Ikea buys six German wind farms', *Financial Times* (9 September 2010), p. 23; Cecilie Rohwedder, 'Big UK chains tout local produce', *Wall Street Journal* (17 March 2011), p. 25; Peter Marsh, 'Big Names in clothing eco-label plan', *Financial Times* (1 March 2011).

21 Paul Tyrrel, 'Technology lets buyers unravel the ethics behind the label', *Financial Times* (16 September 2010), p. 16.

22 Examples taken from Jonathan Leake, 'Sea life massacred for Tesco tuna tins', *Sunday Times* (9 January 2011), S1, p. 13; 'Cornish pasty's 25-mile journey from the factory to the Tesco store next door', *Daily Mail* (30 May 2010), p. 5; Chris Brooke, 'The pound shop polo that went all round the world', *Daily Mail* (2 September 2010), p. 5.

23 Seel Alan S. Brown, 'The many shades of green', *Mechanical Engineering* (January 2009).

24 Based on information from Marc Gunther, 'Coca-Cola's green crusader', *Fortune* (28 April 28, 2008), p. 150; 'Cold test markets aluminum bottles', (20 February 2008), accessed at www.bevnet.com/news/2008/02-20-2008-Coke.asp; 'Coca-Cola to install 1,800 CO2 Coolers in North America', (30 April 2009), accessed at www.r744.com/articles/2009-04-30-coca-cola-to-install-1800-co2-coolers-in-north-america.php; and 'The Business of recycling', www.thecoca-colacompany.com/citizenship/environment_case_studies.html, accessed July 2010.

25 See '2010 global 100 list', www.global100.org/annual-reviews/2010-global-100-list.html?sort=company; and www.unileverusa.com/sustainability/environment, accessed July 2010.

26 See http://ec.europa.eu/environment/legal/implementation_en.htm, accessed (2 March 2012), and 'What is EMAS?', http://ec.europa.eu/environment/emas/index_en.htm, accessed October 2010.

27 For example, see Nigel F. Piercy, *Market-Led Strategic Change: Transforming the Process of Going to Market*, 4th edn. (Oxford: Elsevier, 2009), Chapter 4; and Piercy and Lane, 'Corporate social responsibility initiatives and strategic marketing imperatives'.

28 Information from Mark Borden, 'The world's 50 most innovative companies: #36: Samsung', *Fast Company* (17 February 2010), p. 90; Laurie Burkitt, 'Samsung courts consumers, marketers', *Forbes* (7 June 2010), accessed at www.forbes.com/global/2010/0607/marketing-apps-consumer-electronics-apple-samsungs-big-spend.html; and Choi He-suk, 'Samsung renews resolve to reform', *Korea Herald* (8 June 2010), accessed at www.koreaherald.com/national/Detail.jsp?newsMLId=20100607001598.

29 Information from Eleftheria Parpis, 'Must love dogs', *Adweek* (18 February 2008) accessed at www.adweek.com/aw/content_display/esearch/e3i14785206d4d123ec32476ca4ac7470d5; and 'The PEDIGREE® adoption drive partners with dog lover Carrie Underwood to help homeless dogs' (12 February 2010), accessed at www.mars.com/global/news-and-media/press-releases/news-releases.aspx?SiteId=94&Id=1767.

[30] See 'Our reason for being', www.patagonia.com/web/us/patagonia.go?slc=en_US&sct=US&assetid=2047, accessed November 2010.

[31] Quotes and other information from Bob Liodice, '10 companies with social responsibility at the core', *Advertising Age* (19 April 2010), p. 88. See also www.nikebiz.com/responsibility/, accessed July 2010.

[32] Mike Hoffman, 'Ben Cohen: Ben & Jerry's homemade, established in 1978', *Inc* (30 April 2001), p. 68; Sindya N. Bhanoo, 'Products that are Earth-and-profit friendly', *New York Times* (12 June 2010), p. B3. See also www.benjerry.com/company/history/, and www.nikebiz.com/responsibility, accessed July 2010.

[33] Information from www.haworth.com/en-us/Products/Furniture/Seating/Desk/Pages/Zody.aspx, accessed October 2010.

[34] Nanette Byrnes, 'Pepsi brings in the health police', *Bloomberg Businessweek* (25 January 2010), pp. 50–51.

[35] Adapted from material found in Jeff Heilman, 'Rules of engagement', *The Magazine of Branded Engagement* (Winter 2009), pp. 7–8.

[36] Elliot Wilson, 'Britain goes to war on bribery', *Daily Mail* (1 April 2011), p. 91; Dionne Searcey, 'UK bribes law has firms in a sweat', *Wall Street Journal* (29 December 2010), p. 6.

[37] 'Graft around the globe', *Bloomberg BusinessWeek* (17–23 May 2010), p. 14; Christopher Hope, 'Britain sinks to new low in corruption index', *Daily Telegraph* (18 November 2009), p. 8; Samuel Brittan, 'Worse evils exist than corruption', *Financial Times* (18 September 2009), p. 15.

[38] Adapted from Piercy. *Market-Led Strategic Change*, pp. 203–204.

[39] See Samuel A. DiPiazza, 'Ethics in action', *Executive Excellence* (January 2002), pp. 15–16; Samuel A. DiPiazza Jr., 'It's all down to personal values' (August 2003), accessed at www.pwcglobal.com; and 'Ethics and business conduct', www.pwc.com/ethics, accessed November 2010.

[40] DiPiazza, 'Ethics in action', p. 15.

[41] David A. Lubin and Daniel C. Esty, 'The sustainability imperative', *Harvard Business Review* (May 2010), pp. 41–50.

VIDEO CASE

Land Rover MyMarketingLab

The automotive industry has seen better days. Many car companies are now facing declining revenues and negative profits. Additionally, because of its primary dependence on products that consume petroleum, the industry has a big environmental black eye, especially companies that primarily makes gas-guzzling trucks and 4×4s.

During the past few years, however, Land Rover has experienced tremendous growth in revenues and profits. It is currently selling more vehicles than ever worldwide. How is this possible for a company that only sells 4×4s? One of the biggest reasons is Land Rover's strategic focus on social responsibility and environmentalism. Land Rover believes that it can meet consumer needs for luxury all-terrain vehicle while at the same time providing a vehicle that is kinder to the environment. As a corporation, it is also working feverishly to reduce its carbon emissions, reduce waste, and reduce water consumption and pollution. With actions like this, Land Rover is successfully repositioning its brand away from the standard perceptions of 4×4s as environmental enemies.

After viewing the video featuring Land Rover answer the following questions about the company's efforts toward social responsibility:

1. Make a list of social criticisms of the car industry. Discuss all of the ways that Land Rover practise sustainable marketing?
2. By the textbook's definition, does Land Rover practise 'sustainable marketing'?
3. Do you believe that Land Rover is sincere in its efforts to be environmentally friendly? Is it even possible for a large 4×4 to be environmentally friendly?

COMPANY CASE

Competing through green engineering: Siemens versus GE

GE'S ECOMAGINATION INITIATIVE

GE (General Electric Corporation) is an American multinational conglomerate operating through four segments: Energy, Technology Infrastructure, Capital Finance and Consumer and Industrial. In 2011, *Fortune* magazine ranked GE the sixth largest firm in the US, as well as the 14th most profitable. However, GE has a history of some of its activities being associated with large-scale air and water pollution, and the company has been accused of being one of the largest creators of toxic waste in the United States. To many, the company has a legacy of environmental damage from its business.

But, in May 2005 GE announced the launch of a programme called 'Ecomagination', intended, in the words of CEO Jeff Immelt 'to develop tomorrow's solutions such as solar energy, hybrid locomotives, fuel cells, lower-emission aircraft engines, lighter and stronger durable materials, efficient lighting, and water purification technology'. GE said in 2008 that it would invest $1.4 billion (€1.1billion) in clean technology research and development as part of its Ecomagination initiative. As of October 2008, the scheme had resulted in 70 green products being brought to market, ranging from halogen lamps to biogas engines. In 2007, GE raised the annual revenue target for its Ecomagination initiative from $20 billion (€15.6 billion) in 2010 to $25 billion (€19.5 billion) following positive market response to its new product lines. In 2010, GE continued to raise its investment by adding $10 billion (€7.8 billion) into Ecomagination over the following five years.

Advertising in the *Financial Times* and the *Wall Street Journal* proclaimed:

> Ecomagination
>
> A GE commitment
>
> At GE, we've discovered an inexhaustible resource. A resource that we believe could help solve the problems of an energy hungry world. It's called imagination, or rather Ecomagination. We're putting ideas into action by creating forward-looking technology for improved environmental performance, greater fuel efficiency, lower emissions and reduced noise. By developing advanced technologies in energy, manufacturing and infrastructure, we can create solutions that are as economically advantageous as they are ecologically sound. Just imagine it.

GE, according to Mr Immelt, had been investing for years in 'clean' technology that reduces the emissions of greenhouse gases, usually by substituting low-carbon fuels for conventional energy sources, or making more efficient use of fossil fuel. The company produces several key technologies in this area: wind turbines, for instance. GE's turnover in wind power will be €2 billion (€1.5 billion) a year, according to the European Wind Energy Association. Cleaner coal is another: GE has technology that allows power plants to convert coal to a form that produces more electricity for less fuel and with fewer carbon dioxide emissions.

In order to qualify for the Ecomagination branding, GE products must 'significantly and measurably improve customers' environmental and operating performance'. An independent environmental consulting company, Green Order, verifies the company's claims. So the move encompasses products as different as the GEnx engine, which will power the Airbus 350 and Boeing 787 and is 15 per cent more energy efficient than its predecessors, and the compact fluorescent light bulb that saves 70 to 80 per cent of energy compared with ordinary light bulbs.

Water also falls under the scheme: GE has started work on the biggest desalination plant in Africa, to provide drinking water for 25 per cent of the population of Algiers. Another key part of the initiative is to attempt to 'green' many products of which environmental implications may not be obvious. For instance, as part of GE's work on materials, the company has developed a new wire coating for use in cars and consumer electronics that does not require certain polluting compounds in its production.

Ecomagination places these technologies under a single brand, with an initial pledge to increase research spending on them to €1.25 billion by 2010, from €600 million in 2004. GE's total research and development budget stands at about €3.9 billion. GE also plans to double its revenues from such technologies from €8 billion in 2004 to more than €15 billion by 2010.

The reasoning behind the drive is clear: Mr Immelt scents a business opportunity. 'Green is green', he tells customers and investors, equating the green of the environment with the green of the dollar. As people and governments become increasingly concerned with environmental issues, more pressure will be brought to bear on GE and its customers to prove their environmental credentials. A soaring oil price and the quest for energy security are equally important factors.

Nuclear power will also play a part. When the Ecomagination brand was conceived about a year before its launch in the US, nuclear power was not included. Now, Mr Immelt has decided to bring GE's nuclear products within the Ecomagination family. 'We are pushing for nuclear power. You cannot believe in energy security and greenhouse gas emissions and not understand that nuclear power has to be part of the future.'

The Ecomagination push will also require GE to cut its greenhouse gas emissions by 1 per cent in absolute terms by 2012. As the company's emissions would have risen by 40 per cent in that period, if growth estimates are correct, this represents a big undertaking. But cutting greenhouse gas emissions can also save money by cutting fuel bills.

Mr Immelt would like his customers to adopt Ecomagination, with co-branding efforts and joint development. Some are already keen to do so. Gustav Humber, Airbus CEO, welcomed measures to make aircraft engines more efficient: 'This is absolutely the right initiative. [Air] transportation is growing at 5 to 6 per cent a year, and that can be at least balanced by the increased environmental friendliness of these products'.

But the push for environmental virtue has practical limits. If a customer were using old, environmentally unsound technology and were unwilling to invest in changing it, would GE try to persuade it otherwise? Mr Immelt does not hesitate: 'Unlikely.' GE will not allow its new-found environmental credentials to stand in the way of business.

Ecomagination also requires greater transparency by the company. Mr Immelt pledges to report GE's impact on the environment in detail. This will please environmental groups, which have campaigned against some of its polluting activities in the past. But will he go as far as some companies and invite an environmentalist on to the board? Again, no hesitation: 'I would doubt that. But I would say if you looked at our citizenship report that we just launched a month or so ago, there is extraordinary detail about our environmental performance'. GE suppliers will be subjected to similar levels of scrutiny, he promised.

By 2007 General Electric revealed that it had doubled sales from environmentally friendly products to €9.4 billion over the previous two years, suggesting that for GE at least corporate America's drive to respond to climate change was beginning to pay off. The company had €39 billion of projects in the pipeline and was on track to meet its target of €15.6 billion in 'green' sales by 2010. According to GE, sales of environmentally friendly products, such as wind turbines, water-purification systems and energy-efficient appliances, rose from €4.7 billion in 2004 to €7.8 billion in 2005 and €9.4 billion in 2007. In the same period, overall sales at GE grew more than 20 per cent to €127 billion.

News of the sharp rise in revenues from 'Ecomagination' came as US companies were scrambling to take advantage of opportunities presented by climate change. Executives at GE, which has lobbied government and the business community for action on the environment, said its Ecomagination sales showed that, far from being a drag on earnings, such strategies can benefit the bottom line. 'I think the idea has traction now,' Mr Immelt said. 'As a business, you have got to be willing to have your own strategy [on climate change].'

The focus on driving revenues from greener products is a priority in Mr Immelt's plan to reduce GE's exposure to low-growth industries and reshape its portfolio towards more profit-able sectors. GE also revealed that the previous year, it invested €700 million of its €29 billion annual research-and-development budget on green projects. Mr Immelt pledged to raise R&D spending on eco-projects to €1.2 billion by the end of the decade. The company also reduced greenhouse gas emissions by 4 per cent in 2006, ahead of its target of lowering them by 1 per cent before 2012.

CRITICS' VIEWS OF ECOMAGINATION

Incredulity had been the reaction of many observers when Mr Immelt had pledged to double GE's revenues from 'green' products to $20 billion by 2010, boost research spending on 'cleaner technologies' and slash its greenhouse gas emissions.

Some labelled it 'greenwash' – a cynical marketing move by a smokestack conglomerate that was notorious in environmental circles for its alleged pollution of New York state's Hudson River in the 1970s and 1980s. Others warned that Mr Immelt would struggle to instill an environmentally minded culture into a company whose genetic make-up was to seek profit at all costs.

For GE being at the front of corporate America's environmental bandwagon has its drawbacks. One of the big criticisms of the company's eco-marketing and advertising campaign, complete with green-tinted website, is that it is just a public relations stunt. Christopher Miller, leader of the US. global warming campaign at Greenpeace, credits GE with raising the profile of environmental issues in the business world but says the green credo is at odds with the company's involvement in industries such as coal and oil and gas. 'There is a certain level of hypocrisy in their actions,' he says.

A corporate conversion to environmental causes as public as GE's carries reputational risks. Eco-sceptics criticise GE's advocacy of environmental issues as a self-serving exercise. 'A lot of Ecomagination is based on a plan to get government to change regulations so that people buy technologies and products that would not otherwise be profitable', says Myron Ebell, of the Washington-based Competitive Enterprise Institute, a free market think-tank.

COMPETITIVE RESPONSES

What is more, GE's leadership in 'green engineering', and hence competitive advantage from the initiative, has been challenged by several major competitors, particularly Siemens in Germany.

In continued fierce rivalry, Siemens, Europe's largest engineering group, locked horns with GE yet again as it claimed Siemens made nearly double the amount of revenues from Environmentally friendly products as its US competitor's much-heralded Ecomagination programme. The German conglomerate said it had revenues of €17 billion last year from such products against €11 billion at GE. Siemens is aiming to earn €25 billion by 2011 against a GE target of €9.5 billion in 2010.

The release of these figures are the first time Siemens has spelled out how much it earns from environmentally friendly products and is a clear admission that GE and other rivals had outflanked the German group in marketing.

The publication of Siemens' target is likely to lead to increased competition over green products among companies over who can sell the most. Companies are increasingly seeing greener products as a way of boosting the bottom line as well as helping the environment. As a percentage of sales, Siemens seems to lead the way, with about 23 per cent of its €72 billion sales last year in environmentally-friendly products, followed by Philips of the Netherlands with about 20 per cent of €27 billion and GE with 15 per cent of its €72 billion non-financial and non-media sales. Philips is aiming for 30 per cent by 2012.

Under new CEO Peter Löscher, Siemens is fighting to free itself of its own legacy of doubtful ethics – a global bribery scandal nearly finished the company in the 2000s. Löscher has focused on mega-trends like green business to assure the company's future. He says that around 400,000 employees today are what Siemans calls 'green-collar workers' – those who produce or market its portfolio of resource-efficient products.

Löscher's strategy for Siemens has led to head-to-head competition with GE, not least in the area of green business. A key part of his strategy, like GE's, is a big bet that green consciousness will fuel future sales. He has branded Siemens a 'green infrastructure giant', emphasising the German company's roots as a leading innovator and the vast growth potential in supplying infrastructure, such as trams, smart power grids and water treatment facilities.

Questions for discussion

1. Give as many examples as you can of how GE and Siemens are defying common social criticisms of marketing.
2. Are GE and Siemens successfully applying concepts of sustainability? Which is the more effective in doing so?
3. Analyse GE and Siemens according to the environmental sustainability portfolio in Figure 20.2.
4. Are the green engineers truly practising enlightened marketing, or are there green policies no more than vested self-interest and a marketing ploy? Give as many examples as you can to justify your answer.
5. Is green engineering likely to provide greater profitability compared to conventional approaches? Explain your answer.

Sources: Fiona Harvey, 'GE looks out for a cleaner profit', *Financial Times* (1 July 2005), p. 13; Francesco Guerrera, 'GE doubles eco-friendly Product Sales', *Financial Times* (24 March 2007), p. 28. Francesco Guerrera, 'Turning green requires a lot of Imagination', *Financial Times* (24 March 2007), p. 28. Richard Milne and Fiona Harvey, 'Siemens tackles GE in Green Push' *Financial Times*, (23 June 2008), www.ft.com. Richard Weiss and Beendikt Kammel, 'How Siemens Got its Geist Back', *Bloomberg Business-Week*, (31 January–6 February 2011), pp. 18–20. See also www.ecomagination .com.

APPENDIX 1: MARKETING PLAN

THE MARKETING PLAN: AN INTRODUCTION

As a marketer, you'll need a good marketing plan to provide direction and focus for your brand, product or company. With a detailed plan, any business will be better prepared to launch a new product or build sales for existing products. Non-profit organisations also use marketing plans to guide their fund-raising and outreach efforts. Even government agencies develop marketing plans for initiatives such as building public awareness of proper nutrition and stimulating local tourism.

The purpose and content of a marketing plan

Unlike a business plan, which offers a broad overview of the entire organisation's mission, objectives, strategy and resource allocation, a marketing plan has a more limited scope. It serves to document how the organisation's strategic objectives will be achieved through specific marketing strategies and tactics, with the customer as the starting point. It is also linked to the plans of other departments within the organisation.

Suppose a marketing plan calls for selling 200,000 units annually. The production department must gear up to make that many units, the finance department must arrange funding to cover the expenses, the human resources department must be ready to hire and train staff, and so on. Without the appropriate level of organisational support and resources, no marketing plan can succeed.

Although the exact length and layout will vary from company to company, a marketing plan usually contains the elements described in Chapter 2. Smaller businesses may create shorter or less formal marketing plans, whereas corporations frequently require highly structured marketing plans. To effectively guide implementation, every part of the plan must be described in great detail. Sometimes a company will post its marketing plan on an internal website, which allows managers and employees in different locations to consult specific sections and collaborate on additions or changes.

The role of research

Marketing plans are not created in a vacuum. To develop successful strategies and action programmes, marketers require up-to-date information about the environment, the competition and the market segments to be served. Often, an analysis of internal data is the starting point for assessing the current marketing situation; this is supplemented by marketing intelligence and research investigating the overall market, the competition, key issues, and threats and opportunities. As the plan is implemented, marketers use a variety of research techniques to measure progress toward objectives and identify areas for improvement if the results fall short of projections.

Finally, marketing research helps marketers learn more about their customers' requirements, expectations, perceptions and satisfaction levels. This deeper understanding is the foundation for building competitive advantage through well-informed segmenting, targeting, differentiating and positioning decisions. Thus, the marketing plan should outline what marketing research will be conducted and how the findings will be applied.

The role of relationships

The marketing plan shows how the company will establish and maintain profitable customer relationships. It also shapes several internal and external relationships. First, it affects how marketing personnel work with each other and with other departments to deliver value and satisfy customers. Second, it affects how the company works with suppliers, distributors and strategic alliance partners to achieve the objectives in the plan. Third, it influences the company's dealings with other stakeholders, including government regulators, the media, and the community at large. All of these relationships are important to the organisation's success, so they should be considered when a marketing plan is being developed.

From marketing plan to marketing action

Companies generally create yearly marketing plans, although some plans cover longer periods of time. Marketers start planning well in advance of the implementation date to allow time for marketing research, thorough analysis, management review and coordination between departments. Then, after each action programme begins, marketers monitor on-going results, compare them with projections, analyse any differences and take corrective steps as needed. Some marketers also prepare contingency plans if certain conditions emerge. Because of inevitable and sometimes unpredictable environmental changes, marketers must be ready to update and adapt marketing plans at any time.

For effective implementation and control, the marketing plan should define how progress toward objectives will be measured. Managers typically use budgets, schedules and performance standards for monitoring and evaluating results. With budgets, they can compare planned expenditures with actual expenditures for a given week, month or other time period. Schedules allow management to see when tasks were supposed to be completed and when they were actually completed. Performance standards track the outcomes of marketing programmes to see whether the company is moving toward its objectives. Some examples of performance standards are market share, sales volume, product profitability and customer satisfaction.

SAMPLE MARKETING PLAN FOR SONIC

This section takes you inside the sample marketing plan for Sonic, a hypothetical start-up company. The company's first product is the Sonic 1000, a multimedia, cellular/Wi-Fi-enabled smartphone. Sonic will be competing with Apple, Nokia, Research in Motion, Motorola, Samsung and other well-established rivals in a crowded, fast-changing marketplace for smartphones that combine communication, entertainment and storage functionality. The marginal definitions explain the purpose and function of each section of the plan.

Executive summary

Executive summary—This section summarises and overviews the main goals, recommendations and points for senior managers who will read and approve the marketing plan. For management convenience, a table of contents usually follows this section.

Sonic is preparing to launch a new multimedia, dual-mode smartphone, the Sonic 1000, in a mature market. Our product offers a competitively unique combination of advanced features and functionality at a value-added price. We are targeting specific segments in the consumer and business markets, taking advantage of opportunities indicated by higher demand for easy-to-use smartphones with expanded communications, entertainment and storage functionality.

The primary marketing objective is to achieve first-year Europe-wide sales of 500,000 units. The primary financial objectives are to achieve first-year sales revenues of €75 million, keep first year losses under €8 million, and break even early in the second year.

Current marketing situation

Sonic, founded 18 months ago by two entrepreneurs with experience in the PC market, is about to enter the mature smartphone market. Multifunction mobile phones, e-mail devices and wireless communication devices are commonplace for both personal and professional photography and allow the user to store images for later retrieval and use. Research shows that the United States has 262 million wireless phone subscribers, and 85 per cent of the population owns a mobile phone. Comparable statistics for the EU are available at http:/epp.eurostat.ec.europa.eu/statistics_explained/index_php/Telecommunication_statistics.

Competition is therefore more intense even as demand flattens, industry consolidation continues, and pricing pressures squeeze profitability. Worldwide, Nokia is the smartphone leader, with 38 per cent of the global market. The runner-up is Research in Motion, maker of the BlackBerry, with 18 per cent of the global market. To gain market share in this dynamic environment, Sonic must carefully target specific segments with features that deliver benefits valued by each customer group.

Market description

Sonic's market consists of consumers and business users who prefer to use a single device for communication, information storage and exchange, and entertainment on the go. Specific segments being targeted during the first year include professionals, corporations, students, entrepreneurs and medical users. Table A1.1 shows how the Sonic 1000 addresses the needs of targeted consumer and business segments.

Buyers can choose among models based on several different operating systems, including systems from Microsoft, Symbian, BlackBerry and Linux variations. Sonic licenses a Linux-based

Market description— Describes the targeted segments in detail and provides context for the marketing strategies and detailed action programmes discussed later in the plan.

Table A1.1   Segment needs and corresponding features/benefits

Targeted segment	Customer needs	Corresponding features/benefits
Professionals (consumer market)	• Stay in touch conveniently and securely while on the go • Perform many function hands-free without carrying multiple gadgets	• Built-in cell phone and push-to-talk feature to communicate anywhere at any time. • Wireless e-mail/Web access from anywhere • Linux operating system that is less vulnerable to hackers • Voice-activated applications are convenient • GPS functionality and camera add value
Students (consumer market)	• Perform many functions hands-free without carrying multiple gadgets • Express style and individuality	• Compatible with numerous applications and peripherals for convenient, cost-effective communications and entertainment • Variety of smartphone cases
Corporate users (business market)	• Security and adaptability for proprietary tasks • Obtain driving directions to business meetings	• Customisable to fit corporate tasks and networks • Linux-based operating system less vulnerable to hackers • Built-in GPS allows voice-activated access to directions and maps
Entrepreneurs (business market)	• Organise and access contacts, schedule details, and business and financial files • Get in touch fast	• Hands-free, wireless access to calendar, address book, information files for checking appointments and data, and connecting with contacts. • Push-to-talk instant calling speeds up communications
Medical users (business market)	• Update, access, and exchange medical records • Photograph medical situations to maintain a visual record	• Removable memory card and hands-free, wireless information recording reduces paperwork and increases productivity • Built-in camera allows fast and easy photography and stores images for later retrieval

system because it is somewhat less vulnerable to attack by hackers and viruses. Hard drives and removable memory cards are popular smartphone options. Sonic is equipping its first entry with an ultrafast, 20-gigabyte removable memory card for information and entertainment storage. This will allow users to transfer photos and other data from the smartphone to a home or office computer. Technology costs are decreasing even as capabilities are increasing which make value-priced models more appealing to consumers and business users with older devices who want to trade up to new, high-end multifunction units.

Product review

Our first product, the Sonic 1000, offers the following standard features with a Linux operating system:

Product review—The product review summarises the main features for all of a company's products, organised by product line, type of customer, market and/or order of product introduction.

- Built-in dual mobile phone/Internet phone functionality and push-to-talk instant calling
- Digital music/video/television recording, wireless downloading and playback
- Wireless Web, e-mail, text messaging and instant messaging
- 3.5-inch colour screen for easy viewing
- Organisation functions, including calendar, address book and synchronisation
- GPS for directions and maps
- Integrated 4-megapixel digital camera
- Ultrafast, 20-gigabyte removable memory card with upgrade potential
- Interchangeable case wardrobe of different colours and patterns
- Voice recognition functionality for hands-free operation

First-year sales revenues are projected to be €75 million, based on sales of 500,000 Sonic 1000 units at a wholesale price of €150 each. During the second year, we plan to introduce the Sonic 2000, also with a Linux operating system, as a higher-end smartphone product offering the following standard features:

- Global phone and messaging compatibility
- Integrated 8-megapixel camera with flash

Competitive review

Competitive review—The purpose of a competitive review is to identify key competitors, describe their market positions and briefly discuss their strategies.

The emergence of lower-priced smartphones, including the Apple iPhone, has increased competitive pressure. Competition from specialised devices for text and e-mail messaging, such as BlackBerry devices, is also a major factor. Key competitors include the following:

- *Nokia.* The market leader in smartphones, Nokia offers a wide range of products for personal and professional use. It purchased the maker of the Symbian operating system and made it into a separate foundation dedicated to improving and promoting this mobile software platform. Many of Nokia's smartphones offer full keyboards, similar to Research in Motion models. Nokia also offers stripped-down models for users who do not require the full keyboard and full multimedia capabilities.
- *Apple.* The stylish and popular iPhone 4S has a 3.5-inch colour screen and is well equipped for music, video and Web access; it also has communication, calendar, contact management and file management functions. Its global positioning system technology can pinpoint a user's location. Also, users can erase data with a remote command if the smartphone is lost or stolen. Apple has only recently added new network providers. The iPhone 5 is priced from €499.
- *RIM.* Lightweight BlackBerry wireless multifunction products are manufactured by Research in Motion and are especially popular among corporate users. RIM's continuous innovation and solid customer service strengthen its competitive standing as it introduces smartphones with enhanced features and communication capabilities. Its newest Blackberry, the Torch 9800, is the company's first touch-screen smartphone that includes a full keyboard. Priced at €199 with a two-year AT&T contract, the Torch competes with its iPhone and Android rivals.

- *Motorola.* Motorola, a global giant, has been losing market share to Apple and Research in Motion because it has slowed the pace of new product introduction. However, Motorola is now showing signs of improvement as it taps into the Android operating system market with its newest smartphone, the Droid X. Boasting an 8-megapixel camera, a 4.3-inch screen, and Google services ranging from voice search to Gmail, the Droid X is priced at €200 (after €100 mail-in rebate and a two-year contract).
- *Samsung.* Value, style, function – Samsung is a strong competitor and offers a variety of smartphones for consumer and business segments. Some of its smartphones are available for specific telecommunications carriers, and some are 'unlocked', ready for any compatible telecommunications network. Its newest smartphones, the Galaxy S series, are available with the top four carriers. The Captivate model features a 4-inch AMOLED touch screen and a 5-megapixel camera for €199 with a two-year contract.

Despite this strong competition, Sonic can carve out a definite image and gain recognition among the targeted segments. Our voice-recognition system for completely hands-free operation is a critical point of differentiation for competitive advantage. Also, offering GPS as a standard feature gives us a competitive edge compared with similarly priced smartphones. Moreover, the product is speedier than most and runs on the Linux operating system, which is an appealing alternative for customers concerned about security.

Channels and logistics review

Sonic-branded products will be distributed through a network of retailers in the top European markets. Some of the most important channel partners are as follows:

- *Office supply superstores.* Staples and other supply superstores will carry Sonic products in stores, in catalogues and online.
- *Computer stores.* Independent computer retailers will carry Sonic products.
- *Electronics speciality stores.* Curry's, Dixons, PC World and other electronic speciality stores will feature Sonic products.
- *Online retailers.* Amazon will carry Sonic products and, for a promotional fee, will give Sonic prominent placement on its homepage during the introduction.

Initially, our channel strategy will focus on Europe according to demand, but we have plans to expand into North America and beyond, with appropriate logistical support.

Strengths, weaknesses, opportunities and threat analysis

Sonic has several powerful strengths on which to build, but our major weakness is a lack of brand awareness and image. The major opportunity is the demand for multimedia smartphones that deliver a number of valued benefits, eliminating the need for customers to carry more than one device. We also face the threat of ever-higher competition from consumer electronics manufacturers, as well as downward pricing pressure.

Strengths

Sonic can build on three important strengths:

1. *Innovative product.* The Sonic 1000 offers a combination of features that would otherwise require customers to carry multiple devices: speedy, hands-free, dual-mode mobile/Wi-Fi telecommunications capabilities; GPS functionality; and digital video/music/television programme storage and playback.
2. *Security.* Our smartphone uses a Linux-based operating system that is less vulnerable to hackers and other security threats that can result in stolen or corrupted data.
3. *Pricing.* Our product is priced lower than many competing multifunction models – none of which offer the same bundle of features – which gives us an edge with price-conscious customers.

Strengths—Strengths are internal capabilities that can help a company reach its objectives.

Weaknesses

Weaknesses—Weaknesses are internal elements that may interfere with a company's ability to achieve its objectives.

By waiting to enter the smartphone market until some consolidation of our competitors has occurred, we have learned from the successes and mistakes of others. Nonetheless, we have two main weaknesses:

1. *Lack of brand awareness.* Sonic has no established brand or image, whereas Apple and others have strong brand recognition. We will address this issue with aggressive promotion.
2. *Physical specifications.* The Sonic 1000 is slightly heavier and thicker than most competing models because it incorporates multiple features, offers sizeable storage capacity, and is compatible with numerous peripheral devices. To counteract this weakness, we will emphasise our product's benefits and value-added pricing, which are two compelling competitive strengths.

Opportunities

Opportunities—Opportunities are external elements that a company may be able to exploit to its advantage.

Sonic can take advantage of two major market opportunities:

1. *Increasing demand for multimedia smartphones with multiple functions.* The market for multimedia, multifunction devices is growing much faster than the market for single-use devices. Growth will accelerate as dual-mode capabilities become mainstream, giving customers the flexibility to make phone calls over mobile or Internet connections. Smartphones are already commonplace in public, work and educational settings, which is boosting primary demand. Also, customers who bought entry-level models are replacing older models with more advanced models.
2. *Cost-efficient technology.* Better technology is now available at a lower cost than ever before. Thus, Sonic can incorporate advanced features at a value-added price that allows for reasonable profits.

Threats

Threats—Threats are current emerging external elements that could potentially challenge a company's performance.

We face three main threats with the introduction of the Sonic 1000:

1. *Increased competition.* More companies are entering the European market with smartphone models that offer some but not all the features and benefits provided by Sonic's product. Therefore, Sonic's marketing communications must stress our clear differentiation and value-added pricing.
2. *Downward pressure on pricing.* Increased competition and market-share strategies are pushing smartphone prices down. Still, our objective of seeking a 10 per cent profit on second-year sales of the original model is realistic, even given the lower margins in this market.
3. *Compressed product life cycle.* Smartphones have reached the maturity stage of their life cycle more quickly than earlier technology products. We have contingency plans to keep sales growing by adding new features, targeting additional segments and adjusting prices as needed.

Objectives and issues

Objectives and issues—A company's objectives should be defined in specific terms so management can measure progress and plan corrective action if needed, to stay on track. This section, describes any major issues that might affect a company's marketing strategy and implementation.

Sonic have set aggressive but achievable objectives for the first and second years of market entry.

- *First-year objectives.* During the Sonic 1000's initial year on the market, we are aiming for unit sales volume of 500,000.
- *Second-year objectives.* Our second-year objectives are to sell a combined total of one million units of our two models and break even early in this period.

Issues

In relation to the product launch, our major issue is the ability to establish a well-regarded brand name linked to meaningful positioning. We will invest heavily in marketing to create a memorable and distinctive brand image projecting innovation, quality and value. We must also measure awareness and response so we can adjust our marketing efforts as necessary.

Marketing strategy

Sonic's marketing strategy is based on a positioning of product differentiation. Our primary consumer target is middle- to upper-income professionals who need one portable device to coordinate their busy schedules, communicate with family and colleagues, get driving directions and be entertained on the go. Our secondary consumer target is secondary/high school, college and postgraduate students who want a multimedia, dual-mode device. This segment can be described demographically by age (16–30) and educational attainment level.

Our primary business target is mid- to large-sized corporations that want to help their managers and employees stay in touch and be able to input or access critical data when not in the office. This segment consists of companies with more than €25 million in annual sales and more than 100 employees. We are also targeting entrepreneurs and small-business owners as well as medical users who want to update or access patients' medical records while reducing paperwork.

Positioning

Using product differentiation, the Sonic is being positioned as the most versatile, convenient and value-added model for personal and professional use. Our marketing will focus on hands-free operation of multiple communication, entertainment and information capabilities that differentiate the Sonic 1000 from its competitors.

> **Positioning**—Positioning built on meaningful differentiation, supported by appropriate strategy and implementation, can help a company build competitive advantage.

Product strategy

The Sonic 1000, including all the features described earlier, will be sold with a one-year warranty. We will introduce a more compact, powerful high-end model (the Sonic 2000) in the second year. Building the Sonic brand is an integral part of our product strategy. The brand and logo (Sonic's distinctive yellow thunderbolt) will be displayed on the product and its packaging and reinforced by its prominence in the introductory marketing campaign.

Pricing strategy

The Sonic 1000 will be introduced at €150 wholesale/€199 estimated retail price per unit. We expect to lower the price of this first model when we expand the product line by launching the Sonic 2000, whose wholesale price will be €175 per unit. These prices reflect a strategy of attracting desirable channel partners and taking share from Nokia, Research in Motion, Motorola and other established competitors.

Distribution strategy

Our channel strategy is to use selective distribution, marketing Sonic smartphones through well-known stores and online retailers. During the first year, we will add channel partners until we have coverage in all major European markets and the product is included in the major electronics catalogues and websites. We will also investigate distribution through mobile-phone outlets maintained by major carriers. In support of our channel partners, Sonic will provide demonstration products, detailed specification hand-outs, and full-colour photos and displays featuring the product. Finally, Sonic plan to arrange special payment terms for retailers that place volume orders.

Marketing communications strategy

By integrating all messages in all media, we will reinforce the brand name and the main points of product differentiation. Research about media consumption patterns will help our advertising agency choose appropriate media and timing to reach prospective customers before and during product introduction. Thereafter, advertising will appear on a regular basis to maintain brand awareness and communicate various differentiation messages. The agency will also coordinate public relations efforts to build the Sonic brand and support the differentiation message. To create buzz, we will host a user-generated video contest on our website. To attract, retain and motivate channel partners for a push strategy, we will use trade sales promotions and personal selling. Until the Sonic brand has been established, our communications will encourage purchases through channel partners rather than from our website.

Marketing research

Marketing research—This section shows marketing research will be used to support development, implementation and evaluation of strategies and action programmes.

Using research, we are identifying the specific features and benefits that our target market segments value. Feedback from market tests, surveys and focus groups will help us develop the Sonic 2000. We are also measuring and analysing customers' attitudes toward competing brands and products. Brand awareness research will help us determine the effectiveness and efficiency of our messages and media. Finally, we will use customer satisfaction studies to gauge market reaction.

Marketing organisation

Marketing organisation—The marketing department may be organsied by function, as in this example, geography, product or customers (or some combination thereof).

Sonic's chief marketing officer, Jane Melody, holds overall responsibility for all marketing activities. Figure A1.1 shows the structure of the eight-person marketing organisation. Sonic has hired Worldwide Marketing to handle national sales campaigns, trade and consumer sales promotions, and public relations efforts.

Action programmes

Action programmes—Action programmes should be coordinated with the resources and activities of other departments, including production, finance and purchasing.

The Sonic 1000 will be introduced in February. The following are summaries of the action programmes we will use during the first six months of next year to achieve our stated objectives.

- *January.* We will launch a €200,000 trade sales promotion campaign and exhibit at the major industry trade shows to educate dealers and generate channel support for the product launch in February. Also, we will create buzz by providing samples to selected product reviewers, opinion leaders, influential bloggers and celebrities. Training staff will work with retail sales personnel at major chains to explain the Sonic 1000's features, benefits and advantages.
- *February.* We will start an integrated print/radio/Internet advertising campaign targeting professionals and consumers. The campaign will show how many functions the Sonic smartphone can perform and emphasise the convenience of a single, powerful handheld device. This multimedia campaign will be supported by point-of-sale signage as well as online-only ads and video tours.
- *March.* As the multimedia advertising campaign continues, we will add consumer sales promotions, such as a contest in which consumers post videos to our website showing

Figure A1.1 Sonic's marketing organisation

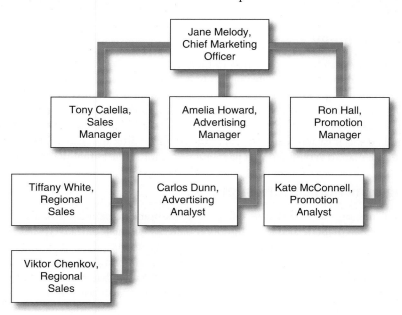

how they use the Sonic in creative and unusual ways. We will also distribute new point of-purchase displays to support our retailers.

- *April.* We will hold a trade sales contest offering prizes for the salesperson and retail organisation that sells the most Sonic smartphones during the four-week period.
- *May.* We plan to roll out a new national advertising campaign this month. The radio ads will feature celebrity voices telling their Sonic smartphones to perform various functions, such as initiating a phone call, sending an e-mail, playing a song or video, and so on. The stylised print and online ads will feature avatars of these celebrities holding their Sonic smartphones.
- *June.* Our radio campaign will add a new voice-over tagline promoting the Sonic 1000 as a graduation gift. We will also exhibit at the twice a year electronics trade show and provide channel partners with new competitive comparison hand-outs as a sales aid. In addition, we will tally and analyse the results of customer satisfaction surveys for use in future promotions and provide feedback for product and marketing activities.

Budgets

Total first-year sales revenue for the Sonic 1000 is projected at €75 million, with an average wholesale price of €150 per unit and a variable cost per unit of €100 for 500,000 units. We anticipate a first-year loss of up to €8 million on the Sonic 1000 model. Break-even calculations indicate that the Sonic 1000 will become profitable after the sales volume exceeds 650,000, which we anticipate early in the product's second year. Our break-even analysis of Sonic's first smartphone product assumes wholesale revenue of €150 per unit, variable cost of €100 per unit and estimated first-year fixed costs of €32,500,000. Based on these assumptions, the break-even calculation is as follows:

$$\frac{€32,500,000}{€150/unit - €100/unit} = 650,000 \text{ units}$$

Budgets—Managers use budgets to project profitability and plan for each marketing, programme's expenditures, scheduling and operations.

Controls

We are planning tight control measures to closely monitor quality and customer service satisfaction. This will enable us to react very quickly to correct any problems that may occur. Other early warning signals that will be monitored for signs of deviation from the plan include monthly sales (by segment and channel) and monthly expenses. Given the market's volatility, we are developing contingency plans to address fast-moving environmental changes, such as new technology and new competition.

MARKETING PLAN TOOLS

Pearson offers two valuable resources to assist you in developing a marketing plan:

- *The Marketing Plan Handbook* by Marian Burk Wood explains the process of creating a marketing plan and includes detailed checklists and dozens of real-world examples.
- *Marketing Plan Pro* is an award-winning software package that includes sample plans, step-by-step guides, an introductory video, help wizards and customisable charts for documenting a marketing plan.

Sources: Background information and market data adapted from Matt Gallagher, 'Blackberry gets smarter', *Red Herring* (3 August 2010), p. 5; Dan Moren and Jason Snell, 'Meet the iPhone 4', *Macworld* (August 2010), pp. 22–23; Walter S. Mossberg, 'Galaxy phones from Samsung are worthy iPhone rivals', *Wall Street Journal* (Eastern Edition) (22 July 2010), pp. D1–D5; Hester Plumridge, 'Nokia dials new number for success', *Wall Street Journal* (Eastern Edition) (21 July 2010), p. C16; Rich Jaroslovsky, 'Motorola's new mojo', *Bloomberg Businessweek* (12 July 2010), p. 72; Edward C. Baig, 'Droid X marks all the right spots; android phone could challenge iphone 4', *USAToday* (1 July 2010), p. 3B; Arik Hesseldahl, 'Nokia's Kallasvuo: we must "move even faster," ' *Businessweek Online* (17 March 2010), p. 1; Ginny Miles, 'The hottest smartphones of the season', *PC World* (September 2009), pp. 44–48; 'Android smart phone shipments grow 886% year-on-year in Q2 2010', www.canalys.com/pr/2010/r2010081.html, accessed December 2011.

APPENDIX 2: MARKETING BY THE NUMBERS

Marketing managers are facing increased accountability for the financial implications of their actions. This appendix provides a basic introduction to measuring marketing financial performance. Such financial analysis guides marketers in making sound marketing decisions and in assessing the outcomes of those decisions.

The appendix is built around a hypothetical manufacturer of consumer electronic products – ConnectPhone. In the past, ConnectPhone has concentrated on making Internet modems. However, the company is now introducing a new type of product – a *media phone* that replaces a household's telephone and provides 'always-on' Internet connectivity and wireless phone access through VoIP (Voice over Internet Protocol) technology. In this appendix, we will analyse the various decisions ConnectPhone's marketing managers must make before and after the new-product launch.

The appendix is organised in *three sections*. The *first section* introduces pricing, break-even, and margin analysis assessments that will guide the introduction of ConnectPhone's new product. The *second section* discusses demand estimates, the marketing budget and marketing performance measures. It begins with a discussion of estimating market potential and company sales. It then introduces the marketing budget, as illustrated through a *pro forma* profit-and-loss statement followed by the actual profit-and-loss statement. Next, we discuss marketing performance measures, with a focus on helping marketing managers to better defend their decisions from a financial perspective. In the *third section*, we analyse the financial implications of various marketing tactics. Each of the three sections ends with a set of quantitative exercises that provide you with an opportunity to apply the concepts you have learned to situations beyond ConnectPhone.

PRICING, BREAK-EVEN AND MARGIN ANALYSIS

Pricing considerations

Determining price is one of the most important marketing-mix decisions. The limiting factors are demand and costs. Demand factors, such as buyer-perceived value, set the price ceiling. The company's costs set the price floor. In between these two factors, marketers must consider competitors' prices and other factors such as reseller requirements, government regulations and company objectives.

Current competing media phone products sell at retail prices between €500 and €1,000. ConnectPhone plans to introduce its new product at a lower price in order to expand the market and to gain market share rapidly. We first consider ConnectPhone's pricing decision from a cost perspective. Then, we consider consumer value, the competitive environment, and reseller requirements.

Determining costs

Recall from Chapter 10 that there are different types of costs. **Fixed costs** do not vary with production or sales level and include costs such as rent, interest, depreciation and clerical and management salaries. Regardless of the level of output, the company must pay these costs. Whereas total fixed costs remain constant as output increases, the fixed cost per unit (or average fixed cost) will decrease as output increases because the total fixed costs are spread across more units of output. **Variable costs** vary directly with the level of production and include costs related to the direct production of the product (such as costs of goods sold – COGS) and many of the marketing costs associated with selling it. Although these costs tend to be uniform for each unit produced, they are called variable because their total varies with the number of units produced. **Total costs** are the sum of the fixed and variable costs for any given level of production.

ConnectPhone has invested €10 million in refurbishing an existing facility to manufacture the new media phone product. Once production begins, the company estimates that it will incur fixed costs of €20 million per year. The variable cost to produce each device is estimated to be €250 and is expected to remain at that level for the output capacity of the facility.

Fixed costs—Costs that do not vary with production of sales level.

Variable costs—Costs that vary directly with the level of production.

Total costs—The sum of the fixed and variable costs for any given level of production.

Setting price based on costs

ConnectPhone starts with the cost-based approach to pricing discussed in Chapter 10. Recall that the simplest method, **cost-plus pricing** (or **mark-up pricing**), simply adds a standard mark-up to the cost of the product. To use this method, however, ConnectPhone must specify expected unit sales so that total unit costs can be determined. Unit variable costs will remain constant regardless of the output, but *average unit fixed costs* will decrease as output increases.

To illustrate this method, suppose ConnectPhone has fixed costs of €20 million, variable costs of €250 per unit, and expects unit sales of one million media phones. Thus, the cost per unit is given by:

Cost-plus pricing (or mark-up pricing)—A standard mark-up to the cost of the product.

$$\text{Unit cost} = \text{variable cost} + \frac{\text{fixed costs}}{\text{unit sales}} = \text{€}250 + \frac{\text{€}20{,}000{,}000}{1{,}000{,}000} = \text{€}270$$

Note that we do *not* include the initial investment of €10 million in the total fixed cost figure. It is not considered a fixed cost because it is not a *relevant* cost. **Relevant costs** are those that will occur in the future and that will vary across the alternatives being considered. ConnectPhone's investment to refurbish the manufacturing facility was a one-time cost that will not reoccur in the future. Such past costs are *sunk costs* and should not be considered in future analyses.

Also notice that if ConnectPhone sells its product for €270, the price is equal to the total cost per unit. This is the **break-even price** – the price at which unit revenue (price) equals unit cost and profit is zero.

Suppose ConnectPhone does not want to merely break-even but rather wants to earn a 25 per cent mark-up on sales. ConnectPhone's mark-up price is:

Relevant costs—Costs that will occur in the future and that will vary across the alternatives being considered.

Break-even price—The price at which total revenue equals total cost and profit is zero.

$$\text{Mark-up price} = \frac{\text{unit cost}}{(1 - \text{desired return on sales})} = \frac{\text{€}270}{1 - 0.25} = \text{€}360$$

This is the price at which ConnectPhone would sell the product to resellers such as wholesalers or retailers to earn a 25 per cent profit on sales.

Another approach ConnectPhone could use is called **return on investment (ROI) pricing** (or **target-return pricing**). In this case, the company *would* consider the initial €10 million investment, but only to determine the euro profit goal. Suppose the company wants a 30 per cent return on its investment. The price necessary to satisfy this requirement can be determined by:

Return on investment (ROI) pricing (or target-return pricing)—A cost-based pricing method that determines price based on a specified rate of return on investment.

$$\text{ROI price} = \text{unit cost} + \frac{\text{ROI} \times \text{investment}}{\text{unit sales}} = \text{€}270 + \frac{0.3 \times \text{€}10{,}000{,}000}{1{,}000{,}000} = \text{€}273$$

That is, if ConnectPhone sells its product for €273, it will realise a 30 per cent return on its initial investment of €10 million.

In these pricing calculations, unit cost is a function of the expected sales, which were estimated to be one million units. But what if actual sales were lower? Then the unit cost would be higher because the fixed costs would be spread over fewer units, and the realised percentage mark-up on sales or ROI would be lower. Alternatively, if sales are higher than the estimated one million units, unit cost would be lower than €270, so a lower price would produce the desired mark-up on sales or ROI. It's important to note that these cost-based pricing methods are *internally* focused and do not consider demand, competitors' prices or reseller requirements. Because ConnectPhone will be selling this product to consumers through wholesalers and retailers offering competing brands, the company must consider mark-up pricing from this perspective.

Setting price based on external factors

Whereas costs determine the price floor, ConnectPhone also must consider external factors when setting price. ConnectPhone does not have the final say concerning the final price of its media phones to consumers – retailers do. So it must start with its suggested retail price and work back. In doing so, ConnectPhone must consider the mark-ups required by resellers that sell the product to consumers.

In general, a euro **mark-up** is the difference between a company's selling price for a product and its cost to manufacture or purchase it. For a retailer, then, the mark-up is the difference between the price it charges consumers and the cost the retailer must pay for the product. Thus, for any level of reseller:

$$\text{Euro markup} = \text{selling price} - \text{cost}$$

Mark-ups are usually expressed as a percentage, and there are two different ways to compute mark-ups – on *cost* or on *selling price*:

$$\text{Mark-up percentage on cost} = \frac{\text{euro markup}}{\text{cost}}$$

$$\text{Mark-up percentage on selling price} = \frac{\text{euro markup}}{\text{euro price}}$$

To apply reseller margin analysis, ConnectPhone must first set the suggested retail price and then work back to the price at which it must sell the product to a wholesaler. Suppose retailers expect a 30 per cent margin and wholesalers want a 20 per cent margin based on their respective selling prices. And suppose that ConnectPhone sets a manufacturer's suggested retail price (MSRP) of €599.99 for its product.

Recall that ConnectPhone wants to expand the market by pricing low and generating market share quickly. ConnectPhone selected the €599.99 MSRP because it is lower than most competitors' prices, which can be as high as €1,000. And the company's research shows that it is below the threshold at which more consumers are willing to purchase the product. By using buyers' perceptions of value and not the seller's cost to determine the MSRP, ConnectPhone is using **value-based pricing**. For simplicity, we will use an MSRP of €600 in further analyses.

To determine the price ConnectPhone will charge wholesalers, we must first subtract the retailer's margin from the retail price to determine the retailer's cost (€600 – (€600 × 0.30) = €420). The retailer's cost is the wholesaler's price, so ConnectPhone next subtracts the wholesaler's margin (€420 – (€420 × 0.20) = €336). Thus, the **mark-up chain** representing the sequence of mark-ups used by firms at each level in a channel for ConnectPhone's new product is as follows:

Suggested retail price:	€600
minus retail margin (30%):	− €180
Retailer's cost/wholesaler's price:	€420
minus wholesaler's margin (20%):	− €84
Wholesaler's cost/ConnectPhone's price:	€336

Mark-up—The difference between a company's selling price for a product and its cost to manufacture or purchase it.

Value-based pricing—Offering just the right combination of quality and good service at a fair price.

Mark-up chain—The sequence of mark-ups used by firms at each level in a channel.

By deducting the mark-ups for each level in the mark-up chain, ConnectPhone arrives at a price for the product to wholesalers of €336.

Break-even and margin analysis

The previous analyses derived a value-based price of €336 for ConnectPhone's product. Although this price is higher than the break-even price of €270 and covers costs, that price assumed a demand of 1 million units. But how many units and what level of euro sales must ConnectPhone achieve to break even at the €336 price? And what level of sales must be achieved to realise various profit goals? These questions can be answered through break-even and margin analysis.

Determining break-even unit volume and euro sales

Based on an understanding of costs, consumer value, the competitive environment and reseller requirements, ConnectPhone has decided to set its price to wholesalers at €336. At that price, what sales level will be needed for ConnectPhone to break even or make a profit on its media phones? **Break-even analysis** determines the unit volume and euro sales needed to be profitable given a particular price and cost structure. At the break-even point, total revenue equals total costs and profit is zero. Above this point, the company will make a profit; below it, the company will lose money. ConnectPhone can calculate break-even volume using the following formula:

Break-even analysis— Analysis to determine the unit volume and euro sales needed to be profitable given a particular price and cost structure.

$$\text{Break-even volume} = \frac{\text{fixed costs}}{\text{price} - \text{variable cost}}$$

The denominator (price – unit variable cost) is called **unit contribution** (sometimes called contribution margin). It represents the amount that each unit contributes to covering fixed costs. Break-even volume represents the level of output at which all (variable and fixed) costs are covered. In ConnectPhone's case, break-even unit volume is:

Unit contribution—The amount that each unit contributes to covering fixed costs – the difference between price and variable costs.

$$\text{Break-even volume} = \frac{\text{fixed costs}}{\text{price} - \text{variable cost}} = \frac{\text{€}20,000,000}{\text{€}336 - \text{€}250} = 232,558.1 \text{ units}$$

Thus, at the given cost and pricing structure, ConnectPhone will break even at 232,559 units.

To determine the break-even euro sales, simply multiply unit break-even volume by the selling price:

$$\text{BE sales} = \text{BE}_{\text{vol}} \times \text{price} = 232,559 \times \text{€}336 = \text{€}78,139,824$$

Another way to calculate euro break-even sales is to use the percentage contribution margin (hereafter referred to as **contribution margin**), which is the unit contribution divided by the selling price:

Contribution margin—The unit contribution divided by the selling price.

$$\text{Contribution margin} = \frac{\text{price} - \text{variable costs}}{\text{price}} = \frac{\text{€}336 - \text{€}250}{\text{€}336} = 0.256 \text{ or } 25.6\%$$

Then,

$$\text{Break-even sales} = \frac{\text{fixed costs}}{\text{contribution margin}} = \frac{\text{€}20,000,000}{0.256} = \text{€}78,125,000$$

Note that the difference between the two break-even sales calculations is due to rounding.

Such break-even analysis helps ConnectPhone by showing the unit volume needed to cover costs. If production capacity cannot attain this level of output, then the company should not launch this product. However, the unit break-even volume is well within ConnectPhone's capacity.

Of course, the bigger question concerns whether ConnectPhone can sell this volume at the €336 price. We'll address that issue a little later.

Understanding contribution margin is useful in other types of analyses as well, particularly if unit prices and unit variable costs are unknown or if a company (say, a retailer) sells many products at different prices and knows the percentage of total sales variable costs represent. Whereas unit contribution is the difference between unit price and unit variable costs, total contribution is the difference between total sales and total variable costs. The overall contribution margin can be calculated by:

$$\text{Contribution margin} = \frac{\text{total sales} - \text{total variable costs}}{\text{total sales}}$$

Regardless of the actual level of sales, if the company knows what percentage of sales is represented by variable costs, it can calculate contribution margin. For example, ConnectPhone's unit variable cost is €250, or 74 per cent of the selling price (€250 ÷ €336 = 0.74). That means for every €1 of sales revenue for ConnectPhone, €0.74 represents variable costs, and the difference (€0.26) represents the contribution to fixed costs. But even if the company doesn't know its unit price and unit variable cost, it can calculate the contribution margin from total sales and total variable costs or from its knowledge of the total cost structure. It can set total sales equal to 100 per cent regardless of the actual absolute amount and determine the contribution margin:

$$\text{Contribution margin} = \frac{100\% - 74\%}{100\%} = \frac{1 - 0.07}{1} = 0.74 = 0.26 \text{ or } 26\%$$

Note that this matches the percentage calculated from the unit price and unit variable cost information. This alternative calculation will be very useful later when analysing various marketing decisions.

Determining 'break-even' for profit goals

Although it is useful to know the break-even point, most companies are more interested in making a profit. Assume ConnectPhone would like to realise a €5 million profit in the first year. How many must it sell at the €336 price to cover fixed costs and produce this profit? To determine this, ConnectPhone can simply add the profit figure to fixed costs and again divide by the unit contribution to determine unit sales:

$$\text{Unit volume} = \frac{\text{fixed costs} - \text{profit goal}}{\text{price} - \text{variable cost}} = \frac{€20,000,000 + €5,000,000}{€336 - €250} = 290,667.7 \text{ units}$$

Thus, to earn a €5 million profit, ConnectPhone must sell 290,698 units. Multiply by price to determine euro sales needed to achieve a €5 million profit:

$$\text{Euro sales} = 290,698 \text{ units} \times €336 = €97,674,528$$

Or use the contribution margin:

$$\text{Sales} = \frac{\text{fixed costs} + \text{profit goal}}{\text{contribution margin}} = \frac{€20,000,000 + €5,000,000}{0.256} = €97,656,250$$

Again, note that the difference between the two break-even sales calculations is due to rounding.

As we saw previously, a profit goal can also be stated as a return on investment goal. For example, recall that ConnectPhone wants a 30 per cent return on its €10 million investment. Thus, its absolute profit goal is €3 million (€10,000,000 × 0.30). This profit goal is treated the same way as in the previous example:

$$\text{Unit volume} = \frac{\text{fixed costs} + \text{profit goal}}{\text{price} - \text{variable cost}} = \frac{\text{€}20{,}000{,}000 + \text{€}3{,}000{,}000}{\text{€}336 - \text{€}250} = 267{,}442 \text{ units}$$

$$\text{Euro sales} = 267{,}442 \text{ units} \times \text{€}336 = \text{€}89{,}860{,}512$$

Or

$$\text{Euro sales} = \frac{\text{fixed costs} + \text{profit goal}}{\text{contribution margin}} = \frac{\text{€}20{,}000{,}000 + \text{€}3{,}000{,}000}{0.256} = \text{€}89{,}843{,}750$$

Finally, ConnectPhone can express its profit goal as a percentage of sales, which we also saw in previous pricing analyses. Assume ConnectPhone desires a 25 per cent return on sales. To determine the unit and sales volume necessary to achieve this goal, the calculation is a little different from the previous two examples. In this case, we incorporate the profit goal into the unit contribution as an additional variable cost. Look at it this way: if 25 per cent of each sale must go toward profits, that leaves only 75 per cent of the selling price to cover fixed costs. Thus, the equation becomes:

$$\text{Unit volume} = \frac{\text{fixed costs}}{\text{price} - \text{variable cost} - (0.25 \times \text{price})} = \frac{\text{fixed cost}}{(0.75 \times \text{price}) - \text{variable cost}}$$

So,

$$\text{Unit volume} = \frac{\text{€}20{,}000{,}000}{(0.75 \times \text{€}336) - \text{€}250} = 10{,}000{,}000 \text{ units}$$

$$\text{Euro sales necessary} = 10{,}000{,}000 \text{ units} \times \text{€}336 = \text{€}3{,}360{,}000{,}000$$

Thus, ConnectPhone would need more than €3 billion in sales to realise a 25 per cent return on sales given its current price and cost structure! Could it possibly achieve this level of sales? The major point is this: although break-even analysis can be useful in determining the level of sales needed to cover costs or to achieve a stated profit goal, it does not tell the company whether it is *possible* to achieve that level of sales at the specified price. To address this issue, ConnectPhone needs to estimate demand for this product.

Before moving on, however, let's stop here and practise applying the concepts covered so far. Now that you have seen pricing and break-even concepts in action as they related to ConnectPhone's new product, here are several exercises for you to apply what you have learned in other contexts.

Marketing by the numbers exercise set one

Now that you've studied pricing, break-even and margin analysis as they relate to ConnectPhone's new-product launch, use the following exercises to apply these concepts in other contexts.

1.1 Sanborn, a manufacturer of electric roof vents, realises a cost of €55 for every unit it produces. Its total fixed costs equal €2 million. If the company manufactures 500,000 units, compute the following:

   (a) unit cost

   (b) mark-up price if the company desires a 10 per cent return on sales

   (c) ROI price if the company desires a 25 per cent return on an investment of €1 million

1.2 An interior decorator purchases items to sell in her store. She purchases a lamp for €125 and sells it for €225. Determine the following:
   (a) euro mark-up

    (b) mark-up percentage on cost

    (c) mark-up percentage on selling price

1.3 A consumer purchases a toaster from a retailer for €60. The retailer's mark-up is 20 per cent, and the wholesaler's mark-up is 15 per cent, both based on selling price. For what price does the manufacturer sell the product to the wholesaler?

1.4 A vacuum manufacturer has a unit cost of €50 and wishes to achieve a margin of 30 per cent based on selling price. If the manufacturer sells directly to a retailer who then adds a set margin of 40 per cent based on selling price, determine the retail price charged to consumers.

1.5 Advanced Electronics manufactures DVDs and sells them directly to retailers who typically sell them for €20. Retailers take a 40 per cent margin based on the retail selling price. Advanced's cost information is as follows:

Unit volume	€20,000,000
DVD package and disc	€2.50/DVD
Royalties	€2.25/DVD
Advertising and promotion	€500,000
Overhead	€200,000

Calculate the following:

(a) contribution per unit and contribution margin

(b) break-even volume in DVD units and euros

(c) volume in DVD units and euro sales necessary if Advanced's profit goal is 20 per cent profit on sales

(d) net profit if 5 million DVDs are sold

DEMAND ESTIMATES, THE MARKETING BUDGET AND MARKETING PERFORMANCE MEASURES

Market potential and sales estimates

ConnectPhone has now calculated the sales needed to break even and to attain various profit goals on its new product. However, the company needs more information regarding demand in order to assess the feasibility of attaining the needed sales levels. This information is also needed for production and other decisions. For example, production schedules need to be developed and marketing tactics need to be planned.

    The **total market demand** for a product or service is the total volume that would be bought by a defined consumer group in a defined geographic area in a defined time period in a defined marketing environment under a defined level and mix of industry marketing effort. Total market demand is not a fixed number but a function of the stated conditions. For example, next year's total market demand for media phones will depend on how much other producers spend on marketing their brands. It also depends on many environmental factors, such as government regulations, economic conditions and the level of consumer confidence in a given market. The upper limit of market demand is called **market potential**.

    One general but practical method that ConnectPhone might use for estimating total market demand uses three variables: (1) the number of prospective buyers; (2) the quantity purchased by an

Total market demand—The total volume that would be bought by a defined consumer group, in a defined geographic area, in a defined time period, in a defined marketing environment, under a defined level and mix of industry marketing effort.

Market potential—The upper limit to market demand.

average buyer per year; and (3) the price of an average unit. Using these numbers, ConnectPhone can estimate total market demand as follows:

$$Q = n \times q \times p$$

where

Q = total market demand
n = number of buyers in the market
q = quantity purchased by an average buyer per year
p = price of an average unit

A variation of this approach is the **chain ratio method**. This method involves multiplying a base number by a chain of adjusting percentages. For example, ConnectPhone's product is designed to replace a household's telephone as well as provide 'always on' Internet access. Thus, only households with broadband Internet access will be able to use the product. Finally, not all Internet households will be willing and able to purchase the new product. ConnectPhone can estimate demand using a chain of calculations like the following:

Chain ratio method—
Estimating market demand by multiplying a base number by a chain of adjusting percentages.

> Total number of European households
>
> × The percentage of households with broadband Internet access
>
> × The percentage of these households willing and able to buy this device

ConnectPhone's Research finds that these are 113 million 'reachable' households in Europe, around 50 per cent of these households have broadband Internet access and 33.1 per cent of households possess the discretionary income needed and are willing to buy a device such as this. Then, the total number of households willing and able to purchase this product is:

$$113 \text{ million households} \times 0.50 \times 0.331 = 18.7 \text{ million households}$$

Households will need only one media phone. Assuming the average retail price across all brands is €750 for this product, the estimate of total market demand is as follows:

$$18.7 \text{ million households} \times 1 \text{ device per household} \times €750 = €14 \text{ billion}$$

This simple chain of calculations gives ConnectPhone only a rough estimate of potential demand. However, more detailed chains involving additional segments and other qualifying factors would yield more accurate and refined estimates. Still, these are only *estimates* of market potential. They rely heavily on assumptions regarding adjusting percentages, average quantity and average price. Thus, ConnectPhone must make certain that its assumptions are reasonable and defendable. As can be seen, the overall market potential in euro sales can vary widely given the average price used. For this reason, ConnectPhone will use unit sales potential to determine its sales estimate for next year. Market potential in terms of units is 18.7 million (18.7 million households × 1 device per household).

Assuming that ConnectPhone wants to attain 2 per cent market share (comparable to its share of the Internet modem market) in the first year after launching this product, then it can forecast unit sales at 18.7 million units × 0.02 = 374,000 units. At a selling price of €336 per unit, this translates into sales of €125,664,000 (374,000 units × €336 per unit). For simplicity, further analyses will use forecasted sales of €125 million.

This unit volume estimate is well within ConnectPhone's production capacity and exceeds not only the break-even estimate (232,559 units) calculated earlier, but also the volume necessary to realise a €5 million profit (290,698 units) or a 30 per cent return on investment (267,442 units). However, this forecast falls well short of the volume necessary to realise a 25 per cent return on sales (10 million units!) and may require that ConnectPhone revise expectations.

To assess expected profits, we must now look at the budgeted expenses for launching this product. To do this, we will construct a pro forma profit-and-loss statement.

The profit-and-loss statement and marketing budget

Pro forma (or projected) profit-and-loss statement (or income statement or operating statement)—A statement that shows projected revenues less budgeted expenses and estimates the projected net profit for an organisation, product or brand during a specific planning period, typically a year.

All marketing managers must account for the profit impact of their marketing strategies. A major tool for projecting such profit impact is a **pro forma** (or projected) **profit-and-loss statement** (also called an **income statement** or **operating statement**). A pro forma statement shows projected revenues less budgeted expenses and estimates the projected net profit for an organisation, product or brand during a specific planning period, typically a year. It includes direct product production costs, marketing expenses budgeted to attain a given sales forecast, and overhead expenses assigned to the organisation or product. A profit and loss statement typically consists of several major components (see Table A2.1):

- *Net sales* – gross sales revenue minus returns and allowances (for example, trade, cash, quantity and promotion allowances). ConnectPhone's net sales for 2013 are estimated to be €125 million, as determined in the previous analysis.
- *Cost of goods sold* – (sometimes called *cost of sales*) – the actual cost of the merchandise sold by a manufacturer or reseller. It includes the cost of inventory, purchases and other costs associated with making the goods. ConnectPhone's cost of goods sold is estimated to be 50 per cent of net sales, or €62.5 million.
- *Gross margin (or gross profit)* – the difference between net sales and cost of goods sold. ConnectPhone's gross margin is estimated to be €62.5 million.
- *Operating expenses* – the expenses incurred while doing business. These include all other expenses beyond the cost of goods sold that are necessary to conduct business. Operating expenses can be presented in total or broken down in detail. Here, Connect-Phone's estimated operating expenses include *marketing expenses* and *general and administrative expenses*.

Marketing expenses include sales expenses, promotion expenses and distribution expenses. The new product will be sold through ConnectPhone's sales force, so the company budgets €5 million for sales salaries. However, because sales representatives earn a 10 per cent commission on sales, ConnectPhone must also add a variable component to sales expenses of €12.5 million (10 per cent of €125 million net sales), for a total budgeted sales expense of €17.5 million. ConnectPhone sets its advertising and promotion to launch this product at €10 million. However, the company also budgets 4 per cent of sales, or €5 million, for cooperative advertising allowances to retailers who promote ConnectPhone's new product in their advertising. Thus, the total budgeted advertising and promotion expenses are €15 million (€10 million for advertising plus €5 million in co-op allowances). Finally, ConnectPhone budgets 10 per cent of net sales, or €12.5 million, for freight and delivery charges. In all, total marketing expenses are estimated to be €17.5 million + €15 million + €12.5 million = €45 million.

Table A2.1 Pro forma profit-and-loss statement for the 12-month period ended 31 December 2013

			% of Sales
Net sales		€125,000,000	100%
Cost of good margin		62,500,000	50%
Gross margin		€62,500,000	50%
Marketing expenses:			
Sales expenses	€17,500,000		
Promotion expenses	15,000,000		
Freight	12,500,000	45,000,000	36%
General and administrative expenses:			
Managerial salaries and expenses	€2,000,000		
Indirect overhead	3,000,000	5,000,000	4%
Net profit before tax		€12,500,000	

General and administrative expenses are estimated at €5 million, broken down into €2 million for managerial salaries and expenses for the marketing function and €3 million of indirect overhead allocated to this product by the corporate accountants (such as depreciation, interest, maintenance and insurance). Total expenses for the year, then, are estimated to be €50 million (€45 million marketing expenses + €5 million in general and administrative expenses).

- *Net profit before taxes* – profit earned after all costs are deducted. ConnectPhone's estimated net profit before taxes is €12.5 million.

In all, as Table A2.1 shows, ConnectPhone expects to earn a profit on its new product of €12.5 million in 2013. Also note that the percentage of sales that each component of the profit-and-loss statement represents is given in the right-hand column. These percentages are determined by dividing the cost figure by net sales (that is, marketing expenses represent 36 per cent of net sales determined by €45 million ÷ €125 million). As can be seen, ConnectPhone projects a net profit return on sales of 10 per cent in the first year after launching this product.

MARKETING PERFORMANCE MEASURES

Now let's fast-forward a year. ConnectPhone's product has been on the market for one year and management wants to assess its sales and profit performance. One way to assess this performance is to compute performance ratios derived from ConnectPhone's **profit-and loss statement** (or **income statement** or **operating statement**).

Whereas the pro forma profit-and-loss statement shows *projected* financial performance, the statement given in Table A2.2 shows ConnectPhone's *actual* financial performance based on actual sales, cost of goods sold and expenses during the past year. By comparing the profit-and-loss statement from one period to the next, ConnectPhone can gauge performance against goals, spot favourable or unfavourable trends, and take appropriate corrective action.

The profit-and-loss statement shows that ConnectPhone lost €1 million rather than making the €12.5 million profit projected in the pro forma statement. Why? One obvious reason is that net sales fell €25 million short of estimated sales. Lower sales translated into lower variable costs associated with marketing the product. However, both fixed costs and the cost of goods sold as a percentage of sales exceeded expectations. Hence, the product's contribution margin was 21 per cent rather than the estimated 26 per cent. That is, variable costs represented 79 per cent of sales (55 per cent for cost of goods sold, 10 per cent for sales commissions, 10 per cent for freight and 4 per cent for co-op allowances). Recall that contribution margin can be calculated by subtracting that fraction from one (1 − 0.79 = 0.21). Total fixed costs were €22 million, €2 million more than estimated. Thus, the sales that ConnectPhone needed to break even given this cost structure can be calculated as:

$$\text{Break-even sales} = \frac{\text{fixed costs}}{\text{contribution margin}} = \frac{€22,000,000}{0.21} = €104,761,905$$

If ConnectPhone had achieved another €5 million in sales, it would have earned a profit.

Although ConnectPhone's sales fell short of the forecasted sales, so did overall industry sales for this product. Overall industry sales were only €2.5 billion. That means that ConnectPhone's **market share** was 4 per cent (€100 million/€2.5 billion = 0.04 or 4%), which was higher than forecasted. Thus, ConnectPhone attained a higher-than-expected market share but the overall market sales were not as high as estimated.

Analytic ratios

The profit-and-loss statement provides the figures needed to compute some crucial **operating ratios** – the ratios of selected operating statement items to net sales. These ratios let marketers

Profit-and-loss statement (or income statement or operating statement)—A statement that shows actual revenues less expenses and net profit for an organisation, product or brand during a specific planning period, typically a year.

Market share—Company sales divided by market sales.

Operating ratios—The ratios of selected operating statement items to net sales.

Table A2.2 Profit-and-loss statement for the 12-month period ended 31 December 2012

			% of Sales
Net sales		€100,000,000	100%
Cost of goods sold		55,000,000	55%
Gross margin		€45,000,000	45%
Marketing expenses:			
Sales expenses	€15,000,000		
Promotion expenses	14,000,000		
Freight	10,000,000	39,000,000	39%
General and administrative expenses:			
Managerial salaries and expenses	$2,000,000		
Indirect overhead	5,000,000	7,000,000	7%
Net profit before tax		(€1,000,000)	(1%)

compare the firm's performance in one year to that in previous years (or with industry standards and competitors' performance in that year). The most commonly used operating ratios are the gross margin percentage, the net profit percentage, and the operating expense percentage. The inventory turnover rate and return on investment (ROI) are often used to measure managerial effectiveness and efficiency.

Gross margin percentage—The percentage of net sales remaining after cost of goods sold – calculated by dividing gross margin by net sales.

The **gross margin percentage** indicates the percentage of net sales remaining after cost of goods sold that can contribute to operating expenses and net profit before taxes. The higher this ratio, the more a firm has left to cover expenses and generate profit. ConnectPhone's gross margin ratio was 45 per cent:

$$\text{Gross margin percentage} = \frac{\text{gross margin}}{\text{net sales}} = \frac{€45,000,000}{€100,000,000} = 0.45 = 45\%$$

Note that this percentage is lower than estimated, and this ratio is seen easily in the percentage of sales column in Table A2.2. Stating items in the profit-and-loss statement as a per cent of sales allows managers to quickly spot abnormal changes in costs over time. If there was previous history for this product and this ratio was declining, management should examine it more closely to determine why it has decreased (that is, because of a decrease in sales volume or price, an increase in costs, or a combination of these). In ConnectPhone's case, net sales were €25 million lower than estimated, and cost of goods sold was higher than estimated (55 per cent rather than the estimated 50 per cent).

Net profit percentage—The percentage of each sales euro going to profit – calculated by dividing net profits by net sales.

The **net profit percentage** shows the percentage of each sales euro going to profit. It is calculated by dividing net profits by net sales:

$$\text{Net profit percentage} = \frac{\text{net profit}}{\text{net sales}} = \frac{-€1,000,000}{€100,000,000} = -0.01 = -1.0\%$$

This ratio is easily seen in the per cent of sales column. ConnectPhone's new product generated negative profits in the first year, not a good situation given that before the product launch net profits before taxes were estimated at more than €12 million. Later in this appendix, we will discuss further analyses the marketing manager should conduct to defend the product.

Operating expense percentage—The portion of net sales going to operating expenses – calculated by dividing total expenses by net sales.

The **operating expense percentage** indicates the portion of net sales going to operating expenses. Operating expenses include marketing and other expenses not directly related to marketing the product, such as indirect overhead assigned to this product. It is calculated as follows:

$$\text{Operating expense percentage} = \frac{\text{total expenses}}{\text{net sales}} = \frac{€46,000,000}{€100,000,000} = 0.46 = 46\%$$

This ratio can also be quickly determined from the per cent of sales column in the profit-and-loss statement by adding the percentages for marketing expenses and general and administrative expenses (39% + 7%). Thus, 46 euro cents of every sales euro went to operations. Although ConnectPhone wants this ratio to be as low as possible, and 46 per cent is not an alarming amount, it is of concern if it is increasing over time or if a loss is realised.

Another useful ratio is the **inventory turnover rate** (also called **stockturn rate** for resellers). The inventory turnover rate is the number of times an inventory turns over or is sold during a specified time period (often one year). This rate tells how quickly a business is moving inventory through the organisation. Higher rates indicate that lower investments in inventory are made, thus freeing up funds for other investments. It may be computed on a cost, selling price or unit basis. The formula based on cost is:

Inventory turnover rate (or stockturn rate)—The number of times an inventory turns over or is sold during a specified time period (often one year) – calculated based on costs, selling price or units.

$$\text{Inventory turnover rate} = \frac{\text{cost of goods sold}}{\text{average inventory at cost}}$$

Assuming ConnectPhone's beginning and ending inventories were €30 million and €20 million, respectively, the inventory turnover rate is:

$$\text{Inventory turnover rate} = \frac{€55,000,000}{(€30,000,000 + €20,000,000)/2} = \frac{€55,000,000}{€25,000,000} = 2.2$$

That is, ConnectPhone's inventory turned over 2.2 times in 2013. Normally, the higher the turnover rate, the higher the management efficiency and company profitability. However, this rate should be compared to industry averages, competitors' rates and past performance to determine if ConnectPhone is doing well. A competitor with similar sales but a higher inventory turnover rate will have fewer resources tied up in inventory, allowing it to invest in other areas of the business.

Companies frequently use return on investment (ROI) to measure managerial effectiveness and efficiency. For ConnectPhone, ROI is the ratio of net profits to total investment required to manufacture the new product. This investment includes capital investments in land, buildings, and equipment (here, the initial €10 million to refurbish the manufacturing facility) plus inventory costs (ConnectPhone's average inventory totalled €25 million), for a total of €35 million. Thus, ConnectPhone's ROI for this product is:

$$\text{Return on investment} = \frac{\text{net profit before taxes}}{\text{investment}} = \frac{-€1,000,000}{€35,000,000} = -0.286 = -2.86\%\%$$

ROI is often used to compare alternatives, and a positive ROI is desired. The alternative with the highest ROI is preferred to other alternatives. ConnectPhone needs to be concerned with the ROI realised. One obvious way ConnectPhone can increase ROI is to increase net profit by reducing expenses. Another way is to reduce its investment, perhaps by investing less in inventory and turning it over more frequently.

Marketing profitability metrics

Given the above financial results, you may be thinking that ConnectPhone should drop this new product. But what arguments can marketers make for keeping or dropping this product? The obvious arguments for dropping the product are that first-year sales were well below expected levels and the product lost money, resulting in a negative return on investment.

So what would happen if ConnectPhone did drop this product? Surprisingly, if the company drops the product, the profits for the total organisation will decrease by €4 million! How can that be? Marketing managers need to look closely at the numbers in the profit and loss statement to determine the *net marketing contribution* for this product. In ConnectPhone's case, the net marketing contribution for the product is €4 million, and if the company drops this product, that contribution will disappear as well. Let's look more closely at this concept to illustrate how marketing managers can better assess and defend their marketing strategies and programmes.

Net marketing contribution

Net marketing contribution (NMC), along with other marketing metrics derived from it, measures *marketing* profitability. It includes only components of profitability that are controlled by marketing. Whereas the previous calculation of net profit before taxes from the profit-and-loss statement includes operating expenses not under marketing's control, NMC does not. Referring back to ConnectPhone's profit-and-loss statement given in Table A2.2, we can calculate net marketing contribution for the product as:

$$\text{NMC} = \text{net sales} - \text{cost of goods sold} - \text{marketing expenses}$$
$$= €100 \text{ million} - €55 \text{ million} - €41 \text{ million} = €4 \text{ million}$$

The marketing expenses include sales expenses (€15 million), promotion expenses (€14 million), freight expenses (€10 million) and the managerial salaries and expenses of the marketing function (€2 million), which total €41 million.

Thus, the product actually contributed €4 million to ConnectPhone's profits. It was the €5 million of indirect overhead allocated to this product that caused the negative profit. Furthermore, the amount allocated was €2 million more than estimated in the pro forma profit-and-loss statement. Indeed, if only the estimated amount had been allocated, the product would have earned a *profit* of €1 million rather than losing €1 million. If ConnectPhone drops the product, the €5 million in fixed overhead expenses will not disappear – it will simply have to be allocated elsewhere. However, the €4 million in net marketing contribution *will* disappear.

Marketing return on sales and investment

To get an even deeper understanding of the profit impact of marketing strategy, we'll now examine two measures of marketing efficiency – *marketing return on sales* (marketing ROS) and *marketing return on investment* (marketing ROI).

Marketing return on sales (or **marketing ROS**) shows the per cent of net sales attributable to the net marketing contribution. For our product, ROS is;

$$\text{Marketing ROS} = \frac{\text{net marketing contribution}}{\text{net sales}} = \frac{€4,000,000}{€100,000,000} = 0.04 = 4\%$$

Thus, out of every €100 of sales, the product returns €4 to ConnectPhone's bottom line. A high marketing ROS is desirable. But to assess whether this is a good level of performance, ConnectPhone must compare this figure to previous marketing ROS levels for the product, the ROSs of other products in the company's portfolio, and the ROSs of competing products.

Marketing return on investment (or **marketing ROI**) measures the marketing productivity of a marketing investment. In ConnectPhone's case, the marketing investment is represented by €41 million of the total expenses. Thus, marketing ROI is:

$$\text{Marketing ROI} = \frac{\text{net marketing contribution}}{\text{marketing expenses}} = \frac{€4,000,000}{€41,000,000} = 0.0976 = 9.76\%$$

As with marketing ROS, a high value is desirable, but this figure should be compared with previous levels for the given product and with the marketing ROIs of competitors' products. Note from this equation that marketing ROI could be greater than 100 per cent. This can be achieved by attaining a higher net marketing contribution and/or a lower total marketing expense. In this section, we estimated market potential and sales, developed profit-and-loss statements and examined financial measures of performance. In the next section, we will discuss methods for analysing the impact of various marketing tactics. However, before moving on to those analyses, here's another set of quantitative exercises to help you apply what you've learned to other situations.

Marketing by the numbers exercise set two

2.1 Determine the market potential for a product that has 50 million prospective buyers who purchase an average of 3 per year at an average price of €25. How many units must a company sell if it desires a 10 per cent share of this market?

2.2 Develop a profit-and-loss statement for the Westgate division of North Industries. This division manufactures light fixtures sold to consumers through home improvement and hardware stores. Cost of goods sold represents 40 per cent of net sales. Marketing expenses include selling expenses, promotion expenses and freight. Selling expenses include sales salaries totalling €3 million per year and sales commissions (5 per cent of sales). The company spent €3 million on advertising last year, and freight costs were 10 per cent of sales. Other costs include €2 million for managerial salaries and expenses for the marketing function and another €3 million for indirect overhead allocated to the division.

  (a) Develop the profit-and-loss statement if net sales were €20 million last year.

  (b) Develop the profit-and-loss statement if net sales were €40 million last year.

  (c) Calculate Westgate's break-even sales.

2.3 Using the profit-and-loss statement you developed in question 2.2(b), and assuming that Westgate's beginning inventory was €11 million, ending inventory was €7 million and total investment was €20 million including inventory, determine the following:

  (a) gross margin percentage

  (b) net profit percentage

  (c) operating expense percentage

  (d) inventory turnover rate

  (e) return on investment (ROI)

  (f) net marketing contribution

  (g) marketing return on sales (marketing ROS)

  (h) marketing return on investment (marketing ROI)

  Is the Westgate division doing well? Explain your answer.

FINANCIAL ANALYSIS OF MARKETING TACTICS

Although the first-year profit performance for ConnectPhone's new product was less than desired, management feels that this attractive market has excellent growth opportunities. Although the sales of ConnectPhone's product were lower than initially projected, they were not unreasonable given the size of the current market. Thus, ConnectPhone wants to explore new marketing tactics to help grow the market for this product and increase sales for the company.

For example, the company could increase advertising to promote more awareness of the new product and its category. It could add salespeople to secure greater product distribution. ConnectPhone could decrease prices so that more consumers could afford its product. Finally, to expand the market, ConnectPhone could introduce a lower-priced model in addition to the higher-priced original offering. Before pursuing any of these tactics, ConnectPhone must analyse the financial implications of each.

Increase advertising expenditures

Although most consumers understand the Internet and telephones, they may not be aware of media phones. Thus, ConnectPhone is considering boosting its advertising to make more people aware of the benefits of this device in general and of its own brand in particular.

What if ConnectPhone's marketers recommend increasing national advertising by 50 per cent to €15 million (assume no change in the variable cooperative component of promotional expenditures)? This represents an increase in fixed costs of €5 million. What increase in sales will be needed to break even on this €5 million increase in fixed costs?

A quick way to answer this question is to divide the increase in fixed cost by the contribution margin, which we found in a previous analysis to be 21 per cent:

$$\text{Increase in sales} = \frac{\text{increase in fixed costs}}{\text{contribution margin}} = \frac{€5,000,000}{0.21} = €23,809,524$$

Thus, a 50 per cent increase in advertising expenditures must produce a sales increase of almost €24 million to just break even. That €24 million sales increase translates into an almost 1 percentage point increase in market share (1 per cent of the €2.5 billion overall market equals €25 million). That is, to break even on the increased advertising expenditure, ConnectPhone would have to increase its market share from 4 per cent to 4.95 per cent (€123,809,524/€2.5 billion = 0.0495 or 4.95% market share). All of this assumes that the total market will not grow, which might or might not be a reasonable assumption.

Increase distribution coverage

ConnectPhone also wants to consider hiring more salespeople in order to call on new retailer accounts and increase distribution through more outlets. Even though ConnectPhone sells directly to wholesalers, its sales representatives call on retail accounts to perform other functions in addition to selling, such as training retail salespeople. Currently, ConnectPhone employs 60 sales reps who earn an average of €50,000 in salary plus 10 per cent commission on sales. The product is currently sold to consumers through 1,875 retail outlets. Suppose ConnectPhone wants to increase that number of outlets to 2,500, an increase of 625 retail outlets. How many additional salespeople will ConnectPhone need, and what sales will be necessary to break even on the increased cost?

Workload method—An approach to determining sales force size based on the workload required and the time available for selling.

One method for determining what size sales force ConnectPhone will need is the **workload method**. The workload method uses the following formula to determine the sales force size:

$$\text{NS} = \frac{\text{NC} \times \text{FC} \times \text{LC}}{\text{TA}}$$

where

NS = number of salespeople
NC = number of customers
FC = average frequency of customer calls per customer
LC = average length of customer call
TA = time an average salesperson has available for selling per year

ConnectPhone's sales reps typically call on accounts an average of 20 times per year for about 2 hours per call. Although each sales rep works 2,000 hours per year (50 weeks per year × 40 hours per week), they spent about 15 hours per week on non-selling activities such as administrative duties and travel. Thus, the average annual available selling time per sales rep per year is 1,250 hours (50 weeks × 25 hours per week). We can now calculate how many sales reps ConnectPhone will need to cover the anticipated 2,500 retail outlets:

$$\text{NS} = \frac{2,500 \times 20 \times 2}{1,250} = 80 \text{ salespeople}$$

Therefore, ConnectPhone will need to hire 20 more salespeople. The cost to hire these reps will be €1 million (20 salespeople × €50,000 salary per sales person).

What increase in sales will be required to break even on this increase in fixed costs? The 10 per cent commission is already accounted for in the contribution margin, so the contribution margin remains unchanged at 21 per cent. Thus, the increase in sales needed to cover this increase in fixed costs can be calculated by:

$$\text{Increase in sales} = \frac{\text{increase in fixed cost}}{\text{contribution margin}} = \frac{€1,000,000}{0.21} = €4,761,905$$

That is, ConnectPhone's sales must increase almost €5 million to break even on this tactic. So, how many new retail outlets will the company need to secure to achieve this sales increase? The average revenue generated per current outlet is €53,333 (€100 million in sales divided by 1,875 outlets). To achieve the nearly €5 million sales increase needed to break even, ConnectPhone would need about 90 new outlets (€4,761,905 divided by €53,333 = 89.3 outlets), or about 4.5 outlets per new rep. Given that current reps cover about 31 outlets apiece (1,875 outlets/60 reps), this seems very reasonable.

Decrease price

ConnectPhone is also considering lowering its price to increase sales revenue through increased volume. The company's research has shown that demand for most types of consumer electronics products is elastic – that is, the percentage increase in the quantity demanded is greater than the percentage decrease in price.

What increase in sales would be necessary to break even on a 10 per cent decrease in price? That is, what increase in sales will be needed to maintain the total contribution that ConnectPhone realised at the higher price? The current total contribution can be determined by multiplying the contribution margin by total sales:

Current total contribution = contribution margin × sales = 0.21 × €100 million = €21 million

Price changes result in changes in unit contribution and contribution margin. Recall that the contribution margin of 21 per cent was based on variable costs representing 79 per cent of sales. Therefore, unit variable costs can be determined by multiplying the original price by this percentage: €336 × 0.79 = €265.44 per unit. If price is decreased by 10 per cent, the new price is €302.40. However, variable costs do not change just because price decreased, so the contribution and contribution margin decrease as follows:

	Old	New (reduced 10%)
Price	€336	€302.40
– Unit variable cost	€265.44	€265.44
= Unit contribution	€70.56	€36.96
Contribution margin	€70.56/€336 = 0.21 or 21%	€36.96/€302.40 = 0.12 or 12%

So a 10 per cent reduction in price results in a decrease in the contribution margin from 21 per cent to 12 per cent. To determine the sales level needed to break even on this price reduction, we calculate the level of sales that must be attained at the new contribution margin to achieve the original total contribution of €21 million:

New contribution margin × new sales level = original total contribution

So,

$$\text{New sales level} = \frac{\text{original contribution}}{\text{new contribution margin}} = \frac{€21,000,000}{0.12} = €175,000,000$$

Therefore, sales must increase by €75 million (€175 million – €100 million) just to break even on a 10 per cent price reduction. This means that ConnectPhone must increase market share to 7 per cent (€175 million/€2.5 billion) to achieve the current level of profits (assuming no increase in the total market sales). The marketing manager must assess whether or not this is a reasonable goal.

Extend the product line

Cannibalisation — The situation in which one product sold by a company takes a portion of its sales from other company products.

As a final option, ConnectPhone is considering extending its product line by offering a lower-priced model. Of course, the new, lower-priced product would steal some sales from the higher-priced model. This is called **cannibalisation** – the situation in which one product sold by a company takes a portion of its sales from other company products. If the new product has a lower contribution than the original product, the company's total contribution will decrease on the cannibalised sales. However, if the new product can generate enough new volume, it is worth considering.

To assess cannibalisation, ConnectPhone must look at the incremental contribution gained by having both products available. Recall in the previous analysis we determined that unit variable costs were €265.44 and unit contribution was just over €70. Assuming costs remain the same next year, ConnectPhone can expect to realise a contribution per unit of approximately €70 for every unit of the original product sold. Assume that the first model offered by ConnectPhone is called MP1 and the new, lower-priced model is called MP2. MP2 will retail for €400, and resellers will take the same mark-up percentages on price as they do with the higher-priced model. Therefore, MP2's price to wholesalers will be €224 as follows:

Retail price:	€400
minus retail margin (30%):	– €120
Retailer's cost/wholesaler's price:	€280
minus wholesaler's margin (20%):	– €56
Wholesaler's cost/ConnectPhone's price	€224

If MP2's variable costs are estimated to be €174, then its contribution per unit will equal €50 (€224 – €174 = €50). That means for every unit that MP2 cannibalises from MP1, ConnectPhone will *lose* €20 in contribution toward fixed costs and profit (that is, contribution$_{MP2}$ – contribution$_{MP1}$ = €50 – €70 = – €20). You might conclude that ConnectPhone should not pursue this tactic because it appears as though the company will be worse off if it introduces the lower-priced model. However, if MP2 captures enough *additional* sales, ConnectPhone will be better off even though some MP1 sales are cannibalised. The company must examine what will happen to *total* contribution, which requires estimates of unit volume for both products.

Originally, ConnectPhone estimated that next year's sales of MP1 would be 600,000 units. However, with the introduction of MP2, it now estimates that 200,000 of those sales will be cannibalised by the new model. If ConnectPhone sells only 200,000 units of the new MP2 model (all cannibalised from MP1), the company would lose €4 million in total contribution (200,000 units × €20 per cannibalised unit = €4 million) – not a good outcome. However, ConnectPhone estimates that MP2 will generate the 200,000 of cannibalised sales plus an *additional* 500,000 unit sales. Thus, the contribution on these additional MP2 units will be €25 million (i.e. 500,000 units × €50 per unit = €25 million). The net effect is that ConnectPhone will gain €21 million in total contribution by introducing MP2. The following table compares ConnectPhone's total contribution with and without the introduction of MP2:

	MP1 only	MP1 and MP2
MP1 contribution	600,000 units × €70 = €42,000,000	400,000 units × €70 = €28,000,000
MP2 contribution	0	700,000 units × €50 = €35,000,000
Total contribution	€42,000,000	€63,000,000

The difference in the total contribution is a net gain of €21 million (€63 million – €42 million). Based on this analysis, ConnectPhone should introduce the MP2 model because it results in a positive incremental contribution. However, if fixed costs will increase by more than €21 million as a result of adding this model, then the net effect will be negative and ConnectPhone should not pursue this tactic.

Now that you have seen these marketing tactic analysis concepts in action as they related to ConnectPhone's new product, here are several exercises for you to apply what you have learned in this section in other contexts.

Marketing by the numbers exercise set three

3.1 Kingsford, Inc. sells small plumbing components to consumers through retail outlets. Total industry sales for Kingsford's relevant market last year were €80 million, with Kingsford's sales representing 10 per cent of that total. Contribution margin is 25 per cent. Kingsford's sales force calls on retail outlets and each sales rep earns €45,000 per year plus 1 per cent commission on all sales. Retailers receive a 40 per cent margin on selling price and generate average revenue of €10,000 per outlet for Kingsford.

   (a) The marketing manager has suggested increasing consumer advertising by €300,000. By how much would euro sales need to increase to break even on this expenditure? What increase in overall market share does this represent?

   (b) Another suggestion is to hire three more sales representatives to gain new consumer retail accounts. How many new retail outlets would be necessary to break even on the increased cost of adding three sales reps?

   (c) A final suggestion is to make a 20 per cent across-the-board price reduction. By how much would euro sales need to increase to maintain Kingsford's current contribution?

   (d) Which suggestion do you think Kingsford should implement? Explain your recommendation.

3.2 PepsiCo sells its soft drinks in approximately 400,000 retail establishments, such as supermarkets, discount stores and convenience stores. Sales representatives call on each retail account weekly, which means each account is called on by a sales rep 52 times per year. The average length of a sales call is 75 minutes (or 1.25 hours). An average salesperson works 2,000 hours per year (50 weeks per year × 40 hours per week), but each spends 10 hours a week on non-selling activities, such as administrative tasks and travel. How many salespeople does PepsiCo need?

3.3 Hair Zone manufactures a brand of hair-styling gel. It is considering adding a modified version of the product – a foam that provides a stronger hold. Hair Zone's variable costs and prices to wholesalers are:

	Current hair gel	New foam product
Unit selling price	2.00	2.25
Unit variable costs	.85	1.25

Hair Zone expects to sell 1 million units of the new styling foam in the first year after introduction, but it expects that 60 per cent of those sales will come from buyers who normally purchase Hair Zone's styling gel. Hair Zone estimates that it would sell 1.5 million units of the gel if it did not introduce the foam. If the fixed cost of launching the new foam will be €100,000 during the first year, should Hair Zone add the new product to its line? Why or why not?

GLOSSARY

Action programmes—Action programmes should be coordinated with the resources and activities of other departments, including production, finance and purchasing.

Adapted global marketing—An international marketing strategy that adjusts the marketing strategy and mix elements to each international target market, bearing more costs but hoping for a larger market share and return.

Administered VMS—A vertical marketing system that coordinates successive stages of production and distribution, through the size and power of one of the parties.

Adoption process—The mental process through which an individual passes from first hearing about an innovation to final adoption.

Advertising agency—A marketing services firm that assists companies in planning, preparing, implementing and evaluating all or portions of their advertising programmes.

Advertising budget—The euros and other resources allocated to a product or a company advertising programme.

Advertising media—The vehicles through which advertising messages are delivered to their intended audiences.

Advertising objective—A specific communication *task* to be accomplished with a specific *target* audience during a specific period of *time*.

Advertising strategy—The strategy by which the company accomplishes its advertising objectives. It consists of two major elements: creating advertising messages and selecting advertising media.

Advertising—Any paid form of non-personal presentation and promotion of ideas, goods or services by an identified sponsor.

Affordable method—Setting the promotion budget at the level management thinks the company can afford.

Age and life-cycle segmentation—Dividing a market into different age and life-cycle groups.

Agent—A wholesaler who represents buyers or sellers on a relatively permanent basis, performs only a few functions and does not take the goods.

Allowance—Promotional money paid by manufacturers to retailers in return for an agreement to feature the manufacturer's products in some way.

Alternative evaluation—The stage of the buyer decision process in which the consumer uses information to evaluate alternative brands in the choice set.

Approach—A salesperson meets the customer for the first time.

Attitude—A person's consistently favourable or unfavourable evaluations, feelings and tendencies toward an object or idea.

Baby boomers—The 78 million people born during years following the Second World War and lasting until 1964.

Base-point pricing—A geographical pricing strategy in which the seller designates some city as a base point and charges all customers the freight cost from that city to the customer.

Behavioural segmentation—Dividing a market into segments based on consumer knowledge, attitudes, uses or responses to a product.

Belief—A descriptive thought that a person holds about something.

Benchmarking—The process of comparing one company's products and processes to those of competitors or leading firms in other industries to identify best practices and find ways to improve quality and performance.

Benefit segmentation—Dividing the market into segments according to the different benefits that consumers seek from the product.

Blogs—Online journals where people post their thoughts, usually on a narrowly defined topic.

Brand extension—Extending an existing brand name to new product categories.

Brand—A name, term, sign, symbol, design, or a combination of these, that identifies the products or services of one seller or group of sellers and differentiates them from those of competitors.

Brand equity—The differential effect that knowing the brand name has oncustomer response to the product or its marketing.

Break-even analysis—Analysis to determine the unit volume and euro sales needed to be profitable given a particular price and cost structure.

Break-even price—The price at which total revenue equals total cost and profit is zero.

Break-even pricing (target return pricing)—Setting price to break even on the costs of making and marketing a product or setting price to make a target return.

Broker—A wholesaler who does not take title to goods and whose function is to bring buyers and sellers together and assist in negotiation.

Budgets—Managers use budgets to project profitability and plan for each marketing programme's expenditures, scheduling and operations.

Business analysis—A review of the sales, costs and profit projections for a new product to find out whether these factors satisfy the company's objectives.

Business buyer behaviour—The buying behaviour of organisations that buy goods and services for use in the production of other products and services that are sold, rented or supplied to others.

Business buying process—The decision process by which business buyers determine which products and services their organisations need to purchase and then find, evaluate and choose among alternative suppliers and brands.

Business portfolio—The collection of businesses and products that make up the company.

Business promotions—Sales promotion tools used to generate business leads, stimulate purchases, reward customers and motivate salespeople.

Business-to-business (B-to-B) online marketing—Businesses using online marketing to reach new business customers, serve current customers more effectively and obtain buying efficiencies and better prices.

Business-to-consumer (B-to-C) online marketing—Businesses selling goods and services online to final consumers.

Buyer-readiness stages—The stages consumers normally pass through on their way to a purchase, including awareness, knowledge, liking, preference, conviction and, finally, the actual purchase.

Buyers—People in an organisation's buying centre who make an actual purchase.

Buying centre—All the individuals and units that play a role in the purchase decision-making process.

Buzz marketing—Cultivating opinion leaders and getting them to spread information about a product or a service to others in their communities.

By-product pricing—Setting a price for by-products to make the main product's price more competitive.

Cannibalisation—The situation in which one product sold by a company takes a portion of its sales from other company products.

Captive product pricing—Setting a price for products that must be used along with a main product, such as blades for a razor and games for a computer game console.

Catalogue marketing—Direct marketing through print, video or digital catalogues that are mailed to select customers, made available in stores, or presented online.

Category killer—A giant speciality store that carries a very deep assortment of a particular line and is staffed by knowledgeable employees.

Causal research—Marketing research to test hypotheses about cause-and-effect relationships.

Chain ratio method—Estimating market demand by multiplying a base number by a chain of adjusting percentages.

Chain stores—Two or more outlets that are commonly owned and controlled.

Channel conflict—Disagreement among marketing channel members on goals, roles and rewards – who should do what and for what rewards.

Channel level—A layer of intermediaries that performs some work in bringing the product and its ownership closer to the final buyer.

Click-and-mortar companies—Traditional brick-and-mortar companies that have added online marketing to their operations.

Click-only companies—The so-called dot-coms, which operate online only and have no brick-and-mortar market presence.

Closing—A salesperson asks the customer for an order.

Co-branding—The practice of using the established brand names of two different companies on the same product.

Cognitive dissonance—Buyer discomfort caused by postpurchase conflict.

Commercial online databases—Collections of information available from online commercial sources or accessible via the Internet.

Commercialisation—Introducing a new product into the market.

Communication adaptation—A global communication strategy of fully adapting advertising messages to local markets.

Competition-based pricing—Setting prices based on competitors' strategies, prices, costs and market offerings.

Competitive advantage—An advantage over competitors gained by offering greater customer value, either by having lower prices or providing more benefits that justify higher prices.

Competitive marketing intelligence—The systematic collection and analysis of publicly available information about consumers, competitors and developments in the marketing environment.

Competitive marketing strategies—Strategies that strongly position the company against competitors and give the company the strongest possible strategic advantage.

Competitive review—The purpose of a competitive review is to identify key competitors, describe their market positions and briefly discuss their strategies.

Competitive-parity method—Setting the promotion budget to match competitors' outlays.

Competitor analysis—The process of identifying key competitors; assessing their objectives, strategies, strengths and weaknesses, and reaction patterns; and selecting which competitors to attack or avoid.

Competitor-centred company—A company whose moves are mainly based on competitors' actions and reactions.

Complex buying behaviour—Consumer buying behaviour characterised by high consumer involvement in a purchase and significant perceived differences among brands.

Concentrated (niche) marketing—A market-coverage strategy in which a firm goes after a large share of one or a few segments or niches.

Concept testing—Testing new-product concepts with a group of target consumers to find out if the concepts have strong consumer appeal.

Consumer buyer behaviour—The buying behaviour of final consumers – individuals and households that buy goods and services for personal consumption.

Consumer market—All the individuals and households that buy or acquire goods and services for personal consumption.

Consumer product—A product bought by final consumers for personal consumption.

Consumer promotions–Sales promotion tools used to boost short-term customer buying and involvement or enhance long-term customer relationships.

Consumer-generated marketing–Brand exchanges created by consumers themselves – both invited and uninvited – by which consumers are playing an increasing role in shaping their own brand experiences and those of other consumers.

Consumerism–An organised movement of citizens and government agencies to improve the rights and power of buyers in relation to sellers.

Consumer-oriented marketing–A principle of sustainable marketing that holds a company should view and organise its marketing activities from the consumer's point of view.

Consumer-to-business (C-to-B) online marketing–Online exchanges in which consumers search out sellers, learn about their offers and initiate purchases, sometimes even driving transaction terms.

Consumer-to-consumer (C-to-C) online marketing–Online exchanges of goods and information between final consumers.

Contract manufacturing–A joint venture in which a company contracts with manufacturers in a foreign market to produce a product or provide a service.

Contractual VMS–A vertical marketing system in which independent firms at different levels of production and distribution join together through contracts.

Contribution margin–The unit contribution divided by the selling price.

Convenience product–A consumer product that customers usually buy frequently, immediately and with minimal comparison and buying effort.

Convenience store–A small store, located near a residential area, that is open long hours seven days a week and carries a limited line of high-turnover convenience goods.

Conventional distribution channel–A channel consisting of one or more independent producers, wholesalers and retailers, each a separate business seeking to maximise its own profits, even at the expense of profits for the system as a whole.

Corporate (brand) website–A website designed to build customer goodwill, collect customer feedback and supplement other sales channels rather than sell the company's products directly.

Corporate VMS–A vertical marketing system that combines successive stages of production and distribution under single ownership – channel leadership is established through common ownership.

Cost-based pricing–Setting prices based on the costs for producing, distributing and selling the product plus a fair rate of return for effort and risk.

Cost-plus pricing (or mark-up pricing)–A standard mark-up to the cost of the product.

Creative concept–The compelling 'big idea' that will bring the advertising message strategy to life in a distinctive and memorable way.

Crowdsourcing–Inviting broad communities of people – customers, employees, independent scientists and researchers and even the public at large – into the new-product innovation process.

Cultural environment–Institutions and other forces that affect society's basic values, perceptions, preferences and behaviours.

Culture–The set of basic values, perceptions, wants and behaviours learned by a member of society from family and other important institutions.

Customer (or market) sales force structure–A sales force organisation in which salespeople specialise in selling only to certain customers or industries.

Customer database–An organised collection of comprehensive data about individual customers or prospects, including geographic, demographic, psychographic and behavioural data.

Customer equity–The total combined customer lifetime values of all of the company's customers.

Customer insights–Fresh understandings of customers and the marketplace derived from marketing information that become the basis for creating customer value and relationships.

Customer lifetime value–The value of the entire stream of purchases that the customer would make over a lifetime of patronage.

Customer relationship management (CRM)– The overall process of building and maintaining profitable customer relationships by delivering superior customer value and satisfaction.

Customer satisfaction–The extent to which a product's perceived performance matches a buyer's expectations.

Customer value analysis–An analysis conducted to determine what benefits target customers value and how they rate the relative value of various competitors' offers.

Customer value-based pricing–Setting price based on buyers' perceptions of value rather than on the seller's cost.

Customer-centred company–A company that focuses on customer developments in designing its marketing strategies and delivering superior value to its target customers.

Customer-centred new-product development–New-product development that focuses on finding new ways to solve customer problems and create more customer-satisfying experiences.

Customer-managed relationships–Marketing relationships in which customers, empowered by today's new digital technologies, interact with companies and with each other to shape their relationships with brands.

Customer-perceived value–The customer's evaluation of the difference between all the benefits and all the costs of a marketing offer relative to those of competing offers.

Customer-value marketing–A principle of sustainable marketing that holds a company should put most of its resources into customer-value-building marketing investments.

Deciders–People in an organisation's buying centre who have formal or informal power to select or approve the final suppliers.

Decline stage–The PLC stage in which a product's sales decline.

Deficient products–Products that have neither immediate appeal nor long-term benefits.

Demand curve–A curve that shows the number of units the market will buy in a given time period, at different prices that might be charged.

Demands–Human wants that are backed by buying power.

Demographic segmentation—Dividing the market into segments based on variables such as age, gender, family size, family life cycle, income, occupation, education, religion, race, generation and nationality.

Demography—The study of human populations in terms of size, density, location, age, gender, race, occupation and other statistics.

Department store—A retail organisation that carries a wide variety of product lines – each line is operated as a separate department managed by specialist buyers or merchandisers.

Derived demand—Business demand that ultimately comes from (derives from) the demand for consumer goods.

Descriptive research—Marketing research to better describe marketing problems, situations or markets, such as the market potential for a product or the demographics and attitudes of consumers.

Desirable products—Products that give both high immediate satisfaction and high long-term benefits.

Differentiated (segmented) marketing—A market-coverage strategy in which a firm decides to target several market segments and designs separate offers for each.

Differentiation—Differentiating the market offering to create superior customer value.

Direct investment—Entering a foreign market by developing foreign-based assembly or manufacturing facilities.

Direct marketing—Direct connections with carefully targeted individual consumers to both obtain an immediate response and cultivate lasting customer relationships.

Direct marketing channel—A marketing channel that has no intermediary levels.

Direct-mail marketing—Direct marketing by sending an offer, announcement, reminder or other item to a person at a particular physical or virtual address.

Direct-response television (DRTV) marketing—Direct marketing via television, including direct-response television advertising (or infomercials) and home shopping channels.

Discount—A straight reduction in price on purchases during a stated period of time or of larger quantities.

Discount store—A retail operation that sells standard merchandise at lower prices by accepting lower margins and selling at higher volume.

Disintermediation—The cutting out of marketing channel intermediaries by product or service producers or the displacement of traditional resellers by radical new types of intermediaries.

Dissonance-reducing buying behaviour—Consumer buying behaviour in situations characterised by high involvement but few perceived differences among brands.

Distribution centre—A large, highly automated warehouse designed to receive goods from various plants and suppliers, take orders, fill them efficiently and deliver goods to customers as quickly as possible.

Diversification—Company growth through starting up or acquiring businesses outside the company's current products and markets.

Downsizing—Reducing the business portfolio by eliminating products or business units that are not profitable or that no longer fit the company's overall strategy.

Dynamic pricing—Adjusting prices continually to meet the characteristics and needs of individual customers and situations.

Economic community—A group of nations organised to work toward common goals in the regulation of international trade.

Economic environment—Economic factors that affect consumer purchasing power and spending patterns.

Environmental sustainability—Developing strategies and practices that create a world economy that the planet can support indefinitely.

Environmentalism—An organised movement of concerned citizens and government agencies to protect and improve people's current and future living environment.

E-procurement—Purchasing through electronic connections between buyers and sellers – usually online.

Ethnographic research—A form of observational research that involves sending trained observers to watch and interact with consumers in their 'natural environments'.

Event marketing (or event sponsorships)—Creating a brand-marketing event or serving as a sole or participating sponsor of events created by others.

Exchange—The act of obtaining a desired object from someone by offering something in return.

Exclusive distribution—Giving a limited number of dealers the exclusive right to distribute the company's products in their territories.

Execution style—The approach, style, tone, words and format used for executing an advertising message.

Executive summary—This section of a marketing plan summarises and overviews the main goals, recommendations and points for senior managers who will read and approve the marketing plan. For management convenience, a table of contents usually follows this section.

Experience curve (learning curve)—The drop in the average per-unit production cost that comes with accumulated production experience.

Experimental research—Gathering primary data by selecting matched groups of subjects, giving them different treatments, controlling related factors and checking for differences in group responses.

Exploratory research—Marketing research to gather preliminary information that will help define problems and suggest hypotheses.

Exporting—Entering a foreign market by selling goods produced in a company's home country, often with little modification.

Factory outlet—An off-price retailing operation that is owned and operated by a manufacturer and normally carries the manufacturer's surplus, discontinued or irregular goods.

Fad—A temporary period of unusually high sales driven by consumer enthusiasm and immediate product or brand popularity.

Fashion—A currently accepted or popular style in a given field.

Fixed costs—Costs that do not vary with production or sales level.

FOB-origin pricing—A geographical pricing strategy in which goods are placed free on board a carrier; the customer pays the freight from the factory to the destination.

Focus group interviewing—Personal interviewing that involves inviting six to ten people to gather for a few hours with a trained interviewer to talk about a product, service or organisation. The interviewer 'focuses' the group discussion on important issues.

Following up—A salesperson follows up after the sale to ensure customer satisfaction and repeat business.

Franchise organisation—A contractual vertical marketing system in which a channel member, called a franchisor, links several stages in the production-distribution process.

Franchise—A contractual association between a manufacturer, wholesaler or service organisation (a franchisor) and independent businesspeople (franchisees) who buy the right to own and operate one or more units in the franchise system.

Freight-absorption pricing—A geographical pricing strategy in which the seller absorbs all or part of the freight charges to get the desired business.

Gatekeepers—People in an organisation's buying centre who control the flow of information to others.

Gender segmentation—Dividing a market into different segments based on gender.

General need description—The stage in the business buying process in which a buyer describes the general characteristics and quantity of a needed item.

Generation X—The 45 million people born between 1965 and 1976 in the 'birth dearth' following the baby boom.

Geographic segmentation—Dividing a market into different geographical units, such as nations, states, regions, counties, cities or even neighbourhoods.

Geographical pricing—Setting prices for customers located in different parts of the country or world.

Global firm—A firm that, by operating in more than one country, gains R&D, production, marketing and financial advantages in its costs and reputation that are not available to purely domestic competitors.

Good-value pricing—Offering the right combination of quality and good service at a fair price.

Government market—Governmental units that purchase or rent goods and services for carrying out the main functions of government.

Gross margin percentage—The percentage of net sales remaining after cost of goods sold – calculated by dividing gross margin by net sales.

Group—Two or more people who interact to accomplish individual or mutual goals.

Growth stage—The PLC stage in which a product's sales start climbing quickly.

Growth-share matrix—A portfolio-planning method that evaluates a company's SBUs in terms of its market growth rate and relative market share.

Habitual buying behaviour—Consumer buying behaviour characterised by low-consumer involvement and few significantly perceived brand differences.

Handling objections—A salesperson seeks out, clarifies and overcomes any customer objections to buying.

Horizontal marketing system—A channel arrangement in which two or more companies at one level join together to follow a new marketing opportunity.

Idea generation—The systematic search for new-product ideas.

Idea screening—Screening new-product ideas to spot good ideas and drop poor ones as soon as possible.

Income segmentation—Dividing a market into different income segments.

Independent off-price retailer—An off-price retailer that is either independently owned and run or is a division of a larger retail corporation.

Indirect marketing channel—Channel containing one or more intermediary levels.

Individual marketing—Tailoring products and marketing programmes to the needs and preferences of individual customers – also called *one-to-one marketing*, *customised marketing* and *markets-of-one marketing*.

Industrial product—A product bought by individuals and organisations for further processing or for use in conducting a business.

Influencers—People in an organisation's buying centre who affect the buying decision; they often help define specifications and also provide information for evaluating alternatives.

Information search—The stage of the buyer decision process in which the consumer is aroused to search for more information; the consumer may simply have heightened attention or may go into an active information search.

Innovative marketing—A principle of sustainable marketing that requires a company to seek real product and marketing improvements.

Inside sales force—Salespeople who conduct business from their offices via telephone, the Internet or visits from prospective buyers.

Institutional market—Schools, hospitals, nursing homes, prisons and other institutions that provide goods and services to people in their care.

Integrated logistics management—The logistics concept that emphasises teamwork – both inside the company and among all the marketing channel organisations – to maximise the performance of the entire distribution system.

Integrated marketing communications (IMC)—Carefully integrating and coordinating the company's many communications channels to deliver a clear, consistent and compelling message about an organisation and its products.

Intensive distribution—Stocking the product in as many outlets as possible.

Interactive marketing—Training service employees in the fine art of interacting with customers to satisfy their needs.

Intermarket segmentation (cross-market segmentation)—Forming segments of consumers who have similar needs and buying behaviour even though they are located in different countries.

Intermodal transportation—Combining two or more modes of transportation.

Internal databases—Electronic collections of consumer and market information obtained from data sources within the company network.

Internal marketing—Orienting and motivating customer contact employees and supporting service people to work as a team to provide customer satisfaction.

Internet—A vast public web of computer networks that connects users of all types around the world to each other and an amazingly large information repository.

Introduction stage—The PLC stage in which a new product is first distributed and made available for purchase.

Inventory turnover rate (or stockturn rate)—The number of times an inventory turns over or is sold during a specified time period (often one year) – calculated based on costs, selling price, or units.

Joint ownership—A joint venture in which a company joins investors in a foreign market to create a local business in which a company shares joint ownership and control.

Joint venturing—Entering foreign markets by joining with foreign companies to produce or market a product or a service.

Learning—Changes in an individual's behaviour arising from experience.

Licensing—A method of entering a foreign market in which a company enters into an agreement with a licensee in a foreign market.

Lifestyle—A person's pattern of living as expressed in his or her activities, interests and opinions.

Line extension—Extending an existing brand name to new forms, colours, sizes, ingredients or flavours of an existing product category.

Local marketing—Tailoring brands and promotions to the needs and wants of local customer segments – cities, neighbourhoods and even specific stores.

Macroenvironment—The larger societal forces that affect the microenvironment – demographic, economic, natural, technological, political and cultural forces.

Madison & Vine—A term that has come to represent the merging of advertising and entertainment in an effort to break through the clutter and create new avenues for reaching consumers with more engaging messages.

Management contracting—A joint venture in which a domestic firm supplies the management know-how to a foreign company that supplies the capital; the domestic firm exports management services rather than products.

Manufacturers' sales branches and offices—Wholesaling by sellers or buyers themselves rather than through independent wholesalers.

Market challenger—A runner-up firm that is fighting hard to increase its market share in an industry.

Market description—Describes the targeted segments in detail and provides context for the marketing strategies and detailed action programmes.

Market development—Company growth by identifying and developing new market segments for current company products.

Market follower—A runner-up firm that wants to hold its share in an industry without rocking the boat.

Market leader—The firm in an industry with the largest market share.

Market nicher—A firm that serves small segments that the other firms in an industry overlook or ignore.

Market offerings—Some combination of products, services, information or experiences offered to a market to satisfy a need or want.

Market penetration—Company growth by increasing sales of current products to current market segments without changing the product.

Market potential—The upper limit of market demand.

Market segment—A group of consumers who respond in a similar way to a given set of marketing efforts.

Market segmentation—Dividing a market into distinct groups of buyers who have different needs, characteristics or behaviours, and who might require separate products or marketing programmes.

Market share—Company sales divided by market sales.

Market targeting—The process of evaluating each market segment's attractiveness and selecting one or more segments to enter.

Market—The set of all actual and potential buyers of a product or service.

Market-centred company—A company that pays balanced attention to both customers and competitors in designing its marketing strategies.

Marketing channel (or distribution channel)—A set of interdependent organisations that help make a product or service available for use or consumption by the consumer or business user.

Marketing channel design—Designing effective marketing channels by analysing customer needs, setting channel objectives, identifying major channel alternatives and evaluating those alternatives.

Marketing channel management—Selecting, managing and motivating individual channel members and evaluating their performance over time.

Marketing concept—A philosophy that holds that achieving organisational goals depends on knowing the needs and wants of target markets and delivering the desired satisfactions better than competitors do.

Marketing control—Measuring and evaluating the results of marketing strategies and plans and taking corrective action to ensure that the objectives are achieved.

Marketing environment—The actors and forces outside marketing that affect marketing management's ability to build and maintain successful relationships with target customers.

Marketing implementation—Turning marketing strategies and plans into marketing actions to accomplish strategic marketing objectives.

Marketing information system (MIS)—People and procedures for assessing information needs, developing the needed information, and helping decision makers to use the information to generate and validate actionable customer and market insights.

Marketing intermediaries—Firms that help the company to promote, sell and distribute its goods to final buyers.

Marketing logistics (or physical distribution)—Planning, implementing and controlling the physical flow of materials, final goods and related information from points of origin to points of consumption to meet customer requirements at a profit.

Marketing management—The art and science of choosing target markets and building profitable relationships with them.

Marketing mix—The set of tactical marketing tools – product, price, place and promotion – that the firm blends to produce the response it wants in the target market.

Marketing myopia—The mistake of paying more attention to the specific products a company offers than to the benefits and experiences produced by these products.

Marketing organisation—The marketing department may be organised by function, geography, product or customer (or some combination thereof).

Marketing research—The systematic design, collection, analysis and reporting of data relevant to a specific marketing situation facing an organisation.

Marketing return on investment (or marketing ROI)—A measure of the marketing productivity of a marketing investment – calculated by dividing net marketing contribution by marketing expenses.

Marketing return on sales (or marketing ROS)—The percent of net sales attributable to the net marketing contribution – calculated by dividing net marketing contribution by net sales.

Marketing strategy development—Designing an initial marketing strategy for a new product based on the product concept.

Marketing strategy—The marketing logic by which the company hopes to create customer value and achieve profitable customer relationships.

Marketing website—A website that engages consumers in interactions that will move them closer to a direct purchase or other marketing outcome.

Marketing—The process by which companies create value for customers and build strong customer relationships to capture value from customers in return.

Market-penetration pricing—Setting a low price for a new product to attract a large number of buyers and a large market share.

Market-skimming pricing (price skimming)—Setting a high price for a new product to skim maximum revenues layer by layer from the segments willing to pay the high price; the company makes fewer but more profitable sales.

Mark-up—The difference between a company's selling price for a product and its cost to manufacture or purchase it.

Mark-up chain—The sequence of mark-ups used by firms at each level in a channel.

Maturity stage—The PLC stage in which a product's sales growth slows or levels off.

Merchant wholesaler—An independently owned wholesale business that takes title to the merchandise it handles.

Microenvironment—The actors close to the company that affect its ability to serve its customers - the company, suppliers, marketing intermediaries, customer markets, competitors and publics.

Micromarketing—Tailoring products and marketing programmes to the needs and wants of specific individuals and local customer segments; It includes *local marketing* and *individual marketing*.

Millennials (or Generation Y)—The 83 million children of the baby boomers, born between 1977 and 2000.

Mission statement—A statement of the organisation's purpose – what it wants to accomplish in the larger environment.

Modified rebuy—A business buying situation in which the buyer wants to modify product specifications, prices, terms or suppliers.

Motive (drive)—A need that is sufficiently pressing to direct the person to seek satisfaction of the need.

Multi-channel distribution system—A distribution system in which a single firm sets up two or more marketing channels to reach one or more customer segments.

Natural environment—Natural resources that are needed as inputs by marketers or that are affected by marketing activities.

Need recognition—The first stage of the buyer decision process, in which the consumer recognises a problem or need.

Needs—States of felt deprivation.

Net marketing contribution (NMC)—A measure of marketing profitability that includes only components of profitability controlled by marketing.

Net profit percentage—The percentage of each sales euro going to profit – calculated by dividing net profits by net sales.

New product—A good, service or idea that is perceived by some potential customers as new.

New task—A business buying situation in which the buyer purchases a product or service for the first time.

New-product development—The development of original products, product improvements, product modifications and new brands through the firm's own product development efforts.

Non-personal communication channels—Media that carry messages without personal contact or feedback, including major media, atmospheres and events.

Objective-and-task method—Developing the promotion budget by (1) defining specific promotion objectives, (2) determining the tasks needed to achieve these objectives and (3) estimating the costs of performing these tasks. The sum of these costs is the proposed promotion budget.

Observational research—Gathering primary data by observing relevant people, actions and situations.

Occasion segmentation—Dividing the market into segments according to occasions when buyers get the idea to buy, actually make their purchase or use the purchased item.

Off-price retailer—A retailer that buys at less-than-regular wholesale prices and sells at less than retail. Examples are factory outlets, independents and warehouse clubs.

Online advertising—Advertising that appears while consumers are browsing the Web, including display ads, search-related ads, online classifieds and other forms.

Online focus groups—Gathering a small group of people online with a trained moderator to chat about a product, service or organisation and gain qualitative insights about consumer attitudes and behaviour.

Online marketing research—Collecting primary data online through Internet surveys, online focus groups, Web-based experiments or tracking consumers' online behaviour.

Online marketing—Efforts to market products and services and build customer relationships over the Internet.

Online social networks—Online social communities - blogs, social networking websites or even virtual worlds - where people socialise or exchange information and opinions.

Operating expense percentage—The portion of net sales going to operating expenses – calculated by dividing total expenses by net sales.

Operating ratios—The ratios of selected operating statement items to net sales.

Opinion leader—A person within a reference group who, because of special skills, knowledge, personality or other characteristics, exerts social influence on others.

Opportunities—Opportunities are external elements that a company may be able to exploit to its advantage.

Optional product pricing—The pricing of optional or accessory products along with a main product.

Order-routine specification—The stage of the business buying process in which the buyer writes the final order with the chosen supplier(s), listing the technical specifications, quantity needed, expected time of delivery, return policies and warranties.

Outside sales force (or field sales force)—Salespeople who travel to call on customers in the field.

Packaging—The activities of designing and producing the container or wrapper for a product.

Partner relationship management—Working closely with partners in other company departments and outside the company to jointly bring greater value to customers.

Percentage-of-sales method—Setting the promotion budget at a certain percentage of current or forecasted sales or as a percentage of the unit sales price.

Perception—The process by which people select, organise and interpret information to form a meaningful picture of the world.

Performance review—The stage of the business buying process in which the buyer assesses the performance of the supplier and decides to continue, modify or drop the arrangement.

Personal communication channels—Channels through which two or more people communicate directly with each other, including face to face, on the phone, via mail or e-mail, or even through an Internet 'chat'.

Personal selling—Personal presentation by the firm's sales force for the purpose of making sales and building customer relationships.

Personality—The unique psychological characteristics that distinguish a person or group.

Pleasing products—Products that give high immediate satisfaction but may hurt consumers in the long term.

Political environment—Laws, government agencies and pressure groups that influence and limit various organisations and individuals in a given society.

Portfolio analysis—The process by which management evaluates the products and businesses that make up the company.

Positioning statement—A statement that summarises company or brand positioning. It takes this form: *To (target segment and need) our (brand) is (concept) that (point of difference)*.

Positioning—Arranging for a product to occupy a clear, distinctive and desirable place relative to competing products in the minds of target consumers. Positioning built on meaningful differentiation, supported by appropriate strategy and implementation, can help a company build competitive advantage.

Postpurchase behaviour—The stage of the buyer decision process in which consumers take further action after purchase based on their satisfaction or dissatisfaction with a purchase.

Pre-approaching—A salesperson learns as much as possible about a prospective customer before making a sales call.

Presenting—A salesperson tells the 'value story' to the buyer, showing how the company's offer solves the customer's problems.

Price elasticity of demand—A measure of the sensitivity of demand to changes in price.

Price—The amount of money charged for a product or a service; the sum of the values that customers exchange for the benefits of having or using the product or service.

Primary data—Information collected for the specific purpose at hand.

Pro forma (or projected) profit-and-loss statement (or income statement or operating statement)—A statement that shows projected revenues less budgeted expenses and estimates the projected net profit for an organisation, product or brand during a specific planning period, typically a year.

Problem recognition—The first stage of the business buying process in which someone in the company recognises a problem or need that can be met by acquiring a good or a service.

Product adaptation—Adapting a product to meet local conditions or wants in foreign markets.

Product bundle pricing—Combining several products and offering the bundle at a reduced price.

Product concept—The idea that consumers will favour products that offer the most quality, performance and features and that

the organisation should therefore devote its energy to making continuous product improvements.

Product development—Developing the product concept into a physical product to ensure that the product idea can be turned into a workable market offering.

Product invention—Creating new products or services.

Product life cycle (PLC)—The course of a product's sales and profits over its lifetime. It involves five distinct stages: product development, introduction, growth, maturity and decline.

Product line pricing—Setting the price steps between various products in a product line based on cost differences between the products, customer evaluations of different features and competitors' prices.

Product line—A group of products that are closely related because they function in a similar manner, are sold to the same customer groups, are marketed through the same types of outlets, or fall within given price ranges.

Product mix (or product portfolio)—The set of all product lines and items that a particular seller offers for sale.

Product position—The way the product is defined by consumers on important attributes – the place the product occupies in consumers' minds relative to competing products.

Product quality—The characteristics of a product or service that bear on its ability to satisfy stated or implied customer needs.

Product review—The product review summarises the main features for all of a company's products, organised by product line, type of customer, market and/or order of product introduction.

Product sales force structure—A sales force organisation in which salespeople specialise in selling only a portion of the company's products or lines.

Product specification—The stage of the business buying process in which the buying organisation decides on and specifies the best technical product characteristics for a needed item.

Product—Anything that can be offered to a market for attention, acquisition, use or consumption that might satisfy a want or need.

GLOSSARY

Product/market expansion grid—A portfolio-planning tool for identifying company growth opportunities through market penetration, market development, product development or diversification.

Production concept—The idea that consumers will favour products that are available and highly affordable and that the organisation should therefore focus on improving production and distribution efficiency.

Profit-and-loss statement (or income statement or operating statement)—A statement that shows actual revenues less expenses and net profit for an organisation, product or brand during a specific planning period, typically a year.

Promotion mix (or marketing communications mix)—The specific blend of promotion tools that the company uses to persuasively communicate customer value and build customer relationships.

Promotional pricing—Temporarily pricing products below the list price, and sometimes even below cost, to increase short-term sales.

Proposal solicitation—The stage of the business buying process in which the buyer invites qualified suppliers to submit proposals.

Prospecting—A salesperson or company identifies qualified potential customers.

Psychographic segmentation—Dividing a market into different segments based on social class, lifestyle or personality characteristics.

Psychological pricing—Pricing that considers the psychology of prices, not simply the economics; the price says something about the product.

Public relations (PR)—Building good relations with the company's various publics by obtaining favourable publicity, building up a good corporate image, and handling or heading off unfavourable rumours, stories and events.

Public—Any group that has an actual or potential interest in or impact on an organisation's ability to achieve its objectives.

Pull strategy—A promotion strategy that calls for spending a lot on consumer advertising and promotion to induce final consumers to buy a particular product, creating a demand vacuum that 'pulls' a product through the channel.

Purchase decision—The buyer's decision about which brand to purchase.

Push strategy—A promotion strategy that calls for using the sales force and trade promotion to push a product through channels. A producer promotes a particular product to channel members, who in turn promote it to final consumers.

Reference prices—Prices that buyers carry in their minds and refer to when they look at a given product.

Relevant costs—Costs that will occur in the future and that will vary across the alternatives being considered.

Retailer—A business whose sales come *primarily* from retailing.

Retailing—All the activities involved in selling goods or services directly to final consumers for their personal, non-business use.

Return on advertising investment—The net return on advertising investment divided by the costs of the advertising investment.

Return on investment (ROI) pricing (or target-return pricing)—A cost-based pricing method that determines price based on a specified rate of return on investment.

Return on marketing investment (or marketing ROI)—The net return from a marketing investment divided by the costs of the marketing investment.

Sales 2.0—The merging of innovative sales practices with Web 2.0 technologies to improve sales force effectiveness and efficiency.

Sales force management—Analysing, planning, implementing and controlling sales force activities.

Sales promotion—Short-term incentives to encourage the purchase or sale of a product or a service.

Sales quota—A standard that states the amount a salesperson should sell and how sales should be divided among the company's products.

Salesperson—An individual representing a company to customers by performing one or more of the following activities: prospecting, communicating, selling, servicing, information gathering and relationship building.

Salutary products—Products that have low appeal but may benefit consumers in the long term.

Sample—A segment of the population selected for marketing research to represent the population as a whole.

Secondary data—Information that already exists somewhere, having been collected for another purpose.

Segmented pricing—Selling a product or service at two or more prices, where the difference in prices is not based on differences in costs.

Selective distribution—The use of more than one but fewer than all the intermediaries who are willing to carry the company's products.

Selling concept—The idea that consumers will not buy enough of the firm's products unless it undertakes a large-scale selling and promotion effort.

Selling process—The steps that salespeople follow when selling, which include prospecting and qualifying, pre-approaching, approaching, presenting and demonstrating, handling objections, closing and following up.

Sense-of-mission marketing—A principle of sustainable marketing that holds a company should define its mission in broad social terms rather than narrow product terms.

Service inseparability—Services are produced and consumed at the same time and cannot be separated from their providers.

Service intangibility—Services cannot be seen, tasted, felt, heard or smelled before they are bought.

Service perishability—Services cannot be stored for later sale or use.

Service profit chain—The chain that links service firm profits with employee and customer satisfaction.

Service retailer—A retailer whose product line is actually a service, including hotels, airlines, banks, colleges and many others.

Service variability—The quality of services may vary greatly depending on who provides them and when, where and how.

Service—An activity, benefit or satisfaction offered for sale that is essentially intangible and does not result in the ownership of anything.

Share of customer—The portion of the customer's purchasing that a company gets in its product categories.

Shopper marketing—Using in-store promotions and advertising to extend brand equity to 'the last mile' and encourage favourable in-store purchase decisions.

Shopping centre—A group of retail businesses built on a site that is planned, developed, owned and managed as a unit.

Shopping product—A consumer product that the customer, in the process of selecting and purchasing, usually compares on such attributes as suitability, quality, price and style.

Social class—Relatively permanent and ordered divisions in a society whose members share similar values, interests and behaviours.

Social marketing—The use of commercial marketing concepts and tools in programmes designed to influence individuals' behaviour to improve their well-being and that of society.

Societal marketing concept—The idea that a company's marketing decisions should consider consumers' wants, the company's requirements, and the long-term interests of consumers and society.

Societal marketing—A principle of sustainable marketing that holds a company should make marketing decisions by considering consumers' wants, the company's requirements, consumers' long-run interests and society's long-run interests.

Spam—Unsolicited, unwanted commercial e-mail messages.

Speciality product—A consumer product with unique characteristics or brand identification for which a significant group of buyers is willing to make a special purchase effort.

Speciality store—A retail store that carries a narrow product line with a deep assortment within that line.

Standardised global marketing—An international marketing strategy that basically uses the same marketing strategy and mix in all of a company's international markets.

Store brand (or private brand)—A brand created and owned by a reseller of a product or service.

Straight product extension—Marketing a product in a foreign market without any change.

Straight rebuy—A business buying situation in which the buyer routinely reorders something without any modifications.

Strategic group—A group of firms in an industry following the same or a similar strategy.

Strategic planning—The process of developing and maintaining a strategic fit between the organisation's goals and capabilities and its changing marketing opportunities.

Strengths—Strengths are internal capabilities that can help a company reach its objectives.

Style—A basic and distinctive mode of expression.

Subculture—A group of people with shared value systems based on common life experiences and situations.

Supermarket—A large, low-cost, low-margin, high-volume, self-service store that carries a wide variety of grocery and household products.

Superstore—A store much larger than a regular supermarket that offers a large assortment of routinely purchased food products, non-food items and services.

Supplier development—Systematic development of networks of supplier-partners to ensure an appropriate and dependable supply of products and materials for use in making products or reselling them to others.

Supplier search—The stage of the business buying process in which the buyer tries to find the best vendors.

Supplier selection—The stage of the business buying process in which the buyer reviews proposals and selects a supplier or suppliers.

Supply chain management—Managing upstream and downstream value-added flows of materials, final goods and related information among suppliers, the company, resellers and final consumers.

Survey research—Gathering primary data by asking people questions about their knowledge, attitudes, preferences and buying behaviour.

Sustainable marketing—Socially and environmentally responsible marketing that meets the present needs of consumers and businesses while also preserving or enhancing the ability of future generations to meet their needs.

SWOT analysis—An overall evaluation of the company's strengths (S), weaknesses (W), opportunities (O) and threats (T).

Systems selling (or solutions selling)—Buying a packaged solution to a problem from a single seller, thus avoiding all the separate decisions involved in a complex buying situation.

Target costing—Pricing that starts with an ideal selling price and then targets costs that will ensure that the price is met.

Target market—A set of buyers sharing common needs or characteristics that the company decides to serve.

Team selling—Using teams of people from sales, marketing, engineering, finance, technical support and even upper management to service large, complex accounts.

Team-based new-product development—An approach to developing new products in which various company departments work closely together, overlapping the steps in the product development process to save time and increase effectiveness.

Technological environment—Forces that create new technologies, creating new product and market opportunities.

Telephone marketing—Using the telephone to sell directly to customers.

Territorial sales force structure—A sales force organisation that assigns each salesperson to an exclusive geographic territory in which that salesperson sells the company's full line.

Test marketing—The stage of new-product development in which the product and its proposed marketing programme are tested in realistic market settings.

Third-party logistics (3PL) provider—An independent logistics provider that performs any or all of the functions required to get a client's product to market.

Threats—Threats are current or emerging external elements that could potentially challenge a company's performance.

Total costs—The sum of the fixed and variable costs for any given level of production.

Total market demand—The total volume that would be bought by a defined consumer group, in a defined geographic area, in a defined time period, in a defined marketing environment, under a defined level and mix of industry marketing effort.

Trade promotions—Sales promotion tools used to persuade resellers to carry a brand, give it shelf space, promote it in advertising and push it to consumers.

Undifferentiated (mass) marketing—A market-coverage strategy in which a firm decides to ignore market segment differences and go after the whole market with one offer.

Uniform-delivered pricing—A geographical pricing strategy in which the company charges the same price plus freight to all customers, regardless of their location.

Unit contribution—The amount that each unit contributes to covering fixed costs - the difference between price and variable costs.

Unsought product—A consumer product that the consumer either does not know about or knows about but does not normally consider buying.

Users—Members of the buying organisation who will actually use the purchased product or service.

Value chain—The series of internal departments that carry out value-creating activities to design, produce, market, deliver and support a firm's products.

Value delivery network—A network composed of the company, suppliers, distributors and, ultimately, customers who 'partner' with each other to improve the performance of the entire system in delivering customer value.

Value proposition—The full positioning of a brand - the full mix of benefits on which it is positioned.

Value-added pricing—Attaching value-added features and services to differentiate a company's offers and charging higher prices.

Value-based pricing—Offering just the right combination of quality and good service at a fair price.

Variable costs—Costs that vary directly with the level of production.

Variety-seeking buying behaviour—Consumer buying behaviour characterised by low consumer involvement but significant perceived brand differences.

Vertical marketing system (VMS)—A distribution channel structure in which producers, wholesalers and retailers act as a unified system. One channel member owns the others, has contracts with them, or has so much power that they all cooperate.

Viral marketing—The Internet version of word-of-mouth marketing: websites, videos, e-mail messages or other marketing events that are so infectious that customers will want to pass them along to friends.

Wants—The form human needs take as they are shaped by culture and individual personality.

Warehouse club—An off-price retailer that sells a limited selection of brand name grocery items, appliances, clothing and a hodge-podge of other goods at deep discounts to members who pay annual membership fees.

Weaknesses—Weaknesses are internal elements that may interfere with a company's ability to achieve its objectives.

Wheel-of-retailing concept—A concept that states that new types of retailers usually begin as low-margin, low-price, low-status operations but later evolve into higher-priced, higher-service operations, eventually becoming like the conventional retailers they replaced.

Whole-channel view—Designing international channels that take into account the entire global supply chain and marketing channel, forging an effective global value delivery network.

Wholesaler—A firm engaged *primarily* in wholesaling activities.

Wholesaling—All the activities involved in selling goods and services to those buying for resale or business use.

Word-of-mouth influence—Personal communications about a product between target buyers and neighbours, friends, family members and associates.

Workload method—An approach to determining sales force size based on the workload required and the time available for selling.

Zone pricing—A geographical pricing strategy in which the company sets up two or more zones. All customers within a zone pay the same total price; the more distant the zone, the higher the price.

SUBJECT INDEX

COMPANY INDEX